Lecture Notes in Computer Science 1843

Edited by G. Goos, J. Hartmanis and J. van Leeuwen

D1807421

Lecture Notes in Computer Science   1843
Edited by G. Goos, J. Hartmanis and J. van Leeuwen

Springer
Berlin
Heidelberg
New York
Barcelona
Hong Kong
London
Milan
Paris
Singapore
Tokyo

David Vernon (Ed.)

Computer Vision – ECCV 2000

6th European Conference on Computer Vision
Dublin, Ireland, June 26 – July 1, 2000
Proceedings, Part II

Springer

Series Editors

Gerhard Goos, Karlsruhe University, Germany
Juris Hartmanis, Cornell University, NY, USA
Jan van Leeuwen, Utrecht University, The Netherlands

Volume Editor

David Vernon
5 Edwin Court, Glenageary, Co. Dublin, Ireland
E-mail: vernon@ieee.org

Cataloging-in-Publication Data

Die Deutsche Bibliothek - CIP-Einheitsaufnahme

Computer vision : proceedings / ECCV 2000, 6th European Conference on
Computer Vision, Dublin, Ireland, June 26 - July 1, 2000. David
Vernon (ed.). - Berlin ; Heidelberg ; New York ; Barcelona ; Hong Kong ;
London ; Milan ; Paris ; Singapore ; Tokyo : Springer
Pt. 2 . - (2000)
  (Lecture notes in computer science ; Vol. 1843)
  ISBN 3-540-67686-4

CR Subject Classification (1998): I.4, I.3.5, I.5, I.2.9-10

ISSN 0302-9743
ISBN 3-540-67686-4 Springer-Verlag Berlin Heidelberg New York

Springer-Verlag is a company in the BertelsmannSpringer publishing group.
© Springer-Verlag Berlin Heidelberg 2000
Printed in Germany

Typesetting: Camera-ready by author
Printed on acid-free paper   SPIN 10722044   06/3142   5 4 3 2 1 0

Preface

Ten years ago, the inaugural European Conference on Computer Vision was held in Antibes, France. Since then, ECCV has been held biennially under the auspices of the European Vision Society at venues around Europe. This year, the privilege of organizing ECCV 2000 falls to Ireland and it is a signal honour for us to host what has become one of the most important events in the calendar of the computer vision community.

ECCV is a single-track conference comprising the highest quality, previously unpublished, contributed papers on new and original research in computer vision. This year, 266 papers were submitted and, following a rigorous double-blind review process, with each paper being reviewed by three referees, 116 papers were selected by the Programme Committee for presentation at the conference.

The venue for ECCV 2000 is the University of Dublin, Trinity College. Founded in 1592, it is Ireland's oldest university and has a proud tradition of scholarship in the Arts, Humanities, and Sciences, alike. The Trinity campus, set in the heart of Dublin, is an oasis of tranquility and its beautiful squares, elegant buildings, and tree-lined playing-fields provide the perfect setting for any conference.

The organization of ECCV 2000 would not have been possible without the support of many people. In particular, I wish to thank the Department of Computer Science, Trinity College, and its head, J. G. Byrne, for hosting the conference secretariat. Gerry Lacey, Damian Gordon, Niall Winters, Mary Murray, and Dermot Furlong provided unstinting help and assistance whenever it was needed. Sarah Campbell and Tony Dempsey in Trinity's Accommodation Office were a continuous source of guidance and advice. I am also indebted to Michael Nowlan and his staff in Trinity's Information Systems Services for hosting the ECCV 2000 web-site. I am grateful too to the staff of Springer-Verlag for always being available to assist with the production of these proceedings. There are many others whose help – and forbearance – I would like to acknowledge: my thanks to all.

Support came in other forms too, and it is a pleasure to record here the kind generosity of the University of Freiburg, MV Technology Ltd., and Captec Ltd., who sponsored prizes for best paper awards.

Finally, a word about conferences. The technical excellence of the scientific programme is undoubtedly the most important facet of ECCV. But there are other facets to an enjoyable and productive conference, facets which should engender conviviality, discourse, and interaction; my one wish is that all delegates will leave Ireland with great memories, many new friends, and inspirational ideas for future research.

April 2000   David Vernon

Conference Chair

D. Vernon

Conference Board

H. Burkhardt	University of Freiburg, Germany
B. Buxton	University College London, United Kingdom
R. Cipolla	University of Cambridge, United Kingdom
J.-O. Eklundh	KTH, Stockholm, Sweden
O. Faugeras	INRIA, Sophia Antipolis, France
B. Neumann	University of Hamburg, Germany
G. Sandini	University of Genova, Italy

Programme Committee

L. Alvarez	University of Las Palmas, Spain
N. Ayache	INRIA, Sophia Antipolis, France
R. Basri	Weizmann Institute, Israel
M. Black	Xerox Palo Alto Research Center, USA
A. Blake	Microsoft Research, United Kingdom
P. Bouthemy	IRISA/INRIA, Rennes, France
M. Brady	University of Oxford, United Kingdom
H. Buxton	University of Sussex, United Kingdom
S. Carlsson	KTH, Stockholm, Sweden
H. Christensen	KTH, Stockholm, Sweden
L. Cohen	Université Paris IX Dauphine, France
J. Crowley	INRIA, Rhône-Alpes, France
R. Deriche	INRIA, Sophia Antipolis, France
M. Dhome	Blaise Pascal University, France
W. Enkelmann	IITB, Karlsruhe, Germany
W. Förstner	University of Bonn, Germany
D. Forsyth	University of California, Berkeley, USA
P. Fua	EPFL, Switzerland
G. Granlund	Linköping University, Sweden
R. Hartley	General Electric, USA
D. Hogg	Leeds University, United Kingdom
P. Johansen	DIKU, Denmark
H. Knutsson	Linköping University, Sweden
M. Kunt	EPFL, Switzerland
T. Lindeberg	KTH, Stockholm, Sweden
J. Malik	University of California, Berkeley, USA
S. Maybank	University of Reading, United Kingdom
R. Mohr	Xerox Research Centre Europe
D. Murray	Oxford University, United Kingdom

P. Perona	California Institute of Technology, USA
	& University of Padova, Italy
L. Quan	INRIA, Rhône-Alpes, France
J. Santos-Victor	Instituto Superior Técnico, Lisbon, Portugal
A. Shashua	The Hebrew University of Jerusalem, Israel
G. Sparr	Lund University, Sweden
R. Szeliski	Microsoft Research, USA
C. Taylor	Manchester University, United Kingdom
B. ter Haar Romeny	University Medical Center, Utrecht, The Netherlands
M. Tistarelli	University of Genova, Italy
B. Triggs	INRIA, Rhône-Alpes, France
A. Verri	University of Genova, Italy
L. van Gool	Katholiek University, Leuven, Belgium
J. Villanueva	Autonomous University of Barcelona, Spain
D. Weinshall	The Hebrew University of Jerusalem, Israel
A. Zisserman	University of Oxford, United Kingdom
S. Zucker	Yale University, USA

Additional Referees

J. Andersen
K. Astrom
J. August
S. Balcisoy
R. Baldrich
C. Barillot
K. Barnard
A. Bernardino
X. Binefa
J. Bioucas Dias
A. Broadhurst
P. Bonton
J. Costeira
A. Criminisi
L. de Agapito
E. Dam
P. Deléglise
H. Delingette
D. Demirdjian
E. Di Berarnardo
A. R. Dick
T. W. Drummond
A. Fitzgibbon
D. Fleet
L. Florack
O. Fogh
A. Frangi
J. Gaspar
A. Gasteratos
A. S. Georghiades
J. Goldberger
L. Goncalves
V. Govindu
N. Gracias
P. Gros

E. Grossmann
E. Grosso
S. Haker
D. Hall
H. Haussecker
E. Hayman
K. Henriksen
L. Herda
A. Heyden
R. Horaud
P. Huggins
F. Jurie
C. Kervrann
J.-T. Lapresté
I. Laptev
J.-M. Lavest
B. Lamiroy
T. Leung
M. Lillholm
F. Lumbreras
J. MacCormick
J. Maciel
G. Malandain
R. Manzotti
E. Marchand
J. Marques
E. Martí
J. Martnez
E. Mémin
P.R. Mendonca
G. Metta
M. E. Munich
M. Nielsen
J.-M. Odobez
N. Olsen

S. Olsen
T. Pajdla
F. Panerai
K. Pedersen
X. Pennec
P. Pérez
R. Plaenkers
J. P. W. Pluim
J. Puzicha
S. Remy
M. Richetin
J. Rittscher
G. Rives
R. Rosenholtz
J. Saludes
F. Schaffalitzky
J. Serrat
C. Silva
C. Sminchisescu
Y. Song
J. Staal
P. Sturm
J. Sullivan
T. Thórhallsson
R. Torre
B. van Ginneken
M. Vanrell
X. Varona
F. Vergnenegre
T. Vetter
M. Vincze
J. Vitrià
Y. Weiss
M. Welling

Contents of Volume II

Segmentation & Grouping II

Visual Motion

Contents of Volume I

Recognition & Modelling II

Structure from Motion I

Shape

Structure from Motion / Shape / Image Features

Structure from Motion II

Active, Real-Time, & Robot Vision

Partitioned Sampling, Articulated Objects, and Interface-Quality Hand Tracking

John MacCormick[1] and Michael Isard[2]

[1] Dept. of Eng. Science, University of Oxford, Parks Road, Oxford OX1 3PJ, UK
jmac@robots.ox.ac.uk, http://www.robots.ox.ac.uk/~jmac
[2] Compaq Systems Research Center, 130 Lytton Ave, Palo Alto, CA 94301, USA
misard@pa.dec.com

1 Introduction

Partitioned sampling is a technique which was introduced in [17] for avoiding the high cost of particle filters when tracking more than one object. In fact this technique can reduce the curse of dimensionality in other situations too. This paper describes how to use partitioned sampling on articulated objects, obtaining results that would be impossible with standard sampling methods. Because partitioned sampling is the statistical analogue of a hierarchical search, it makes sense to use it on articulated objects, since links at the base of the object can be localised before moving on to search for subsequent links.

A new concept relating to particle filters, termed the *survival rate* is introduced, which sheds light on the efficacy of partitioned sampling. The domain of articulated objects also highlights two important features of partitioned sampling which are discussed here for the first time: firstly, that the number of particles allocated to each partition can be varied to obtain the maximum benefit from a fixed computational resource; and secondly, that the number of likelihood evaluations (the most expensive operation in vision-based particle filters) required can be halved by taking advantage of the way the likelihood function factorises for an articulated object.

Another important contribution of the paper is the presentation of a vision-based "interface-quality" hand tracker: a self-initialising, real-time, robust and accurate system of sufficient quality to be used for complex interactive tasks such as drawing packages. The tracker models the hand as an articulated object and partitioned sampling is the crucial component in achieving these favourable properties. The system tracks a user's hand on an arbitrary background using a standard colour camera, in such a way that the hand can be employed as a 4-dimensional mouse (planar translation and the orientations of the thumb and index finger).

Hand gesture recognition is the subject of much research, for a wide variety of applications and by a plethora of methods. Kohler and Schröter [13] give a comprehensive survey. We are not aware of any hand tracking system which combines the speed, robustness, accuracy and simple hardware requirements of the system described here. Among the more successful systems which recover continuous parameters (rather than recognising gestures from a discrete "vocabulary"), some use a stereo rig (e.g. [5, 20]), some are not real time (e.g. [3, 9]), while others do not appear to have sufficient accuracy for the applications envisaged here (e.g. [1, 2, 8, 11, 12]). Of these, [1, 11] are the closest to our system in terms of the method used. In both cases, the tracking is good enough to permit navigation through a virtual environment, but not for the fine adjustment of interactive visual tools (e.g. drawing at pixel accuracy).

2 Partitioned sampling and the efficiency of particle filters

Partitioned sampling is a way of applying particle filters (also known as the Condensation algorithm e.g. [11]) to tracking problems with high-dimensional configuration spaces, without incurring the large computational cost that would normally be expected in such problems. In this section we first review particle filters, then explain why the large computational cost arises, and finally describe the basic idea behind partitioned sampling.

2.1 Particle filters

Consider a tracking problem with configuration space $\mathcal{X} \subset \mathbb{R}^d$. Recall that Condensation expresses its belief about the system at time t by approximating the posterior probability distribution $p(\mathbf{x}|\mathcal{Z}^t)$, where $\mathcal{Z}^t$ is the history of observations $\mathbf{Z}^1, \ldots \mathbf{Z}^t$ made at each time step, and $\mathbf{x} \in \mathcal{X}$. The distribution $p(\mathbf{x}|\mathcal{Z}^t)$ is approximated using a *weighted particle set* $(\mathbf{x}_i, \pi_i)_{i=1}^n$, which can be interpreted as a sum of δ-functions centred on the $\mathbf{x}_i$ with real, non-negative weights π_i (one requires that $\sum_i \pi_i = 1$). Each time step of the Condensation algorithm is just an update according to Bayes' formula, implemented using operations on particle sets which can be shown to have the desired effects (as $n \to \infty$) on the underlying probability distributions. One step of Condensation can be conveniently represented on a diagram as follows:

$$ \boxed{p(\mathbf{x}|\mathcal{Z}^{t-1})} \longrightarrow \fbox{$\sim$} \longrightarrow \left\langle * h(\mathbf{x}'|\mathbf{x}) \right\rangle \longrightarrow \left\langle \times f(\mathbf{Z}^t|\mathbf{x}') \right\rangle \longrightarrow \boxed{p(\mathbf{x}'|\mathcal{Z}^t)} \quad (1) $$

where the $\sim$ symbol denotes resampling, $*$ denotes convolving with dynamics, and $\times$ denotes multiplication by the observation density. Specifically, the resampling operation $\sim$ maps $(\mathbf{x}_i, \pi_i)_{i=1}^n$ to $(\mathbf{x}'_i, 1/n)_{i=1}^n$, where each $\mathbf{x}'_i$ is selected independently from the the $\{\mathbf{x}_1, \ldots \mathbf{x}_n\}$ with probability proportional to π_i. This operation has no effect on the distribution represented by the particle set, but often helps to improve the efficiency with which it is represented. The dynamical convolution operation $*$ maps $(\mathbf{x}_i, \pi_i)_{i=1}^n$ to $(\mathbf{x}'_i, \pi_i)_{i=1}^n$, where $\mathbf{x}'_i$ is a random draw from the conditional distribution $h(\mathbf{x}'|\mathbf{x}_i)$. Its effect on the distribution represented by the particle set is to transform a distribution $p(\mathbf{x})$ into $\int h(\mathbf{x}'|\mathbf{x})p(\mathbf{x})d\mathbf{x}$. Finally, the multiplication operation $\times$ maps $(\mathbf{x}_i, \pi_i)_{i=1}^n$ to $(\mathbf{x}_i, \pi'_i)_{i=1}^n$, where $\pi'_i \propto \pi_i f(\mathbf{Z}^t|\mathbf{x}_i)$. Its probabilistic effect is to transform a distribution $p(\mathbf{x})$ into the distribution proportional to $p(\mathbf{x})f(\mathbf{Z}^t|\mathbf{x})$. Hence, the overall effect of diagram (1) on the distribution $p(\mathbf{x}|\mathcal{Z}^{t-1})$ is to transform it into the distribution proportional to $f(\mathbf{Z}^t|\mathbf{x}') \int h(\mathbf{x}'|\mathbf{x})p(\mathbf{x}|\mathcal{Z}^{t-1})d\mathbf{x}$ — precisely the Bayes update rule for dynamical diffusion governed by $h(\mathbf{x}'|\mathbf{x})$ and likelihood function $f(\mathbf{Z}^t|\mathbf{x}')$.

2.2 The survival diagnostic and survival rate

In assessing the efficacy of particle filters we have found two quantities to be of use: the *survival diagnostic* $\mathcal{D}$ and the *survival rate* α. The survival diagnostic[1] is defined for a particle set $(\mathbf{x}_i, \pi_i)_{i=1}^n$ as

$$\mathcal{D} = \left(\sum_{i=1}^{n} \pi_i^2 \right)^{-1}. \tag{2}$$

Intuitively, it can be thought of as indicating the number of particles which would survive a resampling operation. Two extreme cases make this clear. If $\pi_1 = 1$ and all the other weights are zero, then $\mathcal{D} = 1$ — only one particle will survive the resampling. On the other extreme, if every weight is equal to $1/n$, then $\mathcal{D} = n$. In this case, every particle would be chosen exactly once by an ideal resampling operation, so all n particles would survive.[2] Any particle set lies somewhere between these two extremes. The survival diagnostic indicates whether tracking performance is reliable or not: a low value of $\mathcal{D}$ indicates that estimates (e.g. of the mean) based on the particle set may be unreliable, and that there is significant danger of the tracker losing lock on its target. The difficult problem of assessing the performance of particle filters is discussed in the statistical literature (e.g. [4, 6, 7, 14]) and no single approach has met with resounding success. In our experience, the survival diagnostic is as useful as any other indicator and has the significant advantage of having negligible computational cost.

Whereas the survival diagnostic is a property of a given particle set, the *survival rate* is a property of a given prior $p(\mathbf{x})$ and posterior $p'(\mathbf{x})$. Specifically, the survival rate is given by

$$\alpha = \left(\int p'(\mathbf{x})^2 / p(\mathbf{x}) \, d\mathbf{x} \right)^{-1}. \tag{3}$$

(See theorem 2 of [7] for another use of this quantity.) Again, a special case is instructive. Suppose p is a uniform distribution on a set $\mathcal{X}_p \subset \mathcal{X}$ of volume V_p, and that p' is also uniform, on a smaller subset $\mathcal{X}_{p'} \subset \mathcal{X}_p$ of volume $V_{p'}$. Then p'/p is equal to $V_p/V_{p'}$ everywhere on $\mathcal{X}_{p'}$, so that $\alpha = V_{p'}/V_p$. That is,

---

[1] Doucet [6] calls it the *estimated effective sample size*. See also [4].

[2] In fact, if truly random resampling is employed, a certain fraction of the particles would not survive even in this case. But in practice one uses a deterministic version of the resampling operation which selects every particle the appropriate number of times.

the survival rate is just the ratio of the volume of the posterior to the volume of the prior. It turns out that this interpretation is valid in more general cases too. Let $l(\mathbf{x}) = p'(\mathbf{x})/p(\mathbf{x})$ be the likelihood function and define a particle set $(\mathbf{x}_i, \pi_i)$ which represents p' by letting the $\mathbf{x}_i$ be i.i.d. draws from $p(\mathbf{x})$ and setting $\pi_i = l(\mathbf{x}_i)$. Then it can be shown (see appendix) that for large n,

$$\mathcal{D} \approx \alpha n. \tag{4}$$

This explains our terminology: α is called the survival rate because when multiplied by n it is approximately the number of particles expected to survive a resampling. Hence we expect the overall tracking performance to be related to the survival rate at each time step: if the survival rate is too low, the tracker will be in danger of producing inaccurate estimates or losing lock altogether.

Example Figure 1 shows an example of a survival rate α calculated for a contour likelihood in a real image. In this particular example, in which the configuration space is the one-dimensional interval $[-150, 150]$, the value of α was calculated numerically as 0.20. (In more realistic multi-dimensional examples, typical values of α are much lower than this.) Equation (4) can also be verified directly by simulations for this simple example.

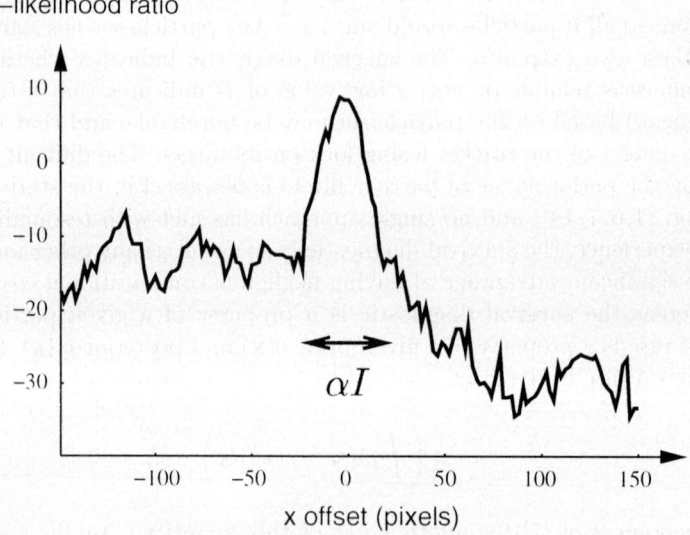

Fig. 1. Survival rate. A contour likelihood of the kind used in section 3.1 is graphed for a range of offsets in the x-direction from a template. Taking a uniform prior p on the interval $I = [-150, 150]$, the survival rate α for this particular likelihood function can be calculated numerically as 0.20. This corresponds to the "volume" αI indicated on the graph.

2.3 More dimensions means more particles

The survival rate concept makes it easy to see why particle filters require so many extra particles to achieve the same level of performance as the dimension of the configuration space increases. An informal argument runs as follows. Fix (by trial and error, if necessary) a value $\mathcal{D}_{\min}$ which represents the minimum acceptable survival diagnostic for successful tracking of a given object with a given steady-state prior $p(\mathbf{x})$ on a configuration space $\mathcal{X}$. Then according to (4), we should take $n \geq \mathcal{D}_{\min}/\alpha$ to achieve $\mathcal{D} \geq \mathcal{D}_{\min}$, where α is the survival rate for this particular problem. Now consider tracking two such objects. By the definition of the survival rate (3), it is easy to see the survival rate for the two-object problem is α^2, so that to achieve the same level of tracking performance (i.e. the same minimum survival diagnostic) we must take $n \geq \mathcal{D}_{\min}/\alpha^2$. Since typically $\alpha \ll 1$, this is a substantial additional requirement. Note this does not contradict the well-known result that the variance of standard Monte Carlo estimators is independent of the dimension of the configurations space. The general recipe of "sample from a prior, then weight by a likelihood" can be regarded as a type of importance sampling, and it is well-known that importance sampling scales badly with dimension. [18] gives a lucid explanation of these phenomena.

Partitioned sampling essentially eliminates the need for these additional particles. The intuition that α is the ratio of the posterior and prior volumes gives a hint as to how this problem could be solved. Take the simple case of tracking 2 objects A and B, whose configurations are described respectively by the one-dimensional variables $x_A, x_B \in [0, 1]$. Suppose the survival rate for the one-object problem is α: then as remarked above, we have a survival rate $\alpha' = \alpha^2$ for the two-object problem. Figure 2 shows a schematic representation of the situation. The intuition behind partitioned sampling is that instead of searching the entire unit square for the lightly shaded area α', we can divide the search into two stages: first, a search of the horizontal axis only, which will attempt to populate the dark shaded area α. This step will have survival rate α. Second, we try to populate the lightly shaded area. This second step will also have survival rate of approximately α, since the *relative* area of the dark shade to light shade is α'/α. This is the key idea behind partitioned sampling. It remains to show how we can "populate" certain parts of the configuration space with particles in the desired manner. This is done using an operation on particle sets called weighted resampling.

2.4 Weighted resampling

Let $g(\mathbf{x})$ be a strictly positive, continuous function on $\mathcal{X}$ called the *weighting function*. The weighted resampling function is analogous to the importance function used in standard importance sampling [19]. Weighted resampling with respect to g is an operation on a particle set which "populates" the peaks of g with particles, without altering the distribution actually represented by the particle set. Given a particle set $(\mathbf{x}_i, \pi_i)_{i=1}^n$, weighted resampling produces a new set $(\mathbf{x}'_i, \pi'_i)_{i=1}^n$ as follows. First define some "importance" weights $\rho_i =$

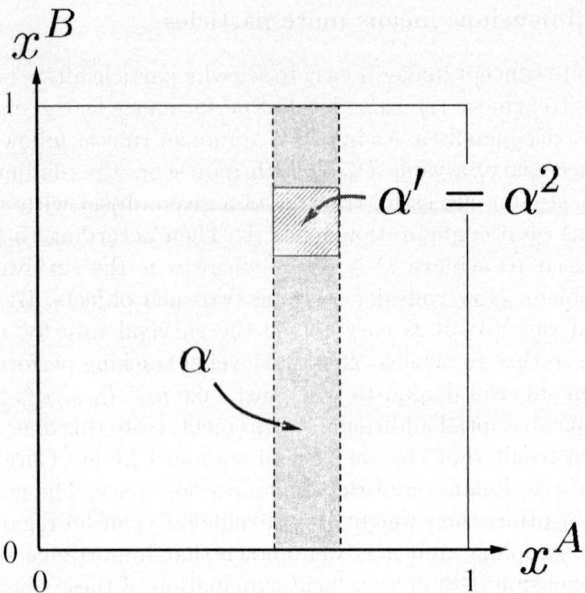

Fig. 2. Intuition behind partitioned sampling. To locate the peak of a 2D likelihood function, which has area $\alpha' = \alpha^2$, the search is split into two stages, each of which has survival rate α. The first stage populates the dark shaded area with particles, and the second stage populates the light shaded area.

$g(\mathbf{x}_i)/\sum_{j=1}^{n} g(\mathbf{x}_j)$. Next, select indices $k_1, k_2, \ldots k_n$ by setting $k_i = j$ with probability ρ_j, independently for $i = 1, \ldots n$. Finally, set $\mathbf{x}'_i = \mathbf{x}_{k_i}$ and $\pi'_i = \pi_{k_i}/\rho_{k_i}$. This last choice of weights has the effect of precisely counteracting the extent to which the particles were "biased" by the importance weights. A proof that the weighted resampling operation does not alter the underlying distribution can be found in [15]. On a Condensation diagram, the operation of weighted resampling with respect to g is denoted $\sim g$.

2.5 Partitioned sampling

Partitioned sampling is a generic term for the strategy which consists of dividing the state space into two or more "partitions", and sequentially applying the dynamics for each partition followed by an appropriate weighted resampling operation. For example, the two-object problem described above could be implemented as the following condensation diagram:

$$
\boxed{p(\mathbf{x}|\mathcal{Z}^{t-1})} \longrightarrow \boxed{\sim} \longrightarrow \langle *h_A(\mathbf{x}'|\mathbf{x}) \rangle \longrightarrow \boxed{\sim g}
$$
$$
\longrightarrow \langle *h_B(\mathbf{x}''|\mathbf{x}') \rangle \longrightarrow \langle \times f(\mathbf{Z}^t|\mathbf{x}'') \rangle \longrightarrow \boxed{p(\mathbf{x}|\mathcal{Z}^t)}
$$

(5)

where we have assumed the dynamics can be decomposed as

$$h(\mathbf{x}''|\mathbf{x}) = \int_{\mathbf{x}'} h_B(\mathbf{x}''|\mathbf{x}')h_A(\mathbf{x}'|\mathbf{x})d\mathbf{x}'. \tag{6}$$

The algorithm is formally valid for any choice of h_A, h_B satisfying (6), and for any g; the objective of partitioned sampling is to use one's intuition about the problem to choose a decomposition of the dynamics, and a weighting function g, which are beneficial. In the example shown in figure 2, the overall strategy is to populate the dark shaded region first, so h_A should be such that some particles are diffused into dark region, g should be peaked in the dark region, and h_B should be such that particles already in the dark region are not diffused out of it. A natural choice, therefore, is to take h_A to be the dynamics for object A, g to be a likelihood function for the location of object A only, and h_B to be the dynamics for object B. This was the approach taken by the authors of [17].

3   Partitioned sampling for articulated objects

Although the preceding discussion was phrased for clarity in terms of multiple objects, partitioned sampling is not restricted to improving the efficiency of multiple object tracking. In fact, it can be used whenever the following conditions hold.

- The configuration space $\mathcal{X}$ can be partitioned as a Cartesian product $\mathcal{X} = \mathcal{X}_1 \times \mathcal{X}_2$.
- The dynamics h can be decomposed as $h = h_1 * h_2$, where h_2 acts on $\mathcal{X}_2$. This means that if $\mathbf{x} = (\mathbf{x}_1, \mathbf{x}_2)$ and $\mathbf{x}' = (\mathbf{x}'_1, \mathbf{x}'_2)$ with $\mathbf{x}_i, \mathbf{x}'_i \in \mathcal{X}_i$, and $\mathbf{x}'$ is a random draw from $h_2(\cdot|\mathbf{x})$, then $\mathbf{x}'_1 = \mathbf{x}_1$. Informally, the second partition of the dynamics does not change the value of the projection of any particle into the first partition of the configuration space.[3] We refer to this later as property $(\star)$.
- A weighting function g_1 defined on $\mathcal{X}_1$ is available, which is peaked in the same region as the posterior restricted to $\mathcal{X}_1$.

There is also an obvious generalisation to $k > 2$ partitions: the configuration space is partitioned as $\mathcal{X} = \mathcal{X}_1 \times \ldots \times \mathcal{X}_k$, the dynamics as $h = h_1 * \ldots * h_k$ with each h_j acting on $\mathcal{X}_j \times \ldots \times \mathcal{X}_k$, and we have weighting functions $g_1, g_2, \ldots g_{k-1}$ with each g_j peaked in the same region as the posterior restricted to $\mathcal{X}_j$.

One example of such a system is an articulated object. The example given in this paper is of a hand tracker which models the fist, index finger and thumb as an articulated rigid object with three joints. The partitioned sampling algorithm

---

[3] This condition is stronger than necessary, but a more general discussion would obscure the important idea.

used for this application is shown in the following Condensation diagram:

$$
\begin{array}{l}
\boxed{p(\mathbf{x}|\mathcal{Z}^{t-1})} \longrightarrow \boxed{\sim} \longrightarrow \langle *h_{\mathrm{f}}(\mathbf{x}'|\mathbf{x}) \rangle \longrightarrow \boxed{\sim f_{\mathrm{f}}} \\[4pt]
\longrightarrow \langle *h_{\mathrm{th1}}(\mathbf{x}''|\mathbf{x}') \rangle \longrightarrow \boxed{\sim f_{\mathrm{th1}}} \\[4pt]
\longrightarrow \langle *h_{\mathrm{th2}}(\mathbf{x}'''|\mathbf{x}'') \rangle \longrightarrow \boxed{\sim f_{\mathrm{th2}}} \\[4pt]
\longrightarrow \langle *h_{\mathrm{i}}(\mathbf{x}''''|\mathbf{x}''') \rangle \longrightarrow \langle \times f(\mathbf{Z}|\mathbf{x}'''') \rangle \longrightarrow \boxed{p(\mathbf{x}''''|\mathcal{Z}^t)}
\end{array}
\tag{7}
$$

The subscript 'f' stands for "fist", 'th1' for "first thumb joint", 'th2' for "second thumb joint", and 'i' for "index finger". So the configuration space is partitioned into 4 parts:

- $\mathcal{X}_{\mathrm{f}} \equiv$ scale, orientation, and x and y translation of the fist
- $\mathcal{X}_{\mathrm{th1}} \equiv$ joint angle of base of thumb
- $\mathcal{X}_{\mathrm{th2}} \equiv$ joint angle of tip of thumb
- $\mathcal{X}_{\mathrm{i}} \equiv$ joint angle of index finger

The dynamics are decomposed as $h = h_{\mathrm{f}} * h_{\mathrm{th1}} * h_{\mathrm{th2}} * h_{\mathrm{i}}$ with the last three operations consisting of a deterministic shift plus Gaussian diffusion within the appropriate partition only. Note that although $\mathcal{X}$ is a shape space of splines, it is not described by the linear parameterisation normally used for such shape spaces. Instead it is parameterised by the 7 physical variables listed above (scale, orientation, x and y translation, and the 3 joint angles), so that any $\mathbf{x}$ is an element of $\mathbb{R}^7$.

3.1   Likelihood function and weighting functions

It remains to specify the measurement likelihood $f(\mathbf{Z}|\mathbf{x})$. Recall that the parameters $\mathbf{x}$ correspond to a B-spline in the image. A one-dimensional grey-scale edge operator is applied to the normal lines to this B-spline at 28 points (8 on the main hand, 6 on each of the thumb joints and 8 on the index finger). Each of the 28 resulting "edges" (actually points which are the nearest above-threshold responses of a 1D operator) has a normal distance ν_i from the B-spline, which would be zero if the model fitted the image edges perfectly. By assuming (i) the deviations of the model from the template shape are Gaussian, (ii) that such deviations are independent on different normal lines, and (iii) there is a fixed probability of finding no edge, it is easy to see that the form of $f(\mathbf{Z}|\mathbf{x})$ should be

$$
\log f(\mathbf{Z}|\mathbf{x}) \propto \mathrm{const} + \sum_m \nu_m{}^2,
\tag{8}
$$

where the constant was set by hand for this application. We can also exploit the fact that the portion of a normal line on the *interior* of the B-spline should be skin-coloured. This is reflected by adding to (8) the output of correlating the (colour) normal line pixel values with a colour template. Full details on densities of the form (8) can be found in [15, 16], for example.

Recall there are 28 measurement lines on the hand template: 8 on the fist, 6 on each of the thumb joints and 8 on the index finger. Since the likelihood factorises as a product of likelihoods for individual measurement lines, this gives us a convenient way to re-express the likelihood:

$$f(\mathbf{Z}|\mathbf{x}) = f_f(\mathbf{Z}_f|\mathbf{x}_f)\, f_{th1}(\mathbf{Z}_{th1}|\mathbf{x}_f, \mathbf{x}_{th1})\, f_{th2}(\mathbf{Z}_{th2}|\mathbf{x}_f, \mathbf{x}_{th1}, \mathbf{x}_{th2})\, f_i(\mathbf{Z}_i|\mathbf{x}_f, \mathbf{x}_i) \quad (9)$$

where, for example, $\mathbf{Z}_f$ are the measurements on the 8 fist locations, $\mathbf{x}_f$ are the components of $\mathbf{x}$ which specify the configuration of the fist, and similarly for the other subscripts.

The factorisation (9) immediately suggests the use of f_f, f_{th1} and f_{th2} as weighting functions, since they should be peaked at the correct locations of the fist and thumb joints respectively. This is precisely what the implementation does; hence the presence of f_f, f_{th1} and f_{th2} on diagram (7).

3.2 Dividing effort between the partitions

An important advantage of partitioned sampling is that the number of particles devoted to each partition can be varied. Partitions which require a large number of particles for acceptable performance can be satisfied without incurring additional effort in the other partitions. For instance, in the hand tracking application, the fist often moves rapidly and unpredictably whereas the joint angles of finger and thumb tend to change more slowly. Hence we use $n_1 = 700$ particles for the fist partition, but only $n_2 = n_3 = 100$ particles for the two thumb partitions and $n_4 = 90$ for the index finger partition. A glance at diagram (7) shows this produces a substantial saving, since at every time-step we avoid calculating $f_{th1}(\mathbf{Z}_{th1}|\mathbf{x})$, $f_{th2}(\mathbf{Z}_{th2}|\mathbf{x})$ and $f_i(\mathbf{Z}_i|\mathbf{x})$ for over 600 values of $\mathbf{x}$ that would otherwise have been required.

Note that the analysis of section 2.3, in terms of survival rates, cannot necessarily be used to determine the optimum allocation of particles between the partitions. If the dynamics and observations in each partition are completely independent, and inaccuracies in the estimated parameters for each partition are equally costly, then one can show that the number of particles in each partition should be inversely proportional to the survival rate for that partition. However, these conditions are never satisfied for an articulated object. Indeed, almost the opposite is true in the hand-tracking case. For one thing, since the intended application is a drawing tool based on the position of the finger tip, inaccuracies of many pixels are acceptable in the fist position, provided only that lock is not lost on the finger tip. However, even small errors in the finger tip position will degrade the performance of the drawing tool greatly. Thus one might think that the majority of particles should be devoted to the finger tip partition.

Two factors militate against this conclusion, however. One is that the precise location of the finger tip is in fact determined by an auxiliary least-squares fitting operation mentioned later; hence the imperative for accuracy in this partition is not so great. Second, it is of overwhelming importance that lock is not lost on the fist, because the search lines for locating finger and thumb are placed relative to the fist. Experiment showed that this factor is the most crucial, which is why the majority of particles are devoted to the fist partition.

So far we have not been able to develop a coherent theory for choosing how to allocate the particles between partitions in such cases, and can only recommend careful experimentation. Some insight can be gained by studying simulated data, however. Figure 3 shows the results of tracking a simulated articulated chain with several links. The state space is divided into one partition for each link, and a fixed number of particles was divided between these in various ways. The graphs show the variance (in pixels^2) of the end-point of the articulated object, as estimated by partitioned sampling averaged over 200 frames. Several different runs were made for each set of parameter values; the curves shown are the best-fit (least-squares) quartics through all data points. Figure 3(a) is for a 3-link object whose dynamics have equal variance at each link. A total of 300 particles were available; 100 were allocated to the final partition and the remaining particles divided between the first two partitions. Because the dynamics and likelihood function are the same for each partition, the survival rates are similar for each partition, and as we might expect, the minimum variance is achieved by equally dividing these particles between the first two partitions.

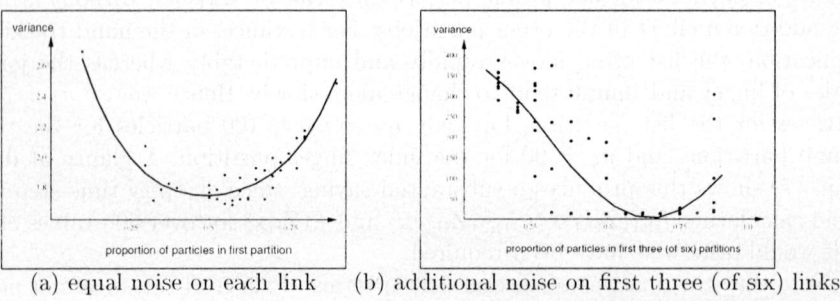

(a) equal noise on each link   (b) additional noise on first three (of six) links

Fig. 3. Allocating resources to different partitions. *(a) Because the variance of the dynamics for each link is equal, the survival rate for each partition is approximately the same and the best allocation of particles is to distribute them evenly between partitions. (b) Now the variance of the dynamics on early partitions is 9 times higher than the later ones, so the survival rates on early partitions are lower and it is best to devote a higher proportion of the particles to these partitions.*

Figure 3(b) is a more extreme example. Now there are 6 links, and the first three links have dynamics which are much "noisier" than the last three links. Specifically, the first three links have the same dynamics $h_{123}(\cdot|\mathbf{x})$ and the last three share a different conditional density $h_{456}(\cdot|\mathbf{x})$ for their dynamics. The densities h_{123}, h_{456} were Gaussian with $\mathrm{var}(h_{123}) = 9\mathrm{var}(h_{456})$. Because of the higher variance of the dynamics, the survival rate for particles in the first three partitions is lower than those in the last three; hence we expect that it will be most efficient to devote the majority of particles to the first three partitions. This is indeed the case; from the graph it appears that the best results are achieved when 60-70% of the particles are devoted to the first three partitions. Notice the extremely high variances for many data points outside this range: these are caused by the tracker losing lock on the early partitions.

3.3 Articulated objects can be evaluated twice as fast

In the particular case in which the overall likelihood $f(\mathbf{Z}|\mathbf{x})$ can be expressed as a product (9) of the weighting functions and another easily calculated function (in this case, f_i), the diagram (7) can be given a simpler form which uses standard resampling rather than weighted resampling:

$$
\begin{array}{c}
\boxed{p(\mathbf{x}|\mathcal{Z}^{t-1})} \longrightarrow \langle *h_{\mathrm{f}}(\mathbf{x'}|\mathbf{x}) \rangle \longrightarrow \langle \times f_{\mathrm{f}} \rangle \longrightarrow \ulcorner \sim \urcorner \\[6pt]
\longrightarrow \langle *h_{\mathrm{th1}}(\mathbf{x''}|\mathbf{x'}) \rangle \longrightarrow \langle \times f_{\mathrm{th1}} \rangle \longrightarrow \ulcorner \sim \urcorner \\[6pt]
\longrightarrow \langle *h_{\mathrm{th2}}(\mathbf{x'''}|\mathbf{x''}) \rangle \longrightarrow \langle \times f_{\mathrm{th2}} \rangle \longrightarrow \ulcorner \sim \urcorner \\[6pt]
\longrightarrow \langle *h_{\mathrm{i}}(\mathbf{x''''}|\mathbf{x'''}) \rangle \longrightarrow \langle \times f_{\mathrm{i}} \rangle \longrightarrow \boxed{p(\mathbf{x''''}|\mathcal{Z}^{t})}
\end{array}
\tag{10}
$$

One can check the equivalence by just writing out in detail the algorithm described by each diagram. The key is property ($\star$) mentioned in section 3: e.g. the "fist" component $\mathbf{x}_{\mathrm{f}}$ of a particle does not change after the fist partition, so the value of f_{f} for the particle does not change either. In other words, the evaluation of any given importance function commutes with the dynamics from subsequent partitions.

The reformulation of (7) as (10) is important because the computational expense of the hand tracking largely resides in evaluating the likelihood functions. Using diagram (7), the likelihood of each measurement line (except those on the index finger) is evaluated twice — once as part of a weighting function, and once as part of the final likelihood function. In diagram (10), each measurement line is examined only once.

3.4 Other details

Initialisation and re-initialisation are handled by the ICondensation mechanism of [11]. Various standard tools, such as background subtraction (which can be performed on an SGI Octane very cheaply using the alpha-blending hardware), and least-squares fitting of an auxiliary spline to the tip of the index finger, are used to refine the performance of the tracker. Details of these tools can be found in our technical report [10].

4 Results: a vision-based drawing package

The hand tracker described in the previous section was implemented on an SGI Octane with a single 175MHz R10000 CPU. Using 700 samples for the hand base, 100 samples for each of the thumb joints and 90 samples for the index finger, the tracker consumes approximately 75% of the machine cycles, which allows real-time operation at 25Hz with no dropped video frames even while other applications are running on the machine. The tracker is robust to clutter (figure 4), including skin-coloured objects (figure 5). The position of the index finger is located with considerable precision (figure 5) and the two articulations in the thumb are also recovered with reasonable accuracy (figure 6).

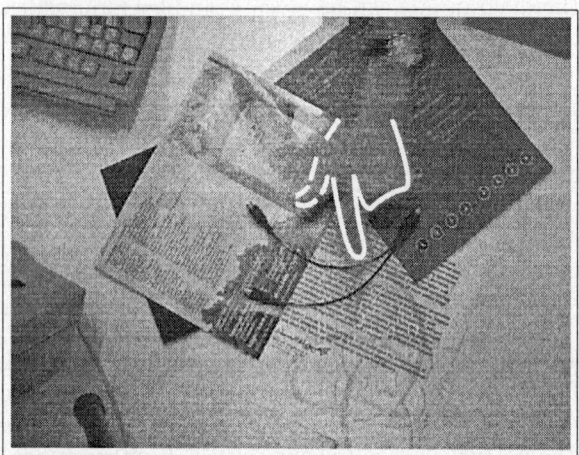

Fig. 4. Heavy clutter *does not hinder the hand tracker. Even moving the papers on the desk to invalidate the background subtraction does not prevent the Condensation tracker functioning. The fingertip localisation is less robust, however, and jitter increases in heavily cluttered areas.*

We have developed a simple drawing package to explore the utility of a vision-based hand tracker for user-interface tasks. The tracking achieved is sufficiently good that it can compete with a mouse for freehand drawing, though (currently) at the cost of absorbing most of the processing of a moderately powerful workstation. It is therefore instructive to consider what additional strengths of the vision system we can exploit to provide functionality which could not be reproduced using a mouse.

The current prototype drawing package provides only one primitive, the freehand line. When the thumb is extended, the pointer draws, and when the thumb is placed against the hand the virtual pen is lifted from the page. Immediately we can exploit one of the extra degrees of freedom estimated by the tracker, and use the orientation of the index finger to control the width of the line be-

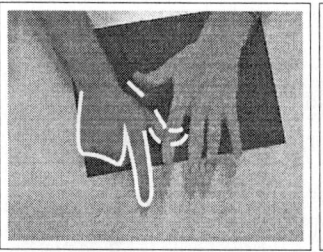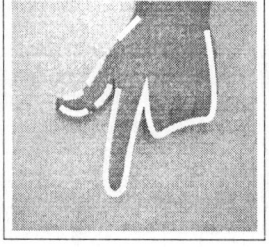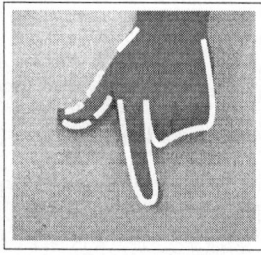

Fig. 5. Left: **Skin-coloured objects** *do not distract the tracker. Here two hands are present in the image but tracking remains fixed to the right hand. If the right hand were to leave the field of view the tracker would immediately reinitialise on the left hand.* Middle and right: **The index finger** *is tracked rotating relative to the hand body. The angle of the finger is estimated with considerable precision, and agile motions of the fingertip, such as scribbling gestures, can be accurately recorded.*

ing produced. When the finger points upwards on the image, the pen draws with a default width, and as the finger rotates the width varies from thinner (finger anti-clockwise) to thicker (finger clockwise) — see figure 7. The scarcity of variable-thickness lines in computer-generated artwork is a testament to the difficulty of producing this effect with a mouse.

The fact that a camera is observing the desk also allows other intriguing features not directly related to hand-tracking. We have implemented a natural interface to translate and rotate the virtual workspace for the modest hardware investment of a piece of black paper (figure 8). The very strong white-to-black edges from the desk to the paper allow the paper to be tracked with great precision using a simple Kalman filter, at low computational cost. Translations and rotations of the paper are then reflected in the virtual workspace, a very satisfying interface paradigm. While one hand draws, the other hand can adjust the workspace to the most comfortable position. Figure 9 is a still from a movie which shows the system in action; this movie is available at [15]. In the future it should be possible to perform discrete operations such as switching between drawing tools using simple static gesture recognition on one of the hands. Tracking both hands would allow more complex selection tasks, for example continuous zooming, or colour picking.

5   Conclusion

It has been shown that the technique of partitioned sampling can be applied to articulated objects. A new concept termed the "survival rate" of particles in a particle filter was used to explain why partitioned sampling works, and some special features of the application to articulated objects were exploited for significant computational improvements. Although some progress has been made, the question of how to allocate a fixed number of particles between partitions has

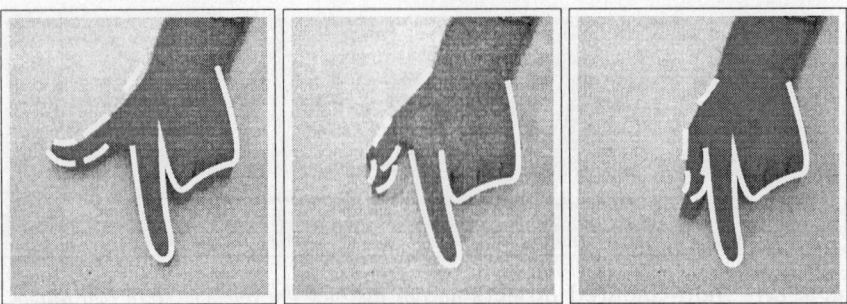

Fig. 6. The two degrees of freedom of the thumb *are tracked. The thumb angles are not very reliably estimated. This is probably partly because the joints are short, and so offer few edges to detect, and more importantly because the shape model gives a poor approximation to the thumb when it opposes. The gross position of the thumb can be extracted consistently enough to provide a stable switch which can be used analogously to a mouse button.*

not been answered coherently and this must be the subject of future work. Another open problem, not previously mentioned, is that our current "articulated partitioned" approach takes no account of the tree structure of the object: every link must be sampled as a chain even though the physical structure is a tree. Our present approach is valid mathematically, but it would be more appropriate, and possibly more efficient, to take account of the tree structure.

A hand-tracking system using partitioned sampling on articulated objects was described. It is of sufficient quality for very demanding interactive tasks. The main features of the system are robustness (from the Condensation algorithm), instantaneous initialisation and near-perfect responsiveness (from importance sampling based on colour segmentation) and inexpensive addition of extra degrees of freedom (from partitioned sampling). The system runs on a single-processor workstation with a standard colour camera and no additional hardware. Even in the simple drawing package described it is easily possible to produce figures which could not comfortably be produced with a mouse, and to do so using natural gestures and a natural, changing desk environment. We believe this system has significant implications for the everyday use of virtual environments with interactive computer vision.

A Appendix

An informal proof of (4) follows; more details can be found in [15]. Recall the scenario of section 2.2: a particle set $(\mathbf{x}_i, \pi_i)_{i=1}^{n}$ has been formed with prior (or "proposal density") $p(\mathbf{x})$ and weighted by likelihood $p'(\mathbf{x})/p(\mathbf{x})$, resulting in a

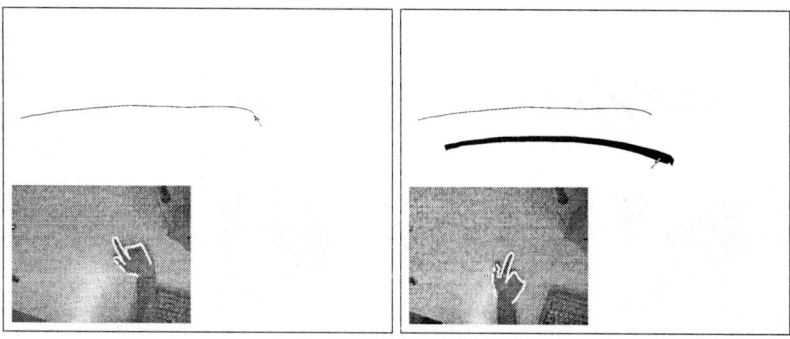

Fig. 7. Line thickness *is controlled using the orientation of the index finger. The top image shows a line drawn with the index finger pointing to the left, producing a thin trace. In the bottom image the finger pointed to the right and the line is fatter. Of course if the finger angle varies while the line is being drawn, a continuous variation of thickness is produced.*

posterior $p'(\mathbf{x})$. Some simple calculations give

$$
\begin{aligned}
\mathcal{D} &= \left(\sum_{i=1}^{n} \pi_i^{(n)^2} \right)^{-1} && \text{by definition of } \mathcal{D}, \text{ equation (2)} \\
&\approx \left(\sum_{i=1}^{n} \tfrac{1}{n^2} p'(\mathbf{x}_i^{(n)})^2 / p(\mathbf{x}_i^{(n)})^2 \right)^{-1} && \text{by defn of the } \pi_i, \text{ and comment below} \\
&\approx \left(\tfrac{1}{n} \int p'(\mathbf{x})^2 / p(\mathbf{x})\, d\mathbf{x} \right)^{-1} && \text{as the } \mathbf{x}_i^{(n)} \text{ are drawn from } p(\mathbf{x}) \\
&= \left(\int p'(\mathbf{x})^2 / p(\mathbf{x})\, d\mathbf{x} \right)^{-1} \times n \\
&= \alpha n
\end{aligned}
$$

The second line uses the fact (see [15]) that for large n, the normalisation constant for the weights is approximately $1/n$ — so $\pi_i \approx p'(\mathbf{x}_i)/(np(\mathbf{x}_i))$.

References

1. S. Ahmad. A usable real-time 3D hand tracker. In *28th Asilomar Conference on Signals, Systems and Computers*. IEEE Computer Society Press, 1995. Available from www.icsi.berkeley.edu/~ahmad.
2. A. Blake and M.A. Isard. 3D position, attitude and shape input using video tracking of hands and lips. In *Proc. Siggraph*, pages 185–192. ACM, 1994.
3. L. Brettzner and T. Lindeberg. Use your hand as a 3D mouse. In *Proc. 5th European Conf. Computer Vision*, volume 1, pages 141–157, Freiburg, Germany, 1998. Springer Verlag.
4. J. Carpenter. P. Clifford. and P. Fearnhead. An improved particle filter for non-linear problems. Technical report, Dept. of Statistics, University of Oxford, 1997. Available from www.stats.ox.ac.uk/~clifford/index.html.
5. R. Cipolla and N.J. Hollinghurst. Human-robot interface by pointing with uncalibrated stereo vision. *J. Image and Vision Computing*, 14(3):171–178, 1996.

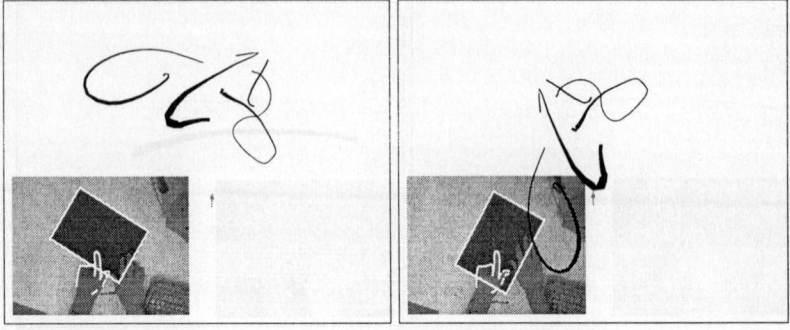

Fig. 8. Moving around the virtual workspace *is accomplished by following the tracked outline of a physical object. The piece of black paper can be tracked with a simple Kalman filter, and the virtual drawing follows the translations and rotations of the paper. The virtual workspace has been rotated anti-clockwise between the top and bottom frames. This is a very natural interface which can be used while drawing.*

6. A. Doucet. On sequential simulation-based methods for Bayesian filtering. Technical Report CUED/F-INFENG/TR310, Dept. of Engineering, University of Cambridge, 1998. Available from www.stats.bris.ac.uk:81/MCMC/pages/list.html.
7. J. Geweke. Bayesian inference in econometric models using Monte Carlo integration. *Econometrica*, 57:1317–1339, 1989.
8. H.P. Graf, E. Cosatto, D. Gibbon, M. Kocheisen, and E. Petajan. Multi-modal system for locating heads and faces. In *Proc. 2nd Int. Conf. on Automatic Face and Gesture Recognition*, pages 88–93, 1996.
9. T. Heap and D. Hogg. Wormholes in shape space: Tracking through discontinuous changes in shape. In *Proc. 6th Int. Conf. on Computer Vision*, 1998.
10. M. Isard and J. MacCormick. Hand tracking for vision-based drawing. Technical report, Visual Dynamics Group, Dept. Eng. Science, University of Oxford, 2000. Available from www.robots.ox.ac.uk/~vdg.
11. M.A. Isard and A. Blake. ICondensation: Unifying low-level and high-level tracking in a stochastic framework. In *Proc. 5th European Conf. Computer Vision*, pages 893–908, 1998.
12. R. Kjeldsen and J. Kender. Toward the use of gesture in traditional user interfaces. In *Proc. 2nd Int. Conf. on Automatic Face and Gesture Recognition*, pages 151–156, 1996.
13. Marcus Kohler and Sven Schröter. A Survey of Video-based Gesture Recognition: Stereo and Mono Systems. Technical Report 693, Informatik VII, University of Dortmund/Germany, August 1998. Available from ls7-www.cs.uni-dortmund.de/~kohler.
14. J. Liu and R. Chen. Sequential Monte Carlo methods for dynamic systems. *J. Amer. Statist. Assoc.*, 93, 1998. In press. Available from www-stat.stanford.edu/~jliu.
15. J. MacCormick. *Probabilistic modelling and stochastic algorithms for visual localisation and tracking*. PhD thesis, University of Oxford, 2000. Available from www.robots.ox.ac.uk/~jmac/research/thesis/.
16. J. MacCormick and A. Blake. A probabilistic contour discriminant for object localisation. In *Proc. 6th Int. Conf. on Computer Vision*, pages 390–395, 1998.

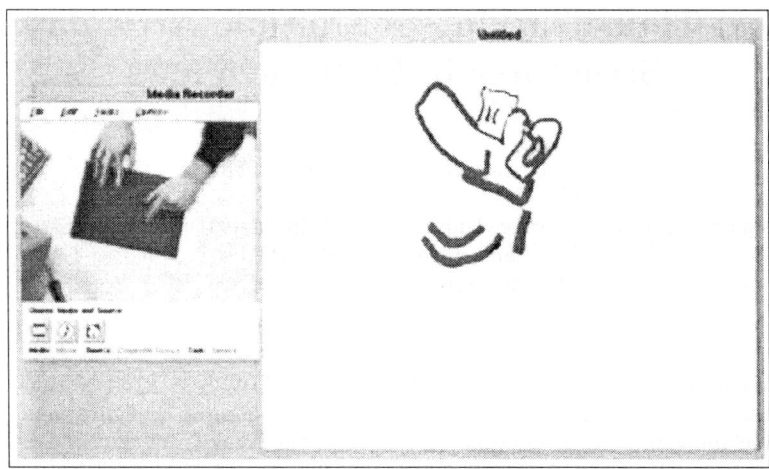

Fig. 9. The drawing package in action. *This screen shot shows a cartoon character drawn using the drawing package; note the variable-width lines. A movie clip showing this figure being created is available at [15]. The scene on the left is the camera's view; it is shown for information only and is not employed by the user.*

17. J. MacCormick and A. Blake. A probabilistic exclusion principle for tracking multiple objects. In *Proc. 7th International Conf. Computer Vision*, pages 572–578, 1999.
18. D. Mackay. Introduction to Monte Carlo methods. In M. Jordan, editor, *Learning in Graphical Models*. MIT Press, 1999. Available as ftp://wol.ra.phy.cam.ac.uk/pub/mackay/erice.ps.gz.
19. B.D. Ripley. *Stochastic simulation.* New York: Wiley, 1987.
20. C. Wren and A. Pentland. Dynamic modeling of human motion. In *Third IEEE International Conference on Automatic Face and Gesture Recognition*, Nara, Japan, April 1998.

Real-Time Tracking of Multiple Articulated Structures in Multiple Views

Tom Drummond and Roberto Cipolla

Department of Engineering, University of Cambridge Trumpington Street,
Cambridge, UK, CB2 1PZ
{twd20, cipolla}@eng.cam.ac.uk

Abstract. This paper describes a highly flexible approach to real-time frame-rate tracking in complex camera and structures configurations, including the use of multiple cameras and the tracking of multiple or articulated targets. A powerful and general method is presented for expressing and solving the constraints which exist in these configurations in a principled manner. This method exploits the geometric structure present in the Lie group and Lie algebra formalism to express the constraints that derive from structures such as hinges or a common ground plane. This method makes use of the adjoint representation to simplify the constraints which are then applied by means of Lagrange multipliers.

1 Introduction

The tracking of known three-dimensional objects is useful for numerous applications, including motion analysis, surveillance and robotic control tasks. This paper presents a novel approach to visual tracking in complex camera and structure configurations, including the use of multiple cameras and the tracking of multiple structures with constraints or of articulated structures. Earlier work in the tracking of rigid bodies [1] which employs a Lie group and Lie algebra formalism is exploited in order to simplify the difficulties that arise in these more complex situations and thus provide a real-time frame-rate tracking system.

The paper first reviews work on the tracking of rigid bodies and then describes the Lie group and Lie algebra formalism used within the rigid body tracking system which is used as the basis for more complex configurations. It then shows how this formalism provides a powerful means of managing complex multi-component configurations; the transformation of measurements made in differing co-ordinate frames is simplified as is the expression of constraints (e.g. hinge or slide) that are present in the system. These constraints can then be imposed by means of Lagrange multipliers. Results from experiments with real-time frame-rate systems using this framework are then presented and discussed.

1.1 Model-based tracking

Because a video feed contains a very large amount of data, it is important to extract only a small amount of salient information if real-time frame (or field) rate performance is to be achieved [2]. This observation leads to the notion of *feature based* tracking [3] in which processing is restricted to locating strong image features such as contours [4, 5].

A number of successful systems have been based on tracking the image contours of a known model. Lowe [6] used the Marr-Hildreth edge detector to extract edges from the image which were then chained together to form lines. These lines were matched and fitted to those in the model. A similar approach using the Hough transform has also been used [7]. The use of two-dimensional image processing incurs a significant computational cost and both of these systems make use of special purpose hardware in order to achieve frame rate processing.

An alternative approach is to render the model first and then use sparse one-dimensional search to find and measure the distance to matching (nearby) edges in the image. This approach has been used in RAPID [8], CONDENSATION [9] and other systems [10, 11, 12]. The efficiency yielded by this approach allows all these systems to run in real-time on standard workstations. The approach is also used here.

Using either of these approaches, most systems (except CONDENSATION) then compute the pose parameters by linearising with respect to image motion. This process is reformulated here in terms of the Lie group SE(3) and its Lie algebra (see [13, 14] for a good introduction to Lie groups and their algebras). This formulation is a natural one to use since SE(3) exactly represents the space of poses that form the output of a system which tracks a rigid body. Differential quantities such as velocities and small motions in the group then correspond to the Lie algebra of the group (which is the tangent space to the identity). Thus the representation provides a canonical method for linearising the relationship between image motion and pose parameters. Further, this approach can be generalised to other transformation groups and has been successfully applied to deformations of a planar contour using the groups GA(2) and P(2) [15].

Outliers are a key problem that must be addressed by systems which measure and fit edges. They frequently occur in the measurement process since additional edges may be present in the scene in close proximity to the model edges. These may be caused by shadows, for example, or strong background scene elements. Such outliers are a particular problem for the traditional least-squares fitting method used by many of the algorithms. Methods of improving robustness to these sorts of outliers include the use of RANSAC [16], factored sampling [9] or regularisation, for example the Levenberg-Marquadt scheme used in [6]. The approach used here employs iterative re-weighted least squares (a robust M-estimator).

There is a trade-off to be made between robustness and precision. The CONDENSATION system, for example, obtains a high degree of robustness by taking a large number of sample hypotheses of the position of the tracked structure with a comparatively small number of edge measurements per sample. By contrast, the system presented here uses a large number of measurements for a single position hypothesis and is thus able to obtain very high precision in its positional estimates. This is particularly relevant in tasks such as visual servoing since the dynamics and environmental conditions can be controlled so as to constrain the robustness problems, while high precision is needed in real-time in order for the system to be useful.

Occlusion is also a significant cause of instabilities and may occur when the object occludes parts of itself (self occlusion) or where another object lies between the camera and the target (external occlusion). RAPID handles the first of these problems by use of a pre-computed table of visible features indexed by what is essentially a view-sphere. By contrast, the system presented here uses graphical rendering techniques [17] to dynamically determine the visible features and is thus able to handle more complex situations (such as objects with holes) than can be tabulated on a view-sphere.

External occlusion can be treated by using outlier rejection, for example in [16] which discards primitives for which insufficient support is found, or by modifying statistical descriptions of the observation model (as in [18]). If a model is available for the intervening object, then it is possible to use this to re-estimate the visible features [19, 7]. Both of these methods are used within the system presented here.

1.2 Articulated Structures

A taxonomy of non-rigid motion is given in [20]. This paper is only concerned with what is classified as *articulated motion*, which can be characterised as comprising rigid components connected by simple structures such as hinges, slides etc.

Lowe [21] also considered articulated motion, which was implemented by means of internal model parameters which are stored in a tree structure. By contrast, the approach presented here uses a symmetric representation in which the full pose of each rigid component is stored independently. Constraints are then imposed on the relationships between component pose estimates. A similar approach has been taken for tracking people [22] which relies on prior extraction of accurate silhouettes in multiple synchronised views of each frame which are then used to apply forces on the components of the three dimensional model.

2 Tracking a Rigid Structure in a Single View

This section will review the rigid body tracking system which is used as a basis for the extensions which are presented in this paper. The approach used here for tracking a known 3-dimensional structure is based upon maintaining an estimate of the camera projection matrix, P, in the co-ordinate system of the structure. This projection matrix is represented as the product of a matrix of internal camera parameters:

$$K = \begin{bmatrix} f_u & s & u_0 \\ 0 & f_v & v_0 \\ 0 & 0 & 1 \end{bmatrix} \tag{1}$$

and a Euclidean projection matrix representing the position and orientation of the camera relative to the target structure:

$$E = \begin{bmatrix} R\ t \end{bmatrix} \qquad \text{with } RR^T = I \text{ and } |R| = 1 \tag{2}$$

The projective co-ordinates of an image feature are then given by

$$\begin{pmatrix} u \\ v \\ w \end{pmatrix} = P \begin{pmatrix} x \\ y \\ z \\ 1 \end{pmatrix} \tag{3}$$

with the actual image co-ordinates given by

$$(\begin{smallmatrix} \tilde{u} \\ \tilde{v} \end{smallmatrix}) = \begin{pmatrix} u/w \\ v/w \end{pmatrix} \tag{4}$$

Rigid motions of the camera relative to the target structure between consecutive video frames can then be represented by right multiplication of the projection matrix by a Euclidean transformation of the form:

$$M = \begin{bmatrix} R & t \\ 0\ 0\ 0 & 1 \end{bmatrix} \tag{5}$$

These M, form a 4×4 matrix representation of the group SE(3) of rigid body motions in 3-dimensional space, which is a 6-dimensional Lie Group. The generators of this group are typically taken to be translations in the x, y and z directions and rotations about the x, y and z axes, represented by the following matrices:

$$G_1 = \begin{bmatrix} 0\ 0\ 0\ 1 \\ 0\ 0\ 0\ 0 \\ 0\ 0\ 0\ 0 \\ 0\ 0\ 0\ 0 \end{bmatrix}, G_2 = \begin{bmatrix} 0\ 0\ 0\ 0 \\ 0\ 0\ 0\ 1 \\ 0\ 0\ 0\ 0 \\ 0\ 0\ 0\ 0 \end{bmatrix}, G_3 = \begin{bmatrix} 0\ 0\ 0\ 0 \\ 0\ 0\ 0\ 0 \\ 0\ 0\ 0\ 1 \\ 0\ 0\ 0\ 0 \end{bmatrix}, \tag{6}$$

$$G_4 = \begin{bmatrix} 0\ 0\ 0\ 0 \\ 0\ 0\ -1\ 0 \\ 0\ 1\ 0\ 0 \\ 0\ 0\ 0\ 0 \end{bmatrix}, G_5 = \begin{bmatrix} 0\ 0\ 1\ 0 \\ 0\ 0\ 0\ 0 \\ -1\ 0\ 0\ 0 \\ 0\ 0\ 0\ 0 \end{bmatrix}, G_6 = \begin{bmatrix} 0\ -1\ 0\ 0 \\ 1\ 0\ 0\ 0 \\ 0\ 0\ 0\ 0 \\ 0\ 0\ 0\ 0 \end{bmatrix}$$

These generators form a basis for the vector space (the Lie algebra) of derivatives of SE(3) at the identity. Group elements can be obtained from the generators via the exponential map:

$$M = \exp(\alpha_i G_i) \tag{7}$$

Thus, if M represents the transformation of the structure between two adjacent video frames, then the task of the tracking system becomes that of finding the α_i that describe the inter-frame transformation. Since the motion will be small, M can be approximated by the linear terms:

$$M \approx I + \alpha_i G_i \tag{8}$$

Consequently, the motion is approximately a linear sum of that produced by each of the generators. The partial derivative of projective image co-ordinates with respect the ith generating motion can be computed as:

$$\begin{pmatrix} u' \\ v' \\ w' \end{pmatrix} = P G_i \begin{pmatrix} x \\ y \\ z \\ 1 \end{pmatrix} \tag{9}$$

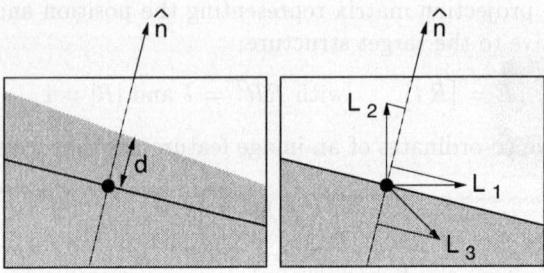

Fig. 1. Computing the normal component of the motion and generator vector fields

with

$$L_i = \begin{pmatrix} \tilde{u}' \\ \tilde{v}' \end{pmatrix} = \begin{pmatrix} \frac{u'}{w} - \frac{uw'}{w^2} \\ \frac{v'}{w} - \frac{vw'}{w^2} \end{pmatrix} \tag{10}$$

giving the motion in true image co-ordinates. A least-squares approach can then be used to fit the observed motion of image features between adjacent frames. This process is detailed in Section 2.1.

The features used in this work for tracking are the edges that are present in the model. These are strong features that can be reliably found in the image because they have a significant spatial extent. Furthermore, this means that a number of measurements can be made along each edge, and thus they may be accurately localised within an image. This choice also makes it possible to take advantage of the aperture problem (that the component of motion of an edge, tangent to itself, is not observable locally), since it allows the use of one-dimensional search along the edge normal (see Figure 1). The normal component of the motion fields, L_i are then also computed (as $f_i = L_i \cdot \hat{n}$) and d can be fitted as a linear combination of the projections of the f_i.

In order to track the edges of the model as lines in the image, it is necessary to determine which (parts of) lines are visible at each frame and where they are located relative to the camera. This work uses binary space partition trees [17] to dynamically determine the visible features of the model in real-time. This technique allows accurate frame rate tracking of complex structures such as the ship part shown in Figure 2. As rendering takes place, the stencil buffer is used to locate the visible parts of each edge by querying the buffer at a series of points along the edge prior to drawing the edge. Where the line is visible, tracking nodes are assigned to search for the nearest intensity discontinuity in the video feed along the edge normal (see Figure 4).

Figure 3 shows system operation. At each cycle, the system renders the expected view of the object (a) using its current estimate of the projection matrix, P. The visible edges are identified and tracking nodes are assigned at regular intervals in image co-ordinates along these edges (b). The edge normal is then searched in the video feed for a nearby edge (c). Typically $m \approx 400$ nodes are

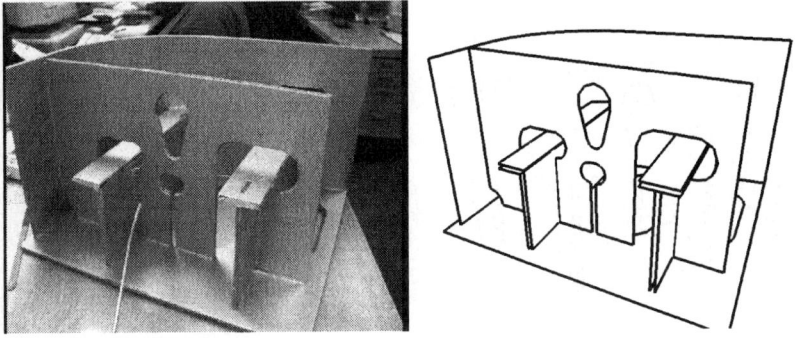

Fig. 2. Image and CAD model of ship part

assigned and measurements made in this way. The system then projects this m-dimensional measurement vector onto the 6-dimensional subspace corresponding to Euclidean transformations (d) giving the least squares estimate of the motion, M. The Euclidean part of the projection matrix, E is then updated by right multiplication with this transformation (e). Finally, the new projection matrix P is obtained by multiplying the camera parameters K with the updated Euclidean matrix to give a new current estimate of the local position (f). The system then loops back to step (a).

2.1   Computing the Motion

Step (d) in the process involves the projection of the measurement vector onto the subspace defined by the Euclidean transformation group. This subspace is given by the f_i^ξ which describe the magnitude of the edge normal motion that would be observed in the image at the ξth node for the ith group generator. These can be considered as a set of m-dimensional vectors which describe the

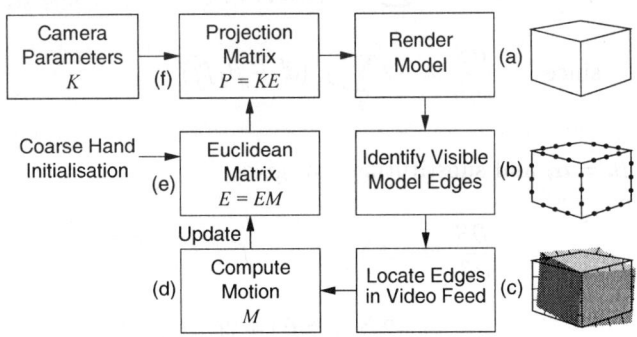

Fig. 3. Tracking system operation

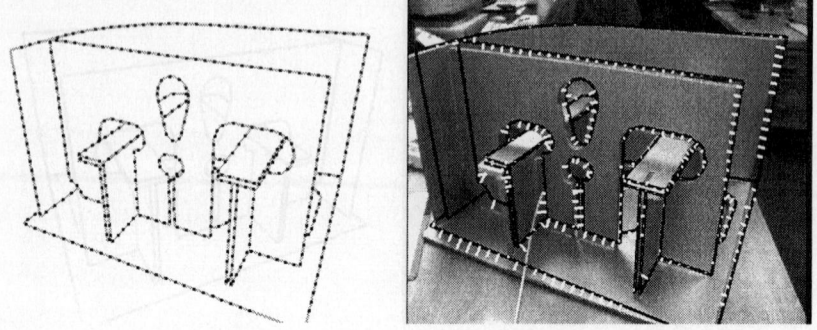

Fig. 4. Tracking nodes are assigned and distances measured

motion in the image for each mode of Euclidean transformation. The system then projects the m-vector corresponding to the measured distances (to the observed edges) onto the subspace spanned by the transformation vectors. The geometric transformation of the part which best fits the observed edge positions can be found by minimising the square error between the transformed edge position and the actual edge position (in pixels). This process is performed as follows:

$$v_i = \sum_\xi d^\xi f_i^\xi \tag{11}$$

$$C_{ij} = \sum_\xi f_i^\xi f_j^\xi \tag{12}$$

$$\alpha_i = C_{ij}^{-1} v_j \tag{13}$$

(with Einstein summation convention over Latin indices used throughout this paper). It can be seen that setting $\beta_i = \alpha_i$ gives the minimum (least-squares) solution to

$$S = \sum_\xi (d^\xi - \beta_i f_i^\xi)^2 \tag{14}$$

since
$$\frac{\partial S}{\partial \beta_i} = -2 \sum_\xi f_i^\xi (d^\xi - \beta_j f_j^\xi) \tag{15}$$

and setting $\beta_i = \alpha_i$ and substituting (13) gives

$$\frac{\partial S}{\partial \beta_i} = -2 \sum_\xi f_i^\xi d^\xi - f_i^\xi f_j^\xi C_{jk}^{-1} \sum_{\xi'} f_k^{\xi'} d^{\xi'} \tag{16}$$

$$= -2 \sum_\xi (f_i^\xi d^\xi) + 2 C_{ij} C_{jk}^{-1} \sum_{\xi'} f_k^{\xi'} d^{\xi'} \tag{17}$$

$$= 0 \tag{18}$$

Fig. 5. Frames from video of tracking sequence: The CAD model of the ship part is superimposed on the video image using the estimate of the projection matrix.

The α_i thus define a linear approximation to the Euclidean motion which minimises the sum squared error between the model and the observed lines. When more complex configurations are examined, it becomes important to consider how the sum squared error varies when $\beta_i \neq \alpha_i$. Setting $\beta_i = \alpha_i + \varepsilon_i$, (15) gives

$$\frac{\partial S}{\partial \beta_i} = 0 + 2 \sum_\xi f_i^\xi f_j^\xi \varepsilon_j \tag{19}$$

$$= 2 C_{ij} \varepsilon_j \tag{20}$$

and integrating gives

$$S = S_0 + \varepsilon_i C_{ij} \varepsilon_j \qquad \text{where } S_0 = S|_{\varepsilon=0} \tag{21}$$

All that remains for the rigid body tracker is to compute the matrix for the motion of the model represented by the α_i and apply it to the matrix E in (2) which is done by using the exponential map.

$$E_{t+1} = E_t \, \exp(\textstyle\sum_i \alpha_i G_i) \tag{22}$$

The system is therefore able to maintain an estimate of E (and hence P) by continually computing the coefficients α_i of inter-frame motions (see Figure 5). This method has also been extended to include the motion of image features due to the change in internal camera parameters and thus provide a method for on-line camera calibration [23]. In practice the simple least squares algorithm is not robust to outliers so the terms in (11) and (12) are reweighted by a decaying function of d^ξ to obtain a robust M-estimator. The reweighting causes the algorithm to become iterative (since d^ξ varies with each iteration) but convergence in all but extreme conditions is very fast and only one iteration is used per video frame/field.

3   Complex configurations

The rigid body tracking system presented in the previous section is now used as the basis of an approach which is designed to operate in more complex configurations. A novel framework for constructing tracking systems within these configurations is now presented, which takes advantage of the formulation and computational operation of the rigid body tracker. Such configurations arise in a number of ways,

Multiple cameras: It is often desirable to use more than one camera to obtain information about a scene since multiple view configurations can provide higher pose precision (especially when a large baseline is used) and also increase the robustness of the tracker.

Multiple targets: There are many situations in which knowing the relationship between the camera and a single target is insufficient. This occurs particularly when the position of the camera is not of direct interest. In these situations, it is often desirable to measure the relationship between two or more targets that are present in the scene, for example between two vehicles and the road, or between a robot tool and its workpiece.

Articulated targets: Many targets of interest are not simple rigid bodies, but contain internal degrees of freedom. This work is restricted to considering targets which comprise a number of rigid components connected by hinges or slides etc.

The simplest way to handle these configurations is merely to run multiple instances of the rigid body tracker concurrently, one per component per camera. Thus, for example three cameras viewing two structures would require six concurrent trackers. Unfortunately, this naïve approach can introduce many more degrees of freedom into the system than are really present. In this example, even if the cameras and structures can move independently, there are only 24 degrees of freedom in the world, whereas the system of six trackers contains 36. In general, this is a bad thing since problems such as ill-conditioning and high search complexity are more prevalent in high dimensional systems and also because the solution thus generated can exhibit inconsistencies. The natural approach to this problem is to impose all of the constraints that are known about the world upon the tracking system.

4 Applying Constraints

Multiple Cameras: In the case in which multiple cameras are used to view a scene, it may be that the cameras are known to be rigid relative to one another in space. In this case, there are 6 constraints that can be imposed on the system for every camera additional to the first.

Multiple structures: Where the system is being used to track multiple structures, it is often the case that other constraints apply between the structures. For example two cars will share a common ground-plane, and thus a system in which two vehicles observed from an airborne camera will have three constraints that apply to the raw twelve dimensions present in the two trackers, reflecting the nine degrees of freedom present in the world.

Articulated structures: This is really a special case of constrained multiple structures, except that there are usually more constraints. A hinged structure, for example has seven degrees of freedom (six for position in the world and one for the angle of the hinge). When the two components of the structure are independently tracked, there are five hinge constraints which apply to the system.

Because these constraints exist in the world, it is highly desirable to impose them on the system of trackers. Each of the trackers generates an estimate for the motion of one rigid component in a given view, α_i in (13) as well as a matrix C_{ij} in (12) which describes how the error varies around that estimate. Thus the goal is to use both of these pieces of information from each tracker to obtain a global maximum a-posteriori estimate of the motion subject to satisfying the known constraints. This raises three issues which must be addressed:

1. Measurements from different trackers are made in different co-ordinate frames.
2. How can the constraints be expressed?
3. How can they then be imposed?

4.1   Co-ordinate frames

The first difficulty is that the α_i and the C_{ij} are quantities in the Lie algebra deriving from the co-ordinate frame of the object being tracked. Since these are not the same, in general, for distinct trackers, a method for transforming the α_i and C_{ij} from one co-ordinate frame to another is needed. Specifically, this requires knowing what happens to the Lie algebra of SE(3) under $\mathbb{R}^3$ co-ordinate frame changes. Since these frame changes correspond to elements of the Lie group SE(3), this reduces to knowing what happens to the Lie algebra of the group under conjugation by elements of the group. This is (by definition) the adjoint representation of the group which is a $n \times n$ matrix representation, where n is the dimensionality of the group (six in the case of SE(3)). The adjoint representation, $\mathrm{ad}(M)$, for a matrix element of SE(3), M, can easily be computed by considering the action of M on the group generators, G_i, by conjugation:

$$MG_iM^{-1} = \sum_j \mathrm{ad}(M)_{ij}G_j \tag{23}$$

If (with a slight abuse of notation) $M = [R|t]$, this is given by

$$\mathrm{ad}(M) = \begin{bmatrix} R & 0 \\ [t_\wedge]R & R \end{bmatrix} \quad \text{where } [t_\wedge]_{ij} = \varepsilon_{ijk}t_k \tag{24}$$

To see that these 6×6 matrices do form a representation of SE(3), it is only necessary to ensure that multiplication is preserved under the mapping into the adjoint space (that $\mathrm{ad}(M_1)\,\mathrm{ad}(M_2) = \mathrm{ad}(M_1M_2)$) which can easily be checked using the identity $R_1[t_{2\wedge}]R_1^{-1} = [R_1t_{2\wedge}]$. Thus if M transforms points from co-ordinate frame 1 into frame 2, then $\mathrm{ad}(M)$ transforms a vector in the Lie algebra of frame 1 into the Lie algebra of frame 2. Using this, the quantities in equations (11) – (13) can be transformed as follows (see Figure 6(a–b)):

$$\alpha' = \mathrm{ad}(M)\,\alpha \qquad (25)$$

$$C' = \mathrm{ad}(M)\,C\,\mathrm{ad}(M)^T \qquad (26)$$

$$v' = \mathrm{ad}(M)^{-T}v \qquad (27)$$

4.2 Expressing constraints

It is useful to have a generic method for expressing the constraints that are present on the given world configuration since this increases the speed with which models for new situations may be constructed. In the Lie algebra formalism, it is very easy to express the constraints that describe a hinge, a slide or the existence of a common ground plane since the relationship between the motion in the algebra and the constraints is a simple one.

The presence of a hinge or common ground plane are holonomic constraints which reduce the dimensionality of the configuration space by five and three respectively. This results in a seven or nine dimensional sub-manifold representing legal configurations embedded within the raw twelve dimensional configuration manifold. The tangent space to this submanifold corresponds to the space of velocities which respect the constraint. This means that at each legal configuration there is a linear subspace of legal velocities, which implies that the constraints on the velocities must be both linear and homogeneous (since zero velocity results in a legal configuration). Thus if β_1 and β_2 correspond to the motions of the two rigid components (in their Lie algebras) then the constraints must take the form

$$\beta_1 \cdot c_1^i + \beta_2 \cdot c_2^i = 0 \qquad (28)$$

There must be five such c_1 and c_2 for the hinge or three for the common ground plane. As a simple example, consider the case of a hinge in which the axis of rotation passes through the origin of component 1's co-ordinate frame and lies along its z axis. When the motions of the two parts are considered in 1's frame, then their translations along all three axes must be the same as must their rotations about the x and y axes; only their rotations about the z axis can differ. Since component 2's motion can be transformed into 1's co-ordinate frame using the adjoint representation of the co-ordinate transformation, the constraints now take the form

$$\beta_1 \cdot c_1^i + \beta_2' \cdot c_2^i = 0 \qquad (29)$$

where $\beta_2' = \mathrm{ad}(E_1^{-1}E_2)\beta_2$ is the motion of component 2 in 1's frame. In this example, the c_1 and c_2 vectors for the five constraints become particularly simple:

$$c_1^i = \begin{bmatrix} 1 \\ 0 \\ 0 \\ 0 \\ 0 \\ 0 \end{bmatrix}, \begin{bmatrix} 0 \\ 1 \\ 0 \\ 0 \\ 0 \\ 0 \end{bmatrix}, \begin{bmatrix} 0 \\ 0 \\ 1 \\ 0 \\ 0 \\ 0 \end{bmatrix}, \begin{bmatrix} 0 \\ 0 \\ 0 \\ 1 \\ 0 \\ 0 \end{bmatrix}, \begin{bmatrix} 0 \\ 0 \\ 0 \\ 0 \\ 1 \\ 0 \end{bmatrix} \qquad (1 \le i \le 5) \tag{30}$$

with $c_2^i = -c_1^i$. In the case of a common ground plane in 1's x-y plane, only constraints 3, 4 and 5 are needed. If the hinge or ground plane are placed elsewhere then the adjoint representation can be used to transform the constraints by considering a Euclidean transformation that takes this situation back to the simple one.

4.3 Imposing the constraints

Since the constraints have a particularly simple form, finding the optimal β_1 and β_2' is also an easy matter. This is done by modifying the least-squares fitting procedure used for the single tracker, which is adapted so that the motion which gives the least square error *subject to satisfying the constraints* is found. Given the α and C computed in (11)–(13), then (21) gives the increase in sum squared error if the motion β is used in place of α as $(\beta - \alpha)C(\beta - \alpha)$. Thus, given the independent solutions for the two motions (α_1, C_1) and (α_2', C_2') the aim is to find β_1 and β_2' such that

$$(\beta_1 - \alpha_1)C_1(\beta_1 - \alpha_1) + (\beta_2' - \alpha_2')C_2'(\beta_2' - \alpha_2') \tag{31}$$

is minimised subject to

$$\beta_1 \cdot c_1^i + \beta_2' \cdot c_2^i = 0 \tag{32}$$

This is a constrained optimisation problem and ideal for solving by means of Lagrange multipliers. Thus the solution is given by the constraints in (32) and

$$\nabla\left((\beta_1 - \alpha_1)^T C_1(\beta_1 - \alpha_1) + (\beta_2' - \alpha_2')^T C_2'(\beta_2' - \alpha_2')\right) + \lambda_i \nabla\left(\beta_1^T c_1^i + \beta_2'^T c_2^i\right) = 0 \tag{33}$$

with ∇ running over the twelve dimensions of $\binom{\beta_1}{\beta_2'}$. This evaluates to

$$\begin{pmatrix} 2C_1(\beta_1 - \alpha_1) \\ 2C_2(\beta_2' - \alpha_2') \end{pmatrix} + \lambda_i \begin{pmatrix} c_1^i \\ c_2^i \end{pmatrix} = 0 \tag{34}$$

Thus $\quad \beta_1 = \alpha_1 - \tfrac{1}{2}C_1^{-1}\lambda_i c_1^i$

and $\quad \beta_2' = \alpha_2' - \tfrac{1}{2}C_2'^{-1}\lambda_i c_2^i \tag{35}$

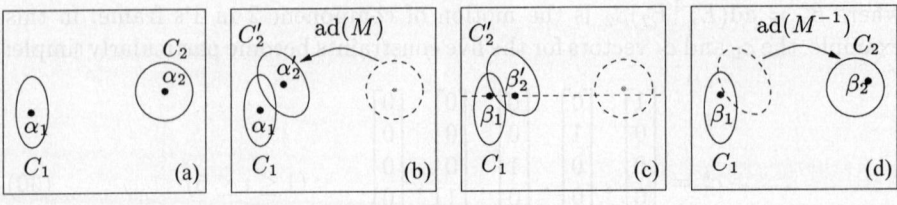

Fig. 6. Applying the constraints: Estimates and errors are computed for motions 1 and 2 (a), the estimate and error of motion 2 are mapped into 1's co-ordinate frame (b), the constraint is applied there (c) and then the new estimate of motion 2 is mapped back into its own frame (d).

Substituting (32) back into (35) gives

$$c_1^i \cdot \alpha_1 + c_2^i \cdot \alpha_2' - \tfrac{1}{2}\lambda_j \left(c_1^i \cdot C_1^{-1}c_1^j + c_2^i \cdot C_2'^{-1}c_2^j\right) = 0 \tag{36}$$

So the λ_i are given by

$$A_{ij} = c_1^i \cdot C_1^{-1}c_1^j + c_2^i \cdot C_2'^{-1}c_2^j \tag{37}$$

$$l_i = 2\left(c_1^i \cdot \alpha_1 + c_2^i \cdot \alpha_2'\right) \tag{38}$$

$$\lambda_i = A_{ij}^{-1}l_j \tag{39}$$

The λ_i can then be substituted back into (35) to obtain β_1 and β_2' (see Figure 6(c)), from which β_2 can also be obtained by $\beta_2 = \mathrm{ad}(E_2^{-1}E_1)\beta_2'$ (see Figure 6(d)). The β can then be used to update the configurations of the two rigid parts of the hinged structure giving the configuration with the least square error that also satisfies the constraints.

5 Results

A system was developed to test the tracking of a simple articulated structure (shown in Figure 7(a)). This system operates in real-time at PAL frame-rate (25Hz) on an SGI O2 (225 MHz R10K). The structure consists of two components, each 15cm square, joined along one edge by a hinge. This structure is a difficult one to track since there are barely enough degrees of freedom in the image of the structure to constrain the parameters of the model. A series of experiments were conducted to examine the precision with which the system can estimate the angle between parts of the model with and without the hinge constraints imposed. The hinge of the part was oriented at a series of known angles and for each angle a set of measurements were taken with and without the constraints imposed. The amount by which the rotational and translational constraints (measured at the hinge) are violated by the unconstrained tracker was also measured.

Ground truth ($\pm 1^o$)	Constrained	Unconstrained	R error	T error
80°	$79.2^o \pm 0.12^o$	—— Tracking Failed ——		
90°	$90.29^o \pm 0.14^o$	$94.46^o \pm 0.53^o$	2.97^o	2.32cm
100°	$99.3^o \pm 0.11^o$	$102.56^o \pm 0.32^o$	4.55^o	2.76cm
110°	$110.07^o \pm 0.11^o$	$111.34^o \pm 0.34^o$	5.75^o	3.23cm
120°	$119.31^o \pm 0.05^o$	$119.09^o \pm 0.2^o$	3.95^o	1.43cm
130°	$130.15^o \pm 0.08^o$	$128.77^o \pm 0.18^o$	1.38^o	1.35cm

In all cases, the estimate produced by the constrained tracker was within 1° of the ground truth. The unconstrained (12 DoF) tracker was much less accurate in general, and also reported substantial errors in violation of the known constraints. The variance in the angle estimate gives an indication of the stability of the tracker and it can be seen that the use of constraints improves this significantly. Figure 7(b) shows the behaviour of the unconstrained tracker. Because of the difficulty in finding the central crease, this tracker becomes weakly conditioned and noise fitting can introduce large errors.

This system was then extended to track the structure with an additional square component and hinge (see Figure 8(a)). The system is able to track the full configuration of the structure, even when the central component is fully hidden from view (see Figure 8(b)). In this case, the observed positions of the two visible components are sufficient to determine the location of the hidden part. Further, the indirect constraints between the two end parts of the structure serve to improve the conditioning of the estimation of their positions.

A system was also developed to show that constraints of intermediate complexity such as the existence of a common ground plane can be implemented within this framework. The system can dynamically impose or relax the common ground plane constraint. The objects to be tracked are shown in Figure 9(a) and Figure 9(b) shows how the tracker behaves when the constraint is deliberately violated; the output of the system still respects the constraint and is forced to find a compromise between the two components.

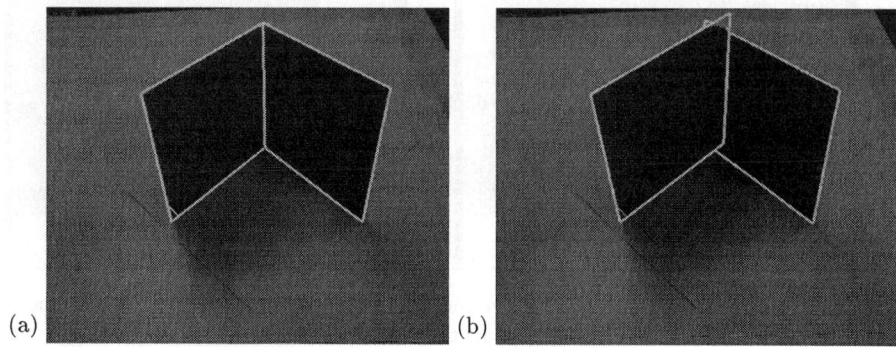

(a) (b)

Fig. 7. Hinge tracking with and without constraints

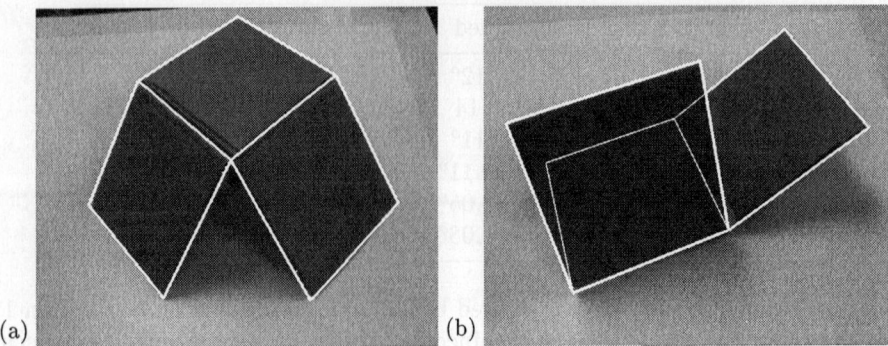

(a) (b)

Fig. 8. Double hinge structure: The tracker can infer the position of a hidden component from the constraints

Finally, a multi-camera system was developed using three cameras multiplexed using the red, green and blue components of a 4:2:2 digital signal to track the pose of a rigid structure (the ship part). With 3 cameras operating simultaneously (on a complex structure) the achieved frame rate dropped to 20Hz (this is believed to be due to speed limitations of the GL rendering hardware used in the tracking cycle. This 3 camera configuration is found to be much more stable and robust, maintaining a track over sequences that have been found to cause the single camera tracker to fall into a local minimum. These instabilities occur in a sparse set of configurations (e.g. when a feature rich plane passes through the camera and also in near-affine conditions when such a plane is fronto-parallel to the camera). By employing multiple cameras it becomes extremely difficult to contrive a situation that is critical in all camera views simultaneously.

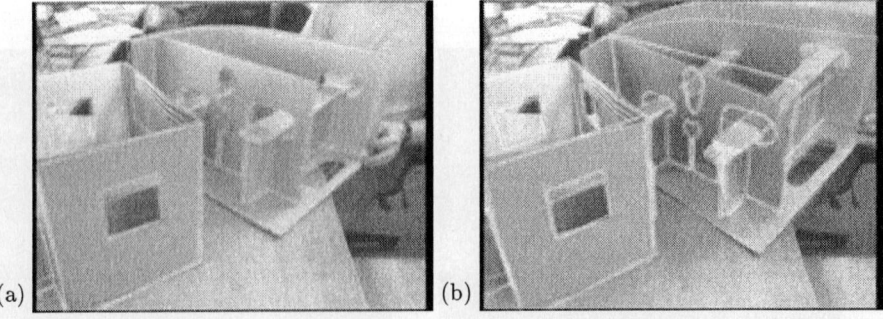

(a) (b)

Fig. 9. Two structures with common ground plane constraint: When the world violates the constraint, the tracker attempts to fit the constrained model. In this example, the tracker has fitted some parts of both models

6 Conclusion

The use of Lie algebras for representing differential quantities within a rigid body tracker has facilitated the construction of systems which operate in more complex and constrained configurations. Within this representation, it is easy to transform rigid body tracking information between co-ordinate frames using the adjoint representation, and also to express and impose the constraints corresponding to the presence of hinges or a common ground plane. This yields benefits in terms of ease of programming and implementation, which in turn make it readily possible to achieve real-time frame rate performance using standard hardware.

References

[1] T. Drummond and R.Cipolla. Real-time tracking of complex structures for visual servoing. In *PreProceedings of Vision Algorithms: Theory and Practice*, pages 91–98, Corfu, Greece, 21–22 September 1999. Also to appear in Springer Lecture Notes in Computer Science.

[2] C. Harris. Geometry from visual motion. In A. Blake, editor, *Active Vision*, chapter 16, pages 263–284. MIT Press, 1992.

[3] G. Hager, G. Grunwald, and K. Toyama. Feature-based visual servoing and its application to telerobotics. In V. Graefe, editor, *Intelligent Robotic Systems*. Elsevier, 1995.

[4] D. Terzopoulos and R. Szeliski. Tracking with Kalman snakes. In A. Blake, editor, *Active Vision*, chapter 1, pages 3–20. MIT Press, 1992.

[5] R. Cipolla and A. Blake. *Active Vision*, chapter Geometry from Visual Motion, pages 189–202. 1992.

[6] D. G. Lowe. Robust model-based motion tracking through the integration of search and estimation. *International Journal of Computer Vision*, 8(2):113–122, 1992.

[7] P. Wunsch and G. Hirzinger. Real-time visual tracking of 3-D objects with dynamic handling of occlusion. In *Proceedings of the 1997 International Conference on Robotics and Automation*, pages 2868–2873, 1997.

[8] C. Harris. Tracking with rigid models. In A. Blake, editor, *Active Vision*, chapter 4, pages 59–73. MIT Press, 1992.

[9] M. Isard and A. Blake. CONDENSATION - conditional density propagation for visual tracking. *International Journal of Computer Vision*, 29(1):5–28, 1998.

[10] N. Daucher, M. Dhome, J. T. Lapresté, and G. Rives. Modelled object pose estimation and tracking by monocular vision. In *Proceedings of the British Machine Vision Conference*, pages 249–258, 1993.

[11] A. D. Worrall, G. D. Sullivan, and K. D. Baker. Pose refinement of active models using forces in 3D. In J. Eklundh, editor, *Proceedings of the Third European Conference on Computer vision (ECCV'94)*, volume 2, pages 341–352, May 1994.

[12] E. Marchand, P. Bouthemy, F. Chaumette, and V. Moreau. Robust real-time visual tracking using a 2D-3D model-based approach. In *Proceedings of ICCV'99*, volume 1, pages 262–268, Kerkyra, Greece, 20–27 September 1999.

[13] V.S. Varadarajan. *Lie Groups, Lie Algebras and Their Representations*. Number 102 in Graduate Texts in Mathematics. Springer-Verlag, 1974.

[14] D.H. Sattinger and O.L. Weaver. *Lie groups and algebras with applications to physics, geometry, and mechanics.* Number 61 in Applied Mathematical Sciences. Springer-Verlag, 1986.

[15] T. Drummond and R. Cipolla. Visual tracking and control using Lie algebras. In *Proceedings of IEEE Conference on Computer Vision and Pattern Recognition*, volume 2, pages 652–657, Fort Collins, Colorado, 23–25 June 1999. IEEE.

[16] M. Armstrong and A. Zisserman. Robust object tracking. In *Proceedings of Second Asian Conference on Computer Vision*, pages 58–62, 1995.

[17] M. Paterson and F. Yao. Efficient binary space partitions for hidden surface removal and solid modeling. *Discrete and Computational Geometry*, 5(5):485–503, 1990.

[18] J. MacCormick and A. Blake. Spatial dependence in the observation of visual contours. In *Proceedings of the Fifth European Conference on Computer vision (ECCV'98)*, pages 765–781, 1998.

[19] M. Haag and H-H. Nagel. Tracking of complex driving manoeuvres in traffic image sequences. *Image and Vision Computing*, 16:517–527, 1998.

[20] J. K. Aggarwal, Q. Cai, W. Liao, and B. Sabata. Nonrigid motion analysis: articulated and elastic motion. *Computer Vision and Image Understanding*, 70(2):142–156, 1998.

[21] D. G. Lowe. Fitting parameterised 3-D models to images. *IEEE T-PAMI*, 13(5):441–450, 1991.

[22] Q. Delamarre and O. Faugeras. 3D articulated models and multi-view tracking with silhouttes. In *Proceedings of ICCV'99*, volume 2, pages 716–721, Kerkyra, Greece, 20–27 September 1999.

[23] T. Drummond and R. Cipolla. Real-time tracking of complex structures with on-line camera calibration. In *Proceedings of British Machine Vision Conference 1999*, volume 2, pages 574–583, Nottingham, 13–16 September 1999. BMVA.

Pedestrian Detection from a Moving Vehicle

D.M. Gavrila

Image Understanding Systems, DaimlerChrysler Research,
Wilhelm Runge St. 11, 89081 Ulm, Germany,
email: dariu.gavrila@DaimlerChrysler.com, WWW: www.gavrila.net

Abstract. This paper presents a prototype system for pedestrian detection on-board a moving vehicle. The system uses a generic two-step approach for efficient object detection. In the first step, contour features are used in a hierarchical template matching approach to efficiently "lock" onto candidate solutions. Shape matching is based on Distance Transforms. By capturing the objects shape variability by means of a template hierarchy and using a combined coarse-to-fine approach in shape and parameter space, this method achieves very large speed-ups compared to a brute-force method. We have measured gains of several orders of magnitude. The second step utilizes the richer set of intensity features in a pattern classification approach to verify the candidate solutions (i.e. using Radial Basis Functions). We present experimental results on pedestrian detection off-line and on-board our Urban Traffic Assistant vehicle and discuss the challenges that lie ahead.

1 Introduction

We are developing vision-based systems for driver assistance on-board vehicles [7]. Safety and ease-of-use of vehicles are the two central themes in this line of work. This paper focusses on the safety aspect and presents a prototype system for the detection of the most vulnerable traffic participants: pedestrians. To illustrate the magnitude of the problem, consider the numbers for Germany: more than 40.000 pedestrians were injured in 1996 alone due to collisions with vehicles [6]. Of these, more than 1000 were fatal injuries. Our long-term goal is to develop systems which, if not avoid these accidents altogether, at least minimize their severity by employing protective measures in case of upcoming collisions.

An extensive amount of computer vision work exists in the area of "Looking-at-People", see [8] for a recent survey. The pedestrian application on-board vehicles is particulary difficult for a number of reasons. The objects of interest appear in highly cluttered backgrounds and have a wide range of appearances, due to body size and poses, clothing and outdoor lighting conditions. They stand typically relatively far away from the camera, and thus appears rather small in the image, at low resolution. A major complication is that because of the moving vehicle, one does not have the luxury to use simple background subtraction methods to obtain a foreground region containing the human. Furthermore, there are hard real-time requirements for the vehicle application which rule out any brute-force approaches.

The outline of this paper is as follows. After reviewing past work on pedestrian detection, in Section 2, we present an efficient two-step approach to this problem. The Chamfer System, a system for shape-based object detection based on multi-feature hierarchical template matching, is described in Section 3. The following Section 4 deals with a Radial Basis Function (RBF)-based verification method employed to dismiss false-positives. Special measures are taken to obtain a "high-quality" training set. Section 5 lists the experiments on pedestrian detection; it is followed by a discussion of the challenges that lie ahead, in Section 6. We conclude in Section 7.

2   Previous Work

Most work on pedestrian detection [8] has taken a learning-based approach, bypassing a pose recovery step altogether and describing human appearance in terms of simple low-level features from a region of interest. One line of work has dealt specifically with scenes involving people walking laterally to the viewing direction. Periodicity has provided a quite powerful cue for this task, either derived from optical flow [17] or raw pixel data [5]. Heisele and Wöhler [10] describe ways to learn the characteristic gait pattern using a Time-Delay Neural Network with local receptive fields; their method is not based on periodicity detection and extends to arbitrary motion patterns.

A crucial factor determining the success of the previous learning methods is the availability of a good foreground region. Standard background subtraction techniques are of little avail because of a moving camera; here, independent motion detection techniques can help [17], although they are difficult to develop, themselves. Yet, given a correct initial foreground region, some of the burden can be shifted to tracking. For example, work by Baumberg and Hogg [2] applied Active Shape Models, based on B-splines, for tracking pedestrians. The interesting feature of this approach is that the Active Shape Models only deform in a way consistent with the training set; they can be combined with scale-space matching techniques to increase their coverage in image space [3]. In other work [10], color clusters are tracked over time; a pre-selection technique is used to identify the clusters that might correspond to the legs. Work by Curio et al. [4] uses a general- purpose tracker based on the Hausdorff distance to track the edges of the legs. Rigoll, Winterstein and Müller [18] perform Kalman filtering on a HMM-based representation of pedestrians.

A complementary problem is to detect pedestrians whilst they stand still. A system that can detect pedestrians in static images is described in [15]. It basically shifts windows of various sizes over the image, extracts an overcomplete set of wavelet features from the current window, and applies a Support Vector Machine (SVM) classifier to determine whether a pedestrian is present or not.

The proposed system is, like [15], applied on pedestrian detection in static images. However, the brute-force window sliding technique used there is not feasible for real-time vision onboard vehicles, because of the large computational cost involved. We propose a shape-based system that does not require a region of interest, yet can very quickly "lock" onto desired objects, using an efficient coarse-to-fine technique based on distance transforms. The pattern classification approach is only applied at the second stage, for verification, allowing realtime performance. The resulting system is generic can been applied to other object recognition tasks as well.

3 Detection: The Chamfer System

We now discuss the basics and extensions of the Chamfer System, a system for realtime shape-based object detection.

3.1 Basics

At the core of the proposed system lies shape matching using distance transforms (DT) [11]. Consider the problem of detecting pedestrians in an image (Figure 1a). Various object appearances are modeled with templates such as in Figure 1b. Matching template T and image I involves computing the feature image of I, (Figure 1c) and applying a distance transform to obtain a DT-image (Figure 1d).

A distance transform converts a binary image, which consists of feature and non-feature pixels, into an image where each pixel value denotes the distance to the nearest feature pixel. A variety of DT algorithms exist, differing in their use of a particular distance metric and the way local distances are propagated. The *chamfer* transform, for example, computes an approximation of the Euclidean distance using integer arithmetic, typically in raster-scan fashion [1].

After computing the distance transform, the relevant template T is transformed (e.g. translated) and positioned over the resulting DT image of I; the matching measure $D(T, I)$ is determined by the pixel values of the DT image which lie under the "on" pixels of the transformed template. These pixel values form a distribution of distances of the template features to the nearest features in the image. The lower these distances are, the better the match between image and template at this location. There are a number of matching measures that can be defined on the distance distribution, one possibility is to use simple averaging. Other more robust (and costly) measures reduce the effect of missing features (i.e. due to occlusion or segmentation errors) by using the average truncated distance or the f-th quantile value (the *Hausdorff* distance), e.g. [11].

For efficiency purposes, we use in our work the average chamfer distance

$$D_{chamfer}(T, I) \equiv \frac{1}{|T|} \sum_{t \in T} d_I(t) \tag{1}$$

where $|T|$ denotes the number of features in T and $d_I(t)$ denotes the chamfer distance between feature t in T and the closest feature in I.

In applications, a template is considered matched at locations where the distance measure $D(T, I)$ is below a user-supplied threshold θ

$$D(T, I) < \theta \tag{2}$$

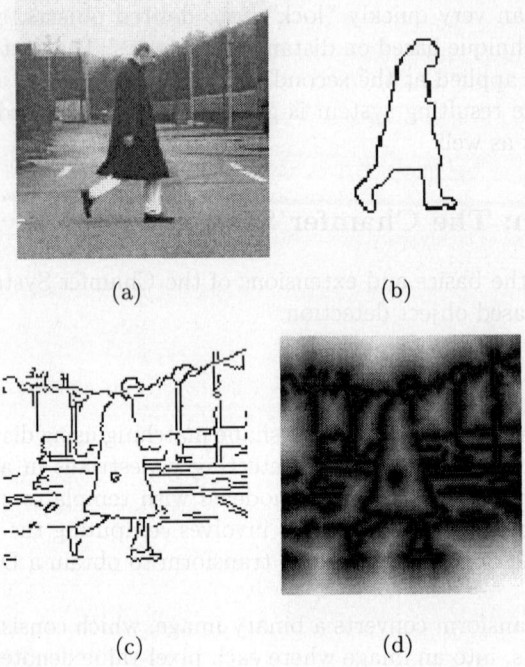

(a) (b)

(c) (d)

Fig. 1. (a) original image (b) template (c) edge image (d) DT image

The advantage of matching a template with the DT image rather than with the edge image is that the resulting similarity measure will be smoother as a function of the template transformation parameters. This enables the use of an efficient search algorithm to lock onto the correct solution, as will be discussed shortly. It also allows some degree of dissimilarity between a template and an object of interest in the image.

3.2 Extensions

The main contribution of the Chamfer System is the use of a template hierarchy to efficiently match whole sets of templates. These templates can be geometrical transformations of a reference template, or, more general, be examples capturing the set of appearances of an object of interest (e.g. pedestrian). The underlying idea is to derive a representation off-line which exploits any structure in this template distribution, so that, on-line, matching can proceed optimized. More specifically, the aim is to group similar templates together and represent them two entities: a "prototype" template and a distance parameter. The latter needs to capture the dissimilarity between the prototype template and the templates it represents. By matching the prototype with the images, rather than the individual templates, a typically significant speed-up can be achieved on-line. When applied recursively, this grouping leads to template hierarchy, see Figure 2.

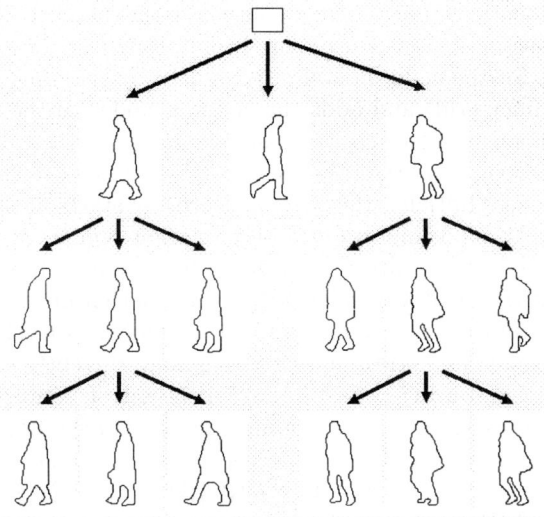

Fig. 2. A hierarchy for pedestrian shapes (partial view)

The above ideas are put into practice as follows. Offline, a template hierarchy is generated automatically from available example templates. The proposed algorithm uses a bottom-up approach and applies a partitional clustering algorithm at each level of the hierarchy. The input to the algorithm is a set of templates $t_1, ..., t_N$, their dissimilarity matrix (see below) and the desired partition size K. The output is the K-partition and the prototype templates $p_1, ..., p_K$ for each of the K groups $S_1, ..., S_K$. The K-way clustering is achieved by iterative optimization. Starting with an initial (random) partition, templates are moved back and forth between groups while the following objective function E is minimized

$$E = \sum_{k=1}^{K} \max_{t_i \in S_k} D(t_i, p_k^*) \qquad (3)$$

Here, $D(t_i, p_k^*)$ denotes the distance measure between the i-th element of group k and the prototype for that group at the current iteration, p_k^*. The distance measure is the same as the one used for matching (e.g. chamfer or Hausdorff distance). Entry $D(i, j)$ is the ijth member of the dissimilarity matrix, which can be computed fully before grouping or only on demand.

One way of choosing the prototype p_k^* is to select the template with the smallest maximum distance to the other templates. A low E-value is desirable since it implies a tight grouping; this lowers the distance threshold that will be required during matching (see also Equation 5) which in turn likely decreases the number of locations which one needs to consider during matching. Simulated annealing [13] is used to perform the minimization of E.

Online, matching can be seen as traversing the tree structure of templates. Each node corresponds to matching a (prototype) template p with the image at some particular locations. For the locations where the distance measure between template and image is below a user-supplied threshold θ_p, one computes new interest locations for the children nodes (generated by sampling the local neighborhood with a finer grid) and adds the children nodes to the list of nodes to be processed. For locations where the distance measure is above the threshold, search does not propagate to the sub-tree; it is this pruning capability that brings large efficiency gains. Initially, the matching process starts at the root and the interest locations lie on a uniform grid over relevant regions in the image. The tree can be traversed in breadth-first or depth-first fashion. In the experiments, we use depth-first traversal, which has the advantage that one needs to maintain only $L - 1$ sets of interest locations, with L the number of levels of the tree.

Let $\mathbf{p}$ be the template corresponding to the node currently processed during traversal at level l and let $C = \{\mathbf{t_1}, ..., \mathbf{t_c}\}$ be the set of templates corresponding to its children nodes. Let δ_p be the maximum distance between $\mathbf{p}$ and the elements of C.

$$\delta_p = \max_{t_i \in C} D(\mathbf{p}, \mathbf{t_i}) \qquad (4)$$

Let σ_l be the size of the underlying uniform grid at level l in grid units, and let μ denote the distance along the diagonal of a single unit grid element. Furthermore, let τ_{tol} denote the allowed shape dissimilarity value between template and image at a "correct" location. Then by having

$$\theta_p = \tau_{tol} + \delta_p + \frac{1}{2}\mu\sigma_l \qquad (5)$$

one has the desirable property that, using untruncated distance measures such as the chamfer distance, one can assure that the coarse-to-fine approach using the template hierarchy will not miss a solution. The thresholds one obtains by Equation (5) are very conservative, in practice one can use lower thresholds to speed up matching, at the cost of possibly missing a solution (see Experiments).

4 Verification: RBF-based pattern classification

As result of the initial detection step, we obtain a (possibly empty) set of candidate solutions. The latter are described by a template id and the particular image location where the match was found. The verification step consists of revisiting the original image, extracting a rectangular window region corresponding to the bounding box of the template matched, normalizing the window for scale, and employing a local approximator based on Radial Basis Functions (RBFs) [16] to classify the resulting $M \times N$ pixel values.

While training the RBF classifier, RBF centers are set in feature space by an agglomerative clustering procedure applied on the available training data. Linear ramps, rather than Gaussians, are used as radial functions, for efficiency purposes. Two radius parameters specify each such ramp, the radius where the ramp initiates (descending from the maximum probability value) and the radius where the ramp is cut off (after which probability value is set 0). These parameters are set based on the distance to the nearest reference vector of the same class and to that of the nearest reference vector of one of the other classes, in a manner described in [14]. The recall stage of the RBF classifier consists of summing probabilities that an unknown feature vector corresponds to a particular class, based on the contributions made by the various RBF centers.

One quickly realizes that the two classes involved (i.e. pedestrian and non-pedestrian) have quite different properties. The pedestrian class is comparably well localized in feature space, while the non-pedestrian class is wide spread-out. Our aim is to accurately model the target class, the pedestrians, while mapping the vast region of non-pedestrian is both impractical and unnecessary. The only instances of the non-pedestrian class really needed are those which lie close to the imaginary border with the target class. In order to find these, an incremental bootstrapping procedure is used, similar to [15]. This procedure adapts at each iteration the RBF classifier based on its performance of a new batch of no-target data. It only adds the non-target class examples which were classified incorrectly to the training set; then, it retrains the RBF classifier.

We take incremental bootstrapping a step further and integrate the detection system into the loop, reflecting the actual system coupling between detection and verification. Each batch of new non-target data is thus prefiltered by the detection unit, which will introduce a useful additional bias towards samples close to the imaginary target vs. non-target border in feature space.

5 Experiments

Experiments with pedestrian detection were performed off-line as well as on-board the Urban Traffic Assistant (UTA) demo vehicle.

We compiled a database of about 1250 distinct pedestrian shapes at a given scale; this number doubled when mirroring the templates across the y-axis. On this set of templates, an initial four-level pedestrian hierarchy was built, following the method described in the previous Section. In order to obtain a more compact representation of the shape distribution and provide some means for generalization, the leaf level was discarded, resulting in the three-level hierarchy used for matching (e.g. Figure 2) with about 900 templates at the new leaf level, per scale. Five scales were used, with range 70-102 pixels.

A number of implementation choices improved the performance and robustness of the Chamfer System, e.g. the use oriented edge features, template subsampling, multi-stage edge segmentation thresholds and ground plane constraints. Applying SIMD processing (MMX) to the main bottlenecks of the system, distance transform computation and correlation, resulted in a speed-up of factor 3-4. See [9].

Our preliminary experiments on a dataset of 900 images with no significant occlusion (distinct from the sequences used for training) showed detection rates in the 60-90 % range using the Chamfer System alone. With this setting, we obtained a handful of false detections solutions per image, of which approximately 90 % were rejected by the RBF classifier, at a cost of falsely rejecting 15 % of the pedestrians correctly detected by the Chamfer System.

Figure 3 illustrates some candidate solutions generated by the Chamfer System. Figure 4 shows intermediate results; matches at various levels of the template hierarchy are illustrated in white, grey and black for the first, second and leaf level, respectively. We undertook various statistics on our dataset, one of which is shown in Figure 5. It shows the cumulative distribution of average chamfer distance values on the path from the root to the "correct" leaf template. The correct leaf template was chosen as the one among the training examples to be most similar with the shape labeled by the human for a particular image. It was Figure 5, rather than Equation (5), that was used to determine the distance thresholds at the nodes of the template hierarchy. For example, from Figure 5 it follows that by having distance thresholds of 5.5, 4.1 and 3.1 for nodes at the first, second and leaf level of the hierarchy, each level passes through about 80% of the correct solutions. Figure 5 provides in essence an indication of the quality of the hierarchical template representation (i.e. how well the templates at the leaf level represent the shape distribution and good the clustering process is).

In general, given image width W, image height H, and K templates, a brute-force matching algorithm would require $W \times H \times K$ correlations between template and image. In the presented hierarchical approach both factors $W \times H$ and K are pruned (by a coarse-to-fine approach in image space and in template space). It is not possible to provide an analytical expression for the speed-up, because it depends on the actual image data and template distribution. Nevertheless, for this pedestrian application, we measured speed-ups of three orders of magnitude.

The Urban Traffic Assistant (UTA) vehicle (Figure 7) is the DaimlerChrysler testbed for driver assistance in the urban environment [7]. It showcases the broader Intelligent Stop & Go function, i.e. the capability to visually "lock" onto a leading vehicle and autonomously follow it, while detecting relevant elements of the traffic infrastructure (e.g. lane boundaries, traffic signs, traffic lights). Detected objects are visualized in a 3-D graphical world in a way that mimicks the configuration in the real world. See Figure 7a. The pedestrian module is a recent addition to UTA. It is being tested on traffic situations such as shown in Figure 8, where, suddenly, a pedestrian crosses the street. If the pedestrian module is used in isolation, the system runs at approximately 1 Hz on a dual-Pentium 450 MHz with MMX; 3-D information can be derived from the flat-world assumption. In the alternate mode of operation the stereo-module in UTA is used to provide a region of interest for the Chamfer System; this enables a processing speed of about 3 Hz.

For updated results (including video clips) the reader is referred to the author's WWW site **www.gavrila.net**.

6 Discussion

Though we have been quite successfull with the current prototype pedestrian system, evidently, we only stand at the beginning of solving the problem with the degree of reliability necessary to actually deploy such a system. A number of issues remain open in the current system. Starting with the Chamfer System, even though it uses a multi-stage edge segmentation technique, matching is still dependend on a reasonable contour segmentation. Furthermore, the proposed template-based technique will not be very suitable for detecting pedestrians very close to the camera. Currently, a multi-modal shape tracker is being developed (i.e. [12]) to integrate results over time and improve overall detection performance; single-image detection rates of 50% might not be problematic after all. Regarding the verification stage, the choice for a RBF classifier is probably not a determining factor; it would be indeed interesting to compare its performance with that of a Support Vector Machine [15].

The experiments indicated that detection performance varied considerably over parts of our database, according to the degree of contrast. Once the database is extended to include partially occluded pedestrians, or pedestrians at night, this variability is only going to increase, increasing the challenge how to report the detection performance in a representative manner. Also, larger test sets will be needed; we will have an enlarged pedestrian database of 5000 images with ground truth (i.e. labeled pedestrian shapes) in the near future.

7 Conclusions

This paper presented a working prototype system for pedestrian detection onboard a moving vehicle. The system used a generic two-step approach for efficient object detection. The first step involved contour features and a hierarchical template matching approach to efficiently "lock" onto candidate solutions. The second step utilized the richer set of intensity features in a pattern classification approach to verify the candidate solutions (i.e. using Radial Basis Functions). We found that this combined approach was able to deliver quite promising results for the difficult problem of pedestrian detection. With further work on (e.g. temporal integration of results, integration with stereo/IR) we hope to come closer to the demanding performance rates that might be required for actual deployment of such a system.

8 Acknowledgements

The author would like to thank Frank Lindner for making the RBF classifier software available.

References

1. H. Barrow et al. Parametric correspondence and chamfer matching: Two new techniques for image matching. In *Proc. of the International Joint Conference on Artificial Intelligence*, pages 659–663, 1977.
2. A. Baumberg and D. Hogg. An efficient method for contour tracking using active shape models. In *Proc. of the IEEE Workshop on Motion of Non-Rigid and Articulated Objects*, pages 194–199, Austin, 1994.

Fig. 3. Pedestrian detection results obtained by the Chamfer System

Fig. 4. Intermediate matching results for a 3-level template hierarchy: templates matched succesfully at levels 1, 2, 3 (leaf) are shown in white, grey, and black, respectively.

3. T. Cootes, C. Taylor, D. Cooper, and J. Graham. Active shape models - their training and applications. *Computer Vision and Image Understanding*, 61(1):38–59, 1995.
4. C. Curio, J. Edelbrunner, T. Kalinke, C. Tzomakas, C. Bruckhoff, T. Bergener, and W. von Seelen. Walking pedestrian detection and classification. In *Proc. of the Deutsche Arbeitsgemeinschaft fr Mustererkennung*, pages 78–85, Bonn, Germany, 1999.
5. R. Cutler and L. Davis. Real-time periodic motion detection, analysis and ap-

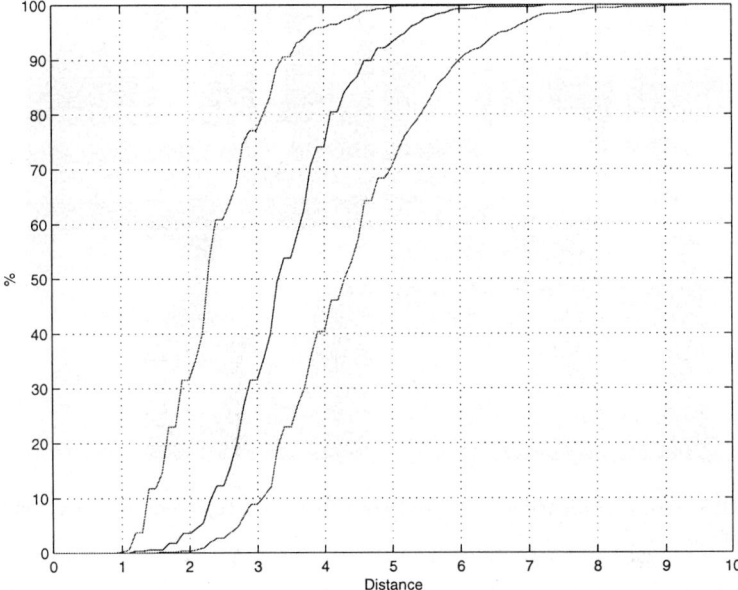

Fig. 5. Cumulative distribution of average chamfer distance values on the path from the root to the "correct" leaf template: first (right curve), second (middle curve) and leaf level (left curve).

plications. In *Proc. of the IEEE Conference on Computer Vision and Pattern Recognition*, pages 326–331, Fort Collins, U.S.A., 1999.

6. Infosystem der Deutschen Verkehrssicherheitsrates. Unfallstatistik fussgänger. In *www.bg-dvr.de*, 1996.

7. U. Franke, D. Gavrila, S. Görzig, F. Lindner, F. Pätzhold, and C. Wöhler. Autonomous driving goes downtown. *IEEE Intelligent Systems*, 13(6):40–48, 1998.

8. D. Gavrila. The visual analysis of human movement: A survey. *Computer Vision Image Understanding*, 73(1):82–98, 1999.

9. D. Gavrila and V. Philomin. Real-time object detection for "smart" vehicles. In *Proc. of the International Conference on Computer Vision*, pages 87–93, Kerkyra, Greece, 1999.

10. B. Heisele and C. Woehler. Motion-based recognition of pedestrians. In *Proc. of the International Conference on Pattern Recognition*, 1998.

11. D. Huttenlocher, G. Klanderman, and W.J. Rucklidge. Comparing images using the hausdorff distance. *IEEE Transactions on Pattern Analysis and Machine Intelligence*, 15(9):850–863, 1993.

12. M. Isard and A. Blake. Condensation - conditional density propagation for visual tracking. *International Journal of Computer Vision*, 1998.

13. S. Kirkpatrick, Jr. C.D. Gelatt, and M.P. Vecchi. Optimization by simulated annealing. *Science*, 220:671–680, 1993.

14. U. Kressel, F. Lindner, C. Wöhler, and A. Linz. Hypothesis verification based on classification at unequal error rates. In *Proc. of ICANN*, 1999.

15. C. Papageorgiou and T. Poggio. A pattern classification approach to dynamical

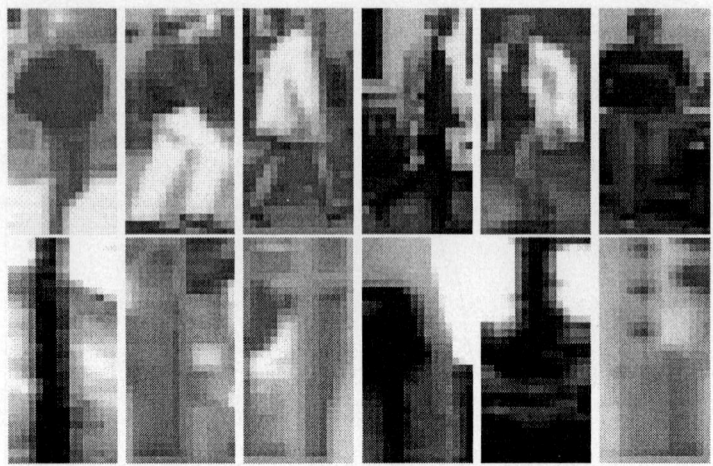

Fig. 6. RBF-based verification: accepted (top row) and rejected (bottom row) candidate solutions

object detection. In *Proc. of the International Conference on Computer Vision*, pages 1223–1228, Kerkyra, Greece, 1999.

16. T. Poggio and F. Girosi. Networks for approximation and learning. *Proc. of the IEEE*, 78(9):1481–1497, 1990.

17. R. Polana and R. Nelson. Low level recognition of human motion. In *Proc. of the IEEE Workshop on Motion of Non-Rigid and Articulated Objects*, pages 77–82, Austin, 1994.

18. G. Rigoll, B. Winterstein, and S. Mller. Robust person tracking in real scenarios with non-stationary background using a statistical computer vision approach. In *Proc. of Second IEEE Int. Workshop on Visual Surveillance*, pages 41–47, Fort Collins, USA, 1999.

(a)

(b)

Fig. 7. The Urban Traffic Assistant (UTA) demonstration vehicle: (a) inside and (b) outside view

Fig. 8. A potentially dangerous traffic situation: a pedestrian suddenly crossing the street

Vision-Based Guidance and Control of Robots in Projective Space

Andreas Ruf and Radu Horaud

INRIA Rhône-Alpes, MOVI
655, avenue de l'Europe
38330 Grenoble (Montbonnot St.Martin), France
`Andreas.Ruf@inrialpes.fr`, `Radu.Horaud@inrialpes.fr`,
`http://www.inrialpes.fr/movi/people/Ruf`

Abstract. In this paper, we propose a method using stereo vision for visually guiding and controlling a robot in projective three-space. Our formulation is entirely projective. Metric models are not required and are replaced with projective models of both the stereo geometry and the robot's "projective kinematics". Such models are preferable since they can be identified from the vision data without any a-priori knowledge. More precisely, we present constraints on projective space that reflect the visibility and mobility underlying a given task. Using interaction matrix that relates articulation space to projective space, we decompose the task into three elementary components: a translation and two rotations. This allows us to define trajectories that are both visually and globally feasible, i.e. problems like self-occlusion, local minima, and divergent control no longer exist. In this paper, we will not adopt a straight-foward image-based trajectory tracking. Instead, a directly computed control that combines a feed-forward steering loop with a feed-back control loop, based on the Cartesian error of each of the task's components.

1 Introduction

The robot vision problem has driven much research in computer vision, but although many approaches have been proposed, visual servoing has not yet made the step from "the labs to the fabs" and scientific progress is still being made. Changes in the way the system is modelled are currently stimulating such progress.

Most position-based approaches are based on CAD models and precise calibration of cameras and robots. Open-loop control is then sufficient for global operation on tasks defined in workspace. In contract, image-based approaches [5] are based on approximate local linear models of the robot-image interaction, so closed-loop control allows local operations on tasks defined in image space. These classical approaches are essentially based on, respectively, geometric and differential metric models of the robot vision system.

Recent research in computer vision has made significant progress in modeling multi-camera systems, thanks to the use of projective geometry. One of the most interesting results is three-dimensional projective reconstruction [8] based on "uncalibrated" stereo vision [6]: The stereo camera provides an instantaneous representation of depth, 3D structure and 3D motion, but only up-to a projective transformation. As such representations are independent of metric geometry, a prior metric calibration and CAD-models can sometimes be dispensed with.

Most research in this area, although this has turn out to be difficult, focuses on recovering additionally the metric calibration [15]. Only few researchers [14] have proposed robot vision systems that are based on non-metric models. In particular, very little work tries to use the projective stereo rigs directly, despite their appeal as dynamic sensors for 3D structure and motion [7].

In this paper, we study such a projective robot vision system presented recently [11]. Although, the effectiveness in image-based visual servoing has already been demonstrated [12], here we exploit the 3D capabilities of stereo and formulate a directly computed control in projective space. This allows us to overcome the most important problems of the image-based approach [3], namely: self-occlusion, local minima, and lack of global convergence.

Overview of the Paper and on the State-of-the-Art

In section 2 we sketch the background of our approach. Consult [11] for full detail. In section 3, we define mobility constraints in projective space, including several 1-dof motions – "visual" and hence "virtual"mechanisms – which later are used to formulate parameterized trajectory functions. Previous work, such as [2], considers only a single camera and thus has to use Rouleaux surfaces as constraints, i.e. a cylinder for a revolution or a prism for a translation. In contrast, considering stereo and projective three-space allows virtual mechanisms to be defined from a minimal number of constraints on very simple primitives, e.g. two 3D-points for a revolution to be defined.

In section 4, we calculate such constraints for a 6-dof reaching-task and decompose it into three visual mechanisms which respect the mobility and visibility of the task. This construction relies on local information on the interaction between joint-space and projective space but not on position-based information. Parametric trajectory functions are then defined to describe the desired reaching motion. In previous work on visual servoing[1] , trajectory generation is often explicit and related to camera-space, whereas task-space would be more appropriate. Furthermore, it relies heavily on metric knowledge. In subsection 4.2, we describe how visibility of the faces of a tool-object implies constraints on the trajectory parameters. Most previous work on visibility uses local reactive methods in order to avoid image borders or obstacles. In contrast, we consider the often neglected but important problem of object self-occlusion and obtain occlusion-free trajectories in closed-form.

In section 5, we describe a directly computed control, consisting of a feed-forward part, which guides the motion along a globally valid and visually feasible trajectory, and a feed-back part, which drives a Cartesian configuration-error to zero. Recent research shows a tendency towards integrating 3D- or pose information into the initially image-based approaches [5]. The aim is a control-error that no longer reflects a linear image motion, but a 3D rigid motion [10]. In current approaches, the calculation of such Cartesian errors is independent from control calculation and does not use the interaction matrix. Hence, they rely on a metric calibration which, if it is a coarse one, will hardly affect stability, but will affect trajectories and will degrade performance. In our approach, the 3-dof Cartesian error and the direct control are the result of one and the same calculation based on the interaction matrix and on the trajectory constraints. Moreover, our projective formalism is independent of metric system parameters and works with the most general model, i.e. with an interaction matrix relating robot joint-space to projective space.

Finally, in section 6, we present experiments using simulations based on real data. We demonstrate the efficiency of our method in a classical benchmark and evaluate the performance. **Notation.** Bold type $\mathbf{H}, \mathbf{T}$ is used for matrices, bold italic $\boldsymbol{A}, \boldsymbol{a}$ for vectors, and Roman a, ν, θ, k_1 for real numbers, scale factors, angles, coefficients, etc. Column vectors are written as $\boldsymbol{A}$, $\boldsymbol{k}$, and row vectors as the transpose $\boldsymbol{a}^\top$, $\boldsymbol{h}^\top$, where uppercase stand for spatial points, and lowercase $\boldsymbol{a}$, $\boldsymbol{m}$ for planes or image points.

2 Preliminaries

Stereo Vision in Projective Space. Given two pinhole cameras that have constant intrinsic parameters and that are rigidly mounted onto a stereo rig. Their epipolar geometry is constant and allows a pair of 3×4 projection matrices $\mathbf{P}, \mathbf{P}'$ to be defined [8]. Then, the left and right images $\boldsymbol{m}, \boldsymbol{m}' \in \mathbb{P}^2$ of a 3D Euclidean point $\boldsymbol{N}$ have a reconstruction $\boldsymbol{M} \in \mathbb{P}^3$ in projective space which is related to a Euclidean one by the $3D$ homography $\mathbf{H}_{PE}$ and an unknown scalar ρ in each point:

$$\begin{bmatrix} \zeta \, \boldsymbol{m} \\ \zeta' \boldsymbol{m}' \end{bmatrix} = \begin{bmatrix} \mathbf{P} \\ \mathbf{P}' \end{bmatrix}^{6 \times 4} \boldsymbol{M}, \qquad \rho \begin{bmatrix} X \\ Y \\ Z \\ 1 \end{bmatrix}_N = \begin{bmatrix} \mathbf{K}^{-1} & 0 \\ \boldsymbol{a}_\infty^\top & 1 \end{bmatrix}_{\mathbf{H}_{PE}}^{4 \times 4} \boldsymbol{M}. \tag{1}$$

The 4×4 matrix $\mathbf{H}_{PE}$ is constant and contains the unknown calibration, the affine one in the infinity-plane $(\boldsymbol{a}_\infty^\top \ 1)$, and the metric one in the (left) intrinsic parameters $\mathbf{K}$, upper-triangular. Implicitly, this defines a projective frame in which the reconstruction is done and which can be imagined as five points rigidly linked with the stereo head.

An object undergoing in Euclidean space the displacement $\mathbf{T}_{RT}$ appears in projective space to undergo the conjugate projective motion $\mathbf{H}_{RT}$ (2), a 4×4 homography well-defined from at least five object-points $\boldsymbol{M}' = \gamma \mathbf{H}_{RT} \boldsymbol{M}$. We will always normalize them to $\det(\mathbf{H}_{RT}) = 1$, as $\det(\mathbf{T}_{RT}) = 1$, and call them "projective displacement":

$$\mathbf{H}_{RT} = \gamma \, \mathbf{H}_{PE}^{-1} \, \mathbf{T}_{RT} \, \mathbf{H}_{PE}, \qquad \det \mathbf{H}_{RT} = 1, \text{ i.e. } \gamma = 1. \tag{2}$$

This conjugacy to the Lie group $SE(3)$ allows a corresponding conjugate Lie algebra to be defined, whose elements are denoted by $\hat{\mathbf{H}}_{RT}$, while $\hat{\mathbf{T}}_{RT}$ denote those of the Lie algebra $se(3)$.

$$\hat{\mathbf{H}}_{RT} = \mathbf{H}_{PE}^{-1} \, \hat{\mathbf{T}}_{RT} \, \mathbf{H}_{PE}, \qquad \exp(\hat{\mathbf{H}}_{RT}) = \mathbf{H}_{RT}. \tag{3}$$

For a homography $\mathbf{H}$ acting on points, its dual, now acting on planes, is $\mathbf{H}^{-\top}$, where plane-vectors are written as columns $\mathbf{a}$. An element $\hat{\mathbf{H}}_{RT}$ of the Lie algebra is a tangent operator acting on points, which has a corresponding tangent operator $-\hat{\mathbf{H}}_{RT}^{\top}$ acting on plane-vectors $\mathbf{a}$.

Since the action of the projective displacement group preserves the scale ρ hidden in the projective coordinates, the orbit of vectors in $\mathbb{R}^4$ are in fact hyperplanes of $\mathbb{R}^4$, characterized by $\rho = (\mathbf{a}_\infty^\top \; 1)\mathbf{M}$. Thanks to this, a projective motion $\mathbf{H}_{RT}(t)\mathbf{M}$ of a point has the velocity $\dot{\mathbf{M}}$ (4), and dually, a plane $\mathbf{H}_{RT}^{-\top}(t)\mathbf{a}$ has a velocity $\dot{\mathbf{a}}$ (5), both well-defined up-to an individual scalar ρ. Analogous to $se(3)$, these velocities can be calculated using the projective operator $\hat{\mathbf{H}}_{RT}$ tangent to $\mathbf{H}_{RT}(t)$ at t, or its dual.

$$\mathbf{M}(t) = \mathbf{H}_{RT}(t)\mathbf{M}, \qquad \dot{\mathbf{M}} = \hat{\mathbf{H}}_{RT}\mathbf{M}, \tag{4}$$

$$\mathbf{a}(t) = \mathbf{H}_{RT}^{-\top}(t)\mathbf{a}, \qquad \dot{\mathbf{a}} = -\hat{\mathbf{H}}_{RT}^{\top}\mathbf{a}. \tag{5}$$

Below, the relationships between points, lines, planes and their duals are briefly stated. For a point or a line through two points $\mathbf{A}_i$, their dual is determined by the null-space or kernel (ker) defined in (6). Geometrically, they are respectively 3- or 2-planes $\mathbf{a}_i^\top$ with the point or the line being their intersection.

$$\begin{bmatrix} \mathbf{a}_1^T \\ \mathbf{a}_2^T \\ \mathbf{a}_3^T \end{bmatrix} \begin{bmatrix} \mathbf{A}_1 \end{bmatrix} = 0, \qquad \begin{bmatrix} \mathbf{a}_1^T \\ \mathbf{a}_2^T \end{bmatrix} \begin{bmatrix} \mathbf{A}_1 \; \mathbf{A}_2 \end{bmatrix} = 0. \tag{6}$$

Robot Kinematics in Projective Space [11]. Consider an uncalibrated stereo rig observing a robot manipulator and capturing the end-effector's motion by continuously reconstructing some marked points on it (Fig. 4). The projective motion $\mathbf{H}_q(\mathbf{q})$ as a function of the vector $\mathbf{q}$ of joint variables is a product of the projective motions of each of the joints. These are either projective rotations $\mathbf{H}_R(\theta)$ of a revolute joint, or projective translations $\mathbf{H}_T(\tau)$ of a prismatic joint (7), [11]. Both are generically denoted as $\mathbf{H}_j(q_j)$ for joint j. Mathematically, they are conjugate representations of the classical one-parameter Lie groups $SO(2)$ and $\mathbb{R}^1$. They have Lie algebras conjugate to the classical Lie algebra $so(2)$ and $\mathbb{R}^1$, which have respective representations as 4×4 matrices, $\hat{\mathbf{H}}_R$ and $\hat{\mathbf{H}}_T$.

$$\hat{\mathbf{H}}_R = \mathbf{H}_J^{-1} \begin{bmatrix} 0 & -1 & 0 & 0 \\ 1 & 0 & 0 & 0 \\ 0 & 0 & 0 & 0 \\ 0 & 0 & 0 & 0 \end{bmatrix} \mathbf{H}_J, \qquad \hat{\mathbf{H}}_T = \mathbf{H}_J^{-1} \begin{bmatrix} 0 & 0 & 0 & 0 \\ 0 & 0 & 0 & 0 \\ 0 & 0 & 0 & 1 \\ 0 & 0 & 0 & 0 \end{bmatrix} \mathbf{H}_J. \tag{7}$$

The similarity $\mathbf{H}_J$ is different for each joint and contains the joint's position and orientation, as well as a part of the calibration matrix $\mathbf{H}_{PE}$. These two contributions are difficult to separate in general.

Since the conjugacy preserves the underlying algebraic structure, the projective representations can be manipulated without resolving the similarity, i.e.

without calibration. Therefore, respective formulae for going from " algebra-to-group" (9) and from "group-to-algebra" (8) can be shown to have closed forms analogous to the Euclidean ones:

$$\mathbf{H}_R(\theta) = \mathbf{I} + \sin\theta\hat{\mathbf{H}}_R + (1 - \cos\theta)\hat{\mathbf{H}}_R^2, \qquad \mathbf{H}_T(\tau) = \mathbf{I} + \tau\hat{\mathbf{H}}_T, \tag{8}$$

$$\hat{\mathbf{H}}_R = \tfrac{1}{2\sin\theta}\left(\mathbf{H}_R - \mathbf{H}_R^{-1}\right), \qquad\qquad\qquad \hat{\mathbf{H}}_T = \tfrac{1}{2\tau}\left(\mathbf{H}_T - \mathbf{H}_T^{-1}\right). \tag{9}$$

In practice, the benefits of these equations are as follows. On the one hand, an observed trial motion $(\mathbf{H}_j(q_j) \in$ group) of a single joint i allows the corresponding operator $(\hat{\mathbf{H}}_j \in$ algebra) to be recovered, representing projectively its kinematics. On the other hand, for given joint values q_j (θ_j or τ_j), the six joint operators $\hat{\mathbf{H}}_j$ constitute a projective kinematic model, and the forward kinematics $\mathbf{H}_q(\boldsymbol{q}) = \bar{\mathbf{H}}_6(\boldsymbol{q})$ can be calculated projectively as the product-of-exponentials (10), where each exponential has one of the above analytic forms (9):

$$\bar{\mathbf{H}}_j(\boldsymbol{q}) = \exp(q_1\hat{\mathbf{H}}_1)\cdots\exp(q_j\hat{\mathbf{H}}_j). \tag{10}$$

The robotics literature calls such a model "zero-reference" as it refers to origin $\boldsymbol{q} = 0$ of joint-space. For $\boldsymbol{q}(t)$ being a joint-space motion starting at zero, the partial derivatives of $\bar{\mathbf{H}}_i$ in $\boldsymbol{q}$ allow the end-effector's velocity $\dot{\mathbf{H}}_q = \dot{\mathbf{H}}_q(t)$ to be written linearly as a sum of the joint operators (11). Consequently, this expression for the interaction between joint- and projective motion equally allows for the Jacobians $\mathbf{J}_H$ of projective point- or plane velocities, $\dot{M}$ or $\dot{a}$, to be written in matrix form (12).

$$\dot{\mathbf{H}}_q = \dot{q}_1\hat{\mathbf{H}}_1 + \cdots + \dot{q}_6\hat{\mathbf{H}}_6, \qquad \text{where } \hat{\mathbf{H}}_j = \partial\mathbf{H}_q/\partial q_j\big|_{\boldsymbol{q}=0} \tag{11}$$

$$\dot{M} = \left[\hat{\mathbf{H}}_1 M_1, \ldots, \hat{\mathbf{H}}_6 M_1\right]^{4\times 6} \dot{\boldsymbol{q}}, \qquad \dot{a} = \left[-\hat{\mathbf{H}}_1^\top a_1, \ldots, -\hat{\mathbf{H}}_6^\top a_1\right]^{4\times 6} \dot{\boldsymbol{q}} \tag{12}$$

An image-based visual servoing could so be formulated in terms of image-velocities $\dot{s}$ and the Jacobian $\mathbf{J}_G(m)$ (13) of the perspective projection map $s = G(m) = (\frac{m_1}{m_3}, \frac{m_2}{m_3})^\top$. In contrast, we will remain in projective three-space and use $\dot{M}$ instead of $\dot{s}$ and $\mathbf{J}_G$.

$$\dot{s} = \begin{bmatrix} \frac{1}{m_3} & 0 & -\frac{m_1}{m_3^2} \\ \frac{1}{m_3} & 0 & -\frac{m_2}{m_3^2} \end{bmatrix}_{\mathbf{J}_G}^{2\times 3} \mathbf{P}\dot{M}. \tag{13}$$

3 Projective Mechanisms

In this section, we express primitive motions in terms of "virtual mechanisms", constraints on the mobility of points and planes in projective three-space. Solving these constraints for a joint-space motion and the resulting projective motion amounts to a local "decoupling" of the general projective kinematic model into such projective mechanisms. Formulating the problem in the visual domain allows these constraints to reflect the geometry underlying the current task (section

4.1), to express visibility conditions (section 4.2) and feasible trajectories (section 4.3), and to directly compute the joint-velocities actually driving the visual mechanisms (section 5.2). **Translation along an Axis.** Suppose a direction of translation given in terms of an axis through two points A_1, A_2. Their dual is a pencil of planes spanned by any two planes $a_1^\top, a_2^\top$ that intersect in the above axis (6). A rigid motion for which the velocities of both planes vanish is a pure translation along the given axis, and this is the only such rigid motion. Since the projective kinematic model – here the plane-operators $-\hat{H}_j^\top$ for each joint j – allows all rigid motions and respective plane-velocities to characterize, one can look for the only joint-space motion $\hat{q}_T$ for which these plane-velocities vanish. This is formalized by requiring $\dot{q} = \hat{q}_T$ to be in the kernel in (14), with ν arbitrary scalar. The corresponding one-dimensional group of projective translations is then described by its operator $\hat{H}_T$ which can be obtained as a linear combination based on $\hat{q}_T$:

$$\nu \, \hat{q}_T = \ker \begin{bmatrix} -\hat{H}_1^\top a_1, \; \dots, \; -\hat{H}_6^\top a_1 \\ -\hat{H}_1^\top a_2, \; \dots, \; -\hat{H}_6^\top a_2 \end{bmatrix}, \qquad \hat{H}_T = \hat{q}_{T1}\hat{H}_1 + \cdots + \hat{q}_{T6}\hat{H}_6. \quad (14)$$

Revolutions around an Axis. Given two points A_1, A_2 on an axis and the point-operators $\hat{H}_j$ for each joint j. Among all rigid motions, here expressed as joint-space motions, the one $\hat{q}_R$ for which the velocities of both points, i.e. the sums of $\hat{H}_j A_1$ and $\hat{H}_j A_2$, vanish, results in a revolution $\hat{H}_R$ around the axis connecting the points. Thus, it can be written as the kernel in (15) with free scalar ν. The operator $\hat{H}_R$ (15) corresponding to $\hat{q}_R$ generates the corresponding one-dimensional projective rotation group, the eigenvalues of which allow the scale of ν to be normalized to radians.

$$\nu \, \hat{q}_R = \ker \begin{bmatrix} \hat{H}_1 A_1, \; \dots, \; \hat{H}_6 A_1, \\ \hat{H}_1 A_2, \; \dots, \; \hat{H}_6 A_2 \end{bmatrix}, \qquad \hat{H}_R = (\hat{q}_{R1}\hat{H}_1 + \cdots + \hat{q}_{R6}\hat{H}_6), \quad (15)$$

where ν is chosen such that $\hat{H}_R$ has eigenvalues $i, -i$.

Revolution around a Point in a Plane. Another way to visually constrain a revolution is as follows: Suppose the action of the revolution on a given plane $a_1^\top$ to be a "planar" rotation, i.e. the plane turns "in-place", and suppose additionally one point A_1 on the axis. Among all joint-space motions, i.e. among all rigid motions, the one $\hat{q}_P$ for which both velocities, one resulting from point-velocities $\hat{H}_j A_j$ and one resulting from the plane-velocities $-\hat{H}_j^\top a_1$, vanish, is the above described "planar" revolution $\hat{H}_P$. The axis of this revolution passes through A_1 and is perpendicular to $a_1^\top$. It can be written as the kernel in (16), and is recombined and normalized to the point-operator $\hat{H}_P$ of the corresponding one-dimensional projective rotation group:

$$\nu \, \hat{q}_P = \ker \begin{bmatrix} -\hat{H}_1^\top a_1, \; \dots, \; -\hat{H}_6^\top a_1 \\ \hat{H}_1 A_1, \; \dots, \; \hat{H}_6 A_1 \end{bmatrix}, \qquad \hat{H}_P = (\hat{q}_{P1}\hat{H}_1 + \cdots + \hat{q}_{P6}\hat{H}_6), \quad (16)$$

where ν is chosen such that $\hat{H}_P$ has eigenvalues $i, -i$.

Actually, the above postulated equivalence between joint-space motions and rigid (projective) motions holds only in case of the robot being fully actuated. In case of under-actuation, the kernel becomes empty if the projective mechanism corresponds to the missing degree-of-freedom. In case of a singularity, the kernel is of a higher dimension. It comprises a fixing motion which yields a zero movement for all points and points, and possibly the projective mechanisms itself, which can be detected easily. So, either there exists currently no joint-space motion corresponding to the projective mechanism or there exists a family of such. This direct relationship between robot singularities and mobility, as defined in the visual (projective) domain, is highly useful for singularity avoidance in visual servoing.

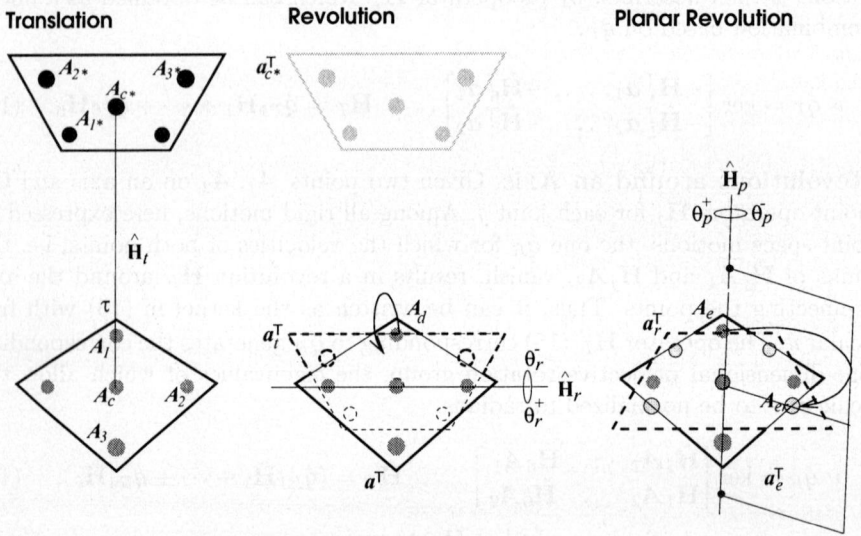

Fig. 1. Three partitions of a task.

4 Trajectories

In this section, the idea is to rewrite a given alignment task in terms of three primitive motions and to extend this to a reaching motion guided by trajectories that are visually and globally feasible. The task is partitioned in section 4.1 into a translation of a central point, followed by a hinge-like rotation of the face onto the target face, and finally rotation of the markers within the face plane onto their target positions (Fig. 1). Although the partitioning results in the primitive motions being "in-sequence", the way they are constructed ensures that a subsequent motions do not disturb the results of the preceding ones. For instance, both rotations are about the center point, thus it remains unaffected,

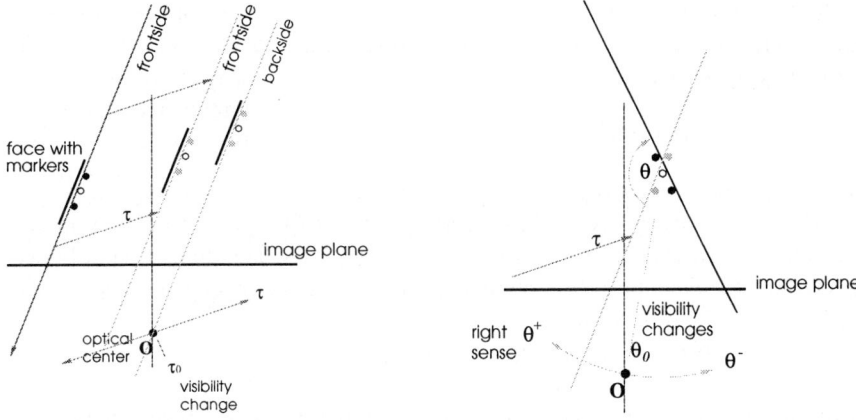

Fig. 2. Translation to τ_0 where visibility changes.

Fig. 3. Rotation of the face in the sense which preserves visibility.

and the final rotation moves points only within a plane, but the face as a plane remains unaffected. Consequently, the three motions can be driven independently without the general characteristics of the trajectories (section 4.3) being affected. These "Cartesian motions", as they are called in robotics, are a superposition of a straight-line trajectory of a central point with a rotation about this point. A feed-forward control of such trajectories, as done in section 5, assures global validity of the visual control and allows for permanent visibility of the face, as developed in section (4.2).

4.1 Partitioning

In this section, we describe the computational geometry used to translate the geometry underlying the task into constraints on projective mechanisms (section 3), where a task is given by the current and the target position of the markers, A and A_*, and the current and target position of the face plane, $a^\top$ and $a_*^\top$. The result will be three projective mechanisms, i.e. their operators $\hat{H}_t$, $\hat{H}_r$, $\hat{H}_p$ and their joint-space equivalents $\hat{q}_t$, $\hat{q}_r$, $\hat{q}_p$, corresponding to the three primitive motions of the task.

The **first component (translation of center)** is to choose one marker or the marker's midpoint as a center point A_c and to partition the task into a translation (Fig. 1 left), modulo a rotation H_s of the face around the center. The respective operator $\hat{H}_t$ is obtained by applying (14) to the center's current and target position, A_c and A_{c*}. A "distance-to-target" is the amplitude τ of this translation. It is obtained by solving (17) for τ, which represents the intersection of A_c's straight-line path with a transversal plane $a_{c*}^\top$ through A_{c*} (Fig. 1, left).

$$a_{c*}^\top \left(\mathbf{I} + \tau \, \hat{\mathbf{H}}_t \right) A_c = 0, \qquad \tau = -\frac{a_{c*}^\top A_c}{a_{c*}^\top \hat{\mathbf{H}}_t A_c}. \qquad (17)$$

Then, the translation can be "removed" from the task by applying the projective translation $\mathbf{H}_t(\tau) = \mathbf{I} + \tau\hat{\mathbf{H}}_t$ "backwards" onto the target primitives, which after that are subscripted with $_t$.

$$A_{it} = \mathbf{H}_t(-\tau)A_{i*}, \qquad a_t = \mathbf{H}_t^{-\top}(-\tau)a_* \qquad (18)$$

The removal in the "backwards" sense results in the residual task being expressed by new target primitives, A_{it} and $a_t^\top$, and in the subsequent rotations being expressed for the current position of the primitives. This also implies them being expressed for the current robot configuration, which is crucial for the direct control in section 5 to be valid.

The **second component (hinge of two planes)** is a rotation around the axis of two planes: the initial and the translated target face, $a^\top$ and $a_t^\top$. In this way, the rotational part $\mathbf{H}_s$ of the task is split into two, a rotation $\mathbf{H}_r(\theta_r)$ onto the target plane (Fig. 1, center), modulo a residual rotation $\mathbf{H}_p$ within this plane (Fig. 1 right). The respective operator $\hat{\mathbf{H}}_r$ is obtained by applying (15) to two points on the axis. An "angle-to-target" is determined by solving (19) for θ_r, which represents the intersection of the new target plane $a_t^\top$ with the circular path of a point A_d on the face. The resulting first-order trigonometric equation in θ_r and with coefficients p_0, p_s, p_c (20) has an analytic solution θ_r^-, θ_r^+ which is found[1] after half-angle substitution as the arctan in the roots α, β of two quadratic equations (21).

$$a_t^\top \left(\mathbf{I} + \sin\theta_r\hat{\mathbf{H}}_r + (1 - cos\theta_r)\hat{\mathbf{H}}_r^2 \right) A_d = 0, \qquad (19)$$

$$p_0 + p_s \sin\theta_r + p_c \cos\theta_r = 0, \qquad (20)$$

$$\theta_r^+ = \arctan(\alpha(p_0, p_s, p_c), \beta(p_0, p_s, p_c)), \qquad \theta_r^- = \pi - \theta_r^+ \qquad (21)$$

Again, the rotation is removed by applying the projective rotation $\mathbf{H}_r(-\theta_r)$ backwards, now to the $_t$-primitives, resulting in new target primitives then subscripted with $_r$.

$$A_{ir} = \mathbf{H}_r(-\theta_r)A_{it}, \qquad a_r = \mathbf{H}_r^{-\top}(-\theta_r)a_t \qquad (22)$$

The **third component (rotation within plane)** is planar revolution $\mathbf{H}_p(\theta_p)$ of the face around A_c to finally move the markers onto their target positions A_{ir}. The respective operator $\hat{\mathbf{H}}_p$ is obtained by applying (16) to $a^\top$ and A_c. The angle θ_P requires intersecting the circular path of a point A_e with a transversal plane $a_e^\top$ through the corresponding target point A_{er} (Fig. 1, right), in analogy to (19).

4.2 Visibility

In general, naive projective coordinates are "unoriented". So, the front- and back-side of the face are distinguishable, and visibility is undecidable. However,

---

[1] For the sake of briefty, full technical detail had to be omitted.

projective displacements preserve the scalar ρ of an orbit (section 2), and so the sign of projective coordinates of both, points and planes. Therefore, it is decidable in this case from the sign of their product wether a point changes side with respect to a plane. For the face plane $a^\top$ and the optical center O, this amounts to detecting changes in the face's visibility from the sign of $a^\top \cdot O$. For the above introduced one-parameter motions, such an event is precisely characterized by an amplitude τ_0 (Fig. 3), or a pair of angles θ_0^+, θ_0^- (Fig. 3), as obtained from (17) or (19) applied to the optical center.

In terms of trajectories and their components this means the following. If the translation is towards and beyond τ_0, a respective reorientation of the face is required before the feed-forward reaches τ_0 (Fig. 3). If the rotation is either leaving or entering the interval $\left[\theta_0^-, \theta_0^+\right]$, the visibility changes and a respective translation of the face is required before the feed-forward reaches a θ_0 (Fig. 3). The above concerns only the rotation $\mathbf{H}_r$, since visibility remains unaltered under planar rotation $\mathbf{H}_p$. Additionally, such "side-of-plane" arguments are heavily used in the implementations of sections 4.1 and 4.3 in order to determine the "right" sense of θ_r (21). This is required to avoid the back-face being turned towards the camera (Fig. 3) or the face being moved backside-up onto the target (Fig. 1). Please note also that in presence of the second camera, the above arguments apply independently to both of them, such that the most conservative thresholds τ_o, θ_0 have to be taken.

4.3 Generation

Now, we formalize in (23) a family of Cartesian trajectories $\mathbf{H}_d(\sigma)$ allowing to simultaneously execute the three independent parts of the task (Fig. 6). Three functions $\mu_t(\sigma)$, $\mu_r(\sigma)$, $\mu_p(\sigma)$ in a common abscissa σ (24) allow to modify the characteristics of the trajectories and to incorporate the visibility constraints. In analogy to the product-of-exponentials (10), the projective mechanisms have to be multiplied in reverse order (23) for the desired trajectories to emerge. Intuitively, the translation is the left-most one, since the rotations must not affect its direction nor the position of the center. The hinge is the second one, since the planar rotation must not affect the face as a plane:

$$\mathbf{H}_d\left(\tau(\sigma), \theta_r(\sigma), \theta_p(\sigma)\right) = \exp(\tau(\sigma)\hat{\mathbf{H}}_t) \, \exp(\theta_r(\sigma)\hat{\mathbf{H}}_r) \, \exp(\theta_p(\sigma)\hat{\mathbf{H}}_p), \quad (23)$$
$$\tau(\sigma) = \mu_t(\sigma)\tau, \qquad \theta_r(\sigma) = \mu_r(\sigma)\theta_r, \qquad \theta_p(\sigma) = \mu_p(\sigma)\theta_p. \quad (24)$$

Here, the μ are monotonically growing functions $[0, t_*] \rightarrow [0, 1]$ subject to visibility constraints between μ_r and μ_t. More formally, if $\mathbf{H}_r^{-\top}(\theta_r(\sigma)a$ is visible then $\mu_t(\sigma) < \tau_0$, and $\mu_t(\sigma) > \tau_0$ otherwise. Vice versa, if $\mathbf{H}_t^{-\top}(\tau(\sigma))a_*$ is visible then $\mu_r(\sigma) < \theta_0$, and $\mu_r(\sigma) > \theta_0$ otherwise. Note that $\mu_p(\sigma)$ is always unconstrained. Either of these cases can be used to drive a feed-forward in either τ or θ_r while constraining the other correspondingly. Additionally, the overall behaviour can be modified. For instance, a linear decay of time-to-goal arises for $\mu(\sigma) = \sigma$, whereas an exponential decay as in classical feed-back loops arises for $\mu(\sigma) = 1 - \exp(-\frac{\sigma}{t_*})$. An initial very flat plateau in the respective μ allows trajectories like rotation-first, translation-first, planar-first to be implemented.

Although robot guidance based on trajectory tracking and a feed-back law is now perfectly feasible, we will further exploit the above established direct relations between joint-space motions, projective mechanisms, Cartesian trajectories, and velocities in projective-space in order to come up in the next section with a directly computed control.

5   Control

In this section, we devise a twofold scheme for a directly calculated visual servo control. On the one hand, there is a feed-forward steering loop which drives the robot along trajectories restricted by visibility and other mobility constraints. On the other hand, there is a feed-back servoing loop which drives a 3-dof or 2-dof Cartesian control-error down to zero. The video feed-back from the stereo cameras serves as input to both loops, which actually are just two interpretations of one and the same calculation. As a result, the servoing no longer generates a linear image motion, but a "Cartesian" motion in three-space. In order to apply directly the results of the previous sections, the projective kinematic model has to be generalized to come up for varying robot configurations.

5.1   Generalized Projective Kinematics of a Moving Robot

The kinematic model presented so far is only valid around the zero of the robot. As the robot moves so do its joints, and their operators change, respectively. Hence, the generalized projective kinematics will consists of operators $\hat{\mathbf{H}}_j\big|_{\boldsymbol{Q}}$ which are expressed in function of the current configuration $\boldsymbol{Q}$ of the robot, and it will refer to the joint-space shifted by $\boldsymbol{q}(t) - \boldsymbol{Q}$. This is well-known in robotics and is utilized in Cartesian velocity control rather commonly. Here, the formulation has to be extended to the projective model, where the arguments of the respective proofs are essentially based on the properties of conjugate forms. The equations are stated in (25) and are intuitively explained as follows: for each joint j, first its own displacement, expressed by the truncated forward kinematics $\bar{\mathbf{H}}_j = \bar{\mathbf{H}}_j(\boldsymbol{Q})$ (10), must be undone, then the initial operator $\hat{\mathbf{H}}_j$ is applied as beforehand, and after that the joint must return to $\boldsymbol{Q}$. The Jacobian for the current position $\boldsymbol{M}(t)$ of a projective point equally uses the current operator values

$$ \hat{\mathbf{H}}_j\big|_{\boldsymbol{Q}} = \bar{\mathbf{H}}_j \cdot \hat{\mathbf{H}}_j \cdot \bar{\mathbf{H}}_j^{-1}, \qquad \mathbf{J}_H\big|_{\boldsymbol{Q}} = \left[\hat{\mathbf{H}}_1\big|_{\boldsymbol{Q}} \boldsymbol{M}(t), \cdots, \hat{\mathbf{H}}_6\big|_{\boldsymbol{Q}} \boldsymbol{M}(t) \right]^{4\times6} . \quad (25) $$

To summarize, we have a general model for the projective kinematics and the Jacobian of a projective point in form of an analytical expression in $\boldsymbol{Q}$, i.e. in configuration space. It is a sound linear model of the instantaneous interaction between joint-space and projective space. In consequence, as long as this general model is applied in sections 3 and 4, the resulting joint-space motions $\hat{\boldsymbol{q}}$ are valid and can be used for a direct control to be calculated.

5.2 Direct Control

In visual servoing, a task is commonly represented in terms of a target image, e.g. by a number of image points s_{i*} or equivalently by their 3D-reconstructions[2] A_{i*} in case of stereo. As soon as the current positions $A_i(t)$ do overlap the target, the task has been achieved. Classically, the control is computed by means of the inverse Jacobian (12) applied to an error-vector $A_i(t) - A_{i*}$ in the point-coordinates or in their image-coordinates $s_i(t) - s_{i*}$ (13), respectively [11]. As a result of this local linear approximation, the convergence and stability highly depends on the conditioning of the Jacobian matrix.

In our approach, the task is extended to guided motion towards the target. On the one hand, the constraints (section 4.1) on the motion in the current positions $A_i(t)$ assure the trajectories to emerge as desired (23). On the other hand, the projective kinematic model $\hat{H}_i\big|_Q$ expressed for the robot's current configuration allows for direct calculation of the control from the constrained solutions $\hat{q}_t, \hat{q}_r, \hat{q}_p$. Above that, they give rise to a "distance-to-target" along the trajectory as well as a corresponding 3-dof Cartesian feed-back error $(\tau, \theta_r, \theta_p)$. Therefore, the direct control can be calculated as the gain-weighted sum (26).

$$e = (\tau, \theta_r, \theta_p)^\top, \quad -\dot{e} = (\lambda_t, \lambda_r, \lambda_p)\, e, \quad \dot{q} = \begin{bmatrix} \hat{q}_t & \hat{q}_r & \hat{q}_p \end{bmatrix} \dot{e}, \tag{26}$$

$$\mathbf{H}_e(\dot{e}) \approx \exp(\lambda_t \tau \hat{\mathbf{H}}_t + \lambda_r \theta_r \hat{\mathbf{H}}_r + \lambda_p \theta_p \hat{\mathbf{H}}_p), \quad \text{for } \theta_r, \theta_p \text{ small.} \tag{27}$$

However, this version "**directTHREE**" of the direct control is valid only for the gains being small, or for the control being recalculated at high frequencies. There is a systematic "integration-error" between the trajectories $\mathbf{H}_e$ (27) as they are controlled and $\mathbf{H}_d$ (23) as they are desired. However, the experiments show that already **directTHREE** allows for directly servoing a complicated reaching task without the deviations becoming too strong.

By construction, the feed-forward is such that the center is undergoing a pure translation, and that the face is undergoing a pure rotation $\mathbf{H}_s = \exp(\theta_s \hat{\mathbf{H}}_s)$ around the center (section 4.1). This part of the direct control is valid, since the summed operators can be shown to integrate as desired (28). However, the operators of the two rotations $\hat{\mathbf{H}}_r, \hat{\mathbf{H}}_p$ integrate differently than their sum does (29). Therefore, a sound formulation "**directTWO**" of the direct control will be derived that consists of a single effective rotation $\hat{q}_s$ and that controls only a 2-dof feed-back error $(\tau, \theta_s)^\top$ (30).

$$\exp^{(\lambda_t \tau \hat{\mathbf{H}}_t)} \exp^{(\lambda_s \theta_s \hat{\mathbf{H}}_s)} = \exp^{(\lambda_t \tau \hat{\mathbf{H}}_t + \lambda_s \theta_s \hat{\mathbf{H}}_s)}, \text{ but} \tag{28}$$

$$\exp^{(\lambda_r \theta_r \hat{\mathbf{H}}_r)} \exp^{(\lambda_p \theta_p \hat{\mathbf{H}}_p)} \neq \exp^{(\lambda_r \theta_r \hat{\mathbf{H}}_r + \lambda_p \theta_p \hat{\mathbf{H}}_p)} \tag{29}$$

$$e = (\tau, \theta_s)^\top, \quad -\dot{e} = (\lambda_t, \lambda_s)\, e, \quad \dot{q} = \begin{bmatrix} \hat{q}_t & \hat{q}_s \end{bmatrix} \dot{e}, \quad \hat{\mathbf{H}}_s = \Sigma_{j=1}^k \hat{q}_{sj} \hat{\mathbf{H}}_j, \tag{30}$$

In order to calculate $\hat{\mathbf{H}}_s$ and $\hat{q}_s$, e.g. for constant $\frac{\lambda_r}{\lambda_p}$, we make use of the fact that both $\hat{\mathbf{H}}_r$ and $\hat{\mathbf{H}}_p$ are rotations about the center, i.e. they are elements of

---

[2] Again, we allow for the general case of a projective reconstruction.

the respective matrix representation of $so(3)$. The solution is provided by the Campbell-Baker-Hausdorff formula known in Lie-group theory [13]. It has in case of $so(3)$ an algebraic solution in closed form. For two given operators, it relates their product-of-exponentials to the exponential of an (infinite) sum of higher order Lie brackets $[\hat{\mathbf{H}}_r, \hat{\mathbf{H}}_p]^3$ of the operators. In contrast to [4], where a truncated approximation of such a sum is used, the closed form solution (31), (32) can be found in our case. Thanks to the operators being just conjugate forms of $so(3)$, this solution can be calculated directly from the projective operators, as sketched below:

$$e^{(\theta_r \hat{\mathbf{H}}_r)} e^{(\theta_p \hat{\mathbf{H}}_p)} = e^{(\theta_s \hat{\mathbf{H}}_s)}, \quad \hat{\mathbf{H}}_s = (\sin \tfrac{\theta_s}{2})^{-1} \left(a\hat{\mathbf{H}}_r + b\hat{\mathbf{H}}_p + c\left[\hat{\mathbf{H}}_r, \hat{\mathbf{H}}_p\right] \right), \quad (31)$$

$$a = \sin \tfrac{\theta_r}{2} \cos \tfrac{\theta_p}{2}, \quad b = \cos \tfrac{\theta_r}{2} \sin \tfrac{\theta_p}{2}, \quad c = \sin \tfrac{\theta_p}{2} \sin \tfrac{\theta_r}{2}. \tag{32}$$

Note additionally, that only a and b in (32) have a cosine term, so the first-order approximation in (27) is valid.

6 Experiments

In this section, we validate and evaluate the above theoretical results on a classical benchmark test: a rotation of 180° around the optical axis or the stereo rig's roll axis in our case (Fig. 4). This configuration is known to be a degenerate one in the monocular case [3]. Additionally, a potential self-occlusion is enforced by the face being oriented transversally with respect to the image planes. Besides that, the dimensions correspond to those of our experimental system and the projective kinematic data has been taken from a recent self-calibration experiment [12].

First, three classical stereo servoing laws are tried (Fig. 5): pseudo-inverse of the stacked Jacobians [7], their block-wise pseudo-inverse [9], and a straightforward servoing for plain 3D points in Euclidean three-space (like (10) but in space). The second one, which basically sums two independent monocular controls, diverges while moving towards infinity. The other two laws run into the self-occlusion while more or less translating towards the target, but get draped in the local minimum. Both manage to escape slowly due to some accidental perturbation, but this is unpredictable. Then, they turn the face almost in-place, again through an occlusion, before finally converging.

Second, trajectory generation from section 4 is tested. Figure 6 shows the solutions found using (23), where all the $\mu(\sigma)$ are chosen linear. In Fig. 7 a rather steep μ_t is chosen to favor the translation first. The self-occlusion has been avoided successfully, as evident in the figures which are rendered from a central view-point close to the stereo one. Besides this illustrative example, the control experiments establish a thorough validation of reliability as well as an extensive evaluation of the precision of the trajectories (Figs. (11), (10)), since

---

[3] $[\hat{\mathbf{H}}_r, \hat{\mathbf{H}}_p] = \hat{\mathbf{H}}_r \hat{\mathbf{H}}_p - \hat{\mathbf{H}}_p \hat{\mathbf{H}}_r = \hat{\mathbf{H}}_{PE}^{-1} \hat{\mathbf{T}}_r \hat{\mathbf{T}}_p - \hat{\mathbf{T}}_p \hat{\mathbf{T}}_r \mathbf{H}_{PE} = \hat{\mathbf{H}}_{PE}^{-1} [\hat{\mathbf{T}}_r, \hat{\mathbf{T}}_p] \mathbf{H}_{PE}$, with $\hat{\mathbf{T}}_{r,p}$ having the classical anti-symmetric form of $so(3)$ as upper 3×3 block.

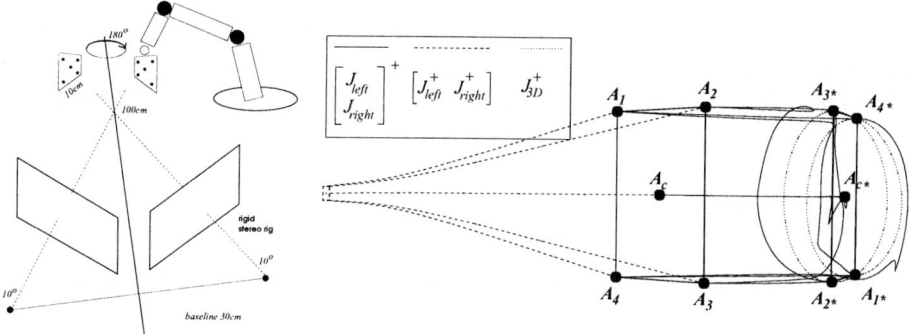

Fig. 4. Experimental setup.   **Fig. 5.** Failure of classical stereo visual servoing

each iteration of the direct control can be interpreted as a newly generated feed-forward trajectory.

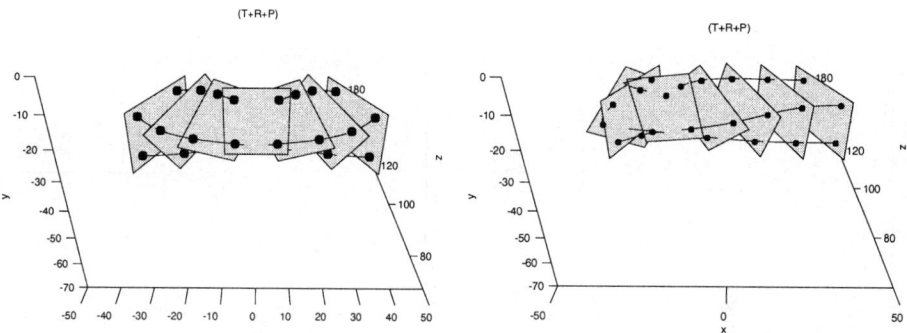

Fig. 6. Trajectories: visibility is preserved.   **Fig. 7.** Trajectories: early translation.

Third, the two control laws are compared with respect to the bias intrinsic to **directTHREE** (27). Figure 8 shows this as a very small deviation of their image trajectories. More remarkable is the center point's deviation from the desired straight-line trajectory. This deviation is also found in Figure 9, but it is vanishing with the gain decreasing. A first conjecture is that this deviation is due to linearization error arising when integration of a Cartesian velocities $\hat{H}$ is desired (23) but a joint-velocities $\hat{q}$ is actually driven, which are only very locally in exact correspondence. This is confirmed by the innermost trajectory for which the joint-velocities were limited to 5° in order to limit this cause of deviations.

Fourth, both control-errors (26), (30) are confirmed to have exponential convergence rate (Figs. 10, 11). In the case of **directTHREE** (11), we compare the Cartesian-error $(\tau, \theta_r, \theta_p)$ as calculated in our projective control scheme with Euclidean ground-truth. The angular errors do strictly overlap, whereas the decay

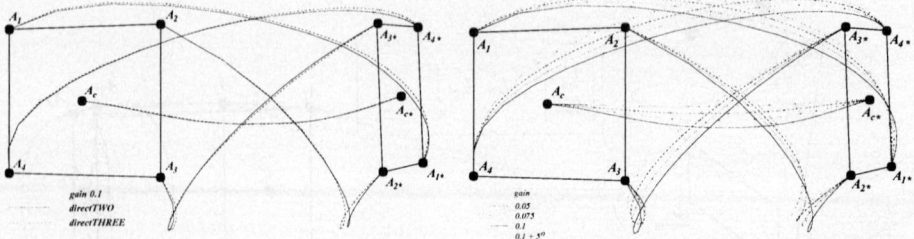

Fig. 8. directTHREE versus directTWO.   **Fig. 9.** Various gains + joint-speed limit.

of the projective translation error τ seems much steeper. However, this difference is only an apparent one caused by the unknown scale ρ. In fact, it is absorbed by a reciprocal scaling of $\hat{q}_t$, such that the performance and behavior of the control remains unaffected by this ambiguity. In figure 10, the results of the **directTWO** law are compared, once with and once without the joint-velocity limit. The curve of θ_s clearly reflects the task's overall rotation of 180°, which beforehand was spread among the two rotational motions in θ_r, θ_p.

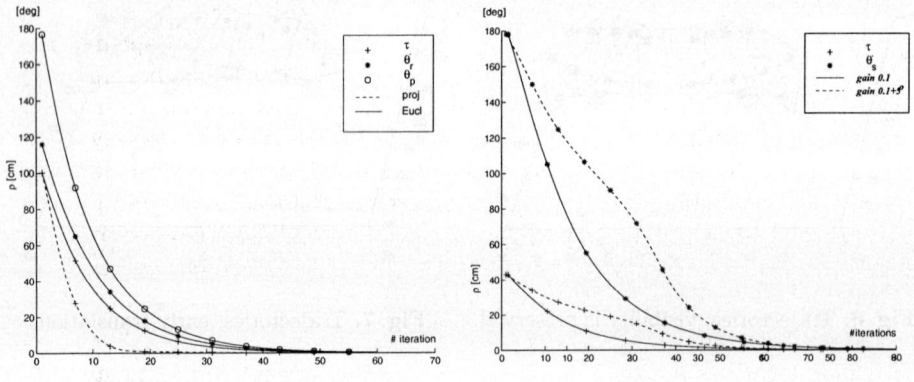

Fig. 10. directTWO: control-error.   **Fig. 11.** directTHREE: control-error.

Fifth, figure 12 shows the error in the markers' image coordinates. It clearly has no longer an exponential decay, not even a monotonic one. The zero-line actually reflects the center's straight horizontal trajectory. Finally, the corresponding trajectories in joint-space are given in figures 13, once without and once with the 5° limit. Apparently it is the initially high velocities of q_1 and q_3 which are the cause for the above mentioned drift away from the straight line.

7   Discussion

In this paper we described a new method for robot visual guidance based on non-metric representations of both the stereo system and the robot's kinematics. The

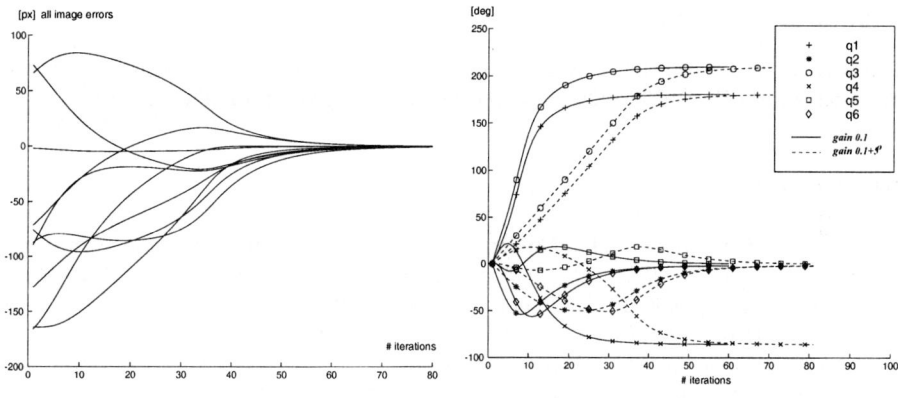

Fig. 12. Image errors.   **Fig. 13.** Joint-space motion.

paper is build on top of two main bodies of work: (i) the well-known framework for representing 3-D visual information in projective space and (ii) the motion representation of rigid bodies and articulated mechanism using 3-D projective transformations. The latter was recently introduced by the authors.

Traditionally, visual robot control used Euclidean pose to estimate an image-to-robot Jacobian together with a Euclidean kinematic model to transform desired Cartesian velocities into robot joint-velocities. These are derived from image data and the inverse of the image-Jacobian. Here, we went directly "from the image to the joints" using a sound projective model for robot motions as seen by an uncalibrated stereo rig. The advantage over the Euclidean approach is that exact knowledge of the robot's mechanics is not required. Moreover, the projective models can be estimated quite precisely on-line and on-site simply by observing the elementary joint motions with a stereo rig.

Above that, we studied in detail the general task of reaching B starting from A, where locations A and B are described by their images. We formulated the decompositon of such a task into three elementary motions which satisfy several constraints: the features must be visible in the images all along the trajectory and the motion must be feasible by the manipulator. We showed how to design such trajectories and how to drive them efficiently in practice.

The method was validated and evaluated on a classical benchmark test for visual servoing, namely a 180^0 turn of the end-effector, which most existing techniques based only on image-error measurements fail to succeed.

Our work extends the state-of-the-art in visual servoing from calibrated or poorly calibrated cameras to uncalibrated stereo rigs, where the robot motion and kinematics as well as the reaching trajectory are represented by projective transformations. We believe that the latter is a promising framework for describing articulated mechanisms and their associated constrained motions from image observations alone and without any prior knowledge about the geometric configuration at hand.

Acknowledgements

The authors are very grateful towards the EC for financial support through the Marie-Curie fellowship FMBICT972281, and the Esprit LTR project VIGOR 26247.

References

1. E. Berry, P. Martinet, and J. Gallice. Trajectory generation by visual servoing. In *Proc. of the IEEE/RSJ Intl. Conf. on Intelligent Robots and Systems (IROS'97)*, volume 2, pages 1066–1072, Grenoble, France, September 1997.
2. F. Chaumette. *Visual Servoing*, volume 7 of *World Scientific Series in Robotics and Automated Systems*, chapter Classification and Realization of the Different Vision-based Tasks, pages 199–228. World Scientific, Singapour, 1993.
3. F. Chaumette. Potential problems of stability and convergence in image-based and position-based visual servoing. In *The Confluence of Vision and Control*, number 237 in LNCIS. Springer-Verlag, 1996.
4. T. Drummond and R. Cipolla. Visual tracking and control using Lie algebras. In *Proc. of IEEE Conf. on Computer Vision and Pattern Recognition (CVPR'1999)*, volume 2, pages 652–657, Ft. Collins, CO, June 1999.
5. B. Espiau, F. Chaumette, and P. Rives. A new approach to visual servoing in robotics. *IEEE Trans. on Robotics and Automation*, 8(3):313–326, June 1992.
6. O. D. Faugeras. What can be seen in three dimensions with an uncalibrated stereo rig. In *Proc. 2nd European Conference on Computer Vision (ECCV'92)*, pages 563–578. Springer Verlag, Santa Margherita Ligure, Italy, May 1992.
7. G. Hager. A modular system for robust positioning using feedback from stereo vision. *IEEE Trans. on Robotics and Automation*, 13(4):582 – 595, August 1997.
8. R. I. Hartley. Projective reconstruction and invariants from multiple images. *IEEE Trans. on Pattern Analysis and Machine Intelligence*, 16(10):1036–1041, October 1994.
9. R. Horaud, F. Dornaika, and B. Espiau. Visually guided object grasping. *IEEE Transactions on Robotics and Automation*, 14(4):525–532, August 1998.
10. E. Malis, F. Chaumette, and S. Boudet. 2 1/2 d visual servoing. *IEEE Trans. on Robotics and Automation*, 15(2):238–250, April 1999.
11. A. Ruf and R. Horaud. Rigid and articulated motion seen with an uncalibrated stereo rig. In *Proc. of the 7th International Conference on Computer Vision (ICCV'99)*, pages 789 – 796, Korfu, Greece, September 1999.
12. A. Ruf, F. Martin, B. Lamiroy, and R. Horaud. Visual control using projective kinematics. In *Proc. of 9th International Symposium on Robotics Research (ISRR'99)*, page to appear, Snowbird, UT, October 1999. Springer-Verlag.
13. J. Selig. *Geometrical Methods in Robotics*. Springer, 1996.
14. M. Spratling and R. Cipolla. Uncalibrated visual servoing. In E. T. R. B. Fisher, editor, *British Machine Vision Conference (BMVC'96)*, pages 545–554, 1996.
15. A. Zisserman, P. A. Beardsley, and I. D. Reid. Metric calibration of a stereo rig. In *Proc. IEEE Workshop on Representation of Visual Scenes*, pages 93–100, Cambridge, Mass., June 1995.

Segmentation & Grouping I

Segmentation & Grouping I

A General Method for Unsupervised Segmentation of Images Using a Multiscale Approach

Alvin H.Kam and William J.Fitzgerald

Signal Processing Laboratory
University of Cambridge Engineering Department
Trumpington Street, Cambridge CB2 1PZ,
United Kingdom
[ahswk2,wjf]@eng.cam.ac.uk

Abstract. We propose a general unsupervised multiscale approach towards image segmentation. The novelty of our method is based on the following points: firstly, it is general in the sense of being independent of the feature extraction process; secondly, it is unsupervised in that the number of classes is not assumed to be known a priori; thirdly, it is flexible as the decomposition sensitivity can be robustly adjusted to produce segmentations into varying number of classes and fourthly, it is robust through the use of the *mean shift* clustering and Bayesian multiscale processing. Clusters in the joint spatio-feature domain are assumed to be properties of underlying classes, the recovery of which is achieved by the use of the mean shift procedure, a robust non-parametric decomposition method. The subsequent classification procedure consists of Bayesian multiscale processing which models the inherent uncertainty in the joint specification of class and position via a Multiscale Random Field model which forms a Markov Chain in scale. At every scale, the segmentation map and model parameters are determined by sampling from their conditional posterior distributions using Markov Chain Monte Carlo simulations with stochastic relaxation. The method is then applied to perform both colour and texture segmentation. Experimental results show the proposed method performs well even for complicated images.

1   Introduction

The segmentation of an image into an unknown number of distinct and in some way homogeneous regions is a difficult problem and remains a fundamental issue in low-level image analysis. Many different methodologies has been proposed but a process that is highly unsupervised, flexible and robust has yet to be realised.

In this paper, we propose a general unsupervised multiscale approach towards image segmentation. The strength of our method is based on the following points: (i) it is general in the sense of being independent of the feature extraction process; consequently, the algorithm can be applied to perform different types of segmentation without modification, be it grey-scale, texture, colour based etc.

(ii) it is unsupervised in that the number of classes is not assumed to be known a priori (iii) it is flexible as the decomposition sensitivity can be robustly adjusted to produce segmentations into varying number of classes (iv) it is robust through the use of the *mean shift* clustering and Bayesian multiscale processing (v) dramatic speed-ups of computation can be achieved using appropriate processor architecture as most parts of the algorithm are highly parallellised.

The complete algorithm consists of a two-step strategy. Firstly, salient features which correspond to clusters in the feature domain, are regarded as manifestations of classes, the recovery of which is to be achieved using the mean shift procedure [5], a kernel-based decomposition method, which can be shown to be the generalised version of the k-means clustering algorithm [3].

Secondly, upon determining the number of classes and the properties of each class, we proceed towards the problem of classification. Unfortunately, classification in the image segmentation context is afflicted by uncertainties which render most simple techniques ineffective. To be more certain of the class of a pixel requires averaging over a larger area, which unfortunately makes the location of the boundary less certain. In other words, localisation in class space conflicts directly with the simulteneous localisation in position space. This has been rigorously shown by Wilson and Spann [15] to be a consequence of the relationship between the signals of which images are composed and the symbolic descriptions, in terms of classes and properties, which are the output of the segmentation process. These effects of uncertainties can however be minimised by the use of representations employing multiple scales.

Motivated by this rationale, we adopted a Bayesian multiscale classification paradigm by modelling the inherent uncertainty in the joint specification of class and position via the Multiscale Random Field model [1]. This approach provides context for the classification at coarser scales before achieving accurate boundary tracking at finer resolutions.

2 The Mean Shift Procedure

The mapping of real images to feature spaces often produces a very complex structure. Salient features whose recovery is necessary for the solution of the segmentation task, correspond to clusters in this space. As no a priori information is typically available, the number of clusters/classes and their shapes/distributions have to be discerned from the given image data.

The uniqueness of image analysis in this clustering context lies in the fact that features of neighbouring data points in the spatial domain are strongly correlated. This is due to the fact that typical images do not consist of random points but are manisfestations of entities which form contiguous regions in space. Following this rationale, we represent the image to be segmented in a n-dimensional feature space. Position and feature vectors are then concatenated to obtain a joint spatio-feature domain of dimension $d = n + 2$. Our approach thus includes the crucial spatial locality information typically missing from most clustering approaches to image segmentation. All features are then normalised by dividing with its standard deviation to eliminate bias due to scaling.

This joint spatio-feature domain can be regarded as samples drawn from an unknown probability distribution function. If the distribution is represented with a parametric model (e.g. Gaussian mixture), severe artifacts may be introduced as the shape of delineated clusters is constrained. Non-parametric cluster analysis however, uses the modes of the underlying probability density to define cluster centres and the valleys in the density to define boundaries separating the clusters.

Kernel estimation is a good practical choice for non-parametric clustering techniques as it is simple and for kernels obeying mild conditions, the estimation is asymptotically unbiased, consistent in a mean-square sense and uniformly consistent in probability [5]. Furthermore, for unsupervised segmentation, where flexibility and interpretation are of utmost importance, any rigid inference of 'optimal' number of clusters may not be productive. By using a kernel-based density estimation approach and controlling the kernel size, a method is developed which is capable of decomposing an image into the number of classes which corresponds well to a useful partitioning for the application at hand. Alternatively, we can produce a set of segmentations for the image (corresponding to different number of classes) with each one reflecting the decomposition of the image under different feature resolution.

2.1 Density Gradient and the Mean Shift Vector

Let $\{\mathbf{X}_i\}_{i=1\ldots N}$ be the set of N image vectors in the d-dimensional Euclidean space R^d. The multivariate kernel density estimate obtained with kernel $K(\mathbf{x})$ and window radius h, computed at point $\mathbf{x}$ is defined as:

$$\hat{f}(\mathbf{x}) = \frac{1}{Nh^d} \sum_{i=1}^{N} K\left(\frac{\mathbf{x} - \mathbf{X}_i}{h}\right) \tag{1}$$

The use of a differential kernel allows us to define the estimate of the density gradient estimate as the gradient of the kernel density estimate (1):

$$\hat{\nabla} f(\mathbf{x}) \equiv \nabla \hat{f}(\mathbf{x}) = \frac{1}{Nh^d} \sum_{i=1}^{N} \nabla K\left(\frac{\mathbf{x} - \mathbf{X}_i}{h}\right) \tag{2}$$

The Epanechnikov kernel [13], given by:

$$K_{\mathrm{E}}(\mathbf{x}) = \begin{cases} \frac{1}{2} c_{\mathrm{d}}^{-1}(d+2)(1 - \mathbf{x}^T \mathbf{x}) & \text{if } \mathbf{x}^T \mathbf{x} < 1 \\ 0 & \text{otherwise} \end{cases} \tag{3}$$

has been shown to be the simplest kernel to possess properties of asymptotic unbiasedness, mean-square and uniform consistency for the density gradient estimate [5]. In this case, the density gradient estimate becomes:

$$\hat{\nabla} f_{\mathrm{E}}(\mathbf{x}) = \frac{N_{\mathbf{x}}}{N(h^d c_{\mathrm{d}})} \frac{d+2}{h^2} \left[\frac{1}{N_{\mathbf{x}}} \sum_{\mathbf{X}_i \in S_h(\mathbf{x})} (\mathbf{X}_i - \mathbf{x}) \right] \tag{4}$$

where the region $S_h(\mathbf{x})$ is a hypersphere (uniform kernel) of radius h centred on $\mathbf{x}$, having the volume $h^d c_d$ and containing $N_\mathbf{x}$ data points. The last term in (4):

$$M_h(\mathbf{x}) = \frac{1}{N_\mathbf{x}} \sum_{\mathbf{X}_i \in S_h(\mathbf{x})} (\mathbf{X}_i - \mathbf{x}) \tag{5}$$

is called the sample *mean shift*. The quantity $\frac{N_\mathbf{x}}{N(h^d c_d)}$ is the kernel density estimate computed with the uniform kernel $S_h(\mathbf{x})$, $\hat{f}_U(\mathbf{x})$ and thus we can write (4) as:

$$\hat{\nabla} f_E(\mathbf{x}) = \hat{f}_U(\mathbf{x}) \frac{d+2}{h^2} M_h(\mathbf{x}) \tag{6}$$

which yields:

$$M_h(\mathbf{x}) = \frac{h^2}{d+2} \frac{\hat{\nabla} f_E(\mathbf{x})}{\hat{f}_U(\mathbf{x})} \tag{7}$$

Equation (7) depicts the mean shift vector as a normalised density gradient estimate. This implies that the vector always points towards the direction of the maximum increase in density and hence it can define a path leading to a local density maximum. The normalised gradient in (7) also brings about a desirable adaptive behaviour, with the mean shift step being large for low density regions and decreases as $\mathbf{x}$ approaches a mode.

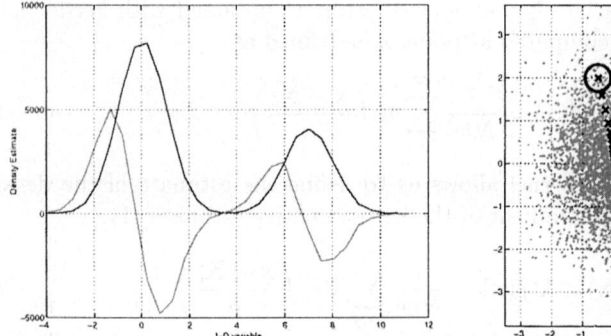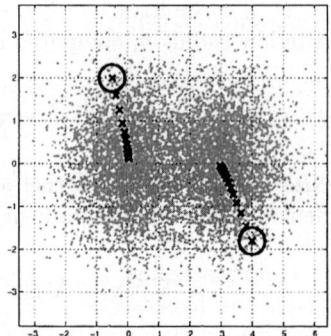

Fig. 1. On the left: Consider the density estimation plot (in blue) of a hypothetical 1-D feature. The gradient or derivative of the density plot is shown in red. It is obvious that the density gradient always points in the direction of maximum increase in density (bear in mind that left-to-right along the 1-D axis constitutes positive movement). On the right: As the mean shift vector is proportional to the density gradient estimate, successive computations of the mean shift define a path leading to a local density maximum (shown here for a 2-D feature)

While it is true that the mean shift vector $M_h(\mathbf{x})$ has the direction of the gradient estimate at $\mathbf{x}$, it is not apparent that the density estimate at the successive locations of the mean shift procedure is a monotonic increasing sequence. The following theorem, however, assures the convergence:

Theorem. Let $\hat{f}_{\mathrm{E}} = \left\{ \hat{f}_k \left(\mathbf{Y}_k, K_{\mathrm{E}} \right) \right\}_{k=1,2,\dots}$ be the sequence of density estimates obtained using the Epanechnikov kernel and computed at the points $(\mathbf{Y}_k)_{k=1,2,\dots}$ defined by the sucessive locations of the mean shift procedure with a uniform kernel. The sequence is convergent.

Proof of this theorem can be found in [4].

2.2 Mean Shift Clustering Algorithm

The mean shift clustering algorithm consists of successive computation of the mean shift vector, $M_{\mathrm{h}}(\mathbf{x})$ and translation of the window $S_{\mathrm{h}}(\mathbf{x})$ by $M_{\mathrm{h}}(\mathbf{x})$. Each data point thus becomes associated with a point of convergence which represents a local mode of the density in the d-dimensional space. Iterations of the procedure thus gives rise to a 'natural' clustering of the image data, based solely on their mean shift trajectories.

The procedure in its original form, is meant to be applied to each point in the data set. This approach is not desirable for practical applications especially when the data set is large as is typical for images. The conventional mean shift procedure has a complexity of $O(N^2)$ for a set of N data points. A more realistic approach consist of a probabilistic mean shift algorithm as proposed in [4] whose complexity is of $O(mN)$, with $m \ll N$, as outlined below:

1. *Define a random tessellation of the space with $m \ll N$ hyperspheres $S_{\mathrm{h}}(\mathbf{x})$.* To reduce computational load, a set of m points called the sample set, is randomly selected from the data. It is proposed that two simple constraints are imposed on the sample set: firstly, the distance between any two points in the sample set should not be smaller than h, the radius of the hypersphere, $S_{\mathrm{h}}(\mathbf{x})$. Secondly, sample points should not lie in sparsely populated regions. A region is defined as sparsely populated whenever the number of points inside the hypersphere is below a certain threshold T_1. The distance and density constraints automatically determine the size m of the sample set. Hyperspheres centred on the sample set cover most of the data points. These constraints can of course be relaxed if processing time is not a critical issue.

2. *The mean shift procedure is applied to the sample set.* A set containing m cluster centre candidates is defined by the points of convergence of the m mean shift procedures. As the computation of the mean shift vectors is based on almost the entire data set, the quality of the gradient estimate is not diminished by the use of sampling.

3. *Perturb the cluster candidates and reapply the mean shift procedure.* Since a local plateau can prematurely stop the iterations, each cluster centre candidate is perturbed by a random vector of small norm and the mean shift procedure is left to converge again.

4. *Derive the cluster centres* $\mathbf{Y}_1, \mathbf{Y}_2, ..., \mathbf{Y}_p$ *from the cluster centre candidates.* Any subset of cluster centre candidates which are less than distance h from each other defines a cluster centre. The cluster centre is the mean of the cluster centre candidates in the subset.

5. *Validate the cluster centres.* Between any two cluster centres $\mathbf{Y}_i$ and $\mathbf{Y}_j$, a significant valley should occur in the underlying density. The existence of the valley is tested for each pair $(\mathbf{Y}_i, \mathbf{Y}_j)$. The hypersphere $S_\mathrm{h}(\mathbf{x})$ is moved with step h along the line defined by $(\mathbf{Y}_i, \mathbf{Y}_j)$ and the density is estimated using the Epanechnikov kernel, K_E along the line. Whenever the ratio between $\min\left[\hat{f}(\mathbf{Y}_i), \hat{f}(\mathbf{Y}_j)\right]$ and the minimum density along the line is larger than a certain threshold, T_2, a valley is assumed between $\mathbf{Y}_i$ and $\mathbf{Y}_j$. If no valleys are found, the cluster centre of lower density, $(\mathbf{Y}_i$ or $\mathbf{Y}_j)$ is removed from the set of cluster centres.

The clustering algorithm makes use of three parameters: the kernel radius, h, which controls the sensitivity of the decomposition, the threshold T_1, which imposes the density constraint on the sample set and T_2, corresponding to the minimum acceptable peak-valley ratio. The parameters T_1 and T_2 generally have a weak influence on the final results. In fact, all our experimental results as performed on 256×256 resolution images were obtained by fixing $T_1 = 50$ and $T_2 = 1.2$. As the final objective of a segmentation is often application specific, top-down a priori information controls the kernel radius h, resulting in data points having trajectories that merge into appropriate number of classes. Alternatively, the 'optimal' radius can be obtained as the centre of the largest operating range which yields the same number of classes. Finally, cluster centres which are sufficient close (distance being less then h apart) in the n-dimensional 'feature-only' space (remember, $n = d - 2$) are merged in order to group similar features which are spatially distributed.

Fig. 2. Flexibility of mean shift clustering in determining the number of classes. From left: Image of 'house' and its corresponding segmentations using $h = 0.2$ (47 classes), $h = 0.4$ (15 classes) and $h = 0.8$ (8 classes) in the 5-dimensional normalised Euclidean space. The classification strategy is implemented using techniques detailed in Sect. 3 and 4

We shall assume these validated cluster centres to be manifestations of underlying class properties for our image segmentation task, with each class thus represented by an n-dimensional feature vector. We then proceed with a multiscale Bayesian classification algorithm outlined below. A Bayesian approach is used because the notion of likelihood can be determined naturally from the computation of dissimilarity measures between feature vectors. Moreover, priors can be effectively used to represent information regarding segmentation results of coarser scales when segmentation is being performed for finer resolutions.

3 The Multiscale Random Field Model

A multiscale Bayesian classification approach is implemented using the Multiscale Random Field (MSRF) model [1]. In this model, let the random field Y be the image that must be segmented into regions of distinct statistical behaviour. The behaviour of each observed pixel is dependent on a corresponding unobserved class in X. The dependence of observed pixels on their class is specified through the probability $p(Y = y|X = x)$, or the likelihood function. Prior knowledge about the size and shapes of regions will be modelled by the prior distribution $p(X)$.

X is modelled by a pyramid structure multiscale random field. $X^{(0)}$ is assumed to be the finest scale random field with each site corresponding to a single image pixel. Each site at the next coarser scale, $X^{(1)}$, corresponds to a group of four sites in $X^{(0)}$. And the same goes for coarser scales upwards. Thus, the multiscale classification is denoted by the set of random fields, $X^{(n)}, n = 0, 1, 2, ...$.

The main assumption made is that the random fields form a Markov Chain from coarse to fine scale, that is:

$$p\left(X^{(n)} = x^{(n)}|X^{(l)} = x^{(l)}, l > n\right) = p\left(X^{(n)} = x^{(n)}|X^{(n+1)} = x^{(n+1)}\right) \quad (8)$$

In other words, it is assumed that for $X^{(n)}$, $X^{(n+1)}$ contain all relevant information from previous coarser scales. We shall further assume that the classification of sites at a particular scale is dependent only on the classfication of a local neighbourhood at the next coarser scale. This relationship and the chosen neighbourhood structure are depicted in Fig. 3.

3.1 Sequential Maximum A Posteriori (SMAP) Estimation

In order to segment the image Y, one must accurately estimate the site classes in X. Generally, Bayesian estimators attempt to minimise the average cost of an errorneous segmentation. This is done by solving the optimisation problem:

$$\hat{x} = \arg\min_x E\left(C(X, x)|Y = \mathbf{y}\right) \quad (9)$$

where $C(X, x)$ is the cost of estimating the 'true' segmentation X by the approximate segmentation x. The choice of functional C is of crucial importance as it determines the relative importance of errors. Ideally, a desirable cost function should assign progressively greater cost to segmentations with larger regions of

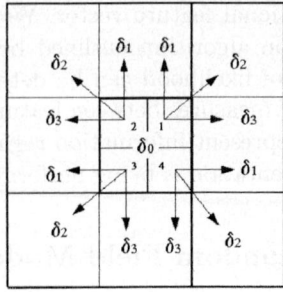

Fig. 3. Blocks 1,2,3 and 4 are of scale n and have a common parent at scale $n+1$, i.e. δ_0, which they are dependent on. The arrows show additional dependence on their parent's neighbours: δ_1, δ_2 and δ_3.

misclassified pixels. To achieve this goal, the following cost function has been proposed [1]:

$$C_{\text{SMAP}} = \frac{1}{2} + \sum_{n=0}^{L} 2^{n-1} C_n(X, x) \tag{10}$$

where:

$$C_n(X, x) = 1 - \prod_{i=n}^{L} \delta\left(X^{(i)} - x^{(i)}\right) \tag{11}$$

The behaviour of C_{SMAP} is solely a function of the coarsest scale that contains a misclassified site. The solution is given by:

$$\hat{x}^{(n)} = \arg\max_{x^{(n)}} \left\{ p\left(X^{(n)} = x^{(n)} | X^{(n+1)} = \hat{x}^{(n+1)}, Y = \mathbf{y}\right) + \varepsilon\left(x^{(n)}\right) \right\} \tag{12}$$

where ε is a second order term which may be bounded by:

$$0 \le \varepsilon(x^{(n)}) \le \max_{x^{(n-1)}} p\left(X^{(n-1)} = x^{(n-1)} | X^{(n)} = x^{(n)}, Y = \mathbf{y}\right) << 1 \tag{13}$$

Using Bayes rule and ignoring the contribution of ε, one obtains the following equation:

$$\hat{x}^{(n)} = \begin{cases} \arg\max_{x^{(L)}} \left\{ p\left(Y = \mathbf{y} | X^{(L)} = x^{(L)}\right) p(X^{(L)} = x^{(L)}) \right\} & \text{for } n = L \\ \arg\max_{x^{(n)}} \left\{ p\left(Y = \mathbf{y} | X^{(n)} = x^{(n)}\right) p(X^{(n)} = x^{(n)} | X^{(n+1)} = \hat{x}^{(n+1)}) \right\} & \text{for } n < L \end{cases} \tag{14}$$

where L is the coarsest scale of the multiscale pyramid. The solution is initialised by determining the maximum a posteriori (MAP) estimate of the coarsest scale field given the image Y. The MAP segmentation at the next finer scale, $\hat{x}^{(n)}$ is then found by computing the MAP estimate of $X^{(n)}$, given $\hat{x}^{(n+1)}$ and the image Y, hence the name sequential MAP (SMAP) estimator. For our experiments, we assumed a uniform prior for $X^{(L)}$ but in general, any suitable priors may be used.

3.2 Likelihood and Prior Probability Functions

We will assume that at a particular scale, the observed sites are *conditionally independent* given their classes:

$$p\left(Y = \mathbf{y}|X^{(n)} = x^{(n)}\right) = \prod_{s \in S^{(n)}} p\left(Y_s = \mathbf{y}_s|X_s^{(n)} = x_s^{(n)}\right) \tag{15}$$

where the index s denotes individual sites at scale n, $\mathbf{y}_s$ represents the 'averaged' feature vector of observed site Y_s and $x_s^{(n)}$ correspond to segmentation classes which have values taken from $\Lambda = \{1, 2, ..., c\}$, where c is the total number of classes.

The multiscale averaging to generate $\mathbf{y}_s$ at each scale is achieved using the lowpass subimages of Kingsbury's complex wavelet decomposition (KCWD) [10] of each feature component of $\mathbf{y}$. The advantage of KCWD over the more conventional discrete wavelet transform for multiscale representation of features lies in the remarkable shift invariance property of the former approach. To illustrate, the figure below shows grey-level feature averaging of 'lenna' using the lowpass subimages of KCWD:

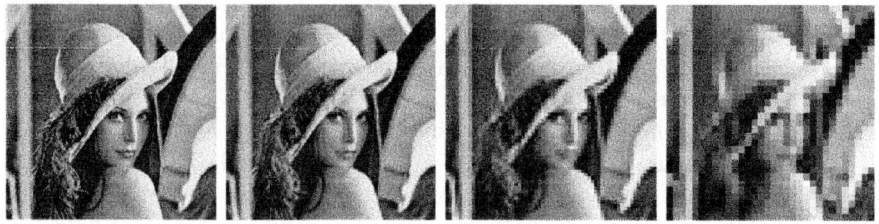

Fig. 4. Grey-level feature averaging of 'lenna' using the lowpass subimages of Kingsbury's complex wavelet decompostion at scales (from left) $n = 0, 1, 2$ and 3 respectively, with excellent shift invariance

We choose to model $p(Y_s = \mathbf{y}_s|X_s^{(n)} = x_s^{(n)})$ as a Gaussian distribution:

$$p\left(Y_s = \mathbf{y}_s|X_s^{(n)} = x_s^{(n)}\right) \propto \frac{1}{\sigma_n} \exp\left\{-\frac{1}{2\sigma_n^2} \left\|\mathbf{y}_s, x_s^{(n)}\right\|^2\right\} \tag{16}$$

where $\|\cdot\|$ denotes Euclidean distance. The variance parameter σ_n typically increases with segmentation resolution, which agrees with the increased class uncertainties at finer scales.

From our assumptions on the label field X, we have:

$$p\left(X^{(n)} = x^{(n)}|X^{(n+1)} = \hat{x}^{(n+1)}\right) = \prod_{s \in S^{(n)}} p\left(X_s^{(n)} = x_s^{(n)}|X_{\delta s}^{(n+1)} = \hat{x}_{\delta s}^{(n+1)}\right) \tag{17}$$

where δs denotes the neighbourhood structure shown in Fig. 3. We choose the following form for the right-hand-side term above:

$$p\left(X_s^{(n)} = m | X_{\delta s_0}^{(n+1)} = i, X_{\delta s_1}^{(n+1)} = j, X_{\delta s_2}^{(n+1)} = k, X_{\delta s_3}^{(n+1)} = l\right) =$$

$$\frac{\alpha_n}{9}\left(3\delta_{m,i} + 2\delta_{m,j} + 2\delta_{m,k} + 2\delta_{m,l}\right) + \frac{1 - \alpha_n}{c} \quad (18)$$

where $\delta_{m,n}$ represents the unit delta function. The scale dependent parameter $\alpha_n \in [0,1]$, determines the probability that the class of the fine scale site remains the same as that of one of the coarser scale local neighbourhood. Conversely, $1 - \alpha_n$ is the probability that a new class will be randomly chosen from the remaining classes.

3.3 Parameter Estimation

In order for the method to be adaptive to the segmentation at hand, the MSRF model parameters has to be estimated at each scale. A Markov Chain Monte Carlo (MCMC) sampling approach is used in a predetermined sequential scan to sample the model parameters and the segmentation map from their conditional distributions in a specific order. The conditional distributions of the segmentation map and the model parameters are difficult functions to maximise because they are multimodal and the vast combined parameter spaces are composed of both continuous and discrete subspaces. The Metropolis-Hastings algorithm [7], [11] is a robust MCMC optimisation algorithm which is ideally suited to be applied to these types of problem.

The stochastic relaxation process of simulated annealing [6] is used. At initial high temperatures, the probability of acceptance is very high but it reduces with the gradual cooling of the annealing temperature to reach the global maximum at very low temperatures. The first step consist of sampling the class field. The conditional distribution, from equations (15) and (17), is given by:

$$p\left(X^{(n)} = x^{(n)} | X^{(n+1)} = \hat{x}^{(n+1)}, Y = \mathbf{y}, \sigma_n, \alpha_n\right) \propto$$

$$\left\{\prod_{s \in S^{(n)}} \left[p(Y_s = \mathbf{y}_s | X_s^{(n)} = x_s^{(n)}, \sigma_n) p(X_s^{(n)} = x_s^{(n)} | X_{\delta s}^{(n+1)} = \hat{x}_{\delta s}^{(n+1)}, \alpha_n)\right]\right\}^{\frac{1}{T_t}}$$

$$(19)$$

where T_t is the annealing temperature at iteration t of the algorithm and the distributions for the likelihood and prior terms are given by (16) and (18) respectively.

For the sampling of σ_n and α_n, the respective conditional distributions are:

$$\sigma_n : p(\sigma_n | X^{(n)} = x^{(n)}, Y = \mathbf{y}) \propto$$

$$\left\{\left[\prod_{s \in S^{(n)}} p(Y_s = \mathbf{y}_s | X_s^{(n)} = x_s^{(n)}, \sigma_n)\right] p(\sigma_n | X_s^{(n)} = x_s^{(n)})\right\}^{\frac{1}{T_t}} \quad (20)$$

$$\alpha_n : p(\alpha_n | X^{(n)} = x^{(n)}, X^{(n+1)} = \hat{x}^{(n+1)}) \propto$$

$$\left\{ \left[\prod_{s \in S^{(n)}} p(X_s^{(n)} = x_s^{(n)} | X_{\delta s}^{(n+1)} = \hat{x}_{\delta s}^{(n+1)}, \alpha_n) \right] p(\alpha_n | X_{\delta s}^{(n+1)} = \hat{x}_{\delta s}^{(n+1)}) \right\}^{\frac{1}{T_t}}$$

$$(21)$$

with the likelihood terms given by equations (16) and (18) for σ_n and α_n respectively. Non-informative or reference priors [9] were used for all experiments.

Our choice of the likelihood and prior probability distributions also makes it possible for the dissimilarity term of (16) and the delta function terms of (18) to be calculated for each segmentation class prior to the MCMC sampling procedure. Therefore, these terms need to be computed only once and not repeatedly for each iteration of the Metropolis-Hastings algorithm. This greatly decreases the overall computation time. More importantly, as the computation of conditional distributions at each site is independent of each other at a particular iteration, dramatic speed-ups of calculations can be achieved using systems with highly parallel architecture.

There has been much debate of how convergence might relate to the annealing schedule used. Theoretically, the logarithmic schedule of [6] is guaranteed to converge in infinite time. In practice, this is not implementable. We have adopted a linear schedule which produces robust convergence in a relatively short time.

We now apply the complete algorithm to perform the challenging tasks of **colour** and **texture** segmentation.

4   Colour Segmentation

Colour correlates with the class identity of an object because pigments form part of the appearance of an object and thus provide vital cues for segmentation purposes. In our paper, the perceptually uniform CIE L*a*b* space is used to represent colour features. It is generated by linearly transforming the RGB colour space to the XYZ colour space followed by a non-linear transformation. The non-linear transformation is determined by relation to a nominally white object-colour stimulus which gives the tristimulus values (X_n, Y_n, Z_n). The lightness L^* is given by:

$$L^* = \begin{cases} 116(Y/Y_n)^{\frac{1}{3}} - 16 & \text{for } (Y/Y_n) > 0.008856 \\ 903.3(Y/Y_n) & \text{for } (Y/Y_n) \leq 0.008856 \end{cases} \tag{22}$$

The values a*,b* are given as follows:

$$a^* = 500 \{f(X/X_n) - f(Y/Y_n)\} \tag{23}$$

$$b^* = 200 \{f(Y/Y_n) - f(Z/Z_n)\} \tag{24}$$

where:

$$f(t) = \begin{cases} t^{\frac{1}{3}} & \text{for } t > 0.008856 \\ 7.787t + \frac{16}{116} & \text{for } t \leq 0.008856 \end{cases} \tag{25}$$

The distance between two colours as evaluated in L*a*b* space is simply the Euclidean distance between them:

$$\Delta E_{L^*a^*b^*} = \sqrt{(\Delta L^*)^2 + (\Delta a^*)^2 + (\Delta b^*)^2} \tag{26}$$

The CIE L*a*b* is as close to be perceptually linear as any colour space is expected to get. Thus the distance measure in (26) effectively quantifies the perceived difference between colours.

Figures 5 and 6 show some typical colour segmentation results using our algorithm. To determine the number of classes, mean shift clustering using $h = 0.7$ (in the normalised 5-dimensional Euclidean space) were used for all experiments to demonstrate that the kernel radius h is a robust parameter that does not require tedious 'trial-and-error' tinkering to achieve desired results for each image.

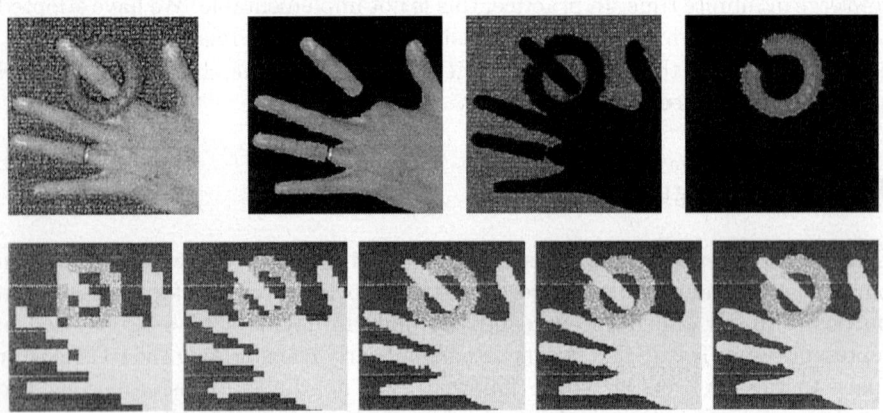

Fig. 5. First row: The 'hand' image and the three classes segmented by the algorithm. Second row: Segmentation results shown at every intermediate scale corresponding to (from left) $n = 4, 3, 2, 1$ and 0 respectively

Segmentation of the 'hand' image shown in figure 5 shows the algorithm being able to easily distinguish the human hand and the blue doughnut-like object from the textured background. As shown by the segmentation result at each scale, processing at coarse scales gives context to the segmentation based on which processing at finer resolution achieves boundary refinement accuracy.

Figure 6 shows more colour segmentation results. For the 'jet' image, the toy jet-plane, its shadow and the background are picked out by the algorithm despite

Fig. 6. First row: The 'jet' and 'parrot' image and their corresponding segmentations. Second row: The 'house' and 'fox' image and their corresponding segmentations

the considerable colour variability of each object. Segmentation of the 'parrot' image reveals a fairly smooth partitioning with all major colours bounded by reasonably accurate boundaries. The algorithm also produces a meaningful segmentation of the 'house' image with the sky, walls, window frames, lawn and trees/hedges isolated as separate entities. The 'fox' image poses a tricky problem with its shadows and highlights but the algorithm still performs reasonably well in isolating the fox from the background although there is inevitable misclasification at the extreme light and dark regions of the fox due the L*a*b* features used. Generally, for all the images, the well-defined region contours reflect the excellent boundary tracking ablility of the algorithm while smooth regions of homogeneous behaviour are the result of the multiscale processing.

5 Texture Segmentation

The figure below [12] illustrates a texture feature extraction model. Basically $x(m, n)$ is the input texture image which is filtered by $h(k, l)$, a frequency and orientation selective filter, the output of which passes a local energy function (consisting of a non-linear operator, $f(.)$ and a smoothing operator, $w(k, l)$) to produce the final feature image, $v(m, n)$. Basically, the purpose of the filter, $h(k, l)$, is extraction of spatial frequencies (of a particular scale and orientation) where one or more textures have high signal energy and the others have low energy. A quadrature mirror wavelet filter bank, used in an undecimated version of an adaptive tree-structured decomposition scheme [2], perform this task for our experiments on textures.

Numerous non-linearity operators, $f(.)$, have been applied in the literature, the most popular being the magnitude, $|x|$, the squaring, $(x)^2$ and the rectified sigmoid, $|\tanh(\alpha x)|$. It has been found that squaring in conjuction with the

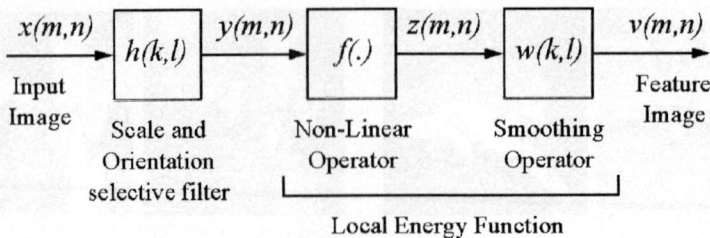

Fig. 7. Block diagram of the texture feature extraction model

logarithm after the smoothing to be the best operator pair for unsupervised segmentation from a set of tested operator pairs [14]. For this reason, this operator pair is used for our experiments.

Several smoothing filters are possible for $w(k, l)$ and the Gaussian lowpass filter is one candidate. The Gaussian lowpass filter has joint optimum resolution in the spatial and spatial frequency domains, with its impulse response given by:

$$w_G(k, l) = \frac{1}{2\pi\sigma_s^2} \exp\left\{-\frac{(k^2 + l^2)}{2\sigma_s^2}\right\} \qquad (27)$$

If we want to estimate the local energy of a signal with low spatial frequency, the smoothing filter must have a larger region-of-support and vice versa. Hence, the smoothing filter size may be set to be a function of the band centre frequency, f_0. With f_0 normalised $(-\frac{1}{2} \leq f_0 \leq \frac{1}{2})$, it has been suggested [8] that:

$$\sigma_s = \frac{1}{2\sqrt{2}|f_0|} \qquad (28)$$

This smoothing filter is also scaled so as to produce unity gain in order for the mean of the filter's output to be identical to that of its input.

For dimension reduction and extraction of saliency, *principal component analysis* is performed on the raw wavelet features, $v(m, n)$. The final feature space for the texture segmentation task consists of two dimensions of textural features (the top two principal components, which typically contribute more than 85% of the total variances of the wavelet features) and one dimension of luminance.

Figure 8 shows some texture segmentation results. Again, as in colour segmentation, mean shift clustering with kernel radius $h = 0.7$ is used to determine the number of classes. For the 'brodatz' image, the algorithm is able to distinguish all 5 textures of the Brodatz texture mosaic and produced a highly accurate segmentation map. The segmentation of the SAR image, 'sar' depicts remarkable preservation of details as well as accurate boundary detection. The image 'manassas', an aerial view of the city of Manassas, Virginia provides an interesting challenge to the algorithm, which as shown, is able to successfully isolate densely populated areas from roads and flat plains. The leopard of the image 'leo' is also successfully segmented from background grass and scrubs; 'misclassified' regions constitute shadows and relatively large homogeneous regions of black spots on the legs.

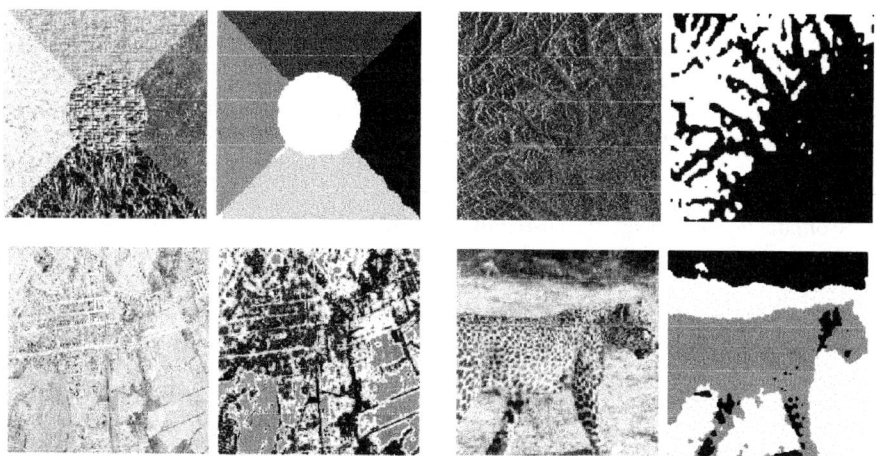

Fig. 8. First row: The 'brodatz' and 'sar' image and their corresponding segmentations. Second row: The 'manassas' and 'leo' image and their corresponding segmentations

6   Summary and Discussion

In this paper, we have proposed a general multiscale approach for unsupervised image segmentation. The method is general due to its independence of the feature extraction process and unsupervised in that the number of classes is not known a priori. The algorithm is also highly flexible due to its ability to control segmentation sensitivity and robust through the use of the mean shift procedure and multiscale processing.

The mean shift procedure has been proven to perform well in detecting clusters of complicated feature spaces of many real images. By controlling the kernel size, the procedure is capable of producing classes whose associative properties correspond well to a meaningful partitioning of an image. The Multiscale Random Field model makes effective use of the inherent trade-off between class and position uncertainty which is evident through the excellent boundary tracking performance. This multiscale processing reduces computational costs by keeping computations local and yet produces results that reflect the global properties of the image.

The proposed method has been shown to perform well for colour and texture segmentation of various images. It produces desirable segmentations with smooth regions of homogeneous behaviour and accurate boundaries. We believe these segmentations possess a high degree of utility especially as precursors to higher level tasks of scene analysis or object recognition.

References

1. Bouman, C. , Shapiro, M.: A Multiscale Random Field Model for Bayesian Image Segmentation. IEEE Trans. Image Process. **3**(2) (1994) 162–177
2. Chang, T. , Kuo, C.J.: Texture Analysis and Classification with a Tree-Structured Wavelet Transform. IEEE Trans. Image Process. **2**(4) (1993) 429–441
3. Cheng, Y.: Mean Shift, Mode Seeking, and Clustering. IEEE Trans. Pattern Anal. Machine Intell. **17**(8) (1993) 770–799
4. Comaniciu, D. , Meer, P.: Distribution Free Decomposition of Multivariate Data. 2nd Intern. Workshop on Statist. Techniques in Patt. Recog., Sydney, Australia. (1998)
5. Fukunaga, K. , Hosteler, L.D.: The Estimation of the Gradient of a Density Function, with Applications in Pattern Recognition. IEEE Trans. Info. Theory **21** (1975) 32–40
6. Geman, S. , Geman, D.: Stochastic Relaxation, Gibbs Distributions and the Bayesian Restoration of Images. IEEE Trans. Pattern Anal. Machine Intell. **6**(6) (1984) 721–741
7. Hastings, W.K.: Monte Carlo Sampling Methods using Markov Chains and their Applications. Biometrika **57** (1970) 97–109
8. Jain, A.K. , Farrokhnia, F.: Unsupervised Texture Segmentation using Gabor Filters. Pattern Recognition. **24**(12) (1991) 1167–1186
9. Jeffreys, H.: Theory of Probability. Oxford University Press (1939)
10. Kingsbury, N.: The Dual-Tree Complex Wavelet Transform: A New Technique for Shift Invariance and Directional Filters. IEEE Dig. Sig. Proc. Workshop, DSP98, Bryce Canyon, paper no. 86. (1998)
11. Metropolis, N. , Rosenbluth, A.W. , Rosenbluth, M.N.: Equation of State Calculations by Fast Computing Machines. Journal of Chem. Phys. **21** (1953) 1087–1092
12. Rangen, T. , Husoy, J.H.: Multichannel Filtering for Image Texture Segmentation. Opt. Eng. **8** (1994) 2617–2625
13. Silverman, B.W.: Density Estimation for Statistics and Data Analysis. Chapman and Hall, London. (1986)
14. Unser, M. , Eden, M.: Non-linear Operators for Improving Texture Segmentation based on Features Extracted by Spatial Filtering. IEEE Trans. Syst., Man and Cyb. **20** (1990) 804–815
15. Wilson, R. , Spann, M.: Image Segmentation and Uncertainty. Research Studies Press Ltd., Letchworth, Hertfordshire, U.K. (1988)

Image Segmentation by Nonparametric Clustering Based on the Kolmogorov-Smirnov Distance

Eric J. Pauwels[1][2] and Greet Frederix[2][3]

[1] Centre for Mathematics and Computer Science (CWI),
Kruislaan 413, 1098 SJ Amsterdam, The Netherlands
`Eric.Pauwels@cwi.nl`
[2] ESAT-PSI, K.U.Leuven, K. Mercierlaan 94,
B-3001 Heverlee, Belgium
`Eric.Pauwels@esat.kuleuven.ac.be`
[3] Dept. of Mathematics, K.U.Leuven, Celestijnenlaan 200 B,
B-3001 Heverlee, Belgium
`Greet.Frederix@esat.kuleuven.ac.be`

Abstract. In this paper we introduce a non-parametric clustering algorithm for 1-dimensional data. The procedure looks for the simplest (i.e. smoothest) density that is still compatible with the data. Compatibility is given a precise meaning in terms of the Kolmogorov-Smirnov statistic. After discussing experimental results for colour segmentation, we outline how this proposed algorithm can be extended to higher dimensions.

1   Motivation and overview

The quest for robust and autonomous image segmentation has rekindled the interest of the computer vision community in the generic problem of *data clustering* (see e.g. [3, 6, 15, 1, 2, 16]). The underlying rationale is rather straightforward: As segmentation algorithms try to divide the image into regions that are fairly homogeneous, it stands to reason to map the pixels into various feature-spaces (such as colour- or texture-spaces) and look for clusters. Indeed, if in some feature-space pixels are lumped together, this obviously means that, with respect to these features, the pixels are similar. By the same token, image regions that are perceptually salient will map to clusters that (in at least some feature-spaces) are clearly segregated from the bulk of the data.

Unfortunately, the clustering problems encountered in segmentation applications are particularly challenging, as neither the number of clusters, nor their shape is known in advance. Moreover, clusters are frequently unbalanced (i.e. have widely different sizes) and often distinctly non-Gaussian (e.g. skewed). This heralds serious difficulties for most "classical" clustering algorithms that often assume that the number of clusters is known in advance (e.g. K-means), or even that the shape of the data-density is explicitly specified up to a small number of parameters that can be estimated from the data (e.g. Gaussian Mixture Models (*GMM*)).

Furthermore, strategies to estimate the number of clusters prior to, or concurrent with, the actual clustering are of limited value as they tend to be biased towards solutions that favour spherical or elliptical clusters of roughly the same size. The root for this bias is to be found in the fact that almost all cluster-validity criteria compare variation *within* to variation *between* clusters (for more details we refer to standard texts such as [9, 11, 10]).

To circumvent the problems outlined above, we focus on clustering based on **non-parametric density estimation** (for prior work, see e.g. [3, 15]). In contradistinction to *parametric* density estimation (such as *GMM*), no explicit parametric form of the density is put forward, and the data-density is obtained by convolving the dataset by a density-kernel. More precisely, given an d-dimensional dataset $\{\mathbf{x}_i \in I\!\!R^d;\ i = 1\ldots n\}$ a density $f(\mathbf{x})$ is obtained by convolving the dataset with a unimodal density-kernel $K_\sigma(\mathbf{x})$:

$$f(\mathbf{x}) = \frac{1}{n} \sum_{i=1}^{n} K_\sigma(\mathbf{x} - \mathbf{x}_i), \tag{1}$$

where σ is the size-parameter for the kernel, measuring its spread. Although almost any unimodal density will do, one typically takes K_σ to be a (rotation-invariant) Gaussian density with σ^2 specifying its variance:

$$K_\sigma(\mathbf{x}) = \left(\frac{1}{2\pi\sigma^2}\right)^{d/2} e^{-\|\mathbf{x}\|^2/2\sigma^2}. \tag{2}$$

After convolution we identify clusters by using *gradient ascent* (hill-climbing) to pinpoint local maxima of the density f. This procedure ends up assigning each point to a nearby density-maximum, thus carving up the data-set in compact and dense clumps.

However, it is obvious that unless the width σ is judiciously picked within a fairly narrow range, this procedure will result in either too many (if σ is chosen too small) or too few clusters (if σ is set too large). Although a huge bulk of the work on density-estimation concerns itself with this problem of choosing an "optimal" value for σ (e.g. see the book by Thompson and Tapia [18]), it is fair to say that it remains extremely tricky to try and estimate optimal (or even acceptable) clustering parameters.

For this reason we propose a different approach: We start from a sub-optimal (too small) choice for σ, and then modify the resulting density f directly. The proposed modification (which will be detailed in Section 3) is based on the *Kolmogorov-Smirnov statistic* and the resulting criterion has therefore a precise and easy to grasp meaning, which does not involve arbitrarily chosen parameters.

The rest of this paper is organised as follows. In Section 2 we will argue that performance of clustering is improved if the dimensionality of the problem can be meaningfully reduced. Rather than trying to combine all the information in one huge feature-vector, we will champion the view that it makes sense to look at as simple a feature as reasonable. This amounts to projecting the high-dimensional data-set on low-dimensional subspaces and is therefore similar in spirit to *Projection Pursuit*, a technique used in data analysis, where projections on low-dimensional subspaces (1- or 2-dimensional) are used to gain insight into the structure of high-dimensional data.

One particularly interesting and useful case of the aforementioned dimension reduction is that of clustering one-dimensional data, which boils down to partitioning the corresponding histogram. This topic is discussed extensively in Section 3 for several reasons. First, although one can argue that this is just a special case of the general n-dimensional clustering problem, the topology of a 1-dimensional (non-compact) space (such as $\mathbb{R}$) is unique in that it allows a *total order*. As a consequence, the mathematical theory is well understood and yields sharp results. Furthermore, the 1-dimensional case furnishes us with a useful stepping stone towards the more complex high-dimensional case that will be discussed in Section 5. Finally, Section 4 will report on results obtained for colour segmentation.

2 High-dimensional versus low-dimensional clustering

Like most statistical procedures, clustering in high-dimensional spaces suffers from the dreaded *curse of dimensionality*. This is true in particular, for density estimation, as even for large data sets, high-dimensional space is relatively empty.

As a consequence the reliability and interpretability of the resulting clustering may be improved whenever it is possible to reduce the dimensionality of the problem. In particular, this argument indicates that it is often ill-advised to artificially increase the dimensionality of the problem by blindly concatenating feature-vectors into high-dimensional datapoints. More precisely, if there is no theoretical or prior indication that features are mutually dependent, it is advisable to cluster them separately. The reason for this is straightforward: if features $x_1, x_2, \ldots, x_n$ are independent, then their joint probability density function factorizes into a product of 1-dimensional densities:

$$f(x_1, x_2, \ldots, x_n) = f_1(x_1)f_2(x_2)\ldots f_n(x_n), \tag{3}$$

and interesting structure in the joint density f will also be apparant in (one of) the marginal densities f_i. For instance, computing the mean and variance of the gray-values in a small window about every pixel produces two features at each pixel. However, for an unconstrained image there is no reason why these two features would be dependent. Therefore, it makes sense to cluster them separately, rather than confounding the problem by focussing exclusively on their joint distribution.

In particular, there are a number of perceptually relevant dichotomies (e.g. **dark versus bright, horizontal versus vertical, direction versus randomness, coloured** versus gray, textured versus flat, etc.) that can be captured mathematically in a relatively straightforward fashion, but that nevertheless yield important clues for segmentation. This means that it makes sense to start studying 1-dimensional densities (simple histograms) and this will be our main point of focus for most of this paper.

Indeed, one of the motivations for this work is the observation that lots of effort in computer learning and artificial intelligence focuses on ways of finding transformations (often non-linear ones) that vastly reduce the *dimensionality* of the problem. The assumption is that in many cases there is a relatively small set of so-called *latent variables* that capture the intrinsic structure of the problem and by determining the intrinsic dimensionality of the data, these (hidden) variables are brought to the fore. Exponents of this approach are classical methodologies such as *principal component analysis* (PCA) and multi-dimensional scaling, but also more recent developments of similar flavour such as *projection pursuit* (PP), *generative topographic mapping* (GTM), Kohonen's *self-organising maps* (SOM) and *independent component analysis* (ICA). The latter is actually looking for transformations that decouple different components such that the factorisation in eq.(3) is — at least approximately — realised.

3 Histogram Segmentation and 1-Dimensional Clustering

3.1 The Empirical Distribution Function

In this section we will concentrate on finding clusters in a sample $x_1, \ldots, x_n$ of 1-dimensional data. In principle, clustering 1-dimensional data by segmenting the histogram should be fairly straightforward: all we need to do is locate the peaks (local maxima) and valleys (local minima) of the data density (for which the histogram is an estimator) and position the cluster boundaries at the local minima. However, the problem is that the number and position of these local minima will strongly depend on the width of the histogram bins. An appropriate choice for this parameter is difficult to make.

For this reason we have decided to use the *cumulative density function* (also called the *distribution function*) as the tool of choice for segmentation, since it allows a *non-parametric approach* (see below). We recall that for a stochastic variable X with density function f, the cumulative density (distribution) F is defined in terms of the probability P by

$$F(x) := P(X \leq x) = \int_{-\infty}^{x} f(u) \, du$$

Of course, in most cases of interest the underlying density f is unknown and we proceed by using the *empirical distribution* F_n, which for a sample $X_1, \ldots, X_n$ is given by

$$F_n(x) = \frac{\#\{i \, : \, X_i \leq x\}}{n} \tag{4}$$

One can prove (see eg.[12]) that F_n is an adequate estimator of F, as for instance

$$F_n(x) \longrightarrow F(x) \qquad \text{as} \qquad n \longrightarrow \infty.$$

at every *continuity point x of F*.

Compared to the histogram, the empirical distribution has a number of advantages. First, it is parameter-free as it is completely determined by the data itself and there is no need to judiciously pick values for critical parameters such as bin-width. Second, working with the cumulative density rather than with the density itself has the added benefit of stability. Indeed, the integration operation which transforms f into F smooths out random fluctuations, thereby highlighting the more essential characteristics. And last but not least, using the distribution allows us to invoke the Kolmogorov-Smirnov statistic, a powerful non-parametric test that can be used to compare arbitrary densities. This theme will be elaborated further in the next section.

3.2 Non-parametric Density Estimation using Kolmogorov-Smirnov

To make good on our promise to proceed in a non-parametric fashion, we proceed by asking ourselves the question: *What is the smoothest density g that is compatible with the data, in the sense that the corresponding cumulative distribution G is not significantly different from the empirical distribution F_n?* This is basically a reformulation of *Occam's razor* and in that sense akin to the MDL-principle that has made several appearances in this context. To tackle this question we note that, recast in the appropriate mathematical parlance, it reads as follows (see Fig. 1): Find the density g that solves the following constrained minimisation problem:

$$\text{minimize} \quad \Phi(g) \equiv \int_{I\!R} (g'(x))^2 \, dx, \qquad \text{subject to} \qquad \sup_x |G(x) - F_n(x)| \le \epsilon_n,$$

$$(5)$$

where ϵ_n is the critical value for the Kolmogorov-Smirnov statistic at an appropriate significance level, e.g. 5% (details regarding the Kolmogorov-Smirnov statistic can be found in section 3.3).

As there is no straightforward closed form solution to this problem, we proceed by invoking a *gradient descent* procedure,

$$\frac{\partial g}{\partial t} = -D\Phi(g), \qquad (6)$$

but this calls for a precise definition of the gradient of a functional. This concept is studied extensively in funtional analysis and we briefly remind the reader of the relevant definition (for more details, see e.g. Troutman[19], p. 44). To motivate the approach we recall that in classical calculus, the rate of change of a function in a specified direction is obtained by taking the inner-product of the gradient and the unit-vector in the specified direction. Exactly the same procedure can be used for functionals: The standard inner product on function spaces is given by

$$< f, g > = \int_{I\!R} f(x)g(x) \, dx$$

and the functional equivalent of a directional derivative is provided by the important concept of the *Gâteaux derivative of Φ at g in the direction of v:*

$$D_v\Phi(g) := \lim_{\epsilon \to 0} \frac{\Phi(g + \epsilon v) - \Phi(g)}{\epsilon} = \frac{\partial}{\partial \epsilon} \Phi(g + \epsilon v)\bigg|_{\epsilon=0} \qquad (7)$$

Under quite mild regularity conditions one can prove that for each g there is a unique function w_g such that for all v, $D_v\Phi(g) = < w_g, v >$. This function is called the *gradient of Φ at g* and denoted by $D\Phi(g)$, resulting in the suggestive formula

$$D_v\Phi(g) = < D\Phi(g), v > \qquad \text{(for all } v) \qquad (8)$$

which is formally identical to the corresponding formula in standard vector calculus relating the gradient to an arbitrary directional derivative.

It is now straightforward to compute the gradient for the functional in (5). Plugging the explicit form of the functional Φ into eq.(7) yields:

$$D_v\Phi(g) = \lim_{\epsilon \to 0} \frac{1}{\epsilon} \int_{\mathbb{R}} [(g' + \epsilon v')^2 - g'^2]\, dx$$

$$= \lim_{\epsilon \to 0} \frac{1}{\epsilon} \int_{\mathbb{R}} [(2\epsilon g' v' + \epsilon^2 v'^2]\, dx$$

$$= 2 \int_{\mathbb{R}} g' v'\, dx$$

Next, using integration by parts and the assumption that the density function g and its derivatives vanish at infinity (a reasonable assumption for a density modelling a histogram), it immediately follows that

$$D_v\Phi(g) = -2 < g'', v > \quad \text{whence,} \quad D\Phi(g) = -2\frac{\partial^2 g}{\partial x^2}$$

Therefore the gradient-descent method for the functional Φ gives rise to the heat equation:

$$\frac{\partial g}{\partial t} = c\frac{\partial^2 g}{\partial x^2}, \qquad (c \text{ appropriate conductivity coefficient}) \qquad (9)$$

which suggests the following **strategy** to search for a minimum in eq. (5): Take an initial (fine-grained, i.e. small bins) estimate $g = g_0$ for the density, e.g. by constructing a histogram with small bins, or using a kernel estimator (as in (1)) with σ sufficiently small. Next, subject g by plugging it into diffusion equation (9) with g_0 as initial condition. After each diffusion step, compute the cumulative density

$$G(x) = \int_{-\infty}^{x} g(u)\,du$$

by (numerically) integrating g. Now stop the diffusion the moment the constraint in (5) is violated and use the final g as the estimate for the density for which valleys and peaks can be determined.

Although this approach has been implemented and yields very satisfactory results, we hasten to point out that there is no guarantee that the evolution equation (9) actually ends up at a minimum (even a local one). The reason for this is that although the functional is quadratic, the diffusion is stopped as soon as it hits (domain-boundary specified by) the constraint. In most cases it will be possible to further reduce the functional Φ by sliding along the constraint.

In fact, one obvious way for doing this would be to make the diffusion coefficient c in eq(9) dependent on the Kolmogorov-Smirnov difference:

$$\rho(x) = |G(x) - F_n(x)|$$

yielding a non-linear diffusion:

$$\frac{\partial g}{\partial t} = c(\rho(x)) \frac{\partial^2 g}{\partial x^2}, \qquad \text{where e.g.} \quad c(\rho) = \exp\left(-\frac{\rho^2}{\epsilon_n^2 - \rho^2}\right) \quad (0 \le \rho \le \epsilon_n).$$

$$(10)$$

The conductivity coefficient c is engineered to behave like a Gaussian function near the origin, but to drop smoothly to zero when the difference ρ approaches the critical distance ϵ_n. This ensures that the diffusion is stopped wherever the smoothed density is about to violate the constraint, whereas it can proceed unhampered in locations where the Kolmogorov-Smirnov difference is still sufficiently small. In the actual implementation we used an even simpler computational scheme to guarantee the same effect: whenever the evolving distribution hits the KS-boundary the conductance-coefficient c in the region sandwiched between the two flanking minima was set to zero. This halts the smoothing in that region, but allows further reduction in complexity at other locations.

The sole drawback is that the diffusion tends to displace minima, so that for an accurate location it might be worthwhile to locally refit. Alternatively, one can simply pick the location of the actual minimal value (of the original data) in a small neighbourhood of the suggested minimum or trace it back to the original data.

3.3 Confidence Band based on Kolmogorov-Smirnov Statistic

To implement the rationale underlying eq. (5) and amplified in the preceding section we still need to specify a principled way to determine the amount of acceptable deviation $|G(x) - F_n(x)|$. To this end we introduce the *Kolmogorov-Smirnov* statistic which directly compares distribution functions (eg. see [17]). More precisely, if $F_n(x)$ is the cumulative distribution for a sample of size n drawn from F, the Kolmogorov-Smirnov test-statistic is defined to be the L^∞-distance between the two functions:

$$D_n = \sup_{x \in \mathbb{R}} |F_n(x) - F(x)|$$

$$(11)$$

for which the p-value can be computed using:

$$P(D_n > \xi) = Q_{KS}(\sqrt{n}\xi),$$

$$(12)$$

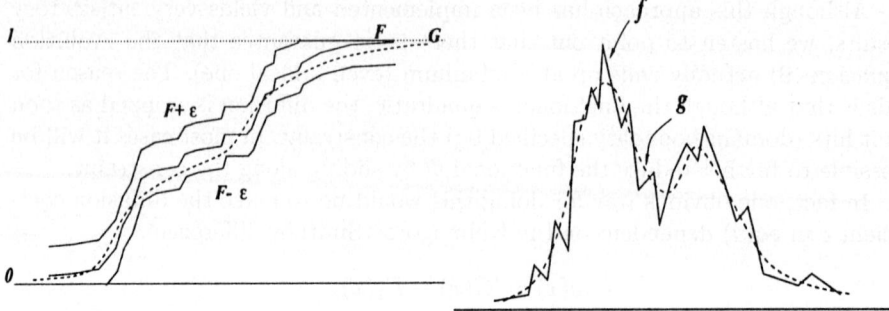

Fig. 1. Segmenting densities (histograms) using the cumulative density. *Left:* The empirical cumulative density F_n flanked by its Kolmogorov-Smirnov confidence bands $F_n \pm \epsilon_n$, together with the smoothed cumulative density G that fits within the band. *Right:* The corresponding densities (obtained by differentiation).

where

$$Q_{KS}(\xi) = 2 \sum_{k=1}^{\infty} (-1)^{k+1} e^{-2k^2 \xi^2}.$$

(A reference can be found in Mood et.al. [12]). However, the alternating character makes this series expansion rather unwieldy to use, and we therefore hark back to Good [8] who proved the following approximation. First, define the one-sided difference

$$D_n^+ = \sup_x (F_n(x) - F(x)) \qquad \text{and} \qquad D_n^- = \sup_x (F(x) - F_n(x)),$$

then Good showed that under the null-hypothesis (i.e. if F_n does indeed correspond to a sample taken from the underlying distribution F), both statistics D_n^+ and D_n^- are identically distributed and tend to the following asymptottic distribution (for n sufficiently large):

$$4n D_n^{+2} \sim \chi_2^2. \tag{13}$$

This approximation is eminently useful as it provides us with an handle to compute the boundary ϵ_n in eq.(5). More precisely, we pick ϵ_n so that under the null-hypothesis, it is unlikely that the KS-distance exceeds ϵ_n:

$$P(D_n^+ > \epsilon_n) = \alpha \qquad \text{where e.g. } \alpha = 0.05 \text{ or } 0.1. \tag{14}$$

Selecting a critical point c_α for the χ_2^2-distribution such that $P(\chi_2^2 > c_\alpha) = \alpha$ we see that the probability in eq.(14) can be rewritten as $P(4n D_n^{+2} > 4n \epsilon_n^2) = \alpha$ whence $\epsilon_n^2 = c_\alpha / 4n$. We therefore conclude that the bound ϵ_n in eq.(5) is determined by

$$\epsilon_n = \frac{1}{2} \sqrt{\frac{c_\alpha}{n}} \qquad \text{where} \quad P(\chi_2^2 > c_\alpha) = \alpha. \tag{15}$$

The only point that needs further amplification concerns the fact that we are interested in statistics on the two-sided distance D, whereas eq. (15) yields bounds on the one-sided distances D^+ or D^-. However, since

$$P(D > \xi) = P((D^+ > \xi) \text{ or } (D^- > \xi))$$
$$\leq P(D^+ > \xi) + P(D^- > \xi)$$
$$= 2 P(D^+ > \xi)$$

Hence, we see that we get a (conservative) confidence bound if we set ϵ_n in eq.(5) to be equal to

$$\epsilon_n = \frac{1}{2} \sqrt{\frac{c_{\alpha/2}}{n}} \quad \text{where} \quad P(\chi_2^2 > c_{\alpha/2}) = \alpha/2. \tag{16}$$

3.4 Comparison to Fitting Gaussian Mixture Models

Fitting a *Gaussian Mixture Model* (GMM) is probably the most popular method to partition a histogram into a unknown number of groups. If the number of clusters is known in advance, one can take recourse to the well-known *Expectation-Maximisation algorithm* (EM) [4] to estimate the corresponding parameters (ie. mean, variance and prior probabilities of each group). However, caution is called for as the sensitivity of the EM-algorithm to its initialisation is well-documented: Initially assigning a small number of "outliers" to the wrong group (albeit with small probability) often lures the algorithm to an erroneous local likelihood minimum, from which it never recovers.

The second problem has to do with the fact that the number of groups isn't known in advance and needs to be determined on the fly. Obviously, maximum likelihood methods are unable to extract the number of clusters as the likelihood increases monotonically with the number of clusters. One possibility, proposed by Carson et.al. [2], is to use a criterion based on *Minimum Description Length* (MDL). The idea is combine the likelihood of the data with respect to a (Gaussian mixture) model with a penalty term that grows with the number of parameters that need to be determined to fit the model. More precisely, for a sample $\mathbf{x}$ of size n they choose the number K of components in the Gaussian mixture (determined by parameters θ) by maximisizing

$$L(\theta \mid \mathbf{x}) - \beta \frac{m_K}{2} \log n \tag{17}$$

where m_K is the number of free parameters needed for a model with K Gaussian (d-dimensional) mixture components:

$$m_K = (K - 1) + Kd + K \frac{d(d + 1)}{2}.$$

(The significance of the β-factor will be discussed presently).

There are two, potentially serious, problems. First, there are the aforementioned problems regarding the instabilities inherent to the EM-algorithm. But even if the EM-algorithm is successful in identifying the underlying mixture, there is the need for an adhoc factor β to balance out the contribution from both cost-terms in eq.(17), as they may differ by an order of magnitude.

One could of course object that the fudge-factor β is comparable to the parameter α that needs to be fixed in the KS-approach. But there is an important difference: unlike β, the factor α specifying the confidence level has a clear and operational meaning in terms of the risk of committing a type-I error and this risk needs to be fixed in any statistical approach to data-analysis.

In all fairness we need to point out that there is one situation in which the EM-algorithm yields a more satisfying result than the non-parametric approach. Whenever we have two Gaussian densities that encroach on one another, there is a possibility that the global density shows two ill-separated bumps without a clearcut minimum. In such cases EM has little difficulty extracting the individual Gaussians (granted of course, that the number of Gaussians is specified beforehand). As there is no minimum in the original density, our method will have no alternative but to lump the Gaussians together in one cluster.

Having said that, it is also worthwhile to point out that there are situations where EM will fail to deliver the goods while the non-parametric approach has no difficulty whatsoever The simplest example is a uniformly distributed density. In an attempt to come up with a good approximation to this flat density, the EM-algorithm has no other option but to insert a variable number of Gaussians, resulting in a excessive fractioning of the cluster.

In **conclusion** we can say the EM-algorithm for GMM is a typical example of a parametric approach to density estimation. As such it enjoys an advantage over a non-parametric approach (such as the one detailed in this paper) whenever there is clear evidence that the underlying data-distribution is well modeled by the proposed parametrised density. However, in typical image-segmentation problems such an assumption is seldomly warranted and consequently, EM is almost invariably outperformed by the proposed non-parametric histogram segmentation.

4 Some Experimental Results

We also tested this strategy on a number of challenging colour images (see Figs. 2). In keeping with the spirit of our approach we project each image on the axes of a number of different colour-spaces (such as RGB, rgb, and opponent-colours). This yields for each image 9 histograms which are all segmented. The resulting histogram clusterings can easily be scored by marking whether there is more than one cluster (uninteresting) and if so, how well-separated and pronounced these clusters are (e.g. by comparing their mean distance to their variance). In the experiments reported below we display for each image the two most salient histograms. More precisely, the original colour images (left), together with two histograms obtained by projection on an appropriate colour-axis (the choice of which is image dependent) and the resulting image segmentation based on the segmentation of the histogram. It is clear that combining the information from the different projections often yields very acceptable segmentation results.

To enhance the robustness of the segmentation we apply two simple pre-processing steps:

1. Slight diffusion of the colours in the original image; apart from reducing noise it introduces some sort of spatial correlation into the statistics and therefore compensates for the fact that spatial information is completely lost when mapping pixels into colour-spaces.

2. Global perturbation of the 1-dimensional data by adding independent Gaussian noise to all the datapoints:

$$\tilde{x}_i = x_i + \delta_i$$

where $\delta_i \sim N(0, \sigma^2)$ are independent and the standard deviation σ is taken to be a fraction of the data range R:

$$\sigma = \gamma R \qquad \text{(typically, } \gamma = 0.01\text{).}$$

The reason for introducing this perturbation is that it resolves ties and removes artifacts due to quantisation, thus improving the final results.

It goes without saying that segmentation based on a single 1-dimensional histogram will only reflect a particular visual aspect (if any at all), and as such only has a very limited range of applicability. However, we contend that as different aspects are highlighted by different histograms, combinations of the regions thus obtained will yield complementary information.

This topic will be taken up in a forthcoming paper but for now, let us just point out that it is helpful to think of the segmentation results for the one-dimensional histograms as some sort of *spatial binding*. If for some feature pixels are mapped into the same region, then they are in effect "bound together" in the sense that, with respect to that particular feature, they are very similar. In this way, each different projection (feature) imposes its own binding-structure on the pixels and pixels that are often "bound together" in the same region therefore accrue a lot of mutual spatial correlation. This spatial correlation structure can be used to improve segmentation or to suggest to the user a number of different possible segmentations, the correlation structure detailing for each of them their statistical support.

5 Extensions to higher dimensions

The main thrust of the argument in this paper was based on the Kolmogorov-Smirnov distance, and it is therefore of interest to note that there is multi-dimensional extension of sorts for the KS-statistic. This opens up the possibility to extend this approach to higher dimensions, always bearing in mind of course that the dimension should not be inflated without proper reason.

The generalisation of the distribution function for a d-dimensional stochastic variable $\mathbf{X}$ is straightforward:

$$F(\mathbf{x}) := P(\mathbf{X} \leq \mathbf{x}) = P(X_1 \leq x_1, \ldots, X_d \leq x_d) \tag{18}$$

For the sake of brevity, we limit ourselves here to formulating the relevant theorem (for more details, see [20]):

For any $\epsilon > 0$ there exists a sufficiently large n_0 such that for $n > n_0$ the inequality

$$P\left\{ \sup_{\mathbf{x}} |F(\mathbf{x}) - F_n(\mathbf{x})| > \epsilon \right\} < 2e^{-a\epsilon^2 n} \tag{19}$$

holds true, where a is any constant smaller than 2.

Notice how this result falls short of mathematical solidity and elegance enjoyed by the 1-dimensional result (12). First of all, having to deal with an inequality rather than an equality means that we are only given an upperbound for the probability. Furthermore, as stated above, the result is akward to use as it pontificates the existence of an appropriate sample size (n), given a KS-distance ϵ. However, in practice the sample size is fixed in advance and there is little scope for an asymptotic expansion. In fact, for most realistic sample sizes, the specified upper bound is much larger than 1 and therefore of little use.

These theoretical proviso's notwithstanding, there is no good reason why a strategy similar to the one expounded in section 3 cannot be explored in higher dimensions, if we are willing to shoulder a higher computational burden. More specifically we propose the following algorithm to cluster d-dimensional data.

Algorithm Given a sample $\mathbf{x}_1, \ldots, \mathbf{x_n}$ in $\mathbb{R}^d$;

1. Compute for each $\mathbf{x}_i$ the empirical distribution function $F_n(\mathbf{x}_i) = \#\{\mathbf{x}_k \mid \mathbf{x}_k \leq \mathbf{x}_i\}/n$ (the ordering relation is defined component-wise, as in eq.(18)). Next, pick a small initial value for σ;
2. Use eq.(1) to construct the kernel-estimate f_σ for the density. In order to evaluate the KS-statistic we need the corresponding cumulative density F_σ which can be obtained by integration:

$$F_\sigma(\mathbf{x}) = \frac{1}{n} \sum_{i=1}^{n} \int_{-\infty}^{\mathbf{x}} K_\sigma(\xi - \mathbf{x}_i)\, d\xi \tag{20}$$

If the kernel K_σ is a rotation-invariant Gaussian (2) (actually the most common choice), then its integral can be straightfowardly expressed in terms of products of the error-function $\mathtt{erf(x)}$, and (20) therefore yields an explicit expression.

3. Compute the KS-distance between the proposed distribution F_σ and the empirical one supported by the actual data:

$$D(F_\sigma) = \sup_{i} |F_\sigma(\mathbf{x}_i) - F_n(\mathbf{x}_i)|$$

4. To assess how (un)acceptable this result is we need to compute the p-value for $D(F_\sigma)$, ie. we need to compute the probability that a sample from F_σ will yield a value at least as large as $D(F_\sigma)$. To this end we draw M samples of size n from F_σ and construct for each of them the corresponding empirical $F_n^{(m)}, (m = 1, \ldots, M)$ and the associated distance $D^{(m)}$. Ranking $D(F_\sigma)$ relative to the sequence $\{D^{(m)}; \ m = 1, \ldots, M\}$ yields an estimate for the required p-value. (Note that since F_σ is based on a convolution (1), sampling from this distribution is straigthforward: first pick a data-point $\mathbf{x}_i$ at random and next, sample from the Gaussian K_σ centered at $\mathbf{x}_i$.)

5. Finally, if the p-value thus obtained indicates that there is still room to further increase σ (ie. to further smooth f), do so and return to step 2. Notice how we can change σ *globally* (which amounts to a global smoothing), or *locally* at those locations where KS-difference indicates that there is further leeway for data-smoothing. This is the multi-dimensional equivalent of the non-linear smoothing proposed in eq.(10).

6   Conclusion and outlook

In this paper we have introduced a non-parametric clustering algorithm for *1-dimensional* data. The procedure looks for the *simplest (i.e. smoothest) density that is still compatible with the data*. Compatibility is given a precise meaning in terms of the *Kolmogorov-Smirnov* statistic. This approach is therefore genuinely nonparametric and does not involve fixing arbitrary cost- or fudge-factors.

We have argued that it often makes sense to look for salient regions by investigating projections on appropriate 1-dimensional feature-spaces, which are inspected for evidence of clusters. We note in passing that this provides us with a operational tool for automatic and data-driven selection of promising features: a feature is deemed interesting (for the image under scrutiny) whenever it gives rise to a non-trivial clustering. Finally, we have outlined how the results obtained in the 1-dimensional case can be generalised to higher-dimensional settings.

Acknowledgement The authors gratefully acknowledges partial support by the Belgian Fund for Scientific Research (F.W.O. Vlaanderen), under grant G.0366.98 and KULeuven VIS-project.

References

1. C. Carson, S. Belongie, H. Greenspan, and J. Malik: *Region-Based Image Querying*. Proc. of CVPR'97 Workshop on Content-Based Access of Image and Video Libraries.
2. C. Carson, S. Belongie, H. Greenspan, and J. Malik: *Blobworld: Image Segmentation using Expectation-Maximization and its application to Image Querying*. Submitted to PAMI.
3. G. Coleman and H.C. Andrews: *Image segmentation by clustering*. Proc. IEEE 67, 1979, pp. 773-785.

4. A.P. Dempster, N.M. Laird and D.R. Rubin : *Maximum Likelihood from Incomplete Data via the EM Algorithm.* J. Royal Statist. Soc.Ser B, 39 (1977), pp. 1-38.

5. R.O. Duda and P.E. Hart: *Pattern Classification and Scene Analysis.* Wiley 1973.

6. H. Frigui and R. Krishnapuram: *Clustering by Competitive Agglomeration.* Pattern Recognition, Vol. 30, No. 7, ppe. 1109-1119, 1997.

7. K. Fukunaga: *Introduction to Statistical Pattern Recognition.* Academic Press, 1990.

8. I.J. Good and R.A. Gaskins: *Nonparametric roughness penalties for probability densities.* Biometrika 58, 255-77, 1971.

9. A.K. Jain and R.C. Dubes: *Algorithms for Clustering Data.* Prentice Hall, 1988.

10. Leonard Kaufman and Peter J. Rousseeuw: *Finding Groups in Data: An Introduction to Cluster Analysis.* J. Wiley and Sons, 1990.

11. Brian S. Everitt: *Cluster Analysis.* Edward Arnold, 1993.

12. A. Mood, F. Graybill, D. Boes: *Introduction to the Theory of Statistics.* McGraw-Hill, 1974, 3rd Edition.

13. E.J. Pauwels, P. Fiddelaers and F. Mindru: *Fully Unsupervised Clustering using Center-Surround Receptive Fields with Applications to Colour-Segmentation.* Proc. of the 7th. International Conference on Computer Analysis of Images and Patterns. Kiel, Germany, Sept 10-12, 1997.

14. E.J. Pauwels and G. Frederix: *Non-parametric Clustering for Segmentation and Grouping.* Proc. of International Workshop on Very Low Bitrate Video Coding VLBV'98, Urbana, IL, Oct. 1998. pp. 133-136.

15. E.J. Pauwels and G. Frederix: *Finding Salient Regions in Images. Computer Vision and Image Understanding,* Vol. 75, Nos 1/2, July/August 1999, pp. 73-85.

16. J. Shi and J. Malik: *Normalized Cuts and Image Segmentation.* Proc. IEEE Conf. oon Comp. Vision and Pattern Recognition, San Juan, Puerto Rico, Jun

17. W. Press, B. Flannery, S. Teukolsky, W. Vetterling: *Numerical Recipes.* Cambridge University Press, 1989.

18. J.R. Thompson and R.A. Tapia: *Nonparametric Function Estimation, Modeling and Simulation.* SIAM, 1990.

19. John L. Troutman: *Variational Calculus with Elementary Convexity.* UTM, Springer-Verlag, 1983.

20. V.N. Vapnik: *The Nature of Statistical Learning Theory.* Springer, 1995.

Fig. 2. Original colour images (left), together with two histograms obtained by projection on an appropriate colour-axis (the choice of which is image dependent) and the resulting image segmentation based on the segmentation of the histogram.

Euclidean Group Invariant Computation of Stochastic Completion Fields Using Shiftable-Twistable Functions

John W. Zweck and Lance R. Williams

Dept. of Computer Science
University of New Mexico
Albuquerque, NM 87131, USA.

Abstract. We describe a method for computing the likelihood that a completion joining two contour fragments passes through any given position and orientation in the image plane, that is, a method for completing the boundaries of partially occluded objects. Like computations in primary visual cortex (and unlike all previous models of contour completion in the human visual system), our computation is Euclidean invariant. This invariance is achieved in a biologically plausible manner by representing the input, output, and intermediate states of the computation in a basis of shiftable-twistable functions. The spatial components of these functions resemble the receptive fields of simple cells in primary visual cortex. Shiftable-twistable functions on the space of positions and directions are a generalization of shiftable-steerable functions on the plane.

1 Introduction

Any computational model of human visual information processing must reconcile two apparently contradictory observations. First, computations in primary visual cortex are largely *Euclidean invariant*—an arbitrary rotation and translation of the input pattern of light falling on the retina produces an identical rotation and translation of the output of the computation. Second, simple calculations based on the size of primary visual cortex (60 mm × 80 mm) and the observed density of cortical hypercolumns (4/mm^2) suggest that the discrete spatial sampling of the visual field is exceedingly sparse [24]. The apparent contradiction becomes clear when we ask the following questions: How is this remarkable invariance achieved in computations performed by populations of cortical neurons with broadly tuned receptive fields centered at so few locations? Why doesn't our perception of the world change dramatically when we tilt our head by 5 degrees?[1]

---

[1] Ulf Eyesel asks a related question in a recent *Nature* paper [5]:

"On average, a region of just 1 mm^2 on the surface of the cortex will contain all possible orientation preferences, and, accordingly, can analyze orientation for one small area of the visual field. This topographical arrangement allows closely spaced objects with different orientations to interact. But it also means

(a)   (b)

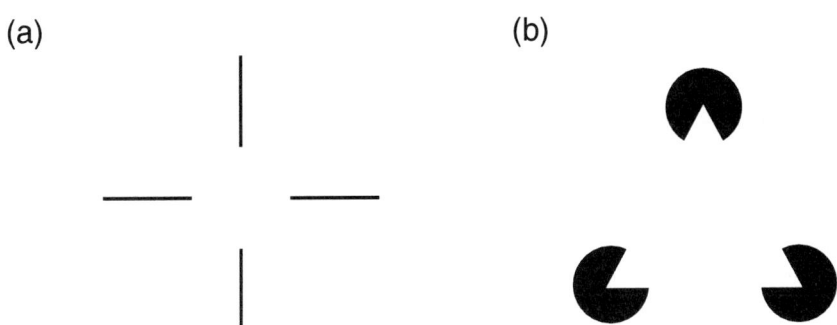

Fig. 1. (a) Ehrenstein Figure (b) Kanizsa Triangle

One of the main goals of our research is to show how the sparse and seemingly haphazard nature of the sampling of the visual field can be reconciled with the Euclidean invariance of visual computations. To realize this goal, we introduce the notion of a shiftable-twistable basis of functions on the space, $\mathbf{R}^2 \times S^1$, of positions and directions. This notion is a generalization of the notion of a shiftable-steerable basis of functions on the plane, $\mathbf{R}^2$, introduced by Freeman, Adelson, Simoncelli, and Heeger in two seminal papers [6, 18]. Freeman and Adelson [6] clearly appreciated the importance of the issues raised above when they devised the notion of a steerable basis to implement rotationally invariant computations. In fact, for computations in the plane the contradictions discussed above were largely resolved with the introduction by Simoncelli *et al.* [18] of the shiftable-steerable pyramid transform, which was specifically designed to perform Euclidean invariant computations on $\mathbf{R}^2$. The basis functions in the shiftable-steerable pyramid are very similar to simple cell receptive fields in primary visual cortex. However, many computations in V1 and V2 likely operate on functions of the space of positions and directions, $\mathbf{R}^2 \times S^1$, rather than on functions of the plane, $\mathbf{R}^2$ (e.g., [8, 9, 13, 16, 17, 21, 22, 25]). Consequently, we propose that shiftability-twistability (in addition to shiftability-steerability) is the property which binds sparsely distributed receptive fields together functionally to perform Euclidean invariant computations in visual cortex.

In this article, we describe a new algorithm for completing the boundaries of partially occluded objects. This algorithm is based on a computational theory of contour completion in primary and secondary visual cortex developed in recent years by Williams and colleagues [19–22]. Like computations in V1 and V2, and unlike previous models of illusory contour formation in the human visual system, our computation is Euclidean invariant. This invariance is achieved by

that a continuous line across the whole visual field would be cortically depicted in a patchy, discontinuous fashion. How can the spatially separated elements be bound together functionally?"

representing the input, output, and intermediate states of the computation in a basis of shiftable-twistable functions.

Mumford [15] proposed that the probability distribution of natural shapes can be modeled by particles traveling with constant speed in directions given by Brownian motions. More recently, Williams and Jacobs [21] defined the *stochastic completion field* to be the distribution of particle trajectories joining pairs of position and direction constraints, and showed how it could be computed in a neural network.

The neural network described in [22] is based on Mumford's observation that the evolution in time of the probability density function (p.d.f.) representing the position, (x, y), and direction, θ, of the particle can be modeled as a set of independent advection equations acting in the (x, y) dimension coupled in the θ dimension by the diffusion equation [15]. Unfortunately, solutions of this *Fokker-Planck* equation computed by numerical integration on a rectangular grid do not exhibit the robust invariance under rotations and translations which characterizes the output of computations performed in primary visual cortex. Nor does any other existing model of contour completion, sharpening, or saliency (e.g., [8, 9, 13, 16, 17, 21, 22, 25]).

Our new algorithm computes stochastic completion fields in a Euclidean invariant manner. Figure 2 (left) is a picture of the stochastic completion field due to the Kanizsa Triangle stimulus in Figure 1(b). Figure 2 (right) shows the stochastic completion field due to a rotation and translation of the (input) Kanizsa Triangle. The Euclidean invariance of our algorithm can be seen by observing that the (output) stochastic completion field on the right in Figure 2 is itself a rotation and translation of the stochastic completion field on the left, by the same amount.

2 Relevant Neuroscience

Our new Euclidean invariant algorithm was motivated, in part, by the following experimental findings. To begin with, the receptive fields of simple cells, which have been traditionally described as edge (or bar) detectors, can be accurately modeled using two-dimensional Gabor functions [3, 14], which are the product of a Gaussian (localized in position) and a harmonic grating (localized in orientation and spatial frequency). Gabor functions are well suited to the purpose of encoding visual information, since, by the Heisenberg Uncertainty Principle, they are the unique functions which are maximally localized in both space and frequency.

The sampling of the visual field in V1 is quite sparse—there are about about 100×100 hypercolumns, with receptive fields of about 5 scales and 16 orientations in each hypercolumn. Neglecting size (and phase), a simple cell receptive field can be parameterized by its position and orientation. The spatial distribution of these two parameters, known as *orientation preference structure*, is an attempt (on the part of evolution) to smoothly map the three-dimensional parameter space, $\mathbf{R}^2 \times S^1$, of edge positions and orientations onto the two-dimensional surface, of the

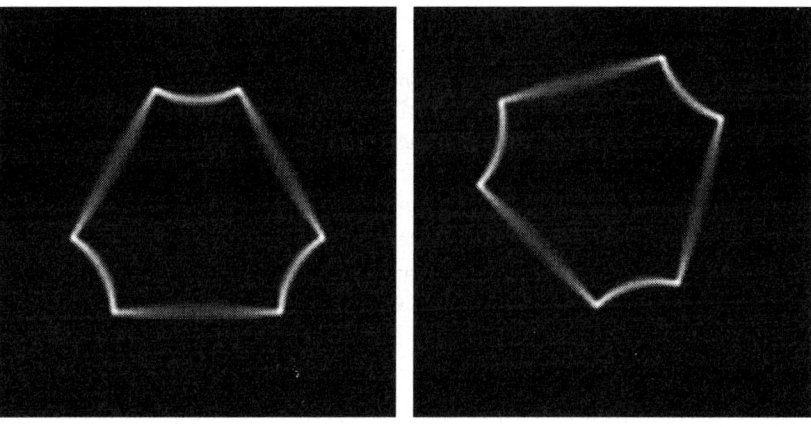

Fig. 2. Stochastic completion fields: Of Kanizsa Triangle (*left*) and after the initial conditions have been rotated and translated (*right*)

visual cortex, $\mathbf{R}^2$. Due to the differences in dimensionality, orientation preference structure is punctuated by so-called *pinwheels*, which are the singularities in this mapping [1].

As a first approximation, a neuron's response to an arbitrary grey-level image can be modeled as the L^2-inner product of the image with the neuron's receptive field. These experimental observations suggested to Daugman [4] that an ensemble of simple cell receptive fields can be regarded as performing a wavelet transform of the image, in which the responses of the neurons correspond to the transform coefficients and the receptive fields correspond to the basis functions.

Recent experiments have demonstrated that the response of simple cells in V1 can be modulated by stimuli outside the classical receptive fields. Apart from underscoring the limitations of the classical (linear) model, they suggest a function for the long-range connections which have been observed between simple cells. For example, in a recent experiment, Gilbert [7] has demonstrated that a short horizontal bar stimulus can modulate the response of simple cells whose receptive fields are located at a significant horizontal distances from the bar, and which have a similar orientation preference to the bar. Non-linear long-range effects have also been observed in secondary visual cortex. For example, von der Heydt *et al.*[10] reported that the firing rate of certain neurons in V2 increases when their "receptive fields" are crossed by illusory contours (of specific orientations) which are induced by pairs of bars flanking the receptive field. Significantly, these neurons do not respond to these same bars presented in isolation—they only respond to pairs.[2]

---

[2] These experiments suggests that the source and sink fields, which are intermediate representations in Williams and Jacobs model of illusory contour formation, could be

Although our new contour completion algorithm does not provide a model for illusory contour formation in the brain which is realistic in every respect, it does have several features which are biologically plausible, none of which are found in previous algorithms, e.g., [8, 9, 13, 16, 17, 21, 22, 25]. These features are that (1) all states of the computation be represented in a wavelet-like basis of functions which are localized in both space and frequency (spatial localization allows the computation to be performed in parallel); (2) the computation operates on the coefficients in the wavelet-like transform and can be implemented in a neural network; (3) the computation is Euclidean invariant; and (4) it is accomplished using basis functions with centers lying on a (relatively) sparse grid in the image plane.

3 Shiftable-Twistable Bases

Many visual and image processing tasks are most naturally formulated in the continuum and are invariant under a group of symmetries of the continuum. The Euclidean group, of rotations and translations, is one example of a continuous symmetry group. However, because discrete lattices are not preserved by the action of continuous symmetry groups, the natural invariance of a computation can be easily lost when it is performed in a discrete network. In this section we will introduce the notion of a shiftable-twistable basis and show how it can be used to implement discrete computations on the continuous space of positions and directions in a way which preserves their natural invariance.

In image processing, the input and output are functions on $\mathbf{R}^2$, and the appropriate notion of the invariance of computations is *Euclidean invariance*— any rotation and translation of the input should produce an identical rotation and translation of the output. Simoncelli *et al.* [6, 18] introduced the notion of a shiftable-steerable basis of functions on $\mathbf{R}^2$, and showed how it can be used to achieve Euclidean invariance in discrete computations for image enhancement, stereo disparity measurement, and scale-space analysis.

Given the nature of simple cell receptive fields, the input and output of computations in primary visual cortex are more naturally thought of as functions defined on the continuous space, $\mathbf{R}^2 \times S^1$, of positions, $\mathbf{x} = (x, y)$, in the plane, $\mathbf{R}^2$, and directions, θ, in the circle, S^1. For such computations the appropriate notion of invariance is determined by those symmetries, $T_{\mathbf{x}_0, \theta_0}$, of $\mathbf{R}^2 \times S^1$, which perform a shift in $\mathbf{R}^2$ by $\mathbf{x}_0$, followed by a twist in $\mathbf{R}^2 \times S^1$ through an angle, θ_0. A *twist* through an angle, θ_0, consists of two parts: (1) a rotation, R_{θ_0}, of $\mathbf{R}^2$ and (2) a translation in S^1, both by θ_0. The symmetry, $T_{\mathbf{x}_0, \theta_0}$, which is called a *shift-twist transformation*[3], is given by the formula,

$$T_{(\mathbf{x}_0, \theta_0)}(\mathbf{x}, \theta) = (R_{\theta_0}(\mathbf{x} - \mathbf{x}_0), \theta - \theta_0). \tag{3.1}$$

---

represented by populations of simple cells in V1, and that the stochastic completion field, which is the product of the source and sink fields, could be represented in V2.

[3] The relationship between shift-twist transformations and computations in V1 was described by Williams and Jacobs in [21] and more recently by Kalitzin *et al.* [12] and Cowan [2].

A visual computation on $\mathbf{R}^2 \times S^1$ is called *shift-twist invariant* if, for all $(\boldsymbol{x}_0, \theta_0) \in$ $\mathbf{R}^2 \times S^1$, a shift-twist of the input by $(\boldsymbol{x}_0, \theta_0)$ produces an identical shift-twist of the output.

Correspondingly, we define a *shiftable-twistable basis*[4] of functions on $\mathbf{R}^2 \times S^1$ to be a set of functions on $\mathbf{R}^2 \times S^1$ with the property that whenever a function, $P(\boldsymbol{x}, \theta)$, is in their span, then so is $P(T_{\boldsymbol{x}_0, \theta_0}(\boldsymbol{x}, \theta))$, for every choice of $(\boldsymbol{x}_0, \theta_0)$ in $\mathbf{R}^2 \times S^1$. As such, the notion of a shiftable-twistable basis on $\mathbf{R}^2 \times S^1$ generalizes that of a shiftable-steerable basis on $\mathbf{R}^2$.

Shiftable-twistable bases can be constructed as follows. First we recall Simoncelli's concept of the shiftability of a function, which is closely related to the Shannon-Whittaker Sampling Theorem. A periodic function, $\psi(x)$, of period X, is *shiftable* if there is an integer, K, such that the shift of ψ by an arbitrary amount, x_0, can be expressed as a linear combination of K basic shifts of ψ, i.e., if there exist *interpolation functions*, $b_k(x_0)$, such that

$$\psi(x - x_0) = \sum_{k=0}^{K-1} b_k(x_0) \, \psi(x - k\Delta) , \qquad (3.2)$$

where $\Delta = X/K$ is the basic shift amount. The simplest shiftable function in one dimension is a pure harmonic signal, $e^{i\omega x}$, in which case $K = 1$. More generally, Simoncelli *et al.* [18] proved that any band-limited function is shiftable. In fact, if the set of non-zero Fourier series frequencies of ψ is (a subset of) $B = \{\omega_0, \omega_0 + 1, \ldots, \omega_0 + K - 1\}$, then ψ can be shifted using the K interpolation functions, $b_k(x_0) = b(x_0 - k\Delta)$, where $b(x)$ is the complex conjugate of the perfect bandpass filter constructed from the set of K frequencies, B. In particular, note that the interpolation functions only depend on the set of non-zero frequencies of ψ, and not on ψ itself.

Strictly speaking, since they are not band-limited, functions such as Gabors are not shiftable. Nevertheless, for all intents and purposes, they can be shifted by choosing the set, B, to consist of all Fourier series frequencies, ω, of ψ, such that the Fourier amplitude, $|\hat{\psi}(\omega)|$, is *essentially non-zero* (i.e., it exceeds some small threshold value). Such functions will be called *effectively shiftable*.

Let $\Psi(\boldsymbol{x}, \theta)$ be a function on $\mathbf{R}^2 \times S^1$ which is periodic (with period X) in both spatial variables, $\boldsymbol{x}$. In analogy with the definition of a shiftable-steerable function on $\mathbf{R}^?$, we say that Ψ is *shiftable-twistable* on $\mathbf{R}^2 \times S^1$ if there are integers, K and M, and interpolation functions, $b_{\boldsymbol{k}, m}(\boldsymbol{x}_0, \theta_0)$, such that, for each $(\boldsymbol{x}_0, \theta_0) \in \mathbf{R}^2 \times S^1$, the shift-twist of Ψ by $(\boldsymbol{x}_0, \theta_0)$ is a linear combination of a finite number of basic shift-twists of Ψ by amounts $(k\Delta, m\Delta_\theta)$, i.e., if

$$\Psi(T_{\boldsymbol{x}_0, \theta_0}(\boldsymbol{x}, \theta)) = \sum_{\boldsymbol{k}, m} b_{\boldsymbol{k}, m}(\boldsymbol{x}_0, \theta_0) \, \Psi(T_{k\Delta, m\Delta_\theta}(\boldsymbol{x}, \theta)) . \qquad (3.3)$$

Here $\Delta = X/K$ is the *basic shift amount* and $\Delta_\theta = 2\pi/M$ is the *basic twist amount*. The sum in equation (3.3) is taken over all pairs of integers, $\boldsymbol{k} = (k_x, k_y)$, in the range, $0 \leq k_x, k_y < K$, and all integers, m, in the range, $0 \leq m < M$. For many shiftable-twistable bases, the interpolation functions, $b_{\boldsymbol{k}, m}(\boldsymbol{x}_0, \theta_0)$, are defined in terms of Simoncelli's one-dimensional interpolation functions, $b_k(x_0)$.

---

[4] We use this terminology even though the basis functions need not be linearly independent.

The simplest example of a shiftable-steerable basis is the Gaussian-Fourier basis, $G_{k,\omega}$, which is the product of a shiftable-steerable basis of Gaussians in x and a Fourier series basis in θ. Let $g(x) = \frac{1}{\nu}e^{-\|x\|^2/2\nu^2}$ be a radial Gaussian of standard deviation, ν. We regard g as a periodic function of period, X, which is chosen to be much larger than ν, so that g defines a smooth periodic function. For each frequency, ω, we define $G_\omega(x,\theta) = g(x)e^{i\omega\theta}$. Also, given a choice of a shift amount, Δ, so that $K = X/\Delta$ is an integer, we define the *Gaussian-Fourier basis functions*, $G_{k,\omega}$, by

$$G_{k,\omega}(x,\theta) = g(x - k\Delta)\, e^{i\omega\theta} \ . \tag{3.4}$$

The following proposition implies that the Gaussian-Fourier basis is shiftable-twistable.

Proposition 1. *The periodic function, G_ω, (of period X) is effectively shiftable-twistable. More precisely, let $M = 1$ and let K be the number of essentially non-zero Fourier series coefficients of the factor, $g_X(x) = e^{-x^2/2\nu^2}$, of $g(x)$. Then,*

$$G_\omega(T_{x_0,\theta_0}(x,\theta)) = \sum_k b_{k,\omega}(x_0,\theta_0)\, G_{k,\omega}(x,\theta) \ , \tag{3.5}$$

where the interpolation functions are given by

$$b_{k,\omega}(x_0,\theta_0) = e^{-i\omega\theta_0}\, b_k(x_0) \ . \tag{3.6}$$

Here $b_k(x_0) = b(x_0 - k\Delta)$, where $b(x_0)$ is the complex conjugate of the perfect bandpass filter constructed from the set of K^2 essentially non-zero Fourier series coefficients, η, of $g(x)$.

For certain computations, the input can be easily represented in a Gaussian-Fourier basis. For example, suppose that the input is modeled as a linear combination of fine scale three-dimensional Gaussians, centered at arbitrary points, (x_0,θ_0), in $\mathbf{R}^2 \times S^1$. Since the input is the product of a Gaussian in x and a Gaussian in θ it can be represented in a *single scale* Gaussian-Fourier basis as follows. First, the Gaussian in θ is represented in the Fourier basis using the standard analysis and synthesis formulae for Fourier series. Second, if the two-dimensional input Gaussians in x are chosen to be shifts of the basis function, $g(x)$, then we can use Proposition 1 to represent the input Gaussians in x in the Gaussian basis.

A somewhat more biologically plausible basis is the *complex directional derivative of Gaussian (CDDG)-Fourier basis*, which is very similar to the previous example, except that the Gaussian, $g(x)$, is replaced by its complex directional derivative in the direction of the complex valued vector, $[1,i]^{\mathrm{T}}$. The CDDG looks more like the receptive field of a simple cell in V1 than a Gaussian does. Also the CDDG is a wavelet, whereas the Gaussian is not.

4 Stochastic Completion Fields

In their computational theory of illusory contour formation, Williams and Jacobs [21] argued that, given a prior probability distribution of possible completion shapes, the visual system computes the local image plane statistics of the distribution of all possible completions, rather than simply the most probable completion. This view is in accord with human experience—some illusory contours are more salient than others, and some appear sharper than others. They defined the notion of a stochastic completion field to model illusory contours in a probabilistic manner. The stochastic completion field is a probability density function (p.d.f.) on the space, $\mathbf{R}^2 \times S^1$, of positions, $\boldsymbol{x} = (x, y)$, in the plane, $\mathbf{R}^2$, and directions, θ, in the circle, S^1. It is defined in terms of a set of position and direction constraints representing the beginning and ending points of a set of contour fragments (called *sources* and *sinks*), and a prior probability distribution of completion shapes, which is modeled as the set of paths followed by particles traveling with constant speed in directions described by Brownian motions [15]. The magnitude of the *stochastic completion field*, $C(\boldsymbol{x}, \theta)$, is the probability that a completion from the prior probability distribution will pass through $(\boldsymbol{x}, \theta)$ on a path joining two of the contour fragments. Williams and Jacobs [21] showed that the stochastic completion field could be factored into a *source field* and a *sink field*. The source field, $P'(\boldsymbol{x}, \theta)$, represents the probability that a contour beginning at a source will pass through $(\boldsymbol{x}, \theta)$ and the sink field, $Q'(\boldsymbol{x}, \theta)$, represents the probability that a contour beginning at $(\boldsymbol{x}, \theta)$ will reach a sink. The completion field is

$$C(\boldsymbol{x}, \theta) = P'(\boldsymbol{x}, \theta) \cdot Q'(\boldsymbol{x}, \theta) . \tag{4.1}$$

The source (or sink) field itself is obtained by integrating a probability density function, $P(\boldsymbol{x}, \theta; t)$, over all positive times, t, where $P(\boldsymbol{x}, \theta; t)$ represents the probability that a particle beginning at a source reaches $(\boldsymbol{x}, \theta)$ at time t,

$$P'(\boldsymbol{x}, \theta) = \int_0^\infty P(\boldsymbol{x}, \theta; t) dt . \tag{4.2}$$

Mumford [15] observed that P evolves according to a Fokker-Planck equation of the form,

$$\frac{\partial P}{\partial t} = -\cos\theta \frac{\partial P}{\partial x} - \sin\theta \frac{\partial P}{\partial y} + \frac{\sigma^2}{2} \frac{\partial^2 P}{\partial \theta^2} - \frac{1}{\tau} P , \tag{4.3}$$

where the initial probability distribution of sources (or sinks) is described by $P(\boldsymbol{x}, \theta; 0)$. This partial differential equation can be viewed as a set of independent *advection* equations in $\boldsymbol{x} = (x, y)$ (the first and second terms) coupled in the θ dimension by the *diffusion* equation (the third term). The advection equations translate probability mass in direction θ with unit speed, while the diffusion term models the Brownian motion in direction, with *diffusion parameter*, σ. The combined effect of these three terms is that particles tend to travel in straight lines, but over time they drift to the left or right by an amount proportional to

σ^2. Finally, the effect of the fourth term is that particles decay over time, with a half life given by the *decay constant*, τ. This represents our prior expectation on the length of gaps—most are quite short. In [22] stochastic completion fields were computed by solving the Fokker-Planck equation using a standard finite differencing scheme on a regular grid.

5   Description of Algorithm

One of the main goals of this paper is to derive a discrete numerical algorithm to compute stochastic completion fields in a shift-twist invariant manner. This invariance is achieved by first evolving the Fokker-Planck equation in a shiftable-twistable basis of $\mathbf{R}^2 \times S^1$ to obtain representations of the source and sink fields in the basis, and then multiplying these representations in a shift-twist invariant manner to obtain a representation of the completion field in a shiftable-twistable basis.

We observe that a discrete Dirac basis, consisting of functions, $\Psi_{k,m}(x,\theta) = \delta(x - k\Delta)\,\delta(\theta - m\Delta_\theta)$, where (k,m) is a triple of integers, is not shiftable-twistable. This is because a Dirac function located off the grid of Dirac basis functions is not in their span.

A major shortcoming of previous contour completion algorithms [8, 9, 13, 16, 17, 21, 22, 25] is that they perform computations in this basis. As a consequence, initial conditions which do not lie directly on the grid cannot be accurately represented. This problem is often skirted by researchers in this area by choosing input patterns which match their choice of sampling rate and phase. For example, Li [13] used only six orientations (including $0°$) and Heitger and von der Heydt [9], only twelve (including $0°$, $60°$ and $120°$). Li's first test pattern was a line of orientation, $0°$, while Heitger and von der Heydt used a Kanizsa Triangle with sides of $0°$, $60°$, and $120°$ orientation. There is no reason to believe that the experimental results they show would be the same if their input patterns were rotated by as little as $5°$.[5]

In addition to the problem of representing the input, the computation itself must be Euclidean invariant. Stochastic completion fields computed using the finite differencing scheme of [22] exhibit marked anisotropic spatial smoothing due to the manner in which 2D advection is performed on a grid (see Figures 4,5 and 6). Although probability mass advects perfectly in either of the two principal coordinate directions, mass which is moving at an angle to the grid gradually disperses, since, at each time step, bilinear interpolation is used to place the mass on the grid.

For reasons of simplicity, in this paper, we chose to compute stochastic completion fields in a Gaussian-Fourier basis.[6] The initial conditions for the Fokker-

---

[5] Nor are we blameless in this respect. Williams and Jacobs [21, 22] used 36 directions (including $0°$, $60°$ and $120°$) and demonstrated their computation with a Kanizsa Triangle with sides of $0°$, $60°$ and $120°$ orientation.

[6] The computation can also be performed in more biologically plausible shiftable-twistable bases, the simplest of which is the CDDG-Fourier basis.

Planck initial value problem are modeled by fine scale, three-dimensional Gaussians, whose centers are determined by the locations and directions of the edge fragments to be completed. We use the single scale method discussed in Section 3 to represent the initial conditions in the basis.

To solve the Fokker-Planck equation, we express its solution in terms of the basis functions, $G_{k,\omega}(x,\theta)$, as

$$P(x,\theta\,;t) \;=\; \sum_{k,\omega} \; c_{k,\omega}(t)\, G_{k,\omega}(x,\theta) \;, \qquad\qquad (5.1)$$

where the coefficients, $c_{k,\omega}(t)$, depend on time. Then, we derive a linear transformation, $c(t+\Delta t) = (\mathbf{A}\circ\mathbf{D})c(t)$, to evolve the coefficient vector in time. This transformation is the composition of an advection transformation, $\mathbf{A}$, which has the effect of transporting probability mass in directions θ, and a diffusion-decay transformation, $\mathbf{D}$, which implements both the diffusion of mass in θ, and the decay of mass over time. Representations of source or sink fields in the basis are obtained by integrating the coefficient vector, $c(t)$, over time, where the initial coefficient vector represents the initial sources or sinks.

The shiftability-twistability of the basis functions is used in two distinct ways to obtain shift-twist invariant source and sink fields. First, it enables any two initial conditions, which are related by an arbitrary transformation, T_{x_0,θ_0}, to be represented equally well in the basis. Second, it is used to derive a shift-twist invariant advection transformation, $\mathbf{A}$, thereby eliminating the grid orientation artifacts described above. In summary, given a desired resolution at which to represent the initial conditions, our new algorithm produces source and sink fields, at the given resolution, which transform appropriately under arbitrary Euclidean transformations of the input image. In contrast, in all previous contour completion algorithms, the degree of failure of Euclidean invariance is highly dependent on the resolution of the grid, and can be quite large relative to the grid resolution.

The final step in our shift-twist invariant algorithm is to compute the completion field (the product of the source and sink fields) in a shiftable-twistable basis. The particular basis used to represent completion fields is the same as the one used to represent the source and sink fields, except that the variance of the Gaussian basis functions in $\mathbf{R}^2$ needs to be halved. The need to use a slightly different basis to represent completion fields is not biologically implausible, since the experimental evidence described in Section 2 suggests that the neural locus of the source and sink fields could be V1, while completion fields are more likely located in V2.

6 The Solution of the Fokker-Planck Equation

In this section we derive a shift-twist invariant linear transformation, $c(t+\Delta t) = (\mathbf{A}\circ\mathbf{D})c(t)$, of the coefficient vector which evolves the Fokker-Planck equation in a shiftable-twistable basis. The derivation holds for any shiftable-twistable basis constructed from shiftable-twistable functions of the form, $\Psi_\omega(x,\theta) = \psi(x)e^{i\omega\theta}$, for some function, $\psi(\boldsymbol{x})$. Since the transformation, $\mathbf{A} \circ \mathbf{D}$, will only involve interactions between functions, $\psi(\boldsymbol{x})$, at different positions $k\Delta$, and not at different scales or orientations, the basis functions and coefficients will be denoted by $\Psi_{\boldsymbol{k},\omega}$ and $c_{\boldsymbol{k},\omega}(t)$ respectively.[7]

To derive an expression,

$$c_{\boldsymbol{\ell},\eta}(t + \Delta t) = \textstyle\sum_{\boldsymbol{k},\omega} \mathbf{A}_{\boldsymbol{\ell},\eta\,;\,\boldsymbol{k},\omega}(\Delta t)\, c_{\boldsymbol{k},\omega}(t)\,, \tag{6.1}$$

for the advection transformation, $\mathbf{A}$, in the basis, $\Psi_{\boldsymbol{k},\omega}$, we exploit the fact that spatial advection can be done perfectly using shiftable basis functions, $\psi_{\boldsymbol{k}}(\boldsymbol{x})$, in $\mathbf{R}^2$, and the continuous variable, $\theta \in S^1$. Suppose that P is given in the form,

$$P(\boldsymbol{x}, \theta;\, t) = \textstyle\sum_{\boldsymbol{k},\omega} c_{\boldsymbol{k},\omega}(t)\, \psi_{\boldsymbol{k}}(\boldsymbol{x})\, e^{i\omega\theta} = \textstyle\sum_{\boldsymbol{k}} \check{c}_{\boldsymbol{k},\theta}(t)\, \psi_{\boldsymbol{k}}(\boldsymbol{x})\,, \tag{6.2}$$

where $\check{c}(t)$ is related to $c(t)$ by the standard synthesis formula for Fourier series, $\check{c}_{\boldsymbol{k},\theta} = \sum_\omega c_{\boldsymbol{k},\omega} e^{i\omega\theta}$, which we denote by $\check{c} = \mathbf{F}^{-1} c$. Then the translation of P in direction, θ, at unit speed, for time, Δt, is given by

$$P(\boldsymbol{x}, \theta;\, t + \Delta t) = P(\boldsymbol{x} - \Delta t[\cos\theta, \sin\theta]^{\mathrm{T}}, \theta;\, t) \tag{6.3}$$

$$= \sum_{\boldsymbol{k}} \check{c}_{\boldsymbol{k},\theta}(t)\, \psi_{\boldsymbol{k}}(\boldsymbol{x} - \Delta t[\cos\theta, \sin\theta]^{\mathrm{T}})\,, \tag{6.4}$$

where the second equation follows from equation (6.2). The shiftability of ψ then implies that

$$\check{c}_{\boldsymbol{\ell},\theta}(t + \Delta t) = \textstyle\sum_{\boldsymbol{k}} \check{\mathbf{A}}_{\boldsymbol{\ell},\theta;\boldsymbol{k},\theta}(\Delta t)\, \check{c}_{\boldsymbol{k},\theta}(t)\,, \tag{6.5}$$

where

$$\check{\mathbf{A}}_{\boldsymbol{\ell},\theta;\boldsymbol{k},\theta}(\Delta t) = b_{\boldsymbol{\ell}-\boldsymbol{k}}(\Delta t[\cos\theta, \sin\theta]^{\mathrm{T}})\,. \tag{6.6}$$

Finally, the advection transformation, $\mathbf{A}$, in the basis, $\Psi_{\boldsymbol{k},\omega}$, is given by the similarity transformation, $\mathbf{A} = \mathbf{F}\check{\mathbf{A}}\mathbf{F}^{-1}$, where $\mathbf{F}$ denotes the standard analysis formula for Fourier series, $(\mathbf{F}f)(\omega) = \frac{1}{2\pi}\int_0^{2\pi} f(\theta) e^{-i\omega\theta}\, d\theta$. Since $c = \mathbf{F}\check{c}$ we have the following result.

Theorem 1. *In the basis, $\Psi_{\boldsymbol{k},\omega}$, the advection transformation, $\mathbf{A}$, is given by*

$$c_{\boldsymbol{\ell},\eta}(t + \Delta t) = \textstyle\sum_{\boldsymbol{k},\omega} \hat{b}_{\boldsymbol{\ell}-\boldsymbol{k},\eta-\omega}(\Delta t)\, c_{\boldsymbol{k},\omega}(t)\,, \tag{6.7}$$

where

$$\hat{b}_{\boldsymbol{k},\eta}(\Delta t) = \tfrac{1}{2\pi}\int_0^{2\pi} b_{\boldsymbol{k}}(\Delta t[\cos\theta, \sin\theta]^{\mathrm{T}})\, e^{-i\eta\theta}\, d\theta\,. \tag{6.8}$$

In particular, the transformation, $\mathbf{A}$, is shift-twist invariant and is a convolution operator on the vector space of coefficients, $c_{\boldsymbol{k},\omega}$.

---

[7] Since we are using Fourier series in θ the transformation, $\mathbf{D}$, can be implemented in a shift-twist invariant manner by applying a standard finite differencing scheme to the coefficients.

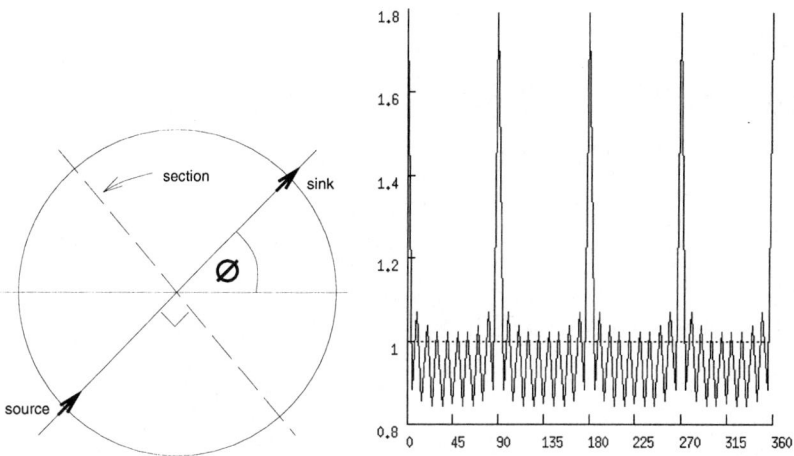

Fig. 3. The geometry of the straight line completion field experiment (*left*). Graph (*right*) of the mean along a section normal to the straight line completion field as a function of the direction, ϕ, for our new algorithm (*dashed line*) and for the algorithm of [22] (*solid line*)

Theorem 1 implies that the computation of source and sink fields can be performed in a recurrent neural network using a fixed set of units as described in [22]. Since the advection transformation, **A**, is a convolution operator on the space of coefficients, for efficiency's sake we implemented both **A** and **D** in the 3D Fourier domain of the coefficient vector. In this domain, **A** is given by a diagonal matrix and **D** by a circulant tridiagonal matrix.

7 Experimental Results

We present three experiments demonstrating the Euclidean invariance of our algorithm. In each experiment, the Gaussian-Fourier basis consisted of $K = 160$ translates in each spatial variable of a Gaussian (of period $X = 40.0$ units), and harmonic signals of $N = 92$ frequencies in the angular variable, for a total of 2.355×10^6 basis functions. Pictures of completion fields were obtained by analytically integrating over θ and rendering the completion field on a 256×256 grid.

We compare the new algorithm with the finite differencing scheme of [22]. For the method of [22], the $40.0 \times 40.0 \times 2\pi$ space was discretized using a 256×256 spatial grid with 36 discrete orientations, for a total of 2.359×10^6 Dirac basis functions. The intent was to use approximately the same number of basis functions for both algorithms. The initial conditions were represented on the grid using tri-linear interpolation and pictures of the completion fields were obtained by summing over the discrete angles. The same parameters were used for both algorithms. The decay constant was $\tau = 4.5$ and the time increment, $\Delta t = 0.1$.

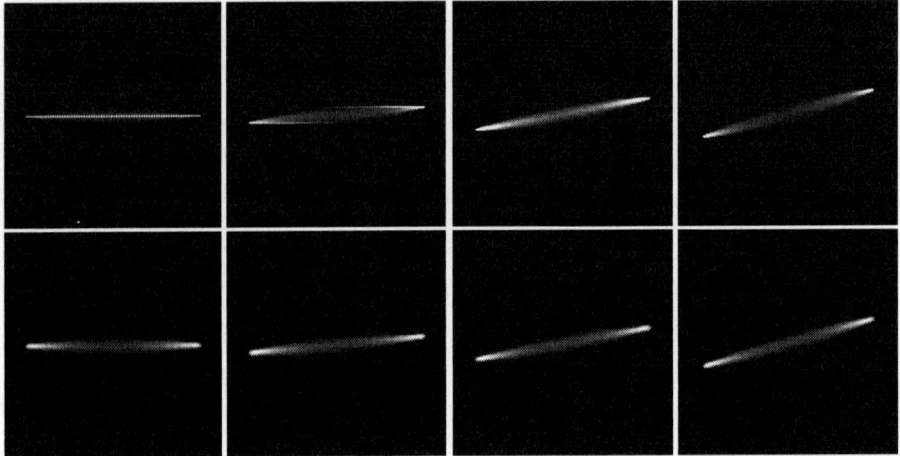

Fig. 4. Straight line completion fields due to an initial stimulus consisting of two points on a circle with direction, ϕ, normal to the circle, for $\phi = 0°, 5°, 10°, 15°$ (*left to right*). The completion fields were computed using the algorithm of [22] (*top row*) and using the new algorithm (*bottom row*)

The diffusion parameter was $\sigma = 0.08$ for the first and second experiments and $\sigma = 0.14$ for the third.[8] In Figures 4, 5 and 6 the completion fields constructed using the algorithm of [22] are in the top row, while those constructed using the new algorithm are in the bottom row.

In the first experiment, we computed straight line completion fields joining two diametrically opposed points on a circle of radius, 16.0, with initial directions normal to the circle. That is, given an angle, ϕ, the initial stimulus consisted of the two points, $(\pm 16.0 \cos \phi, \pm 16.0 \sin \phi, \phi)$, see Figure 3 (left). The completion fields are shown in Figure 4, with those in the top row, computed using the method of [22], clipped above at 2×10^{-6}.

To compare the degree of Euclidean invariance of the two algorithms, we extracted a section of each completion field along the diameter of the circle normal to the direction of the completion field. In Figure 3 (right), we plot the mean of each section as a function of the angle ϕ. The dashed line indicates the means computed using the new algorithm, and the solid line shows the means computed using the algorithm of [22].[9] The fact that the dashed line graph is constant provides solid evidence for the Euclidean invariance of the new algorithm. The solid line graph demonstrates the two major sources of the lack of Euclidean invariance in the method of [22]. First, the rapid oscillation of

---

[8] The diffusion parameter, σ, was required to be larger in the third experiment because of the high curvature circles in the Kanizsa triangle figure.

[9] The angles, ϕ, were taken in 5° increments from 0° to 45°. For illustration purposes the ϕ-axis was extended to 360° so as to reflect the symmetry of the grid. Both graphs were normalized to have average value one.

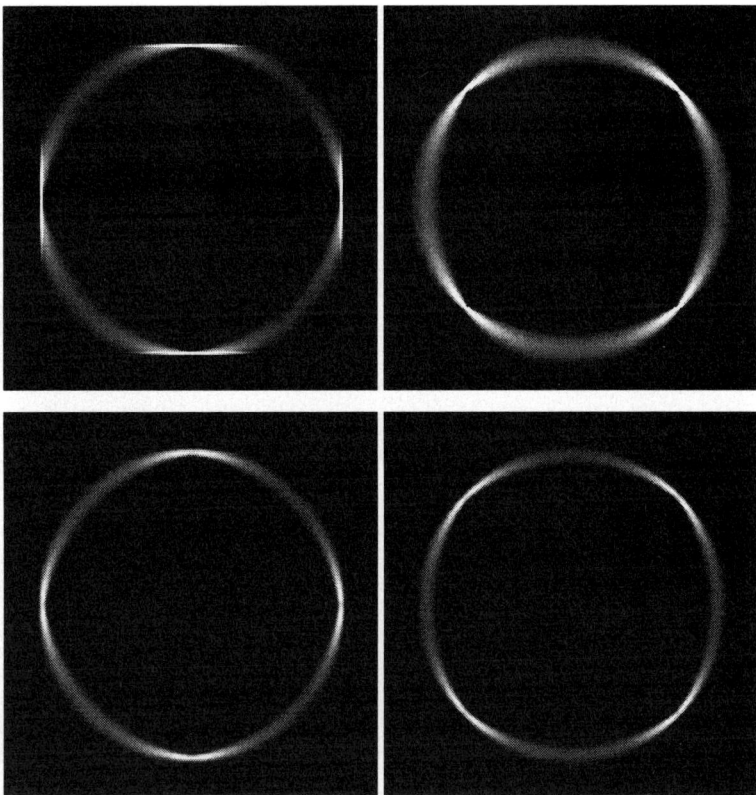

Fig. 5. Completion fields due to the Ehrenstein initial stimulus in Figure 1(a) (*left column*) and with the initial conditions rotated clockwise by 45° (*right column*). The completion fields were computed using the algorithm of [22] (*top*) and using the new algorithm (*bottom*)

period 10° is due to the initial conditions coming in and out of phase with the angular grid. This 10° periodicity can be seen in the periodicity of the general shape of the completion fields in the top row of Figure 4. Second, the large spikes at 90° intervals are due to the anisotropic manner in which the advection transformation was solved on the spatial grid. These large spikes correspond to the very bright horizontal line artifacts in the first two completion fields in the top row of Figure 4.

In the second experiment, we computed completion fields due to rotations of the Ehrenstein initial stimulus in Figure 1(a). Pictures of the completion fields are shown in Figure 5.[10] The left column shows the completion fields due to the Ehrenstein stimulus in Figure 1(a), while in the right column the

---

[10] Because of the periodicity in the spatial variables, x, to avoid wrap around in this experiment, for the new algorithm the computation was performed on a $80.0 \times 80.0 \times 2\pi$ space with $K = 320$.

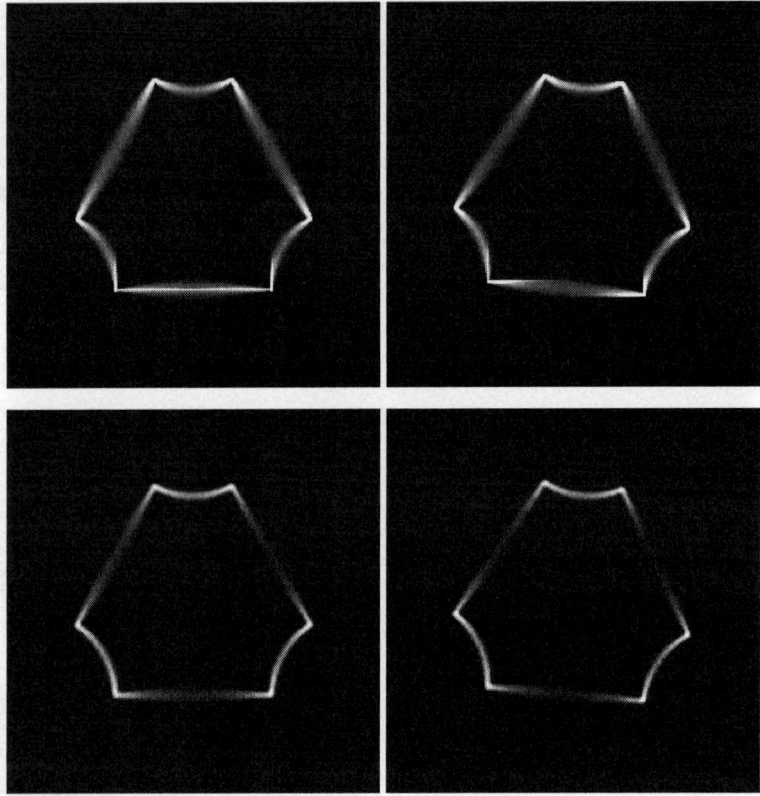

Fig. 6. Completion fields due to the Kanizsa triangle initial stimulus in Figure 1(b) (*left column*) and with the initial conditions rotated clockwise by 5° (*right column*). The completion fields were computed using the algorithm of [22] (*top*) and using the new algorithm (*bottom*)

initial conditions have been rotated clockwise by 45°. The completion fields computed using the method of [22] were clipped above at 1.25×10^{-8}. For our final experiment, we compute completion fields due to rotations and translations of the Kanizsa Triangle stimulus in Figure 1(b). Completion fields are shown in Figure 2, which was discussed in the Introduction, and in Figure 6. The left column of Figure 6 shows completion fields due to the Kanizsa Triangle in Figure 1(b). In the right column the initial conditions have been rotated clockwise by 5°. The completion fields computed using the method of [22] were clipped above at 9×10^{-5}.

The completion fields in the bottom rows of Figures 5 and 6, and in Figure 2, demonstrate the Euclidean invariance of our new algorithm. This is in marked contrast with the obvious lack of Euclidean invariance in the completion fields in the top rows of Figures 5 and 6. The visible straight line artifacts in these completion fields, which are oriented along the coordinate axes, are due to the anisotropic nature of the advection process in the algorithm of [22], and (to a lesser extent), to the way in which the initial conditions were represented on the grid.

8 Conclusion

An important initial stage in the analysis of a scene requires completion of the boundaries of partially occluded objects. Williams and Jacobs introduced the notion of the stochastic completion field which measures the probability distribution of completed boundary shapes in a given scene. In this article we have described a new, parallel, algorithm for computing stochastic completion fields. As is required of any computational model of human visual information processing, our algorithm attempts to reconcile the apparent contradiction between the Euclidean invariance of human early visual computations on the one hand, and the observed sparseness of the discrete spatial sampling of the visual field by primary and secondary visual cortex on the other hand. The new algorithm reconciles these two contradictions by performing the computation in a basis of separable functions with spatial components similar to the receptive fields of simple cells in primary visual cortex. In particular, the Euclidean invariance of the computation is achieved by exploiting the shiftability and twistability of the basis functions.

In this paper, we have described three basic results. First, we have generalized Simoncelli *et al.'s* notion of shiftability and steerability in $\mathbf{R}^2$ to a more general notion of shiftability and twistability in $\mathbf{R}^2 \times S^1$. The notion of shiftability and twistability mirrors the coupling between the advection and diffusion terms in the Fokker-Planck equation, and at a deeper level, basic symmetries in the underlying random process characterizing the distribution of completion shapes. Second, we described a new method for numerical solution of the Fokker-Planck equation in a shiftable-twistable basis. Finally, we used this solution to compute stochastic completion fields, and demonstrated, both theoretically and experimentally, the invariance of our computation under translations and rotations of the input pattern.

References

1. Blasdel, G., and Obermeyer, K., Putative Strategies of Scene Segmentation in Monkey Visual Cortex, *Neural Networks*, **7**, pp. 865-881, 1994.
2. Cowan, J.D., Neurodynamics and Brain Mechanisms, *Cognition, Computation and Consciousness*, Ito, M., Miyashita, Y. and Rolls, E., (Eds.), Oxford UP, 1997.
3. Daugman, J., Uncertainty Relation for Resolution in Space, Spatial Frequency, and Orientation Optimized by Two-dimensional Visual Cortical Filter, *J. Opt. Soc. Am. A*, **2**, pp.1160-1169, 1985.
4. Daugman, J., Complete Discrete 2-D Gabor Transforms by Neural Networks for Image Analysis and Compression, *IEEE Trans. Acoustics, Speech, and Signal Processing* **36**(7), pp. 1,169-1,179, 1988.

5. Eyesel, U. Turning a Corner in Vision Research, *Nature*, **399**, pp. 641-644, 1999.
6. Freeman, W., and Adelson, E., The Design and Use of Steerable Filters, IEEE Trans. PAMI, **13** (9), pp.891-906, 1991.
7. Gilbert, C.D., Adult Cortical Dynamics, *Physiological Review*, **78**, pp. 467-485, 1998.
8. Grossberg, S., and Mingolla, E., Neural Dynamics of Form Perception: Boundary Completion, Illusory Figures, and Neon Color Spreading, *Psychological Review*, **92**, pp. 173-211, 1985.
9. Heitger, R. and von der Heydt, R., A Computational Model of Neural Contour Processing, Figure-ground and Illusory Contours, *Proc. of 4th Intl. Conf. on Computer Vision*, Berlin, Germany, 1993.
10. von der Heydt, R., Peterhans, E. and Baumgartner, G., Illusory Contours and Cortical Neuron Responses, *Science*, **224**, pp. 1260-1262, 1984.
11. Iverson, L., Toward Discrete Geometric Models for Early Vision, Ph.D. dissertation, McGill University, 1993.
12. Kalitzin, S., ter Haar Romeny, B., and Viergever, M., Invertible Orientation Bundles on 2D Scalar Images, in *Scale-Space Theory in Computer Vision*, ter Haar Romeny, B., Florack, L., Koenderink, J. and Viergever, M., (Eds.), Lecture Notes in Computer Science, **1252**, 1997, pp. 77-88.
13. Li, Z., A Neural Model of Contour Integration in Primary Visual Cortex, *Neural Computation*, **10**(4), pp. 903-940, 1998.
14. Marčelja, S. Mathematical Description of the Responses of Simple Cortical Cells, *J. Opt. Soc. Am.*, **70**, pp. 1297-1300, 1980.
15. Mumford, D., Elastica and Computer Vision, *Algebraic Geometry and Its Applications*, Chandrajit Bajaj (ed.), Springer-Verlag, New York, 1994.
16. Parent, P., and Zucker, S.W., Trace Inference, Curvature Consistency and Curve Detection, *IEEE Transactions on Pattern Analysis and Machine Intelligence*, **11**, pp. 823-889, 1989.
17. Shashua, A. and Ullman, S., Structural Saliency: The Detection of Globally Salient Structures Using a Locally Connected Network, *2nd Intl. Conf. on Computer Vision*, Clearwater, FL, pp. 321-327, 1988.
18. Simoncelli, E., Freeman, W., Adelson E. and Heeger, D., Shiftable Multiscale Transforms, *IEEE Trans. Information Theory*, **38**(2), pp. 587-607, 1992.
19. Thornber, K.K. and Williams, L.R., Analytic Solution of Stochastic Completion Fields, *Biological Cybernetics* **75**, pp. 141-151, 1996.
20. Thornber, K.K. and Williams, L.R., Orientation, Scale and Discontinuity as Emergent Properties of Illusory Contour Shape, *Neural Information Processing Systems* **11**, Denver, CO, 1998.
21. Williams, L.R., and Jacobs, D.W., Stochastic Completion Fields: A Neural Model of Illusory Contour Shape and Salience, *Neural Computation*, **9**(4), pp. 837-858, 1997, (also appeared in *Proc. of the 5th Intl. Conference on Computer Vision (ICCV '95)*, Cambridge, MA).
22. Williams, L.R., and Jacobs, D.W., Local Parallel Computation of Stochastic Completion Fields, *Neural Computation*, **9**(4), pp. 859-881, 1997.
23. Williams, L.R. and Thornber, K.K., A Comparison of Measures for Detecting Natural Shapes in Cluttered Backgrounds, *Intl. Journal of Computer Vision*, **34** (2/3), pp. 81-96, 1999.
24. Wandell, B.A., *Foundations of Vision*, Sinauer Press, 1995.
25. Yen, S. and Finkel, L., Salient Contour Extraction by Temporal Binding in a Cortically-Based Network, *Neural Information Processing Systems* **9**, Denver, CO, 1996.

Active, Real-Time, & Robot Vision

Segmentation & Grouping

Vision Systems Engineering & Evaluation

Bootstrap Initialization of Nonparametric Texture Models for Tracking

Kentaro Toyama[1] and Ying Wu[2]

[1] Microsoft Research, Redmond, WA 98052, USA
kentoy@microsoft.com
[2] University of Illinois (UIUC), Urbana, IL 61801, USA
yingwu@ifp.uiuc.edu

Abstract. In *bootstrap initialization* for tracking, we exploit a weak prior model used to track a target to learn a stronger model, without manual intervention. We define a general formulation of this problem and present a simple taxonomy of such tasks.

The formulation is instantiated with algorithms for bootstrap initialization in two domains: In one, the goal is tracking the position of a face at a desktop; we learn color models of faces, using weak knowledge about the shape and movement of faces in video. In the other task, we seek coarse estimates of head orientation; we learn a person-specific ellipsoidal texture model for heads, given a generic model. For both tasks, we use nonparametric models of surface texture.

Experimental results verify that bootstrap initialization is feasible in both domains. We find that (1) independence assumptions in the learning process can be violated to a significant degree, if enough data is taken; (2) there are both domain-independent and domain-specific means to mitigate learning bias; and (3) repeated bootstrapping does not necessarily result in increasingly better models.

1 Introduction

Often, we know something about the target of a tracking task in advance, but specific details about the target will be unknown. For example, in desktop interfaces, we are likely to be interested in the moving ellipsoid that appears in the image, but we may not know the user's skin color, 3D shape, or the particular geometry of the facial features. If we could learn this additional information during tracking, we could use it to track the same objects more accurately, more efficiently, or more robustly.

This problem, which we call *bootstrap initialization for tracking* arises whenever the target object is not completely known *a priori*. In Section 2, we propose an abstract formulation of bootstrap initialization. Section 3 offers a taxonomy of bootstrap initialization problems and reviews previous work. Sections 4 and 5 discuss experiences with two domains in which the learned models are nonparametric models of target texture. We take the Bayesian perspective that models represent a tracking system's "belief" about the target. Experiments show how different data sampling techniques affect learning rate and quality (Section 5).

2   Bootstrap Initialization Formulation

Given a prior belief about the target (inherited from the system designer), the goal of bootstrap initialization is to learn a more useful model of the target, using only information gained during actual tracking. We now introduce an abstract framework for this concept. Reference to Figure 1 will clarify the notation.

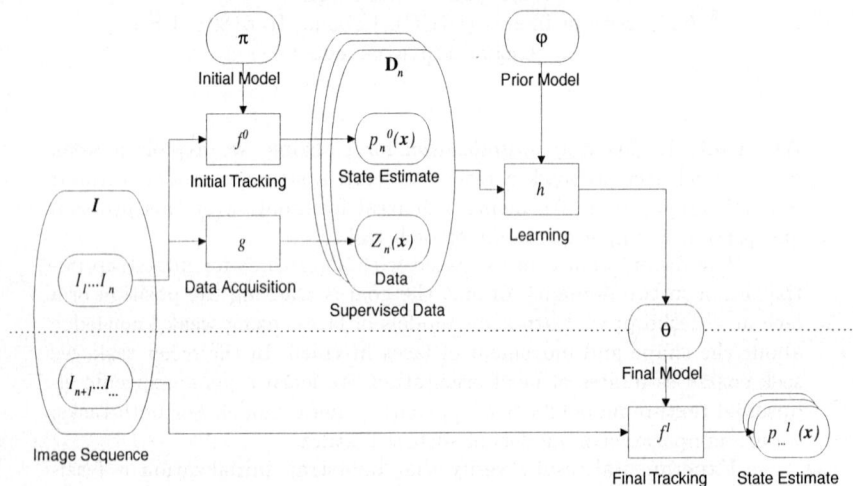

Fig. 1. Abstract formulation of bootstrap initialization.

The goal of tracking is the recovery of the configuration of the target, $\mathbf{x}_m \in \mathcal{X}$, at time t_m, given a model of the target, a sequence of images, $\mathcal{I}_m = \{I_1 \ldots I_m\}$ (where I_i is the image taken at time t_i).

Automatic initialization is impossible without some starting belief about the target. So, we assume that there is an *initial model*, π, that can be used to track targets with some reliability. This means that there is some prespecified, *initial tracking function*, $f_\pi^0(\mathcal{I}_m)$, which, given a sequence of images and an initial model, returns a distribution, $p_m^0(\mathbf{x})$, for the probable configurations that the target assumes at time t_m. (We will assume that tracking functions return distribution functions and that should it be necessary, some way to choose a single estimate $\tilde{\mathbf{x}}$, given $p_m^0(\mathbf{x})$, is also specified.) The initial model represents a belief about the target that the system designer passes on to the algorithm, *e.g.*, the target is blue, it is round, it matches template A, etc. We leave the form of the initial model intentionally vague; what matters is the existence of an f_π^0 that incorporates the information contained in π. The initial model need not be particularly reliable, as long as it correlates to some degree with characteristics of the target that distinguish it from non-target objects.

For bootstrap initialization, we also posit a data *acquisition function*, $g(\mathcal{I}_m)$, which takes an image sequence and returns observations, $\mathbf{Z}_m(\mathbf{x})$, defined over the state space. Note that $\mathbf{Z}$ maps target states to observations. The observations are of the type that will be relevant to the *final model*, the model to be acquired.

The final model is represented by $\boldsymbol{\theta}$. $\boldsymbol{\theta}$ will contain all of the information relevant to the *final tracking function*. Knowing $\boldsymbol{\theta}$ allows the final tracking function, $f_{\boldsymbol{\theta}}^1(\mathcal{I}_m)$, to output $p_m^1(\mathbf{x})$. We assume that the final model itself has some prior, denoted ϕ, which contains the same *type* of information contained in $\boldsymbol{\theta}$. That is, $f_{\phi}^1(\mathcal{I}_m)$ – ϕ not $\boldsymbol{\theta}$ – makes sense, although it may not provide good tracking output. In general, we will be concerned with determining a final model for time $t > t_n$, for $n \geq 1$.

Next, let a pair of corresponding observations and tracking output be denoted $\mathbf{D}_i = (p_i^0(\mathbf{x}), \mathbf{Z}_i(\mathbf{x}))$. By expressing its degree of belief in intervals of $\mathcal{X}$, $p_i^0(\mathbf{x})$ effectively provides supervision that points out which values in the range of $\mathbf{Z}_i(\mathbf{x})$ are more or less reliable as training data. Thus, $\mathbf{D}_i$ represents a single instance of supervised data annotated by the initial tracking function.

Let $\mathcal{D}_n = (\mathbf{D}_1, \ldots, \mathbf{D}_n)$. These are fed to a learning function, $h(\mathcal{D}_n, \phi)$, which takes the available data and learns the final model.

This framework has been structured broadly enough to encompass existing forms of bootstrap initialization. As an example, consider a recursive estimation scheme such as the Kalman filter. In our framework, the Kalman filter corresponds to the following: $n = 1$, $f^1 = f^0$, the models π, ϕ, and $\boldsymbol{\theta}$ contain state and covariance parameters, $\phi = \pi$, and h updates ϕ to $\boldsymbol{\theta}$. Because $f^1 = f^0$, and π and $\boldsymbol{\theta}$ share similar structure, the Kalman filter can (and does) iterate bootstrap initialization by setting $\pi_i = \boldsymbol{\theta}_{i-1}$.

The preference for the function $f_{\boldsymbol{\theta}}^1$ over f_{π}^0 supplies the entire *raison d'être* for bootstrap initialization; we expect at least one of the following to be true:

- $f_{\boldsymbol{\theta}}^1$ is more accurate than f_{π}^0, *e.g.*, for ground truth target configuration $\mathbf{x}^*$,

$$\| \arg\max_{\mathbf{x}} p^1(\mathbf{x}) - \mathbf{x}^* \| < \| \arg\max_{\mathbf{x}} p^0(\mathbf{x}) - \mathbf{x}^* \|,$$

- $f_{\boldsymbol{\theta}}^1$ can be computed more efficiently than f_{π}^0,
- $f_{\boldsymbol{\theta}}^1$ is more robust than $f_{\boldsymbol{\theta}}^1$, or
- $f_{\boldsymbol{\theta}}^1$ is otherwise preferable to f_{π}^0.

We anticipate that in most applications, the forms of $\mathbf{x}$, π, ϕ, $\boldsymbol{\theta}$, f^0, and f^1 will be well understood. Thus, the interesting problems in bootstrap initialization are in the design of the acquisition function, g, and the learning function, h.

3 Taxonomy and Related Work

To help restrict our attention to a small subset of bootstrap problems we will consider a taxonomy for the common types of initialization problems in tracking. We propose a classification of initialization problems based on the following axes:

- Does the final model learn information about **the object geometry or the surface texture** of the target?

- Does the final model involve information about **static or dynamic** properties of the target?
- Is the final model **parametric or nonparametric**?
- Does the learning take place **adaptively or in batch mode**?
- Is the information contained in the initial and final **models same or different**?

Very little prior work addresses automatic initialization for the sake of tracking, but there is a body of related work that fits the bootstrap initialization paradigm.

Classic structure from motion algorithms can be thought to learn the static (rigid) geometry of an object, often outside of any explicit parametrization. Most such work is cast as a batch problem, and rarely as an initialization step for tracking, but there are exceptions. In some facial pose tracking work, for example, 3D points on the face are adaptively estimated (learned) using Extended Kalman Filters [1, 9]. Care must be used to structure the EKF correctly [4], but doing so ensures that as the geometry is better learned, tracking improves, as well.

Other research focuses on learning textural qualities. Again, in the domain of facial imagery, there is work in which skin color is modeled as a parametrized mixture of n Gaussians in some color space [11, 12]. Work here has covered both batch [11] and adaptive [12] learning with much success. The preferred learning algorithm for parameter learning in these instances is expectation-maximization.

Although color distributions are a gross quality of object texture, learning of localized texture is also of interest. Work here focuses on intricate facial geometry and texture, using an array of algorithms to recover fine detail [7].

Finally, there is research in learning of dynamic geometry – the changing configuration (pose or articulation) of a target. The most elementary type occurs with the many variations of the Kalman filter, which "learns" a target's geometric state [3]. In these cases, the value of the learned model is fleeting, since few targets ever maintain fixed dynamics. More interesting learning focuses on models of motion. Existing research includes learning of multi-state motion models of targets which exhibit a few discrete patterns of motion [8, 13].

Our work focuses on bootstrap initialization of nonparametric models for the static texture of faces. In contrast with previous work, we explicitly consider issues of automatic learning during tracking without manual intervention.

4 Nonparametric Texture Models

In our first example, we consider learning a skin-color distribution model of a subject's face, using a contour tracking algorithm to offer samples of target skin color. We use this model for color-based tracking of facial position.

In the second, we learn a person-specific 3D texture model of a subject's head, using a generic model to provide supervisory input. The 3D model is used to estimate approximate head orientation, given head location in an image.

The models we use will be nonparametric in the sense adopted by common statistical parlance. For example, the skin-color distributions are modeled by histograms. Strictly speaking, histograms have a finite number of parameters equal to the number of bins, but they can also be considered discrete approximations to elements of a nonparametric function space. Likewise, the 3D texture models we use are discrete approximations to a continuous surface model of texture.

4.1 Color PDF

Tracking of faces using color information is popular both for its speed and simplicity. Previous techniques require manual initialization or parameter tuning in order to achieve optimal performance [11, 17]. At best, a manually initialized model adapts over time [12]. Below, we consider automatic initialization of a color model that bootstraps from prior knowledge about object shape and movement.

Framework Instantiation We will assume that the goal is estimation of $\mathbf{x} = (x, y, s)$, the position and scale of an approximately upright face at a desktop computer.

The initial model, π, encapsulates *a priori* knowledge of user's heads at a PC. In particular, they are likely to project edges shaped like an ellipse at a limited range of scales, and they are likely to exhibit motion from time to time. Given this knowledge and an incoming image sequence, $\mathcal{I}_m$, the initial tracking function, f^0, performs adjacent frame differencing (with decay [5]) on frames I_m and I_{m-1} to detect moving edges and follows this with simple contour tracking [3] to track the most salient ellipse.

The acquisition function, $g(\mathcal{I}_m)$, returns the following observation function: $\mathbf{Z}_m(\mathbf{x}) = I_m(\mathbf{x})$ – the mapping from state to observation simply returns the RGB pixel value of the pixel at the center of the tracked ellipse in the current image (other schemes such as averaging among a set of pixels are also possible and may reduce noise).

Finally, we consider the form of the prior, ϕ, and posterior, θ, of the final model. Both are represented by normalized histograms, which serve as approximations to the pdf of skin-color. The histogram itself will be represented by a Dirichlet distribution. The reasons for this choice will be explained in the next section. Observed pixel values will be represented by the random variable $\mathbf{U} \in \mathcal{U}$.

Given a likelihood function for skin color, it is a simple matter to define a final tracking function that tracks a single face in an image by computing spatial moments [11, 12].

Bootstrap Initialization Algorithm We now describe our bootstrap initialization algorithm for learning color pdfs of skin, assuming we have a body of data, $\mathcal{D}$, from some frames of tracking.

First, we can cast the goal of bootstrap initialization in this case to be $p(\mathbf{U}|\mathcal{D}_n, \phi)$ (recall that $\mathcal{D}_n$ the body of supervised data acquired between time

t_1 and t_n). We can determine $p(\mathbf{U}|\mathcal{D}_n, \phi)$ if we know the final model, $p(\boldsymbol{\theta}|\mathcal{D}_n, \phi)$. The latter can be computed by Bayes' Rule:

$$p(\boldsymbol{\theta}|\mathcal{D}, \phi) = \frac{p(\boldsymbol{\theta}|\phi)p(\mathcal{D}|\boldsymbol{\theta}, \phi)}{p(\mathcal{D}|\phi)}, \tag{1}$$

where the marginal likelihood, $p(\mathcal{D}|\phi)$, is given by

$$p(\mathcal{D}|\phi) = \int p(\mathcal{D}|\boldsymbol{\theta}, \phi)p(\boldsymbol{\theta}|\phi)d\boldsymbol{\theta}. \tag{2}$$

We can then compute $p(\mathbf{U}|\mathcal{D}, \phi)$ by marginalizing over $\boldsymbol{\theta}$,

$$p(\mathbf{U}|\mathcal{D}, \phi) = \int p(\mathbf{U}|\boldsymbol{\theta}, \phi)p(\boldsymbol{\theta}|\mathcal{D}, \phi)d\boldsymbol{\theta}. \tag{3}$$

In general, neither the posterior probability in Equation 1 nor the integral in Equation 3 are easy to compute, since expressions for $p(\mathcal{D}|\boldsymbol{\theta}, \phi)$ and $p(\boldsymbol{\theta}|\phi)$ can be arbitrarily complex. Fortunately, there are approximations that simplify the analysis. We discretize $\mathcal{U}$ and assume that our distributions can be captured by *conjugate distributions* [2], which provide tractable, analytical solutions under certain assumptions about the models.

First, we discretize the observed variable, $\mathbf{U}$, such that it can assume any of r possible values, $\mathbf{u}^1, \ldots, \mathbf{u}^r$. Assume that the final model parameters are given by $\boldsymbol{\theta} = \{\theta_1, \ldots \theta_r\}$, with $\theta_k \geq 0$, and $\sum_{k=1}^{r} \theta_k = 1$, and that the likelihood function for $\mathbf{U}$ is given by

$$p(\mathbf{U} = \mathbf{u}^k|\boldsymbol{\theta}, \phi) = \theta_k, \tag{4}$$

for $k = 1, \ldots, r$. Clearly, we can represent any pdf to arbitrary precision by varying r. In our case, we use 32^3 bins, where each of the RGB color channels is quantized into 32 discrete values.

If the data, $\mathcal{D}_n$ can be reduced to n independent observations of $\mathbf{U}$, the process of observation is a multinomial sampling, where a sufficient statistic [2] is the number of occurrences of each θ_k in $\mathcal{D}_n$. As mentioned earlier, we force the algorithm to choose one observation per frame as follows: For each $\mathbf{D}_i$, we choose the pixel at $\mathbf{Z}_{\mathbf{x}'}$, where $\mathbf{x}' = \arg\max_{\mathbf{x}} p^0(\mathbf{x})$. Then, if we let N_k be equal to the total number of occurrences of θ_k in the data ($N = \sum_{k=1}^{r} N_k$), then

$$p(\mathcal{D}_n|\boldsymbol{\theta}, \phi) = \prod_{k=1}^{r} \theta_k^{N_k}. \tag{5}$$

What remains now is to determine the form of the prior, $p(\boldsymbol{\theta}|\phi)$. We choose *Dirichlet distributions*, which when used as a prior for this example, have several nice properties. Among them are the fact that (1) a Dirichlet prior ensures a Dirichlet posterior distribution, and (2) there is a simple form for estimating $p(\mathbf{U}|\mathcal{D}, \phi)$, which is our eventual goal. The Dirichlet distribution is as follows:

$$p(\boldsymbol{\theta}|\phi) = \text{Dir}(\boldsymbol{\theta}|\alpha_1, \ldots, \alpha_r) \tag{6}$$

$$\equiv \frac{\Gamma(\alpha)}{\prod_{k=1}^{r} \Gamma(\alpha_k)} \prod_{k=1}^{r} \theta_k^{\alpha_k - 1}, \tag{7}$$

where α_k is a "hyperparameter" for the prior, with $\alpha_k > 0$, $\alpha = \sum_{k=1}^{r} \alpha_k$, and $\Gamma(\cdot)$ is the Gamma function [2].

Properly, a Dirichlet distribution is a unimodal distribution on a $(r - 1)$-dimensional simplex. When used to represent a distribution of a single variable with r bins, it can be interpreted as a distribution of distributions. In our case, we use it to model the distribution of possible distributions of $\mathbf{U}$, where $p(\mathbf{U} = \mathbf{u}^k | \mathcal{D}, \phi)$ is the expected probability of $\mathbf{u}^k$ integrated over $\boldsymbol{\theta}$ (Equation 9). Examples of Dirichlet distributions for $r = 2$ (also known as Beta distributions) are given in Figure 2.

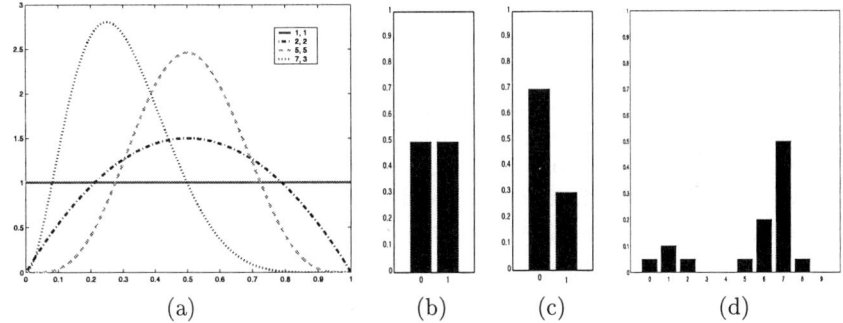

Fig. 2. Examples of (a) 2-parameter Dirichlet functions (Beta functions) and (b,c) their corresponding 2-bin histograms. A 10-parameter Dirichlet function could represent the histogram in (d).

As distributions of distributions, Dirichlet distributions contain more information than a single pdf alone. For example, while the pdf shown in Figure 2(b) is the expected pdf for any Beta distribution with $\alpha_1 = \alpha_2$, the Beta distribution also gives us information about our confidence in that pdf. Specifically, as $\alpha = \alpha_1 + \alpha_2$ increases, our confidence in the expected pdf increases as well. This is illustrated by the increased peakedness corresponding to increasing α in Figure 2(a).

With this prior, the posterior becomes

$$p(\boldsymbol{\theta}|\mathcal{D}, \phi) = \text{Dir}(\boldsymbol{\theta}|\alpha_1 + N_1, \ldots, \alpha_r + N_r), \tag{8}$$

and the probability distribution for $\mathbf{U}_{n+1}$ is

$$p(\mathbf{U}_{n+1} = \mathbf{u}^k | \mathcal{D}, \phi) = \int \theta_k p(\boldsymbol{\theta}|\mathcal{D}, \phi) d\boldsymbol{\theta} = \frac{\alpha_k + N_k}{\alpha + N}. \tag{9}$$

The surprising consequence of the discretization of $\boldsymbol{\theta}$ and the assumption of the Dirichlet prior is the simple form of Equation 9. Effectively, we need only count the number of samples in the data for each bin of the histogram. Also, note how the expression appeals to our intuition: First, if $\alpha_k = 1$ for all k (a flat, low-information prior, which we use in our implementation), then the probability of observing $\mathbf{u}^k$ is $(N_k + 1)/(N + r)$, which asymptotically approaches the fraction that $\mathbf{u}^k$ is observed in the data. Second, as the number of observations increases, the effect of the prior diminishes; in the limit, the influence of the prior vanishes. Lastly, we find a particularly intuitive form for expressing our prior beliefs. Our relative sense for how often each of the $\mathbf{u}^k$ occurs is decided by the relative values of α_k, and the confidence with which we believe in our prior is determined by their sum, α.

4.2 3D Feature-Mapped Surface

In our second example, we consider the task of estimating a person's approximate head pose, given head location in an image. We distinguish "head pose" from "facial pose" by the range of applicability: facial pose is restricted to images where most of the face is visible.

In contrast to pose-tracking techniques that give precise pose estimates for close-up, well-lit facial images of known subjects [6, 9, 14–17], we consider coarse, but robust, estimation of pose for unknown subjects under a variety of circumstances. By using a generic model to provide initial pose estimates, we can learn a new model that is tailored to that person.

Framework Instantiation The output is $\mathbf{x} = (r_x, r_y, r_z)$, the rotational pose of a person's head. We will assume that other parameters (position and scale, for example) have been recovered by other means [3, 10].

In this case, the initial model, $\boldsymbol{\pi}$, the final model, $\boldsymbol{\theta}$, and the prior for the final model, $\boldsymbol{\phi}$ all take the same form: We model heads as ellipsoids with a set of points on the surface. Each point, indexed by j $(1 \leq j \leq m)$, is represented by its coordinates, $\mathbf{q}_j$ (lying on the ellipsoid surface), and a pdf representing the belief probability, $p_j(\mathbf{z}|\mathbf{x})$ – the belief that given a particular pose, the point j will project observation $\mathbf{z}$. Model points are placed at the intersections of regularly-spaced latitudinal and longitudinal lines, where "north pole" coincides with the front of the head (see Figure 3(a)).

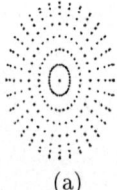  

(a)   (b)   (c)

Fig. 3. (a) Model point distribution; (b) rotation-invariant sum of Gabor wavelets for determining local edge density; (c) coefficients for a learned model viewed exactly frontally, for one kernel.

The domain of the pdfs stored at model points form a feature vector space. An element of this space, $\mathbf{z}$, is a 5-element feature vector consisting of the transform coefficients when five convolution kernels are applied to a pixel in the image. For a model point j, $\mathbf{z}^j$ is the feature vector for the pixel on which point j would project via scaled orthographic projection (assuming fixed orientation $\mathbf{x}$). The kernels extract information about local "edge density," which tends to be consistent for corresponding points of people's heads across different illumination conditions [19].

The acquisition function, g, returns the observation function $\mathbf{Z}$, where $\mathbf{Z}(\tilde{\mathbf{x}})$ is the concatenation of the feature vectors, $\{\mathbf{z}^j\}$, observed at points in the image which correspond to the orthographically projected points, $\{j\}$, of the model when oriented with pose $\tilde{\mathbf{x}}$ (for $1 \leq j \leq m$). For model points j that occur in the hemisphere not facing the image plane, $\mathbf{z}^j$ is undefined.

Because the underlying models are the same, the tracking functions, f^0 and f^1 are identical. In particular, they simply compute the maximum likelihood pose. Given a cropped image of a head, the image is first rescaled to a canonical size and histogram-equalized. The resulting image is convolved with the five templates described above. Finally, we compute

$$\mathbf{x}^* = \arg\max_{\mathbf{x}} p(\mathbf{x}|\mathbf{Z}) = \arg\max_{\mathbf{x}} p(\mathbf{Z}|\mathbf{x}), \qquad (10)$$

using Bayes' Rule, where we ignore the normalization constant and assume a constant, low-information prior over possible head poses. More detail on the pose estimation algorithm is presented elsewhere [19].

Bootstrap Initialization Algorithm Given a set of pose-observation pairs, $\mathcal{D}$, where the pose pdfs are generated using a generic head model, bootstrapping a person-specific model proceeds as follows.

Let $\mathbf{s}_j = \{\mathbf{z}_i^j : $ the j-th element of $\mathbf{Z}_i(\arg\max_{\mathbf{x}} p_i^0(\mathbf{x})), \forall i\}$. That is, $\mathbf{s}_j$ represents the set of all observations that would project to model point j, if, for each pose-observation pair, the pose estimated to have the maximum likelihood is used.

Once all of the data is collected for each model point, j, we estimate the pdf for that point. In our implementation, we approximate the pdf with a single Gaussian whose mean and covariance coincide with that for $\mathbf{s}_j$. This is consistent with a Bayesian approximation of the model pdfs with a low-information prior, ϕ, which contains Gaussian pdfs with zero mean and very large, constant covariances at each model point. The data at each model point is thus assumed to be indepedent of data at other points – this is not the case, but experiments suggest independence serves as a reasonable approximation.

5   Results and Analysis

Both learning algorithms were implemented as described above. Initial results indicate that the bootstrapping algorithms work as expected – in both cases, the final model is learned without manual intervention, when only an initial model was available.

Annotation within:	$0° - 45°$		$45° - 90°$		$90° - 135°$		$135° - 180°$	
Model Type	Rot Y	Rot X	Rot Y	Rot X	Rot Y	Rot X	Rot Y	Rot X
person-specific	10.4	5.7	14.8	6.8	16.9	5.9	28.5	8.7
generic model	19.2	12.0	33.6	16.3	38.0	15.7	47.5	13.2
bootstrap 1	14.2	8.7	23.2	12.2	26.5	9.7	49.7	13.9
bootstrap 2	14.7	8.3	22.1	13.2	25.8	10.4	46.5	13.9
bootstrap 3+	14.5	9.0	25.1	15.2	26.6	11.7	50.5	14.4
preproc+bs1	13.9	8.8	22.9	12.4	26.3	9.7	49.4	14.0

Fig. 4. Average estimation errors.

For the skin-color initialization task, Figure 7 shows an example input image (a) and the corresponding skin-color map (b) using the final model learned over 60 frames during 2 seconds of tracking.

For the head-pose task, Figure 4 displays average error rates over 4 different angular ranges. The values indicate errors averaged over runs on 10 separate sequences of people recorded by different cameras, under different illumination conditions, and at varying distances from the camera. "Ground truth" pose was determined by hand because many of the data sequences were from prerecorded video. For testing purposes, all errors of the algorithm are measured with respect to the annotation.

Because texture is more stable on the face than in hair, results were far more accurate when all or part of the face was actually visible. Thus, we report errors averaged over four regions of the pose space. The columns in Figure 4 show the range for which errors were averaged. These numbers indicate the difference in rotation about the y-axis between the annotated face normal and the camera's optical axis. A typical result for a single individual is shown in Figure 5(a).

The results suggest that no unreasonable approximations have been made – bootstrapping works as expected. Nevertheless, because our algorithms are based on independence assumptions which do necessarily hold, we examine the effect that algorithmic choices have on the final outcome.

5.1 Data Dependencies

Both of the learning algorithms presented are based on the assumption that data is acquired independently and without bias from the distribution the models try to capture. How likely and how important is it that these assumptions hold?

In the case of generating learning examples from tracking, the acquired data is unlikely to represent independent samples for several reasons. First, the image sequences involved in tracking generally exhibit little change from frame to frame. We thus anticipate that data from adjacent frames will exhibit considerable temporal dependencies. Second, initial tracking functions are unlikely to track the target with high accuracy or precision (hence the need for bootstrap initialization at all). Thus, a certain amount of noise is expected to corrupt the training data. What is worse is if the initial tracking function (or the initial

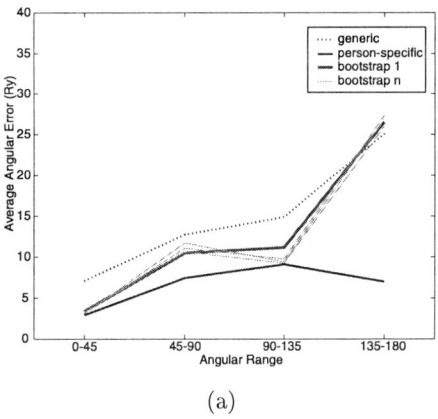 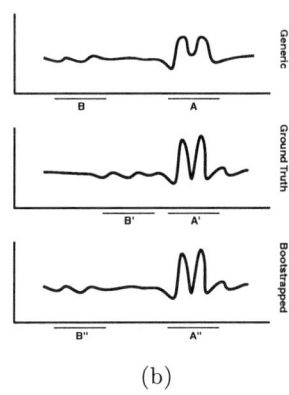

(a) (b)

Fig. 5. (a) Differences in estimation errors for generic model (top line) and bootstrap-iterated models (middle lines) for a typical subject. For comparison, the results for a person-specific model trained using manually annotated data are given as well (bottom line). (b) 1-D schematic representation of models. See Section 5.

model on which it is based) presents a consistent bias in its estimates, which propagates to the data. The acquisition function may also introduce biases in a similar manner.

Reducing Effects of Temporal Coherence: Dependencies due to temporal coherence can be reduced in one of two ways. An intuitive approach is to sample data at random instances in time that are a sufficient interval apart. A "sufficient interval" would be on the order of time such that tracked states appear conditionally independent. For example, in learning the skin-color model, instead of taking samples at 30Hz, we could sample at intervals determined by a Poisson process with intensity adjusted to sample every 0.3 seconds or so. In Figure 6(a), we plot the entropy, $H(X) = -\sum_{\mathbf{x}} p^1(\mathbf{x}) \log p^1(\mathbf{x})$, of the final model for skin color against the total number of data samples, where the lines represent variation in sampling frequency. We expect the entropy to converge as more samples are incorporated. We note that taking samples at lesser frequency increases the learning rate *per datum*, suggesting that temporal coherence can be broken through subsampling.

Alternatively, data can be taken over a long enough period of time that a representative sequence of tracking contexts (*i.e.*, spanning a wide range of target configurations and environmental contexts) is observed. Although the data may not be locally independent, the sufficient statistics of the data set should approximate those of a large, randomly sampled set. This behavior is evident in all of the plots in Figure 6, where the final models appear to converge to similar models, regardless of sampling frequency. The inversion in learning rates between Figure 6(a) and (b) suggests that one can trade off amount of data to process with time required to collect data.

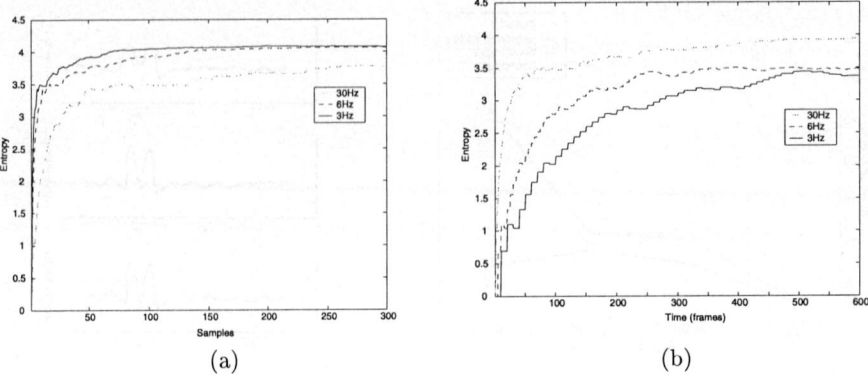

Fig. 6. Entropy of final model plotted against number/time of data samples. In (a), the x-axis represents number of data samples; in (b), the time required to collect the samples.

Weighting Data: Some of the problems with data acquisition may be alleviated if the initial tracking function returns a confidence value for its output. If we read these confidence values as indicators of the *effective sample size* that a particular datum represents, we can weight its contribution to the final model.

For both examples, we can simply multiply each piece of data by a value proportional to its confidence. It seems strange to say that a single datum can represent more than one sample, so for both skin-color and head texture models, we normalize all weights such that they fall in the interval $[0.0, 1.0]$. For the skin-color model, we use the residual from ellipse tracking to weight each set of observations (better fits correspond to greater confidence). In the case of the head-texture model, we weight by the normalized likelihood of the maximum likelihood pose, which is interpretable as an actual probability.

Performance improves for both cases. Results for the skin-color model are shown in Figure 7. Note how the pixel distribution is most concentrated in skin-colored regions in (c) because samples which were taken when tracking was unreliable were suppressed. This is in contrast to (b), where each sample was weighted evenly.

Reducing Bias from Tracking and Acquisition Functions: The problem we are least able to overcome is bias in the initial tracking function and the acquisition function, since they provide the supervisory data, $(p^0(\mathbf{x}), \mathbf{z}(\mathbf{x}))$. In the abstract, there is very little we can do to eliminate such a bias. But, there may be domain-specific solutions which help alleviate the problem.

For example, the skin-color model learns a pdf consisting of mostly skin color, together with a small contribution from pixels taken inadvertently from the background. If we can learn the distribution of background pixels, we can eliminate these with a Bayesian decision criterion to determine whether a given

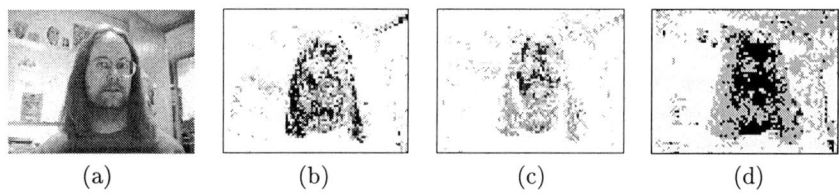

$$\begin{array}{cccc} \text{(a)} & \text{(b)} & \text{(c)} & \text{(d)} \end{array}$$

Fig. 7. (a) A raw image, as input to the final tracking function. (b-c) likelihood of pixel skin-color, based on learned final model (likelihoods scaled so that highest is darkest), with total weight of training data size kept constant: (b) 1 sample from each frame; (c) data weighted by ellipse residual (1 sample from each frame, for 70% of frames). (d) Bayesian decision to separate foreground from background: Black pixels mark foreground pixels; gray pixels mark potential foreground pixels which are more likely to be background.

pixel value, $\mathbf{u}^k$ is more likely to be skin or background. That is, $\mathbf{u}^k$ is skin if

$$p(\text{skin}|\mathbf{u}^k) > p(\text{bg}|\mathbf{u}^k) \tag{11}$$

$$p(\mathbf{u}^k|\text{skin})p(\text{skin}) > p(\mathbf{u}^k|\text{bg})p(\text{bg}), \tag{12}$$

where $p(\mathbf{u}^k|\text{skin})$ is acquired from Equation 9, $p(\mathbf{u}^k|\text{bg})$ can be acquired similarly by simply sampling pixels outside of the tracked ellipse (in practice, we collect entire frames of pixels from just a few frames), and $p(\text{skin})$ and $p(\text{bg})$ are set based on the relative area that they are expected to occupy in an image containing a face. See Figure 7(d) for an example in which only those pixels which occur frequently on the face, but very infrequently in the background are considered skin color. Modeling both skin and background as mixtures of a handful of Gaussians achieves a similar result [12], but without the granularity possible with a nonparametric model.

In the head orientation example, our original generic model exhibits a slight orientational bias – in Figure 3(c), a slight turn of the head to the left is visible. We can eliminate this bias by finding the angle at which the model appears most symmetrical and averaging the model with its reflection. Doing so does in fact reduce some of the error generated by the final model (see Figure 4, Row 6 vs. any of Rows 3-5).

Repeated Bootstrapping Finally, we mention the possibility of repeated bootstrapping. Clearly, if one model can be used to learn a second model, any combination of the first two models could be used to learn a third model. In Figure 1, f^1 and $\theta(\mathbf{x})$ replace f^0 and $p^0(\mathbf{x})$, and bootstrap initialization iterates.

Strangely, in both of our examples, repeated bootstrapping does not appear to improve the final models. For learning skin-color, repeated bootstrapping is good for adapting to a changing color model [12], but for a fixed distribution, there is nothing more to be gained by going beyond the asymptotically learned color models. This is not surprising, since we have chosen to gather enough data in the first iteration to learn a good model.

Figures 4 and 5(a), show that even for the head-texture case, bootstrapping beyond the first iteration does not appear to improve pose estimates.

Figure 5(b) shows a one-dimensional schematic of what we believe is taking place. The x-axis shows the angular position on the model and the y-axis gives the extracted feature value. The top figure shows a generic model, the middle figure shows the ground truth model, and the bottom graph shows the bootstrapped model.

Pose estimation is equivalent to being given a short, noisy segment of the bottom function (the observation) and trying to find the best match displacement in the top function. In the case when we are trying to find a match to a uniquely-varying part of the model, such as Segment A', the corresponding segment is accurately localized (Segment A). This corresponds to cases when the front or side views (angular ranges 0-135) are being presented. Bootstrapping helps in this instance because the characteristics of the real model are transferred to the bootstrapped model.

When the observation segment is more homogeneous as in Segment B', the match is likely to be affected by noise and other small differences in the generic model, making matching inaccurate (Segment B). The bootstrapped model then merely recaptures the initial estimation error. This behavior was observed in many of the test images, where the bootstrapped model inhereted a tendency to misestimate back-of-head poses by a significant and *consistent* amount.

It is not clear whether the ineffectiveness of repeated bootstrapping should be expected in other similar cases of bootstrap initialization. One distant counterexample is the remarkable success of iterated bootstrapping in learning linear subspace models of faces [18].

6 Conclusion

We have presented bootstrap initialization, an abstract framework for using one model to guide the initialization of another model during tracking. We presented two examples of bootstrap initialization for tracking, using nonparametric models of target surface texture. In the first, we acquired a strong skin-color model of a user's face, given a weak edge-based model of user shape. In the second, we refined a generic model of head texture to suit a particular individual. Preliminary experiments show the potential for bootstrap initialization in tracking applications; in both cases, initial implementations were able to learn a bootstrapped model without undue concern for data dependencies in the acquired training data.

Additional experiments provided evidence toward the following tentative conclusions:

- Independence assumptions in the acquired training data can be violated to a great degree. Movement of target objects creates enough variation that the sufficient statistics of training data taken over an extended period of time closely match those of an ideally sampled data set.

- Dependencies in data can be removed through both generic and domain-specific strategies. Final models are better learned by taking advantage of such tactics.
- Repeated bootstrapping does not necessarily result in improved models.

In future work, we expect to delve deeper into theoretical limits of bootstrap initialization and more broadly into other tracking domains.

References

1. A. Azarbayejani and A. Pentland. Recursive estimation of motion, structure, and focal length. *IEEE Trans. Patt. Anal. and Mach. Intel.*, 17(6), June 1995.
2. J.M. Bernardo and A.F.M. Smith. *Bayesian Theory.* John Wiley, Chichester, 1994.
3. S. Birchfield. Elliptical head tracking using intensity gradients and color histograms. In *Proc. Computer Vision and Patt. Recog.*, pages 232–237, 1998.
4. A. Chiuso and S. Soatto. 3-D motion and structure causally integrated over time: Theory (stability) and practice (occlusions). Technical Report 99-003, ESSRL, 1999.
5. J.W. Davis and A.F. Bobick. The representation and recognition of action using temporal templates. In *CVPR97*, pages 928–934, 1997.
6. D. DeCarlo and D. Metaxas. The integration of optical flow and deformable models with applications to human face shape and motion estimation. In *Proc. Computer Vision and Patt. Recog.*, pages 231–238, 1996.
7. P. Fua and C. Miccio. From regular images to animated heads: a least squares approach. In *Proc. European Conf. on Computer Vision*, pages 188–202, 1998.
8. M. Isard and A. Blake. ICondensation: Unifying low-level and high-level tracking in a stochastic framework. In *Proc. European Conf. on Computer Vision*, pages I:893–908, 1998.
9. T. S. Jebara and A. Pentland. Parametrized structure from motion for 3D adaptive feedback tracking of faces. In *Proc. Computer Vision and Patt. Recog.*, 1997.
10. J. MacCormick and A. Blake. A probabilistic exclusion principle for tracking multiple objects. In *Proc. Int'l Conf. on Computer Vision*, pages I:572–578, 1999.
11. N. Oliver, A. Pentland, and F. Berard. LAFTER: Lips and face real time tracker. In *Proc. Computer Vision and Patt. Recog.*, 1997.
12. Y. Raja, S. J. McKenna, and S. Gong. Tracking and segmenting people in varying lighting conditions using colour. In *Proc. Int'l Conf. on Autom. Face and Gesture Recog.*, pages 228–233, 1998.
13. D. Reynard, A. Wildenberg, A. Blake, and J. Marchant. Learning dynamics of complex motions from image sequences. In *Proc. European Conf. on Computer Vision*, pages 357–368, 1996.
14. A. Schoedl, A. Haro, and I. A. Essa. Head tracking using a textured polygonal model. In *Proc. Wkshp on Perceptual UI*, pages 43–48, 1998.
15. R. Stiefelhagen, J. Yang, and A. Waibel. Tracking eyes and monitoring eye gaze. In *Proc. Wkshp on Perceptual UI*, Banff, Canada, 1997.
16. H. Tao and T. S. Huang. Bezier volume deformation model for facial animation and video tracking,. In *Proc. IFIP Workshop on Modeling and Motion Capture Techniques for Virtual Environments (CAPTECH'98)*, November 1998.
17. K. Toyama. 'Look Ma, no hands!' Hands-free cursor control with real-time 3D face tracking. In *Workshop on Perceptual User Interfaces*, 1998.
18. T. Vetter, M. J. Jones, and T. Poggio. A bootstrapping algorithm for learning linear models of objects classes. In *Proc. Computer Vision and Patt. Recog.*, pages 40–46, 1997.
19. Y. Wu, K. Toyama, and T. S. Huang. Wide-range, person- and illumination-insensitive head orientation estimation. In *Proc. Int'l Conf. on Autom. Face and Gesture Recog.*, 2000.

Quasi-Random Sampling for Condensation

Vasanth Philomin, Ramani Duraiswami, and Larry Davis

Computer Vision Laboratory
Institute for Advanced Computer Studies
University of Maryland, College Park, MD 20742, USA
{vasi, ramani, lsd}@umiacs.umd.edu
http://www.umiacs.umd.edu/{~vasi, ~ramani, ~lsd}

Abstract. The problem of tracking pedestrians from a moving car is a challenging one. The Condensation tracking algorithm is appealing for its generality and potential for real-time implementation. However, the conventional Condensation tracker is known to have difficulty with high-dimensional state spaces and unknown motion models. This paper presents an improved algorithm that addresses these problems by using a simplified motion model, and employing quasi-Monte Carlo techniques to efficiently sample the resulting tracking problem in the high-dimensional state space. For N sample points, these techniques achieve sampling errors of $O(N^{-1})$, as opposed to $O(N^{-1/2})$ for conventional Monte Carlo techniques. We illustrate the algorithm by tracking objects in both synthetic and real sequences, and show that it achieves reliable tracking and significant speed-ups over conventional Monte Carlo techniques.

1 Introduction

Since its introduction, the Condensation algorithm [1] has attracted much interest as it offers a framework for dynamic state estimation where the underlying probability density functions (pdfs) need not be Gaussian. The algorithm is based on a Monte Carlo or sampling approach, where the pdf is represented by a set of random samples. As new information becomes available, the posterior distribution of the state variables is updated by recursively propagating these samples (using a motion model as a predictor) and resampling. An accurate dynamical model is essential for robust tracking and for achieving real-time performance. This is due to the fact that the process noise of the model has to be made artificially high in order to track objects that deviate significantly from the learned dynamics, thereby increasing the extent of each predicted cluster in state space. One would then have to increase the sample size to populate these large clusters with enough samples. A high-dimensional state space (required for tracking complex shapes such as pedestrians) only makes matters worse. Isard et al. [2] use two separate trackers, one in the Euclidean similarity space and the other in a separate deformation space, to handle the curse of dimensionality.

Our need for a tracking algorithm was for tracking moving objects (such as pedestrians) from a *moving* camera for applications in driver assistance systems and vehicle guidance that could contribute towards traffic safety [4, 3]. The problem of pedestrian detection has been addressed in [3] and [5], but without temporal integration of results. We believe that temporal integration of results is essential for the demanding performance rates that might be required for the actual deployment of such a system. This tracking problem, however, is complicated because there is significant camera motion, and objects in the image move according to unpredictable/unknown motion models. We want to make no assumptions about how the camera is moving (translation, rotation, etc.) or about the viewing angle. Hence it is not practically feasible to break up the dynamics into several different motion classes ([6, 7]) and learn the dynamics of each class and the class transition probabilities. We need a general model that is able to cope with the wide variety of motions exhibited by both the camera and the object, as well as with the shape variability of the object being tracked.

A common problem that is often overlooked when using the Condensation tracker in higher dimensions is that typical implementations rely on the system supplied rand() function, which is almost always a linear congruential generator. These generators, although very fast, have an inherent weakness that they are not free of sequential correlation on successive calls, i.e. if k random numbers at a time are used to generate points in k-dimensional space, the points will lie on $(k - 1)$-dimensional planes and will not fill up the k-dimensional space. Thus the sampling will be sub-optimal and even inaccurate. Another problem with these generators arises when the modulus operator is used to generate a random sequence that lies in a certain range. Since the least significant bits of the numbers generated are much less random than their most significant bits, a less than random sequence results [8]. Even if one uses a 'perfect' pseudo-random number generator, the sampling error for N points will only decrease as $O(N^{-1/2})$ as opposed to $O(N^{-1})$ for another class of generators (see Section 2).

We must thus deal with the problems of high dimensionality, motion models of unknown form, and sub-optimal random number generators, while at the same time attempt to achieve satisfactory performance. For accuracy, the sampling must be fine enough to capture the variations in the state space, while for efficiency, the sampling must be performed at a relatively small number of points. In mathematical terms, the goal is to reduce the variance of the Monte Carlo estimate.

Various techniques (such as importance sampling [2] and stratified sampling [9]) have been proposed to improve the efficiency of the representation. In importance sampling, auxiliary knowledge is used to sample more densely those areas of the state space that have more information about the posterior probability. Importance sampling depends on already having some approximation to the posterior (possibly from alternate sensors), and is effective only to the extent that this approximation is a good one. In stratified sampling, variance reduction is achieved by dividing the state space into sub-regions and filling them with unequal numbers of points proportional to the variances in those subregions. However, this is not practical in spaces of high dimensionality since dividing a space into K segments along each dimension yields K^d subregions, too large a number when one has to estimate the variances in each of these subregions.

A promising extension to Condensation that addresses all the issues discussed above is the incorporation of quasi-Monte Carlo methods [8, 10]. In such methods, the sampling is not done with random points, but rather with a carefully chosen set of quasi-random points that span the sample space so that the points are maximally far away from each other. These points *improve the asymptotic complexity of the search* (number of points required to achieve a certain sampling error), can be *efficiently generated*, and are *well spread in multiple dimensions*. Our results indicate that significant improvements due to these properties are achieved in our implementation of a novel Condensation algorithm using quasi-Monte Carlo methods. Note that quasi-random sampling is complementary to other sampling techniques used in conjunction with the Condensation algorithm, such as importance sampling, partitioned sampling [11], partial importance sampling [7], etc., and can readily be combined with these for better performance.

This paper is organized as follows: Section 2 gives a brief introduction to quasi-random sequences and their properties, including a basic estimate of sampling error for quasi-Monte Carlo methods, and establishes their relevance to the Condensation algorithm. We also indicate how such sequences can be generated and used in practice. In Section 3 we describe a modified Condensation algorithm that addresses the issues of an unknown motion model, robustness to outliers, and use of quasi-random points for efficiency. In Section 4 we apply this algorithm to some test problems and real video sequences, and compare its performance with an algorithm based on pseudo-random sampling. The results demonstrate the lower error rate and robustness of our algorithm for the same number of sampling points. Section 5 concludes the paper.

2 Quasi-Random Distributions

2.1 Sampling and Uniformity

Functionals associated with problems in computer vision often have a complex structure in the parameter space, with multiple local extrema. Furthermore, these extrema can lie in regions of involved or convoluted shape in the parameter space. Alternatively, the functionals may have a collapsed structure and have support on a sub-dimensional manifold in the space (perhaps indicating an error in modeling or in the choice of parameters). If the sampling is to be successful in recovering the functional in such cases, the distributions of the sample points and their subdimensional projections must satisfy certain properties. Intuitively, the points must be distributed such that any subvolume in the space should contain points in proportion to its volume (or other appropriate measure). This property must also hold for projections onto a manifold.

Quasi-random sequences are a deterministic alternative to random sequences for use in Monte Carlo methods, such as integration and particle simulations of transport processes. The discrepancy of a set of points in a region is related to the notion of uniformity. Let a region with unit volume have N points distributed in it. Then, for uniform point distributions, any subregion with volume α would have αN points in it. The difference between this quantity and the actual number

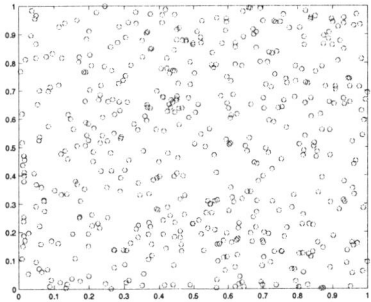 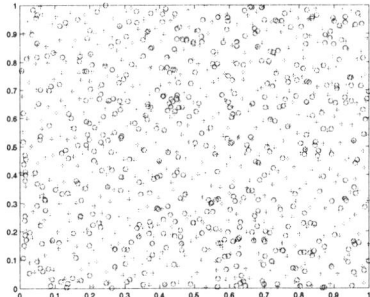

(a) 512 points in $(0,1)^2$ generated with Matlab's pseudo-random number generator.

(b) 512 points from the Sobol' sequence denoted by $(+)$ overlaid on top of (a)

Fig. 1. Distributions of pseudo-random points (a) and quasi random points overlaid (b). Observe the clustering of the pseudo-random points in some regions and the gaps left by them in others. The quasi-random points in (b) leave no such spaces and do not form clusters.

of points in the region is called the "discrepancy." Quasi-random sequences have low discrepancies and are also called low-discrepancy sequences. The error in uniformity for a sequence of N points in the k-dimensional unit cube is measured by its discrepancy, which is $O((\log N)^k N^{-1})$ for a quasi-random sequence, as opposed to $O((\log \log N)^{1/2} N^{-1/2})$ for a pseudo-random sequence [15].

Figure 1 compares the uniformity of distributions of quasi-random points and pseudo-random points. Figure 1(a) shows a set of random points generated in $(0,1)^2$ using a pseudo-random number generator. If the distribution of points were uniform one would expect that *any* region of area larger than $1/512$ would have at least one point in it. As can be seen, however, many regions considerably larger than this are not sampled at all, while points in other portions of the region form rather dense clusters, thus oversampling those regions. Thus from an information gathering perspective the sampling is sub-optimal. Figure 1(b) shows Sobol' quasi-random points overlaid on the pseudo-random points. These points do not clump together, and fill the spaces left by the pseudo-random points.

A good introduction to why quasi-random distributions are useful in Monte Carlo integration is provided by Press et al. [8]. As far as application of the technique to optimization or sampling is concerned, Niederreiter [10] provides a mathematical treatment of this issue. The goal is to sample the space of parameters with sufficient fineness so that we are close enough to every significant maximum or minimum, and can be assured that the approximation to the functional in any given region is bounded, and is well characterized by the number of points chosen for sampling, N. We will motivate and state below the results for the quasi-random points. For a more mathematical and formal treatment, consult [10, 17]

Given N points, for the sampling to be effective, each point should be optimally far from the others in the set so that a truly representative picture of the function being sampled is arrived at. Intuitively, if the points are sufficiently close, the approximation to the underlying functional at any point will be bounded. This can be made precise by the multidimensional analogue of Rolle's theorem. The value of a function at some point x_2 can be approximated by its value at a neighboring point x_1 according to

$$f(x + \delta) = f(x) + \nabla f|_\xi \cdot \delta, \qquad \text{for some } \xi \quad \text{such that } |\xi| \leq |\delta| \qquad (1)$$

where $x_2 = x_1 + \delta$.

Thus for sufficiently smooth functions, our sampling of the function will be subject to errors on the order of δ, where δ is characterized by the inter-sample point distance. The mathematical quantity *"dispersion"* was introduced by Niederreiter [10] to account for this property of a set of sample points. Given a set of points, the dispersion is defined by the following construction: place balls at each of the sample points with radii sufficiently large to intersect the balls placed at the other points, so that the whole space is covered. We can now define the average dispersion as the average radius of these balls, and the maximal dispersion by the maximum radius. The sampling error is thus characterized by the value of the dispersion of the set of sample points.

As shown in [10], low-discrepancy distributions of points have low dispersions, and hence provide lower sampling errors (see Equation (1)) in comparison with point sets with higher discrepancies.

2.2 Generating Quasi-Random Distributions

Now that we have seen that quasi-random distributions are likely to be useful for numerical problems requiring random sampling, the question is whether such distributions exist, and how one constructs them. Several distributions of quasi-random points have been proposed. These include the Halton, Fauré, Sobol', and Niederreiter family of sequences. Several of these have been compared as to their discrepancy and their suitability for high-dimensional Monte Carlo calculations [14, 15]. The consensus appears to be that the Sobol' sequence is good for problems of moderate dimension ($k \leq 7$), while the Niederreiter family of sequences seems to do well in problems of somewhat higher dimension. For problems in very large numbers of dimensions ($k > 100$), the properties of these distributions, and strategies for reducing their discrepancies to theoretical levels, are active areas of research [17].

The Sobol' and the Niederreiter sequences of order 2, which can be generated using bit shifting operations, are the most efficient. For reasons of brevity, their generation algorithms are not discussed here; the readers are referred to [13, 16]. The complexity of these quasi-random generators is comparable to that of standard pseudo-random number generation schemes, and there is usually no performance penalty for using them.

3 The Modified Tracking Algorithm

In the standard formulation of the Condensation algorithm [1], the sample positions $s_t^{(n)}$ at time t are obtained from the previous approximation to the posterior $\{(s_{t-1}^{(n)}, \pi_{t-1}^{(n)})\}$, $\pi_{t-1}^{(n)}$ being the probabilities, using the motion model $p(\mathbf{X}_t / \mathbf{X}_{t-1})$ as a predictor. The dynamics is usually represented as a second-order auto-regressive process, where each of the dimensions of the state space is modelled by an independent one-dimensional oscillator. The parameters of the oscillators are typically learned from training sequences that are not too hard to track [19, 20, 6, 7]. To learn multi-class dynamics, a discrete state component labelling the class of motion is appended to the continuous state vector x_t to form a "mixed" state, and the dynamical parameters of each class and the state transition probabilities are learned from example trajectories. However, for the complicated motions exhibited by pedestrians walking in front of a moving car, it is not easy to identify different classes of motions that make up the actual motion. Moreover, we would like to make no assumptions about how the camera is moving (translation, rotation, etc.) or about the viewing angle. We need a general model that is able to cope with the wide variety of motions exhibited by both the camera and the object being tracked, as well as the shape variability of the object. We propose using a zero-order motion model with large process noise high enough to account for the greatest expected change in shape and motion, since we now have a method of efficiently sampling high-dimensional spaces using quasi-random sequences.

Given the sample set $\{(s_{t-1}^{(n)}, \pi_{t-1}^{(n)})\}$ at the previous time step, we first choose a base sample $s_{t-1}^{(i)}$ with probability $\pi_{t-1}^{(i)}$. This yields a small number of highly probable locations, say M, the neighborhoods of which we must sample more densely. This has the effect of reducing δ when the Jacobian term in Equation (1) is locally large, thereby achieving a more consistent distribution of error over the domain (importance sampling). If there were just one region requiring a dense concentration, an invertible mapping from a uniform space to the space of equal importance could be constructed, as given below in Equation (3) for the case of a multi-dimensional Gaussian. Since we have M regions, the importance function cannot be constructed in closed form. One therefore needs an alternative strategy for generating from the quasi-random distribution, a set of points that samples important regions densely.

We have devised a simple yet effective strategy that achieves these objectives. Let the M locations have centers $\mu^{(j)}$ and variances $\sigma^{(j)}$ based on the process noise, where these quantities are k-dimensional vectors. We then overlay $M + 1$ distributions of quasi-random points over the space, with the first M distributions made Gaussian, centered at $\mu^{(j)}$ and with diagonal variance $\sigma^{(j)}$ (3). Finally, we also overlay a $(M + 1)$th distribution that is spread uniformly over the entire state space. This provides robustness against sudden changes in shape and motion. The total number of points used is N, where

$$N = N_1 + N_2 + \ldots + N_{M+1}, \tag{2}$$

the sample size in the Condensation algorithm. We have in effect chosen $\mathbf{s}_t^{(n)}$ by sampling from $p(\mathbf{X}_t/\mathbf{X}_{t-1} = \mathbf{s}_{t-1}^{(i)})$.

The conversion from a uniform quasi-random distribution to a Gaussian quasi-random distribution is achieved using the mapping along the lth dimension

$$y_{jl} = \mu_l^{(j)} + \sqrt{2}\sigma_l^{(j)} \, \mathrm{erf}^{-1}\left((2\xi_l - 1)\right), \qquad (3)$$

where erf^{-1} is the inverse of the error function given by

$$\mathrm{erf}(z) = \frac{2}{\sqrt{\pi}} \int_0^z e^{-t^2} \, dt,$$

and ξ_l represents the quasi-randomly distributed points in $[0, 1]$.

Finally, we measure and compute the probabilities $\pi_t^{(n)} = p(\mathbf{Z}_t/\mathbf{X}_t = \mathbf{s}_t^{(n)})$ for these new sample positions in terms of the image data $\mathbf{Z}_t$. We use a measurement density based on the multi-feature distance transform algorithm (see [3] for details) that has been successfully used for detecting pedestrians from static images. Therefore

$$\log p(\mathbf{Z}_t/\mathbf{X}_t) = \log p\,(\mathbf{Z}/\mathbf{X}) \propto \left\{ -\frac{1}{M} \sum_{i=1}^{M} d_{typed}^2(z_i, I) \right\},$$

where the z_i's are measurement points along the contour, I is the image data, and $d_{typed}(z_i, I)$ denotes the distance between z_i and the closest feature of the same type in I. We use oriented edges discretized into eight bins as the features in all our experiments.

4   Results

In order to investigate the effectiveness of quasi-random sampling we performed experiments using a simple synthetic example, as well as real video sequences of pedestrians taken from moving cars. Both sets of experiments demonstrated the expected improvements due to the use of quasi-random sampling. We describe these below.

4.1   Synthetic Experiments

We constructed the following simple tracking problem to illustrate the effectiveness of using quasi-random sampling as opposed to pseudo-random sampling for the Condensation tracker. The motion of an ellipse of fixed aspect ratio (ratio of axes)

$$\left(\frac{x - x_c\,(t)}{a\,(t)}\right)^2 + \left(\frac{y - y_c\,(t)}{\alpha a(t)}\right)^2 = 1 \qquad (4)$$

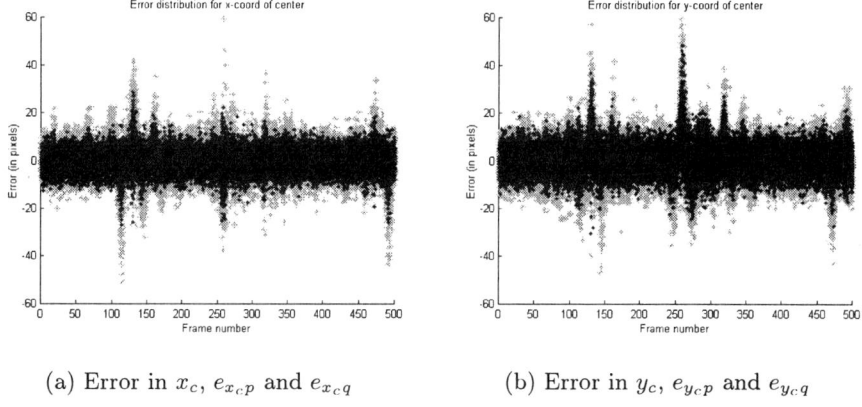

(a) Error in x_c, e_{x_cp} and e_{x_cq} (b) Error in y_c, e_{y_cp} and e_{y_cq}

Fig. 2. Error distributions vs. frame number. Light - PseudoRandom; Dark - QuasiRandom.

was simulated using a second-order harmonic oscillator model (4) independently in each of the ellipse parameters x_c, y_c and a. The ellipse translates and scales as a result of the combination of their motions. Reasonable values for the parameters of the oscillators were chosen manually.

We ran the tracking algorithm described in Section 3, first with a standard pseudo-random number generator and then with the quasi-random number generator for a given value of N (the Condensation sample size). The tracking algorithm generates estimates for the ellipse parameters at each time step, namely $\hat{x}_{cp}(t), \hat{y}_{cp}(t)$ and $\hat{a}_p(t)$ in the pseudo-random case and $\hat{x}_{cq}(t), \hat{y}_{cq}(t)$ and $\hat{a}_q(t)$ in the quasi-random case, from which the errors in the estimates $e_{x_cp}(t), e_{y_cp}(t), e_{ap}(t)$ (pseudo-random case) and $e_{x_cq}(t), e_{y_cq}(t), e_{aq}(t)$ (quasi-random case) are obtained. A consistent and reliable value of the error in each dimension was obtained by performing M Monte Carlo trials with each type of generator (for quasi-random, using successive points from a single quasi-random sequence) for each N. All plots shown here are for a sequence of length 500 frames and for 50 trials. Figure 2 shows the errors in the estimates of the center of the ellipse in all the 50 trials. The errors for both type of generators are plotted on top of each other. One can clearly see that the standard pseudo-random number generator leads to higher errors at almost every time step. To get a feel for how the sample size of the tracker affects the error rates resulting from the two sampling methods, the mean of the root mean square errors and the standard deviation over the entire sequence are plotted against N on a log-log scale (base 2).

Figure 3 shows the plots of the average rmse and standard deviation errors in the estimation of the center coordinates of the ellipse, x_c and y_c. From these experiments, as well as those described below, it can be seen that quasi-random sequences generally result in lower errors than standard random sequences. Fur-

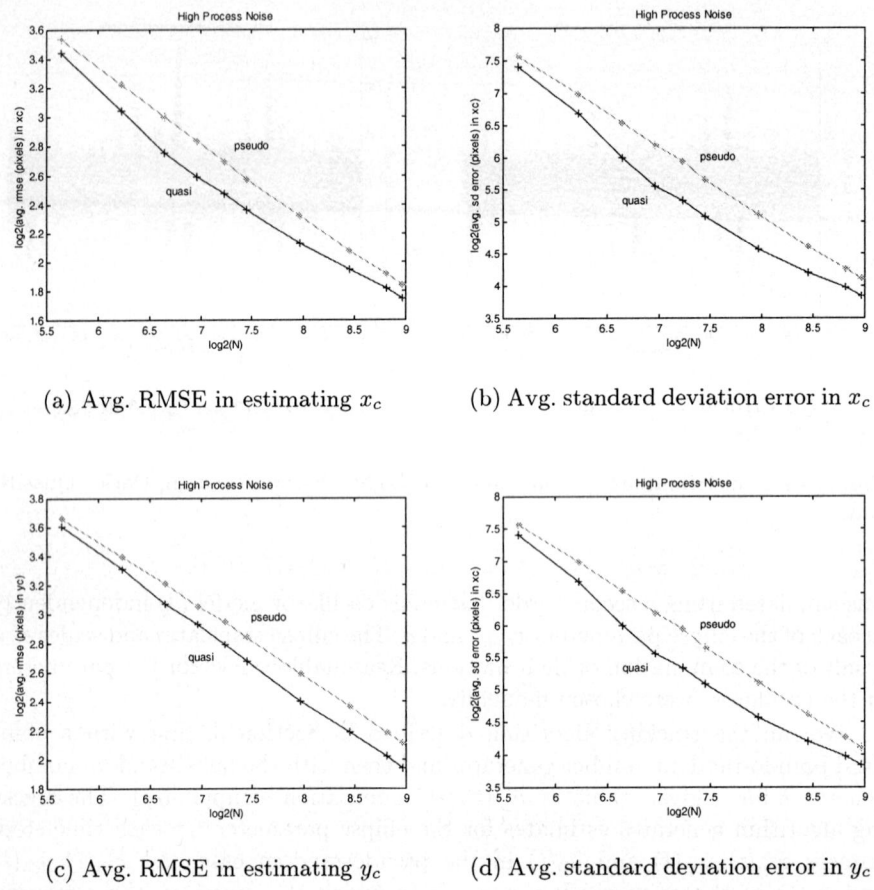

(a) Avg. RMSE in estimating x_c (b) Avg. standard deviation error in x_c

(c) Avg. RMSE in estimating y_c (d) Avg. standard deviation error in y_c

Fig. 3. Log-log plot of estimation error vs. N (sample size). * - PseudoRandom, + - QuasiRandom.

thermore, for low values of N, the errors for quasi-random sampling drop faster as the number of samples is increased, but as N gets very large, a saturation condition is reached, and a further increase in the sample size does not lead to comparable drops in the error rates, although they are still lower than in the pseudo-random case. These graphs thus show that for a given tolerance to error, quasi-random sampling needs a significantly smaller number of sample points (between $1/3$ and $1/2$ as many), thereby speeding up the execution of the algorithm considerably.

Figure 4 shows similar plots for the low process noise case, where the effects of using quasi-random sampling are slightly reduced compared to the high process noise case. Finally, Figure 5 (not a log-log plot) shows the behavior of the error rates with increasing process noise for a fixed value of N. As the process noise

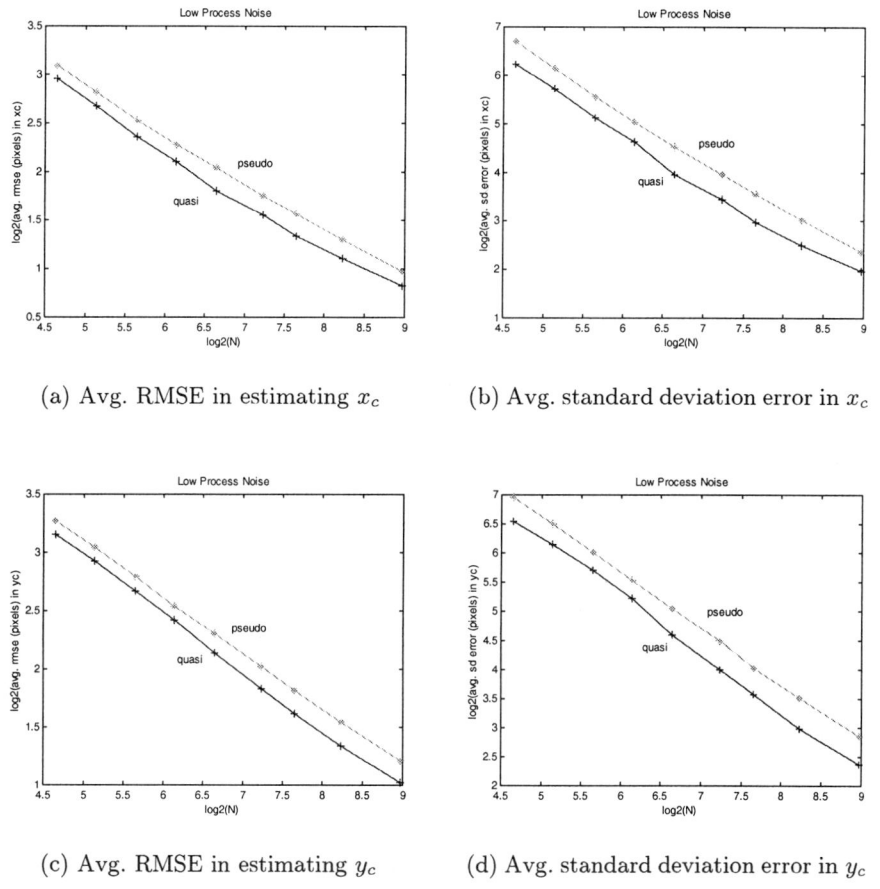

(a) Avg. RMSE in estimating x_c

(b) Avg. standard deviation error in x_c

(c) Avg. RMSE in estimating y_c

(d) Avg. standard deviation error in y_c

Fig. 4. Log-log plot of estimation error vs. N (sample size). * - PseudoRandom, + - QuasiRandom.

increases, the superiority of quasi-random sampling becomes clearer and both the rmse and sd errors for pseudo-random sampling increase much more rapidly than their quasi-random counterparts.

We have thus seen that using quasi-random sampling as the underlying random sampling technique in particle filters can lead to a significant improvement in the performance of the tracker. Even in a simplistic 3-D state space case such as that presented in this section, there is a sizable difference in the error rates. Furthermore, quasi-random sampling is actually more powerful in higher dimensions, as will be qualitatively demonstrated in the following section. We also note that adding noise to the simulations only helps the quasi-random case, since there are more clusters corresponding to multiple hypotheses which need to be populated efficiently.

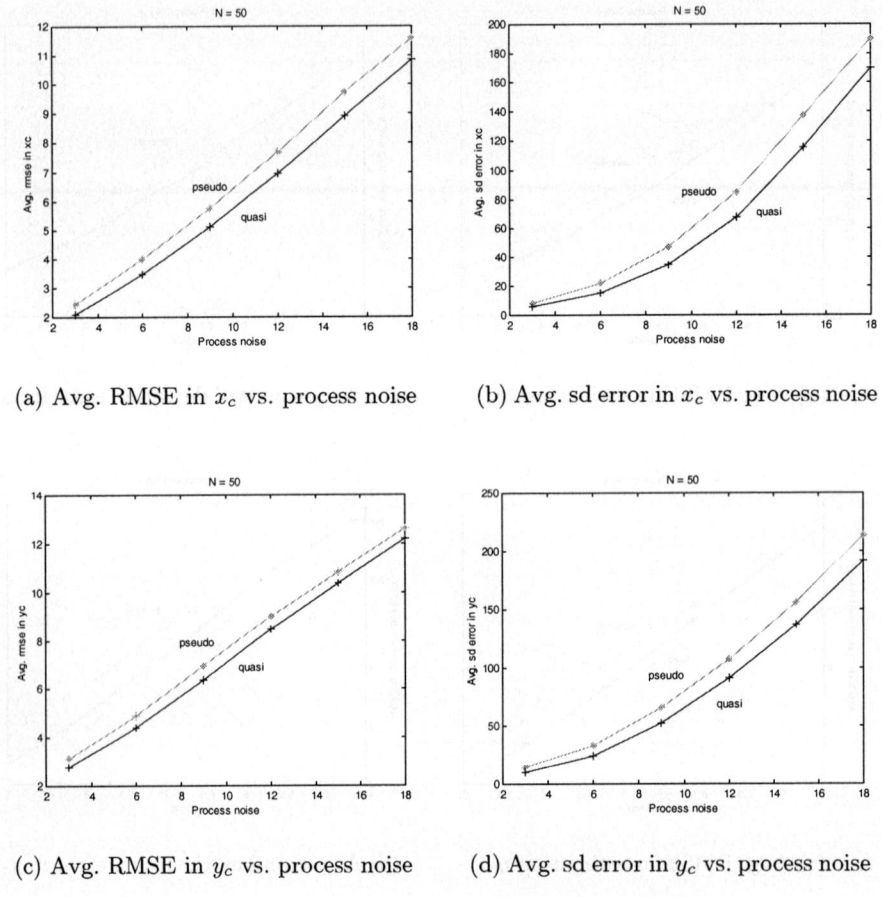

(a) Avg. RMSE in x_c vs. process noise   (b) Avg. sd error in x_c vs. process noise

(c) Avg. RMSE in y_c vs. process noise   (d) Avg. sd error in y_c vs. process noise

Fig. 5. Estimation error vs. process noise (fixed N). * - PseudoRandom, + - QuasiRandom.

4.2 Tracking pedestrians from a moving vehicle

We now present some results on tracking pedestrians from a moving vehicle using the techniques discussed above. First, a statistical shape model of a pedestrian was built using automatically segmented pedestrian contours from sequences obtained by a stationary camera (so that we can do background subtraction). We use well-established computer vision techniques (see [22] and [23]) to build a LPDM (Linear Point Distribution Model). We fit a NURB (Non-Uniform Rational B-spline) to each extracted contour using least squares curve approximation to points on the contour [21]. The control points of the NURBs are then used as a shape vector and aligned using weighted Procrustes analysis, where the control points are weighted according to their consistency over the entire training

(a)   (b)

Fig. 6. Tracking failures using standard pseudorandom sampling. Dark - Highest probability state estimate; Light - Mean state estimate. The quasi-random tracker was successful using the same number of samples.

set. The dimensionality is then reduced by using Principal Component Analysis (PCA) to find an eight-dimensional space of deformations. Hence, the total dimension of x_t (the state variable) is 12 (4 for the Euclidean similarity parameters and 8 for the deformation parameters). We used $N = 2000$ samples and the tracker was initialized in the first frame of the sequence using the pedestrian detection algorithm described in [3]. We introduced 10% of random samples at every iteration to account for sudden changes in shape and motion. We applied the tracker to several Daimler-Chrysler pedestrian sequences and found that the quasi-random tracker was able to successfully track the pedestrians over the entire sequence. The tracker was also able to recover very quickly from failures due to sudden changes in shape or motion or to partial occlusion. On the other hand, the pseudo-random tracker was easily distracted by clutter and was unable to recover from some failures. Figure 6 shows some frames where the pseudo-random tracker drifts and fails. For the same sequences with the same sample size, the quasi-random tracker was able to track successfully. Figures 7 and 8 show the tracker output for two pedestrian sequences using the quasi-random tracker. In each frame, both the state estimate with the maximum probability and the mean state estimate are shown.

5 Conclusions

In this paper, we have addressed the problem of using the Condensation tracker for high-dimensional problems by incorporating quasi-Monte Carlo methods into the conventional algorithm. We have also addressed the problem of making the tracker work efficiently in situations where the motion models are unknown. The superiority of quasi-random sampling was demonstrated using both synthetic

146

Fig. 7. Tracking results for Daimler-Chrysler pedestrian sequence using quasi-random sampling. Dark - Highest probability state estimate; Light - Mean state estimate.

Fig. 8. Tracking results for Daimler-Chrysler pedestrian sequence using quasi-random sampling. Dark - Highest probability state estimate; Light - Mean state estimate.

and real data. Promising results on pedestrian tracking from a moving vehicle were obtained using these techniques.

Monte Carlo techniques are used in other areas of computer vision where there is a need for optimization or sampling. The use of quasi-random points can be readily extended to these areas and should result in improved efficiency or speed-up of algorithms.

Acknowledgements

The partial support of ONR grant N00014-95-1-0521 is gratefully acknowledged. The authors would also like to thank Azriel Rosenfeld, Dariu Gavrila, Michael Isard, Jens Rittscher and Fernando Le Torre for their useful suggestions and comments.

References

1. M. Isard and A. Blake. Contour tracking by stochastic propagation of conditional density. Proc. European Conf. on Computer Vision, pages 343-356, 1996.
2. M. Isard and A. Blake. ICONDENSATION: Unifying low-level and high-level tracking in a stochastic framework. Proc. European Conf. on Computer Vision, vol. 1, pp. 893-908, 1998.
3. D. Gavrila and V. Philomin. Real-time object detection for "smart" vehicles. Proc. IEEE International Conf. on Computer Vision, vol. 1, pp. 87-93, 1999.
4. D. Gavrila and V. Philomin. Real-time object detection using distance transforms. Proc. Intelligent Vehicles Conf., 1998.
5. M. Oren, C. Papageorgiou, P. Sinha, E. Osuna, and T. Poggio. Pedestrian detection using wavelet templates. Proc. IEEE International Conf. on Computer Vision, pp. 193-199, 1997.
6. A. Blake, B. North and M. Isard. Learning multi-class dynamics. *Advances in Neural Information Processing Systems* **11**, in press.
7. J. Rittscher and A. Blake. Classification of human body motion. Proc. IEEE International Conf. on Computer Vision, pp. 634-639, 1999.
8. W. H. Press, S. A. Teukolsky, W. T. Vetterling and B. P. Flannery. *Numerical Recipes: The Art of Scientific Computing.* 2nd Edition, Cambridge University Press, Cambridge, UK.
9. J. Carpenter, P. Clifford and P. Fearnhead. An improved particle filter for nonlinear problems. *IEE Proc. Radar, Sonar and Navigation* **146**, pp. 2-7, 1999.
10. H. Niederreiter. *Random Number Generation and Quasi-Monte Carlo Methods.* SIAM, Philadelphia, PA, 1992.
11. J. MacCormick and A. Blake. A probabilistic exclusion principle for tracking multiple objects. Proc. IEEE International Conf. on Computer Vision, vol. 1, pp. 572-578, 1999.
12. B. L. Fox. Algorithm 647: Implementation and relative efficiency of quasirandom sequence generators. *ACM Transactions on Mathematical Software* **12**, pp. 362-376, 1986.
13. P. Bratley and B. L. Fox. Algorithm 659: Implementing Sobol's quasirandom sequence generator. *ACM Transactions on Mathematical Software* **14**, pp. 88-100, 1988.

14. P. Bratley, B. L. Fox, and H. Niederreiter. Implementation and tests of low-discrepancy sequences. *ACM Transactions on Modeling and Computer Simulation* **2**, pp. 195-213, 1992.

15. W. J. Morokoff and R. E. Caflisch. Quasi-random sequences and their discrepancies. *SIAM J. Sci. Comput.* **15**, pp. 1251-1279, 1994.

16. P. Bratley, B. L. Fox, and H. Niederreiter. Algorithm 738: Programs to generate Niederreiter's low-discrepancy sequences. *ACM Transactions on Mathematical Software* **20**, pp. 494-495, 1994.

17. B. Moskowitz and R. E. Caflisch. Smoothness and dimension reduction in quasi-Monte Carlo methods. *Math. Comput. Modelling* **23**, pp. 37-54, 1996.

18. M. J. Black and A. D. Jepson. Recognizing temporal trajectories using the Condensation algorithm. Proc. IEEE International Conf. on Automatic Face and Gesture Recognition, 1998.

19. D. Reynard, A. Wildenberg, A. Blake and J. Merchant. Learning dynamics of complex motions from image sequences. Proc. European Conf. on Computer Vision, pp. 357-368, 1996.

20. B. North and A. Blake. Learning dynamical models using Expectation-Maximisation. Proc. IEEE International Conf. on Computer Vision, pp. 384-389, 1998.

21. L. Piegl and W. Tiller. *The NURBS Book.* Springer-Verlag, 1995.

22. T. F. Cootes, C. J. Taylor, A. Lanitis, D. H. Cooper, and J. Graham. Building and using flexible models incorporating grey-level information. Proc. IEEE International Conf. on Computer Vision, pp. 242-246, 1993.

23. A. Baumberg and D. C. Hogg. Learning flexible models from image sequences. Proc. European Conf. on Computer Vision, 1994.

Tracking Discontinuous Motion Using Bayesian Inference

Jamie Sherrah and Shaogang Gong

Queen Mary and Westfield College
Department of Computer Science
London E1 4NS UK
jamie|sgg@dcs.qmw.ac.uk

Abstract. Robustly tracking people in visual scenes is an important task for surveillance, human-computer interfaces and visually mediated interaction. Existing attempts at tracking a person's head and hands deal with ambiguity, uncertainty and noise by intrinsically assuming a consistently continuous visual stream and/or exploiting depth information. We present a method for tracking the head and hands of a human subject from a single view with no constraints on the continuity of motion. Hence the tracker is appropriate for real-time applications in which the availability of visual data is constrained, and motion is discontinuous. Rather than relying on spatio-temporal continuity and complex 3D models of the human body, a Bayesian Belief Network deduces the body part positions by fusing colour, motion and coarse intensity measurements with contextual semantics.

1 Introduction

Tracking human body parts and motion is a challenging but essential task for modelling, recognition and interpretation of human behaviour. In particular, tracking of at least the head and hands is required for gesture recognition in human-computer interface applications such as sign-language recognition. Existing methods for markerless tracking can be categorised according to the measurements and models used [9]. In terms of measurements, tracking usually relies on intensity information such as edges [10, 2, 17, 5], skin colour and/or motion segmentation [24, 14, 11, 16], or a combination of these with other cues including depth [13, 25, 19, 1]. The choice of model depends on the application of the tracker. If the tracker output is to be used for some recognition process then a 2D model of the body will suffice [16, 11]. On the other hand, a 3D model of the body may be required for generative purposes, to drive an avatar for example, in which case skeletal constraints can be exploited [25, 19, 5], or deformable 3D models can be matched to 2D images [10, 17].

Colour-based tracking of body parts is a relatively robust and inexpensive approach. Nevertheless the loss of information involved induces problems of noise, uncertainty, and ambiguity due to occlusion and distracting "skin-coloured" background objects. The two most difficult problems to deal with when tracking the head and hands are occlusion and correct hand association. Occlusion occurs when a hand passes in front of the face or intersects with the other hand. Hand association requires that the hands found in the current frame be matched correctly to the left and right hands. Most existing attempts at tracking cope with these problems using temporal prediction and/or depth information. Temporal prediction intrinsically assumes temporal order and continuity in measured data, therefore a consistent, sufficiently high frame rate is required. The use of depth information requires more than one camera and solution of the correspondence problem which is computationally non-trivial.

We argue that robust, real-time human tracking systems must be designed to work with a source of *discontinuous visual information*. Any vision system operates under constraints that attenuate the bandwidth of visual input. In some cases the data may simply be unavailable, in other cases computation time is limited due to finite resources. A further and more significant computational constraint is associated with complexity and stability of behavioural models. Exhaustive modelling of the world would be prohibitively complex; rather it is more realistic to establish economical models or *beliefs* about the environment which are iteratively updated by visual observations. Since the models are not exhaustive, not all visual information requires processing. In fact, it may be undesirable to absorb all available visual information into belief structures because instability, or "catastrophic unlearning", may result. Therefore a robust vision system should be based on selective attention to filter out irrelevant information and use only salient visual stimuli to update its beliefs [23]. While selective attention is traditionally considered in the spatial domain, in this work we cast the notion into the temporal domain in order to relax the underlying constraint of temporal order and continuity required in tracking visual events over time.

We achieve the goal of tracking discontinuous human body motion by replacing the problem of spatio-temporal prediction with reasoning about body-part associations based on contextual knowledge. Our approach uses *Bayesian Belief Networks* (BBNs) to fuse high-level contextual knowledge with sensor-level observations. Belief networks are an effective vehicle for combining user-supplied semantics with conflicting and noisy observations to deduce an overall consistent interpretation of the scene. BBNs have been used previously as a framework for tracking multiple vehicles under occlusion using contextual information [4]. In [18], a naive BBN was used to characterise and classify objects in a visual scene. For tracking body parts under discontinuous motion the BBN framework is ideal because unlike other tracking methods such as Kalman filtering or CONDENSATION [12] that explicitly model the dynamics through change, Belief Networks model absolute relationships between variables and can make deductive leaps given limited but significant evidence. Nevertheless, the accumulated beliefs still implicitly reflect all currently observed evidence over time. We demonstrate that through iterative revision of hypotheses about associations of hands with skin-coloured image regions, such an *atemporal belief-based tracker* is able to recover from almost any form of track loss. In Section 2 we describe the context, assumptions and measurements used by the body tracker. In Section

3 we present the framework for combining these observations with contextual knowledge using BBNs. An experimental comparison of our tracker with a dynamic tracker and a non-contextual tracker is presented in Section 4, and the conclusion is given in Section 5.

2   Tracking Discontinuous Motion from 2D Observations

The merits of any given behavioural modelling method are established according to the purpose for which it is used, therefore it is appropriate at this point to introduce the context for our tracking approach and the assumptions made. We are interested in modelling individual and group behaviours for visually mediated interaction using only a single 2D view, therefore depth information is unavailable. Behaviour models are used to interpret activities in the scene and change the view to focus on regions of interest. Therefore we have the luxury of not requiring full 3D tracking of the human body parts, which would rely on expensive matching to unreliable intensity observations. On the other hand, the system is required to simultaneously track several people which generally results in a variable and relatively low frame rate. From our experience with these conditions, a person's hand, for example, can often move from rest to a distance half the length of their body between one frame and the next! Also, in images of manageable resolution containing several people (all images used in this work are 320×240 pixels), the hands may occupy regions as small as ten pixels or less wide, making appearance-based methods unreliable.

To illustrate the nature of the discontinuous body motions under these conditions, Figure 1 shows the head and hands positions and accelerations (as vectors) for two video sequences, along with sample frames. The video frames were samples at 18 frames per second (fps). Even so, there are many significant temporal changes in both the magnitude and orientation of the acceleration of the hands. It may be unrealistic to attempt to model the dynamics of the body under these circumstances. We propose that under the following assumptions, the ambiguities and uncertainties associated with tracking a person's discontinuous head and hand movement can be overcome using only information from a single 2D view without modelling the full dynamics of the human body:

1. the subject is oriented roughly towards the camera for most of the time.
2. the subject is wearing long sleeves.
3. reasonably good colour segmentation of the head and hands is possible, and
4. the head and hands are the largest moving skin colour clusters in the image.

The robust visual cues used for tracking are now described, followed by a description of the head-tracking and bootstrapping methods.

2.1   Computing Visual Cues

Real-time vision systems have two chief practical requirements: computational efficiency and robustness. Computational constraints exclude the use of expensive optimisation methods, while robustness requires tolerance of assumption

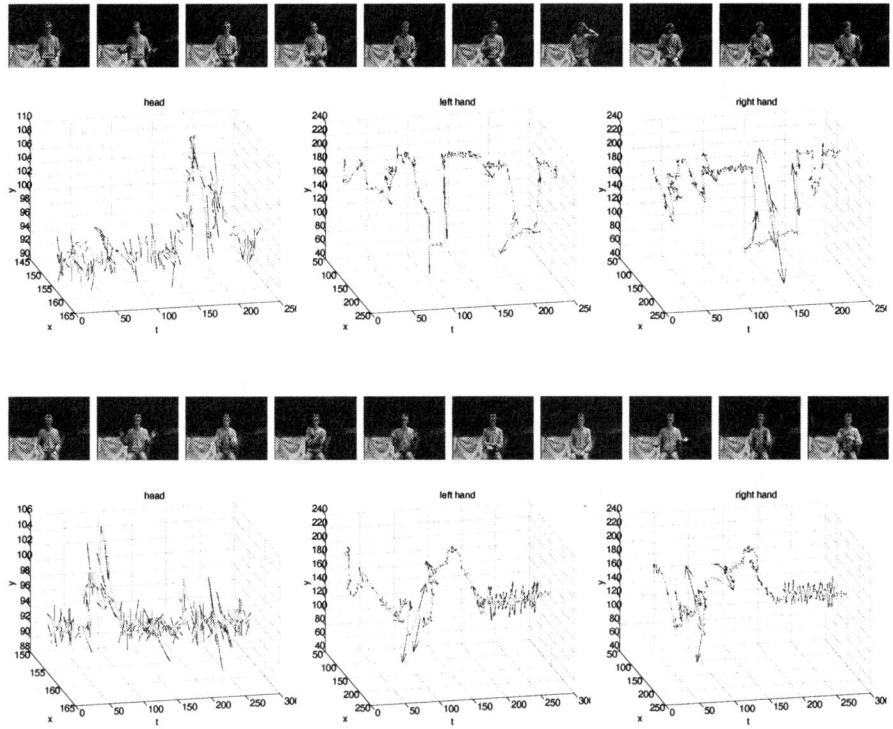

Fig. 1. Two examples of behaviour sequences and their tracked head and hand positions and accelerations. At each time frame, the 2D acceleration is shown as an arrow with arrowhead size proportional to the acceleration magnitude. From left to right, the plots correspond to the head, left hand and right hand.

violation. To meet these requirements we adopt a philosophy of perceptual fusion: independent, relatively inexpensive visual cues are combined to benefit from their mutual strengths and achieve some invariance to their assumptions [7]. The cues that are used to drive our body tracker are skin colour, image motion and coarse intensity information, namely hand orientation. Pixel-wise skin colour probability has been previously shown to be a robust and inexpensive visual cue for identification and tracking of people under varying lighting conditions [22]. Skin colour probabilities can be computed for an image and thresholded to obtain a binary skin image, an example is shown in Figure 2(b). Here image motion is naively computed as the thresholded difference between pixel intensities in successive frames; an example is shown in Figure 2(c).

Skin colour and motion are natural cues for focusing attention and processing resources on salient regions in the image. Note that although distracting noise and background clusters appear in the skin image, these can be eliminated at a low level by "AND"ing directly with motion information. However, fusion of these cues at this low level of processing is premature due to loss of information.

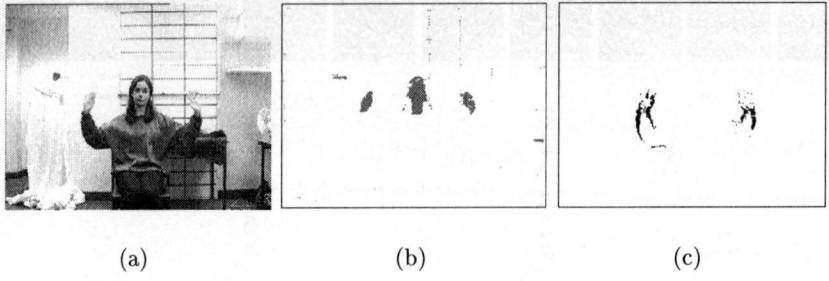

(a)   (b)   (c)

Fig. 2. Example of visual cues measured from video stream. (a) original image; (b) binary skin colour image; and (c) binary motion image.

The problem of associating the correct hands over time can usually be solved using spatial constraints. However, situations arise under occlusion in which choosing the nearest skin-coloured cluster to the previous hand position results in incorrect hand assignment. Therefore the problem cannot be solved purely using colour and motion information. In the absence of depth information or 3D skeletal constraints, we use intensity information to assist in resolving incorrect assignment. The intensity image of each hand is used to obtain a very coarse measurement of hand orientation which is robust even in low resolution imagery. The restricted kinematics of the human body are loosely modelled to exploit the fact that only certain hand orientations are likely at any position in the image relative to the head.

The accumulation of a statistical hand orientation model is illustrated in Figure 3. Assuming that the subject is facing the camera, the image is divided coarsely into a grid of histogram bins. We then artificially synthesise a histogram of likely hand orientations for each 2D position of the hand in the image projection relative to the head position. To do this, a 3D model of the human body is used to exhaustively sample the range of possible arm joint angles in up-right posture. Assuming that the hand extends parallel to the forearm, the 2D projection is made to obtain the appearance of hand orientation and position in the image plane, and the corresponding histogram bin is updated. During tracking, the quantised hand orientation is obtained according to the maximum response from a bank of oriented Gabor filters, and the tracked hand position relative to the tracked head position is used to index the histogram and obtain the likelihood of the hand orientation given the position.

2.2 Head Tracking using Mean Shift

The first two constraints to be exploited are that the head is generally larger than the hands in the image, and that head movement is significantly more stable and moderate than hand motion. We track the head directly using an iterated

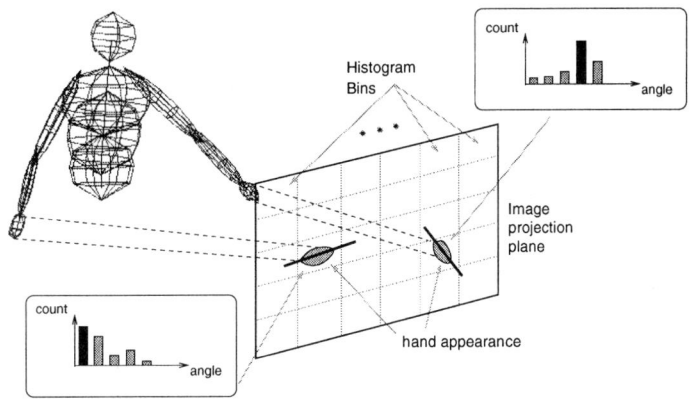

Fig. 3. Schematic diagram of the hand orientation histogram process.

mean shift algorithm [3]. This method converges on the local mode of the skin probability distribution. Despite its simplicity, the algorithm is very robust to occlusion by hands. The head is modelled as a rectangular region containing skin pixels. A search region is defined such that it is centred on the head box but is slightly larger. Given an initial/previous position $(c_x(t), c_y(t))$, the algorithm is to iteratively calculate the spatial mean of skin pixels in the rectangular search region and shift the box to be centred on that estimated mean until it converges, as expounded in Figure 4.

```
loop:
  − c_x(t − 1) = c_x(t),  c_y(t − 1) = c_y(t)
  − c_x(t) = (1/n_skin) Σ_{p∈S} p_x
    c_y(t) = (1/n_skin) Σ_{p∈S} p_y
    where p = (p_x, p_y) is a pixel, S is the set of skin pixels in
    the search region and n_skin = |S|.
  − Set search region centre to (c_x(t), c_y(t)).
until c_x(t) = c_x(t − 1) and c_y(t) = c_y(t − 1).
```

Fig. 4. The mean shift algorithm for tracking the head box.

After convergence, the size of the head box is set according to the following heuristic:

$$w = \sqrt{n_{skin}} \tag{1}$$

$$h = 1.2w \qquad\qquad (2)$$

Note that the search region must be slightly larger than the head rectangle to avoid continual shrinking of the box, and to allow significant movement of the head without loss of track.

2.3 Local Skin Colour Clusters

Under the assumption that the head and hands form the largest moving connected skin coloured regions in the image, tracking the hands reduces to matching the previous hand estimate to the skin clusters in the current frame. This association can be performed either at the pixel level or at a "cluster" level. At the pixel level, hands are tracked using local search via updating of spatial hand box means and variances (size). At the cluster level, a connected components algorithm is used to find all spatially connected sets of coloured pixels, which are subsequently treated as discrete entities. We have chosen to use the cluster representation for three reasons:

- The pixel-level approach requires estimation of spatial means and variances of pixels which are quite sensitive to outliers. Even if medians are used instead of means, the hand box sizes are very sensitive to noise.
- The local tracking approach requires heuristic search parameters, and is generally invalid for discontinuous motion since the hands may move a significant distance from one frame to the next.
- Reasoning about hand associations is easier using the higher-level cluster representation.

We used a connected components algorithm that has computational complexity linear in the number of skin pixels to obtain a list of skin clusters in the current frame. The components are drawn only from those portions of the region outside of an exclusion region defined by the head tracker box. The exclusion region is slightly larger than the head box due to protruding necklines or ears that can be mistaken for potential hand clusters. Clusters containing only a few pixels are assumed to be noise and removed. Finally the clusters are sorted in descending order of their skin pixel count for subsequent use.

2.4 Initialisation

Tracking is initialised by using skin colour to focus on areas of interest, then performing a multi-scale, multi-position identity-independent face search within these regions using a Support Vector Machine (SVM) [20]. An example is shown in Figure 5. The SVM has been trained only on frontal and near-frontal faces, so it is assumed that the subject is initially facing approximately towards the camera. The mean shift head tracker is then initialised on the detected face region. Since the hands tracker only uses temporal association as a secondary cue, full tracking of the body can begin immediately after this partial initialisation.

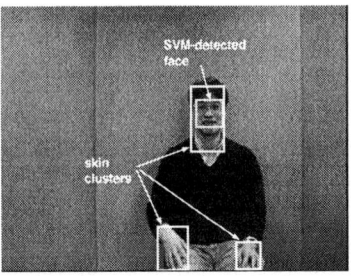

Fig. 5. Example of the tracker initialisation using an SVM.

3 Reasoning about Body-Parts Association using Bayesian Inference

Given only the visual cues described in the previous section, the problem is now to determine the association of skin colour clusters to the left and right hands. One can consider this situation to be equivalent to watching a mime artist wearing a white face mask and white gloves in black clothing and a black background (see Figure 2(b)). Further, only discontinuous information is available as though a strobe light were operating, creating a "jerky" effect (see Figure 6(a)). Under these conditions explicit modelling of body dynamics inevitably makes too strong an assumption about image data. Rather, the tracking can be performed better and more robustly through a process of deduction. This requires full exploitation of both visual cues and high-level contextual knowledge. For instance, we know that at any given time a hand is either (1) associated with a skin colour cluster, or (2) it occludes the face (and is therefore "invisible" using only skin colour) as in Figures 6(b) and 6(c), or (3) it has disappeared from the image as in Figure 6(d). When considering both hands, the possibility arises that both hands are associated with the same skin colour cluster, as when one clasps the hands together for example, shown in Figure 6(e).

Clearly a mechanism is required for reasoning about the situation. In the next section, Bayesian Belief Networks (BBNs) are introduced as a mechanism for performing inference, after which we describe how BBNs have been applied to our tracking problem.

3.1 Bayesian Belief Networks

The obvious method of incorporating semantics into our tracking problem would be through a fixed set of rules. However there are two unpleasantries associated with this approach: brittleness and global lack of consistency. Hard rule-bases are notoriously sensitive to noise because once a decision has been made based on some fixed threshold, subsequent decision-making is isolated from the contending unchosen possibilities. Sensitivity to noise is undesirable in our situation since we are dealing with very noisy and uncertain image data. The rule-based approach can also suffer from global consistency problems because commitment to a single decision precludes feedback of higher-level knowledge to refine lower-level uncertain observations or beliefs.

An alternative approach to reasoning is based on soft, probabilistic decisions. Under such a framework all hypotheses are considered to some degree but with an associated probability. Bayesian Belief Networks provide a rigorous framework for combining semantic and sensor-level reasoning under conditions of uncertainty [21, 8]. Given a set of variables $\mathbf{W}$ representing the scenario[1], the assumption is that all our knowledge of the current state of affairs is encoded in the joint distribution of the variables conditioned on the existing evidence, $P(\mathbf{w}|\mathbf{e})$. Explicit modelling of this distribution is unintuitive and often infeasible. Instead, conditional independencies between variables can be exploited to sparsely specify the joint distribution in terms of more tangible conditional distributions between variables.

A BBN is a directed acyclic graph that explicitly defines the statistical (or "causal") dependencies between all variables[2]. These dependencies are known a

---

[1] Regarding notation, upper-case is used to denote a random variable, lower-case to denote its instantiation, and boldface is used to represent sets of variables.
[2] Therefore the statistical independencies are implicitly defined as well.

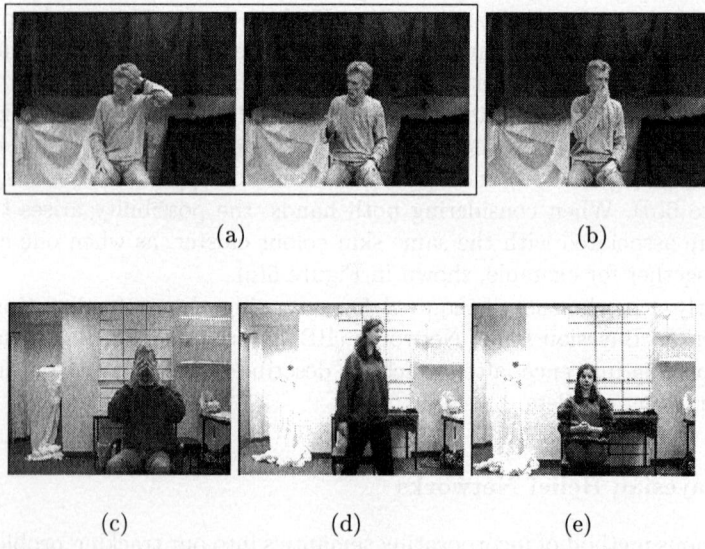

Fig. 6. Examples of the difficulties associated with tracking the body. (a) motion is discontinuous between frames; (b) one hand occludes the face; (c) both hands occlude the face; (d) a hand is invisible in the image; and (e) the hands occlude each other.

priori and used to create the network architecture. Nodes in the network represent random variables, while directed links point from conditioning to dependent variables. For a link between two variables, $X \rightarrow Y$, the distribution $P(y|x)$ in the absence of evidence must be specified beforehand from contextual knowledge. As evidence is presented to the network over time through variable instantiation, a set of beliefs are established which reflect both prior and observed information:

$$BEL(x) = P(x|e) \tag{3}$$

where $BEL(x)$ is the belief in the value of variable X given the evidence $\mathbf{e}$. Updating of beliefs occurs through a distributed message-passing process that is made possible via exploitation of local dependencies and global independencies. Hence dissemination of evidence to update currently-held beliefs can be performed in a tractable manner to arrive at a globally consistent evaluation of the situation.

A BBN can subsequently be used for prediction and queries regarding values of single variables given current evidence. However, if the most probable joint configuration of several variables given the evidence is required, then a process of *belief revision*[3] (as opposed to belief updating) must be applied to obtain the most probable explanation of the evidence at hand, $\mathbf{w}^*$, defined by the following criterion:

$$P(\mathbf{w}^*|\mathbf{e}) = \overset{\max}{\mathbf{w}} \ P(\mathbf{w}|\mathbf{e}) \tag{4}$$

where $\mathbf{w}$ is any instantiation of the variables $\mathbf{W}$ consistent with the evidence $\mathbf{e}$, termed an *explanation* or *extension* of $\mathbf{e}$, and $\mathbf{w}^*$ is the most probable explanation/extension. This corresponds to the locally-computed function expressing the local belief in the extension:

$$BEL^*(x) = \overset{\max}{\mathbf{w}'_X} \ P(x, \mathbf{w}'_X|\mathbf{e}) \tag{5}$$

where $\mathbf{W}'_X = \mathbf{W} - X$.

3.2 Tracking by Inference

The BBN for tracking hands is shown in Figure 7. Abbreviations are: LH = left hand, RH = right hand, LS = left shoulder, RS = right shoulder, B1 = skin cluster 1, B2 = skin cluster 2. There are 19 variables, $\mathbf{W} = \{X_1, X_2, \ldots, X_{19}\}$. The first point to note is that some of the variables are conceptual, namely X_1, X_2, X_5 and X_9, while the remaining variables correspond to image-measurable quantities, $\mathbf{e} = \{X_3, X_4, X_6, X_7, X_8, X_{10}, \ldots, X_{19}\}$. All quantities in the network are or have been transformed to discrete variables. The conditional probability distributions attributed to each variable in the network are specified beforehand using either domain knowledge or statistical sampling. At each time step, all of the measurement variables are instantiated from observations. B1 and B2 refer

---

[3] The difference between belief updating and belief revision comes about because in general, the values for variables X and Y that maximise their joint distribution are not the values that maximise their individual marginal distributions.

to the two largest skin clusters in the image (apart from the head), obtained as per Section 2.3. Absence of clusters is handled by setting the variables X_5 and X_9 to have zero probability of being a hand. The localised belief revision method is then employed until the network stabilises and the most probable joint explanation of the observations is obtained:

$$P(\mathbf{w}^* | \{x_3, x_4, x_6, x_7, x_8, x_{10}, \ldots, x_{19}\}) = \overset{\max}{\mathbf{w}} \ P(\mathbf{w} | \{x_3, x_4, x_6, x_7, x_8, x_{10}, \ldots, x_{19}\}) \tag{6}$$

This yields the most likely joint values of X_1 and X_2, which can be used to set the left and hand box position.

Note that the network structure is not singly connected, due to the loops formed through X_1 and X_2. Consequently the simple belief revision algorithm of Pearl [21] cannot be used due to non-convergence. Instead, we apply the more general inference algorithm of Lauritzen and Spiegelhalter [15, 6, 8]. This inference method transforms the network to a *join tree*, each node of which contains a sub-set of variables called a *clique*. The transformation to the join tree needs to be performed only once off-line. Inference then proceeds on the join tree via a message-passing mechanism similar to the method proposed by Pearl. The complexity of the propagation algorithm is proportional to the span of the join tree and the largest state space size amongst the cliques. The variables and their dependencies are now explained as follows.

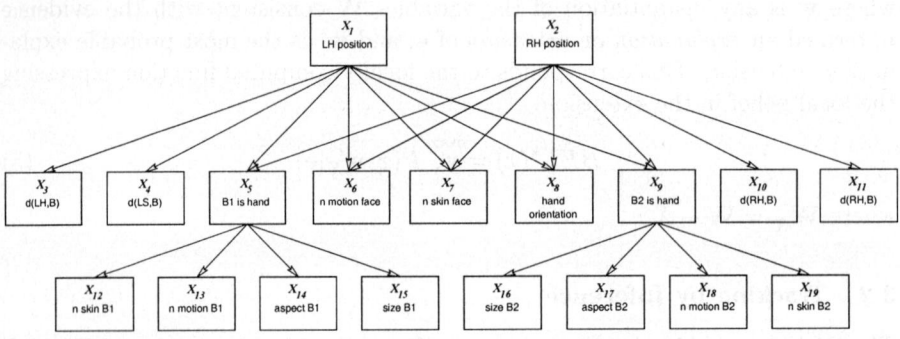

Fig. 7. A Bayesian Belief Network representing dependencies amongst variables in the human body-parts tracking scenario.

X_1 **and** X_2**:** the primary hypotheses regarding the left and right hand positions respectively. These variables are discrete with values {CLUSTER1, CLUSTER2, HEAD} which represent skin cluster 1, skin cluster 2 and occlusion of the head respectively. Note that disappearance of the hands is not modelled here for simplicity.

X_3**;** X_{10}**:** the distance in pixels of the previous left/right-hand box position from the currently hypothesised cluster. The dependency imposes a weak spatiotemporal constraint that hands are more likely to have moved a small distance than a large distance from one frame to the next.

X_4; X_{11}: the distance in pixels of the hypothesised cluster from the left/right shoulder. The shoulder position is estimated from the tracked head box. This dependency specifies that the hypothesised cluster should lie within a certain distance of the shoulder as defined by the length of the arm.

X_5, X_{12}, X_{13}, X_{14}, X_{15}; X_9, X_{16}, X_{17}, X_{18}, X_{19}: these variables determine whether each cluster is a hand. X_5 and X_9 are boolean variables specifying whether or not their respective clusters are hands or noise. The variables have an obvious dependency on X_1 and X_2: if either hand is a cluster, then that cluster must be a hand. The descendants of X_5 and X_9 provide evidence that the clusters are hands. X_{12} and X_{19} are the number of skin pixels in each cluster, which have some distribution depending on whether or not the cluster is a hand. X_{13} and X_{18} are the number of motion pixels in each cluster, expected to be high if the cluster is a hand. Note that these values can still be non-zero for non-hands due to shadows, highlights and noise on skin-coloured background objects. X_{14} and X_{17} are the aspect ratios of the clusters which will have a certain distribution if the cluster is a hand, but no constraints if the cluster is not a hand. X_{15} and X_{16} are the spatial areas of the enclosing rectangles of the clusters. For hands, these values have a distribution in terms relative to the size of the head box, but for non-hands there are no expectations.

X_6 and X_7: the number of moving pixels and number of skin-coloured pixels in the head exclusion box respectively. If either of the hands is hypothesised to occlude the head, we expect more skin pixels and some motion.

X_8: orientation of the respective hand, which depends to some extent on its spatial position in the screen relative to the head box. This orientation is calculated for each hypothesised hand position, and the histogram described in Section 2.1 is used to assign a conditional probability.

Under this framework, all of the visual cues can be considered *simultaneously* and consistently to arrive at a most probable explanation for the positions of both hands. BBNs lend the benefit of being able to "explain away" evidence, which can be of use in our network. For example, if the belief that the right hand occludes the face increases, this decreases the belief that the left hand also occludes the face because it explains any motion of growth in the number of skin pixels in the head region. This comes about through the indirect coupling of the hypotheses X_1 and X_2 and the fixed amount of probability attributable to any single piece of evidence. Hence probabilities are consistent and evidence is not "double counted" [21].

4 Experimental Evaluation

An experimental evaluation of the atemporal belief-based tracker is now presented. First, examples of the tracker's behaviour are given, then a comparison is performed between the BBN tracker and two other tracking methods. Note that to make our point about the difficulty of discontinuous motion more poignant, we captured all video data at a relatively high frame rate of 18 fps and used off-line processing.

4.1 Tracker Performance Examples

Selected frames from four different video sequences consisting of 141 to 367 frames per sequence are shown in Figure 8. Each sub-figure shows frames from one sequence temporally ordered from left to right, top to bottom. It is important to note that the frames are not consecutive. In each image a box frames the head and each of the two hands. The hand boxes are labelled left and right, showing the correct assignments. In the first example, Figure 8(a), the hands are accurately tracked before, during and after mutual occlusion. In Figure 8(b), typical coughing and nose-scratching movements bring about occlusion of the head by a single hand. In this sequence the two frames marked with "A" are adjacent frames, exhibiting the significant motion discontinuity that can be encountered. Although the frame rate was high, this discontinuity came about due to disk swapping during video capture. Nevertheless the tracker was able to correctly follow the hands. In Figure 8(c) the subject undergoes significant whole body motion to ensure that the tracker works while the head is constantly moving. With the hands alternately occluding each other and the face in a tumbling action, the tracker is still able to follow the body parts. In the third-to-last frame both hands simultaneously occlude the face. The example of Figure 8(d) has the subject partially leaving the screen twice to fetch and then offer a book. Note that in the frames marked "M" one hand is not visible in the image. Since this case is not explicitly modelled by the tracker, occlusion with the head or the other hand is deduced. After these periods of disappearance, the hand is once again accurately tracked.

4.2 Comparison with Dynamic and Non-Contextual Trackers

We compared the atemporal belief-based tracker experimentally with two other tracking methods:

dynamic: assuming temporal continuity exists between frames over time and linear dynamics, this method uses Kalman filters for each body part to match boxes at the pixel level between frames.

non-contextual: similar to the belief-based method, this method assumes temporal continuity but does not attempt to model the dynamics of the body parts. The method matches skin clusters based only on spatial association without the use of high-level knowledge.

It is difficult to compare the tracking methods fairly in this context. Comparison of the average deviation from the true hand and head positions would be misleading because of the all-or-nothing nature of matching to discrete clusters.

163

Fig. 8. Examples of discontinuous motion tracking.

Another possible criterion is the number of frames until loss-of-track, but this is somewhat unfair since a tracker may lose lock at the start of the sequence and then regain it for the rest of the sequence. The criterion we chose for comparison is the total number of frames on which at least one body part was incorrectly tracked, or the hands were mismatched. The comparison was performed on 14 sequences containing two different people totalling 3300 frames.

Table 1 shows the number of frames incorrectly tracked by each method, in absolute terms and as a percentage of the total number of frames. The belief-based tracker performs significantly better than the other two methods, even though the data was captured at a high frame rate. Therefore the benefits of using contextual knowledge to track discontinuous motion by inference rather than temporal continuity are significant. One would expect even better improvements if low frame-rate data were used. The most common failure modes for the belief-based and non-contextual trackers were incorrect assignment of the left and right hands to clusters, and locking on to background noise when one hand was occluded. The dynamic tracker often failed due to inaccurate temporal prediction of the hand position. Two examples of this failure are shown in consecutive frames in Figure 9. Although one could use more sophisticated dynamic models, it is very unlikely they will ever be able to feasibly capture the full gamut of human behaviour, let alone accurately predict under heavily discontinuous motion. For example, the body-parts tracker in [25] switches in appropriate high-level models of behaviour for improved tracking, but the computational cost increases with the number of possible behaviours modelled. In terms of processing speed, all trackers had approximately the same performance. The average frame rate was about 4 fps on a PII 330 using 320x240 images.

method	incorrect frames	
	number	%
belief-based	439	13
dynamic	728	22
non-contextual	995	30

Table 1. Comparative results of the three tracking methods.

5 Conclusion

Observations of body motion in real-time systems can often be jerky and discontinuous. Contextual knowledge can be used to overcome ambiguities and uncertainties in measurement. We have presented a method for tracking discontinuous motion of multiple occluding body parts of an individual from a single 2D view. Rather than modelling spatio-temporal dynamics, tracking is performed by reasoning about the observations using a Bayesian Belief Network. The BBN

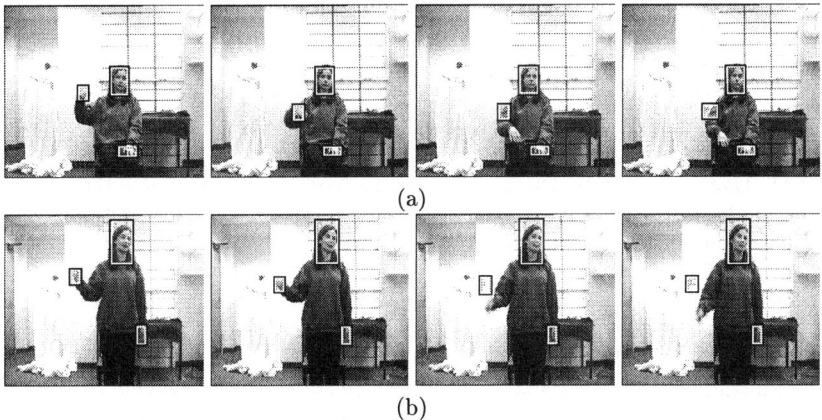

(a)

(b)

Fig. 9. Two examples of the failure of the dynamic Kalman filter tracker.

framework performs bottom-up and top-down message passing to fuse both conceptual and sensor-level quantities in a consistent manner. Hence the visual cues of skin colour, image motion and local intensity orientation are fused with contextual knowledge of the human body. The inference-based tracker was tested and compared with dynamic and non-contextual approaches. The results indicate that fusion of all available information at all levels significantly improves the robustness and consistency of tracking.

We wish to extend this work in two ways. First, the tracker can be made adaptive so that no parameters need to be changed when different people are tracked. Second, the current tracker assumes that there is only one person in the field of view, but we wish to use the tracker in scenes containing several people. We will investigate how trackers can be instantiated as people enter the scene, and how the tracker networks can be causally coupled so that skin clusters can be explained away by one network and not considered by the other networks.

References

1. Y. Azoz, L. Devi, and R. Sharma. Tracking hand dynamics in unconstrained environments. In *Proc. 3rd IEEE Int. Conf. on Automatic Face and Gesture Recognition*, pages 247–279, Japan, 1998.
2. Andrew Blake and Michael Isard. *Active Contours*. Springer-Verlag, 1998.
3. Gary R. Bradski. Computer vision face tracking for use in a perceptual user interface. *Intel Technology Journal*, 2nd Quarter, 1998.
4. Hilary Buxton and Shaogang Gong. Visual surveillance in a dynamic and uncertain world. *Artificial Intelligence*, 78:431–459, 1995.
5. T. Cham and J. Rehg. Dynamic feature ordering for efficient registration. In *IEEE Int. Conf. on Computer Vision*, volume 2, pages 1084–1091, Greece, Sept. 1999.
6. E. Charniak. Bayesian networks without tears. *AI Magazine*, 12(4):50–63, 1991.

7. James J. Clark and Alan L. Yuille. *Data Fusion for Sensory Information Processing Systems*. Kluwer Academic Publishers, 1990.

8. Robert G. Cowell, A. Philip Dawid, Steffen L. Lauritzen, and David J. Spiegelhalter. *Probabilistic Networks and Expert Systems*. Springer-Verlag, NY, 1999.

9. D. M. Gavrila. The visual analysis of human movement - a survey. *Computer Vision and Image Understanding*, 73(1), 1999.

10. D.M. Gavrila and L.S. Davis. 3-D model-based tracking of human motion in action. In *Proceedings of the IEEE Conference on Computer Vision and Pattern Recognition*, pages 73–80, 1996.

11. Kazuyuki Imagawa, Shan Lu, and Seiji Igi. Color-based hands tracking system for sign language recognition. In *Proc. 3rd IEEE Int. Conf. on Automatic Face and Gesture Recognition*, pages 462–467, Nara, Japan, 1998.

12. M. Isard and A. Blake. CONDENSATION – conditional density propagation for visual tracking. *International Journal of Computer Vision*, 29(1):5–28, 1998.

13. C. Jennings. Robust finger tracking with multiple cameras. In *Proc. of Int. Workshop on Recognition, Analysis and Tracking of Faces and Gestures in Real-Time Systems*, pages 152–160, Corfu, Greece, September 1999. IEEE Computer Society.

14. N. Jojic, M. Turk, and T. Huang. Tracking self-occluding articulated objects in dense disparity maps. In *IEEE Int. Conf. on Computer Vision*, volume 1, pages 123–130, Greece, Sept. 1999.

15. S. Lauritzen and D. Spiegelhalter. Local computations with probabilities on graphical structures and their application to expert systems. In G. Shafer and J. Pearl, editors, *Readings in Uncertain Reasoning*, pages 415–448. Morgan Kauffmann, 1990.

16. J. Martin, V. Devin, and J. Crowley. Active hand tracking. In *Proc. 3rd IEEE Int. Conf. on Automatic Face and Gesture Recognition*, pages 573–578, Japan, 1998.

17. D. Metaxas. Deformable model and HMM-based tracking, analysis and recognition of gestures and faces. In *Proc. of Int. Workshop on Recognition, Analysis and Tracking of Faces and Gestures in Real-Time Systems*, pages 136–140, Greece, Sept. 1999. IEEE Computer Society.

18. Darnell J. Moore, Irfan A. Essa, and Monson H. Hayes III. Exploiting human actions and object context for recognition tasks. In *IEEE International Conference on Computer Vision*, volume 1, pages 80–86, Corfu, Greece, September 1999.

19. Eng-Jon Ong and Shaogang Gong. A dynamic human model using hybrid 2D-3D representations in hierarchical PCA space. In *British Machine Vision Conference*, volume 1, pages 33–42, Nottingham, UK, September 1999. BMVA.

20. E. Osuna, R. Freund, and F. Girosi. Training support vector machines: An application to face detection. In *IEEE Conference on Computer Vision and Pattern Recognition*, pages 130–136, 1997.

21. Judea Pearl. *Probabilistic Reasoning in Intelligent Systems: Networks of Plausible Inference*. Morgan Kaufmann, San Mateo, CA, 1988.

22. Y. Raja, S. J. McKenna, and S. Gong. Tracking and segmenting people in varying lighting conditions using colour. In *Proc. 3rd IEEE Int. Conf. on Automatic Face and Gesture Recognition*, pages 228–233, Nara, Japan, 1998.

23. Herbert Simon. Rational choice and the structure of the environment. *Psychological Review*, 63:129–138, 1956.

24. C. Wren, A. Azarbayejani, T. Darrell, and A. Pentland. Pfinder: Real-time tracking of the human body. *IEEE Trans. on PAMI*, 19(7):780–785, July 1997.

25. C. Wren and A. Pentland. Understanding purposeful human motion. In *IEEE Int. Workshop on Modelling People*, pages 19–25, Corfu, Greece, September 1999.

Direction Control for an Active Docking Behaviour Based on the Rotational Component of Log-Polar Optic Flow

Nick Barnes[1] and Giulio Sandini[2]

[1] Computer Vision and Machine Intelligence Lab (CVMIL),
Department of Computer Science and Software Engineering,
University of Melbourne, Victoria, 3010, AUSTRALIA
nmb@cs.mu.oz.au
[2] Laboratory for Integrated Advanced Robotics (LIRA-Lab),
Department of Communication Computer and Systems Science,
University of Genova, Via Opera Pia, 13, Genova, 16145, ITALY
sandini@dist.unige.it

Abstract. Docking is a fundamental requirement for a mobile robot in order to be able to interact with objects in its environment. In this paper we present an algorithm and implementation for a special case of the docking problem for ground-based robots. We require the robot to dock with a fixated environment point where only visual information is available. Specifically, camera pan/tilt information is unknown, as is the direction of motion with respect to the object and the robot's velocity. Further, camera calibration is unavailable. The aim is to minimise the difference between the camera optical axis and the robot heading direction. This constitutes a behaviour for controlling robot direction based on fixation. This paper presents a full mathematical derivation of the method and implementation used. In its most general form, the method requires partial segmentation of the optical flow field. The experiments presented, however, assume partial knowledge as to whether points are closer to the camera than the fixation point or further away. There are many scenarios in robotic navigation where such assumptions are typical working conditions. We examine two cases: convex objects; and distant background/floor. The solution presented uses only the rotational component of optical flow from a log-polar sensor. Results are presented with real image and ray-traced image sequences. The robot is controlled based on a single component of optical flow over a small portion of the image, and thus is suited to real-time implementation.

Keywords: Active vision and real-time vision, vision-guided mobile robots, and docking.

1   Introduction

Docking is a fundamental requirement for a mobile robot to interact with objects in its environment. In order to perform operations such manipulation (e.g.

autonomous fork-lifts [8]), or industrial assembly [12, 9], a mobile robot must be able to dock. In this paper, we present the derivation and implementation of an active behaviour for controlling robot heading direction to support docking with a fixated environment point. Only visual information is required (i.e. pan/tilt information, and robot's heading direction and velocity are unknown). Further, camera calibration is not required. This method does not require knowledge of the object, other than a constraint on the distribution of the depth of points relative to the fixation point. Previously, we demonstrated that it was sufficient that the object be convex and centred in the image, or that the majority of background points be behind the fixated object [2]. This method can be used as a behaviour that is independent of fixation and high-level planning. The robot need only fixate on a point in the desired heading direction and invoke the behaviour, and then the robot will turn as required. This is elegant from an architectural viewpoint for general docking, but also facilitates systems where fixation is entirely separate from platform control. For example, consider a situation where fixation is controlled by a human operator with a camera attached to a head-set and no information is available about the head-set position.

This research will be integrated with our existing mobile robot system for circumnavigation [3], which uniquely identifies objects and moves around them. Integration of docking will facilitate close inspection and manipulation.

Fixation systems control camera direction to keep the projection of a scene point that is moving relative to the camera in a fixed position in the image. Fixation is fundamental to active vision, and as such there are many approaches available (e.g. [15, 16]). Fixation can be used to facilitate perception of general motion [7]. Research with human subjects has shown that pedestrians can use fixation to gain information about their instantaneous heading direction [6].

Docking is a difficult problem, that is often handled with hardware solutions such as tactile sensors [13], or by using extensive knowledge about the visual properties of the object and camera [1, 3, 13]. Santos-Victor and Sandini [18] present an active approach to docking for a mobile robot that corrects heading direction, however, this assumes that the docking surface is planar.

2 The Log-Polar Sensor

Schwartz [19, 20] derived an analytical formulation of biological vision systems based on experimental measures of the mapping from the retina to the visual cortex of monkeys. Visual data is transformed from the retinal plane in polar coordinates (ρ, θ) to log-polar Cartesian coordinates (ξ, γ) in the cortical plane. The relation can be expressed:

$$\xi = log_a \frac{\rho}{\rho_0}, \gamma = q\eta, \tag{1}$$

where (ρ, η) are the polar coordinates of a point on the retinal plane and ρ_0, q, and a are constants determined by the physical layout of the sensor. Thus,

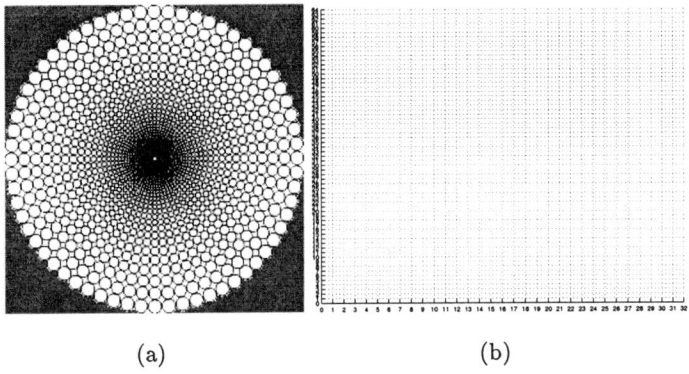

Fig. 1. The log-polar sensor samples 64 evenly spaced angles, at 32 radii. The sensing elements increase in size toward the periphery. (a) sensor geometry; (b) image geometry.

sensing elements appear in a non-uniform distribution, with a high density at the central fovea, and continuously decreasing density toward the periphery.

A CMOS implementation simulating this type of sensor has been realised [14]. Figure 1 shows a log-polar image and its Cartesian reconstruction, illustrating the high-resolution at the fovea, and low resolution in the image periphery.

Jain [11] pointed out the advantages of using optical flow from a log-polar complex mapping for depth recovery from a translating camera with known motion parameters. The benefits of space-variant sensors for calculation of time-to-impact have also been demonstrated [14, 21]. The method presented here demonstrates advantages for control of motion orthogonal to the image axis. The log-polar sensor parameterisation enables closed-loop robot heading direction control based directly on the rotational component of log-polar optical flow.

3 Theoretical Background

Consider a robot moving in three space, with a velocity vector $W = (W_x, W_y, W_z)$ (see Figure 3). A camera mounted on the robot can move about all three axes with rotational velocities of $= \omega = (\theta, \phi, \psi)$, about (x, y, z) respectively.

Consider a point P on an object in the camera field of view, specified in camera coordinates (x, y, z). Sandini and Tisarelli [17] derive the motion of P as rotational and translational components as follows. From the inverse perspective transform, the projected point on the image plane given a focal length F is:

$$P = [x, y] = \frac{F}{z}[x, y], \tag{2}$$

Differentiating (2) with respect to time, we may decompose the velocity vector into a component due to camera translation and due to camera rotation:

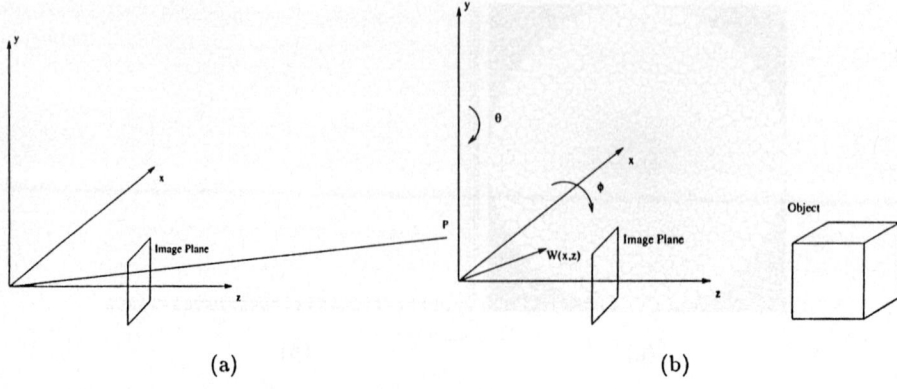

Fig. 2. (a) The coordinate system for a robot that moves in 3 space. (b) The coordinate system for the ground-based robot.

$$V = V_t + V_r$$

$$V_t = \left[\frac{xW_z - FW_x}{Z}, \frac{yW_z - FW_y}{Z}\right],$$ (3)

$$V_r = \left[\frac{xy\phi - [x^2 + F^2]\theta + y\psi}{F}, \frac{[y^2 + F^2]\phi - xy\theta - x\psi}{F}\right]$$ (4)

Now we derive equations for general motion observed by a log-polar sensor, following Tistarelli and Sandini [21]. The velocity in the image plane can be described in terms of radial and angular coordinates:

$$\dot{\rho} = \frac{xu + yv}{\rho} = u\cos\eta + v\sin\eta$$ (5)

$$\dot{\eta} = \frac{xv + yu}{\rho^2} = \frac{v\cos\eta - u\sin\eta}{\rho}$$ (6)

Substituting the motion equations (3) and (4):

$$\dot{\rho} = \left(\frac{xW_z - FW_x}{Z} + \frac{xy\psi - [x^2 + F^2]\theta + Fy\phi}{F}\right)\cos\eta + \left(\frac{yW_z - FW_y}{Z} + \frac{[y^2 + F^2]\psi - xy\theta - Fx\phi}{F}\right)\sin\eta$$ (7)

$$\dot{\eta} = \frac{1}{\rho}\left[\left(\frac{yW_z - FW_y}{Z} + \frac{xy\psi - [x^2 + F^2]\theta + Fy\phi}{F}\right)\cos\eta - \left(\frac{xW_z - FW_x}{Z} + \frac{xy\psi - [x^2 + F^2]\theta + Fy\phi}{F}\right)\sin\eta\right]$$ (8)

By substituting $x = \rho\cos\eta$ and $y = \rho\sin\eta$:

$$\dot{\rho} = \frac{1}{Z}[\rho W_z - F(W_x\cos\eta + W_y\sin\eta)] + \left(\frac{\rho^2}{F}\right)(\psi\sin\eta - \theta\cos\eta)$$ (9)

$$\dot{\eta} = \frac{F}{\rho}\left[\left(\frac{W_x}{Z} + \theta\right)\sin\eta + \left(\phi - \frac{W_y}{Z}\right)\cos\eta\right] - \phi.$$ (10)

However, the retinal sensor performs a logarithmic mapping as shown in Equation (1), thus we have [21]:

$$\dot{\xi} = [\frac{1}{Z}[W_z - \frac{F}{\rho}(W_x \cos \frac{\gamma}{q} + W_y \sin \frac{\gamma}{q})] + (\frac{\rho}{F} + \frac{F}{\rho})(\phi \sin \frac{\gamma}{q} - \theta \cos \frac{\gamma}{q})]log_a e, \quad (11)$$

$$\dot{\gamma} = \frac{qF}{\rho}[(\frac{W_x}{Z} + \theta) \sin \frac{\gamma}{q} + (\phi - \frac{W_y}{Z}) \cos \frac{\gamma}{q}] - q\psi. \quad (12)$$

Now let us consider the case of a ground-based robot that has a camera mounted on a pan-tilt platform, with no capacity for rotation about the optical axis (Figure 3). Thus, the robot moves with motion vector $\boldsymbol{W} = (W_x, W_z)$, and the camera has an angular velocity vector $\boldsymbol{\omega} = (\theta, \phi)$, given a combination of robot and pan/tilt platform motion. Consider also that the robot camera fixates independently on a target point in the environment. The pan and tilt velocities and absolute direction of the head are unknown, as is the absolute direction of the robot. Assume, without loss of generality, that the target object lies along the z axis, where the origin is a fixed to the robot along the optical axis.

We would like the robot to dock with the fixation point. To achieve this goal, the robot must adjust its heading direction such that W_x is zero. For a ground-based robot, the magnitude of W_y is not important. The issue of controlling the magnitude of velocity has been addressed previously [14, 21].

If the robot is tracking a point in the environment, then from [21], we have:

$$\theta = \frac{-W_x}{D}, \phi = \frac{W_y}{D}, \quad (13)$$

where D is the distance to the point of fixation.

Substituting Equations (13) into Equations (11) and (12) to eliminate θ and ϕ, removing the redundant ψ, we obtain:

$$\dot{\xi} = [\frac{W_z}{Z} + \frac{1}{D}(\frac{\rho}{F} + \frac{F}{\rho}[1 - \frac{D}{Z}])(W_x \cos \frac{\gamma}{q} - W_y \sin \frac{\gamma}{q})]log_a e, \quad (14)$$

$$\dot{\gamma} = \frac{qF}{\rho D}(1 - \frac{D}{Z})(W_y \cos \frac{\gamma}{q} - W_x \sin \frac{\gamma}{q}). \quad (15)$$

For Equation (15), if the object is not a long way above the ground relative to the robot-to-object distance, then the W_y residual from camera tilt will be small. Further, consider log-polar image region in which $\cos \frac{\gamma}{q}$ is close to zero, and $\sin \frac{\gamma}{q}$ is maximal, as shown in Figure 3 and specified in Equation (16).

$$\frac{\pi}{2} \frac{+}{-} k \bigcup \frac{3\pi}{2} \frac{+}{-} k, \quad (16)$$

where k is a constant specifying the width of the sensor region over which the mean is taken. Provided k is small, the coefficient of W_y is close to zero.

Thus, we may approximate $\dot{\gamma}$ in this region as:

$$\dot{\gamma} = \frac{qF}{\rho D}(\frac{D}{Z} - 1)W_x \sin\frac{\gamma}{q}. \quad (17)$$

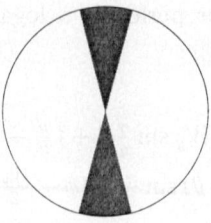

Fig. 3. W_x dominates $\dot{\gamma}$ over the region shown in Equation (16).

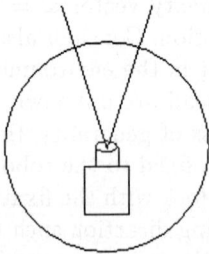

Fig. 4. The intersection of the camera field of view and a sphere centred at the camera focal point with a radius the size of the fixation distance. The sign of $\dot{\gamma}$ is dependent on which side of this volume the world point appears.

From Equation 17, we can see that $\dot{\gamma}$ is directly proportional to W_x for this part of the image. The sign of $\dot{\gamma}$ is dependent on the sign of W_x and whether $D > Z$ for the given point. With no assumptions about scene formation $D > Z$ is unknown for any image point. Ideally, we could adjust the heading direction in either direction and check if $\dot{\gamma}$ reduces also. However, for the optical flow method used, the magnitude of $\dot{\gamma}$ can vary greatly for similar values of W_x, and so the second order derivative of motion cannot be determined with sufficient accuracy.

Note that in the region at the sides of the image, where $\cos\frac{x}{q}$ is maximal, the effect on $\dot{\xi}$ of W_x will be maximal, however, for robot motion that is largely towards the object, $\dot{\xi}$ will be dominated by the expansion component, W_z, and so is less well suited than $\dot{\gamma}$ for direct use for control.

3.1 Geometric constraints

As a log-polar sensor has high resolution at the fovea, and this resolution decreases toward the periphery, it is natural to fixate the object of interest at the centre of the image, i.e. the optical axis should point towards the object.

By definition, $D > Z$ for a given point P if the distance from the camera focal point is greater than that of the fixation point. By assuming the fixation point lies along the optical axis, we may define the region that is closer to the camera than the fixation point. It is the region contained within the intersection of the cone defining camera visibility, and a sphere centred at the focal point, with radius equal to the fixation distance (see Figure 4). See [2] for an analysis.

In order to deduce robot heading angle relative to the optical axis we must be able to segment the visible scene into parts contained within this cone, or beyond it. A segmentation-based solution may be possible, however, in order to maintain processing speed, we assume constraints on scene geometry that allow $\dot{\gamma}$ to be used directly. Many assumptions are possible for particular situations, however, we wish to maintain the generality of the system. Two possible assumptions that have general application for ground-based mobile robots are:

1. The fixated object is convex and large in the image. Thus, most visible points are behind the fixation point from the robot's view point.
2. The fixation point is on the ground, such that all image points below it are ground points that are closer to the robot, and the majority of points above the object are background, and so behind the object. (This assumes the space between the object and the robot is not cluttered with other objects).

To clarify the theory above, Figure 5 shows optical flow for the motion discussed, and for several types of component motions.

4   Implementation

Many methods are available for calculating optical flow, with different strengths and weaknesses. See [4] for a comprehensive review of methods, and [10] for a review of the performance of these methods. Two major considerations drive our choice of method for calculating optical flow:

- Mobile robot docking is an on-line task, so any method must be capable of real-time performance; and,
- Our basic assumption on scene geometry does not facilitate the use of model-based methods.

The first consideration requires a fast method that avoids excessive computation. It should not deal with the whole image if a restricted part of the image will suffice. Although overall navigation performance must be robust to avoid unnecessary deviations, the optical flow method need not produce exact results. We avoided methods involving flow reconstruction, and instead used local flow calculation, relying on aggregation over part of the image to handle noise.

If knowledge is available about geometry of the docking surface, then methods can be applied that are based on assumptions such as that the surface is a first order function of image coordinates [22]. However, we wish to investigate a more general case where the only assumed knowledge is the approximate distance of points with respect to the fixation point.

The method chosen was that of Uras *et. al.* [23], which does not require assumptions about surface shape, is simple enough for fast implementation and is competitive in terms of accuracy [10]. Other fast local methods may also be appropriate. The method uses a local solution to the second order derivative:

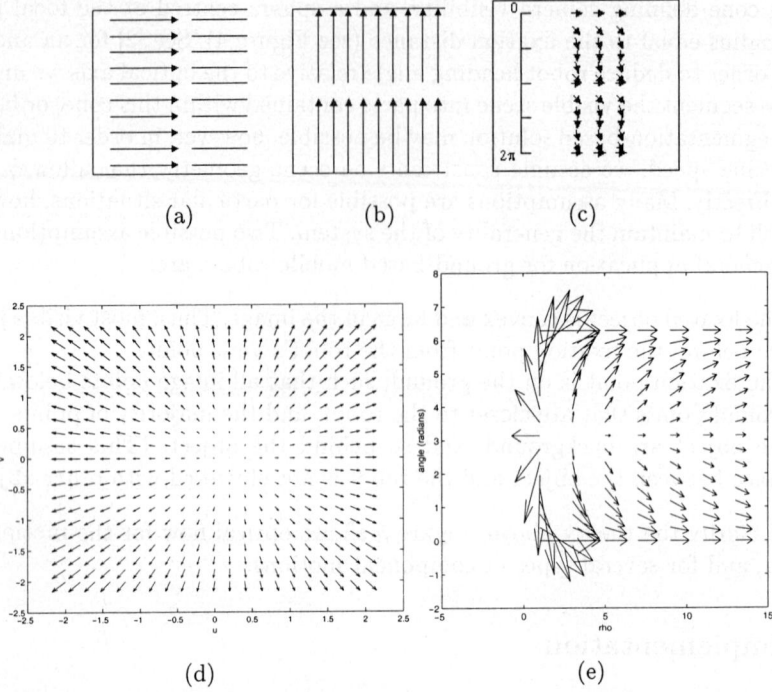

Fig. 5. Optical flow in polar coordinates. (a) The object moving closer to the camera. (b) Clockwise rotation in the plane. (c) Robot translation perpendicular to the image axis, while fixating on a point in front of the object. (d) Flow in Cartesian coordinates resulting from translation perpendicular to the image axis combined with motion toward the object, while fixating in front of the object. (e) In log-polar coordinates.

$$\begin{bmatrix} I_{xx} & I_{yx} \\ I_{xy} & I_{yy} \end{bmatrix} \begin{pmatrix} V_1 \\ V_2 \end{pmatrix} + \begin{pmatrix} I_{tx} \\ I_{ty} \end{pmatrix} = \begin{pmatrix} 0 \\ 0 \end{pmatrix}. \tag{18}$$

In a log-polar image, values for optical flow can be calculated at each pixel. However, only angles where W_x dominates $\dot{\gamma}$ are used, as specified in Equation (16). Further, the log-polar sensor is a multi-scale device. The distance from the centre of the image at which the flow will have the most favourable signal to noise ratio is dependent on the flow scale. The flow was taken between two values ρ_u and ρ_l which were set manually dependent on geometry of the particular situation. Automated setting of scale is not addressed in this paper.

We largely ignored noise in the flow calculation to facilitate speed, aiming instead for tolerance of noise in the input flow. We used the sign of the mean of $\dot{\gamma}$ (see Equation 17) to control heading direction, in a closed loop.

Note that there must be sufficient net optical flow for the signal-to-noise ratio to be adequate for robust control. For this to be the case, the depth between the fixation point and the other image points must not be small with respect to the robot-to-object distance. For the second assumption, of a small object on the floor in a room, net flow will generally be sufficient given a distant background. However, as the robot moves close, the object may become large in the image so that little background is visible. Hardware final docking solutions may be appropriate at this stage (e.g. [1]). Alternatively, for the convex object assumption, the object must not be small with respect to the robot-to-object distance.

$$\mu = \sum_{\rho=\rho_l}^{\rho_u} \sum_{\gamma=\frac{\pi}{2}-k}^{\frac{\pi}{2}+k} \dot{\gamma} + \sum_{\rho=\rho_l}^{\rho_u} \sum_{\gamma=\frac{3\pi}{2}-k}^{\frac{3\pi}{2}+k} \dot{\gamma} \qquad (19)$$

5 Results

We present experiments with real and simulated image sequences. All images are 256x256 Cartesian images that are subsampled into log-polar coordinates according to Equation (1). The simulated sequences show closed loop system performance. We have not yet completed the implementation on our mobile platform, however, we have taken real image sequences that confirm that real data does behave in the same manner as the simulated data. Thus, the system should perform correctly when the loop is closed.

5.1 Ray traced robot simulations

Image sequences of textured objects were generated using the POV-Ray ray tracing package. These sequences generate noisy optical flow patterns as flow calculation incurs many of the difficulties that apply to real images. Simulation allow us to examine precise cases, enabling full evaluation of the mathematical theory. For example, it is difficult to ensure that the fixation point remains constant on the surface of a plane using real data.

For these experiments we used a robot simulator. The simulator takes an image every p msec, moving forward only with fixed velocity. The heading direction can be changed by applying an angular velocity. This is represented as an average value for the time interval. Thus, for an applied angular velocity of a radians per msec, the robot will turn ap radians during the interval.

Early simulated results have been presented previously [2]. The results presented here show more extensive trials of relevant situations.

Convex Object Assumption The algorithm was tested on two convex objects, using the assumption that all points are behind the fixation point. Figure 6(a) shows the first object, and (b) and (c) show the heading direction with respect to the optical axis against total distance travelled. The robot overshoots the zero heading direction in both cases. This is due partly to the fact that it is getting close to the object. It should be noted that the depth variation within the object is small in comparison with the distance from the object, the resulting flow is

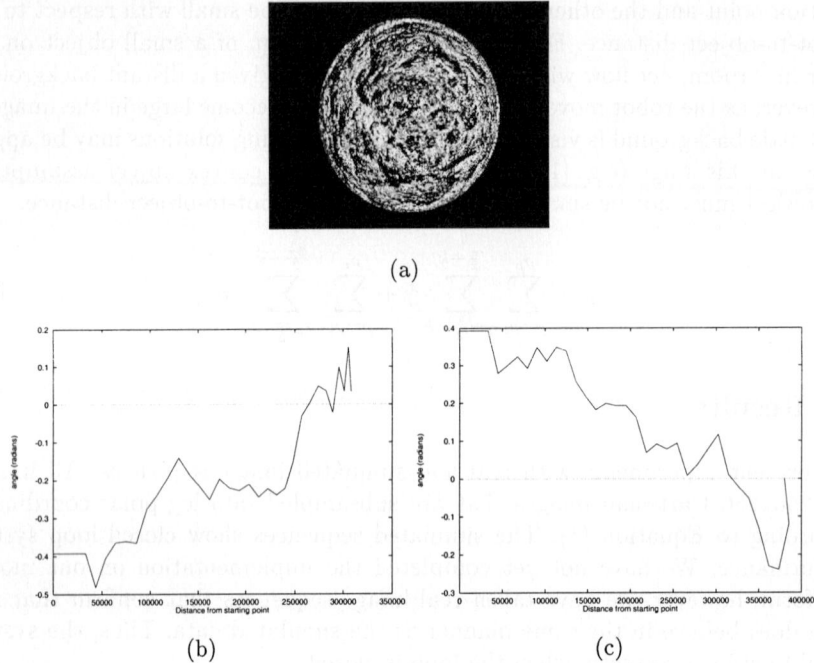

(a)

(b)   (c)

Fig. 6. Docking with a stone-surfaced ellipsoid. (a) The object. (b) Docking when the initial direction of motion is at $\frac{\pi}{8}$ radians to the optical axis. (c) Initial direction of motion is at $\frac{\pi}{8}$ radians to the optical axis in the opposite direction.

also small, resulting in the noise seen in the experiment. Similar results were found for a convex polyhedral object with a brick-like surface.

Background assumption The second case is where the robot fixates on a small object in the foreground, and we assume that all points above the object are background (see Figure 7 (a)). The lower half of the image is floor, and a planar wall covers most of the upper half. This is a plausible setup for a ground-based robot attempting to dock with an object in a room with a background wall, and a flat floor. In this case, the system assessed only points in the upper part of the image. The floor could also have been used, however this configuration was chosen to be consistent with that used for the real image sequences. Figure 7(b) and (c) show plots of heading direction angle. In this case, convergence was faster and more stable, because the image points for which $\dot{\gamma}$ was calculated are further behind the object. Similar performance was also demonstrated with ray-traced images where all the points were in front of the fixation point.

Although theoretically, the algorithm should be able to correct heading direction with a planar surface, trials performed were unable to support this.

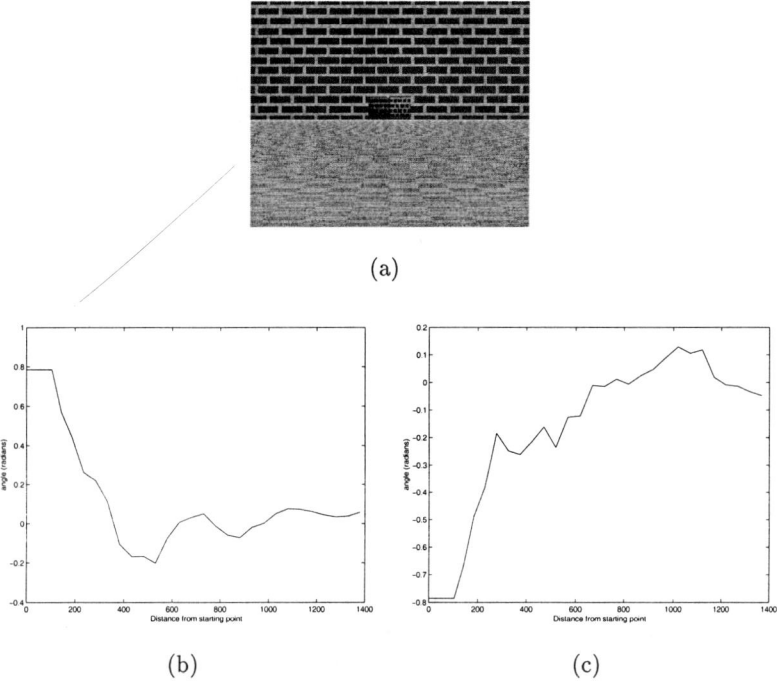

(a)

(b)   (c)

Fig. 7. Docking with an object with a distant background. (a) At the starting point, the object is small in the image, with a floor plane for all points below the object, and a background wall for all points behind the object. (b) Docking when motion begins at $\frac{\pi}{4}$ radians to the optical axis. (c) Docking when motion begins at $\frac{-\pi}{4}$ radians.

Mathematically there is a net rotational flow, however, in practice it appears this component is too small to be reliably extracted due to noise in this case.

5.2 Real Images

The object shown in Figure 8 object moved in a straight line along a rail. While it moved it was fixated by the LIRA head [5], using a colour-based binocular fixation method under development at the LIRA-lab. The images shown were taken from one of the cameras. Two types of image sequence were taken:

- The object moves from the right to the left of the image, toward the robot.
- The object moves from the left to the right of the image, toward the robot.

Figure 8 shows a sequence where the object moves at an angle such that in the coordinate system of Figure 3, W_x would be positive. With the object moving, motion is similar to when the robot moves, but the background is far away. This exemplifies the assumption that all above the object is background.

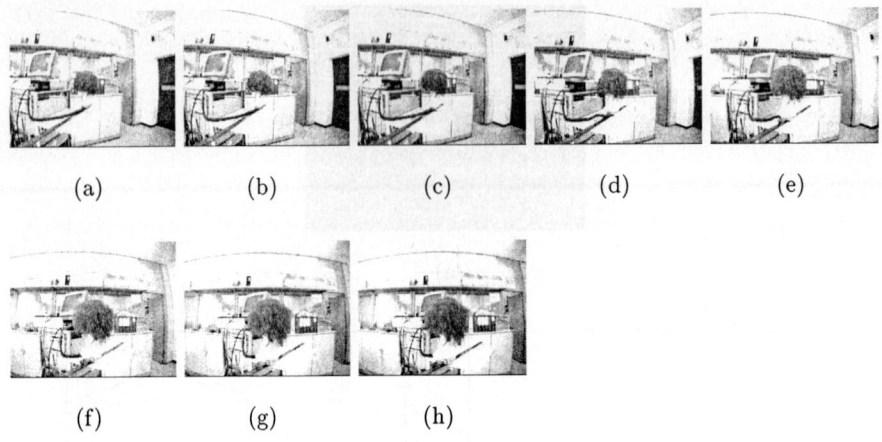

(a) (b) (c) (d) (e)

(f) (g) (h)

Fig. 8. A clown mask is fixated as it moves along a rail from right to left.

Figure 9 shows log-polar versions of the Cartesian images of Figure 8 (c) and (d), and the resulting log-polar optic flow. The scale of motion for this sequence is large, so the symmetric regions where $\dot\gamma$ was taken were towards the periphery of the image. Figure 10 shows the mean of $\dot\gamma$ for this sequence. Figure 11 shows a similar sequence, where the rail is at an angle with respect to the camera such that W_x would be negative. Figure 12 shows the mean of $\dot\gamma$.

These sequences show the sign of the mean changes with the direction of W_x. Due to slow recording of images, and minimum movement requirements between frames for the fixation algorithm, the changes between the images are large. More stable results can be expected with a higher sampling rate.

6 Conclusion

In this paper, we derived an algorithm which could be used to control heading direction for docking with an independently fixated object based on a class of assumptions about general scene properties. We demonstrated the algorithm's effectiveness on simulated and real images. This algorithm could be used as the basis of a docking behaviour, whereby a mobile robot need only fixate on a point and invoke the behaviour and it will move toward the point.

As this paper is early research in an interesting area, there is more work to be done. We are currently implementing this algorithm on a mobile robot to close the loop with real images. Further, as log-polar images are multi-scale, on-line automated determination of the optimal scale for heading control would be useful. Finally, this method is based on assumptions about the scene, even if these are high-level assumptions. Image segmentation into regions that are closer than the fixation point or otherwise would allow docking without scene knowledge.

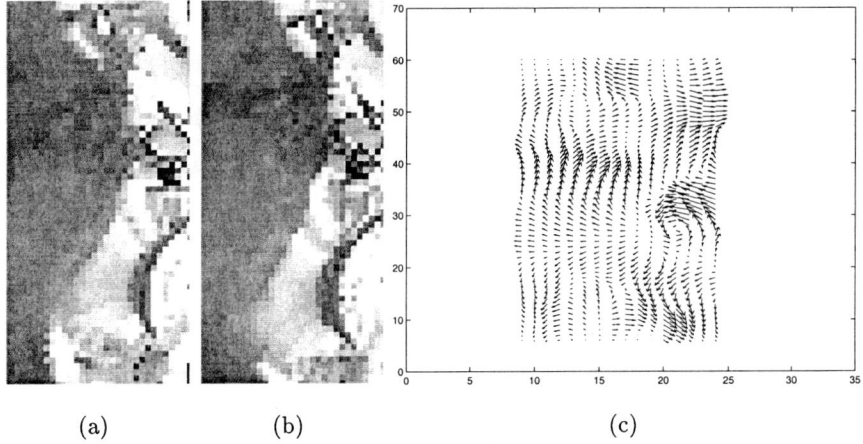

(a)   (b)   (c)

Fig. 9. Log-polar images of (c) and (d) in Figure 8, and the resulting optical flow.

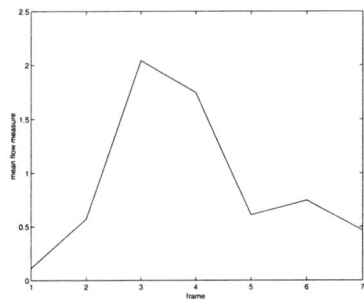

Fig. 10. Mean value of $\dot{\gamma}$ for the image sequence of Figure 8.

Acknowledgements

The authors gratefully acknowledge Dr. Giorgio Metta for his assistance in the implementation reported in this paper. This work was supported in part by grants from The Queen's Trust for Young Australians, The Ian Potter Foundation, and an Australian Research Council (ARC) Small Grant, and in part by grants from the European Union: VIRGO and ROBVISION.

References

1. R C Arkin and D MacKenzie. Temporal coordination of perceptual algorithms for mobile robot navigation. *IEEE Trans on Robotics and Automation*, 10(3):276–286, June 1994.

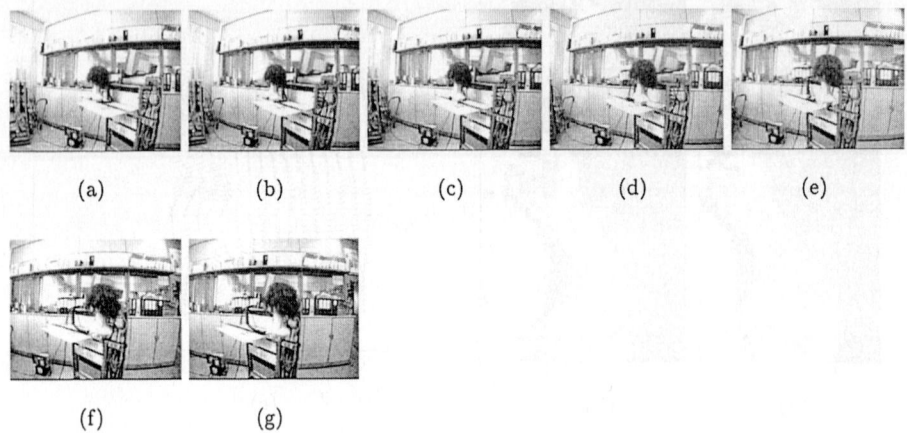

(a)   (b)   (c)   (d)   (e)

(f)   (g)

Fig. 11. The second image sequence, the motion is from left to right.

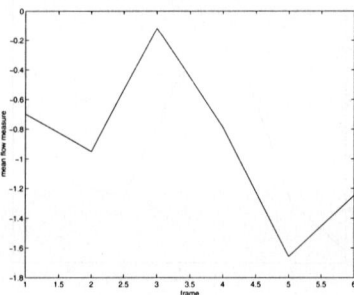

Fig. 12. Mean value of $\dot{\gamma}$ for the image sequence of Figure 11.

2. N Barnes and G Sandini. Active docking based on the rotational component of log-polar optic flow. In W-H Tsai and H-J Lee, editors, *ACCV Proceedings of the Asian Conference on Computer Vision*, pages 955–960, 2000.
3. N M Barnes and Z Q Liu. Vision guided circumnavigating autonomous robots. *Int. Journal of Pattern Recognition and Machine Intelligence*, 2000. in press.
4. S S Beauchemin and J L Barron. The computation of optical flow. *ACM Computing Surveys*, 27(3):433–467, 1996.
5. C Capurro, F Panerai, and E Grosso. The lira-lab head: mechanical design and control. Technical Report LIRA-TR 3/93, LIRA-Lab, DIST, Via Opera Pia, 13, University of Genova, Genova, Italy, August 1993.
6. J E Cutting, R F Wang, M Fluckliger, and B Baumberger. Human heading judgements and object-based motion information. *Vision Research*, 39:1079–1105, 1999.
7. C Fermuller. Navigational preliminaries. In *Active Perception*, pages 103–150. Lawrance Erlbaum Assoc., Hillsdale, NJ, 1993.

8. G Garibotto, S Masciangelo, M Ilic, and P Bassino. Service robotics in logistic automation: Robolift: Vision based autonomous navigation of a conventional fork-lift for pallet handling. In *8th International Conference on Advanced Robotics. Proceedings. ICAR'97*, pages 781–6, 1997.

9. A Hormann and U Rembold. Development of an advanced robot for autonomous assembly. In *IEEE Int. Conf. on Robotics and Automation*, pages 2452–7, 1991.

10. D J Fleet J L Barron and S S Beauchemin. Performance of optical flow techniques. *International Journal of Computer Vision*, 12(1):43–77, 1994.

11. R C Jain, L Barlett, and N O'Brian. Motion stereo using egomotion complex logarithmic mapping. *IEEE Trans. on Pattern Analysis and Machine Intelligence*, PAMI-9(2):356–369, Mar. 1987.

12. T C Leuth, U M Nassal, and U Rembold. Reliability and integrated capabilities of locomotion and manipulation for autonomous robot assembly. *Robotics and Automous Systems*, 14:185–198, 1995.

13. K Mandel and N A Duffie. On-line compensation of mobile robot docking errors. *IEEE Int. Journal of Robotics and Automation*, RA-3(6):591–598, Dec. 1987.

14. P Questa and G Sandini. Time to contact computation with a space-variant retina-line c-mos sensor. In *Proceedings of the International Conference on Intelligent Robots and Systems*, Osaka, Japan, 1996.

15. D Raviv and M Herman. A unified approach to camera fixation and vision based road following. *IEEE Trans. on Systems, Man and Cybernetics*, 24(8):1125–1141, Aug. 1994.

16. G Sandini, F Gandolfo, E Grosso, and M Tistarelli. Vision during action. In *Active Perception*, pages 151–190. Lawrance Erlbaum Assoc., Hillsdale, NJ, 1993.

17. G Sandini and M Tistarelli. Active tracking strategy for monocular depth inference over multiple frames. *IEEE Trans. on Pattern Analysis and Machine Intelligence*, 12(1):13–27, January 1990.

18. J Santos-Victor and G Sandini. Visual behaviours for docking. *Computer Vision and Image Understanding*, 67(3):223–28, Sept. 1997.

19. E L Schwartz. Spatial mapping in the primate sensory projection: Analytical structure and the relevance to perception. *Biological Cybernetics*, 25:181–194, 1977.

20. E L Schwartz. A quantitive model of the functional architecture of human striate cortex with application to visual illustration and cortical texture analysis. *Biological Cybernetics*, 37:63–76, 1980.

21. M Tistarelli and G Sandini. On the advantages of polar and log-polar mapping for direct estimation of time-to-impact from optical flow. *IEEE Trans. on Pattern Analysis and Machine Intelligence*, 15(4):401–410, April 1993.

22. H Tunley and D Young. First order optic flow from log-polar sampled images. In J-O Eklundh, editor, *European Conference on Computer Vision '94*, 1994.

23. S Uras, F Girosi, A Verri, and V Torre. A computational approach to motion perception. *Biological Cybernetics*, 60:79–87, 1988.

The Construction of 3 Dimensional Models Using an Active Computer Vision System

P. J. Armstrong[1] and J. Antonis[2]

[1]School of Mechanical and Manufacturing Engineering,
Queen's University Belfast.
Ashby Building, Stranmillis Road, Belfast, BT9 5AH.
pj.armstrong@qub.ac.uk
[2]School of Mechanical and Manufacturing Engineering,
Queen's University Belfast.
Ashby Building, Stranmillis Road, Belfast, BT9 5AH.
jan.antonis@usa.net

Abstract. The initial development and assessment of an active computer vision system is described, which is designed to meet the growing demand for 3 dimensional models of real-world objects. Details are provided of the hardware platform employed, which uses a modified gantry robot to manoeuvre the system camera and a purpose-built computer controlled turntable on which the object to be modelled is placed. The system software and its computer control system are also described along with the occluding contour technique developed to automatically produce initial models of objects. Examples of models constructed by the system are presented and experimental results are discussed, including results which indicate that the occluding contour technique can be used in an original manner to identify regions of the object surface which require further modelling and also to determine subsequent viewpoints for the camera.

1 Introduction

An active computer vision system can be described as a vision system in which the camera, or cameras, are moved in a controlled and purposive manner in order to capture images from different viewpoints. In many cases the purpose is to fixate on a feature of a moving target in order to track the target in real time [1]. In other cases, features in the environment are located in order to provide information for the real-time navigation of a robot or robot vehicle [2]. Research relating to both these applications has tended to concentrate on the development of high-speed, multiple degree of freedom platforms on which the camera, or cameras, are mounted [3,4].

Another potential application of active vision, which has received less attention, is the construction of 3 dimensional models of objects by using a moving camera to "explore" the surface of the object. Here the requirement is not for a high-speed camera platform, but for a platform which can position the camera accurately and for an accurate method of converting images into a 3 dimensional model of the object in a real-world co-ordinate system. Such fundamental differences suggest that a separate line of research is required to support the development of practical active vision systems for 3 dimensional modelling. This would undoubtedly be worthwhile as the demand for 3 dimensional models is growing and will continue to grow with the more widespread use of 3 dimensional CAD and computer graphics software.

One key role for a system which can produce 3 dimensional models would be the reverse engineering of manufactured parts. Often the latter do not have an associated CAD model, yet there are many situations where one would be useful, as a basis for designing and manufacturing a similar or modified part. It is also common for the design of parts to be altered during the period between initial design and production and it would be desirable if the final version of the part could be used to update the original model. In addition a potential role for reverse engineering exists in the manufacture of moulds and dies, where traditionally crafted masters have been used in the production process. If a CAD model were created from the crafted master then modern CNC machines could be used more frequently to manufacture the tool [5]. In the case of jewellery and other decorative objects, the availability of CAD models would allow new designs to be created without the use of crafted masters [6]. Apart from reverse engineering it is evident that there is a growing demand for realistic models of both manufactured and natural objects for multimedia, film and virtual reality environments. Clearly computer graphics applications seldom need models as accurate and detailed as models required for CAD purposes and the realistic reproduction of surface properties, such colour and texture, is equally important.

To date the requirement for 3 dimensional models has been met by commercially available laser scanners and co-ordinate measuring machines (CMMs). However, the use of a CMM to digitise sufficient points to create a 3 dimensional model is a laborious task, which is difficult to automate. Conventional CMMs are also unsuitable for soft or flexible objects and return no information on the properties of a surface other than its geometry. The use of a laser scanner can also be problematic, since it may not be possible to access some regions of the object's surface, the performance of the scanner is dependent on surface properties and details of surface characteristics such as colour and texture are difficult to acquire. In theory computer vision could provide a superior approach. The co-ordinates of surface points could be obtained quickly, efficiently and in an automated manner. Soft and flexible objects could be modelled and surface characteristics including colour and texture could be reproduced if necessary.

For the most part, work on the use of computer vision for constructing 3 dimensional models has relied on images obtained from multiple static cameras [7] or a static camera with the object rotated on a turntable [8,9]. Some research has been reported on the use of continuously moving cameras to obtain 3 dimensional data by tracking occluding contours [10] or to determine object structure from the known motion of the camera [11]. Various methods have also been proposed to define the optimum viewpoints (camera positions and orientations) for model construction [9,12], but there is a lack of experimental work to assess the methods proposed.

The current paper reports the initial results of a research programme to develop a practical active vision system for automated 3 dimensional modelling. The prototype system was to be built to model objects which would fit within a 100 mm cube and the system was to be assembled from relatively low cost components, in the first instance. The intention was that the system would be able to manoeuvre a camera to view any part of an object's visible surface and, critically, higher resolution data would be obtained, when required, by moving the camera towards the object. The target application would be reverse engineering which would place a stringent demand on the accuracy of the results. However it was recognised that failure to achieve this may mean that the system is still suitable for less demanding applications in computer graphics and animation.

2 The Active Vision System

Since it would be necessary to move a camera around an object and accurate positioning of the camera was required, this suggested the use of a gantry robot. A relatively low cost 4-axis gantry robot was sourced which formed the basis of the camera platform. In order to provide the system with additional flexibility a high-resolution turntable was designed and built. The robot's computer control system was extended to incorporate control of the turntable. The initial step-up is shown schematically in Figure 1.

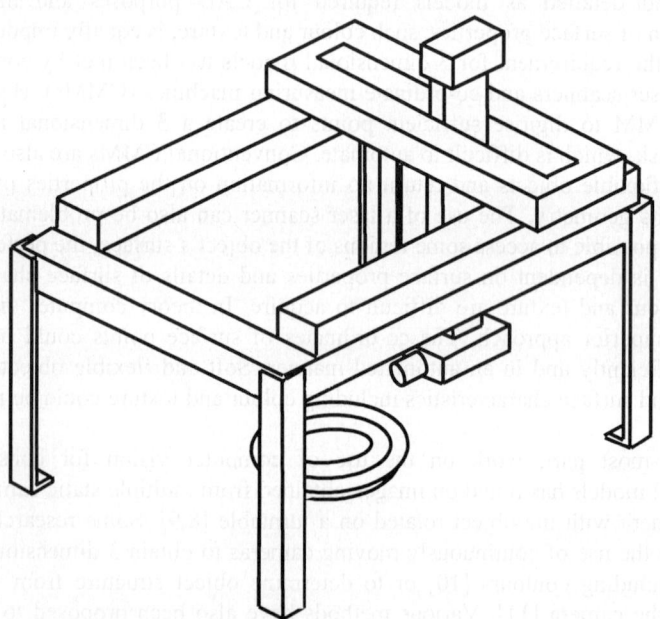

Fig. 1. Schematic Diagram of Gantry Robot and Turntable

As shown in the diagram, an object to be modelled is placed on the turntable and viewed by a colour CCD camera mounted on the robot arm. In order to enable the camera to view the top of the object a fifth (pitch) axis drive was designed, built and integrated into the robot's control system. The camera and pitch axis drive are shown in Figure 2.

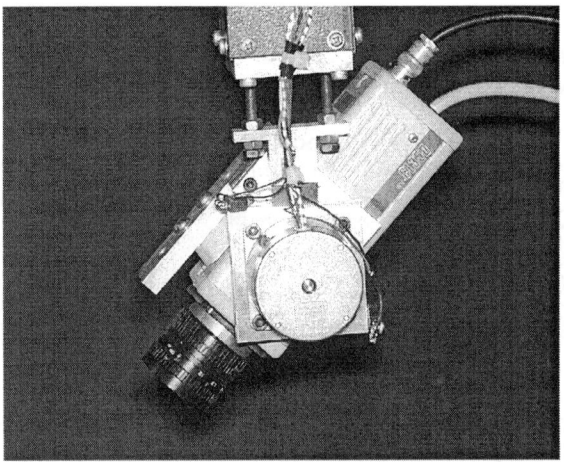

Fig. 2. Camera and Pitch Axis Drive

It was decided that two computers (both standard PCs) would be used to control the overall system, as shown in Figure 3. A colour digitiser was installed in computer 1 and, as shown, this computer is responsible for image analysis. Computer 2 is assigned to viewpoint control which is implemented through a combination of camera and turntable movements.

As indicated in Figure 3 the system was set up so that a sequence of predefined viewpoints can be specified. Computer 2 then moves the turntable and/or the camera to create each viewpoint in turn. Once both are in position, computer 1 is instructed to capture an image. It then sends a request to computer 2 to move the system to the next predefined viewpoint. Alternatively the next viewpoint can be computed as part of the image analysis process, so that the system will effectively operate in a closed loop. Ultimately computer 1 assembles and outputs the surface point data which is used to create a 3 dimensional model of the object.

Communication was established between the two computers and software written to affect the two-way transmission of instructions and data. All time-critical software, such as the image analysis procedures, was written in Visual C++. Software which was not time-critical, including the viewpoint control program, was written in Visual Basic for speed of development. Software was also written to provide a Windows standard interface on both machines for user input and output.

3 Constructing Initial 3 Dimensional Models

An approach was adopted whereby the system first provides surface point data for an initial model using a set of predefined viewpoints. The intention was that this model would be used to identify regions of the surface which required further modelling and also, ideally, to specify the viewpoints from which this data should be obtained.

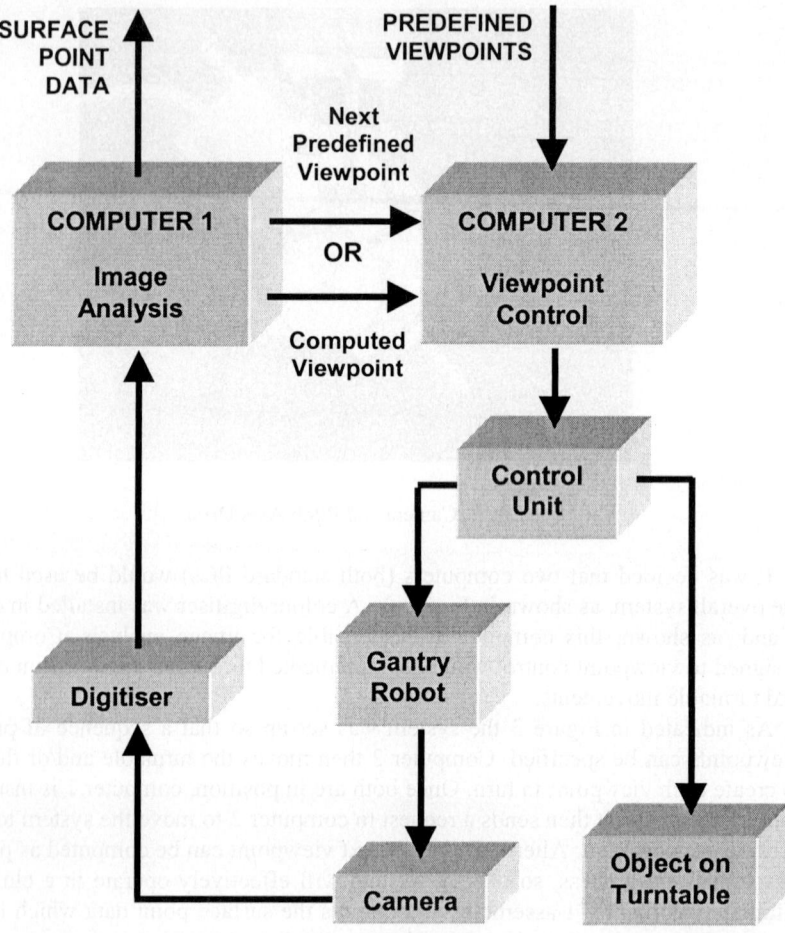

Fig. 3. Computer Control and Image Analysis System

As assessment of the various techniques used to extract 3 dimensional data from captured images was carried out, including stereo, structured light approaches and shape from X. It was concluded, as others have maintained, that no technique is generally applicable, but that a combination of techniques can be used to compensate the disadvantages of individual techniques. An occluding contour approach was chosen as the preferred technique for generating the initial model. The obvious disadvantage is that regions of the object's surface which are doubly concave cannot be modelled. In fact the system models both planar regions and doubly concave regions as planar regions. Hence it is necessary to label all regions returned as planar as requiring further investigation. Although not implemented to date, it is envisaged that the modelling of such regions will use a colour encoded structured light approach which uses stereo instead of triangulation [13]. In effect this means that a coloured structured light pattern is used to provide easily matched features in the stereo images.

(In practice the single camera in the active vision system will be used to capture the two "stereo" images from laterally displaced viewpoints.) The proposed structured light technique has been tested experimentally, as an adjunct to the current research project, and the results obtained have been encouraging.

The occluding contour approach developed for the system operates as follows. An image of the object is captured from a series of predefined viewpoints. Each image is obtained with the object back-lit and the image is thresholded to produce a silhouette. The occluding contour is extracted by locating points on the edge of the silhouette (the visible rim).

The workspace within which the object has been placed is assumed to be divided into a "stack" of horizontal planes, as shown in Figure 4(a). When an occluding contour is extracted it is projected onto each "workspace plane" in turn. In Figure 4(b) the object is a sphere and the occluding contour is a circle. When projected onto a horizontal workspace plane, the projection will be an ellipse. (The process can also be regarded as one whereby the ellipse is formed from the intersection of the cone emanating from the focal point of the camera, which must enclose the object, and the workspace plane, which must also enclose the object). As further contours are projected onto each plane, they will define an "enclosing area" within which the object must exist. This is shown in Figure 4(c), where the enclosing area will tend towards the circular cross-section of the sphere as further contours are projected on to the workspace plane.

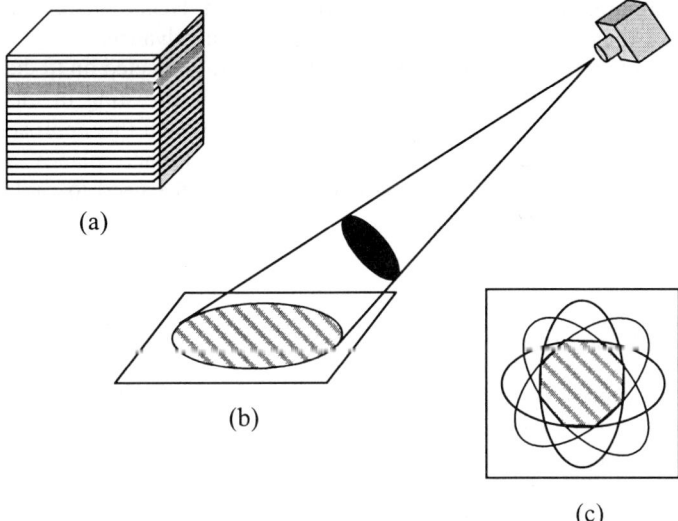

(a)

(b)

(c)

Fig. 4. Conceptual Diagram of the Occluding Contour Technique

When a contour is projected onto a workplace plane, it is represented by a series of line segments between projected points on the visible rim. As shown in Figure 5(a), the projection of a further contour means that the intersection points between the contours have to be located. The intersection points are then used along with the appropriate projected edge points to define the enclosing area.

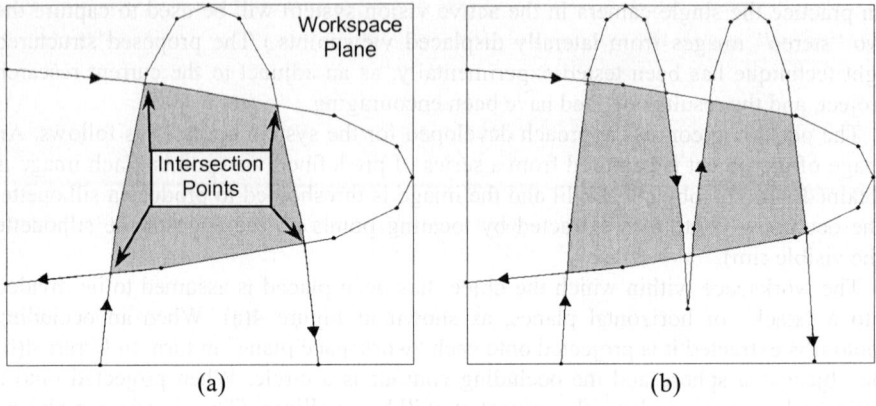

Fig. 5. Defining the Enclosing Area(s)

A heuristic technique was devised to locate the intersection points between projected contours. Various eventualities had to be covered, such as the situation shown in Figure 5(b), and to resolve some ambiguities the handedness of each contour had to be recorded along with the sequence of edge points. The technique used was found to be robust and the choice of intersection points to define enclosing areas has a major advantage over the commonly used voxel approach [14] since a priori quantization in the horizontal plane is not required. Hence the resolution of the horizontal co-ordinates of the model will not be limited in advance.

When the contours from all predefined viewpoints are projected on to the full stack of workspace planes, a 3 dimensional model is formed consisting of the edge and intersection points which define the enclosing areas. Although this approach requires quantization in the vertical direction, additional workspace planes and hence additional enclosing areas can easily be defined without the need to capture further images.

4   Calibration

A thorough calibration programme was carried out to enable the system to produce object surface points in world co-ordinates. For this purpose a world co-ordinate system was specified with its origin at the centre of the turntable. Transformations were then defined and evaluated between the world co-ordinate system and the turntable, camera and robot co-ordinate systems. The camera calibration task required to produce the camera/robot transformation was the most demanding step in this process. Camera calibration was carried out using a modified implementation of the method developed by Tsai [15,16]. This involved measuring various intrinsic and extrinsic camera parameters including the position of the camera's principal point, which was located with the aid of a low intensity laser. A calibration object was also required and this consisted of a glass plate which was sprayed matt white and marked with a 14 by 20 matrix of solid black squares. The precise locations of the corners of the squares were found using a travelling microscope.The Tsai coplanar method requires images of the calibration object to be captured from a wide range of viewpoints. Software was written to position the robot at a sequence of viewpoints and automatically capture and analyse images of the calibration plate. A red spot was marked on a square close to the centre of the plate, so that each square could be identified when the camera's field of view covered only part of the plate. After each image was captured, the Sobel operator was used to locate the edges of the black squares, as shown in Figure 6. Linear regression was then employed to fit lines to all edges and the corners were located by finding the intersection points between the lines. A matrix manipulation package was used to process the matrices containing the image and real-world co-ordinates of the corner points, along with the measured camera parameters. This yielded coefficient values for the camera/robot transformation matrix.

Fig. 6. Calibration Pattern Edge Detection

5 Initial Results

The system was used to produce initial 3 dimensional models of a wide range of objects in the form of collections of surface point co-ordinates or "data clouds". Each data cloud was then passed to a software package which created a surface model, either by fitting triangular patches or by fitting NURBS surfaces. An example is shown in Figure 7 of a hemisphere which was modelled by the system and rendered using triangular meshes (Figure 7(a)) and NURBS surfaces (Figure 7(b)).

An examination of the proximity of the raw data points to the NURBS surface model produced the graph shown in Figure 8, which shows that 90% of the data points are within 50 microns of the surface.

A series of tests was undertaken to establish the success or otherwise of the calibration exercise. Figure 9 shows two views of a NURBS surface model of a 1 inch BS bolt produced by the system. The standard pitch of the thread is 2.54 mm and the pitch as measured from the model differs by only 15.3 microns.

Among the more complex objects modelled by the system were a set of chess pieces which had been produced by a Flexible Manufacturing System installed in the University. Figure 10 shows 3 dimensional models of the king and the rook created by the active vision system and rendered, in this case, using triangular meshes.

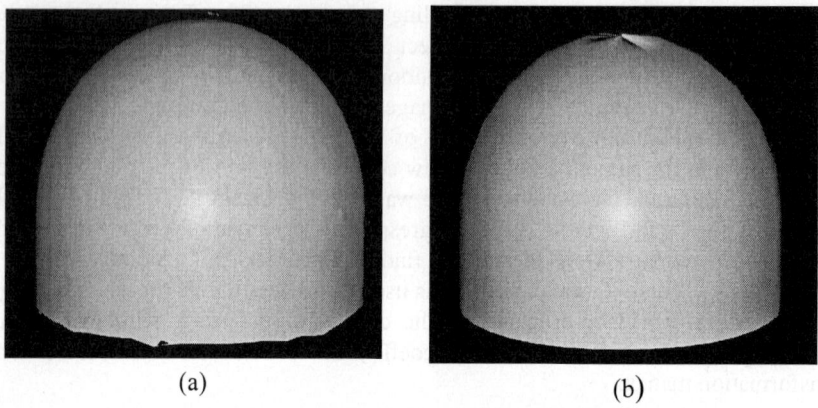

(a)   (b)

Fig. 7. Rendered Models of Hemisphere

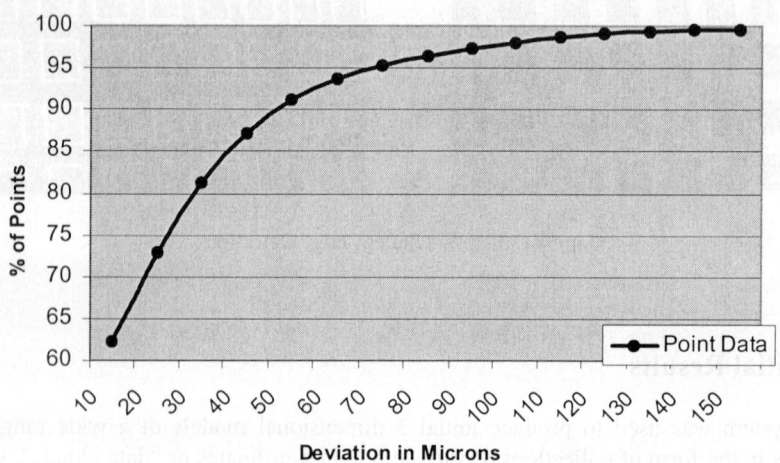

Fig. 8. Deviation of Data Points from Surface of NURBS Model.

As an indication that the models produced are at least suitable for computer graphics applications, Figure 11 shows a scene where a surface texture has been added to the chess piece models. They have then been placed on a manually drawn 3 dimensional model of a chessboard.

6 Viewpoint Planning

As noted previously, further modelling may be necessary for one of two reasons. Either a planar surface has been detected which may be concave or a region of fine detail requires closer examination at a higher level of resolution. In the first instance, candidates are regions where the local surface curvature is low and in the second instance candidates are regions where the local surface curvature is high or where, in the extreme case, discontinuities occur. When contour intersection points on the perimeter of enclosing areas (see Figure 5) are examined it is evident that the local density of points is low when surface curvature is low and high when surface curvature is high. Hence it is postulated that the local density of intersection points can be used to identify potentially concave regions (low density) and regions requiring higher resolution modelling (high density).

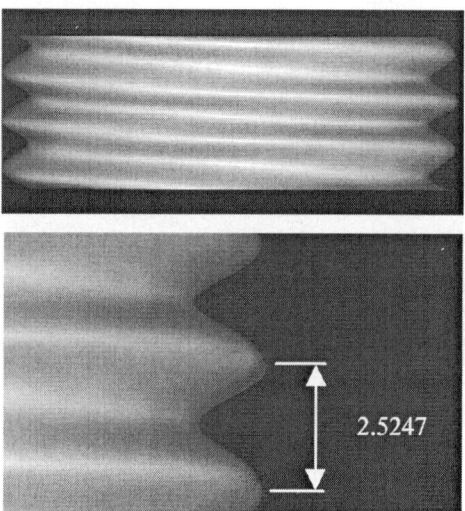

Fig. 9. Model of 1 inch Bolt

Fig. 10. Models of Chess Pieces

Fig. 11. Model of Chessboard Scene

In order to measure the local density of the intersection points a mask was designed to compute a weighted sum of the intersection points within a small region centred on each point in turn. The results are then filtered to identify regions where the mask output is either high or low. The overall process is referred to as "point density filtering" and its application to a range of objects suggests that it can provide the basis of a method for identifying the regions which require further modelling. Figure 12 shows the results of applying point density filtering to a model of a half- cylinder (shown in Figure 12(a)). All points are displayed in Figure 12(b). However, when the filter is biased towards high density points, Figure 12(c) is produced which highlights the curved rear surface of the half-cylinder and the surface discontinuities at the vertical edges. When the filter is biased towards low density points, the planar top and front surfaces are highlighted.

In practice, further modelling would be performed on those regions with the highest and the lowest point densities, in the first instance. In the case of the half-cylinder, this would mean generating high resolution data for the two vertical edges, which in turn would enhance the accuracy of the model. It would also mean that the proposed structured light facility would be applied to the front and top surfaces, since they both return low point densities.

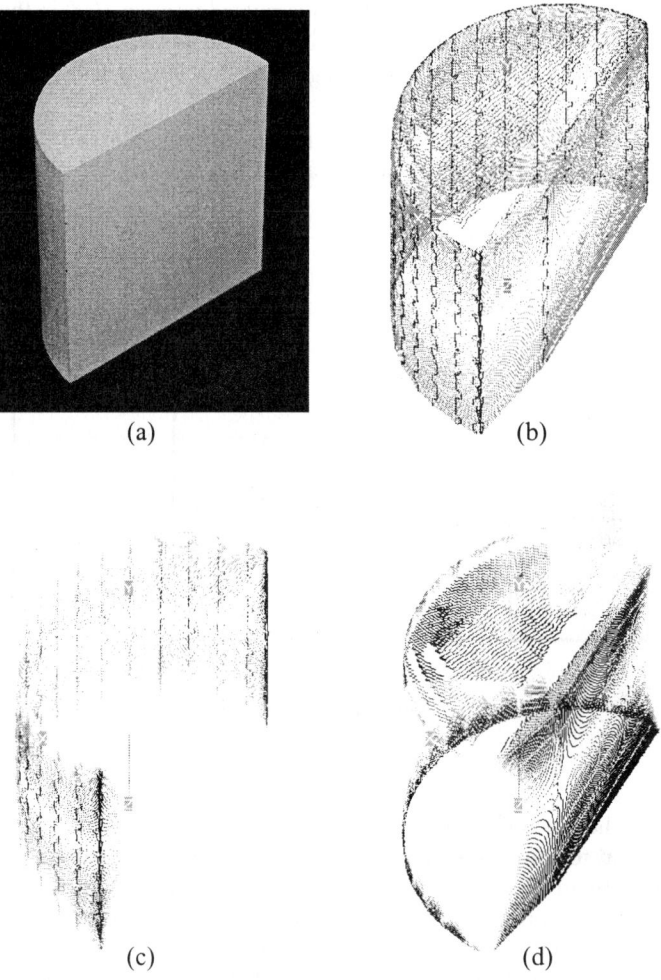

(a)   (b)

(c)   (d)

Fig. 12. Application of Point Density Filtering

A further procedure was devised to estimate the optimum viewpoints for subsequent modelling. In cases where regions requiring higher resolution data have been identified, the optimum viewpoint for each region is the one which places that region on the visible rim. This can be obtained by rotating the data point model in computer memory and recording the model's orientation when the maximum number of intersection points from the chosen region appears on the visible rim. If orthogonal projection is assumed, the optimum viewing direction will in fact coincide with the direction of a tangent which touches the surface of the object at the centre of the region concerned.

In Figure 13 a high density region has been chosen on one of the half-cylinder's vertical edges. The figure shows the number of intersection points from this region which appear on the visible rim, as the model is rotated through 360° in the horizontal plane. As the case should be, the graph indicates that the edge will remain on the visible rim while the viewing angle is changed through 90°. It will then reappear at the visible rim on the other side of the object after an absence of 90° and will remain there for a further 90°. The graph provides sufficient information to select a sequence of viewpoints (in the horizontal plane) suitable for a close-up view of the vertical edge.

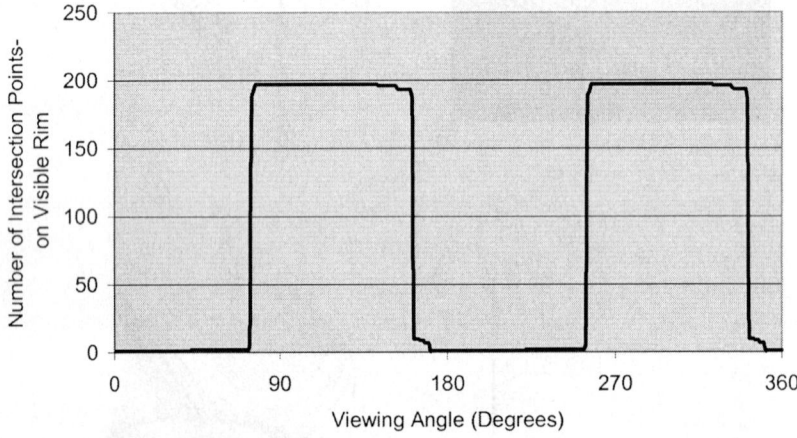

Fig. 13. Optimum Angles for High Resolution Viewpoints

In the case where a region of low intersection point density has been found, the nominal direction for projecting and viewing a structured light pattern will coincide with the direction of a normal to the object surface at the centre of the region concerned. Hence the procedure described above can be employed and the resulting viewing direction is then simply rotated through 90 degrees.

In Figure 14, a low density region has been chosen on the half-cylinder's planar front surface. If the model is rotated through 360° in the horizontal plane as before, the graph shows the number of intersection points from this region which are visible when the viewing direction is normal to the surface. As should be the case, the graph indicates that there is a unique optimum angle which occurs when the viewing direction is normal to the half-cylinder's planar front surface. The projection and viewing directions for the structured light facility should be chosen so that the angle between them is bisected by the nominal direction indicated by the graph.

7 Discussion of Results

Progress to date with the active vision system has enabled a wide range of models to be produced for assessment purposes. The accuracy achieved suggests that the system would be suitable for computer graphics applications and that it may be suitable for reverse engineering applications. The occluding contour technique employed does not place a limit, a priori, on resolution and further work will be undertaken to define the level of accuracy which is achievable. At present, the system is clearly only capable of modelling convex surfaces and the proposed method of refining models by using higher resolution close range images has not yet been fully implemented. However, it has been shown that the projected contour intersection points can be used as a basis for automatically identifying surface regions for further modelling and also for suggesting the viewpoints which should be employed. Hence viewpoints which place surface features and details on the visible rim for close range viewing can be computed and potentially concave regions can be identified and a nominal direction for applying structured light obtained. Further work is required, however, to fully develop this technique, including removal of the constraint which restricts viewing directions to the horizontal plane.

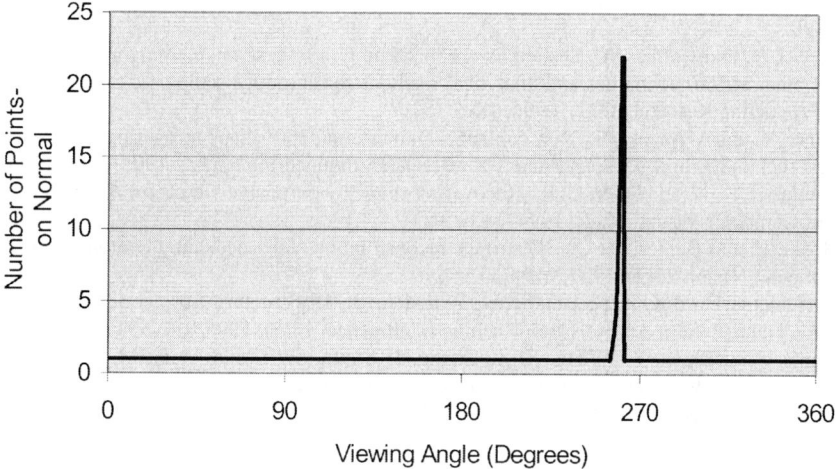

Fig. 14. Optimum (Nominal) Angle for Projecting and Viewing Structured Light.

An objective of the current work was to develop a low cost system and no difficulties have been experienced with the modified robot, custom-built turntable and standard computing hardware employed. However, it is evident that the basic CCD camera incorporated in the system will limit future development and will prevent the system from being used for reverse engineering purposes. At present image resolution can only be varied within the range of the camera's limited depth of field and initial results suggest that calibration accuracy deteriorates as the camera is moved towards the object. A more versatile camera will therefore be substituted and calibration repeated in advance of further development. The general principles established and techniques devised during the first phase of the project will, however, be retained since it is believed that the active vision system described in the paper can be the basis of a practical automated 3 dimensional modelling tool.

References

1. Uhlin, T., Nordlund, P., Maki, A. and Eklundh, J.O., Towards an active visual observer. Proc. 5th Int. Conf. on Computer Vision, Cambridge, MA, USA, 20-23 Jun. 1995, 679-686.
2. Reid, I.D. and Beardsley, P.A., Self-alignment of a binocular robot. Proc. 6th British Machine Vision Conf., BMVC, Birmingham, UK, 11-14 Sept. 1995, 635-640.
3. Ferrier, N.J., Harvard Binocular Head. Proc. Applications of Artificial Intelligence X: Machine Vision and Robotics, Orlando, FL, USA, 22-24 April 1992, 2-13.
4. Batista, J., Peixoto, P. and Araujo, H., Real-time visual behaviors with a binocular active vision system. Proc. 1996 IEEE/SICE/RSJ Int. Conf. on Multisensor Fusion and Integration for Intelligent Systems, Washington, DC, USA, 8-11 Dec.1996, 663-670.
5. Yang, J., Lee, N. L. and Menq, C. H., Application of computer vision in reverse engineering for 3D coordinate acquisition, Proc. of the ASME Int. Mechanical Engineering Congress and Exposition, San Francisco, CA, USA, 12-17 Nov.1995, 143-156.
6. Ippolito, R., Iuliano, L. and Gatto, A., Integrated reverse engineering, rapid prototyping and investment casting in the jeweller's craft, Proc. 11th Int. Conf. on Computer-Aided Production Engineering, Institution of Mechanical Engineers, London, 20-21 Sept. 1995, 85-90.
7. Ip, W.L.R. and Loftus, M., Shaded image machining: a reverse engineering approach using computer vision techniques and analytical methods to reproduce sculptured surfaces. Int. J. of Production Research 34(7), 1996, 1895-1916.
8. Niitsu, Y. and Miyazaki, S., Non-contact 3-Dimensional 360° shape measuring system using light section method. J. Japan Society for Precision Engineering 62(12), 1996, 1790-1794.
9. Kutulakos, K. N. and Dyer, C. R., Recovering shape by purposive viewpoint adjustment. Int. J. of Computer Vision, 12(2), 1994, 113-136.
10. Boyer, E. and Berger, M. O., 3D surface reconstruction using occluding contours. Int. J. of Computer Vision 22(3), 1997, 219-233.
11. Chaumette, F., Boukir, s., Bouthemy, P. and Juvin, D. Structure from controlled motion. IEEE Trans. Pattern Analysis and Machine Intelligence. 18(5), 1996, 492-504.
12. Banta, J. E., Zhien, Y., Wang, X. Z., Zhang, J., Smith, M. T. and Abidi, M. A. Best-next-view algorithm for three-dimensional scene reconstruction using range images. Proc. Intelligent Robots and Computer Vision XIV; Algorithms, Techniques, Active Vision, and Materials Handling, Philadelphia, PA, USA, 23-26 Oct. 1995, 418-429.
13. Chen, C. S., Hung, Y. P., Chiang, C. C. and Wu, J. L. Range data acquisition using color structured lighting and stereo vision. Image and Vision Computing, 15(6), 1997, 445-456.
14. Martin, W. N. and Aggarwal, J. K. Volumetric descriptions of objects from multiple views. IEEE Trans. Pattern Analysis and Machine Intelligence, 1983, 5(2), 150-158.
15. Tsai, R. Y., A versatile camera calibration technique for high-accuracy 3D machine vision metrology using off-the-shelf TV cameras and lenses. IEEE J. of Robotics and Automation, 3(4), 1987, 323-344.
16. Heikkilä, J. and Silvén, O., A four-step camera calibration procedure with implicit image correction, Proc. IEEE Computer Society Conf. on Computer Vision and Pattern Recognition, San Juan, Puerto Rico, 17-19 June 1997, 1106-1112.

Significantly Different Textures: A Computational Model of Pre-attentive Texture Segmentation

Ruth Rosenholtz

Xerox PARC, 3333 Coyote Hill Rd., Palo Alto, CA 94304, rruth@parc.xerox.com

Abstract. Recent human vision research [1] suggests modelling pre-attentive texture segmentation by taking a set of feature samples from a local region on each side of a hypothesized edge, and then performing standard statistical tests to determine if the two samples differ significantly in their mean or variance. If the difference is significant at a specified level of confidence, a human observer will tend to pre-attentively see a texture edge at that location. I present an algorithm based upon these results, with a well specified decision stage and intuitive, easily fit parameters. Previous models of pre-attentive texture segmentation have poorly specified decision stages, more unknown free parameters, and in some cases incorrectly model human performance. The algorithm uses heuristics for guessing the orientation of a texture edge at a given location, thus improving computational efficiency by performing the statistical tests at only one orientation for each spatial location.

1 Pre-attentive Texture Segmentation

Pre-attentive texture segmentation refers to the phenomenon in human vision in which two regions of texture quickly (i.e. in less than 250 ms), and effortlessly segregate. Observers may perceive a boundary or edge between the two regions.

In computer vision, we would like to find semantically meaningful boundaries between different textures. One way of estimating these boundaries is to find boundaries that would be found by a human observer. The boundaries thus defined should be sufficient for most computer vision applications. Whether a human observer can distinguish two textures depends upon whether the discrimination is pre-attentive or attentive. The experimental literature tells us far more about pre-attentive segmentation than attentive discrimination.

Researchers have suggested both feature- and filter-based models of pre-attentive texture segmentation. Many of the feature-based models have been statistical in nature. Julesz [2] suggested that pre-attentive segmentation is determined by differences in the 2nd-order statistics of the texture, or differences in the 1st-order statistics of "textons" such as line terminators and corners [3]. Beck, Prazdny, & Rosenfeld [4] suggested that texture segmentation is based upon differences in the first-order statistics of stimulus features such as orientation, size, and contrast. However, these theories do not indicate how these differences might be quantified, or what properties of the statistics might be used. Furthermore, such models have not typically been implemented such that they could be tested on actual images.

Filter-based models [e.g. 5, 6, 7, 8] have suggested that texture segmentation is determined by the responses of spatial-frequency channels, where the channels contain both linear filtering mechanisms and various non-linearities. Malik & Perona's model [7] provides the most developed example of this type of model. It involves linear bandpass filtering, followed by half-wave rectification, non-linear inhibition and excitation among channels and among neighboring spatial locations, filtering with large-scale Gaussian first derivative filters, and a decision based upon the maximum response from the final filtering stage.

These models often contain many unknown parameters. What weights specify the inhibition and excitation among the different filter responses? What scale should one use for the Gaussian 1st- derivative filters? Perhaps most importantly, such models often contain an arbitrary, unspecified, threshold for determining the existence of a perceived edge between two textures. Many of these filter-based models are notoriously vague about the final decision stage. Furthermore, such models don't give us much insight into which textures will segment, since the comparison carried out by the model is often obscured by the details of the filtering, non-linearities, and image-based decision stage. What is the *meaning* of the texture gradient computed in the penultimate stage of the Malik & Perona model?

This paper describes a working texture segmentation algorithm that mimics human pre-attentive texture segmentation. Section 2 reviews recent human vision experiments [1], which were aimed at studying what first-order statistics determine texture segmentation. These results suggest that modelling pre-attentive texture segmentation by standard statistical tests for a difference in mean and standard deviation of various features such as orientation and contrast. Section 3 reviews previous models of pre-attentive texture segmentation in light of these results, and discusses the relationship to other edge detection and image segmentation algorithms. Section 4, presents a biologically plausible, filter-based algorithm based upon the experimental results in Section 2 and those of Kingdom & Keeble [9]. Section 5 presents results of this algorithm on artificial and natural images.

2 Recent Experimental Results in Pre-attentive Texture Segmentation

In [1], I studied segmentation of orientation-defined textures such as those shown in Figure 1. In each of the three experiments, observers viewed each texture pair for 250 ms, and the task was to indicate whether the boundary between the two textures fell to the left or right of the center of the display.

If, as Beck et al [4] suggested, texture segmentation of orientation-defined textures is based upon differences in the 1st-order statistics of orientation, to what 1st-order statistics does this refer? If the difference in mean orientation is the crucial quantity, two textures should segment if this difference lies above a certain threshold, independent of other properties of the orientation distributions. A more plausible possibility is that the determining factor is the *significance* of the difference in mean orientations. The significance of the difference takes into account the variability of the textures, so that two homogeneous textures with means differing by 30 degrees may segment, while two heterogeneous textures with the same difference in mean may not. Perhaps observers can also segment two textures that differ only in their variability. Other parameters of the distribution might also be relevant, such as the

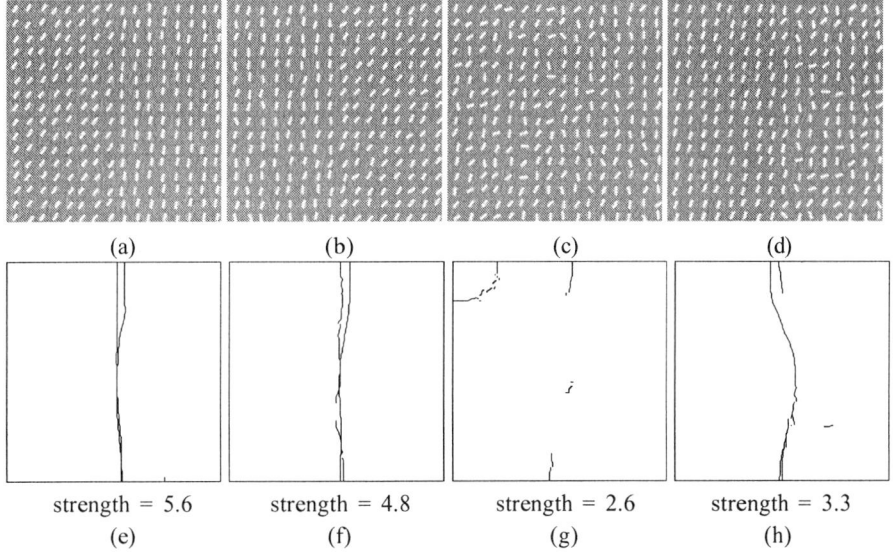

(a)	(b)	(c)	(d)

strength = 5.6	strength = 4.8	strength = 2.6	strength = 3.3
(e)	(f)	(g)	(h)

Figure 1: Three orientation-defined textures (a, b, c, d) and the significant edges found by our algorithm (e, f, g, h). The "strength" gives the average value of the test statistic at all locations for which the edge was significant. For (e, f, g), compare this with 2.04, the 82% threshold for a difference in mean orientation. For (h), compare the strength with 2.5, the 82% threshold for a difference in orientation variability.

skew or kurtosis. Alternatively, observers might be able to segment two textures given any sufficiently large difference in their first-order statistics.

The first experiment asked observers to segment two textures that differed only in their mean orientation. Each texture had orientations drawn from a *wrapped normal* distribution [10]. The experiment determined the threshold difference in mean orientation, at which observers can correctly localize the texture boundary 82% of the time, for 4 different values of the orientation standard deviation. Figure 2a shows the results. Clearly observers can segment two textures differing only in their mean orientation. Furthermore, the difference in mean required to perform the segmentation task depends upon the standard deviation.

The second experiment determined whether or not observers could pre-attentively segment textures that differed only in the variance of their orientation distributions. For two possible baseline standard deviations, the experiment measured the threshold increment in standard deviation at which observers could correctly localize the texture boundary 82% of the time. Observers could segment textures differing only in their variance, and Figure 2b shows the thresholds found. The difference in variance required depends upon the baseline standard deviation.

The third experiment tested segmentation of a unimodal wrapped-normal distribution from a discrete, bimodal distribution with the same mean orientation and variance. This experiment measured percent correct performance, for 4 possible spacings of the modes of the bimodal distribution. The results are shown in Figure 2c. All observers

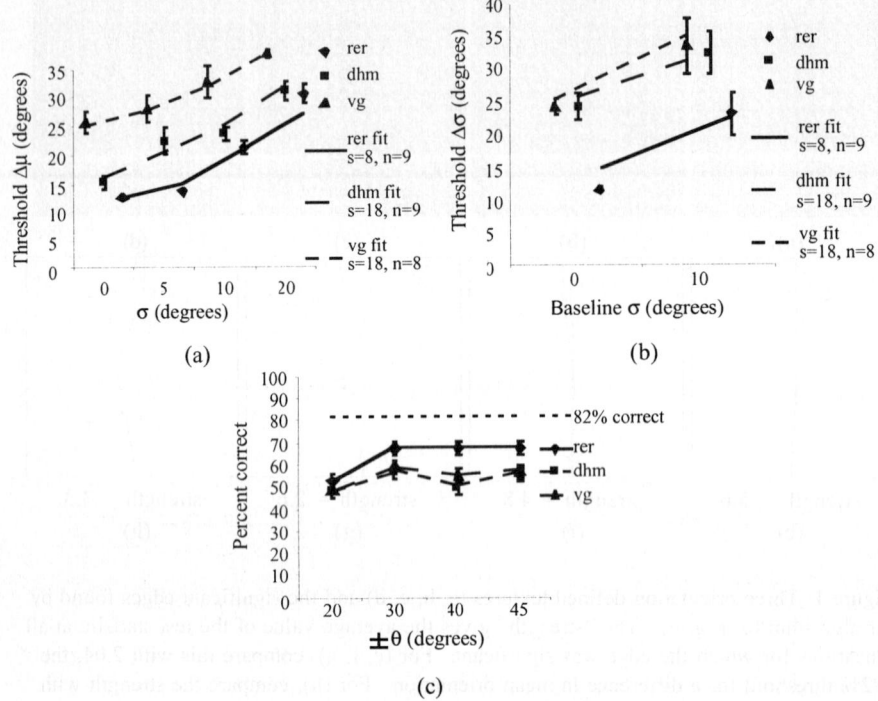

Figure 2: Results of psychophysical experiments and modelling. Symbols plus error bars indicate data; curves indicate the fit of the model to that data. (See text.) In (a) and (b) data for the 3 observers and best fit curves have been shifted horizontally to facilitate viewing.

performed well below the 82% correct required in Experiments 1 and 2, with only RER (the author) performing significantly above chance. These results do not rule out the possibility that observers may segment textures differing in statistics other than their mean and variance. However, the inability to segment textures that differ so greatly suggests that observers do not make use of the full first-order statistics in performing this task.

These results suggest a model of pre-attentive texture segmentation of orientation-defined textures. Figure 3 depicts the stages of this model. The observer first extracts noisy estimates of orientation, with the internal noise distributed according to a

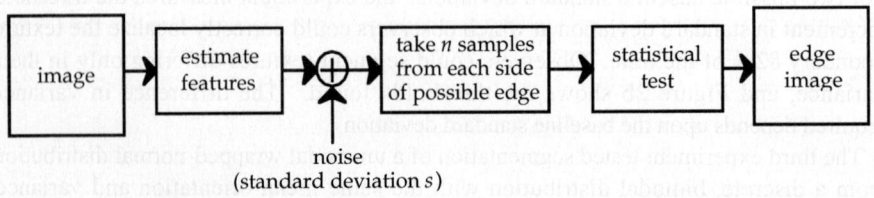

Figure 3: Diagram of our computational model of texture segmentation.

wrapped normal distribution, with some standard deviation s. The observer then collects n orientation estimates from each side of a hypothesized edge. If the two sets of samples differ significantly, at the $\alpha=0.82$ confidence level, in either their mean orientation or variance, then the observer sees a boundary. As implemented, this model uses the standard Watson-Williams test for a significant difference in mean orientation, and the Watson-Williams and Mardia test for a significant difference in orientation variance [10]. Section 4 discusses these tests in more detail.

This model, then, has two free parameters: the internal noise standard deviation, s, and the number of samples, n. The curves Figure 2a-b show the fit of this model to the experimental data, and the legend indicates the best-fit values of these parameters. For any given observer, this model provides a good fit of the thresholds for segmentation both of textures differing only in mean orientation, and textures differing only in orientation variance. Furthermore, the fit to the data of each of the three observers yields roughly the same value for the number of samples, n, suggesting that the size of the integration region may not vary much across observers. In modelling experimental results on homogeneous textures such as those used in these experiments, the n samples may be taken from anywhere in the texture. However, previous work suggests that the visual system performs local texture segmentation computations, with samples taken from regions adjacent to the hypothesized edge [see, e.g., 8, 11]. The fit to the data of the two less experienced subjects, DHM and VG, yields roughly the same value for the internal noise parameter, s. The fit to the data of experienced observer RER yields a lower value for this parameter, consistent with evidence that learning, for low-level perceptual tasks such as this one, may be mediated by a reduction of internal noise [12].

It appears, then, that for these orientation-defined textures, a good model for segmentation extracts noisy orientation estimates, then tests for a significant difference between the distributions of estimates using standard parametric statistical tests. For the purposes of this paper, I assume that a similar model describes segmentation based upon features besides orientation, such as contrast, color, etc. As of yet there is little experimental evidence addressing this point. Section 4 presents a texture segmentation algorithm based upon this model, using orientation and contrast as the texture features.

3 Previous Work: Texture Segmentation Models and Algorithms

To summarize the experimental results discussed in the previous section, a texture segmentation algorithm should be able to segment textures differing in mean orientation or in orientation variability. The segmentation difficulty should increase with increasing variability, in a way described by standard statistical tests. The segmentation algorithm should not find an edge when two textures have the same mean and variance, yet one is bimodally distributed and the other is unimodal.

Most filter-based models of pre-attentive texture segmentation will find an edge when the two textures differ in their mean orientation. Though these algorithms do not explicitly perform a statistical test for the difference in mean orientation, many of them will replicate the findings that edges become weaker as the variance increases [e.g. 7, 8]. It remains to be seen whether performance will degrade in a way that matches the experimental findings. If it does not, then these algorithms require more than one threshold -- the threshold would need to vary with orientation variance. Furthermore, my suggested model has two intuitive parameters, s and n, easily determined by a fit to the data. To the extent that previous models have *implicitly* performed a sort of statistical test, it may prove difficult to fit such models to the data. Space concerns prohibit our displaying results from Bergen/Landy [8] and Malik/Perona [7]. However, in our experience, as the variability of the texture increases, both algorithms find a large number of spurious edges, and Bergen/Landy may generate spurious edges at a finer scale than the true edge. Both models fail to find an edge when the textures differ only in variance.

A number of standard clustering techniques will cluster in such a way as to maximize the difference in mean relative to the variability of each cluster, or some other standard statistical measure [13, 14, 15]. However, clustering techniques require that the user specify the number of clusters. My edge detection algorithm will test for edges without knowledge of the number of edges.

Ruzon & Tomasi [16] perform color edge detection using the Earth Mover's Distance (EMD) as a measure of the difference between two distributions of color samples. This work uses a more complicated statistical test for an edge, like the algorithm presented here – this paper does not analyze the relationship between their EMD and standard statistical tests. Voorhees & Poggio [17] also use a more complicated distance measure between two textures, extracting blobs from the textures, then using a non-parametric statistical test to compare the textures. However, not all textures lend themselves to easy blobs extraction. Furthermore, the experimental results discussed in Section 2 show that the non-parametric test in [17] will find edges where human observers do not pre-attentively perceive them [1], a criticism that also holds for the χ^2 measure of [14].

At each location, Ruzon & Tomasi test for an edge in a number of different directions. This requires a great deal of computation. Section 4.5 presents heuristics for testing for an edge at only one orientation.

Elder [18] and Marimont & Rubner [19], working in standard, luminance-based edge detection, perform a statistical test for whether an edge exists at a given location, but they use a global measure of the variability, and thus will yield unexpected results when the variance changes over the image.

Some of the closest previous work comes from Fesharki & Hellestrand [20], who perform edge detection by using a Student's t-test to test for a significant difference in mean luminance. Similarly, Weber & Malik [21] test for motion boundaries, by using standard parametric statistical tests.

4 The Texture Segmentation Algorithm

4.1 Statistical Tests for a Significant Difference in Mean or Spread

My texture segmentation algorithm declares the presence of an edge if certain basic texture features differ significantly in their mean or spread. For the purposes of this paper, the algorithm extracts the features of orientation and contrast. This subsection describes the statistical tests used by the algorithm for these two kinds of features.

Testing for a Difference in Mean Orientation. Given two samples of orientation estimates, the Watson-Williams test [10] indicates whether the mean orientations of the two samples differ significantly. Assume the two independent random samples of the same size, n, and denote them $\{\phi_i\}_{i=1}^n$ and $\{\psi_i\}_{i=1}^n$. The Watson-Williams test assumes two samples drawn from *von Mises* distributions with the same *concentration parameter*, κ. The von Mises distribution for directional data has many of the nice features of the normal distribution for linear data. It is quite similar to the wrapped normal distribution used in Section 2, and for many purposes they may be considered equivalent [10]. The higher the concentration parameter, the more concentrated the distribution about the mean orientation – i.e. the lower the spread of the distribution. The Watson-Williams test is ideally for κ larger than 2 -- roughly equivalent to an angular standard deviation of less than 22 degrees.

We first compute the components of the *mean resultant vectors*:

$$\overline{C}_1 = \frac{1}{n}\sum_i \cos 2\phi_i, \quad \overline{S}_1 = \frac{1}{n}\sum_i \sin 2\phi_i, \quad \overline{C}_2 = \frac{1}{n}\sum_i \cos 2\psi_i, \quad \overline{S}_2 = \frac{1}{n}\sum_i \sin 2\psi_i$$

From this, we compute the length of the jth mean resultant vector:

$$\overline{R}_j = \sqrt{\overline{C}_j^2 + \overline{S}_j^2}$$

We also compute the length of the resultant vector for the combined data sample:

$$\overline{R} = \sqrt{\overline{C}^2 + \overline{S}^2}, \text{ where } \overline{C} = (\overline{C}_1 + \overline{C}_2)/2 \text{ and } \overline{S} = (\overline{S}_1 + \overline{S}_2)/2$$

The test statistic is

$$F_\mu = 2\left(1 + \frac{3}{8\tilde{\kappa}}\right)(n-1)\frac{\overline{R}_1 + \overline{R}_2 - 2\overline{R}}{2 - \overline{R}_1 - \overline{R}_2} \tag{1}$$

where $\tilde{\kappa}$ is the value of the concentration parameter estimated from the two samples.

Under the null hypothesis of no edge, F_μ is approximately distributed according to an F distribution, tabulated in standard statistics books. If F_μ is larger than the tabulated value for significance level α and degrees of freedom $(1, 2n-2)$, the difference in mean orientation is significant at level α. Throughout this paper, $\alpha = 0.82$.

Testing for a Difference in Orientation Variability. The Watson & Williams test, modified by Mardia [see 10], tests for a difference in concentration parameter. Assuming two samples, both of size n, drawn from von Mises distributions, with the mean resultant length of the combined sample greater than 0.70 (equivalently, an angular deviation of less than 22 degrees), the test statistic is:

$$F_\kappa = \frac{(1 - \overline{R}_1)}{(1 - \overline{R}_2)} \tag{2}$$

or $1/F_\kappa$, whichever is >1. Under the null hypothesis that the two samples have the same concentration, F_κ is approximately distributed according to an F distribution. To test for an edge of a given significance, α, one compares F_κ with the value in the $\alpha/2$ F distribution table, with degrees of freedom $(n-1, n-1)$. If the statistic is larger than the value from the table, the difference in concentration parameter is statistically significant.

Testing for a Difference in Mean Contrast. The standard Student's *t*-test tests for a significant difference in mean for linear variables such as contrast. Assuming two samples, both of size *n*, drawn from normal distributions with unknown but equal variance, the test statistic is

$$t = (\bar{x}_1 - \bar{x}_2)\sqrt{n} \, / \sqrt{s_1^2 + s_2^2} \tag{3}$$

where $\bar{x}_j$ and s_j are the *j*th sample mean and standard deviation, respectively. Under the null hypothesis that the two samples are drawn from the same distribution, this statistic is distributed according to a Student's *t* distribution, tabulated in standard statistics books. If the absolute value of *t* is larger than $t_{\alpha/2}$ from these tables, the difference in mean is significant at significance level α.

Testing for a Difference in Contrast Variance. To test for a significant difference in variance, for a linear variable such as contrast, one uses a standard *F* test. Again assuming two samples, each of size *n*, drawn from normal distributions, the test statistic is

$$F_\sigma = \frac{s_1^2}{s_2^2} \tag{4}$$

or $1/F_\sigma$, whichever is greater than 1. Under the null hypothesis that the two samples are drawn from distributions with the same variance, this statistic is once again distributed according to an *F* distribution. For a given significance, α, the difference in variance is significant if F_σ is larger than the value in the statistics table for this significance, with degrees of freedom $(n-1, n-1)$.

General Comments. Note that the two tests for an orientation edge may also be used for any texture feature that is circularly distributed, i.e. for which a value *k* is equivalent to a value *k* mod *m*, for some *m*. The two tests for a contrast edge may be used for any one-dimensional, linearly distributed texture feature. Similar tests exist for multi-dimensional data.

Before going on to describe the rest of the texture segmentation algorithm, consider what processing occurs in each of these four statistical tests. In each case, computing the statistic involves first taking the average of one or more functions of the feature estimates. For example, the orientation tests require first computing the mean resultant vectors, by taking the average of the cosine and sine of twice the orientation. In all 4 cases, the final test statistic involves some function of these averages. This suggests that an algorithm that computes these test statistics will involve first (1) computing a set of feature images, then (2) integrating some function(s) of these images over some integration region, and finally (3) computing the test statistics and testing for the presence of an edge. These stages correspond to those of the model depicted in Figure 3. Additional details of these stages are given below.

4.2 Extract Texture Features

For the purposes of this paper, my algorithm extracts the features of orientation and contrast. The use of contrast as a feature deserves some discussion. Several researchers [6, 7] have argued that segmentation of texture patterns such as those studied by Julesz [2] is determined by the "contrast" features extracted by center-surround filters such as Difference-of-Gaussian (DOG) filters. Others [3, 22] have suggested that one must extract more complicated features such as junctions and line endings. This remains an unresolved issue, but for many examples there is little difference between these two approaches. In addition, my algorithm assumes that segmentation of contrast-defined textures is determined by the significance of the differences between the mean and standard deviation of the contrast, as with orientation. This has yet to be demonstrated experimentally. Finally, the fit of the model to the orientation data from [1] yields estimates of the various model parameters, and the same would need to be done for other texture features, if one wishes to mimic human performance. My philosophy here is to extrapolate the orientation segmentation model to contrast textures, test it on various images, and look forward to additional psychophysics to resolve some of the above issues.

The algorithm extracts the features of orientation and contrast using biologically plausible spatial-frequency channel operations. For orientation, this amounts to using steerable filtering [23] to extract estimates of orientation. Steerable filtering produces two images at each scale, representing $\cos(2\theta)$ and $\sin(2\theta)$, where θ is the orientation, locally. These are precisely the functions of orientation one needs in order to compute the mean resultant vectors required by the statistical tests in Eqns. 1 and 2. For contrast, we follow [7], filtering with first- and second-derivative DOG filters, followed by half-wave rectification, and a local max operation. The local max is intended to give a single, phase-invariant measure of local contrast.

The algorithm extracts orientation and contrast at a number of different scales. For orientation, we use the oriented Gaussian pyramid from [8]. Thus the scales for orientation filtering differ by a factor of two. For contrast, we use the more densely sampled scales of [7].

The algorithm processes each scale and feature independently. As necessary, it adds noise to the feature estimates, so as to match the internal noise parameter in fits to human data. The orientation estimation procedure contains inherent noise equivalent to the internal noise for the two more naïve observers in Figure 2, so the algorithm requires no added noise. For contrast, we have no fit to human data, and have experimented with a number of possible amounts of added noise. In the examples shown here, use an added noise with variance $\sigma^2 = 150$.

4.3 Collect Samples of Feature Estimates and Compute the Relevant Statistics

Next, the algorithm hypothesizes that an edge, with a particular orientation, exists at a particular location in the image. It then tests this hypothesis by running the various statistical tests described above.

As mentioned in the discussion of these statistical tests, the first step in calculating each of the statistics is to compute averages of various functions of the feature values.

Therefore, the step in the model in which the observer collects n feature samples from each side of a hypothesized edge is equivalent to integrating some functions of the feature values over a local integration region. The algorithm integrates using a Gaussian window.

Previous work by Kingdom & Keeble [9] suggests that, for orientation, the size of the integration region is a constant multiple of the width of the oriented lines that make up the texture. Alternatively, one may think of the region size as being a constant multiple of the support of the filters used to extract orientation estimates. For finer features, the region is proportionally smaller than for coarser features. Once again, the algorithm described here assumes that the same principle holds for features other than orientation.

The fit to the experimental data in Figure 2 indicated that human observers seemed to collect orientation estimates from $n=9$ elements on each side of the hypothesized edge. Based upon the width and spacing of the line elements used in the experimental displays, this implies that human observers collect samples from a circular region of diameter approximately 5 times the support of their oriented filters. The algorithm uses an integration region for contrast features of a similar size relative to the center-surround filters used to extract contrast.

4.4 Combine Results into a Single Edge Map

The results of the previous steps give us an image for each scale, feature type, and statistical test (mean and spread). Each image indicates, for each location, the presence or absence of a significant edge of the given type. The value of the statistic gives an indication of the strength of the edge. One could stop at this stage, or there are various things one could do to clean up these edge maps and combine them into a single map. "False" variance edges tend to occur next to edges due to a difference in mean, since a region which spans the edge will have a higher variance than neighboring regions which include only one texture. Therefore, the algorithm inhibits variance edges near significant difference-in-mean edges. It combines edge images across scales using a straightforward "or" operation. If an edge is significant at any scale, it is significant, regardless of what happens at any other scale. Finally, texture edges tend to be more poorly localized than luminance edges, due to their statistical nature. Texture edges, in the examples in this paper, are typically statistically significant in a band about 2 texels wide. One can "thin" edges by finding the maximum of the test statistic in the direction of the edge, as done for the results presented here.

4.5 How to Hypothesize an Edge

Edge detection methods that involve taking the gradient of the mean of some feature value [e.g. 24, 7, and many others] have the advantage that they are "steerable" [23]. This means that such methods can take only a horizontal and a vertical derivative, and infer the direction in which the derivative – and thus the edge strength – is maximized. Edge detection methods that involve more complex comparisons of the features on each side of the edge [e.g. 16] typically require that one check each possible orientation for the presence of an edge. This process is time consuming. Thus in this

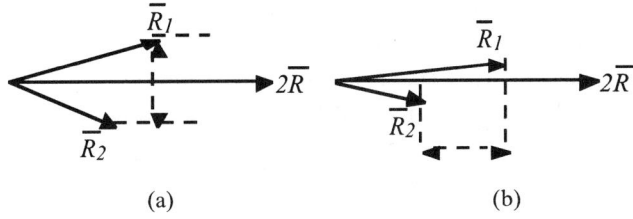

Figure 4: Relationship between mean resultant vectors and heuristics for guessing edge direction (see text).

subsection I ask whether one can make a good guess as to the most likely orientation of an edge at each location, and test only that edge orientation.

This subsection presents a set of heuristics for guessing the edge orientation, one for each statistical test s. For each s, one would like to test only one orientation for an edge at each location, yet find edges at the same locations as if one had tested all possible orientations. Therefore, for each s, one desires a steerable function, f_s, of the feature values, such that *if there exists an orientation such that test s indicates a significant edge, test s will indicate a significant edge at the orientation that maximizes f_s*. If these conditions hold, one may easily find the orientation, θ_{edge}, that maximizes f_s, and be assured that if test s would find a significant edge at that location, it will find one at orientation θ_{edge}.

For each test, s, I present a function f_s that is the Gaussian 1st-derivative of some function of the feature values. The maximizing orientation of such f_s is given by the direction of the gradient. The heuristics presented produced the desired behaviour over 99% of the time in Monte Carlo simulations. Thus these heuristics provide a reliable way of avoiding the computational complexity of testing each possible edge orientation at each spatial location.

Heuristic for a Mean-Orientation Edge. As mentioned above, the orientation estimation stage returns two images for each scale, representing $\cos(2\theta)$ and $\sin(2\theta)$, where θ is the local orientation estimate at that scale. First, rotate all orientation estimates by angle β, such that the mean resultant vector for the combined sample has an orientation of $0°$. This generates the image:

$$\sin(2\theta - \beta) = \sin(2\theta)\cos(\beta) - \cos(2\theta)\sin(\beta)$$

Next, take the Gaussian 1st-derivative of this image in the horizontal and vertical directions. The direction of the gradient provides a guess for the edge direction. The intuition follows:

Figure 4a shows example resultant vectors, rotated to the canonical position, for the case in which the two distributions have the same concentration but different mean orientations. The Gaussian 1st-derivative computes essentially the difference between the y-components of the two resultant vectors. The length of the resultant vector gives a measure of the concentration of the distribution. The orientation of the resultant vectors indicates an estimate of the mean orientations of the underlying distributions. For given lengths of the two mean resultant vectors, $\bar{R}_1$ and $\bar{R}_2$, the vertical distance between their tips will be larger the larger the difference in angle between them, and for a given difference in angle, the vertical distance will be smaller the shorter their lengths. The same is true of the test statistic, F_μ, thus the intuition that this heuristic should give us a reasonable guess for the direction of the edge.

Heuristic for an Orientation-Variability Edge. Again rotate the orientation estimates such that the resultant vector for the combined sample has an orientation of $0°$. This time, compute the image:

$$\cos(2\theta - \beta) = \cos(2\theta)\cos(\beta) + \sin(2\theta)\sin(\beta)$$

Again, take Gaussian 1st-derivatives of this image. The direction of the gradient provides the guess for the edge direction. The intuition follows:

Figure 4b shows example resultant vectors for the case in which the underlying distributions differ only in their concentration parameter. The horizontal distance between the tips of these resultant vectors gives a measure of the difference between the two concentration parameters. The test statistic (see Eqn. 2) takes a ratio of the resultant vector lengths, as opposed to a difference, but the difference serves well when it comes to guessing the direction of the edge.

Heuristic for a Mean-Contrast Edge. Here we steer the Gaussian 1st-derivative of contrast. The direction of the gradient, which gives the direction with the largest change in mean contrast, provides the guess for the edge direction.

In this case, one can make a stronger statement: The direction of the gradient of mean contrast indicates the direction in which the test statistic reaches its maximum. Thus the direction of the gradient always provides the best guess for the edge direction. Recall that the test statistic for a difference in mean contrast is:

$$t = (\bar{x}_1 - \bar{x}_2)\sqrt{n} / \sqrt{s_1^2 + s_2^2}$$

The gradient indicates the direction in which $(\bar{x}_1 - \bar{x}_2)$ is maximized. The only way that t could reach a maximum in a different direction is if that direction reduced the denominator more than the numerator. It is a simple matter of algebra to show that an edge direction with smaller $(\bar{x}_1 - \bar{x}_2)$ in fact also yields a larger $\sqrt{s_1^2 + s_2^2}$, thus reducing the test statistic. Due to space concerns, we do not reproduce the proof here. The intuition follows: Suppose that in the direction of the gradient, $\bar{x}_1 > \bar{x}_2$. When the direction of the hypothesized edge changes, m samples from the first set transfer to the second, and vice versa. Since the difference between the two means decreases, the change in direction adds, on average, smaller elements to the 1st set, and takes away larger elements. But such a manipulation will increase the sum of the variances of the sets, since it adds small elements to the set with the larger mean, and vice versa.

Heuristic for a Contrast-Variance Edge. First calculate the mean, μ, of both sample sets. Then compute the image

$$(x_i - \mu)^2$$

Again, steer the Gaussian 1st-derivative of this function, and the direction of its maximum gives us our guess for the edge direction.

This heuristic estimates the variance of each sample set, and uses the difference between these variances as a measure of the strength of the edge in a given direction. The test statistic takes a ratio of the two variance estimates, as opposed to a difference, but the difference serves well when it comes to guessing the direction of the edge, and is easily steered.

5 Results and Discussion

All of the examples in this paper used the same version of the algorithm, with parameters set as described above. Figure 1 shows the results on four images much like those used in the experiments described in Section 2. The first three texture pairs differ in mean orientation by 25°. Low variability textures, as in Figure 1a, allow observers to localize the boundary well over 82% of the time. In Figure 1b, a larger orientation variance makes the difference in mean just above the 82% correct threshold. In Figure 1c, the increased variance makes the difference in mean well below threshold – observers would have great difficulty localizing this edge.

Figures 1e-1g show the results of our algorithm on these three texture pairs. The results will often show a number of edges laid on top of each other, when edges are found at a number of different scales or by more than one of the 4 statistical tests. The algorithm correctly finds a strong boundary in the first image, a weaker one in the second image, and essentially no edge in the third.

Figure 1d shows an image in which the two textures differ only in the spread of their orientations. This difference is above the thresholds found in Experiment 2, and it should be possible to see the boundary. Our algorithm finds the boundary, as shown in Figure 1h.

Many texture segmentation experiments and theories have revolved around images like those in Figure 5. Malik & Perona [7] tested their algorithm on such images, and used it to predict the segmentability of these texture pairs. Their predictions agreed with the experimental data of Gurnsey & Browse [25]. (Malik & Perona also compared the results of their algorithm with those of Krose [26]. However, Krose studied a visual search task, in which observers looked for an "odd man out." It is inappropriate to compare those results with results of segmentation of images such as those in Figure 5, for reasons given in [25].) The results of my algorithm, shown in

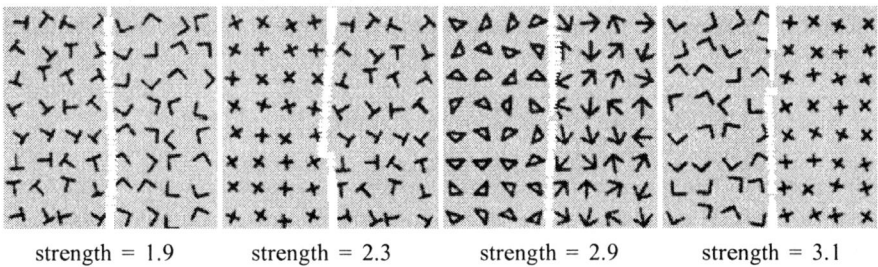

strength = 1.9   strength = 2.3   strength = 2.9   strength = 3.1

Figure 5: Four texture pairs from [7], with the edges found by our algorithm. The strength gives the average value of the mean-contrast test statistic for each edge, and should be compared with the threshold value, 1.42. Only mean-contrast edges were significant.

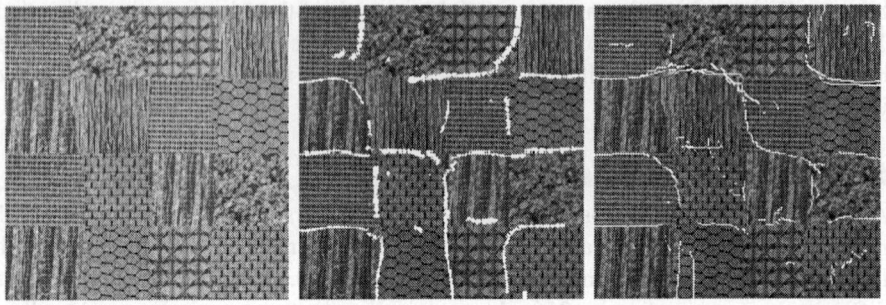

Figure 6: Patchwork of natural textures (a), along with the contrast (b) and orientation (c) edges found by our algorithm.

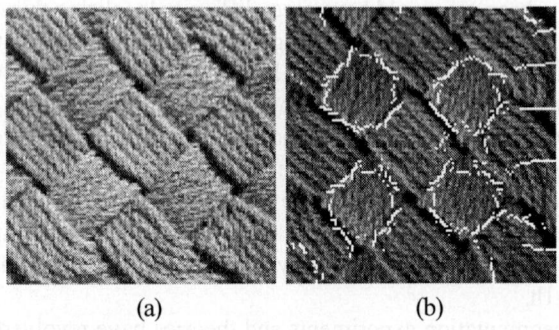

(a)   (b)

Figure 7: Results on a natural image.

Figure 5, agree with those of [25].

Figure 6a shows an array of real textures, stitched together. Note that the true boundaries between the textures are *not* straight. The algorithm does quite well at extracting contrast edges (Figure 6b), often closely following the boundaries. It performs less well near corners, where assumptions about the number of textures present in a region are violated. Few of the textures in this image have strong orientation, providing a challenge to finding orientation edges, yet we still see reasonable results, as shown in Figure 6c. The algorithm predicts no pre-attentive segmentation for texture pairs with no edge shown between them. Figure 7 shows a highly oriented natural image, for which the algorithm extracts strong orientation edges.

This paper has presented an algorithm for mimicking pre-attentive texture segmentation. The algorithm bridges the gap between earlier statistical and filter-based models. It has essentially two intuitive key parameters, the internal noise in the feature estimates and the integration scale, and obtains values of those parameters from fits to experimental data in [1, 9]. Performing tests for an edge more complicated than a gradient has traditionally led to increased computational cost due to a need to test for an edge at multiple orientations. The heuristics presented here essentially allow the algorithm's statistical tests to be "steered."

References

1 R. Rosenholtz. What statistics determine segmentation of orientation-defined textures? *Perception (Suppl.)*, 26:111, 1997.

2 B. Julesz. Experiments in the visual perception of texture. *Sci. Amer.*, 232:34-43, 1975.

3 B. Julesz. Texton gradients: the texton theory revisited. *Biol. Cybern.*, 54:245-51, 1986.

4 J. Beck, K. Prazdny, & A. Rosenfeld. A theory of textural segmentation. In *Human & Machine Vision*, Beck, Hope, & Rosenfeld, eds. (New York: Academic Press), 1983.

5 M. R. Turner. Texture discrimination by Gabor functions. *Biol. Cybern.,* 55:71-82, 1986.

6 J. Bergen & E. Adelson. Early vision and texture perception. *Nature*, 333:363-4, 1988.

7 J. Malik & P. Perona. Preattentive texture discrimination with early vision mechanisms. *J. Opt. Soc. Am.. A.*, 7(5):923-32, 1990.

8 J. R. Bergen & M. S. Landy. Computational modeling of visual texture segregation. In *Computational models of visual perception*, Landy & Movshon, eds. (Cambridge, MA: MIT Press), 1991.

9 F. A. A. Kingdom & D. R. T. Keeble. On the mechanism for scale invariance in orientation-defined textures. *Vision Research*, 39:1477-89, 1999.

10 E. Batschelet. *Circular statistics in biology*. (London: Academic Press), 1981.

11 H. C. Nothdurft. Sensitivity for structure gradient in texture discrimination tasks. *Vision Research*, 25:1957-68, 1985.

12 B. A. Dosher & Z.-L. Lu. Mechanisms of perceptual learning. *Investigative Ophthalmology & Visual Science (Suppl.)*, 39(4):912, 1998.

13 R. Duda & P. Hart. *Pattern classification and scene analysis*. (New York: Wiley), 1973.

14 J. Puzicha, T. Hoffman, J. Buhmann. Non-parametric similarity measures for unsupervised texture segmentation and image retrieval. *Proc. CVPR*, pp. 267-72, Puerto Rico, June, 1997.

15 J. Shi & J. Malik. Self-inducing relational distance and its application to image segmentation. *Proc. ECCV*, pp. 528-43, Freiburg, Germany, June, 1998.

16 M. A. Ruzon & C. Tomasi. Color edge detection with the compass operator. *Proc. CVPR*, pp. 160-6, Fort Collins, CO, June, 1999.

17 H. Voorhees & T. Poggio. Computing texture boundaries from images. *Nature*, 333:364-7, 1988.

18 J. H. Elder & S. W. Zucker. Local scale control for edge detection and blue estimation. *Proc. ECCV*, pp. 57-69, 1996.

19 D. H. Marimont & Y. Rubner. A probabilistic framework for edge detection and scale selection. *Proc. ICCV*, pp. 207-14, Bombay, India, January, 1998.

20 M. N. Fesharki & G. R. Hellestrand. A new edge detection algorithm based on a statistical approach. *Proc. ISSIPNN*, 1:21-4, 1994.

21 J. Weber & J. Malik. Scene partitioning via statistic-based region growing. Tech. report UCB/CSD-94-817, Comp. Sci. Div. (EECS), Univ. of California, Berkeley, 1994.

22 E. Barth, C. Zetzsche, F. Giulianini, & I. Rentschler. Intrinsic 2D features as textons. *J. Opt. Soc. Am. A.*, 15(7):1723-32, 1998.

23 W. T. Freeman & E. H. Adelson. The design and use of steerable filters. *IEEE PAMI*, 13(9):891-906, 1995.

24 R. M. Haralick. Digital step edges from zero crossings of the 2nd directional derivative. *IEEE PAMI*, 6(1):58-68, 1984.

25 R. Gurnsey & R. Browse. Micropattern properties and presentation conditions influencing visual texture discrimination. *Percept. Psychophys.*, 41:239-52, 1987.

26 B. Krose. Local structure analyzers as determinants of preattentive pattern discrimination. *Biol. Cybern.*, 55:289-98, 1987.

Calibrating Parameters of Cost Functionals

Laurent Younes

CMLA (CNRS, URA 1611)
Ecole Normale Supérieure de Cachan
61, avenue du Président Wilson
F-94 235 Cachan CEDEX
email: younes@cmla.ens-cachan.fr
Tel: 33.1.47.40.59.18, Fax: 33.1.47.40.59.01

Abstract. We propose a new framework for calibrating parameters of
energy functionals, as used in image analysis. The method learns parameters from a family of correct examples, and given a probabilistic
construct for generating wrong examples from correct ones. We introduce a measure of frustration to penalize cases in which wrong responses
are preferred to correct ones, and we design a stochastic gradient algorithm which converges to parameters which minimize this measure of
frustration. We also present a first set of experiments in this context,
and introduce extensions to deal with data-dependent energies.

keywords: Learning, variational method, parameter estimation, image reconstruction, Bayesian image models

1 Description of the method

Many problems in computer vision are addressed through the minimization of
a cost functional U. This function is typically defined on a large, finite, set
Ω (for example the set of pictures with fixed dimensions), and the minimizer
of $x \mapsto U(x)$ is supposed to conciliates several properties which are generally
antithetic.

Indeed, the energy is usually designed as a combination of several terms, each
of them corresponding to a precise property which must be satisfied by the optimal solution. As an example among many others, let us quote probably the most
studied cost functional in computer vision, namely the Mumford/Shah energy
(cf. [5]), which is used to segment and smooth an observed picture. Expressed
in a continuous setting, it is the combination of three terms, one which ensures
that the smoothed picture x, defined on a set $D \subset I\!\!R^2$ is not too different from
the observed one ξ, another which states that the derivative of the smoothed
picture is small, except, possibly, on a discontinuity set Δ, and a last one which
ensures that the discontinuity set has small length. These terms are weighted by
parameters, yielding an energy function of the kind

$$U(x) = \int_D (\xi(s) - x(s))^2 ds + \alpha \int_{D \setminus \Delta} |\nabla_s x| * 2 ds + \beta \mathcal{H}(\Delta) \tag{1}$$

where $\mathcal{H}(\varDelta)$ is Haussdorf measure of the discontinuity set.

In this paper, we consider cost functionals of the kind

$$U(x) = U_0(x) + \sum_{i=1}^{d} \theta_i U_i(x)$$

where the θ_i are positive parameters. Whatever vision task this functional is dedicated to (restoration, segmentation, edge detection, matching, pattern recognition, ...), it is acknowledged that variations in the values of the parameters have significant effects on the qualitative properties of the minimizer. Very often, these parameters are fixed by trial and error, while experimenting the optimization algorithm. We here propose a systematic way for tuning them, based on a learning procedure.

The method is reminiscent to the qualitative box estimation procedure which has been introduced by Azencott in [1]. It relies on some *a priori* knowledge which is available to the designer. The basic information can be expressed under the statement: *For some configurations x and y in Ω, one should have $U(x) \geq U(y)$.* In other terms, y is a "better" solution than x.

When this is known for a number of pairs of configurations, $\{(x_k, y_k), k = 1, \dots, N\}$, we get a system of constraints which take the form, for $k = 1, \dots, N$:

$$U_0(y_k) - U_0(x_k) + \sum_{i=1}^{d} \theta_i (U_i(y_k) - U_i(x_k)) \leq 0$$

If we let $\theta = (\theta_1, \dots, \theta_d)$, $\varDelta_{ki} = U_i(y_k) - U_i(x_k)$, and $\varDelta_k = (\varDelta_{k1}, \dots, \varDelta_{kd})$, this can be written

$$\varDelta_{0k} + \langle \theta, \varDelta_k \rangle \leq 0, k = 1, \dots, N,$$

$\langle ., . \rangle$ being the usual inner product on $\mathbb{R}^d$.

Solving such a system of linear inequalities can be performed by a standard simplex algorithm. However, when the system has no solution (which is likely to occur if there are many inequalities, and/or if they are deduced for the observation of noisy real data), it is difficult to infer from the simplex method which parameter should be selected. We thus define a new cost functional in the parameters, or *measure of frustration*, which is large when the inequalities are not satisfied: denote by α^+ the positive part of a real number α, and set

$$F_0(\theta) = \sum_{k=1}^{N} [\varDelta_{0k} + \langle \theta, \varDelta_k \rangle]^+$$

It is practically more convenient to use a smooth approximation of this function, so that we let, for $\lambda > 0$

$$F_\lambda(\theta) = \frac{1}{2} \sum_{k=1}^{N} q_\lambda [\varDelta_{0k} + \langle \theta, \varDelta_k \rangle]$$

with $q_\lambda(\alpha) = \lambda \log \left(e^{\frac{\alpha}{\lambda}} + e^{-\frac{\alpha}{\lambda}} \right) + \alpha$. Given properly selected examples, the minimization of F_λ is the core of our estimation procedure. We therefore study some related properties.

2 Properties of the function F_λ

Proposition 1. *For all $\lambda \geq 0$, F_λ is a convex function of θ. Moreover,* $\lim_{\lambda \to 0+} F_\lambda(\theta) = F_0(\theta)$.

This is more or less obvious and left to the reader. Let us, however, write down the derivatives of F_λ, for $\lambda > 0$, since they will be used in the sequel (recall that the first derivative is a vector and the second derivative a $d \times d$ symmetric matrix). One has:

$$F'_\lambda(\theta) = \sum_{k=1}^{N} \left(1 + \tanh \left[\frac{1}{\lambda} (\Delta_{0k} + \langle \theta , \Delta_k \rangle) \right] \right) \Delta_k \tag{2}$$

$$F''_\lambda(\theta) = \frac{1}{\lambda} \sum_{k=1}^{N} \left(1 - \tanh^2 \left[\frac{1}{\lambda} (\Delta_{0k} + \langle \theta , \Delta_k \rangle) \right] \right) \Delta_k .^t \Delta_k \tag{3}$$

Denote by Σ_Δ the covariance matrix of the Δ_k, namely $\Sigma_\Delta = \sum_{k=1}^{N} \Delta_k .^t \Delta_k$.

Proposition 2. *The matrix Σ_Δ is positive definite if and only if, for all $\lambda > 0$, the function F_λ is strictly convex, and if and only if, for some $\lambda > 0$, the function F_λ is strictly convex*

Proof. If, for some $\lambda > 0$, and for some θ, $F''_\lambda(\theta)$ is not definite positive, there exists a vector $u \in \mathbb{R}^d$ such that $^t u.F''_\lambda(\theta).u = 0$. But one has

$$^t u.F''_\lambda(\theta).u = \frac{1}{\lambda} \sum_{k=1}^{N} \left(1 - \tanh^2 \left[\frac{1}{\lambda} (\Delta_{0k} + \langle \theta , \Delta_k \rangle) \right] \right) \langle u , \Delta_k \rangle^2$$

and this expression can vanish only if, for all k, $\langle u , \Delta_k \rangle = 0$, but this implies that $^t u \Sigma_\Delta u = 0$ so that Σ_Δ cannot be definite.

Conversely, if Σ_Δ is not positive, one shows similarly that there exists u such that $\langle u , \Delta_k \rangle = 0$ for all k, but this implies that, for any $\lambda > 0$, for any θ and any $t \in \mathbb{R}$, $F_\lambda(\theta + tu) = F_\lambda(\theta)$ so that F_λ cannot be strictly convex.

Thus, non convexity is equivalent to the existence of a fixed linear relation among $\Delta_{k1}, \ldots, \Delta_{kd}$.

We now address the question of the existence of a minimum of F_λ. We assume $\lambda > 0$ and strict convexity, ie $\Sigma_\Delta > 0$. The convex function F_λ has no minimum if and only if it has a direction of recession, ie. if and only if there exists a vector $u \in \mathbb{R}^d$ such that, for all θ, $t \mapsto F_\lambda(\theta + tu)$ is decreasing. By studying the derivative of this function, we can show that, in order to have a direction of recession, there must exist some u such that $\langle \Delta_k , u \rangle \leq 0$ for all k, with a strict inequality for some k in order to have strict convexity. If u provides a direction of recession, then $t.u$ will be a solution of the original set of inequalities as soon as t is large enough. This is a very unconvenient feature, since, in particular, it will completely cancel out the role of U_0. Such a situation is in fact caused a lack of information in the original set of examples $(x_k, y_k), k = 1, \ldots, N$, in the sense that this set fails to provide situations in which the role of U_0 has some impact.

3 Learning from examples

3.1 Objective function from small variations

We now provide a framework in which this simple technique can be applied when some examples of "correct configurations" are available. They may come, either from simulated, synthetic data, or from real data which have been processed by an expert. The idea is to generate random perturbations of the correct configurations and to estimate the parameters so that the perturbed configurations have a higher energy than the correct ones.

Let us first assume, that a single configuration y_0 is provided. Our goal is thus to design the parameters so that y_0 will be, in some local sense, a minimizer of the energy. The key of the learning process is to define a process which generates *random perturbations* of a given configuration. This process of course depends on the application, and should provide a sufficiently large range of new configurations from the initial one. Formally, it will be associated to a transition probability $P(y_0, .)$ on Ω, which will produce variations of the correct configuration y_0. Assume this is done K times independently, and that a sample $x_1, \ldots, x_K$ has been drawn from this probability. From the fact that y_0 is a good configuration, we assume that, for all k, $U(y_0) - U(x_k) \leq 0$. Slightly changing the notation, define $\Delta(y_0, x)$ to be the vector composed with the $U_i(y_0) - U_i(x)$ for $i = 1, \ldots, d$ and $h(y_0, x) = U_0(y_0) - U_0(x)$. The previous method leads to minimize

$$F_\lambda^K(\theta) = \frac{1}{2} \sum_{k=1}^{K} q_\lambda[h(y_0, x_k) + \langle \theta, \Delta(y_0, x_k) \rangle]$$

Now, when K tends to infinity, the limit of F_λ^K/K is almost surely given by (since the samples are drawn independently)

$$F_\lambda(\theta) = \frac{1}{2} \mathbf{E}_{y_0} \{ q_\lambda[h(y_0, x_k) + \langle \theta, \Delta(y_0, x_k) \rangle] \}$$

where $\mathbf{E}_{y_0}$ is the expectation with respect to the probability $P(y_0, .)$. This functional becomes our measure of frustration, which should be minimized in order to calibrate θ.

Assume now that several examples are provided, under the form of a learning set $y_1, \ldots, y_N$: the new objective function is

$$F_\lambda(\theta) = \frac{1}{2} \sum_{j=1}^{N} \mathbf{E}_{y_j} \{ q_\lambda[h(y_j, x_k) + \langle \theta, \Delta(y_j, x_k) \rangle] \}$$

3.2 Minimizing F_λ

To simplify the notation, we restrict again to the case of a single example y_0. We still have the fact that, for any λ, the function F_λ is convex, with first derivative

$$F_\lambda'(\theta) = \mathbf{E}_{y_0}\left\{\left(1 + \tanh\left[\frac{1}{\lambda}(h(y_0,.) + \langle\theta, \Delta(y_0,.)\rangle)\right]\right)\Delta(y_0,.)\right\} \quad (4)$$

According to the discussion of section 2, the transition probability P should, to avoid directions of recession, explore a sufficiently large neighborhood of y_0, to provide enough information on the variations of U. Because of this, it is likely that the gradient in (4) cannot be efficiently computed, neither analytically nor numerically. To minimize F_λ in such a case, we use a stochastic gradient learning procedure, which we describe now:

Learning procedure

0. Start with some initial value θ_0
1. At time n, θ_n being the current parameter, draw at random a sample X^n from the transition probability $P(y_0,.)$, and set

$$\theta_{n+1} = \theta_n - \gamma_{n+1}\left(1 + \tanh\left[\frac{1}{\lambda}(h(y_0, X^n) + \langle\theta, \Delta(y_0, X^n)\rangle)\right]\right)\Delta(y_0, X^n)$$

$$(5)$$

where $(\gamma_n, n \geq 1)$ is a decreasing sequence of positive gains satisfying $\sum_n \gamma_n = +\infty$ and $\sum_n \gamma_n^2 < +\infty$.

Standard results in stochastic approximation (see [2], for example), show that, in the absence of direction of recession, the sequence (θ_n) generated by this algorithm almost surely converges to the minimizer of F_λ.

If there are more than one example $y_1, \ldots, y_M$, the previous algorithm simply has to be modified by taking, at each step, y_0 at random in the set $\{y_1, \ldots, y_M\}$.

3.3 Remark

Notice that, under its most general form, and when the perturbations explore a large set of configurations, there is very little chance that there exists a parameter set for which all the constraints are truly satisfied, that is for which the energy of the correct configurations y_j are smaller than the energies of all the perturbations which might be generated by $P(y_j,.)$. This could be made possible by designing an energy with a very large number of terms, which will then essentially work as an associative memory (like an Hopfield neural net [4]), in which the correct configurations are *stored*, but this certainly is not a desirable feature of an energy function in image processing. A more efficient goal is to learn some common important trends of the correct configurations, and not all their peculiarities, in which case having some residual frustration is not a problem.

4 Illustration

4.1 Description

We illustrate this methodology with binary example. Let Ω be the set of configurations $x = (x_s, s \in S := \{1, \ldots, M\}^2)$ with $x_s = 0$ or 1 for all s. We define an energy $U(x)$ on Ω as follows.

Let $U_0(x) = \sum_s x_s$. For a radius $r > 0$ and a direction $\alpha \in [0, 2\pi[$, we define an energy term $U_{\alpha, r}$ which operates as an edge analyzer in the direction α, with scale r.

For $s = (i, j) \in S$, let $\mathcal{B}_s(r)$ be the discrete ball of center s and radius r, ie. set of all $s' = (i', j') \in S$ such that $(i - i')^2 + (j - j')^2 \leq r^2$. For each direction α, divide this ball in two parts $\mathcal{B}_s^+(r, \alpha)$ and $\mathcal{B}_s^-(r, \alpha)$ according to the sign of $(i - i') \cos \alpha + (j - j') \sin \alpha$, then define

$$U_{r,\alpha}(x) = \sum_{s \in S} \left| \sum_{s' \in \mathcal{B}_s^+(r,\alpha)} x_{s'} - \sum_{s' \in \mathcal{B}_s^-(r,\alpha)} x_{s'} \right|$$

Finally, select a series of pairs (r_i, α_i) for $i = 1, \ldots, d$, and set

$$U(x) = \theta_0 U_0(x) + \sum_{i=1} \theta_i U_{r_i, \alpha_i}(x)$$

Our experiment will consist in learning the parameters $\theta_0, \ldots, \theta_d$ on the basis of a single image y_0, and then try to analyze which features of the image have emerged in the final model. Notice that we have added a parameter, θ_0, for the first term U_0, which is also estimated. If there exist parameters such that $U(x) > U(y_0)$ for all configurations x which can be generated by $P(y_0, .)$, the extraneous parameter is redundant (only its sign matters), and this creates a direction of recession for the minimized functional. But such a case did not seem to happen in the present set of experiments, so that, even with one additional parameter, the measure of frustration did remain strictly convex.

For learning, the perturbations $P(y_0, .)$ consist in adding of deleting balls of random centers and radii to the configuration y_0. To validate the estimated parameters, we run an energy minimization algorithm (simulated annealing with exponentially fast decay of temperature) with different starting configurations (including the learned image y_0 itself) to see whether y_0 is close to the minimizing solutions.

4.2 Experiments

We have used three pictures (disc, square and triangle, see fig. 1), and estimated parameters independently for each picture. The results were quite different for each image.

The disc-picture seems to have been perfectly stored, in the sense of an associative memory, by the learned parameters: starting with any initial picture, the final restored picture is a disc, with only minor variations. This is not surprising, in fact, since the energy function is itself based on disc-shaped analyzers.

The square picture is stabilized by the restoration algorithm, again with minor variations, so that the estimation has suceeded in making this picture (almost) a local minimum of the energy. However, starting from other configurations does not always result in a white square on a dark background, and a phenomenon reminiscent of phase transition can be observed (see fig. 5). This is due to the fact that, in the square picture, the number of white pixels is almost equal to the number of black pixels.

Finally, the triangle picture is not even stabilized by the restoration algorithm. It is in fact significantly modified, as shown in fig. 6. As stated before, it would not be difficult to design an energy with additional terms in order to perfectly store the triangle. It is however more interesting to stay with a given energy, and analyse which features for the triangle picture have been learned. This can be seen in fig. 7, where the restored picture from a uniformly white input clearly has nothing to do with a triangle, but shares essential local features, in particular regarding the orientations of the boundaries.

Fig. 1. Pictures of disc, square, triangle

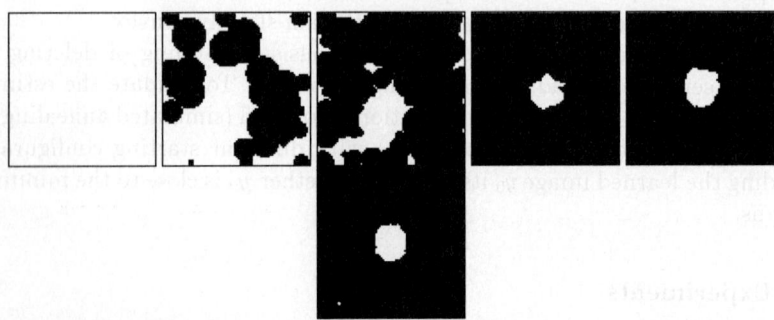

Fig. 2. Starting with a white picture with parameters estimated from the disc

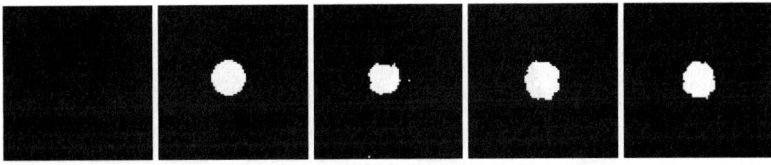

Fig. 3. Starting with a black picture with parameters estimated from the disc

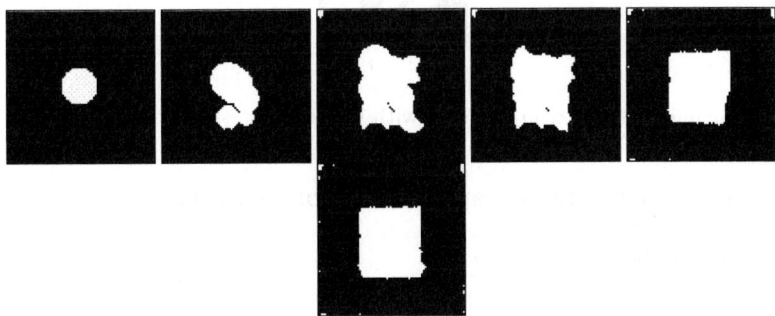

Fig. 4. Starting from the disc with parameters estimated from the square

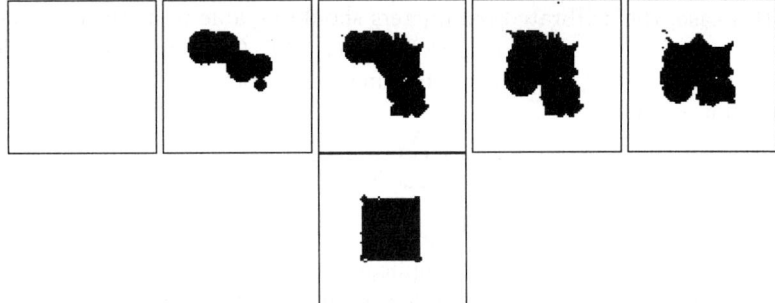

Fig. 5. Starting with a white picture with parameters estimated from the square, exhibiting a phase-transition-like phenomenon

Fig. 6. Output of the restoration algorithm, initialized with the triangle, and using parameters estimated from the triangle

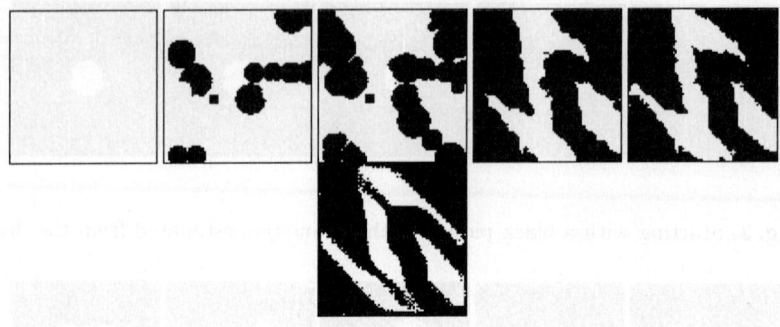

Fig. 7. Starting with the white picture with parameters estimated from the triangle

5   Extension to data-dependent cost functions

5.1   Generalities

In a typical use of energy minimization methods for image analysis, one (or several terms) in the energy depends on an extraneous configuration of observed data ξ, like the first term in equation (1). Such situations directly arise from the Bayesian framework which has been introoduced in [3], and applied many times since then.

In this case, the calibrated parameters should be able to adapt to variations of the data, and $\theta_1, \ldots, \theta_d$ should be functions of ξ. One simple way to address this is to model each θ_i as a linear combination of some fixed functions of ξ, as in regression analysis:

$$\theta_i = \sum_{j=1}^{K} \beta_{ij} \Phi_j(\xi)$$

The functions Φ_j are fixed in the learning procedure. They should be relevant statistics of the data, for the given application. From a formal point of view, we are back to the framework of section 3.2, with the new energy terms

$$\tilde{U}_{ij}(\xi, y) = \Phi_j(\xi) U_i(y)$$

and parameters β_{ij}. However, in this case, it is clear that learning can only be performed on the basis of sufficiently large number of correct analyses, of the kind $(\xi_1, y_1), \ldots, (\xi_N, y_N)$, since we are going to estimate functions of the variable ξ.

An alternative to choosing fixed functions Φ_j is to set $\Phi_j = \Phi(h_j + \langle W_j, \xi \rangle)$ where $h_j \in \mathbb{R}$ and W_j is a vector of same dimension as ξ, which also have to be estimated. Here Φ is a fixed function, typically sigmoidal. It is not hard to adapt the stochastic gradient descent algorithm to deal with this model, which will have more learning power than the initial linear combinations. The counterpart of this is that the measure of frustration is not convex anymore.

We now illustrate this approach by considering a simple unidimensional framework.

5.2 A 1D example

We consider the issue of smoothing a function $\xi : [0, 1] \mapsto I\!R$. Fixing a discretization step $\delta = 1/M$, we let $\xi_k = \xi(k\delta)$ and consider the cost function

$$U(\xi, x) = \sum_{k=1}^{N} (\xi_k - x_k)^2 + \lambda \sum_{i=2}^{N} (x_k - x_{k-1})^2$$

where x is the unknown smooth signal.

To calibrate the parameters, we let $(\Phi_1(\xi), \ldots, \Phi_p(\xi))$ be regularly spaced quantiles of the distribution of $(\xi_k - \xi_{k-1})$ and look for λ in the form

$$\lambda = \sum_{i=1}^{p} \lambda_i \Phi_i(\gamma)$$

The learning dataset is generated by first simulating the smooth signal x by random linear combinations of cosine functions on $[0, 1]$:

$$x(t) = \sum_{p=1}^{K} \alpha_p \cos(\omega_p t + \phi_p)$$

where the α_p, ω_p and ϕ_p are random; ξ is obtained from x by adding a gaussian white noise of random variance σ^2. The random perturbations in the learning procedure consisted in adding a small variantion to one or several x_k's.

The learning procedure achieved the estimation of λ as a linear function of the distribution of the $\xi_i - \xi_{i-1}$. It is an odd function of the quantiles, which implies that it is not affected if a constant value is added to $\xi_i - \xi_{i-1}$ (ie. a linear term added to ξ_i). It can be very tightly approximated by the polynomial $250q^7 + 3.1 * q$, which means that $\sum_q \lambda(q)$ is a linear combination of the 8th centered moment and the variance of the $\xi_i - \xi_{i-1}$.

The cost function U has been minimized on test data generated independently, and some results are shown in fig. 8.

6 Conclusion

In this paper, we have developed a new learning framework for calibrating parameters of energy functionals, as used in image analysis. Given a probabilistic way for building wrong examples from correct ones, we have introduced a stochastic gradient algorithm which consistently estimates parameters, in order to minimize a measure of frustration designed to wrong examples to have a larger energy than correct ones. An extension of the method in the case of data-dependent energies have been proposed, resulting in an adaptive set of parameters reacting to the statistical distribution of the data. The approach has been illustrated by a preliminar series of experiments.

We are now aiming at developing this approach to deal with realistic imaging problems. We are, in particular, studying image segmentation energies, and developing 2D perturbations to learn parameters.

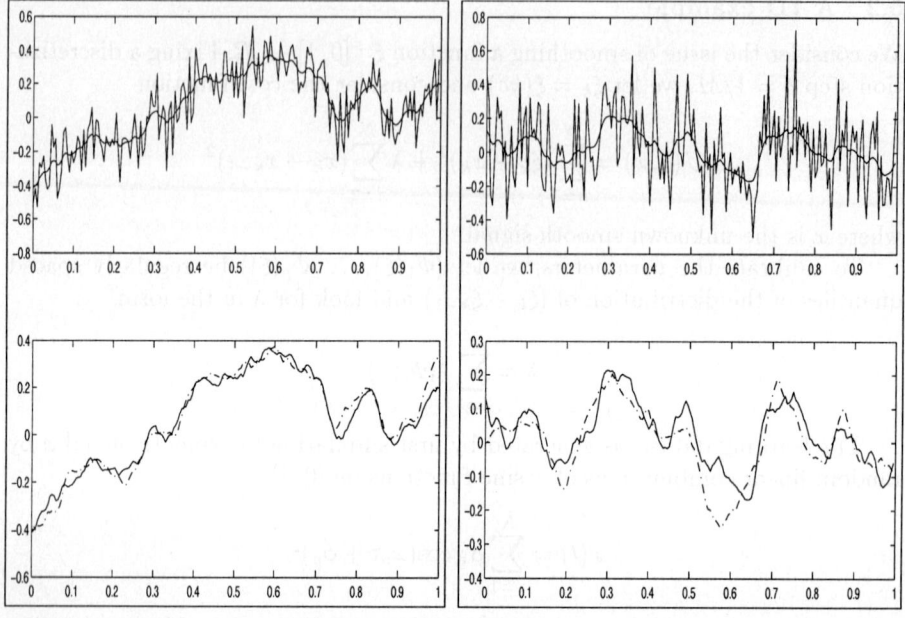

Fig. 8. Smoothing 1D data. Left and right: two distinct examples; up: observed and estimated signals; down: true and estimated signals.

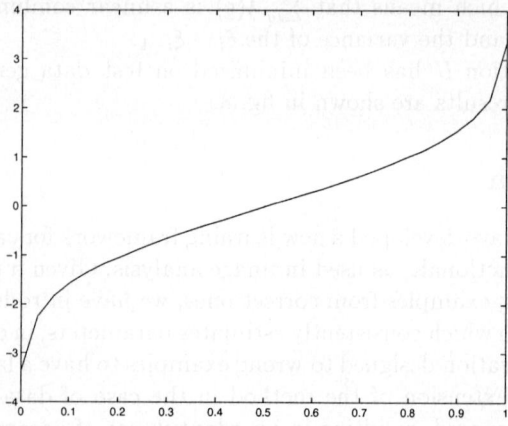

Fig. 9. Plot of the λ_i vs. the quantiles

References

1. R. AZENCOTT, *Image analysis and markov fields,* in Proc. of the Int. Conf. on Ind. and Appl. Math, SIAM, Paris, 1987.

2. A. BENVENISTE, M. MÉTIVIER, AND P. PRIOURET, *Algorithmes Adaptatifs et Approximations Stochastiques, Théorie et Application,* Masson, 1987.

3. S. GEMAN AND D. GEMAN, *Stochastic relaxation, gibbs distributions, and the bayesian restoration of images,* IEEE Trans. PAMI, 6 (1984), pp. 721–741.

4. J. J. HOPFIELD, *Neural networks and physical systems with emergent collective computational abilities,* Proc. Nat. Acad. Sci. USA, 79 (1982), pp. 2554–2558. Biophysics.

5. D. MUMFORD AND SHAH, *Optimal approximation by piecewise smooth functions and variational problems,* Comm. Pure and Appl. Math., XLII (1988).

Coupled Geodesic Active Regions
for Image Segmentation: A Level Set Approach

Nikos Paragios[1] and Rachid Deriche[2]

[1] Siemens Corporate Research,
Imaging and Visualization Department,
755 College Road East, Princeton, NJ 08540, USA
E-mail: nikos@scr.siemens.com

[2] I.N.R.I.A.
B.P. 93, 2004 Route des Lucioles,
06902 Sophia Antipolis Cedex, France
E-mail: der@sophia.inria.fr

Abstract. This paper presents a novel variational method for image segmentation that unifies boundary and region-based information sources under the Geodesic Active Region framework. A statistical analysis based on the Minimum Description Length criterion and the Maximum Likelihood Principle for the observed density function (image histogram) using a mixture of Gaussian elements, indicates the number of the different regions and their intensity properties. Then, the boundary information is determined using a probabilistic edge detector, while the region information is estimated using the Gaussian components of the mixture model. The defined objective function is minimized using a gradient-descent method where a level set approach is used to implement the resulting PDE system. According to the motion equations, the set of initial curves is propagated toward the segmentation result under the influence of boundary and region-based segmentation forces, and being constrained by a regularity force. The changes of topology are naturally handled thanks to the level set implementation, while a coupled multi-phase propagation is adopted that increases the robustness and the convergence rate by imposing the idea of mutually exclusive propagating curves. Finally, to reduce the required computational cost and the risk of convergence to local minima, a multi-scale approach is also considered. The performance of our method is demonstrated on a variety of real images.

1 Introduction

The segmentation of a given image is one of the most important techniques for image analysis, understanding and interpretation.

Feature-based image segmentation is performed using two basic image processing techniques: the **boundary-based segmentation** (which is often referred as edge-based) relies on the generation of a strength image and the ex-

225

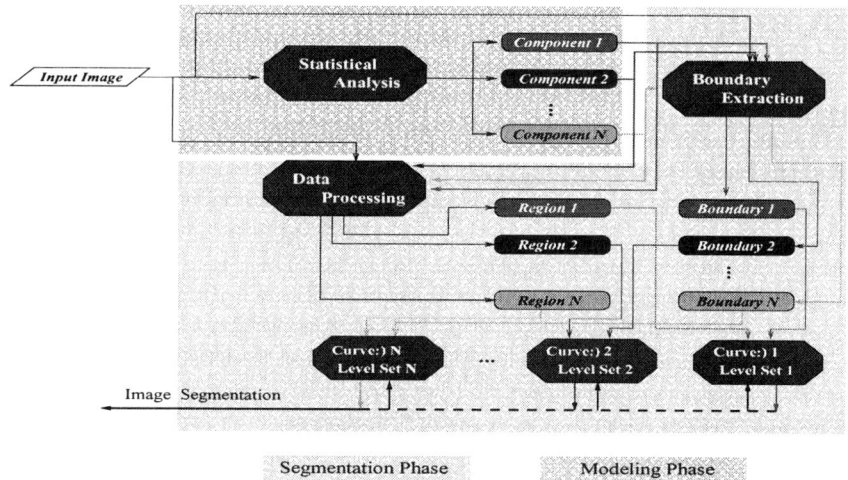

Fig. 1. Multi-phase Coupled Geodesic Active Regions for Image Segmentation: **the flow chart**.

traction of prominent edges, while the **region-based segmentation** relies on the homogeneity of spatially localized features and properties.

- Early approaches for **boundary-based** image segmentation have used local filtering techniques such as edge detection operators. However, such approaches have difficulty in establishing the connectivity of edge segments. This problem has been confronted by employing Snake/Balloons models [6, 12] which also require a good initialization step. Recently, the geodesic active contour model has been introduced [3, 13] which combined with the level set theory [14] deals with the above limitation resulting in a very elegant and powerful segmentation tool.

- The **region-based** methods are more suitable approaches for image segmentation and can be roughly classified into two categories: The region-growing techniques [2] and the Markov Random Fields based approaches [9]. The region growing methods are based on split-and-merge procedures using statistical homogeneity tests [7, 26]. Another powerful region-based tool, which has been widely investigated for image segmentation, is the Markov Random Fields (MRF) [10]. In that case the segmentation problem is viewed as a statistical estimation problem where each pixel is statistically dependent only on its neighbors so that the complexity of the model is restricted.

- Finally, there is a significant effort **to integrate boundary-based with region-based segmentation approaches** [4, 21, 26]. The difficulty lies on the fact that even though the two modules yield complementary information, they involve conflicting and incommensurate objectives. The region-based methods attempt to capitalize on homogeneity properties, whereas boundary-based ones use the non-homogeneity of the same data as a guide.

In this paper, a unified approach for image segmentation is presented that is based on the propagation of regular curves [4, 5, 23, 24, 26] and is exploited from the **Geodesic Active Region** model [19, 20]. This approach is as an extension of our previous work on supervised texture segmentation [18, 20].

This approach is depicted in [**fig.** (1)] and is composed of two stages. The first stage refers to a modeling phase where the observed histogram is approximated using a mixture of Gaussian components. This analysis is based on the Minimum Description Length criterion and the Maximum Likelihood Principle, denotes the regions number as well as their statistics, since a Gaussian component is associated to each region. Then, the segmentation is performed by employing the Geodesic Active Region model. The different region boundaries are determined using a probabilistic module that seeks for local discontinuities on the statistical space that is associated with the image features. This information is combined with the region one, resulting in a geodesic active region-based segmentation framework. The defined objective function is minimized with respect to the different region boundaries (multiple curves) using a gradient descent method, where the obtained equations are implemented using the level set theory that enables the ability of dealing automatically with topological changes. Moreover, as in [25, 5, 23], a coupling force is introduced to the level set functions that imposes the constraint of a non-overlapping set of curves. Finally, the objective function is used within the context of a coarse to fine multi-scale approach that increases the convergence rate and decreases the risk of converging to a local minimum.

The reminder of this paper is organized as follows. In section 2 the Geodesic Active Region model which is the basis of the proposed approach is shortly presented. The problem of determining the number of regions and their intensity properties is considered in section 3. The proposed segmentation framework is introduced in section 4, while its implementation issues are addressed in section 5. Finally, conclusions and discussion appear in section 6.

2 Geodesic Active Regions

The Geodesic Active Region [15] model was originally proposed in [16] to deal with the problem of supervised texture segmentation and was successfully exploited in [19] to deal with the the motion estimation and tracking problem.

This model will be shortly presented for a simple image segmentation case with two hypotheses (h_A, h_B) (bi-modal). In order to facilitate the notation, let us make some definitions:

- Let I be the input frame.
- Let $\mathcal{P}(\mathcal{R}) = \{\mathcal{R}_A, \mathcal{R}_B\}$ be a partition of the frame domain into two non-overlapping regions $\{\mathcal{R}_A \cap \mathcal{R}_B = \emptyset\}$.
- And, let $\{\partial \mathcal{R}\}$ be the boundaries between $\mathcal{R}_A$ and $\mathcal{R}_B$.

The Geodesic Active Region model assumes that for a given application some *information regarding the real region boundaries* and some *knowledge about the desired intensity properties of the different regions* are available. For example, let $[p_C(I(s))]$ be the *boundary density function* that measures the probability of a given pixel being at the boundaries between the two regions. Additionally, let $[p_A(I(s)), p_B(I(s))]$ be the conditional intensity density functions with respect to the hypothesis h_A and h_B.

Then, the optimization procedure refers to a frame partition problem [determined by a curve that is attracted by the region boundaries] based on *the observed data, the associated hypotheses and their expected properties.* This partition according to the Geodesic Active Region model is given by:

$$
E(\partial\mathcal{R}) = \alpha \underbrace{\int_0^1 g \left(\overbrace{\underbrace{p_C(I(\partial\mathcal{R}(c)))}_{boundary\ probability}}^{boundary\ attraction} \right) \overbrace{\left| \partial\dot{\mathcal{R}}(c) \right|}^{regularity} dc}_{Boundary\ Term}
$$

$$
+ (1-\alpha) \underbrace{\iint_{\mathcal{R}_A} g \left(\overbrace{\underbrace{p_A(I(x,y))}_{h_A\ probability}}^{\mathcal{R}_A\ fitting\ measurement} \right) dx dy + (1-\alpha) \iint_{\mathcal{R}_B} g \left(\overbrace{\underbrace{p_B(I(x,y))}_{h_B\ probability}}^{\mathcal{R}_B\ fitting\ measurement} \right) dx dy}_{Region\ Term}
$$

where $\partial\mathcal{R}(c) : [0,1] \to \mathcal{R}^2$ is a parameterization of the region boundaries in a planar form, $\alpha \in [0,1]$ is a positive constant balancing the contribution of the two terms, and $g()$ is a positive monotonically decreasing function (*e.g.* Gaussian).

The interpretation of the above objective function is clear, since

a curve is demanded $[\partial\mathcal{R}]$ that:
- is **regular** [regularity], of minimal length and is attracted by the real boundaries between the regions $\mathcal{R}_A$ and $\mathcal{R}_B$ [**eq.** (2): boundary attraction] : **Boundary Term**,
- and defines a partition of the image that optimizes the segmentation map by maximizing the *a posteriori* segmentation probability [20]: **Region Term**.

The minimization of this function is performed using a gradient descent method. If $u = (x, y)$ is a point of the initial curve, then the curve should be deformed at this point using the following equation:

$$
\frac{\partial u}{\partial t} = \left[\underbrace{(1-\alpha)\left[g\left(p_A(I(u))\right) - g\left(p_B(I(u))\right)\right]}_{region-based\ force} + \right.
$$

$$
\left. \underbrace{\alpha\left(g(p_C(I(u)))\mathcal{K}(u) - \nabla g(p_C(I(u))) \cdot \mathcal{N}(u)\right)}_{boundary-based\ force} \right] \mathcal{N}(u)
$$

The obtained PDE motion equation has two kind of *forces* acting on the curve, both in the direction of the normal inward normal,

– **Region force**
This force aims at shrinking or expanding the curve to the direction that maximizes the *a posteriori* segmentation probability according to the observation set and the expected intensity properties of the different regions.
– **Boundary force**
The force aims at shrinking the curve towards the boundaries between the different regions being constrained by the curvature effect.

3   Regions and their Statistics

In order to simplify the notation and to better and easily introduce the proposed model, let us make some definitions:

– Let $H(I)$ be the observed density function (histogram) of the input image,
– Let $\mathcal{P}(\mathcal{R}) = \{\mathcal{R}_i : i \in [1, N]\}$ be a partition of the image into N non-overlapping regions, and let $\partial\mathcal{P}(\mathcal{R}) = \{\partial\mathcal{R}_i : i \in [1, N]\}$ be the region boundaries,
– And, let h_i be the segmentation hypothesis that is associated with the region $\mathcal{R}_i$.

The key hypothesis that is made to perform segmentation relies on the fact that the image is composed of homogeneous regions. In other words, we assume that the the intensity properties of a given region (local histogram) can be determined using a Gaussian distribution and hence the global intensity properties of the image (image histogram) refer to a mixture of Gaussian elements.

Let $p(.)$ be the probability density function with respect to the intensity space of the image I (normalized image histogram $H(I)$). If we assume that this probability density function is homogeneous, then an intensity value x is derived by selecting a component k with *a priori* probability P_k and then selecting this value according to the distribution of this element $p_k()$. This hypothesis leads to a mixture model of Gaussian elements

$$p(x) = \sum_{k=1}^{N} P_k \, p_k(x), \quad p_k(x) = \frac{1}{\sqrt{2\pi}\sigma_k} e^{-\frac{(x-k)^2}{2\sigma_k^2}}$$

This mixture model consists of a vector Θ with $3N - 1$ unknown parameters $\Theta = \{(P_k, \mu_k, \sigma_k) : k \in [1, ..., N]\}$: (i) The number of components $[N]$, (ii) the *a priori* probability of each component $[P_k]$, (iii) and, the mean $[\mu_k]$ and the standard deviation $[\sigma_k]$ of each component.

Hence, there are two key problems to be dealt with: the determination of the components number and the estimation of the unknown parameters Θ of these components. These problems are solved simultaneously using the Minimum Description Length (MDL) criterion [22] and the Maximum Likelihood Principle (ML) [8]. Thus, given the data sample and all possible approximations using Gaussian Mixture models, the MDL principle is to select the approximation which minimizes the length of the mixture model as well as the approximation error using this model. In other words with more complex mixture models, the

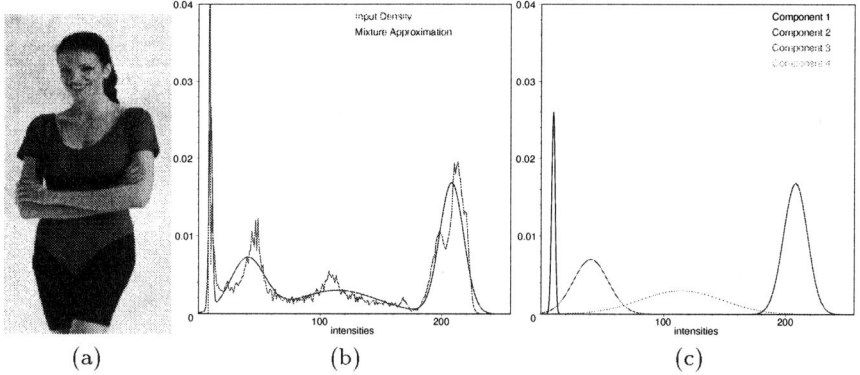

Fig. 2. (a) Input Image, (b) Image Histogram and its approximation: *Components Number: 4, Mean Approximation Error: 1.04641e-05, Iterations Number: 117,* (c) Region Intensity Properties [*Component 1:* black pants, *Component 2:* background, *Component 3:* (hair, t-shirt), *Component 4:* skin].

approximation is better and the error is minimized but at the same time the cost induced by the model is significant since more parameters are required for its description. Thus, a compromise between the components number and the approximation error has to be obtained.

This is done using the MDL principle, where initially a single node Gaussian mixture is assumed. Then, the number of mixture modes is increased and an estimation of the mixture parameters is performed. These parameters are used to determine the MDL measurement for the current approximation. If the obtained measurement is smaller than then one given by the approximation with a smaller number components, then the number of components is increased. Finally, the approximation the gives the minimum value for the MDL measurement is selected. The performance of this criterion is demonstrated in [**fig.** (2, 6)].

4 Image Segmentation

Given the region number as well their expected intensity properties, we can proceed to the segmentation phase. Two different modules are involved, a boundary and a region-based.

4.1 Determining the Boundary Information

The first objective is to extract some information regarding the real boundaries of each region. This can be done by employing an edge detector, thus by seeking for high gradient values on the input image. Given the hypothesis that this image is composed of homogeneous regions, this method will provide reliable global boundary information. However, this information is blind, since its nature cannot be determined. In other words, a pixel with important gradient value (boundary pixel) cannot be attributed to the boundaries of a specific region $[\partial \mathcal{R}_i]$.

Here, an alternative method is proposed to determine the boundary-based information [17]. Let s be a pixel of the image, $N(s)$ a partition of its local neighborhood, and the $N_R(s)$ and $N_L(s)$ be the regions associated with this partition.

Moreover, let $p_{B_k}(I(N(s)))$ be the boundary probability density function with respect to the k hypothesis, $[p(I(N(s))|B_k)]$ be the conditional boundary probability and $[p(I(N(s))|\bar{B}_k)]$ be the conditional non-boundary probability. Then, using the Bayes rule and making some assumptions regarding the global *a priori* boundary probability [17] it can be easily shown that the probability for a pixel s being at the boundaries of k region, given a neighborhood partition $N(s)$ is given by,

$$p_{B_k}(s) = \frac{p(I(N(s))|B_k)}{p(I(N(s))|B_k) + p(I(N(s))|\bar{B}_k)}$$

The conditional boundary/non-boundary probabilities can be estimated directly from known quantities (see [17] for details). Thus,

k Boundary Condition:
If s is a k boundary pixel, then there is a partition $[N_L(s), N_R(s)]$ where the most probable assignment for the "left" local region is k and for the "right" j $[j \neq k]$, or vice-versa,

k Non-Boundary Condition:
On the other hand, if s is not a k boundary pixel, then for every possible neighborhood partition the most probable assignment for the "left" as well as for the "right" local region is k, or i and j where $\{i, j\} \neq k$.

As a consequence, the conditional k boundary/non-boundary probability density functions are given by,

$$p(I(N(s))|B_k) = \underbrace{p_k(I(N_R(s)))\ p_j(I(N_L(s)))}_{N_R(s)\in\mathcal{R}_k\cap N_L(s)\in\mathcal{R}_j} + \underbrace{p_j(I(N_R(s)))\ p_k(I(N_L(s)))}_{N_R(s)\in\mathcal{R}_j\cap N_L(s)\in\mathcal{R}_k}$$

$$p(I(N(s))|\bar{B}_k) = \underbrace{p_k(I(N_R(s)))\ p_k(I(N_L(s)))}_{N_L(s)\in\mathcal{R}_i\cap N_R(s)\in\mathcal{R}_j} + \underbrace{p_i(I(N_R(s)))\ p_j(I(N_{LS}))}_{N_L(s)\in\mathcal{R}_k\cap N_R(s)\in\mathcal{R}_k}$$

where $\{i, j\}$ can be identical and

- $p_k(I(N_R(s)))$ is the probability of "right" local region $[N_R(s)]$ being at the k region, given the observed intensity values within this region $[I(N_R(s))]$,
- $p_j(I(N_L(s)))$ is the probability of "left" local region $[N_L(s)]$ being at the j region, given the observed intensity values within this region $[I(N_L(s))]$.

Given the definition of the probability for a pixel s being a k boundary point, the next problem is to define the neighborhood partition. We consider four different partitions of the neighborhood and the local neighborhood regions are considered to be 3×3 directional windows. We estimate the boundary probability for all partitions by using the mean values over these windows, and set the boundary information $[p_{B,k}(s)]$ for the given pixel s with respect to the k using the partition with the maximum boundary probability. The same procedure is followed for all regions, given their intensity properties (Gaussian component) resulting on N boundary-based information images $[p_{B,k}(s) : k \in [1, N]]$. A demonstration of the extracted boundary information using this framework can be found in [**fig. (3)**].

4.2 Setting the Energy

The proposed method has made implicitly the assumption that the image is composed of N regions and a given pixel s lies always between two regions $[\mathcal{R}_i, \mathcal{R}_{k_i}]$. However, given the initial curves [regions] positions, some image pixels might not belong to any region. Moreover, other image pixels might be attributed to several regions.

To deal with this problem, a temporal *spending* region $\mathcal{R}_0$ has to be considered. This region **(i) does not correspond to a real hypothesis** (it is composed from pixel with different hypotheses origins), **(ii) does not have a predefined intensity character** (it depends from the latest segmentation map) and **(iii) has to be empty when convergence is reached**. The next problem is to define the intensity properties of this region, thus the probability density function $p_0()$. This can be done by seeking the non-attributed image pixels and estimating directly from the observed intensity values the probability density function $p_0()$.

Then, the segmentation task can be considered within the geodesic active region framework where the region information is expressed directly from the Gaussian elements of the mixture model $[p_i()]$ estimated in the observed image $[p_i(I(s))]$. Thus, the proposed framework consists of minimizing following objective function,

$$
\left\{
\begin{aligned}
E(\mathcal{P}(\mathcal{R})) = {} & \alpha \sum_{i=0}^{N} \iint_{\mathcal{R}_i} \underbrace{g\left(p_i\left(I(x,y)\right), \sigma_R\right)}_{region\ fitting} dx\,dy + \\
& (1-\alpha) \sum_{i=1}^{N} \int_0^1 \underbrace{g\left(p_{B,i}\left(\partial\mathcal{R}_i(c_i)\right), \sigma_B\right)}_{boundary\ attraction} \underbrace{|\partial\dot{\mathcal{R}}_i(c_i)|}_{regularity\ constraint} dc_i
\end{aligned}
\right.
$$

where $\partial\mathcal{R}_i(c_i)$ is a parameterization of the region $\mathcal{R}_i$ boundaries into a planar form, and $g(x, \sigma)$ is a Gaussian function.

Within this framework the set of the unknown variables consists of the different region boundaries (curves) $[\partial\mathcal{R}_i]$. The interpretation of the defined objective function is the same with the one presented in section 2 for the bi-modal Geodesic Active Region framework.

4.3 Minimizing the Energy

The defined objective function is minimized using a gradient descent method. Thus, the system of the Euler-Lagrange motion equations with respect to the different curves (one for each region) is given by:

$$
\left\{
\begin{aligned}
& \forall\, i \in [1, N], \\
& \frac{\partial}{\partial t}\partial\mathcal{R}_i = \alpha \underbrace{\left[g(p_i(I(\partial\mathcal{R}_i)), \sigma_R) - g(p_{k_i}(I(\partial\mathcal{R}_i)), \sigma_R)\right]\mathcal{N}_i(\partial\mathcal{R}_i)}_{Region-based\ force} + \\
& (1-\alpha)\underbrace{\left(g(p_{B,i}(\partial\mathcal{R}_i), \sigma_B)\mathcal{K}_i(\partial\mathcal{R}_i) + \nabla g(p_{B,i}(\partial\mathcal{R}_i), \sigma_B) \cdot \mathcal{N}_i(\partial\mathcal{R}_i)\right)\mathcal{N}_i(\partial\mathcal{R}_i)}_{Boundary-based\ force}
\end{aligned}
\right.
$$

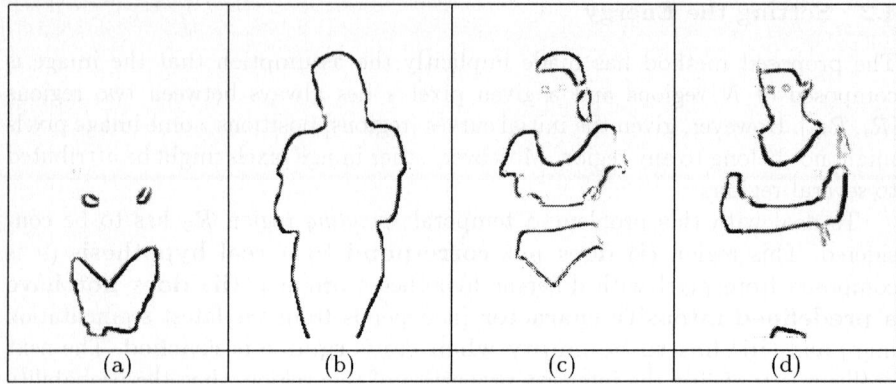

Fig. 3. Boundary information with respect to the different regions for the woman image [**fig.** (2.a)]. (a) *Region 1 (black pants)*, (b) *Region 2 (background)*, (c) *Region 3 (hair, t-shirt)*, (d) *Region 4 (skin)*.

where $\mathcal{K}_i$ (resp. $\mathcal{N}_i$) is the Euclidean curvature (resp. normal) with respect to the curve $\partial\mathcal{R}_i$.

Moreover, the assumption that **the pixel** $\partial\mathcal{R}_i$ **lies between the regions** $\mathcal{R}_i$ **and** $\mathcal{R}_{k_i}$ **was done implicitly** to provide the above motion equations and the probability $p_{k_i}()$ is given by,

$$p_{k_i}(s) = \begin{cases} p_0(s), & if \ s \notin \cup_{j=1,j\neq i}^{N} [\mathcal{R}_j] \\ p_m(s), & m := \max\{p_m(s) : m \in [1, N], m \neq i, s \in \mathcal{R}_m\} \end{cases}$$

Thus, if the given pixel is not attributed to any region, then the spending region distribution $p_0(.)$ is used to determine the k_i hypothesis. On the other hand, if this pixel is already attributed to one, or more than one regions, then the most probable hypothesis is used.

These motion equations have the same interpretation with the one presented in section 2. Moreover, they refer to **a multi-phase curve propagation since several curves are propagated simultaneously.** In other words, each region is associated with a motion equation and the propagation of a single or multi-component initial curve. However, within this system of motion equations there is no interaction between the propagations of the different curves.

4.4 Level Set Implementation

The obtained motion equations are implemented using the pioneering work of Osher and Sethian [14], the level set theory where the central idea is to represent the moving front $\partial\mathcal{R}(c,t)$ as the zero-level set $\{\phi(\partial\mathcal{R}(c,t),t) = 0\}$ of a function ϕ. This representation of $\partial\mathcal{R}(c,t)$ is implicit, parameter-free and intrinsic. Additionally, it is topology-free since different topologies of the zero level-set do not imply different topologies of ϕ. It is easy to show, that if the moving front evolves according to $\left[\frac{\partial}{\partial t}\partial\mathcal{R}(c,t) = F(\partial\mathcal{R}(c,t)) \mathcal{N}\right]$ for a given function F, then the embedding function ϕ deforms according to $\left[\frac{\partial}{\partial t}\phi(p,t) = F(p) \ |\nabla\phi(p,t)|\right]$ For this level-set representation, it is proved that the solution is independent of the embedding function ϕ, and in most of the cases is initialized as a signed distance function.

Thus, the system of motion equations that drives the multi-phase curve propagation for segmentation is transformed into a system of multiple surfaces evolution given by,

$$
\left\{
\begin{array}{l}
\forall\, i \in [1, N], \\
\dfrac{\partial}{\partial t}\phi_i(s) = \alpha\left(g(p_i(I(s)), \sigma_R) - g(p_{k_i}(I(s)), \sigma_D)\right) |\nabla\phi_i(s)| + \\
\qquad\qquad (1-\alpha)\left(g(p_{B,i}(s), \sigma_B)\mathcal{K}_i(s)\,|\nabla\phi_i(s)| + \nabla g(p_{B,i}(s), \sigma_B)\cdot\nabla\phi_i(s)\right)
\end{array}
\right.
$$

4.5 Coupling the Level Sets

The use of the level set methods provides a very elegant tool to propagate curves where their position is recovered by seeking for the zero level set crossing points. Moreover, the state of given pixel with respect to a region hypothesis can be easily determined since if it belongs to the region, then the corresponding level set value is negative. On the other hand if it does not belong to it, then the corresponding value is positive. Additionally, since we consider signed distance functions for the level set implementation, a step further can be done by estimating the distance of the given pixel from each curve. This information is very valuable during the multi-phase curve propagation cases where the overlapping between the different curves is prohibited.

However, the overlapping between the different curves is almost an inevitable situation at least during the initialization step. Moreover, the case where an image pixel has not been attributed to any hypothesis may occurs. Let us now assume that a pixel is attributed initially to two different regions (there are two level set functions with negative values at it). Then, as in [25, 5, 23], a constraint that discourages a situation of this nature can be easily introduced, by **adding an artificial force (always in the normal direction)** to the corresponding level set motion equations that penalizes pixels with multiple labels (they are attributed to multiple regions). Moreover, a similar force can be introduced to discourage situations where pixels are not attributed to any regions. This can be done by modifying the level set motion equations as,

$$
\left\{
\begin{array}{l}
\forall\, i \in [1, N], \\[4pt]
\dfrac{\partial}{\partial t}\phi_i(s) = \beta \underbrace{\sum_{j\in[1,N]} H_i(i, \phi_j(s))\,|\nabla\phi_i(s)|}_{Coupling\ force} + \\[12pt]
\qquad\qquad \gamma \underbrace{\left[g\left(p_i(I(s)), \sigma_R\right) - g\left(p_{k_i}(I(s)), \sigma_R\right)\right]|\nabla\phi_i(s)|}_{Region\ force} + \\[12pt]
\qquad\qquad \delta \underbrace{\left(g(p_{B,i}(s), \sigma_B)\mathcal{K}_i(s) + \nabla g(p_{B,i}(s), \sigma_B)\cdot\dfrac{\nabla\phi_i(s)}{|\nabla\phi_i(s)|}\right)|\nabla\phi_i(s)|}_{Boundary\ force}
\end{array}
\right.
$$

where β, γ, δ are positive constants $[\beta + \gamma + \delta = 1]$, and the function $H_i(, \phi())$ is given by

$$H_i(m, \phi_n(s)) = \begin{cases} 0, & \text{if } m = i \\ -sign(\phi_j(s)), & \text{if } m \neq i \end{cases}$$

Let us now interpret the new artificial force that has been added to the motion equation i, for a given pixel s:

Expanding Effect:
If this pixel does not belong to any region, then the new force is negative, equal to $f_c = -(N-1)|\nabla \phi_i|$ and aims at expanding the region $\mathcal{R}_i$ to occupy this pixel (the appearance of non-attributed pixels is discouraged).

Shrinking Effect:
On the other hand, if this pixel has been already attributed to another region $[\mathcal{R}_k]$, then the level set $[\phi_k]$ will contribute with a positive force that aims at shrinking the region $\mathcal{R}_i$ (the overlapping is discouraged).

Although the selection of the function $[H_i(\phi())]$ seems to fulfill the required conditions (mutually exclusive propagating curves, non overlapping, no "empty" pixels), it encounters some problems. Thus, the non-attributed pixels are penalized with the same manner to the ones that have been attributed to multiple regions. Finally, the defined coupling function is discontinuous which is a not desirable property since it creates stability problems during the level set evolution.

To summarize, the coupling function has to be redefined by taking into account the following considerations:

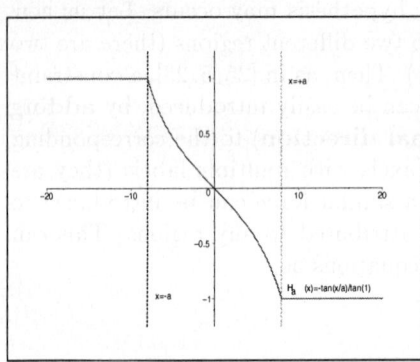

Fig. 4. The trigonometric basis of the level set coupling function.

i. A pixel that is already attributed to a region j and is far away from $\partial \mathcal{R}_j$, should strongly discourage the evolution of the level set $\phi_i()$ to include this pixel in $\mathcal{R}_i$,

ii. A pixel which belongs to the region $\mathcal{R}_j$ and is close to its boundaries can be reached or be liberated by $\partial \mathcal{R}_j$ during the next few iterations, and hence, the coupling force introduced by the j level set function should "tolerate" a temporal overlapping.

Thus, inspired by the properties of the trigonometric functions, the coupling force is defined as,

$$H_i(j, \phi_j(s)) = \begin{cases} 0, & \text{if } j = i \\ H_a(\phi_j(s)), & \text{if } j \neq i \text{ and } \phi_j(s) \geq 0 \\ \frac{1}{N-1} H_a(\phi_j(s)), & \text{if } j \neq i \text{ and } [\cap_{\{k=1, k \neq i\}}^N \phi_k(s) > 0] \end{cases}$$

where the basis function $H_a(x)$ is shown in [**fig.** (4)] and is given by:

$$H_a(x) = - \begin{cases} +1, & \text{if } x > a \\ -1, & \text{if } x < -a \\ \frac{1}{\tan(1)} \tan(x/a), & \text{if } |x| \leq a \end{cases}$$

In any case, the selection of this function is still an open issue and for the time being we are investigating other forms for it.

To interpret this force via the new function, a level set function $[\phi_i()]$ and a pixel location $[s]$ are considered,

i. If s is already attributed to another region, then there is an hypothesis j for which $\phi_j(s) \leq 0$ which will contribute with a positive value (shrinking effect) to the coupling force that is proportional to the distance of this pixel from the boundaries of $\mathcal{R}_j$,

ii. A similar interpretation can be done if this pixel is not attributed to any region (expanding effect). However, for this case the coupling force has to be normalized because it is not appropriate to penalize with the same way the situation of overlapping and the case in which the given pixel is not attributed to one of the regions. At the same time this force is plausible if and only if this pixel is not attributed to any region $\left[\cap_{\{k=1, k \neq i\}}^{N} \phi_k(s) > 0 \right]$.

5   Implementation Issues

However, analyzing the obtained motion equations, some hidden problems might be observed due to the fact that the region forces are estimated using a single intensity-based probability value. However, for real image segmentation cases there is always an overlap between the Gaussian components that characterize the different regions. Furthermore, due to presence of noise, isolated intensity values incoherent with the region properties can be found within it. As a consequence, it is quite difficult to categorize a pixel, based on its very local data (single intensity value).

To cope with these problems, a circular window approach can be used, as proposed in [26]. Hence, a centralized window is defined locally and the region-based force is estimated as the mean value of the region-based forces of the window pixels [**fig.** (5, 7,8)]. However, here opposite to [26] where all the window pixels were equally considered, the distance between the window pixels and the window center is used, and these pixels contribute to the region with weights inversely proportional to their distances.

A more elegant solution can be obtained by considering a multi-scale approach. It is well known that the use of *multi-scale* techniques reduces significantly the required computational cost of the minimization process and performs a smooth operation to the objective function that reduces the risk of converging to local minima. The main idea consists in defining a consistent coarse-to-fine *multi-grid* contour propagation by using contours which are constrained to be piecewise constant over smaller and smaller pixel subsets [11]. The objective

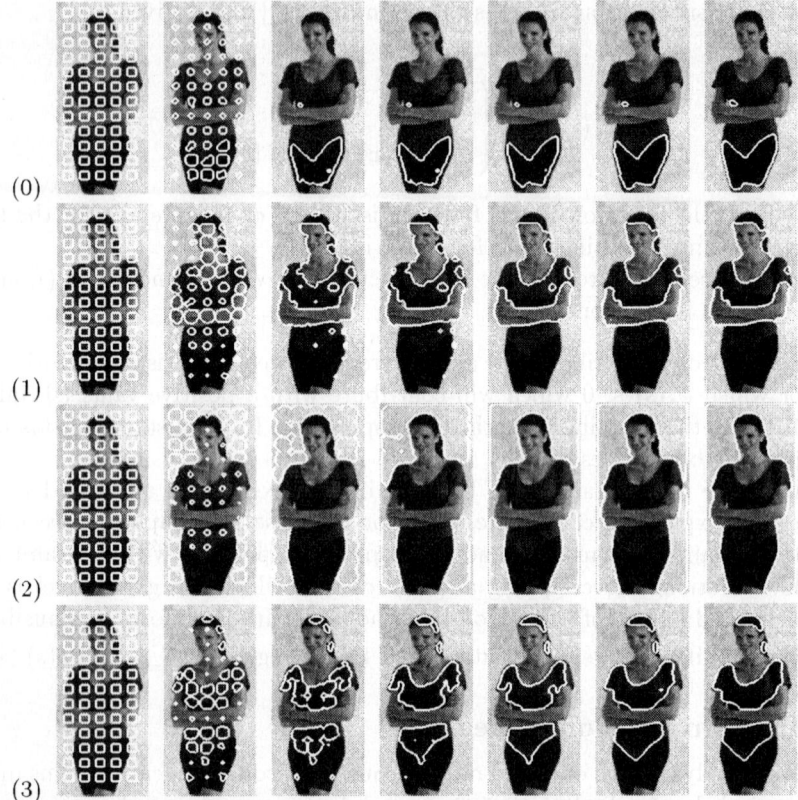

Fig. 5. Segmentation for the woman image [**fig.** (2.a)]. Multi-phase Curve Propagation. A random initialization step is used with a large number of spoiled regions. The initial regions are the same for all hypothesis. (1) *Region 1 (black pants)*, (2) *Region 2 (skin)*, (3) *Region 3 (background)*, (d) *Region 4 (hair, t-shirt)*.

function which is considered at each level is then automatically derived from the original finest scale energy function. Additionally, the finest data space is used at each level, and there is no necessity for constructing a multi-resolution pyramid of the data. More details about the multi-scale implementation of the proposed segmentation framework can be found at [17, 15].

As for the selection of the model parameters, we have observed that in most of the cases the region force is more reliable since it is estimated over blocks. On the other hand, the boundary force ensures the regularity of the propagating curves. Finally, the coupling force is considered less, with a progressive way since it has been introduced artificially and has a complementary role. Taking into account these remarks the following settings are used [$\beta \approx 0.20, \gamma \approx 0.35, \delta \approx 0.45$]. Finally, as it concerns the α parameter of the coupling function it is determined using the band size of the Narrow Band algorithm [1] which is used to implement the evolution of the level set functions.

To summarize, the proposed approach,

 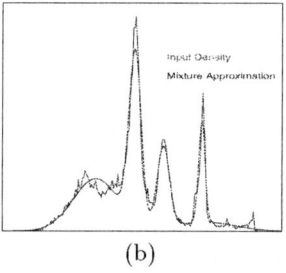 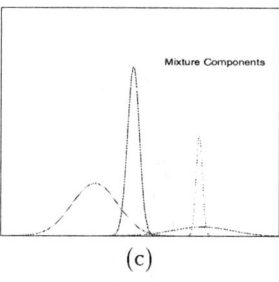

(a)   (b)   (c)

Fig. 6. (a) Input Image, (b) Image Histogram and its approximation: *Components Number: 5, Mean Approximation Error: 2.283931e-06, Iterations Number: 421,* (c) Region Intensity Properties.

- Initially, determines the number of regions and their intensity properties,
- Then, estimates the boundary-probabilities with respect to the different hypotheses,
- Finally, performs segmentation by the propagation of a "mutually exclusive" set of regular curves under the influence of boundary and region-based segmentation forces.

6   Discussion, Summary

In this paper[1], a new multi-phase level set approach for un-supervised image segmentation has been proposed. Very promising experimental results were obtained using real images [**fig.** (5,7,8)] of different nature (outdoor, medical, etc.).

As far the computational cost of the proposed method is concerned (an ULTRA-10 Sun Station with 256 MB Ram and a processor of 299 MHZ was used) we can make the following remarks; the modeling phase is very fast almost real time. On the other hand, the segmentation phase is very expensive. The extraction of the boundary information takes approximately 3 to 5 seconds for a 256×256 image with four different regions, while the propagation phase is more expensive due to the fact that there are multiple level set evolutions in parallel. Thus, for a 256×256 image (Coronal image [**fig.** (8)]) with a random initialization step, the propagation phase takes approximately 20 seconds. However, this cost is strongly related with the regions number, the initial curve positions and the parameters of the level set evolution. This cost is significantly decreased by the use of the multi-scale approach (three to five times).

Summarizing, in this paper a new variational framework has been proposed to deal with the problem of image segmentation. The main contributions of the proposed image segmentation model are the following:

- An adaptive method that determines automatically the regions number and their intensity properties,

---

[1] A detailed version of this article can be found at [17], while more experimental results (in MPEG format) are available at:

       http://www-sop.inria.fr/robotvis/personnel/nparagio/demos

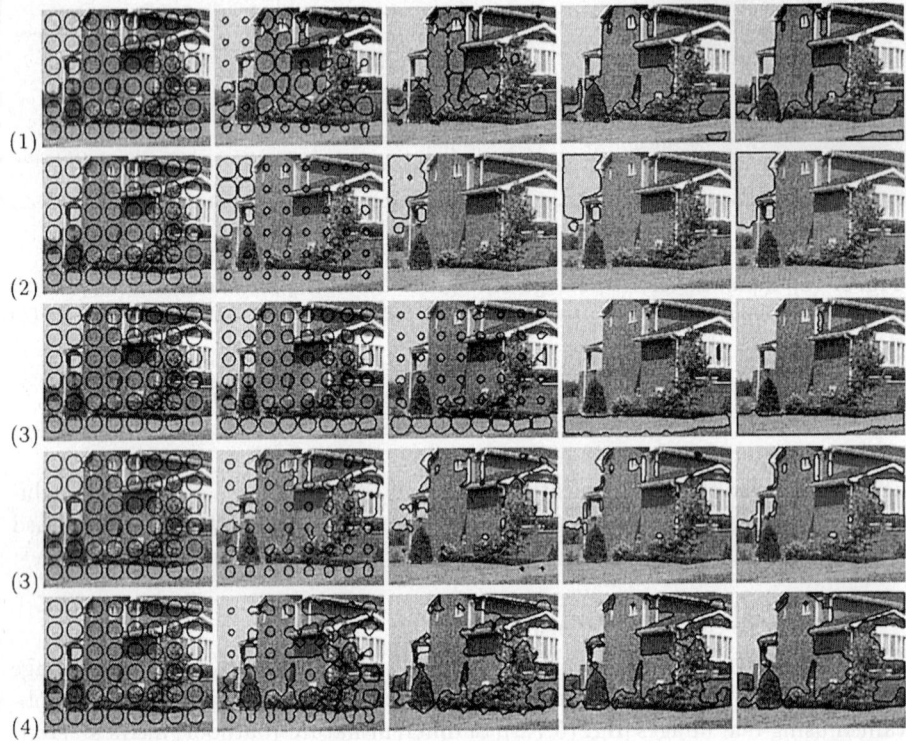

Fig. 7. The segmentation of the house image into five regions. Curve propagation: left to right. (a) House walls, (2) Sky, (b) Ground, (4) Windows, (5) Small trees, flowers, shadows.

- A variational image segmentation framework that integrates boundary and region-based segmentation modules and connects the optimization procedure with the the curve propagation theory,
- The implementation of this framework within level set techniques resulting on a segmentation paradigm that can deal automatically with changes of topology and is free from the initial conditions,
- The interaction between the different curves [regions] propagation using an artificial coupling force that imposes the concept of mutually exclusive propagating curves, increases the convergence rate, and eliminates the risk of convergence to a non-proper solution,
- And, the consideration of the proposed model in a multi-scale framework, which deals with the presence of noise, increases the convergence rate, and decreases the risk of convergence to a local minimum.

As far the future directions of this work, the incorporation to the model of a term that accounts for some prior knowledge with respect to expected segmentation map is a challenge (constrained geodesic active regions).

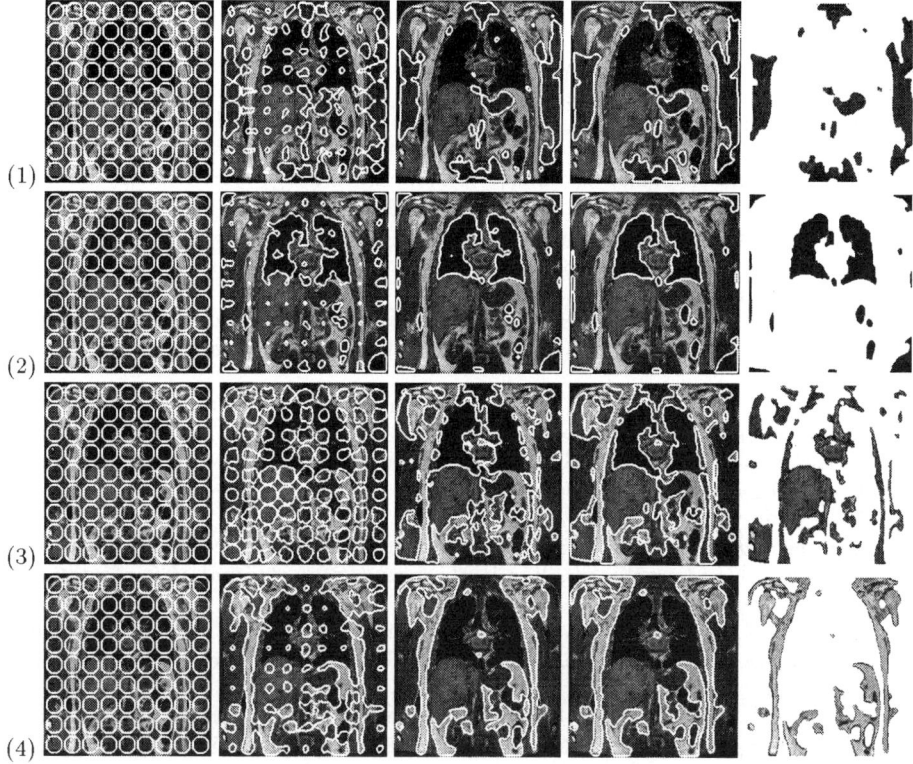

Fig. 8. Segmentation in five regions of a Coronal Medical image.

Acknowledgments

This work has been carried out during the appointment (doctoral research) of the first author with the Computer Vision and Robotics Group (RobotVis) of I.N.R.I.A. Sophia Antipolis from October 1, 1996 to November 1, 1999 and was funded in part under the VIRGO research network (EC Contract No ERBFMRX-CT96-0049) of the TMR Program.

References

1. D. Adalsteinsson and J. Sethian. A Fast Level Set Method for Propagating Interfaces. *Journal of Computational Physics*, 118:269–277, 1995.
2. R. Adams and L. Bischof. Seeded Region Growing. *IEEE Transactions on Pattern Analysis and Machine Intelligence*, 16:641–647, 1994.
3. V. Caselles, R. Kimmel, and G. Sapiro. Geodesic active contours. In *IEEE ICCV*, Boston, USA, 1995.
4. A. Chakraborty, H. Staib, and J. Duncan. Deformable Boundary Finding in Medical Images by Integrating Gradient and Region Information. *IEEE Transactions on Medical Imaging*, 15(6):859–870, 1996.
5. T. Chan and L. Vese. An Active Contour Model without Edges. In *International Conference on Scale-Space Theories in Computer Vision*, pages 141–151, 1999.

6. D. Cohen. On active contour models and balloons. *CVGIP: Image Understanding*, 53:211–218, 1991.

7. D. Comaniciu and P. Meer. Mean Shift Analysis and Applications. In *IEEE ICCV*, pages 1197–1203, Corfu, Greece, 1999.

8. R. Duda and P. Hart. *Pattern Classification and Scene Analysis*. John Wiley & Sons, Inc., 1973.

9. D. Geiger and A. Yuille. A common framework for image segmentation. *International Journal of Computer Vision*, 6:227–243, 1991.

10. S. Geman and D. Geman. Stochastic Relaxation, Gibbs Distributions, and the Bayesian Restoration of Images. *IEEE Transactions on Pattern Analysis and Machine Intelligence*, 6:721–741, 1984.

11. F. Heitz, P. Perez, and P. Bouthemy. Multiscale minimization of global energy functions in some visual recovery problems. *CVGIP: Image Understanding*, 59:125–134, 1994.

12. M. Kass, A. Witkin, and D. Terzopoulos. Snakes: Active contour models. *International Journal of Computer Vision*, 1:321–332, 1988.

13. S. Kichenassamy, A. Kumar, P. Olver, A. Tannenbaum, and A. Yezzi. Gradient flows and geometric active contour models. In *IEEE ICCV*, pages 810–815, Boston, USA, 1995.

14. S. Osher and J. Sethian. Fronts propagating with curvature-dependent speed : algorithms based on the hamilton-jacobi formulation. *Journal of Computational Physics*, 79:12–49, 1988.

15. N. Paragios. *Geodesic Active Regions and Level Set Methods: Contributions and Applications in Artificial Vision*. PhD thesis, University of Nice/ Sophia Antipolis, Jan. 2000.

16. N. Paragios and R. Deriche. Geodesic Active Regions for Texture Segmentation. Research Report 3440, INRIA, France, 1998. http://www.inria.fr/RRRT/RR-3440.html.

17. N. Paragios and R. Deriche. Coupled Geodesic Active Regions for image segmentation. Research Report 3783, INRIA, France, Oct. 1999. http://www.inria.fr/RRRT/RR-3783.html.

18. N. Paragios and R. Deriche. Geodesic Active Contours for Supervised Texture Segmentation. In *IEEE CVPR*, Colorado, USA, 1999.

19. N. Paragios and R. Deriche. Geodesic Active regions for Motion Estimation and Tracking. In *IEEE ICCV*, pages 688–674, Corfu, Greece, 1999.

20. N. Paragios and R. Deriche. Geodesic Active regions for Supervised Texture Segmentation. In *IEEE ICCV*, pages 926–932, Corfu, Greece, 1999.

21. T. Pavlidis and Y. Liow. Integrating region growing and edge detection. *IEEE Transactions on Pattern Analysis and Machine Intelligence*, 12:225–233, 1990.

22. J. Rissanen. Modeling by the Shortest Data Description. *Automatica*, 14:465–471, 1978.

23. C. Samson, L. Blanc-Feraud, G. Aubert, and J. Zerubia. A Level Set Model for image classification. In *International Conference on Scale-Space Theories in Computer Vision*, pages 306–317, 1999. http://www.inria.fr/RRRT/RR-3662.html.

24. A. Yezzi, A. Tsai, and A. Willsky. A Statistical Approach to Snakes for Bimodal and Trimodal Imagery. In *IEEE ICCV*, pages 898–903, Corfu, Greece, 1999.

25. H.-K. Zhao, T. Chan, and S. Osher. A variational level set approach to multiphase motion. *Journal of Computational Physics*, 127:179–195, 1996.

26. S. Zhu and A. Yuille. Region Competition: Unifying Snakes, Region Growing, and Bayes/MDL for Multiband Image Segmentation. *IEEE Transactions on Pattern Analysis and Machine Intelligence*, 18:884–900, 1996.

Level Lines as Global Minimizers of Energy Functionals in Image Segmentation

Charles Kervrann, Mark Hoebeke, and Alain Trubuil

INRA - Biométrie, Domaine de Vilvert
78352 Jouy-en-Josas, France
{ck,mh,at}@jouy.inra.fr

Abstract. We propose a variational framework for determining global minimizers of rough energy functionals used in image segmentation. Segmentation is achieved by minimizing an energy model, which is comprised of two parts: the first part is the interaction between the observed data and the model, the second is a regularity term. The optimal boundaries are the set of curves that globally minimize the energy functional. Our motivation comes from the observation that energy functionals are traditionally complex, for which it is usually difficult to precise global minimizers corresponding to "best" segmentations. Therefore, we focus on basic energy models, which global minimizers can be explicitly determined. In this paper, we prove that the set of curves that minimizes the image moment-based energy functionals is a family of level lines, i.e. the boundaries of level sets (connected components) of the image. For the completeness of the paper, we present a non-iterative algorithm for computing partitions with connected components. It leads to a sound initialization-free algorithm without any hidden parameter to be tuned.

1 Introduction

One of the primary goals of early vision is to segment the domain of an image into regions ideally corresponding to distinct physical objects in the scene. While it has been clear that image segmentation is a critical problem, it has proven difficult to precise segmentation criteria that capture non-local properties of an image and to develop efficient algorithms for computing segmentations. There is a wide range of image segmentation techniques in the literature. Many of them rely on the design and minimization of an energy function which captures the interaction between models and image data [10,2,21,15,27]. Conventional segmentation techniques generally fall into two distinct classes, being either boundary-based or region-based. The former class looks at the image discontinuities near objects boundaries, while the latter examines the homogeneity of spatially localized features inside objects boundaries. Based on these properties, each of these has characteristic advantages and drawbacks. Nevertheless, several methods combine both approaches [29,7,5,12].

Region-based approaches are our main interest. In contrast to boundary-based methods, region-based approaches try to find partitions of the image pixels into zones the most homogeneous possible corresponding to coherent image properties such as brightness, color and texture. Homogeneity is traditionally measured by a given global objective function and hard decisions are made only when information from the whole image is examined at the same time. In that case, the boundaries are the set of curves that minimizes a global energy function. Past approaches have centered on formulating the problem as the minimization of a functional involving the image intensity and edge functions. Some energy models are based on a discrete model of the image, such as Markov random fields [10, 15, 27] or a *Minimum Description Length* (MDL) representation [15, 8], whereas variational models are based on a continuous model of the image [2, 21, 20, 19, 26]. More recently, Zhu attempted to unify snakes, region growing and energy/Bayes/MDL within a general framework [29]. Finally, Blake and Zisserman [2] and Mumford and Shah [21] have written about most aspects of this approach to segmentation and have proposed various complex functionals whose minima correspond to segmented images. In a recent review, Morel and Solimini [19] have, indeed, shown that most approaches aim at optimizing a cost functional which is the combination of three terms: one which ensures that the smoothed image approximates the observed one, another which states that the gradient of the smoothed image should be small, except on a discontinuity set, and a last one which ensures that the discontinuity set has a small length. In other respects, while these different approaches offer powerful theoretical frameworks and minimizers exist [19, 29, 26], it is often computationally difficult to minimize the associated functions. Typically, some embedding procedure, like graduate-non-convexity [2] , is used to avoid bad local minima of cost functionals. A fairly complete analysis is available only for a simplified version of the Mumford and Shah model that approximates a given image with piecewise constant functions [19]. Moreover, in the area of region-based approaches, layers approaches attempted to use both region and boundary information [8]. But the number of layers and the values associated with the layers must be known *a priori* or estimated using ad-hoc methods or prohibitive Expectation-Maximization procedures.

The main obstacle of energy model based approaches is to find more effective and faster ways of estimating the boundaries and values for regions minimizing the energy than those presently available. This motivates the search for global minimizers of energy functionals commonly used in image segmentation. The key contribution of this paper is to provide basic energy models, which global minimizers can be explicitly determined in advance. Accordingly, energy minimization methods and iterative algorithms are not necessary to solve the optimization problem. The energy model introduced in a discrete setting by Beaulieu and Goldberg [1] and reviewed by Morel and Solimini [19] has been the starting point for our own work. This model tends to obtain a partition with a small number of regions and small variances without *a priori* knowledge on the image. The cost function allows to partition the image into regions, though in a more restrictive manner than previous approaches [21, 2, 15, 29] since it can generate irregular boundaries [19]. In [1], the energy is efficiently minimized using a split-and-merge algorithm. Here, our approach is completely different to determine global minimizers of similar energy models. The present investigation is based on a variational model. In Section 2, we prove that the set of curves that minimizes a particular class of energy models is a family of level lines defined from level sets of the image. We list some prior models (Markov connected component fields, entropy prior) which are consistent with this theoretical framework. In this sense, the method is deterministic and equivalent to a procedure that selects the "best" level lines delimiting object boundaries. The rest of the paper is organized as follows. A description of the initialization-free segmentation algorithm is included in Section 3. In Section 4, experiments on several examples demonstrate the effectiveness of the approach.

2 The framework

One approach to the segmentation problem has been to try to globally minimize what we call the "energy" of the segmentation. These energy models are usually used in conjunction with Bayes's theorem. Most of the time, the energy is designed as a combination of several terms, each of them corresponding to a precise property which much be satisfied by the optimal solution. The models have two parts: a *prior model* E_p and a *data model* E_d. The prior term is sometimes called the "regularizer" because it was initially conceived to make the problem of minimizing the data model well-posed.

2.1 Minimization problem

Our theoretical setting is the following. Let us consider a real-value function I, i.e. the image, whose domain is denoted $S : [0, a] \times [0, b]$. In many situations, it is convenient to consider images as real-valued functions of continuous variables. We define the solution to the segmentation problem as the global minimum of a regularized criterion over all regions.

Let $s = (x, y) \in S$ an image pixel, $\Omega_i \subset S$, $i = 1, \ldots, P$, an non-empty image domain or object and $\partial \Omega_i$ its boundary. We associate with the unknown domains Ω_i the following regularized objective function, inspired from [1, 11]:

$$
\begin{cases}
E_\lambda(f, \Omega_1, \ldots, \Omega_P) = E_d(f, \Omega_1, \ldots, \Omega_P) + \lambda\, E_p(\Omega_1, \ldots, \Omega_P) \\
E_d(f, \Omega_1, \ldots, \Omega_P) = \sum_{i=1}^{P} E_d(f, \Omega_i)
\end{cases}
\tag{1}
$$

where f is any integrable function, for instance the convolution of the image I with any filter, $E_p(\Omega_1, \ldots, \Omega_P)$ is a penalty functional and $\lambda > 0$ is the regularization parameter. Some choices of f have been recently listed in [12]. Here, we just consider the possibility of examining the image at various scales using a Gaussian smoothing of the image, including the case of zero variance, i.e. $f = I$ and the case of anisotropic diffusion [14].

Equation (1) is the most general form of energy we can optimize globally at present. We present two appropriate energy models for segmentation which attempt to capture homogeneous regions with unknown constant intensities. It will be clear that none of these models captures all the important scene variables but may be useful to provide a rough analysis of the scene.

LEAST SQUARES CRITERION: In this modeling, implicitly, a Gaussian distribution for the noise is assumed [19, 29]. The data model is usually defined as

$$E_d(f, \Omega_1, \ldots, \Omega_P) = \sum_{i=1}^{P} \int_{\Omega_i} (f(x, y) - \overline{f}_{\Omega_i})^2 \, dx dy \qquad (2)$$

where $\overline{f}_{\Omega_i}$ denotes the average of f over Ω_i. This means that one observes a corrupted function $f = f_{\text{true}} + \varepsilon$, where ε is a zero-mean Gaussian white noise and f_{true} is supposed piecewise constant, i.e.

$$f_{\text{true}}(s) = \sum_{i=1}^{P} \overline{f}_{\Omega_i} \, \mathcal{I}(s \in \Omega_i) \quad \text{where} \quad |\Omega_i| = \int_{\Omega_i} dx dy, \qquad (3)$$

and $\mathcal{I}(\cdot)$ is the indicator function. The standard deviation is assumed to be constant over the entire image. The image domain S is split into unknown P disjoint regions $\Omega_1, \cdots, \Omega_P$.

CONTRAST STATISTIC CRITERION: One may be interested in identifying boundaries corresponding to sharp contrast in the image. We define the contrast of a boundary by the difference between the average value of f per unit area on the inside of the boundary and the outside of the object, that is the background Ω_P [23]. Formally, the corresponding data model is

$$E_d(f, \Omega_1, \ldots, \Omega_P) = -\sum_{i=1}^{P-1} (\overline{f}_{\Omega_i} - \overline{f}_{\Omega_P})^2. \qquad (4)$$

Regions are assumed to be simple closed curves superimposed on the background. This data model does appear to have a fairly wide application potential, especially in medical image analysis and confocal microscopy, where the regions of interest appear as bright objects relative to the dark background.

For the sake of clarity, we restrict ourselves to the first case, i.e. the LEAST SQUARES CRITERION, and give major results for the other criterion.

Our aim is now to define objects in f. Therefore, we define the following class C_P, $P \geq 1$ of admissible objects

$$C_P = \{(\Omega_1, \ldots, \Omega_{P-1}) \subset S \text{ are regular, closed and connected } ; \ \cup_{i=1}^{P} \Omega_i = S ;$$
$$1 \leq i, j \leq P, \ i \neq j \implies \Omega_i \cap \Omega_j = \emptyset ; \}$$

where the subsets $(\Omega_1, \ldots, \Omega_{P-1})$ are the objects of the image and Ω_P is the background. When $P = 1$, there is no object in the image. An optimal segmentation of image f over C_P is by definition a global minimum of the energy (when exists)

$$(\Omega_1^\star, \ldots, \Omega_{P^\star}^\star) = \inf_{P \geq 1} \inf_{(\Omega_1, \ldots, \Omega_P) \in C_P} E_\lambda(f, \Omega_1, \ldots, \Omega_P) . \qquad (5)$$

A direct minimization with respect to all unknown domains Ω_i and parameters $\bar{f}_{\Omega_i}$ is a very intricate problem [2, 21, 19, 29]. In the next section, we prove that the object boundaries are level lines of function f if the penalty function E_p only encourages the emergence of a small number of regions. In our context, an entropy prior or Markov connected component fields-based prior are used to reduce the number of regions. The parameter λ can be then interpreted as a scale parameter that only tunes the number of regions [19].

2.2 Minimizer description and level lines

Our estimator is defined by (when exists)

$$(\widehat{\Omega}_1, \ldots, \widehat{\Omega}_{\widehat{P}}) \;=\; \operatorname{argmin}_{P \geq 1} \operatorname{argmin}_{(\Omega_1, \ldots, \Omega_P) \in C_P} E_\lambda(f, \Omega_1, \ldots, \Omega_P). \qquad (6)$$

The question of the existence of an admissible global minimum for energies like Mumford and Shah's energy [21] is a difficult problem (see [19] for more details). Here, our aim is not to investigate conditions for having an admissible global minimum. In what follows, we make an *ad-hoc* assumption ensuring the existence of an unique minimum of the energy [11].

Minimizer description. We propose the following lemma

<u>LEMMA 1</u> *If there exists an unique admissible global minimum and that no pathological minimum exists [11], then the set of curves that globally minimizes the energy is a subset of level lines of f:*

$$f_{|\partial \Omega_i} \;\equiv\; \mu_i, \qquad i = 1, \ldots, \widehat{P} - 1 .$$

i.e. the border $\partial \Omega_i$ of each Ω_i is a boundary of a level set of f.

Proof of Lemma 1 Without loss of generality, we prove Lemma 1 for one object Ω and a background Ω^c, where Ω^c denotes the closure of the complementary set of Ω. For two sets A and B, denote $\int_{A \; B} f \overset{\triangle}{=} \int_A f - \int_B f$. Let Ω_δ be a small perturbation of Ω, i.e. the Hausdorff distance $d_\infty(\Omega_\delta, \Omega) \leq \delta$. Then, we have

$$\int_{\Omega_\delta - \Omega} \mathbb{1} = \underbrace{|\Omega_\delta| - |\Omega|}_{\triangle(|\Omega|)} \text{ and } \left(\int_{\Omega_\delta} f\right)^2 - \left(\int_\Omega f\right)^2 = 2 \int_\Omega f \int_{\Omega_\delta - \Omega} f + \left(\int_{\Omega_\delta - \Omega} f\right)^2 (7)$$

and the following image moments:

$$m_0 = \int_\Omega \mathbb{1}, \quad m_1 = \int_\Omega f, \quad m_2 = \int_\Omega f^2, \quad K_0 = \int_S \mathbb{1}, \quad K_1 = \int_S f, \quad K_2 = \int_S f^2. (8)$$

The difference between the involved energies is equal to

$$\underbrace{E_\lambda(f, \Omega_\delta, \Omega_\delta^c) - E_\lambda(f, \Omega, \Omega^c)}_{\triangle E_\lambda(f, \Omega, \Omega^c)} = \underbrace{E_d(f, \Omega_\delta, \Omega_\delta^c) - E_d(f, \Omega, \Omega^c)}_{\triangle E_d(f, \Omega, \Omega^c)} + \lambda \underbrace{E_p(\Omega_\delta, \Omega_\delta^c) - E_p(\Omega, \Omega^c)}_{\triangle E_p(\Omega, \Omega^c)}.$$

$$(9)$$

Table 1. Coefficients A_0 and A_1 associated to the two segmentation criteria.

	A_0	A_1
LEAST SQUARE CRITERION	$\dfrac{m_1^2}{m_0^2} - \dfrac{(K_1-m_1)^2}{(K_0-m_0)^2}$	$-\dfrac{2m_1}{m_0} + \dfrac{2(K_1-m_1)}{K_0-m_0}$
CONTRAST STATISTIC CRITERION	$\dfrac{2m_1^2}{m_0^3} - \dfrac{2(K_1-m_1)^2}{(K_0-m_0)^3}$ $-\dfrac{2m_1(1-2m_0)(K_1+m_1)}{m_0^2(K_0-m_0)^2}$	$-\dfrac{2m_1}{m_0^2} + \dfrac{2(K_1-m_1)^2}{(K_0-m_0)^2}$ $+\dfrac{2(K_1-2m_1)}{m_0(K_0-m_0)}$

In Appendix, it is shown that for $\Delta(|\Omega|) \rightarrow 0$, $\Delta E_{\mathrm{d}}(f, \Omega, \Omega^c)$ is equal to

$$\Delta E_{\mathrm{d}}(f, \Omega, \Omega^c) = \Delta(|\Omega|)\,(A_0 + A_1 f) + O(\Delta(|\Omega|)^2) \qquad (10)$$

where A_0 and A_1 are computed from image moments given in (8). For the two criteria described in Section 2.1, the coefficients are listed in table 1. Suppose we can write $\Delta E_{\mathrm{p}}(\Omega, \Omega^c)$ as

$$\Delta E_{\mathrm{p}}(\Omega, \Omega^c) = \Delta(|\Omega|)\,(B_0 + B_1 f) + O(\Delta(|\Omega|)^2). \qquad (11)$$

Let s_0 be a fixed point of the border $\partial\Omega$. Choose Ω_δ such that $\partial\Omega_\delta = \partial\Omega$ except on a small neighborhood of s_0. The energy having a minimum for Ω, $f(s_0)$ needs to be solution of the following equation

$$\Delta E_\lambda(f, \Omega, \Omega^c) = \Delta(|\Omega|)\,[(A_0 + \lambda B_0) + (A_1 + \lambda B_1)f(s_0)] + O(\Delta(|\Omega|)^2) = 0. \quad (12)$$

By pre-multiplying (12) by $\Delta(|\Omega|)^{-1}$ and passing to the limit $\Delta(|\Omega|) \rightarrow 0$, we obtain

$$(A_0 + \lambda B_0) + (A_1 + \lambda B_1)f(s_0) = 0. \qquad (13)$$

Equation (13) has an unique solution. The coefficients $(A_0 + \lambda B_0)$ and $(A_1 + \lambda B_1)$ do depend on neither s_0 nor $f(s_0)$, and $A_0 + \lambda B_0 \neq 0$. The function f is continuous and $\partial\Omega$ is a connected curve. Therefore $f(s_0)$ is constant when s_0 covers $\partial\Omega$. $\square$

In conclusion, we proved that the global minimizer is a subset of iso-intensity curves of the image provided that $E_\lambda(f, \Omega_1, \ldots, \Omega_P)$ is explained by second-order image moments. In the next section, we list two penalty functionals relying on the Markov connected component fields and entropy theories, which are consistent with Lemma 1 and (11).

Image representation by level sets. In consequence of Lemma 1, object borders can be determined by boundaries of level sets. Meanwhile, it turns out that the basic information of an image (or function f) is contained in the family of its binary shadows or *level sets*, that is, in the family of sets $\mathcal{S}_\eta$ defined by

$$\mathcal{S}_\eta = \{s \in S : f(s) \geq \eta\} \qquad (14)$$

for all values of η in the range of f [16]. In contrast to edge representation, the family of level sets is a complete representation of f [18]. This representation is invariant with respect to any increasing contrast change and so robust to illumination conditions changes. In general, the threshold set is made up of connected components based both on the image gray levels and spatial relations between pixels. To extract a connected component of a level set $\mathcal{S}_\eta$, we threshold the image at the gray level η and extract the components of the binary image we obtain. A more efficient technique has been described in [18]. A recent variant of this representation is proposed in [3, 18] by considering the boundary of level sets, that is the *level lines*. This representation does not differ with respect to the set of level sets. As a consequence of the inclusion property of level sets, the level lines do not cross each other's. In the following, we basically consider that a connected component is an object Ω_i and the level lines are just a set of η-isovalue pixels at the borders $\partial\Omega_i$ of connected components.

2.3   Forms of prior models

One of the difficulties in the Bayesian approach is to assign the prior law to reflect our prior knowledge about the solution. Besides, in consequence of Lemma 1, the set of penalty functionals is limited. The contribution of a given pixel to the prior does not depend on the relation with neighbors and the resulting regions may have noisy boundaries. Here, the proposed penalty functionals are not necessary convex but only enable to select the right number of regions. Instead of fixing *a priori* the cardinality of the segmentation, which is a highly arbitrary choice, it seems more natural to control the emergence of regions by an object area-based penalty or by an information criterion weighted by a scale parameter λ.

Markov connected component fields. A new class of Gibbsian models with potentials associated to the connected components or homogeneous parts has been introduced in [17]. For these models, the neighborhood of a pixel is not fixed as for Markov random fields, but given by the components which are adjacent to the pixel. These models are especially applicable for images where a relatively few number of gray levels occur, and where some prior knowledge is available about size and shape characteristics for the connected components [27]. The Markov connected component fields possess certain appealing Markov properties which have been established in [17].

Here we considered a Markov connected component field which the probability density function is proportional to

$$\exp \underbrace{\sum_{i=1}^{P-1} \alpha|\Omega_i| + \beta(P-1)^{\zeta-1} + \gamma|\Omega_i|^2}_{E_{\mathrm{p}}(\Omega_1,\dots,\Omega_P)}. \tag{15}$$

The parameter γ controls the size of the components since the squared area of the union of two components is greater than the sum of the squared areas of each component. The size of the components is however also influenced by the parameter α together with the parameters β and ζ which controls the number of components. The potential $E_p(\Omega_1, \ldots, \Omega_P)$ is the more general functional we can use since the boundaries of connected components cannot be penalized in our framework. These potentials can be separately used to select the right number of regions by setting $\alpha, \beta, \gamma = \{0, 1\}$.

In Section 2.2, we proved Lemma 1 for one object Ω and a background Ω^c. Using the same notations, we easily write

$$\Delta E_p(\Omega, \Omega^c) = \alpha\,\Delta(|\Omega|) + \gamma\left(|\Omega_\delta|^2 - |\Omega|^2\right) = \Delta(|\Omega|)\left(\alpha + 2\gamma m_0\right) + \gamma\,\Delta(|\Omega|)^2. \quad (16)$$

Accordingly, we obtain $B_0 = (\alpha + 2\gamma m_0)$ and $B_1 = 0$, which is consistent with Lemma 1 and (11) if no pathological events (e.g. topological changes) occurs.

The application of Markov connected component fields is somewhat more computationally demanding than the application of Markov random fields. By the local Markov property the calculations for an update of a site in a single site updating algorithm only involves the components adjacent to this site. Our work may be regarded as an preliminary exploitation of the theoretical framework described by Møller *et al* [17] in image segmentation.

Entropy prior. The entropy function has been widely used as a prior in a Bayesian context for image restoration. Here, the entropy of the segmented image is written as follows [9]

$$E_p(\Omega_1, \ldots, \Omega_P) = -\sum_{i=1}^{P} p_i \ln p_i = -\sum_{i=1}^{P} \frac{|\Omega_i|}{|S|} \ln \frac{|\Omega_i|}{|S|} \quad (17)$$

where the p_is represent the histogram values, $|\Omega_i|$ the cardinality of region Ω_i and $|S|$ the cardinality of the image domain. The value p_i is the number of occurrence of the gray level value $\overline{f}_{\Omega_i}$ in the segmented image. The histogram entropy is minimized for a Dirac distribution corresponding to one single class in the segmented image. In image segmentation, we want to obtain a histogram sharper than the histogram of the initial image, so the entropy should be minimized [9]. The actual reduction of number of classes is obtained from the information prior $E_p(\Omega_1, \ldots, \Omega_P)$. Using the notations introduced in Section 2.2, we write

$$\Delta E_p(\Omega, \Omega^c) = \frac{\Delta(|\Omega|)}{|S|} \ln \frac{|S| - |\Omega|}{|\Omega|} + O(\Delta(|\Omega|)^2). \quad (18)$$

Accordingly, we obtain $B_0 = \frac{1}{|S|} \ln \frac{|S|-|\Omega|}{|\Omega|}$ and $B_1 = 0$, which is consistent with Lemma 1 and (11).

2.4 Properties of the energy models

In this section, we complete the analysis of energy models and discuss the connections with image partitioning algorithms.

Upper bound of the objects number. It appears, most of the time, that variations in the values of the parameters λ have significant effects on the qualitative properties of the minimizer [28]. We show that the maximum number of objects is explicitly influenced by λ.

LEMMA 2 *If there exists an optimal segmentation defined by (1) and (2) then the optimal number P^* of objects is upper bounded by*

$$P_{\max} = 1 + (\lambda \; |\Omega_{\min}|)^{-1} \int_S (f(x,y) - \overline{f_S})^2 dx dy$$

if $E_p(\Omega_1, \ldots, \Omega_P) = \sum_{i=1}^{P-1} |\Omega_i|, \quad i.e. \; \alpha = 1, \; \beta = \gamma = 0.$

Proof of Lemma 2 :

$$\lambda \sum_{i=1}^{P^*-1} |\Omega_i^*| \leq E_\lambda(f, \Omega_1^*, \ldots, \Omega_{P^*}^*) \leq E_\lambda(f, S) = \int_S (f(x,y) - \overline{f_S})^2 dx dy.$$

If $|\Omega_i| \geq |\Omega_{\min}|$, we have $(P^* - 1)|\Omega_{\min}| \leq \sum_{i=1}^{P^*-1} |\Omega_i^*| \leq \lambda^{-1} \int_S (f(x,y) - \overline{f_S})^2 \; dx dy$

and $P^* \leq 1 + (\lambda \; |\Omega_{\min}|)^{-1} \int_S (f(x,y) - \overline{f_S})^2 \; dx dy$ $\qquad\qquad\square$

Connection to snakes and geodesic active contour models. Let $v_i(s) = (x_i(s), y_i(s))$ denote a point on the common boundary $\partial \Omega_i$ (parametrized by $s \in [0,1]$) of a region Ω_i and the background Ω_P. We suppose

$$E_\lambda(\Omega_1, \cdots, \Omega_P) = \sum_{i=1}^{P} \int_{\Omega_i} (f(x,y) - \overline{f}_{\Omega_i})^2 \; dx dy + \lambda \sum_{i=1}^{P-1} |\Omega_i| \; .$$

The time t dependent position of the boundary $\partial \Omega_i$ can be expressed parametrically by $v_i(s,t)$. The motion of the boundary $\partial \Omega_i$ is governed by the Euler-Lagrange differential equation [29]. For any point $v_i(s,t)$ on the boundary $\partial \Omega_i$ we obtain.

$$\frac{dv_i(s,t)}{dt} = -\frac{\delta E_\lambda(f, \Omega_i, \Omega_P)}{\delta v_i(s)} = \left[(f(x,y) - \overline{f}_{\Omega_i})^2 + \lambda - (f(x,y) - \overline{f}_{\Omega_P})^2 \right] n(v_i(s)) \; (19)$$

where $n(v_i(s))$ is the unit normal to $\partial \Omega_i$ at point $v_i(s,t)$. This equation can be seen as a degenerate case of the *region competition* algorithm described by Zhu *et al.* [29] where λ is analogous to a pressure term [13, 6]. The solving of the Euler-Lagrange equations for each region can be complex and the *region competition* algorithm (see [29]) finds a local minima. Using the level-set formulation [22, 4, 24], suitable numerical schemes have been derived for solving propagating equations. However, in both cases, seed regions must be provided by the user or randomly put across the image, and mean values $\overline{f}_{\Omega_i}$ are updated at each step of the iterative algorithm. In this paper, we directly determined the steady solutions associated with the motion equation given in (19).

3   Segmentation algorithm

In practical imaging, both the domain S and the range of f are discrete sets. The segmentation algorithm we propose is automatic and does require neither the number of regions nor any initial value for regions. This algorithm is not a region growing algorithm as described in [25, 1, 19] since all objects are built once and for all according to (14). Energy minimization is performed once all admissible objects have been registered. To implement our level set image segmentation, a four step method is used.

LEVEL SET CONSTRUCTION   The first step completes a crude mapping of each image pixel on a given level set. At present, we uniformly quantize the function $f \in [f_{min}, f_{max}]$ in $K = \{4, 8, 16, 32\}$ equal-sized and non-overlapping intervals $\{[l_1, h_1[, \ldots, [l_K, h_K]\}$. Given this set of levels, we then assign one of the levels to each pixel s: s is assigned to $[l_j, h_j[$ if $l_j \leq f(s) < h_j$.

OBJECT EXTRACTION   A crude way to build pixels sets corresponding to objects is to proceed to a connected components labeling and to associate each label with an object Ω_i. The background Ω_P corresponds to the complementary set of objects Ω_i. The list of connected components of each of these then forms the list of objects $\{\Omega_1, \ldots \Omega_T\}$ where T is the maximum number of connected components such as $|\Omega_i| \geq |\Omega_{\min}|$ and $P \leq T \leq P_{\max}$.

Though this process may work in the noise-free case, in general we would also need some smoothing effect of the connected components labeling. So we consider a size-oriented morphological operator acting on sets that consists in keeping all connected components of the output of area larger than a limit Ω_{min}.

CONFIGURATION DETERMINATION   The connected components are then combined during the third step to form objects configurations. Having the objects list $\{\Omega_1, \ldots \Omega_T\}$, configurations can be built by enumeration of all possible object combinations, i.e. 2^T configurations. Each possible configuration can then be represented by a binary number b_i which is the binary expansion of i ($0 \leq i \leq 2^T - 1$). The binary value of each bit in b_i determines the presence or absence of a given object in the configuration.

ENERGY COMPUTATION   Each configuration represents a set of objects which in turn is a set of pixels. Energy calculations take the image intensities of the original (not quantized) image at each of these pixels to establish mean and approximation error. Note that energies corresponding to each object are computed once and stored, and energy corresponding to the background is efficiently updated for each configuration. The configuration that globally minimizes the energy functional corresponds to the optimal segmentation. The time necessary to perform image segmentation essentially depends on the length of the object list, i.e. the number T of connected components. Nevertheless, all configurations are independent and could be potentially evaluated on suitable parallel architectures.

4   Experimental results

We are interested in the use of the technique in the context of medical and aerial imagery and confocal microscopy. Our system successfully segmented various images into a few regions. For the bulk of the experiments, we used a slightly restricted form, in which the data model is given by (2) and, for the sake of clarity, we restrict ourselves to use a single potential at one and the same time, i.e. $E_{\mathrm{p}}(\Omega_1, \ldots, \Omega_P) = P - 1$ or $E_{\mathrm{p}}(\Omega_1, \ldots, \Omega_P) = \sum_{i=1}^{P-1} |\Omega_i|$. The last prior model can be re-defined to find large regions with low/high intensity in the image (see Figs. 2–3). Similar results were obtained using an entropy prior. The algorithm parameters were set as follows: $K = 4, 8, 16$ or 32, and regions which areas $|\Omega_i| < 0.01 \times |S|$ are discarded. Most segmentations took approximately about 4-10 seconds on a 296MHz workstation. Two sets of simulations were conducted on synthetic as well as real-world images to evaluate the performance of the algorithm. In experiments, the image intensities have been normalized into the range $[0, 1]$.

Figure 1a shows an artificially computed 256×256 image representing the superposition of two bidimensional Gaussian functions located respectively at $s_0 = (64, 128)$ and $s_1 = (160, 128)$ with variance of $\sigma_0 = 792$ and $\sigma_1 = 1024$. Figure 1b shows the result of the uniform quantization operation applied on Fig. 1a ($K = 32$). The levels lines associated with the quantized image are displayed on Fig. 1c. Note that level sets of area too small are suppressed. Figures 1d-f show how the penalization parameter influences the segmentation results when $E_{\mathrm{p}}(\Omega_1, \ldots, \Omega_P) = \sum_{i=1}^{P-1} |\Omega_i|$. The white borders denote the boundaries of the objects resulting from the segmentation.

We have applied the same algorithm to an aerial 256×256 image depicted the region of Saint-Louis during the rising of the Mississipi and Missouri rivers in July 1993 (Fig. 2a). We are interested in extracting dark regions labelled using $\overline{f}_{\Omega_i}$ in this image. The level lines corresponding to $K = 8$ are shown on Fig. 2b. The approach has successfully extracted significant dark regions and labeled in "white" urban areas, forests and fields as "background" (Fig. 2c).

An example in 2D medical imaging is shown on Fig. 3. Figure 3c shows the results of the above method when applied to outline the endocardium of a heart image obtained using Magnetic Resonance. This figure illustrates how our method selects the number of segments in a 2D medical MR image (179×175 image). The level lines are shown in Fig. 3b and the region of interest is successfully located using $K = 8$ and $\lambda = 0.01$.

Confocal systems offer the chance to image thick biological tissue in 2D+t or 3D dimensions. They operate in the bright-field and fluorescence modes, allowing the formation of high-resolution images with a depth of focus sufficiently small that all the detail which is imaged appears in focus and the out-of-focus information is rejected. Some of the current applications in biological studies are in neuron research. We have tested the proposed algorithm on 2D confocal microscopy 256×240 images (Fig. 4a), courtesy of INSERM 413 IFRMP n^o23 (Rouen, France). Figure 4a depicts a triangular cell named "astrocyte". These cells generally take the place of died neuron cells. In Figs.4b-c, the seg-

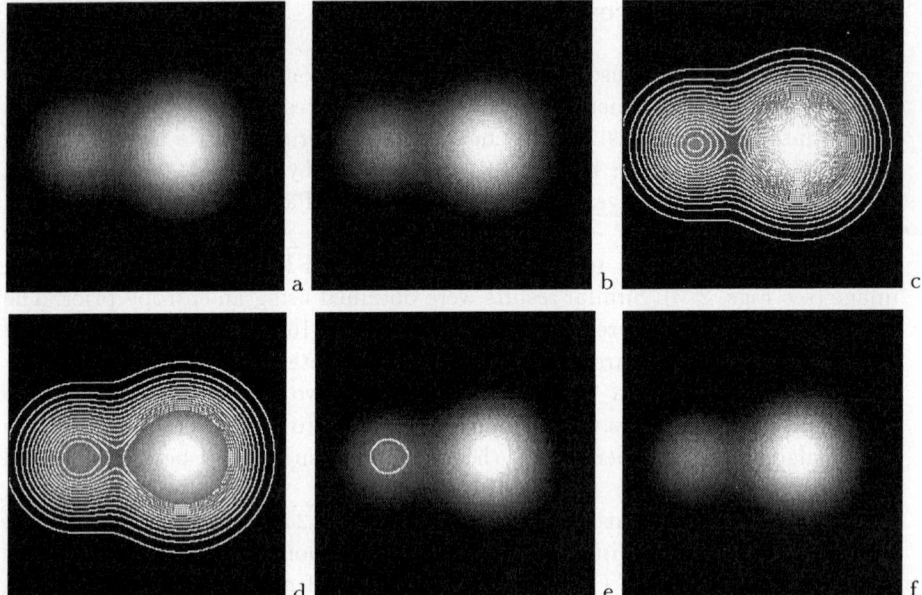

Fig. 1. *Segmentation results of a synthetic image. a) original image ; b) uniformly quantized image ($K = 32$) ; c) level lines superimposed on the quantized image ; d) segmentation with $\lambda = 0.01$; e) segmentation with $\lambda = 0.1$ – two detected objects; f) segmentation with $\lambda = 1.0$ – one detected object.*

mentation of one single cell is shown. We have preliminary filtered the image using anisotropic diffusion [14]. The boundaries of the cell components are quite accurately delineated in Fig. 4b ($K = 8$, $\lambda = 0.001$).

5   Conclusion and perspectives

In this paper we have proposed basic energy functionals for the segmentation of regions in images, and we proved that the minimizer of our energy models can be explicitly determined. The minimization requires no initialization, and is highly parallelizable. A total CPU time of a few seconds for segmenting a 256×256 image on a workstation makes the method attractive for many time-critical applications. The contribution of this approach has been illustrated on synthetic as well as real-world images. The energies are of a very general form and always globally optimizable by the same algorithm. The framework offers many other possibilities for further modeling. We are currently studying an adaptive quantization technique instead of the uniform quantization used at present to estimate the objects. Finally, the extension of the approach to volumetric images (confocal microscopy) and multi-spectral images is also of interest. In this setting, the structure of the algorithm would be largely the same, although there are a number of points which would need to be examined closely.

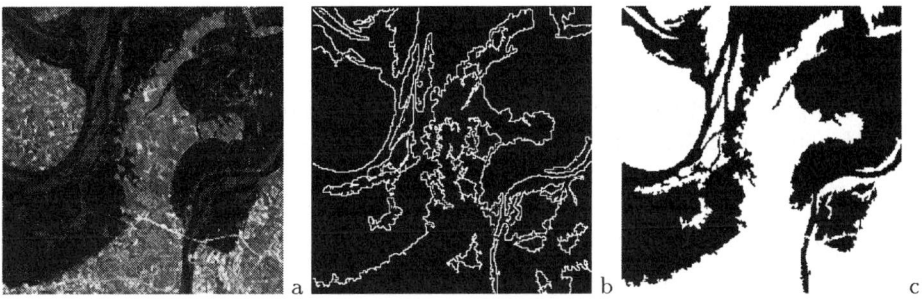

Fig. 2. *Segmentation results of an aerial image* ($\lambda = 0.001$). *Left: original image. Middle: level lines computed from the quantized image* ($K = 8$). *Right: label map.*

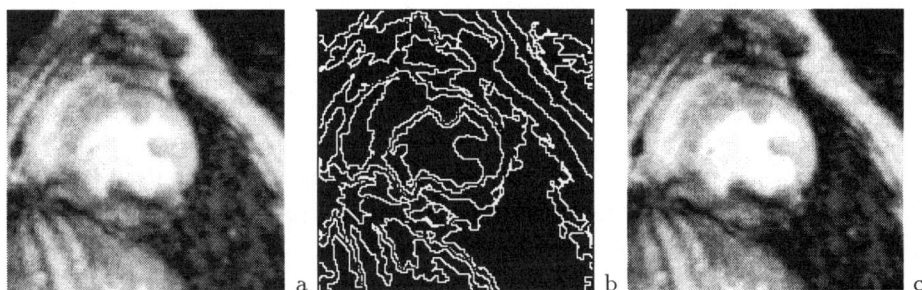

Fig. 3. *Segmentation results of a MR image* ($\lambda = 0.01$). *Left: original image. Middle: level lines computed from the quantized image* ($K = 8$). *Right: boundaries of the object of interest superimposed on the original image.*

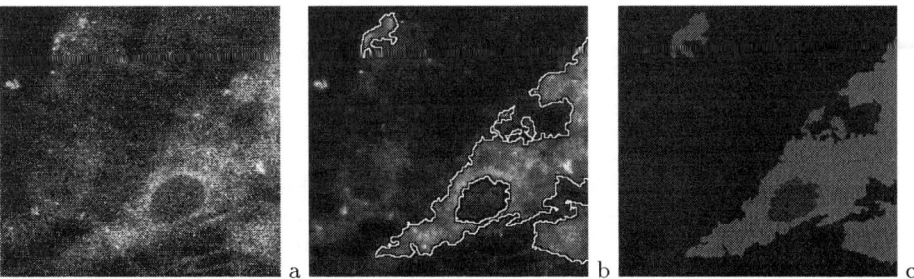

Fig. 4. *Segmentation in 2D confocal microscopy* ($\lambda = 0.001$). *Left: original image. Middle: boundaries superimposed on a adaptively filtered image* ($K = 8$). *Right: label map.*

A Computation of the energy variation for the LEAST SQUARES CRITERION

We compute the energy variation for one object Ω and a background Ω^c, where Ω^c denotes the closure of the complementary set of Ω. The data model is

$$E_d(f, \Omega, \Omega^c) = \int_\Omega (f(x,y) - \overline{f_\Omega})^2 \, dxdy + \int_{\Omega^c} (f(x,y) - \overline{f_{\Omega^c}})^2 \, dxdy. \quad (20)$$

For two sets A and B, denote $\int_{A-B} f \triangleq \int_A f - \int_B f$. Let Ω_δ be a small perturbation of Ω, i.e. the Hausdorff distance $d_\infty(\Omega_\delta, \Omega) \leq \delta$. Then, we define

$$\underbrace{\int_{\Omega_\delta - \Omega} \mathbb{1}}_{\Delta(|\Omega|)} = |\Omega_\delta| - |\Omega| \quad \text{and} \quad \left(\int_{\Omega_\delta} f\right)^2 - \left(\int_\Omega f\right)^2 = 2\int_\Omega f \int_{\Omega_\delta - \Omega} f + \left(\int_{\Omega_\delta - \Omega} f\right)^2 (21)$$

The difference between the involved energies is equal to $\Delta E_d(f, \Omega, \Omega^c) = E_d(f, \Omega_\delta, \Omega_\delta^c) - E_d(f, \Omega, \Omega^c) = T_1 + T_2 + T_3 + T_4$, with

$$T_1 = \int_{\Omega_\delta} f^2 - \int_\Omega f^2, \qquad T_2 = -\frac{1}{|\Omega_\delta|}\left(\int_{\Omega_\delta} f\right)^2 + \frac{1}{|\Omega|}\left(\int_\Omega f\right)^2,$$

$$T_3 = \int_{S - \Omega_\delta} f^2 - \int_{S - \Omega} f^2, \qquad T_4 = -\frac{1}{|S| - |\Omega_\delta|}\left(\int_{S-\Omega_\delta} f\right)^2 + \frac{1}{|S| - |\Omega|}\left(\int_{S-\Omega} f\right)^2.$$

Using (21) and passing to the limit $\Delta(|\Omega|) \to 0$, i.e. $|\Omega_\delta| \simeq |\Omega|$, we obtain (higher order terms are neglected)

$$T_1 = -T_3 = \int_{\Omega_\delta - \Omega} f^2,$$

$$T_2 = -\frac{2}{|\Omega|}\int_{\Omega_\delta - \Omega} f \int_\Omega f - \frac{1}{|\Omega|}\left(\int_{\Omega_\delta - \Omega} f\right)^2 + \frac{1}{|\Omega|^2}\int_{\Omega_\delta - \Omega}\mathbb{1}\left(\int_\Omega f\right)^2,$$

$$T_4 = \frac{2}{|S| - |\Omega|}\int_{\Omega_\delta - \Omega} f \int_{S - \Omega} f - \frac{1}{|S| - |\Omega|}\left(\int_{\Omega_\delta - \Omega} f\right)^2 \qquad (22)$$
$$-\frac{1}{(|S| - |\Omega|)^2}\int_{\Omega_\delta - \Omega}\mathbb{1}\left(\int_{S - \Omega} f\right)^2.$$

Define the image moments $m_0 = \int_\Omega \mathbb{1}$, $m_1 = \int_\Omega f$, $K_0 = \int_S \mathbb{1}$, $K_1 = \int_S f$.

Using the *mean value theorem for double integral*, which states that if f is continuous and A is bounded by a simple curve, then for some point s_0 in A we have $\int_A f(s)dA = f(s_0) \cdot |A|$ where $|A|$ denotes the area of S, it follows that

$$\Delta E_d(f, \Omega, \Omega^c) = \overbrace{\left[\frac{m_1^2}{m_0^2} - \frac{(K_1 - m_1)^2}{(K_0 - m_0)^2}\right]}^{A_0}\int_{\Omega_\delta - \Omega}\mathbb{1} + \overbrace{\left[-\frac{2m_1}{m_0} + \frac{2(K_1 - m_1)}{K_0 - m_0}\right]}^{A_1} f(s_0)\int_{\Omega_\delta - \Omega}\mathbb{1}$$
$$-\left[\frac{1}{m_0} + \frac{1}{K_0 - m_0}\right]f(s_0)^2\left(\int_{\Omega_\delta - \Omega}\mathbb{1}\right)^2. \qquad (23)$$

References

1. J. Beaulieu and M. Goldberg. Hierarchy in picture segmentation: a stepwise optimization approach. *IEEE Trans. Patt. Anal. and Mach. Int.*, 11(2):150–163, 1989.
2. A. Blake and A. Zisserman. *Visual Reconstruction*. MIT Press, Cambridge, Mass, 1987.
3. V. Caselles, B. Coll, and J. Morel. Topographic maps. *preprint CEREMADE*, 1997.
4. V. Caselles, R. Kimmel, and G. Sapiro. Geodesic active contours. *Int J. Computer Vision*, 22(1):61–79, 1997.
5. A. Chakraborty and J. Duncan. Game-theoretic integration for image segmentation. *IEEE Trans. Patt. Anal. and Mach. Int.*, 21(1):12–30, 1999.
6. L. Cohen. On active contour models and balloons. *CVGIP: Image Understanding*, 53(2):211–218, 1991.
7. L. Cohen. Deformable curves and surfaces in image analysis. In *Int. Conf. Curves and Surfaces*, Chamonix, France, 1996.
8. T. Darrell and A. Pentland. Cooperative robust estimation using layers of support. *IEEE Trans. Patt. Anal. and Mach. Int.*, 17(5):474–487, 1995.
9. X. Descombes and F. Kruggel. A markov pixon information approach for low-level image description. *IEEE Trans. Patt. Anal. and Mach. Int.*, 21(6):482–494, 1999.
10. S. Geman and D. Geman. Stochastic relaxation, gibbs distributions, and the bayesian restoration of images. *IEEE Trans. Patt. Anal. and Mach. Int.*, 6(6):721–741, 1984.
11. J. Istas. *Statistics of processes and signal-image segmentation*. University of Paris VII, 1997.
12. I. Jermyn and H. Ishikawa. Globally optimal regions and boundaries. In *Int. Conf. on Comp. Vis.*, pages 904–910, Kerkyra, Greece, September 1999.
13. M. Kass, A. Witkin, and D. Terzopoulos. Snakes: active contour models. *Int J. Computer Vision*, 12(1):321–331, 1987.
14. C. Kervrann, M. Hoebeke, and A. Trubuil. A level line selection approach for object boundary estimation. In *Int. Conf. on Comp. Vis.*, pages 963–968, Kerkyra, Greece, September 1999.
15. Y. Leclerc. Constructing simple stable descriptions for image partitioning. *Int J. Computer Vision*, 3:73–102, 1989.
16. G. Matheron. *Random Sets and Integral Geometry*. John Wiley, New York, 1975.
17. J. Møller and R. Waagepertersen. Markov connected component fields. *Adv. in Applied Probability*, pages 1–35, 1998.
18. P. Monasse and F. Guichard. Scale-space from a level line tree. In *Int. Conf. on Scale-Space Theories Comp. Vis.*, pages 175–186, Kerkyra, Greece, September 1999.
19. J. Morel and S. Solimini. *Variational Methods in Image Segmentation*. Birkhauser, 1994.
20. D. Mumford. The Bayesian rationale for energy functionals. *Geometry-Driven Diffusion in Domputer Vision*, pages 141–153, Bart Romeny ed., Kluwer Academic, 1994.
21. D. Mumford and J. Shah. Optimal approximations by piecewise smooth functions and variational problems. *Communication on Pure and applied Mathematics*, 42(5):577–685, 1989.
22. S. Osher and J. Sethian. Fronts propagating with curvature dependent speed: algorithms based on the hamilton-jacobi formulation. *J. Computational Physics*, 79:12–49, 1988.

23. F. O'Sullivan and M. Qian. A regularized contrast statistic for object boundary estimation – implementation and statistical evaluation. *IEEE Trans. Patt. Anal. and Mach. Int.*, 16(6):561–570, 1994.

24. N. Paragios and R. Deriche. Coupled geodesic active regions for image segmentation: a level set approach. In *Euro. Conf. on Comp. Vis.*, Dublin, Ireland, 2000.

25. T. Pavlidis and Y. Liow. Integrating region growing and edge detection. *IEEE Trans. Patt. Anal. and Mach. Int.*, 12:225–233, 1990.

26. C. Schnörr. A study of a convex variational diffusion approach for image segmentation and feature extraction. *J. Math. Imaging and Vision*, 3(8):271–292, 1998.

27. J. Wang. Stochastic relaxation on partitions with connected components and its application to image segmentation. *IEEE Trans. Patt. Anal. and Mach. Int.*, 20(6):619–636, 1998.

28. L. Younes. Calibrating parameters of cost functionals. In *Euro. Conf. on Comp. Vis.*, Dublin, Ireland, 2000.

29. S. Zhu and A. Yuille. Region competition: unifying snakes, region growing, and bayes/MDL for multiband image segmentation. *IEEE Trans. Patt. Anal. and Mach. Int.*, 18(9):884–900, 1996.

A Probabilistic Interpretation of the Saliency Network

Michael Lindenbaum * and Alexander Berengolts **

Computer Science Department, Technion,
Haifa 32000, ISRAEL

Abstract. The calculation of salient structures is one of the early and basic ideas of perceptual organization in Computer Vision. Saliency algorithms aim to find image curves, maximizing some deterministic quality measure which grows with the length of the curve, its smoothness, and its continuity. This note proposes a modified saliency estimation mechanism, which is based on probabilistically specified grouping cues and on length estimation. In the context of the proposed method, the well-known saliency mechanism, proposed by Shaashua and Ullman [SU88], may be interpreted as a process trying to detect the curve with maximal expected length.

The new characterization of saliency using probabilistic cues is conceptually built on considering the curve starting at a feature point, and estimating the distribution of the length of this curve, iteratively. Different saliencies, like the expected length, may be specified as different functions of this distribution. There is no need however to actually propagate the distributions during the iterative process.

The proposed saliency characterization is associated with several advantages: First, unlike previous approaches, the search for the "best group" is based on a probabilistic characterization, which may be derived and verified from typical images, rather than on pre-conceived opinion about the nature of figure subsets. Therefore, it is expected also to be more reliable. Second, the probabilistic saliency is more abstract and thus more generic than the common geometric formulations. Therefore, it lends itself to different realizations of saliencies based on different cues, in a systematic rigorous way. To demonstrate that, we created, as instances of the general approach, a saliency process which is based on grey level similarity but still preserve a similar meaning. Finally, the proposed approach gives another interpretation for the measure than makes one curve a winner, which may often be more intuitive to grasp, especially as the saliency levels has a clear meaning of say, expected curve length.

1 Introduction

The human visual system (HVS) is capable of filtering images and finding the important visual events so that its limited computational resources may be focused on them and used efficiently. This discrimination between the important

---

* email address:mic@cs.technion.ac.il
** email address:aer@cs.technion.ac.il

parts of the image, denoted "figure", and the less important parts, denoted "background", is done before the objects in the image are identified, and using general rules (or cues) indicating what is likely to be important [Wer50].

Presented, for example, with a binary image containing points and/or curves (such as those resulting from edge detection), it turns out that this perceptual process prefers to choose for figure, a subset of points lying on some long, smooth and dense curve.

To account for this phenomenon with a computational theory [Mar82], Shaashua and Ullman suggested a particular measure, denoted saliency, that is a particular quantification of the desirable smoothness and length properties. They have shown that indeed, the image subsets, associated with high saliency are those considered as more important by common human subjective judgment [SU88]. One important advantage of this computational theory is that this global optimization may be formulated as a dynamic programming task and consequently may be carried out as an iterative process running on a network of simple processors getting only local information. This makes the theory attractive because the proposed process is consistent with common neural mechanisms.

The saliency measure of [SU88] was re-analyzed recently as well, revealing some deficiencies. A generalization, stating that every saliency measure which satisfy some conditions set in [SU88], can be optimized in the same way, was suggested in [AM98]. Other measures of saliency, based on non-iterative local support [GM93], eigenvectors of an affinity matrix [SB98] and stochastic models for particle motion [WJ96] were suggested as well. A survey on different saliency methods is described in [WT98]. The aim of the work on saliency remains to explain perceptual phenomena such as Figure from Ground abilities and illusory contours perception, but also to provide a computer vision tool for intermediate level sorting and filtering of the image data. Work on Figure from Ground discrimination such as [HH93,HvdH93,AL98], do not address explicitly the saliency issue but, implicitly, calculate a (binary) saliency as well.

Having its origin in an attempt to explain a perceptual phenomena, most of the work on saliency does not emphasize the justification for the HVS preference of long smooth curves. It just tries to find a computational mechanism that produces such preference. Note that the particular saliency measure proposed in [SU88] is one particular quantification of the intuitively phrased desired properties. It may be (slightly) modified (by say, replacing the curvature value by twice its value), yielding a measure which is as plausible and computationally efficient, but leading to a different choice of the most salient curve.

For perceptual modeling, the "best" saliency measure may be decided by psychophysical experimentation. For computer vision applications, however, optimizing the saliency measure requires first to agree on a quantitative criterion. The initial motivation of this work is to provide an interpretation and another justification of the original saliency concept.

We show here how saliency like measures may be derived within a more general framework, namely the quantification of grouping reliability using probabilities. The method is conceptually built on considering the curve starting at a feature point, and estimating the distribution of the length of this curve, iteratively. Different saliencies, like the expected length, may be specified as different functions of this distribution. Although central to the explanation of the method, there is no need, in practice, to propagate the actual distribution during the iterative process, which indeed would have required a substantial computational effort.

The proposed view and corresponding algorithm is different than that considered in [SU88] (for example, with regard to the treatment of virtual (non-feature) points), but it shares the iterative dynamic programming like algorithm. When phrased in terms of our algorithm, the original saliency of [SU88] corresponds to a curvature/distance based grouping cue. Maximizing it at a point corresponds to maximizing the expected length of the curve on which this point lies. This way, the traditional saliency measure gets a different interpretation, of looking for objects associated with maximal expected perimeter.

The new characterization of saliency using probabilistic cues is associated with the following advantages:

1. reliability — Basing the search for the "best group" on the probabilistic characterization, which may be derived from typical images, (using ground truth), rather than on pre-conceived opinion about the nature of figure subsets is expected to give better choices of significant groups.
2. generality — the probabilistic saliency is more abstract and thus more generic than the original geometric formulation. Therefore, it lends itself to different realizations of saliencies based on different cues. To demonstrate that, we run the same saliency method with two different cues: low curvature and grey level similarity.
3. another perspective — consider the SU saliency not only by its original curvature based interpretation, but also by its probabilistic interpretation gives another interpretation for the measure than makes one curve a winner, and may often be more intuitive to grasp, especially as the saliency levels has a clear meaning of say, expected curve length.

The paper continues as follows. First, in section 2, we present the length distribution concept, and show how different saliency measures may be built upon it. The proposed saliency process is described in section 3, where we consider the iterative calculation, some shortcuts allowing not to calculate or to keep the actual distribution, convergence issues, and the formulation of the SU saliency as an instance of the new saliency. Some experiments, demonstrating the different types of saliencies resulting from the proposed saliency algorithm, are described in section 4.

2 Probabilistic Saliency

2.1 Length distributions

Let x_i be a directional feature point in the image (e.g. an edgel). Such a point may or may not belong to some curve which extends l_+ length units to one side and l_- length units to the other side. Here we consider these lengths as random variables associated with the feature x_i, and characterize them by the distributions $\mathbf{D}_+^i(l)$ and $\mathbf{D}_-^i(l)$, respectively. The meaning of treating the lengths as random variables is discussed below. The direction, used to keep the order in the curve, is specified relative to say, the direction of the gradient at this feature point, and may take one of the two $\{+, -\}$ values. The parts of the curve lying in the positive and negative directions are denoted positive and negative extensions, respectively. Our basic intuition is that points with long extensions, correspond to larger objects and deliver more significant information about the content of the image. Therefore we shall try to find those feature points associated with the $\mathbf{D}_+^i(l)$ and $\mathbf{D}_-^i(l)$ distributions, which put more weight on longer l values.

When no connectivity information is available, all features are not known to belong to any curve. Then, all distributions are concentrated on very short lengths, corresponding to the length of the corresponding feature themselves. For simplicity, we assume that all these initial distributions are identical and denote this initial distribution by $\mathbf{D}^*(l)$.

2.2 Length distribution update rules

Consider two features, x_i and x_j, which belong to some curve, such that x_j lies in the positive extension of x_i. Suppose that $\mathbf{D}_+^j(l)$ is known. Then, $\mathbf{D}_+^i(l)$ can be written as

$$\mathbf{D}_+^i(l) = \mathbf{D}_+^{j \to i}(l) = \mathbf{D}_+^j(l - l_{ij}) \tag{1}$$

where l_{ij} is the distance from x_i to x_j (on the curve). This follows by observing that a positive extension of length l associated with x_j implies that the length of the positive extension of x_i is $l + l_{ij}$. The notation $\mathbf{D}_+^{j \to i}(l)$ explicitly emphasizes that this is an inference of the length distribution associated with the i−th feature from the known distribution associated with the j−th feature.

In the common situation in image analysis, we can never be sure that two features lie on the same curve. In a non-model-based context, we can only estimate the probability for this event based on local information such as perceptual organization cues [Low85]. Let $c(x_j)$ denote the curve on which x_j lies and let P_{ij} be the probability $Prob\{x_i \in c(x_j)\}$. This probability, denoted as "the grouping cue" is expected to be inferred from perceptual information. Specifying the affinity value between the two feature points x_i and x_j, in this probabilistic abstract way, allows to calculate a saliency like measure, based on different grouping cues and not only on the co-circularity cue used in [SU88]. As we shall see, this probabilistic formulation provides a common meaning for the different saliencics associated with the different cues, independently of the different types of information they employ.

The cue value $Prob\{x_i \in c(x_j)\}$ may be regarded as a characteristic of a binary random variable determining whether x_i and x_j are connected. Consider a path $\Gamma = \{x_1, x_2, \ldots, x_N\}$ starting at the feature point x_1, such that x_{i+1} is on the positive extension of x_i, $i = 1, \ldots, N - 1$. The length of the connected path which starts at x_1 depends on the outcome of all binary random variables characterizing the connectedness of the pairs x_i, x_{i+1}. Therefore, this length may be considered as a random variable itself. The distribution of this random variable characterizes the support that x_i gets from its positive extension.

Consider now an algorithm trying to find a path between the feature points, and some hypothesis about a particular path, in which the feature x_j lies on the positive extension of the feature x_i. If the length distribution $\mathbf{D}_+^j(l)$ is known then the expected value of the length distribution $\mathbf{D}_+^i(l)$, is

$$\hat{\mathbf{D}}_+^{j \to i}(l) = P_{ij}\mathbf{D}_+^j(l - l_{ij}) + (1 - P_{ij})\mathbf{D}^*(l). \tag{2}$$

Note that $\hat{\mathbf{D}}_+^{j \to i}(l)$ is not the expected length of the positive extension length (which is a scalar), but rather, an *expected distribution* (out of the simple distribution of length distributions specified by the random connection between x_i and x_j), which is a distribution itself. Note also that this is an estimate of the length distribution of the positive extension of x_i, under a particular hypothesis regarding the path. The possibility that x_i belongs to some other path (or curve) which does not contain x_j is not taken into account. Therefore the only options for x_i are either to be connected to this curve or to be disconnected from anything (in the positive direction). An alternative formulation, where all curves to which x_i may belongs are taken into account, leads to a Bayesian estimate of $\mathbf{D}_+^i(l)$. See section 5 for a discussion of this alternative and its relation to the saliency like approach developed in [WJ96].

Suppose now that a path $\Gamma = \{x_1, x_2, \ldots, x_N\}$ starts at the feature point x_1, such that x_{i+1} is on the positive extension of x_i, $i = 1, \ldots, N-1$. Then, the length distribution associated with x_1 may be recursively calculated: $\mathbf{D}_+^N(l) = \mathbf{D}^*(l)$, $\hat{\mathbf{D}}_+^{N-1}(l) = \hat{\mathbf{D}}_+^{N \to N-1}(l)$, $\ldots$, until $\hat{\mathbf{D}}_+^1(l)$ is finally estimated. A distribution estimated this way, from a path of length N, is denoted (when we we want to make it explicit), $\hat{\mathbf{D}}_{+N}^i(l)$.

2.3 Probabilistic Saliency

Let $Q[\mathbf{D}_+^i(l)]$ be a (scalar) quality measure computable from the length distribution, and quantifying, in some way, the desired property of a long curve. Typical measures may be the average length or other moments. This measure serves as a one-sided-saliency, and we shall look for features points maximizing it and for curves containing such points. Note that every feature point is associated with two one-sided saliencies, corresponding to the two directions. Some possible choices for the saliency are

Maximum one-sided expected length — A straightforward saliency measure is the expected value of the extension length random variable, which is denoted expected length and is easily calculated from its distribution.

Maximum two-sided expected length — Unless the curve is close and very tightly connected. maximizing the expected length in the two directions is done independently for the two sides. Then, the sum of these one-sided saliencies at a point is just the expected length of the curve on which the point lies.

Maximum confidence one-sided curve — Some common object recognition process, which rely on curve invariants, need some continuous curve from the object. In such scenario, some reasonably long curve associated with high reliability is preferred over a longer curve with lower reliability. Here, the preferred curve is characterized by a distribution concentrating around one value, in contrast to an uncertain estimate, characterized by a closer to uniform distribution.

In the rest of this paper, the one-sided expected length saliency is usually used. although one example, demonstrating the advantages of the confidence emphasizing approaches is considered in the experiments. The expected length is the measure corresponding to SU saliency and its interpretation is simple and clear. We shall also see that it has algorithmic advantages.

For feature points on closed curves, the meaning of the saliency as expected length is distorted, because the length of points of the curve is counted twice or more (after a sufficient number of iterations). The increase of the saliency of close curves is often considered desirable because closer curves have usually higher significance over their open counterparts with the same length [SU88]. Calculating the expected length for closed curves can be done using the technique described in [AB98] and shall not be repeated here.

3   The probabilistic saliency optimization process

The aim of the optimization process is, for every feature point, to find a path, starting at this point and maximizing the saliency of that point (calculated relative to this path).

(We should mention here that the proposed method is similar, in principle, to that proposed by Shaashua and Ullman (see [SU88,AB98]), and is brought here only because some details differ (due to the use of distributions) and for completeness. We tried to use similar notations when possible. The calculation of saliency in the sense of [SU88], for a sparse set of feature points (i.e. without virtual feature points) was considered also in [AM98].)

Calculating this optimum is easy for short paths (e.g. $N = 1, 2$) but is generally exponential in N. Fortunately, it may be calculated by a simple iterative process using dynamic programming if the quality criterion (or saliency) is extensible [SU88]. That is, if the saliency associated with the best (length N) path starting from x_i satisfies

$$Q[\mathbf{D}_{+N}^i(l)] = \max_j F\left(q_{ij}, \mathbf{D}_{+(N-1)}^j(l)\right)$$

where q_{ij} is a quantity calculated from the feature points x_i and x_j, $\mathbf{D}_{+(N-1)}^j(l)$ is the distribution associated with the best (length $N - 1$) path, associated with the highest saliency, starting from x_j, and the maximization is done over all neighbors x_j of x_i. Note that this condition is a bit more general that that suggested in [SU88], as the new saliency calculation may use the distribution and not only a function of it. In fact, all information about the best path may be used as well, as the more general condition is that the optimal solution contains within in optimal solutions to subproblem instances [CLR90]. Note that the expected length is an extensible quality criterion.

3.1 The iterative process

Preprocessing:
A neighborhood is specified for every feature point.

At the k-th iteration $(k = 1, 2, 3, \ldots)$
For every feature point x_i

1. For all neighbors x_j $j = 1, 2, 3 \ldots$ of x_i
   (a) calculate the grouping cue P_{ij}.
   (b) update the length distribution $\mathbf{D}_+^{j \to i}(l)$ using eq. (2), and calculate $Q[\mathbf{D}_+^{j \to i}(l)]$.
2. Choose the neighbor x_j maximizing the quality measure and update the length distribution to $\mathbf{D}_+^{j \to i}(l)$.

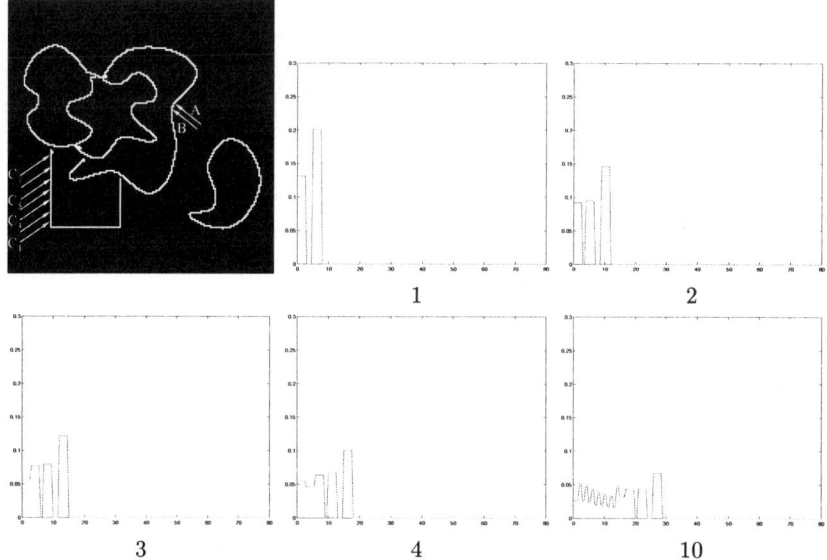

Fig. 1. The one sided length distribution at the point C_3 (in the top left illustration), plotted for 1,2,3,4 and 10 iterations. Note that for such a smooth curve (a straight line segment), the distribution quickly develops a significant weight for the large values.

The procedure starts when all feature points are associated with the basic distribution $\mathbf{D}_+^*(l)$. For saliencies prefering long curves, the process behaves as follows: At the first stage, every feature point x_i chooses the best perceptually connected neighbor x_j, so that P_{ij} is maximal for it, "improves" its distribution, and increase its saliency. At the next iterations, the prefered neighbor is chosen not only by its perceptual affinity but also by its own saliency, as generated in the previous iterations. See Figure 1, illustrating the development of the length distribution associated with a particular point and Figure 2 which describe some (roughly) stable distribution obtained after many iterations.

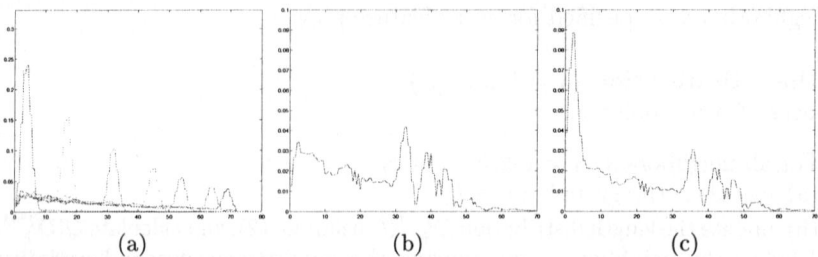

(a)   (b)   (c)

Fig. 2. The left graph (a) describes some distributions corresponding to the different points $C_1, \dots, C_7$ (in the previous Figure) after 80 iterations. Note that points which are close to the end (C_1 is the closest) cannot develop large value, and correspond to the distributions with peaks on small l values. The point A is gets support from a smooth curve and is associated with a distribution having significant weight in the high values (b). The point B is weakly connected to A, and therefore, its distribution is an average of the initial distribution, focusing on low values and that of A, which makes its roughly bimodal (c).

Apart from building the length distributions, the process also specifies, for every feature point, the next feature point on its extension. Thus, starting from salient points, the iterative process finds also the long, well connected, curves which contributed and supported this high saliency.

3.2 Shortcuts

Apparently, one deficiency of the proposed saliency is the need to update a length distribution for every feature point, which is costly in time and space. To alleviate this problem we suggest to store and update only the statistics required to calculate the prefered saliency. For example, For calculating the expected length quality measure, let $E^*[l]$ be the expected length associated with the distribution $\mathbf{D}_+^*(l)$. Then, the distribution update rule is changed to the following expected length update rule

$$E[l]_+^i = E[l]_+^{j \to i} = P_{ij}(l_{ij} + E[l]_+^j) + (1 - P_{ij})E^*[l]$$

Other statistics (e.g. variance) may be propagated similarly, and there is usually no need to propagate the entire

3.3 Optimality and Convergence

By the same arguments made in standard dynamic programming and in [SU88], after N iterations, the length distribution of the i-th feature is associated with the maximal saliency. The maximum is over all possible curves of length N starting in the i-th feature point. This optimization happens for all feature points simultaneously. One (or more) of them will also achieve the global saliency measure. Therefore, the process finds also the maximal quality curve, as measured by the saliency of its endpoint.

After N iterations, all the open paths of length N or less, which start at x_i make their maximal contribution. If N is set as the number of feature points in the image, then the process should converge after N iterations. The exception is of course closed curves, which are equivalent to infinite chains. We show now that even for closed curves the length distribution converges. The proof takes follows some principles from [AB98].

Consider, for example, a feature point on a closed path of length N_c. Let this point be the i-th point and let the direction be such that this i-th point updates its distribution based on the $(i+1)$-th point. Until the N_c-th iteration, the closure does not effect the distribution associated with the feature point. At the N_c-th iteration, the saliency of the i-th point may be written as

$$
\begin{aligned}
\mathbf{D}^i_{+N_c}(l) &= (1 - P_{i,i+1})\mathbf{D}^*(l) + P_{i,i+1}\mathbf{D}^{i+1}_{+(N_c-1)}(l - l_{i,i+1}) \\
&= (1 - P_{i,i+1})\mathbf{D}^*(l) + P_{i,i+1}(1 - P_{i+1,i+2})\mathbf{D}^*(l - l_{i,i+1}) \\
&\quad + P_{i,i+1}P_{i+1,i+2}\mathbf{D}^{i+2}_{+(N_c-2)}(l - l_{i,i+1} - l_{i+1,i+2}) \\
&= \dots \\
&= (1 - \Pi_{j=0}^{N_c-1}P_{i+j,i+j+1})\bar{\mathbf{D}}^*(l) + \Pi_{j=0}^{N_c-1}P_{i+j,i+j+1}\mathbf{D}^i_{+0}(l - \textstyle\sum_{j=0}^{N_c-1}l_{i+j,i+j+1}) \\
&= (1 - \alpha)\bar{\mathbf{D}}^*(l) + \alpha\mathbf{D}^i_{+0}(l - L) \\
&= (1 - \alpha)\bar{\mathbf{D}}^*(l) + \alpha\mathbf{D}^*_+(l - L)
\end{aligned}
$$

$$(3)$$

$\bar{\mathbf{D}}^*(l)$ is an average distribution of $\mathbf{D}^*(l), \mathbf{D}^*(l - l_{i,i+1}), \mathbf{D}^*(l - l_{i,i+1} - l_{i+1,i+2}), \dots$ (with non-equal coefficients), $L = \sum_{j=0}^{N_c-1}l_{i+j,i+j+1}$, and $\alpha = \Pi_{j=0}^{N_c-1}P_{i+j,i+j+1}$. Note that while the distribution of the i-th feature point is no longer the initial distribution, this update is not reflected yet in the way it supports itself through the closed curve. From the next iterations however, the change of the i-th feature point histogram will be reflected in this support, and after N_c additional iterations the histogram will change to

$$
\begin{aligned}
\mathbf{D}^i_{+2N_c}(l) &= (1 - \alpha)\bar{\mathbf{D}}^*(l) + \alpha\mathbf{D}^i_{+N_c}(l - L) \\
&= (1 - \alpha)\bar{\mathbf{D}}^*(l) + \alpha[(1 - \alpha)\bar{\mathbf{D}}^*(l - L) + \alpha\mathbf{D}^*_+(l - 2L)]
\end{aligned}
\quad (4)
$$

After $K \cdot N_c$ iterations,

$$
\mathbf{D}^i_{+KN_c}(l) = (1 - \alpha)\sum_{k=0}^{K}\alpha^k\bar{\mathbf{D}}^*(l - kL) + \alpha^K\mathbf{D}^*_+(l - KL) \quad (5)
$$

Consider now any finite moment or order m associated with the length distribution. Note that $\mathbf{D}^*_+(l - kL)$ (and $\bar{\mathbf{D}}^*(l - kL)$) has zero weight on any length

l higher than kL. Therefore, after the KN_c-the iteration, this moment, denoted $M^i_{+KN_c}$, is bounded:

$$M^i_{+KN_c} \leq (1-\alpha)\sum_{k=0}^{K}\alpha^k(kL)^m + \alpha^K(KL)^m$$
$$= (1-\alpha)L^m\sum_{k=0}^{K}\alpha^k k^m + L^m\alpha^K K^m \qquad (6)$$

For any reasonable cue, $\alpha = \Pi_{j=0}^{N_c-1}P_{i+j,i+j+1}$ is strictly smaller than one and the bounds on the moments converges. The moments themselves are increasing with K, and therefore converge, and hence the distribution converge.

3.4 Relation to the original SU saliency

The original saliency measures, proposed in [SU88], meant to mimic the human visual system (HVS) behavior and to model the priority it gives to long smooth curves, even when they are fragmented. Our approach, on the other hand, is based on a statistical characterization of grouping cues, which is believed to be available. It is well known that the HVS is very successful in grouping tasks, therefore, the statistics of grouping cues must have been learned and incorporated into its grouping mechanisms. Thus, it is expected that our method will also give results, which are compatible with the HVS preferences. For cues based on co-circularity, which is the principle used in [SU88], the results of both methods are expected to be similar.

We shall show now that in the context of curvature/distance based cue, the SU algorithm corresponds to an instance of our algorithm: The saliency of the $i-$th feature, specified in [SU88] is updated by the local rule

$$E_i^{(n+1)} = \sigma_i + \rho_i\max(E_j^{(n)}f_{ij})$$

where the maximum is taken over all the features in the neighborhood of the $i-$th feature, and

- $E_i^{(n)}$ is the saliency of the i-th feature after the $n-$th iteration,
- σ_i is a "local saliency" which is set as a positive value (e.g. 1) for every real feature,
- ρ_i is a penalty for gaps which is set to one in features (no gap) and to a lower value when the feature is virtual. Finally,
- f_{ij} is a "coupling constant" which decreases with the local curvature.

In the framework of [SU88] features could be "real" (where we have, say, an edge point), or "virtual" where there is no local image based evidence for an edge. This choice allows to hypothesize an image independent and1g1g parallel local architecture which is a plausible model for a perceptual process. A virtual feature does not add to saliency and therefore is associated with null σ_i. It should also attenuate the currently existing saliency and is therefore associated with lower than one ρ_i parameter.

In our framework, all features are real. For them, the co-circularity may be interpreted as a measure for the grouping probability: by the general assumption that smooth curves are likely, a low curvature implies that connection is more probable then high curvature. Thus, for real feature points, the SU update formulae may be interpreted as

$$E_i^{(n+1)} = 1 + \max(E_j^{(n)} P_{ij}). \tag{7}$$

The ability to continue the curve over gaps is interpreted as follows: Suppose that the three feature points x_i, x_j, x_k are consecutive along the curve, are chosen as such by the SU algorithm, and let x_j be a virtual feature point. Then, the SU saliency of x_i is (roughly) $E_i^{(n+1)} = 1 + f_{ij}E_j^{(n)} = 1 + f_{ij}f_{jk}\rho_k E_k^{(n-1)} = 1 + P_{ik}E_k^{(n-1)}$. Thus, the effect of a missing point may be replaced by a lower probability $P_{i,k} = f_{ij}f_{jk}\rho_k$. The probability of the feature point x_i to be part of the curve $c(x_k)$ on which x_k lies, is indeed lower when there is a gap between x_i and x_k. Moreover, the process of calculating a cue between two distant points may be considered as an explicit search for a path between them, which minimizes a cost function.

Recall now (from section 3.2) that the expected length propagates as

$$\begin{aligned} E[l]_+^i &= (1 - P_{ij})E^*[l] + P_{ij}(l_{ij} + E[l]_+^j) \\ &= E^*[l] + P_{ij}(l_{ij} - E^*[l] + E[l]_+^j) \end{aligned} \tag{8}$$

which, for inter-pixel distance of l_{ij} equal to the expected length of one edgel $E^*[l]$, and both equal to 1, yields

$$E[l]_+^i = 1 + P_{ij}E[l]_+^j \tag{9}$$

Therefore we conclude that the co-circularity and the gap attenuation, used in SU saliency, may be interpreted as measures of the grouping probability used here, and that the overall saliency maximized there, is, according to this interpretation, the expected length.

There are also other differences, but they are technical, and result from our use of directional feature points, implying that we can work with the actual features, and not with the arcs between the features as done in [SU88].

4 Implementation and Experiments

In contrast with [SU88,AB98], we considered only real (non-virtual) feature points. They were oriented using the gradients direction. The positive (negative) extension neighbors of every feature point were all (real) neighboring feature points, s.t. the vector $x_i x_j$ is making an angle in $[\pi/6, 5\pi/6]$ ($[-5\pi/6, -\pi/6]$) with the gradient. The neighborhood was usually a disk of radius 10 pixels. The initial length distribution was set to have equal weights on the values $0, 1$ and 2.

Traditional co-circularity cue. First we considered the classical cue, using curvature (or weighted angle differences). Following [SU88], we set the cue as

$$P_{ij} = \exp\{\|x_{ij}\|^2/50\} \cdot \exp\{-\tan(GradAngleDiff/2)\},$$

where *GradAngleDiff* is just the difference between the two gradient angles in the two points. Note that as the distances between a feature points and its neighbors is no longer constant, we added a preference to short distances. Interestingly this dependency needs to reduce the cue faster than $\exp\{\|x_{ij}\|\}$ because otherwise the process always prefers the far neighbors. (Going to that neighbor through another, closer neighbor, gives a lower expected length, which follows directly from the update rules.)

We view this experimental work as an intermediate stage, because the actual probabilities are not those determined by this parametric form. Our current work focuses on measuring these cues empirically.

Here (Figures 3,4 are two examples of the implementation. They include the original image (synthetic and real), the edge points detected with standard DRF (Khoros) operator, the two one-sided saliencies and their sum, and the thresholded saliency. Note that the saliency image has a concrete meaning: it is the expected length on which the point lies. For the one sided case for example, if one starts from a point associated with saliency of 38 (a typical value for the strong curves, on say, the lizard back), he can expect to find about 38 neighbors on the curve in one of the directions.

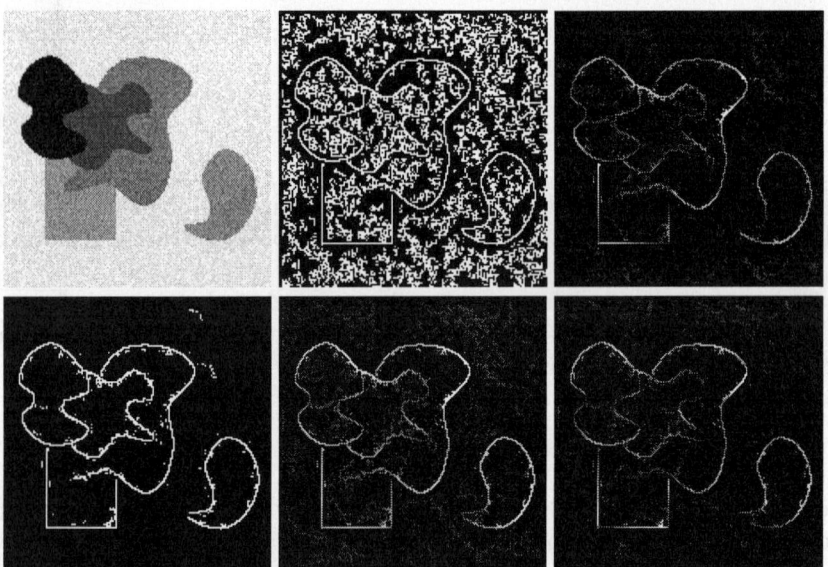

Fig. 3. A typical saliecy calculation with an **angle** cue done on a heavily corrupted noise: (starting from upper left, clockwise) The original image, edges, positive and negative saliencies, sum of saliency, thresholded saliency.

Saliency with a Grey Level Cue. Next we took the same saliency process and just changed the cue, which now, measure the similarity in grey levels and not the smoothness of the curve. Specifically, we set

$$P_{ij} = \exp\{\|x_{ij}\|^2/50\} \frac{1}{1 + \frac{30\,GreyLevelDiff^2}{GradSize(i)GradSize(j)}}.$$

The $GreyLevelDiff$ is the difference in grey levels between the two feature points, and $GradSize(i)$ is the gradient size at x_i. See Figure 5. Note that most unwanted additions to the thresholded saliency image are in inner points where the grey level is similar and random high gradients exist. Note also that the saliency value has the same meaning: expected length of the curve (either to one side or to both). Actually, the results were better than we expected and in a sense outperform the use of the angle-based cue. We intend to investigate this issue farther and with real images as well. To conclude, this experiment demonstrates that a saliency process which is similar, in principle, to that proposed in [SU88], can work also with other sources of information.

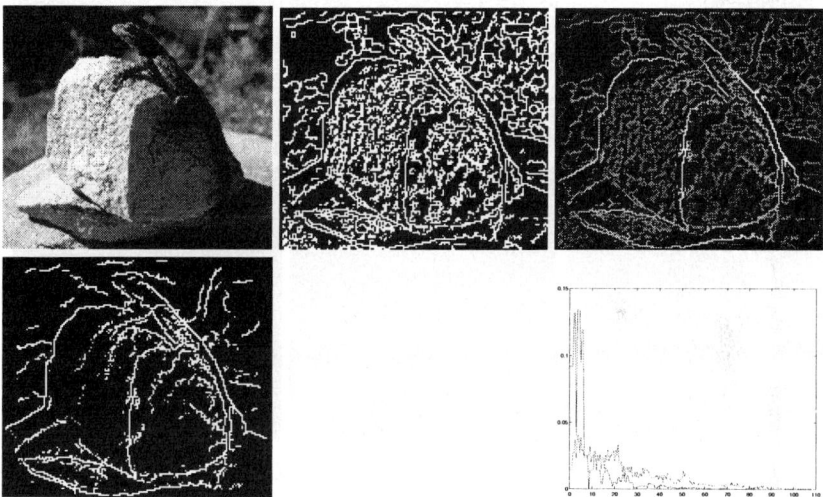

Fig. 4. Saliency calculation for a real, complex, image: (From upper left, clockwise) original image, edges, sum of positive and negative saliencies, two length distributions associated with a stone point (dark) and the lizard back (lighter), and thresholded saliency.

A Saliency measure emphasizing confidence. It may happen that a relatively weakly connected sequence of edgles will yield a substantial expected length (or SU) saliency. Indeed this was the case, for example, in the real "lizard" image, where many points on the texture were associated with large saliency. Thus, a quality measure emphasizing the connectedness over the long length may be preferred. One such measures is the "expected square root length", specified as $\sum_l \mathbf{D}_+^i(l)\sqrt{l}$, which prefers shorter curves associated with higher confidence: consider, for example, two length distributions, one giving a full weight to the length $l = 10$ and another sharing the weight between $l = 0$ and $l = 20$. While the expected length associated with the distributions is identical, the expected square root length clearly prefers the more "concentrated" distribution where full confidence is given to the $l = 10$ value, and give it a saliency value of $\sqrt{10}$ which is larger by a factor of $\sqrt{2}$ than the saliency associated with the other distribution. Indeed we found that such saliency may have advantages when working on real images (see Figure 6).

Note however that such saliency has one severe theoretical deficiency: it is not extensible, and thus global maximization is not guaranteed.

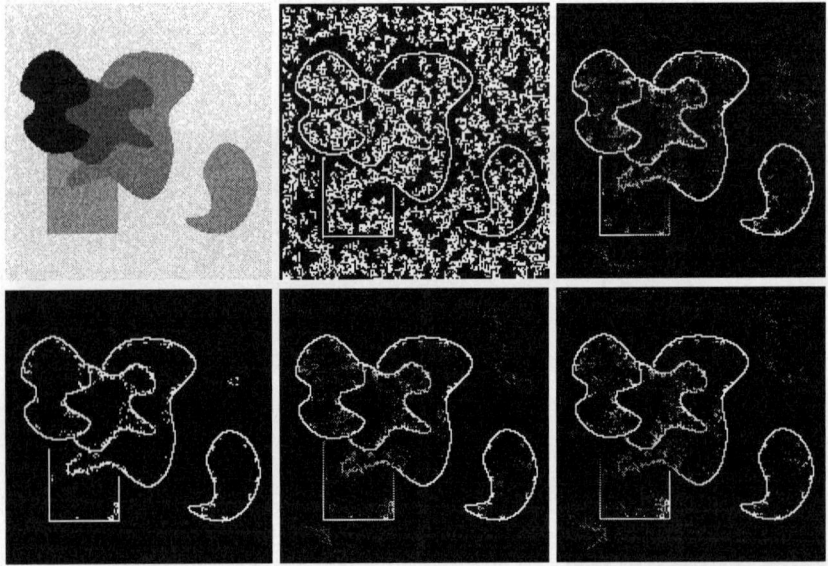

Fig. 5. A typical saliency calculation with an **Grey Level** cue done on a heavily corrupted noise: (starting from upper left, clockwise) The original image, edges, positive and negative saliencies, sum of saliency, thresholded saliency.

5 Discussion

This note presented a framework and an algorithm for calculating a well defined saliency measure which is based on estimating the length distribution and the expected length of curves. The work was motivated by the SU saliency [SU88], which, in our opinion, was build on good principles but lacked in interpretation, at least for computer vision practitioners. One result of the proposed work is that, when interpreting high curvature and gaps as factors, which decrease the probability to connect, then the SU saliency calculates the expected length of the curve on which every pointy lies. This is of course in agreement with [AB98] where the saliency of a straight line of length l and no gaps is found to be l.

The work is now in progress and we are exploring many interesting issues related to the proposed saliency mechanism. One interesting question is whether we can make the saliency invariant to scale (at least in the sense that the ratio between saliencies of two different curves stay the same over scale), and thus solve one of the problems raised in [AB98]. This is possible in principle because we are no longer limited to the curvature cue but can design other cues as well. An even more interesting question is whether there is extensible useful saliency quality function of the distribution, which is different than the expected value (or weighted expected value). The variance, for example, is not such a function, because it is not necessary that the path of length N associated with, say, the least variance, contains a path of length $N-1$ associated with the lowest variance as well.

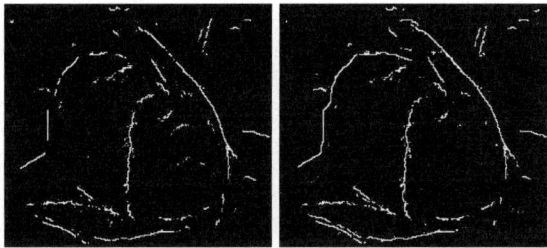

Fig. 6. Comparison between the expected value saliency (left) and the square root expected saliency (right). Both saliencies were thresholded so that only the points associated with saliency in the top 10 % are marked. The square root measure preserves more un-fragmented figure and contains less background texture (although the differences are not that large). This was the case also for other thresholds.

The claimed added advantage of higher reliability is not fully proved yet in this paper. Our current goal is to develop methods for characterizing the probability P_{ij} empirically and for constructing cues which are associated with a higher reliability than simply measuring the curvature. We expect to gain in the overall reliability when such cues are constructed.

The interpretation of cues as probabilities was considered in [WJ96], where the stochastic motion of a particle was used to model completion fields and elicits a saliency process as well (as observed in [WT98]). The saliency induced by this process is different than that suggested in [SU88] mainly because it is not associated with a single "best" curve but with some average of all curves in the image. Interestingly, a modified form of the proposed saliency form may be created by updating the length distribution not according to the best curve but according to the average of all curves with weights, which are just the corresponding probabilities. This way we get an alternative estimate of the length distribution (and the expected length). Which one is better? As we see it, the saliency method that we proposed here, (and that of [SU88]) is a maximum likelihood approach to saliency and length estimation, because it calculates the saliency relative to the best parameter. (This "parameter" is a path in this case). The second approach is essentially Bayesian and allows to get contributions from many alternatives. Note that both methods can be used to calculate the expected length estimate. We actually expect the second, Bayesian, method to give more visually pleasing saliency plots. Observe however, that it does not provide an estimate of the best path with it.

6   Acknowledgments

This research was supported by the fund for the promotion of research at the Technion.

References

[AB98]   T.D. Alter and R. Basri. Extracting salient curves from images: An analysis of the saliency network. *IJCV*, 27(1):51–69, March 1998.

[AL98]   A. Amir and M. Lindenbaum. Ground from figure discrimination. In *CVPR98*, pages 521–527, 1998.

[AM98]   Laurent Alquier and Philippe Montesinos. Representation of linear structures using perceptual grouping. In *Presented in The 1st workshop on Perceptual Organization in Computer Vision*, 1998.

[CLR90]   T.H. Cormen, C.E. Leiserson, and R.L. Rivest. *Introduction to Algorithms*. MIT Press, 1990.

[GM93]   G. Guy and G.G. Medioni. Inferring global perceptual contours from local features. In *CVPR93*, pages 787–787, 1993.

[HH93]   Laurent Herault and Radu Horaud. Figure-ground discrimination: A combinatorial optimization approach. *PAMI*, 15(9):899–914, Sep 1993.

[HvdH93]   Friedrich Heitger and Rudiger von der Heydt. A computational model of neural contour processing: Figure-ground segregation and illusory contours. In *ICCV-93, Berlin*, pages 32–40, 1993.

[Low85]   David G. Lowe. *Perceptual Organization and Visual Recognition*. Kluwer Academic Publishers, 1985.

[Mar82]   D. Marr. Vision: A computational investigation into the human representation and processing of visual information. In *W.H. Freeman*, 1982.

[SB98]   S. Sarkar and K.L. Boyer. Quantitative measures of change based on feature organization: Eigenvalues and eigenvectors. *CVIU*, 71(1):110–136, July 1998.

[SU88]   Amnon Sha'ashua and Shimon Ullman. Structural saliency: The detection of globally salient structures using locally connected network. In *ICCV-88*, pages 321–327, 1988.

[Wer50]   Max Wertheimer. Laws of organization in perceptual forms. In Willis D. Ellis, editor, *A Source Book of Gestalt Psychology*, pages 71–88, 1950.

[WJ96]   L.R. Williams and D.W. Jacobs. Local parallel computation of stochastic completion fields. In *CVPR96*, pages 161–168, 1996.

[WT98]   L. Williams and K. Thornber. A comparison of measures for detecting natural shapes in cluttered backgrounds. In *ECCV98*, 1998.

Layer Extraction
with a Bayesian Model of Shapes

P. H. S. Torr[1], A. R. Dick[2], and R. Cipolla[2]

[1] Microsoft Research, 1 Guildhall St, Cambridge CB2 3NH, UK
philtorr@microsoft.com
[2] Department of Engineering, University of Cambridge, Cambridge CB2 1PZ, UK
{ard28,cipolla}@eng.cam.ac.uk

Abstract. This paper describes an automatic 3D surface modelling system that extracts dense 3D surfaces from uncalibrated video sequences. In order to extract this 3D model the scene is represented as a collection of layers and a new method for layer extraction is described. The new segmentation method differs from previous methods in that it uses a specific prior model for layer shape. A probabilistic hierarchical model of layer shape is constructed, which assigns a density function to the shape and spatial relationships between layers. This allows accurate and efficient algorithms to be used when finding the best segmentation. Here this framework is applied to architectural scenes, in which layers commonly correspond to windows or doors and hence belong to a tightly constrained family of shapes.

Keywords: Structure from motion, Grouping and segmentation.

1 Introduction

The aim of this work is to obtain dense 3D structure *and* texture maps from an image sequence, the camera matrices (calibration and location) having been recovered using previously developed methods [3, 4, 12, 15]. The computed structure can then be used as the basis for building 3D graphical models. This representation can be used as a basis for compression, new view rendering, and video editing. A typical example sequence is shown in Figure 1 and the computed model in Figure 9.

Although extracting scene structure using stereo has been actively researched, the accurate recovery of the depth for each pixel remains only partially solved. For instance, one approach to the dense stereo problem is the voxel based approach [14] in which the scene volume is first discretized into voxels, and then a space carving scheme applied to find the voxels that lie on the surfaces of the objects in the scene. The disadvantage of the voxel carving method is that the surfaces produced from homogeneous regions are "fattened" out to a shape known as the Photo Hull [14]. Rather than generate voxels in 3D some algorithms operate in the image by testing different disparities for each pixel e.g.

Koch *et al* [9]. The problem with these approaches are that they do not treat all the images equally and work well only for small baselines.

Generally dense stereo algorithms work well in highly textured regions, but perform poorly around occlusion boundaries and in untextured regions. This is because there is simply not enough information in these untextured regions to recover the shape. In this paper we propose a general framework for overcoming this by the utilization of prior knowledge.

A vehicle for encoding this prior knowledge is the decomposition of the image into layers [1, 2, 8, 17–19]. Each layer corresponds to a surface in the scene, hence the decomposition of the scene into layers acknowledges the conditional dependence of the depths for adjacent pixels in an image. Detecting the different surfaces (layers) within the scene offers a compact and physically likely representation for the image sequence. The main problem is that such a decomposition is difficult to achieve in general. This is because the parametrization of the layer itself is problematic. For each layer the parametrization is composed of three parts: (a) the parameteric form of the 3D surface giving rise to the layer, (b) its spatial extent within the image and (c) its texture map. Generally it is easy to construct the former e.g. in [1, 8, 18] it is assumed that the surfaces are planar, in [2, 17] the surfaces are encoded by a plane together with a per pixel parallax, in [19] only smoothness of depth is assumed. The latter two however are more difficult to parametrize. One approach is to ignore the spatial cohesion altogether and simply model the whole image as a mixture model of the layers [1, 8, 19]. Whilst this simplifies the problem of estimating the layers affording the use of iterative algorithms like EM, it is not a realistic model of layer generation e.g. a homogeneous region which contains little depth or motion information could be broken up in any way and assigned to different layers with no increase in the mixture model's likelihood.

A now classical method for modelling the spatial dependence of layer memberships of adjacent pixels is by use of Markov Random Fields (MRFs) [7]. There are several disadvantages with this approach: first is that using an MRF model leads to very difficult optimization problems that are notoriously slow to converge. Second, sampling from an MRF distribution does not produce things that look like images of the real world, which might lead one to think that using this as a prior is a bad idea. Third, the MRF is pixel based which can lead to artefacts. The MRF only implicitly defines the prior probability distribution in that the normalization factor cannot be readily computed. What would be preferable would be an explicit prior for the segmentation, which would allow more direct minimization of the error function, for instance by gradient descent.

Within this paper a prior for the shape of the layers is constructed and illustrated for architectural scenes. Architectural scenes are particularly amenable to the construction of priors, as layers will typically correspond to such things as windows or doors which for which an informative prior distribution can be constructed (e.g. they are often planar with regular outline). Although architectural scenes are chosen to illustrate the basic principles the method proposed is representative of *a general approach* to segmentation. Taking inspiration from [6], rather than using an implicit model for the prior probability of a segmentation an explicit model is defined and used. A solution to the final problem (c), that of finding the texture map, is also found by considering the texture as a set of hidden variables.

The layout of the paper is as follows. The parameters used to represent the shape and texture of a scene are defined in Section 2. A posterior probability measure is also introduced here for estimating the optimal parameter values for a scene from a set of images and prior information. As shape is now represented parametrically, layer extraction becomes a problem of *model selection*, i.e. determining the number and type of these parameters required to model the scene. In Section 3 a method is developed for choosing automatically which model is most appropriate for the current scene, based on goodness of fit to the images and the idea of model simplicity. Section 4 then deals with the details of implementing this method. In Section 5 it is demonstrated that this technique can decide which individual shape model is appropriate for each layer, which overall model best fits the collection of layers in the scene, and how many layers are present in the scene, given a coarse initialisation. Concluding remarks are given in Section 6.

2 Problem formulation

A scene is modelled as a collection of layers. A scene model has a set of parameters represented by a vector $\boldsymbol{\theta}$, which can be decomposed into shape parameters $\boldsymbol{\theta}_S$ and texture parameters $\boldsymbol{\theta}_T$ such that $\boldsymbol{\theta} = \boldsymbol{\theta}_S \bigcup \boldsymbol{\theta}_T$. Each layer is defined as a deformable template in three space; the shape parameters $\boldsymbol{\theta}_S$ comprise the location and orientation of each template together with the boundary (a variable number of parameters for each layer depending on which model $\mathcal{M}$ is selected). A grid is defined on the bounded surface of each layer, and each point on this grid is assigned an intensity value forming a texture map on the 3D layer. The intensity at each grid point is a variable of $\boldsymbol{\theta}_T$. The projection matrix to a given image, a noise process, and $\boldsymbol{\theta}$ provide a complete generative model for that image. Each point in the model can be projected into the image and the projected intensity compared with that observed, from which the likelihood of the model can be computed. If priors are assigned to the parameters then the posterior likelihood can be computed.

Within this paper a dominant plane is assumed to fill most of the scene (such as a wall of the building), with several offset objects (such as windows, doors and pillars). An example of such a scene is given in Figure 1. The background plane $\mathcal{L}_0$ is modelled as the plane $z = 0$ with infinite extent (thus having no shape parameters). The other layers $\mathcal{L}_1 \ldots \mathcal{L}_m$ are modelled as deformable templates as now described.

2.1 The shape parameters

At present there are four types of layer model $\mathcal{M}$ available, which allow the modelling of a wide variety of architectural scenes. These are $\mathcal{M}_1$ a rectangle (6

Fig. 1. *Three images of the type of scene considered. A gateway and two indentations are offset from the background plane of the wall.*

parameters), $\mathcal{M}_2$ an arch (7 parameters), $\mathcal{M}_3$ a rectangle with bevelled (sloped) edges (7 parameters), and $\mathcal{M}_4$ an arch with bevelled edges (8 parameters). The 8 parameter model $\mathcal{M}_4$ has position coordinates (x, y), scale parameters a and b, orientation ω, an arch height c, depth from the background plane d and bevel width r. The arch in $\mathcal{M}_2$ and $\mathcal{M}_4$ is completely specified by c as it is modelled using a semi-ellipse. The other layer models are constrained versions of this model, as shown in Figure 2.

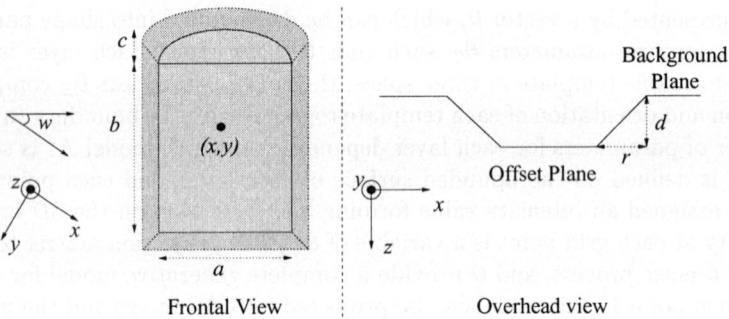

Fig. 2. *Top and cross-sectional views of the most general shape primitive. The other primitives are special cases of this one—the non-bevelled arch has $r = 0$, the bevelled rectangle has $c = 0$ and the non-bevelled rectangle has $r = 0, c = 0$. The coordinate axes shown for each view are translated versions of the 3D world coordinate system.*

Layers in architectural scenes are highly constrained not only in their individual shape, but also in their spatial relationship to each other. Hence a single parameter can often be used to represent a feature common to several primitives, such as the common y position of layers belonging to a single row. These global parameters are known as *hyperparameters* [5], as the entities that they model are themselves parameters. The introduction of hyperparameters makes the model hierarchical as illustrated in the directed acyclic graph (DAG) Figure 3. The hyperparameters defined in Table 1 are later used to represent our belief that primitives occur in rows, but there are many other possibilities.

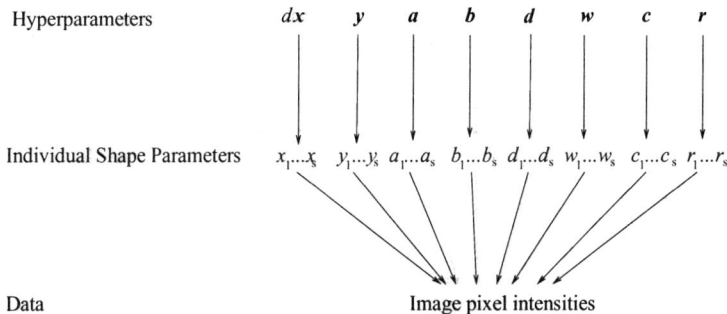

Fig. 3. *The hierarchical shape model. Hyperparameters model functions of the individual shape parameters. The camera projection matrices, and lighting conditions, could also be modelled as hyperparameters based on the data and shape parameters, but in this paper they are given as prior information.*

To sum up, architectural scenes containing a background layer $\mathcal{L}_0$, together with a set of offset layers $\mathcal{L}_i$, $i = 1 \ldots m$ are to be modelled. Each offset layer has an associated model $\mathcal{M}_j$, $j = 1 \ldots 4$. The individual shape parameters and the hyperparameters together define the shape of the model, and can be represented as a parameter vector $\boldsymbol{\theta}_S$; next the texture paramters $\boldsymbol{\theta}_T$ are defined.

2.2 Texture Parameters

The set of layers defined above define a surface. Next this surface is discretized and a two dimensional coordinate system defined on it. At each point $\mathbf{X}$ on this surface an unknown brightness parameter $i(\mathbf{X})$ (between 0 and 255) is defined. These brightness parameters form the texture parameter vector $\boldsymbol{\theta}_T$.

2.3 Evaluating the Likelihood

The shape parameters (number of layers and their associated parameters) and the texture parameters give the total parameter vector $\boldsymbol{\theta}$. In order to estimate this its posterior probability must be maximized:

$$p(\boldsymbol{\theta}|\mathbf{DI}) = p(\mathbf{D}|\boldsymbol{\theta}\mathbf{I})p(\boldsymbol{\theta}|\mathbf{I}) \qquad (1)$$

where $\mathbf{I}$ is the prior information (such as the camera matrices etc.) and $\mathbf{D}$ is the set of input images. This is a product of the likelihood and prior. To perform the optimization gradient descent is used. This would prove prohibitive if all

Table 1. *Example set of hyperparameters. Knowledge about overall scene structure can be imposed by assigning a probability distribution to each hyperparameter.*

$d\mathbf{x}$	The spacing of x-axis position of the primitives
$\mathbf{y}$	The y-axis position of the primitives
$\mathbf{a}$	The horizontal scale of the primitives
$\mathbf{b}$	The vertical scale of the primitives
$\mathbf{d}$	The depth of the primitives
ω	The orientation of the primitives
$\mathbf{c}$	The arch height of the primitives
$\mathbf{r}$	The bevel width of the primitives

the paramaters had to be searched simultaneously. Fortunately the task can be decomposed into several easier optimizations: first the shape parameters of each layer can be optimized independently, second only the shape parameters need to be optimized explicitly. It is now shown how to estimate the optimal set of texture parameters given these shape parameters.

Given the shape parameters and projection matrices, it is now assumed that the projected intensity of $\mathbf{X}$ is observed with noise $i(\mathbf{X}) + \epsilon$, where ϵ has a Gaussian distribution mean zero and standard deviation σ_ϵ. The parameter $i(\mathbf{X})$ can then be found such that it minimizes the sum of squares $\min_{i(\mathbf{X})} \sum_{j=1}^{j=m} \left(i(\mathbf{x}^j) - i(\mathbf{X}) \right)^2$ where $i(\mathbf{x}^j)$ is the intensity at $\mathbf{x}^j$, and $\mathbf{x}^j$ is the projection of $\mathbf{X}$ into the jth image. The likelihood for a given value of $i(\mathbf{X})$ is

$$p(\mathbf{D}|i(\mathbf{X})) = \prod_j \frac{1}{\sqrt{2\pi}\sigma_\epsilon} \exp -\frac{1}{2} \left(\frac{i(\mathbf{x}^j) - i(\mathbf{X})}{\sigma_\epsilon} \right)^2 \tag{2}$$

Using Equation (2) under the assumption that the errors ϵ in all the pixels are independent, the likelihood over all pixels can then be written:

$$p(\mathbf{D}|\boldsymbol{\theta}_T\boldsymbol{\theta}_S\mathbf{I}) = \prod_i \prod_j \frac{1}{\sqrt{2\pi}\sigma_\epsilon} \exp -\frac{1}{2} \left(\frac{i(\mathbf{x}_i^j) - i(\mathbf{X}_i)}{\sigma_\epsilon} \right)^2 \tag{3}$$

where $\mathbf{x}_i^j$ is the projection of the ith scene point into the jth image. This summation is over all the discretized scene points (lying on the surfaces of the layers) $\mathbf{X}_i$.

2.4 Evaluating the priors

Prior knowledge of parameter values is encoded in the prior probability term of Equation (1), $p(\boldsymbol{\theta}|\mathbf{I}) = p(\boldsymbol{\theta}_S\boldsymbol{\theta}_T|\mathbf{I}) = p(\boldsymbol{\theta}_S|\mathbf{I})$, as the value of the texture parameters is determined by the shape parameters and the images. The shape parameter vector $\boldsymbol{\theta}_S = (\alpha, \beta)$ contains both individual shape parameters α and hyperparameters β. Hence the prior probability $p(\boldsymbol{\theta}_S|I) = p(\alpha\beta|I) = p(\alpha|\beta I)p(\beta|I)$.

Table 2. *Hyperpriors encoding a row of identical primitives. $U[a,b]$ is the uniform distribution over the interval $[a,b]$. $N(a,b)$ is the normal distribution with mean a and standard deviation b. A column of primitives is similarly constrained, by imposing a hyperprior on $\mathbf{x}$ and $\mathbf{dy}$. The model typically has a spatial extent of [-0.5, 0.5] in the x and y axes of the world coordinate system; hence a standard deviation of 0.005 corresponds to 2 or 3 pixels in a typical image of the scene.*

β	$p(\beta)$	$p(\alpha\|\beta)$
$\mathbf{dx}$	$U[0.2, 0.4]$	$N(\mathbf{dx}, 0.005)$
$\mathbf{y}$	$U[-0.4, 0.4]$	$N(\mathbf{y}, 0.005)$
$\mathbf{a}$	$U[0.1, 0.2]$	$N(\mathbf{a}, 0.005)$
$\mathbf{b}$	$U[0.1, 0.2]$	$N(\mathbf{b}, 0.005)$
$\mathbf{d}$	$U[-0.1, 0.1]$	$N(\mathbf{d}, 0.005)$
ω	$N(0, \pi/12]$	$N(\omega, \pi/12)$
$\mathbf{c}$	$U[0.01, 0.2]$	$N(\mathbf{c}, 0.005)$
$\mathbf{r}$	$U[0.01, 0.1]$	$N(\mathbf{r}, 0.005)$

The term $p(\beta|I)$, known as a *hyperprior*, expresses a belief in the overall structure of the scene, while $p(\alpha|\beta I)$ determines how individual shapes in the scene are expected to vary within the overall structure. To express complete prior ignorance about the scene structure, each prior probability may be assigned a uniform distribution bounded by the range of the cameras' fields of view. The correct distribution for each hyperparameter should ideally be learnt automatically from previous data sets; however at present they are manually initialised. An example of a set of hyperpriors for a row of identical shapes is given in Table 2. Samples from this distribution are given in Figure 4.

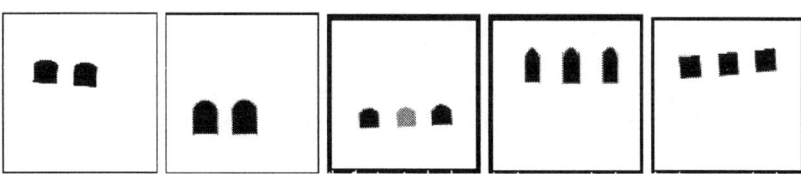

Fig. 4. *Samples drawn from the hyperprior distribution for a row of identical primitives given in table 2, using two and three primitives. The intensity at each point is proportional to the depth offset from the background layer.*

3 Model selection

In Section 2 a set of parameters was defined, and the posterior probability (Equation (1)) was introduced as a means of estimating the optimal parameter values for a given model. However a more fundamental problem remains: how to decide which model (i.e. which set of parameters) best represents a scene? This is the problem of *model selection*, described in this section.

The goal of model selection is to choose the most probable of a finite set of models $\mathbf{M}_j, j = 1..n$, given data $\mathbf{D}$ and prior information $\mathbf{I}$. Using Bayes rule the probability of each model can be expressed as

$$p(\mathbf{M}_j|\mathbf{DI}) = \frac{p(\mathbf{D}|\mathbf{M}_j\mathbf{I})p(\mathbf{M}_j|\mathbf{I})}{p(\mathbf{D}|\mathbf{I})}. \tag{4}$$

The denominator $p(\mathbf{D}|\mathbf{I})$ is constant for all models and hence is used only as a normalisation constant to ensure that $\sum_{j=1}^{n} p(\mathbf{M}_j|\mathbf{DI}) = 1$. The prior probability $p(\mathbf{M}_j|\mathbf{I})$ can be used to encode any prior preference one has for each model. In the absence of any such prejudice this is uniform, and model selection depends primarily on the *evidence*

$$p(\mathbf{D}|\mathbf{M}_j\mathbf{I}) = \int p(\mathbf{D}|\boldsymbol{\theta}_j\mathbf{M}_j\mathbf{I})p(\boldsymbol{\theta}_j|\mathbf{M}_j\mathbf{I})d\boldsymbol{\theta}_j \tag{5}$$

where $\boldsymbol{\theta}_j$ is the set of parameters belonging to model $\mathbf{M}_j$.

For this problem, the data $\mathbf{D}$ is simply a set of images of the scene. The prior information $\mathbf{I}$ is the projection matrix for each camera, and a noise model for projection into each image (Section 2.3). The parameter vector $\boldsymbol{\theta}_j$ contains shape and texture parameters, as described in Section 2. Considering these separately, the evidence becomes

$$p(\mathbf{D}|\mathbf{M}_j\mathbf{I}) = \int \int p(\mathbf{D}|\alpha_j\beta_j\boldsymbol{\theta}_{Tj}\mathbf{M}_j\mathbf{I})p(\alpha_j\beta_j\boldsymbol{\theta}_{Tj}|\mathbf{M}_j\mathbf{I})d\alpha_j d\beta_j \tag{6}$$

$$= \int \int p(\mathbf{D}|\alpha_j\mathbf{M}_j\mathbf{I})p(\alpha_j|\beta_j\mathbf{M}_j\mathbf{I})p(\beta_j|\mathbf{M}_j\mathbf{I})d\alpha_j d\beta_j. \tag{7}$$

The β_j term is dropped from the first factor of this equation, the *likelihood* of the data, as the probability of the data $\mathbf{D}$ is dependent only on the individual shape parameters α_j. The texture parameters are not considered here as they are completely determined by the shape parameters and the images.

3.1 Evaluation of the evidence

It is impractical to perform the integration of Equation (6) for any but the simplest models. However previous work (e.g. [13, 16, 10]) has shown that an approximation to the evidence is sufficient for model selection. Five possible approximations are briefly described here. Consider first the inner integral,

$$\int p(\mathbf{D}|\alpha_j\mathbf{M}_j\mathbf{I})p(\alpha_j|\beta_j\mathbf{M}_j\mathbf{I})p(\beta_j|\mathbf{M}_j\mathbf{I})d\alpha_j. \tag{8}$$

In any useful inference problem the likelihood fuction obtained from the data will be much more informative than the prior probabilities—if not, there is little to be gained by using the data. Hence the likelihood function has a sharp peak (relative to the prior distribution) around its maximum value, as shown in Figure 5(a). The entire integral is therefore well approximated by integrating a neighbourhood of the maximum likelihood estimate of α_j. For convenience the log likelihood, $\log L(\alpha_j)$, which is a monotonic function of the likelihood and hence is maximised at the same value, is considered rather than the likelihood itself. A second order approximation of $\log L(\alpha_j)$ about its mode α_{jML} is

$$\log L(\alpha_j) \cong \log L(\alpha_{jML}) + \frac{1}{2}(\alpha_j - \alpha_{jML})^T \mathbf{H}(\alpha_{jML})(\alpha_j - \alpha_{jML}), \quad (9)$$

where $\mathbf{H}(\alpha_{jML})$ is the hessian of $\log L$ evaluated at its mode. This corresponds to approximating the likelihood in this region by a multivariate Gaussian with covariance matrix $\boldsymbol{\Sigma}_\alpha = -\mathbf{H}^{-1}(\alpha_{jML})$:

$$L(\alpha_j) \cong L(\alpha_{jML}) \exp\left[-\frac{1}{2}(\alpha_j - \alpha_{jML})^T \boldsymbol{\Sigma}_\alpha^{-1}(\alpha_j - \alpha_{jML})\right] \quad (10)$$

Assuming that $p(\alpha_j | \beta_j \mathbf{M}_j \mathbf{I}) \cong p(\alpha_{jML} | \beta_j \mathbf{M}_j \mathbf{I})$ in this region, the integrand of Equation (8) reduces to

$$\int \exp\left[-\frac{1}{2}(\alpha_j - \alpha_{jML})^T \boldsymbol{\Sigma}_\alpha^{-1}(\alpha_j - \alpha_{jML})\right] d\alpha_j = (2\pi)^{k_\alpha/2} \sqrt{\det(\boldsymbol{\Sigma}_\alpha)} \quad (11)$$

where k_α is the number of shape parameters, as a Gaussian must integrate to 1. Hence the integral of Equation (8) is approximately

$$L(\alpha_{jML})(2\pi)^{k_\alpha/2} \sqrt{\det \boldsymbol{\Sigma}_\alpha} p(\alpha_{jML} | \beta_j \mathbf{M}_j \mathbf{I}) p(\beta_j | \mathbf{M}_j \mathbf{I}) \quad (12)$$

and the evidence is approximated as

$$p(\mathbf{D}|\mathbf{M}_j\mathbf{I}) \cong L(\alpha_{jML})(2\pi)^{k_\alpha/2} \sqrt{\det \boldsymbol{\Sigma}_\alpha} \int p(\alpha_{jML} | \beta_j \mathbf{M}_j \mathbf{I}) p(\beta_j | \mathbf{M}_j \mathbf{I}) d\beta_j \quad (13)$$

The remaining integral can be similarly approximated; now the parameter values α_{jML} are the "data" being used to estimate the hyperparameters β_j. The final expression for the evidence is therefore

$$p(\mathbf{D}|\mathbf{M}_j\mathbf{I}) \cong L(\alpha_{jML}) p(\alpha_{jML} | \beta_{jML} \mathbf{M}_j \mathbf{I}) p(\beta_{jML} | \mathbf{M}_j \mathbf{I}) (2\pi)^{k/2} \sqrt{\det \boldsymbol{\Sigma}_\alpha \det \boldsymbol{\Sigma}_\beta}. \quad (14)$$

where k is the total number of parameters, $\boldsymbol{\Sigma}_\beta$ is the covariance matrix of the hyperparameters with respect to the shape parameters and β_{jML} is the set of hyperparameters which maximise $p(\alpha_{jML} | \beta_j \mathbf{M}_j \mathbf{I})$. The terms to the right of the likelihood approximate the fraction of the volume of prior probability space enclosed by the maximum likelihood peak, and are known collectively as an *Occam factor* [10, 16].

282

3.2 Occam factors

An Occam factor encodes the idea of Occam's Razor for model selection: a simpler model (usually one with fewer parameters) should be preferred to a more complex one, unless the more complex one explains or fits the data significantly better. Information theoretic techniques such as Minimum Description Length (MDL) encoding [1] enforce this preference by penalising models according to the information required to encode them. The Bayesian approach to model selection naturally incorporates an identical penalty in the evaluation of the evidence as the product of a likelihood and an Occam factor. As extra parameters are intro-

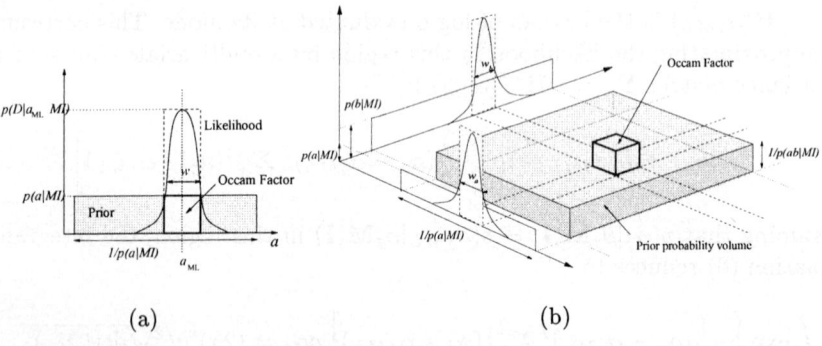

(a)   (b)

Fig. 5. *Occam factor for (a) one and (b) two independent parameters with uniform independent priors. For a single variable, the likelihood is approximated as $p(\mathbf{D}|a_{ML}\mathbf{MI})$ and the Occam factor is $w/p(a|\mathbf{MI})$. In the case of two variables the likelihood is $p(\mathbf{D}|a_{ML}b_{ML}\mathbf{MI})$ and the Occam factor is $w_a w_b/p(ab|\mathbf{MI})$. In each case the Occam factor approximates the fraction of the volume of prior probability (the shaded volume) occupied by the maximum likelihood probability peak.*

duced into the model, the fraction of the volume of parameter space occupied by the peak surrounding the maximum likelihood estimate inevitably decreases, as illustrated in Figure 5 for the simple case of 1 and 2 parameter models. Because the volume of prior probability over the entire parameter space must always be 1, this decrease in occupied volume translates to a decrease in prior probability, assuming that prior probability is reasonably uniform over the parameter space.

3.3 Other approximations to the evidence

The Occam factor is one of many possible model selection criteria. By disregarding it completely, evidence evaluation reduces to a maximum likelihood (ML) estimation. This includes no preference for model parsimony and hence will always select the best fitting model regardless of its complexity. If the prior terms $p(\alpha_{jML}|\beta_{jML}\mathbf{M}_j\mathbf{I})$ and $p(\beta_{jML}|\mathbf{M}_j\mathbf{I})$ are known to be almost uniform, Schwarz[13] suggests approximating them with diffuse normal distributions, and approximating $\sqrt{\det \boldsymbol{\Sigma}_\alpha \det \boldsymbol{\Sigma}_\beta}$ by $N^{\frac{-k}{2}}$, where N is the number of observations and k is the number of parameters in the model. This forms the Bayesian Information Criterion (BIC) measure of evidence

$$\log(p(\mathbf{D}|\mathbf{M}_j\mathbf{I})) \cong \log L(\alpha_{jML}) - \frac{k}{2}\log N. \tag{15}$$

A non Bayesian penalty term, the AIC has the form

$$\log(p(\mathbf{D}|\mathbf{M}_j\mathbf{I})) \cong \log L(\alpha_{jML}) - 2k \tag{16}$$

and hence penalises models according to the number of parameters they include. Finally if the posterior distribution is very peaked, the MAP estimate of each model may be the same order of magnitude as the evidence, in which case one would expect it to perform just as well for model selection. Each of these criteria is compared in section 5.

4 Implementation issues

4.1 Initialisation

The purpose of the initialisation stage is to provide a rough estimate of the number of planes to be modelled, and their position, scale, depth and orientation. First, each image is warped by a transformation $\mathbf{A}_j$ so that the layer $\mathcal{L}_0$ is aligned. Approximate projection matrices are found by estimating each camera pose from $\mathbf{A}_j$, as in [15]. A dense parallax field is obtained by applying a wavelet transform to each warped image, and performing multiresolution matching in the phase domain [11]. The correspondences obtained from each pair of images are fused robustly to obtain depth estimates for each point, from which initial layer estimates can be hypothesised [4].

Initial parameter estimates are obtained by fitting the simplest model, a 6 parameter rectangle, to each region (see Figure 6). The centre of the rectangle is positioned at the centroid of the region. The horizontal and vertical scales are set to the average distance of each of the extrema of the region from the centroid, the depth is given by the depth of the centroid and the orientation is assumed to be vertical (i.e. $\omega = 0$). The projection matrices generated by this system have a typical reprojection error of order 1 pixel.

4.2 Search for the maximum likelihood parameters

A multiresolution gradient descent search is used to locate the maximum likelihood parameters α_{jML} for each possible shape model. The image is recursively convolved with a Gaussian filter and downsampled by a factor of 2 horizontally and vertically to obtain a multiresolution representation. The search is initialised

a)   b)

Fig. 6. *(a) A poor initial reconstruction (compare with Figure 9) based only on stereo between two images, and (b) initial layer estimates based on three images. The layers are bounded by the black lines and meet the zero layer at the white lines. Each major offset layer is detected, but their shape and size are estimated poorly.*

at the coarsest level, and the estimate found is used to seed the search at a finer level. At each level the model is sampled more densely to maintain a constant sample rate of approximately one point per image pixel. Experience shows that two or three levels of resolution are sufficient, and the search typically converges in less than 100 iterations.

5 Results

5.1 Model selection for the shape parameters

Initially the model selection algorithm is assessed by trying to identify the correct shape for a single layer. Starting from the parameters found during initialisation (section 4), the gradient descent method described in Section 4.2 is used to find the model $\mathcal{M}_1$ maximum likelihood shape parameters α_{ML1} for that layer. This parameter set is then used to initialise the search for the set α_{ML} for each of the models $\mathcal{M}_2$, $\mathcal{M}_3$ and $\mathcal{M}_4$ in turn. Model selection is then performed using 5 measures: Occam Factors (OF), maximum likelihood (ML), Bayesian Information Criterion (BIC), Akaike Information Criterion (AIC) and MAP likelihood evaluation. Results are given in Figure 7.

Model $\mathcal{M}_1$: Rectangle

Because the layer of the door is well represented by the rectangle model with 6 parameters, the maximum likelihood parameters for more complex models are the same, and the ML measure is not altered for different models. Each other measure selects $\mathcal{M}_1$ because it includes the fewest parameters.

Model $\mathcal{M}_2$: Arch

Models $\mathcal{M}_1$ and $\mathcal{M}_3$, which do not contain arches, are clearly inadequate for this layer. The maximum likelihood of models $\mathcal{M}_2$ and $\mathcal{M}_4$ is very similar, so again the maximum likelihood measure is ambiguous while the other measures all select the simpler model $\mathcal{M}_2$.

Model $\mathcal{M}_3$: Bevelled Rectangle

Models $\mathcal{M}_1$ and $\mathcal{M}_2$, which do not incorporate bevelling, fit the indentation poorly at its sloped edges. Models $\mathcal{M}_3$ and $\mathcal{M}_4$ have similar likelihoods, so $\mathcal{M}_3$ is chosen by all measures except ML.

Model $\mathcal{M}_4$: Bevelled Arch

In this case only the most complex model adequately describes the data. It is chosen by all measures depsite its complexity, as the likelihood of the data for this model is significantly higher than for other models.

For each model, each model selection measure is clearly dominated the likelihood term. The OF, BIC, AIC and MAP measures all give similar results and appear adequate for preventing model overfitting. However the Occam factor is more theoretically sound than the other measures and incurs little extra computational expense, and is therefore preferred.

5.2 Model selection for the hyperparameters

Having selected a shape model for each layer in the scene, it is possible to discern not only between individual shapes, but also between configurations of shapes. As a simple test case, the evidence for a set of layers having no geometric alignment ($p(\beta)$ uniform, and $p(\alpha|\beta)$ uniform) is compared with the evidence for their belonging to a row of primitives, with priors given in Table 2. In this section, evidence is measured only using the Occam factor.

Gateway scene:

Figure 8(a) gives the layer models selected for each layer in the scene. In Figure 8(b) the evidence for each combination of two or more layers belonging to a row of identical primitives (black bars) is compared to the evidence for their being a uniformly distributed collection of shapes (white bars). No prior preference is expressed for either of these models. Clearly any combination of layers which includes the gateway is more likely to be part of a random scene, as the gateway is quite dissimilar in size and shape to the indentations. However the evidence for the two indentations taken by themselves belonging to a row is much higher than for their belonging to a general structure. Having detected this regularity, the indentations can be represented using 8 parameters (7 for one indentation, and the x position of the other) rather than 14. If such regularity can be detected in several collections of shapes, it can in turn be used to form hypotheses about higher level structure, such as the architectural style of the building as a whole.

Gothic church scene:

Figure 8(d) gives the evidence for several combinations of layers from the segmentation in Figure 8(c) belonging to a row as opposed to an arbitrary structure. There is a clear preference for a model with no regularity when the layers chosen include both windows and columns. However when only the windows are tested, the row model is clearly preferred, depsite the window parameters being slightly different due to some fitting errors caused by ambiguity near the boundary of each layer. Similarly the row model was preferred for the three columns, again allowing both a compact representation of the scene and the possibility of higher level inference about the scene strucure.

Model $\mathcal{M}_1$: Rectangle

Measure	Model			
$(\times 10^4)$	$\mathcal{M}_1$	$\mathcal{M}_2$	$\mathcal{M}_3$	$\mathcal{M}_4$
OF	**1.4781**	1.4787	1.4785	1.4797
ML	**1.4731**	**1.4731**	**1.4731**	**1.4731**
BIC	**1.4764**	1.4775	1.4775	1.4786
AIC	**1.4743**	1.4745	1.4745	1.4747
MAP	**1.4750**	1.4753	1.4753	1.4757

Model $\mathcal{M}_2$: Arch

Measure	Model			
$(\times 10^4)$	$\mathcal{M}_1$	$\mathcal{M}_2$	$\mathcal{M}_3$	$\mathcal{M}_4$
OF	2.5870	**2.5678**	2.5872	2.5691
ML	2.5817	**2.5618**	2.5807	**2.5618**
BIC	2.5850	**2.5657**	2.5842	2.5662
AIC	2.5829	**2.5632**	2.5821	2.5634
MAP	2.5837	**2.5641**	2.5829	2.5643

Model $\mathcal{M}_3$: Bevelled Rectangle

Measure	Model			
$(\times 10^3)$	$\mathcal{M}_1$	$\mathcal{M}_2$	$\mathcal{M}_3$	$\mathcal{M}_4$
OF	8.2704	8.2789	**8.1750**	8.1785
ML	8.2201	8.2169	**8.1139**	**8.1139**
BIC	8.2536	8.2453	**8.1524**	8.1582
AIC	8.2213	8.2183	**8.1153**	8.1155
MAP	8.2385	8.2378	**8.1353**	8.1376

Model $\mathcal{M}_4$: Bevelled Arch

Measure	Model			
$(\times 10^4)$	$\mathcal{M}_1$	$\mathcal{M}_2$	$\mathcal{M}_3$	$\mathcal{M}_4$
OF	2.3682	2.3623	2.3588	**2.3512**
ML	2.3628	2.3561	2.3528	**2.3444**
BIC	2.3661	2.3599	2.3566	**2.3488**
AIC	2.3640	2.3575	2.3542	**2.3460**
MAP	2.3649	2.3586	2.3552	**2.3472**

Fig. 7. *Evidence evaluation for single shapes. From left to right in each row: negative log evidence for this shape being an instance of each shape model, worst fit shape, best fit shape. Occam factor (OF), Maximum likelihood (ML), Bayesian Information Criterion (BIC), Akaike Information Criterion (AIC) and MAP probability measures are given. The model selected by each measure is in bold face.*

287

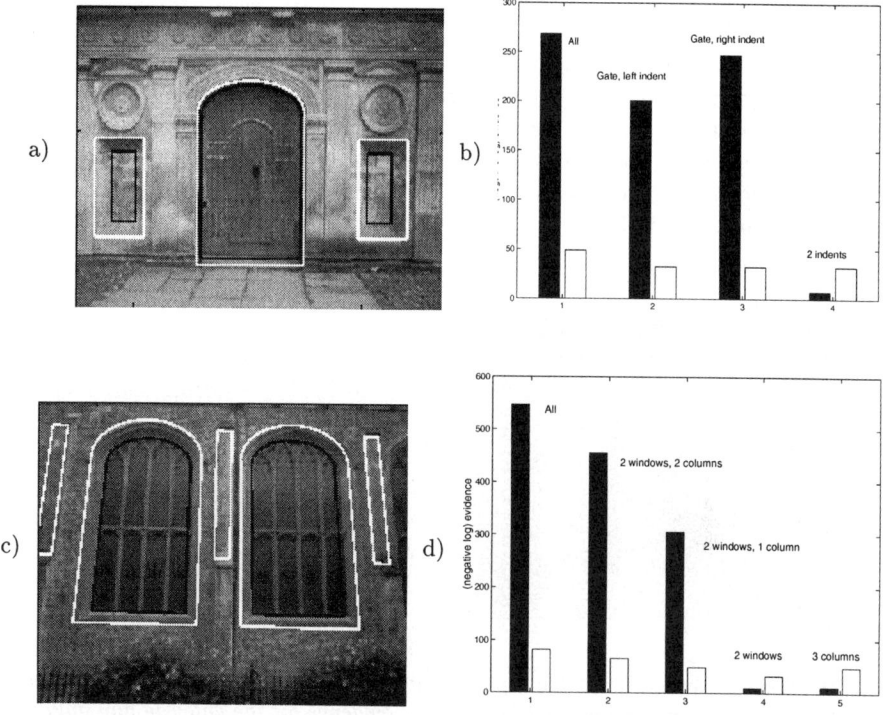

Fig. 8. *Testing for rows of similar shapes. The black bar is the (negative log) evidence for the shapes belonging to the row model; the white bar is the evidence for shapes having no regularity (see Section 5.2). Evidence has been normalised by subtracting out common factors.*

Fig. 9. *Recovered 3D surface of the Caius gateway scene.*

5.3   Selecting the number of layers

Comparison of the evidence can determine the number of layers present in a scene as well as their shape. Figure 10 gives the evidence for the gateway scene being modelled by 3, 2 and 1 primitives, which is clearly maximised for the 3 primitive case. The subsequent addition of a spurious primitive such as a depth 0 rectangle decreases the Occam factor while the likelihood remains constant, and hence is not selected.

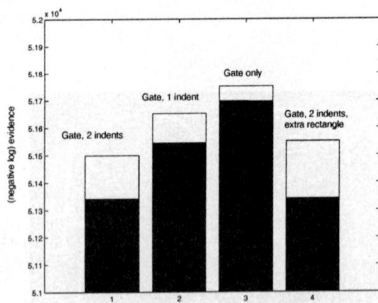

Fig. 10. *Negative log evidence for different numbers of layers in the gateway scene. From left to right: evidence for 3 detected layers, evidence for the gateway and only one indentation, evidence for the gateway only, evidence for all layers including spurious rectangle (shown above). The 3 and 4 layer models are clearly preferred to those with 1 and 2 layers; the 3 layer model is selected as it has a higher Occam factor.*

6   Conclusion

This paper presents a novel approach to layer extraction with the aim of creating a 3D model of the images that accurately reflects prior belief. This has been effected by a Bayesian approach with explicit, rather than implicit modelling of the distribution over segmentations. Given a hypothesised segmentation it is shown how to evaluate its likelihood and how to compare it with other hypotheses. A variety of model selection measures are considered, all but the most basic of which prove adequate to prevent model overfitting for the architectural scenes on which this approach is demonstrated. The Occam factor is recommended as is more accurate and theoretically sound while incurring minimal extra computational cost.

The hierarchical nature of the shape model means that it is easily extended to more complex scenes than those presented here. Future work will extend the number and type of shape primitives modelled, and the number of levels in the hierarchical shape model. For example, it should be possible to infer both the minimal parametrisation and the architectural style (e.g. Gothic, Georgian, modern bungalow) of the scene. A fully automatic initialisation scheme will use these hierarchical models to constrain an initial search for primitives in each image.

References

1. S. Ayer and H. Sawhney. Layered representation of motion video using robust maximum-likelihood estimation of mixture models and mdl encoding. In *International Conference on Computer Vision*, pages 777–784, 1995.
2. S. Baker, R. Szeliski, and P. Anandan. A layered approach to stereo reconstruction. In *IEEE Computer Vision and Pattern Recognition*, pages 434–441, 1998.
3. R. Cipolla, D. Robertson, and E. Boyer. Photobuilder – 3d models of architectural scenes from uncalibrated images. In *IEEE Int. Conf. on Multimedia Computing and Systems*, 1999.
4. A.R. Dick and R. Cipolla. Model refinement from planar parallax. In *Proc. 10th British Machine Vision Conference (BMVC'99)*, volume 1, pages 73–82, Nottingham, 1999.
5. A. Gelman, J. Carlin, H. Stern, and D. Rubin. *Bayesian Data Analysis*. Chapman and Hall, Boston, 1995.
6. U. Grenander, Y. Chow, and D.M. Keenan. *HANDS. A Pattern Theoretical Study of Biological Shapes*. Springer-Verlag. New York, 1991.
7. F. Heitz and P. Bouthemy. Multimodal motion estimation and segmentation using markov random fields. In *Proc. 10th Int. Conf. Pattern Recognition*, pages 378–383, 1991.
8. A. Jepson and M. Black. Mixture models for optical flow computation. In *IEEE Computer Vision and Pattern Recognition*, pages 760–766. IEEE, 1993.
9. R. Koch, M. Pollefeys, and L. Van Gool. Multi viewpoint stereo from uncalibrated video sequences. In *European Conference on Computer Vision*, pages 55–71, 1998.
10. D. J. C. MacKay. Bayesian interpolation. *Neural Computation*, 4(3):415–447, 1992.
11. J. Magarey and N. Kingsbury. Motion estimation using a complex-valued wavelet transform. *IEEE Trans. Signal Processing*, 46(4):1069–1084, April 1998.
12. M. Pollefeys, R. Koch, and L. VanGool. Self-calibration and metric reconstruction in spite of varying and unknown internal camera parameters. In *International Conference on Computer Vision*, pages 90–95, 1998.
13. G. Schwarz. Estimating dimension of a model. *Ann. Stat.*, 6:401–464, 1978.
14. S. Seitz and C. Dyer. A theory of shape by space carving. In *International Conference on Computer Vision*, pages 307–314, 1999.
15. H.Y. Shum, M. Han, and R. Szeliski. Interactive construction of 3d models from panoramic mosaics. In *IEEE Computer Vision and Pattern Recognition*, pages 427–433, 1998.
16. D. S. Sivia. *Data Analysis: A Bayesian Tutorial*. Oxford University Press, Oxford, 1996.
17. P. Torr, R. Szeliski, and P. Anandan. An integrated bayesian approach to layer extraction from image sequences. In *International Conference on Computer Vision*, pages 983–990, 1999.
18. J. Wang and E. H. Adelson. Layered representation for motion analysis. In *IEEE Computer Vision and Pattern Recognition*, pages 361–366, 1993.
19. T. Weiss and E. H. Adelson. A unified mixture framework for motion segmentation. In *IEEE Computer Vision and Pattern Recognition*, pages 321–326, 1996.

Model-Based Initialisation for Segmentation

Johannes Hug, Christian Brechbühler, and Gábor Székely

Swiss Federal Institute of Technology, ETH Zentrum
CH-8092 Zürich, Switzerland
{jhug | brech | szekely}@vision.ee.ethz.ch

Abstract. The initialisation of segmentation methods aiming at the localisation of biological structures in medical imagery is frequently regarded as a given precondition. In practice, however, initialisation is usually performed manually or by some heuristic preprocessing steps. Moreover, the same framework is often employed to recover from imperfect results of the subsequent segmentation. Therefore, it is of crucial importance for everyday application to have a simple and effective initialisation method at one's disposal. This paper proposes a new model-based framework to synthesise sound initialisations by calculating the most probable shape given a minimal set of statistical landmarks and the applied shape model. Shape information coded by particular points is first iteratively removed from a statistical shape description that is based on the principal component analysis of a collection of shape instances. By using the inverse of the resulting operation, it is subsequently possible to construct initial outlines with minimal effort. The whole framework is demonstrated by means of a shape database consisting of a set of corpus callosum instances. Furthermore, both manual and fully automatic initialisation with the proposed approach is evaluated. The obtained results validate its suitability as a preprocessing step for semi-automatic as well as fully automatic segmentation. And last but not least, the iterative construction of increasingly point-invariant shape statistics provides a deeper insight into the nature of the shape under investigation.

1 Introduction

The advent of the "Active Vision" paradigm in the 1980s came along with the idea of using model-based prior knowledge to simplify and stabilise the treatment of a specific vision problem. Since then, all kinds of active shape models have emerged in many application areas in various forms such as Snakes [10], deformable templates [23] or active appearance models [2]. The amount of prior knowledge included in these models varies from simple general smoothness assumptions to very detailed knowledge about the shape and the image data to be expected. In the field of medical imaging, the usage of statistical shape models has found widespread use [3, 21, 12, 13], since the notion of biological shape seems to be best defined by a statistical description of a large population.

Even though these statistical methods have proven to be fairly stable and reliable, there are cases where they fail completely in finding at least an approximation of the correct object boundary. If a certain application asks for absolutely flawless segmentations, alternative or supplemental frameworks must be applied to compensate for the missing functionality. On the one hand, we could employ semi-automatic [6, 10, 17, 8] or manual segmentation tools that rely on a human operator providing the missing information. On the other hand, we may initialise the fully automatic procedure such that the correct solution is just nearby the initial configuration. Since almost all semi-automatic methods rely on suitable initialisations as well, the provision of a reasonable starting point seems to be a valuable extension of both approaches. Our main goal is therefore to provide a possibly interactive initialisation method that still takes into account the prior knowledge of the shape as far as possible.

In order to keep the amount of required user input as small as possible, simple and intuitive interaction metaphors are of crucial importance for the design of such a tool. Since the most simple and probably most feasible interaction metaphor is still the adjustment of individual points lying on the boundary of the object under investigation, we are subsequently looking for a small number of points describing the overall shape of the object to be segmented — analogous to coarse control polygons of hierarchical shape descriptions that have recently been proposed in the field of modelling and animation [7, 24]. Such a "coarse control polygon" should capture as much prior shape knowledge as possible. And there should be a way to calculate the most "natural" fine scale shape given the correct arrangement of the control vertices.

Our shape database should therefore be able to answer the following three questions: Which points along the object boundary are best suited for a compact and robust description of the shape? How many control vertices must be included in the coarsest control polygon? And how should the full resolution object be predicted so as to provide a reasonable initial outline?

In search of answers to these questions, we have decided to pursue the following strategy: Using statistical shape analysis, we examine the remaining variability of shape, if the variation coded by the position of individual points is progressively subtracted. The coarsest control polygon necessary to capture the main shape characteristics is complete as soon as the remaining variability is small with respect to the working range of the subsequent segmentation method. And the most probable shape for a given control polygon can then be calculated by just inverting the process of subtracting the variation of control vertices.

2 Experimental Set-up

In order to have a compact statistical shape description at our disposal, we employ a representation that is based on a principal component analysis (PCA) of all object instances in our database. This approach, first proposed by Cootes and Taylor in [4], has the very useful property to reflect the shape variations occurring within the population by a complete set of basis vectors. These basis vectors span a linear shape space containing all the instances of our collection. This enables us to apply the whole framework of linear algebra to make the statistic point-wise invariant. Furthermore, the properties of such a shape description are well understood and appropriately documented [11].

In addition to a statistical description method, we need a population of several object instances representing our model-based foreknowledge. The PCA is therefore applied to a collection of 71 hand segmented outlines of the corpus callosum on mid-sagittal MR-slices. Five randomly selected examples of this database are illustrated in Fig. 1. All aspects of the model building process regarding this population are described in detail in [22].

Since we aim at working with a vertex-based control polygon at interactive speed, the original representation based on elliptic Fourier descriptors [20, 14, 21] has been converted to a polygonal representation by equidistantly sampling the parameter space of the outline. For the following analysis, we assume that the underlying arc-length based curve parameterisation with normalised parameter starting point provides a sufficiently good correspondence between the individual specimen. All experiments we performed suggest that the achieved correspondence is not faultless but sufficiently precise for our intentions (see also [11]). In order to normalise the model contours, we represented the vertex positions as usual with respect to an anatomical coordinate system given by the AC-PC line. Experience shows that these anatomical landmarks can easily be located and are very stable with respect to the corpus callosum.

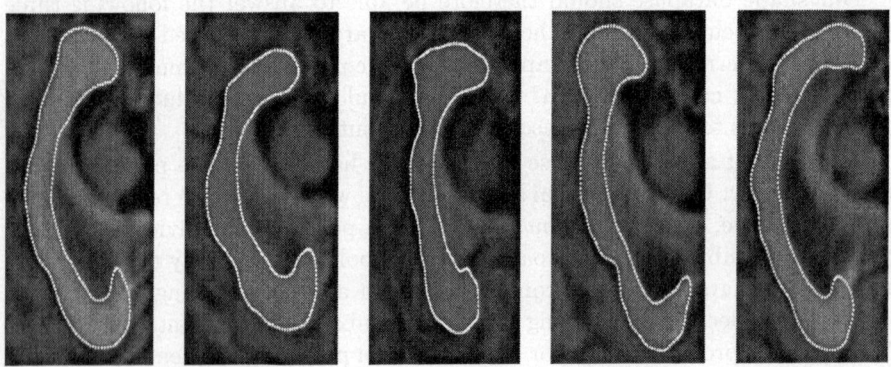

Fig. 1. Five randomly selected corpora callosa from our collection that consists of 71 examples.

In the following, Section 3 reviews shortly the statistical shape analysis using principal components and fixes the mathematical notation. In Section 4, we discuss in detail the aforementioned progressive subtraction of variation, and Section 5 describes subsequently the inversion of this operation. The initialisation procedure founding on the presented framework is evaluated in Section 6 for both interactive and fully automatic mode of operation. Finally, Section 7 concludes this report and outlines the next steps towards a highly robust initialisation oracle.

3   Shape Analysis using Principal Components

The basic idea of statistical shape analysis using principal components consists in separating and quantifying the main variations of shape that occur within a population of several instances exemplifying the same object. More precisely, a PCA defines a linear transformation that decorrelates the parameter signals of the original shape population by projecting the objects into a linear shape space spanned by a complete set of orthogonal basis vectors. If the parameter signals are highly correlated, then the coarse scale variations of shape are described by the first few basis vectors, whereas fine details are captured by the remaining ones. Furthermore, if the joint distribution of the parameters describing the shape is Gaussian, then a reasonably weighted linear combination of the basis vectors results in a shape that is similar to the existing ones. On the other hand, if the joint distribution of the parameters is highly non-Gaussian or if the dependencies of the parameter signals are non-linear, then other decomposition methods such as the independent component analysis [9] should be employed.

As already mentioned, the considered population consists of $N + 1 = 71$ corpus callosum instances, given as polygonal models $\mathbf{p}_i = [x_i^{[1]}, y_i^{[1]}, \ldots, x_i^{[M]}, y_i^{[M]}]^T$ with $M = 256$ points. Since we will later compare statistic-based initialisations to the ground truth given by one object instance, we always exclude this particular instance from the statistic for cross-validation. To simplify the formalism, we centre the parameter signals of the shapes beforehand by calculating an average model $\overline{\mathbf{p}}$ and an instance specific difference vector $\Delta \mathbf{p}_i$:

$$\overline{\mathbf{p}} = \frac{1}{N} \sum_{i=1}^{N} \mathbf{p}_i, \qquad \Delta \mathbf{p}_i = \mathbf{p}_i - \overline{\mathbf{p}}, \qquad \Delta P = [\Delta \mathbf{p}_1 \cdots \Delta \mathbf{p}_N] \qquad (1)$$

Note, the $N = 70$ difference vectors span only a 69-dimensional space; the missing dimension obviously originates from the linear dependence $\sum_{i=1}^{N} \Delta \mathbf{p}_i = 0$. The corresponding covariance matrix $\Sigma \in \mathbb{R}^{2M \times 2M}$ is consequently rank-deficient. As has been pointed out in [5], this circumstance can be exploited to speed up the calculation of the 69 valid eigenvalues and eigenvectors: Instead of calculating the full eigensystem of the covariance matrix Σ, the multiplication of the eigenvectors of a smaller matrix $\check{\Sigma}$ with ΔP leads to the correct principal components:

$$\check{\Sigma} = \frac{1}{N-1} \Delta P^T \Delta P \stackrel{PCA}{=} \check{U} \Lambda' \check{U}^T, \quad \Lambda' = \mathrm{diag}(\lambda_1, \ldots, \lambda_{N-1}, 0)$$

$$U' = [\mathbf{u}_1 \cdots \mathbf{u}_{N-1} \mathbf{u}_N] = \psi \left(\Delta P \, \check{U} \right), \quad \psi(A) = \text{Normalise columns of A} \qquad (2)$$

As an alternative that is not equally fast but conceptually more elegant, we propose to work in a subspace with a complete set of basis vectors to find the eigensystem of our data. To do so, we project the difference vectors $\Delta \mathbf{p}_i$ into a lower dimensional space whose basis M is constructed by the Gram-Schmidt orthonormalisation χ:

$$M = [\mathbf{m}_1 \cdots \mathbf{m}_{N-1}] = \chi(\Delta \mathbf{p}_1, \ldots, \Delta \mathbf{p}_{N-1}), \qquad \Delta \tilde{\mathbf{p}}_i = M^T \Delta \mathbf{p}_i \qquad (3)$$

Note, one arbitrary $\Delta\mathbf{p}_i$ must be dropped for the construction of M, and $\Delta\tilde{\mathbf{p}}_i$ denotes the projection of $\Delta\mathbf{p}_i$ into the subspace spanned by M. The covariance matrix $\tilde{\Sigma}$ and the resulting PCA given by the eigensystem of $\tilde{\Sigma}$ can subsequently be calculated according to:

$$\tilde{\Sigma} = \frac{1}{N-1}\sum_{i=1}^{N} \Delta\tilde{\mathbf{p}}_i\,\Delta\tilde{\mathbf{p}}_i^T \overset{\text{PCA}}{=} \tilde{U}\Lambda\tilde{U}^T, \qquad \Lambda = \mathrm{diag}(\lambda_1,\ldots,\lambda_{N-1}) \quad (4)$$

The principal components defining the eigenmodes *in shape space* are then given by back-projecting the eigenvectors $\tilde{U}$: $\quad U = [\mathbf{u}_1 \,\cdots\, \mathbf{u}_{N-1}] = M\tilde{U}$. Each object instance can be represented as a linear combination $\mathbf{p}_i = \overline{\mathbf{p}} + U\mathbf{b}_i$ of these eigenmodes, where $\mathbf{b}_i = [b_i^{[1]},\ldots,b_i^{[N-1]}]^T$. In order to calculate the uncorrelated coordinates $\mathbf{b}_i$ of each object instance, we project the difference vectors $\Delta\mathbf{p}_i$ into the eigenspace: $\quad \mathbf{b}_i = U^T\Delta\mathbf{p}_i$.

The first four eigenmodes resulting from the PCA of our population are displayed in Fig. 3(a). The shapes representing the first eigenmode on the left are calculated by adding the weighted first eigenvector $\mathbf{u}_1$ to the average model $\overline{\mathbf{p}}$. The following three shape variations to the right of the first one are calculated correspondingly.

4 Progressive Elimination of Variation

Given a statistical analysis as defined above, we consider the following situation: After having defined the shape coordinate system by locating the AC-PC line, the initialisation of a new object instance starts with the average model $\overline{\mathbf{p}}$, as illustrated in Fig. 2(a) on the left. Let us assume for the moment that the aforementioned coarse control polygon consists of the three marked vertices on the outline of the mean shape. To generate an initial approximation of the object, we define now a set of boundary conditions for the global shape by moving the control vertices to an approximately correct position. Given these constraints and our prior knowledge of the shape, we wish to choose that outline for initialisation which is most natural in that case. In the following two sections we will show, how this most probable outline can be found.

Since we hope that some control vertices carry more shape information than others, we approach the whole problem iteratively. In a first step, we calculate the most probable shape that satisfies only the boundary conditions provided by the most important control vertex. For the second most important control point we use subsequently the resulting outline as initial configuration. This process is then repeated until we can satisfy all the boundary conditions. Since we do not yet know how to determine the most important control vertex, we will first investigate the computation of the most probable shape given the position of an *arbitrary* point. This will be the subject of the next subsection. The problem of finding the points carrying most shape information will be discussed afterwards in subsection 4.3.

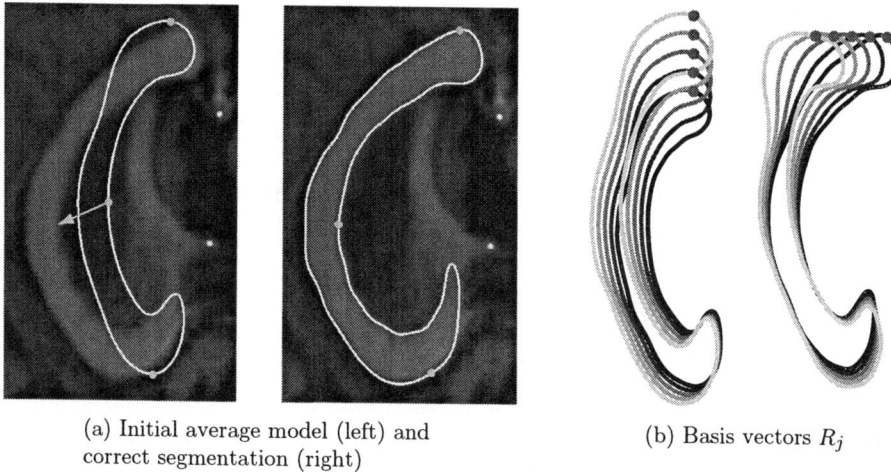

(a) Initial average model (left) and
correct segmentation (right)

(b) Basis vectors R_j

Fig. 2. (a) Boundary conditions for an initial outline are established by prescribing a position for each coarse control vertex. (b) Shape variations caused by adding the two basis vectors R_j to the average model, inducing x- and y-translations of point j, respectively. The various shapes are obtained by evaluating $\overline{\mathbf{p}} + \omega\, U\, \mathbf{r}_k$ with $\omega \in \{-2, \ldots, 2\}$ and $k \in \{x_j, y_j\}$.

4.1 Shape-based Basis Vectors for one Point

To start with, we must translate our conceptual goal into mathematical terms. Since the most probable shape is given by the mean model $\overline{\mathbf{p}}$ in the context of PCA, we can reinterpret the notion of "choosing the most probable outline" as "choosing the shape with minimal deviation from the mean". And this means nothing else than choosing the model with minimal Mahalanobis-distance D_m, the common metric in eigenspaces.

The key idea enabling the solution of our first problem can now be summarised as follows: We must find two vectors *in the space of variation* that describe decoupled x- and y-translations of a given point j with minimal variation, respectively. In other words, these two vectors should cause a unit translation of vertex j in either x- or y-direction, and they should have minimal Mahalanobis-length D_m. If we have found them, we can satisfy all possible boundary conditions caused by one vertex with minimal variation by just adding the two appropriately weighted "basis" vectors to the mean. This problem gives rise to the following constrained optimisation:

Let $\mathbf{r}_{x_j}$ and $\mathbf{r}_{y_j}$ denote the two unknown basis vectors causing unit x- and y- translation of point j, respectively. The Mahalanobis-length D_m of these two vectors is then given by:

$$D_m(\mathbf{r}_k) = (\tilde{U}\mathbf{r}_k)^T \tilde{\Sigma}^{-1}\tilde{U}\mathbf{r}_k = \mathbf{r}_k^T \Lambda^{-1}\mathbf{r}_k = \sum_{e=1}^{N-1} \frac{\left(r_k^{[e]}\right)^2}{\lambda_e}, \qquad k \in \{x_j, y_j\} \quad (5)$$

Taking into account that x_j and y_j depend only on two rows of U, we define the sub-matrix U_j according to the following expression:

$$\begin{bmatrix} x_j \\ y_j \end{bmatrix} = \begin{bmatrix} \overline{x}_j \\ \overline{y}_j \end{bmatrix} + \begin{bmatrix} u_{2j-1\,\circ} \\ u_{2j\,\circ} \end{bmatrix} \mathbf{b} = \begin{bmatrix} \overline{x}_j \\ \overline{y}_j \end{bmatrix} + U_j\,\mathbf{b}, \qquad u_{j\,\circ} = j^{\text{th}} \text{ row of } U \quad (6)$$

In order to minimise the Mahalanobis-distance D_m subject to the constraint of a separate x- or y-translation by one unit, we establish — as is customary for constrained optimisation — the Lagrange function L:

$$L(\mathbf{r}_k, \mathbf{l}_k) = \sum_{e=1}^{N-1} \frac{\left(r_k^{[e]}\right)^2}{\lambda_e} - \mathbf{l}_k^T\,[U_j \mathbf{r}_k - \mathbf{e}_k], \qquad \mathbf{e}_{\{x_j, y_j\}} = \{\begin{bmatrix} 1 \\ 0 \end{bmatrix}, \begin{bmatrix} 0 \\ 1 \end{bmatrix}\} \quad (7)$$

The vectors $\mathbf{l}_{x_j}$ and $\mathbf{l}_{y_j}$ contain as usual the required Lagrange multipliers. To find the minimum of $L(\mathbf{r}_k, \mathbf{l}_k)$, we calculate the derivatives with respect to all elements of $\mathbf{r}_{x_j}$, $\mathbf{r}_{y_j}$, $\mathbf{l}_{x_j}$, and $\mathbf{l}_{y_j}$ and set them equal to zero:

$$\left.\begin{array}{l} \dfrac{\delta L(\mathbf{r}_k, \mathbf{l}_k)}{\delta \mathbf{r}_k} \overset{!}{=} 0 \\[2ex] \dfrac{\delta L(\mathbf{r}_k, \mathbf{l}_k)}{\delta \mathbf{l}_k} \overset{!}{=} 0 \end{array}\right\} \begin{bmatrix} \frac{2}{\lambda_1} & & \vdots & \\ & \ddots & \vdots & -U_j^T \\ & & \frac{2}{\lambda_{N-1}} & \vdots \\ \cdots & \cdots & \cdots & \cdots \\ U_j & & \vdots & 0 \end{bmatrix} \begin{bmatrix} \vdots & \vdots \\ \mathbf{r}_{x_j} & \mathbf{r}_{y_j} \\ \vdots & \vdots \\ \cdots & \cdots \\ \mathbf{l}_{x_j} & \mathbf{l}_{y_j} \end{bmatrix} = \begin{bmatrix} \vdots & \vdots \\ 0 & 0 \\ \vdots & \\ \cdots & \cdots \\ \mathbf{e}_{x_j} & \mathbf{e}_{y_j} \end{bmatrix} \quad (8)$$

If the basis vectors and the Lagrange multipliers are combined according to $R_j = [\mathbf{r}_{x_j}\ \mathbf{r}_{y_j}]$ and $L_j = [\mathbf{l}_{x_j}\ \mathbf{l}_{y_j}]$, Eq. (8) can be rewritten as two linear matrix equations:

$$2\Lambda^{-1}R_j = U_j^T L_j \quad (9)$$

$$U_j R_j = I \quad (10)$$

The two basis vectors $\mathbf{r}_{x_j}$ and $\mathbf{r}_{y_j}$ resulting from simple algebraic operations (resolve (9) for R_j and replace R_j in (10) by the result, use to resulting equation to find $L_j = 2[U_j \Lambda U_j^T]^{-1}$ and substitute for L_j in (9)) are then given by:

$$R_j = [\mathbf{r}_{x_j}\ \mathbf{r}_{y_j}] = \Lambda\,U_j^T\,[U_j\,\Lambda\,U_j^T]^{-1} \quad (11)$$

While $\mathbf{r}_{x_j}$ describes the translation of x_j by one unit with constant y_j and minimal shape variation, $\mathbf{r}_{y_j}$ alters y_j correspondingly. The resulting effect caused by adding these shape-based basis vectors to the average model is illustrated in Fig. 2(b). The most probable shape $\check{\mathbf{p}}$ given the displacement $[\Delta x_j, \Delta y_j]^T$ of control vertex j is consequently determined by

$$\check{\mathbf{p}} = \overline{\mathbf{p}} + U R_j \begin{bmatrix} \Delta x_j \\ \Delta y_j \end{bmatrix}. \quad (12)$$

Another possibility to find the two basis vectors R_j consists in exploiting the least-squares property of the Moore-Penrose pseudo-inverse. The basic idea in this context is to solve the highly under-determined linear system $U_j \mathbf{r}_k = \mathbf{e}_k$ (representing the prescribed constraints) by calculating the pseudo-inverse $U_j^\#$. Since we are not looking for the normal least-squares solution but for the one with minimal Mahalanobis-distance, we have to introduce a weighting of the rows of U_j, in order to map the problem into normal Euclidean space, where the minimal solution is then given by the generalised inverse. As shown in Appendix A, this approach leads to the same basis vectors R_j and validates Eq. (11), since there is only one unique element in the hyper-plane of all solutions that has minimum Mahalanobis-norm.

4.2 Point-wise Subtraction of Variation

In the previous subsection we have seen how to choose the most probable shape given the position of one specific control vertex j. Before we can now proceed to the next control point, we must ensure that subsequent shape modifications will not alter the previously adjusted vertex j. To do so, we must remove those components from the statistic that cause a displacement of this point. Unfortunately, we cannot apply a projection for this purpose, since the basis vectors R_j are not orthogonal in the shape space. Therefore, we propose to subtract the variation coded by the point j from each instance i, and to rebuild the statistic afterwards. For the first part of this operation, we must subtract the basis vectors R_j weighted by the example-specific displacement $[\Delta x_j, \Delta y_j]_i^T$ from the parameter representation $\mathbf{b}_i$ of each instance i:

$$\mathbf{b}_i^{\hat{j}} = \mathbf{b}_i - R_j \begin{bmatrix} \Delta x_j \\ \Delta y_j \end{bmatrix}_i = \mathbf{b}_i - R_j\, U_j\, \mathbf{b}_i = (I - R_j\, U_j)\, \mathbf{b}_i, \quad \forall i \in \{1,..,N\} \quad (13)$$

Doing so for all instances, we obtain a new description of our population which is invariant with respect to the point j (denoted by $\circ^{\hat{j}}$). The variability in this point-normalised population is expected to be smaller compared to the original collection. In order to verify this assumption and to rebuild the statistic, we apply anew a PCA to the normalised set of instances $\{\mathbf{b}_i^{\hat{j}} \mid i \in \{1,\ldots,N\}\}$. Note, the eigenspace shrinks by two dimensions since we removed two degrees of freedom. The resulting principal components, denoted by $U^{\hat{j}}$, confirm the expected behaviour and validate also the removal of the variation of point j. The first four one-point invariant eigenmodes are illustrated in Fig. 3(b).

4.3 Point Selection Strategy

The point-wise elimination of variability presented above can subsequently be repeated for several points, until the remaining variability is small enough with respect to the working range of the subsequent segmentation algorithm. In order to achieve optimal results and to find the most compact control polygon, we should now explore the strategy for the selection of control points. Since we

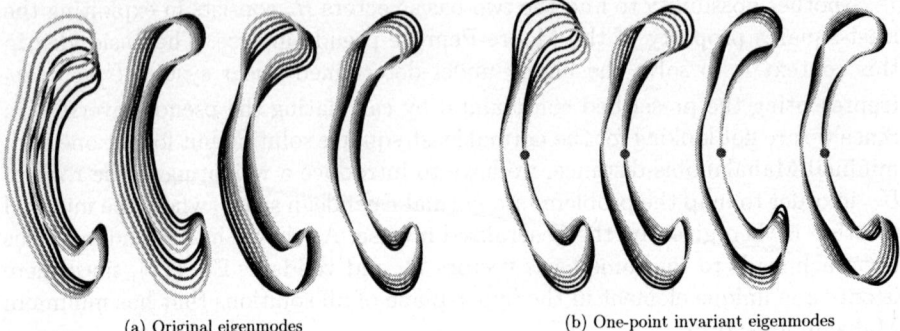

(a) Original eigenmodes   (b) One-point invariant eigenmodes

Fig. 3. (a) The first four eigenmodes of 70 corpus callosum instances. The various shapes are obtained by evaluating $\overline{\mathbf{p}} + \omega\sqrt{\lambda_k}\mathbf{u}_k$ with $\omega \in \{-2, \ldots, 2\}$ and $k \in \{1, \ldots, 4\}$. (b) The first four one-point invariant eigenmodes after subtracting the first principal landmark. The various shapes are obtained by evaluating $\overline{\mathbf{p}} + \omega\sqrt{\lambda_k^{\hat{j}}}\mathbf{u}_k^{\hat{j}}$ with $\omega \in \{-2, \ldots, 2\}$ and $k \in \{1, \ldots, 4\}$.

aim to choose those vertices that carry as much shape information as possible, we should select the points according to their "reduction potential". A control vertex holds a large reduction potential, if the remaining variability after its elimination is small.

To make the following formalism as precise as possible, we introduce some additional definitions at this point: Firstly, we will subsequently refer to the kth point being removed from the statistic as the kth *principal landmark*. Secondly, let the sequence $\hat{s}_k = \{\hat{j}_1, \ldots, \hat{j}_k\}$ denote the set of point-indices of those k principal landmarks that have been removed from the statistic in the given order. And last but not least, the superscript $\circ^{\hat{s}_k}$ is used for the value of $\circ$, if the principal landmarks $\hat{s}_k$ have been removed.

Using this formalism, the reduction potential P of vertex j_k, being a candidate to serve as the kth principal landmark, can be defined as follows:

$$P(j_k) = -\sum_{l=1}^{N-1-2(k-1)} \left(\tilde{\sigma}_l^2\right)^{\hat{s}_k} = -\text{tr}(\tilde{\Sigma}^{\hat{s}_k}) = -\text{tr}(\Lambda^{\hat{s}_k}), \quad \hat{s}_k = \{\hat{j}_1, \ldots, \hat{j}_k\} \quad (14)$$

Figure 4(a) shows the reduction potential for all the points of the original model. In order to remove as much variation as possible, we choose consequently that point as the first principal landmark that holds the largest reduction potential: $j_1 = \max_j[P(j)]$. The selected vertex and the resulting point-invariant statistic after its elimination have already been shown in Fig. 3(b).

If we apply this selection and elimination step twice again, we end up with the second and third principal landmark. The corresponding eigenmodes and the selected points are depicted in Fig. 5. The decreasing deviations from the mean indicate that the variation within the population is progressively reduced by this operation. The observation of the overall variance subject to progressive

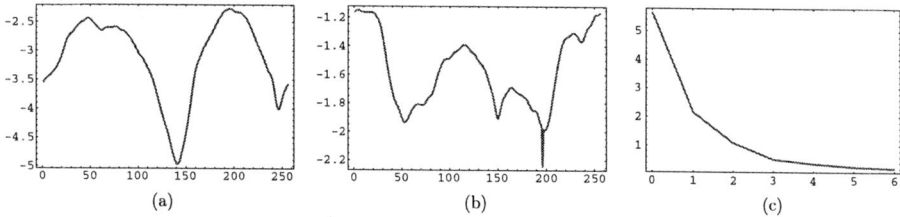

(a)   (b)   (c)

Fig. 4. (a) & (b) Reduction potentials for the selection of (a) the first and (b) the second principal landmark. For each point j in the abscissa, the reduction potential $P(j)$ is displayed. Note, the first principal landmark $j_1 = 196$ has minimal reduction potential in (b), because subtracting the same point twice has no effect at all. (c) The overall variance $\mathrm{tr}(\tilde{\Sigma}^{\hat{s}_k})$ of the population depending on the number of subtracted principal landmarks.

point removal (see Fig. 4(c)) verifies this hypothesis and shows that the variability decreases surprisingly fast in the beginning. Later on, after three vertices have been processed, the decline levels out and the benefit of each additional principal landmark becomes fairly small. This finding suggests that the main shape characteristics of a corpus callosum can be captured by only three or four principal landmarks.

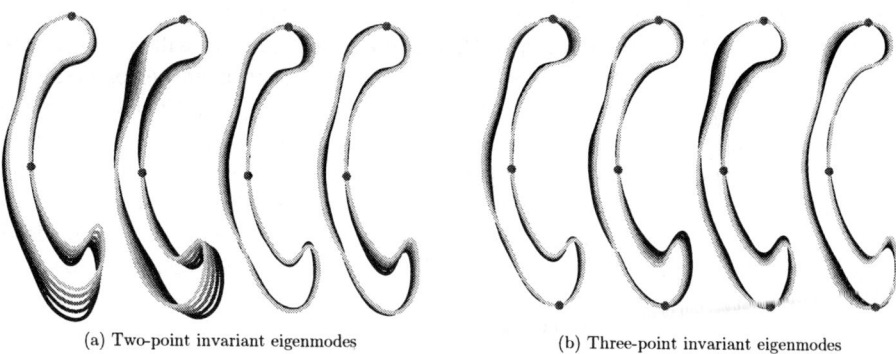

(a) Two-point invariant eigenmodes   (b) Three-point invariant eigenmodes

Fig. 5. Remaining variability after vertex elimination of (a) two and (b) three principal landmarks.

5 Initial Shapes for Segmentation

The progressive application of the point selection and removal process enables now the construction of the most compact *principal control polygon*, consisting of the first few principal landmarks. Analogous to traditional parametric curve representations, each control point has two associated *principal basis functions*

(UR_j) that are globally supported. The final outline $\check{p}_l$ based on a principal control polygon with l vertices is then given by the inverse operation of the construction, that is, by the combination of the mean shape $\overline{p}$ and all the weighted principal basis functions $R_{j_k}^{\hat{s}_{k-1}}$:

$$\check{p}_l = \overline{p} + \sum_{k=1}^{l} U^{\hat{s}_{k-1}} R_{j_k}^{\hat{s}_{k-1}} \begin{bmatrix} \Delta x_{j_k} \\ \Delta y_{j_k} \end{bmatrix} \tag{15}$$

Note that the weights $[\Delta x_{j_k}, \Delta y_{j_k}]^T$ for the basis vectors $U^{\hat{s}_{k-1}} R_{j_k}^{\hat{s}_{k-1}}$ depend on the shape defined by the previous principal landmarks $\hat{s}_{k-1}$. Therefore, if any control point j_k is modified and the less important landmarks shall remain in their position, the weights $\{[\Delta x_{j_{k+1}}, \Delta y_{j_{k+1}}]^T, \ldots, [\Delta x_{j_l}, \Delta y_{j_l}]^T\}$ must be recalculated in the correct order of vertex removal. To emphasise the hierarchical structure of our formalism and to simplify the algorithmic implementation, we recommend to use the following recursive definition instead of equation (15):

$$\check{p}_0 = \overline{p} \; , \qquad \check{p}_k = \check{p}_{k-1} + U^{\hat{s}_{k-1}} R_{j_k}^{\hat{s}_{k-1}} \begin{bmatrix} \Delta x_{j_k} \\ \Delta y_{j_k} \end{bmatrix} \tag{16}$$

With this shape-based curve representation $\check{p}$, the last piece has fallen into place. By utilising a minimal principal control polygon with associated basis functions, we are now able to fulfil all our original objectives: The initialisation of a new shape instance results in the simple adjustment of a small number of points, taking into account all our prior knowledge of the shape.

In order to validate the quality of the proposed method, we will subsequently show some results of cross-validation experiments that have been performed with each shape instance in our database. It goes without saying that the test instance has always been removed from the statistic. The initialisations to be presented have been generated by moving the principal landmarks into the positions of the corresponding points on the outline of the respective test object. A selection of the results of these experiments is illustrated in Fig. 6 and can be summarised as follows: The initial average model in Fig. 6(a) converges efficiently towards an approximation of the correct shape whilst the control vertices are adjusted. In most of our examples, only three or four principal landmarks are necessary to provide a reasonably good initialisation. The consideration of more than five or six points does not significantly improve the quality of the initial shape. In some cases, the initialisation even deteriorates slightly, if too much control vertices are employed. This behaviour may also indicate some deficiencies of the underlying correspondence function. To show a representative cross-section of the achieved results, Fig. 6(b) displays four truly randomly chosen experiments, where four principal landmarks have been adjusted.

6 Interactive and Automatic Initialisation

The major question remaining to be answered is, whether the proposed framework proves its worth in practical application as well. Although we have not yet

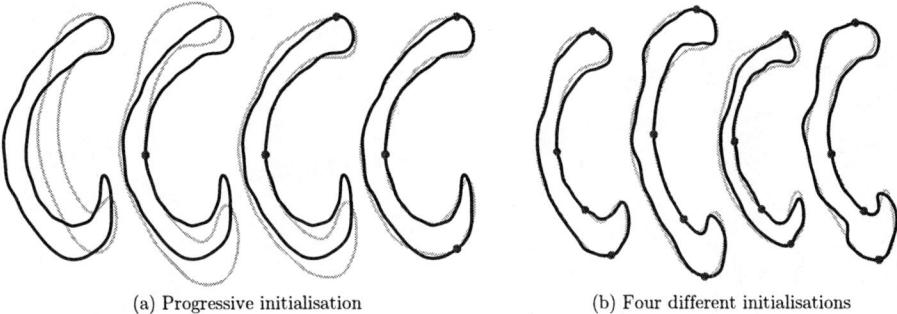

(a) Progressive initialisation   (b) Four different initialisations

Fig. 6. (a) Generation of an initial outline for segmentation; shape instance in black and fitted initialisations in gray with an increasing number of fitted principal landmarks. (b) Initial shapes with four adjusted principal landmarks for the segmentation of four randomly chosen instances.

gained any experience in everyday clinical application, our experimental results are fairly convincing. Tests have been performed for both interactive and fully automatic initialisation.

The interactive approach simply uses the underlying shape basis as a highly specialised curve representation. The required adjustments of the principal landmarks must be provided by a human operator. Since the recalculation of the outline can be done at interactive speed, the instant feedback supports the operator in finding an appropriate initialisation within a few seconds. In most of the cases, three principal landmarks are sufficient to define a coarse initialisation. At most three additional control vertices can then be used to refine the characteristic details of the shape. Figure 7(a) shows one possible initialisation based on six manually adjusted principal landmarks.

By exploiting the statistical prior knowledge of the shape once again, we can even eliminate the remaining interaction: For each principal landmark j_k, we calculate the covariance matrix $\Sigma_{j_k}^{\hat{s}_k-1}$ in order to determine its positional variability. On the assumption that a landmark is Gaussian distributed, we can then compute a confidence ellipse that contains the corresponding control point with probability $\chi_2^2(c) = P(|\boldsymbol{\omega}| < c)$ (see e.g. [1]). The new auxiliary variable $\boldsymbol{\omega}$ is, as usual in this context, a standardised random vector with normal distribution: $\omega_i \sim \mathcal{N}(0,1) \wedge \boldsymbol{\omega} \sim \mathcal{N}(0,I)$. Since it is well known that $\chi_2^2(3) = P(|\boldsymbol{\omega}| < 3) \approx 99\%$, we can construct the main axes a_{j_k} and b_{j_k} of the confidence ellipse that contains the principal landmark with a probability of 99% by the following linear transformation of $\boldsymbol{\omega}$:

$$a_{j_k} = \sqrt{\Sigma_{j_k}^{\hat{s}_k-1}}\boldsymbol{\omega}_{\parallel}, \quad b_{j_k} = \sqrt{\Sigma_{j_k}^{\hat{s}_k-1}}\boldsymbol{\omega}_{\perp}; \quad \boldsymbol{\omega}_{\parallel} = 3\begin{bmatrix}1\\0\end{bmatrix}, \quad \boldsymbol{\omega}_{\perp} = 3\begin{bmatrix}0\\1\end{bmatrix} \quad (17)$$

Figure 7(b) shows these confidence ellipses for all considered control vertices. As expected, the length of the axes a_{j_k} and b_{j_k} declines with increasing k, according to the smaller variances in the underlying statistics.

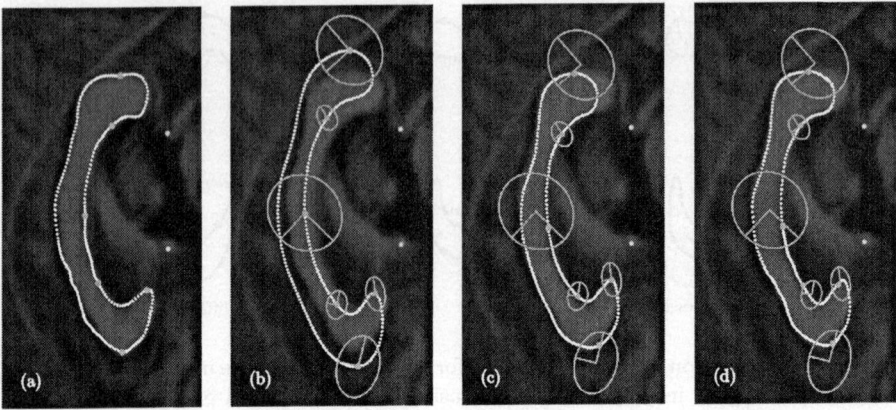

Fig. 7. (a) Interactive initialisation by manual adjustment of six principal landmarks. (b) Initial average model with the confidence ellipses of the control vertices. (c) & (d) Automatic initialisation by the sequential optimisation of the matching function G_k for (c) three and (d) six principal landmarks.

For an automatic initialisation, we can subsequently use these confidence intervals as the region of interest with respect to an optimisation of the fit. The goal function of such an optimisation should measure the correspondence between the shape $\check{\mathbf{p}}_k$ to be optimised and the actual image data I. In order to simplify and accelerate the optimisation process, we propose to fit only one principal landmark at a time, analogous to manual initialisation. By employing a very popular matching function based on the image gradient ∇I, we end up with the following goal function G_k:

$$G_k(\Delta x_{j_k}, \Delta y_{j_k}) = \sum_{e=1}^{M} \| \nabla I[\, \check{\mathbf{p}}_k^{[e]}(\Delta x_{j_k}, \Delta y_{j_k})\,]\,\|, \qquad I : \text{Image data} \qquad (18)$$

Note that G_k depends on the results of the previously optimised principal landmarks $\hat{s}_{k-1}$, since the centre of the confidence ellipse k is given by $\check{\mathbf{p}}_{k-1}^{[j_k]}$. A closer inspection of the goal functions G_k within the confidence ellipse k shows that the most important goal functions G_1, G_2, and G_3 exhibit several local minima and maxima. But apart from this minor difficulty, their overall behaviour is fairly smooth and regular. However, due to the hierarchical dependencies, it is essential to reliably locate the global maximum. Therefore, we propose the following simple optimisation scheme: In a first step, we sample the goal function within the bounding box of the confidence ellipse on a coarse grid, in order to find the local neighbourhood of the global optimum. Having done so, we apply the Newton-Raphson method to find the proper optimum. Since the computation of a Newton-Raphson iteration includes the calculation of first and second derivatives, we recommend to fit a bivariate Taylor polynom of fourth degree around the estimated optimum, instead of relying on discrete derivatives.

This optimisation scheme has proven to be robust and it finds reliably the global optimum with high sub-pixel accuracy. The time taken to optimise one principal landmark amounts to about one second on an SGI O_2. Figure 7(d) shows the result of the initialisation, if the optimisation is sequentially applied to six principal landmarks. With the exception of the Splenium of the corpus callosum, the resulting outline is very close to the optimum. A comparison between the final outline and the manual initialisation in Fig. 7(a) shows two differences: On the one hand, the automated method obviously detects the border of the shape with higher precision. On the other hand, manual initialisation seems to be superior with respect to an overall fit to the image data. Although we could speculate that the better estimate induces a higher distortion of the correspondence function, we suspect that the superior performance has another reason: The manual approach simply finds a better solution regarding the problem of optimising the position of all principal landmarks at once. The automatic optimisation of this problem is much more difficult due to the dependencies of the goal functions G_k and has not yet been investigated.

7 Conclusion and Future Research

In search of a stable initialisation oracle that is based on a small number of points, we presented a new way to make a statistical shape description point-wise invariant. The inverse of the resulting operation generates initial configurations for subsequent segmentation by choosing the most probable shape given the estimated control polygon. The whole framework has been evaluated by means of a shape population consisting of 71 corpus callosum instances. To demonstrate its practical benefit, we implemented both an interactive and a fully automatic initialisation method. The achieved results are satisfying and validate its suitability for our initialisation purposes. Furthermore, we gained a deeper insight into the nature of the shape under investigation by finding the most compact shape description given by the principal control polygon with associated principal basis functions.

Additional work has to be done in order to evaluate and improve the practical application of the proposed shape analysis. In the context of interactive initialisation, we must explore the influence of the point selection strategy on the user's ability to locate the prescribed vertices in the image. Since we choose the principal landmarks purely on the basis of a statistical measure, problems may arise in locating the correct position of the points in the image to be segmented. Hence, another point selection strategy could be based on the analysis of *local* shape and image characteristics. Control vertices with salient local curve features or locations with stable image characteristics could serve as landmarks well suited for automatic or interactive localisation. Such point selection oracles should be combined with our statistical selection strategy. Moreover, the automatic initialisation should be improved by optimising all the control vertices at once.

Last but not least, model-based initialisations for surfaces should be provided as well, in order to overcome the limitations imposed by the two-dimensional segmentation approach, if three dimensional data sets are available. And if we broaden the horizons beyond the borders of computer vision, we surmise that our framework could be of great value for the interactive animation of various natural objects.

8 Acknowledgements

We would like to express our sincere gratitude to the BIOMORPH consortium (BIOMORPH, EU-BIOMED2 project no BMH4-CT96-0845) for providing the data and the manual segmentation of the 71 corpora callosa.

A Derivation of the Basis Vectors R_j by Means of the Pseudo-Inverse

Another approach to find the two basis vectors $\mathbf{r}_{x_j}$ and $\mathbf{r}_{y_j}$ causing unit translation in x- and y-direction with minimal Mahalanobis-distance D_m involves the calculation of the generalised Moore-Penrose pseudo-inverse [16, 18]. To derive a solution with this concept, we use only the prescribed constraints as a starting point:

$$U_j R_j = I \tag{19}$$

Since U_j is a $2 \times (N-1)$ matrix, the linear system of equations in (19) is highly *under-determined*. Such a system either has no solution or there will be an $(N-3)$ dimensional family of solutions. In the second case, one can show that there is a unique element in the hyper-plane of all solutions which has minimum 2-norm [19]. It is well known that this least-squares solution can be found by calculating the generalised Moore-Penrose pseudo-inverse $U_j^{\#}$. The resulting vectors R_j with minimal Euclidean norm are then given by

$$R_j = U_j^{\#} I = U_j^{\#} . \tag{20}$$

Unfortunately, we are not looking for the solution with minimal 2-norm but for the one with minimal Mahalanobis-distance D_m. For this reason, we introduce the Mahalanobis-norm $\| \circ \|_m$ that can be expressed in terms of the traditional Euclidean norm:

$$\|\mathbf{x}\|_m = \|\sqrt{\Lambda}^{-1} \mathbf{x}\|_2 \tag{21}$$

If we are able to calculate the least-squares solution with respect to this Mahalanobis-norm, we have automatically found the solution with minimal Mahalanobis-distance, since

$$\|\mathbf{x}\|_m^2 = \|\sqrt{\Lambda}^{-1} \mathbf{x}\|_2^2 = \left(\sqrt{\Lambda}^{-1} \mathbf{x}\right)^T \left(\sqrt{\Lambda}^{-1} \mathbf{x}\right) = \mathbf{x}^T \Lambda^{-1} \mathbf{x} = D_m . \tag{22}$$

By exploiting relation (21), we can map the minimisation of the Mahalanobis-norm to the normal least-squares problem with respect to the Euclidean norm. The required transformation results in a weighting of the columns of U_j by the square root of the corresponding eigenvalues Λ:

$$\min_{R_j} \|R_j\|_m : \quad U_j R_j = I \quad \longmapsto \quad \min_{\breve{R}_j} \|\breve{R}_j\|_2 : \quad \left(U_j\sqrt{\Lambda}\right)\breve{R}_j = I \quad (23)$$

$$R_{j_{\min}} = \sqrt{\Lambda}\breve{R}_{j_{\min}} = \sqrt{\Lambda}\left(U_j\sqrt{\Lambda}\right)^{\#} \quad (24)$$

As illustrated in Eq. (24), the minimal m-norm vectors $R_{j_{\min}}$ are then given by the scaled version of the least-squares solution $\breve{R}_{j_{\min}}$ that is uniquely determined by the pseudo-inverse of $(U_j\sqrt{\Lambda})$. By exploiting subsequently the relation $A^{\#} = A^T\left[AA^T\right]^{-1}$ that holds for $m \times n$ matrices A with $(m < n)$ and rank$(A) = m$ (see [15]), we end up with a fairly familiar result:

$$R_j = \sqrt{\Lambda}\left(U_j\sqrt{\Lambda}\right)^{\#} = \sqrt{\Lambda}\left(\sqrt{\Lambda}U_j^T\left[U_j\Lambda U_j^T\right]^{-1}\right) \quad (25)$$

References

1. Andrew Blake and Michael Isard. *Active Contours*. Springer, first edition, 1998. ISBN 3-54-076217-5.
2. T. F. Cootes, G. J. Edwards, and C. J. Taylor. Active appearance models. In *Proceedings 5th European Conference on Computer Vision*, volume 2, pages 484–498. Springer, 1998. ISBN 3-540-64613-2.
3. T. F. Cootes, A. Hill, C. J. Taylor, and J. Haslam. The use of active shape models for locating structures in medical images. In H. H. Barrett and A. F. Gmitro, editors, *Information Processing in Medical Imaging*, pages 33–47. Springer, June 1993.
4. T. F. Cootes and C. J. Taylor. Active shape models - "Smart Snakes". In *Proceedings British Machine Vision Conference*, pages 266–275, Leeds, 1992. Springer. ISBN 3-540-19777-X.
5. T. F. Cootes and C. J. Taylor. Statistical models of appearance for computer vision. Technical report, University of Manchester, Wolfson Image Analysis Unit, Imaging Science and Biomedical Engineering, Manchester M13 9PT, United Kingdom, September 1999. http://www.wiau.man.ac.uk.
6. M. A. Fischler, J. M. Tenenbaum, and H. C. Wolf. Detection of roads and linear structures in low-resolution aerial imagery using a multisource knowledge integration technique. *Computer Graphics and Image Processing*, 15:201–233, 1981.
7. David R. Forsey and Richard H. Bartels. Hierarchical B-spline refinement. In *Computer Graphics Proceedings SIGGRAPH 1988*, pages 205–212. Addison-Wesley, 1988.
8. J. Hug, C. Brechbühler, and G. Székely. Tamed Snake: A Particle System for Robust Semi-automatic Segmentation. In *Medical Image Computing and Computer-Assisted Intervention - MICCAI'99*, number 1679 in Lecture Notes in Computer Science, pages 106–115. Springer, September 1999.

9. Aapo Hyvärinen. Independent component analysis by minimization of mutual information. Technical Report A46, Helsinki University of Technology, Department of Computer Science and Engineering, Laboratory of Computer and Information Science, Rakentajanaukio 2 C, FIN-02150 Espoo, Finland, August 1997. http://www.cis.hut.fi/~aapo.

10. M. Kass, A. Witkin, and D. Terzopoulos. Snakes: Active contour models. In *Proceedings 1st International Conference on Computer Vision*, pages 259–268, June 1987.

11. András Kelemen. *Elastic Model-Based Segmentation of 2-D and 3-D Neuroradiological Data Sets*. PhD thesis, Swiss Federal Institute of Technology Zürich, Switzerland, 1998. ETH Dissertation No. 12907.

12. András Kelemen, Gábor Székely, and Guido Gerig. Three-dimensional model-based segmentation. In *IEEE International Workshop on Model-Based 3D Image Analysis*, pages 87–96, January 1998.

13. András Kelemen, Gábor Székely, and Guido Gerig. Elastic Model-Based Segmentation of 3-D Neuroradiological Data Sets. *IEEE Transactions on Medical Imaging*, 18(10):828–839, October 1999.

14. F. P. Kuhl and C. R. Giardina. Elliptic Fourier features of a closed contour. *Computer Vision, Graphics, and Image Processing*, 18:236–258, March 1982.

15. Frieder Kuhnert. *Pseudoinverse Matrizen und die Methode der Regularisierung*. Teubner, first edition, 1976.

16. E. H. Moore. On the reciprocal of the general algebraic matrix (abstract). *Bulletin of the American Mathematical Society*, 26:394–395, 1920.

17. E. N. Mortensen, B. Morse, and W. A. Barret. Adaptive boundary detection using live-wire two-dimensional dynamic programming. *Computers in Cardiology*, pages 635–638, October 1992.

18. R. Penrose. A generalized inverse for matrices. *Proceedings Cambridge Philosophical Society*, 51:406–413, 1955.

19. R. Penrose. On best approximate solutions of linear matrix equations. *Proceedings Cambridge Philosophical Society*, 52:17–19, 1956.

20. E. Persoon and K. S. Fu. Shape discrimination using Fourier descriptors. *IEEE Transactions on Systems, Man and Cybernetics*, 7(3):170–179, March 1977.

21. Lawrence H. Staib and James S. Duncan. Boundary finding with parametrically deformable models. *IEEE Transactions on Pattern Analysis and Machine Intelligence (PAMI)*, 14(11):1061–1075, November 1992.

22. Gábor Székely, András Kelemen, Christian Brechbühler, and Guido Gerig. Segmentation of 2-D and 3-D objects from MRI volume data using constrained elastic deformations of flexible Fourier contour and surface models. *Medical Image Analysis*, 1(1):19–34, 1996.

23. A. Yuille, D. Cohen, and P. Hallinan. Feature extraction from faces using deformable templates. In *Proceedings Conference on Computer Vision and Pattern Recognition*, pages 104–109, 1989.

24. Denis Zorin, Peter Schröder, and Wim Sweldens. Interactive multiresolution mesh editing. In *Computer Graphics Proceedings SIGGRAPH 1997*, pages 259–268. Addison-Wesley, 1997.

Statistical Foreground Modelling for Object Localisation

Josephine Sullivan[1], Andrew Blake[2], and Jens Rittscher[1]

[1] Dept. of Engineering, Oxford University, Oxford OX2 3PJ, UK.
{sullivan, jens}@robots.ox.ac.uk,
WWW home page: http://www.robots.ox.ac.uk/~vdg
[2] Microsoft Research Ld., 1 Guildhall Street, Cambridge CB2 3NH, UK.
ablake@microsoft.com

Abstract. A Bayesian approach to object localisation is feasible given suitable likelihood models for image observations. Such a likelihood involves statistical modelling — and learning — both of the object foreground and of the scene background. Statistical background models are already quite well understood. Here we propose a "conditioned likelihood" model for the foreground, conditioned on variations both in object appearance and illumination. Its effectiveness in localising a variety of objects is demonstrated.

1 Introduction

Following "pattern theory" [15, 21], we regard an image of an object as a function $I(\mathbf{x})$, $\mathbf{x} \in \mathcal{D} \subset \mathcal{R}^2$, generated from a template image $\bar{I}(\mathbf{x})$ over a support $\bar{S}$ that has undergone certain distortions. Much of the distortion is accounted for as a warp of the template $\bar{I}(\mathbf{x})$ into the image by a warp mapping T_X:

$$\bar{I}(\mathbf{x}) = I(T_X(\mathbf{x})), \ \mathbf{x} \in \bar{S}, \tag{1}$$

where T_X is parameterised by $X \in \mathcal{X}$ over some configuration space $\mathcal{X}$, for instance planar affine warps. We adopt the convention that $X = 0$ is the template configuration so that T_X is the identity map when $X = 0$.

Using the warp framework, "analysis by synthesis" can be applied to generate the posterior distribution for X. Given a prior distribution $p_0(X)$ for the configuration X, and an observation likelihood $L(X) = p(Z|X)$ where $Z \equiv Z(I)$ is some finite-dimensional representation of the image I, then the posterior density for X is given by

$$p(X|Z) \propto p_0(X)p(Z|X). \tag{2}$$

This can be done very effectively by *factored sampling* [16] which produces a weighted "particle-set" $\{(s^{(1)}, \pi_1), \ldots, (s^{(N)}, \pi_N)\}$, of size N that approximates the posterior [7]. From this approximation of the distribution fusion of inference about X from different sensors, over time and across scales. It also allows a structured way of incorporating prior knowledge to the algorithm.

Much of the challenge with the pattern theory approach is in constructing a suitable matching score. Examples of non-Bayesian approaches include correlation scores [9, 4, 10, 17] and mutual information [27]. But factored sampling, calls for a Bayesian approach in which both the foreground and background image statistics are modelled [14]. In particular, modelling a likelihood $p(Z|X)$ in terms of the foreground/background statistics of receptive field outputs is employed in *Bayesian Correlation* [26]. Although background statistics for Bayesian Correlation, and their independence properties, are quite well understood [11, 22, 1, 28, 6, 25] foreground statistics are more complex.

Foreground statistics should be characterised by the response of a receptive field *conditioned* on its location relative to the object and on the object's pose. This can be achieved by performing template subtraction. This increases the specifity and selectivity between background and foreground over the method of adhoc foreground "partitioning" implemented in [26]. The weakness of the latter approach is demonstrated in figure 1. Even when receptive fields are mutually independent over the background, independence need not necessarily hold over the foreground. It was hoped that the new foreground measurements would also be decorrelated and/or independent. However, it turns out that the statistical dependencies between measurements are not greatly affected by the template subtraction. This paper proposes a more acutely tuned foreground likeli-

Fig. 1. Simple foreground partitioning gives poor selectivity. An *decoy* object produces an alternative likelihood peak of sufficient strength that the mean configuration (black contour) is substantially displaced from the true location of the head. (white contours represent the posterior distribution; wider contours indicate higher likelihood for the face object.)

hood, *conditioned* explicitly on variability of pose and illumination, that pays greater respect to the deterministic properties of the object's geometric layout.

2   Modelling Image Observations

In the framework presented here, image intensities are observed via a bank of filters, isotropic ones in the examples shown here, though steerable, oriented filters [23] would also be eminently suitable. The likelihood of such observations depends both on foreground and background statistics [26] and this approach is reviewed below, before looking more carefully at foreground models in the following section.

2.1 Filter Bank

The observation $Z = Z(I)$ is to be a fixed, finite dimensional representation of the image I, consisting of a vector $Z = (z_1, \ldots, z_K)$ whose components

$$z_k = \int_{S_k} W_{x_k}(\mathbf{x}) I(\mathbf{x}) d\mathbf{x}, \tag{3}$$

are an inner product of the image with a filter function W_{x_k}, over a finite support S_k. In [26] it was argued that a suitable choice of filter function is a Laplacian of Gaussian $W_{\mathbf{x}}$, centred at $\mathbf{x}$:

$$W_{\mathbf{x}}(\mathbf{x}') = \nabla^2 G_\sigma(\mathbf{x}' - \mathbf{x})$$

with hexagonally tesselated, overlapping supports as in figure 2. The scale parameter of

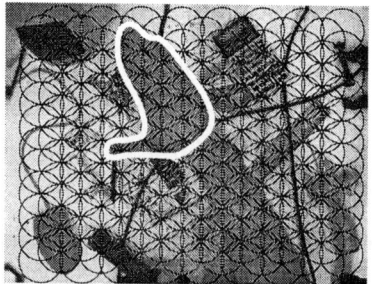

Fig. 2. Tessellation of filter supports. Filters are arranged in a hexagonal tessellation, as shown, with substantial overlap (support radius $r = 40$ pixels illustrated).

the Gaussian is σ and it is adequate to truncate the Gaussian to a finite support of radius $r = 3\sigma$. The tessellation scheme was arrived at [26] by requiring the densest packing of supports while maintaining statistical de-correlation between filters over background scene texture. In practice, at that separation, filter responses are not only decorrelated but also, to a good approximation, independent over the background.

2.2 Probabilistic Modelling of Observations

The observation (ie output value) z from an individual filter is generated by integration over a support-set S such as the circular one in figure 3, which is generally composed of both a background component $B(X)$, and a foreground component $F(X)$:

$$z|X = \underbrace{\int_{B(X)} W(\mathbf{x}) I(\mathbf{x}) \, d\mathbf{x}}_{\text{MAIN NOISE SOURCE}} + \int_{F(X)} W(\mathbf{x}) I(\mathbf{x}) \, d\mathbf{x}. \tag{4}$$

Densities $p^{\mathcal{B}}(z|\rho)$ and $p^{\mathcal{F}}(z|\rho)$, $0 < \rho < 1$ for the background and foreground components of mixed supports must be learned. Then, a particular object hypothesis X is

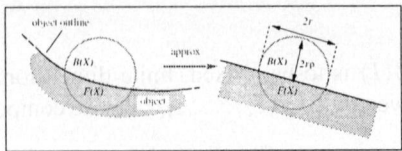

Fig. 3. Foreground and background filter components A circular support set S is illustrated here, split into subsets $F(X)$ from the foreground and $B(X)$ from the background. Assuming that the object's bounding contour is sufficiently smooth, the boundary between foreground and background can be approximated as a straight line. The support therefore divides into segments with offsets $2r\rho$ and $2r(1-\rho)$ for background and foreground respectively.

evaluated as a global likelihood score $p(Z|X)$, based on components $z_1, \ldots, z_K$ which need to have either a known mutual dependence or, simpler still, be statistically independent. Then the observation likelihood can be constructed as a product

$$p(Z|X) = \prod_{k=1}^{K} p(z_k|X). \tag{5}$$

containing terms $p(z_k|X)$ in which the density $p(z_k|X)$ depends, to varying degrees according to the value of X, on each of the learned densities $p^{\mathcal{F}}$ and $p^{\mathcal{B}}$ for the foreground and the background model. This places the requirement on the filter functions W_{X_k}, that they should generate such mutually independent z_k. As mentioned in section 2.1, this is known to be true for z_k over the background. Here we aim to establish independence also over the foreground.

3 Modelling the Foreground Likelihood

The modelling of background components is straightforward [26], simply inferring a density for responses z from a training set of filter outputs z_n, calculated from supports S_n dropped at random over an image [26]. Then $p^{\mathcal{B}}(z|\rho)$ can be learned for some finite set of ρ-values, and interpolated for the ρ-continuum. A similar approach can be used for the foreground case $p^{\mathcal{F}}$ but with some important additional complexities however.

3.1 Spatial Pooling

The distribution $p^{\mathcal{B}}(z|\rho)$ is learned from segments dropped down at random, anywhere on the background. Over the foreground, and in the case that $\rho = 0$, $p^{\mathcal{F}}(z|\rho)$ is similarly learned from a circular support, dropped now at any location wholly inside the training object. However, whenever $\rho > 0$, the support $F(X)$ must touch the object outline; therefore $p^{\mathcal{F}}(z|\rho)$ has to be learned entirely from segments touching the outline. Thus, for $\rho = 0$, statistics are pooled over the whole of the object interior — "spatial pooling", whereas for $\rho > 0$ statistics pooling is restricted to occur over narrow bands, of width $2r(1-\rho)$, running around the inside of the template contour.

Spatial pooling dilutes information contained in the gross spatial arrangement of the grey-level pattern. Sometimes this provides adequate selectivity for the observation likelihood, particularly when the object outline is distinctive, such as the outline of a hand as in figure 2. The outline of a face, though, is less distinctive. In the extreme case of a circular face, and using isotropic filters, rotating the face would not produce any change in the pooled response statistics. In that case, the observation likelihood would carry no information about (2D) orientation. One approach to this problem is to include some anisotropic filters in the filter bank, which would certainly address the rotational indeterminacy. Another approach [26] to enhancing selectivity is to subdivide the interior $\mathcal{F}$ of the object as $\mathcal{F} = \mathcal{F}_0 \cup \dots \cup \mathcal{F}_{N_F}$, and construct individual distributions $p^{\mathcal{F}_i}(z|\rho = 0)$ for each subregion $\mathcal{F}_i$. However, the choice of the number and shape of subregions is somewhat arbitrary. It would be much more satisfying to find a way of increasing selectivity that is tailored specifically to foreground structure, rather than imposing an arbitrary subdivision, and that is what we seek to do in this paper.

3.2 Warp Pooling

In principle the foreground density $p^{\mathcal{F}}$ depends on the full warp T_X. This means that $p^{\mathcal{F}}(z|\rho)$ must be learned not simply from one image, but from a training set of images containing a succession of typical transformations of the object, and this is reasonable enough. In principle, the learned $p^{\mathcal{F}}$ should be parameterised not merely by $\rho(X)$, as was the case for the background, but by the full, multi-dimensional configuration X itself, and that is not computationally feasible. One approach to this problem is that if these variations cannot be modelled parametrically, they can nonetheless be pooled into the general variability represented by $p^{\mathcal{F}}(z|\rho)$. However, such "warp pooling" dilutes the available information about X, especially given that it is combined with spatial pooling as above.

3.3 Foreground Distribution

The predictable behaviour of filter responses over natural scenes, which applies well to background modelling, could not necessarily be expected to apply for foreground models. Filter response over background texture assumes a characteristic kurtotic form, well modelled as by an exponential (Laplace) distribution [6]. The foreground,

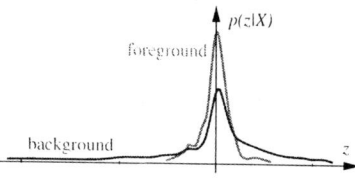

Fig. 4. Foreground and background distributions for support radius $r = 20$ pixels. The background distribution has higher kurtosis, having extended tails.

being associated with just a single object, is less variable and does not have extended tails (figure 4). Hence the exponential distribution that applies well to the background [6] is inapplicable and a normal distribution is more appropriate.

As for independence, filter outputs over the background are known to be uncorrelated at a displacement of r or 3σ but this need not necessarily hold over the foreground. Nonetheless, autocorrelation experiments done over the foreground have produced evidence of good independence for $\nabla^2 G$ filters, as in figure 6 (b).

4 Conditioned Foreground Likelihood: Warping and Illumination Modelling

It was demonstrated in section 1 that greater selectivity is needed in the foreground model. Generally this can be approached by reducing the degree of pooling in the learning of $p^{\mathcal{F}}$. A previous attempt at this inhibited spatial pooling by subdivision, but this is not altogether satisfactory, as explained in the previous section. The alternative investigated here simultaneously diminishes both warp pooling and spatial pooling. It involves warping a template image $\bar{I}$, onto the test image I and taking the warped $T_X(\bar{I})$ to be the mean of the distribution for I. This warping scheme is described in the next section, together with a further elaboration to take account of illumination variations.

4.1 Approximating Warps

Two-dimensional warps T_X could be realised with some precision, as thin plate splines [8]. A more economical, though approximate, approach is proposed here. First the warped outline contour is represented as a parametric spline curve [2], over a configuration-space $\mathcal{X}$, define to be a sub-space of the spline space. Then the warp of the *interior* of the object is approximated as an affine transform by *projecting* the configuration X onto a space of planar-affine transformations [7, ch 6]. The fact that this affine transformation warps the interior only approximately is absorbed by pooling approximation error, during learning, into the foreground distribution $p^{\mathcal{F}}$. The resulting warp of the interior then loses some *specificity* but is still "fair" in that the variability is fairly represented by probabilistic pooling. (A similar approach was taken with pooled camera calibration errors in mosaicing [24].)

To summarise, the warp model is bipartite: an accurate mapping of outline contour coupled with an approximate (affine) mapping of the interior. The precision of the mapped contour ensures that foreground/background discrimination is accurate, and this is essential for precise contour localisation. The approximate nature of the interior mapping is however acceptable because it is used only for intensity compensation in which, especially with large filter scale σ, there is some tolerance.

4.2 Single Template Case

Given a hypothesised warp T_X, the output $z(\mathbf{x})$ of a filter $W_\mathbf{x}$ centred at $\mathbf{x}$ is modelled as

$$z(\mathbf{x}) = \langle W_\mathbf{x}, T_X \cdot \bar{I} + \mathbf{n} \rangle = \langle W_\mathbf{x}, T_X \cdot \bar{I} \rangle + \langle W_\mathbf{x}, \mathbf{n} \rangle \tag{6}$$
$$= \tilde{z}(\mathbf{x}, X) + Y_\mathbf{x}$$

where $\tilde{z}(\mathbf{x}, X)$ is the predicted filter output and where $Y_\mathbf{x}$ is a random variable, whose distribution is to be learned, assumed to be symmetric with zero mean. It is the residue (6) of the predicted intensity from the image data and is likely to have a narrow distribution if prediction is reasonably effective as in figure 5. Thus the distribution p_Y is far more restrictive than $p^{\mathcal{F}}$. Using the $Y_\mathbf{x}$'s instead of the $z(\mathbf{x})$'s in the calculation of the global likelihood $p(Z|X)$ results in more powerful and specific detection.

(a) Template   (b) Image Data   (c) Differenced Image

Fig. 5. Template subtraction.(a) The white contour marks the outline of the intensity template $\bar{I}$. When subtracted from an image I (b), the residue (c) is relatively small, as indicated by the dark area over the face.

Note that the predicted output $\tilde{z}(\mathbf{x}, X)$ can be approximated as

$$\tilde{z}(\mathbf{x}, X) \approx (T_X \cdot W_\mathbf{x} * \bar{I})(\mathbf{x})$$

which is computationally advantageous as the filtered template $W_\mathbf{x} * \bar{I}$ can be computed in advance. The approximation is valid provided T_X is not too far from being a Euclidean isometry. (An affine transformation, which is of course non-Euclidean, will change a circular filter support S, and this generates some error.)

4.3 Light Source Modelling

A family of templates $\bar{I}_1, \ldots, \bar{I}_K$ is generated corresponding to K lighting conditions, and typically $K = 4$ to span a linear space of shadow-free, Lambertian surfaces under variable lighting [5]. So the image data is can be modelled as $I = T_X(\boldsymbol{\alpha} \cdot \bar{I}) + \mathbf{n}$. Now the predicted filter outputs are defined to be

$$\tilde{z}(\mathbf{x}, X, \boldsymbol{\alpha}) = \langle W_{\mathbf{x}}, T_X(\boldsymbol{\alpha} \cdot \bar{\mathbf{I}}) \rangle = \sum_k \alpha_k \langle W_{\mathbf{x}}, T_X \cdot \bar{I}_k \rangle$$

$$= \sum_k \alpha_k \tilde{z}_k(\mathbf{x}, X) \tag{7}$$

Illumination modelling in this way makes for better prediction allowing the distribution of the residual p_Y to become even narrower (see figure 8).

4.4 Joint and Marginal Distributions for Illumination-Compensated Foreground

In order to preserve the validity of (5), the independence of the $Y_{\mathbf{x}}$ for sufficiently separated $\mathbf{x}$ should be checked. For instance, the correlation

$$C[\mathbf{x}, \mathbf{x}'] = \mathcal{E}[Y_{\mathbf{x}}, Y_{\mathbf{x}'}].$$

should $\to 0$ sufficiently fast as $|\mathbf{x} - \mathbf{x}'|$ increases. As figure 6 shows, the correlation

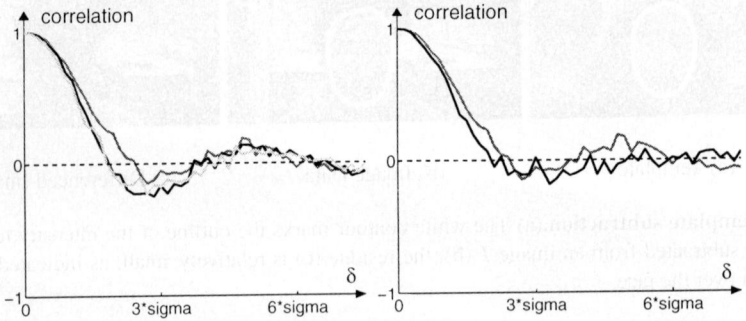

Fig. 6. Foreground correlation. The correlation between filter outputs at various displacements is shown (black) for $Y_{\mathbf{x}}$, the resuidual between the image data and the template and this is very similar to the correlation of the $z(\mathbf{x})$ (grey), and the $Y'_{\mathbf{x}}$ obtained by taking illumination factors into account (light grey). Right: the foreground correlation (grey) is similar to background correlation (black).

has fallen close to zero at a displacement of r, giving independence of adjacent outputs for the support-tessellation of figure 2. Correlation functions for foreground and background are broadly similar and so fit the same grid of filters. Finally, de-correlation is a necessary condition for statistical independence but is not sufficient. Independence properties can be effectively visualised via the conditional histogram [25]. Figure 7 displays histograms which estimate $p(Y_{\mathbf{x}}, Y_{\mathbf{x}'} | |\mathbf{x} - \mathbf{x}'| = \delta)$ where $\delta = \sigma, 2\sigma, 3\sigma$ and $\mathbf{x}$ and $\mathbf{x}'$ are diagonally displaced ($r = 3\sigma$). The greylevel in each histogram represents the frequency in each bin. White indicates high frequency and black none. From these it is clear that at the grid separation $r = 3\sigma$, $Y_{\mathbf{x}}, Y_{\mathbf{x}'}$ are largely independent. It might

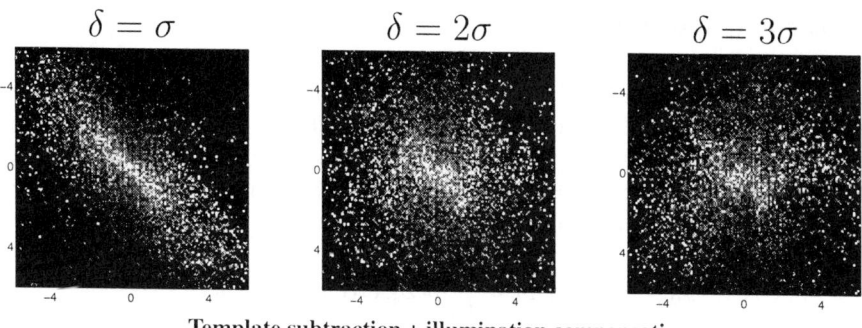

$\delta = \sigma$ $\delta = 2\sigma$ $\delta = 3\sigma$

Template subtraction + illumination compensation

Fig. 7. Joint conditional histograms of pairs of filter responses. As δ increases the structure of the histograms decreases. When $\delta = \sigma$ the white diagonal ridge indicates the correlation between the filter responses. While at $\delta = 3\sigma$ this ridge has straightened and diffused. The two rows of figures are extremely similar and show that the template subtraction and illumination compensation have at most a marginal effect as regards whitening the data.

have been expected that template subtraction, especially with illumination compensation, would have significantly decreased correlation of the foreground but that was not the case. Where there is a significant effect is in the marginal distribution for $p^{\mathcal{F}}$ which becomes significantly narrower, as figure 8 shows.

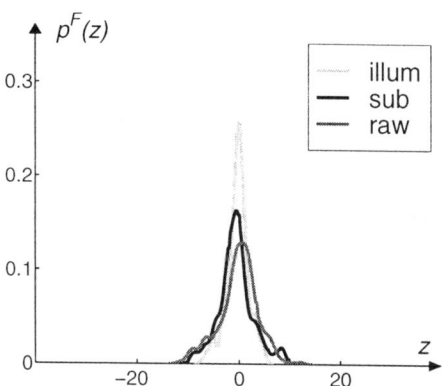

Fig. 8. Illumination compensation narrows $p_Y(Y_\mathbf{x})$. Each of the graph displays p_Y or $p^{\mathcal{F}}(z)$ learnt from data at different stages of preprocessing, Grey:raw filter responses ($p^{\mathcal{F}}(z)$), Black:template subtracted residual responses and Light Grey:template subtracted plus illumination compensated residual responses.

This is a measure of the increased selectivity of modelling the foreground with template subtraction, especially when this is combined with illumination compensation.

5 Learning and Inference

The goal is to infer the value of X from $p(X|Z)$ via Bayes' Rule and the constructed likelihood function $p(Z|X)$. If the test data was labelled with the value of the α of the illumination/object inference would be straight forward. Modelling the illumination results in the fact that we have instead $p(Z|X,\alpha)$. In principle the correct way to proceed would be to integrate α out of $p(Z|X,\alpha)$ to construct

$$L(X) = p(Z|X) = \int_\alpha p(Z|X,\alpha)p_0(\alpha|X)d\alpha \qquad (8)$$

However, due to the probable dimensionality of α and the computational expense of exhaustively calculating $p(Z|X,\alpha)$ it is not feasible to compute this integration numerically. In fact maximisation of $p(Z|X,\alpha)$ over α in place of integration is an well known alternative that is simply an instance of the model selection problem. A factor $G(Z,X)$ known as the "generacity" factor (and has elsewhere been known as the "Occam" factor [20]) is a measure of robustness [12] of the inferred $\hat{\alpha}$ — the stability of Z with respect to fluctuations in α:

$$G(Z,X) = \frac{\int_\alpha p(Z|X,\alpha)p_0(\alpha|X)d\alpha}{p(Z|X,\hat{\alpha}(X,Z))} \qquad (9)$$

The generacity G is then the additional weight that would need to be applied to the maximised likelihood

$$\hat{L}(X) \equiv L(X,\hat{\alpha})$$

to infer the posterior distribution for X:

$$p(X|Z) \propto \hat{L}(X)G(Z,X)p_0(X). \qquad (10)$$

If $G(Z,X)$ does not vary greatly then it is reasonable to use $\hat{L}(X)$ instead of $p(Z|X)$.

5.1 MLE for Illumination Parameters

As stated it has been assumed that the residual variable Y_x in 6 is drawn from the stationary distribution p_Y. The likelihood function for particular values of X and α is the product of three separate components, the likelihood of the hypothesised background, foreground and mixed measurements as:

$$L(X,\alpha) = p(Z|X,\alpha) = \prod_{i\in\mathcal{I}_F} p_Y(Y_{\mathbf{x}_i},\alpha) \prod_{i\in\mathcal{I}_B} p^B(z_i) \prod_{i\in\mathcal{I}_M} p(z_i|\rho(X)) \qquad (11)$$

$$= L_F(X,\alpha)L_B(X)L_M(X)$$

where $\mathcal{I}_{\{F,B,M\}}$ are the sets containing the foreground, background and mixed measurements. In the implementation of template subtraction and illumination compensation only the foreground measurements are affected. Therefore only L_F is dependent upon α.

317

Intuitively it would seem reasonable to solve for α by maximising L_F in 11 with respect to α:

$$\hat{\alpha}(Z, X) = \arg\max_{\alpha} L_F(X, \alpha) \tag{12}$$

and then proceed with α fixed as $\hat{\alpha}$ and $p(Z|X, \alpha)$ is used. A functional form of p_Y is needed though in order to be able to differentiate equation 12. From figure 8 it is plausible to assume that p_Y is a zero mean Gaussian with variance γ^2. It then follows that

$$L_F(X, \alpha) \sim \mathrm{MVN}(\mathbf{0}, \gamma^2 I_{K \times K}) \tag{13}$$

where $I_{K \times K}$ is the identity matrix and MVN stands for the multi-variate normal distribution. Obviously maximisation of equation 13 is equivalent to the least squares minimisation

$$\hat{\alpha}(Z, X) = \arg\min_{\alpha} \sum_{n} (z(\mathbf{x}_i) - \tilde{z}(\mathbf{x}_i, X, \alpha))^2 \tag{14}$$

Thus in the factored sampling algorithm for inferring X the following is implemented. For each hypothesis X_h a corresponding MLE $\hat{\alpha}_h$ is calculated and the likelihood $L(Z|X)$ is approximated by $L(Z|X, \hat{\alpha}_h)$.

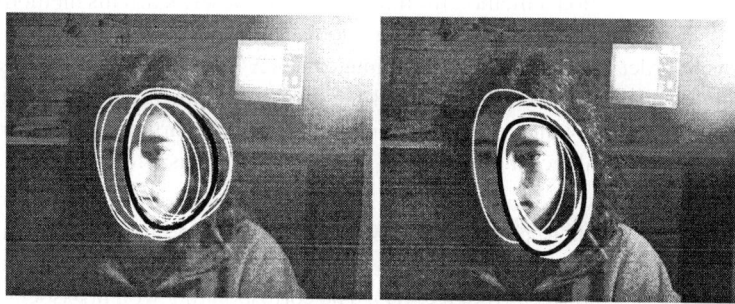

No illumination Modelling

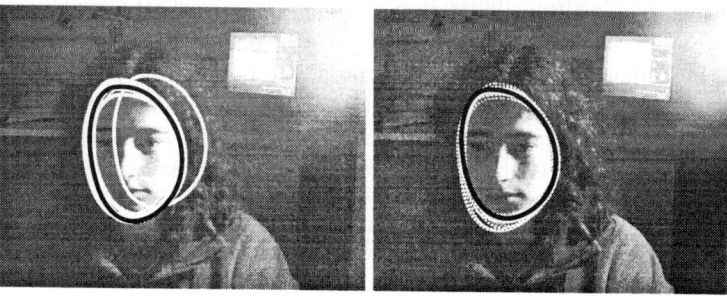

Illumination Modelling

Fig. 9. Illumination modelling improves detection results. Layered sampling at two levels (r=40 and 20 pixels) with the *conditioned* foreground likelihood model in which illumination is not modelled and it is. In the latter case α is inferred by its MLE value. The gross change in the illumination conditions foils the naive *conditioned* foreground likelihood.

For the experiments performed in figure 9, the MLE method is used to infer α. However, it remains to be confirmed experimentally that $G(Z|X)$ remains more or less constant. In this experiment a shadow basis was formed by taking three images with the point light source to the left, right and behind of the subject. Then a sequence of 267 frames in which the light source moved around the subject was used as test data. In every fifth frame the face person was searched for using layered sampling with the *conditioned* foreground likelihood, independent of the results from the previous search. Two levels of layered sampling were applied ($r = 40, 20$) and 900 samples at each level. The prior for the object's affine configuration space was uniform over $x, y-$translation and Gaussian over the other parameters allowing the contour to scale to $\pm 20\%$ horizontally, vertically or diagonally and rotate 20 degrees from its original position. (Each of the 6 parameters were treated independently). Using the proposed method the face was successfully located at each frame. However, when illumination was not modelled detection was not always successful. Two frames in which this happened are shown in figure 9. To see the results of the whole sequence please see **http://www.robots.ox.ac.uk/ sullivan/Movies/FaceIlluminated.mpg**.

5.2 Sampling Illumination Parameters

In the previous subsection a method for inferring α was described. This method though is not Bayesian. The alternative is to extend the state vector to $X' = (X, \alpha)$ and to sample this in order to obtain a particle estimate of $p(X'|Z)$. This however, is likely to be computationally burdensome because of the increased dimensionality and also due to the broad prior from which α must be drawn. Usually no particular prior for α will be known and in accordance a uniform one will be generally used.

The alternative is to use an importance sampling function [18] $g_X(\alpha)$ that restricts α to its likely range. It is possible to incorporate this importance function into the factored sampling process as follows. Draw a sample X_h from $p_0(X)$. Given this fixed value of X draw a sample α_h from $g_{X_h}(\alpha)$. The corresponding weight associated with the particle $X'_h = (X_h, \alpha_h)$ is $L(X'_h)/g_{X_h}(\alpha_h)$ (the denominator is the correction factor applied to compensate for the bias shown towards certain α values).

The most important question has yet to be answered. From where can an appropriate importance function $g(\alpha)$ be found ? In fact we don't have to look any further than the partial likelihood function L_F. From equation 13 this can be approximated by a multi-variate normal distribution with diagonal covariance matrix. This then implies that α given a fixed value of X is also a multi-variate normal distribution whose covariance matrix and mean can be easily calculated. Allowing this distribution to be $g(\alpha)$ results in an importance function that can be sampled from exactly and greatly narrows the range of possible α values.

6 Results and Conclusions

Results of localisation by factored sampling, using the new *conditioned* foreground likelihood are shown next, and compared with the "partitioned foreground" approach

319

of [26]. Each figure displays an image plus the particle representation of the posterior distribution for the configuration of the target object. For clarity, just the 15 most highly weighted particles are displayed. The weight of each particle being represented, on a log scale, by the width of the contour. The black contour represents the mean configuration of the particle set. Three different sets of experiments were carried out. Firstly it was checked if the new likelihood was prone to highlighting the same false positives as the partitioned likelihood and this is investigated with the decoy test. Then does the new method work for face detection and finally can it detect other textured objects.

The decoy test In figure 1, it was shown using a face decoy that the partitioned foreground model was prone to ghost object hypotheses. Results of this experiment with the new, conditioned foreground likelihood are shown in figure 10. Note the effect on the mean configuration (the black contour): for the partitioned foreground, the mean lies between the two peaks in the posterior. With the conditioned likelihood the posterior is unimodal however, as evidenced by the coincidence of the mean configuration with the main particle cluster. Experiments were carried out at one scale level $r = 40$ and using 1200 particles, uniformly distributed, the translational component of the prior being drawn deterministically (ie on a regular grid), for efficiency. For computational

Partitioned foreground   **Conditioned likelihood**

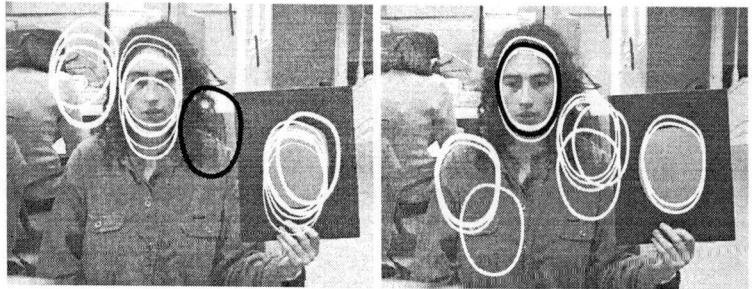

Fig. 10. Conditioned foreground likelihood eliminates ghosting. Foreground partitioning produces a bimodal posterior distribution (plainly visible from the position of the mean contour) while conditioned foreground gives a unimodal distribution.

efficiency, multi-scale processing can be applied via "layered sampling" [26] and this is demonstrated with person-specific models, for two different people, in figure 11. The prior for the affine configuration space is uniform over $x, y-$translation and Gaussian over the other parameters allowing the contour to scale to $\pm20\%$ horizontally, vertically or diagonally and rotate 20 degrees from its original position. (Each of the 6 configuration space parameters are treated independently) This prior is used for the rest of the experiments unless otherwise stated.

Fig. 11. Layered sampling demonstrated for individuals, using individual-specific models this figure. The prior for the position in the face is uniform in the $x, y-$translation over the image. The search takes place over two scales ($r = 20, 10$) implemented via layered sampling, using 1500 samples in each layer.

Generalisation Experimentally, a model trained on one individual turns out to be capable of distinguishing the faces of a range of individuals from general scene background. The experiment used the learnt model from figure 11 (a) and applied it to the images displayed in figure 12. Once again two levels of layered sampling were applied ($r = 20, 10$), now increasing the number of samples increased to 3000. This perfor-

Fig. 12. Generalisation of face detection. Training on a single face generates a model that is still specific enough to discriminate each of a variety of faces against general scene background.

mance is achieved without resorting to the more complex, multi-object training procedure of 7.1, though it remains to test what improvements in multi-object training would bring.

Detecting various textured objects Finally, the conditioned foreground likelihood model has been tested on a variety of other objects, as in figure 13. Note that even in the case of a the textured vase resting against a textured sofa, the vase object is successfully localised. Given that the boundary edge of the vase is not distinct, edge based methods would not be expected to work well here. (Layered sampled was applied at scales $r = 20, 10$ pixels with 1200 particles in each layer.) The prior in the clown example allows for a greater rotation, while in the shoe example the prior has been narrowed.

Fig. 13. Textured inanimate objects can also be localised by the algorithm. Special note should be taken of the detection of the vase against the textured sofa.

7   Discussion and Future Work

7.1   Modelling Object Variability

In addition to lighting variations, a further generalisation is to allow object variations. For example, in the case of faces, varying physiognomy and/or expression. This could be dealt with in conventional fashion [19] by training from a set $I_1^*, I_2^*, \ldots$ covering both object and illumination variations, and using Principal Components Analysis (PCA) to generate templates $\bar{I}_1, \ldots, \bar{I}_K$ that approximately spans the training set. Then the methodology of the previous section can be followed as before.

Alternatively, it may be the case that the training set is explicitly labelled with illumination conditions $k = 1, \ldots, K$ and basis-object index $j = 1, \ldots, M$, in which case the training set is organised as $\{I_{jk}\}$ and these could be used directly as templates $\{\bar{I}_{jk}\}$. Then a general image is

$$I = \sum_{j,k} \alpha_{jk} \bar{I}_{jk} = \sum_{j,k} \beta_j \gamma_k \bar{I}_{jk}$$

where γ_k weights light-sources and β_j weights basis objects. Thus the KM weights α_{jk} applied to the templates decompose as $\beta_j \gamma_k$, and so have just $K + M$ degrees of freedom. This is a familiar type of bilinear organisation, the "style and content" decomposition [13], that occurs also with the decomposition of facial expression and pose [3]. Imposing the bilinear constraint that $\alpha = \beta \gamma^\top$, which stabilises the estimation of α, can be performed as usual by SVD.

In this bilinear situation, the earlier model (7) is extended to take account of light source variations as follows.

$$\tilde{z}(\mathbf{x}, X, A) = \sum_{j,k} \alpha_{jk} \tilde{z}_{j,k}(\mathbf{x}, X) \qquad (15)$$

where

$$\tilde{z}_{j,k}(\mathbf{x}, X) = \langle W_{\mathbf{x}}, T_X \cdot \bar{I}_{j,k} \rangle .$$

and A is a matrix whose entries are α_{jk}.

Acknowledgements. We are grateful for the support of the EU (JR) and the EPSRC (JS).

References

1. R. Baddeley. Searching for filters with interesting output distributions: an uninteresting direction to explore?. *Network*, 7(2):409–421, 1996.
2. R.H. Bartels, J.C. Beatty, and B.A. Barsky. *An Introduction to Splines for use in Computer Graphics and Geometric Modeling.* Morgan Kaufmann, 1987.
3. B. Bascle and A. Blake. Separability of pose and expression in facial tracking and animation. In *Proc. 6th Int. Conf. on Computer Vision*, pages 323–328, 1998.
4. B. Bascle and R. Deriche. Region tracking through image sequences. In *Proc. 5th Int. Conf. on Computer Vision*, pages 302–307, Boston, Jun 1995.
5. P.N. Belhumeur and D.J. Kriegman. What is the set of images of an object under all possible illumination conditions. *Int. J. Computer Vision*, 28(3):245–260, 1998.
6. A.J. Bell and T.J. Sejnowski. Edges are the independent components of natural scenes. In *Advances in Neural Information Processing Systems*, volume 9, pages 831–837. MIT Press, 1997.
7. A. Blake and M. Isard. *Active contours.* Springer, 1998.
8. F.L. Bookstein. Principal warps:thin-plate splines and the decomposition of deformations. *IEEE Trans. on Pattern Analysis and Machine Intelligence*, 11(6):567–585, 1989.
9. P.J. Burt. Fast algorithms for estimating local image properties. *Computer Vision, Graphics and Image Processing*, 21:368–382, 1983.
10. T.F. Cootes, C.J. Taylor, D.H. Cooper, and J. Graham. Active shape models — their training and application. *Computer Vision and Image Understanding*, 61(1):38–59, 1995.
11. D.J. Field. Relations between the statistics of natural images and the response properties of cortical cells. *J. Optical Soc. of America A.*, 4:2379–2394, 1987.
12. W.T. Freeman. The generic viewpoint assumption in a framework for visual perception. *Nature*, 368:542–545, 1996.
13. W.T. Freeman and J.B. Tenenbaum. Learning bilinear models for two-factor problems in vision. In *Proc. Conf. Computer Vision and Pattern Recognition*, pages 554–560, June 1997.
14. D. Geman and B. Jedynak. An active testing model for tracking roads in satellite images. *IEEE Trans. on Pattern Analysis and Machine Intelligence*, 18(1):1–14, 1996.
15. U. Grenander. *Lectures in Pattern Theory I, II and III.* Springer, 1976–1981.
16. U. Grenander, Y. Chow, and D.M. Keenan. *HANDS. A Pattern Theoretical Study of Biological Shapes.* Springer-Verlag. New York, 1991.
17. G.D. Hager and K. Toyama. Xvision: combining image warping and geometric constraints for fast tracking. In *Proc. 4th European Conf. Computer Vision*, pages 507–517, 1996.
18. J.M. Hammersley and D.C. Handscomb. *Monte Carlo methods.* Methuen, 1964.
19. A. Lanitis, C.J. Taylor, and T.F. Cootes. A unified approach to coding and interpreting face images. In *Proc. 5th Int. Conf. on Computer Vision*, pages 368–373, 1995.
20. D.J.C. MacKay. *Bayesian Methods for Adaptive Models.* PhD thesis, California Institute of Technology, 1992.

21. D. Mumford. Pattern theory: a unifying perspective. In D.C. Knill and W. Richard, editors, *Perception as Bayesian inference*, pages 25–62. Cambridge University Press, 1996.
22. B.A. Olshausen and D.J. Field. Emergence of simple-cell receptive field properties by learning a sparse code for natural images. *Nature*, 381:607–609, 1996.
23. P. Perona. Steerable-scalable kernels for edge detection and junction analysis. *J. Image and Vision Computing*, 10(10):663–672, 1992.
24. S.M. Rowe and A. Blake. Statistical mosaics for tracking. *J. Image and Vision Computing*, 14:549–564, 1996.
25. E.P. Simoncelli. Modeling surround suppression in V1 neurons with a statistically-derived normalization model. In *Advances in Neural Information Processing Systems*, volume 11, page in press. MIT Press, 1997.
26. J. Sullivan, A. Blake, M. Isard, and J. MacCormick. Object localization by bayesian correlation. In *Proc. 7th Int. Conf. on Computer Vision*, volume 2, pages 1068–1075, 1999.
27. P. Viola and W.M. Wells. Alignment by maximisation of mutual information. In *Proc. 5th Int. Conf. on Computer Vision*, pages 16–23, 1993.
28. S.C. Zhu and D. Mumford. GRADE: Gibbs reaction and diffusion equation. *IEEE Trans. on Pattern Analysis and Machine Intelligence*, 19(11):1236–1250, 1997.

Nautical Scene Segmentation Using Variable Size Image Windows and Feature Space Reclustering

P.Voles, A.A.W. Smith, and M.K. Teal

Machine Vision Group, Bournemouth University, UK
{pvoles, asmith, mteal}@bournemouth.ac.uk

Abstract This paper describes the development of a system for the segmentation of small vessels and objects present in a maritime environment. The system assumes no a priori knowledge of the sea, but uses statistical analysis within variable size image windows to determine a characteristic vector that represents the current sea state. A space of characteristic vectors is searched and a main group of characteristic vectors and its centroid found automatically by using a new method of iterative reclustering. This method is an extension and improvement of the work described in [9]. A Mahalanobis distance measure from the centroid is calculated for each characteristic vector and is used to determine inhomogenities in the sea caused by the presence of a rigid object. The system has been tested using several input image sequences of static small objects such as buoys and small and large maritime vessels moving into and out of a harbour scene and the system successfully segmented these objects.

1 Introduction

Maritime vessels are today faced with the threat of piracy. Piracy is usually associated with the old swash buckling films and consequently we do not consider piracy in the modern age, however several incidents of piracy happen each day, particularly in the Mallaca straights and the South China Sea areas. Here fast RIB craft (Rigid Inflatable Boats) approach the stern of a large cargo ship, even super-tankers, and scale the ship using simple rope ladders. The small numbers of crew that these ships have on duty means pirate detection needs to be automated. Current Radar systems are of limited use in these situations as RIB craft are small almost non-metallic and consequently have poor radar returns and as such radar systems find them difficult to detect. To overcome this problem an image processing system is under development.

The maritime scene, however, has been found to be extremely complex to analyse [1], [2], producing large number of motion cues making identification and tracking in the visual environment complex. The system being developed here concentrates on the task of extracting the maritime vessels and other static nautical objects (buoys, mooring buoys, piers, etc.) from the sea to aid the recognition and tracking process. To accomplish this task three integrated algorithms have been developed, namely (i) variable size image window analysis, (ii) statistical analysis by reclustering and (iii) region segmentor. The variable window analysis determines a set of overlapping image windows and, for each image window, calcualtes the energy, entropy, homogeneity and contrast. This vector effectively forms a four-dimensional feature for each image window. The statistical analyser uses a new method of iterative reclustering of the feature space to determine the centroid of vectors representing the main feature in the scene (sea) [7]. The region segmentor calculates the Mahalanobis distance between the values of the feature centroid in each image window which identifies outliers from the mean. These outliers are potentially regions that contain inhomogeneities, effectively forming a feature map [3], which may indicate the presence of a rigid object. These extracted regions effectively form regions of interest (ROI) in the image, and the region segmentor identifies these ROI's in the original image sequence using white rectangular boxes.

Figure 1. Typical nautical scene.

2 Window Analysis

The segmentation of a maritime scene is complicated by the fact that waves cause noise (undesirable regions of interest) that does not have a Gaussian distribution, and consequently traditional ways of filtering are ineffective. The main properties of this noise are spatial dependent i.e. its appearance. Fig. 1 shows a typical maritime scene and we can see that the noise is not distributed uniformly in the image, a noise 'pattern' is formed which can clearly be seen in the bottom of the image.

Commonly used texture techniques (as described in many texts such as [10]) proved to be unsuccessful in describing the distribution of these noise patterns as they differ from scene to scene and frame to frame. However, from looking at a typical nautical scene, we observe a plane (sea level) that is almost parallel to the camera axis.

The bottom of the image contains that part of the sea that is closest to the camera, while the horizon is made up of points at infinity on the sea level plane [4]. Therefore, the resolution of observation is larger for any objects that are close to the bottom of image than for objects that are closer to the horizon. This also holds true for the noise patterns. Using this observation we can see that a variable size image window segmentation technique will require finer (smaller) image windows as we approach the horizon, but courser (larger) image windows could be used closer to the bottom of the image. The variable image analysis algorithm is passed the position of the image horizon and an initial window size.

Overlapping image windows are determined by growing the window size from an initial 16 by 16 pixels on the horizon line towards the bottom line of the image at a rate of 6% per window line. For our experiments we used rates from 5% to 10% depending on the camera angle under which the scenes are observed. The image windows are allowed to overlap by 33%. This effectively positions a grid on the sea plane as shown in Fig. 2. If we consider perspectivity then the correct shape of the projected grid tiles should be trapezoidal. This brings a complication to the process because we would have to use bilinear or other perspective transformation for each of the windows to transform it into a rectangle. These transformations are computationally intensive. However, it has been found that rectangles provide a good approximation of trapezoidal segments. The size of the windows and the amounts of overlays are stretched accordingly so the windows cover a whole region under observation and there are no uncovered 'blind spots' on the sides and at the bottom of the image.

Each window is then resized to the size of the smallest windows (a window near the horizon) by using either simple re-sampling or bilinear interpolation. Bilinear interpolation gives better results but is slower, while simple re-sampling gives poorer results but is much faster and for most applications is sufficient. The final task of the variable window analysis is to calculate the following statistical values[5] for each image window:

$$energy = \sum_{r=0}^{R} \sum_{c=0}^{C} P(r,c)^2 . \tag{1}$$

$$entropy = \sum_{r=0}^{R} \sum_{c=0}^{C} \log(P(r,c)) \cdot P(r,c) . \tag{2}$$

$$homogeneity = \sum_{r=0}^{R} \sum_{c=0}^{C} \frac{P(r,c)}{1+|r-c|} . \tag{3}$$

$$contrast = \sum_{r=0}^{R} \sum_{c=0}^{C} (r - c)^2 \cdot P(r,c) \ . \tag{4}$$

where r, c are row and column indexes, $P(r,c)$ is the pixel value at position r,c and R, C are the image window boundaries. The calculated values are arranged to form a 4-element vector, giving N 4-element feature vectors, where N is the total number of windows in the segmentation.

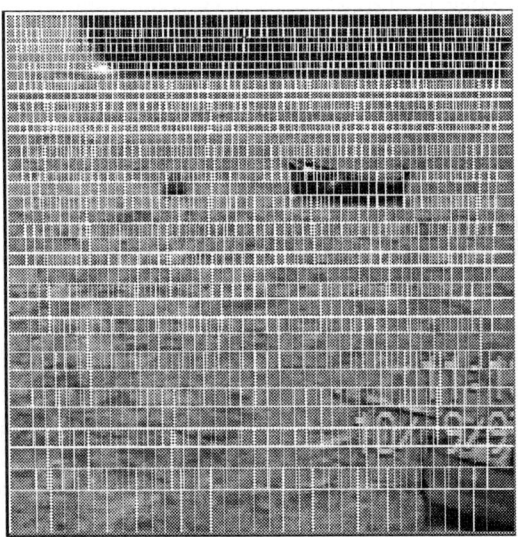

Figure 2. Variable Image Windows overlaid on the sea, minimum window size of 16 x 16 pixels with 33% overlap and an expansion rate of 6%.

3 Statistical Analyser

We can consider the vectors calculated from the variable window analysis as a population of points in a 4-dimensional feature space. The statistical analyser determines a set of characteristic features that could be used to describe the current sea state. This set is represented by a main cluster in the feature space.The previous algorithm used to find the main cluster is described in [9]. This algorithm uses histograms that are constructed for each of the four previously described characteristics. It divides the smoothed data histograms into subparts by local minima and assigns the largest subpart to the main cluster. This method does not perform well for smaller numbers of feature vectors. In these cases it becomes difficult to find the correct local minima because of the lack of data needed to create meaningful histograms. Another disadvantage is the presence of many thresholds whose settings influence the results significantly.

A new method is introduced that helps to approximate the distribution of the unlabelled feature vector data in feature space. The method takes feature vectors generated at the previous stage of the algorithm (variable size image windows analysis) as an input and it iteratively determines the centroid and the covariance matrix for the data in the main cluster. The problem here is that there is no useful knowledge about the data due to the nature of the problem (each scene segmented in the previous stage of the algorithm can be significantly different from the previous one in terms of sea appearance and presence of objects). The only usable knowledge is that there is a certain main cluster in the feature space which comprises the vectors corresponding to major features in the scene (presumably the sea). These vectors are relatively close to one another. Other vectors (outliers) represent regions where objects are in the scene and these vectors are relatively far from the main cluster and it's centroid. Unfortunately, due to the nature of the problem, we cannot use learning and classification algorithms (as described in Shalkoff [6]) as the feature data can change its values disobeying any rule at all. The distributions of feature data change from scene to scene and the only usable information is the presence of the main cluster and possible outliers.

We assume that the main cluster contains the majority of vectors and that these vectors are relatively close to one another. Other vectors or groups of vectors (representing the objects) are positioned relatively far from this main cluster. Therefore, if we calculate the centroid of all the vectors in the distribution by using the mean, or better, median then we can assume that this centroid of all vectors is not far from the centroid of only the vectors in main cluster. That is, because there are many vectors close together whose position will bias (or attract) the position of the centroid determined as the median of all vectors in the feature space. Experiments have proved that median performed better than mean because median is not influenced by a small number of outlying vectors. The next step after determining the centroid of the whole distribution in feature space is to choose which vectors actually fall into the main cluster. We assume that the main cluster lies within the boundary that corresponds to the mean distance of all the vectors from the determined centroid. Thus, the resulting group of vectors has a centroid corresponding to the median of all vectors in the distribution and includes vectors with distance's less than the mean distance of all the vectors in the distribution in the feature space.

The next step is similar to the one described above: once again, we determine the median centroid but now we use only the vectors lying within the mean distance from the previous centroid. We recalculate the mean distance from the newly calculated centroid for all the vectors in the group. The new main cluster consists of the vectors that lie within the new mean distance from the new centroid.

This process is repeated iteratively. The number of iterations is not significantly large as after each step the group of selected vectors shrinks significantly, especially if the main cluster is packed tightly together. Practical experiments proved that one to three iterations are sufficient.

We use the Mahalanobis measure to determine the distances among feature vectors:

$$k = (\vec{x} - \vec{\mu}) \cdot C^{-1} \cdot (\vec{x} - \vec{\mu})^T \ . \tag{5}$$

where k is the distance, $\vec{x}$ is the feature vector, $\vec{\mu}$ is the centroid and C^{-1} is the inverse of covariance matrix. The reason for using the Mahalanobis distance is that the data is highly correlated. The Mahalanobis distance used in this method is slightly modified - the centroid used in the formula is not determined as a mean but as a median. The reason for that, as stated above, is the avoidance of outliers. This method only determines the main cluster and it's centroid approximately but as we haven't got any prior knowledge about the data it is sufficient to determine the outliers that represent the regions with objects in the scene. Experiments proved that the separation of outliers from the main cluster vectors is by means of orders (value of Mahalanobis distance of outliers from the centroid is by a few orders higher than the distance of vectors in the main cluster) even for highly scattered feature vectors. Another important property of the method is the fact that it does not shift the centroid of the feature vectors significantly if the data is relatively consistent and does not contain any outliers.

The main advantage of the algorithm is that there is no need for prior knowledge to approximate the distribution of the vectors in the main cluster. Another important advantage is the absence of any thresholds. The only value that is to be set is the number of iterations and as stated above, one to three iterations are sufficient. Figures 3a-3f show two iterations of the reclustering process in 2D projections of the feature space.

The statistical analyser applies the method described above onto the feature vectors determined by variable size image windows analysis and it determines the Mahalanobis distance from the main cluster centroid for each of the vectors.

4 Region Segmentor

The statistical analyser has calculated the distances of the feature vectors from the centroid of the main cluster which represents the main feature in the image (presumably the sea), the region segmentor must now determine those image windows whose feature vectors have Mahalanobis distance above the set up threshold. The values of the Mahalanobis distance for each vector provide a measure of the likelihood of an image window being an object, the greater the distance value the more the likelihood of it being a vessel or other man-made object. Figure 5 shows the result of transforming the values of the Mahalanobis distance measure back into the image plane, the darker the image window, the greater the likelihood of that tile being a region of interest. The Mahalanobis distances are now scanned and the rate of change of the distance is calculated. If the rate of change is below a threshold value, the Mahalanobis distance is replaced with the minimum of that region. Finally Mahalanobis distances which have minimum values correspond to be the primary feature in the scene, namely

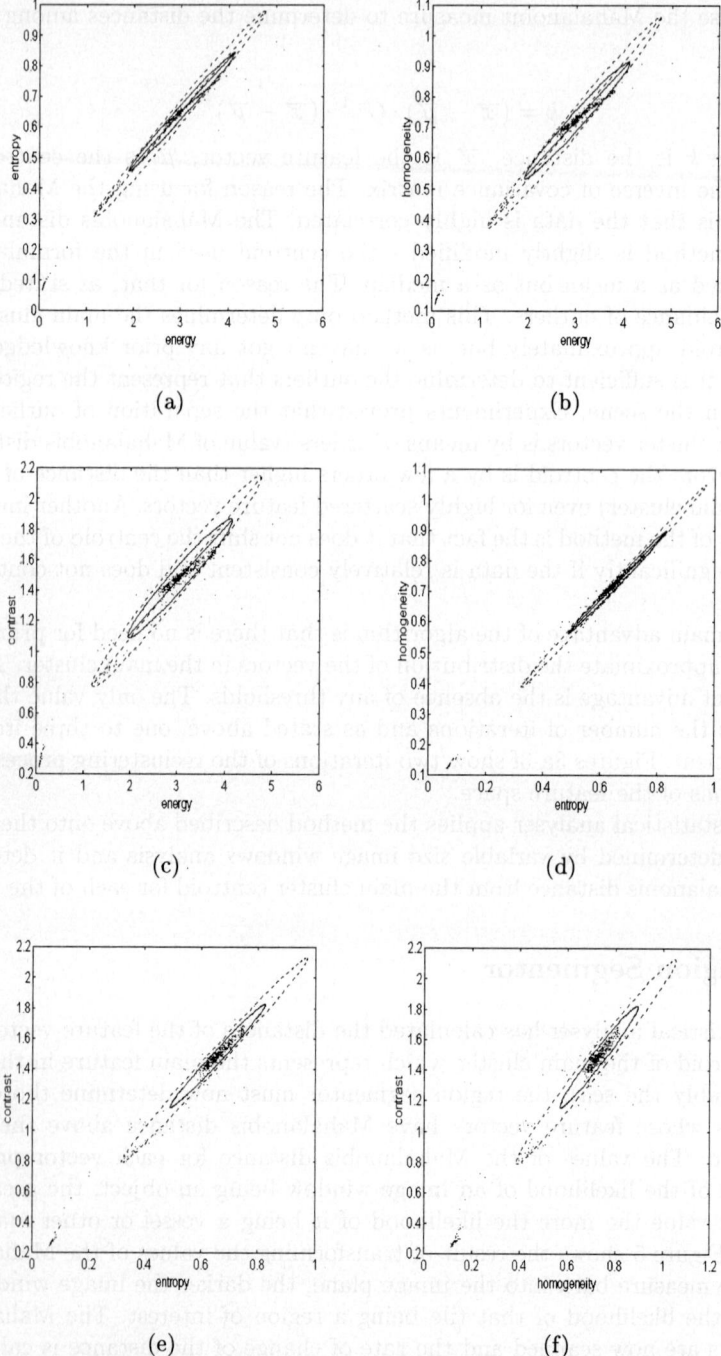

(a) (b)

(c) (d)

(e) (f)

Figure 3. 2D projections of feature space showing the re-alignment of the elipsoid representing the main cluster (dashed line - 1st iteration, solid line 2nd iteration).

the sea (Fig. 4). The determination of the primary feature works even if the object covers the majority of the scene. The main feature then represents the object and outliers, determined by a large distance value, represent either sea or other smaller objects.

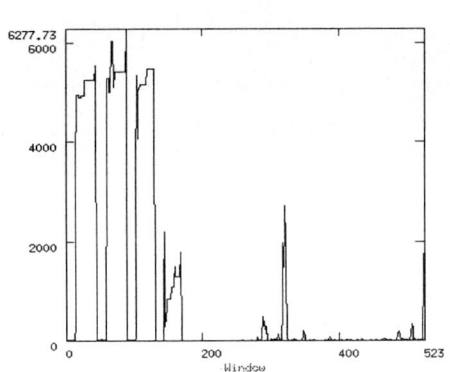

Figure 4. Mahalanobis distance of feature vectors from the centroid of the main cluster after process of homogenizing (distance values are substituted by local minima).

5 Discussion

A static camcorder was set up at the entrance to Portsmouth harbour and an image sequence showing small motor vessels and in particular RIBs moving out of the harbour was filmed. From this sequence a 1500 frame clip was digitised to disk at a rate of 10 frames per second. A second sequence was filmed at Poole harbour showing yachts and buoys moving in the scene and a third showing a medium sized vessel approaching a pier.

The error rate of the segmentation was determined as a ratio between number of frames where the segmentation was incorrect (i.e., rigid objects present in scene were not found or false regions without any objects were marked) and total number of frames in each sequence. This ratio is stated in percentage terms.

Figures 6a and 6b show the Portsmouth scene where a larger motor vessel led a procession of five smaller motor vessel out of the harbour. The algorithm correctly segmented the motor vessels 91% of the time, however, as the vessels moved across the scene several segmented regions were merged. This particular sequence included a number of RIBs.

Figures 7a and 7b show the Poole scene where small and large yachts were moving into and out of the harbour entrance together with a small buoy. The

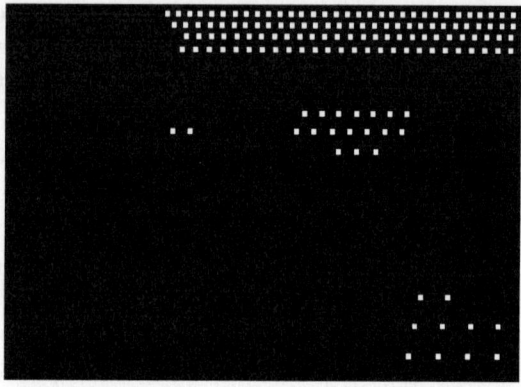

Figure 5. Mahalanobis distance transformed back to image plane. Blobs are positioned at the centers of windows used in segmentation. Brightness of the blob corresponds to the likelihood of object beeing present in the window.

system segmented out the yachts 95% of the time, however, again as vessels crossed, the segmented regions were merged. The system did however, incorrectly segment the buoy 15% of the time but this is still an improvement on the results shown in [9].

Figure 7a shows that algorithm has found only the bottom of the large yacht. The reason for this is, that the algorithm is segmenting only the sea. It ignores everything above the shore. Thus, this algorithm serves only as a partial solution of maritime scene segmentation task.

Figures 8a and 8b show the ability of the system to correctly segment either static and moving objects in the scene even if these cover large areas of the image.

6 Conclusion

A method for segmenting static man-made objects and small vessels moving in a maritime scene has been developed and has been shown to provide reliable segmentation results for a number of maritime scenes. The algorithm uses simple mathematical operators to build a statistical character of the sea. A new method of feature space re-clustering is has been introduced for statistical analysis, based on the work first described in [9].

One advantage of the algorithm is the use of only the current image in the segmentation process, the algorithm does not rely on any change between consecutive images to provide the regions of interest. It does not rely on any prior knowledge about the characteristics representing the sea. It efficiently eliminates the noise caused by the motion of the sea, and has demonstrated within the constraints of the project that this is both scene and time independent.

However, the algorithm as it stands requires initial start positions for the horizon and the minimum window size which must be passed to the algorithm at the start of processing. It also requires the threshold value for separating the main feature from outliers which is the main drawback at the moment. It does not give an exact and final identification about any objects in the scene, it provides only a measure of the objects presence.

Future enhancements to the algorithm are aimed at addressing automating the horizon identification, determining a function for homogenising the Mahalanobis distance measure to preserve outliers and using connectivity analysis to produce improved object detection. The future development is also oriented to find and process the temporal correspondence of the detected regions in the sequence.

Another important enhancement to the algorithm is aimed at substituting the final thresholding of the Mahalanobis distances with a clustering algorithm that connects the regions with similar Mahalanobis distances. A good description of such a clustering algorithm is given in [8].

References

1. Sanderson, J.G., Teal, M.K., Ellis, T.J.: Identification and Tracking in Maritime Scenes. IEE Int. Conference on Image Processing and its applications. (1997) Vol. 2 463–467
2. Smith, A.A.W., Teal, M.K.: Identification and Tracking of Maritime Objects in Near-Infrared Image Sequences for Collision Avoidance. IEE 7th Int. Conference on Image Processing and its applications. (1999) Vol. 1 250–254
3. Campbell, .N.W., Thomas, B.T.: Segmentation of natural images using self organising feature maps. British Machine Vision Conference Proceedings. (1996) 223–232
4. Mohr, R., Triggs, B.: Projective geometry for image analysis. A tutorial given at ISPRS in Vienna. (1996)
5. Jain, R., Kasturi, R., Schunck, B.G.: Machine Vision. (1995) 234–241
6. Schalkoff, R.: Pattern Recognition, Statistical, Structural and Neural Approaches. John Wiley & Sons Inc. (1992).
7. Sanderson, J.G., Teal, M.K., Ellis, T.J.: Characterisation of a Complex Maritime Scene using Fourier Space Analysis to Identify Small Craft. 7th IEE Int. Conference on Image Processing and its applications (1999) Vol. 2 803–807.
8. Shapiro, L.S.: Affine analysis of image sequences. Cambridge University Press (1995).
9. Voles, P., Smith, A.A.W., Teal, M.K.: Segmentation of Nautical Scenes Using the Statistical Characteristics of Variable Size Image Windows. accepted for CVPRIP 2000.
10. Sonka, M., et al.: Image Processing, Analysis and Machine Vision. Thomson Computer Press (1993)

(a)   (b)

Figure 6. Procession of small motor vessels (a) frame 200, (b) frame 1100.

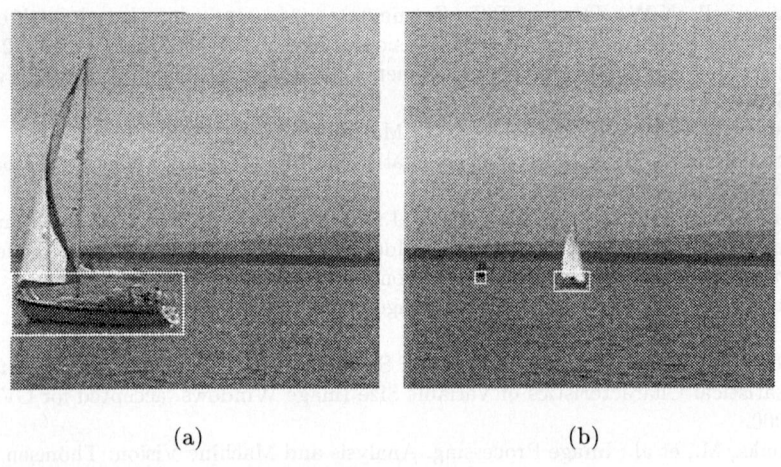

(a)   (b)

Figure 7. Large and small yachts and a buoy, (a) frame 300, (b) frame 900.

335

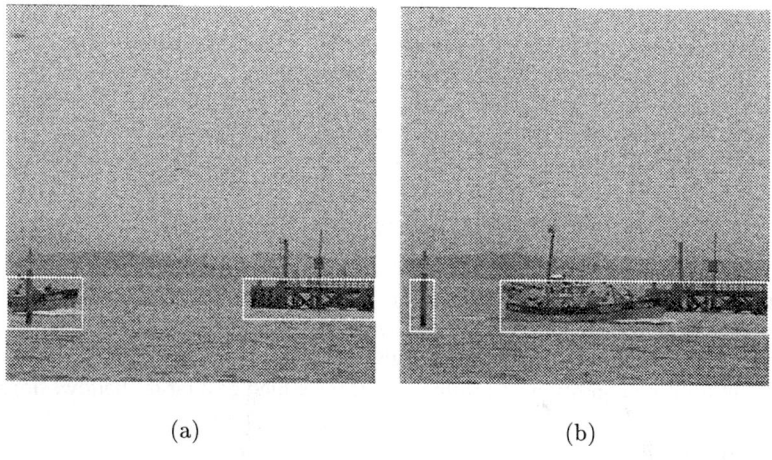

(a)   (b)

Figure 8. Medium sized vessel approaching a pier, (a) frame 100, (b) frame 200.

A Probabilistic Background Model for Tracking

J. Rittscher[1], J. Kato[1], S. Joga[2], and A. Blake[3]

[1] University of Oxford, Department of Engineering Science, Parks Road, Oxford OX1 PJ3, UK
[2] École Nationale Supérieure des Télécommunications, 46 rue Barrault,
75634 Paris Cedex 13, France
[3] Microsoft Research ,1 Guildhall Street, Cambridge, CB2 3NH, UK

Abstract. A new probabilistic background model based on a Hidden Markov Model is presented. The hidden states of the model enable discrimination between foreground, background *and* shadow. This model functions as a low level process for a car tracker. A particle filter is employed as a stochastic filter for the car tracker. The use of a particle filter allows the incorporation of the information from the low level process via importance sampling. A novel observation density for the particle filter which models the statistical dependence of neighboring pixels based on a Markov random field is presented. The effectiveness of both the low level process and the observation likelihood are demonstrated.

1 Introduction

The main requirement of a vision system used in automatic surveillance is robustness to different lighting conditions. Lighting situations which cast large shadows are particularly troublesome (see figure 1) because discrimination between foreground and background is then difficult. As simple background subtraction or inter-frame differencing schemes are known to perform poorly a number of researchers have addressed the problem of finding a probabilistic background model [6, 17, 10, 13, 20]. Haritaoglu *et al.* [6] only learn the minimal and maximal grey-value intensity for every pixel location. The special case of a video camera mounted on a pan-tilt head is investigated in [17]. Here a Gaussian mixture model is learnt. Paragios and Deriche [13] demonstrate that a background foreground/segmentation based on likelihood ratios can be elegantly incorporated into a PDE Level Set approach. In order to acquire training data for these methods it is necessary to observe a static background without any foreground objects. Toyama *et al.* [20] address the problem of background maintenance by using a multi-layered approach. The intensity distribution over time is modelled as an autoregressive process of order 30. This seems to be an unnecessarily complex model for a background process. None of the above models are able to discriminate between background, foreground, and shadow regions. In the present paper we propose a probabilistic background model based on a Hidden Markov Model (HMM). This model has two advantages. Firstly it is no longer necessary to select training data. The different hidden states allow the learning of distributions for foreground and background areas from a mixed sequence. By adding a third state it is possible to extend the model so that it can discriminate shadow regions. The background model is introduced in section 2.

In addition to the low level process it is necessary to build a high level process that can track the vehicles. Probabilistic trackers based on a particle filters [7] are known to be robust and can be extended to tracking multiple objects [11]. The benefit of using a particle filter is that the tracker can recover from failures [7]. But very importantly the use of a particle filter also allows a way to utilise the information of the low level process modelled by the HMM. The propagated distribution for the previous time-step $t-1$ is effectively used as a prior for time t. It is very difficult to fuse two sources of prior information. However, importance sampling, as introduced in [8], can be used to incorporate the information obtained from the low level process. Instead of applying the original algorithm an importance sampling scheme which is linear in time [16] is used here. The importance function itself is generated by fitting a rectangle with parameters X_I to the pixels which are classified as foreground pixels (see figure 5) and using a normal distribution with fixed variance and mean X_I as the importance function. The remaining challenge is to build an observation likelihood for the particle filter which takes account of spatial dependencies of neighbouring pixels. The construction of this observation likelihood is discussed in in section 3. We demonstrate that by employing a Markov random field it is possible to model these statistical dependencies.

Such a car tracking system has to be able to compete with existing traffic monitoring systems. Beymer *et al.* [2] built an very robust car tracker. Their tracking approach is based on feature points and works in most illumination conditions. The disadvantage of the system is that it is necessary to run a complex grouping algorithm in order to solve the data association problem. The use of additional algorithms would be necessary to extract information about the shape of the cars. By modelling cars as rectangular regions it would be possible to infer about their size and allow classification into basic categories. Koller *et al.* [10] as well as Ferrier [4] *et al.* already demonstrated applications of contour tracking to traffic surveillance. [10] extracts a contour extraction from features computed from inter-frame difference images as well as the grey value intensity images themselves. In the case of extreme lighting conditions as shown in figure 1 this system is likely to get distracted. Approaches which model vehicles as three dimensional wire frame objects [18, 12, 15] are of course less sensitive to extreme lighting conditions. The main drawback of modelling vehicles as three dimensional objects is that the tracking is computationally expensive. The challenge is to design a robust real-time system which allows the extraction shape information.

2   A probabilistic background model

In addition to being able to discriminate between background and foreground it is also necessary to detect shadows. Figure 2 clearly shows that the grey-value distributions of the shadow differs significantly from the intensity distributions in the foreground and background regions. This is the motivation for treating the shadow region separately. Since all three distributions have a large overlap it is of course not possible to construct a background model which is purely based on intensity values. However another source of information is available: the temporal continuity. Once a pixel is inferred to be in a foreground region it is expected to be within a foreground region for some time. An suitable model to impose such temporal continuity constraints is the Hidden Markov Model (HMM) [14]. The grey-value intensities over time for one specific pixel location is to be modelled as a single HMM, independent of the neighbouring pixels. This is

Fig. 1. A traffic surveillance example. *This is a typical camera image from a traffic surveillance camera. Notice that especially for dark coloured cars intensity differences between foreground and background are small. In order to track the cars robustly it is necessary to detect the shadows as well as the cars.*

of course an unrealistic independence assumption. The spatial dependencies of neighbouring pixel locations will be modelled by the higher level process (see section 3). The reader should note that the specific traffic surveillance situation (see figure 1) is particularly suited to investigate this class of model because the speed of the cars does not vary greatly. It is therefore possible to learn parameters which will determine the expected duration a pixel belongs to a foreground, shadow or background region.

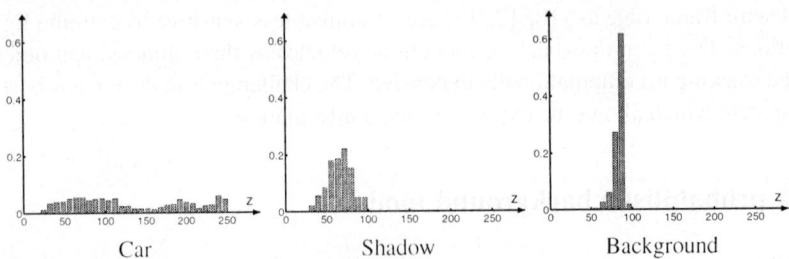

Fig. 2. Intensity histograms of the different regions. *Intensity values for single pixel positions were collected from a 30 seconds long video sequence and manually classified into the regions: foreground, shadow or background. The intensity histograms of the different regions clearly show a large amount of overlap. A method which is purely based on grey-value intensities is therefore inadequate for this problem.*

The model parameters of the HMM with N states are the initial state distribution $\pi = \{\pi_i\}$, the state transition probability distribution $A = \{a_{i,j}\}$, and the emission or observation probability for each state $p_f(z), p_b(z)$ and $p_s(z)$. The set of parameters defining the HMM model will be abbreviated as $\omega := (A, \pi, p_f, p_s, p_b)$. Standard texts include [14, 9]. Based on the intensity histograms of figure 2 the emission models of the background and shadow regions are modelled as Gaussian densities. Since very little about the distribution of the colours of vehicles is known, the observation probability of the foreground region is taken to be uniform. Hence

$$p_f(z) = \frac{1}{256}, \quad p_s(z) = \frac{1}{\sqrt{2\pi\sigma_s^2}} e^{-\frac{(z-\mu_s)^2}{2\sigma_s^2}}, \quad \text{and} \quad p_b(z) = \frac{1}{\sqrt{2\pi\sigma_b^2}} e^{-\frac{(z-\mu_b)^2}{2\sigma_b^2}}.$$

(1)

It is of course possible to employ more complex emission models. In section 2.2 it will be shown that is in fact necessary to use a more complex model for the observations.

2.1 Parameter learning

For a given training sequence the model parameters are estimated by using a maximum likelihood approach. Because the model has hidden parameters an expectation maximisation (EM) type approach is used. In this particular case the Baum Welch algorithm [9] is applied as a learning algorithm. Because EM-type algorithms are not guaranteed to find the global maximum and are very sensitive to initialisation it is necessary to explain how the initialisation is done. In order to find an initialisation method the

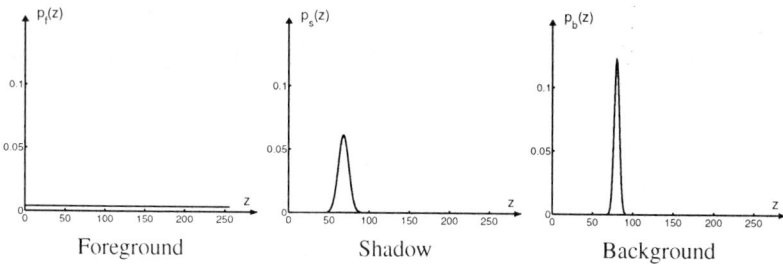

Fig. 3. Learnt emission models. *Shown is a set of emission models for one pixel location. The distributions p_f, p_s and p_b model the intensity distributions for all three states foreground, shadow and background. It should be noted that the emission models can vary between pixel locations.*

following time constants are defined: τ_b - the typical time duration a pixel belongs to the background, and τ_s, τ_f the typical duration for shadow and foreground. Let λ_b, λ_s, and λ_f be the proportion of the time spent in background, shadow and foreground, with $\lambda_f + \lambda_s + \lambda_b = 1$. All these parameters are determined empirically. Using these definitions an intuitive transition matrix can be chosen as

$$A = \begin{pmatrix} 1 - \tau_b^{-1} & \tau_b^{-1}\Lambda_{sf} & \tau_b^{-1}\Lambda_{fs} \\ \tau_s^{-1}\Lambda_{bf} & 1 - \tau_s^{-1} & \tau_s^{-1}\Lambda_{bs} \\ \tau_f^{-1}\Lambda_{bs} & \tau_s^{-1}\Lambda_{sb} & 1 - \tau_f^{-1} \end{pmatrix},$$

(2)

where $\Lambda_{ij} = \lambda_i/(\lambda_i+\lambda_j)$. The initial state distribution π is chosen to be $\pi = \{\lambda_b, \lambda_s, \lambda_f\}$. The mean of the observation density for the background state μ_b can be estimated to be the mode of the intensities at a given pixel since $\lambda_b \gg \lambda_s$ and $\lambda_b \gg \lambda_f$. The variance σ_b^2 is determined empirically. The initial parameters of the observation density for the shadow region are based on the assumption that the shadow is darker than the background, i.e.

$$\mu_s = \frac{\mu_f + 2\sigma_b}{2}, \quad \text{and} \quad \sigma_s = \frac{\mu_s}{2}. \tag{3}$$

This ensures that $\mu_s < \mu_b$ in case $\mu_b > 2\sigma_b$, i.e. the background intensities are not as low as intensities in the shadow areas. At each iteration of the Baum Welch algorithm, the backward and forward variables are rescaled for reasons of numerical stability [9]. It is not necessary to learn a transition probability distribution A for every pixel. By learning one transition probability distribution for an observation window the complexity of the learning is reduced considerably. A set of learnt emission models are shown in figure 3. The corresponding transition probability distribution is of the form

$$A = \begin{pmatrix} 0.986 & 0.012 & 0.001 \\ 0.013 & 0.884 & 0.101 \\ 0.033 & 0.025 & 0.941 \end{pmatrix}, \tag{4}$$

A close inspection of these transition probabilities reveals that during learning dark cars are mistaken for shadows. As a consequence the expected duration for being in a foreground state is unrealistically short. For the particular lighting situation (see figure 1) it is possible to solve the problem by adding the constraint $a_{fs} = 0$. This implies that the transition probability from foreground to shadow should be zero. Of course this constraint cannot be applied in the general case. It is therefore necessary to find a more general solution. As a result the parameters of the observation density for the shadow change. Especially the variance σ_S is now smaller $\sigma_S = 41.95$ instead of 44.97. The corresponding transition matrix A is

$$A = \begin{pmatrix} 0.980 & 0.015 & 0.003 \\ 0.013 & 0.897 & 0.891 \\ 0.047 & 0.000 & 0.952 \end{pmatrix}, \tag{5}$$

notice that the values of a_{ff} is increased.

2.2 Two observations improve the model

Initial experiments show that by using only one observation, dark cars are not detected sufficiently well (see figure 4). In order to make the method more robust, it is desirable to reduce the amount of overlap of the observation densities. In particular it is necessary to reduce the ambiguity between dark foreground regions and shadows. These ambiguities can be reduced by introducing a second observation. To be precise the responses of two different filters will be used. The HMM is no longer modelled for every pixel but for sites on a lattice such that the filter supports of the different sites do not overlap. As a first observation a simple 3×3 average is used. It can be observed that background and shadow regions are more homogeneous than foreground regions. It would therefore make sense to introduce a second observation which measures the intensity variation in a small neighbourhood each pixel. In order to test this approach a simple 3×3 Sobel filter mask is used as a second observation. It is possible to show empirically that for this specific data, the responses of the Sobel filter and the mean intensity response at a pixel are uncorrelated. Hence the two observations are considered to be independent. The comparison shown in figure 4 shows that the use of two observations greatly improves the detection of dark cars. Whereas the choice of the average filter is justified the chosen Sobel filter is by no means optimal. A filter which implies computing a higher order derivative of the image data as for example a Laplace filter or even a spatio temporal filter might be a much better alternative.

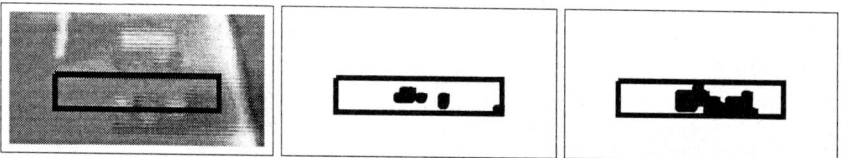

Fig. 4. Using two observations improves the model. *For each time step t every pixel is classified to be in a foreground, background, or shadow region. For visualisation purposes the pixels for which the forward probability $p(z_t, z_{t-1}, Y_t = f | \omega)$ is greater than the forward probability for the alternative states are marked in black. The image on the left shows the raw data. The black box indicates the area in which the model is tested. The two images on the right show the sets of pixels which are classified as foreground pixels. It shows that the classification based on two observations (right) is superior to the method based on only one measurement (middle).*

2.3 Practical Results

In order to test the performance of the model the forward probabilities $p(z_t, z_{t-1}, Y_t | \omega)$ are evaluated for the three different states $Y_t \in \{f, b, s\}$ for each time-step t. The discrete state Y_t for which the forward probability is maximal is taken as a discrete label. By determining discrete labels this classification method discards information which could be used by a higher level process. But for now this should be sufficient to discuss the results obtained with the method. Two typical results are shown in figure 5. A movie which demonstrates the performance of this process can be found in the version of this paper on our web site (http://www.robots.ox.ac.uk/~vdg). The interior of the car is not detected perfectly. But there is clearly enough information to detect the boundaries of the vehicle. In order to illustrate the importance of the state transition probability the matrix A was altered by hand. The results are presented in figure 6 and display clearly that the transition probability plays an important role. The effect is of course most evident when the discrimination based on measurements alone is ambiguous.

3 The car tracker

The remaining challenge is to build a robust car tracker. Probabilistic trackers based on a particle filters [7] are known to be robust and can be extended to tracking multiple

Fig. 5. Results of the background modelling. *The discrete label Y_t for which the forward probability $p(z_t, z_{t-1}, Y_t|\omega)$ is maximal is used as a discrete label for visualisation (see text). Foreground pixels are marked in black, shadow pixels in grey, and background pixels in white. It should be noted that even for dark coloured cars the results are respectable. The labels will then be used by a higher level process to locate the vehicles.*

Fig. 6. Importance of the temporal continuity constraint. *Like in figure 5 the pixels are assigned a discrete label Y_t as which forward probability $p(z_t, z_{t-1}, Y_t|\omega)$ is maximal. In this experiment the transition probability of a model which uses two observations was altered such that all $a_{ij} = 1/3$ in order to explore the importance of the temporal continuity constraint. Each pixel is classified (see text) as foreground (in black), shadow (in grey) or background (white). A comparison with the images shown in figure 5 shows that these results are clearly worse. Obviously the transition probability A plays a crucial role.*

343

objects [11]. In order to build such a tracker it is necessary to model the observation likelihood

$$p(Z|X;\vartheta) \qquad (6)$$

for a set of measurements Z and a hypothesis X. The parameters of the model are denoted by ϑ. For the present purpose it is sufficient to model the outlines of the cars as a perspectively distorted rectangle which will be parameterised by the state vector X. In order to track cars robustly it is not sufficient to take edge measurements as in [7]. [19] showed that detection of the background aids finding the foreground object. The problem is that in this case the measurements Z cannot be assumed to be independent (also see [19]). These conditions lead us to model the likelihood (6) as a conditioned Markov random field (MRF) (see for example [5, 21]). In Gibbs form an MRF can be written as

$$P(Z|X;\vartheta) = \frac{\exp(-H^\vartheta(Z,X))}{\sum_{Z'\in\mathcal{Z}}\exp(-H^\vartheta(Z',X))} \cdot \qquad (7)$$

The denominator of the fraction is known as the partition function of the MRF. The difficulty is now to find a model which is tractable yet still captures the spatial dependence of neighbouring measurements.

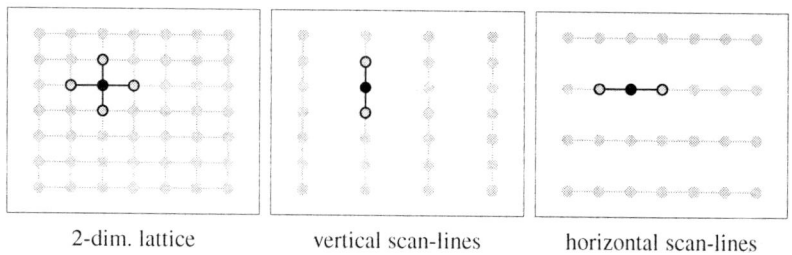

2-dim. lattice   vertical scan-lines   horizontal scan-lines

Fig. 7. Neighbourhood structure of the MRF. *The set of sites on a lattice S is marked by circles. The neighbourhood structure at one particular site s (marked as a filled black circle) is different in each case. The neighbours $r \subset \delta(s)$ of the site s are marked by black circles which are filled grey. The set of cliques are indicated by lines connecting neighbouring sites.*

3.1 Modelling the observation likelihood

As mentioned in the previous section, one difficult problem is to find an energy function H for which the likelihood $P(Z|X;\vartheta)$ can be evaluated efficiently. The energy function H will depend on a lattice S and a corresponding *neighbourhood system* $\delta := \{\delta(s) : s \in S\}$ (see figure 7). The set of cliques will be denoted by $\mathcal{C}$. In order to take the distribution of the measurement z at a given site and the statistical dependence of measurements at neigbouring sites into account we let the energy function

$$H_A^\vartheta(Z,X) = \sum_{s\in A_X} g_A(z_s) + \sum_{(s,r)\in\mathcal{C}\cap A_X^2} \vartheta_A \cdot (z_s - z_r)^2 , \qquad (8)$$

where A_X denotes an area which is either in the foreground or background, i.e. $X \in \{B, F\}$. Since the function g_A models the distribution of the measurement at a given site it would be ideal if one could make use of the emission models which were learnt for the different states of the HMM (see section 2.1). But as it will be shown later the energy function needs to be translational invariant (13) so therefore g_A cannot depend on a particular site s. And in order to compute the partition function efficiently (section 3.3) it is necessary that the functions g_f and g_b are normal distributions. The foreground distribution g_f is therefore chosen to be a normal distribution with a large variance. The background distribution g_f is taken to be the normal with mean μ_f and variance σ_f such that it approximates the the mixture of the background and shadow emission models (1) learnt by the HMM.

The set of sites which belong to a given area A_X depends of course on the hypothesis X. Because the partition function depends also on X it will be necessary to evaluate it for every hypothesis X. It turns out that if the lattice S is two dimensional, the partition function is too expensive to compute. In the following it is explained that it is not possible to approximate the observation likelihood (7). It is therefore necessary to find a simpler model. It is known that under certain conditions the pseudolikelihood function [1, 21], defined as

$$\prod_{s \in S} p(z_s | z_{S \setminus s}; \vartheta) \tag{9}$$

can be used for parameter estimation instead of the Maximum Likelihood approach based on the MRF (7). It can be shown [21] that estimators obtained by maximizing the pseudolikehood can compete in terms of statistical properties with maximum likelihood estimators. Although some authors state that when the variables are weakly correlated, the pseudolikehood is a good approximation to the likelihood [3] it seems to be an open problem under which conditions precisely it can be used as an approximation to the likelihood function. In section 3.2 it will also become clear why the pseudolikehood method cannot be used to estimate X. An alternative is to restrict the MRF to measurements on scan lines taken out of the image. This will simplify the model considerably. The observation likelihoods of the different scan lines will be treated as independent. Based on the grid in figure 11 it is possible to formulate a random field for each of the horizontal $\{h_i\}$ and vertical lines $\{v_i\}$. The likelihood is now of the following form:

$$p(Z|X; \vartheta) = \prod_l \frac{\exp(-(H_B^\vartheta + H_F^\vartheta)(Z, X))}{\sum_{Z \in \mathcal{Z}} \exp(-(H_B^\vartheta + H_F^\vartheta)(Z, X))} , \tag{10}$$

where $\{l\}$ is the set of lines on the grid. The energies H_B^ϑ and H_F^ϑ are defined as in (8) except that the neighbourhood system has changed (see figure 7). The partition function for the set of lines can be written as

$$\sum_{Z \in \mathcal{Z}} \exp(-(H_B^\vartheta + H_F^\vartheta)(Z, X)) = \prod_i \sum_{Z \in \mathcal{Z}_i} \exp(-H_{A(i)}^\vartheta(Z, X)) \tag{11}$$

where for every $i \neq j$ one has $\mathcal{Z}_i \cap \mathcal{Z}_j = \emptyset$. So $\mathcal{Z}$ is union of mutually disjoint sets $\mathcal{Z}_i$. Therefore it is now possible to compute the partition function because it only depends on line segments which are entirely in the foreground or background.

3.2 Learning the parameters of the random field

Learning the model parameters by a maximum likelihood method is computationally expensive [21]. And as mentioned above, maximising the pseudeolikelihood (9) with respect to ϑ leads to an effective estimator for ϑ. For reasons which will be apparent later we consider the pseudolikelihood for a observation window $T \subset S$ which is entirely in the foreground or background. That implies that the conditioning on the hypothesis X can be ignored for this analysis. The energy function of $p(z_s|z_{\delta(s)};\vartheta)$ is in this case equal to the neighbourhood potential. The logarithm of the pseudolikelihood for an observation window $T \subset S$ has the form

$$PL_T(Z;\vartheta) = \sum_{s \in T}\left[g(z_s) + \vartheta V_s(z_s z_{\delta(s)}) - \ln \sum_{z_s}\exp(-\vartheta V_s(z_s z_{\delta(s)}))\right] , \quad (12)$$

where V is defined as $V_s := \sum_{r \in \delta(s)}(z_s - z_r)^2$. The neighbourhood potential must satisfy a special spatial homogeneity condition. The potential is *shift* or *translational invariant* if for all $s, t, u \in S$

$$t \in \delta(s) \longleftrightarrow t + u \in \delta(s + u) \qquad \text{and} \qquad V_{C+u}(z_{s-u}) = V_C(z_s) . \quad (13)$$

Furthermore a parameter ϑ is said to be *identifiable* if for every $\vartheta' \in \theta$ there is a configuration Z such that

$$p(Z;\vartheta) \neq p(Z;\vartheta') . \quad (14)$$

The maximum pseudolikelihood estimator for the observation window T maximises $PL_T(Z,\cdot)$. If the potential is translational invariant and the parameter ϑ is identifiable Winkler [21] (Theorem 14.3.1 on page 240) proves that this estimator is asymptotically consistent when the size of the observation window increases. Winkler also proves that that the log of the pseudolikelihood PL_T is concave. In the present setting it is of course necessary to learn the parameters for the foreground and background energies H_F^ϑ and H_B^ϑ separately. Since the PL_T is concave it is possible to use a standard gradient decent algorithm to find the maximum of the log pseudolikelihood. In order to compute the gradient of the log pseudolikelihood it is desirable that the potential only depends on the parameters linearly. The gradient of the log pseudolikelihood can be written as

$$\nabla PL_T(Z;\vartheta) = \sum_{s \in T}\left[V(z_s z_{\delta(s)}) - E(V(Z_s z_{\delta(s)})|z_{\delta(s)};\vartheta)\right] , \quad (15)$$

where $E(V(Z_s z_{\delta(s)}))$ denotes the conditional expectation with respect to the distribution $p(z_s|z_{\delta(s)};\vartheta)$ on Z_s. The graphs of the pseudolikelihood can be found in figure 8.

3.3 Computing the partition function

The main reason for adapting a one dimensional model was the problem of computing the partition function of the observation likelihood (10). Due to equation (11) it is

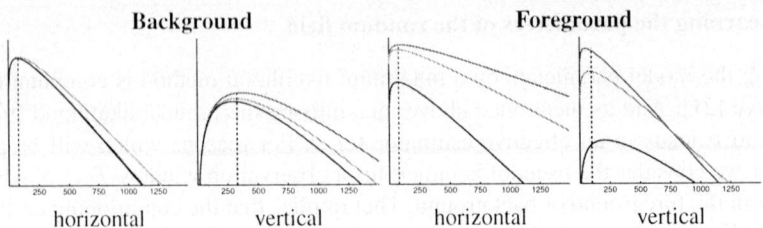

Fig. 8. Pseudolikelihood of training data. *The pseudolikelihood (12) is plotted for different values of ϑ. The distance between neighbouring sites d is set be d = 4 for horizontal and d = 2 for the vertical lines. Because we work on fields, d differs for horizontal and vertical lines. It should be noted that there is a difference between the models. The functions are concave, as expected.*

possible to to compute the partition function by precomputing

$$B_N := \sum_{Z \in \mathcal{Z}} - \exp(H_B^\vartheta(Z)) \quad \text{and} \quad F_N := \sum_{Z \in \mathcal{Z}} - \exp(H_B^\vartheta(Z)) \ , \qquad (16)$$

where vector of measurements Z has length N. Rather than computing the value of the partition function for a particular hypothesis X it is desirable to compute a factor $\alpha(X)$ such that

$$\sum_{Z \in \mathcal{Z}} \exp(-(H_B^\vartheta + H_F^\vartheta)(Z, X)) = \alpha(X)C \ , \qquad (17)$$

where C is some constant. Now the problem of computing B_N and F_N needs to be addressed. The energy functions H_B^ϑ can be written as a quadratic form, i.e. $H_B^\vartheta(Z) = Z^t M Z$. The matrix M is of the form

$$\begin{pmatrix} (\lambda + \vartheta) & -\vartheta & 0 & \cdots & & 0 \\ -\vartheta & (\lambda + 2\vartheta) & -\vartheta & \cdots & & \vdots \\ 0 & 0 & \ddots & \ddots & & 0 \\ \vdots & \vdots & & -\vartheta & (\lambda + 2\vartheta) & -\vartheta \\ 0 & 0 & \cdots & & -\vartheta & (\lambda + \vartheta) \end{pmatrix} \qquad (18)$$

The matrix M is symmetric so it is possible to approximate B_N as

$$B_N = \sum_{Z \in \mathcal{Z}} \exp(-Z^t M Z) \approx \int_{\mathbf{R}^N} exp(-Z^t M Z)\, dZ = (2\pi)^{N/2} \det(M)^{-\frac{1}{2}} \ . \quad (19)$$

Since g_f and g_b are normal distributions this approximation holds for B_N as well as F_N.

3.4 Results

The observation likelihood $p(Z|X)$ as defined in (8) was tested on a set of single images. The results are summarised in figure 9. Whereas the results for horizontal and

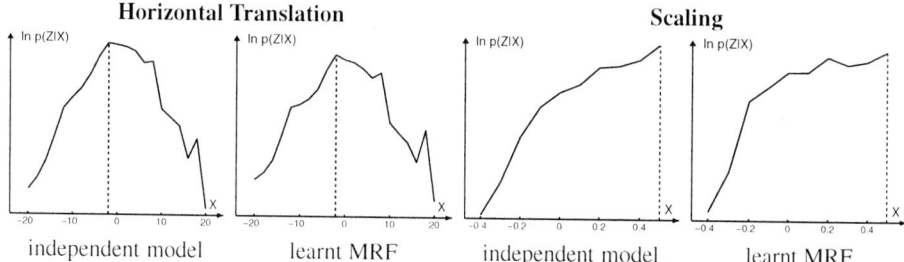

Fig. 9. Log-likelihood for horizontal translation and scaling. *The horizontal translation and scaling of the shape template is illustrated in figure 11. For both the horizontal translation and the scaling the log-likelihood for the independent model ($\vartheta = 0$) (left) and the MRF with the learnt parameter vartheta (see figure 8). The parameters for the intensity distributions g_f and g_s are $\sigma_b^2 = 25, \mu_b = 102, \sigma_f^2 = 600, \mu_b = 128$. The results obtained for the scaling clearly need to be improved. See text for discussion.*

vertical translation are good the results obtained for the scaling of the foreground window are poor. In order to test whether the MRF has any effect ϑ_F and ϑ_B are set to zero which is equivalent to assuming that two neighbouring measurements are independent. The graphs in figure 9 show that the modelling the statistical dependence of neighbouring measurement using the MRF does have an effect. As a first step to improve the model the neighbourhood structure was changed hoping that the interaction terms V_s (12) would have a greater effect. Now every pixel location on a scan lines is a site for the MRF. The resulting energy function is

$$H_A^\vartheta(Z, X) = \sum_{s \in A_X} g_A^s(z_s) + \sum_{\delta(s) \in A_X} \vartheta_A \cdot (z_s - z_{s+d})^2 \ . \tag{20}$$

Only the distance between neighbours depends on a predefined spacing d. The results of this improved method are shown in figures 10 and 11. The fact that the results obtained with the new observation likelihood (20) are better shows that the MRF is very sensitive to the chosen neighbourhood structure. This raises the question if there is any way to determine an optimal neighbourhood structure automatically. The hand-picked MRF we chose might not be the best after all.

A more ambitious step would be to construct a observation likelihood which makes use of the forward probabilities $p(z_t, z_{t-1}, Y_t = f \mid \omega)$. This would complicate the computation of the partition function. But based on the encouraging results we obtained from the HMM (see figure 5) this could lead to a far more powerful model. It can be concluded that the MRF does the right thing but needs to be improved so it can be used in a tracker.

4 Conclusion

Both a new probabilistic background model as well as a observation likelihood for tracking cars are presented. Although the background model is particularly suited to

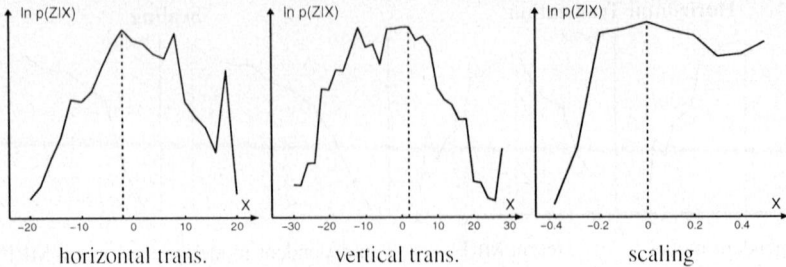

horizontal trans.   vertical trans.   scaling

Fig. 10. Log-likelihoods for the improved model. *Similar to figure 9 the log-likelihoods are shown for horizontal and vertical translation as well as scaling using the improved model defined in (20). The model parameters itself are chosen as in figure 9. Although the maximum for the horizontal translation is not at zero figure 11 demonstrates that the most likely hypothesis leads to a correct localisation.*

the traffic surveillance problem it can be used for a wide range of application domains. The results presented in figure 5 show that the use of this background model could lead to a robust tracker. The observation likelihood itself however still needs to be improved. The contribution this paper makes can be summarised as follows.

Probabilistic background model. Unlike many other background models the model presented here is capable of modelling shadow as well as foreground and background regions. Another considerable advantage of this model is that it is no longer necessary to select the training data. HMMs are a suitable model for this problem as they impose temporal continuity constraints. Although using two observation did improve the results significantly the choice of filters is not optimal. The results presented in figure 6 support the claim that it is crucial to model the transition probabilities correctly.

Car tracker. In order to build a robust car tracker it is necessary to model the inside of the vehicles as well as the background and the statistical dependence of neighbouring pixels. This is possible by modelling an observation density used in a particle filter which is based on an MRF. However it has to be noted that the MRF is very sensitive to the choice of the neighbourhood system. It remains an open problem which neighbourhood system is optimal. The formulation of the MRF based on scan-lines leads to a model which is computationally tractable. It should be noted that the presented observation likelihood is consistent with a Bayesian framework since the measurements do not depend on the hypothesised position of the vehicle. The use of importance sampling makes it possible to feed the information of the low level process into the car tracker in a consistent fashion.

Future work. Since the illumination changes throughout the day it is necessary to derive a criterion when the the parameters of the background model need to be updated. It is furthermore necessary to investigate how the observation density can be improved.

Acknowledgements. We are grateful for the support of the EPSRC and the Royal Society (AB) and the EU (JR).

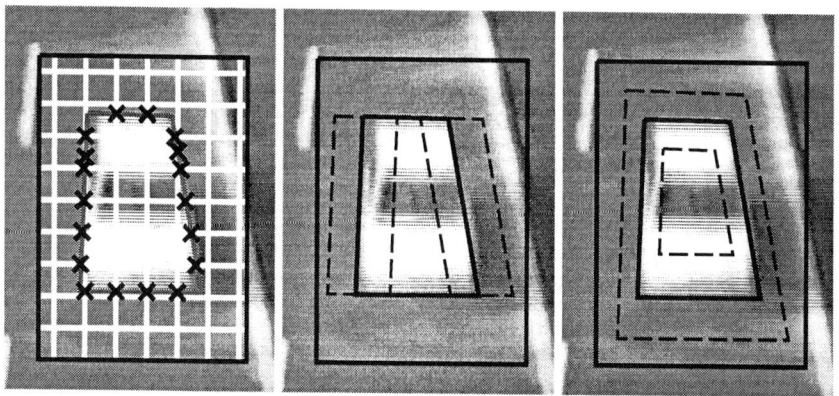

Fig. 11. Observation window and scan lines of the car tracker. *The right image illustrates the grid used by the algorithm. The observation window is marked in black. The measurements are taken on scan-lines (in white). The hypothesised position of the car is shown in dark grey. The other two images illustrate how well the improved model localises. The most likely hypothesis is shown as a solid black line. The dashed lines illustrate the minimal and maximal configurations of the variation. See figures 10 and 9 for the corresponding log-likelihood functions.*

References

[1] J. Besag. Spatial interaction and the statistical analysis of lattice systems. *J. R. Statist. Soc. B*, 36:192–236, 1974.

[2] D. Beymer, P. McLauchlan, B. Coifman, and J. Malik. A real-time computer vision system for measuring traffic pramameters. In *IEEE Conf. Computer Vision and Pattern Recognition, June 1997, Puerto Rico*, 1997.

[3] F. Divino, A. Frigessi, and P. J. Green. Penalized pseudolikelihood inference in spatial interaction models with covariates. *Scandinavian Journal of Statistics (to appear)*, 1998.

[4] N. Ferrier, S. Rowe, and A. Blake. Real-time traffic monitoring. In *Proc. 2nd IEEE Workshop on Applications of Computer Vision*, pages 81–88, 1994.

[5] S. Geman and D. Geman. Stochastic relaxation, Gibbs distributions, and the Bayesian restoration of images. *IEEE Trans. PAMI*, 6:721–741, 1984.

[6] I. Haritaoglu, D. Harwood, and L. S. Davis. W4 - a real time system for detection and tracking people and their parts. In *Proc. Conf. Face and Gesture Recognition, Nara, Japan*, 1998.

[7] M. Isard and A. Blake. Contour tracking by stochastic propagation of conditional density. In *Proc. European Conf. on Computer Vision, Cambridge, UK*, 1996.

[8] M.A. Isard and A. Blake. ICondensation: Unifying low-level and high-level tracking in a stochastic framework. In *Proc. 5th European Conf. Computer Vision*, pages 893–908, 1998.

[9] B.-H. Juang and L.R. Rabiner. Mixture autoregressive hidden markov models for speech signals. *IEEE Trans. Acoustics, Speech, and Signal Processing*, December:1404–1413, 1985.

[10] D. Koller, J. Weber, and J. Malik. Robust multiple car tracking with occlusion reasoning. In *Proc. of ECCV 94, Stockholm, Sweden*, pages 189–196, 1994.

[11] J. MacCormick and A. Blake. A probablilistic exclusion principle for tracking multiple objects. In *Proc. 7th Int. Conf. on Computer Vision*, volume 2, pages 572 – 578, 1999.

[12] S.J. Maybank, A.D. Worrall, and G.D. Sullivan. Filter for car tracking based on acceleration and steering angle. In *Proc. 7th BMVC*, 1996.

[13] N. Paragios and R. Deriche. A PDE-based Level Set Approach for detection and tracking of moving objects. Technical Report 3173, INRIA Sophia Antipolis, 1997.

[14] L. R. Rabiner. A tutorial on hidden Markov models and selected applications in speech recognition. *Proc. IEEE*, 77(2):257–286, February 1989.

[15] P. Remagnino, A. Baumberg, T. Grove, D. Hogg, T. Tan, A. Worrall, and K. Baker. An integratedtraffic and pedestrian model-based vision system. In *Proc. of BMVC '97, Univ. of Essex*, volume 2, pages 380–398, 1997.

[16] J. Rittscher and A. Blake. Classification of human body motion. In *Proc. 7th Int. Conf. on Computer Vision*, pages 634–639, 1999.

[17] S.M. Rowe and A. Blake. Statistical background modelling for tracking with a virtual camera. In *Proc. British Machine Vision Conf.*, volume 2, pages 423–432, 1995.

[18] G.D Sullivan, K.D. Baker, and A.D. Worrall. Model-based vehicle detection and classification using orthographic approximations. In *Proc. of 7th BMVC*, pages 695–704, 1996.

[19] J. Sullivan, A. Blake, M. Isard, and J. MacCormick. Object localisation by Baysian correlation. In *Proc. 7th Int. Conf. on Computer Vision*, volume 2, pages 1068–1075, 1999.

[20] K. Toyama, J. Krumm, B. Brumitt, and B. Meyers. Wallflower: Principles and practice of background maintenance. In *Proc. 7th Int. Conf. on Computer Vision*, pages 255–261, 1999.

[21] G. Winkler. *Image analysis, random fields and dynamics Monte Carlo methods: a mathematical introduction.* Spinger, 1995.

On the Performance Characterisation of Image Segmentation Algorithsm: A Case Study

B Southall[1,2,3], B F Buxton[2], J A Marchant[3], and T Hague[3]

[1] GRASP Laboratory, University of Pennsylvania,
3401 Walnut Street,
Philadelphia, PA 19104, USA
southall@grip.cis.upenn.edu
Tel: +1 215 898 0352 Fax: +1 215 573 2048

[2] Department of Computer Science, University College London, Gower Street,
London, WC1E 6BT, UK
b.buxton@cs.ucl.ac.uk
Tel: +44 20 7679 7294 Fax: +44 20 7387 1397

[3] Silsoe Research Institute, Wrest Park, Silsoe,
Bedfordshire, MK45 4HS, UK
{john.marchant,tony.hague}@bbsrc.ac.uk
Tel: +44 1525 860000 Fax: +44 1525 860156

Abstract. An experimental vehicle is being developed for the purposes of precise crop treatment, with the aim of reducing chemical use and thereby improving quality and reducing both costs and environmental contamination. For differential treatment of crop and weed, the vehicle must discriminate between crop, weed and soil. We present a two stage algorithm designed for this purpose, and use this algorithm to illustrate how empirical discrepancy methods, notably the analysis of type I and type II statistical errors and receiver operating characteristic curves, may be used to compare algorithm performance over a set of test images which represent typical working conditions for the vehicle. Analysis of performance is presented for the two stages of the algorithm separately, and also for the combined algorithm. This analysis allows us to understand the effects of various types of misclassification error on the overall algorithm performance, and as such is a valuable methodology for computer vision engineers.

1 Introduction

Economic and ecological pressures have led to a demand for reduced use of chemical applicants in agricultural operations such as crop and weed treatment. The discipline of precision agriculture strives to reduce the use of agro-chemicals by directing them more accurately and appropriately. The extreme interpretation of this approach is *plant scale husbandry*, where the aim is to treat individual plants according to their particular needs. An experimental horticultural vehicle has been developed to investigate the viability of plant scale husbandry, and previous work [15, 17, 16] has described a tracking algorithm, centred upon an extended Kalman filter, that allows navigation of the vehicle along the rows of crop in the field. This paper presents a simple algorithm for frame-rate segmentation of images for the task of differential plant treatment, together with a thorough evaluation of algorithm performance on data captured from the vehicle. The algorithm comprises two stages. Stage I aims to extract image features which represent plant matter from the soil background, and stage II divides these features into crop and weed classes for treatment scheduling.

The practical application of the algorithm requires that we understand how its performance varies in different operating conditions; Haralick [10] underlines the necessity of the evaluation of computer vision algorithms if the field is to produce methods of practical use to engineers. In this paper, we evaluate the two stages of the algorithm separately and as a result, we are able to gain deeper insight into the performance of the algorithm as a whole. A review of techniques for image segmentation evaluation is presented by Zhang [22], who partitions the methods into three categories; analytical, where performance is judged on the basis of its principles, complexity, requirements and so forth; empirical goodness methods, which compute some manner of "goodness" function such as uniformity within regions, contrast between regions, shape of segmented regions; and finally, empirical discrepancy methods, which compare properties of the segmented image with some ground truth segmentation and computes error measures. Analytic methods may only be useful for simple algorithms or straightforward segmentation problems, and the researcher needs to be confident of the models on which these processes are based if they are to trust the analysis. Empirical goodness methods have the advantage that they do not force the researcher to perform the onerous task of producing ground truth data for comparison with the segmentation, for meaningful results, an appropriate model of "goodness" is required, and in most practical problems if such a model were available, it should be used as part of the algorithm itself. This leaves empirical discrepancy methods, which compare algorithmic output with ground truth segmentation of the test data and quantify the levels of agreement and/or disagreement.

A discrepancy method which is suitable for two-class segmentation problems is receiver operating characteristic (ROC) curve analysis. Rooted in psychophysics and signal detection theory, ROC analysis [8, 21] has proved popular for the comparison of diagnostic techniques in medicine [11, 9], and is gradually gaining currency within the computer vision and image analysis community for the comparative evaluation of algorithms such as colour models [2], edge detectors [1, 5] and appearance identification [6]. Receiver operating characteristic curves typically plot true positive rates against false positive rates as a decision parameter is varied and provide a means of algorithm comparison and evaluation. ROC analysis also allows selection of an operating point which yields the minimum possible Bayes risk [8]. ROC curves will be discussed further below, together with the related maximum realisable ROC (MRROC) curve [14]. Although our algorithm produces a three-way final classification (crop, weed and soil), stages I and II are both binary classifiers, so we can analyse their performance using ROC methods.

We will first outline the segmentation algorithm prior to discussing evaluation of the performance of stages I and II. Final results for the complete algorithm are then presented and discussed in the light of our knowledge of its constituent parts.

2 The segmentation algorithm

The two stage segmentation algorithm is sketched in the following sections; for the sake of brevity, details of the algorithms are not given (these may be found elsewhere [15, 18]), but sufficient information is provided to allow the performance evaluation sections to be understood.

2.1 Stage I: Plant matter extraction

The experimental vehicle is equipped with a monochrome camera that is fitted with a filter which blocks visible light, but allows near infra-red wavelengths to pass. Many researchers, including for example Biller [4], have noted that the contrast between soil and plant matter is greater in the near infra-red wavelengths than the visible, and this allows us to use a grey level threshold to extract pixels which represent plant matter from the images captured by the vehicle as it traverses the field. We use an adaptive interpolating threshold algorithm, to allow for the fact that there is often a brightness gradient across many of the images captured by the vehicle. The cause of such a gradient is most likely the position of the Sun relative to the ground plane and the vehicle's camera, and the interaction of the illuminant with the rough surface of the soil. A simple linear variation in intensity between the upper and lower parts of the image is used to allow for such effects. Accurate modelling of illumination and reflectance effects is a complex issue and not of direct concern to this work. More principled models are known for surface reflectance, such as those due to van Branniken et al [20] or Oren and Nayar [12].

The algorithm is also adaptive to the average brightness of the image, which offers some robustness to changes in illumination as, for example, when the Sun is temporarily masked by a cloud. A mean grey-level is computed for both the top (μ_1) and bottom (μ_2) halves of the image and these two means are used as fixed points to linearly interpolate a mean $\mu(y_f)$ across the vertical pixel coordinates of the image. The classification of output pixels $O(x_f, y_f)$ is then given by the adaptive interpolating thresholding algorithm:

$$O(x_f, y_f) = \begin{cases} \text{P if } I(x_f, y_f) \geq \alpha\mu(y_f) \\ \text{S if } I(x_f, y_f) < \alpha\mu(y_f) \end{cases}, \tag{1}$$

where P denotes plant matter (crop or weed) and S soil. The decision rule of equation 1 is used in a chain-code clustering algorithm [7] whereby groups of neighbouring above-threshold pixels are clustered into "blobs". Each blob is described by the pixel co-ordinates of its centroid in the image, and its size in number of pixels. The process is illustrated in figure 1 which shows an image and the plant matter extracted from it automatically. It can be seen from the figure that some of the plants fracture into multiple blobs. This is largely caused by shadows falling between plant leaves which lead to areas of the plant in the image that lie below the chosen threshold. Another problem that sometimes occurs is that neighbouring plants sometimes become merged into a single feature. Whilst there is little that can be done about the latter problem, the feature clustering technique in stage II of the algorithm aims to address difficulties caused by plant features fracturing.

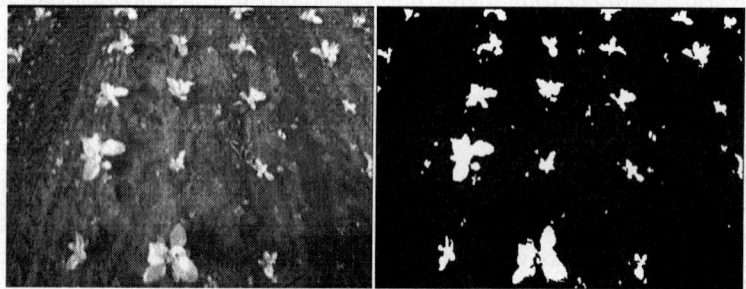

Fig. 1. An image and its automatically extracted plant matter.

2.2 Stage II: Crop/weed discrimination

The image on the left of figure 1 shows that the crop plants grow in a fairly regular pattern in the field, and also that they are generally larger than the weeds. These are the two pieces of information that we exploit in the second stage of the segmentation algorithm, which aims to separate the set of plant matter features (denoted P) into subsets of crop (C) and weed (W). The first step of this stage is to filter the plant matter features on the basis of their size in the image. Justification for this decision is provided by figure 2, where histograms of the feature sizes (in pixels/feature) are plotted for both weed and crop. This data is derived from manually segmented images that we use as our ground truth data throughout this paper. More details of this data are given below.

It can be seen from the histograms that the vast majority (in fact 95%) of the weed blobs have a size of less than 50 pixels, whilst most (90%) of the crop blobs have a size of 50 or pixels or greater. This supports the claim that the weeds are typically smaller than the crop.

Thus, we have a straightforward algorithm that places a threshold on the size s of the image features. This may be expressed as follows:

$$\text{Class(feature)} = \begin{cases} W \text{ if } s(\text{feature}) < \varsigma \\ P \text{ if } s(\text{feature}) \geq \varsigma \end{cases}, \qquad (2)$$

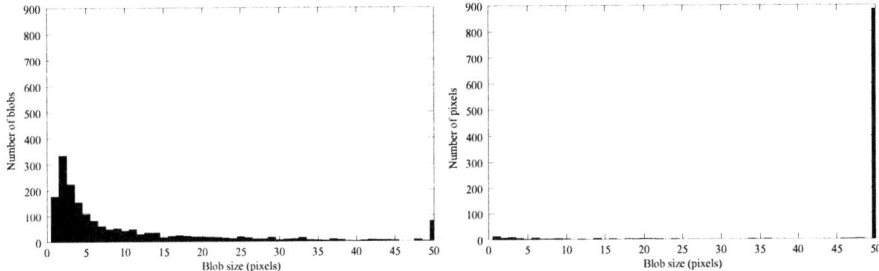

Fig. 2. Blob size histograms. Left: weed blobs. Right: crop blobs. In both histograms, the right-most bin (marked 50) counts all blobs of size ≥ 50. Note that the crop feature histogram, most of the bins are empty, except for the right-most.

where s(feature) is the size of an image feature in pixels, and ς is the size threshold.

The second step of stage II of the algorithm makes use of the regular grid pattern formed by the crop as they are planted in the field. The grid pattern is used as a cue for vehicle navigation [15], where the position of the vehicle relative to the crop grid and the dimensions of the grid are estimated by an extended Kalman filter (EKF) [3]. The EKF also produces a covariance matrix that describes the level of confidence in the current estimate. The state estimate is used to predict the position of each plant within the grid, and an algorithm akin to a validation gate [13] is used to cluster all plant matter features within a certain radius of the predicted crop plant position.

The validation gate has proved to be effective as an outlier rejection mechanism in practical Kalman filtering applications [13]. The algorithm combines the uncertainty on the predicted feature position and the uncertainty attached to the observed data to define a validation region outside of which candidate feature matches are rejected as being outliers. In our algorithm, we take the uncertainty of the estimated plant position and combine it with a user defined region which describes a radius on the ground plane about the plant centroid within which all of the crop plant should lie. This defines an association region in the image inside of which all plant matter features are labelled as crop (C), and outside of which the features are labelled as weed (W). The schematic diagram in figure 3 illustrates the components of the association region, Full details of the algorithm can be found elsewhere [18]. The size of the region which describes the user-defined plant radius is controlled by a single parameter r, the radius on the ground plane within which the crop plant matter should lie. This model implicitly assumes a distribution for the weed matter that gives lower probability of weed occurrence than plant occurrence within the radius r.

3 Evaluation using ROC curves

The receiver operating characteristic (ROC) curve [8] supports the analysis of binary classification algorithms whose performance is controlled by a single

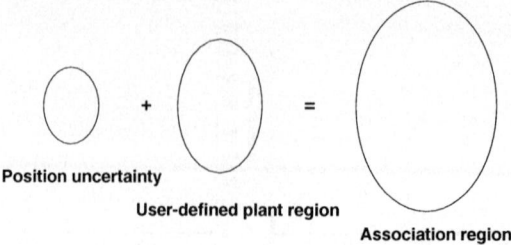

Position uncertainty

User-defined plant region

Association region

Fig. 3. The construction of the association region.

parameter. For each parameter setting, algorithmic output is compared with ground truth data, and four numbers are calculated; TP, the number of "positive" cases correctly classified as positive; TN, the number of "negative" cases correctly classified as negative; FN, the number of positive cases incorrectly classified as negative; and FP, the number of negative cases incorrectly classified as positive. In the statistical literature, FN cases are type I errors, and FP cases type II errors [19]. From these four figures, two independent quantities are constructed, the true positive ratio, TPR = TP/(TP+FN), and the false positive ratio, FPR=FP/(FP+TN). To construct an ROC curve, a set of algorithm parameter values are chosen, and for each of these, the TPR and FPR values are calculated and plotted against each other. The set of TPR,FPR pairs form the ROC curve.

To characterise the performance of our algorithms, we shall use the area underneath the ROC curve. This metric has often been used to compare the performance of different algorithms across the same data sets [2, 1, 6], but we will use it to compare the performance of stage I of our algorithm across a number of test data sets which represent different stages of crop growth and weather conditions that the vehicle is likely to encounter. The performance of stage II across these data sets is assessed using the maximum realisable ROC (MRROC) curve. It is also possible to use the slope of the ROC curve to select a value for the algorithm's controlling parameter which minimises the Bayes risk associated with the decision being made. van Trees [21] provides full details.

3.1 The MRROC curve

In the analysis described above, variation of a single decision parameter in a classification algorithm leads to the formation of the ROC curve. Each point on the curve characterises an instance of the classification algorithm that we call a *classifier*. If a single parameter is undergoing variation, then all of the classifiers lie along the ROC curve. This is the case within stage I of our algorithm, the adaptive interpolating threshold, which has gain parameter α, as defined in equation 1.

When an algorithm has more than one parameter, then it will generate a cloud of classifiers in the ROC space. The convex hull of this cloud is the MRROC curve [14], and the area underneath it reflects the best overall classification performance it is possible to obtain from this group of classifiers. We will use the area under the MRROC curve to compare the operation of stage II of our algorithm, which has two parameters ς and r (the size threshold and clustering radius, respectively), on different data sets. The set of classifiers which provide the best performance is comprised of those that lie on the MRROC curve. Unlike the normal ROC curve which is a function of one decision parameter alone, it is not possible to set the algorithm operating point on the basis of the slope of an MRROC curve.

4 Characterisation of the algorithm

We will now deal with algorithm characterisation, which is the evaluation of algorithmic performance over a range of different data sets. For the purposes of performance evaluation, we require image data sets which are representative of the application, and also a set of labelled images which represent the "true" segmentation of these scenes into the classes of interest to compare with the algorithmic output [22].

4.1 Ground truth image data

Four sequences of images captured from the vehicle were used in off-line tests of the classification algorithm. An example image from each sequence is given in figure 4 (a)–(d). The sequences have been chosen to represent a range of typical crop growth stages and imaging conditions, although this range should by no means be considered exhaustive. The sequence properties are summarised in table 1. The deep shadows seen in figure 4 D are a result of bright sunlight.

Sequence	# images	Crop age	Weed density	Weather
A	960	8 weeks	low	cloudy
B	960	3 weeks	very low	overcast
C	1380	6 weeks	moderate	overcast
D	1280	3 weeks	very low	sunny

Table 1. Properties of the image sequences.

Haralick [10] asserts that performance characterisation requires a test set of statistically independent data. To this end, a subset of each image sequence was chosen such that no two images contain overlapping areas of the ground, which ensures that no two pixels in the test set represent the same patch of soil or plant. For each image in these test sets (a total of 66 images across the four sequences), a ground truth labelling was produced by hand segmenting the image pixels into four classes: crop, weed, soil and doubt. The ground truth images have been produced by hand using standard image editing software, and are subject to error, especially at border pixels where different image regions (crop, weed or soil) are adjacent. Some of these pixels will be incorrectly classified as their adjacent class, whilst some will be of genuinely mixed class. Alexander [2] noted such problems with border pixels and proposed that at the border between

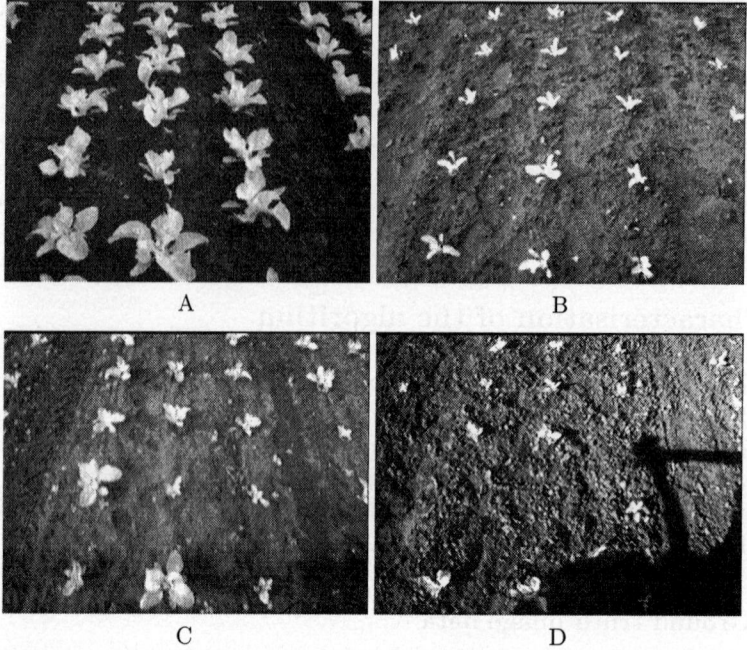

Fig. 4. Examples from the four image sequences A – D.

foreground (in our case plant matter) and background (soil), regions of doubt should be inserted, and the pixels within these doubt regions should be ignored for the purpose of assessing classifiers. All pixels that are on the border of plant matter and soil in the ground truth images are assigned to the doubt class and ignored in the classification assessments.

4.2 Stage I

A set of 27 threshold gain levels was chosen and the algorithm applied to the test images to generate the TPR,FPR pairs that constitute the ROC curve. The area under each of the curves plotted for sequences A – D is given in table 2.

Data Set	Area under ROCC	Area under MRROCC
A	0.9957	0.9974
B	0.9779	0.9997
C	0.9846	0.9996
D	0.9241	0.9993

Table 2. Area underneath ROC curves for algorithm stage I, sequences A–D (left) and for the MRROC curves for algorithm stage II (right).

The performance of stage I on each of the four data sets is reflected by the measures of area underneath the ROC curve shown in table 2. These show that the algorithm performs best on sequence A, where the plants are large and there are few shadows, with sequences C and B following. The lowest overall performance is seen on sequence D, caused by the heavy shadows present (figure 4 D).

4.3 Stage II

As noted above, to compare the performance of stage II of the algorithm on our data sets, we use MRROC analysis. The two parameters ς and r, described in section 2.2, are varied systematically (27 samples of each parameter, yielding a total of 729 classifiers) to produce a cloud of TPR,FPR pairs in the ROC space. The convex hull of these points constitutes the MRROC curve [14], and the area underneath the curve is calculated for each data set and used as a metric for comparison, with better performance indicated as usual by an area closer to 1.

Recall that stage II of the algorithm comprises two steps, a size filtering step followed by feature clustering on the basis of proximity to the crop grid pattern. In the fully automatic algorithm, the input features are provided by stage I, and the grid position by the extended Kalman filter crop grid tracker [15]. In our first experiment, we removed the dependency on both of these algorithms by locating the crop grid by hand, and used the ground truth classified features as our input. In his outline of a performance characterisation methodology Haralick [10] states that testing algorithms on perfect input data is not worthwhile; if the algorithm's performance is less than perfect, then a new algorithm should be devised. In an ideal world, this would be the case, but our the crop/weed discrimination problem is difficult; capturing the large variations in size and shape of each sort of plant devising an algorithm to fit such models to image data will not be easy, so we currently have to settle for an imperfect algorithm that makes mistakes even on perfect data. In this case, testing on perfect input data tells us the best performance that the algorithm can be expected to deliver.

The areas underneath the MRROC curve for each sequence in this experiment are given in the right-hand columns of table 2, whilst a section of the MRROC curve, and the cloud of classifiers in the ROC space, is plotted in figure 5 (where we take crop pixels to be positives and weed pixels to be negatives). In table 2, the performance of the stage II algorithm is seen to be consistent over each sequence, and very close to the ideal of 1 in each case. As noted above, to generate the curve for each sequence, we ran 729 trials of the algorithm over each of the 4 sequences, a time-consuming task. To cut down on computational effort for the fully automatic algorithms, we selected a single ς, r pair for each sequence. The point selected was that closest to the ideal (0,1) point in ROC space. A more principled selection of operating parameters might be possible if the values and costs of correct and incorrect decisions were known. For example, if the farmer wishes to remove all weeds and is willing to risk some crop in this process, the value of true negatives (correctly classified weed) would be high, and the cost of a false positive (weed classified as crop) would be higher than the cost of a false negative (crop classified as weed). If crop fertilisation was a priority, a true positive (correctly identified crop) would be high, and the cost of a false negative

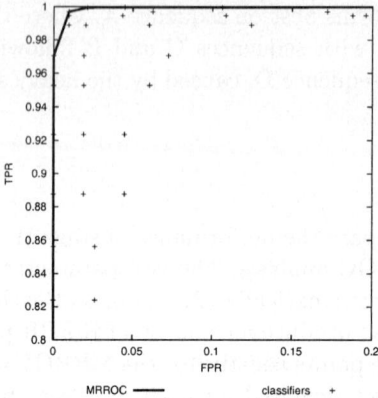

Fig. 5. The MRROC curve for ground truth plant matter segmentations of sequence C.

would be higher than the cost of a false positive. The values of ς and r chosen, together with their corresponding TPR and FPR, are given for each sequence in table 3.

Sequence	ς (pixels)	r (mm)	Parameter Setting		Automatic Tracking	
			TPR	FPR	TPR	FPR
A	100	450	0.9950	0.0	0.9939	0.1564
B	30	100	0.9940	0.0	0.9982	0.0
C	80	100	0.9970	0.0094	0.9981	0.0307
D	30	100	0.9975	0.0638	0.9993	0.2017

Table 3. Operating points for the size filtering and clustering algorithms, and their corresponding TPR and FPR chosen in the parameter setting experiment (left), together with the TPR and FPR realised under automatic tracking (right, and section 4.4).

4.4 Segmentation of ground truth plant images

Before combining stages I and II of the algorithm and analysing overall performance, we test stage II on the *ground truth plant matter images* under automatic tracking by our Kalman filter algorithm [15]. We perform this experiment in order to assess stage II of the algorithm in such a way that is as far as possible independent of the image thresholding algorithm of stage I. The test is not entirely independent of the image processing errors, because they have an effect on the tracker's estimate of the crop grid position that is used in the feature clustering algorithm, but it does allow us to compare the true positive and false positive ratios for crop pixels directly with those found in the parameter selection experiments.

We use the Kalman filter's estimate of the crop grid position in conjunction with the size filtering and feature clustering algorithm of algorithm stage II. After this processing, we have two sets of classified pixels for each image sequence. The first set is C, the ground truth plant matter pixels that have been classified as crop. The second set is W, the ground truth plant matter pixels that have been classified as weed. Given the two sets C and W, we can produce true positive (ground truth crop pixels that are classified C) and false positive (ground truth weed pixels classified as C) ratios for the automatic segmentation. These ratios are given in table 3 in the column marked 'automatic tracking'.

Before we compare the ratios from the tracking experiment with those from the parameter setting experiment, we reiterate the main differences between the two experiments. In the tracking experiment, the association region, within which all features are classified as crop, includes the uncertainty on the grid position, so will be larger than the corresponding region in the parameter setting experiment where the grid position was assumed to be known perfectly. We might expect that, as the association region expands, more image features will fall within it, so both TPR and FPR are likely to rise. The second difference is that the grid position in the tracking experiment is determined automatically by tracking the features derived from image processing, whilst the in the parameter setting experiment, the grid was placed by hand, and will be unaffected by any image processing errors.

If we now compare the tracking and parameter setting figures in table 3, we can see how these two experimental differences manifest themselves for each sequence:

Sequence A: The TPR drops and the FPR rises when the grid is tracked automatically. This sequence is the most difficult to track, because many crop plant features merge together so that feature centroids do not represent plant locations. Poor tracking is almost certainly the cause of the increased errors.

Sequence B: The TPR rises for the automatic tracker, where the association regions will be larger than in the parameter setting experiment owing to the increased uncertainty on plant position. The FPR is unaffected; this is a result of the low weed density in sequence B.

Sequence C: Both TPR and FPR increase under automatic tracking. This will be caused by the larger association region as it incorporates plant position uncertainty from the tracker.

Sequence D: As with sequence C, both TPR and FPR increase. Owing to the strong shadows present in this sequence, automatic tracking is difficult, so the uncertainty on individual plant position will be large; this is reflected in the dramatic rise in FPR.

The figures in table 3 show that the combination of size filtering and feature merging is very effective for classifying crop features, with true positive ratios in excess of 0.99 in for every sequence. The algorithm is less effective at weed pixel classification when tracking is difficult, as in sequences A and D, where the FPR rises to 15% and 20% respectively. This is not surprising because the success on the feature clustering algorithm hinges on the crop grid tracker providing good estimates of the crop position. However, when the tracking is easier, as in sequences B and C, the FPRs are much lower, 0.0% and 3.07% respectively.

4.5 Combining stages I and II

The second segmentation experiment relies wholly on the thresholding and chain-coding algorithms and tests the full automatic segmentation algorithm that combines stages I and II. In the previous experiment, we knew that all the features presented for size filtering and clustering were true plant matter. In this experiment, some soil pixels will be misclassified as plant matter (and labelled C or W), and some plant matter pixels (crop or weed) will be labelled S. A suitable value for the threshold gain α for each sequence was determined from the slope of the ROC curves generated for each sequence [18] by using an empirical estimate of the Bayes costs and values and prior probabilities computed from the test data.

Each of the tables 4 – 7 presents the percentage of the ground truth crop, weed and soil pixels classified as C, W and S, together with the total number of ground truth pixels in each class from the ground truth images of sequences A – D. The numbers of pixels bordering ground truth crop and weed features are also given as an indication of the number of doubt pixels that have been ignored in the classification totals. Each image is composed of 384×288 pixels, although only pixels in the region of the image ($approx 65\%$) that will pass underneath the autonomous vehicle's treatment system (a bar of spray nozzles that runs along the front axis of the vehicle) are classified.

Perusal of the figures in tables 4 – 7 prompts a number of observations:

1. In every sequence, in excess of 98% of the soil pixels are correctly classified as S.
2. In each sequence, more crop pixels are misclassified as S than misclassified as W.
3. In each sequence, more weed pixels are misclassified as S than misclassified as C.
4. In sequences A and C, a greater percentage of crop pixels are correctly classified C than the percentage of weed pixels that are correctly classified as W.
5. In sequences B and D, a greater percentage of weed pixels are correctly classified W than the percentage of crop pixels that are classified C.
6. The number of doubt pixels that border ground truth weed features outnumber the total number of ground truth weed pixels in every test sequence.
7. The total number of ground truth crop pixels outnumber the doubt pixels that border the crop features in every test sequence.

Observations 1, 2 and 3 directly reflect the performance of the adaptive interpolated grey-level thresholding algorithm, which misclassifies a large percentage of the plant matter pixels as soil. This will obviously be the most common misclassification, because plant matter is most often seen against a background of soil rather than other plant matter. The observations do, however, highlight the fact that the plant matter/soil discrimination problem requires more attention if image segmentation is to be improved.

		Classified as			Number of	
		C (%)	W (%)	S (%)	pixels	border pixels
	Crop	95.11	1.28	3.61	331,222	52,688
Ground truth	Weed	10.50	51.88	37.62	505	1,373
	Soil	0.33	0.03	99.64	905,200	-

Table 4. Sequence A segmentation results, percentages of true numbers of crop, weed and soil pixels classified as C, W or S, and the number of pixels that border crop and weed features. There are 16 ground truth images for sequence A.

		Classified as			Number of	
		C (%)	W (%)	S (%)	pixels	border pixels
	Crop	78.90	3.72	17.38	53,514	19,615
Ground truth	Weed	0.0	81.8	18.2	934	3,455
	Soil	0.01	0.04	99.95	1,152,254	-

Table 5. Sequence B segmentation results, percentages of true numbers of crop, weed and soil pixels classified as C, W or S, and the number of pixels that border crop and weed features. There are 17 ground truth images for sequence B.

		Classified as			Number of	
		C (%)	W (%)	S (%)	pixels	border pixels
	Crop	81.72	4.51	13.76	141,075	19,615
Ground truth	Weed	3.93	56.90	39.17	17,160	18,544
	Soil	0.06	0.24	99.7	1,195,308	-

Table 6. Run C segmentation results, percentages of true numbers of crop, weed and soil pixels classified as C, W or S, and the number of pixels that border crop and weed features. There are 17 ground truth images for sequence C.

		Classified as			Number of	
		C (%)	W (%)	S (%)	pixels	border pixels
	Crop	55.00	4.11	40.89	41,411	13,171
Ground truth	Weed	6.31	73.52	20.17	1,046	2,202
	Soil	0.06	1.13	98.81	1,003,418	-

Table 7. Run D segmentation results, percentages of true numbers of crop, weed and soil pixels classified as C, W or S, and the number of pixels that border crop and weed features. There are 16 ground truth images for sequence D.

Observations 4 and 5 suggest that the larger plants seen in image sequences A and C are more easily identified than the smaller plants in sequences B and D. The reasons for this are unclear, but may be related to changes in the infra-red reflectance of the crop plants as they age.

Observations 6 and 7 show that the weed features, which are dominated by border pixels, are typically smaller than the crop features. This has already been illustrated in figure 2 and forms the basis of the size threshold algorithm.

If we ignore the crop and weed ground truth pixels that the segmentation algorithm labels S, we can construct true positive and false positive ratios for the crop and weed pixels that have been classified as plant matter (either C or W). These figures are given for each sequence in table 8 and show that those pixels which *are* identified as plant matter are separated into the crop and weed classes with some success. This allows us to conjecture that if plant matter/soil discrimination were more reliable then figures similar to those in table 3 might be obtained.

Sequence	TPR	FPR
A	0.9639	0.1683
B	0.9550	0.0
C	0.9477	0.0650
D	0.9305	0.0790

Table 8. TPR and FPR for the correctly identified plant matter pixels in sequences A–D.

5   Conclusions

We have used a novel two stage algorithm developed for a horticultural application to illustrate that breaking an algorithm down into its constituent components and testing these individually can provide a better understanding of overall behaviour. Analysis of the test results allows us to conclude that the majority of the errors in the system are propagated forward from stage I of the algorithm. It was seen that II performs effectively on the data that is correctly propagated form stage I, so algorithm development should focus on improving the plant matter/soil segmentation. Empirical discrepancy analysis based on ROC curves and type I and type II statistical errors was used for the individual binary classifiers, and overall tri-partite classification figures given for the full algorithm.

Acknowledgement

This work was funded by the BBSRC.

References

1. I E Abdou. Quantitative methods of edge detection. Technical Report USCIPI Report 830, University of California Image Processing Institute, July 1978.

2. D C Alexander and B F Buxton. Modelling of sinlge mode distributions of colour data using directional statistics. In *Proceedings Computer Vision and Pattern Recognition*, 1997.

3. Y Bar-Shalom and T Fortmann. *Tracking and Data Association*. Academic Press, New York, 1988.

4. H.R. Biller. Reduced input of herbicides by use of optoelectronic sensors. *Journal of Agricultural Engineering Research*, 71:357–362, 1998.

5. K Bowyer, C Kranenburg, and S Dougherty. Edge detector evaluation using empirical ROC curves. In *Proc. CVPR*, volume 1, 1999.

6. G J Edwards, C J Taylor, and T F Cootes. Improving identification performance by integrating evidence from sequences. In *Proc. CVPR*, volume 1, 1999.

7. H Freeman. On the encoding of arbitrary geometric configurations. *IEEE Trans. Elec. Computers*, EC-10:260–268, 1961.

8. D M Green and J A Swets. *Signal Detection Theory and Psychophysics*. John Wiley and Sons, 1966.

9. J A Hanley and B J McNeil. The meaning and use of the area under a receiver operating characteristic (ROC) curve. *Radiology*, 143:29–36, April 1982.

10. R M Haralick. Performance characterization protocol in computer vision. In *DARPA Image Understanding Workshop*, 1994.

11. M G M Hunink, R G M Deslegte, and M F Hoogesteger. ROC analysis of the clinicl, CT and MRI diagnosis of orbital space-occupying lesions. *ORBIT*, 8(3), September 1989.

12. M Oren and S K Nayar. Generalization of the Lambertian model and implications for machine vision. *International Journal of Computer Vision*, 14:227–251, 1995.

13. B Rao. Data association methods for tracking systems. In A Blake and A Yuille, editors, *Active Vision*, chapter 6. MIT Press, 1992.

14. M J J Scott, M Niranjan, and R W Prager. Realisable classifiers: Improving operating performance on variable cost problems. In *Proceedings BMVC 1998*, volume I, pages 306–315, September 1998.

15. B Southall, B F Buxton, and J A Marchant. Controllability and observability: Tools for Kalman filter design. In M S Nixon, editor, *Proceedings 9th British Machine Vision Conference*, volume 1, pages 164–173, September 1998.

16. B Southall, T Hague, J A Marchant, and B F Buxton. Vision-aided outdoor navigation of an autonomous horticultural vehicle. In Henrik I Christensen, editor, *Proceedings 1st International Conference on Vision Systems*. Springer Verlag, January 1999.

17. B Southall, J A Marchant, T Hague, and B F Buxton. Model based tracking for navigation and segmentation. In H Burkhardt and B Neumann, editors, *Proceedings 5th European Conference on Computer Vision*, volume 1, pages 797–811, June 1998.

18. J B Southall. *The design and evaluation of computer vision algorithms for the control of an autonomous horticultural vehicle*. PhD thesis, University of London, 2000.

19. M R Spiegel. *Probability and Statistics*. Schaum's Outline Series. McGraw Hill, 1980.

20. B van Branniken, M Stavridi, and J J Koenderink. Diffuse and specular reflectance from rough surfaces. *Applied Optics*, 37(1):130–139, January 1998.

21. H L van Trees. *Detection, Estimation and Modulation Theory, Part I*. John Wiley and Sons, 1968.

22. Y J Zhang. A survey on evaluation methods for image segmentation. *Pattern Recognition*, 29(8):1335–1346, 1996.

Statistical Significance as an Aid to System Performance Evaluation

Peter Tu and Richard Hartley

Image Understanding Group,
General Electric,
Niskayuna, NY 12309

Abstract. Using forensic fingerprint identification as a testbed, a statistical framework for analyzing system performance is presented. Each set of fingerprint features is represented by a collection of binary codes. The matching process is equated to measuring the Hamming distances between feature sets. After performing matching experiments on a small data base, the number of independent degrees of freedom intrinsic to the fingerprint population is estimated. Using this information, a set of independent Bernoulli trials is used to predict the success of the system with respect to a particular dataset.

1 Introduction

Given an image of a particular target, computer vision recognition systems such as [9] search a large database in order to find a second image of the target. The approach usually takes several steps. The initial image is characterized by a set of features forming a target template. Feature extraction is performed on all candidate images in the database. Each set of candidate features is matched with the template set (this may require some form of registration). A similarity function is used to determine the merit of each match. The candidates with the highest match scores are reported to the user. It is important for developers of such systems to have answers to the following questions:

- As the database grows what will happen to the reliability of the system?
- What is the optimal performance that can be expected for a given datum?
- Is there room for improvement in the system and if so where should future research resources be allocated?

In this work a statistical framework for analyzing these questions is presented in the context of forensic fingerprint identification. Each set of image features is represented by a collection of binary codes. The matching process is viewed as a mechanism which measures the Hamming distance between various codes generated by the template and those generated by a candidate. The number of independent degrees of freedom intrinsic to the population is then measured by performing experiments on a small representative data base. Using this information, the ranking for the true match of a particular template can then be modeled as a series of independent Bernoulli trials. Questions regarding system reliability, scalability and maturity can then be addressed.

In forensic identification the target image is known as a *latent* print such as one found at a crime scene. The database of candidate images are known as *tenprints* and are taken under controlled conditions. Some tenprint databases can have hundreds of millions of entries. Many fingerprint systems such as [6] and [8] use minutiae as their image features. These are points where ridges terminate or bifurcate. They are characterized by their 2D location and an angular measure corresponding to the orientation of the surrounding ridge flow. Stretching by up to 30 percent can take place and there may be false and missing minutiae. The latent is usually just a partial print which can have as few as 5 or 6 minutiae (the average tenprint has over 80). The position of the latent with respect to the tenprint coordinate system is usually unknown. Mechanisms based on approaches such as graph matching [1] and matched filtering [2] are often used to perform the matching between sets of minutiae. Each tenprint is ranked based on the score received during the matching process. If the search is successful, the true mate will receive a rank at or near the top of the list.

By representing minutia structure as sets of binary codes and performing matching experiments on a local database of 300 tenprints the following information will be determined:

- The number of degrees of freedom found in a particular fingerprint code.
- The expected ranking of the true mate for a given latent with respect to a 700,000 print database.
- The level of performance of a particular matching algorithm based on the analysis of 86 latent prints.

1.1 Previous Work

Methods for computing the probability of encountering two identical sets of features from unrelated fingerprints have been found in the works by [4],[5] and [7]. However these approaches assume that only local features are correlated.

Like fingerprints, iris matching has become a viable tool for online identification. In the work by Daugman [3], a single binary code is generated for each iris. Matching can then be accomplished by computing the Hamming distance between codes. Statistical significance is evaluated by measuring the number of independent degrees of freedom that these codes possess. The matching process can then be equated to a series of independent Bernoulli trials which are modeled probabilistically. In this paper, Daugman's approach is extended by generating multiple codes for a single set of features so that the latent and a tenprint need not be registered in advance.

2 Measuring Average Information Content

The purpose of the first experiment is to determine the information contained within a 100x100 pixel region of a fingerprint. Ostenburg's [4] grid system is used to generate a binary code for the region. In this experiment only minutia position is considered. One conclusion that is drawn from this experiment is that minutiae are correlated with one another.

By representing local minutia structure as a binary code, the information contained in a fingerprint can be quantitatively assessed. A similarity function between two sets of minutiae is developed based on the Hamming distance between their binary codes. By extracting a large number of codes and computing the Hamming distances between all pairs of unrelated codes, the relative frequencies of the similarity function can be measured. The parameters for the appropriate probability distribution function of the similarity function can then be estimated. These parameters are used to determine the number of statistical degrees of freedom that are intrinsic to the fingerprint population.

2.1 Minutia Structure to Binary Codes

Given a particular minutia A, a 10 by 10 grid of squares is centered on minutia A and is rotated so as to be aligned with minutia A's orientation. Each square is 10 pixels by 10 pixels in dimension. A binary code is formed by assigning a single bit to each square. If a square contains a minutia other that minutia A, then its bit is set to 1. In this way a binary code is used to represent the local minutia structure around minutia A. See figure 1 for an example of the code extraction process.

Using a database of 300 tenprints, 10 minutiae were selected at random from each print. A code was generated for each minutia resulting in 3000 codes. The relative frequency of each bit can be seen in figures 2 and 3. As one would expect the 8 bits around the center of the grid have a relatively low frequency. These bits are excluded leaving a 92 bit code. From these measurements it was estimated that the probability p that a bit is turned on was uniformly distributed and that

$$p = 0.05381. \tag{1}$$

2.2 Hamming Distance

Given two 92 bit codes $\mathbf{X}$ and $\mathbf{Y}$, the similarity of the two codes can be measured based on the Hamming distance. The Hamming distance is defined as the average value of the exclusive or between each pair of bits in the two codes. A similarity function S which is a maximum for identical codes is defined as:

$$S = 1 - \frac{1}{92} \sum_{k=1}^{92} \mathbf{X}[k] \otimes \mathbf{Y}[k] \tag{2}$$

$$= \frac{1}{92} \sum_{k=1}^{92} \mathbf{H}[k] \tag{3}$$

where

$$\mathbf{H}[k] = \begin{cases} 1 & \text{if } \mathbf{X}[k] = \mathbf{Y}[k] \\ 0 & \text{otherwise} \end{cases}$$

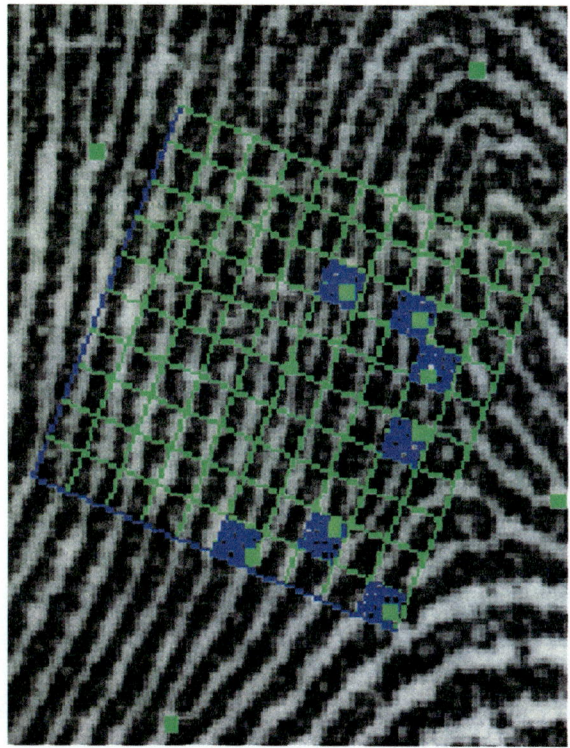

Fig. 1. A minutia is selected and a grid is centered on and oriented with this minutia. The green dots are identified minutiae. The blue marks indicate squares where local minutiae have been found.

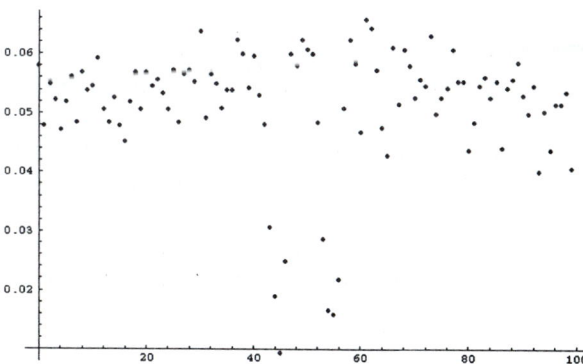

Fig. 2. The bit number versus the probability of the bit being set to 1. As expected the bits near the center of the grid have a lower probability of activation.

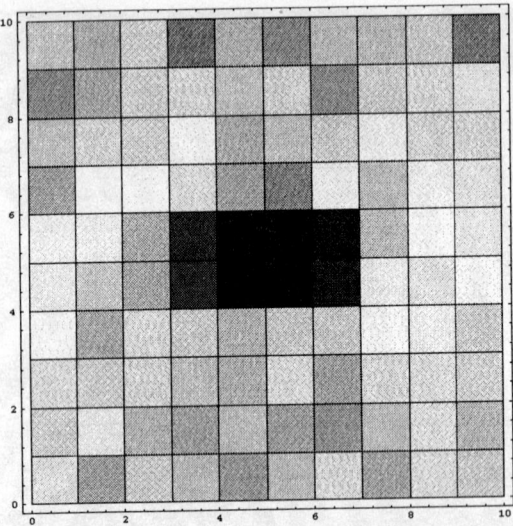

Fig. 3. A grid depicting the probability of a bit being set to 1. The bits near the center of the grid have a lower probability of activation.

Each term of S can be viewed as a Bernoulli trial. For all k, the expected value of $\mathbf{H}[k]$ is equal to α where

$$\alpha = p^2 + (1-p)^2. \tag{4}$$

It follows that

$$\bar{S} = E(S) = \alpha = 0.89817. \tag{5}$$

If the initial assumption is made that all the bits in the code are independent, then it would be expected that

$$\sigma_S = \sqrt{E[(S - \bar{S})^2]} = \sqrt{\frac{\alpha(1-\alpha)}{92}} = 0.031529. \tag{6}$$

The complete independence assumption implies that there are 92 degrees of freedom in the minutia structure. The following tests will show that this assumption is not valid.

Using the 3000 codes, the similarity function S was computed for every pair of unrelated codes. The observed mean and standard deviation of S were:

$$\bar{S}_{obs} = 0.898185 \tag{7}$$

and

$$\sigma_{obs} = 0.033366 \tag{8}$$

The observed mean is very close to the predicted value (equation 5). However the observed standard deviation of S is larger than expected. It is therefore concluded that the true number of degrees of freedom N, which can be found by solving the formula:

$$\sqrt{\frac{\alpha(1-\alpha)}{N}} = \sigma_{obs},\tag{9}$$

is $N \approx 82$.

In other words, taking a measurement of S between two unrelated codes, is equivalent to counting the number of times a weighted coin comes up heads out of N tosses such that the probability of getting heads on an individual toss is equal to α.

Given the estimates of α and N, the probability of observing a value of $S = \frac{m}{92}$ can be computed. The first step is to determine m_1 such that

$$\frac{m_1}{N} = \frac{m}{92}\tag{10}$$

The probability of observing S is calculated by:

$$P(S = \frac{m}{92}) = \frac{N}{92}\frac{N!}{m_1!(N-m_1)!}\alpha^{m_1}(1-\alpha)^{N-m_1}.\tag{11}$$

This equation is based on the standard binomial distribution where N is the number of trials, m_1 is the number of positive results and α is the probability of a positive result on a given trial. The scaling factor $\frac{N}{92}$ is used to compensate for the fact that there are 92 possible results as opposed to just N. Linear interpolation is used since in general m_1 is not an integer. Figure 4 shows the measured frequencies of S along with $P(S)$ computed in equation 11. It turns out that the probability of finding two identical codes is 1:6677 as opposed to 1:19,544 which was computed under the assumption of complete independence.

3 Statistical Significance of a Particular Latent

When searching for the true mate of a particular latent, each tenprint in the database is ranked based on a score given during the matching process. If the search is successful, the true mate will be ranked at or near the top of the list.

In this section an experiment based on an "ideal" matching mechanism, will be performed in order to evaluate a particular latent and its true mate. Using measurements taken from a 300 print database, the odds that a false print will out-rank (i.e. get a higher score than) the true mate will be determined. A prediction of the ranking that the true mate would receive from a 700,000 print search will be made. This will be compared to the results achieved by a real search performed by an in house matching algorithm referred to here as the "MATCHER".

The ideal matching mechanism is modeled as a form of template matching. In this process a set of transformations between the latent and the tenprint coordinate system are generated. Each transformation, which is composed of a translation and a rotation, is applied to the latent print. Once the latent has been

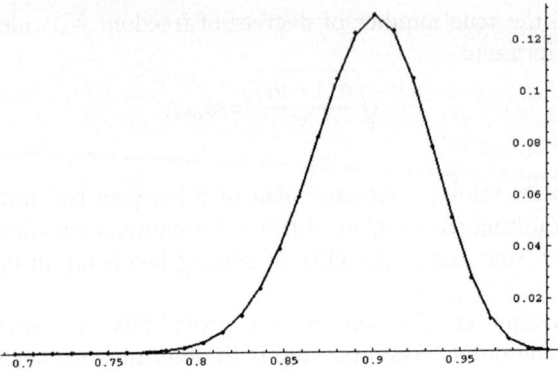

Fig. 4. The dots show the measured frequencies of the similarity function S (defined in equation 3). The solid line is the estimated probability density function shown in equation 11. As can be seen there is almost perfect agreement.

transformed, it is determined whether or not each latent minutia can be matched with a tenprint minutia. This can be viewed as a mechanism for generating a binary code, where bit i is set to 1 iff minutia i can be matched to a tenprint minutia. A merit function M for the transformation is defined as the sum of the bit values divided by the number of bits in the code. The score assigned to the tenprint is set to the merit of the transformation with the highest merit score.

A transformation is generated by aligning a single latent minutia with a single tenprint minutia. The alignment is based on both position and orientation (angle of the dominant ridge flow near the minutia) of the minutia. The latent minutia used to construct the transformation is not used when the merit of the resulting binary code is computed.

Each minutia is defined by an (x, y, ω) coordinate where (x, y) represents position and ω represents orientation. Let (x', y', ω') represent the transformed coordinates of minutia i. The i'th bit for the transformation will be set to 1 iff there exists a tenprint minutia with coordinates (x, y, ω) such that:

$$\sqrt{(x' - x)^2 + (y' - y)^2} \leq \Delta_s \qquad (12)$$

and

$$|\omega' - \omega| \leq \Delta_a \qquad (13)$$

where Δ_s is a spatial threshold and Δ_a is an angular threshold.

By modeling the matching process in this way, it can be argued that a somewhat optimistic prediction will be generated. This is because it is assumed that a rigid transformation can align a latent with its true mate in spite of the fact that stretching of up to 30 percent can occur. If minutia descriptions are the only features used to represent the fingerprint, a true matching algorithm would be forced to use weaker assignment criteria. However variation due to stretching can be reduced by considering additional fingerprint features. Ridge topology is invariant with respect to stretching. The number of ridges that cross a straight line connecting any two points on a fingerprint can be used as a normalized distance measure. Fiducial points such as cores and deltas (singularities in the ridge flow field) can be identified and used to estimate global transformations which compensate for many stretching effects. For these reasons it is argued that rigid template matching is a reasonable model for the matching process.

3.1 Probability Distribution of the Merit Function

We now consider a particular latent print and its true mate as shown in figure 5. The position and orientation of each minutia are represented by a dot and a small line segment. There are 14 minutiae in the latent print. An examiner determined that there are 11 legitimate minutia assignments between the latent and its true mate. A triangulation is applied to the matched minutiae to make it easier to see the assignments. The merit score for the true mate is 10 out of 13 possible matches. It is not 11 out of 14 because one pair of minutiae is always needed to generate a transformation.

In order to determine the spatial and angular thresholds, an affine transform based on a least squares fit between the identified minutia correspondences of the latent and the true mate was computed. The values Δ_s and Δ_a were set as tightly as possible while still allowing the transformed latent minutiae to be matched to their true assignments. An affine transform was used in order to compensate for possible stretching in the print. In this example the thresholds were set to:

$$\Delta_s = 15 \; pixels \tag{14}$$

and

$$\Delta_a = 13.29 \; degrees \tag{15}$$

The next step is to compute a probability distribution function for the merit function M so that predictions can be made regarding a search on a large database for the true mate shown in figure 5 It is important to note that the derived PDF will only be applicable when considering this particular latent print. All possible transformations between the latent and 300 tenprints were generated. It was assumed that the latent print was roughly oriented so that transformations requiring too much rotation were rejected. A transformation was also rejected if the transformed latent minutiae were not contained within the convex hull of the tenprint minutiae. A total of 53,334 transformations were generated.

The probability p that a transformed latent minutia i would be matched with a tenprint minutia was observed to be:

$$p = 0.074. \tag{16}$$

This is the same as saying that the probability of the ith bit being set to 1 is equal to p. Each bit in the code can be viewed as a Bernoulli trial. The expected

Latent   True Mate

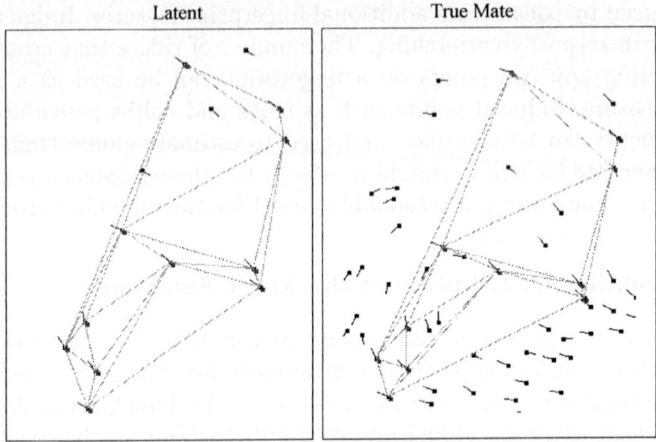

Fig. 5. This figure shows a latent and its true mate. The position and orientation of each minutia is represented by a dot and a small line segment. There are 14 minutiae in the latent print. An examiner determined that there are 11 legitimate minutia assignments. A triangulation is applied to the matched minutiae to make it easier to see the assignments. Note that there are 3 unassigned latent minutiae

value of M is equal to p. If we assume independence between bits in the code and since there are only 13 bits (one minutia is always excluded from the code since it is used to create the transformation), the standard deviation of M would be expected to be:

$$\sigma_M = \sqrt{\frac{p(1-p)}{13}} = 0.072639, \tag{17}$$

However, the measured standard deviation for M was found to be

$$\sigma_{obs} = 0.075057 \tag{18}$$

Since the observed standard deviation is higher than predicted, it is concluded that the latent minutiae are not completely independent. The number of statistical degrees of freedom N is calculated by solving:

$$\sqrt{\frac{p(1-p)}{N}} = \sigma_{obs} \tag{19}$$

and it turns out that

$$N \approx 12 \tag{20}$$

The probability distribution for $M = \frac{m}{13}$ can now be formulated. Let

$$m_1 = \frac{Nm}{13} \tag{21}$$

then

$$P(M = \frac{m}{13}) = \frac{N}{13} \frac{N!}{m_1!(N-m_1)!} p^{m_1}(1-p)^{N-m_1}. \tag{22}$$

Like equation 11 this equation is composed of a scaling factor $\frac{N}{13}$ and a binomial function for N trials and m_1 successes with a probability p of success on an individual trial.

The measured frequencies of M for various values of m along with the predicted probabilities of M derived from equation 22 are shown in table 1

Number of hits	Measured frequency	predicted frequency
0	0.401451	0.366531
1	0.345802	0.353033
2	0.182266	0.185172
3	0.056662	0.067505
4	0.011269	0.017855
5	0.002231	0.003445
6	0.000281	0.000487
7	0.000037	0.000051
8	0.000000	0.000004
9	0.000000	0.000000
10	0.000000	0.000000
11	0.000000	0.000000
12	0.000000	0.000000
13	0.000000	0.000000

Table 1. The first column shows the number of set bits in the code. The second column shows the measured frequency of observing such a code based on test made on a 300 print database. The third column shows the predicted frequencies based on equation 22. As can be seen there is a reasonable agreement between the measured and predicted frequencies.

As previously stated, the merit that could be attributed to the true mate would be $\frac{10}{13}$. Using equation 22 the probability that a code generated by a false print will do as well or better than the true mate is computed to be one in 116,041,312. There were 300 tenprints used to generate 53,334 transformations which means that there were approximately 177 transformations per print. So that one in 652,724 prints could be expected to out rank the true mate. Given a database with 700,000 tenprints, one false print could be expected to have a higher rank than the true mate. This results in an expected ranking of 2 for the true mate. In comparison, the matching algorithm MATCHER attempted to locate the true mate of this example from a real 700,000 print database. The true mate was given a ranking of 3.

4 Evaluation of the MATCHER performance

In order to evaluate the general level of performance of the matching algorithm MATCHER, the previous analysis was applied to a set of 86 latent prints. These prints have been identified as *difficult* to match. In some cases there were less than 10 minutiae to work with. For each latent, the following steps were taken:

1. The true assignments between the latent and its mate were picked by hand.
2. The thresholds Δ_s and Δ_a were automatically set based on the relationship between the latent and its mate.
3. Using measurements on a 300 print database, the PDF for the merit function M associated with the latent was determined.
4. The odds of encountering a false print which would outperform the true mate was computed.
5. The ranking of the true mate with respect to a 700,000 print search was predicted
6. A real 700,000 print search for the true mate was performed using the matching algorithm MATCHER

In figure 6 the predicted and true rankings for this data set have been sorted and placed on a graph so as to generate a set of performance curves.

The MATCHER significantly outperformed the predictions on 7 out of 86 latents. However it did not do as well as expected on 13 out of 86 prints. This is reflected in the gap between the MATCHER performance curve and the predicted performance curve. Table 2 shows the MATCHER and predicted top 10 performances. The MATCHER failed to achieve a large number of top 1s, however at the top 10 level, the MATCHER is only missing 4 prints.

With respect to conclusions that can be drawn regarding the MATCHER performance, there does seem to be some room for improvement. However, the predictions were made using the assumption that latents and tenprints can be matched using a rigid transformation, yet stretching of up to 30 percent can happen and any realistic matcher must compensate for this. For this reason the predicted performance can be viewed as somewhat optimistic.

There were a large number of prints that were deemed unmatchable and this agrees with the current state of diminishing returns on algorithmic performance.

5   Summary and Conclusions

A statistical framework for evaluating a fingerprint recognition system was developed. By performing experiments on a local database it was shown that the features used for matching are not completely independent. It was shown how the matching process can be modeled as a set of independent Bernoulli trials. This lead to the ability to make predictions regarding specific datasets. By comparing estimates of optimal performance with that achieved by the matching algorithm MATCHER, statements regarding the maturity of the system can be made.

Since the fingerprint identification is similar in nature to many computer vision recognition systems, we believe that this approach is broadly applicable. Once the matching process is understood, experiments performed on a modest database may allow researchers to answer questions regarding system reliability and scalability.

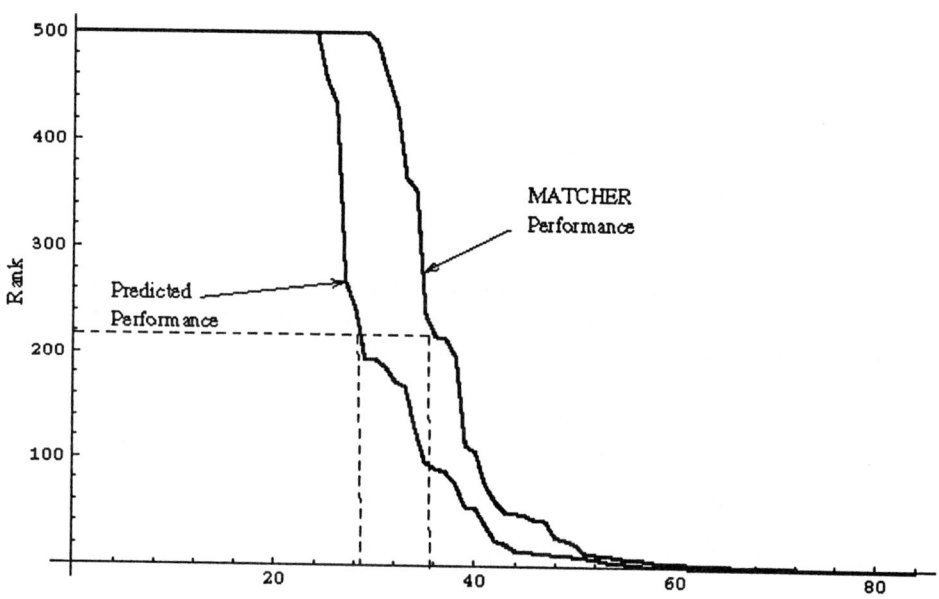

Fig. 6. The graph shows the ordered rankings of the true mates for a 700,000 print database. The two curves represent the predicted performance and the performance of the MATCHER matching algorithm. An interpretation of a point in the graph with horizontal coordinate x and vertical coordinate y is that x true mates had a ranking worse than or equal to rank y. For example, by noting were the two curves intersect the horizontal dashed line, it can be determined that 29 true mates were predicted to have a ranking worse than 220 and that when the MATCHER was run, 36 true mates were found to have a ranking worse than 220. This means that the MATCHER did slightly less well than expected.

Table 2. This table shows the number of top rankings achieved by the MATCHER as compared to the number of predicted top rankings.

	MATCHER	Predicted
Top 1	12	23
Top 2	17	26
Top 3	19	28
Top 4	23	29
Top 5	26	31
Top 6	27	31
Top 7	27	32
Top 8	28	32
Top 9	30	33
Top 10	30	34

Acknowledgments

This work has been supported by Lockheed Martin under the AFIS and shared vision programs. In particular we would like to thank Dr. Art Forman and Mark Cavanagh for their invaluable contributions.

References

1. Ambler A.P., Barrow H.G., Brown C.M., Burstall R.M., Popplestone R.J., 'A versatile computer-controlled assembly system', IJCAI, pages 298-307, 1973.
2. Ballard D.H., Brown C.M., 'Computer Vision', Prentice-Hall, Englewood Cliffs, NJ, 1982.
3. Daugman J.G., "High Confidence Visual Recognition for Persons by a Test of Statistical Independence", PAMI, vol, 15, no. 11, November 1993.
4. Ostenburg J.W., "An inquiry into the nature of proof: the identity of fingerprints", J. forensic Sciences, vol. 9, pp. 413-427, 1964.
5. Ostenburg J. W., Parthasanathy T., Raghavan T.E.S, Sclove S.L., "Development of mathematical formula for the calculation of fingerprint probabilities based on individual characteristics", J. Am. Statistical Assoc., vol. 72, pp. 772-778, Dec., 1977.
6. Ratha N.K., Karu K., Chen S., Jain A.K, 'A real-time matching system for large fingerprint databases', IEEE PAMI, vol. 18, no. 8, pp. 799-813, August 1996.
7. Roddy A.R., Stosz J.D., "Fingerprint Features - Statistical Analysis and System Performance Estimates", Proc. of the IEEE, vol. 85, no. 9, pp. 1390-1421, September 1997.
8. Weber D.M.,'A cost effective fingerprint verification algorithm for commercial applications', Proceedings of the 1992 South African symposium on communications and signal processing COSMIG'92. pp 99-104, published by the IEE.
9. Zisserman A., Forsyth D., Mundy J., Rothwell C., Liu J., Pillow N., '3D Object Recognition Using Invariance', Artificial Intelligence Journal, 78, pp. 239-288, 1995.

Segmentation & Grouping II

Segmentation & Grouping II

New Algorithms for Controlling Active Contours Shape and Topology

H. Delingette and J. Montagnat

Projet Epidaure
I.N.R.I.A.
06902 Sophia-Antipolis Cedex, BP 93, France

Abstract. In recent years, the field of active-contour based image segmentation have seen the emergence of two competing approaches. The first and oldest approach represents active contours in an explicit (or parametric) manner corresponding to the *Lagrangian* formulation. The second approach represent active contours in an implicit manner corresponding to the *Eulerian* framework. After comparing these two approaches, we describe several new topological and physical constraints applied on parametric active contours in order to combine the advantages of these two contour representations. We introduce three key algorithms for independently controlling active contour parameterization, shape and topology. We compare our result to the level-set method and show similar results with a significant speed-up.

1 Introduction

Image segmentation based on active contours has achieved considerable success in the past few years [15]. Deformable models are often used for bridging the gap between low-level computer vision (feature extraction) and high-level geometric representation. In their seminal paper [8], Kass *et al* choose to use a parametric contour representation with a semi-implicit integration scheme for discretizing the law of motion. Several authors have proposed different representations [16] including the use of finite element models [3], subdivision curves [6] and analytical models [17]. Implicit active contour representation were introduced in [13] following [19]. This approach has been developed by several other researchers including "geodesic snakes" introduced in [2].

The opposition between parametric and implicit contour representation corresponds to the opposition between Lagrangian and Eulerian frameworks. Qualifying the efficiency and the implementation issues of these two frameworks is difficult because of the large number of different algorithms existing in the literature. On one hand, implicit representations are in general regarded as being less efficient than parametric contours. This is because the update of an implicit contour requires the update of at least a narrow band around each contour. On the other hand, parametric contours cannot in general achieve any automatic topological changes, also several algorithms have been proposed to overcome this limitation [11, 14, 10].

This paper includes three distinct contributions corresponding to three different modeling levels of parametric active contours:

1. **Discretization**. We propose two algorithms for controlling the relative vertex spacing and the total number of vertices. On one hand, the vertex spacing is controlled through the tangential component of the internal force applied at each vertex. On the other hand, the total number of contour vertices is periodically updated in order to constrain the distance between vertices.
2. **Shape**. We introduce an intrinsic internal force expressions that do not depend on contour parameterization. This force regularizes the contour curvature profile without producing any contour shrinkage.
3. **Topology**. A new algorithm automatically creates or merges different connected components of a contour based on the detection of edge intersections. Our algorithm can handle opened and closed contours.

We propose a framework where algorithms for controlling the discretization, shape and topology of active contours are completely independent of each other. Having algorithmic independence is important for two reasons. First, each modeling component may be optimized separately leading to computationally more efficient algorithms. Second, a large variety of active contour behaviors may be obtained by combining different algorithms for each modeling component.

2 Discretization of active contours

In the remainder, we consider the deformation over time of a two-dimensional parametric contour $\mathcal{C}(u,t) \in \mathbb{R}^2$ where u designates the contour parameter and t designates the time. The parameter u belongs to the range $[0,1]$ with $\mathcal{C}(0,t) = \mathcal{C}(1,t)$ if the contour is closed. We formulate the contour deformation with a Newtonian law of motion:

$$\frac{\partial^2 \mathcal{C}}{\partial t^2} = -\gamma \frac{\partial \mathcal{C}}{\partial t} + f_{\text{int}} + f_{\text{ext}} \tag{1}$$

where f_{int} and f_{ext} correspond respectively to internal and external forces. A contour may include several connected components, each component being a closed or opened contour.

Temporal and spatial discretizations of $\mathcal{C}(u,t)$ are based on finite differences. Thus, the set of N^t vertices $\{\mathbf{p}_i^t\}$, $i = 0 \dots N^t - 1$ represents the contour $\mathcal{C}(u,t)$ at time t. The discretization of equation 1 using centered and right differences for the acceleration and speed term leads to:

$$\mathbf{p}_i^{t+1} = \mathbf{p}_i^t + (1 - 2\gamma)(\mathbf{p}_i^t - \mathbf{p}_i^{t-1}) + \alpha_i(f_{\text{int}})_i + \beta_i(f_{\text{ext}})_i. \tag{2}$$

In order to simplify the notation, we will write $\mathbf{p}_i$ instead of $\mathbf{p}_i^t$ the vertex position at time t. At each vertex $\mathbf{p}_i$, we define a local tangent vector $\mathbf{t}_i$, normal vector $\mathbf{n}_i$, metric parameter ϵ_i and curvature k_i. We propose to define the tangent vector at $\mathbf{p}_i$, as the direction of the line joining its two neighbors: $\mathbf{t}_i = (\mathbf{p}_{i+1} -$

$\mathbf{p}_{i-1})/(2r_i)$ where $r_i = \|\mathbf{p}_{i+1} - \mathbf{p}_{i-1}\|/2$ is the half distance between the two neighbors of $\mathbf{p}_i$. The normal vector $\mathbf{n}_i$ is defined as the vector directly orthogonal to $\mathbf{t}_i$: $\mathbf{n}_i = \mathbf{t}_i^\perp$ with $(x, y)^\perp = (-y, x)$. The curvature k_i is naturally defined as the curvature of the circle circumscribed at triangle $(\mathbf{p}_{i-1}, \mathbf{p}_i, \mathbf{p}_{i+1})$. If we write as ϕ_i, the oriented angle between segments $[\mathbf{p}_{i-1}, \mathbf{p}_i]$ and $[\mathbf{p}_i, \mathbf{p}_{i+1}]$, then the curvature is given by $k_i = \sin(\phi_i)/r_i$. Finally, the metric parameter ϵ_i measures the relative spacing of $\mathbf{p}_i$ with respect to its two neighboring vertices $\mathbf{p}_{i-1}$ and $\mathbf{p}_{i+1}$. If $\mathbf{F}_i$ is the projection of $\mathbf{p}_i$ on the line $[\mathbf{p}_{i-1}, \mathbf{p}_{i+1}]$, then the metric parameter is: $\epsilon_i = \|\mathbf{F}_i - \mathbf{p}_{i+1}\|/(2r_i) = 1 - \|\mathbf{F}_{i+1} - \mathbf{p}_{i-1}\|/(2r_i)$. In another words, ϵ_i and $1 - \epsilon_i$ are the barycentric coordinates of $\mathbf{F}_i$ with respect to $\mathbf{p}_{i-1}$ and $\mathbf{p}_{i+1}$: $\mathbf{F}_i = \epsilon_i \mathbf{p}_{i-1} + (1 - \epsilon_i)\mathbf{p}_{i+1}$.

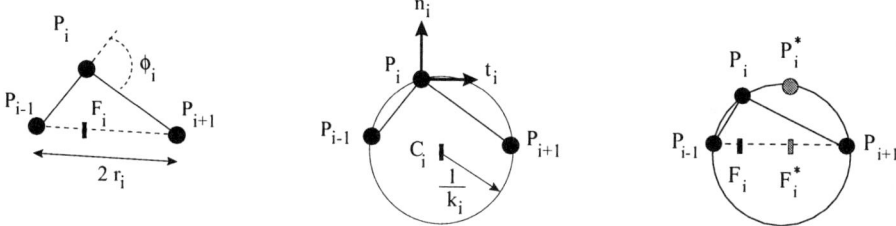

Fig. 1. Left: The geometry of a discrete contour; definition of $\mathbf{t}_i$, $\mathbf{n}_i$, k_i, ϕ_i, and $\mathbf{F}_i$. Right: The internal force associated with the curvature-conservative flow is proportional to $\mathbf{p}_i^* - \mathbf{p}_i$.

Other definitions for the tangent and normal vectors could have been chosen. However, our tangent and normal vectors definitions has the advantage of providing a simple local shape description:

$$\mathbf{p}_i = \epsilon_i \mathbf{p}_{i-1} + (1 - \epsilon_i)\mathbf{p}_{i+1} + L(r_i, \phi_i, \epsilon_i)\mathbf{n}_i, \qquad (3)$$

where $L(r_i, \phi_i, \epsilon_i) = \frac{r_i}{\tan \phi_i}(1 + \mu\sqrt{1 + 4\epsilon(1 - \epsilon)\tan^2 \phi})$ with $\mu = 1$ if $|\phi| < \pi/2$ and $\mu = -1$ if $|\phi| > \pi/2$. Equation 3 simply decomposes vertex position $\mathbf{p}_i$ into a tangential and normal component. The importance of this equation will be revealed in sections 3.

3 Parameterization control

For a continuous active contour $\mathcal{C}(u, t)$, the contour parameterization is characterized by the metric function: $g(u, t) = \|\frac{\partial \mathcal{C}}{\partial u}\|$. If $g(u, t) = 1$ then the parameter of $\mathcal{C}(u, t)$ coincides with the contour arc length. For a discrete contour, the parameterization corresponds to the relative spacing between vertices and is characterized by $g_i = \|\mathbf{p}_i - \mathbf{p}_{i-1}\|$.

For a continuous representation, parameterization is clearly independent of the contour shape. For a discrete contour represented by finite differences, shape and parameterization are not completely independent. The effect of parameterization changes is especially important at parts of high curvature. Therefore, parameterization is an important issue for handling discrete parametric contours. In this section we propose a simple algorithm to enforce two types of parameterization:

1. **uniform parameterization**: the spacing between consecutive vertices is uniform.
2. **curvature-based parameterization**: vertices are concentrated at parts of high curvature. This parameterization tends to optimize the shape description for a given number of vertices.

To modify a contour parameterization, only the tangential component of the internal force should be considered. Indeed, Kimia *et al* [9] have proved that only the normal component of the internal force applied on a continuous contour $\mathcal{C}(u,t)$ has an influence on the resulting contour shape. Therefore, if $\mathbf{t}$, $\mathbf{n}$ are the tangent and normal vector at a point $\mathcal{C}(u,t)$, then the contour evolution may be written as: $\frac{\partial \mathcal{C}}{\partial t} = f_{\text{int}} = a(u,t)\mathbf{t} + b(u,t)\mathbf{n}$. Kimia *et al* [9] show that only the normal component of the internal force $b(u,t)$ modifies the contour shape whereas the metric function $g(u,t) = \|\frac{\partial \mathcal{C}}{\partial u}\|$ evolution is dependent on $a(u,t)$ and $b(u,t)$:

$$\frac{\partial g}{\partial t} = \frac{\partial a(u,t)}{\partial u} + b(u,t)kg. \tag{4}$$

The tangential component of the internal force $a(u,t)\mathbf{t}$ constrains the nature of the parameterization. We propose to apply this principle on discrete parametric contours as well by decomposing the internal force f_{int} into its normal and tangential components: $(f_{\text{int}})_i = (f_{\text{tg}})_i + (f_{\text{nr}})_i$ with $(f_{\text{tg}})_i \cdot \mathbf{n}_i = 0$, and $(f_{\text{nr}})_i \cdot \mathbf{t}_i = 0$. More precisely, since the tangent direction $\mathbf{t}_i$ at a vertex is the line direction joining its two neighbors, we use a simple expression for the tangential component: $(f_{\text{tg}})_i = (\epsilon_i^\star - \epsilon_i)(\mathbf{p}_{i+1} - \mathbf{p}_{i-1}) = 2r_i(\epsilon_i^\star - \epsilon_i)\mathbf{t}_i$ where $\epsilon_i^\star$ is the reference metric parameter whose value depends on the type of parameterization to enforce.

3.1   Uniform vertex spacing

To obtain evenly spaced vertices, we simply choose: $\epsilon_i^\star = \frac{1}{2}$. This tangential force moves each vertex in the tangent direction towards the middle of its two neighbors. When the contour reaches its equilibrium, i.e. when $(f_{\text{tg}})_i = \mathbf{0}$, $\mathbf{p}_i$ is then equidistant from $\mathbf{p}_{i-1}$ and $\mathbf{p}_{i+1}$. It equals to $(f_{\text{tg}})_i = \left(\frac{\partial^2 \mathcal{C}}{\partial u^2} \cdot \mathbf{t}\right)\mathbf{t} = \frac{\partial g}{\partial u}\mathbf{t}$. Because the second derivative vector $\frac{\partial^2 \mathcal{C}}{\partial u^2}$ is the first variation of the weak string internal energy $(\int_u \|\frac{\partial \mathcal{C}}{\partial u}\|^2 du)$, this force is somewhat related to the classical "snakes" approach proposed in [8].

3.2   Curvature based vertex spacing

To obtain an optimal description of shape, it is required that vertices concentrate at parts of high curvature and that flat parts are only described with few vertices. To obtain such parameterization, we present a method where edge length is inversely proportional to curvature. If e_i is the edge joining $\mathbf{p}_i$ and $\mathbf{p}_{i+1}$, then we compute its edge curvature K_i^{i+1} as the mean absolute curvature of its two vertices: $K_i^{i+1} = (|k_i| + |k_{i+1}|)/2$. Then at each vertex $\mathbf{p}_i$, we can compute the local relative variation of absolute curvature $\Delta K_i \in [-1, 1]$ as: $\Delta K_i = (K_i^{i+1} - K_{i-1}^i)/(K_i^{i+1} + K_{i-1}^i)$. To enforce a curvature-based vertex spacing, we compute the reference metric parameter $\epsilon_i^\star$ as: $\epsilon_i^\star = \frac{1}{2} - 0.4 * \Delta K_i$.

When vertex $\mathbf{p}_i$ is surrounded by two edges having the same curvature then $\Delta K_i = 0$ and therefore $\epsilon_i^\star$ is set to $\frac{1}{2}$ which implies that $\mathbf{p}_i$ becomes equidistant from its two neighboring vertices. On the contrary, when the absolute curvature of $\mathbf{p}_{i+1}$ is greater than the absolute curvature of $\mathbf{p}_{i-1}$ then ΔK_i becomes close to 1 and therefore $\epsilon_i^\star$ is close to 0.1 which implies that $\mathbf{p}_i$ moves towards $\mathbf{p}_{i+1}$.

3.3 Results of vertex spacing constraints

To illustrate the ability to decouple parameterization and shape properties, we propose to apply an internal force that modifies the vertex spacing on a contour without changing its shape. We define a *curvature conservative* regularizing force that moves $\mathbf{p}_i$ in the normal direction in order to keep the same local curvature:

$$f_{\mathrm{nr}} = (L(r_i, \phi_i, \epsilon_i^\star) - L(r_i, \phi_i, \epsilon_i))\mathbf{n}_i. \tag{5}$$

This equation has a simple geometric interpretation if we note that the total internal force $f_{\mathrm{int}} = f_{\mathrm{tg}} + f_{\mathrm{nr}}$ is simply equal to $\mathbf{p}_i^\star - \mathbf{p}_i$ where $\mathbf{p}_i^\star$ is the point having the same curvature as $\mathbf{p}_i$ but with a metric parameter $\epsilon_i^\star$. From right of figure 1, we can see that f_{tg} corresponds to the displacement between $\mathbf{F}_i^\star$ and $\mathbf{F}_i$ whereas f_{nr} corresponds to the difference of elevation between $\mathbf{p}_i^\star$ and $\mathbf{p}_i$.

Given an open or closed contour we iteratively apply differential equation 2 with the internal force expression described above. Figure 2 shows an example of vertex spacing constraint enforced on a closed contour consisting of 150 vertices. The initial vertex spacing is uneven. When applying the uniform vertex spacing tangential force ($\epsilon_i^\star = 0.5$), after 1000 iterations, all contour edge lengths become equal within less 5 percent without greatly changing the contour shape, as shown in figure 2 (upper row). The diagram displays the distribution of edge curvature as a function of edge length. Similarly, with the same number of iterations, the contour evolution using the curvature-based vertex spacing force tends to concentrate vertices at parts of high curvature. The corresponding diagram clearly shows that edge length is inversely proportional to edge curvature.

3.4 Contour resolution control

In addition to constraining the relative spacing between vertices, it is important to control the total number of vertices. Indeed, the computational complexity of discrete parametric contours is typically linear in the number of vertices. In order to add or remove vertices, we do not use any global contour reparameterization as performed in the level-set method [19] because of its high computational cost. Instead, we propose to locally add or remove a vertex if the edge length does not belong to a given distance range, similarly to [7, 12]. Our resolution constraint

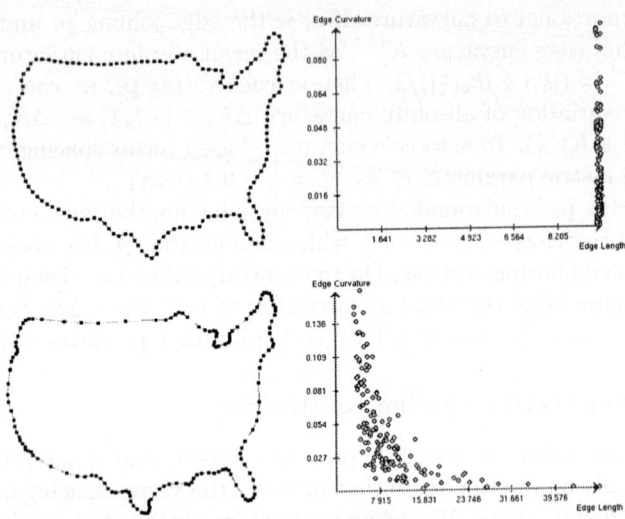

Fig. 2. (**up**) contour after applying the uniform vertex spacing tangential force; (**bottom**) contour after applying the curvature-based vertex spacing constraint.

algorithm proceeds as follows. Given two thresholds s_{min} and s_{max} corresponding to the minimum and maximum edge length, we scan all existing contour edges. If the current edge length is greater than s_{max} and $2 * s_{min}$ then a vertex is added. Otherwise if current edge length is less than s_{min} and if the sum of the current and previous edge length is less than s_{max}, then the current vertex is removed. In general, this procedure is called every $fr_{resolution} = 5$ deformation iterations.

4   Shape regularization

The two internal forces defined in previous section have little influence on the contour shape evolution because they are only related to the contour parameterization. In this section, we deal with the internal force normal component which determines the contour shape regularization. The most widely used internal forces on active contours are the mean curvature motion [13], Laplacian smoothing, thin rod smoothing or spring forces.

Laplacian Smoothing and *Mean Curvature Motion* have the drawback of significantly shrinking the contour. This shrinking effect introduces a bias in the contour deformation since image structures located inside the contour are more likely to be segmented than structures located outside the contour. Furthermore, the amount of shrinking often prevents active contours from entering inside fine structures.

To decrease the shrinking effect, Taubin [20] proposes to apply a linear filter to curves and surfaces in order to reduce the shrinking effect of Gaussian smoothing. However, these two methods only remove the shrinking effect for a given curvature scale. For instance, when smoothing a circle, this circle would stay invariant only for one given circle radius which is related to a set of filtering parameters. Therefore, in these methods, the choice of these parameters are important but difficult to estimate prior to the segmentation process. A regularizing force with higher degrees of smoothness such as the *Thin Rod Smoothing* causes significantly less shrinking since it is based on fourth derivatives along the contour. However, the normal component of this force $-(\frac{\partial^4 C}{\partial u^4} \cdot \mathbf{n})\mathbf{n}$ is dependent on the nature of the parameterization which is a serious limitation.

4.1 Curvature diffusion regularization

We propose to use the second derivative of curvature with respect to arc length as the governing regularizing force:

$$f_{\text{int}} = \frac{d^2 k}{ds^2}\mathbf{n} \tag{6}$$

This force tends to diffuse the curvature along the contour, thus converging towards circles, independently of their radii, for closed contours. For the discretization of equation 6, we do not use straightforward finite differences, since it would lead to complex and potentially unstable schemes. Instead, we propose a geometry-based implementation that is similar to equation 5:

$$f_{\text{nr}} = (L(r_i, \phi_i^\star, \epsilon_i^\star) - L(r_i, \phi_i, \epsilon_i))\mathbf{n}_i \tag{7}$$

where $\phi_i^\star$ is the angle at a point $\mathbf{p}_i^\star$ for which $\frac{d^2 k}{ds^2} = 0$. The geometric interpretation of equation 7 is also straightforward, since the internal force $f_{\text{int}} = f_{\text{tg}} + f_{\text{nr}}$ corresponds to the displacement $\mathbf{p}_i^\star - \mathbf{p}_i$. The angle $\phi_i^\star$ is simply computed by $\phi_i^\star = \arcsin(k_i^\star * r_i)$ where $k_i^\star$ is the curvature at $\mathbf{p}_i^\star$. Therefore, $k_i^\star$ is simply computed as the local average curvature weighted by arc length:

$$k_i^\star = \frac{\|\mathbf{p}_i\mathbf{p}_{i-1}\|k_{i+1} + \|\mathbf{p}_i\mathbf{p}_{i+1}\|k_{i-1}}{\|\mathbf{p}_i\mathbf{p}_{i+1}\| + \|\mathbf{p}_i\mathbf{p}_{i-1}\|}$$

Furthermore, we can compute the local average curvature over a greater neighborhood which results in increased smoothness and faster convergence. If $\sigma_i > 0$ is the *scale* parameter, and $l_{i,i+j}$ is the distance between $\mathbf{p}_i$ and $\mathbf{p}_{i+j}$ then we compute k_i as :

$$k_i^\star = \frac{\sum_{j=1}^{\sigma_i} l_{i,i-j}k_{i+j} + l_{i,i+j}k_{i-j}}{\sum_{j=1}^{\sigma_i} l_{i,i-j} + l_{i,i+j}} \quad \text{with} \quad l_{i,i+j} = \sum_{k=1}^{j} \|\mathbf{p}_{i+k-1}\mathbf{p}_{i+k}\|.$$

This scheme generalizes the *intrinsic polynomial stabilizers* proposed in [5] that required a uniform contour parameterization. Because of this regularizing force is geometrically intrinsic, we can combine it with a curvature-based vertex spacing tangential force, thus leading to optimized computations. Finally, the stability analysis of the explicit integration scheme is linked to the choice of α_i. We have found experimentally, without having a formal proof yet, that we obtain a stable iterative scheme if we choose $\alpha_i \leq 0.5$.

5 Topology constraints

Automatic topology changes of parametric contour has been previously proposed in [11, 14, 10]. In McInerney *et al* approach, all topological changes occur by computing the contour intersections with a simplicial decomposition of space. The contour is reparameterized at each iteration, the intersections with the simplicial domain being used as the new vertices. Recently Lachaud *et al* [10] introduced topologically adaptive deformable surfaces where self-intersections are detected based on distance between vertices. Our algorithm is also based on a regular lattice for detecting all contour intersections. However, the regular grid is not used for changing the contour parameterization and furthermore topology changes result from the application of topological operators. Therefore unlike previous approaches, we propose to completely decouple the physical behavior of active contours (contour resolution and geometric regularity) with their topological behavior in order to provide a very flexible scheme. Finally, our framework applies to closed or opened contours.

A contour topology is defined by the number of its connected components and whether each of its components is closed or opened. Our approach consists in using two basic topological operators. The first operator illustrated in figure 3 consists in merging two contour edges. Depending whether the edges belong to the same connected component or not, this operator creates or remove a connected component. The second topological operator consists in closing or opening a connected component.

Fig. 3. Topological operator applying on (**left**) two edges on the same connected component or (**right**) two different connected components.

Our approach for modifying a contour topology can be decomposed into three stages. The first stage creates a data structure where the collision detection between contour connected components is computationally efficient. The second determines the geometric intersection between edges and the last stage actually performs all topological modifications.

5.1 Data structure for the detection of contour intersections

Finding pairs of intersecting edges has an *a priori* complexity of $O(n^2)$ where n is the number of vertices (or edges). Our algorithm is based on a regular grid of size d and has a complexity linear with the ratio $\mathcal{L}/d$ where $\mathcal{L}$ is the length of the contour. Therefore, unlike the approach proposed in [14], our approach is not region-based (inside or outside regions) but only uses the polygonal description of the contour.

The two dimensional Euclidean space with a reference frame $(\mathbf{o}, \mathbf{x}, \mathbf{y})$ is decomposed into a regular square grid which size d is user-defined. The influence of the grid size d is discussed in section 6.1. In this regular lattice, we define a point of row and column indices r and c as the point of Cartesian coordinates $\mathbf{o}_{\text{grid}} + r\mathbf{x} + c\mathbf{y}$ where $\mathbf{o}_{\text{grid}}$ is the grid origin point. This point is randomly determined each time topology constraints are activated in order to make the algorithm independent of the origin choice. Furthermore, we define a square cell of index (r, c) as the square determined by the four points of indices (r, c), $(r+1, c)$, $(r+1, c+1)$ and $(r, c+1)$.

In order to build the sampled contour, we scan all edges of each connected components. For each edge, we test if it intersects any row or columns of the regular lattice. Since the row and column directions correspond to the directions $\mathbf{x}$ and $\mathbf{y}$ of the coordinate frame, these intersection tests are efficiently computed. Each time an intersection with the row or column direction is found, a *grid vertex* is created and the intersecting contour edge is stored in the *grid vertex*. Furthermore, a *grid vertex* is stored in a *grid edge* structure. A *grid edge* is either a pair of *grid vertices* or a *grid vertex* associated with an end vertex (when the connected component is an opened line). Finally, the *grid edge* is appended to the list of *grid edges* inside the corresponding grid cell.

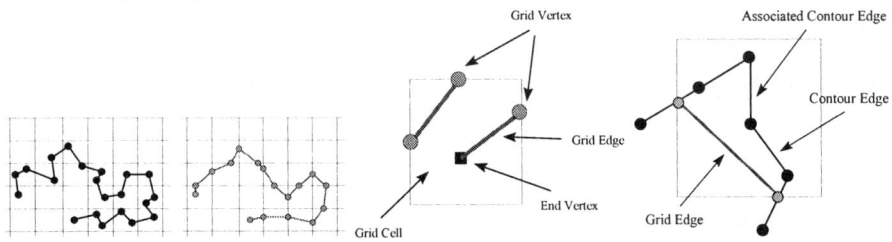

Fig. 4. (left) The original contour with the regular grid the contour decomposed on the regular grid; **(right)** Definition of grid vertex, grid edge, grid cell and contour edge associated with a grid edge.

5.2 Finding intersecting grid edges

In order to optimize memory space, we store all non-empty grid cells inside a hash table, hashed by its row and column indices. The number of grid cells is proportional to the length $\mathcal{L}$ of the contour. In order to detect possible contour intersections, each entry to the hash table is scanned. For each cell containing n grid edges with $n > 1$, we test the intersection between all pairs of grid edges (see figure 4, left). Since each grid edge is geometrically represented by a line segment, this intersection test only requires the evaluation of two dot products.

Once a pair of grid edges has been found to intersect, a pair of contour edges must be associated for the application of topological operators (see section 5.3). Because a contour edge is stored in each grid vertex, one contour edge can be associated with each grid edge. Thus, we associate with each grid edge, the middle of these two contour edges (in terms of topological distance) as shown in figure 4, right.

Our contour edges intersection algorithm has the following properties: (i) if one pair of grid edges intersects then there is at least one pair of contour edges that intersects inside this grid cell; and (ii) if a pair of contour edges intersects and if the corresponding intersecting area is greater than $d * d$ then there is a corresponding pair of intersecting grid edges. In another words, our method does not detect all intersections but is guaranteed to detect all intersection having an area greater than $d * d$. In practice, since the grid origin $\mathbf{o}_{grid}$ is randomly determined each time the topology constraint is enforced, we found that our algorithm detected all intersections that are relevant for performing topology changes.

5.3 Applying topological operators

All pairs of intersecting contour edges are stored inside another hash table for an efficient retrieval. Since in general two connected components intersect each other at two edges, given a pair of intersecting contour edges, we search for the closest pair of intersecting contour edges based on topological distance. If such a pair is found, we perform the following tasks. If both edges belong to the same connected component, then the they are merged if their topological distance is greater than a threshold (usually equal to 8). This is to avoid creating too small connected components. In all other cases, the two edges are merged with the topological operator presented in figure 3. Finally, we update the list of intersecting edge pairs by removing from the hash table all edge pairs involving any of the two contour edges that have been merged.

5.4 Other applications of the collision detection algorithm

The algorithm presented in the previous sections merges intersecting edges regardless of the nature of the intersection. If it corresponds to a self-intersection, then a new connected component is created, otherwise two connected components are merged. As in [14] our framework can prevent the merging of two distinct connected components while allowing the removal of self-intersections. To do so, when a pair of intersecting contour edges belonging to distinct connected components is found, instead of merging this edges, we align all vertices located between intersecting edges belonging to the same connected component (see figure 5). Thus, each component pushes back all neighboring components. In figure 5, right, we show an example of image segmentation where this repulsive behavior between components is very useful in segmenting the two heart atriums.

6 Results

6.1 Topology algorithm cost

We evaluate the performance of our automatic topology adaptation algorithm on the example of figure 6. The contour consisting of 50 vertices, is deformed from a circular shape towards a vertebra in a CT image. The computation time for building the data structure described in section 5.1 is displayed in figure 6,

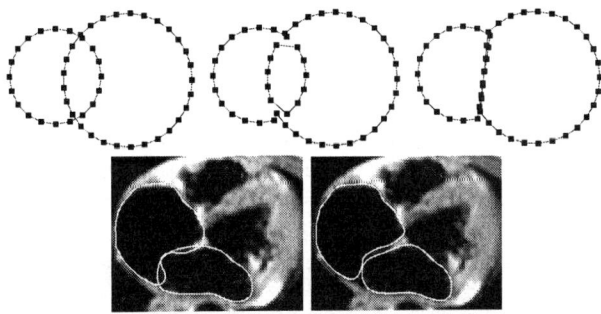

Fig. 5. (from left to right) Two intersecting connected components; after merging the two pairs of intersecting edges; after aligning vertices along the intersecting edges. Example of 2 active contours reconstructing the right and left ventricles in a MR image with a repulsive behavior between each components.

right, as a function of the grid size d. It varies from 175 ms to 1 ms when the grid size increases from 0.17 to 10 image pixels on a Digital PWS 500 Mhz. The computation time for applying the topological operators can be neglected in general. When the grid size is equal to the mean edge distance (around 2 pixels), the computation time needed to detect edge intersections becomes almost equal to the computation time needed to deform the contour during one iteration (4.8 ms).

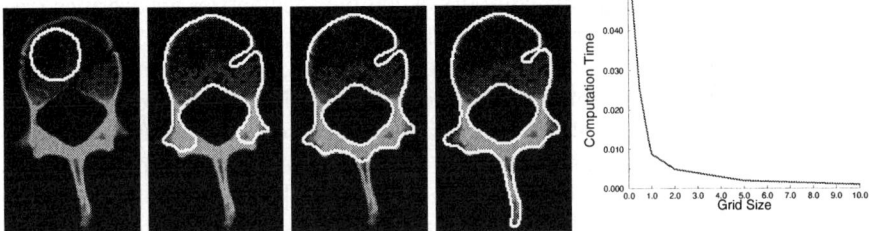

Fig. 6. Segmentation of a vertebra in a CT image; Topology algorithm computation time.

When the grid size increases, the contour sampling on the regular grid becomes sparse and therefore some contour intersections may not be detected. However, we have verified that topological changes still occur if we choose a grid size corresponding to 20 image pixels with contour intersections checked every 20 iterations. In practice, we choose a conservative option with a grid size equal to the average edge length and with a frequency for topology changes of 5 iterations which implies an approximate additional computation time of 20 percent.

6.2 Segmentation example

This example illustrates the segmentation of an aortic arch angiography. Figure 7 shows the initial contour (up left) and its evolution towards the aorta and the main vessels. External forces are computed as a function of vertex distance to a gradient point to avoid oscillations around image edges and are projected on the vertex normal direction. The contour is regularized by a curvature diffusive constraint. The contour resolution constraint is applied every 10 iterations which makes the resampling overhead very low. Topology constraints are computed every 5 iterations on a 4 pixel grid size to fuse the self-intersecting contour parts. Intersections with image borders are computed every 10 iterations and the contour is opened as it reaches the image border.

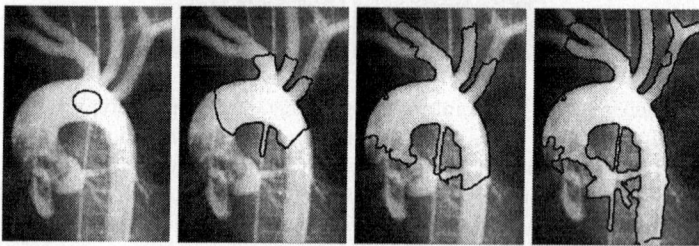

Fig. 7. Evolution of a closed curve towards the aortic arch and the branching vessels.

7 Comparison with the level-set method

The main advantage of the level-set method is obviously its ability to automatically change the contour topology during the deformation. This property makes it well-suited for reconstructing contours of complex geometries for instance tree-like structures. Also, by merging different intersecting contours, it is possible to initialize a deformable contour with a set of growing seeds. However, the major drawbacks of level-sets methods are related to their difficult user interaction and their computational cost, although some speed-up algorithms based on constraining the contour evolution through the Fast-Marching method [19] or by using an asynchronous update of the narrow-band [18] have been proposed. The formal comparison between both parametric and level-set approaches have been recently established in the case of geodesic snakes [1]. In this section, we propose a practical comparison between both approaches including implementation issues.

7.1 Level-set implementation

The level-set function Ψ is discretized on a rectangular grid whose resolution corresponds to the image pixel size. The evolution equation is discretized in space using finite differences in time using an explicit scheme, leading to : $\Psi_{ij}^{t+\Delta t} = \Psi_{ij}^t + \Delta t \nu_{ij} \|\nabla_{ij}\Psi_{ij}^t\|$ [13] where ν_{ij} denotes the propagation speed term and Δt is the discrete time step.

The propagation speed term ν is designed to attract $\mathcal{C}$ towards object boundaries extracted from the image using a gradient operator with an additional regularizing term: $\nu(\mathbf{p}) = \beta(\mathbf{p})(\kappa(\mathbf{p}) + c)$. $\kappa(\mathbf{p})$ denotes the contour curvature at point $\mathbf{p}$ while c is a constant resulting in a balloon force [4] on the contour. Finally, $\beta(\mathbf{p}) \in [0,1]$ is a multiplicative coefficient dependent on the image gradient

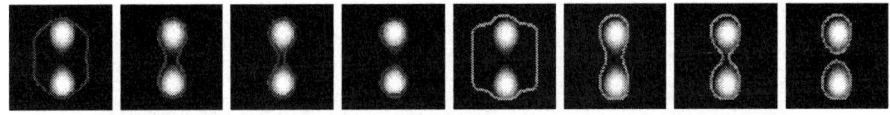

Fig. 8. (Five left figures) Discrete contour deformation; (Five right figures) level-set deformation.

norm at point **p**. When $\mathcal{C}$ moves across pixels of high gradients, this term slows down the level-set propagation. A threshold parameter determines the minimal image boundary strength required to stop a level-set evolution. We speed-up the level-set by using a narrow band method [13] which requires to periodically reinitialize the level-set contour.

In order to compare active contours to level-sets, we compute external forces similar to level-set propagation at discrete contour vertices. First, we use mean curvature motion as the governing internal force and we have implemented for the external force, a balloon force weighted by the coefficient β proposed above. Finally, we were able to use the same gradient threshold in both approaches.

7.2 Torus example

We first propose to compare both approaches on the synthetic image shown in figure 8. This image has two distinct connected components.

A discrete contour is initialized around the two components. A medium grid size (8 pixels resolution) is used and topology constraints are computed every 10 iterations. Throughout the deformation process, vertices are added and removed to have similar edge length along the contour. A corresponding level-set is initialized at the same place that the discrete contour. A 7 pixel wide narrow band appeared to optimize the convergence time. A 0.3 time step is used. It is the maximal value below which the evolving curve is stable.

Figure 8 shows the convergence of the discrete contour (left) and the level-set (right). The discrete contour converges in 0.42 seconds opposed to 3.30 seconds for the level-set, that is a 7.85 acceleration factor in favor of the discrete contour. The difference of computational time is due to the small vertex number used for the discrete contour (varying between 36 and 48 vertices) compared to the much greater number of sites (from 1709 up to 3710) updated in the level-set narrow band.

7.3 Synthetic data

This experiments shows the ability of the discrete contour topology algorithm to follow difficult topology changes. We use a synthetic fractal image showing a number of small connected components. Figure 9, upper row, shows the discrete contour convergence in the image while the bottom row shows the level set convergence.

In both cases, the initial contour is a square located at the image border. It evolves under a deflation force that stops on strong image boundaries. For the

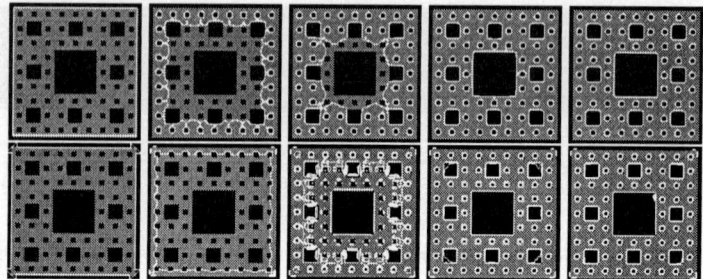

Fig. 9. (upper row) Discrete contour convergence in a fractal image; (bottom row) Level-set convergence in the same image.

discrete contour, a small grid size is used due to the small image structure size (4 pixels grid size and 5 iterations algorithm frequency). A weak regularizing constraint allows the contour to segment the square corners. The contour is checked every 10 iterations to add the necessary vertices. A 0.3 time step is used for the level-set. This high value leads to a rather unstable behavior as can be seen in figure 9. As the level-set contours gradually fills-in the whole image, we have verified that the convergence time is not minimized by using any narrow bands. Again, the speed-up is 3.84 in favor of the discrete contour.

8 Conclusion

We have introduced three algorithms that greatly improve the generality of parametric active contours while preserving their computational efficiency. Furthermore, these algorithms are controlled by simple parameters that are easy to understand. For the internal force, a single parameter α between 0 and 1 is used to set the amount of smoothing. For resolution and topology constraint algorithms, distance parameters must be provided as well as the frequency at which they apply. Given an image, all these parameters can be set automatically to meaningful values providing good results in most cases.

Finally, we have compared the efficiency of this approach with the level set method by implementing parametric geodesic snakes. These experiments seem to conclude that our approach is at least three times as fast as the implicit implementation. Above all, we believe that the most important advantage of parametric active contours is their user interactivity.

References

1. G. Aubert and L. Blanc-Féraud. Some Remarks on the Equivalence between 2D and 3D Classical Snakes and Geodesic Active Contours. *International Journal of Computer Vision*, 34(1):5–17, September 1999.
2. V. Caselles, R. Kimmel, and G. Sapiro. Geodesic Active Contours. *International Journal of Computer Vision*, 22(1):61–79, 1997.

3. I. Cohen, L.D. Cohen, and N. Ayache. Using Deformable Surfaces to Segment 3-D Images and Infer Differential Structures. *Computer Vision, Graphics, and Image Processing: Image Understanding*, 56(2):242–263, September 1992.

4. L.D. Cohen. On Active Contour Models and Balloons. *Computer Vision, Graphics, and Image Processing: Image Understanding*, 53(2):211–218, March 1991.

5. H. Delingette. Intrinsic stabilizers of planar curves. In *third European Conference on Computer Vision (ECCV'94)*, Stockholm, Sweden, June 1994.

6. J. Hug, C. Brechbüler, and G. Székely. Tamed Snake: A Particle System for Robust Semi-automatic Segmentation. In *Medical Image Computing and Computer-Assisted Intervention (MICCAI'99)*, volume 1679 of *Lectures Notes in Computer Science*, pages 106–115, Cambridge, UK, September 1999. Springer.

7. J. Ivins and J. Porrill. Active Region models for segmenting textures and colours. *Image and Vision Computing*, 13(5):431–438, June 1995.

8. M. Kass, A. Witkin, and D. Terzopoulos. Snakes: Active Contour Models. *International Journal of Computer Vision*, 1:321–331, 1988.

9. B. Kimia, A. Tannenbaum, and S. Zucker. On the evolution of curves via a function of curvature i. the classical case. *Journal of Mathematical Analysis and Applications*, 163:438–458, 1992.

10. J.-O. Lachaud and A. Montanvert. Deformable meshes with automated topology changes for coarse-to-fine three-dimensional surface extraction. *Medical Image Analysis*, 3(2):187–207, 1999.

11. F. Leitner and P. Cinquin. Complex topology 3d objects segmentation. In *SPIE Conf. on Advances in Intelligent Robotics Systems*, volume 1609, Boston, November 1991.

12. S. Lobregt and M. Viergever. A Discrete Dynamic Contour Model. *IEEE Transactions on Medical Imaging*, 14(1):12–23, 1995.

13. R. Malladi, J.A. Sethian, and B.C. Vemuri. Shape Modeling with Front Propagation : A Level Set Approach. *IEEE Transactions on Pattern Analysis and Machine Intelligence*, 17(2):158–174, 1995.

14. T. McInerney and D. Terzopoulos. Topologically adaptable snakes. In *International Conference on Computer Vision (ICCV'95)*, pages 840–845, Cambridge, USA, June 1995.

15. T. McInerney and D. Terzopoulos. Deformable models in medical image analysis: a survey. *Medical Image Analysis*, 1(2):91–108, 1996.

16. S. Menet, P. Saint-Marc, and G. Medioni. Active Contour Models: Overview, Implementation and Applications. *IEEE Trans. on Systems, Man and Cybernetics*, pages 194–199, 1993.

17. D. Metaxas and D. Terzopoulos. Constrained Deformable Superquadrics and non-rigid Motion Tracking. In *International Conference on Computer Vision and Pattern Recognition (CVPR'91)*, pages 337–343, Maui, Hawai, June 1991.

18. N. Paragios and R. Deriche. A PDE-based Level-Set Approach for Detection and Tracking of Moving Objects. In *International Conference on Computer Vision (ICCV'98)*, pages 1139–1145, Bombay, India, 1998.

19. J.A. Sethian. *Level Set Methods : Evolving Interfaces in Geometry, Fluid Mechanics, Computer Vision and Materials Science*. Cambridge University Press, 1996.

20. G. Taubin. Curve and Surface Smoothing Without Shrinkage. In *International Conference on Computer Vision (ICCV'95)*, pages 852–857, 1995.

Motion Segmentation by Tracking Edge Information over Multiple Frames

Paul Smith, Tom Drummond, and Roberto Cipolla

Department of Engineering
University of Cambridge
Cambridge CB2 1PZ, UK
{pas1001|twd20|cipolla}@eng.cam.ac.uk
http://www-svr.eng.cam.ac.uk/~pas1001/

Abstract. This paper presents a new Bayesian framework for layered motion segmentation, dividing the frames of an image sequence into foreground and background layers by tracking edges. The first frame in the sequence is segmented into regions using image edges, which are tracked to estimate two affine motions. The probability of the edges fitting each motion is calculated using 1st order statistics along the edge. The most likely region labelling is then resolved using these probabilities, together with a Markov Random Field prior. As part of this process one of the motions is also identified as the foreground motion.

Good results are obtained using only two frames for segmentation. However, it is also demonstrated that over multiple frames the probabilities may be accumulated to provide an even more accurate and robust segmentation. The final region labelling can be used, together with the two motion models, to produce a good segmentation of an extended sequence.

1 Introduction

Video segmentation is a first stage in many further areas of video analysis. For example, there is growing interest in video indexing – where image sequences are indexed and retrieved by their content – and semantic analysis of an image sequence requires moving objects to be distinguished from the background. Further, the emerging MPEG-4 standard represents sequences as objects on a series of layers, and so these objects and layers must be identified to encode a video sequence.

A recent trend in motion segmentation is the use of layers [7, 16]. This avoids some of the traditional multiple-motion estimation problems by assuming that motion within a layer is consistent, but layer boundaries mark motion discontinuities. The motions and layers may be estimated using the recursive dominant motion approach [1, 10], or by fitting many layers simultaneously [11, 15, 16, 17].

Motion estimation is poor in regions of low texture, and here the structure of the image has to play a part. Smooth regions are expected to move coherently, and changes in motion are more likely to occur at edges in the image. A common approach is to use the local image intensity as a prior when assigning pixels to layers [10, 15, 17]. The normalized cuts method of Shi and Malik [12] can combine both the motion and intensity information of pixels into a weighted graph, for which the best partition has then to be found.

Alternatively, the image structure may be considered before the motion estimation stage by performing an initial static segmentation of the frame based on pixel colour or intensity. This reduces the problem to one of identifying the correct motion labelling for the each region. Both Bergen and Meyer [2] and Moscheni and Dufaux [9] have had some success in merging regions with similar motion fields.

This paper concentrates on the edges in an image. Edges are very valuable features to consider, both for motion estimation and segmentation. Object tracking is commonly performed using edge information (in the form of snakes), while image segmentation techniques naturally use the structure cues given by edges. If an image from a motion sequence is already segmented into regions of similar colour or intensity along edges, it is clear that a large proportion of the motion information will come from these edges rather than the interior of regions. This paper shows how this edge information alone is sufficient to both estimate and track motions, and label image regions.

Many papers on motion segmentation avoid the question of occlusion or the ordering of layers. Occluded pixels are commonly treated as outliers which the algorithm has to be able to tolerate, although reasoned analysis and modelling of these outliers can be used to retrieve the layer ordering and identify occluded regions [2, 3, 16]. With the edge-based method proposed in this paper, the problem of occluded pixels is greatly reduced since it is only the occluding boundary, and not the region below, which is being tracked. Furthermore, the relationship between edges and regions inherently also depends on the layer ordering, and this is extracted as an integral part of the algorithm.

This paper describes a novel and efficient framework for segmenting frames from a sequence into layers using edge motions. The theory linking the motions of edges and regions is outlined and a Bayesian probabilistic framework developed to enable a solution for the most likely region labelling to be inferred from edge motions. This work extends the approach first proposed in [14], developing more powerful probabilistic models and demonstrating that evidence may be accumulated over a sequence to provide a more accurate and robust segmentation.

The theoretical and probabilistic framework for analysing edge motions is presented in Sect. 2. The current implementation of this theory is outlined in Sect. 3, with experimental results presented in Sect. 4.

2 Theoretical Framework

Edges in the image are important features since the desired segmentation divides the image along occluding edges of the foreground object (or objects) in the image. Edges are also very good features to consider for motion estimation: they can be found more reliably than corners and their long extent means that a number of measurements may be taken along their length, leading to a more accurate estimation of their motion. However, segmentation ultimately involves regions, since the task is one of labelling image pixels according to the motions. If it is assumed that the image is already segmented into regions along edges, then there is a natural link between the regions and the edges. In this section the relationship between the motion of regions and edges is outlined and a probabilistic framework is developed to enable a region labelling to be estimated from edge data.

2.1 The Image Motion of Region Edges

Edges in an image are due to the texture of objects, or their boundaries in the scene. Edges can also be due to shadows and specular reflections, but these are not considered at this stage. It is assumed that as an object moves all of the edges associated with the object move, and hence edges in one frame may be compared with those in the next and partitioned according to different real-world motions.

The work in this paper assumes that the motion in the sequence is layered i.e. one motion takes place completely in front of another. Typically the layer farthest from the camera is referred to as the background, with foreground layers in front of this. It is also assumed that any occluding boundary (the edge of a foreground object) is visible in the image. With regions in the image defined by the edges, this implies that each region obeys only one motion, and an edge which is an occluding boundary will have the motion of the occluding region. This enables a general rule to be stated for labelling edges from regions:

Labelling Rule: **The layer to which an edge belongs is that of the nearer of the two regions which it bounds.**

2.2 Probabilistic Formulation

There are a large number of parameters which must be solved to give a complete motion segmentation. In this section a Bayesian framework is developed to enable the most likely value of these parameters to be estimated.

The complete model of the segmentation, M, consists of the elements $M = \{\Theta, F, R\}$ where

Θ is the parameters of the layer motion models,
F is the depth ordering of the motion layers,
R is the motion label (layer) for each region.

The region edge labels are not part of the model, but are completely defined by R and F from the Labelling Rule of Sect. 2.1.

Given the image data D (and any other prior information assumed about the world), the task is to find the model M with the maximum probability given this data and priors:[1]

$$\max_{M} P\left(M|D\right) = \max_{RF\Theta} P\left(RF\Theta|D\right). \tag{1}$$

---

[1] Throughout this paper, max is used to also represent argmax, as frequently both the maximum value and the parameters giving this are required.

This can be further decomposed into a motion estimation component and region labelling:

$$\max_{RF\Theta} P\left(RF\Theta|D\right) = \max_{RF\Theta} P\left(\Theta|D\right) P\left(RF|\Theta D\right).\tag{2}$$

At this stage a simplification is made: it is assumed that the maximum *value* (not the model parameters which give this) of (2) is independent of the motion, and thus the motion parameters Θ can be maximised independently of the others. The expression to be maximised is thus

$$\underbrace{\max_{\Theta} P\left(\Theta|D\right)}_{a} \underbrace{\max_{RF} P\left(RF|\Theta D\right)}_{b},\tag{3}$$

where the value of Θ used in term (b) is that which maximises term (a). The two components of (3) can be evaluated in turn: first (a) and then (b).

(a) Estimating the Motions Θ. The first term in (3) estimates the motions between frames, which this may be estimated by tracking features. As outlined in Sect. 2.1, edges are robust features to track and they also provide a natural link to the regions which are to be labelled.

In order to estimate the motion models from the edges it is necessary to know which edges belong to which motion, which is not something that is known a priori. In order to resolve this, another random variable is introduced, e, which is the labelling of an edge: which motion the edge obeys. The motion estimation can then be expressed in terms of an Expectation-Maximisation problem [5]:

$$\begin{cases} P\left(e|\Theta_n D\right) & \text{E-stage} \\ \max_{\Theta_{n+1}} P\left(\Theta_{n+1}|eD\right) P\left(e|\Theta_n D\right) & \text{M-stage}. \end{cases}\tag{4}$$

Starting with an initial guess of the motions, the expected edge labelling is estimated. This edge labelling can then be used to maximise the estimate of the motions, and the process iterates until convergence.

(b) Estimating the Labellings R and F. Having obtained the most likely motions, the remaining parameters of the model M can be maximised. Once again, the edge labels are used as an intermediate step. The motion estimation allows the edge probabilities to be estimated, and from Sect. 2.1 the relationship between edges and regions is known. Term (3b) can be augmented by the edge labelling e, which must then be marginalised, giving

$$\max_{RF} P\left(RF|\Theta D\right) = \max_{RF} \sum_{e} P\left(RF|e\right) P\left(e|\Theta D\right),\tag{5}$$

since R and F are conditionally independent of D given e (which is entirely defined by R and F).

The second term, the edge probabilities, can extracted directly from the motion estimation stage. The first term is more difficult to estimate, and it is easier to recast this using Bayes' Rule, giving

$$P\left(\boldsymbol{RF}|e\right) = \frac{P\left(e|\boldsymbol{RF}\right)P\left(\boldsymbol{RF}\right)}{P\left(e\right)} . \qquad (6)$$

The maximisation is over $\boldsymbol{R}$ and $\boldsymbol{F}$, so $P\left(e\right)$ is constant. It can also be assumed that the priors of $\boldsymbol{R}$ and $\boldsymbol{F}$ are independent, and any foreground motion is equally likely, so $P\left(\boldsymbol{F}\right)$ is constant. The last term, the prior probability of a particular region labelling $P\left(\boldsymbol{R}\right)$, is not constant, which leaves the following expression to be evaluated:

$$\max_{\boldsymbol{RF}} \sum_{e} P\left(e|\boldsymbol{RF}\right) P\left(\boldsymbol{R}\right) P\left(e|\boldsymbol{\Theta D}\right) . \qquad (7)$$

The $P\left(e|\boldsymbol{RF}\right)$ term is very useful. e is only an intermediate variable, and is entirely defined by the region labelling $\boldsymbol{R}$ and the foreground motion $\boldsymbol{F}$. This probability therefore takes on a binary value – it is 1 if that edge labelling is implied and 0 if it is not. The sum in (7) can thus be removed, and the e in the final term replaced by a function of $\boldsymbol{R}$ and $\boldsymbol{F}$ which gives the correct edge labels:

$$\max_{\boldsymbol{RF}} \underbrace{P\left(e\left(\boldsymbol{R},\boldsymbol{F}\right)|\boldsymbol{\Theta D}\right)}_{a} \underbrace{P\left(\boldsymbol{R}\right)}_{b} . \qquad (8)$$

The variable $\boldsymbol{F}$ takes only a discrete set of values (in the case of two layers, only two: either one motion is foreground, or the other). Equation (8) can therefore be maximised in two stages: $\boldsymbol{F}$ can be fixed at one value and the expression maximised over $\boldsymbol{R}$, and the process then repeated with other values of $\boldsymbol{F}$ and the global maximum taken.

The maximisation over $\boldsymbol{R}$ can be performed by hypothesising a complete region labelling and then testing the *evidence* (8a) – calculating the probability of the edge labelling given the regions and the motions – and the *prior* (8b), calculating the likelihood of that particular labelling configuration. An exhaustive search is impractical, and in the implementation presented here region labellings are hypothesised using simulated annealing.

3   Implementation

This section outlines the implementation of the framework presented in Sect. 2 for two layers (foreground and background), with the motions of each modelled by an affine motion. The basic implementation is divided into three sections (see Fig. 1):

1. Find edges and regions in the first frame
2. Estimate the motions and edge probabilities
3. Label the regions and foreground motion

The second two stages can then be continued over subsequent frames and the edge probabilities accumulated.

| (a) Initial static segmentation | (b) Edges labelled as motion 1 or motion 2 | (c) Foreground regions |

Fig. 1. 'Foreman' segmentation from two frames. The foreman moves his head very slightly to the left between frames, but this is enough to accurately estimate the motions and calculate edge probabilities. The foreground motion can then be identified and the regions labelled to produce a good segmentation of the head.

3.1 Finding Edges and Regions

To implement the framework outlined in Sect. 2, regions and edges must first be located in the image. The implementation presented here uses a scheme developed by Sinclair [13] but other edge-based schemes, such the morphological segmentation used in [2], are also suitable.

Under Sinclair's scheme, colour edges are found in the image and seed points for region growing are then found at the locations furthest from these edges. Regions are grown, by pixel colour, with image edges acting as hard barriers. The result is a series of connected, closed region edges generated from the original fragmented edges (see Fig. 1(a)). The edges referred to in this paper are the region boundaries: each boundary between two distinct regions is an edge.

3.2 Estimating the Motions Θ

As described in Sect. 2.2, the problem of labelling the segmented regions can be divided into two stages: first estimating the motions and then the motion and region labelling. In order to estimate the motions, features are tracked from one frame to the next; the obvious features to use are the region edges. The motion is parameterised by a 2D affine transformation, which gives a good approximation to the small inter-frame motions.

Multiple-motion estimation is a circular problem. If it were known which edges belonged to which motion, these could be used to directly estimate the motions. However, edge motion labelling cannot be performed without knowing the motions. In order to resolve this, Expectation-Maximisation (EM) is used [5], implementing the formulation outlined in (4) as described below.

Edge Tracking. Both stages of the EM process make use of group-constrained snake technology [4, 6]. For each edge, tracking nodes are assigned at regular

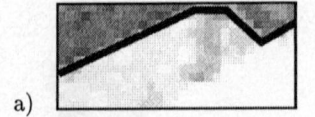

a)   b)

Fig. 2. Edge tracking example. (a) Edge in initial frame. (b) In the next frame the image edge has moved. Tracking nodes are initialised along the model edge and then search normal to the edge to find the new location. The best-fit motion is the one that minimises the squared distance error between the tracking nodes and the edge.

intervals along the edge (see Fig. 2). The motion of these nodes are considered to be representative of the edge motion (there are around $1,400$ tracking nodes in a typical frame). The tracking nodes from the first frame are mapped into the next according to the current best guess of the motion. A 1-dimensional search is then made along the edge normal (for 5 pixels either direction) to find a matching edge pixel based on colour image gradients. The image distance d, between the original node location and its match in the next image, is measured (see Fig. 2(b)).

At each tracking node the expected image motion due to the 2D affine motion θ can be calculated. The best fit solution is the one which minimises the residual:

$$\min_{\theta} \sum_{e} \sum_{t \in e} (d_t - n(\theta, t))^2 \qquad (9)$$

over all edges e and tracking nodes t, where d_t is the measurement and $n(\theta, t)$ the component of the image motion normal to the edge at that image location. This expression may be minimised using least squares, although in practice an M-estimator (see, for example, [11]) is used to provide robustness to outliers.

Maximisation: Estimating the Motions. Given the previous estimate of the motions Θ, all tracking nodes are mapped into the next frame according to both motions. From each of the two possible locations a normal search is performed as described above and the best match found (or 'no match' is reported if none is above a threshold). These distances are combined into the estimate of the affine motion parameters (9) in proportion to the current edge probabilities.

Expectation: Calculating Edge Probabilities. For simplicity, it is assumed that the tracking nodes along each edge are independent and that tracker errors can be modelled by a normal distribution. Experiments have shown Gaussian statistics to be a good fit, and although the independence assumption is less valid (see Sec. 3.3), it still performs satisfactorily for the EM stage.

By assuming independence, the edge probability under each motion is the product of the tracking node probabilities. Each tracking node tries to find a match under each of the two motions, yielding either an error distance d_i or finding no match above a threshold (denoted by $d_i = \otimes$). There are three distinct cases when matching under the two motions: a match is found under both motions, under neither motion, or under only one motion. The probability distributions for each case have been modelled from data by considering an ideal solution.

Match Found Under Both Motions. The errors under both motions are modelled by normal distributions and, a priori, both are equally likely. The probability of a tracker belonging to motion 1 is given by the normalised probability

$$P\left(\text{Motion } 1 | d_1 d_2\right) = \frac{1}{1 + \exp\left(-\frac{1}{2\sigma_1^2}\left(d_2^2 - d_1^2\right)\right)} \tag{10}$$

where, from data, $1/2\sigma_1^2 = 0.3$. The probability of it belonging to motion 2 is, of course, $(1 - P\left(\text{Motion } 1 | d_1 d_2\right))$.

Match Found Under Only One Motion. A Gaussian was found to be a good fit to experimental data:

$$P\left(\text{Motion } 1 | d_1, d_2 = \otimes\right) = \alpha e^{-\beta d_1^2}, \tag{11}$$

with $\alpha = 0.97$ and $\beta = 0.0265$. The same equation holds, but with d_2, if the single match were under motion 2 instead.

No Match Found Under Either Motion. In this case, no information is available and a uniform prior is used:

$$P\left(\text{Motion } 1 | d_1 = d_2 = \otimes\right) = 0.5. \tag{12}$$

Initialisation and Convergence. The EM is initialised with a guess of the two motions Θ. For the first frame, the initial guesses are zero motion (the camera is likely to be stationary or tracking the foreground object) and the mean motion, estimated from the initial errors of all the edges. For subsequent frames, a velocity estimate is used (see Sec. 3.4). For the first iteration of EM, the tracker search path is set at 20 pixels to compensate for a possible poor initialisation.

Convergence is gauged by considering the Maximum A Posteriori labelling of each edge (either motion 1 or motion 2 depending on which is most likely). If no edge changes labelling between two iterations then convergence is assumed. The maximum number of iterations is set at 40, which takes around 3 seconds on a 300MHz Pentium II.

3.3   Labelling Regions R and finding the Layer Order F

Having estimated the most likely motions Θ, the second term of (3) can be maximised. This finds the most likely region labelling and identifies the motion most likely to be foreground. Using (8), this can be performed by hypothesising possible region and foreground motion labellings and calculating their probabilities, selecting the most probable.

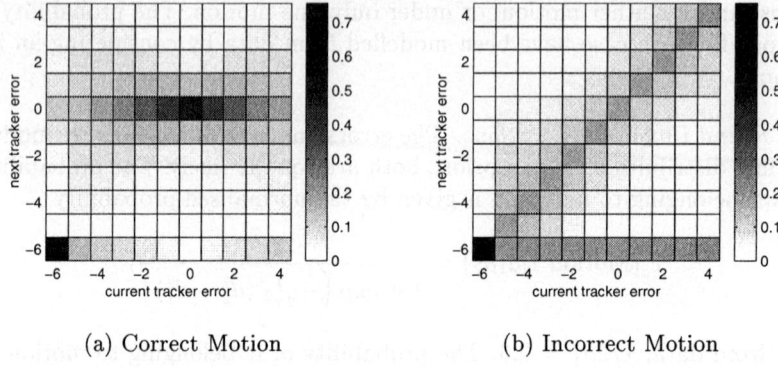

(a) Correct Motion   (b) Incorrect Motion

Fig. 3. Markov chain transition probabilities. These are used to calculate the probability of observing a particular sequence of tracking node errors along an edge. A residual of -6 corresponds to no match being found at that tracker under that motion.

Region Probabilities from Edge Data. Given a hypothesised region labelling and layer ordering, the edges can all be labelled as motion 1 or motion 2 by following the Labelling Rule from Sect. 2.1. The probability of this region labelling given the data (term (8a)) is given by the probability of the edges having these labels.

The edge probabilities used in the EM of Sec. 3.2 made the assumption that tracking node errors were independent. While this is acceptable for the EM, under this assumption the edge probabilities are too confident and can result in an incorrect region labelling solution. As a result, a more suitable edge probability model was developed. Correlations between tracking nodes along an edge can be decoupled using Markov chains, which encode 1st order probabilistic relationships. (Used, for example, by MacCormick and Blake [8] to make their contour matching more robust to occlusion.) These higher-order statistics cannot be used for the EM since they are only valid at (or near) convergence. However, to ensure that the EM solution maximises the Markov chain edge probabilities, the EM switches to the Markov chain model near convergence.

The Markov chain models the relationship between one tracking node and the next along an edge, giving the probability of a tracking node having a certain residual d_i given the residual at the previous tracking node. These transition probabilities were estimated from data for the cases where an edge is matched under the correct motion and under the incorrect motion, and the modelled probabilities can be seen in Fig. 3. It is found that under the correct motion, a low residual distance is likely, and the residuals are largely independent (unless no match is found, in which case it is highly likely that the next tracking node will also find no match). Under the incorrect motion, the residual distances are highly correlated, and there is always a high probability that no match will be found.

There are two models of edge tracking node sequence formation: either motion 1 is correct and motion 2 incorrect, or vice versa. Both are considered equally likely a priori. The chain probability is calculated from the product of the transition probabilities, and it is assumed that the probabilities under the correct and incorrect motions are independent and so the two can be multiplied to give the hypothesis probability. Finally, the two hypothesis probabilities must be normalised by their sum to give the posterior edge probability.

The region probability given the data is the probability that all its edges obey the correct motions. It is assumed that the edges are independent, so (8a) can be evaluated by multiplying together all region edge probabilities under the edge labelling implied by R and F.

Region Prior Term (8b) encodes the a priori region labelling. This is implemented using a Markov Random Field (MRF), where the prior probability of a region's labelling depends on its immediate neighbours. Neighbours are considered in term of the fractional boundary length such that the more of a region's boundary adjoins foreground regions, the more likely the region is to be foreground.

The prior model was estimated from examples of correct region segmentations. An asymmetric sigmoid is a good fit to the data, where it is more likely to have a promontory of foreground in a sea of background than an inlet in the foreground (f is the percentage of foreground boundary around the region):

$$P\left(R\right) = \frac{1}{1 + \exp\left(-10\left(f - 0.4\right)\right)} \tag{13}$$

Solution by Simulated Annealing. In order to minimise over all possible region labellings, simulated annealing (SA) is used. This begins with an initial guess and then repeatedly tries flipping individual region labels one by one to see how the change affects the overall probability. (This is a simple process since a single region label change only causes local changes.)

The annealing process is initialised with a guess based on the edge probabilities. According to Sec. 2.1, foreground regions are entirely surrounded by foreground edges. This can be used as a region-labelling rule, although it is found that it works better if slightly diluted to allow for outliers. The initial region labelling labels as foreground any region with more than 85% of its edges having a high foreground probability.

Taking each region in turn,[2] they are considered both as foreground and as background and the probability of each hypothesis is calculated. In each case, the prior $P\left(R\right)$ can be calculated by reference to the current labels of its neighbours and the evidence calculated from the edge probabilities (using the edge motions implied by the neighbouring region labels and the layer ordering).

---

[2] Each pass of the data labels each region, but the order is shuffled each time to avoid systematic errors.

In the first pass, the region is then assigned by a Monte Carlo approach, i.e. randomly according to the two probabilities. However, the cycle is repeated and as the iterations progress, these probabilities are forced to saturate such that after around 30 iterations, all regions will be being assigned to their most likely motion. The annealing process continues until no changes are observed in a complete pass of the data, which takes about 40 iterations.

The random element in SA enables some local minima to be avoided. However, it was found that local minima were still a problem under any reasonable cooling timetable and, under some situations, the optimal solution was only found around a third of the time. This is solved by repeating the annealing process a number of times: 10 maximisations are performed, which gives a 99% probability of finding the optimal solution. The entire maximisation of (8) takes around 2 seconds on a 300MHz Pentium II.

Determining Depth Ordering F and Optimal Segmentation R Moving between region and edge labels, as in the annealing process, requires the layer ordering F to be known. This identifies the occluding edges of regions, and a different layer ordering can result in a very different segmentation. The most likely ordering, and segmentation, is the one which is most consistent with the edge probabilities i.e. the R, given F, with the highest probability.

The annealing process is thus performed twice, once for each possible value of F, first with motion 1 as foreground and then motion 2 as foreground. The segmentation with the greater posterior probability identifies the most likely foreground motion and the segmentation.

3.4 Multiple Frames

The maximisation outlined in Sects 3.2 and 3.3 can be performed over only two frames with good results (see, for an example, Fig. 1(c)). However, over multiple frames more evidence can be accumulated to give a more robust estimate. It is always the segmentation of frame 1 that is being maximised, so after comparing frame 1 to frame 2, frames 1 and 3 are compared, and then 1 and 4 and so on.

Initialisation The estimated motions and edge probabilities between frames 1 and 2, can be used to initialise the EM stage for the next frame. The motion estimate is that for the previous frame incremented by the velocity between the previous two frames. The edge labelling is initialised to be that implied by the region labelling of the previous frame, and the EM begins at the M-stage.

Combining statistics The probability that an edge obeys motion 1 over n frames is the probability that it obeyed motion 1 in each of the n frames. This can be calculated from the product of the probabilities for that edge over all n frames, if it is assumed that the edge probabilities are independent between frames.

To perform the region and foreground labelling based on the cumulative statistics, the method described in Sec. 3.3 is followed but using the cumulative edge statistics rather than those from just one frame.

Occlusion Over only two frames the problem of occlusion has been ignored as it has little effect on the outcome. When tracking over multiple frames, this becomes a significant problem. The foreground/background labelling for edges, however, allows this problem to be overcome. For each edge labelled as background according to the previous frame's region labelling, the tracking nodes' locations in the current image (under the background motion) are projected back into frame 1 under the foreground motion. If they fall into regions currently labelled as foreground, they are marked as occluded and they do not contribute to the tracking for that edge. All trackers are also tested to see if they project to outside the frame under the current motion and, if so, they are also ignored.

Segmenting a Sequence The segmentation of an entire sequence may be approximated by projecting the foreground regions into the other frames of the sequence according to the foreground motion at each frame. These regions may then be used as a 'template' to cut out the object in each of the subsequent frames (see Figs 5 and 6).

4 Results

Figure 1 shows the segmentation from the standard 'foreman' sequence based on two neighbouring frames. Between frames the head moves a few pixels to the left. The first frame is statically segmented (Fig. 1(a)) and then EM run between this frame and the next to extract the motion estimates. Figure 1(b) shows the edge labels based on how well they fit each motion after convergence. It can be seen that the EM process picks out most of the edges correctly, even though the motion is small. The edges on his shoulders are poorly labelled, but this is due to the shoulders' motion being even smaller than that of the head. The correct motion is selected as foreground with very high confidence (a posterior probability of about 99%) and the final segmentation, Fig. 1(c), is very good despite some poor edge labels. In this case the MRF region prior is a great help in producing a plausible segmentation. On a 300MHz Pentium II, it takes around 7 seconds to produce the motion segmentation from an initial static region segmentation.

The effect of using multiple frames can be seen in Fig. 4. Accumulating the edge probabilities over several frames allows random errors to be removed and edge probabilities to be reinforced. The larger motions between more widely separated frames also removes ambiguity. It can be seen that over time the consensus among many edges on the shoulders is towards the foreground motion. The accumulated edge probabilities have a positive effect on the region segmentation, which settles down after a few frames to a very accurate solution. If the

Fig. 4. Evolution of the 'foreman' segmentation, showing the edge probabilities and segmentations of frames 47–52 as the evidence is accumulated. The edge probabilities become more certain and small errors are removed, resulting in an improved region segmentation.

Fig. 5. Multiple-frame segmentation of the 'tennis' sequence. The camera zooms out while the arm slowly descends. Shown is the original frame 29 and then the foreground segmentation of part of the sequence, showing every 5th frame. The final region labelling is used to segment all frames in a second pass of the data.

segmentation were continued over a large number of frames then the errors from assuming affine motion become would become significant (particularly as the foreman tilts his head back and opens his mouth), and the segmentation would break down. Dealing with non-affine motions is a significant element planned for further work.

Figures 5 and 6 show some frames from extended sequences segmented using this method. In the 'tennis' sequence (Fig. 5) the arm again does not obey the affine motion particularly well (and the upper arm and torso hardly obey it at all), but is still tracked and segmented well over a short sequence of frames. The 'car' sequence, Fig. 6, is atypical – it has a large background motion (around 10 pixels per frame), a hole in the foreground object, and the dominant motion is the foreground. However, it is still segmented very cleanly (including the window) and the correct motion is identified as foreground. In this case the layer ordering is rather unsure over 2 frames (70%/30%), but over many frames the edge labellings are reinforced and the final decision is clearly in favour of the correct labelling. The affine motion fits the side of the car well over a large number of frames.

Fig. 6. Multiple-frame segmentation of the 'car' sequence. The camera pans to the left to track the car. Shown is the original frame 490 and then the foreground segmentation of part of the sequence, showing every 5th frame. The final region labelling is used to segment all frames in a second pass of the data.

5 Conclusions and Future Work

This paper develops and demonstrates a novel Bayesian framework for segmenting a video sequence into foreground and background regions based on tracking the edges of an initial region segmentation between frames. It is demonstrated that edges can be reliably tracked and labelled between frames of a sequence and are sufficient to label regions and the motion ordering.

The EM algorithm is used to simultaneously estimate the two motions and the edge probabilities (which can be robustly estimated using a Markov chain along the edge). The correct foreground motion and region labelling can be identified by hypothesising and testing to maximise the probability of the model given the edge data and a MRF prior. The algorithm runs quickly and the results are very good over two frames. Over multiple frames the edge probabilities can be accumulated resulting in a very accurate and robust region segmentation.

The current implementation considers only two layers under affine motions. Future work will concentrate on extended multi-frame sequences, since over a longer sequence the edge motions cannot be well modelled by an affine motion model. Disoccluded edges also appear, and should be incorporated into the model. Both problems may be solved by using the tracked edges to assist in the resegmentation of future frames in the sequence, which then behave as new 'key frames' for the segmentation process described in this paper. This would allow the system to adapt to non-rigid, non-affine motions over the longer term.

Acknowledgements

This research was funded by a United Kingdom EPSRC studentship, with a CASE award from the AT&T Laboratories, Cambridge, UK. Thanks go to David Sinclair for the use of his image segmentation code and to Ken Wood for many useful discussions.

References

[1] S. Ayer, P. Schroeter, and J. Bigün. Segmentation of moving objects by robust motion parameter estimation over multiple frames. In *Proc. 3rd European Con-*

ference on Computer Vision, volume II, pages 317–327, Stockholm, Sweden, May 1994.

[2] L. Bergen and F. Meyer. Motion segmentation and depth ordering based on morphological segmentation. In *Proc. 5th European Conference on Computer Vision*, volume II, pages 531–547, Freiburg, Germany, June 1998.

[3] M.J. Black and D.J. Fleet. Probabilistic detection and tracking of motion discontinuities. In *Proc. 7th International Conference on Computer Vision*, volume I, pages 551–558, Kerkyra, Greece, September 1999.

[4] A. Blake and M. Isard. *Active Contours*. Springer-Verlag, 1998.

[5] A. P. Dempster, H. M. Laird, and D. B. Rubin. Maximum likelihood from incomplete data via the EM algorithm. *Journal of Royal Statistical Society Series B*, 39:1–38, 1977.

[6] T. Drummond and R. Cipolla. Visual tracking and control using lie algebras. In *Proc. IEEE Conference on Computer Vision and Pattern Recognition '99*, volume 2, pages 652–657, Fort Collins, CO, June 1999.

[7] S. Hsu, P. Anandan, and S. Peleg. Accurate computation of optical flow by using layered motion representations. In *Proc. 12th International Conference on Pattern Recognition*, pages 743–746, Jerusalem, Israel, October 1994.

[8] J. MacCormick and A. Blake. Spatial dependence in the observation of visual contours. In *Proc. 5th European Conference on Computer Vision*, volume II, pages 765–781, Freiburg, Germany, June 1998.

[9] F. Moscheni and F. Dufaux. Region merging based on robust statistical testing. In *Proc. SPIE Visual Communications and Image Processing '96*, Orlando, Florida, USA, March 1996.

[10] J. M. Odobez and P. Bouthemy. Separation of moving regions from background in an image sequence acquired with a mobile camera. In *Video Data Compression for Multimedia Computing*, pages 283–311. Kluwer Academic Publisher, 1997.

[11] H. S. Sawhney and S. Ayer. Compact representations of videos through dominant and multiple motion estimation. *IEEE Transactions on Pattern Analysis and Machine Intelligence*, 18(8):814–830, August 1996.

[12] J. Shi and J. Malik. Motion segmentation and tracking using normalized cuts. In *Proc. 6th International Conference on Computer Vision*, pages 1154–1160, Bombay, India, January 1998.

[13] D. Sinclair. Voronoi seeded colour image segmentation. Technical Report 1999.3, AT&T Laboratories Cambridge, 1999.

[14] P. Smith, T. Drummond, and R. Cipolla. Edge tracking for motion segmentation and depth ordering. In *Proc. 10th British Machine Vision Conference*, volume 2, pages 369–378, Nottingham, September 1999.

[15] P. H. S. Torr, R. Szeliski, and P. Anandan. An integrated Bayesian approach to layer extraction from image sequences. In *Proc. 7th International Conference on Computer Vision*, volume II, pages 983–990, Kerkyra, Greece, September 1999.

[16] J.Y.A Wang. and E.H. Adelson. Layered representation for motion analysis. In *Proc. IEEE Conference on Computer Vision and Pattern Recognition '93*, pages 361–366, New York, NY, June 1993.

[17] Y. Weiss and E. H. Adelson. A unified mixture framework for motion segmentation: Incorporating spatial coherence and estimating the number of models. In *Proc. IEEE Conference on Computer Vision and Pattern Recognition '96*, pages 321–326, San Francisco, CA, June 1996.

Data-Driven Extraction of Curved Intersection Lanemarks from Road Traffic Image Sequences

K. Mück[1], H.-H. Nagel[1,2], and M. Middendorf[1]

[1] Institut für Algorithmen und Kognitive Systeme,
Universität Karlsruhe (TH), Postfach 6980, 76128 Karlsruhe, Germany,
{klaus|nagel|markusm}@ira.uka.de
Phone: +49 721 608–4044; Fax: +49 721 608–6116
[2] Fraunhofer-Institut für Informations- und Datenverarbeitung (IITB),
Fraunhoferstr. 1, 76131 Karlsruhe, Germany

Abstract. Segmentation of optical flow fields, estimated by spatio-temporally adaptive methods, is – under favourable conditions – reliable enough to track moving vehicles at intersections *without using vehicle or road models*. Already a single image plane trajectory per lane obtained in this manner offers valuable information about where *lane markers* should be searched for. Fitting a hyperbola to an image plane trajectory of a vehicle which crosses an intersection thus provides concise geometric hints. These allow to separate images of direction indicators and of stop marks painted onto the road surface from side marks delimiting a lane. Such a 'lane spine hyperbola', moreover, facilitates to link side marks even across significant gaps in cluttered areas of a complex intersection. Data-driven extraction of trajectory information thus facilitates to link *local* spatial descriptions practically across the entire field of view in order to create *global* spatial descriptions. These results are important since they allow to extract required information from image sequences of traffic scenes without the necessity to obtain a map of the road structure and to make this information (interactively) available to a machine-vision-based traffic surveillance system.
The approach is illustrated for different lanes with markings which are only a few pixels wide and thus difficult to detect reliably without the search area restriction provided by a lane spine hyperbola. So far, the authors did not find comparable results in the literature.

1 Introduction

Geometric results derived from (model-based) tracking of road vehicles in traffic image sequences can already be transformed into *conceptual* descriptions of road traffic. The generation of such descriptions from video recordings of road traffic at inner-city intersections – see, e. g., [2–4, 6, 11] – presupposes, however, the availability of knowledge about the spatial lane structure of the intersection. In addition to knowledge about the geometric arrangement of lanes, knowledge about lane attributes is required such as, e. g., which lane might be reserved for left or right turning traffic – see Figure 1 for illustration.

So far, this kind of knowledge had to be provided a-priori by the designer(s) of a system, either by a qualitative interactive extraction from image sequence data or by digitizing a map of the intersection. Even if a city administration provides a map of an intersection comprising all significant lane markings, however, experience has shown that such a map may not be up-to-date.

Fig. 1. The left panel shows a representative frame from a traffic intersection video sequence recording traffic from the incoming arm of road A (upper left quadrant) through the intersection to the outgoing arm of road B at the bottom. The right panel shows another frame from this same sequence, recorded while pedestrians where allowed to walk and no vehicles happen to be in the field of view of the recording video camera. Lane markings have been extracted from this frame.

This state of affairs naturally suggests an attempt to *automatically* extract the lane structure of an intersection from the video sequence recording the road traffic to be analyzed. The next section outlines our approach, followed by a more detailed description in Sections 3 and 4, illustrated by experimental results obtained by an implementation of this approach. Additional experimental results are presented in Section 5. A concise overview of relevant publications is followed by a comparison with our approach and by conclusions in Section 6.

2 Basic Assumptions and Outline of the Approach

Experience with *data-driven* image segmentation approaches – regardless whether edge- or region-oriented – has shown that success at an affordable computational expense depends critically on the exploitation of appropriate *implicit* knowledge about the depicted scene, including its illumination, and about the imaging conditions. We venture that progress results if such implicit knowledge can be explicated and thus made amenable to scrutiny, a precondition for further improvement.

This contribution assumes that vehicles which approach, cross, and leave an intersection stay predominantly within their lane. Image plane trajectories of vehicles thus provide crucial information about the number and geometry of lanes as well as about admitted driving directions. The image region corresponding to a lane can thus be conceived to be a *ribbon* of approximately constant width. The vehicle trajectory constitutes the 'spine' of such a 'lane ribbon'.

Lanes around an innercity intersection are composed in general of three segments: a straight 'approaching' arm, a straight-line or circular-arc segment across the intersection proper, and a straight 'leaving' arm. As will be shown, these characteristics can be captured astonishingly well and concisely by one arm of a hyperbola. The assumed 'hyperbolic spine' of a lane thus constitutes a powerful cue for lane interpolation across the intersection area.

Direction markers painted onto the road surface are expected near the spine of a lane ribbon and parallel to it whereas stopping lines cut nearly perpendicular across the lane ribbon. Sidemarks delimit the lane along the ribbon borders in the approaching and leaving arm segments, but are often omitted within the intersection area itself. All lane markers are assumed to be elongated bright blobs surrounded by dark road surface.

These quite general – but nevertheless essentially appropriate – assumptions can be exploited to the extent that we succeed to extract vehicle trajectories in the image plane *without introducing knowledge about position, orientation, shape, and motion* of vehicles in the scene. Instead, we assume that vehicles can be represented as blobs with sufficient *spatiotemporal* contrast – i. e. not necessarily purely spatial contrast – to segment them from the remainder of the imaged scene. We assume, moreover, that such 'object image candidates (OICs)' *move smoothly* in the image plane.

The transformation of these assumptions into an algorithm for the extraction of lane descriptions from intersection traffic image sequences will be treated in more detail in the next section.

3 Extraction of Lane Spines from Image Sequences

Automatic machine-vision-based traffic surveillance at an intersection avoids several complications if a *single* camera records the *relevant intersection area* (no tracking beyond the field of view of a camera into that of another, more simple camera calibration, no inter-camera correspondence problems, etc.). The price to be paid for this simplification consists in rather small image structures which have to be detected, tracked, and classified, since a large field of view at a given resolution results in small object images. The following discussion treats only the evaluation of *monocular* image sequences.

3.1 Detecting and Tracking the Image of a Moving Road Vehicle

If a vehicle trajectory is expected to provide the information about where in the image one should search for lane markings, then this trajectory must be extracted with a minimum of a-priori knowledge. Detection and tracking of moving

(a)   (b)   (c)   (d)

Fig. 2. The leftmost panel (a) shows an enlarged section around a vehicle to be tracked, cropped from the 375th frame of the sequence illustrated in Figure 1. Panel (b) shows the accepted OF-vectors overlayed to this enlarged section whereas the OIC-mask generated for the first subsequence ending with this frame is shown as an overlay in panel (c). Panel (d) shows OIC-mask contours obtained for this vehicle, overlayed to the 375th frame of this sequence. The OIC-mask position has been advanced from frame m to $m+1$ by the average optical flow vector $\overline{\mathbf{u}_m}$ obtained from the OF-blob determined for this vehicle in frame m. The centers of these OIC-masks form a trajectory obtained by a purely data-driven approach.

vehicles will be investigated by estimation and segmentation of densely populated Optical Flow (OF) fields, despite the considerable computational expenses involved: compared with, e. g., change detection approaches, OF-field segments provide immediately usable information about magnitude and direction of the shift velocity of greyvalue structures. In many cases, such information allows to exclude alternative interpretations of results. If executed properly, moreover, the estimation of OF-fields provides additional information about the reliability of an estimation and, thereby, further supports the algorithmic analysis of any result in doubt.

In view of the rather small image structures to be tracked, we adopted – albeit in a modified manner – a recently published approach towards OF-estimation [13]: optical flow is computed by determination of the eigenvector corresponding to the smallest eigenvalue of the so-called 'Greyvalue Local Structure Tensor' $\overline{\nabla g (\nabla g)^T}$, a weighted average (over a local environment of the current pixel) of the outer product of $\nabla g = (\frac{\partial g}{\partial x}, \frac{\partial g}{\partial y}, \frac{\partial g}{\partial t})^T$, where ∇g denotes the gradient of the greyvalue function $g(x, y, t)$ with respect to image plane coordinates (x, y) and time t. Spatio-temporal adaptation of the filter masks for gradient estimation improves the trade-off between noise reduction and separation of different greyvalue structures.

A 4-connected region of OF-estimates is then selected as an 'OF-blob', provided at each pixel position within such a region

1. the OF-magnitude exceeds a minimum threshold (separation between stationary background and moving vehicles),
2. the smallest eigenvalue of $\overline{\nabla g (\nabla g)^T}$ is smaller than a threshold (i. e. the greyvalue structure remains essentially constant in the OF-direction), and
3. the two larger eigenvalues of $\overline{\nabla g (\nabla g)^T}$ both exceed a minimum threshold (i. e. the greyvalue variation in both spatial directions is sufficient to reliably estimate an OF-vector).

OF-blobs which can be persistently detected at mutually (according to the OF-estimate) compatible image plane locations are aggregated into an 'Object Image Candidate (OIC)' as follows. We assume that the *shape* of a vehicle's image does not change significantly during a subsequence of n ($\simeq 12$) frames. Let $\overline{u_k}$ denote the average OF-vector of the k-th OF-blob within a subsequence ($k = 1, 2, \ldots, n - 1$). The k-th OF-blob is shifted forward by $\sum_{j=k}^{n-1} \overline{u_j}$ (with components of the resulting sum vector rounded to the next integer value) and 'stacked' on top of the OF-blob extracted from the last frame within this subsequence. Among the pixel locations supporting this stack, we retain as an *initial* OIC-mask only those which are covered by at least p % (with, e. g., $p = 45$) of the n possible entries from the stacked OF-blobs. The OIC-contour is then taken as a rough estimate for the image shape of a moving vehicle.

For the first subsequence, $OIC_{1_{\text{initial}}}$ is accepted in this form. In the case of later subsequences, however, consecutive OIC-masks are merged in order to adapt an OIC-mask to possible changes in appearance of an object image. An OIC-mask OIC_{i-1} obtained from the $(i-1)$-th subsequence is shifted by $\overline{u_{(i-1)_n}} + \sum_{j=1}^{n-1} \overline{u_{i_j}}$ to the location of $OIC_{i_{\text{initial}}}$ obtained from the next (i-th) subsequence. The two OIC-masks are stacked, each with the weight (i. e. hit count) determined at its generation. Analogously to the generation of an initial OIC-mask, all pixel locations are retained which received a weight of at least p % of the $2n$ possible entries from the two stacked OIC-masks.

Figure 2 illustrates the generation of an OIC-mask.

3.2 Extraction of the 'Lane Spine'

Fig. 3. Left panel: The OIC-mask contours, shown every 20 half-frames, with small dark 'x' denoting the center of an OIC-Mask. Right panel: The 'lane spine', a hyperbola fitted according to equ. 1 – using every half-frame – to the OIC-mask trajectory shown in the left panel.

As mentioned in Section 2, image plane trajectories of vehicles crossing the intersection illustrated in Figure 1 can in good approximation be described by a hyperbola. In analogy with established practice for ellipses [16], we fit the following polynomial

$$Ax^2 + Bxy + Cy^2 + Dx + Ey + F = 0 \qquad (1)$$

to a sequence of OIC-mask centers such as shown in Figure 3. The free parameter in this homogeneous equation is fixed by the requirement $A - C = 1$, in analogy to the well-known trace requirement $A + C = 1$ for ellipse fitting (see, e. g., [16]). The degenerate case of a straight-line trajectory is automatically detected and treated separately. The axes of the right-handed eigenvector coordinate system of the resulting conic are fixed by requiring that the apex of the hyperbola intersects the first axis and the estimated vehicle trajectory opens into the positive direction of this axis.

4 Extraction of Lane Structures from Image Sequences

In innercity intersections such as those shown in Figure 1, lanes are in general delimited at the sides by bright lines, by sidewalks with a visible curb, or by a surface with color or texture visibly different from the lane surface. We generally expect, therefore, to find edge elements marking the side of a lane image. The problem consists in the challenge to reliably detect a sufficiently large fraction of these edge elements in order to facilitate their concatenation into a coherent lane delimiter. At this point, we introduce a-priori knowledge about (continuous or interrupted) lane side boundary markings in the form of a 'lane model'. In principle, one could define such a model in the (2-D) image plane or in the (3-D) scene. We decided to define the model in the scene, because the dependencies between the 'lane spine' and the hyperbolas representing the lateral lane boundaries are more simply described in the scene. If we know the projective transformation by the camera system, a lane representation in the scene domain can be transformed without any further heuristics into the image plane. Our lane model will be denoted as a 'hyperbolic ribbon'. This hyperbolic ribbon will be fitted to the edge elements tentatively selected as marking the side boundary of a lane image.

4.1 Hyperbolic Ribbon as Lane Model

As mentioned in section 2, the spine of curved intersection lanes can in good approximation be described by a hyperbola. Based on such a 'hyperbolic spine', we are able to construct a ribbon of hyperbolas to describe the lateral delimiters of a curved lane. A lane has one delimiter at the right and one at the left side. So it seems to be enough to construct a ribbon of three hyperbolas. One hyperbola can be defined by five parameters $[m_x, m_y, \theta, a, b]$. The parameters m_x and m_y represent the center point, θ describes the orientation and a, b specify the form

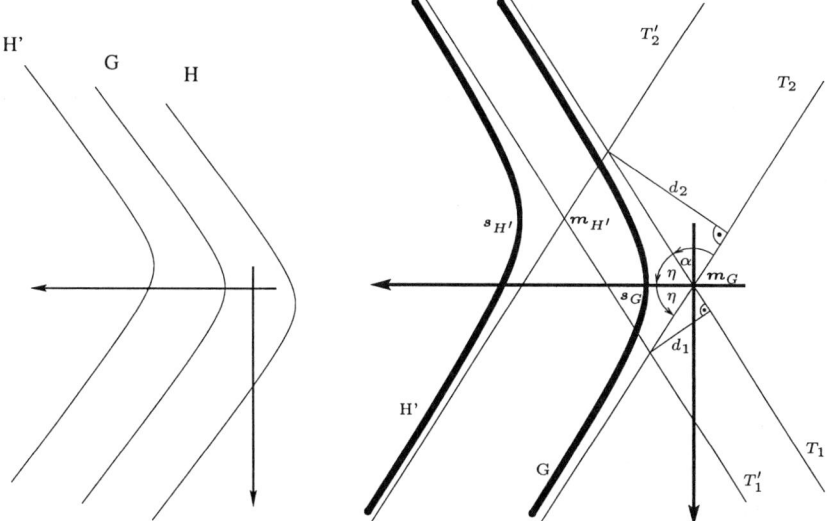

Fig. 4. The left panel depicts the 'lane spine' G as shown in the right panel of Figure 3, together with the two 'lane boundary' hyperbolas H, H'. These three hyperbolas represent a lane as a 'hyperbolic ribbon'. The 'leaving' arm is wider than the 'approaching' arm of the lane, but the asymptotes of all hyperbolas are parallel. The coordinate system shown refers to the lane spine G, i. e. $m_{Gx} = m_{Gy} = 0$ and $\theta_G = 0$. The right panel illustrates how to construct one side of a hyperbolic ribbon with different widths. The center point $m_{H'}$ of the hyperbola H' can be constructed with the normalized directions of the asymptotes T_1 and T_2, the angle $\alpha = \pi - 2\eta$, and a scale factor based on the widths d_1, d_2. The direction and orientation of the hyperbola H' are the same, respectively, as those of the lane spine G, i. e. the normalized directions of the asymptotes T_1', T_2' are the same as the normalized directions of T_1, T_2. The position of the apex $s_{H'}$ is defined by the distance between the apices s_G and $s_{H'}$.

of a hyperbola. A ribbon of three – nominally unrelated – hyperbolas therefore requires the specification of 15 parameters.

The outer hyperbolas can be derived from the hyperbolic spine inside the ribbon with a few basic and useful assumptions about the symmetry of a lane. These assumptions, based on official guidelines for constructing innercity intersections, lead to a large reduction of the number of parameters while defining a hyperbolic ribbon (see Figure 4). All of the following definitions are related to the eigensystem of the lane spine G which is shifted by $(m_x, m_y)^T$ and rotated by θ relative to the coordinate system of the scene, according to the parameters $[m_x, m_y, \theta, a, b]$ of lane spine G:

- *Orientation*: All hyperbolas have the same orientation θ. This reduces the number of parameters from 15 by two to 13.
- *Shape*: Each hyperbola has a pair of asymptotes. These asymptotes represent the straight parts of a lane. We assume, therefore, that all aperture

angles have the same value η with $\tan(\eta) = b/a$. This reduces the number of parameters by two more to 11.

- *Position*: The 'approaching' arm and the 'leaving' arm of a lane at an innercity intersection can differ in their width. The parameters d_1 and d_2 take this observation into account. Figure 4 shows how the center point of the hyperbola H' is moved. It can be computed from the center point of G as follows:

$$m_{H'} = \begin{pmatrix} (d_1 + d_2)/(2\sin(\eta)) \\ (d_1 - d_2)/(2\cos(\eta)) \end{pmatrix}. \tag{2}$$

The position of the center point of the hyperbola H can be computed analogously:

$$m_H = -\begin{pmatrix} (d_1 + d_2)/(2\sin(\eta)) \\ (d_1 - d_2)/(2\cos(\eta)) \end{pmatrix}, \tag{3}$$

Equations 3 and 2 can be derived based on the geometric context shown in the right panel of Figure 4. This reduces the number of parameters further by two parameters to 9.

- *Apex*: The last free parameter defines the position of the apex. This position specifies, too, the acuity of the hyperbola at this point, because the center point, orientation and aperture angle are fixed. A hyperbola G in the normal form

$$\frac{x^2}{a^2} - \frac{y^2}{b^2} = 1 \tag{4}$$

has its apex at $(a, 0)^T$. Multiplying this vector by a factor p moves the apex along the first axis: $(p \cdot a, 0)^T$. At the same time, the hyperbolas have to retain their shape. This can be achieved by multiplying the shape parameter b with the same factor p. The aperture angle η — where $\tan(\eta) = (p \cdot b)/(p \cdot a) = b/a$ — will thus remain unchanged. The distance between the apices $s_{H'}$ and s_G as well as between s_H and s_G is defined by

$$\|s_{H'}s_G\| = \|s_H s_G\| = \tau \cdot \frac{d_1 + d_2}{2}. \tag{5}$$

Usually the width of the curved section of a lane is greater than in the straight lane sections. This can be taken into account by setting τ to values greater than 1. The factors p_H and $p_{H'}$, referring to the lane boundary hyperbolas H and H', respectively, can be computed by solving:

$$p_H \cdot a = a + \frac{d_1 + d_2}{2\sin(\eta)} - \sqrt{\left(\tau \frac{d_1 + d_2}{2}\right)^2 - \left(\frac{d_2 - d_1}{2\cos(\eta)}\right)^2}, \tag{6}$$

$$p_{H'} \cdot a = a - \frac{d_1 + d_2}{2\sin(\eta)} + \sqrt{\left(\tau \frac{d_1 + d_2}{2}\right)^2 - \left(\frac{d_2 - d_1}{2\cos(\eta)}\right)^2}. \tag{7}$$

Using these assumptions, the initial number of 15 parameters can be reduced to only 8 parameters for describing a complete hyperbolic ribbon:

$$< (m_x, m_y)_G^T, \theta_G, a_G, b_G, d_1, d_2, \tau >$$

where the index G refers to the lane spine G.

This model approximates a *lateral lane delimiter* by an infinitely thin line. In order to take the finite width of a lane delimiter into account, we extend the model: we use a hyperbolic ribbon for each lane delimiter, this time parameterized for the width dw of the lane delimiter. The complete lane model can thus be described by the tuple $< (m_x, m_y)_G^T, \theta_G, a_G, b_G, d_1, d_2, \tau, dw_1, dw_2 >$ of parameters. The parameters dw_1, dw_2 represent the width of the left and right lane boundary delimiter, respectively. Two separate parameters are necessary in general since lane delimiters between adjacent lanes may differ in width from those delimiting the road sides.

4.2 Fitting Hyperbolic Ribbons to Edge Elements

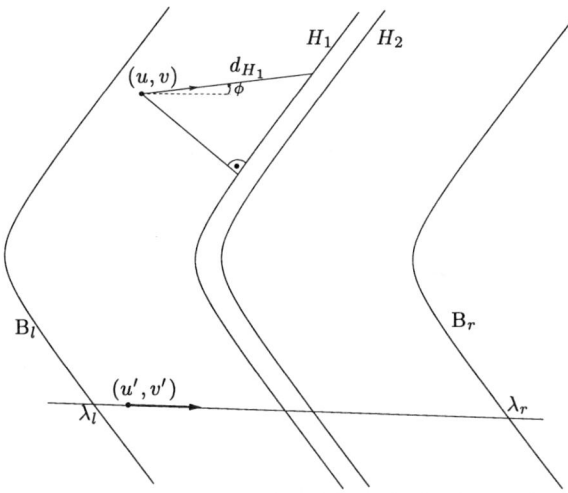

Fig. 5. The hyperbolas H_1 and H_2 model one lateral boundary of a lane. All edge elements inside the hyperbolic tolerance ribbon limited by the hyperbolas B_l and B_r are candidates for the fitting step. An edge element has a position and a direction, so we can interpret an edge element as a line. As shown in the lower part of this Figure, the intersection of this line with the hyperbolas B_l and B_r results in the parameters λ_l and λ_r. If $\lambda_l < 0 < \lambda_r$, the edge element inside the hyperbolic ribbon limited by B_l and B_r will be fitted to the hyperbola H_1, otherwise to H_2. The edge element shown at position $(u, v)^T$ in the upper part of this Figure has the distance d_{H_1} from H_1. This distance measure takes into account the gradient orientation at the point $(u, v)^T$. If we consider an edge element as a line, this distance can be derived by intersecting this line with the hyperbola H_1.

Fitting hyperbolic ribbons to edge elements is based on the approach of [10]. Although the lane model is defined in the scene, the projected image of this model is fitted to the edge elements in the image: the sum of Mahalanobis distances between edge elements and the projected model – parameterized according to the actual parameter estimates (which constitute the components of the filter state vector) – is iteratively optimized. The finally accepted state vector represents the matched lane in the scene.

The estimation process is initialized by the lane spine mentioned above. The widths of the arms of a lane are initially set to the *same* standard value. The typical lane width, the typical width at the curved section of a lane, and the typical width of the lateral lane boundary delimiters can be found in guidelines for constructing innercity intersections. All parameters can thus be initialized by reasonable values.

The distance function takes the gradient orientation of an edge element into account (see Figure 5). Let an edge element $e = (u, v, \phi)^T$ and the hyperbola H be given by

$$e : \begin{pmatrix} x \\ y \end{pmatrix} = \lambda \begin{pmatrix} \cos(\phi) \\ \sin(\phi) \end{pmatrix} + \begin{pmatrix} u \\ v \end{pmatrix}, \tag{8}$$

$$H : Ax^2 + Bxy + Cy^2 + Dx + Ey + F = 0 \tag{9}$$

The signed distance function $d_H(e, x)$ which quantifies the distance between an edge element e and the hyperbola H under the actual state x (with $x = (m_{x_G}, m_{y_G}, \theta_G, a_G, b_G, d_1, d_2, \tau, dw_1, dw_2)^T$) is defined by:

$$d_H(e, x) = \begin{cases} \lambda_1, & |\lambda_1| < |\lambda_2| \\ \lambda_2, & \text{otherwise} \end{cases} \tag{10}$$

with

$$\lambda_1 = \frac{-p/2 + \sqrt{p^2/4 - qr}}{r}, \qquad \lambda_2 = \frac{-p/2 - \sqrt{p^2/4 - qr}}{r},$$

$$r = A\cos^2(\phi) + B\cos(\phi)\sin(\phi) + C\sin^2(\phi),$$

$$p = 2A\cos(\phi)u + B(\cos(\phi)v + \sin(\phi)u) +$$
$$+ 2C\sin(\phi)v + D\cos(\phi) + E\sin(\phi),$$

$$q = Au^2 + Buv + Cv^2 + Du + Ev + F.$$

Note that a negative distance is possible.

The lane is modeled with two lane delimiters. Each of them consists of two outer hyperbolas H_1, H_2 (the hyperbolic spine is only used for the construction of the hyperbolic ribbon, but not for the computation of the distance between edge elements and the projection of the lane model). Fitting all edge elements of the entire image to a lane model will consume too much time. It is necessary, therefore, to decide which edge element should be associated with which hyperbola. The first constraint is satisfied by building a hyperbolic tolerance ribbon around each of the delimiters (see Figure 5). All edge elements inside such a hyperbolic tolerance ribbon between the hyperbolas B_l and B_r are considered candidates for the fitting process. The association of an edge element with the correct hyperbola (H_1 or H_2) is based on the typical greyvalue distribution near a lane delimiter since delimiters are in general brighter than the rest of the lane. An edge element represents this property by the gradient direction at this position: this direction has to be approximately perpendicular to the assigned hyperbola. It is easy to decide whether an edge element has to be associated with the left or the right hyperbola of the delimiter: An edge element considered as a directed line can be intersected with the boundaries of the hyperbolic tolerance ribbon. Let $\lambda_l = d_{B_l}(e, x)$ and $\lambda_r = d_{B_r}(e, x)$ denote the distances of the edge element to the intersections of this line with the hyperbolas B_l and B_r. If $\lambda_l < 0 < \lambda_r$, the edge element will be associated with hyperbola H_1, otherwise with hyperbola H_2 (see Figure 5).

5 Experimental Results

Figure 6 shows two successfully detected lanes with fitted models overlayed. The fitting process describes the lane delimiters essentially correct. A small discrepancy in the curved section of the lane shown in the left panel corresponds to the variation of the lane width as described above.

Both lanes differ in width between their approaching (2.85 m) and their leaving (3.50 m) arms. In addition, the widths at the stop line is a little bit smaller (2.75 m) than in the incoming straight sections of both arms. The lane spine derived for the right lane was a bit off the lane center since the driver of the respective car did not drive strictly along the lane center. The starting state for the right boundary delimiter thus was initialized too far to the right. The fitting process could not fully correct this state initialization. A possible solution for such a problem could consist in exploiting a longer observation of the scene: rather than relying on the first trajectory in order to derive a lane spine, one could select a more appropriate one, based on a statistical analysis of several trajectories.

The left panel of Figure 7 shows *all* hyperbolas used in fitting a lane. The enlarged sections allow to verify the quality of fit in more detail.

The approach has been extended in order to treat *neighboring* lanes with essentially the same parameter set as illustrated by the right panel of Figure 7: assuming equal widths and orientation for both lanes and symmetrical apex displacements for boundary spines, we only need one additional parameter, namely for the width of the common boundary delimiter separating the two neighboring lanes. In this manner, we are able to fit six hyperbolas – which can differ substantially with respect to their position and orientation *in the image plane* – to about 4900 edge elements, using only 11 parameters. A backprojection of lane delimiters extracted in this manner into the road plane and a comparison with official map information about lane markings at the depicted intersection yields good agreement (see Figure 8).

The approach reported up to here has been extended even further in order to cope with situations such as those illustrated by the left upper panel in Figure 9: since this sequence comprises only fifty frames, no vehicle trajectory covers a

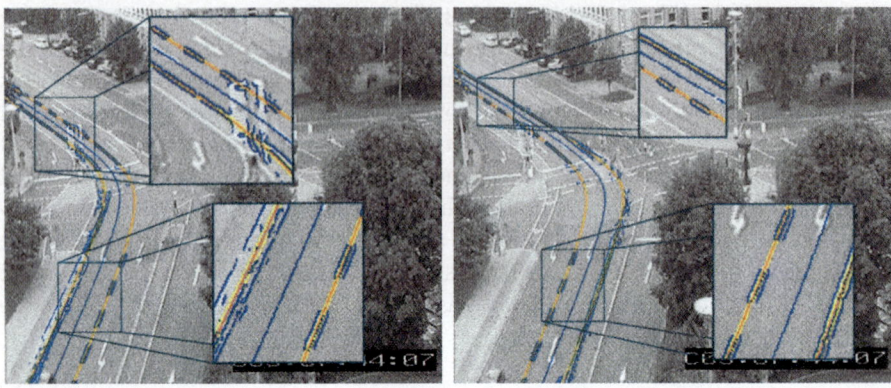

Fig. 6. The left panel shows a fit of a hyperbolic ribbon to the *left* lane, computed according to the approach described in Section 4. The hyperbolic spine is drawn in blue, the hyperbolas in the *centre* of the lane delimiters are painted red, while the hyperbolas which model the *boundaries* of the lane delimiters are painted yellow. All edge elements which are taken into account during the fitting process are painted in blue, too. Within the upper enlarged subwindow, it can be clearly seen that edge elements due to the large traffic sign which occludes part of this lane do not endanger an appropriate fit. The right panel shows a fit of a hyperbolic ribbon to the *right* lane, in analogy to the left panel.

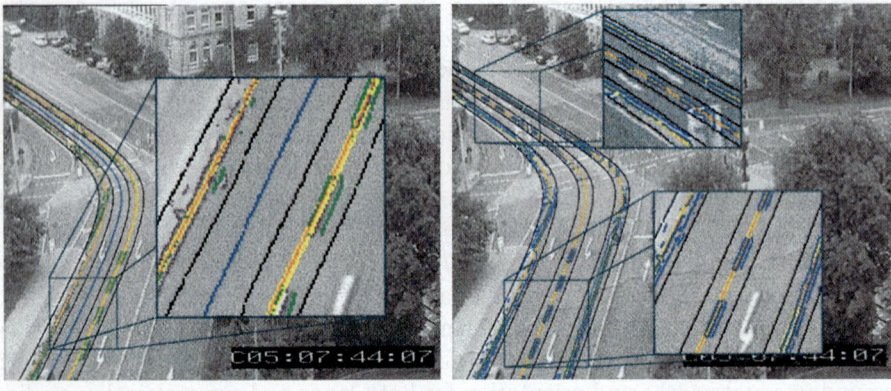

Fig. 7. The left panel shows *all* hyperbolas exploited for the fit to the left lane, together with an enlarged section. The black hyperbolas bound the area in which edge elements are supposed to belong to the enclosed lane delimiter. One can clearly detect the differently (colored in either pink or green) oriented edge elements on the sides of bright blobs corresponding to short lane markings. (Notice the effect of greyvalue overshoot in the scanline direction for a transition between the bright lane markings and the dark background which results in unexpected additional edge elements colored in green, clearly visible in the insets!) The right panel shows a *simultaneous* fit of two hyperbolic lane models side-by-side (using a **joint** parameter set, thus significantly reducing the number of parameters required to describe **both** lanes) to two neighboring lanes.

423

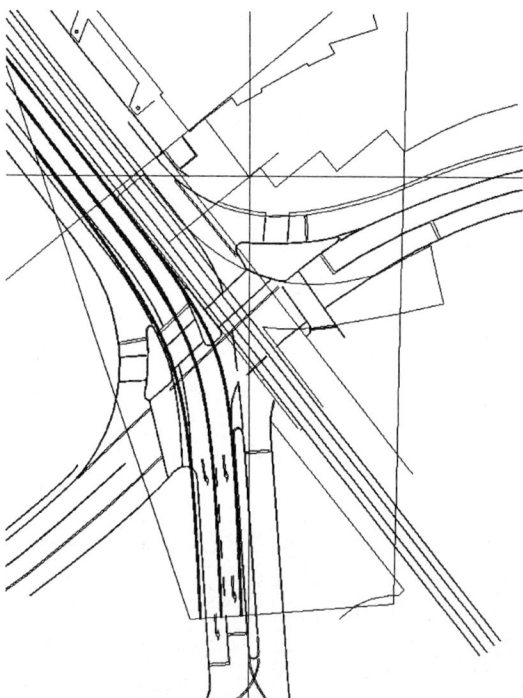

Fig. 8. This image shows the backprojections of two simultaneously fitted lanes (see Figure 7) into a map of the intersection provided by the official land registry. The comparatively small deviations in the lower part of the image are attributed to small systematic errors of the camera calibration. As Figure 7 shows, the lanes were fitted well in the image plane both for the incoming and the leaving arm. It can be seen that the incoming lanes become smaller close to the stopping line in order to allow for an additional 'bicycle lane' for those bicyclists who want to continue straight ahead.

lane across the entire intersection. We thus fit multiple trajectory segments (see the top right panel in Figure 9) from *different* vehicles in neighboring lanes to a *jointly* parameterized *pair* of two neighboring 'lane spine hyperbolas'. The initial estimates for these lane spine hyperbolas are shown in the lower left panel and the final result for the boundary limits in the lower right panel of Figure 9. The remaining deficiency regarding the 'leaving' arm is due to the lack of an appropriate initialization and of sufficient contrast to facilitate a correction in the estimation of lane boundary delimiters. This Figure illustrates both the power and current limits of our approach.

6 Comparison and Conclusions

The idea to exploit data-driven tracking of moving objects in video sequences in order to derive descriptions of developments in the scene has found increasing interest recently, due to methodological improvements in the detection and

424

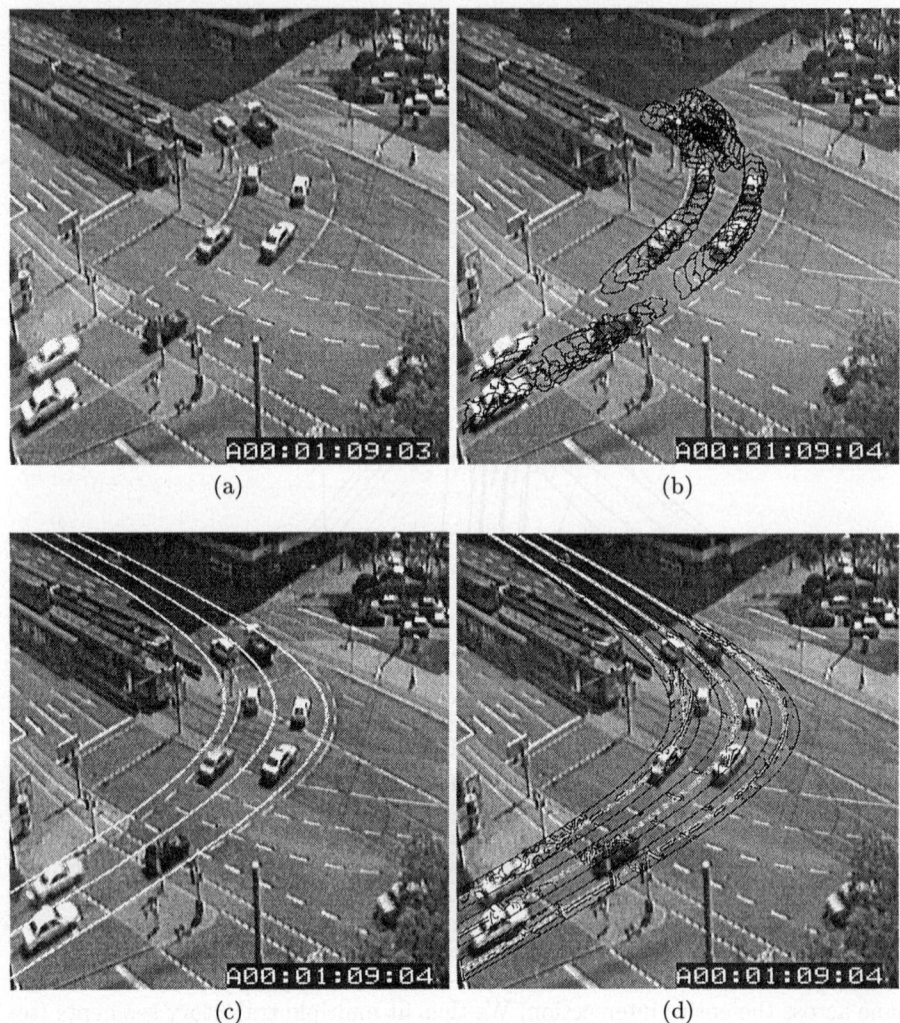

(a)   (b)

(c)   (d)

Fig. 9. The upper left panel (a) shows an overview of another traffic intersection. In the upper right panel (b), object contours of *all* vehicles were overlayed. This variation of the basic method was used due to the shortness – 100 halfframe – of the video sequence. The starting state of the fitting process based on the object contour centroids is shown in panel (c). Despite of the short sequence, the model of two lanes could be fit successfully to the visible lane delimiters (see panel (d)). The quite bad result in the upper left quadrant of the lower right panel (d) is due to missing tracking data – and thus missing object contour centroids – in this area.

tracking of moving objects. The continuous decrease of the price/performance ratio for computers has significantly accelerated research in this area. Recent investigations have concentrated on tracking moving bodies in order to extract significant *temporal events* (see, e. g., [14], [5]) or to build coarse scene models in addition, but based on multiple calibrated cameras [7]. Others use data-driven tracking in order to recover 3D trajectories under the 'ground plane constraint' and exploit the knowledge acquired thereby to control an active camera platform in order to keep a moving body within the field of view of the camera set-up [1].

Lane finding is an important subtask for machine-vision-based control of road vehicles. In such a context, execution time is at a premium, with the effect that preference is given to computationally simple algorithms. As long as a vehicle guided by machine-vision just has to follow an (at most slowly curving) road or to continue straight ahead across an intersection, lane boundaries can be approximated sufficiently well by low-order polynomials of the horizontal image coordinate as studied, for example, by [8]. In [12], similar simple road configurations are investigated for lane keeping purposes by machine-vision. Although [9] addresses this same problem of lane keeping, its author analyzed the image of a slowly curving lane recorded by a video-camera mounted behind the windshield of a driving car and concluded that it can be well approximated *in the image plane* as a hyperbola – essentially due to the effect of perspective projection under the conditions mentioned. In our case, the lane spine is modeled by a hyperbola in the *scene*: the straight line sections enclosing the curved section are due to the lane structure across an intersection in the scene – as opposed to be due to a perspective effect in the image plane associated with a constant curvature lane in the scene. Since we exploit the hyperbolic lane structure in the scene in order to reduce the number of parameters to be estimated for lane boundary delimiters and neighboring lanes, our approach turns out to be able to cope successfully with a considerable number of potentially distractive edge elements.

So far, we did not encounter an example where a vehicle trajectory has been used to extract a global *quantitative* description of multiple lane borders in an image sequence of a nontrivial traffic scene.

We exploit image-plane trajectories of vehicles in order to collect evidence in the image plane about the exact position of side marks in the form of edge segments in very *restricted* image regions, thereby significantly reducing the danger of picking up unwanted edge elements or edge segments. Fitting an hyperbola to vehicle trajectories enables us to interpolate the (frequently 'invisible') part of the lane within an intersection area. *Local* spatial descriptors can thereby be linked along the vehicle trajectory into the remainder of the field of view, thus establishing *global* spatial descriptors. An added attraction of our approach is seen in the fact that the transformation of hyperbolic curves under perspective projection can be studied in closed form. This should facilitate investigations regarding a quantitative transfer of spatial descriptions within an image into spatial *scene* descriptions.

Future research will not only be devoted to increase the robustness of the approach reported here, but also to develop estimation procedures for *initialization* parameters which have so far been set interactively, such as the initial width for a lane. The accumulation of information about lanes from *multiple* vehicle trajectories certainly belongs into this category, too, picking up ideas reported by, e. g., [15].

Robust automatic extraction of lane boundaries should facilitate the detection and classification of additional road markers painted onto a lane. Such a capability allows to determine the 'semantics' of such a lane, for example that it constitutes a lane reserved for left turning traffic – for example, see Figure 7. This information will significantly simplify to characterize traffic behavior at the *conceptual* or even *natural language* level of description.

Acknowledgments

We thank M. Haag for discussions and help during our investigations and for valuable comments on a draft version of this contribution.

Partial support of this research by the Deutsche Forschungsgemeinschaft (DFG) is gratefully acknowledged.

References

1. K.J. Bradshaw, I.D. Reid, and D.W. Murray: "The Active Recovery of 3D Motion Trajectories and Their Use in Prediction", *IEEE Trans. Pattern Analysis and Machine Intelligence*, Vol. PAMI-19, pp. 219–233, 1997.
2. H. Buxton and S. Gong: "Visual Surveillance in a Dynamic and Uncertain World", *Artificial Intelligence*, Vol. 78, pp. 431–459, 1995.
3. S. Dance, T. Caelli, and Z.-Q. Liu: "A Conceptual, Hierarchical Approach to Symbolic Dynamic Scene Interpretation", *Pattern Recognition*, Vol. 29(11), pp. 1891–1903, 1996
4. J.H. Fernyhough, A.G. Cohn, and D.C. Hogg: "Generation of Semantic Regions from Image Sequences", in Proc. *Fourth European Conference on Computer Vision (ECCV'96)*, 15-18 April 1996, Cambridge/UK; B. Buxton and R. Cipolla (Eds.), Lecture Notes in Computer Science LNCS 1065 (Vol. II), pp. 475–484, Springer-Verlag Berlin, Heidelberg, New York 1996.
5. J.H. Fernyhough, A.G. Cohn, and D.C. Hogg: "Building Qualitative Event Models Automatically from Visual Input", Proc. ICCV'98, Bombay/India, pp. 350–355, January 1998.
6. R. Gerber and H.-H. Nagel: "(Mis-?)Using DRT for Generation of Natural Language Text from Image Sequences", in Proc. *Fifth European Conference on Computer Vision*, 2-6 June 1998, Freiburg/Germany; H. Burkhardt and B. Neumann (Eds.), Lecture Notes in Computer Science LNCS 1407 (Vol. II), pp. 255–270, Springer-Verlag Berlin, Heidelberg, New York 1998.
7. W.E.L. Grimson, C. Stauffer, R. Romano, and L. Lee: "Using Adaptive Tracking to Classify and Monitor Activities in a Site", Proc. CVPR'98, pp. 22–29, June 1998.
8. F. Guichard and J. Ph. Tarel: "Curve Finder Combining Perceptual Grouping and a Kalman Like Fitting", Proc. International Conference on Computer Vision ICCV'99, 20–27 September 1999, Kerkyra (Corfu), Greece, pp. 1003–1008.

9. A. Guiducci: "Parametric Model of the Perspective Projection of a Road with Applications to Lane Keeping and 3D Road Reconstruction", Computer Vision and Image Understanding **73**:3 (1999) 414–427.

10. F. Heimes, H.-H. Nagel, and Th. Frank: "Model-Based Tracking of Complex Innercity Road Intersections", *Mathematical and Computer Modelling*, Vol. 22(9-11), pp. 189–203, 1998.

11. R.J. Howarth: "Interpreting a Dynamic and Uncertain World: Task-Based Control", *Artificial Intelligence*, Vol. 100, pp. 5–85, 1998.

12. Ch. Kreucher and S. Lakshmanan: "LANA: A Lane Extraction Algorithm that Uses Frequency Domain Features", IEEE Trans. on Robotics and Automation **15**:2 (1999) 343–350.

13. H.-H. Nagel and A. Gehrke: "Spatiotemporally Adaptive Estimation and Segmentation of OF-Fields", in Proc. *Fifth European Conference on Computer Vision (ECCV'98)*, 2-6 June 1998, Freiburg/Germany; H. Burkhardt and B. Neumann (Eds.), Lecture Notes in Computer Science LNCS <u>1407</u> (Vol. II), pp. 86–102, Springer-Verlag Berlin, Heidelberg, New York 1998.

14. N. Johnson and D. Hogg: "Learning the Distribution of Object Trajectories for Event Recognition", Proc. BMVC'95, pp. 583–592, 1995.

15. M. Mohnhaupt and B. Neumann: "On the Use of Motion Concepts for Top-Down Control in Traffic Scenes", Proc. ECCV'90, Antibes/France, O. Faugeras (Ed.), LNCS 427, pp. 598–600, April 1990.

16. Z. Zhang: "Parameter Estimation Techniques: A Tutorial with Application to Conic Fitting", *Image and Vision Computing*, Vol. 15, pp. 59–76, 1997.

Tracking and Characterization
of Highly Deformable Cloud Structures

Christophe Papin[1], Patrick Bouthemy[1] Etienne Mémin[1], and Guy Rochard[2]

[1] Irisa/Inria, Campus Universitaire de Beaulieu, 35042 Rennes Cedex, France
name.surname@irisa.fr,
[2] Centre de Météorologie Spatiale, Météo France, Avenue de Lorraine, BP 147,
22302 Lannion, France

Abstract. Tracking and characterizing convective clouds from meteorological satellite images enable to evaluate the potential occurring of
strong precipitation. We propose an original two-step tracking method
based on the Level Set approach which can efficiently cope with fre-
quent splitting or merging phases undergone by such highly deformable
structures. The first step exploits a 2D motion field, and acts as a prediction step. The second step can produce, by comparing local and global
photometric information, appropriate expansion or contraction forces on
the evolving contours to accurately locate the cloud cells of interest.
The characterization of the tracked clouds relies on both 2D local motion divergence information and temporal variations of temperature. It
is formulated as a contextual statistical labeling problem involving three
classes "growing activity", "declining activity" and "inactivity".

1   Introduction

The study of the life cycle of strong convective clouds (CC) is an important
issue in the meteorological field. Indeed, such cold clouds often convey hard
weather situations as pouring rains or even tornadoes. We aim at providing
forecasters with new and efficient image processing tools in that context. We
have addressed two major issues: tracking of cold cloud cells and characterization
of their convective activity. To this end, we have developed two original methods
exploiting both motion and photometric information. These methods can also
be of interest beyond the meteorological domain.

Preliminary studies in the meteorological domain have already considered
these issues [1,3]. Since these meteorological phenomena are present in cold
cloud systems, detection of strong convective cloud cells first involves a low
temperature thresholding step in infrared images. In [1,3], relevant cells are
then isolated according to spatial properties (ellipticity factor, distribution of the
spatial gradient of temperature, minimal area,...), and tracking simply results
from the overlap between the prediction of the position of a cell detected at time
$\tau - 1$, using the previously estimated displacement of its gravity center, and a
cell extracted at time τ.

A commonly adopted strategy in computer vision to extract and to track complex objects in an image sequence is to exploit deformable models such as active contours [4, 9]. Starting from an initial position, and using external forces and internal constraints, the contour shape is modified toward the desired solution. However, results are highly sensitive to the initial conditions, and the considered scheme usually prevents from handling shape with significant protrusions. Moreover, topological transformations of the silhouette shape, as merging and splitting of parts, cannot be properly coped with. Different extensions to the active contour techniques have been developed to alleviate these drawbacks, such as introducing particle system [17], exploiting so-called "pedal" curves [18], taking into account region-based informations [10, 20]. However, these shortcomings associated to active contours have been elegantly and efficiently overcome by the Level Set approach introduced by Sethian and Osher [14, 16]. In this mathematical framework, the curve evolution is described through the evolution of an implicit higher-dimensional scalar function. The curve evolution is now described in a fixed coordinate system (Eulerian description) enabling the handling of topological changes. Such an approach or a related formalism has been already exploited in meteorological applications [5, 7, 19]. The tracking of large cloud structures is achieved in [7] following the ideas proposed in [11] to recover the minimal paths over a 3D surface. This method however requires to previously extract the cloud boundaries in the successive considered images. In [19], a particle system [17] is exploited and embedded in an implicit surface formulation. In [5], regions corresponding to convective clouds are extracted by first introducing posterior probabilities associated to the different cloud types. The curves then grow up from user-defined "seed points" to the salient contour shapes.

To make easier the localization of the curve in the next image of the sequence, it seems relevant to exploit motion-based information. The integration of dynamic information has thus been proposed in [6] and quite recently in [12, 15] by adding a motion-based term in the propagation function. Nevertheless, these last methods consider parametric motion models (i.e. 2D affine motion models) which are inappropriate in case of highly deformable structures present in fluid motion such as clouds. In that context, dense motion fields are required to describe the non-linear nature of the cloud motions. Besides, in [12, 15], motion information is in fact introduced to perform motion segmentation.

During its life cycle (growth, stability and decline), a convective cloud cell is likely to undergo different changes of topology such as merging with other neighbouring cells or splitting. Indeed, it seems quite appropriate to follow the Level Set formulation to detect and track these clouds in meteorological satellite images. We propose an original two-stage Level Set method to handle this tracking issue. It introduces the use of dense motion information in a first step acting as a prediction stage. Then, the accurate location of the cloud is achieved in a second step by comparing the local intensity values to an appropriately estimated global temperature parameter representative of the tracked cloud cell. This step can generate appropriate expansion or contraction forces of the evolving contours to localize the boundaries of the cold clouds of interest. This is of primary importance since the predicted position of the cloud cells usually overlap the real ones. Then, to characterize the convective activity of these clouds, we consider the joint evaluation of the local divergence information contained in the 2D estimated velocity field, and of the temporal variations of temperature of the cloud cell points. This leads to qualify the convective activity level of the cloud cell corresponding to its degree of vertical evolution. The characterization stage is formulated as a contextual statistical labeling problem involving three classes: "'growing activity", "declining activity" and "inactivity".

The sequel of this paper is organized as follows. Section 2 outlines the main aspects of the Level Set formulation. Section 3 briefly describes how the cold clouds are primarily detected. In Section 4, we describe our Level Set-based method to track these cold cloud cells. Section 5 deals with the characterization of the convective cells. The efficiency and accuracy of the proposed scheme is demonstrated in Section 6 with results obtained on numerous difficult meteorological situations. Section 7 contains concluding remarks.

2 Level Set formulation

We briefly recall the main aspects of the level set formalism [16]. Let $\eta^i(s, t_0)$ be a set of N closed initial curves in $\mathbb{R}^2$ with $i \in [1, N]$. An implicit representation of these curves is provided by the zero-level set of a scalar function ψ, defined by $z = \psi(\boldsymbol{X}(s), t_0) = \pm d$, where d is the minimal signed distance from the image point, represented by vector $\boldsymbol{X}(s) = [x(s), y(s)]^T$, to the curves $\eta^i(t_0)$ (the convention is plus sign for a location outside the set of curves $\eta^i(t_0)$). In our case, function ψ corresponds to a 3D surface Γ. $\{\eta^i(s, t), i = 1, N\}$ is the family of curves generated by the successive zero-level sets of the surface $\psi(\boldsymbol{X}(s), t)$ moving along its normal directions $\boldsymbol{n} = \frac{\nabla \psi}{|\nabla \psi|}$. For a given level set of ψ, $\psi(\boldsymbol{X}(s), t) = C$, the speed function F at position $\boldsymbol{X}(s)$ represents the component of the vector $\frac{\partial \boldsymbol{X}}{\partial t}$ normal to $\eta^i(s, t)$. Let $F = \frac{\partial \boldsymbol{X}}{\partial t} . \boldsymbol{n}$. Deriving each member of equation $\psi(\boldsymbol{X}(s), t) = C$, and using the expressions of $\boldsymbol{n}$ and F, we obtain the Eulerian formulation of the evolution equation monitoring the successive positions of the surface Γ, evaluated over a fixed grid:

$$\psi_t + F|\nabla \psi| = 0 \tag{1}$$

where $\nabla \psi = (\frac{\partial \psi}{\partial x}, \frac{\partial \psi}{\partial y})$. After each propagation step of the surface Γ according to the speed function F which is given by an iterative numerical resolution scheme, the relation $\psi(\boldsymbol{X}(s), t) = 0$ yields the new position of the family of curves $\eta^i(s, t)$.

The definition of a particular application based on the Level Set approach involves the design of the speed function F.

3 Early detection and initialization

Before considering the tracking of cold cloud cells, let us briefly mention the early detection stage which provides us with the initial positions of curves of interest.

This preliminary detection stage consists in a classical temperature thresholding of the processed infrared satellite images to extract the colder clouds which may contain convective activity. In the very first image of the sequence, the initial curves are all given by the contours of each connected set of pixels with temperature values lower than a given threshold I_{th}. In the current image of the sequence, this procedure is only valid for newly appearing cold clouds. Indeed, if the detected cloud areas are included in already tracked cells, they are removed. For the already tracked cells, we consider as initialization the contours obtained in the previous image and denoted $\eta_{\tau-1}$ (let us note that τ will designate the "physical" time attached to the image sequence whereas t will be used in the evolution process corresponding to the Level Set formulation). Let us note that for convenience temperature and intensity will be assimilated in the sequel (in practice, we use calibrated equivalence tables).

4 Tracking of cold cloud structures

Solving the tracking issue leads to specify the speed function F introduced in equation 1.

The top of a convective cloud is characterized by a low temperature due to its high altitude as a result of vertical displacements, and by spatial intensity gradients of rather small magnitude in the heart of the cloud cell but generally more important in the vicinity of its boundaries. We exploit this a priori knowledge both in the preliminary detection step providing the initial zero level sets as described above, and in the definition of the speed function F. Since we are dealing with moving entities, it appears particularly relevant to exploit dynamic information too. Indeed, predicting the new position of the curves at the next instant brings more robustness (by preventing from false pairing) and more efficiency (by saving iterations and then computational load). Then, a motion estimation step is introduced. We only consider the regions delineated by the closed contours $\eta_{\tau-1}$ as the support of the estimation of the 2D motion field to be used. As stressed in the introduction, we need to compute a dense 2D velocity field. To this end, we have adopted a robust incremental estimation method described in [13], leading to the minimization of a non convex energy function. This energy function involves robust M-estimators applied to the data-driven term based on the optical flow constraint equation, and to a regularization term preserving motion discontinuities. This method combines a hierarchical multigrid minimization with a multiresolution analysis framework. This last point is of key importance to provide accurate estimates in case of cloud displacements of large magnitude which are likely to occur in this application. The estimation of the 2D apparent motion field within selected areas must not be corrupted by the surrounding motions of neighboring lower clouds. We have thus introduced an adaptive subdivision scheme of the image, supplying an initial block partition close to the selected areas. In order to obtain the final velocity field at full resolution, the final size of blocks at full resolution in the minimization process is pixelwise.

We have designed a function F composed of two distinct components, F_1 and F_2, related respectively to dynamic and photometric information. These components will act in a sequential way in the evolution of the tracked curves.

4.1 Dynamic component F_1

The first component F_1 of the speed function F takes into account motion information. It is defined by:

$$F_1(p) = \xi_\omega(p) \ F_{A1} \ \boldsymbol{\omega}(p). \ \boldsymbol{n}(p) - \epsilon\kappa \tag{2}$$

where ξ_ω represents a stopping factor related to the 2D estimated motion field $\boldsymbol{\omega}$ between time $\tau-1$ and τ. F_{A1} is a positive constant greater than one which allows us to speed up convergence. The second term depends on the surface curvature given by $\kappa = \text{div} \ \boldsymbol{n}$. It can be seen as a smoothness term whose influence on the evolving curve depends on the value of parameter ϵ.

F_1 component is considered in a first step and then the photometric component F_2 intervenes. F_1 makes evolve contours according to the projection of $\boldsymbol{\omega}$ on $\boldsymbol{n}$. This component provides a prediction to the photometric tracking step. Compared to a classical motion-based curve registration technique, this formulation allows us to handle in a well-formalized and efficient way problematic events such as splitting, merging, crossing of cloud cells.

The component F_1 is of particular importance in case of small cloud cells, whose apparent displacement magnitude is larger than the size leading to no overlap between two successive positions. Let us mention that their 2D apparent motion is also due to the motion of the surrounding medium, which explains that we can recover their motion using a multiresolution regularization method.

The 2D velocity vector $\boldsymbol{\omega}(p)$ can be used only on the zero-level set, i.e. on the image plane. Therefore, we exploit the geometric Huyghen's principle: the value of $\boldsymbol{\omega}(p)$ at point p is given by the one at pixel $\tilde{p}$ in the image plane, which is the nearest to p. We denote $\hat{\boldsymbol{\omega}}(p)$ the velocity vector exploited at point p given by the one computed at $\tilde{p}$.

Following the same principle, the stopping factor $\hat{\xi}_\omega$ denotes the global "extension" of ξ_ω defined over the whole domain of ψ. We define it as follows:

$$\hat{\xi}_\omega(p) = \delta\left[\Delta d_T(p) \le |\hat{\boldsymbol{\omega}}(p)|\right] \tag{3}$$

where δ is the Kronecker symbol, $\Delta d_T(p) = \sum_{t=1}^{T} |\boldsymbol{d}_t(p)|$ and $\boldsymbol{d}_t(p)$ is the shift vector at pixel p induced by the implicit surface evolution at the tth iteration (for a total of T iterations). The stopping factor is equal to one when the value of $\Delta d_T(p)$ is lower than $|\hat{\boldsymbol{\omega}}(p)|$ and zero otherwise. The contour is stopped as soon as a sufficient number of pixels verify $\hat{\xi}_\omega(p) = 0$. This stopping factor expresses the fact that the total shift applied to the evolving contour at a given point p must be bound by the magnitude of the corresponding estimated velocity vector.

If the hypersurface Γ at iteration $t-1$ is the signed distance to the contours $\eta(t-1)$. By using the Huyghen's principle, updating function ψ to give $\psi(t)$ turns out to be similar for all pixels p_n of the grid belonging to the normal to $\eta(t-1)$ at pixel p. The intersection of the hypersurface Γ to the plane (zOn) is indeed a straight line of slope unity. Finally, we can write $d_t(p) = -(\psi_p(t) - \psi_p(t-1))n$. The contour shift at point p between iteration $t-1$ and t is effective if $d_t(p) > \frac{1}{2}$, since the extraction process providing the current position of the contours after each iteration only yields entire coordinates. An example of results is shown on Figure 1.

4.2 Photometric component F_2

We aim at determining a strategy able to accurately move contours toward the real cold cloud boundaries. To this end, we exploit thermal information (i.e., intensity information in thermal infrared images) over contours. These local temperatures are compared to a global temperature characteristic of the tracked cloud cell at time τ. The sign of the difference of these local and global temperatures determines the way the contour evolves, i.e. the direction of the applied force F_2 at point p. This allows us to explicitly introduce locally contracting or expanding evolution of the contour according to the local configuration at hand, which is of particular importance since the current and desired positions of the curve are supposed to overlap. A somewhat similar flexible mechanism but issued from different considerations has also been proposed quite recently in [2] to extract shapes from background in static images.

The global characteristic temperature of the cloud cell at time τ is estimated as follows. It is predicted from dynamic and thermal information obtained from the previous time instant. We denote the characteristic temperature associated to the ith contour η_τ^i at time τ by θ_i. θ_i is obtained by assuming that the intensity

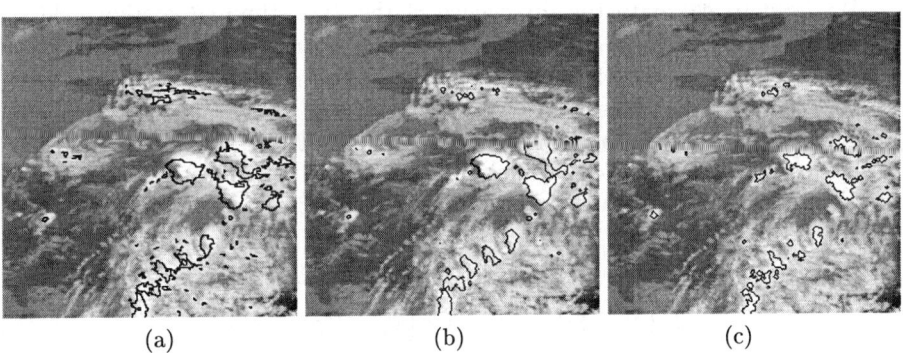

(a)   (b)   (c)

Fig. 1. Contour evolution successively monitored by the two components of the speed function F and their associated stopping factors. Part of infrared Meteosat image acquired on August 10, 1995 at 12h30 TU. (a) Initial contours (overprinted in black). (b) Contours after the first tracking step involving F_1 component. (c) Final contours after successively performing the two tracking steps involving respectively F_1 component and F_2 component.

function verifies the following continuity equation of fluid mechanics:

$$\frac{\partial I}{\partial \tau} + \text{div}(I\boldsymbol{\omega}) = 0 \tag{4}$$

This equation is related to the assumption that expansion or contraction of fluid (associated to a dissipation or to a concentration of matter) corresponds to intensity changes in the image sequence. Recalling that $\text{div}(I\boldsymbol{\omega}) = \boldsymbol{\omega}.\boldsymbol{\nabla}I + I\,\text{div}\,\boldsymbol{\omega}$, and using the expression of the total derivative of I with respect to time $\frac{dI}{d\tau} = \frac{\partial I}{\partial \tau} + \boldsymbol{\omega}.\boldsymbol{\nabla}I$, we can rewrite equation (4) as follows:

$$\frac{dI}{d\tau} + I\,\text{div}\,\boldsymbol{\omega} = 0 \tag{5}$$

Assuming, as in [8], a constant speed over the "particles" trajectories from $\tau - 1$ to τ, we can express intensity I at time τ at the displaced point $p + \boldsymbol{\omega}(p)$ by integrating both members of equation 5, which leads to:

$$I(p + \boldsymbol{\omega}(p), \tau) = I(p, \tau - 1) \exp\left(-\text{div}\,\boldsymbol{\omega}(p)\right) \tag{6}$$

The characteristic temperature θ_i of the cell corresponding to contour η_τ^i can be given by the mean of $I(p + \boldsymbol{\omega}(p), \tau)$ evaluated over region $\mathcal{R}_{\tau-1}^i$ delineated by the contour $\eta_{\tau-1}^i$:

$$\theta_i = \frac{1}{N_i} \sum_{p \in \mathcal{R}_{\tau-1}^i} I(p, \tau - 1) \exp\left(-\text{div}\,\boldsymbol{\omega}(p)\right) \tag{7}$$

where N_i is the number of pixels in $\mathcal{R}_{\tau-1}^i$.

We need to compute the divergence of the 2D estimated motion field. It is expressed by $\text{div}\,\boldsymbol{\omega}(p) = \frac{\partial u(p)}{\partial x} + \frac{\partial v(p)}{\partial y}$, where $\boldsymbol{\omega}(p) = [u(p), v(p)]^T$ is the velocity vector at pixel p. It is derived from the estimated motion field by using appropriate derivative filters.

Solving equation (1) leads to move the set of initial curves toward the new positions of cloud cells. We have designed the following expression of the speed function F_2 composed of a curvature term and a so-called advection term:

$$F_2(p) = \hat{\xi}_I(p) \overbrace{F_{A2}\,\text{sign}\left(\theta_i - I(p)\right)}^{\text{advection term } F_{adv}(p)} -\epsilon\kappa \tag{8}$$

where F_{A2}, θ_i and I respectively denote the constant magnitude of the advection force, the estimated characteristic temperature of the convective cloud cell i, and the intensity function in the infrared satellite image (intensity $I(p)$ here accounts for temperature).

As already mentioned, the definition of the advection term of F_2 allows us to deal with a force either of contraction or of expansion depending on the intensity value $I(p)$. This is further explained and emphasized below.

We need to exploit relevant image-based information to stop the evolution of the curves at the real boundaries of the cloud cells. To this end, we have to define a weighting factor in the speed function F_2, i.e. an image-based factor ξ_I, which will play the role of stopping criterion. The global "extension" of ξ_I, denoting $\hat{\xi}_I$, can be written as:

$$\hat{\xi}_I(p) = \max\left(\delta[F_{adv}^t(p) + F_{adv}^{t-1}(p)], g_I(p) \right) \qquad (9)$$

where $\delta(x) = 0$ if $x = 0$, $\delta(x) = 1$ otherwise, function $g_I(p)$ is given by $g_I(p) = \frac{1}{(1+|\nabla G_\sigma * I(p)|)^2}$ and $F_{adv}^t(p)$ and $F_{adv}^{t-1}(p)$ respectively denote the advection term computed at times t and $t-1$. $\nabla G_\sigma * I(p)$ represents the convolution of the image with a Gaussian smoothing filter. When the evolving contours are located within warm areas (i.e. $I(p) > \theta_i$), they undergo a contraction force which moves them toward a cold cloud cell boundary. After a boundary of a cloud cell is crossed and the curve point is within the cloud cell, $I(p)$ becomes lower than θ_i. This induces a change of the sign of the advection term, and thus defines an expansion force. Since $\delta[F_{adv}^t + F_{adv}^{t-1}]$ becomes equal to 0, the value of $\hat{\xi}_I(p)$ is then given by $g_I(p)$ which can tend to zero if high intensity contrast is present at point p. Hence, we have introduced intensity spatial gradient information in an appropriate way, i.e. only when the evolving curve lies inside a cloud cell of interest. η_τ^i is now moving in the opposite direction, and stops by the first encountered contrasted intensity edges. Owing to the proposed scheme, evolving curves thus cannot be attracted by intensity edges belonging to non relevant clouds or to other visible structures in the image. An example of results obtained after performing successively the two tracking steps respectively involving components F_1 and F_2 is shown on Fig. 1c.

The use of both an appropriate initialization and a motion-based prediction embedded in the first tracking step allows us to provide a real tracking of convective cloud cells over time. We mean that we can effectively and reliably associate the extracted contours from one image to the next one, even in situations with no significant overlap between two corresponding contours.

To save computational time, we make use of the "narrow band" framework introduced in [14]. Moreover, we proceed each narrow band in an independent way. Then, if one of them contains a contour which has reached the desired cloud cell boundaries, the restriction of the function ψ to the corresponding narrow band is frozen, and the computational cost is thus further reduced.

5 Characterization of convective activity and extraction refinement

The clouds located within the closed contours η_τ issued from the tracking stage may include either truly active convective cell (CC), or CC in declining phase, or cold clouds which are not convective clouds. We have to identify regions undergoing strong vertical motion, corresponding either to growing or to declining convective clouds. The vertical development of growing CC is accompanied with a spatial expansion at its top along with a temperature cooling. The opposite occurs for declining CC. Therefore, it seems particularly relevant, in order to qualify and to extract these convective activity areas, to jointly evaluate the degree of divergence of the 2D apparent motion and the tendency of the temporal changes in temperature.

5.1 Discriminant features of convective activity

The first discriminant feature of convective activity is related to the dynamic properties of the cold clouds of interest. It is supplied by the local divergence of the estimated 2D motion field, computed at each point of the tracked cloud cell as explained in Section 4.

The temporal evolution of the cloud temperature provides the second discriminant feature. We evaluate the temporal change of temperature at each point of the tracked cloud by considering the displaced frame difference supplied by the estimated 2D velocity field: $I_\tau(p, w(p)) = I(p + w(p), \tau) - I(p, \tau - 1)$. To take into account motion compensation errors and image noise, we consider in fact a locally average version:

$$\bar{I}_\tau(p, \omega(p)) = \frac{1}{M} \sum_{r \in \mathcal{F}_p} \Big(I(r + \omega(r), \tau) - I(r, \tau - 1) \Big) \tag{10}$$

where $\mathcal{F}_p$ is a local window centered on pixel p and containing M pixels. An example of joint evaluation of local motion divergence and temporal temperature variation can be found in Fig. 2. We can note the characteristic temporal evolution of a convective cloud cell (pointed with an arrow in images (a) and (d)).

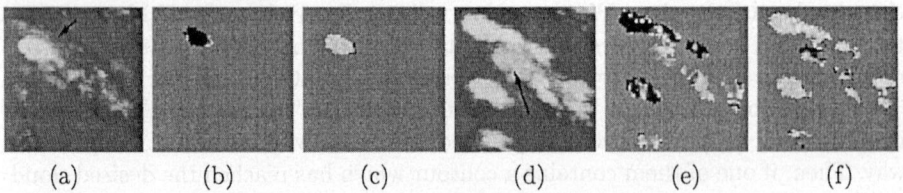

(a)   (b)   (c)   (d)   (e)   (f)

Fig. 2. In columns (a) and (d), part of infrared Meteosat images acquired on August 4, 1995 at 11h00 TU and 13h30 TU. Local motion divergence maps (columns (b) and (e)), computed on convective cloud cells selected after the tracking stage, and the temporal variations of temperature (columns (c) and (f)). Display in Fig. b, c, e and f varies from light grey (highly negative values) to black (highly positive values).

The growing phase (Fig. 2a) presents strong positive values of motion divergence (dark grey in Fig. 2b) and a decrease in temperature (light grey in Fig.

2c). The subsequent declining phase (Fig. 2d) is identified by strong negative divergence values (light grey in Fig. 2e) and a warming up of the cloud top (dark grey in Fig. 2f).

5.2 Extraction of active convective clouds.

We have now to exploit these two discriminant features, i.e. div $w(p)$ and $\bar{I}_\tau(p, w(p))$, to determine the active convective clouds among the tracked cold cloud areas.

The CC characterization scheme is formulated as a labeling problem of these areas. We have adopted a contextual statistical approach based on Bayesian estimation (MAP criterion) associated with Markov Random Field (MRF) models. The MRF framework provides a powerful formalism to specify physical relations between observations o (i.e. temporal changes of temperature, local motion divergences) and the label field e, while easily allowing us to express a priori information on the expected properties of the label field (i.e. spatial regularization). We consider three classes, two classes of activity, growing activity ("*grow* ") and declining activity ("*decl* "), and one of inactivity ("*nact* "). The last one can contain non active clouds but also elements which remain undetermined due to non significant feature values.

Due to the equivalence between MRF and Gibbs distributions, it turns out that this leads to the definition of a global energy function $U(o, e)$. We have designed the following energy function composed of a data-driven term and a regularization term:

$$U(o, e) = \sum_{s \in \mathcal{S}} V_1(o, e) + \alpha_2 \sum_{c \in \mathcal{C}} V_2(e) \qquad (11)$$

where V_1 and V_2 are local potentials, s is a site (here, a pixel), and $\mathcal{C}$ represents all the binary cliques c (i.e. cliques formed by two sites) associated with the considered second-order neighborhood system on the set of sites (pixels). α_2 controls the relative influence of the data-driven term and of the regularization term.

As a matter of fact, we consider the two features introduced above in a combined way through the following product:

$$\mu(s) = \operatorname{div} w(s) \times \bar{I}_\tau\big(s, \ w(s)\big) \qquad (12)$$

The adequacy between a given label and the computed quantity $\mu(s)$ is governed by the sign and the magnitude of $\mu(s)$. If the two discriminant features present opposite signs at site s ($\mu(s) < 0$), this reveals convective activity, either growing activity (div $w(s) > 0$ and $\bar{I}_\tau < 0$) or declining one (div $w(s) < 0$ and $\bar{I}_\tau > 0$). To further distinguish labels "*grow* " and "*decl* ", we examine the sign of div $w(s)$. If div $w(s) < 0$, potential V_1 will favour the label "*decl* ", otherwise the label "*grow* " will be preferred. $\mu(s) > 0$ is not related to a specific physical meaning and label "*nact* " will be favoured. The potential V_1 is defined at site s by:

$$V_1(o(s), e(s)) = \begin{cases} \text{sign}[\text{div } \boldsymbol{\omega}(s)]f(\mu) + \frac{1}{2} & \text{if } e(s) = grow \\ -\text{sign}[\text{div } \boldsymbol{\omega}(s)]f(\mu) + \frac{1}{2} & \text{if } e(s) = decl \\ -f(\mu) + \frac{1}{2} & \text{if } e(s) = nact \end{cases} \quad (13)$$

where $f(x)$ is a smooth stepwise function. We have chosen $f(x) = \frac{1}{\pi}\arctan(k\pi x)$. Potential V_2 in the regularization term is defined by $V_2[e(r), e(s)] = -\beta$ if $e(r) = e(s)$ and $V_2[e(r), e(s)] = \beta$ otherwise, where r and s are two neighbour sites. V_2 favours compact areas of same label. This formulation leads to the minimization of the global energy function $U(o, e)$, which is solved iteratively using the deterministic relaxation algorithm ICM.

The tracking process is concerned with all the cloud areas issued from the detection stage and not only with those from the characterization stage for the following reason. A large convective system can contain different zones of distinct activity which may evolve quickly over time. This temporal evolution does not allow us to perform a relevant and significant tracking of cloud cells displaying a real convective activity. Tracking cold clouds and characterizing in a second stage their convective activity appears to be more stable and physically more meaningful.

6   Results

We have carried out numerous experiments on real complex examples involving Meteosat infrared or water vapor images. Here, we report representative results obtained after each stage of the proposed scheme. Figures 3 and 4 illustrate the tracking stage, figure 5 the characterization stage.

For display convenience, pixels corresponding to low temperature will be represented by white intensities, and conversely. Figure 3 contains three different meteorological situations. For each, we supply the initial contours corresponding to the cold clouds detected in the previous image (central row) and the final locations of the cold clouds (lower row). We can observe that the tracking is quite accurate even in case of large displacements, (first example in the left column of Fig. 5) or in case of the formation of holes within a cloud cell (third example, in the right column of Fig. 3). Let us point out that forecasters are particularly interested by the accurate and reliable determination of colder areas of convective clouds, which are generally quite uniform. Thus, the stopping criterion we have designed stops the inner part of the evolving curve at the first encountered well-contrasted intensity edges. The consequence is that resulting contours may be located inside cloud cells.

Examples of tracking of cloud cells over time are shown in Fig. 4. We can point out the accuracy and the temporal coherence of the obtained results, which is of key importance for forecasters, depicting successive meteorological satellite images over Italy and Sardigna. These warm European areas (dark grey level) are the source of convective activity. At 10h30 TU, small cloud cells over Italy reach higher altitude and are correctly detected in time. They grow, merge, and progressively other surrounding cells undergo the same process. At 14h00 TU (last column, last row), a convective cloud cell becomes too warm with respect to the characteristic temperature estimated from the previous image, and consistently disappears. The characterization of the convective activity of

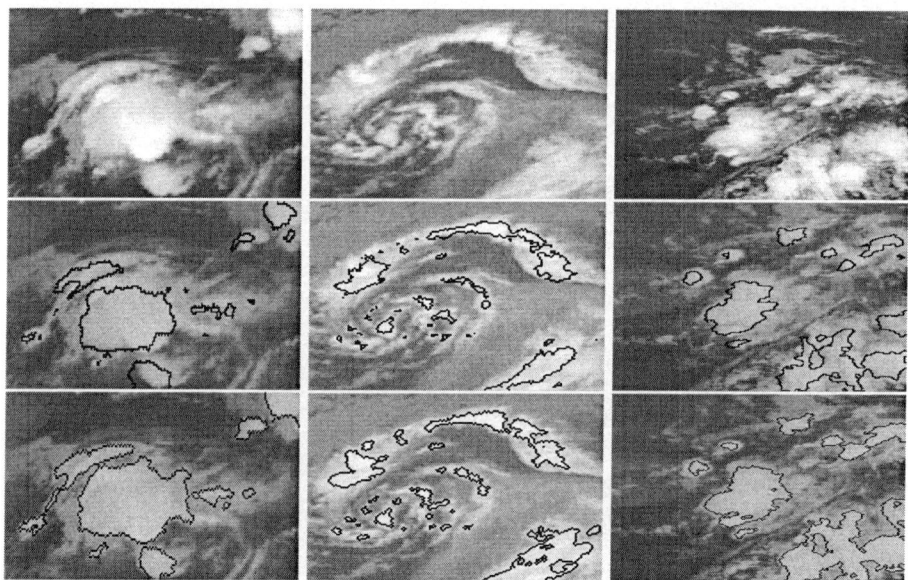

Fig. 3. Evolution of the cloud contours in the tracking stage. Upper row: original infrared images; central row: initial positions corresponding to those determined in the previous image; lower row: final positions of cloud contours. From left to right: part of Meteosat infrared images on August 24, 1995, at 18h30 TU, August 28, 1995, at 4h30 TU, and August 10, 1995 at 21h00 TU. Contours are overprinted in black.

the tracked clouds shown in Fig. 4 is reported on Fig. 5. Six successive results obtained after the characterization stage are supplied. Dark grey corresponds to active clouds in a growing phase. On the opposite, CC in a declining state are labeled in light grey. At the beginning of the sequence, the central cloud cell undergoes a strong vertical motion and the whole corresponding area is corrected labeled as "growing activity". Progressively, this cloud cell becomes less and less active, and the dark grey area shrinks toward its core. In the same time, a declining zone develops up to contain almost the entire area. The same parameter values are considered for all these experiments. Concerning the tracking stage, we set $F_{A1} = 10$, $F_{A2} = 10$, $\epsilon = 3$, and the width of the narrow band is 8 pixels. Temperature threshold I_{th} is $-35°C$. In the characterization stage, we set $k = 5$, $\beta = 0.1$ and $\alpha_2 = 3$. The choice of parameter values associated to the tracking stage only affects the speed of convergence and not the accuracy of results. Parameter values related to the characterization stage only influence the labeling of the uncertain activity areas (i.e. containing weak discriminant

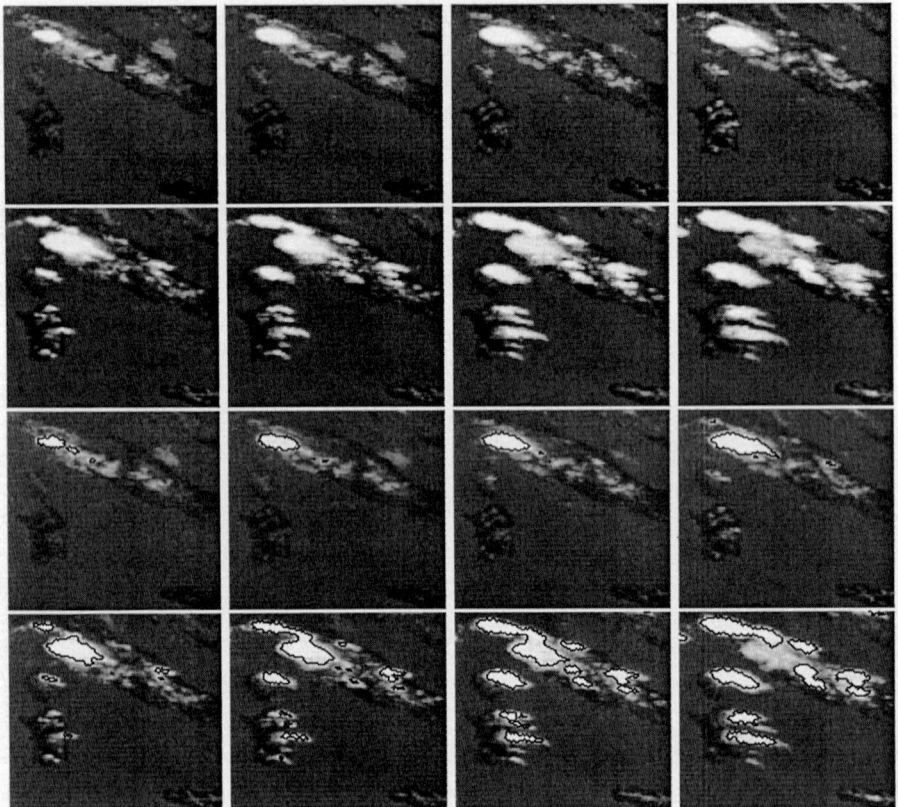

Fig. 4. Results of the tracking stage over a sequence of Meteosat infrared images (two first rows). Illustration of the temporal coherence of the tracking stage of cold clouds. Final contours are overprinted on the original images (two last rows). Part of Meteosat images acquired on August 4, 1995 from 10h30 to 14h00 TU.

feature magnitudes) and it was found that their setting was not critical. The tracking stage has been evaluated by forecasters on several real representative situations (including those reported in this paper) and appeared quite accurate. An extended experimental validation of the characterization stage is just about to be completed by a French meteorological center on the basis of a daily analysis by a forecaster in an operational context. First results are already convincing. The computational time is in accordance with operational requirements since Meteosat satellite images are acquired every thirty minutes. CPU time behaves as a linear function of the number of processed pixels (involved in the narrow band technique). It takes about six minutes for a quantity of processed pixels in the narrow bands equal to 128×128 on a Sun Ultra 60 workstation.

7 Conclusion

We have proposed in this paper an original and efficient framework to detect, track and characterize convective cold clouds from meteorological satellite im-

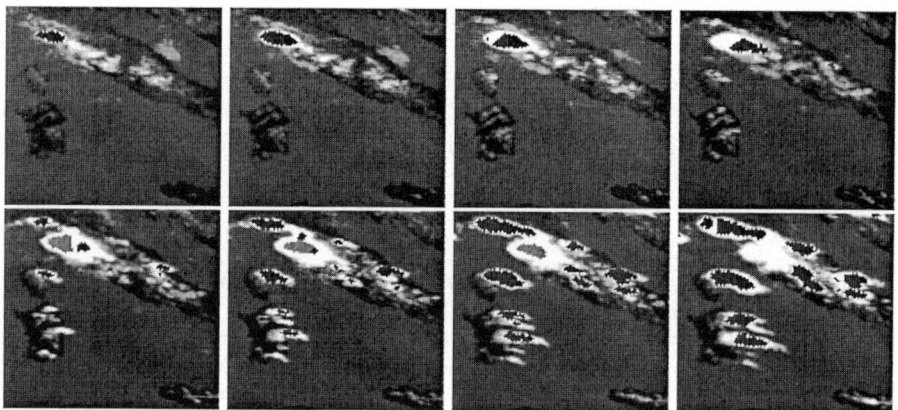

Fig. 5. Characterization stage applied to Meteosat infrared images. Labeling results are overprinted on the original images: in dark, resp. light, grey: growing, resp. declining, convective clouds. Part of Meteosat images acquired on August 4, 1995 from 10h30 TU to 14h00 TU.

ages. It involves two main stages, the tracking stage relying on the Level Set formalism, and the characterization stage stated as a statistical contextual labeling issue. This approach is quite relevant to properly process such highly deformable structures which are often subject to splitting or merging phases during their life cycle. We have designed a two-step tracking scheme exploiting both motion and photometric information in an adequate way. The first step exploits a 2D estimated motion field, and supplies a proper prediction to the second one. The former moves contours along the direction of estimated motion while immediately taking into account topological changes contrary to a usual registration step. The second step uses photometric information at a local level and at the cell level, and can create appropriate expansion or contraction forces on the evolving contours to accurately localize in every image the cold clouds of interest.

The characterization stage relies on local measurements involving divergence computed from the estimated 2D motion field and local temporal variations of the tracked clouds. It leads to the minimization of an energy function comprising a spatial regularization term. It allows us to extract, within the clouds delimited in the tracking stage, the regions of significant vertical motion, i.e. the really active convective cloud cells and to distinguish those in a growing phase from those in a declining phase. The computational time, which is usually a drawback of the Level Set approach, is significantly reduced, thanks to the two-step tracking scheme introduced in our method. Besides, the first tracking step, appropriately exploiting motion information, leads to positions of the curve overlapping the real boundaries of the cold clouds of interest. The second tracking step can then start from this prediction since the designed associated speed function allows a curve to evolve in two ways, contraction and expansion. Another advantage of this method is that results do not strongly depend on the choice of the parameter values. Results obtained on numerous difficult real examples demonstrate the temporal coherence and the accuracy of the extracted convective clouds tracked over time, which provides forecasters with an easily understanding of the meteorological situation. Finally, the tracking method introduced in this paper is not specific to the considered application, and could be successfully applied to other kinds of deformable structures.

References

1. Adler, R.F., Negri, A.J.: A satellite infrared technique to estimate tropical convective and stratiform rainfall. J. Appl. Meteor. **27** (1988) 30–51
2. Amadieu, O., Debreuve, E., Barlaud, M., Aubert, G.: Inward and outward curve evolution using level set method. In Proc. of IEEE ICIP, Kobe, September (1999).
3. Arnaud, Y., Desbois, M., Maize, J.: Automatic tracking and characterization of convective systems on Meteosat pictures. J. Appl. Meteor. **1** (1992) 443–493
4. Blake, A., Isard, M.: Active contours. Springer (1998)
5. Brewer, M., Malladi, R., Pankiewicz, G., Conway, B., Tarassenko, L.: Methods for large scale segmentation of cloud images. In Proc. Meteorol. Satellite Data Users' Conf., Bruxelles (1997) 131–138
6. Caselles, V., Coll, B.: Snakes in movement. SIAM J. Numer. Anal., **3(6)** (1996) 2445–2456
7. Cohen, I., Herlin, I.: Tracking meteorological structures through curve(s) matching using geodesic paths. In Proc of 6th IEEE ICCV, Bombay, January (1998) 396–401
8. Corpetti, T., Mémin, E., Pérez, P.: Estimating Fluid Optical Flow. In Proc. of ICPR'2000, Barcelona, September (2000)
9. Kass, M., Witkin, A., Terzopoulos, D.: Snakes: Active contour models. IJCV **1** (1988) 321–331
10. Kervrann, C., Heitz, F.: A hierarchical markov modeling approach for the segmentation and tracking of deformable shapes. Graphical Models and Image Processing **60** (1998) 173–195
11. Kimmel, R., Amir, A., Bruckstein, A.M.: Finding shortest paths on surfaces using level sets propagation. IEEE Trans. on PAMI **17(6)** (1995) 635–640
12. Mansouri, A.R., Konrad, J.: Motion segmentation with level sets. In Proc of IEEE ICIP, Kobe, Japan, September (1999)
13. Mémin, E., Pérez, P.: A multigrid approach for hierarchical motion estimation. In Proc of 6th IEEE ICCV, Bombay, January (1998) 933–938
14. Osher, S., Sethian, J.A.: Fronts propagating with curvature dependent speed: Algorithms based on Hamilton-Jacobi formulation. Journal of Computational Physics **79** (1988) 12–49
15. Paragios, N., Deriche, R.: Geodesic active regions for motion estimation and tracking. In Proc of IEEE ICCV, Kerkyra, Greece, September **1** (1999) 688–694
16. Sethian, J.A.: Level Set Methods. Cambridge University Press (1996)
17. Szeliski, R., Tonnesen, D.: Surface modeling with oriented particle systems. Computer Graphics, SIGGRAPH, **26(2)** (1992) 185–194
18. Vemuri, B.C., Guo, Y.: Snake pedals: Geometric models with physics-based control. In Proc of 6th IEEE ICCV, Bombay, January (1998) 427–432
19. Yahia, H.M., Berroir, J-P., Mazars, G.: Fast and robust level-set segmentation of deformable structures. In Proc. IEEE ICASSP, Seattle, May (1998)
20. Zhu, S.C., Yuille, A.: Region competition: Unifying snakes, region growing, and Bayes/MDL for multiband image segmentation. IEEE Trans. on PAMI **18** (1996) 884–900

Calibration

A Unifying Theory for Central Panoramic Systems and Practical Implications

Christopher Geyer and Kostas Daniilidis

University of Pennsylvania, GRASP Laboratory, Pennsylvania, PA 19104

Abstract. Omnidirectional vision systems can provide panoramic alertness in surveillance, improve navigational capabilities, and produce panoramic images for multimedia. Catadioptric realizations of omnidirectional vision combine reflective surfaces and lenses. A particular class of them, the central panoramic systems, preserve the uniqueness of the projection viewpoint. In fact, every central projection system including the well known perspective projection on a plane falls into this category.

In this paper, we provide a unifying theory for all central catadioptric systems. We show that all of them are isomorphic to projective mappings from the sphere to a plane with a projection center on the perpendicular to the plane. Subcases are the stereographic projection equivalent to parabolic projection and the central planar projection equivalent to every conventional camera. We define a duality among projections of points and lines as well as among different mappings.

This unification is novel and has a a significant impact on the 3D interpretation of images. We present new invariances inherent in parabolic projections and a unifying calibration scheme from one view. We describe the implied advantages of catadioptric systems and explain why images arising in central catadioptric systems contain more information than images from conventional cameras. One example is that intrinsic calibration from a single view is possible for parabolic catadioptric systems given only three lines. Another example is metric rectification using only affine information about the scene.

1 Introduction

Artificial visual systems face extreme difficulties in tasks like navigating on uneven terrain or detecting other movements when they are moving themselves. Paradoxically, these are tasks which biological systems like insects with very simple brains can very easily accomplish. It seems that this is not a matter of computational power but a question of sensor design and representation. The representation of visual information has to be supported by the adequate sensors in order to be direct and efficient. It is therefore surprising that most artificial visual systems use only one kind of sensor: a CCD-camera with a lens.

We believe that the time has come to study the question of representation in parallel to the design of supportive sensing hardware. As in nature these sensors and representations should depend on the tasks and the physiology of the observer. Omnidirectional or panoramic visual sensors are camera designs that enable capturing of a scene with an almost hemi-spherical field of view. Originally introduced mainly for monitoring activities they now are widely used in multimedia and robotics applications. The advantages of omnidirectional sensing are obvious for applications like surveillance, immersive telepresence, videoconferencing, mosaicing, and map building. A panoramic field of view eliminates the need for more cameras or a mechanically turnable camera. We prove in this paper that a class of omnidirectional sensors, the central panoramic systems, can recover information about the environment that conventional models of perspective projection on a plane cannot.

First let us summarize recent activities on omnidirectional vision. A panoramic field of view camera was first proposed by Rees [13]. After 20 years the concept of omnidirectional sensing was reintroduced in robotics [16] for the purpose of autonomous vehicle navigation. In the last five years, several omnidirectional cameras have been designed for a variety of purposes. The rapid growth of multimedia applications has been a fruitful testbed for panoramic sensors [7, 8, 11] applied for visualization. Another application is telepresence [14, 1] where the panoramic sensor achieves the same performance as a remotely controlled rotating camera with the additional advantage of an omnidirectional alert awareness. Srinivasan [2] designed omnidirectional mirrors that preserve ratios of elevations of objects in the scene and Hicks [5] constructed a mirror-system that rectifies planes perpendicular to the optical axis. The application of mirror-lens systems in stereo and structure from motion has been prototypically described in [15, 4]. Our work is hardly related to any of the above approaches. The fact that lines project to conics is mentioned in the context of epipolar lines by Svoboda [15] and Nayar [10].

Omnidirectional sensing can be realized with dioptric or catadioptric systems. Dioptric systems consist of fish-eye lenses while catadioptric systems are combinations of mirrors and lenses. These sensors can be separated into two classifications, determined by whether they have a unique effective viewpoint. Conical and spherical mirror systems as well as most fish-eye lenses do not possess a single vantage-point. Among those that do have a unique effective viewpoint are systems which are composed of multiple planar mirrors and perspective cameras all of whose viewpoints coincide, as well as a hyperbolic mirror in front of a perspective camera, and a parabolic mirror in front of a orthographic camera. The uniqueness of a projection point is equivalent to a purely rotating planar camera with the nice property that a rotated image is a collineation of an original one. Hence, every part of an image arising from such a catadioptric sensor can easily re-warped into the equivalent image of a planar camera looking to the desired direction without knowledge of the depths of the scene. It is worth mentioning that simple dioptric systems — conventional cameras — are included in this class of catadioptric systems because they are equivalent to catadioptric systems with a planar mirror.

In this paper, we present a unifying theory for all central panoramic systems, that means for all catadioptric systems with a unique effective viewpoint. We prove that all cases of a mirror surface—parabolic, hyperbolic, elliptic, planar—

with the appropriate lens—orthographic or perspective—can be modeled with a projection from the sphere to the plane where the projection center is on a sphere diameter and the plane perpendicular to it. Singular cases of this model are stereographic projection, which we show to be equivalent to the projection induced by a parabolic mirror through a orthographic lens, and central projection which is well known to be equivalent to perspective projection.

Given this unifying projection model we establish two kinds of duality: a duality among point projections and line projections and a duality among two sphere projections from two different centers. We show that parallel lines in space are projected onto conics whose locus of foci is also a conic. This conic is the horizon of the plane perpendicular to all of the original lines, but the horizon is obtained via the dual projection. In case of perspective projection all conics degenerate to lines and we have the well known projective duality between lines and points in P^2.

The practical implications are extremely useful. The constraints given by the projection of lines are natural for calibration by lines. We prove that three lines are sufficient for intrinsic calibration of the catadioptric system without any metric information about the environment. We give a natural proof why such a calibration is not possible for conventional cameras showing thus the superiority of central catadioptric systems. The unifying model we have provided allows us to study invariances of the projection. Perhaps most importantly, in the case of parabolic systems we prove that angles are preserved because the equivalent projection—stereographic—is a conformal mapping. This allows us to estimate the relative position of the plane and facilitates a metric rectification of a plane without any assumption about the environment.

In section 2 we prove the equivalence of the catadioptric and spherical projections and develop the duality relationships. In section 3 we present the computational advantages derived from this theory and in section 4 we show our experimental results.

2   Theory of Catadioptric Image Geometry

The main purpose of this section is to prove the equivalence of the image geometries obtained by the catadioptric projection and the composition of projections of a sphere. We first develop the general spherical projection, and then the catadioptric projections, showing in turn that each are equivalent to some spherical projection. Then we will show that two projections of the sphere are dual to each other, and that parabolic projection is dual to perspective projection.

2.1   Projection of the Sphere to a Plane

We introduce here a map from projective space to the sphere to an image plane. A point in projective space is first projected to an antipodal point pair on the sphere. An axis of the sphere is chosen, as well as a point on this axis, but within the sphere. From this point the antipodal point pair is projected to a pair of points on a plane perpendicular to the chosen axis.

Assume that the sphere is the unit sphere centered at the origin, the axis is the z-axis and the point of projection is the point $(0,0,l)$. Let the plane $z = -m$ be the image plane. If $\sim$ is the equivalence relation relating antipodal points on the sphere, then the map from projective space to the sphere $s : P^3(\mathbb{R}) \to S^2/\sim$ is given by

$$s(x,y,z,w) = \left(\pm \frac{x}{r}, \pm \frac{y}{r}, \pm \frac{z}{r} \right)$$

where $r = \sqrt{x^2 + y^2 + z^2}$. To determine the second part of the map, we need only determine the perspective projection to the plane $z = -m$ from the point $(0,0,l)$. Without taking the equivalence relation into account the projection of (x,y,z) is

$$p_{l,m}(x,y,z) = \left(\frac{x(l+m)}{lr-z}, \frac{y(l+m)}{lr-z}, -m \right) .$$

Now applying the equivalence relation we have a map $p_{l,m}^* : P^3(\mathbb{R}) \to \mathbb{R}_\sim^2$,

$$p_{l,m}^*(x,y,z,w) = \left(\pm \frac{x(l+m)}{lr \mp z}, \pm \frac{y(l+m)}{lr \mp z}, -m \right) .$$

Here $\mathbb{R}_\sim^2$ is $\mathbb{R}^2$ with the equivalence relation induced on it by the map $p_{l,m}$ and $\sim$ on the sphere.

If we move the projection plane to $z = -\alpha$, then the relation between the two projections is

$$p_{l,m}^*(x,y,z,w) = \frac{l+m}{l+\alpha} p_{l,\alpha}^*(x,y,z,w) .$$

So they are the same except for a scale factor. Thus if m is not indicated it is assumed that $m = 1$.

Remark. When $l = 1$ and $m = 0$, i.e. the point of projection is the north pole, we obtain

$$p_{1,0}^*(x,y,z,w) = \left(\pm \frac{x}{\sqrt{x^2+y^2+z^2} \mp z}, \pm \frac{y}{\sqrt{x^2+y^2+z^2} \mp z} \right) ,$$

which is a case of stereographic projection [9] (when (x,y,z) is restricted to the sphere). On the other hand, when $l = 0$ and $m = 1$, we have perspective projection:

$$p_{0,1}^*(x,y,z,w) = \left(\frac{x}{z}, \frac{y}{z} \right) .$$

2.2 Catadioptric Projection

In this section we will describe the projections using conical section mirrors. Throughout the section we will refer to figures 2 and 3.

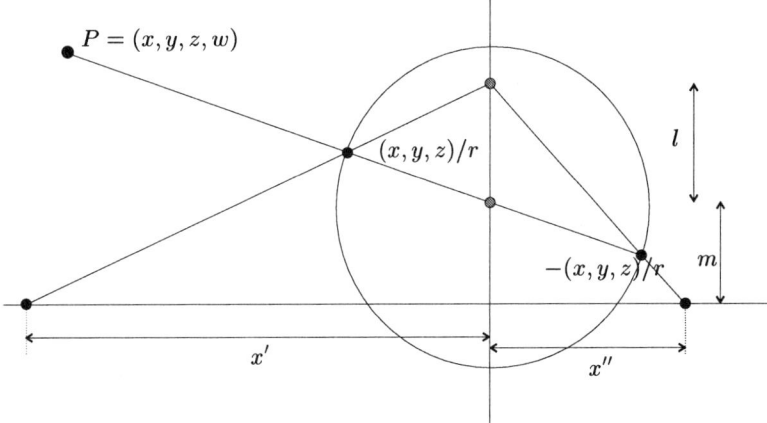

Fig. 1. A point $P = (x, y, z, w)$ is projected via s to two antipodal points $(\pm x, \pm y, \pm z)/r$ on the sphere. The two antipodal points are projected to the image plane $z = -m$ via projection from the point $(0, 0, l)$.

Parabolic Mirror. We call the projection induced by a parabolic mirror to an image plane a parabolic projection. The parabolic projection of a point P in space is the orthographic projection of the intersection of the line PF (where F is the parabola's focus) and the parabola. The orthographic projection is to the image plane perpendicular to the axis of the parabola. Any line (in particular a ray of light) incident with the focus is reflected such that it is perpendicular to the image plane, and (ideally) these are the only rays that the orthographic camera receives.

The projection described is equivalent to central projection of a point to the parabola, followed by standard orthographic projection. Thus we proceed in a similar fashion as we did for the sphere. Assume that a parabola is placed such that its axis is the z-axis, its focus is located at the origin, and p is its focal length. Then

$$S = \left\{ (x, y, z) \mid \frac{1}{4p}(x^2 + y^2) - p = z \right\}$$

is the surface of the parabola. Now define $\sim$ such that if $P, Q \in S$, then $P \sim Q$ if and only if there exists a $\lambda \in \mathbb{R}$ such that $P = \lambda Q$. We now determine the projection $s_p : P^3(\mathbb{R}) \to S/\sim$,

$$s_p(x, y, z, w) = \left(\pm \frac{2px}{r \mp z}, \pm \frac{2py}{r \mp z}, \pm \frac{2pz}{r \mp z} \right) ,$$

where $r = \sqrt{x^2 + y^2 + z^2}$. The next step is to project orthographically to the plane $z = 0$ (the actual distance of the plane to the origin is of course inconsequential). We thereby obtain $q_p^* : P^3(\mathbb{R}) \to \mathbb{R}^2/\sim$ given by

$$q_p^*(x, y, z, w) = \left(\pm \frac{2px}{r \mp z}, \pm \frac{2py}{r \mp z} \right) .$$

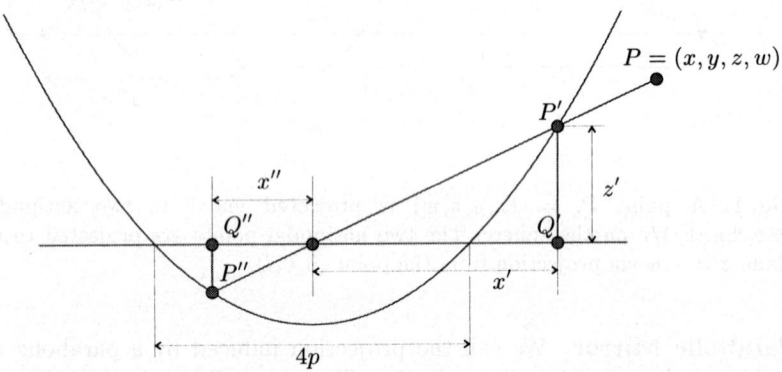

Fig. 2. Cross-section of a parabolic mirror. The image plane is through the focal point. The point in space P is projected to the antipodal points P' and P'', which are then *orthographically* projected to Q' and Q'' respectively.

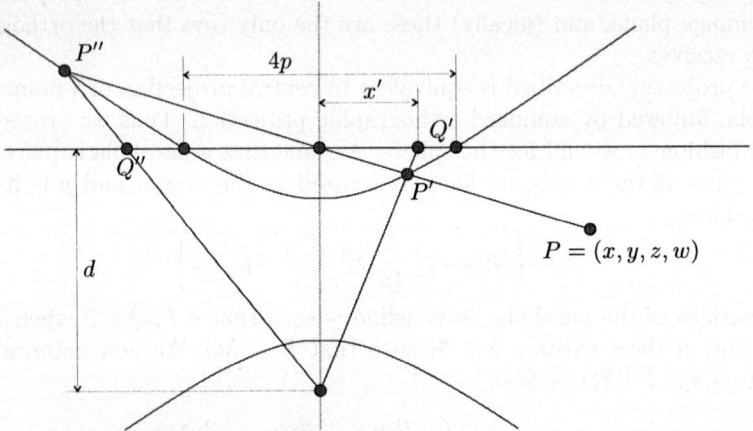

Fig. 3. Cross-section of a hyperbolic mirror, again the image plane is through the focal point. The point in space P is projected to the antipodal points P' and P'', which are then *perspectively* projected to Q' and Q'' from the second focal point.

Again, $\mathbb{R}^2/\!\sim$ is $\mathbb{R}^2$ with the equivalence relation carried over by orthographic projection of the parabola.

Remark. Note that

$$q_p^*(x,y,z,w) = 2p\,p_{1,0}^*(x,y,z,w) = p_{1,2p-1}^*(x,y,z,w) \ .$$

Hyperbolic and Elliptical Mirrors. As with the paraboloid, hyperbolic projection is the result of reflecting rays off of a hyperbolic mirror. Rays incident with one the focal points of the hyperbola are reflected into rays incident with the second focal point. To obtain the projection of a point, intersect the line containing the point and the focal point with the hyperbola. Take the two intersection points and projection them to the image plane. The same applies to ellipses.

Assume a hyperbola is placed such that its axis is the z-axis, one of its foci is the origin, the other $(0,0,-d)$, and its latus rectum is $4p$. Then the surface of the hyperbola is

$$S = \left\{(x,y,z) \ \middle| \ \left(\frac{z+d/2}{a}\right)^2 - \left(\frac{x}{b}\right)^2 - \left(\frac{y}{b}\right)^2 = 1\right\}$$

where

$$a = \frac{1}{2}\left(\sqrt{d^2+4p^2} - 2p\right), \ \text{and} \ b = \sqrt{p\sqrt{d^2+4p^2} - 2p^2} \ .$$

Let $\sim$ be similarly defined for points of S, identifying antipodal points of the hyperbola's surface with respect to the focus. The projection $s_{p,d}(x,y,z,w)$: $P^3(\mathbb{R}) \to S/\!\sim$ may be obtained by intersecting the line through the point and the origin, however it is of too great a length to include here. Nevertheless, once obtained we then proceed by applying a perspective projection of the the antipodal point pair given by $s_{p,d}(x,y,z,w)$ from the point $(0,0,-d)$ to the plane $z=0$, calling this projection $r_{p,d}^* : P^3(\mathbb{R}) \to \mathbb{R}^2/\!\sim$. We find that

$$r_{p,d}^*(x,y,z,w) = \left(\pm\frac{\dfrac{2xdp/\sqrt{d^2+4p^2}}{\dfrac{d}{\sqrt{d^2+4p^2}}r \mp z}}, \pm\frac{\dfrac{2ydp/\sqrt{d^2+4p^2}}{\dfrac{d}{\sqrt{d^2+4p^2}}r \mp z}}\right) \ ,$$

where $r = \sqrt{x^2+y^2+z^2}$.

Remark. Notice that

$$r_{p,d}^*(x,y,z,w) = p^*_{\frac{d}{\sqrt{d^2+4p^2}},\frac{d(1-2p)}{\sqrt{d^2+4p^2}}}(x,y,z,w) \ .$$

For an ellipsoid similarly placed so that its foci are $(0,0,0)$ and $(0,0,-d)$, and latus rectum of $4p$, we have

$$S = \left\{(x,y,z) \ \middle| \ \left(\frac{z+d/2}{a}\right)^2 + \left(\frac{x}{b}\right)^2 + \left(\frac{y}{b}\right)^2 = 1\right\} \ ,$$

where

$$a = \frac{1}{2}\left(\sqrt{d^2 + 4p^2} + 2p\right), \text{ and } b = \sqrt{p\sqrt{d^2 + 4p^2} + 2p^2} \ .$$

We then derive that $t^*_{p,d}(x, y, z, w) : P^3(\mathbb{R}) \to \mathbb{R}^2/\sim$ is given by

$$t^*_{p,d}(x, y, z, w) = \left(\pm \frac{2xdp}{dr \pm z\sqrt{d^2 + 4p^2}}, \pm \frac{2ydp}{dr \pm z\sqrt{d^2 + 4p^2}}\right) \ .$$

Remark. We have that $t^*_{p,d}$ satisfies

$$t^*_{p,d}(x, y, z, w) = r^*_{p,d}(x, y, -z, w) = p^*_{\frac{d}{\sqrt{d^2+4p^2}}, \frac{d(1-2p)}{\sqrt{d^2+4p^2}}}(x, y, -z, w) \ .$$

Thus the ellipse gives the same projection as the hyperbola, modulo a reflection about $z = 0$.

2.3 Equivalence of Catadioptric and Spherical Projections

From the discussion above we may write a general theorem which will allow us to more generally develop the theory of catadioptric image geometry. We have the following central theorem.

Theorem 1 (Projective Equivalence). *Catadioptric projection with a single effective viewpoint is equivalent to projection to a sphere followed by projection to a plane from a point.*

Proof. In the past two sections we have the following relationships for the projection functions:

$$r^*_{p,d}(x, y, z, w) = p^*_{\frac{d}{\sqrt{d^2+4p^2}}, \frac{d(1-2p)}{\sqrt{d^2+4p^2}}}(x, y, z, w) \quad \text{(hyperbola} \longleftrightarrow \text{sphere)} \ ,$$

$$t^*_{p,d}(x, y, z, w) = p^*_{\frac{d}{\sqrt{d^2+4p^2}}, \frac{d(1-2p)}{\sqrt{d^2+4p^2}}}(x, y, -z, w) \quad \text{(ellipse} \longleftrightarrow \text{sphere)} \ ,$$

$$q^*_p(x, y, z, w) = p^*_{1, 2p-1}(x, y, z, w) \quad \text{(parabola} \longleftrightarrow \text{sphere)} \ ,$$

$$\left(\frac{fx}{z}, \frac{fy}{z}\right) = p^*_{0, f}(x, y, z, w) \quad \text{(perspective} \longleftrightarrow \text{sphere)} \ .$$

Each are maps from $P^3(\mathbb{R})$ to $\mathbb{R}^2_\sim$, and for any point in space the relations show that they map to the same point in the image plane. □

We now have a unified theory of catadioptric projection, and in further discussion we need only consider projections of the sphere. In the interest of conciseness we wish to give a name to this class of projections. We write $\pi_{l,m}$ to represent the projective plane induced by the projection $p^*_{l,m}$. Recall that if $l = 1$ then we have the projective plane obtained from stereographic projection, or equivalently parabolic projection. If $l = 0$ then we have the projective plane obtained from perspective projection.

Having demonstrated the equivalence with the sphere we now wish to describe in more detail the structure of the projective plane $\pi_{l,m}$. We therefore describe the images of lines under these projections, therefore the "lines" of the projective planes. But because of the equivalence with the sphere, we may restrict ourselves to studying the projections of great circles and antipodal points. Thus let $s_{l,m}$: $S^2/\!\!\sim\,\to\, \mathbb{R}^2/\!\!\sim$ project points of the sphere to the image plane. Figure 4 shows the projection of the great circle to the image plane, the equator is projected to a circle of radius $\frac{l+m}{l}$; this is the horizon of the fronto-parallel since the equator is the projection of the line at infinity in the plane $z = 0$. The proposition below describes the family of conics which are images of lines.

Proposition 1. *The image of a line is a conic whose major axis (when it exists) intersects the image center. It has the property that it intersects the fronto-parallel horizon antipodally and its major axis intersects the image center.*

Proof. Note first that the intersection of a great circle (which is itself the image of a line in space) with the equator are two points which are antipodal. Their projection to the image plane gives two points which again are antipodal on the image of the equator. The image of the great circle must be symmetric about the axis made by the perpendicular bisector of the two intersection points. This axis contains the image center since the midpoint of the intersection points is the image center.

The actual image may be obtained by taking a cone whose vertex is the point of projection $(0,0,l)$ and which contains the great circle, then intersecting the cone with the image plane. The intersection of a plane and a skew cone is still a conic. □

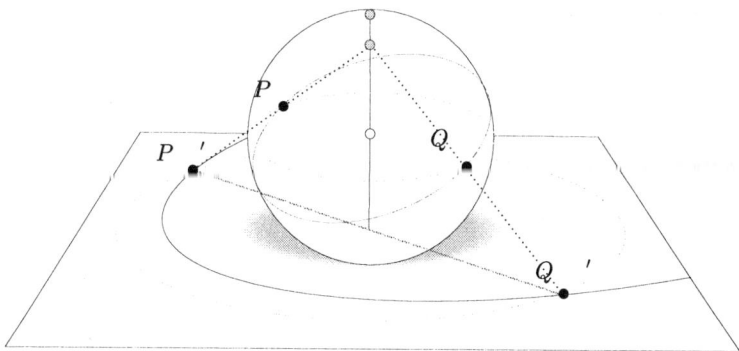

Fig. 4. A line in space is projected to a great circle on the sphere, which is then projected to a conic section in the plane via $p_{l,m}^*$. The equator is mapped to the fronto-parallel horizon, the dotted circle in the plane.

Note that if a conic has the properties in the proposition it is not necessarily the image of a line. There is an additional constraint on the foci of the conic. Let us therefore determine the image of a great circle. Let $\hat{n} = (n_x, n_y, n_z)$ be the normal of a plane containing some great circle. To obtain the quadratic form of the conic section we find the quadratic form of the cone through $(0,0,l)$ and the great circle. To do this we first rotate to a coordinate system (x',y',z') such that the great circle lies in the plane $z' = 0$. Then the vertex of the cone is $(l\sqrt{1-n_z^2},0,ln_z)$. Points of the cone, in the rotated coordinate system, then satisfy

$$
p' \begin{pmatrix} 1 & 0 & \frac{\sqrt{1-n_z^2}}{n_z} & 0 \\ 0 & 1 & 0 & 0 \\ \frac{\sqrt{1-n_z^2}}{n_z} & 0 & \frac{1-\frac{1}{l^2}-n_z^2}{n_z^2} & \frac{1}{ln_z} \\ 0 & 0 & \frac{1}{ln_z} & -1 \end{pmatrix} p'^T \ .
$$

By rotating back to the original coordinate system we have,

$$
p \begin{pmatrix} -n_x^2\alpha - l^2(n_x^2 + n_y^2 n_z^2) & (l^2-1)n_x n_y \alpha & ln_x n_z \alpha \\ (l^2-1)n_x n_y \alpha & -n_y^2\alpha - l^2(n_y^2 + n_x^2 n_z^2) & ln_y n_z \alpha \\ ln_x n_z \alpha & ln_y n_z \alpha & -l^2 n_z^2 \alpha \end{pmatrix} p^T \ ,
$$

where $\alpha = n_z^2 - 1 = n_x^2 + n_y^2$. Let $C_{\hat{n}}$ be the matrix above. From this form we may extract the axes, center, eccentricity and foci, finding that

$$
c = \left(\frac{(l+m)n_x|n_z|}{n_x^2+n_y^2-l^2}, \frac{(l+m)n_y|n_z|}{n_x^2+n_y^2-l^2} \right) \qquad \text{(center)} \ ,
$$

$$
f_{\pm} = \left(\frac{(l+m)n_x(|n_z|\pm\sqrt{1-l^2})}{n_x^2+n_y^2-l^2}, \frac{(l+m)n_y(|n_z|\pm\sqrt{1-l^2})}{n_x^2+n_y^2-l^2} \right) \quad \text{(foci)} \ ,
$$

$$
a = \frac{l(l+m)n_z}{l^2-n_x^2-n_y^2} \qquad \text{(minor axis)} \ ,
$$

$$
b = \frac{l+m}{\sqrt{l^2-n_x^2-n_y^2}} \qquad \text{(major axis)} \ ,
$$

$$
\epsilon = \sqrt{\frac{(1-l^2)(n_x^2+n_y^2)}{l^2-n_x^2-n_y^2}} \qquad \text{(eccentricity)} \ .
$$

Meet and join. We find that the set of "points" of the projective plane $\pi_{l,m}$,

$$
\Pi(\pi_{l,m}) = \left\{ \left(\pm\frac{(l+m)m_x}{l\mp m_z}, \pm\frac{(l+m)m_y}{l\mp m_z} \right) \Big| \hat{n} \in S^2 \right\} \ .
$$

A line is the set of points,

$$
[\hat{n}] = \left\{ (x,y) \ \Big| \ (x\ y)\, C_{\hat{n}} \begin{pmatrix} x \\ y \end{pmatrix} \right\} \ .
$$

Thus the set of "lines" of the projective plane $\pi_{l,m}$,

$$
\Lambda(\pi_{l,m}) = \left\{ [\hat{n}] \ \big| \ \hat{n} \in S^2 \right\} \ .
$$

We may then define the operator meet $\wedge : \Lambda(\pi_{l,m}) \times \Lambda(\pi_{l,m}) \to \Pi(\pi_{l,m})$ to take a pair of lines to their intersection, and the operator join $\vee : \Pi(\pi_{l,m}) \times \Pi(\pi_{l,m}) \to \Lambda(\pi_{l,m})$ to take a pair of points to the line through them.

2.4 Duality

In this section we will show that two projections of the sphere are dual to each other. The antipodal point pairs of one projection are the foci of line images in another projection, and vice versa. When the projection is stereographic (i.e. parabolic) the dual is the usual perspective projection.

We have seen that images of lines are conics, we would like to know if there is anything special about families of line images which intersect the same point. A set of longitudes on the sphere all intersect in two antipodal points, what are their projections? It is clear that the images must all intersect in two points since incidence relationships are preserved, but is there anything special about this particular pencil of conics?

Proposition 2. *The locus of foci of a set of line images, where the great circles corresponding to the lines intersect antipodally, is a conic whose foci are the images of the intersection points.*

Proof. Assume l and m are constant. Choose some point $\hat{m} = (m_x, m_y, m_z)$ on the sphere, by rotational symmetry we may assume without loss of generality that $m_y = 0$. The normals of all lines perpendicular to $\hat{m}$, i.e. those which intersect $\hat{m}$, are

$$(n^\theta_x, n^\theta_y, n^\theta_z) = (m_x \sin\theta, \cos\theta, m_z \sin\theta) \ .$$

Substituting into the formula found for the first focus, we have

$$f^\theta_1 = \left(\frac{(1+m)n^\theta_x \left(n^\theta_z + \sqrt{1-l^2}\right)}{n^{\theta\,2}_x + n^{\theta\,2}_y - l^2}, \frac{(1+m)n^\theta_y \left(n^\theta_z + \sqrt{1-l^2}\right)}{n^{\theta\,2}_x + n^{\theta\,2}_y - l^2} \right)$$

$$= \left(\frac{(1+m)m_x \sin\theta}{\sqrt{1-l^2} - m_z \sin\theta}, \frac{(1+m)\cos\theta}{\sqrt{1-l^2} - m_z \sin\theta} \right) \ .$$

But this is just the projection of $(n^\theta_x, n^\theta_y, n^\theta_z)$ by

$$p^*_{\sqrt{1-l^2},\, l+m-\sqrt{1-l^2}} \ .$$

So let $l' = \sqrt{1-l^2}$ and $m' = l + m - \sqrt{1-l^2}$. Under the projection $p^*_{l',m'}$ the image of the great circle perpendicular to (m_x, m_y, m_z), i.e. the points $\{(n^\theta_x, n^\theta_y, n^\theta_z)\}$, is once again a conic. One of its foci is

$$f'_1 = \left(\frac{(l'+m')m_x \left(m_z + \sqrt{1-l'^2}\right)}{n^2_x - l'^2}, 0 \right) = \left(\frac{(1+m)m_x}{1 - m_z}, 0 \right) \ .$$

This is the image of $(m_x, 0, m_y)$ under $p^*_{l,m}$. □

Define the map $f_{l,m}$ such that given the normal of a line it produces the foci of the line's image. Note that this map is injective and therefore its inverse is well defined. We have the following theorem on duality.

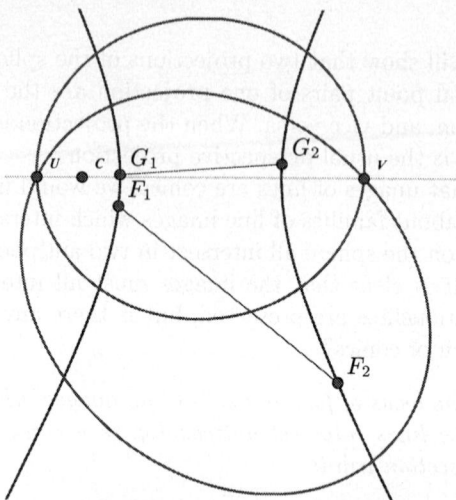

Fig. 5. The two ellipses are projections of two lines in space. Their foci F_1, F_2, and G_1, G_2 respectively lie on a hyperbola containing the foci of *all* ellipses through U and V. The foci of this hyperbola are the points U and V.

Theorem 2 (Duality). *Given the two projective planes* $\pi_1 = \pi_{l,m}$ *and* $\pi_2 = \pi_{l',m'}$ *where* l, m, l' *and* m' *satisfy*

$$l^2 + l'^2 = 1 \quad and \quad l + m = l' + m' \ ,$$

the following is true,

$$f_{l,m} : \Lambda(\pi_1) \to \Pi(\pi_2),$$

$$f_{l,m}^{-1} : \Pi(\pi_2) \to \Lambda(\pi_1),$$

$$f_{l',m'} : \Lambda(\pi_2) \to \Pi(\pi_1),$$

$$f_{l',m'}^{-1} : \Pi(\pi_1) \to \Lambda(\pi_2) \ .$$

In fact the two projective planes π_1 *and* π_2 *are dual. If* l_1, l_2 *are lines of* π_1 *and* p_1, p_2 *are points of* π_1, *then:*

$$f_{l',m'}^{-1}(l_1 \wedge l_2) = f_{l,m}(l_1) \vee f_{l,m}(l_2)$$

$$f_{l,m}(p_1 \vee p_2) = f_{l',m'}^{-1}(p_1) \wedge f_{l',m'}^{-1}(p_2) \ .$$

Proof. The preceding proposition showed that the foci of a pencil of lines $\{l_\lambda\}$ lied on a conic c, where $c \in \Lambda(\pi_2)$. The foci of c were the two points of intersection of the pencil of lines, so $f_{l',m'}(c) = l_{\lambda_1} \wedge l_{\lambda_2}$. But $c = f_{l,m}(l_{\lambda_1}) \vee f_{l,m}(l_{\lambda_2})$, and so

$$f_{l',m'}^{-1}(l_{\lambda_1} \wedge l_{\lambda_2}) = f_{l,m}(l_{\lambda_1}) \vee f_{l,m}(l_{\lambda_2}) \ .$$

The second is true because so is the dual to the proposition, namely that a set of collinear points (in π_1) produce a line whose foci are a single point of π_2. □

Corollary 1. *The projective planes $\pi_{1,0}$ and $\pi_{0,1}$ are dual. The first is obtained from stereographic projection, and the second from perspective projection. The center of every circle in a parabolic projection is a point in the perspective projection; every point of a parabolic projection is a focal point of a line in a perspective projection.*

3 Advantages of Catadioptric Projection

The presented unifying theory of catadioptric projections enables a direct and natural insight on the invariances of these projections. The perspective projection is a degenerate case of a catadioptric projection which fact as we will show directly reveals its inferiority to the other catadioptric projections (parabolic and hyperbolic).

3.1 Recovery of Geometric Properties

We have shown that parabolic projection is equivalent to stereographic projection, as well as being dual to perspective projection. Stereographic projection is a map with several important properties. First the projection of any circle on the sphere is a circle in the plane. In particular the projection of a great circle is a circle. What is also important is that the map is conformal. The angle between two great circles (i.e. the inverse cosine of the dot product of the normals of their planes) is the same angle between the circles which are their projections. This is important because it means for one thing that if two circles are horizons of some planes, and they are orthogonal, then the planes are perpendicular.

Corollary 2. *The angle between great circles on the sphere is equal to the angle between their projections.*

Proof of this fact is given in almost any book on geometry, e.g. [12], and is a direct result of the fact that stereographic projection is a conformal mapping. This implies that the angles between the horizons of two planes is equal to the angle between the two planes; orthogonal planes have orthogonal horizons.

3.2 Calibration

Almost all applications in computer vision require that the imaging sensor's intrinsic parameters be calibrated. The intrinsic parameters include focal length, image center and aspect ratio, as well as any other parameters which determine the projection induced by the sensor such as radial distortion. Sometimes it is possible to calibrate one or more of those parameters with minimal prior information about scene geometry or configuration. For example, it has been shown that radial distortion can be calibrated for, using only the images of lines. The only assumption is that points have been gathered in the image which are projections of points in space lying on some straight line. Using this information not only is it possible to determine the radial distortion parameters, but the image center also may be obtained.

We have shown prior to this work that it is possible to calibrate all of the intrinsic parameters of a parabolic catadioptric sensor, again using only lines. Let us gain some intuition as to why this is true, and why it is not possible to calibrate a normal perspective camera with these simple assumptions.

First examine the perspective case. Assuming that aspect ratio is one, there are two intrinsic parameters, namely the image center and focal length. The image of a line in space is a line in the image plane, and any given line may be uniquely determined by two points. From any image line it is possible only to determine the orientation of the plane containing the line in space and the focal point; the orientation of this plane can be parameterized by two parameters. Given n lines, how many constraints are there and how many unknowns? If for some n the number of constraints exceeds the number of unknowns, then we have a hope of obtaining the unknowns, and thus calibrate the sensor. However, for every line added we gain two more constraints and two more unknowns; we will always be short by three equations. Therefore self-calibration *from lines*, without any metric information, and in one frame is hopeless in the perspective case.

What about the parabolic case? There are a total of three unknowns, focal length and image center (alone giving two unknowns). The projection of any line is a circle, and which is completely specified by as few as three points, therefore three constraints. The orientation of the plane containing the line gives two unknowns. So, for every line that we obtain we reduce the number of unknowns by one. If there are three lines, we have 9 constraints and 9 unknowns, and thus we can perform self-calibration with only three lines.

Finally the hyperbolic case. There are four unknowns and each line adds two for orientation. The projection of a line is a conic which may be specified by five points. Thus when we have two lines we have 8 unknowns and 10 constraints. So, with only two lines the system is over-determined, but nevertheless we can still perform a calibration.

We give here a simple and compact algorithm for calibrating the parabolic projection. It is based on the fact that a sphere whose equator is an image line in the image plane contains the point $(c_x, c_y, 2p)$, where (c_x, c_y) is assumed to be the image center, though initially unknown. This is by symmetry, since the image circle intersects the fronto-parallel plane at points a distance $2p$ from the image center. Thus the intersection of at least three spheres so-constructed will produce the points $(c_x, c_y, \pm 2p)$, giving us both image center and focal length simultaneously.

In the presence of noise, the intersection will not be defined for more than three spheres, yet we may minimize the distance from a point to all of the spheres, i.e. find the point (c_x, c_y, p) such that

$$\sum_{i=1}^{n} \left((d_x^i - c_x)^2 + (d_y^i - c_y)^2 + 4p^2 - r_i^2 \right)^2 \tag{1}$$

is a minimum over all points. Here (d_x^i, d_y^i) is the center of the i-th image circle, and r_i is its radius. The intersection is not defined for fewer than three spheres, since the intersection of two spheres gives only the circle within which the point lies, but not the point itself.

4   Experiment

We present here a short experiment with real data as a proof of concept. We will show how given a single catadioptric image of a plane (left image in Fig. 6) we can recover the intrinsic parameters of the camera and metrically rectify this plane, too. The system used is an off-shelf realization (S1 model, Cyclovision Inc.) of a parabolic catadioptric system invented by Nayar [8]. The algorithm detects edge points and groups them in elliptical arcs using a Delaunay triangulation of the points and a subsequent Hough transform. An ellipse fitting algorithm [3] is then applied on the clustered points. The aspect ratio is eliminated and the ellipses are transformed to circles (Fig. 6, middle). We additionally assume that these lines are coplanar and that they belong to two groups of parallel lines. However, we do not make any assumption about the angles between these lines.

From the parallelism assumption we know that the intersections of the circles are the antipodal projections of vanishing points. The calibration theory developed above tells us that the intersection of the lines connecting the antipodal points gives the image center.

Two vanishing points and the focal point define a plane parallel to the plane viewed. Imagine the horizon of this plane (line at infinity) defined by the two sets of vanishing points. Imagine also a pole on the sphere corresponding to the plane spanned by the horizon and the focal point. The parabolic projection of the horizon is a circle (the horizon conic) and its center is the projection of the pole. However, this pole gives exactly the normal where all the lines lie. This center is the dual point to the line which is the horizon of the perspective projection. Given the calculation (1) the focal length is directly obtained. This focal length is the effective focal length required for any operation in the catadioptric system (we can not decouple the mirror from the lens focal length). We have thus been able to compute image center, focal length, and the normal of a plane without assuming any metric information. We visualize the result on the right of Fig. 6 where we have rectified the ceiling plane so that it looks as if it were fronto-parallel. Unlike the planar perspective case [6] metric rectification of a plane from a single image is possible with a parabolic catadioptric system without any metric information.

5   Conclusion

In this paper, we presented a novel theory on the geometry of central panoramic or catadioptric vision systems. We proved that every projection can be modeled with the projection of the sphere to a horizontal plane from a point on the vertical axis of the sphere. This modeling includes traditional cameras which

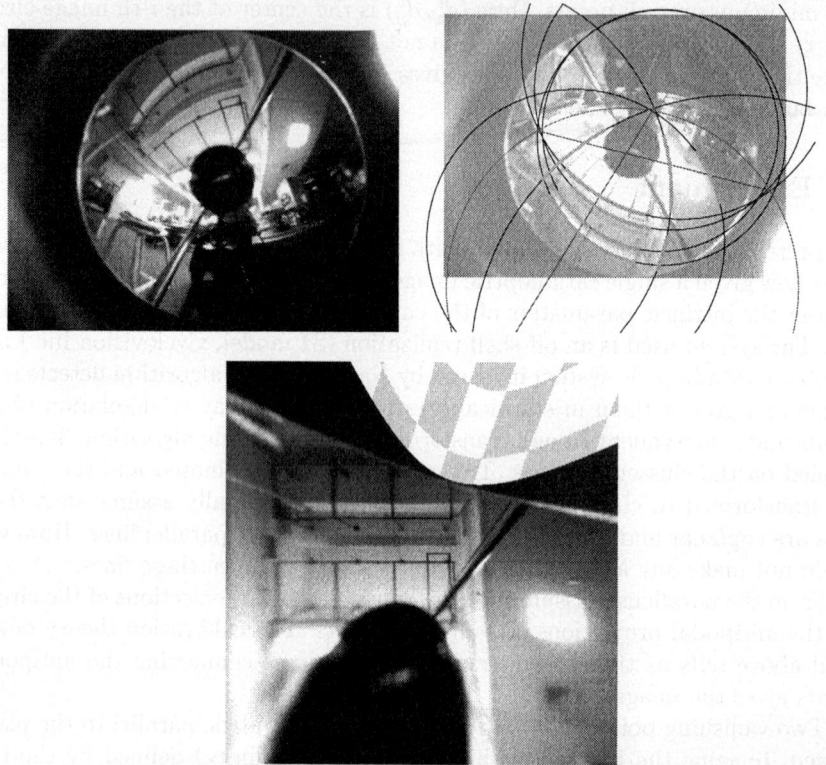

Fig. 6. Top left: Original image of the ceiling recorded by the catadioptric camera slanted approx. 45 deg. with respect to the ceiling. Top right: Two groups of four and three circles, respectively, fitted on the images of the ceiling-edges. The lines through the vanishing points intersect at the image center and all the vanishing points lie on a circle. Bottom middle: Both, the collinearity of the edge elements and the perpendicularity of the edges show a superior performance in estimating intrinsics as well as pan-tilt of the ceiling using only natural landmarks.

are equivalent to a catadioptric projection via a planar mirror. In this case the projection point of our model is the center of the sphere. In the parabolic case, the projection point becomes the north-pole and the projection is a stereography. The conformal mapping properties of the stereography show the power of the parabolic systems. Hyperbolic or elliptical mirrors correspond to projections from points on the vertical diameter within the sphere. We showed that projections of point and lines in space are points and conics, respectively. Due to preservation of the incidence relationship we can regard the conics as projective lines. We showed that these projective lines are indeed dual to the points and vice versa.

Very useful practical implications can be directly derived from this theory. Calibration constraints are natural and we provided a geometric argument why all catadioptric systems except the conventional planar projection can be calibrated from one view. We gave an experimental evidence using a parabolic mirror where we also showed that metric rectification of a plane is possible if we have only affine but not metric information about the environment. We plan to extend our theory to multiple catadioptric views as well as to the study of robustness of scene recovery using the above principles.

References

1. T.E. Boult. Remote reality demonstration. In *IEEE Conf. Computer Vision and Pattern Recognition*, pages 966–967, Santa Barbara, CA, June 23-25, 1998.
2. J.S. Chahl and M.V. Srinivasan. Range estimation with a panoramic sensor. *Journal Opt. Soc. Am. A*, 14:2144–2152, 1997.
3. A. Fitzgibbon, M. Pilu, and R.Fisher. Direct least-square fitting of ellipses. In *Proc. Int. Conf. on Pattern Recognition*, pages 253–257, Vienna, Austria, Aug. 25-30, 1996.
4. J. Gluckman and S.K. Nayar. Ego-motion and omnidirectional cameras. In *Proc. Int. Conf. on Computer Vision*, pages 999–1005, Bombay, India, Jan. 3-5, 1998.
5. A. Hicks and R. Bajcsy. Reflective surfaces as computational sensors. In *CVPR-Workshop on Perception for Mobile Egents, Fort Collins, CO, June 26*, 1999.
6. D. Liebowitz and A. Zisserman. Metric rectification for perspective images of planes. In *IEEE Conf. Computer Vision and Pattern Recognition*, pages 582–488. Santa Barbara, CA, June 23-25, 1998.
7. V. Nalwa. Bell labs 360-degree panoramic webcam. News Release, http://www.lucent.com/press/0998/980901.bla.html, 1998.
8. S. Nayar. Catadioptric omnidirectional camera. In *IEEE Conf. Computer Vision and Pattern Recognition*, pages 482–488, Puerto Rico, June 17-19, 1997.
9. T. Needham. *Visual Complex Analysis*. Clarendon Press, Oxford, 1997.
10. S.A. Nene and S.K. Nayar. Stereo with mirrors. In *Proc. Int. Conf. on Computer Vision*, pages 1087–1094, Bombay, India, Jan. 3-5, 1998.
11. Y. Onoe, K. Yamazawa, H. Takemura, and N. Yokoya. Telepresence by real-time view-dependent image generation from omnidirectional video streams. *Computer Vision and Image Understanding*, 71·588–592, 1998.
12. D. Pedoe. *Geometry: A comprehensive course*. Dover Publications, New York, NY, 1970.
13. D. W. Rees. Panoramic television viewing system. United States Patent No. 3, 505, 465, Apr. 1970.
14. D. Southwell, A. Basu, and B. Vandergriend. A conical mirror pipeline inspection system. In *Proc. IEEE Int. Conf. on Robotics and Automation*, pages 3253–3258, 1996.
15. T. Svoboda, T. Pajdla, and V. Hlavac. Epipolar geometry for panoramic cameras. In *Proc. 6th European Conference on Computer Vision*, pages 218–231, 1998.
16. Y. Yagi, S. Kawato, and S. Tsuji. Real-time omnidirectional image sensor (copis) for vision-guided navigation. *Trans. on Robotics and Automation*, 10:11–22, 1994.

Binocular Self-Alignment and Calibration from Planar Scenes

Joss Knight and Ian Reid[*]

Department of Engineering Science
University of Oxford
Oxford OX1 3PJ, UK
[joss,ian]@robots.ox.ac.uk

Abstract. We consider the problem of aligning and calibrating a binocular pan-tilt device using visual information from controlled motions, while viewing a degenerate (planar) scene.

By considering the invariants to controlled motions about pan and elevation axes while viewing the plane, we show how to construct the images of points at infinity in various visual directions. First, we determine an ideal point whose visual direction is orthogonal to the pan and tilt axes, and use this point to align the rig to its own natural reference frame. Second, we show how by combining stereo views we can construct further points at infinity, and determine the left-right epipoles, without computing the full epipolar geometry and/or projective structure. Third, we show how to determine the infinite homography which maps ideal points between left and right camera images, and hence solve for the two focal lengths of the cameras. The minimum requirement is three views of the plane, where the head undergoes one pan, and one elevation.

Results are presented using both simulated data, and real imagery acquired from a 4 degree-of-freedom binocular rig.

1 Introduction

It has been recognised for some time that self-calibration of a mobile camera is often possible from image information alone, and various algorithms have been presented in the literature, addressing different aspects of the problem [7, 8, 14, 20]. Almost all of the these algorithms involve (either directly or indirectly) computing any or all of the epipolar geometry, the camera locations and the projective structure of the scene viewed, and fail when this cannot be achieved. This occurs if the scene viewed is planar, for example.

Recently, Triggs [21] has shown that five views of a *planar* (*ie.* degenerate) scene are, in principle, sufficient for self calibration. This is a notable result since in this case the scene structure is related between images by a 2D homographic transformation, the fundamental matrix is under-determined, and

---
[*] This work is supported by the UK's Engineering and Physical Sciences Research Council through a studentship to JGHK, an Advanced Research Fellowship to IDR, and through grant GR/L58668.

back-projection of image points to obtain projective structure is not possible. The disadvantage of Triggs' method is that it relies on a bundle adjustment procedure with no clear-cut initialisation.

In this paper we are concerned with the same problem for a binocular rig viewing the planar scene. Clearly from Triggs' result we could infer naively that five binocular views would be sufficient to determine the intrinsics of each camera. However this approach neglects the constraints imposed by the stereo rig, and does not solve the problem of initialising the iterative minimisation. Instead, we make two (reasonable) assumptions about our binocular rig: (i) its internal geometry is unchanging (including unchanging camera internal parameters, although they may be different for the two cameras); and (ii) controlled rotations of the rig are possible – in particular, we can perform zero-pitch screw motions (*ie.* rotations around an axis with no translation along the axis). Consequently, we prove a number of useful results related to self-calibration of the rig. In particular:

- We consider the invariants to a zero-pitch screw motion from a geometrical point of view, and how they relate to the invariants of a 2D image-to-image homography induced by a plane, or rotation about the camera optical centre;
- Using these invariants we show how to construct the image locations of points at infinity irrespective of scene degeneracy. One such point turns out to have visual direction orthogonal to the rotation axes and is therefore a natural alignment reference;
- We show how by combining multiple views of the scene plane, we can construct further points at infinity (and incidentally compute the epipolar geometry of the head);
- We use the constructed points at infinity to determine the infinite homography relating points at infinity between cameras, and in certain cases, the camera parameters.

In summary, we obtain a method to determine a closed-form solution for the infinite homography, and hence two focal lengths from three stereo views of a plane. Additionally (since we can compute the epipolar geometry), we can backproject points to obtain the plane at infinity.

We demonstrate these results with respect to a typical binocular pan-tilt head used for autonomous navigation (Fig. 1), an application in which the knowledge of the relationships between the world and camera images (the calibration) is crucial.

The use of invariants stems from previous work in self-alignment of a stereo head, where the head is rotated so that the cameras are parallel and their optical axes lie perpendicular to both the pan and elevation axes. This is important since it provides a means by which the accurate *relative* angles provided by joint encoders may be upgraded to absolute measurements. The original work [10, 16] looked at invariants to motion in 3D projective space, easily recoverable for non-degenerate scenes. We show how, without needing to calibrate the cameras or calculate epipolar geometry, 2D invariants can provide the same alignment

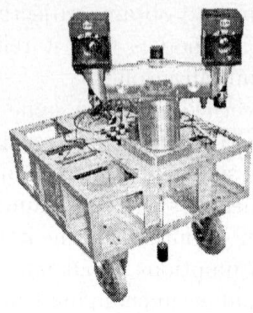

Fig. 1. A typical stereo pan-tilt head, mounted on a mobile robot

information even when degeneracy is present, and we present results to confirm the accuracy of this procedure. We also note and test the ability of the same algorithm to align the head if the degeneracy present is that of the motion of the camera (it rotates about its optical centre) rather than of the scene.

1.1 Relationship to Previous Work

Related previous work on self-calibration of stereo rigs can be found in [1, 2, 16, 23]. In [1, 2] the authors are concerned with obtaining *affine* calibration, that is to say, the location of the plane at infinity, under zero-pitch screw motions, occasionally also termed 'planar motions'. [23] extended this to general motion and full Euclidean calibration ([5, 9] gave further theoretical results and algorithms). [16] used similar ideas from projective geometry but solved the related problem of self-alignment, as defined above.

All of this work is predicated on the ability to compute projective structure and/or the (projective) locations of the cameras, by viewing a general scene. Here we concentrate on the problem of viewing a planar scene, but restrict ourselves, like [1, 2, 16], to zero-pitch screws. We show that self-alignment using image invariants is simpler and more robust than that achieved by [16], and how it can for a typical stereo head be applied to any scene, planar or not.

The most prominent and general work on planar calibration is clearly that of Triggs [21], but others have considered the same problem. By assuming various scene constraints, most usually known metric structure or known orthogonality, [11, 19, 22] all develop simple, flexible monocular calibration methods which are not reliant on initial guesses at the calibration values. We make no assumptions about the scene viewed, other than its planarity, but do require the special motions stereo heads provide. However note that in constrast to [6, 13, 18] which describe methods for self-calibration of active pan-tilt devices, we do *not* assume that the absolute motion is known (e.g. exact angle of rotation about the optic centre), only that it is of the form of a zero-pitch screw.

1.2 Paper Organisation

Section 2 of this paper establishes the geometric groundwork for the work and
the associated mathematical theory, proving the results listed above. In §3 we
present detailed experiments in self-alignment using both real and simulated
data, and give results which validate the self-calibration theory. Conclusions are
drawn in §4.

2 Theory and Implementation

2.1 Background and Notation

Each camera is modelled by a linear, central projection model (so non-linear
effects such as radial distortion are neglected) with its intrinsic parameters encoded by an upper triangular matrix

$$K = \begin{bmatrix} f & \delta & u_0 \\ 0 & \alpha f & v_0 \\ 0 & 0 & 1 \end{bmatrix} . \tag{1}$$

World points and planes are represented as homogeneous 4-vectors and written as upper-case bold characters (X, Π), image points and lines are represented
as homogeneous 3-vectors and written as lower-case bold characters (x, l). Matrices are written in teletype (K, H).

We denote left and right camera images by subscripts l and r, and different
stereo pairs (henceforth referred to as *views*) by integers. So a homography
mapping points from left to right would be denoted by H_{lr}, and from the left
image in view 1 to that in view 2 by $H_{l_1 l_2}$.

Any rigid transformation of a scene may be represented as a *screw* consisting
of a rotation about an axis and a translation along the axis. The *pitch* of the screw
defines the distance of this translation, and we are particularly concerned with
the case where the pitch is zero. Note that zero-pitch screw motion should not
be confused with degenerate rotation about the origin involving no translation
whatsoever. The zero-pitch case permits translation orthogonal to the rotation
axis.

Scene structure can be classified as projective if it is known up to an arbitrary 3D homographic transformation of the 'true' Euclidean structure. Affine
structure, for which the concepts of parallelism and mid-points make sense, can
be obtained from projective structure using knowledge of the location of the
plane at infinity. Affine structure may be upgraded to Euclidean using knowledge of the camera intrinsics K or equivalently the image of the absolute conic
$\omega = K^{-\top}K^{-1}$ or its dual $\omega^* = KK^\top$.

2.2 Motion Invariants

Figure 2(a) shows a camera rotating about some axis in space with zero pitch,
as is the case when our binocular head rotates about just one of its axes.

466

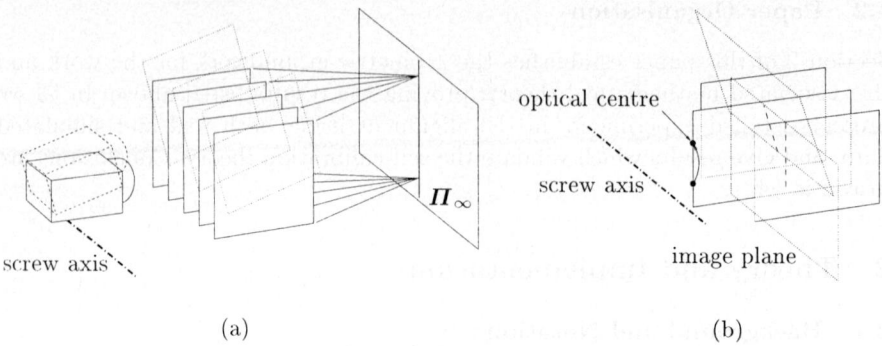

optical centre

screw axis

screw axis

Π_∞

image plane

(a)   (b)

Fig. 2. Planes and line at infinity invariant to rotation

It is evident from the figure that during the motion, each member of the set, or pencil, of planes perpendicular to the screw axis rotates into itself and is therefore preserved under the motion. Since the planes are parallel, the axis of the pencil, the line of common intersection of the planes, lies on the plane at infinity Π_∞, and is invariant to the motion. Likewise the rotation axis itself is invariant to the motion.

Figure 2(b) shows the same situation with the camera represented as an optical centre and image plane. Every point on the invariant plane that passes through the optic centre projects to the same line on the image plane, dashed in the figure. Thus in the case of zero-pitch screw motion, whatever the relationship between images before and after the motion, it will have an invariant line which is the projection of the invariant line at infinity.

Let us now restrict ourselves specifically to the case of a planar scene. The images before and after the motion are related by a plane-induced homography H. The invariant plane through the optic centre passes through the scene plane in an invariant line. There is also an invariant point, the intersection of the screw axis with the scene plane. These invariants have the following algebraic interpretation:

The eigenvectors of the plane-induced homography H *under zero-pitch screw motion consist of (i) a real eigenvector, which is the image of the intersection of the screw axis and the scene plane and (ii) a complex conjugate pair, which span the image of the invariant line on the plane, and so also the image of the invariant line at infinity.*

Images are also related by a 2D homography if the screw axis passes through the camera optical centre. Our argument for the invariant line is universally valid for zero-pitch screw motion, so this homography must also have a complex conjugate pair of eigenvectors which span the invariant line. In this case the real eigenvector becomes the image of the screw axis (which is imaged in a point).

2.3 Constructing Points at Infinity

Two Motions, One Camera. We have shown that if a camera undergoes zero-pitch screw motion, we can calculate an image line invariant to the motion that is the projection of an invariant line at infinity orthogonal to the screw axis. If the camera now undergoes two such motions about different axes, the two resulting invariant lines will intersect in a point orthogonal to both axes. We can therefore conclude:

> *A zero-pitch screw motion about two non-parallel axes suffices to construct the image projection of a point at infinity whose visual direction is orthogonal to both axes.*

A direct consequence is that fixating this point will result in alignment of the camera's optic axis orthogonal to the two rotation axes. This is the problem addressed in [16], but the new result holds for a single camera (of course it also holds for a binocular rig), for planar scenes, and does not require the computation of epipolar geometry and/or scene structure as an intermediate step meaning it is potentially more robust. We require only that we know the relationship between *images* before and after the motion (a fundamental matrix if there is no degeneracy, or a homography if there is).

We can therefore summarise the algorithm for self-alignment of a stereo pan-tilt head for the special cases of degenerate (planar) scenes, and degenerate motions (the camera rotates about its optical centre), for which the image relationship is a homography:

To self-align a stereo head in the presence of degeneracy:

1. Obtain three images of the scene, one in the initial 'wake-up' position, one following a small rotation about the elevation axis, and one following a small rotation about the pan axis. The rotation must retain matchable image features between views, so between $2°$ and $10°$ is sensible for typical cameras.
2. Calculate inter-image homographies between the three images. In our experiments we use robust matching of corner features between images, and a non-linear minimisation to calculate H that minimises reprojection error.
3. Eigendecompose each H and obtain the complex conjugate eigenvectors, v_1 and v_2. Each motion yields one invariant line λ_{tilt}, λ_{pan}, which are computed from the eigenvectors of the appropriate homography as $\lambda = (v_1 + v_2) \times i(v_1 - v_2)$.
4. Fixate the intersection of the lines $x = \lambda_{\text{tilt}} \times \lambda_{\text{pan}}$. This can be done without calibration information by visually servoing to the point as in [10].

Note that for a binocular system, the above algorithm can be performed for each of the left and right cameras separately. We verify the algorithm experimentally in section 3.

One Motion, Two Cameras. Our reasoning to this point is valid for a monocular system. Now consider the case of two cameras on a stereo rig viewing the scene, and undergoing the same motion (so their relative positions remain fixed), as in Fig. 3. For each camera there is a different invariant plane through the optic centre, but each intersects in the same line at infinity, so the invariant lines in each image are matched lines at infinity. This is true whether or not the scene is planar.

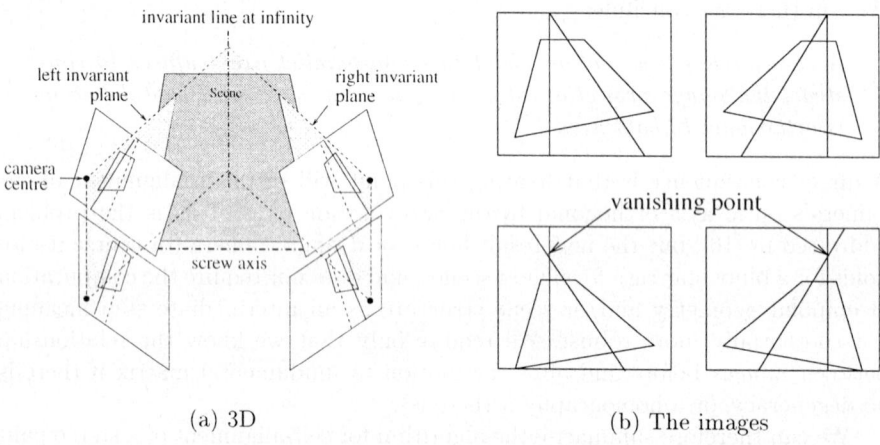

(a) 3D   (b) The images

Fig. 3. Stereo view of a planar scene. Note the left and right invariant planes are parallel and perpendicular to the screw axis, but perspective has been increased here so that they intersect within the figure

If the scene is indeed planar, the invariant planes intersect the scene in two parallel lines. These lines intersect on the vanishing line of the plane, where it meets the plane at infinity, its 'horizon'. We can image both lines in each camera, as shown in Fig. 3(b), by transferring each line to the other image using the homography H_{lr}. The intersection of these image lines, then, is the image of the point on the scene plane's horizon.

This brings up an interesting simplification of self-alignment when the scene consists of the ground plane. For a typical stereo pan-tilt head the pan axis is perpendicular to the ground plane. So the ground plane's vanishing line is also perpendicular to the pan axis. All that is required is to make a single rotation of the head about the elevation axis, and construct the point on the scene horizon as above. This point is then both perpendicular to the pan axis, and to the elevation axis (it lies on the invariant line to the elevation), and so is the fixation point we require for alignment.

Constructing this vanishing point will generally not work for a stereo rig undergoing a pan, since, typically, the camera centres of such a rig will lie on the same pan-invariant plane, making the left and right invariant lines images of the same line on the scene plane.

Two Motions, Two Cameras. Now if we have a stereo rig undergoing two motions there will be two invariant lines for each camera, and their intersection will be a matched point at infinity which is in general *not* on the scene plane.

2.4 Combining Views for Planar Scenes

The relationship between the left and right cameras is fixed during the controlled motions, and this enables us to treat the motions as, interchangeably, either motions of the cameras, or motions of the scene. As Fig. 4 shows, two views of one scene plane are equivalent to a single view of two planes that are (in general) not coincident. This suggests that we can combine image features from the two views as if they were from one view. Note that the scene is no longer degenerate so, for instance, the fundamental matrix can now be determined (§2.7).

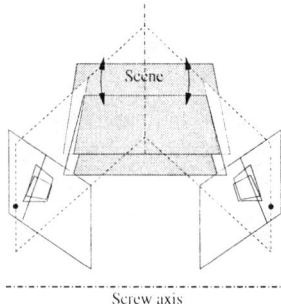

Fig. 4. Camera-centred representation of zero-pitch screw motion

Obtaining Additional Vanishing Points. We observed that a single motion of a binocular rig in a planar scene (in most cases excluding a pan) enables us to construct the image of a point on the scene's horizon, its intersection with the plane at infinity. For this we need an initial view (1) and an elevated view (2). If we also have a panned view (3) we can transfer this vanishing point from view 1 to this view using the planar homographies $H_{l_1 l_3}$ and $H_{r_1 r_3}$. Combining points in all three views, we now have one view of three planes, and a point on the vanishing line of each. Two of them will lie on the elevation-invariant line but the third will not.

2.5 Recovering the Left-Right Infinite Homography, $H_{\infty lr}$

We have established that from three binocular views of a plane related by an elevation followed by a pan we can construct four matched points at infinity. One is the fixation point for alignment (§2.3), the others are points on the vanishing line of the plane in each view (§2.4). We know that $H_{\infty lr}$ is the same in every view; therefore normally four matched points at infinity in the three views would be enough to calculate $H_{\infty lr}$. Unfortunately, three of the points lie on the same line, the line invariant to the elevation.

However the epipole is also a corresponding point for *any* plane-induced homography and so may be used as the fourth point. The epipole can be determined from the planar homographies of the three views without computing the fundamental matrix by observing that the epipole in the right image must be invariant to the matrix $H_{l_1 r_1} H_{l_2 r_2}^{-1}$ [15]. The epipole is the non-degenerate eigenvector of this matrix.

Further rotations and further views can help provide a more accurate estimate of $H_{\infty lr}$: wherever a view is related to another by an elevation, a point on the plane's vanishing line in that view can be calculated, and transferred into other views using plane-to-plane homographies. We have tested a four view method involving one pan and two elevations which results in a total of six distinct matched points at infinity.

2.6   Finding the Camera Internal Parameters

It is well known that the infinite homography H_∞, which maps points at infinity between two images i and j, provides a number of constraints on the images of the absolute conic for those cameras $\omega_{i,j}$, and hence on the internal parameters $K_{i,j}$ [3, 8, 12]. A number of calibration methods take advantage of these constraints directly (cameras related by rotation R):

$$H_\infty = K_j R K_i^{-1}$$
$$\Rightarrow \omega_j = H_\infty^{-\top} \omega_i H_\infty^{-1} \ .$$

If $K_i = K_j$ then one constraint on K such as zero skew ($\delta = 0$ in (1)) enables us to solve for the four remaining unknowns, however in general one cannot assume that the cameras will have identical calibration.

In order to use the infinite homography constraint effectively in our case where we have $H_{\infty lr}$, we solve for the two focal lengths, constraining all other parameters to typical values ($\delta = 0$, (u_0, v_0) = the image centre, and $\alpha = 1$ in (1)). Since these are reasonable assumptions for typical cameras, they do not impact greatly on the accuracy of the focal length estimates, and can be relaxed during a subsequent bundle adjustment phase if required. As they stand, inexact camera parameters can still be used in many tasks such as aiding rapid fixation of a stereo head. [4] shows how to apply the calibration constraints in a simple, linear manner.

2.7   Obtaining Projective Structure and the Plane at Infinity

Although in general our aim has been to achieve as much as possible without computing the explicit epipolar geometry, there is nothing to stop us combining views to this end. After combination we have one stereo view of two (or more) planes, and we can therefore compute the epipolar geometry, using for example,

Pritchett's method [15] (see §2.5). The fundamental matrix can be computed from any left-right plane-induced homography H_{l,r_i} and the epipole e, as $F = [H_{l,r_i} e] \times H_{l,r_i}$ [17].

Projective camera matrices can be computed from F and scene structure generated by backprojection. Unsurprisingly, experiments show that the structure generated by this method is of reasonable quality as long as the rotations are as large as possible.

Naturally we can also backproject the points and lines at infinity we have constructed. From three views we will then have a sufficient number of these to calculate the plane at infinity. For example, it is the null space of the three points on the vanishing line of the scene plane in each view. Knowledge of the plane at infinity enables us to update projective structure to affine, and to Euclidean if we include the calculated calibration.

Given projective structure it might appear we could proceed with the 3D alignment and calibration method of [10, 16]. Unfortunately, the 3D relationships between different views can only be calculated if scene structure is nondegenerate; for planar data they are underconstrained. Even if it were possible to proceed with the 3D method, it would not take full advantage of the constraint that the images are related by 2D homographies.

3 Results

Lens distortion was not modelled in the simulations and was corrected for in real data tests. For our cameras the correction in some cases helped to improve the number of point matches obtained, but in other respects the benefit to the accuracy of results was small.

3.1 Alignment

The alignment algorithm was tested both in simulation and for real data. For the simulation, a cube or plane was generated at random orientations at a fixed distance from the cameras consisting of 200 points at random positions, and the cameras were given random elevation and vergence (within bounds). The rotation angles were 3°. The results are shown in the graphs of Fig. 5. The graphs show the standard deviation of the vergence error σ_θ and that of the elevation error σ_ϕ plotted against noise standard deviation σ_n in pixels. Each plot shows results for a general planar scene, the ground plane method of §2.3, and the motion degeneracy case where the scene is general but we assume the head axes pass through the camera optical centres (so the degenerate alignment algorithm still applies). We also examined the effect of varying the number of feature points available to the algorithm from 200, with σ_n fixed at 0.5 pixels.

The results are encouraging. In real images, noise is rarely over 1 pixel standard deviation, yet we find the error stays below 1°, which is certainly good enough for most tasks. The two-view method off the ground plane seems to work almost as well as the general method, with a worse elevation error but a

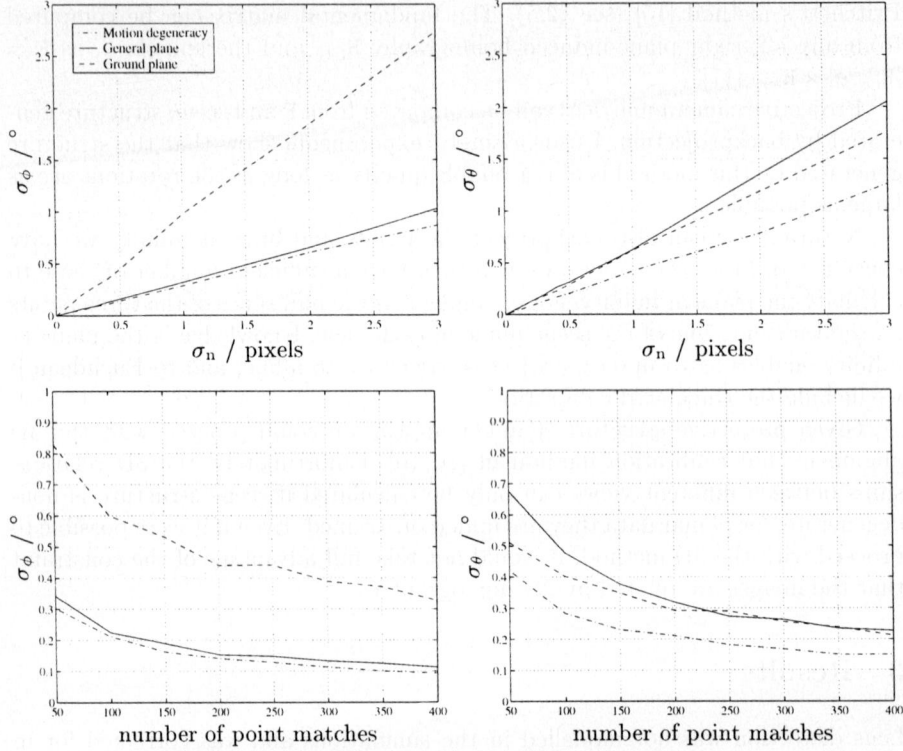

Fig. 5. Alignment simulation results

similar vergence. This is as expected, since the vergence calculation comes from the same technique as the general planar method, while the elevation accuracy relies on the intersection of two image lines which may well be close to parallel and so poorly conditioned (the more distant the plane, the more parallel the vertical invariant lines will appear to each camera).

The algorithm is sensitive to an insufficiency of matched point data, but accuracy is still better than 1° with fairly typical image noise (0.5 pixels) when there are just 50 point matches.

The algorithm was tested on the real scenes of Fig. 6, and the mean error over several tests with different initial orientations of the head (some of which were quite extreme) was taken. Figures 6(a) and 6(b) show the non-degenerate scenes tested, the first having greater depth of structure compared to scene distance, meaning a 2D homography would fit the data less well because of the offset between the rotation axes and the camera centres. Figures 6(c) and 6(d) show the scenes tested for planar alignment, the latter being the ground plane, which was also tested on the two view ground plane alignment algorithm. The lines in the images are the invariant lines.

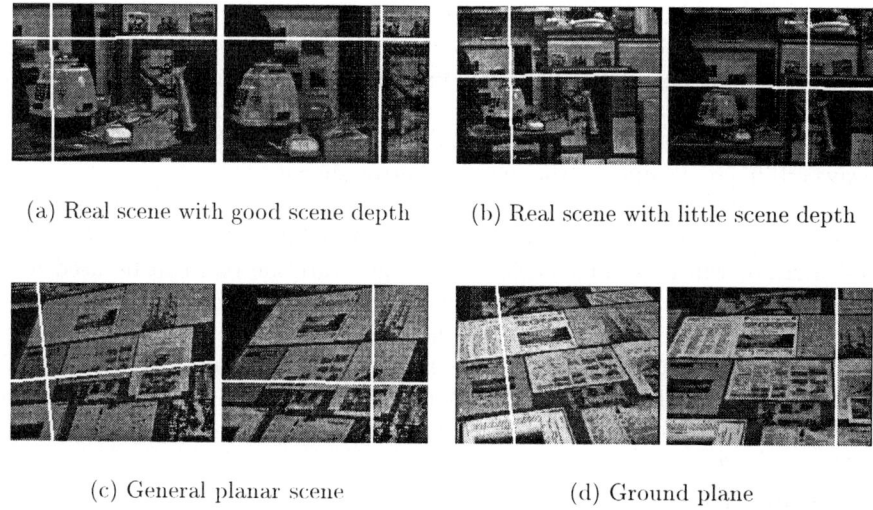

(a) Real scene with good scene depth   (b) Real scene with little scene depth

(c) General planar scene   (d) Ground plane

Fig. 6. Real scenes for alignment tests

Table 1. Alignment results for real data. ϕ refers to elevation, θ_l and θ_r to left and right vergence. Results were obtained by averaging performance over a number of tests.

Figure	Algorithm	Fixation Point	ϕ error (°)	θ_l error (°)	θ_r error (°)
6(a)	Motion degeneracy	in image	0.40	0.29	0.34
	(good scene depth)	off-image	1.58	1.41	1.26
6(b)	Motion degeneracy	in image	0.52	1.58	0.61
	(less scene depth)	off-image	2.40	1.68	0.80
6(c)	General planar	in image	0.78	0.89	0.41
		off-image	0.86	2.12	0.93
6(d)	General planar	off-image	2.09	2.13	0.70
6(d)	Ground plane	off-image	4.71	1.00	0.63

Table 1 shows the alignment results for the real data tests. We have separated the results into mean error when the fixation point was within the image and when it was not. This is because fixating a point off-image without prior knowledge of camera calibration incurs additional inaccuracy unrelated to the alignment algorithm. In the case of the ground plane, the fixation point was always off-image, leading to the increased error shown.

Taking this into account, the results seem to agree with simulation, and suggest the algorithm is genuinely practical. Most interesting, perhaps, is that for our head, which is fairly typical, the degenerate method can be used with good accuracy even where there is considerable structure in the scene because of the near degenerate motion of the head (the head axes pass close enough to the cameras to assume the cameras rotate about their optical centres). We can therefore calculate sufficiently accurate homographic image relationships between views for the algorithm to work well.

3.2 Calibration

Calibration tests were carried out on simulated planar data generated in the same way as in the alignment tests. Figure 7 shows the mean focal length error e_f for each camera as a percentage of the true value.

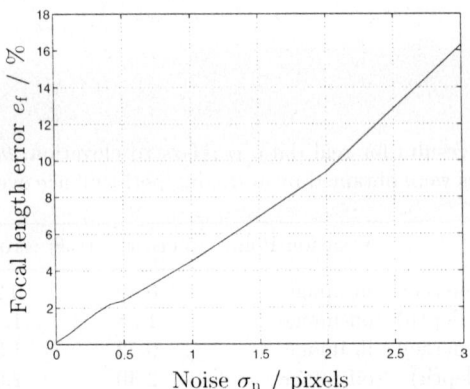

Fig. 7. Calibration simulation results

Calibration was tested on the real scene of Fig. 6(c). We were able to obtain focal length estimates with errors of 16% for the left camera and 15% for the right. Generally, the results were biased towards an overestimate, and somewhat worse than the simulation suggested. Presumably this has to do with the inaccuracy inherent in point matching, a problem which may be solved by the use of direct methods to calculate the homographies. Also, due to the limited size of our scene plane we were forced to restrict the angle of rotation of the head between views, with consequent reduction in the accuracy of the epipole calculation (see the comments of §2.7). The performance could be refined with some sensible adjustments to the algorithm (for instance rejecting results unless there were sufficient point matches), and of course additional views would increase the accuracy.

As expected, using just three views this linear algorithm is not accurate, but it does definitely provide an adequate starting point for bundle adjustment. For calibration we used larger rotations ($8°$–$10°$). Tests showed both alignment and calibration improved the larger the rotation, as long as lack of overlap did not cause too few matches between views. This problem could be overcome by using intermediate images.

4   Summary and Conclusions

We have analysed the invariants and constraints imposed by a stereo pan-tilt head rotating about its axes individually, in a planar scene. We have shown how to construct point matches at infinity in spite of the scene degeneracy, and how to use these to calculate the infinite homography between the left and right camera images given three binocular views of the scene plane, two related by a pan motion, and two related by an elevation. This homography can then be decomposed to give the focal lengths of each camera. Experiments show these focal length estimates to be sufficiently good to be used in a variety of contexts.

One of the points constructed at infinity lies in a direction orthogonal to both head axes. We have used this for self-alignment of the cameras, and shown the algorithm working well in real scenes. In addition we have noted that for a typical stereo head where the rotation axes lie close to the camera optical centres, the relationship between camera images during a rotation will be homographic even in non-degenerate scenes, and the self-alignment algorithm will therefore work equally well. Our experiments have shown that for typical scenes, alignment using this degenerate method works as well as the non-degenerate method of [10, 16], with the advantage of greatly reduced computational expense.

References

1. P. A. Beardsley, I. D. Reid, A. Zisserman, and D. W. Murray. Active visual navigation using non-metric structure. In *Proc. 5th Int'l Conf. on Computer Vision, Boston*, pages 58–65, 1995.
2. P. A. Beardsley and A. Zisserman. Affine calibration of mobile vehicles. In R. Mohr and W. Chengke, editors, *Proc. Joint Europe-China Workshop on Geometrical Modelling and Invariants for Computer Vision, Xi'an, China*, 1995.
3. L. de Agapito, E. Hayman, and I. Reid. Self-calibration of a rotating camera with varying intrinsic parameters. In *Proc. 9th British Machine Vision Conf., Southampton*, volume 1, pages 105–114, 1998.
4. L. deAgapito, R.I. Hartley, and E. Hayman. Linear calibration of a rotating and zooming camera. In *Proc. of the IEEE Conf. on Computer Vision and Pattern Recognition*, pages I:15–21, 1999.
5. Frédéric Devernay and Olivier Faugeras. From projective to euclidean reconstruction. In *Proc. of the IEEE Conf. on Computer Vision and Pattern Recognition, CA*, 1996.

6. F. Du and M. Brady. Self-calibration of the intrinsic parameters of camera for active vision systems. In *Proc. of the IEEE Conf. on Computer Vision and Pattern Recognition*, 1993.

7. O. D. Faugeras, Q.-T. Luong, and S. J. Maybank. Camera self-calibration: Theory and experiments. In *Proc. 2nd European Conf. on Computer Vision, Santa Margharita Ligure, Italy*, pages 321–334, 1992.

8. Richard I. Hartley. Self-calibration of stationary cameras. *International Journal of Computer Vision*, 22(1):5–23, 1997.

9. Radu Horaud and Gabriella Csurka. Self-calibration and euclidean reconstruction using motions of a stereo rig. In *Proc. 6th Int'l Conf. on Computer Vision, Bombay*, pages 96–103, 1998.

10. Joss Knight and Ian Reid. Active visual alignment of a mobile stereo camera platform. In *Proc. International Conference on Robotics and Automation, San Francisco*, 2000.

11. D. Liebowitz and A. Zisserman. Combining scene and auto-calibration constraints. In *Proc. 7th Int'l Conf. on Computer Vision, Corfu*, pages 293–300, 1999.

12. Q.-T. Luong and T. Viéville. Canonic representations for the geometries of multiple projective views. In *Proc. 3rd European Conf. on Computer Vision, Stockholm*, pages 589–599, 1994.

13. P.F. McLauchlan and D.W. Murray. Active camera calibration for a Head-Eye platform using the variable State-Dimension filter. *IEEE Transactions on Pattern Analysis and Machine Intelligence*, 18(1):15–22, 1996.

14. M. Pollefeys, R. Koch, and L. VanGool. Self-calibration and metric reconstruction in spite of varying and unknown internal camera parameters. In *Proc. 6th Int'l Conf. on Computer Vision, Bombay*, pages 90–95, 1998.

15. P. Pritchett and A. Zisserman. Matching and reconstruction from widely separated views. In *Proc. European Workshop on 3D Structure from Multiple Images of Large-Scale Environments, Freiburg*, pages 78–92, 1998.

16. I. D. Reid and P. A. Beardsley. Self-alignment of a binocular head. *Image and Vision Computing*, 1996.

17. D. Sinclair, H. Christensen, and C. Rothwell. Using the relation between a plane projectivity and the fundamental matrix. In *Proc. Scandinavian Image Analysis Conf.*, 1995.

18. G. Stein. Accurate internal camera calibration using rotation, with analysis of sources of error. In *Proc. 5th Int'l Conf. on Computer Vision, Boston*, pages 230–236, 1995.

19. P.F. Sturm and S.J. Maybank. On plane-based camera calibration: A general algorithm, singularities, applications. In *Proc. of the IEEE Conf. on Computer Vision and Pattern Recognition*, pages I:432–437, 1999.

20. B. Triggs. Autocalibration and the absolute quadric. In *Proc. of the IEEE Conf. on Computer Vision and Pattern Recognition*, pages 609–614, 1997.

21. Bill Triggs. Autocalibration from planar scenes. In *Proc. 5th European Conf. on Computer Vision, Freiburg*, volume 1, pages 89–105, 1998. Extended version available at http://www.inrialpes.fr/movi/people/Triggs/publications.html.

22. Z.Y. Zhang. Flexible camera calibration by viewing a plane from unknown orientations. In *Proc. 7th Int'l Conf. on Computer Vision, Corfu*, pages 666–673, 1999.

23. A. Zisserman, P. A. Beardsley, and I. D. Reid. Metric calibration of a stereo rig. In *Proc. IEEE Workshop on Representations of Visual Scenes, Boston*, pages 93–100, 1995.

The Rôle of Self-Calibration in Euclidean Reconstruction from Two Rotating and Zooming Cameras

Eric Hayman, Lourdes de Agapito, Ian D. Reid, and David W. Murray *

Department of Engineering Science, University of Oxford
Parks Road, Oxford OX1 3PJ, UK
{hayman,lourdes,ian,dwm}@robots.ox.ac.uk
http://www.robots.ox.ac.uk/ActiveVision/

Abstract. Reconstructing the scene from image sequences captured by moving cameras with varying intrinsic parameters is one of the major achievements of computer vision research in recent years. However, there remain gaps in the knowledge of what is reliably recoverable when the camera motion is constrained to move in particular ways. This paper considers the special case of multiple cameras whose optic centres are fixed in space, but which are allowed to rotate and zoom freely, an arrangement seen widely in practical applications. The analysis is restricted to two such cameras, although the methods are readily extended to more than two.

As a starting point an initial self-calibration of each camera is obtained independently. The first contribution of this paper is to provide an analysis of near-ambiguities which commonly arise in the self-calibration of rotating cameras. Secondly we demonstrate how their effects may be mitigated by exploiting the epipolar geometry. Results on simulated and real data are presented to demonstrate how a number of self-calibration methods perform, including a final bundle-adjustment of all motion and structure parameters.

1 Introduction

A configuration of cameras which occurs commonly in a number of imaging applications is that of multiple well-separated cameras whose optic centres are fixed in space, but which freely and independently (i) rotate about their optical centres and (ii) zoom in and out. This arrangement is used in surveillance and in broadcasting (particularly outside broadcasting), and is a pattern for acquiring models for virtual and augmented reality, where full or partial panoramas are taken from different positions around a building, for example.

What are the ways of handling the combined imagery from, say, two such uncalibrated cameras to recover a Euclidean reconstruction of a static scene? The least committed approach might be to generate a projective reconstruction, enforcing the zero

* This work is supported by the UK Engineering and Physical Science Research Council through Grant GR/L58668 (D.W.M) and an Advanced Research Fellowship (I.D.R.), by the Norwegian Research Council (E.H.) and by the Spanish Ministry of Education and Science (L.A.).

translation constraint within the images from a single camera, but then using overall a self-calibration algorithm for general motion, such as those of Pollefeys et al. [11], Heyden and Åström [9] or Hartley et al. [7]. A practical disadvantage is that general motion methods require locating the plane at infinity, but a broader criticism is that the motion is far from general.

The most committed (and perhaps most obvious) approach is to self-calibrate each rotating camera independently, for which methods have been described in the literature [3, 2, 12, 13]. The task of reconstruction is then reduced to the more familiar one of structure from multiple views using calibrated cameras. Although dealing with each camera separately is attractive since it reduces the problem to a set of smaller, less complex ones, this method is likely to give poor results if the initial self-calibration is inaccurate. Moreover it is clearly not using all the available information.

The results in this paper provide two pieces of information which inform the solution from the spectrum of those available.

- There are some near-ambiguities in self-calibration of rotating cameras which can have a large effect both on the camera intrinsics and a reconstruction obtained from them. These effects are present when the self-calibration problem is ill-conditioned, in particular with small motions, large focal lengths, short image sequences and a poor spread of image features. They can be mitigated by modelling them correctly.
- Modelling the appropriate degree of inter-camera coupling is desirable. It proves useful to exploit the epipolar geometry not only to recover the relative positions of the two cameras, but also to refine the self-calibration of both sets of intrinsic parameters.

Two very different measures are used to characterize performance. The rms *reconstruction error* measures the distance between points in two rescaled and aligned Euclidean reconstructions. The rms *reprojection error* measures the faithfulness of reconstruction in the image: a low value implies that coplanarity and collinearity are well preserved, but it provides little information regarding the preservation of angles.

Results from any point in the spectrum of solutions may always be used to initialize a bundle-adjustment over all scene points and motion parameters, minimizing reprojection error. However, in addition to its cost implications for on-line use, bundle-adjustment is susceptible to convergence to local minima. The latter is critical in this context where a number of near-ambiguities are present since bundle-adjustment tends to make only very small changes to the motion parameters. Hence even if the reprojection error is reduced, there is by no means a guarantee of a significant change in reconstruction error. One goal of this work is to find algorithms which are good enough either to make bundle-adjustment unnecessary or to provide better initial estimates to increase the chance of convergence to the correct solution within it.

After introducing briefly the theory of self-calibration of rotating and zooming cameras in Section 2 we investigate precisely what information can and cannot be reliably extracted from such algorithms in Section 3. In particular we describe two near-ambiguities which commonly arise. In Section 4 we review the structure from motion algorithm of two calibrated views which we modify to resolve the ambiguities while minimizing epipolar transfer error. Experiments on synthetic and real data are presented in Section 5.

2 Self-Calibrating Rotating and Zooming Cameras: Review

The imaging process is modelled by the pinhole camera model so that in the ith image, the projection $\mathbf{x}_i$ of a point $\mathbf{X}$ in the scene is described by the relation $\mathbf{x}_i = P_i \mathbf{X}$ where $\mathbf{x}_i$ and $\mathbf{X}$ are both given in homogeneous coordinates, implying that all vectors, matrices and equations are only defined up to an unknown scale factor. P_i is a 3×4 projection matrix which may be decomposed as $P_i = K_i (R_i \ \mathbf{t}_i)$ where R_i and $\mathbf{t}_i$ describe the transformation between a coordinate frame attached to the scene and a camera centred coordinate system. K_i is the matrix of intrinsic parameters in image i and has the usual form

$$K = \begin{pmatrix} \alpha_u & s & u_0 \\ 0 & \alpha_v & v_0 \\ 0 & 0 & 1 \end{pmatrix} . \tag{1}$$

α_u and α_v are the focal lengths in the u and v directions, $(u_0 \ v_0)$ are the coordinates of the principal point, and s is a parameter that describes the skew between the two axes of the CCD array.

In the case of a camera rotating about its optic centre, $\mathbf{t} = \mathbf{0}$, the final coordinate of $\mathbf{X} = (X \ Y \ Z \ 1)^\top$ is immaterial, and the projection equation simplifies to $\mathbf{x}_i = K_i R_i (X \ Y \ Z)^\top$. Different images taken from the same rotating camera relate to each other by homographies which take the form

$$\mathbf{x}_j = H_{ij} \mathbf{x}_i = K_j R_j R_i^{-1} K_i^{-1} \mathbf{x}_i = K_j R_{ij} K_i^{-1} \mathbf{x}_i . \tag{2}$$

The inter-image homographies H_{ij} may be calculated directly from image measurements, for instance from point or line correspondences. Various techniques for this calculation are available, ranging from fast linear methods minimizing an algebraic error, via non-linear methods which minimize the geometric transfer error, to a bundle-adjustment in the motion and structure parameters, the structure comprises points on a mosaic.

Eliminating R_{ij} from equation (2) yields

$$\left(K_j K_j^\top \right) = H_{ij} \left(K_i K_i^\top \right) H_{ij}^\top , \tag{3}$$

which can also be derived by projecting a point on the plane at infinity, $\mathbf{X} = (X \ Y \ Z \ 0)^\top$, into a camera with a non-zero fourth column in P_i. The observed inter-image homographies H_{ij} are thus the homographies induced by the plane at infinity, and equation (3) is known as the *infinite homography constraint*. $\boldsymbol{\omega}^* = K_i K_i^\top$ is the dual of the image of the absolute conic (DIAC).

Given the homographies, H_{ij}, equation (3) provides constraints on the intrinsic parameters. If the camera intrinsics are constant throughout the sequence, the constraint reduces to that of Hartley in [6], the DIAC may be computed linearly, and the matrix K is found from it by Cholesky decomposition.

For varying intrinsics, de Agapito et al. [3] solve equation (3) in a manner similar to that of Pollefeys et al. [11] for cameras undergoing general motion. In a non-linear optimization the cost function

$$\mathcal{D} = \sum_{i=1}^{n} \| K_i K_i{}^{\top} - H_{0i} K_0 K_0{}^{\top} H_{0i}{}^{\top} \|_F^2 \qquad (4)$$

is minimized, where the elements of $K_i, i = 0...n$, are the unknown parameters. To eliminate the unknown scale factors, $K_i K_i{}^{\top}$ and $H_{0i} K_0 K_0{}^{\top} H_{0i}{}^{\top}$ are normalized so that their Frobenius norms are equal to one. An advantage of this approach is that any constraints on the intrinsic parameters, such as zero skew or known aspect ratio may be applied directly. Alternatively, parameters such as the aspect ratio or principal point can be solved for, but constrained to be constant throughout the sequence. A similar approach was adopted by Seo and Hong [12], but under known skew and principal point they note that the focal lengths can be computed linearly from equation (3).

In a later work [2] de Agapito et al. proposed a fast linear method for calculating all intrinsic parameters by employing an algebraic trick, used previously in another context by Armstrong et al. [1]. They dealt not with the DIAC, but with its *inverse*, the image of the absolute conic (IAC), ω. Under the assumption of zero skew the IAC is given by

$$\omega = K^{-\top} K^{-1} = \begin{pmatrix} 1/\alpha_u^2 & 0 & -u_0/\alpha_u^2 \\ 0 & 1/\alpha_v^2 & -v_0/\alpha_v^2 \\ -u_0/\alpha_u^2 & -v_0/\alpha_v^2 & 1 + u_0^2/\alpha_u^2 + v_0^2/\alpha_v^2 \end{pmatrix}. \qquad (5)$$

Inverting the infinite homography constraint, $\omega_j = H_{ij}{}^{-\top} \omega_i H_{ij}^{-1}$, provides linear constraints on the IAC in frame i by setting the (1,2) element of ω_j to zero. Further constraints are available from additional assumptions on the intrinsic parameters, in particular, a known aspect ratio and/or a known principal point.

Most recently, optimal results have been obtained by de Agapito et al. [4] by performing a final bundle-adjustment in the motion and structure parameters.

2.1 Recovering Rotation Matrices and Euclidean Projection Matrices

For reconstruction, Euclidean projection matrices of the form $P_i = (\bar{P}_i \ 0) = (K_i R_i \ 0)$ are required. The 3×3 left sub-matrices, $\bar{P}_i$, are recovered from the projective homographies as $H_{0i} K_0$. Rotation matrices, referred to the initial frame, may be found by QR decomposition of $\bar{P}_i$.

A more direct approach for finding rotations would be to use the recovered K_i matrices directly in the equation $R_i = K_i^{-1} H_{0i} K_0$. However, it can be unwise to apply this equation in combination with the non-linear self-calibration method of [3], especially when the principal point is constrained to be constant throughout the sequence in the minimization. The reason is that with fewer parameters in the model, the R_i recovered from $K_i^{-1} H_{0i} K_0$ are less close to orthonormal. Even fitting an orthonormal matrix to R_i by setting the singular values of its SVD to unity does not guarantee that this rotation matrix is the correct one, especially since it is an algebraic error (a Frobenius norm) that is minimized when projecting $K_i^{-1} H_{0i} K_0$ onto the 3-dimensional space of orthonormal matrices. This method could therefore give poor motion recovery and have dire consequences for Euclidean reconstruction. Rays would be back-projected incorrectly, and a large reprojection error ensue. In this work we therefore adopt the approach based on QR decomposition when using the non-linear self-calibration algorithm.

Since the linear self-calibration method of [2] is not parameterized directly in terms of camera intrinsics, it does not suffer from the problems of non-orthonormal matrices, and the two approaches for recovering R_i are equivalent.

With pan-tilt cameras rotations are described by two rather than three parameters. A practical treatment of the decomposition of rotation matrices into these two parameters is provided in [8].

3 Ambiguities in Self-Calibration

Self-calibration is an ill-conditioned problem. Significant advances have been made since the work of Maybank and Faugeras, but there are a few underlying ambiguities which can have a large effect on results in configurations which poorly constrain the solution, coupled changes in the parameters in the model are barely observable. We consider two ambiguities present in the case of rotating cameras. It would be more correct to call these *near*-ambiguities: as opposed to true ambiguities which arise from certain motions and scenes [14, 17], ours are only apparent because perspective effects in the cameras are less prominent under some camera configurations. A discussion of their relevance to reconstruction, motivated by experimental results, is provided in Section 6.

3.1 The Ambiguity between the Angle of Rotation and the Focal Length

For small rotations there is an ambiguity between the rotation and the focal length, and it is difficult to distinguish between small rotations with a large focal length and larger rotations with a small focal length. The ambiguity is easily seen by differentiating the calibrated non-homogeneous projection equation $\mathbf{x} = (\alpha/Z)\mathbf{X}$. Remembering that there is no translation, and secondly that the focal length α is a function of time, differentiation yields the following image motion in the x-direction

$$\dot{x} = +\alpha\Omega_Y - y\Omega_Z + \frac{x}{\alpha}(x\Omega_Y - y\Omega_X) + \frac{\dot{\alpha}x}{\alpha}, \qquad (6)$$

where $\mathbf{x}$ and $\mathbf{X}$ are expressed in camera centred frames and Ω is the angular velocity.

Cyclorotation and the *relative* change in focal length can be recovered from the terms $-y\Omega_Z$ and $\dot{\alpha}x/\alpha$ respectively (the latter is zoom-induced looming motion). However, the first term $\alpha\Omega_Y$, a uniform motion in the image due to the component of rotation perpendicular to the optic axis, contains an ambiguity between focal length and rotation. The third term $(x/\alpha)(x\Omega_Y - y\Omega_X)$, which also arises from the component of rotation perpendicular to the optic axis, provides some disambiguating information, but the term is likely to be small except at the edges of the image. Unfortunately this is also where the optical properties of the lens are poorest. Notice too that the disambiguating information is weakest for large focal lengths. Compounding these difficulties is that in practical applications, sequences taken at large α are less likely to contain significant rotation. Since motion is being integrated over time, this ambiguity persists over a sequence of images.

In experiments we find that the ambiguity is much more pronounced when the principal point is allowed to vary in the self-calibration algorithm: with more parameters, the model is more likely to fit to the noise rather than the underlying true solution. However, if the sequence is ill-conditioned, the ambiguity is also noticeable even if the principal point is constrained to a constant location.

3.2 The Principal Point/Rotation Ambiguity

A similar analysis (again using the x-dimension of the image motion) shows that it is difficult to distinguish between a shift in the principal point along x and a rotation of the camera about y. If δu is the error in the estimation of the principal point, and α is the focal length, the erroneous rotation is $\sim \delta u/\alpha$ about y. This is an ambiguity between parameters from a single image.

Another way of describing this ambiguity is that a large focal length perspective projection is hard to distinguish from a spherical projection where the principal point is meaningless.

3.3 Experiments

Figures 1 and 2 illustrate these ambiguities using both simulated and real image data. The "bookshelf" sequence [3], was gathered by zooming while moving the vergence and elevation axes of one camera of a stereo head (equivalent to pan and tilt, up to an ordering of the the kinematic chain) so that the optic axis traced a right-circular cone. Point features were detected and matched, and homographies derived. Figure 1 shows the resulting mosaic. Simulated point data were synthesized similarly. Levenberg-Marquardt was used to minimize $\mathcal{D}$ in equation (4) allowing the principal point and focal length to vary over the sequence during minimization. (That is, in the minimization there are different values to be found for each frame, rather than a single value to be found for the whole sequence.)

In each set of results the first two plots show the recovered and veridical focal length and principal point. The + symbols in the third plots show the recovered camera motion in terms of elevation and vergence angles. These are roughly circular, but there is a good deal of scatter about the best-fit circle.

In earlier work it was supposed that this scatter arose from noise [3]. However it turns out to be almost entirely due to the principal-point/rotation ambiguity. Using the ground truth value for the position of the principal point, the elevation and vergence angles are corrected and re-plotted as × symbols. These form near perfect circles.

However, the scale of the motion is still incorrect. This is due to the ambiguity between focal length/motion. Table 1 illustrates this point with the recovered scale of focal length and motion compared to the ground truth: multiplied together they give a number very close to unity.

Fig. 1. A Mosaic constructed from the bookshelf sequence during which the camera panned and tilted while the lens zoomed.

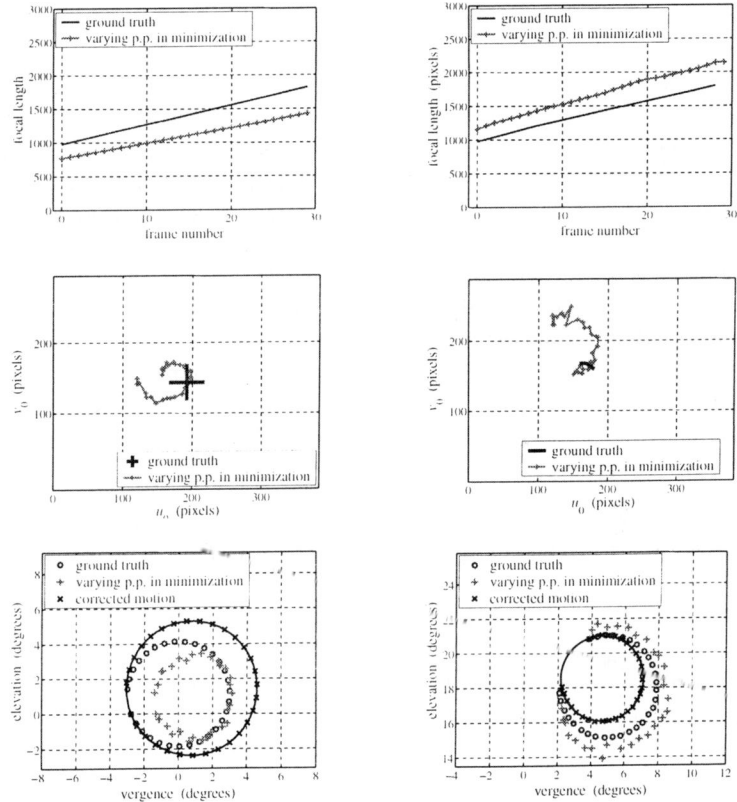

Fig. 2. Correcting the elevation and vergence angles by accepting the principal-point/rotation ambiguity. Parts (a) uses simulated data, (b) real data. Both sequences use a linearly increasing focal length and motion with cone half angle $3°$.

	Recovered α / true α	Radius of recovered motion / radius of true motion	Product of the two
Synthetic data, varying α	0.7819	1.2789	1.000
Real images, varying α	1.198	0.826	0.989

Table 1. Verification of the ambiguity between focal length and motion exhibited in Figure 2.

4 Improving Self-Calibration via the Epipolar Geometry

We now turn to the second theme of the paper; using the appropriate degree of coupling between the two rotating cameras to improve the self-calibration of each, and then also improve the reconstruction. The methods utilize epipolar geometry and it is convenient first to review the work of, among others, Longuet-Higgins [10] and Zhang [16].

4.1 Stereo from Calibrated Cameras: Review

The geometry of two calibrated views is encapsulated in the essential matrix, E [10]. Corresponding image points $\mathbf{x}$ and $\mathbf{x}'$ in the first and second views are related by $\mathbf{x}'^\top E \mathbf{x} = 0$ where $E = [\mathbf{t}]_\times R$, and $[\mathbf{t}]_\times$ is the skew-symmetric form of the translation vector, $\mathbf{t}$, describing the location of the optic centre of the second camera in the coordinate frame of the first. R is the relative rotation of the two cameras. E has five degrees of freedom, three for the rotation and two for translation up to scale. Since $[\mathbf{t}]_\times$ is rank two, so is E, and the nullspace of E is $\mathbf{t}$. R may be recovered from E and $\mathbf{t}$ using quaternions.

The solution is refined with an algorithm due to Zhang [16] which uses the *uncalibrated* image measurements directly. For uncalibrated views the fundamental matrix, F, plays a similar role to E, and the two matrices relate as $F = K'^{-\top} E K^{-1}$ where K and K' are the intrinsic parameters for the first and second camera respectively. F is calculated directly from image measurements. An initial estimate of F is provided by the linear 8-point algorithm. The fundamental matrix is refined by minimizing a cost function with geometric significance, the distance between points and epipolar lines,

$$
\mathcal{E} = \sum_k d^2(\mathbf{x}'^k, F\mathbf{x}^k) + d^2(\mathbf{x}^k, F^\top \mathbf{x}'^k), \quad d(\mathbf{x}^k, F^\top \mathbf{x}'^k) = \frac{\mathbf{x}^{k\top} F \mathbf{x}'^k}{\sqrt{(F\mathbf{x}'^k)_1^2 + (F\mathbf{x}'^k)_2^2}}
$$

(7)

where the superscripts denote a particular point correspondence and $(F\mathbf{x}'^k)_j$ is the jth component of the vector $(F\mathbf{x}'^k)$. Thus, given F and the calibration matrices, E may be recovered and decomposed. The five parameters in R and $\mathbf{t}$ are then refined using the same geometric measure as above. $\mathbf{t}$ is parameterized by a point on the unit sphere, and R by a rotation vector[1].

Having computed R, $\mathbf{t}$ and the self-calibration of each camera the scene may now readily be reconstructed, using not just the images from one stereo pair, but also further images. The projection matrices from the first and second cameras, P and P', in images i and i' respectively take the form

$$
P_i = K_i R_i \begin{pmatrix} I & \mathbf{0} \end{pmatrix} \quad \text{and} \quad P'_{i'} = K'_{i'} R'_{i'} \begin{pmatrix} R & \mathbf{t} \end{pmatrix} .
$$

(8)

3D points are found by the intersection of rays back-projected using these camera matrices. We will evaluate this algorithm in the experimental section.

---

[1] Zhang also performs a final bundle-adjustment over these five parameters and the 3D structure.

4.2 Constraints from the Epipolar Geometry of Two Rotating Cameras

The method given above uses only a single stereo pair to compute R and t and is clearly discarding a lot of information. Although we now have sufficient information to obtain a Euclidean reconstruction from the entire sequence, the result will be heavily biased towards the first pair.

Besides, since the fundamental matrix has seven degrees of freedom, and the essential matrix only five, it is possible to solve for two further parameters in K and K' just from the single pair. This is indeed done by Hartley in [5] and Pollefeys *et al.* in [11] who use linear methods to solve for the focal lengths assuming the principal points, aspect ratios and skew are known. However, in our case the special geometry may be used to greater effect by relating additional frames in either sequence to the original frame via the inter-image homographies.

We now write the epipolar constraint between correspondence k in image i from the first camera and image i' from the second as

$$\mathbf{x'}_{i'}^{k}{}^{\top} F_{ii'} \mathbf{x}_i^k = 0 \ . \tag{9}$$

As before, quantities without a dash refer to camera 1 and those with a dash to camera 2, subscripts relate to the frame number and superscripts to point correspondences. Choosing a reference frame from either camera gives

$$F_{00} = K_0'{}^{-\top} [\mathbf{t}]_\times R K_0^{-1} \ . \tag{10}$$

The fundamental matrix between two further images i and i' from each rotating camera relate to F_{00} as

$$F_{ii'} = H_{i'}'{}^{-\top} F_{00} H_i^{-1} \ . \tag{11}$$

Parameterizing $F_{ii'}$ in terms of F_{00}, points from several image pairs are used to refine our estimate of F_{00}, and thus also R and t. This is the second reconstruction algorithm we will investigate. The cost function minimized is the sum of epipolar distances over all measured points and also all images pairs,

$$\mathcal{F} = \sum_{i,i'} \sum_k d^2(\mathbf{x'}_{i'}^k, F_{ii'} \mathbf{x}_i^k) + d^2(\mathbf{x}_i^k, F_{ii'}{}^{\top} \mathbf{x'}_{i'}^k) \ . \tag{12}$$

Any combinations of i and i' may be chosen, provided image correspondences are available. Since $\mathcal{F}$ is a cost function with geometric significance there is a strong correlation with the reprojection error, but it is not the optimal error.

4.3 Improving Self-Calibration and Reconstruction

Now, since $H_i = K_i R_i K_0^{-1}$ we have that

$$F_{ii'} = K_{i'}'{}^{-\top} R_{i'}' [\mathbf{t}]_\times R R_i{}^{\top} K_i^{-1} \ . \tag{13}$$

Thus, estimates of (i) the relative camera positions R and t in a reference frame, (ii) the intrinsic parameters in both cameras at each frame in the sequence, and (iii) the rotations between frames within sequences from either camera, yield an estimate of the fundamental matrix $F_{ii'}$ between further frames of cameras 1 and 2. The goodness of this *modelled* fundamental matrix may then be measured with the cost function $\mathcal{F}$ in equation (12). Not only may further image pairs be used to provide further constraints on R and t, further parameters may be solved for. Effectively we are constraining the inter-image homographies together with fundamental matrices. This insight provides the basis of the methods we derive for improving the self-calibration, and thus also the reconstruction.

We now introduce two methods of self-calibration refinement, depending on which ambiguities of Section 3 we wish to resolve. To parameterize the unknowns we write the *true* matrix of intrinsic parameters as

$$K_i = \begin{pmatrix} \frac{1}{\beta}\hat{\alpha}_i & 0 & (u_0)_i \\ 0 & \frac{1}{\beta}\hat{\alpha}_i & (v_0)_i \\ 0 & 0 & 1 \end{pmatrix} \tag{14}$$

where $\hat{\alpha}_i$ is the *measured* focal length recovered from independent self-calibration of the rotating cameras, and where β is the unknown overall scale factor of the focal lengths of this camera over the entire sequence. Skew is assumed to be zero and the aspect ratio to be either known from the outset or recovered during self-calibration of each rotating camera. We also assume in both methods that the rotation matrices within a single camera have only two degrees of freedom, taking the form

$$R = R_y(\theta)R_x(\phi) . \tag{15}$$

This is justifiable since pan-tilt cameras are restricted to this kind of motion (the ordering of R_y and R_x depends on the particular kinematic chain).

Method (1) deals only with the ambiguity between focal length and angle of rotation described in Section 3.1. Thus we solve for seven parameters, five for the motion and two for the overall scale of the focal lengths, β and β'. The true principal point (u_0, v_0) is assumed to be known from the self-calibration. The method is predicated on the assumption that rotations are small enough to model the ambiguity between focal length and rotation by requiring the *true* rotation matrix R_i to relate to the *measured* angles $\hat{\theta}_i$ and $\hat{\phi}_i$ as

$$R_i = R_y(\beta\hat{\theta}_i)R_x(\beta\hat{\phi}_i) . \tag{16}$$

Method (2) seeks also to resolve the ambiguity between principal point and motion described in Section 3.2, and thus the number of parameters is $7 + 2n + 2n'$ where n and n' are the number of images from the two cameras. Method (2) models R_i by subtracting the erroneous motion caused by the ambiguity between rotations and motion of the principal point,

$$R_i = R_y\left(\beta\left(\hat{\theta}_i - \frac{u_0 - \hat{u}_0}{\hat{\alpha}_i}\right)\right) R_x\left(\beta\left(\hat{\phi}_i - \frac{v_0 - \hat{v}_0}{\hat{\alpha}_i}\right)\right) \tag{17}$$

where $(\hat{u}_0, \hat{v}_0)$ is the *measured* principal point from self-calibration of a rotating camera whereas (u_0, v_0) is its true value. The idea behind method (2) is based on the experimental results of Section 3.3 where erroneous motion of the principal point is removed and the ambiguity between focal length and motion accounts for the remaining discrepancy from the ground truth.

4.4 Implementation Issues

Combining the information from two types of input, namely homographies and epipolar geometry, in order to provide accurate self-calibration and reconstruction places emphasis in methods (1) and (2) on retaining as much information from the initial self-calibration as possible. Two important issues are therefore *initialization* and *applying priors*.

In our current implementation an initial estimate of, β, and similarly β', are obtained by re-solving for only this single parameter in the non-linear self-calibration method. The prior is then found by investigating the curvature matrix $J^\top J$, where J is the Jacobian. In this case $J^\top J$ is a 1×1 matrix. In fact, experiments with a prior chosen more arbitrarily, and with β and β' initialized at unity, also worked well.

Furthermore, if the principal point was allowed to vary in the initial self-calibration, the correction devised in section 3.3 may be applied to initialize the principal point and motion in refinement methods (1) and (2). However, that example used ground truth of the principal point in the correction. Since such information is not available here, we initialize the principal point either at the centre of the image plane or with that obtained from the non-linear self-calibration method where the principal point is maintained at a fixed but unknown value throughout the sequence.

In our experiments we noticed that method (2) converges much more slowly than method (1). Therefore we choose only to use method (2) to refine the output from method (1).

4.5 Refining the Solution Using Bundle-Adjustment

The motion and structure parameters may be refined using a large non-linear minimization over all parameters, making use of the sparse form of the Jacobian. The cost function for the optimization is the reprojection error over all points and views,

$$C = \sum_{\text{views}} \sum_{\text{points}} \|\mathbf{x} - K (R \ \mathbf{t}) \mathbf{X}\|^2 \qquad (18)$$

which provides a maximum likelihood estimate of the structure and motion. Each point $\mathbf{X}$ in the structure has either two or three degrees of freedom depending on whether it is visible from both cameras or only a single camera.

Bundle-adjustment is thus guaranteed to reduce the reprojection error, but not necessarily the reconstruction error. Of course the reconstruction gained is a valid Euclidean one in the sense that the projection matrices have the required form if parameterized as $P = K(R \ \mathbf{t})$, but it may easily "look" more projective than Euclidean in that angles are skew, and length ratios are not preserved correctly. It would be naïve to expect bundle-adjustment to automatically cope with the inherent ambiguities which are present, the more so as it is prone to convergence to local rather than global minima. The parameters tend to change only by small amounts, and the final set of parameters differ little from the initial estimate.

5   Experiments and Results

Experiments were conducted first on simulated data to allow controlled investigation of the sensitivity of the reconstruction techniques to varying noise, and varying separation of the two cameras. The data were generated so as to correspond roughly with later experiments on real imagery. The image sizes were 384×288 pixels, and one camera had a focal length ranging from $1000 - 1870$ pixels and a circular motion in the elevation and vergence axes of $4°$. The second camera had a longer focal length, $1250 - 2120$ pixels, and a smaller circular motion of $3°$. The principal point used to generate the data moved between frames with an overall motion of approximately 20 pixels.

The self-calibration and reconstruction algorithms are summarized in Table 2.

Result 1. The principal result is that a significant improvement can indeed be achieved by our method of refining the self-calibration using epipolar geometry. In Figure 3 we compare both the reconstruction error and the reprojection error as a function of image position noise with no refinement of the self-calibration (using single and multiple views to calculate R and **t**); and with refinement using method (1) of Section 4.3 which only handles the focal length/rotation ambiguity. Priors on the scale factor were obtained automatically from the method of Section 4.4.

Result 2. The performance of the algorithms with varying separation of the two cameras is shown in Figure 4. As before, a significant improvement may be obtained with our novel methods, especially when the cameras are close together, pointing in a similar average direction.

Whereas Result 1 used linear methods of recovering the homographies, and the linear method of initial self-calibration, and Levenberg-Marquardt for the minimization of the refinement cost function, and so is the fastest approach, this second experiment explores the other extreme. It uses bundle-adjusted homographies, the non-linear (LM) self-calibration, non-linear refinement, and finally bundle-adjusts the entire solution, solving for the focal length, principal point and two rotation parameters per camera, assuming square pixels. Furthermore, a longer image sequence (30 rather than 20 images) and more point correspondences (300 rather than 50 matches between images) were used. Again the refined method works much better than non-refined, and adding a final bundle-adjustment gives only a small further improvement. Notice that the results

Algorithm outline	
Description	Label used in keys of graphs
A. Self-calibrate each camera individually	
B. Compute R and **t** from a single image pair	No refinement, single image pair
OR compute R and **t** from multiple image pairs	No refinement, multiple image pairs
C. Refine solution from B by resolving focal length/rotation ambiguity	Method (1)
D. (optional) Refine solution from C by resolving focal length/rotation and principal point/rotation ambiguities.	Method (2)
E. (optional) Bundle-adjustment, initialized at above solution	Bundle-adjustment

Table 2. The algorithms evaluated in the experiments.

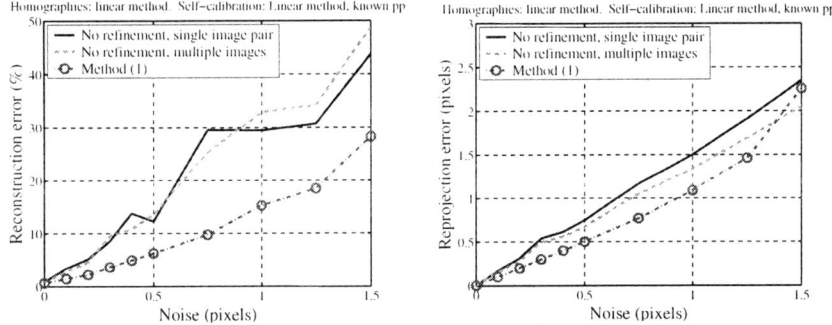

Fig. 3. The reconstruction and reprojection errors of different levels of noise, showing that the refinement of the self-calibration using epipolar geometry provides a significant improvement. (The angle between the principal directions of the cameras was fixed at $20°$.)

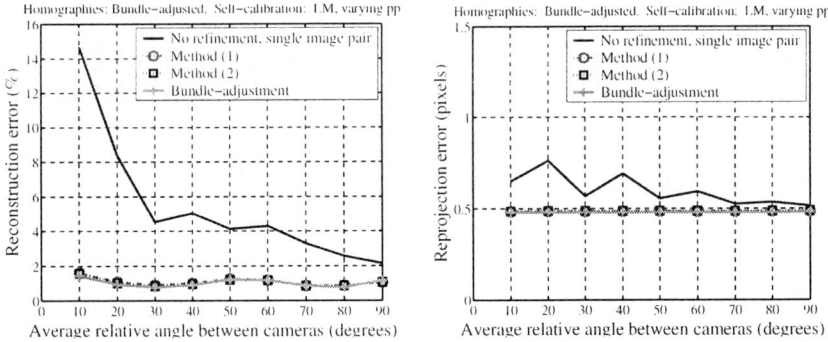

Fig. 4. The performance of the reconstruction techniques for different relative positions of the two cameras. Both cameras perform small rotational motions about some initial direction, the angle between the principal directions of the two cameras is plotted on the x-axis. In this experiment the noise was constant at $\sigma = 0.5$ pixels.

from method (2), which handles both ambiguities (focal length/rotation and principal point/rotation) is virtually indistinguishable from those from method (1) which handles only the former.

Result 3. Figure 5 demonstrates the sensitivity of bundle-adjustment to the initial estimate. A Euclidean bundle-adjustment is initialized with the output from the initial self-calibration, first with varying and then with fixed principal point in the minimization, and also with the output from our refinement method (2). Only small changes in parameters occur, and the reduction in reconstruction error is minimal.

5.1 Real Data

Two zoom sequences of a point grid, were taken with one of the cameras on a stereo head, using the common elevation and one of the vergence axes to generate the motion.

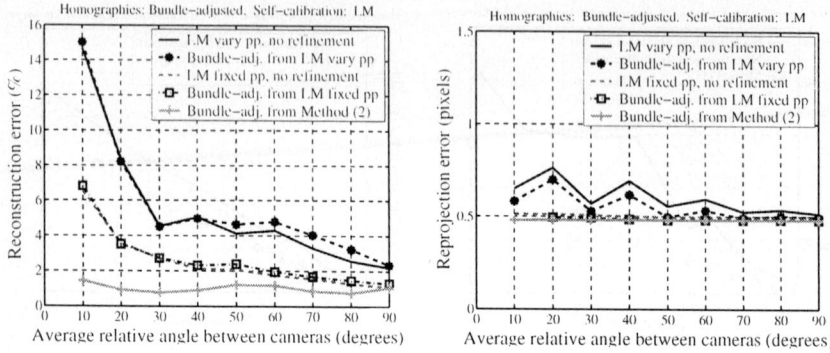

Fig. 5. A good initial estimate is crucial for bundle-adjustment. Using the present method for initialization yields much better results than when the bundle-adjustment is applied directly after self-calibration.

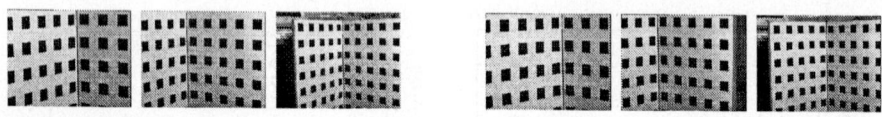

Fig. 6. The first, tenth and last images of the 20 frames of the sequences used from each camera. That the sequences were taken from viewpoints very close together is reflected in the similarity between the sequences.

Since we know the structure of the grid, we may measure results accurately, and the quality of the ensuing reconstruction is easily visualized. In the first sequence the focal length was varied between 1400 and 800 pixels (i.e. zooming out) with a circular motion of half-cone $2.5°$. In the second the focal length decreased from 1700 to 1100 pixels, and the circular motion was $2°$. Between the sequences the head was moved to provide a finite baseline. The angle between the scene and the two optic centres was approximately $10°$. The first, tenth and last images from a 20 image sequence are shown in Figure 6.

The motion in these sequences is very small, and the initial self-calibration was found to vary considerably depending on which algorithms were used to calculate the homographies and self-calibration, and how many images were used. Results from three experiments are summarized in Table 3, and Figure 7 shows reconstructions of the scene with and without refinement. Again, the novel methods presented in this paper provide a very significant improvement.

6 Conclusions

In this paper we have shown how systematic inaccuracies in the self-calibration of rotating cameras apparent in [3] can be accounted for by the ambiguities inherent in rotating motion fields. These effects are particularly keenly felt when small motions, large focal lengths, short image sequences and a poor spread of image features are involved.

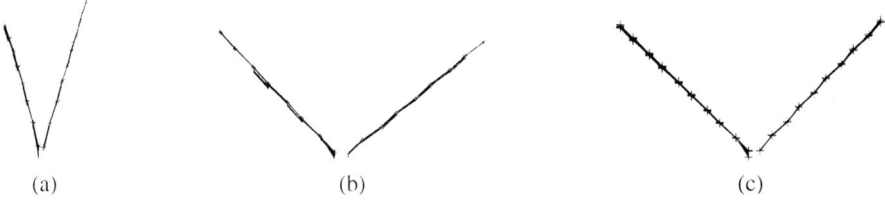

(a)   (b)   (c)

Fig. 7. Plan views of the reconstructed scene. (a) represents the fourth row of Table 3, using homographies calculated from the linear method, and the relative motion from a single image pair with no refinement. (b) demonstrates refinement method (1) applied to this reconstruction (row 6 in the table). (c) was obtained using bundle-adjusted homographies and a final bundle-adjustment of the motion and structure on the output from method (2) (row 10 in the table).

No. of images	Homography calculation	Self-calibration algorithm	Refinement method	Angle between planes	Reconstruction error (%)	Reprojection error (pixels)
5	Linear	Linear, known pp	Single image, no ref.	53.0	81.7	0.544
5	Linear	Linear, known pp	Multiple images, no ref.	52.7	79.0	0.489
5	Linear	Linear, known pp	Method (1)	109.7	19.9	0.298
8	Linear	Linear, known pp	Single image, no ref.	33.3	110.2	0.422
8	Linear	Linear, known pp	Multiple images, no ref.	93.4	8.3	0.316
8	Linear	Linear, known pp	Method (1)	95.7	8.0	0.259
20	Bundle-adj.	LM, varying pp	Single image, no ref.	98.8	9.2	0.336
20	Bundle-adj.	LM, varying pp	Method (1)	88.1	3.2	0.349
20	Bundle-adj.	LM, varying pp	Method (2)	88.8	3.0	0.361
20	Bundle-adj.	LM, varying pp	Bundle-adj.	90.6	2.8	0.327

Table 3. Results of reconstruction of the calibration grid.

The paper has also demonstrated that the epipolar geometry between multiple rotating cameras can and should be exploited to refine the initial self-calibration of the sets of intrinsic parameters, and hence to improve recovered scene structure. The improvements can be substantial.

By experiment, it has been shown too that, by itself, a Euclidean bundle-adjustment cannot resolve the ambiguities. Methods such as those presented here are required to initialize the adjustment. Interestingly, especially for those concerned with on-line time-sensitive implementations, the initialized position is often good enough for bundle-adjustment to make rather little improvement. In current work we are exploring the reduction of the parameters in bundle-adjustment just to those which appear poorly estimated from independent self-calibration of each camera. However it appears that the cost function surface of the reprojection error is still peppered with local minima.

The ambiguity between focal length and rotation is apparent as the bas-relief ambiguity in sequences with general motion, and can rapidly lead to disastrous results [15]. The reconstructed scene appears skewed relative to the true configuration, and length ratios are not preserved, implying that the upgrade from projective to Euclidean structure has not been successful. This is precisely the kind of behaviour we observe here (eg. Fig 7(a)) with reconstructions from multiple rotating cameras if the ambiguity between focal length and rotation is not resolved. It is found that the near ambiguity between principal point and motion does not have as great an impact on the resulting Euclidean reconstruction, and resolving its effects are more difficult.

In future work we intend to extend the analysis to multi-focal constraints. This has the added benefit of better constrained matching.

References

[1] M. Armstrong, A. Zisserman, and R. Hartley. Self-calibration from image triplets. In *Proc. European Conf. on Computer Vision*, LNCS 1064/5, pages 3–16. Springer-Verlag, 1996.

[2] L. de Agapito, R. I. Hartley, and E. Hayman. Linear calibration of a rotating and zooming camera. In *Proc. IEEE Conference on Computer Vision and Pattern Recognition, Fort Collins, Colorado*, 1999.

[3] L. de Agapito, E. Hayman, and I. D. Reid. Self-calibration of a rotating camera with varying intrinsic parameters. In *Proc. BMVC*, pages 105–114, 1998.

[4] L. de Agapito, E. Hayman, and I. D. Reid. Self-calibration of rotating and zooming cameras. Technical Report TR 0225/00, University of Oxford, 2000.

[5] R. I. Hartley. Estimation of relative camera positions for uncalibrated cameras. In *Proc. European Conf. on Computer Vision*, LNCS 588, pages 579–587. Springer-Verlag, 1992.

[6] R. I. Hartley. Self-calibration of stationary cameras. *International Journal of Computer Vision*, 22(1):5–23, February 1997.

[7] R. I. Hartley, E. Hayman, L. de Agapito, and I. D. Reid. Camera calibration and the search for infinity. In *Proc. 7th International Conference on Computer Vision, Kerkyra, Greece*, 1999.

[8] E. Hayman, J. K. Knight, and D. W. Murray. Self-alignment of an active head from observations of rotation matrices. To appear in *Proc. International Conference on Pattern Recognition*, 2000.

[9] A. Heyden and K. Åström. Euclidean reconstruction from image sequences with varying and unknown focal length and principal point. In *Proc. of the IEEE Conf. on Computer Vision and Pattern Recognition*, 1997.

[10] H.C. Longuet-Higgins. A computer algorithm for reconstructing a scene from two projections. *Nature*, 293:133–135, 1981.

[11] M. Pollefeys, R. Koch, and L. Van Gool. Self calibration and metric reconstruction in spite of varying and unknown internal camera parameters. In *Proc. 6th Int'l Conf. on Computer Vision, Bombay*, pages 90–96, 1998.

[12] Y. Seo and K. Hong. Auto-calibration of a Rotating and Zooming Camera. In *Proc. of IAPR workshop on Machine Vision Applications*, pages 17–19, November 1998.

[13] Y. Seo and K. Hong. About the self-calibration of a rotating and zooming camera: Theory and practice. In *Proc. International Conference on Computer Vision*, 1999.

[14] P. Sturm. Critical motion sequences for monocular self-calibration and uncalibrated Euclidean reconstruction. In *Proc. IEEE Conference on Computer Vision and Pattern Recognition, Puerto Rico*, pages 1100–1105, June 1997.

[15] R. Szeliski and S. B. Kang. Shape ambiguities in structure from motion. In *Proc. 4th European Conf. on Computer Vision, Cambridge*, pages 709–721, 1996.

[16] Z. Zhang. A new multistage approach to motion and structure estimation: From essential parameters to euclidean motion via fundamental matrix. Technical Report TR2910, INRIA Sophia-Antipolis, June 1996.

[17] A. Zisserman, D. Liebowitz, and M. Armstrong. Resolving ambiguities in auto-calibration. *Philosophical Transactions of the Royal Society of London, SERIES A*, 356(1740):1193–1211, 1998.

Hand-Eye Calibration from Image Derivatives *

Henrik Malm, Anders Heyden

Centre for Mathematical Sciences, Lund University
Box 118, SE-221 00 Lund, Sweden
email: henrik,heyden@maths.lth.se

Abstract. In this paper it is shown how to perform hand-eye calibration using only the normal flow field and knowledge about the motion of the hand. The proposed method comprise a simple way to calculate the hand-eye calibration when a camera is mounted on a robot. Firstly, it is shown how the orientation of the optical axis can be estimated from at least two different translational motions of the robot. Secondly, it is shown how the other parameters can be obtained using at least two different motions containing also a rotational part. In both stages, only image gradients are used, i.e. no point matches are needed. As a by-product, both the motion field and the depth of the scene can be obtained. The proposed method is illustrated in experiments using both simulated and real data.

1   Introduction

Computer vision and autonomous systems have been fields of active research during the last years. One of the interesting applications is to combine computer vision techniques to help autonomous vehicles performing their tasks. In this paper we are aiming at an application within robotics, more specifically, using a camera mounted on the robot arm to aid the robot in performing different tasks. When a camera is mounted by an operator onto the robot arm, it cannot be assumed that the exact location of the camera with respect to the robot is known, since different cameras and mounting devices can be used. It might even be necessary to have a flexible mounting device in order to be able to perform a wide variety of tasks. This problem, called hand-eye calibration, will be dealt with in this paper.

Hand-eye calibration is an important task due to (at least) two applications. Firstly, in order to have the vision system guiding the robot to, for example, grasp objects, the orientation of the different coordinate systems are essential to know. Secondly, when the robot is looking at an object and it is necessary to take an image from a different viewpoint the hand-eye calibration is again necessary. We will throughout the paper assume that the robot-hand calibration is known, which implies that the relation between the robot coordinate system and the hand coordinate system is known. This assumption implies that we may take

---

* This work has been supported by the Swedish Research Council for Engineering Sciences (TFR), project 95-64-222

advantage of the possibility to move the hand of the robot in any predetermined way with respect to the robot coordinate system. In fact, this possibility will be used as a key ingredient in the proposed method for hand-eye calibration. We will furthermore assume that the camera is calibrated, i.e. that the intrinsic parameters are known. The problem of both recovering the hand-eye calibration and the robot-hand calibration has been treated in [3, 13, 12].

Hand-eye calibration has been treated by many researchers, e.g. [10, 11, 2, 4]. The standard approach relies on (i) a known reference object (calibration object) and (ii) the possibility to reliably track points on this reference object in order to obtain corresponding points between pairs of images. This approach leads to the study of the equation $AX = XB$, where A, X and B denote 4×4 matrices representing Euclidean transformations. A and B denote the transformations between the first and second position of the robot hand (in the robot coordinate system) and the camera (in the camera coordinate system - estimated from point correspondences) respectively and X denotes the transformation between the hand coordinate system and the camera coordinate system, i.e. the hand-eye calibration.

The hand-eye calibration problem can be simplified considerably by using the possibility to move the robot in a controlled manner. In [8] this fact has been exploited by first only translating the camera in order to obtain the rotational part of the hand-eye transformation and then making motions containing also a rotational part in order to obtain the translational part of the hand-eye calibration. This approach makes it also possible to cope without the calibration grid, but it is necessary to be able to detect and track points in the surrounding world.

We will go one step further and solve the hand-eye calibration problem without using any point correspondences at all. Instead we will use the normal flow (e.g. the projection of the motion field along the normal direction of the image gradients - obtained directly from the image derivatives) and the possibility to make controlled motions of the robot. We will also proceed in two steps; (i) making (small) translational motions in order to estimate the rotational part of the hand-eye calibration and (ii) making motions containing also a rotational part in order to estimate the translational part. We will show that it is sufficient, at least theoretically, to use only two translational motions and two motions also containing a rotational part. The idea to use only the normal flow (instead of an estimate of the optical flow obtained from the optical flow constraint equation and a smoothness constraint) has been used in [1] to make (intrinsic) calibration of a camera. In this paper we will use this approach to make hand-eye (extrinsic) calibration.

Our method for hand-eye calibration boils down to recovering the motion of the camera, using only image derivatives, when we have knowledge about the motion of the robot hand. This work has a lot in common with the work by Horn and Weldon [6] and Negahdaripour and Horn [9], where the same kind of intensity constraints are developed. We use, however, an active approach which allows us to choose the type of motions so that, for example, the unknown depth parameter Z can be effectively eliminated. The equations are developed with the goal of a complete hand-eye calibration in mind and so that they effectively uses the information obtained in the preceding steps of the algorithm.

The paper is organized as follows. In Section 2 a formal problem formulation will be given together with some notations. The hand-eye calibration problem will be solved in Section 3, where the estimate of the rotational part will be given in Section 3.1 and the estimate of the translational part will be given in Section 3.2. Some preliminary experimental results on both synthetic and real images will be given in Section 4 and some conclusions and directions of further research will be given in Section 5.

2 Problem Formulation

Throughout this paper we represent the coordinates of a point in the image plane by small letters (x, y) and the coordinates in the world coordinate frame by capital letters (X, Y, Z). In our work we use the pinhole camera model as our projection model. That is the projection is governed by the following equation were the coordinates are expressed in homogeneous form,

$$
\lambda \begin{bmatrix} x \\ y \\ 1 \end{bmatrix} = \begin{bmatrix} \gamma f & sf & x_0 \\ 0 & f & y_0 \\ 0 & 0 & 1 \end{bmatrix} [\, R \mid -Rt \,] \begin{bmatrix} X \\ Y \\ Z \\ 1 \end{bmatrix} . \tag{1}
$$

Here, f denotes the focal length, γ and s the aspect ratio and the skew and (x_0, y_0) the principal point. These are called the **intrinsic parameters**. Furthermore, R and t denote the relation between the camera coordinate system and the object coordinate system, where R denotes a rotation matrix and t a translation vector, i.e. a Euclidean transformation. These are called the **extrinsic parameters**.

In this study of hand-eye calibration we assume that the camera is calibrated, i.e. that the intrinsic parameters are known, and that the image coordinates of the camera have been corrected for the intrinsic parameters. This means that the camera equation can be written as in (1) with $f = 1$, $\gamma = 1$, $s = 0$ and $(x_0, y_0) = (0, 0)$. With these parameters the projection simply becomes

$$
\begin{cases} x = \dfrac{X}{Z}, \\ y = \dfrac{X}{Z}, \end{cases} \tag{2}
$$

where the object coordinates have been expressed in the camera coordinate system.

The hand-eye calibration problem boils down to finding the transformation $H = (R, t)$ between the robot hand coordinate system and the camera coordinate system, see Figure 1. In the general case this transformation has 6 degrees of freedom, 3 for the position, defined by the 3-vector t and 3 for the orientation, defined by the orthogonal matrix R. We will solve these two parts separately, starting with the orientation.

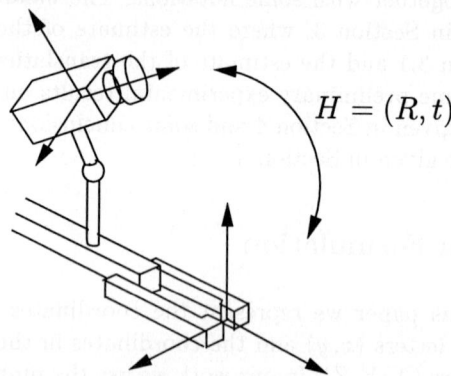

$$H = (R, t)$$

Fig. 1. The relation between the robot coordinate system and the camera coordinate system.

To find the orientation of the camera we will calculate the direction $D = (D_X, D_Y, D_Z)$, in the camera coordinate system, of at least two known translations of the robot hand, in the robot hand coordinate system. The relation between these directions in the two different coordinate systems will give us the orientation, R, between the two coordinate systems in all the 3 degrees of freedom.

For the position we would like to find the translation $T = (T_X, T_Y, T_Z)$ between the robot hand coordinate system and the camera coordinate system as seen in the robot coordinate system. Translation of the robot hand coordinate system will not give any information about T, as Ma also pointed out in [8]. Therefore, we will instead use rotations to find T. The procedure for this will be fully explained below in Section 3.2.

The main goal of our approach is to be able to do a complete hand-eye calibration without at any point having to extract any features and match them between images. To this end we use the notion of normal flow. The normal flow is the apparent flow of intensities in the image plane through an image sequence, i.e. the orthogonal projection of the motion field onto the image gradient. We will look at only two subsequent images in the current method. We will below briefly derive the so called *optical flow constraint equation* which is the cornerstone in our method. Note that our usage of the term normal flow means the motion of the intensity patterns, defined by the spatial and temporal image intensity derivatives, E_x, E_y and E_t, is not the same as the estimate of the motion field obtained from the optical flow constraint equation and a smoothness constraint.

If we think of an image sequence as a continuous stream of images, let $E(x, y, t)$ be the intensity at point (x, y) in the image plane at time t. Let $u(x, y)$ and $v(x, y)$ denote components of the motion field in the x and y directions respectively. Using the constraint that the gray-level intensity of the object is (locally) invariant to the viewing angle and distance we expect the following equation to be fulfilled.

$$E(x + u\delta t, y + v\delta t, t + \delta t) = E(x, y, t) \ . \tag{3}$$

That is, intensity at time $t + \delta t$ at point $(x + u\delta x, y + v\delta y)$ will be the same as the intensity at (x, y) at time t. If we assume that the brightness vary smoothly with x, y and t we can expand (3) in a Taylor series giving

$$E(x, y, t) + \delta x \frac{\partial E}{\partial x} + \delta y \frac{\partial E}{\partial y} + \delta t \frac{\partial E}{\partial t} + e = E(x, y, t) \ . \tag{4}$$

Here, e is is the error term of order $\mathcal{O}((\delta t)^2)$. By cancelling out $E(x, y, t)$, dividing by δt and taking the limit as $\delta t \to 0$ we receive

$$E_x u + E_y v + E_t = 0 \ , \tag{5}$$

where

$$\begin{cases} u = \dfrac{\delta x}{\delta t}, \\ v = \dfrac{\delta y}{\delta t} \ , \end{cases} \tag{6}$$

which denotes the motion field. The equation (5) is often used together with a smoothness constraint to make an estimation of the motion field, see e.g. [5]. In our method we will, however, not need to use such a smoothness constraint. Instead we will use what we know about the current motion and write down expressions for $u(x, y)$ and $v(x, y)$. By constraining the flow (u, v) in this way we will be able write down linear systems of equations of the form (5) which we can solve for the unknowns contained in the expressions for u and v. These unknowns will be shown to be in direct correspondence to the vectors D and T above, that is, to the unknowns of the hand-eye transformation.

3 Hand-Eye Calibration

In this section we will, in two steps, explain in detail our method. We will as the first step start with the orientation part of the transformation H. This is crucial since the result in this part will be used to simplify the calculations of the position part.

3.1 The Orientation of the Camera

The orientation of the camera will be obtained by translating the robot hand in at least two known separate directions in the robot hand coordinate system. As mentioned above we aim at stating expressions for the field components u and v. These expressions will contain the unknown direction D in the camera coordinate system of the current translation. To make the procedure as easy as possible we will choose the directions of the translations so that they coincide with two of the axes of the robot hand coordinate system. Then we know that the perceived directions in camera coordinate system exactly correspond to these two axes in robot hand coordinate system. The direction of the third axis can be obtained from the vector product or by making a third translation.

Following a way of expressing the motion field explained also in e.g. [7] and [5], we will start by expressing the motion of a point $P = (X, Y, Z)$ in a the object coordinate system, which coincide with the camera coordinate system. Let $V = (\dot{X}, \dot{Y}, \dot{Z})$ denote the velocity of this point.

Now we translate the robot hand along one axis in the robot hand coordinate system. Let $D = (D_x, D_y, D_z)$ denote the translation of the point P in the camera coordinate system. Then

$$(\dot{X}, \dot{Y}, \dot{Z}) = -(D_x, D_y, D_z) \ . \tag{7}$$

The minus sign appears because of the fact that we actually model a motion of the camera, but instead move the points in the world. The projection of the point P is governed by the equations in (2). Differentiating these equation with respect to time and using (6) we obtain

$$\begin{cases} u = \dot{x} = \dfrac{\dot{X}}{Z} - \dfrac{X\dot{Z}}{Z^2} = -\dfrac{1}{Z}(D_X - xD_Z), \\ v = \dot{y} = \dfrac{\dot{Y}}{Z} - \dfrac{Y\dot{Z}}{Z^2} = -\dfrac{1}{Z}(D_Y - yD_Z) \ , \end{cases} \tag{8}$$

where the projection equations (2) and (7) have been used. The equation (8) gives the projected motion field in the image plane expressed in the translation D given in the camera coordinate system. This is the motion field that we will use together with optical flow constraint equation (5).

Inserting (8) in (5) gives, after multiplication with Z,

$$-E_x D_X - E_y D_Y + (E_x x + E_y y)D_Z + E_t Z = 0 \ . \tag{9}$$

The spatial derivatives are here taken in the first image, before the motion, so they will not depend on the current translation D. E_t on the other hand will depend on D. Let N denote the number of pixels in the image. We obtain one equation of the form (9) for every pixel in the image. If we look at the unknowns of this set of equations, we have one unknown depth parameter, Z, for each pixel and equation, but the translation parameters (D_x, D_y, D_z) is the same in every pixel. Therefore the linear system of equations of the form (9) taken over the whole image has N equations and $N + 3$ unknowns. Let A denote the system matrix of this system of equations.

To obtain more equations of the form (9) but only 3 more unknowns we make another translation but now in a direction along another axis in the robot hand coordinate system. Let $\bar{D} = (\bar{D}_x, \bar{D}_y, \bar{D}_z)$ denote this new translation direction in the camera coordinate system. Then the new equations of the form (9) becomes

$$-E_x \bar{D}_X - E_y \bar{D}_Y + (E_x x + E_y y)\bar{D}_Z + \bar{E}_t Z = 0 \ . \tag{10}$$

Notice that E_x and E_y is the same as in (9) but E_t have changed to $\bar{E}_t$. The depth parameters $Z(x, y)$ in (10), which is the depth at point (x, y) in the original reference image, is the same as in the equations (9) resulting form the first motion. The only new unknowns are the new translation vector $\bar{D} = (\bar{D}_x, \bar{D}_y, \bar{D}_z)$. Let $\bar{A}$ be the system matrix of this new system of equations resulting from the second translation. Put together the equations from system A and system $\bar{A}$ in a new linear system M. This system will now have $2N$ equations but only $N + 6$ unknowns.

Primarily, we are only interested in the unknowns D and $\bar{D}$. To make the system M more stable with respect to these unknowns, and also in order to reduce the number of equations, we will eliminate Z in M. Pair together the equations that correspond to the same pixel in the first reference image. Then Z can be eliminated from (9) and (10) giving

$$- E_x \bar{E}_t D_X - E_y \bar{E}_t D_Y + (E_x x + E_y y)\bar{E}_t D_Z + E_x E_t \bar{D}_X + \\ + E_y E_t \bar{D}_Y + (E_x x + E_y y)E_t \bar{D}_Z = 0 \quad (11)$$

Taking the equations of the form (11) for each pixel in the first image a new linear system M' is obtained with N equations and only the 6 direction components as unknowns. Observe that the estimates of the directions D and $\bar{D}$ give the known directions of the robot hand, v and $barv$, in the camera coordinate system. The rotational part of the hand-cye calibration can easily be obtained from the fact that it maps the directions v and $barv$ to the directions D and $\bar{D}$ and is represented by an orthogonal matrix.

Another approach would be to use also a third translational motion of the robot hand, resulting in three different equations like (9) containing 9 different translation parameters and N depths. Eliminating the depths for each pixel gives two linearly independent equations in the 9 translational parameters for each pixel, i.e. in total $2N$ equations in 9 parameters. Observe also that an estimate of the depth of the scene can be obtained by inserting the estimated translation parameters into the constraints (9). Note that for pixels where $E_t = 0$ the depths can not be estimate from (9) since the coefficient for Z is equal to 0.

3.2   The Position of the Camera

To find the position of the camera in relation to the robot hand, rotational motions have to be used. Pure translational motions will not give any information about the translation between the robot hand and the camera. We will now write down the motion field $(u(x,y), v(x,y))$ for the rotational case in a similar fashion as we did for the translational case.

Describe the motion of the points in the camera coordinate system by a rotation around an axis that does not have to cross the focal point of the camera. Let $\Omega = (\Omega_X, \Omega_Y, \Omega_Z)$ denote the direction of this axis of rotation and $P = (X, Y, Z)$ the coordinates of a point in the camera coordinate system. Furthermore, let the translation between the origin of the robot hand coordinate system and the focal point be described by the vector $T = (T_x, T_Y, T_Z)$, see Figure 2. This is the vector that we want to calculate.

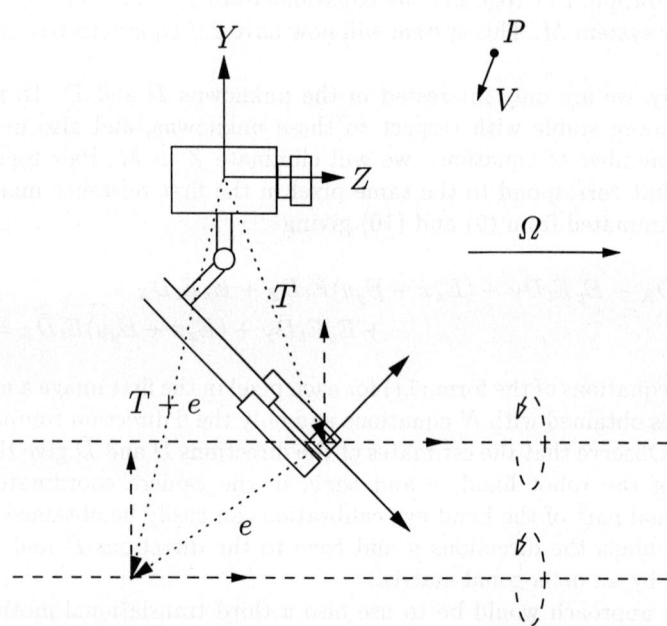

Fig. 2. Rotation around the direction $\Omega = (0, 0, 1)$. The X-axis is pointing out from the picture. The orientation of the camera is here only a rotation around the X-axis, for simplicity. The dashed coordinate systems corresponds to the first and second centers of the rotations.

Let the axis of rotation cross the origin of the robot hand coordinate system. Then the velocity $V = (\dot{X}, \dot{Y}, \dot{Z})$ of the point P in the camera coordinate system resulting from a rotation around this axis will be equal to $-\Omega \times (P - T)$, i.e.

$$\begin{cases} \dot{X} = -\Omega_Y(Z - T_Z) + \Omega_Z(Y - T_Y) = -\Omega_Y Z + \Omega_Z Y + \Omega_Y T_Z - \Omega_Z T_Y, \\ \dot{Y} = -\Omega_Z(X - T_X) + \Omega_X(Z - T_Z) = -\Omega_Z X + \Omega_X Z + \Omega_Z T_X - \Omega_X T_Z, \\ \dot{Z} = -\Omega_X(Y - T_Y) + \Omega_Y(X - T_X) = -\Omega_X Y + \Omega_Y X + \Omega_X T_Y - \Omega_Y T_X \ . \end{cases}$$
$$(12)$$

Here, the equations have been rewritten to the form of a rotation around an axis that crosses the focal point plus a term that can be interpreted as a translation in the camera coordinate system. Using the velocity vector (12) and equations (2) and (8) the motion field now becomes

$$\begin{cases} u = \Omega_X xy - (1 + x^2)\Omega_Y + \Omega_Z y + x\Omega_Y \dfrac{T_X}{Z} - (x\Omega_X + \Omega_Z)\dfrac{T_Y}{Z} + \Omega_Y \dfrac{T_Z}{Z}, \\ v = \Omega_X(1 + y^2) - \Omega_Y xy + \Omega_Z x + (\Omega_Z + y\Omega_Z)\dfrac{T_X}{Z} - y\Omega_X \dfrac{T_Y}{Z} - \Omega_X \dfrac{T_Z}{Z} \ . \end{cases}$$
$$(13)$$

This field will be plugged into the optical flow constraint equation (5). Since we know the axis of rotation, the first three terms of the equations for u and v are known. Let

$$E'_t = E_t + E_x \left(\Omega_X xy - \Omega_Y(1 + x^2) + \Omega_Z y \right) + E_y \left(\Omega_X(1 + y^2) - \Omega_Y xy + \Omega_Z x \right)$$
$$(14)$$

Here, E'_t is a known quantity and the motion field (13) plugged into (5) can be written as (after multiplication with Z)

$$AT_X + BT_Y + CT_Z + ZE'_t = 0,$$
$$(15)$$

where

$$\begin{cases} A = E_x \Omega_Y x + E_y(\Omega_Z + y\Omega_Y), \\ B = -E_x(x\Omega_X + \Omega_Z) - E_y \Omega_X y, \\ C = E_x \Omega_Y - E_Y \Omega_X \ . \end{cases}$$
$$(16)$$

This resembles the equations obtained in Section 3.1. We will also here eliminate the depth Z by choosing a new motion. A difference is that in this case we are not only interested in the direction of the vector T, but also the length of T. To be able to calculate this the center of rotation will be moved away from the origin of the robot hand a known distance $e = (e_X, e_Y, e_Z)$ and a new rotation axis $\bar{\Omega}$ is chosen. This leads to a new equation of the form (15)

$$\bar{A}(T_X + e_X) + \bar{B}(T_Y + e_Y) + \bar{C}(T_Z + e_Z) + Z\bar{E}'_t = 0 \ .$$
$$(17)$$

Here, $\bar{A}, \bar{B}, \bar{C}$ and $\bar{E}'_t$ corresponds to (19) and (14) for the new rotation axis $\bar{\Omega}$. Pairing together (15) and (17) and eliminating the depth Z gives

$$(\bar{E}'_t A - E'_t \bar{A})T_X + (\bar{E}'_t B - E'_t \bar{B})T_Y + (\bar{E}'_t C - E'_t \bar{C})T_Z = E'_t(\bar{A}e_X + \bar{B}e_Y + \bar{C}e_Z)$$
$$(18)$$

We have one equation of this kind for each of the N pixels in the image and only 3 unknowns. Solving the over-determined linear equation system using least-squares gives us the translational part of the hand-eye transformation in the camera coordinate system. It is then a simple task to transfer this translation to the robot hand coordinate system if wanted.

The direction of the second rotation axis $\bar{\Omega}$ do not necessarily have to be different from the first Ω. For example, choosing $\Omega = \bar{\Omega} = (0,0,1)$, i.e. the rotation axis is parallel to the optical axis, we get

$$\begin{cases} A = \bar{A} = E_y, \\ B = \bar{B} = -E_x, \\ C = \bar{C} = 0 \ . \end{cases} \tag{19}$$

Equation (18) then reduces to

$$E_y(\bar{E}'_t - E'_t)T_X - E_x(\bar{E}'_t - E'_t)T_Y = E'_t(E_y e_X - E_x e_Y) \tag{20}$$

where

$$\begin{aligned} E'_t &= E_t + E_x y + E_y x, \\ \bar{E}'_t &= \bar{E}_t + E_x y + E_y x \ . \end{aligned} \tag{21}$$

This equation system gives a way of calculating T_X and T_Y, but T_Z is lost and must be calculated in another manner. To calculate T_Z we can, for example, instead choose $\Omega = \bar{\Omega} = (1,0,0)$ which gives a linear system in T_Y and T_Z.

4 Experiments

In this section the hand-eye calibration algorithm is tested in practice on both synthetic and real data. On the synthetic sequence the noise sensitivity of the method is examined.

4.1 Synthetic Data

A synthetic image E was constructed using a simple raytracing routine. The scene consists of the plane $Z + \frac{X}{2} = 10$ in camera coordinate system. The texture on the plane is described by $I(X,Y) = \sin(X) + \sin(Y)$ in a coordinate system of the plane with origin at $O = (0,0,10)$ in the camera coordinate system, see Figure 3. The extension of the image plane is from -1 to 1 in both the X and Y direction. The image is discretized using a step-size of $\delta x = 0.01$ and $\delta y = 0.01$, so that the number of pixels is equal to $N = 201 \times 201$.

The spatial derivatives, E_x and E_y, has in the experiments been calculated by convolution with the derivatives of a Gaussian kernel. That is $E_x = E * G_x$ and $E_y = E * G_y$ where

$$G_x = -\frac{1}{2\pi\sigma^4} x e^{-\frac{x^2+y^2}{2\sigma^2}}, \quad G_y = -\frac{1}{2\pi\sigma^4} y e^{-\frac{x^2+y^2}{2\sigma^2}} \ . \tag{22}$$

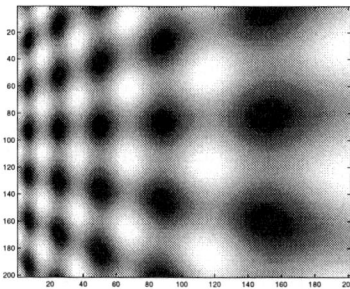

Fig. 3. An image from the computer generated sequence

The temporal derivatives were calculated by simply taking the difference of the intensity in the current pixel between the first and the second image. Before this was done, however, the images was convolved with a standard Gaussian kernel, of the same scale as the spatial derivatives above. The effect of the scale parameter σ has not been fully evaluated yet, but the experiments indicate that σ should be chosen with respect to the magnitude of the motion. If the motion is small, σ should also be chosen rather small. In the experiments on the orientation part, a value of σ between 0.5 and 3 was used. In the position part values higher than 3 was usually used.

Orientation We have used three translations at each calculation to get a linear system with $3N$ equations and 9 unknowns. The use of two translations, as described in the Section 3.1, gives a system with N equations and 6 unknowns, which seemed equally stable. The resulting direction vectors

$$(D_X, D_Y, D_Z, \bar{D}_X, \bar{D}_Y, \bar{D}_Z, \bar{\bar{D}}_X, \bar{\bar{D}}_Y, \bar{\bar{D}}_Z)$$

of some simulated translations are shown in Table 1. The result has been normalized for each 3-vector.

As a reference, the directions were also calculated using the current method with exact spatial and temporal derivatives for each motion, i.e. by calculating the derivatives analytically and then using these to set up the linear system of equations of the form (11). These calculations gave perfect results, in full accordance with the theory. In Table 1 the variable t indicates the time and corresponds to the distance that the robot hand has been moved. The value of t is the length of the translation in robot hand coordinate system. An apparent motion in the image of the size of one pixel corresponds in these experiments to approximately $t = 0.15$. In the first column, $t = 0$ indicates that the exact derivatives are used.

The experiments shows that the component of the translation in the Z direction is most difficult to obtain accurately. The value of this component is often underestimated. Translations in the XY- plane, however, always gave near perfect results. Translations along a single axis also performed very well, including the Z-axis.

Table 1. Results of the motion estimation using the synthetic image data. The parameter t indicates the length of the translation vector in the robot hand coordinate system.

$t = 0$	$t = 0.05, \sigma = 0.5$	$t = 0.1, \sigma = 0.5$	$t = 0.2, \sigma = 1$	$t = 0.3, \sigma = 1.5$
0.5774	0.5826	0.5829	0.5846	0.5896
0.5774	0.5826	0.5885	0.6054	0.6289
0.5774	0.5667	0.5603	0.5401	0.5067
0.7071	0.7078	0.7078	0.7094	0.7094
0.7071	0.7064	0.7064	0.7045	0.7036
0	0.0012	0.0063	0.0211	0.0411
0	0.0019	0.0067	0.0236	0.0513
1	1.0000	1.0000	0.9996	0.9981
0	0.0014	0.0049	0.0157	0.0346

The method is naturally quite sensitive to noise since it based fully on approximations of the intensity derivatives. The resulting direction of some simulated translations is shown in Table 2 together with the added amount of Gaussian distributed noise. The parameter σ_n corresponds to the variation of the added noise. This should be put in relation to the intensity span in the image, which for the synthetic images is -2 to 2. If the image is a standard gray-scale image with 256 grey-levels, $\sigma_n = 0.02$ corresponds to approximately one grey-level of added noise.

Table 2. Results of the motion estimation using images with added Gaussian noise. The parameter σ_n indicates the variation of the added noise. The intensity span in the image is from -2 to 2.

$t = 0$ $\sigma_n = 0$	$t = 0.1$ $\sigma_n = 0.01$	$t = 0.1$ $\sigma_n = 0.02$	$t = 0.1$ $\sigma_n = 0.03$	$t = 0.1$ $\sigma_n = 0.05$
0.5774	0.5899	0.5833	0.5928	0.5972
0.5774	0.5944	0.6016	0.6088	0.6132
0.5774	0.5465	0.5457	0.5272	0.5171
0.7071	0.7083	0.7030	0.7074	0.7025
0.7071	0.7058	0.7109	0.7066	0.7117
0	0.0145	0.0208	0.0180	0.0054
0	0.0132	0.0185	0.0145	0.0118
1	0.9998	0.9997	0.9999	0.9999
0	0.0117	0.0132	0.0094	0.0036

Position The algorithm for obtaining the translational part of the hand-eye transformation was tested using the same kind of synthetic images as in the preceding section. The experiments shows that the algorithm is sensitive to the magnitude of the angle of rotation and to the choice of the vector e.

The algorithm performs well when using equation (20) to obtain T_X and T_Y. Using this equation with $T = (1,1,1)$, $e = (3,2,1)$ and the angle of rotation being $\theta = \pi/240$, we get $T_X = (1.0011)$ and $T_Y = (1.0254)$. With $T = (7,9,5)$, $e = (3,1,0)$ and $\theta = \pi/240$, we get $T_X = 7.0805$ and $T_Y = 8.9113$. In these examples the scale of the Gaussian kernels was chosen as high as $\sigma = 6$.

The component T_Z is however more difficult obtain accurately. Using $\Omega = \bar{\Omega} = (0,0,1)$ as mentioned at the end of Section 3.2 and the same T, e and θ as in the latter of the preceding examples, we get $T_Y = 9.1768$ and $T_Z = 5.2664$. This represents an experiment that worked quite well. Choosing another e and θ, the result could turn out much worse. More experiments and a deeper analysis of the method for obtaining the position is needed to understand the instabilities of the algorithm.

4.2   Real Data

To try the method on a real hand-eye system, we used a modified ABB IRB2003 robot which is capable of moving in all 6 degrees of freedom. The camera was mounted by a ball head camera holder on the hand of the robot so that the orientation of the camera could be changed with respect to the direction of the robot hand coordinate system.

The two scenes, A and B, that has been used in the experiments, consist of some objects placed on a wooden table. Scene A is similar to scene B, except for some additional objects, see Figure 4.

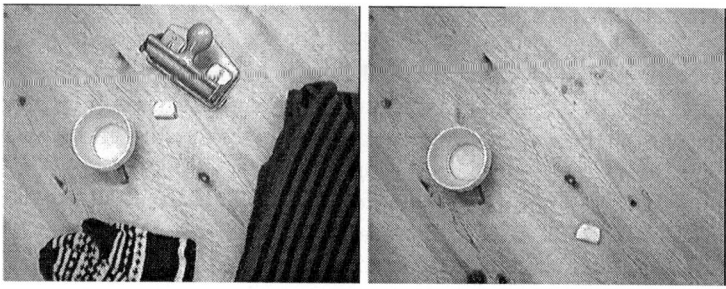

Fig. 4. Two images from the real sequences A (left) and B (right)

Three translations were used for each scene. In the first translation the robot hand was moved along its Z-axis towards the table, in the second along the X-axis and in the third along the Y-axis. The orientation of the camera was approximately a rotation of $-\frac{\pi}{4}$ radians around the Z-axis with respect to the robot hand coordinate system. Therefore, the approximate normed directions of the translations as seen in the camera coordinate system were $D = (0,0,1)$, $\bar{D} = \frac{1}{\sqrt{2}}(-1,1,0)$ and $\bar{\bar{D}} = \frac{1}{\sqrt{2}}(1,1,0)$.

The results of calculating the direction vectors in sequence A and B, using the method in Section 3.1, are presented in Table 3. The derivatives were in these experiments calculated using $\sigma = 2$. The motion of the camera was not very precise and it is possible, for example, that the actual motion in sequence B for the translation along the Z-axis also contained a small component along the X-axis. More experiments on real image sequences are needed to fully evaluate the method.

Table 3. The approximate actual motion compared with the calculated motion vectors from sequence A and B respectively. The direction vectors are normed for each 3-vector.

Approx. actual motion	Calculated motion seq. A	Calculated motion seq. B
0	0.1415	0.4068
0	0.0225	0.1499
1	0.9897	0.9011
-0.7071	-0.5428	-0.6880
0.7071	0.8345	0.7184
0	0.0943	0.1028
0.7071	0.7138	0.6492
0.7071	0.7001	0.7590
0	0.0183	0.0495

5 Conclusions and Future Work

We have in this paper proposed a method for hand-eye calibration using only image derivatives, the so called normal flow field. That is, we have only used the gradients of the intensity in the images and the variation of intensity in each pixel in an image sequence. Using known motions of the robot hand we have been able to write down equations for the possible motion field in the image plane in a few unknown parameters. By using the optical flow constraint equation together with these motion equations we have written down linear systems of equations which could be solved for the unknown parameters. The motion equations was constructed so that the unknown parameters correspond directly to the unknowns of the transformation H between the camera coordinate system and the robot hand coordinate system.

The work was divided in two parts, one for the orientation, i.e. the rotation of camera with respect to the robot hand coordinate system, and one for the position of the camera, i.e. the translation between the camera coordinate system and the robot hand coordinate system. Some preliminary experiments has been made on synthetic and real image data.

The theory shows that a hand-eye calibration using only image derivatives should be possible but the results of the experiments on real data are far from the precision that we would like in a hand-eye calibration. This is, however, our first study of these ideas and the next step will be to find ways to make the motion estimation more stable in the same kind of setting. One thing to look into is the usage of multiple images in each direction so that, for example, a more advanced approximation of the temporal derivatives can be used.

References

1. T. Brodsky, C. Fernmuller, and Y. Aloimonos. Self-calibration from image derivatives. In *Proc. Int. Conf. on Computer Vision*, pages 83–89. IEEE Computer Society Press, 1998.
2. J. C. K. Chou and M. Kamel. Finding the position and orientation of a sensor on a robot manipulator using quaternions. *International Journal of Robotics Research*, 10(3):240–254, 1991.
3. F. Dornaika and R. Horaud. Simultaneous robot-world and hand-eye calibration. *IEEE Trans. Robotics and Automation*, 14(4):617–622, 1998.
4. R. Horaud and F. Dornaika. Hand-eye calibration. In *Proc. Workshop on Computer Vision for Space Applications, Antibes*, pages 369–379, 1993.
5. B. K. P. Horn. *Robot Vision*. MIT Press, Cambridge, Mass, USA, 1986.
6. B. K. P. Horn and E. J. Weldon Jr. Direct methods for recovering motion. *Int. Journal of Computer Vision*, 2(1):51–76, June 1988.
7. H. C. Longuet-Higgins and K. Prazdny. The interpretation of a moving retinal image. In *Proc. Royal Society of London B*, volume 208, pages 385–397, 1980.
8. Song De Ma. A self-calibration technique for active vision systems. *IEEE Trans. Robotics and Automation*, 12(1):114–120, February 1996.
9. S. Negahdaripour and B. K. P. Horn. Direct passive navigation. *IEEE Trans. Pattern Analysis Machine Intelligence*, 9(1):168–176, January 1987.
10. Y. C. Shiu and S. Ahmad. Calibration of wrist-mounted robotic sensors by solving homogeneous transform equations of the form $ax = xb$. *IEEE Trans. Robotics and Automation*, 5(1):16–29, 1989.
11. R. Y. Tsai and R. K. Lenz. A new technique for fully autonomous and efficient 3d robotics hand/eye calibration. *IEEE Trans. Robotics and Automation*, 5(3):345–358, 1989.
12. H. Zhuang, Z. S. Roth, and R. Sudhakar. Simultaneous robot/world and tool/flange calibration by solving homogeneous transformation equation of the form $ax = yb$. *IEEE Trans. Robotics and Automation*, 10(4):549–554, 1994.
13. H. Zhuang, K. Wang, and Z. S. Roth. Simultaneous calibration of a robot and a hand-mounted camera. *IEEE Trans. Robotics and Automation*, 11(5):649–660, 1995.

Medical Image Understanding

Multimodal Elastic Matching of Brain Images

Alexis Roche[1], Alexandre Guimond[1,2], Nicholas Ayache[1], and Jean Meunier[2]

[1] INRIA Sophia Antipolis - Epidaure Project
2004 Route des Lucioles BP 93
06902 Sophia Antipolis Cedex, France
[2] Département d'Informatique et recherche opérationnelle,
Université de Montréal, CP 6128 succ Centre-Ville,
Montréal QC H3C 3J7, Canada

Abstract. This paper presents an original method for three-dimensional elastic registration of multimodal images. We propose to make use of a scheme that iterates between correcting for intensity differences between images and performing standard monomodal registration. The core of our contribution resides in providing a method that finds the transformation that maps the intensities of one image to those of another. It makes the assumption that there are at most two functional dependences between the intensities of structures present in the images to register, and relies on robust estimation techniques to evaluate these functions. We provide results showing successful registration between several imaging modalities involving segmentations, T1 magnetic resonance (MR), T2 MR, proton density (PD) MR and computed tomography (CT).
keywords: Multimodality, Elastic registration, Intensity correction, Robust estimation, Medical imaging.

1 Introduction

Over the last decade, automatic registration techniques of medical images of the head have been developed following two main trends: 1) registration of multimodal images using low degree transformations (rigid or affine), and 2) registration of monomodal images using high-dimensional volumetric maps (elastic or fluid deformations). The first category mainly addresses the fusion of complementary information obtained from different imaging modalities. The second category's predominant purpose is the evaluation of either the anatomical evolution process present in a particular subject or of anatomical variations between different subjects.

These two trends have evolved separately mainly because the combined problem of identifying complex intensity correspondences along with a high-dimensional geometrical transformation defines a search space arduous to traverse. Recently, three groups have imposed different constraints on the search space, enabling them to develop automatic multimodal non-affine registration techniques. All three methods make use of block matching techniques to evaluate local translations. Two of them use mutual information (MI) [30, 17] as a similarity measure and the other employs the correlation ratio [23].

An important aspect when using MI as a registration measure is to compute the conditional probabilities of one image's intensities with respect to those of the other. To do so, Maintz *et al.* [18] proposed to use conditional probabilities after rigid matching of the images as an estimate of the real conditional probabilities after local transformations. Hence, the probabilities are evaluated only once before fluid registration. However, Gaens *et al.* [11] argued that the assumption that probabilities computed after affine registration are good approximations of the same probabilities after fluid matching, is unsuitable. They also proposed a method in which local displacements are found so that the global MI increases at each iteration, permitting incremental changes of the probabilities during registration. Their method necessitates the computation of conditional probabilities over the whole image for every voxel displacement. To alleviate themselves from such computations owing to the fact that MI requires many samples to estimate probabilities, Lau *et al.* [16] have chosen a different similarity measure. Due to the robustness of the correlation ratio with regards to sparse data [23], they employed it to assess the similarity of neighbouring blocks. Hence no global computation is required when moving subregions of the image.

Our method distinguishes itself by looking at the problem from a different angle. In the last years, our group has had some success with monomodal image registration using the demons method [27, 28], an optical flow variant when dealing with monomodal volumetric images. If we were able to model the imaging processes that created the images to register, and assuming these processes are invertible, one could transform one of the images so that they are both represented in the same modality. Then, we could use our monomodal registration algorithm to register them. We have thus developed a completely automatic method to transform the different structures intensities in one image so that they match the intensities of the corresponding structures in another image, and this without resorting to any segmentation method.

The rational behind our formulation is that there is a functional relationship between the intensity of a majority of structures when imaged with different modalities. This assumption is partly justified by the fact that the Woods criterion [31] as well as the correlation ratio [23], which evaluate a functional dependence between the intensities of the images to match, have been used with success in the past, and sometimes lead to better results than MI, which assumes a more general relation [22, 21].

The idea of estimating an intensity transformation during registration is not new in itself. For example, Feldmar *et al.* [10] as well as Barber [1] have both published methods in which intensity corrections are proposed. These methods restrict themselves to affine intensity corrections in a monomodal registration context. We propose here a procedure based on one or two higher degree polynomials found using a robust regression technique to enable the registration of images from different modalities.

The remaining sections of this paper are organized in the following manner. First, we detail our multimodal elastic registration method. We then describe what kind of images were used to test the method and how they were acquired. Next, results obtained by registering different images obtained from several modalities are presented and discussed. We conclude this paper with a brief discussion on future research tracks.

2 Method

Our registration algorithm is iterative and each iteration consists of two parts. The first one transforms the intensities of anatomical structures of a source image S so that they match the corresponding structures intensities of a target image T. The second part regards the registration of S (after intensity transformation) with T using an elastic registration algorithm.

In the following, we first describe the three-dimensional geometrical transformation computation and then the intensity transformation computation. We believe this ordering is more convenient since it is easier to see what result must provide the intensity transformation once the geometrical transformation procedure is clarified.

2.1 Geometrical Transformation

Many methods have been developed to deform one brain so its shape matches that of another [29]. The one used in the present work is an adaptation of the demons algorithm [27, 28]. Adjustments were performed based on empirical observations as well as on theoretical grounds which are discussed below. For each voxel with position x in T, we hope to find the displacement $v(x)$ so that x matches its corresponding anatomical location in S. In our algorithm, the displacements are computed using the following iterative scheme,

$$v_{n+1}(x) = G_\sigma \otimes \left(v_n + \frac{S \circ h_n(x) - T(x)}{||(\nabla S \circ h_n)(x)||^2 + [S \circ h_n(x) - T(x)]^2}(\nabla S \circ h_n)(x) \right),$$

$$(1)$$

where G_σ is a Gaussian kernel, $\otimes$ denotes the three-dimensional convolution, $\circ$ denotes the composition and the transformation $h(x)$ is related to the displacement by $h(x) = x + v(x)$. As is common with registration methods, we also make use of multilevel techniques to accelerate convergence. Details about the number of levels and iterations as well as filter implementation issues are addressed in Section 4. We here show how our method can be related to other registration methods, notably the minimization of the sum of squared difference (SSD) criterion, optical flow and the demons algorithm.

Relation with SSD Minimization In this framework, we find the transformation h that minimizes the sum of squared differences between the transformed source image and the target image. The SSD between the two images for a given transformation h applied to the source is defined as

$$SSD(h) = \frac{1}{2} \sum_{x=1}^{N} [S \circ h(x) - T(x)]^2.$$

$$(2)$$

The minimization of Equation (2) may be performed using a gradient descent algorithm. Thus, differentiating the above equation we get

$$\nabla SSD(h) = -[S \circ h(x) - T(x)](\nabla S \circ h)(x).$$

The iterative scheme is then of the form,

$$h_{n+1} = h_n + \alpha[S \circ h_n(x) - T(x)](\nabla S \circ h_n)(x),$$

where α is the step length. This last equation implies,

$$v_{n+1} = v_n + \alpha[S \circ h_n(x) - T(x)](\nabla S \circ h_n)(x). \tag{3}$$

If we set α to a constant value, this method corresponds to a steepest gradient descent. By comparing Equation (3) to Equation (1), one sees that our method sets

$$\alpha = \frac{1}{||(\nabla S \circ h_n)(x)||^2 + [T(x) - S \circ h_n(x)]^2} \tag{4}$$

and applies a Gaussian filter to provide a smooth displacement field. Cachier et al. [6, 20] have shown that using Equation (4) closely relates Equation (1) with a second order gradient descent of the SSD criterion, in which each iteration n sets h_{n+1} to the minimum of the SSD quadratic approximation at h_n. We refer the reader to these articles for a more technical discussion on this subject as well as for the formula corresponding to the true second order gradient descent.

Relation with Optical Flow T and S are considered as successive time samples of an image sequence represented by $I(x, t)$, where $x = (x_1, x_2, x_3)$ is a voxel position in the image and t is time. The displacements are computed by constraining the brightness of brain structures to be constant in time, so that the following equality holds [14]:

$$\frac{\partial I}{\partial t} + v \cdot \nabla_x I = 0. \tag{5}$$

Equation (5) is however not sufficient to provide a unique displacement for each voxel. By constraining the displacements to always lie in the direction of the brightness gradient $\nabla_x I$, we get:

$$v(x) = -\frac{\partial I(x, t)/\partial t}{||\nabla_x I(x, t)||^2} \nabla_x I(x, t). \tag{6}$$

In general, the resulting displacement field does not have suitable smoothness properties. Many regularization methods have been proposed to fill this purpose [2]. One that can be computed very efficiently was proposed by Thirion [28] in his description of the demons registration method using a complete grid of demons. It consists of smoothing each dimension of the vector field with a Gaussian filter. He also proposed to add $[\partial I(x, t)/\partial t]^2$ to the denominator of Equation (6) for numerical stability when $\nabla_x I(x, t)$ is close to zero, a term which serves the same purpose as α^2 in the original optical flow formulation of Horn and Schunck [14]. As is presented by Bro-Nielsen and Gramkow [5], this kind of regularization approximates a linear elasticity transformation model.

With this in mind, the displacement that maps a voxel position in T to its position in S is found using an iterative method,

$$v_{n+1}(x) = G_\sigma \otimes \left(v_n - \frac{\partial I(x,t)/\partial t}{\|\nabla_x I(x,t)\|^2 + [\partial I(x,t)/\partial t]^2} \nabla_x I(x,t) \right). \qquad (7)$$

Spatial derivatives may be computed in several ways [14, 4, 26]. We have observed from practical experience that our method performs best when they are computed from the resampled source image of the current iteration. As shown in Section 2.1, this is in agreement with the SSD minimization. Temporal derivatives are obtained by subtracting the target images from the resampled source image of the current iteration. These considerations relate Equation (7) to Equation (1). The reader should note that the major difference between this method and other optical flow strategies is that regularization is performed *after* the calculation of the displacements in the gradient direction instead of using an explicit regularization potential in a minimization framework.

Relation with the Demons Algorithm Our algorithm actually is a small variation of the demons method [27, 28] using a complete grid of demons, itself closely related to optical flow as described in the previous section. The demons algorithm finds the displacements using the following formula,

$$v_{n+1}(x) = G_\sigma \otimes \left(v_n + \frac{S \circ h_n(x) - T(x)}{\|\nabla T(x)\|^2 + [S \circ h_n(x) - T(x)]^2} \nabla T(x) \right).$$

As can be seen from the last equation, the only difference between our formulation (Equation (1)) and the demons method is that derivatives are computed on the resampled source image of the current iteration. This modification was performed following the observations on the minimization of the SSD criterion.

2.2 Intensity Transformation

Previous to each iteration of the geometrical transformation, an intensity correction is performed on S so that the intensities of its structures match those in T. The displacement field is then updated by replacing S with its intensity corrected version in Equation (1).

The intensity correction process starts by defining the set C of intensity couples from corresponding voxels of T and of the current resampled source image $S \circ h$, which will be designated by S in this section for simplicity. Hence, the set C is defined as

$$C = \left\{ (S(i), T(i)); 1 \leq i \leq N \right\},$$

where N is the number of voxels in the images. $S(i)$ and $T(i)$ correspond to the intensity value of the ith voxel of S and T respectively when adopting the customary convention of considering images as one-dimensional arrays. From there, we show how to perform intensity correction if one or two functional dependences can be assumed between the structures intensities.

Monofunctional Dependence Assumption Our goal is to model the transformation that characterizes the mapping from voxel intensities in S to those in T, knowing that some elements of C are erroneous, i.e. that would not be present in C if S and T were perfectly matched. If we can assume a monofunctional dependence of the intensities of T with regards to those of S as well as additive stationary Gaussian white noise η on the intensity values of T, then we can adopt the model

$$T(i) = f(S(i)) + \eta(i), \tag{8}$$

where f is an unknown function to be estimated. This is exactly the model employed in [22, 21] which leads to the correlation ratio as the measure to be maximized for registration. In that approach, for a given transformation, one seeks the function that best describes T in terms of S. It is shown that, in a maximum likelihood context, the intensity function $\hat{f}$ that best approximates f is a least squares (LS) fit of T in terms of S.

Here the major difference is that we seek a high-dimensional geometrical transformation. As opposed to affine registration where the transformation is governed by the majority of good matches, we have seen in Section 2.1 that using the elastic registration model, displacements are found using mainly local information (i.e. gradients, local averages, etc.). Hence, we can not expect good displacements in one structure to correct for bad ones in another; we have to make certain each voxel is moved properly during each iteration. For this, since the geometrical transformation is found using intensity similarity, the most precise intensity transformation is required. Consequently, instead of performing a standard least squares regression, we have opted for a robust linear regression estimator which will remove outlying elements of C during the estimation of the intensity transformation. To estimate f we use the least trimmed squares (LTS) method followed by a binary reweighted least squares (RLS) estimation [25]. The combination of these two methods provides a very robust regression technique with outliers detection, while ensuring that a maximum of pertinent points are used for the final estimation.

Least Trimmed Squares Computation For our particular problem, we will constrain the unknown function f to be a polynomial function with degree p:

$$f(s) = \theta_0 + \theta_1 s + \theta_2 s^2 + \cdots + \theta_p s^p,$$

where we need to estimate the polynomial coefficients $\theta = [\theta_0, \ldots, \theta_p]$. A regression estimator will provide a $\hat{\theta} = [\hat{\theta}_0, \ldots, \hat{\theta}_p]$ which can be used to predict the value of $T(i)$ from $S(i)$, $\hat{T}(i) = \hat{\theta}_0 + \hat{\theta}_1 S(i) + \hat{\theta}_2 S(i)^2 + \cdots + \hat{\theta}_p S(i)^p$, as well as the residual errors $r(i) = T(i) - \hat{T}(i)$. A popular method to obtain $\hat{\theta}$ is to minimize the sum of squared residual errors,

$$\hat{\theta} = \arg\min_{\theta} \sum_{i=1}^{N} r(i)^2,$$

which leads to the standard LS solution. It is found by solving a linear system using the Singular Value Decomposition (SVD) method. This method is known to be very sensitive to outliers and thus is expected to provide a poor estimate of the monofunctional mapping from S to T. The LTS method solves this problem by minimizing the same sum on a subset of all residual errors, thus rejecting large ones corresponding to outliers,

$$\hat{\theta} = \arg\min_{\theta} \sum_{i=1}^{h} \rho(i),$$

where $\rho(i)$ is the ith smallest value of the set $\{r(1)^2, \ldots, r(N)^2\}$. This corresponds to a standard LS on the c values that best approximates the function we are looking for. Essentially, c/N represents the percentage of "good" points in C and must be at least 50%. A lesser value would allow to estimate parameters that model a minority of point which could then all be outliers. The value of c will vary according to the modalities used during registration. Assigning actual values to c is postponed to Section 4.

Our method for LTS minimization is a simple iterative technique. First, we randomly pick c/N points from C. We then iterate between calculating $\hat{\theta}$ using the standard LS technique on the selected points and choosing the h/N closest points from C. This process is carried until convergence, usually requiring less than 5 iterations and is guaranteed to find at least a local minimum of the LTS criterion [24].

Reweighted Least Squares Computation As discussed in [25], the LTS method is very robust, but it tends to provide an estimate $\hat{\theta}$ that is notably less accurate than that we would obtain with a standard LS in the absence of outliers. The solution may be refined by considering all the points that relate well to the LTS estimate, not only the best $c/N \times 100\%$. An efficient technique to achieve this is the so-called RLS regression [25], which minimizes the sum of squared residuals over all the points that are not "too far" from the LTS estimate,

$$\hat{\theta} = \arg\min_{\theta} \sum_{i=1}^{N} w_i r(i), \quad \text{where} \quad w_i = \begin{cases} 1 & \text{if } r(i) \leq 3\hat{\sigma}, \\ 0 & \text{otherwise}, \end{cases}$$

where $\hat{\sigma}$ is a scale parameter which actually estimates the standard deviation of the Gaussian noise η introduced in Equation (8). Such an estimate can be computed directly from the final value of the LTS criterion,

$$\hat{\sigma} = \sqrt{\frac{K}{c} \sum_{i=1}^{c} \rho(i)}, \quad \text{with} \quad \frac{1}{K} = \int_{-\alpha}^{\alpha} x^2 g(x)\, dx, \tag{9}$$

where $g(x)$ is the Gaussian distribution $N(0,1)$ and α is the $(0.5 + c/2N)^{\text{th}}$ quantile of $g(x)$. In Equation (9), K is a normalization factor introduced because the LTS criterion is not a consistent estimator of σ when the $r(i)$ are distributed like $N(0, \sigma^2)$, except when $c = N$.

Bifunctional Dependence Assumption Functional dependence as expressed in Equation (8) implicitly assumes that two structures having similar intensity ranges in S should also have similar intensity ranges in T. With some combinations of multimodal images, this is a crude approximation. For example, ventricles and bones generally give similar response values in a MR T1 weighted image while they appear with very distinct values in a CT scan. Conversely, white and black matter are well contrasted in a T1 image while corresponding to similar intensities in a CT.

To circumvent this difficulty, we have developed a strategy that enables the mapping of an intensity value in S to not only one, but two possible intensity values in T. This method is a natural extension of the previous method. Instead of computing a single function that maps the intensities of S to those of T, two functions are estimated and the mapping becomes a weighted sum of these two functions.

We start with the assumption that if a point has an intensity s in S, the corresponding point in T has an intensity t that is normally distributed around two possible values depending on s, $f_{\boldsymbol{\theta}}(s)$ and $f_{\boldsymbol{\psi}}(s)$. In statistical terms, this means that, given s, t is drawn from a mixture of Gaussian distribution,

$$P(t|s) = \pi_1(s)N(f_{\boldsymbol{\theta}}(s), \sigma^2) + \pi_2(s)N(f_{\boldsymbol{\psi}}(s), \sigma^2), \tag{10}$$

where $\pi_1(s)$ and $\pi_2(s) = 1 - \pi_1(s)$ are mixing proportions that depend on the intensity in the source image, and σ^2 represents the variance of the noise in the target image. Consistently with the functional case, we will restrict ourselves to polynomial intensity functions, i.e. $f_{\boldsymbol{\theta}}(s) = \theta_0 + \theta_1 s + \theta_2 s^2 + \cdots + \theta_p s^p$, and $f_{\boldsymbol{\psi}}(s) = \psi_0 + \psi_1 s + \psi_2 s^2 + \cdots + \psi_p s^p$.

An intuitive way to interpret this modelling is to state that for any voxel, there is a binary "selector" variable $\epsilon = \{1, 2\}$ that would tell us, if it was observed, which of the two functions $f_{\boldsymbol{\theta}}$ or $f_{\boldsymbol{\psi}}$ actually serves to map s to t. Without knowledge of ϵ, the best intensity correction to apply to S (in the sense of the conditional expectation [19]) is seen to be a weighted sum of the two functions,

$$f(s, t) = P(\epsilon = 1|s, t)f_{\boldsymbol{\theta}}(s) + P(\epsilon = 2|s, t)f_{\boldsymbol{\psi}}(s), \tag{11}$$

in which the weights correspond to the probability that the point be mapped according to either the first or the second function. We see that the intensity correction is now a function of both s and t. Applying Bayes' law, we find that for $\epsilon = \{1, 2\}$:

$$P(\epsilon|s, t) = \frac{P(\epsilon|s)P(t|\epsilon, s)}{P(t|s)},$$

and thus, using the fact that $P(\epsilon|s) = \pi_\epsilon(s)$ and $P(t|\epsilon, s) = G_\sigma(t - f_\epsilon(s))$, the weights are determined by

$$P(\epsilon|s, t) = \frac{\pi_\epsilon(s) \, G_\sigma(t - f_\epsilon(s))}{\pi_1(s) \, G_\sigma(t - f_\theta(s)) + \pi_2(s) \, G_\sigma(t - f_\psi(s))}, \tag{12}$$

where it should be clear from the context that $f_\epsilon \equiv f_\theta$ if $\epsilon = 1$, and $f_\epsilon \equiv f_\psi$ if $\epsilon = 2$.

In order to estimate the parameters of the model, we employ an ad hoc strategy that proceeds as follows. First, θ is estimated using the LTS/RLS method described in section 2.2. The points not used to compute θ, in a number between 0 and $N - c$, are used to estimate ψ still using the same method. Note that if this number is less than $10 \times p$, p being the polynomial degree, functional dependence is assumed and we fall back to the monofunctional assumption.

This provides a natural estimation of the "selector" variable for each voxel: the n_1 points that were used to build f_θ are likely to correspond to $\epsilon = 1$, while the n_2 points used to build f_ψ are likely to correspond to $\epsilon = 2$. Finally, the points that are rejected while estimating ψ are considered as bad intensity matches. A natural estimator for the variance σ^2 is then

$$\hat{\sigma}^2 = \frac{n_1}{n_1 + n_2} \hat{\sigma}_1^2 + \frac{n_2}{n_1 + n_2} \hat{\sigma}_2^2,$$

where $\hat{\sigma}_1^2$ and $\hat{\sigma}_2^2$ are the variances found respectively for f_θ and f_ψ during the RLS regression (See Section 2.2.). Similarly, the mixing proportions are computed according to

$$\hat{\pi}_\epsilon(s) = \frac{n_\epsilon(s)}{n_1(s) + n_2(s)}, \qquad \epsilon = \{1, 2\},$$

in which $n_\epsilon(s)$ is the number of voxels having an intensity s and used to build the function f_ϵ. Notice that in the case where $n_1(s) = n_2(s) = 0$ (i.e. no voxel corresponding to the intensity class s has been taken into account in the computation of f_θ or f_ψ), then we arbitrarily set the mixing proportions to $\hat{\pi}_1(s) = \hat{\pi}_2(s) = 0.5$.

The intensity correction of S can now be performed by reinjecting the estimated parameters in Equations (12) and (11).

3 Data

Most of the data used in the following experiments were obtained from Brain-Web [3, 8, 15, 9]. This tool uses an atlas with a resolution of $1 \times 1 \times 1 \mathrm{mm}^3$ comprising nine segmented regions from which T1, T2 and PD images can be generated. Three images, one of each modality, were generated with the same resolution as the atlas, 5% noise and no intensity non-uniformity. Since they are generated from the same atlas, they represent the same underlying anatomy and are all perfectly matched.

We also made use of a T1 MR image and a CT image, both from different subjects and having a resolution of $1 \times 1 \times 1mm^3$. Both these images were affinely registered with the atlas using the correlation ratio method [23]. To differentiate the T1 image obtained with the atlas from the other T1 image, the latter will be referenced as SCH.

The images all respect the neurological convention, i.e. on coronal and axial slices, the patient's left is on the left side of the image.

4   Results and Discussion

In the following section we present registration results involving images obtained from several different kinds of modalities. First, we show a typical example where monofunctional dependence can be assumed: registration of an atlas with an MR image. Then, more practical examples are shown where images from different modalities are registered and where bifunctional dependence may be assumed.

The multilevel process was performed at three resolution levels, namely 4mm, 2mm and 1mm per voxel. Displacement fields at one level are initialized from the result of the previous level. The initial displacement field v_0 is set to a zero. The Gaussian filter G_σ used to smooth the displacement field has a standard deviation of 1mm. 128 iterations are performed at 4mm/voxel, 32 at 2mm/voxel and 8 at 1mm/voxel. We believe that making use of a better stopping criterion, such as the difference of the SSD values between iterations, would probably improve the results shown below.

4.1   Monofunctional Dependence

We present here the result of registering the atlas with SCH. Since the atlas can be used to generate realistic MR images, it is safe to assume a functional dependence from the intensity of the atlas to that of SCH. Also, since SCH and the atlas are well aligned due to the affine registration, we have roughly estimated that the number of points already well matched are at least $0.80 \times N$, to which we have set the value of c. Since 10 classes are present in the atlas, the polynomial degree chosen was set to 9.

The result of registration is presented in Figure 1. For lack of space, we only show one set of corresponding slices extracted from the 3D images. However, we wish to make clear to the reader that the registration was performed in 3D, *not* slice by slice. More illustrations will be found in [12]. From left to right, the first picture shows an axial slice of the atlas. The second one presents the corresponding slice of SCH (which was chosen as the target image). The third and fourth pictures show the deformed atlas after elastic registration, respectively without and with intensity correction.

As can be seen, large morphometric differences have been corrected. Still, the matching is not perfect which may be observed by comparing the shape of several structures between SCH and the deformed atlas, e.g. the ventricles and the white matter. Registration imperfections are reflected in the intensity corrected image

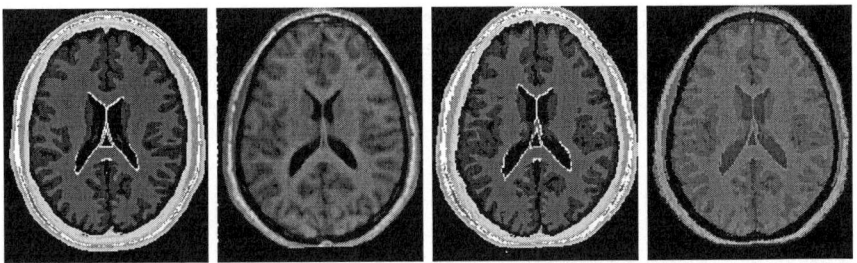

Fig. 1. Axial slices of the atlas to SCH registration result. From left to right: Atlas; SCH; atlas without intensity correction after registration with SCH; atlas with intensity correction after registration with SCH.

(right picture), where one may notice that the CSF intensity is slightly brighter than that in SCH (as can be seen in the ventricles and around the cortex). This problem can also be observed by looking at the intensity transformation function presented in Figure 5. The intensity level corresponding to the CSF is overestimated due to an overlap of the CSF in the atlas with the gray and white matter in SCH, especially around the cortical area which is known to present large variations between subjects.

This is probably an inherent limitation of elastic models when used in the context of inter-subject registration. The strong smoothness constraints imposed by the Gaussian regularization (or related regularization techniques) may prevent the assessment of large and uneven displacements required to match the anatomical structures of different subjects. To allow for larger displacements, another regularization strategy should be used, such as that based on a fluid model [7] or on a non-quadratic potential energy [13].

4.2 Bifunctional Dependence

When registering images from different modalities, monofunctional dependence may not necessarily be assumed. Here, we applied the method described in Section 2.2 where two polynomial functions of degree 12 are estimated. This number was set arbitrarily to a relatively high value to enable important intensity transformations.

Figure 2 presents the result of registering T1 with CT. Using these last two modalities, most intensities should be mapped to gray and only the skull, representing a small portion of the image data, should be mapped to white. After affine registration almost all voxels are well matched. Hence, in this particular case, we have chosen a high value for c set to $0.90 \times N$.

As we can see in Figure 2, the skull, shown in black in the MR image and in white in the CT scan, is well registered and the intensity transformation adequate. The top right graph of Figure 5 presents the functions f_θ and f_ψ found during the registration process. The red line corresponds to f_θ and the blue one to f_ψ. The line width for a given intensity s is proportional to the value of the corresponding $\pi_\epsilon(s)$. The gray values represent the joint histogram after registration. As can be observed on this graph, the polynomials found fit well with the high density clusters of the joint histogram. Still, some points need to be addressed.

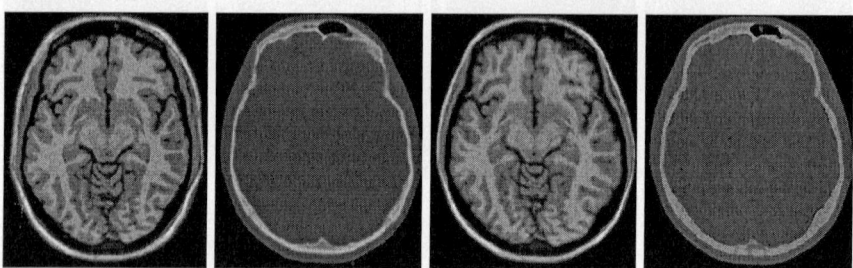

Fig. 2. Axial slices of the T1 to CT registration result. From left to right: T1; CT; T1 without intensity correction after registration with T1; T1 with intensity correction after registration with T1.

We can observe that due to the restricted polynomial degree, f_θ, (shown in red) oscillates around the CT gray value instead of fitting a strait line. This is reflected in the intensity corrected image, where the underlying anatomy can still be observed by small intensity variations inside the skull. This artifact has insubstantial consequences during the registration process since the difference between most of the voxel intensities is zero, resulting in null displacements. The displacements driving the deformation will be those of the skull and the skin contours, and will be propagated in the rest of the image as an effect of smoothing the displacement field.

We also notice that f_ψ (shown in blue), which is mainly responsible for the mapping of the skull, does not properly model the cluster it represents for intensities smaller than 5. The mapping for these intensities is slightly underestimated. This may have two causes. First, as in the previous case, it might be due to the restricted polynomial degree. Second, we can notice that some of the background values in T1 that have an intensity close to 0 are mapped to gray values in the CT which correspond to soft tissues. This means that some of the background in the T1 is matched with the skin in the CT. This has the effect of "pulling" f_ψ closer to the small cluster positioned around (2,65). If the underestimation of f_ψ arises because of the second reason, letting the algorithm iterate longer might provide a better result.

In Figures 3 and 4, we present the result of registering T2 and PD respectively with SCH. The bottom graphs of Figure 5 show the corresponding intensity transformations. For these experiments, c was set to $0.60 \times N$, a value we have found to be effective for these types of modalities after affine registration.

One observation that can be made by looking at the graphs of Figure 5 is that the estimated functions f_θ and f_ψ are quite similar in both cases. This suggests

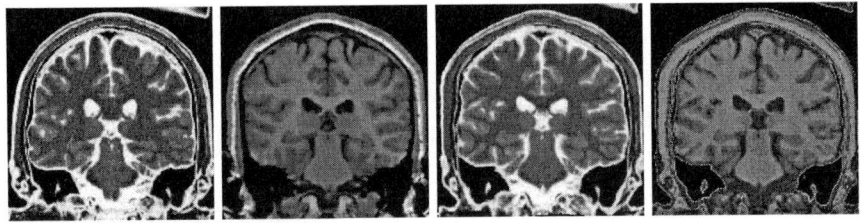

Fig. 3. Coronal slices of the T2 to SCH registration result. From left to right: T2; SCH; T2 without intensity correction after registration with SCH; T2 with intensity correction after registration with SCH.

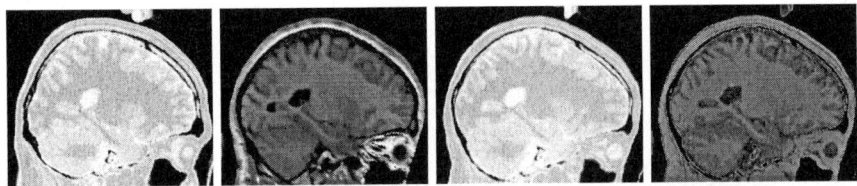

Fig. 4. Sagittal slices of the PD to SCH registration result. From left to right: PD; SCH; PD without intensity correction after registration with SCH; PD with intensity correction after registration with SCH.

that assuming a monofunctional dependence would be relevant. However, the results we obtained when registering T2 with SCH, and PD with SCH, using the monofunctional model were less convincing than when using the bifunctional model [12].

This may be explained by a closer look at our bifunctional intensity modelling. Equation 10 reflects the assumption that if an anatomical point has an intensity s in S, the corresponding point has an intensity t in T that is distributed normally around two possible values depending on s. But it makes no assumption about how the intensities in S are distributed. This models the intensities of S without noise, which may not necessarily be well justified, but enables the use linear regression to estimate the intensity transformation.

The effect of noise in S is reflected in the joint histograms by enlarging clusters along the x axis. This, added to bad matches and partial volume effect, creates many outliers in C and makes the assessment of the true intensity transformation more difficult and more resistant to our robust regression technique. Preprocessing of S using for example anisotropic diffusion may narrow the clusters and provide better results [22].

Adding the estimation of a second function in the bifunctional model helps counter the effect of noise on S. For example, the CSF in the PD image has intensity values ranging from about 200 to 240 and gray matter from about 175 to 210. In SCH, these ranges are about 30 to 70 and 55 to 80 respectively. As can be seen in Figure 5, f_θ models well the gray matter cluster but fails to reflect the

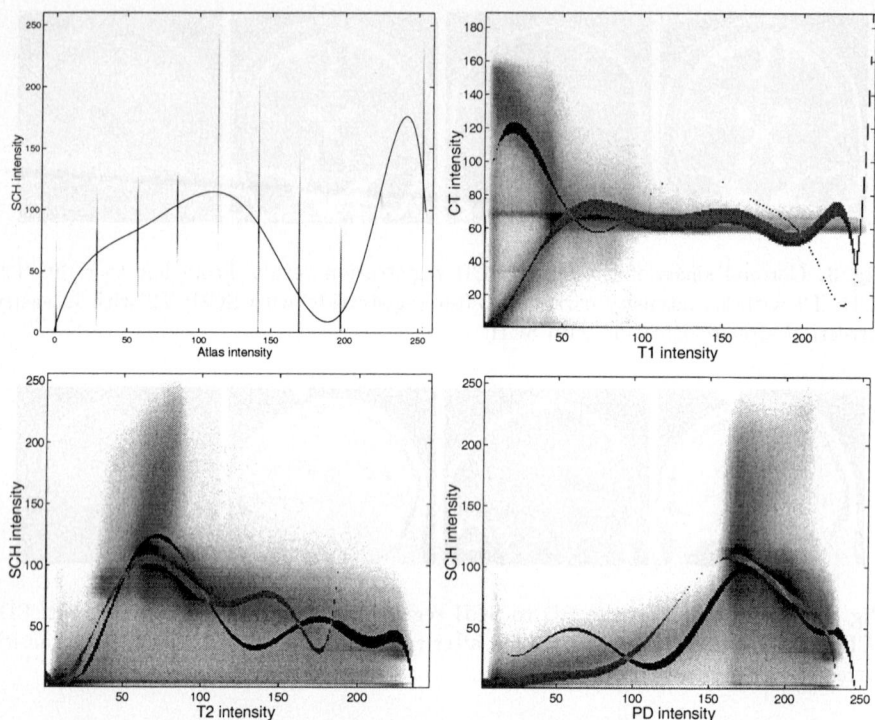

Fig. 5. Graphs of the intensity corrections found in our experiments. From left to right, top to bottom: Atlas to SCH, T1 to CT, T2 to SCH, PD to SCH. In the last three graphs, which correspond to bifunctional models, the red (bright) line represents f_θ and the blue (dark) one f_ψ. The line width for a given intensity value s in the source image corresponds to the value of the corresponding proportion, $\pi_\epsilon(s)$. The gray values represent the joint histogram after registration.

CSF transformation. Estimating the second polynomial f_ψ solves this problem by considering the CSF cluster.

4.3 Displacement field comparison

Since the atlas, the T1, the T2 and the PD images have all been registered with SCH, it is relevant to compare some statistics of the resulting displacement fields to assess if our algorithm provides consistent results across modalities.

We computed statistics regarding the difference between any two of these displacement fields. The length of the vectors of the resulting difference fields were calculated. Each cell of Table 1 presents, for each combination of displacement fields, the median length, the average length with the corresponding standard deviation and the maximum length of the difference field.

The two largest average errors are 1.58 mm and 1.76 mm, and were found when comparing the Atlas-SCH registration with T1-SCH and PD-SCH, respec-

Table 1. Statistics regarding the displacements difference between each type of registration. Each cell presents the median length, the average length with the corresponding standard deviation and the maximum length. All measures are in millimeters.

Difference (mm)	Atlas-SCH T1-SCH	Atlas-SCH T2-SCH	Atlas-SCH PD-SCH	T1-SCH T2-SCH	T1-SCH PD-SCH	T2-SCH PD-SCH
median	1.46	1.13	1.67	1.00	1.01	1.32
average	1.58	1.23	1.76	1.18	1.16	1.40
std. dev.	0.84	0.63	0.79	0.78	0.71	0.68
maximum	6.99	5.14	7.10	7.17	8.08	6.86

tively. This may be explained by the intensity correction bias for the CSF that would tend to attenuate displacements and produce larger errors, a problem invoked in Section 4.1. Aside from these, the average error length varies between 0.97mm and 1.40mm and the median error is between 0.85mm and 1.32mm. These are values in the range of the image resolution of 1.0mm. Note also that all the standard deviations are below this value.

Also, we observe that the results obtained when registering images from different modalities (Atlas-SCH, T2-SCH, and PD-SCH) seem to be consistent with the monomodal registration result (T1-SCH), in which no intensity correction was performed. This suggests that the intensity correction may not cause a sensible degradation of the registration when compared to the monomodal case. We point out, however, that these are global measures that are presented to provide an idea of the differences between the displacement fields. They do not strictly provide a validation of the method, but do show a certain coherence between the different results we obtained.

5   Conclusion

In this paper, we introduced an original method to perform non-rigid registration of multimodal images. This iterative algorithm is composed of two sections: the geometrical transformation and the intensity transformation. We have related the geometrical transformation computation to several popular registration concepts: SSD, optical flow and the demons method. Two intensity transformation models were described which assume either monofunctional or bifunctional dependence between the intensities of the images to match. Both of these models are built using robust estimators to enable precise and accurate transformation solutions. Results of registration were presented and showed that the algorithm performs well for several kinds of modalities including T1 MR, T2 MR, PD MR, CT and segmentations, and provides consistent results across modalities.

A current limitation of the method is that it uses Gaussian filtering to regularize the displacement field. This technique was chosen for its computational efficiency rather than for its physical relevance. In the context of inter-subject registration, other regularization strategies need to be investigated to better account for morphological differences.

References

1. D. C. Barber. Registration of low resolution medical images. *Physics in Medecine and Biology*, 37(7):1485–1498, 1992.

2. J. L. Barron, D. J. Fleet, and S. S. Beauchemin. Performance of optical flow techniques. *International Journal of Computer Vision*, 12(1):43–77, January 1994.

3. Simulated brain database. http://www.bic.mni.mcgill.ca/brainweb/.

4. J. W. Brandt. Improved accuracy in gradient-based optical flow estimation. *International Journal of Computer Vision*, 25(1):5–22, 1997.

5. M. Bro-Nielsen and C. Gramkow. Fast fluid registration of medical images. In K. H. Höhne and R. Kikinis, editors, *Proc. VBC'96*, volume 1131 of *Lecture Notes in Computer Science*, pages 267–276. Springer-Verlag, 1996.

6. P. Cachier, X. Pennec, and N. Ayache. Fast non rigid matching by gradient descent: Study and improvements of the "demons" algorithm. Technical Report 3706, INRIA, June 1999.

7. G. E. Christensen, R. D. Rabbitt, and M. I. Miller. Deformable templates using large deformation kinematics. *IEEE Transactions in Medical Imaging*, 5(10):1435–1447, October 1996.

8. C. A. Cocosco, V. Kollokian, R. K.-S. Kwan, and A. C. Evans. Brainweb: Online interface to a 3D MRI simulated brain database. *NeuroImage, Proc. HBM'97*, 5(4):S425, May 1997.

9. D. L. Collins, A. P. Zijdenbos, V. Kollokian, J. G. Sled, N. J. Kabani, C. J. Holmes, and A. C. Evans. Design and construction of a realistic digital brain phantom. *IEEE Transactions in Medical Imaging*, 17(3):463–468, June 1998.

10. J. Feldmar, J. Declerck, G. Malandain, and N. Ayache. Extension of the ICP algorithm to non-rigid intensity-based registration of 3D volumes. *Computer Vision and Image Understanding*, 66(2):193–206, May 1997.

11. T. Gaens, F. Maes, D. Vandermeulen, and P. Suetens. Non-rigid multimodal image registration using mutual information. In W. M. Wells, A. Colchester, and S. Delp, editors, *Proc. MICCAI'98*, volume 1496 of *Lecture Notes in Computer Science*, pages 1099–1106. Springer-Verlag, 1998.

12. A. Guimond, A. Roche, N. Ayache, and J. Meunier. Multimodal Brain Warping Using the Demons Algorithm and Adaptative Intensity Corrections. Technical Report 3796, INRIA, November 1999.

13. P. Hellier, C. Barillot, E. Mémin, and P. Pérez. Medical image registration with robust multigrid techniques. In *Proc. MICCAI'99*, volume 1679 of *Lecture Notes in Computer Science*, pages 680–687, Cambridge, England, October 1999.

14. B. K. P. Horn and B. G. Schunck. Determining optical flow. *Artificial Intelligence*, 17:185–203, August 1981.

15. R. K.-S. Kwan, A. C. Evans, and G. B. Pike. An extensible MRI simulator for post-processing evaluation. In K. H. Höhne and R. Kikinis, editors, *Proc. VBC'96*, volume 1131 of *LNCS*, pages 135–140. Springer-Verlag, 1996.

16. Y. H. Lau, M. Braun, and B. F. Hutton. Non-rigid 3d image registration using regionally constrainted matching and the correlation ratio. In F. Pernus, S. Kovacic, H.S. Stiehl, and M.A. Viergever, editors, *Proc. WBIR'99*, pages 137–148, 1999.

17. F. Maes, A. Collignon, D. Vandermeulen, G. Marchal, and P. Suetens. Multimodality image registration by maximization of mutual information. *IEEE Transactions in Medical Imaging*, 16(2):187–198, 1997.

18. J. B. A. Maintz, E. H. W. Meijering, and M. A. Viergever. General multimodal elastic registration based on mutual information. In K. M. Hanson, editor, *Medical*

Imaging 1998: Image Processing (MI'98), volume 3338 of *SPIE Proceedings*, pages 144–154, Bellingham (WA), USA, April 1998.

19. A. Papoulis. *Probability, Random Variables, and Stochastic Processes*. McGraw-Hill, Inc., third edition, 1991.

20. X. Pennec, P. Cachier, and N. Ayache. Understanding the "demon's algorithm": 3d non-rigid registration by gradient descent. In *Proc. MICCAI'99*, volume 1679 of *Lecture Notes in Computer Science*, pages 597–605. Springer-Verlag, 1999.

21. A. Roche, G. Malandain, and N. Ayache. Unifying maximum likelihood approaches in medical image registration. *International Journal of Imaging Systems and Technology: Special Issue on 3D Imaging*, 2000. In press.

22. A. Roche, G. Malandain, N. Ayache, and S. Prima. Towards a better comprehension of similarity measures used in medical image registration. In *Proc. MICCAI'99*, volume 1679 of *LNCS*, pages 555–566. Springer-Verlag, September 1999.

23. A. Roche, G. Malandain, X. Pennec, and N. Ayache. The correlation ratio as a new similarity measure for multimodal image registration. In *Proc. MICCAI'98*, volume 1496 of *LNCS*, pages 1115–1124. Springer-Verlag, October 1998.

24. P. J. Rousseeuw and K. Van Driessen. Computing LTS Regression for Large Data Sets. Technical report, Statistics Group, University of Antwerp, 1999.

25. Peter J. Rousseeuw and Annick M. Leroy. *Robust Regression and Outlier Detection*. Wiley series in probability and mathematical statistics. John Wiley & Sons, 1987.

26. E. P. Simoncelli. Design of multi-dimensional derivative filters. In *International Conference on Image Processing*, Austin, USA, November 1994. IEEE.

27. J.-P. Thirion. Fast non-rigid matching of 3D medical images. Technical Report 2547, INRIA, Sophia-Antipolis, 1995.

28. J.-P. Thirion. Image matching as a diffusion process: an analogy with Maxwell's demons. *Medical Image Analysis*, 2(3):243–260, 1998.

29. Arthur W. Toga. *Brain Warping*. Academic Press, 1999.

30. P. Viola and W. M. Wells. Alignment by maximization of mutual information. *International Journal of Computer Vision*, 24(2):137–154, 1997.

31. R. P. Woods, J. C. Mazziotta, and S. R. Cherry. MRI-PET registration with automated algorithm. *Journal of Comp. Assist. Tomography*, 17(4):536–546, 1993.

A Physically-Based Statistical Deformable Model for Brain Image Analysis

Christophoros Nikou[1,2], Fabrice Heitz[1], Jean-Paul Armspach[2], and Gloria Bueno[1,2]

[1] Laboratoire des Sciences de l'Image de l'Informatique et de la Télédétection
Université Strasbourg I (UPRES-A CNRS 7005)
4, boulevard Sébastien Brant, 67400 Illkirch, France
[2] Institut de Physique Biologique, Faculté de Médecine
Université Strasbourg I (UPRES-A CNRS 7004)
4, rue Kirschleger, 67085 Strasbourg CEDEX, France

Abstract. A probabilistic deformable model for the representation of brain structures is described. The statistically learned deformable model represents the relative location of head (skull and scalp) and brain surfaces in Magnetic Resonance Images (MRIs) and accommodates their significant variability across different individuals. The head and brain surfaces of each volume are parameterized by the amplitudes of the vibration modes of a deformable spherical mesh. For a given MRI in the training set, a vector containing the largest vibration modes describing the head and the brain is created. This random vector is statistically constrained by retaining the most significant variation modes of its Karhunen-Loeve expansion on the training population. By these means, the conjunction of surfaces are deformed according to the anatomical variability observed in the training set. Two applications of the probabilistic deformable model are presented: the deformable model-based registration of 3D multimodal (MR/SPECT) brain images without removing non-brain structures and the segmentation of the brain in MRI using the probabilistic constraints embedded in the deformable model. The multi-object deformable model may be considered as a first step towards the development of a general purpose probabilistic anatomical brain atlas.

1 Introduction

In medical image analysis, deformable models offer a unique and powerful approach to accommodate the significant variability of biological structures over time and across different individuals. A survey on deformable models as a promising computer-assisted medical image analysis technique has recently been presented in [7].

We present a 3D statistical deformable model carrying information on multiple anatomical structures (head -skull and scalp- and brain) for multimodal brain image processing. Our goal is to describe the spatial relation between these anatomical structures as well as the shape variations observed over a representative population of individuals. In our approach, the different anatomical structures are represented by physics-based deformable models [13] whose parameters undergo statistical training. The resulting joint statistical deformable model is considered as a first step towards the development of a general purpose probabilistic atlas for various applications in medical image analysis (segmentation, labeling, registration, pathology characterization).

In the proposed approach the considered anatomical structures surfaces are extracted from a training set of 3D MRI. These surfaces are then parameterized by the amplitudes of the vibration modes of a physically-based deformable model [13,10] and a joint model is constructed for each set of structures. The joint model is then statistically constrained by a Karhunen-Loeve decomposition of the vibration modes. By these means, the spatial relation between the head and brain structures, as well as the anatomical variability observed in the training set are compactly described by a limited number of parameters.

Physics-based models enable a hierarchical description of anatomical structures as the ordered superimposition of vibrations (of different frequencies) of an initial mesh. Physically-based parameterizations are also invariant to *small* misregistration in rotation (contrary to Point Distribution Models (PDMs) [4], needing accurate rotation and translation compensation). Let us notice that physically-based models also differ from 3D Fourier descriptors because the latter also need a uniform way to discretize the surface and are not rotation invariant [14].

Two applications of the probabilistic deformable model are presented in this paper:

- The segmentation of the brain from MRIs using the probabilistic constraints embedded in the deformable model.
- The robust deformable model-based rigid registration of 3D multimodal (MR/SPECT) brain images by optimizing an energy function relying on the chamfer distance between the statistically constrained model parts and the image data.

The remainder of this paper is organized as follows: in Section 2, the parameterization of the head and brain structures by the vibration modes of a spherical mesh is presented. The statistical training procedure is described in Section 3. The applications of the probabilistic model to 3D segmentation and to multimodal (MRI/SPECT) image registration are presented in Section 4. Experimental results on real data, with a 50-patients trained model, are presented and commented on in the same section. Finally, conclusions are proposed in Section 5.

2   3D physics-based deformable modeling

To provide a training set, a representative collection of 50 3D MRI volumes of different patients have first been registered to a reference image using an unsupervised robust rigid registration technique [11, 12]. This preliminary step is necessary to provide a consistent initialization for the deformable model for all images in the training step, since the representation is not invariant to rotation (the same alignment is also applied to the patient data processed in Section 4). The head of each volume has then been segmented by simple thresholding and region growing [9].

Both head and brain contours were parameterized by the amplitudes of the vibration modes of a physics-based deformable model. Following the approach of Nastar et al. [10], the model for a given structure consists of 3D points sampled on a spherical surface, following a quadrilateral cylinder topology in order to avoid singularities due to the poles. Each node has a mass m and is connected to its four neighbours with springs of stiffness k. The model nodes are stacked in vector:

$$\mathbf{X}_0 = (x_1^0, y_1^0, z_1^0, ..., x_{N'N}^0, y_{N'N}^0, z_{N'N}^0)^T \tag{1}$$

where N is the number of points in the direction of the geographical longitude and N' is the number of points in the direction of the geographical latitude of the sphere. The physical model is characterized by its mass matrix $\mathbf{M}$, its stiffness matrix $\mathbf{K}$ and its dumping matrix $\mathbf{C}$ and its governing equation may be written as [13]:

$$\mathbf{M\ddot{U}} + \mathbf{C\dot{U}} + \mathbf{KU} = \mathbf{F} \tag{2}$$

where $\mathbf{U}$ stands for the nodal displacements of the initial mesh $\mathbf{X}_0$. The image force vector $\mathbf{F}$ is based on the euclidean distance between the mesh nodes and their nearest contour points [3].

Since equation (2) is of order $3NN'$, where NN' is the total number of nodes of the spherical mesh, it is solved in a subspace corresponding to the truncated vibration modes of the deformable structure [10, 13], using the following change of basis:

$$\mathbf{U} = \mathbf{\Phi\tilde{U}} = \sum_i \tilde{u}_i \phi_i, \tag{3}$$

where $\mathbf{\Phi}$ is a matrix and $\mathbf{\tilde{U}}$ is a vector, ϕ_i is the ith column of $\mathbf{\Phi}$ and $\tilde{u}_i$ is the ith scalar component of vector $\mathbf{\tilde{U}}$. By choosing $\mathbf{\Phi}$ as the matrix whose columns are the eigenvectors of the eigenproblem:

$$\mathbf{K}\phi_i = \omega_i^2 \mathbf{M}\phi_i, \tag{4}$$

and using the standard Rayleigh hypothesis [10], matrices $\mathbf{K}$, $\mathbf{M}$ and $\mathbf{C}$ are simultaneously diagonalized:

$$\begin{cases} \mathbf{\Phi}^T \mathbf{M\Phi} = \mathbf{I} \\ \mathbf{\Phi}^T \mathbf{K\Phi} = \mathbf{\Omega}^2 \end{cases} \tag{5}$$

where $\mathbf{\Omega}^2$ is the diagonal matrix whose elements are the eigenvalues ω_i^2 and $\mathbf{I}$ is the identity matrix.

An important advantage of this formulation is that the eigenvectors and the eigenvalues of a quadrilateral mesh with cylinder topology have an explicit expression [1] and they do not have to be computed by standard slow eigen-decomposition techniques (generally matrices $\mathbf{K}$ and $\mathbf{M}$ are very large). The eigenvalues are given by the equation:

$$\omega_{p,p'}^2 = \frac{4k}{m} \left(\sin^2 \frac{p\pi}{2N} + \sin^2 \frac{p'\pi}{N'} \right) \tag{6}$$

and the eigenvectors are obtained by:

$$\phi_{p,p'} = \left[..., \cos \frac{(2n-1)p\pi}{2N} \cos \frac{2n'p'\pi}{N'}, ... \right]^T \tag{7}$$

with $n \in \{1, 2, ..., N\}$ and $n' \in \{1, 2, ..., N'\}$.

Substituting (3) into (2) and premultiplying by $\mathbf{\Phi}^T$ yields:

$$\ddot{\tilde{\mathbf{U}}} + \tilde{\mathbf{C}}\dot{\tilde{\mathbf{U}}} + \mathbf{\Omega}^2\tilde{\mathbf{U}} = \tilde{\mathbf{F}} \tag{8}$$

where $\tilde{\mathbf{C}} = \mathbf{\Phi}^T\mathbf{C}\mathbf{\Phi}$ and $\tilde{\mathbf{F}} = \mathbf{\Phi}^T\mathbf{F}$.

In many computer vision applications [13], when the initial and the final state are known, it is assumed that a constant load $\mathbf{F}$ is applied to the body. Thus, equation (2) is called the equilibrium governing equation and corresponds to the static problem:

$$\mathbf{K}\mathbf{U} = \mathbf{F} \tag{9}$$

In the new basis, equation (9) is thus simplified to $3NN'$ scalar equations:

$$\omega_i^2\tilde{u}_i = \tilde{f}_i. \tag{10}$$

In equation (10), ω_i designates the ith eigenvalue, the scalar $\tilde{u}_i$ is the amplitude of the corresponding vibration mode (corresponding to eigenvector ϕ_i). Equation (10), indicates that instead of computing the displacements vector $\mathbf{U}$ from equation (9), we can compute its decomposition in terms of the vibration modes of the original mesh.

The number of vibration modes retained in the object description, is chosen so as to obtain a compact but adequately accurate representation. A typical *a priori* value covering many types of standard deformations is the quarter of the number of degrees of freedom in the system [10] (i.e. 25% of the modes are kept). Figure 1 shows the parameterization of head and brain surfaces considered for a subject belonging to the training set, by the 25% lowest frequency modes. Although not providing a high resolution description of the brain surface, this truncated representation provides a satisfactory compromise between accuracy and complexity of the representation. The spherical model is initialized around the structures of interest (fig. 1(a) and 1(d)). The vibration amplitudes are explicitly computed by equation (10), where rigid body modes ($\omega_i = 0$) are discarded and the nodal displacements may be recovered using equation (3). The physical representation $\mathbf{X}(\tilde{\mathbf{U}})$ is finally given by applying the deformations to the initial spherical mesh (fig. 1(b-c) and 1(e-f)):

$$\mathbf{X}(\tilde{\mathbf{U}}) = \mathbf{X}_0 + \mathbf{\Phi}\tilde{\mathbf{U}} \tag{11}$$

Thus, the head and brain surfaces of a particular patient are hierarchically described in terms of vibrations of an initial spherical mesh. The next step consists in applying the above parameterization to each patient of the training set and to perform statistical learning for the head and brain structures.

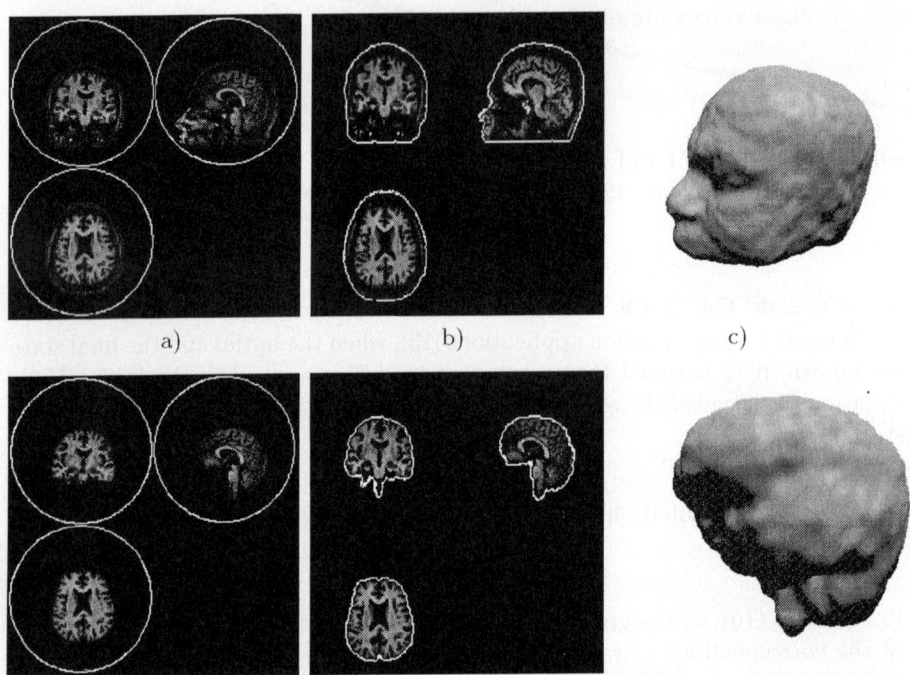

a)　　　　　　　　b)　　　　　　　　c)

Fig. 1. *Head and brain parameterization from 3D MRI. The first column shows in a multiplanar (sagittal, coronal, transversal) view the initial spherical mesh superimposed to the structures to be parameterized. The midlle column presents in a multiplanar view the deformable models at equilibrium (25% of the modes). The last column illustrates 3D renderings of the physically-based models. The rows from top to bottom correspond to: (a)-(c) head and (d)-(f) brain.*

3　Statistical training : the joint model

For each image $i = 1, ..., n$ ($n = 50$) in the training set, a vector $\mathbf{a}_i$ containing the lowest frequency vibration modes, M_H and M_B, describing the head and the brain, respectively, is created:

$$\mathbf{a}_i = (\tilde{\mathbf{U}}_i^H, \tilde{\mathbf{U}}_i^B)^T \qquad (12)$$

where:

$$\tilde{\mathbf{U}}_i^H = (\tilde{u}_1^h, \tilde{u}_2^h, \ldots, \tilde{u}_{M_H}^h)_i \tag{13}$$

$$\tilde{\mathbf{U}}_i^B = (\tilde{u}_1^b, \tilde{u}_2^b, \ldots, \tilde{u}_{M_B}^b)_i \tag{14}$$

with $3(M_H + M_B) < 6NN'$.

Random vector $\mathbf{a}$ is statistically constrained by retaining the most significant variation modes in its Karhunen-Loeve (KL) transform [4,5]:

$$\mathbf{a} = \bar{\mathbf{a}} + \mathbf{Pb} \tag{15}$$

where

$$\bar{\mathbf{a}} = \frac{1}{n} \sum_{i=1}^{n} \mathbf{a}_i \tag{16}$$

is the average vector of vibration amplitudes of the structures belonging to the training set, $\mathbf{P}$ is the matrix whose columns are the eigenvectors of the covariance matrix

$$\mathbf{\Gamma} = \mathbb{E}\left[(\mathbf{a} - \bar{\mathbf{a}})^T(\mathbf{a} - \bar{\mathbf{a}})\right] \tag{17}$$

and

$$\mathbf{b}_i = \mathbf{P}^T(\mathbf{a}_i - \bar{\mathbf{a}}) \tag{18}$$

are the coordinates of $(\mathbf{a} - \bar{\mathbf{a}})$ in the eigenvector basis.

The deformable model is finally parameterized by the m most significant statistical deformation modes stacked in vector $\mathbf{b}$. By modifying $\mathbf{b}$, both head and brain are deformed in conjunction (fig. 2), according to the anatomical variability observed in the training set. The multi-object deformable model describes the spatial relationships between the considered surfaces of a subject as well as their shape variations.

Given the double (head and brain) initial spherical mesh:

$$\mathbf{X}_{INIT} = \begin{pmatrix} \mathbf{X}_0 \\ \mathbf{X}_0 \end{pmatrix}, \tag{19}$$

the statistical deformable model $\mathbf{X}(\mathbf{a})$ is thus represented by:

$$\mathbf{X}(\mathbf{a}) = \mathbf{X}_{INIT} + \overline{\overline{\mathbf{\Phi}}}\mathbf{a} \tag{20}$$

Combining equations (15) and (20) we have:

$$\mathbf{X}(\mathbf{b}) = \mathbf{X}_{INIT} + \overline{\overline{\mathbf{\Phi}}}\bar{\mathbf{a}} + \overline{\overline{\mathbf{\Phi}}}\mathbf{Pb} \tag{21}$$

where:

$$\overline{\overline{\mathbf{\Phi}}} = \begin{pmatrix} \mathbf{\Phi}_H & 0 \\ 0 & \mathbf{\Phi}_B \end{pmatrix}, \quad \mathbf{P} = \begin{pmatrix} \mathbf{P}_{HB} \\ \mathbf{P}_{BH} \end{pmatrix}, \quad \bar{\mathbf{a}} = \begin{pmatrix} \bar{\mathbf{a}}_H \\ \bar{\mathbf{a}}_B \end{pmatrix} \tag{22}$$

In equation (22), the columns of the $3NN' \times 3M_H$ matrix $\mathbf{\Phi}_H$ are the eigenvectors of the spherical mesh describing the head surface and the columns of the $3NN' \times 3M_B$ matrix $\mathbf{\Phi}_B$ are the eigenvectors of the spherical mesh describing the brain surface. Besides, the $3M_H \times m$ matrix $\mathbf{P}_{HB}$ and the $3M_B \times m$ matrix $\mathbf{P}_{BH}$ describe the statistical dependencies of head and brain deformations observed in the training set. Vectors $\bar{\mathbf{a}}_H$ and $\bar{\mathbf{a}}_B$ are of order $3M_H \times 1$ and $3M_B \times 1$ respectively, and vector $\mathbf{b}$ has a low dimension $m \ll 3\,(M_H + M_B)$.

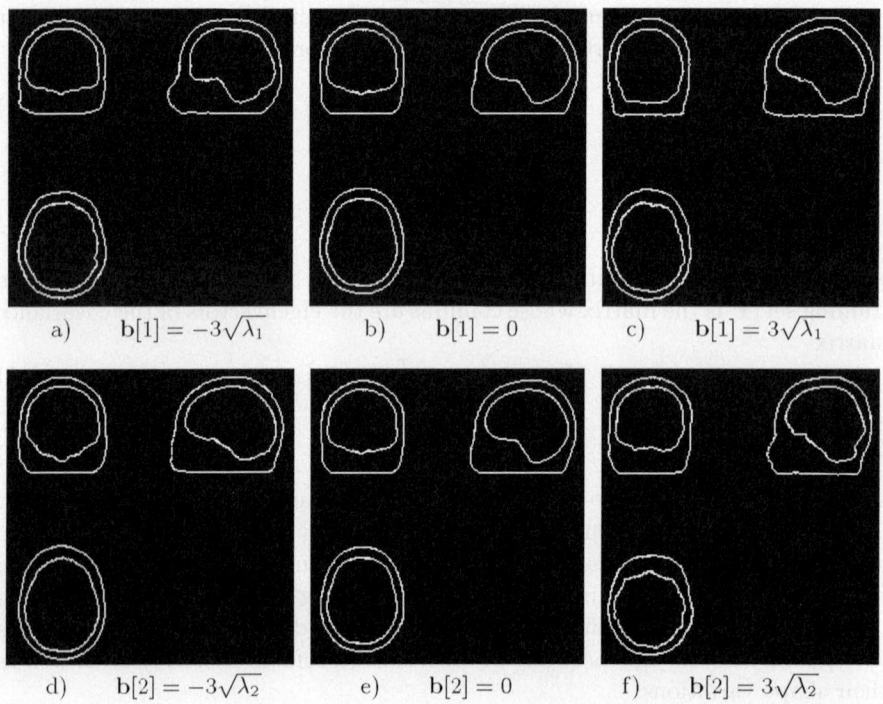

a) $b[1] = -3\sqrt{\lambda_1}$ b) $b[1] = 0$ c) $b[1] = 3\sqrt{\lambda_1}$

d) $b[2] = -3\sqrt{\lambda_2}$ e) $b[2] = 0$ f) $b[2] = 3\sqrt{\lambda_2}$

Fig. 2. *Multiplanar view of the 3D joint model's deformations by varying the first two statistical modes in vector* $\mathbf{b}$ *between* $-\sqrt{\lambda_i}$ *and* $\sqrt{\lambda_i}$, $i = 1, 2$. λ_i *designates the* i^{th} *eigenvalue of the covariance matrix* $\mathbf{\Gamma}$.

As it can be seen in Table 1, with the KL representation, only a few parameters are necessary to describe the variations in the training population (fig. 2). Table 1 shows that, for instance 5 parameters carry approximately 95% of the global information.

The number of degrees of freedom of the original mesh, for both head and brain surfaces, was $2 \times 3NN' = 2 \times 3 \times 100 \times 100 = 60000$. In the vibration modes subspace, this number was reduced to $3(M_H + M_B) = 3 \times (2500 + 2500) = 15000$ and finally in the KL subspace the degrees of freedom were reduced to $m \simeq 5$ achieving a compression ratio of $12000 : 1$. This compression ratio enables a compact description of shape variability, and results in a tractable constrained deformable model for brain image segmentation and registration, as described in the next section.

KL decomposition of joint model variability

λ_k	$\dfrac{\lambda_k}{\sum_{i=1}^{50}\lambda_i}$ (%)	$\dfrac{\sum_{i=1}^{k}\lambda_i}{\sum_{i=1}^{50}\lambda_i}$ (%)
λ_1	51.12	51.12
λ_2	20.54	71.66
λ_3	12.91	84.57
λ_4	7.38	91.95
λ_5	3.16	95.11
$\vdots$	$\vdots$	$\vdots$
λ_{50}	0.00	100.0

Table 1. *Percentage of the global information carried by the different eigenvalues associated with the statistical model. The total number of non-zero eigenvalues is 50.*

4 Applications

Several applications of the statistical model may be considered in brain image processing. The model may be used as a simplified anatomical representation of the images belonging to the training set. If the training set is representative enough of a population, the model may also be used to analyse images of patients not belonging to the training set. To this end, the 50 subjects of our data base were carefully selected, with the aid of an expert neurologist. Besides, the data base is conceived in such a way that it can be incrementally augmented by new elements.

We consider here two applications of the joint statistical model: the segmentation of the brain from 3D MRI and the registration of multimodal (MRI/SPECT) brain images. Before presenting these two applications, let us notice that the equation describing the configuration of the statistical model:

$$\mathbf{X}(\mathbf{b}) = \mathbf{X}_{INIT} + \overline{\overline{\boldsymbol{\Phi}}}\bar{\mathbf{a}} + \overline{\overline{\boldsymbol{\Phi}}}\mathbf{P}\mathbf{b} \tag{23}$$

may be separated into two equations describing the head and brain parts of the model:

$$\mathbf{X}_H(\mathbf{b}) = \mathbf{X}_0 + \boldsymbol{\Phi}_H\bar{\mathbf{a}}_H + \boldsymbol{\Phi}_H\mathbf{P}_{HB}\mathbf{b} \tag{24}$$

$$\mathbf{X}_B(\mathbf{b}) = \mathbf{X}_0 + \boldsymbol{\Phi}_B\bar{\mathbf{a}}_B + \boldsymbol{\Phi}_B\mathbf{P}_{BH}\mathbf{b} \tag{25}$$

Let us also recall that equations (24) and (25) are coupled by the sub-matrices $\mathbf{P}_{HB}$ and $\mathbf{P}_{BH}$ representing the statistical dependencies (spatial relationships) between the two anatomical structures. These submatrices cannot be calculated separately: they are parts of matrix $\mathbf{P}$. The terms $\bar{\mathbf{a}}_H$ and $\bar{\mathbf{a}}_B$ express the mean vibration amplitudes for the head and brain surfaces of the training set, $\mathbf{X}_0$ is the initial spherical mesh and $\boldsymbol{\Phi}_H$ and $\boldsymbol{\Phi}_B$ denote its eigenvectors.

4.1 Brain segmentation

In order to segment the brain from a patient MRI volume, not belonging to the training set, the patient head is first parameterized by the physics-based model. The head structure is easily segmented from its background by simple thresholding and region growing algorithms. The segmented head surface is parameterized by the amplitudes of the vibration modes of a spherical mesh, as already explained in Section 2. The spherical mesh is initialized around the head structure and equation (2) is solved in the modal subspace. The solution for the vibration amplitudes describing the patient head surface is:

$$\tilde{u}_i^h = \frac{1}{\omega_i^2} \tilde{f}_i^h \qquad (26)$$

for $i = 1, ..., 3M_H$. The head surface coordinates are obtained by introducing vector $\tilde{\mathbf{U}}^H = (\tilde{u}_1^h, \tilde{u}_2^h, \ldots, \tilde{u}_{M_H}^h)^T$ in equation (11):

$$\mathbf{X}_H(\tilde{\mathbf{U}}^H) = \mathbf{X}_0 + \boldsymbol{\Phi}_H \tilde{\mathbf{U}}^H \qquad (27)$$

The next step consists in determining the statistical model parameters $\mathbf{b}$ describing "at best" the segmented head surface:

$$\mathbf{X}_H(\mathbf{b}) = \mathbf{X}_0 + \boldsymbol{\Phi}_H \bar{\mathbf{a}}_H + \boldsymbol{\Phi}_H \mathbf{P}_{HB} \mathbf{b} = \mathbf{X}_H(\tilde{\mathbf{U}}^H) \qquad (28)$$

System (28) is overconstrained: there are $3NN'$ equations (the head surface coordinates $\mathbf{X}_H$) and m unknowns (the components of $\mathbf{b}$). Moreover, matrix $\mathbf{P}_{HB}$, describing the head and brain surfaces spatial relation, constrains vector $\mathbf{b}$ to describe *both* head and brain surfaces. Further regularization may be obtained by adding a strain-energy minimization constrain [15]:

$$E_s = \frac{1}{2} \mathbf{b}^T \boldsymbol{\Lambda}^2 \mathbf{b} \qquad (29)$$

where $\boldsymbol{\Lambda} = diag\{\lambda_i\}$ contains the eigenvalues of the covariance matrix $\boldsymbol{\Gamma}$. Strain energy enforces a penalty proportional to the squared eigenvalue associated with each component of $\mathbf{b}$.

The solution of (28) is formulated in terms of minimization of a regularized least squares error:

$$E(\mathbf{b}) = [\mathbf{X}_H(\tilde{\mathbf{U}}^H) - \mathbf{X}_0 - \boldsymbol{\Phi}_H \bar{\mathbf{a}}_H - \boldsymbol{\Phi}_H \mathbf{P}_{HB} \mathbf{b}]^T [\mathbf{X}_H(\tilde{\mathbf{U}}^H) - \mathbf{X}_0 \qquad (30)$$
$$- \boldsymbol{\Phi}_H \bar{\mathbf{a}}_H - \boldsymbol{\Phi}_H \mathbf{P}_{HB} \mathbf{b}] + \alpha \mathbf{b}^T \boldsymbol{\Lambda}^2 \mathbf{b}$$

Differentiating with respect to $\mathbf{b}$, we obtain the strain-minimizing overconstrained least squares solution:

$$\mathbf{b}^* = [(\boldsymbol{\Phi}_H \mathbf{P}_{HB})^T \boldsymbol{\Phi}_H \mathbf{P}_{HB} + \alpha \boldsymbol{\Lambda}^2]^{-1} (\boldsymbol{\Phi}_H \mathbf{P}_{HB})^T [\mathbf{X}_H(\tilde{\mathbf{U}}^H) - \mathbf{X}_0 - \boldsymbol{\Phi}_H \bar{\mathbf{a}}_H]. \qquad (31)$$

A first estimate of the patient's brain surface is then recovered by introducing the estimated parameter $\mathbf{b}^*$ in equation (25), describing the brain part of the statistical model:

$$\mathbf{X}_B(\mathbf{b}^*) = \mathbf{X}_0 + \boldsymbol{\Phi}_B \bar{\mathbf{a}}_B + \boldsymbol{\Phi}_B \mathbf{P}_{BH} \mathbf{b}^* \qquad (32)$$

Equation (32) provides *a good initial prediction of the location of the brain surface*, obtained by exploiting the spatial relationships between head and brain, coded in the learned statistical representation. This feature of the proposed approach significantly alleviates the problem of manual initialization which is a requirement in most of the deformable model-based segmentation methods.

Further improvement of this initial solution may be obtained by alternately optimizing an energy function parameterized by the m components of vector $\mathbf{b}$ [5], in order to fit the part of the model describing the brain, $\mathbf{X}_B$, to a noisy contour map I_c extracted from the MRI image [8]. In our case, the cost function E to be optimized is defined as:

$$E(\mathbf{b}) = \sum_{p \in \mathbf{X}_B(b)|p=1}^{3NN'} \nabla_G * I_c(p) \tag{33}$$

where the operator ∇_G denotes the gradient of a Gaussian kernel. The above cost function simply counts the number of points of the model located on a contour point of the smoothed brain image. Optimization of energy function (33) is obtained by a non linear Gauss-Seidel like algorithm, known as ICM [2]. It has fast convergence properties and only accepts configurations decreasing the cost function.

To summarize, the overall segmentation algorithm is based on the following steps:

1. Parameterization of the head surface using equations (26) and (27).
2. Estimation of the statistical deformation parameters $\mathbf{b}^*$ by solving the regularized overconstrained system (31).
3. Prediction of the brain surface by equation (32).
4. Fine-tuning of the solution by deterministic optimization of cost function (33).

Figure 3 presents a typical example of brain segmentation from a 3D MRI, corresponding to a patient not belonging to the training set. The image in figure 3(a) is a post-operative MRI (thus exhibiting missing data). In figure 3(b) the head surface is segmented and parameterized by the physics-based deformable model (eq. (26) and (27)). In fig. 3(b), the head surface coordinates combined with the probabilistic model provide a good prediction for the brain surface. The statistical model is not affected by missing data because its deformations are constrained by the statistical analysis of the shape variations observed in the training population. The whole segmentation process takes about 5 min cpu time on a standard (HP 9000/C200) workstation for a 128^3 image volume. Most of the computation time concerns head surface parameterization and especially the image forces based on the euclidean distance transform of the 3D MR image [3].

4.2 Multimodal image registration

The second application considered in this paper concerns the rigid registration of multimodal (MR/SPECT) 3D images. Registration of a multimodal image

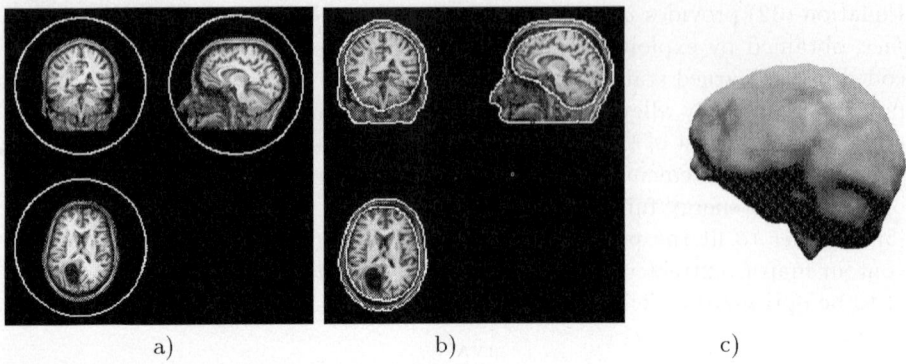

a)   b)   c)

Fig. 3. (a) *A patient MR image with the initial spherical mesh superimposed.* (b) *Prediction of the brain surface using the head surface and the probabilistic deformable model.* (c) *3D rendering of the segmented brain.*

pair consists in estimating the rigid transformation parameters (3D rotation and translation parameters) that have to be applied to the image to be registered (here the SPECT image) in order to match the reference image (here the MRI).

The registration relies on the head structure in the MRI and the brain structure in the SPECT image, which are easy to extract from these two modalities (contrary to the brain structure in MRI). These structures do not overlap but the deformable model represents the relative location of the head and brain contours and accounts for the anatomical variability observed among the training population. The deformable model (restricted here to head and brain surfaces) is used as a probabilistic atlas that constrains the rigid registration of the image pair.

The multimodal rigid registration method relies on the following steps:

1. Segmentation of the head structure in MRI and the brain structure in SPECT from their backgrounds.
2. Brain surface recovery from the MRI using the segmentation algorithm presented in section 4.1
3. Registration of the estimated brain surface with the SPECT brain surface by optimization of a cost function.

The first step is standard preprocessing for background noise elimination. The second step estimates the brain surface from the MRI using the head surface parameterization and the statistical deformable model. By these means, multimodal image registration is also a measure for the accuracy of the segmentation process. Finally, the third step brings into alignment the estimated MRI brain surface and the SPECT image surface by optimization of an objective function having as variables the rigid transformation parameters between the two surfaces. Various cost functions may be used in that step for the registration of binary surfaces. We have applied the following energy function:

$$E(\Theta) = \sum_{p \in I_{SPECT}} I_D(T_\Theta(p)) \qquad (34)$$

where T_Θ is the rigid transformation with parameters $\Theta = \{t_x, t_y, t_z, \theta_x, \theta_y, \theta_z\}$, p is a voxel of the SPECT image surface I_{SPECT} and I_D is the chamfer distance transformation [3] of the part of the statistical model describing the brain. For all of the SPECT surface voxels, equation (34) counts the distance between a SPECT image surface point and its nearest point on the deformable model surface. We have chosen chamfer distance matching because it is fast and it is easily generalized to any surfaces. The whole registration procedure takes about 10 min cpu time on a HP C200 workstation for a 128^3 image volume.

Figure 4 shows an example of a MRI/SPECT registration using the proposed technique. The images in figure 4(a) show the two volumes before registration. The SPECT contours are superimposed onto the MRI to qualitatively evaluate the registration. Figure 4(b) presents the head and brain surface recovery of the MRI using the segmentation algorithm described in the previous section. The matching of the SPECT volume to the part of the model describing the brain is illustrated in fig.4(c). The images in figure 4(d) show the two volumes after registration. As can be seen, although the MRI and SPECT head and brain contours do not overlap, the two images have been correctly registered using the statistical model.

To quantitatively assess the ability of the physics-based statistical deformable model to handle multimodal image pairs, a 3D SPECT image volume has been manually registered to its corresponding MRI volume with the aid of an expert physician. The manually registered SPECT volume was then transformed using translations between −20 and +20 voxels and rotations between −30 and +30 degrees. By these means 25 new images were created. These images were then registered using three different techniques and statistics on the registration errors were computed on the set of 25 different registrations. We have compared our Statistical Deformable Model-based technique (SDM) to the maximization of the Mutual Information (MI) [6] (currently considered as a reference method) and the Robust Inter-image Uniformity criterion (RIU) developed by the authors [11, 12]. Both of the latter techniques have been validated in previous studies and are robust to missing data, outliers and large rotations. For each method, the estimated registration parameters, that is the 3D translations (t_x, t_y, t_z) and rotations (θ_x, θ_y, θ_z) were compared to the true ones to determine the accuracy of the registration. Tables 2 and 3 show the mean, the standard deviation, the median and maximum of the registration errors for the different techniques. As can be seen the proposed SDM approach leads to a registration accuracy which is close to the two other methods.

5   Conclusion and future prospects

We have presented a physically-based 3D statistical deformable model embedding information on the spatial relationships and anatomical variability of mul-

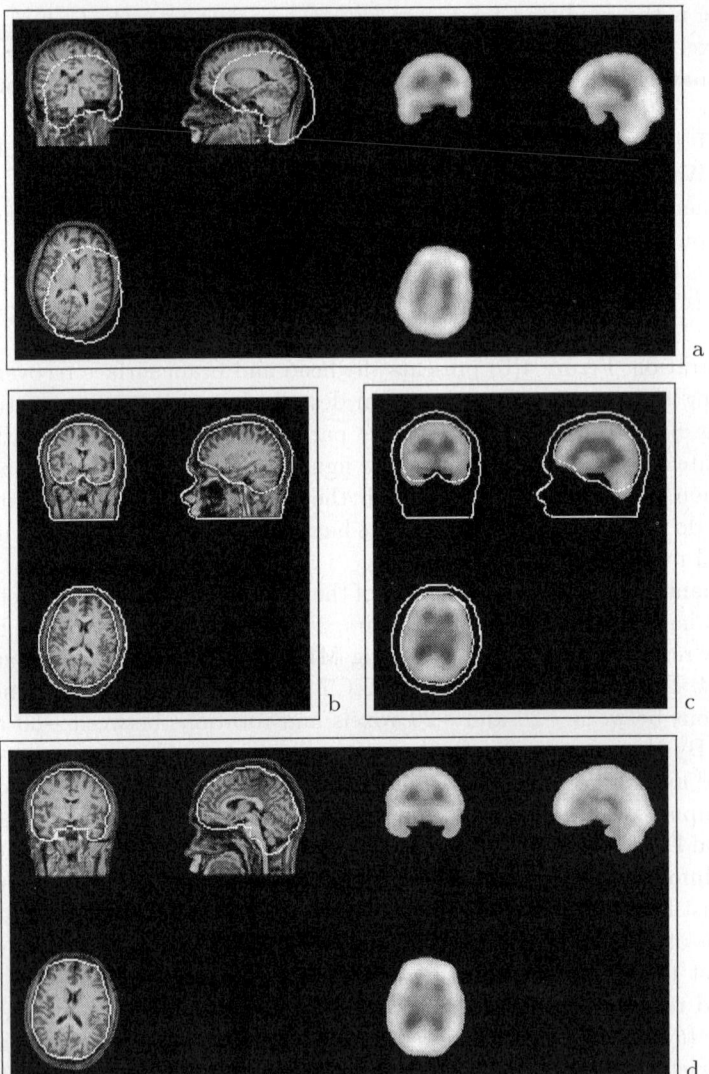

Fig. 4. *MRI/SPECT registration using the deformable model.* **(a)** *MRI and SPECT volumes before registration. The SPECT contours are superimposed onto the MRI to illustrate the misalignment.* **(b)** *Parameterization of the head structure and estimation of the brain surface of the MR image in* **(a)** *using the statistically constrained deformable model.* **(c)** *Registration of the SPECT image to the part of the statistical model describing the brain surface.* **(d)** *MRI and SPECT volumes after registration. The registered SPECT image contours are superimposed onto the MRI to illustrate the alignment of the two images.*

3D MRI/SPECT Registration Errors ($\mu \pm \sigma$)

	MI	RIU	SDM
Δt_x	1.33 ± 1.16	$0.47 \pm 0,41$	0.89 ± 0.43
Δt_y	1.61 ± 1.06	$1.13 \pm 0,90$	0.86 ± 0.88
Δt_z	1.06 ± 1.19	$1.08 \pm 0,74$	1.05 ± 1.02
$\Delta \theta_x$	1.26 ± 1.09	$0.75 \pm 0,56$	1.15 ± 1.11
$\Delta \theta_y$	1.60 ± 0.92	$0.58 \pm 0,44$	1.28 ± 0.87
$\Delta \theta_z$	0.99 ± 0.86	$1.04 \pm 0,78$	1.29 ± 0.67

Table 2. *Multimodal registration of 3D MRI/SPECT images. A 3D SPECT image volume manually pre-registered by an expert to its MRI counterpart was artificially transformed using 25 different translation and rotation parameters. The average and the standard deviation of the registration errors are presented for the different methods. Translation errors are given in voxels and rotation errors in degrees.*

3D MRI/SPECT Registration Errors

	MI	RIU	SDM
median(Δt)	1.35	0.63	0.54
maximum(Δt)	4.24	3.05	2.63
median($\Delta \theta$)	1.14	0.52	1.09
maximum($\Delta \theta$)	4.35	2.47	3.52

Table 3. *Multimodal registration of 3D MRI/SPECT images. A 3D SPECT image volume manually pre-registered by an expert to its MRI counterpart was artificially transformed using 25 different translation and rotation parameters. The median and maximum registration errors for the rigid transformation parameters are presented. See text for technique abbreviations.*

tiple anatomical structures, as observed over a representative population. The particular model developed in this paper was devoted to head and brain representation. Applications of this model included the registration of multimodal image pairs (MRI/SPECT) and the unsupervised segmentation of the brain structure from a given modality (MRI). The major advantage of statistical models is that they naturally introduce *a priori* statistical knowledge that provides useful constraints for ill-posed image processing tasks, such as image segmentation. Consequently they are less affected by noise, missing data or outliers. As an example, the statistical deformable model was applied to the segmentation of the brain structure from post operative images, in which missing anatomical structures lead standard voxel-based techniques to erroneous segmentations. The registration of multimodal brain images was also handled without performing any preprocessing to remove non-brain structures.

One perspective of our work is to extend the model by representing other anatomical structures of the brain (ventricles, corpus callosum, hippocampus, etc.). The statistical deformable model presented in this paper may be considered as a first step towards the development of a general purpose probabilistic anatomical atlas of the brain.

References

1. K. J. Bathe. *Finite element procedures*. Prentice Hall, Englewood Cliffs, New Jersey, 1996.
2. J. Besag. On the statistical analysis of dirty pictures. *Journal of the Royal Statistical Society*, 48(3):259–302, 1986.
3. G. Borgefors. On digital distance transforms in three dimensions. *Computer Vision and Image Understanding*, 64(3):368–376, 1996.
4. T. F. Cootes, C. J. Taylor, and J. Graham. Active shape models - their training and application. *Computer Vision and Image Understanding*, 1(1):38–59, 1995.
5. C. Kervrann and F. Heitz. A hierarchical Markov modeling approach for the segmentation and tracking of deformable shapes. *Graphical Models and Image Processing*, 60(3):173–195, 1998.
6. F. Maes, A. Collignon, D. Vandermeulen, G. Marchal, and P. Suetens. Multimodality image registration by maximization of mutual information. *IEEE Transactions on Medical Imaging*, 16(2):187–198, 1997.
7. T. Mc Inerney and D. Terzopoulos. Deformable models in medical image analysis: a survey. *Medical Image Analysis*, 2(1):91–108, 1996.
8. O. Monga and R. Deriche. 3D edge detection using recursive filtering. *Computer Vision and Image Understanding*, 53(1):76–87, 1991.
9. O. Musse, J. P. Armspach, I. J. Namer, F. Heitz, F. Hennel, and D. Grucker. Data-driven curvilinear reconstruction of 3D MRI: application to cryptogenic extratemporal epilepsy. *Magnetic Resonance Imaging*, 16(10):1227–1235, 1998.
10. C. Nastar and N. Ayache. Frequency-based nonrigid motion analysis: Application to four dimensional medical images. *IEEE Transactions on Pattern Analysis and Machine Intelligence*, 18(11):1069–1079, 1996.
11. C. Nikou, J. P. Armspach, F. Heitz, I.J. Namer, and D. Grucker. MR/MR and MR/SPECT registration of brain images by fast stochastic optimization of robust voxel similarity measures. *Neuroimage*, 8(1):30–43, 1998.
12. C. Nikou, F. Heitz, and J. P. Armspach. Robust registration of dissimilar single and multimodal images. In *Lecture Notes in Computer Science. Proceedings of the 5th European Conference on Computer Vision (ECCV'98)*, volume 2, pages 51–65, Freiburg, Germany, 2-6 June 1998.
13. A. Pentland and S. Sclaroff. Closed-form solutions for physically-based shape modeling and recognition. *IEEE Transactions on Pattern Analysis and Machine Intelligence*, 13(7):730–742, 1991.
14. G. Székely, A. Keleman, A. Brechbuhler, and G. Gerig. Segmentation of 2D and 3D objects from MRI data using constrained elastic deformations of flexible Fourier contour and surface models. *Medical Image Analysis*, 1(1):19–34, 1996.
15. D. Terzopoulos. The computation of visible surface representations. *IEEE Transactions on Pattern Analysis and Machine Intelligence*, 10(4):417–438, 1988.

Minimal Paths in 3D Images and Application to Virtual Endoscopy

Thomas Deschamps[1,2] and Laurent D. Cohen[2]

[1] Medical Imaging Systems Group, LEP,
22, avenue Descartes, BP 15, 94453 Limeil-Brévannes Cedex, France
deschamp@lep-philips.fr, Telephone : 33-1-45 10 68 56, Fax : 33-1-45 10 69 59
[2] Université Paris IX Dauphine, CEREMADE UMR CNRS 7534,
Place du Marechal de Lattre de Tassigny, 75775 Paris Cedex 16, France
cohen@ceremade.dauphine.fr, Telephone : 33-1-44 05 46 78, Fax : 33-1-44 05 45 99

Abstract. This paper presents a new method to find minimal paths in 3D images, giving as initial data one or two endpoints. This is based on previous work [1] for extracting paths in 2D images using Fast Marching [4]. Our original contribution is to extend this technique to 3D, and give new improvements of the approach that are relevant in 2D as well as in 3D. We also introduce several methods to reduce the computation cost and the user interaction.

This work finds its motivation in the particular case of 3D medical images. We show that this technique can be efficiently applied to the problem of finding a centered path in tubular anatomical structures with minimum interactivity, and we apply it to path construction for virtual endoscopy. Synthetic and real medical images are used to illustrate each contribution.

keywords : Deformable Models, Minimal paths, Level Set methods, Medical image understanding, Eikonal Equation, Fast Marching.

1 Introduction

In this paper we deal with the problem of finding a curve of interest in a 3D image. It is defined as a minimal path with respect to a Potential P. This potential is derived from the image data depending on which features we are looking for.

With classical deformable models [2], extracting a path between two fixed extremities is the solution of the minimization of an energy composed of internal and external constraints on this path, needing a precise initialization. Similarly, defining a cost function as an image constraint only, the minimal path becomes the path for which the integral of the cost between the two end points is minimal. Simplifying the model to external forces only, Cohen and Kimmel [1] solved this minimal path problem in 2D with a front propagation equation between the two fixed end points, using the *Eikonal* equation (that physically models wavelight propagation), with a given initial front. Therefore, the first step is to build an image-based measure P that defines the minimality property in the studied image, and to introduce it in the *Eikonal* equation. The second step is to propagate the front on the entire image domain, starting from an initial front restricted to one of the fixed points. The propagation is done using an algorithm called *Fast Marching* [4].

The original contribution of our work is to adapt to 3D images the minimal path technique developed in [1]. We also improve this technique by reducing the computing cost of front propagation. For the particular case of tubular anatomical structures, we also introduce a method to compute a path with a given length with only one point as initialization, and another method to extract a centered path in the object of interest.

Deformable models have been widely used in medical imaging [7]. The main motivation of this work is that it enables almost automatic path tracking routine in 3D medical images for virtual endoscopy inside an anatomical object. An endoscopy consists in threading a camera inside the patient's body in order to examine a pathology. The virtual endoscopy process consists in rendering perspective views along a user-defined trajectory inside tubular structures of human anatomy with CT or MR 3D images. It is a non-invasive technique which is very useful for learning and preparing real examinations, and it can extract diagnostic elements from images. This new method skips the camera and can give views of region of the body difficult or impossible to reach physically (e.g. brain vessels). A major drawback in general remains when the user must define all path points manually. For a complex structure (small vessels, colon,...) the required interactivity can be very tedious. If the path is not correctly built, it can cross an anatomical wall during the virtual fly-through.

Our work focuses on the automation of the path construction, reducing interactions and improving performance, given only one or two end points as inputs. We show that the Fast Marching method can be efficiently applied to the problem of finding a path in virtual endoscopy with minimum interactivity. We also propose a range of choices for finding the right input potential P.

In section 2, we summarize the method detailed in [1] for 2D images. In section 3, we extend this method to 3D, and we detail each improvement made on the front propagation technique. In section 4, we explain how to extract centered paths in tubular structures. And in section 5, we apply our method to colon and brain vessels.

2 The Cohen-Kimmel Method in 2D

2.1 Global Minimum for Active Contours.

We present in this section the basic ideas of the method introduced by Cohen and Kimmel (see [1] for details) to find the global minimum of the active contour energy using minimal paths. The energy to minimize is similar to classical deformable models (see [2]) where it combines smoothing terms and image features attraction term (Potential P):

$$E(C) = \int_{\Omega} \left\{ w_1 \|C'(s)\|^2 + w_2 \|C''(s)\|^2 + P(C(s)) \right\} ds . \tag{1}$$

where $C(s)$ represents a curve drawn on a 2D image, Ω is its domain of definition $[0, L]$, and L is the length of the curve. It reduces the user initialization to giving the two end points of the contour C. In [1], the authors have related this problem to the new paradigm of the level-set formulation. In particular, its Euler equation is equivalent to the geodesic active contours [8]. They introduced a model which improves energy minimization because the problem is transformed in a way to find the global minimum, avoiding being sticked in local minima.

Most of the classical deformable contours have no constraint on the parameterization s, thus allowing different parameterization of the contour C to lead to different results. In [1], contrary to the classical snake model (but similarly to geodesic active contours), s represents the arc-length parameter. Considering a simplified energy model without a second derivative term leads to the expression

$$E(C) = \int_\Omega \{w + P(C(s))\} ds \ . \tag{2}$$

We now have an expression in which the internal forces are included in the external potential. The regularization is now achieved by the constant $w > 0$. Given a potential $P > 0$ that takes lower values near desired features, we are looking for paths along which the integral of $\tilde{P} = P + w$ is minimal. We can define the surface of minimal action U, as the minimal energy integrated along a path between a starting point p_0 and any point p:

$$U(p) = \inf_{\mathcal{A}_{p_0,p}} E(C) = \inf_{\mathcal{A}_{p_0,p}} \left\{ \int_\Omega \tilde{P}(C(s)) ds \right\} \ . \tag{3}$$

where $\mathcal{A}_{p_0,p}$ is the set of all paths between p_0 and p. The minimal path between p_0 and any point p_1 in the image can be easily deduced from this action map. Assuming that potential P is always positive, the action map will have only one local minimum which is the starting point p_0, and the minimal path will be found by a simple back-propagation on the energy map. Thus, contour initialization is reduced to the selection of the two extremities of the path.

2.2 Fast Marching Resolution.

In order to compute this map U, a front-propagation equation related to equation (3) is solved : $\frac{\partial C}{\partial t} = \frac{1}{\tilde{P}} \overrightarrow{n}$. It evolves a front starting from an infinitesimal circle shape around p_0 until each point inside the image domain is assigned a value for U. The value of $U(p)$ is the time t at which the front passes over the point p. Then it notifies the shortest path energy to reach the start point from any point in the image.

The fast marching technique, introduced by Sethian (see [4]), was used by Cohen and Kimmel [1] noticing that the map U satisfies the Eikonal equation:

$$\|\nabla U\| = \tilde{P} \ . \tag{4}$$

Classic finite difference schemes for this equation tend to overshoot and are unstable. Sethian [4] has proposed a method which relies on a one-sided derivative that looks in the up-wind direction of the moving front, and thereby avoids the over-shooting of finite differences. At each pixel (i, j), the unknown u satisfies:

$$(\max\{u - U_{i-1,j}, u - U_{i+1,j}, 0\})^2 +$$
$$(\max\{u - U_{i,j-1}, u - U_{i,j+1}, 0\})^2 = \tilde{P}_{i,j}^2 . \tag{5}$$

giving the correct viscosity-solution u for $U_{i,j}$. The improvement made by the *Fast Marching* is to introduce order in the selection of the grid points. This order is based on the fact that information is propagating *outward*, because action can only grow due to the quadratic equation (5).

The algorithm is detailed in 3D in next section in table 2. The *fast marching* technique selects at each iteration the *Trial* point with minimum action value. This technique of considering at each step only the necessary set of grid points was originally introduced for the construction of minimum length paths in a graph between two given nodes in [6].

Thus it needs only one pass over the image. To perform efficiently these operations in minimum time, the *Trial* points are stored in a min-heap data structure (see details in [4]). Since the complexity of the operation of changing the value of one element of the heap is bounded by a worst-case bottom-to-top proceeding of the tree in $O(\log_2 N)$, the total work is about $O(N \log_2 N)$ for the *fast marching* on a N points grid.

3   3D Minimal Path Extraction

We are interested in this paper in finding a curve in a 3D image. The application that motivates this problem is detailed in section 5. It can also have many other applications. Our approach is to extend the minimal path method of previous section to finding a path $C(s)$ in a 3D image minimizing the energy:

$$\int_\Omega \tilde{P}(C(s)) ds . \tag{6}$$

where $\Omega = [0, L]$, L being the length of the curve. We first extend the Fast marching method to 3D to compute the minimal action U. We then introduce different improvements for finding the path of minimal action between two points in 2D as well as in 3D. In the examples that illustrate the approach, we see various ways of defining the potential P.

3.1   3D Fast-Marching

Similarly to previous section, the minimal action U is defined as

$$U(p) = \inf_{\mathcal{A}_{p_0, p}} \left\{ \int_\Omega \tilde{P}(C(s)) ds \right\} . \tag{7}$$

where $\mathcal{A}_{p_0,p}$ is now the set of all 3D paths between p_0 and p. Given a start point p_0, in order to compute U we start from an initial infinitesimal front around p_0. The 2D scheme equation (5) developed in [5] is extended to 3D, leading to :

$$
\begin{aligned}
(\max\{u - U_{i-1,j,k}, u - U_{i+1,j,k}, 0\})^2 + \\
(\max\{u - U_{i,j-1,k}, u - U_{i,j+1,k}, 0\})^2 + \\
(\max\{u - U_{i,j,k-1}, u - U_{i,j,k+1}, 0\})^2 = \tilde{P}_{i,j,k}^2 \; .
\end{aligned}
\tag{8}
$$

giving the correct viscosity-solution u for $U_{i,j,k}$. Considering the neighbors of grid point (i,j,k) in 6-connexity, we study the solution of the equation (8) in table 1.

Algorithm for 3D Up-Wind Scheme

We note $\{A_1, A_2\}$, $\{B_1, B_2\}$ and $\{C_1, C_2\}$ the three couples of opposite neighbors of $\{i,j,k\}$ with the ordering $U_{A_1} \leq U_{A_2}$, $U_{B_1} \leq U_{B_2}$, $U_{C_1} \leq U_{C_2}$, and $U_{A_1} \leq U_{B_1} \leq U_{C_1}$. Three different cases are to be examined sequentially:

1. Considering that we have $u \geq U_{C_1} \geq U_{B_1} \geq U_{A_1}$, the equation derived is

$$
(u - U_{A_1})^2 + (u - U_{B_1})^2 + (u - U_{C_1})^2 = \tilde{P}^2 \; .
\tag{9}
$$

   Computing the discriminant Δ_1 of equation (9) we have two cases
   - If $\Delta_1 \geq 0$, u should be the largest solution of equation (9);
     - If the hypothesis $u > U_{C_1}$ is wrong, go to 2;
     - If this value is larger than U_{C_1}, go to 4;
   - If $\Delta_1 < 0$, it means that at least C_1 has an action too large to influence the solution and that the hypothesis $u > U_{C_1}$ is false. Go to 2;

2. Considering that $u \geq U_{B_1} \geq U_{B_1}$ and $u < U_{C_1}$, the equation derived is

$$
(u - U_{A_1})^2 + (u - U_{B_1})^2 = P^2 \; .
\tag{10}
$$

   Computing the discriminant Δ_2 of equation (10) we have two cases
   - If $\Delta_2 \geq 0$, u should be the largest solution of equation (10);
     - If the hypothesis $u > U_{B_1}$ is wrong, go to 3;
     - If this value is larger than U_{B_1}, go to 4;
   - If $\Delta_2 < 0$, B_1 has an action too large to influence the solution. It means that $u > U_{B_1}$ is false. Go to 3;

3. Considering that $u < U_{B_1}$ and $u \geq U_{A_1}$, we finally have $u = U_{A_1} + P$. Go to 4;

4. Return u.

Table 1. Solving locally the upwind scheme

We extend the Fast Marching method, introduced in [4] and used by Cohen and Kimmel [1] to our 3D problem. The algorithm is detailed in table 2.

3.2 Several Minimal Path Extraction Techniques

In this section, different procedures to obtain the minimal path between two points are detailed. After discussing the previous backpropagation method, we

---

Algorithm for 3D Fast Marching

- Definition:
    - *Alive* is the set of all grid points at which the action value has been reached and will not be changed;
    - *Trial* is the set of next grid points to be examined and for which an estimate of U has been computed using algorithm of Table 1;
    - *Far* is the set of all other grid points, for which there is not yet an estimate for U;
- Initialization:
    - *Alive* set is confined to the starting point p_0;
    - *Trial* - the initial front is confined to the neighbors of p_0;
    - *Far* is the set of all other grid points;
- Loop:
    - Let $(i_{min}, j_{min}, k_{min})$ be the *Trial* point with the smallest action U;
    - Move it from the *Trial* to the *Alive* set (i.e. $U_{i_{min},j_{min},k_{min}}$ is frozen);
    - For each neighbor (i, j, k) (6-connexity in 3D) of $(i_{min}, j_{min}, k_{min})$:
        * If (i, j, k) is *Far*, add it to the *Trial* set and compute U using table 1;
        * If (i, j, k) is *Trial*, recompute the action $U_{i,j,k}$, and update it if the new value computed is smaller.

Table 2. *Fast marching* algorithm

study how we can limit the front propagation to a subset of the image domain, for speeding-up execution. We illustrate the ideas of this section on two synthetic examples of 3D front propagation in figures 1 and 3. To make the following ideas easier to understand, we show examples in 2D in this section. Examples of minimal paths in 3D real images are presented for the application in Section 5.

Minimal path by back-propagation The minimal action map U computed according to the discretization scheme of equation (7) is similar to convex, in the sense that its only local minimum is the global minimum found at the front propagation start point p_0 where $U(p_0) = 0$. The gradient of U is orthogonal to the propagating fronts since these are its level sets. Therefore, the minimal action path between any point p and the start point p_0 is found by sliding back the map U until it converges to p_0. It can be done with a simple steepest gradient descent, with a predefined descent step, on the minimal action map U, choosing $p_{n+1} = p_n - \text{step} \times \nabla U(p_n)$. See in figure 1-middle the action map corresponding to a binarized potential defined by high values in a spiral rendered in figure 1-middle. The path found between a point in the center of the spiral and another point outside is shown in figure 1-right by transparency.

Partial front propagation. An important issue concerning the back-propagation technique is to constrain the computations to the necessary set of pixels for one path construction. Finding several paths inside an image from the same seed point is an interesting task, but in the case we have two fixed extremities as input for the path construction, it is not necessary to propagate the front on

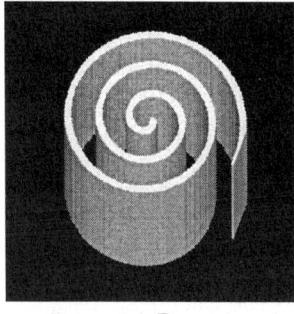  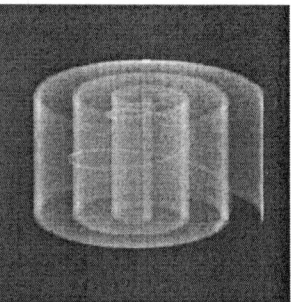

Potential P = spire   action map with P = spire   3D path in the spire

Fig. 1. Examples on synthetic potentials

all the image domain, thus saving computing time. In figure 2 is shown a test on an angiographic image of brain vessels. We can see that there is no need to propagate further the points examined in figure 2-right, the path found being exactly the same as in figure 2-middle where front propagation is done on all the image domain. We used a potential $P(\mathbf{x}) = |\nabla G_\sigma * I(\mathbf{x})| + w$, where I is the original image (512^2 pixels, displayed in figure 2-left), G_σ a Gaussian filter of variance $\sigma = 2$, and $w = 1$ the weight of the model. In figure 2-right, the partial front propagation has visited less than 35% of the image. This ratio depends mainly on the length of the path tracked.

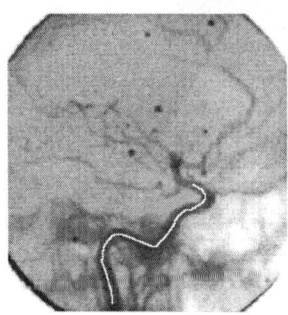 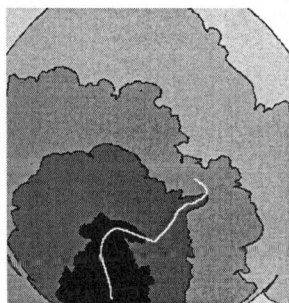 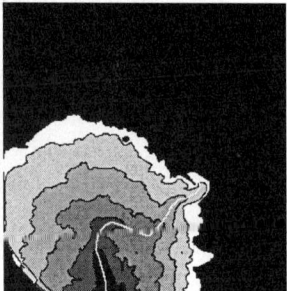

Fig. 2. Comparing complete front propagation with partial front propagation method on a digital subtracted angiography (DSA) image

Simultaneous partial front propagation The idea is to propagate simultaneously a front from each end point p_0 and p_1. Lets consider the first grid point p where those fronts collide. Since during propagation the action can only grow, propagation can be stopped at this step. Adjoining the two paths, respectively between p_0 and p, and p_1 and p, gives an approximation of the exact minimal action path between p_0 and p_1. Since p is a grid point, the exact minimal path might not go through it, but in its neighborhood. Basically, it exists a real point p^*, whose nearest neighbor on the Cartesian grid belongs to the minimal path. Therefore, the approximation done is sub-pixel and there is no need to propagates further.

It has two interesting benefits for front propagation:

- It allows a parallel implementation of the algorithm, dedicating a processor to each propagation;
- It decreases the number of pixels examined during a partial propagation by
  - $\frac{(2R)^2}{2 \times R^2} = 2$ in 2D (figure 3-right);
  - $\frac{(2R)^3}{2 \times R^3} = 4$ in 3D (figure 3-left).

because with the potential $P = 1$, the action map is the Euclidean distance.

Note that it can also compute the Euclidean distance to a set of points by initializing U to be 0 at these points.

In figure 4 is displayed a test on a digital subtracted angiography (DSA) of brain vessels. The potential used is $P(\mathbf{x}) = |I(\mathbf{x}) - C| + w$, where I is the original image (256^2 pixels, displayed in figure 4-left), C a constant term (mean value of the start and end points gray levels), and $w = 10$ the weight of the model. In figure 4-middle, the partial front propagation has visited up to 60% of the image. With a colliding fronts method, only 30% of the image is visited (see figure 4-right), and the difference between both paths found is sub-pixel.

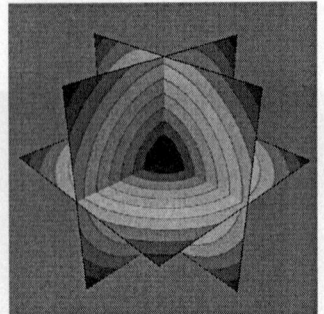
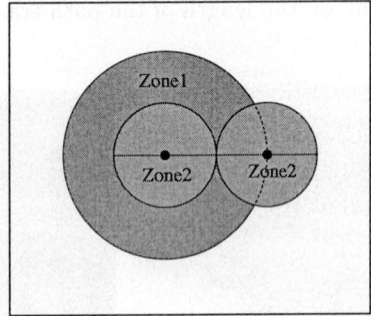

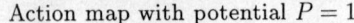

Action map with potential $P = 1$ Comparing both methods on potential $P = 1$

Fig. 3. Propagation with potential $P = 1$

One end point propagation We have shown the ability of the front propagation techniques to compute the minimal path between two fixed points. In some cases, only one point should be necessary, or the needed user interaction for setting a second point is too tedious in a 3D image. We have derived a method that builds a path given only one end point and a maximum path length. The technique is similar to that of subsection 3.2, but the new condition will be to stop propagation when a path corresponding to a chosen Euclidean distance is extracted. A test of this path length condition is shown on figure 5 which is a DSA image of brain vessels. We have seen with figure 3-left that propagating a front with potential $P = 1$ computes the Euclidean distance to the start point.

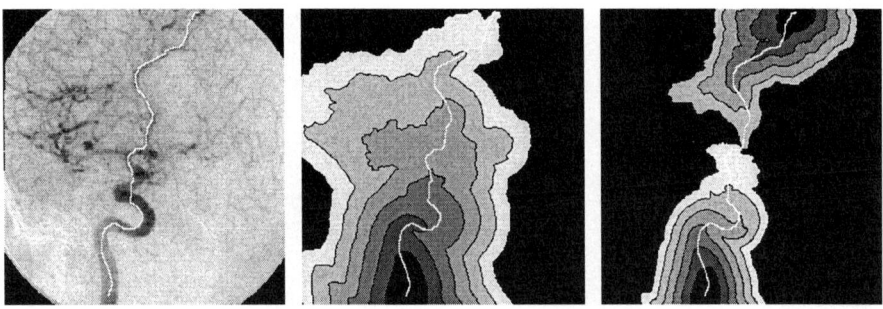

Fig. 4. Comparing the partial front propagation with the colliding fronts method on a DSA image

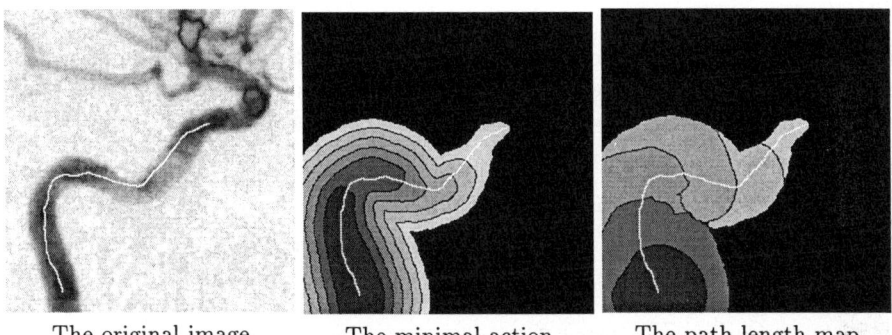

| The original image | The minimal action | The path length map |

Fig. 5. Computing the Euclidean path length simultaneously

Therefore, we use simultaneously an image-based potential P_1, for building the minimal path and a potential $P_2 = 1$ for computing the path length.

While we are propagating the front corresponding to P_1 on the image domain, at each point p examined we compute both minimal actions for P_1 (shown in figure 5-middle) and for P_2 (shown in figure 5-right). In this case the action corresponding to P_2 is an approximate Euclidean length of the minimal path between p and p_0.

4 The Path Centering Method

In this section we derive a technique to track paths that are centered in a tubular shape, using the front propagation methods. To illustrate this problem, we use the example shown on figure 6-left, which is a binarized image of brain vessels. Using our classical front propagation, the minimal path extracted is tangential to the edges, as shown in figure 6-middle, superimposed on the action map computed. This is due to the fact that length is minimized. This path is not tuned for problems which may require a centered path, and we will see in next section that it can be necessary for virtual endoscopy. In some cases it is possible to get the shape of the object in which we are looking for a path. One way of

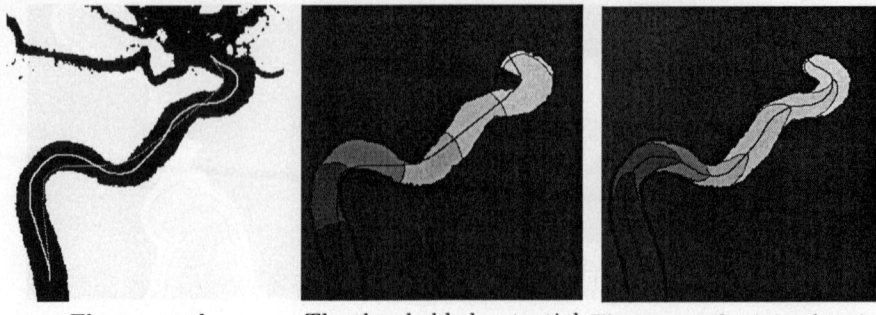

The two paths   The thresholded potential   The centered minimal action

Fig. 6. Comparing classic and centered paths

making this shape available is to use the front propagation itself as shown in Figure 9. This is more detailed in [9]. If we have the shape of our object, we can use a front propagation method to compute the distance to its edges using a potential defined by

$$P(i,j) = 1 \ \forall (i,j) \in \{object\} \ .$$
$$P(i,j) = \infty \ \forall (i,j) \in \{Background\} \ .$$
$$P(i,j) = 0 \ \forall (i,j) \in \{Interface\} \ .$$

When this distance map, noted $\mathcal{E}$, is computed, it is used to create a potential P' which weights the points in order to propagate faster a new front in the centre of the desired regions. Choosing a value d to be the minimum acceptable distance to the walls, we propose the following potential:

$$P'(\mathbf{x}) = \{|d - \min(\mathcal{E}(\mathbf{x}); d)|\}^{\gamma} \text{ with } \gamma \geq 1 \ . \tag{11}$$

According to this new penalty, the final front propagates faster in the center of the vessel. This can be observed by looking at the shape of the iso-action lines of the centered minimal action shown in figure 6-right. Finally, one can observe in figure 6-left that the path avoids the edges and remains in the center of the vessel, while the former path tangential to edges. This method can be related to robotic problems like optimal path planning (see [4] for details), essentially because the potential shown in figure 6-left is binary. But there is no reason to limit the application of this algorithm to a binary domain. Thus, for continuously varying potential P, we use the same method. In section 5, we present results on real 3D data applied to virtual endoscopy, where the problem is to find shortest paths on weighted domains.

5 Application to Virtual Endoscopy

In previous sections we have developed a series of issues in front propagation techniques. We study now the particular case of virtual endoscopy, where extraction of paths in 3D images is a very tedious task.

5.1 The Role of Virtual Endoscopy

Visualization of volumetric medical image data plays a crucial part for diagnosis and therapy planning. The better the anatomy and the pathology are understood, the more efficiently one can operate with low risk. Different possibilities exist for visualizing 3D data: three 2D orthogonal views (see figure 7), maximum intensity projection (MIP, and its variants), surface and volume rendering. In particular, virtual endoscopy allows by means of surface/volume rendering

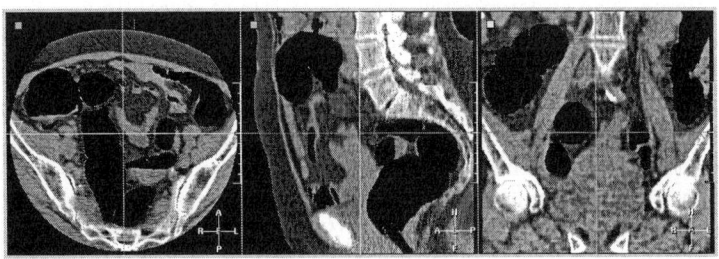

Fig. 7. Three orthogonal views of a volumetric CT data set of the colon

techniques to visually inspect regions of the body that are dangerous and/or impossible to reach physically with a camera. A virtual endoscopic system is usually composed of two parts:

1. A Path construction part, which provides the successive locations of the fly-through the tubular structure of interest (see figure 8-left);
2. Three dimensional viewing along the endoscopic path (see figure 8-right).

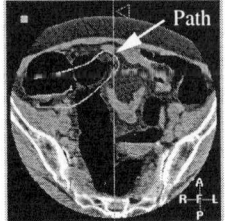
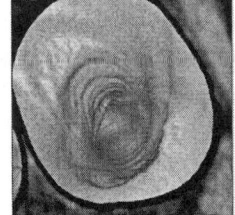

Original CT slice + path   Endoscopic view

Fig. 8. Interior view of a colon, reconstructed from a defined path

A major drawback in general remains when the path construction is left to the user who manually has to "guide" the virtual endoscope/camera. The required interactivity on a 3D image can be very tedious for complex structures such as the colon. Since the anatomical objects have often complex topologies, the path passes in and out of the three orthogonal planes. Consequently the right location is accomplished by alternatively entering the projection of the wanted point in each of the three planes. Then, the path is approximated between the user defined points by lines or Bezier splines, and if the number of points is not enough, it can easily cross an anatomical wall. Path construction in 3D images is thus a very critical task and precise anatomical knowledge of the structure is needed to set a suitable trajectory, with the minimum required interactivity.

Numerous techniques [10],[11] try to automate this path construction process by using a skeletonization technique as a pre-processing. It requires first to segment the object in order to binarize the image, then it extracts the skeleton of this volume. The skeleton often consists in lots of discontinuous trajectories, and post-processing is necessary to isolate and smooth the final path. But those methods can lead to critical cases: if there is a stenosis in the tubular structure, the binarization can produce two separate objects, where a skeletonization is inefficient. The front propagation techniques studied in this paper propose an alternative to the tedious manual path construction by building paths in 3D images with minimum interactivity. In contrast to other methods, it does not require any pre- or post-processing. We first apply this method to the case of virtual endoscopy in a colon CT dataset, then we extend it to a brain MR dataset.

5.2 Application to Colonoscopy

All tests are performed on a volumetric CT scan of size $512 \times 512 \times 140$ voxels, shown in figure 7. We define a potential P from the 3D image $I(x)$ that is minimal inside the anatomical shapes where end points are located. We chose the potential $P(x) = |I(x) - I_{mean}|^{\alpha} + w$, where an average grey level value I_{mean} of the colon is obtained with an histogram. From this definition, P is lower inside the colon in order to propagate the front faster. Also, edges are enhanced with a non-linear function ($\alpha > 1$) since the path to be extracted is in a large object that has complex shape and very thin edges. Then, using this potential, we propagate inside the colon creating a path between a couple of given points. In fact, the colon being a closed object with two extremities, one can use the Euclidean path length stopping criterion as explained in subsection 3.2. This allows to give only one end point. The figure 9 shows the result of the fast marching technique with a unique starting point belonging to the colon and an Euclidean path length criterion of 500 mm. This path has been computed in 10 seconds (in CPU time) on an UltraSparc 30 with a 300 MHz monoprocessor. However, this potential does not produce paths relevant for virtual endoscopy. Indeed, paths should remain not only in the anatomical object of interest but as far as possible from its edges. In order to achieve this target, we use the centering potential method as detailed in section 4. This approach needs a *shape* information. This information is provided by the previous front propagation. From its definition, the front sticks to the anatomical shapes as shown in figure 9. This is related to the use of Fast Marching algorithm to extract a surface for segmentation [3]. It gives a rough segmentation of the colon and provides a good information and a fast-reinitialization technique to compute the distance to the edges. Using this

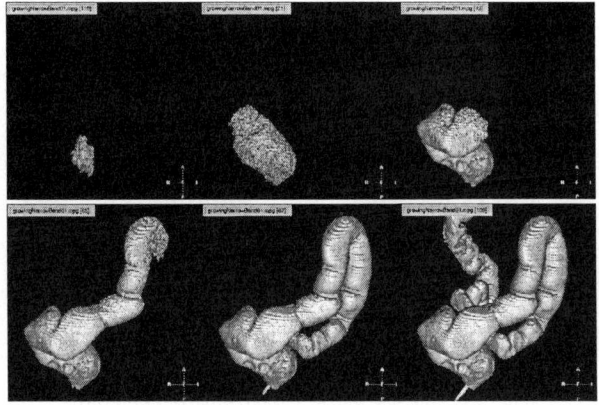

Fig. 9. Successive steps of front propagation inside the colon volume

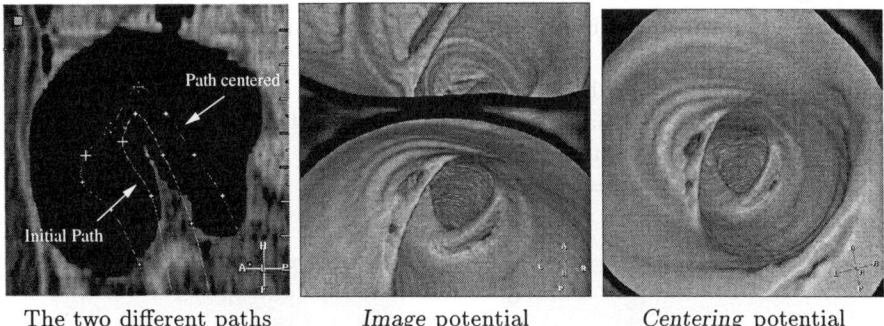

The two different paths   *Image* potential   *Centering* potential

Fig. 10. Centering the path in the colon

thresholded map as a potential that indicates the distance to the walls, we can correct the initial path as shown in figure 10-left. Both 3D paths are projected on the 2D slice for visualization. As expected, the new path remains more in the middle of the colon. The two different cross-sections in figures 10-middle and 10-right display the view of the interior of the colon from both paths at the u-turn shown in figure 10-left. This effect of centering the path enhances dramatically the rendering of the video sequence of virtual endoscopy obtained. [1] With the initial potential, the path is near the wall, and we see the u-turn, whereas with the new path, the view is centered into the colon, giving a more correct view of the inside of the colon.

Therefore, the two end points can be connected correctly, giving a path staying inside the anatomical object. The results are displayed in two 3D views in figure 11. But for virtual colonoscopy, it is often not necessary to set the two end points within the anatomical object.

---

[1] This video will be shown at the presentation, and is available at http://www.ceremade.dauphine.fr/~cohen/ECCV00.

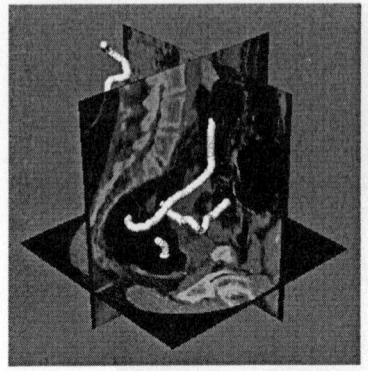 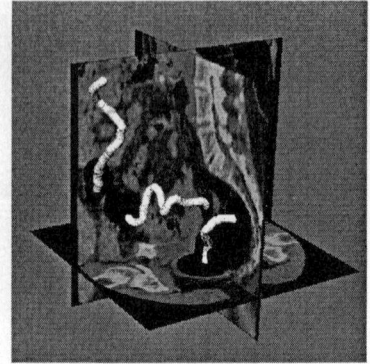

Fig. 11. 3D Views of a path inside the colon

5.3 Application to a Brain MRA Image

Tests were performed on brain vessels in a magnetic resonance angiography
(MRA) scan. The problem is different, because there is only signal from blood.
All other structures have been removed. The main difficulty here lies in the
variations of the dye intensity. The path shown from two viewpoints tracks (see
figure12) the superior sagittal venous canal, using a nonlinear function of the
image dye intensity $(P(x) = |I(x) - 100|^2 + 1)$.

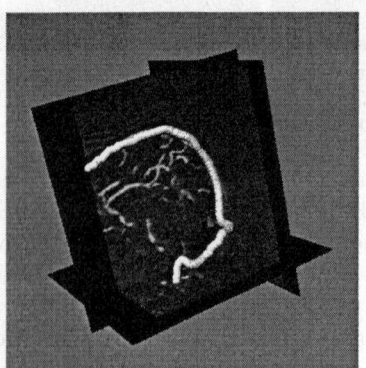 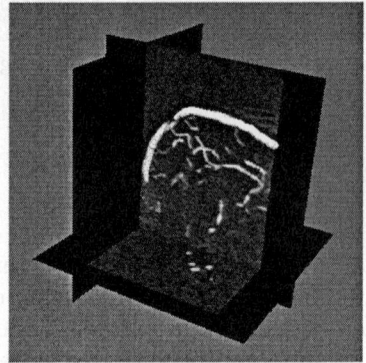

Fig. 12. Path tracking in brain vessels in a MR-Angiographic volume.

6 Conclusion

In this paper we presented a fast and efficient algorithm that computes a 3D path
of minimal energy. This is particularly useful in medical image understanding
for guiding endoscopic viewing.

This work was the extension to 3D of a level-set technique developed in [1]
for extracting paths in 2D images, given only the two extremities of the path
and the image as inputs, with a front propagation equation.

We improved this front propagation equation by creating new algorithms which decrease the minimal path extraction computing cost, and reduce user interaction in the case of path tracking inside tubular structures. We showed that those techniques can be efficiently applied to the problem of finding a path in tubular anatomical structures for virtual endoscopy with minimum interactivity. In particular we extracted centered paths inside a CT dataset of the colon, and in a MR datasets of the brain vessels. We have proved the benefit of our method towards manual path construction, and skeletonization techniques, showing that only a few seconds are necessary to build a complete trajectory inside the body, giving only one or two end points and the image as inputs.

References

1. Cohen, L.D., Kimmel, R.: Global Minimum for Active Contour Models: A Minimal Path Approach. International Journal of Computer Vision. **24** (1997) 57–78
2. Kass, M., Witkin, A., Terzopoulos, D.: Snakes: Active contour models. International Journal of Computer Vision. **4** (1988) 321–331
3. Malladi, R., Sethian, J.A.: A Real-Time Algorithm for Medical Shape Recovery. Proceedings of International Conference on Computer Vision. (1998) 304–310
4. Sethian J.A.: Level set methods: Evolving Interfaces in Computational Geometry, Fluid Mechanics, Computer Vision and Materials Sciences. Cambridge University Press (1999)
5. Rouy, E., Tourin, A.: A Viscosity Solution Approach to Shape-From-Shading. SIAM Journal of Numerical Analysis. **29** (1992) 867–884
6. Dijkstra, E.W.: A note on two problems in connection with graphs. Numerische Mathematic. **1** (1959) 269–271
7. McInerney, T., Terzopoulos, D.: Deformable Models in Medical Image Analysis, A Survey. Medical Image Analysis. **2** (1996)
8. Caselles, V., Kimmel, R., Sapiro, G.: Geodesic active contours. Proceedings of International Conference on Computer Vision. (1995) 694-699
9. Deschamps, T., Cohen, L.D.: Minimal path in 3D images and application to virtual endoscopy. Les Cahiers du Cérémade, Université Paris Dauphine. (2000)
10. Yeorong, G., Stelts, D.R., Jie, W., Vining, D.J.: Computing the centerline of a colon: a robust and efficient method based on 3D skeletons. Proceedings of IEEE Nuclear Science Symposium Conference Record. **23** (1993) 786–794
11. Choiu, R.C.H., Kaufman, A.E., Zhengrong, L., Lichan, H., Achniotou, M.: An interactive fly-path planning using potential fields and cell decomposition for virtual endoscopy. Proceedings of IEEE Nuclear Science Symposium Conference Record. **46** (1999) 1045–1049

Calibration

Medical Image Understanding

Visual Motion

Kruppa Equation Revisited:
Its Renormalization and Degeneracy

Yi Ma*, René Vidal, Jana Košecká, and Shankar Sastry

Department of Electrical Engineering and Computer Sciences
University of California at Berkeley, Berkeley, CA 94720-1774
{mayi, rvidal, janka, sastry}@robotics.eecs.berkeley.edu

Abstract. In this paper, we study general questions about the solvability of the Kruppa equations and show that, in several special cases, the Kruppa equations can be renormalized and become *linear*. In particular, for cases when the camera motion is such that its rotation axis is *parallel* or *perpendicular* to translation, we can obtain linear algorithms for self-calibration. A further study of these cases not only reveals generic difficulties with degeneracy in conventional self-calibration methods based on the nonlinear Kruppa equations, but also clarifies some incomplete discussion in the literature about the solutions of the Kruppa equations. We demonstrate that Kruppa equations do not provide sufficient constraints on camera calibration and give a complete account of exactly what is missing in Kruppa equations. In particular, a clear relationship between the Kruppa equations and *chirality* is revealed. The results then resolve the discrepancy between the Kruppa equations and the necessary and sufficient condition for a unique calibration. Simulation results are presented for evaluation of the sensitivity and robustness of the proposed linear algorithms.

Keywords: Camera self-calibration, Kruppa equations, renormalization, degeneracy, chirality.

1 Introduction

The problem of camera self-calibration refers to the problem of obtaining intrinsic parameters of a camera using only information from image measurements, without any *a priori* knowledge about the motion between frames and the structure of the observed scene. The original question of determining whether the image measurements *only* are sufficient for obtaining intrinsic parameters of a camera was initially answered in [11]. The proposed approach and solution utilize invariant properties of the image of the so called absolute conic. Since the absolute conic is invariant under Euclidean transformations (*i.e.*, its representation is independent of the position of the camera) and depends only on the camera intrinsic parameters, the recovery of the image of the absolute conic is

---

* This work is supported by ARO under the MURI grant DAAH04-96-1-0341.

then equivalent to the recovery of the camera intrinsic parameter matrix. The constraints on the absolute conic are captured by the so called Kruppa equations initially discovered by Kruppa in 1913. In Section 3, we will provide a much more concise derivation of the Kruppa equations.

Certain algebraic and numerical approaches for solving the Kruppa equations were first discussed in [11]. Some alternative and additional schemes have been explored in [7, 17]. Nevertheless, it has been well-known that, in the presence of noise, these Kruppa equation based approaches are not guaranteed to provide a good estimate of the camera calibration and many erroneous solutions will occur [1]. Because of this, we decide to revisit the Kruppa equation based approach in this paper. More specifically, we address the following two questions:

1. Under what conditions do the Kruppa equations become degenerate or ill-conditioned?

2. When conditions for degeneracy are satisfied, how do the self-calibration algorithms need to be modified?

In this paper, we show that the answer to the former question is rather unfortunate: for camera motions such that the rotation axis is *parallel or perpendicular* to the translation, the Kruppa equations become degenerate. This explains why conventional approaches to self-calibration based on the (nonlinear) Kruppa equations often fail. Most practical images are, in fact, taken through motions close to these two types. The parallel case shows up very frequently in motion of aerial mobile robots such as an helicopter. The perpendicular case is interesting in robot navigation, where the main rotation of the on-board camera is yaw and pitch, whose axes *are* perpendicular to the direction of robot heading. Nevertheless, in this paper, we take one step further to show that when such motions occur, the corresponding Kruppa equations can be *renormalized* and become *linear!* This fact allows us to correct (or salvage) classical Kruppa equation based self-calibration algorithms so as to obtain much more stable linear self-calibration algorithms, other than the pure rotation case known to Hartley [4]. Our study also clarifies and completes previous analysis and results in the literature regarding the solutions of the Kruppa equations [17]. This is discussed in Section 3.2.

Relations to Previous Works: Besides the Kruppa equation based self - calibration approach, alternative methods have also been studied extensively. For example some of them use the so called **absolute quadric constraints** [16], **modulus constraints** [13] and **chirality constraints** [5]. Some others restrict to special cases such as stationary camera [4] or to time-varying focal-length [6, 14]. We hope that, by a more detailed study of the Kruppa equations, we may gain a better understanding of the relationships among the various self-calibration methods. This is discussed in Section 3.3.

2 Epipolar Geometry Basics

To introduce the notation, we first review in this section the well-known epipolar geometry and some properties of fundamental matrix to aid the derivation and study of Kruppa equations.

The **camera motion** is represented by (R, p) where R is a rotation matrix as an element in the special orthogonal group $SO(3)$ and $p \in \mathbb{R}^3$ is a three dimensional vector representing the translation of the camera. That is, (R, p) represents a rigid body motion as an element in the special Euclidean group $SE(3)$. The three dimensional coordinates (with respect to the camera frame) of a generic point q in the world are related by the following Euclidean transformation:

$$q(t_2) = R(t_2, t_1)q(t_1) + p(t_2, t_1), \quad \forall t_1, t_2 \in \mathbb{R}. \tag{1}$$

We use the matrix $A \in \mathbb{R}^{3 \times 3}$ to represent the **intrinsic parameters** of the camera, which we also refer to as the **calibration matrix** of the camera. In this paper, without loss of generality, we will assume $\det(A) = 1$, *i.e.*, A is an element in the special linear group $SL(3)$. $SL(3)$ is the group consisting of 3×3 real matrices with determinant equal to 1. This choice of A is slightly different from (and more general than) the traditional choice in the literature, but, mathematically, it is more natural to deal with. Then the (uncalibrated) **image x** (on the image plane in $\mathbb{R}^3$) of the point q at time t is given through the following equation:

$$\lambda(t)\mathbf{x}(t) = Aq(t), \quad \forall t \in \mathbb{R}. \tag{2}$$

where $\lambda(t) \in \mathbb{R}$ is a scalar encoding the **depth** of the point q. Note that this model does not differentiate the **spherical** or **perspective** projection.

Since we primarily consider the two-view case in this paper, to simplify the notation, we will drop the time dependency from the motion $(R(t_2, t_1), p(t_2, t_1))$ and simply denote it as (R, p), and also use $\mathbf{x}_1, \mathbf{x}_2$ as shorthand for $\mathbf{x}(t_1), \mathbf{x}(t_2)$ respectively. Also, for a three dimensional vector $p \in \mathbb{R}^3$, we can always associate to it a **skew symmetric matrix** $\hat{p} \in \mathbb{R}^{3 \times 3}$ such that $p \times q = \hat{p}q$ for all $q \in \mathbb{R}^3$.[1]

Then it is well known that the two image points $\mathbf{x}_1$ and $\mathbf{x}_2$ must satisfy the so called **epipolar constraint**:

$$\mathbf{x}_1^T A^{-T} R^T \hat{p} A^{-1} \mathbf{x}_2 = 0. \tag{3}$$

The matrix $F = A^{-T} R^T \hat{p} A^{-1} \in \mathbb{R}^{3 \times 3}$ is the so called **fundamental matrix** in Computer Vision literature. When $A = I$, the fundamental matrix simply becomes $R^T \hat{p}$ which is called **essential matrix** and plays a very important role in motion recovery [10]. The following simple but extremely useful lemma will allow us to write the fundamental matrix in a more convenient form:

Lemma 1 (Hat Operator). *If $p \in \mathbb{R}^3$ and $A \in SL(3)$, then $A^T \hat{p} A = \widehat{A^{-1} p}$.*

Proof: Since both $A^T \widehat{(\cdot)} A$ and $\widehat{A^{-1}(\cdot)}$ are linear maps from $\mathbb{R}^3$ to $\mathbb{R}^{3 \times 3}$, using the fact that $\det(A) = 1$, one may directly verify that these two linear maps are equal on the bases: $(1, 0, 0)^T, (0, 1, 0)^T$ or $(0, 0, 1)^T$. ∎

---

[1] In the computer vision literature, such a skew symmetric matrix is also often denoted as $p_\times$. But we here use the notation consistent to robotics and matrix Lie group theory, where $\hat{p}$ is used to denote to elements in the Lie algebra $so(3)$ of $SO(3)$.

This simple lemma will be frequently used throughout the paper. By this lemma, we have:

$$F = A^{-T} R^T \hat{p} A^{-1} = A^{-T} R^T A^T A^{-T} \hat{p} A^{-1} = A^{-T} R^T A^T \hat{p'} \qquad (4)$$

where $p' = Ap \in \mathbb{R}^3$ is the so called **epipole**. This equation in fact has a more fundamental interpretation: an uncalibrated camera in a calibrated world is mathematically equivalent to a calibrated camera in an uncalibrated world (for more details see [9]). As we will soon see, the last form of the fundamental matrix in the above equation is the most useful one for deriving and solving the Kruppa equations.

3 The Kruppa Equations

Without loss of generality, we may assume that both the rotation R and translation p are non-trivial, *i.e.*, $R \neq I$ and $p \neq 0$ hence the epipolar constraint (3) is not degenerate and the fundamental matrix can be estimated. The camera self-calibration problem is then reduced to recovering the symmetric matrix $\omega = A^{-T} A^{-1}$ or $\omega^{-1} = A A^T$ from fundamental matrices. It can be shown, even if we have chosen A to be an arbitrary element in $SL(3)$, A can only be recovered up to a rotation, *i.e.*, as an element in the quotient space $SL(3)/SO(3)$, for more details see [9]. Note that $SL(3)/SO(3)$ is only a 5-dimensional space. From the fundamental matrix, the epipole vector p' can be directly computed (up to an arbitrary scale) as the null space of F. Given a fundamental matrix $F = A^{-T} R^T A^T \hat{p'}$, its **scale**, usually denoted as λ, is defined as the norm of p'. If $\lambda = \|p'\| = 1$, such a F is called a **normalized fundamental matrix**.[2] For now, we assume that the fundamental matrix F happens to be normalized.

Suppose the standard basis of $\mathbb{R}^3$ is $e_1 = (1,0,0)^T, e_2 = (0,1,0)^T, e_3 = (0,0,1)^T \in \mathbb{R}^3$. Now pick any rotation matrix $R_0 \in SO(3)$ such that $R_0 p' = e_3$. Using Lemma 1, we have $\hat{p'} = R_0^T \hat{e_3} R_0$. Define matrix $D \in \mathbb{R}^{3 \times 3}$ to be:

$$D = F R_0^T = A^{-T} R^T A^T R_0^T \hat{e_3} = A^{-T} R^T A^T R_0^T (e_2, -e_1, 0). \qquad (5)$$

Then D has the form $D = (\xi_1, \xi_2, 0)$ with $\xi_1, \xi_2 \in \mathbb{R}^3$ being the first and second column vectors of D. We then have $\xi_1 = A^{-T} R^T A^T R_0^T e_2, \xi_2 = -A^{-T} R^T A^T R_0^T e_1$. Define vectors $\eta_1, \eta_2 \in \mathbb{R}^3$ as $\eta_1 = -R_0^T e_1, \eta_2 = R_0^T e_2$, then it is direct to check that ω^{-1} satisfies:

$$\xi_1^T \omega^{-1} \xi_1 = \eta_2^T \omega^{-1} \eta_2, \quad \xi_2^T \omega^{-1} \xi_2 = \eta_1^T \omega^{-1} \eta_1, \quad \xi_1^T \omega^{-1} \xi_2 = \eta_1^T \omega^{-1} \eta_2. \qquad (6)$$

We thus obtain three homogeneous constraints on the matrix ω^{-1}, the inverse (dual) of the matrix (conic) ω. These constraints can be used to compute ω^{-1} hence ω.

The above derivation is based on the assumption that the fundamental matrix F is normalized, *i.e.*, $\|p'\| = 1$. However, since the epipolar constraint is homogeneous in the fundamental matrix F, it can only be determined up to an arbitrary

---

[2] Here $\| \cdot \|$ represents the standard 2-norm.

scale. Suppose λ is the length of the vector $p' \in \mathbb{R}^3$ in $F = A^{-T} R^T A^T \widehat{p'}$. Consequently, the vectors ξ_1 and ξ_2 are also scaled by the same λ. Then the ratio between the left and right hand side quantities in each equation of (6) is equal to λ^2. This gives two equations on ω^{-1}, the so called **Kruppa equations** (after its initial discovery by Kruppa in 1913):

$$\lambda^2 = \frac{\xi_1^T \omega^{-1} \xi_1}{\eta_2^T \omega^{-1} \eta_2} = \frac{\xi_2^T \omega^{-1} \xi_2}{\eta_1^T \omega^{-1} \eta_1} = \frac{\xi_1^T \omega^{-1} \xi_2}{\eta_1^T \omega^{-1} \eta_2}. \tag{7}$$

Alternative means of obtaining the Kruppa equations are by utilizing algebraic relationships between projective geometric quantities [11] or via SVD characterization of F [3]. Here we obtain the same equations from a quite different approach. Equation (7) further reveals the geometric meaning of the Kruppa ratio λ^2: it is the square of the length of the vector p' in the fundamental matrix F. This discovery turns out to be quite useful when we later discuss the renormalization of Kruppa equations. In general, each fundamental matrix provides *at most two* algebraic constraints on ω^{-1}, *if* the two equations in (7) happen to be independent. Since the symmetric matrix ω has five degrees of freedom, in general *at least three* fundamental matrices are needed to uniquely determine ω. Nevertheless, as we will soon see, this is *not* the case for many special camera motions.

Comment 1 *One must be aware that solving Kruppa equations for camera calibration is not equivalent to the camera self-calibration problem in the sense that there may exist solutions of Kruppa equations which are not solutions of a "valid" self-calibration. Given a non-critical set of camera motions, the associated Kruppa equations do not necessarily give enough constraints to solve for the calibration matrix A. See Section 3.3 for a complete account.*

The above derivation of Kruppa equations is straightforward, but the expression (7) depends on a particular choice of the rotation matrix R_0 – note that such a choice is not unique. However, there is an even simpler way to get an equivalent expression for the Kruppa equations in a matrix form. Given a normalized fundamental matrix $F = A^{-T} R^T A^T \widehat{p'}$, it is then straightforward to check that $\omega^{-1} = AA^T$ must satisfy the following equation:

$$F^T \omega^{-1} F = \widehat{p'}^T \omega^{-1} \widehat{p'}. \tag{8}$$

We call this equation the **normalized matrix Kruppa equation**. It is readily seen that this equation is equivalent to (6). If F is not normalized and is scaled by $\lambda \in \mathbb{R}$, *i.e.*, $F = \lambda A^{-T} R^T A^T \widehat{p'}$,[3] we then have the **matrix Kruppa equation**:

$$F^T \omega^{-1} F = \lambda^2 \widehat{p'}^T \omega^{-1} \widehat{p'}. \tag{9}$$

This equation is equivalent to the scalar version given by (7) and is independent of the choice of the rotation matrix R_0. In fact, the matrix form reveals that the nature of Kruppa equations is nothing but **inner product invariants** of the group $ASO(3)A^{-1}$ (for more details see [9]).

---

[3] Without loss of generality, from now on, we always assume $\|p'\| = 1$.

3.1 Solving Kruppa Equations

Algebraic properties of Kruppa equations have been extensively studied (see e.g. [11,17]). However, conditions on dependency among Kruppa equations obtained from the fundamental matrix have not been fully discovered. Therefore it is hard to tell in practice whether a given set of Kruppa equations suffice to guarantee a unique solution for calibration. As we will soon see in this section, for very rich classes of camera motions which commonly occur in many practical applications, the Kruppa equations will become degenerate. Moreover, since the Kruppa equations (7) or (9) are highly nonlinear in ω^{-1}, most self-calibration algorithms based on directly solving these equations suffer from being computationally expensive or having multiple local minima [1,7]. These reasons have motivated us to study the geometric nature of Kruppa equations in order to gain a better understanding of the difficulties commonly encountered in camera self-calibration. Our attempt to resolve these difficulties will lead to simplified algorithms for self-calibration. These algorithms are linear and better conditioned for these special classes of camera motions.

Given a fundamental matrix $F = A^{-T} R^T A^T \widehat{p'}$ with p' of unit length, the normalized matrix Kruppa equation (8) can be rewritten in the following way:

$$\widehat{p'}^T (\omega^{-1} - ARA^{-1}\omega^{-1}A^{-T}R^T A^T)\widehat{p'} = 0. \tag{10}$$

According to this form, if we define $C = A^{-T}R^T A^T$, a linear (Lyapunov) map $\sigma : \mathbb{R}^{3\times 3} \to \mathbb{R}^{3\times 3}$ as $\sigma : X \mapsto X - C^T XC$, and a linear map $\tau : \mathbb{R}^{3\times 3} \to \mathbb{R}^{3\times 3}$ as $\tau : Y \mapsto \widehat{p'}^T Y\widehat{p'}$, then the solution ω^{-1} of equation (10) is exactly the (symmetric real) kernel of the composition map:

$$\tau \circ \sigma : \quad \mathbb{R}^{3\times 3} \xrightarrow{\sigma} \mathbb{R}^{3\times 3} \xrightarrow{\tau} \mathbb{R}^{3\times 3}. \tag{11}$$

This interpretation of Kruppa equations clearly decomposes effects of the rotational and translational parts of the motion: if there is no translation $i.e.$, $p = 0$, then there is no map τ; if the translation is non-zero, the kernel is enlarged due to the composition with map τ. In general, the symmetric real kernel of the composition map $\tau \circ \sigma$ is 3 dimensional – while the kernel of σ is only 2 dimensional (see [9]). The solutions for the unnormalized Kruppa are much more complicated due to the unknown scale λ. However, we have the following lemma to simplify things a little bit.

Lemma 2. *Given a fundamental matrix $F = A^{-T} R^T A^T \widehat{p'}$ with $p' = Ap$, a real symmetric matrix $X \in \mathbb{R}^{3\times 3}$ is a solution of $F^T XF = \lambda^2 \widehat{p'}^T X\widehat{p'}$ if and only if $Y = A^{-1}XA^{-T}$ is a solution of $E^T YE = \lambda^2 \widehat{p}^T Y\widehat{p}$ with $E = R^T \widehat{p}$.*

Using Lemma 1, the proof of this lemma is simply algebraic. This simple lemma, however, states a very important fact: given a set of fundamental matrices $F_i = A^{-T} R_i^T A^T \widehat{p_i'}$ with $p_i' = Ap_i, i = 1,\ldots,n$, there is a one-to-one correspondence between the set of solutions of the equations: $F_i^T XF_i = \lambda_i^2 \widehat{p_i'}^T X\widehat{p_i'}, i = 1,\ldots,n$

and the set of solutions of the equations: $E_i^T Y E_i = \lambda_i^2 \widehat{p}_i^T Y \widehat{p}_i, i = 1, \ldots, n$ where $E_i = R_i^T \widehat{p}_i$ are essential matrices associated to the given fundamental matrices. Note that these essential matrices are determined only by the camera motion. Therefore, the conditions of uniqueness of the solution of Kruppa equations only depend on the camera motion. Our next task is then to study *how* the solutions of Kruppa equations depend on the camera motion.

3.2 Renormalization and Degeneracy of Kruppa Equations

From the derivation of the Kruppa equations (7) or (9), we observe that the reason why they are nonlinear is that we do not usually know the scale λ. It is then helpful to know under what conditions the matrix Kruppa equation will have the same solutions as the normalized one, *i.e.*, with λ set to 1. Here we will study two special cases for which we are able to know directly what the missing λ is. The fundamental matrix can then be *renormalized* and we can therefore solve the camera calibration from the normalized matrix Kruppa equations, which are linear! These two cases are when the rotation axis is *parallel* or *perpendicular* to the translation. That is, if the motion is represented by $(R, p) \in SE(3)$ and the unit vector $u \in \mathbb{R}^3$ is the axis of R,[4] then the two cases are when u is parallel or perpendicular to p. As we will soon see, these two cases are of great theoretical importance: Not only does the calibration algorithm become linear, but it also reveals certain subtleties of the Kruppa equations and explains when the nonlinear Kruppa equations are most likely to become ill-conditioned.

Lemma 3. *Consider a camera motion $(R, p) \in SE(3)$ where $R = e^{\widehat{u}\theta}$, $\theta \in (0, \pi)$ and the axis $u \in \mathbb{R}^3$ is parallel or perpendicular to p. If $\gamma \in \mathbb{R}$ and positive definite matrix Y are a solution to the matrix Kruppa equation: $\widehat{p}^T R Y R^T \widehat{p} = \gamma^2 \widehat{p}^T Y \widehat{p}$ associated to the essential matrix $R^T \widehat{p}$, then we must have $\gamma^2 = 1$. Consequently, Y is a solution of the normalized matrix Kruppa equation: $\widehat{p}^T R Y R^T \widehat{p} = \widehat{p}^T Y \widehat{p}$.*

Proof: Without loss of generality we assume $\|p\| = 1$. For the parallel case, let $x \in \mathbb{R}^3$ be a vector of unit length in the plane spanned by the column vectors of $\widehat{p}$. All such x lie on a unit circle. There exists $x_0 \in \mathbb{R}^3$ on the circle such that $x_0^T Y x_0$ is maximum. We then have $x_0^T R Y R^T x_0 = \gamma^2 x_0^T Y x_0$, hence $\gamma^2 \leq 1$. Similarly, if we pick x_0 such that $x_0^T Y x_0$ is minimum, we have $\gamma^2 \geq 1$. Therefore, $\gamma^2 = 1$. For the perpendicular case, since the columns of $\widehat{p}$ span the subspace which is perpendicular to the vector p, the eigenvector u of R is in this subspace. Thus we have: $u^T R Y R^T u = \gamma^2 u^T Y u \Rightarrow u^T Y u = \gamma^2 u^T Y u$. Hence $\gamma^2 = 1$ if Y is positive definite. $\blacksquare$

Combining Lemma 3 and Lemma 2, we immediately have:

Theorem 1 (Renormalization of Kruppa Equations). *Consider an unnormalized fundamental matrix $F = A^{-T} R^T A^T \widehat{p'}$ where $R = e^{\widehat{u}\theta}$, $\theta \in (0, \pi)$ and the axis $u \in \mathbb{R}^3$ is parallel or perpendicular to $p = A^{-1} p'$. Let $e = p'/\|p'\|$. Then if $\lambda \in \mathbb{R}$ and a positive definite matrix ω are a solution to the matrix Kruppa equation: $F^T \omega^{-1} F = \lambda^2 \widehat{e}^T \omega^{-1} \widehat{e}$, we must have $\lambda^2 = \|p'\|^2$.*

---

[4] R can always be written of the form $R = e^{\widehat{u}\theta}$ for some $\theta \in [0, \pi]$ and $u \in \mathbb{S}^2$.

This theorem claims that, for the two types of special motions considered here, there is no solution for λ in the Kruppa equation (9) besides the true scale of the fundamental matrix. Hence we can decompose the problem into finding λ first and then solving for ω or ω^{-1}. The following theorem allows to directly compute the scale λ for a given fundamental matrix:

Theorem 2 (Renormalization of Fundamental Matrix). *Given an unnormalized fundamental matrix $F = \lambda A^{-T} R^T A^T \widehat{p'}$ with $\|p'\| = 1$, if $p = A^{-1}p'$ is parallel to the axis of R, then λ^2 is $\|F\widehat{p'}F^T\|$, and if p is perpendicular to the axis of R, then λ is one of the two non-zero eigenvalues of $F\widehat{p'}^T$.*

Proof: Note that, since $\widehat{p'}\widehat{p'}^T$ is a projection matrix to the plane spanned by the column vectors of $\widehat{p'}$, we have the identity $\widehat{p'}\widehat{p'}^T\widehat{p'} = \widehat{p'}$. First we prove the parallel case. It is straightforward to check that, in general, $F\widehat{p'}F^T = \lambda^2 \widehat{AR^Tp}$. Since the axis of R is parallel to p, we have $R^Tp = p$ so that $F\widehat{p'}F^T = \lambda^2\widehat{p'}$. For the perpendicular case, let $u \in \mathbb{R}^3$ be the axis of R. By assumption $p = A^{-1}p'$ is perpendicular to u. Then there exists $v \in \mathbb{R}^3$ such that $u = \widehat{p}A^{-1}v$. Then it is direct to check that $\widehat{p'}v$ is the eigenvector of $F\widehat{p'}^T$ corresponding to the eigenvalue λ. $\blacksquare$

Then for these two types of special motions, the associated fundamental matrix can be immediately normalized by being divided by the scale λ. Once the fundamental matrices are normalized, the problem of finding the calibration matrix ω^{-1} from normalized matrix Kruppa equations (8) becomes a simple *linear* one! A normalized matrix Kruppa equation in general imposes *three* linearly independent constraints on the unknown calibration matrix given by (6). However, this is *no longer the case* for the special motions that we are considering here.

Theorem 3 (Degeneracy of Kruppa Equations). *Consider a camera motion $(R,p) \in SE(3)$ where $R = e^{\widehat{u}\theta}$ has the angle $\theta \in (0,\pi)$. If the axis $u \in \mathbb{R}^3$ is parallel or perpendicular to p, then the normalized matrix Kruppa equation: $\widehat{p}^T RY R^T\widehat{p} = \widehat{p}^TY\widehat{p}$ imposes only two linearly independent constraints on the symmetric matrix Y.*

Proof: For the parallel case, by restricting Y to the plane spanned by the column vectors of $\widehat{p}$, it is a symmetric matrix $\tilde{Y}$ in $\mathbb{R}^{2\times2}$. The rotation matrix $R \in SO(3)$ restricted to this plane is a rotation $\tilde{R} \in SO(2)$. The normalized matrix Kruppa equation is then equivalent to $\tilde{Y} - \tilde{R}\tilde{Y}\tilde{R}^T = 0$. Since $0 < \theta < \pi$, this equation imposes exactly two constraints on the three dimensional space of 2×2 real symmetric matrices. The identity $I_{2\times2}$ is the only solution. Hence the normalized Kruppa equation imposes exactly two linearly independent constraints on Y.

For the perpendicular case, since u is in the plane spanned by the column vectors of $\widehat{p}$, there exist $v \in \mathbb{R}^3$ such that (u,v) form an orthonormal basis of the plane. Then the normalized matrix Kruppa equation is equivalent to:

$$\widehat{p}^T RY R^T\widehat{p} = \widehat{p}^TY\widehat{p} \Leftrightarrow (u,v)^T RY R^T(u,v) = (u,v)^TY(u,v). \tag{12}$$

Since $R^Tu = u$, the above matrix equation is equivalent to two equations $v^T RYu = v^TYu, v^T RY R^Tv = v^TYv$. These are the only two constraints given by the normalized Kruppa equation. $\blacksquare$

According to this theorem, although we can renormalize the fundamental matrix when rotation axis and translation are parallel or perpendicular, we only get two independent constraints from the resulting (normalized) Kruppa equation corresponding to a single fundamental matrix. Hence for these motions, in general, we still need three such fundamental matrices to uniquely determine the unknown calibration. On the other hand, if we do not renormalize the fundamental matrix in these cases and directly use the unnormalized Kruppa equations (7) to solve for calibration, the two nonlinear equations in (7) are in fact algebraically dependent! Therefore, one can only get one constraint, as opposed to the expected two, on the unknown calibration ω^{-1}. This is summarized in Table 1.

Table 1. Dependency of Kruppa equation on angle $\phi \in [0, \pi)$ between the rotation and translation.

Cases	Type of Constraints	# of Constraints on ω^{-1}
$(\phi \neq 0)$ and $(\phi \neq \frac{\pi}{2})$	Unnormalized Kruppa Equation	2
	Normalized Kruppa Equation	3
$(\phi = 0)$ or $(\phi = \frac{\pi}{2})$	Unnormalized Kruppa Equation	1
	Normalized Kruppa Equation	2

Although, mathematically, motion involving translation either parallel or perpendicular to the rotation is only a zero-measure subset of $SE(3)$, they are very commonly encountered in applications: Many images sequences are usually taken by moving the camera around an object in trajectory composed of **planar motion** or **orbital motion**, in which case the rotation axis and translation direction are likely perpendicular to each other. Another example is a so called **screw motion**, whose rotation axis and translation are parallel. Such a motion shows up frequently in aerial mobile motion. Our analysis shows that, for these types of motions, even if the sufficient conditions for a unique calibration are satisfied, a self-calibration algorithm based on directly solving the Kruppa equations (7) is likely to be ill-conditioned [1]. To intuitively demonstrate the practical significance of our results, we give an example in Figure 1. Our analysis reveals that in these cases, it is crucial to renormalize the Kruppa equation using Theorem 3: once the fundamental matrix or Kruppa equations are renormalized, not only is one more constraint recovered, but we also obtain linear (normalized Kruppa) equations.

Comment 2 (Solutions of the Normalized Kruppa Equations) *Claims of Theorem 3 run contrary to the claims of Propositions B.5 hence B.9 in [17]: In Proposition B.5 of [17], it is claimed that the solution space of the normalized Kruppa equations when the translation is parallel or perpendicular to the rotation axis is* **two** *or* **three** *dimensional. In Theorem 3, we claim that the solution space is always* **four** *dimensional. Theorem 3 does not cover the case when the rotation angle θ is π. However, if one allows the rotation to be π, the solutions of normalized Kruppa equations are even more complicated. For example, we know $e^{\hat{u}\pi}\hat{p} = -\hat{p}$ if u is of unit length and parallel to p (see [8]). Therefore, if $R = e^{\hat{u}\pi}$, the corresponding normalized Kruppa*

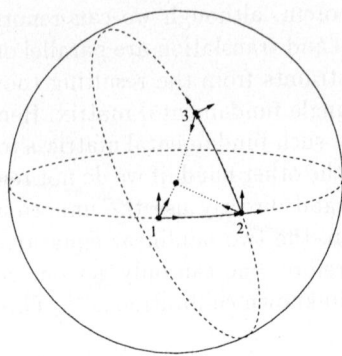

Fig. 1. Two consecutive orbital motions with independent rotations: even if pairwise fundamental matrices among the three views are considered, one only gets at most $1 + 1 + 2 = 4$ effective constraints on the camera intrinsic matrix if the three matrix Kruppa equations are *not* renormalized. After renormalization, however, we may get back to $2 + 2 + 2 \geq 5$ constraints.

equation is completely degenerate and imposes no constraints at all on the calibration matrix.

Comment 3 (Number of Solutions) *Although Theorem 2 claims that for the perpendicular case λ is one of the two non-zero eigenvalues of $F\widehat{p'}^{T}$, unfortunately, there is no way to tell which one is the right one – simulations show that it could be either the larger or smaller one. Therefore, in a numerical algorithm, for given $n \geq 3$ fundamental matrices, one needs to consider all possible 2^n combinations. According to Theorem 1, in the noise-free case, only one of the solutions can be positive definite, which corresponds to the the true calibration.*

3.3 Kruppa Equations and Chirality

It can be shown that if the scene is *rich enough* (with to come), then the necessary and sufficient condition for a unique camera calibration (see [9]) says that two general motions with rotation around different axes already determine a unique Euclidean solution for camera motion, calibration and scene structure. However, the two Kruppa equations obtained from these two motions will only give us *at most four* constraints on ω, which is not enough to determine ω which has *five* degrees of freedom. We hence need to know what information is missing from the Kruppa equation. State alternatively, can we get extra independent constraints on ω from the fundamental matrix other than the Kruppa equation?

The proof of Theorem 2 suggests another equation can be derived from the fundamental matrix $F = \lambda A^{-T} R^T A^T \widehat{p'}$ with $\|p'\| = 1$. Since $F\widehat{p'}F^T = \lambda^2 \widehat{AR^T p}$, we can obtain the vector $\alpha = \lambda^2 A R^T p = \lambda^2 A R^T A^{-1} p'$. Then it is obvious that the following equation for $\omega = A^{-T} A^{-1}$ holds:

$$\alpha^T \omega \alpha = \lambda^4 p'^T \omega p'. \tag{13}$$

Notice that this is a constraint on ω, not like the Kruppa equations which are constraints on ω^{-1}. Combining the Kruppa equations given in (7) with (13) we have:

$$\lambda^2 = \frac{\xi_1^T \omega^{-1} \xi_1}{\eta_2^T \omega^{-1} \eta_2} = \frac{\xi_2^T \omega^{-1} \xi_2}{\eta_1^T \omega^{-1} \eta_1} = \frac{\xi_1^T \omega^{-1} \xi_2}{\eta_1^T \omega^{-1} \eta_2} = \sqrt{\frac{\alpha^T \omega \alpha}{p'^T \omega p'}}. \tag{14}$$

Is the last equation algebraically independent of the two Kruppa equations? Although it seems to be quite different from the Kruppa equations, it is in fact dependent on them. This can be shown either numerically or using simple algebraic tools such as Maple. Thus, it appears that our effort to look for extra *independent, explicit* constraints on A from the fundamental matrix has failed.[5] In the following, we will give an explanation to this by showing that not all ω which satisfy the Kruppa equations may give *valid* Euclidean reconstructions of both the camera motion and scene structure. The extra constraints which are missing in Kruppa equations are in fact captured by the so called **chirality constraint**, which was previously studied in [5]. We now give a clear and concise description between the relationship of the Kruppa equations and chirality.

Theorem 4 (Kruppa Equations and Chirality). *Consider a camera with calibration matrix I and motion (R, p). If $p \neq 0$, among all the solutions $Y = A^{-1}A^{-T}$ of the Kruppa equation $E^T Y E = \lambda^2 \widehat{p}^T Y \widehat{p}$ associated to $E = R^T \widehat{p}$, only those which guarantee $ARA^{-1} \in SO(3)$ may provide a **valid Euclidean reconstruction** of both camera motion and scene structure in the sense that any other solution pushes some plane $N \subset \mathbb{R}^3$ to the plane at infinity, and feature points on different sides of the plane N have different signs of recovered depth.*

Proof: The images $\mathbf{x}_2, \mathbf{x}_1$ of any point $q \in \mathbb{R}^3$ satisfy the coordinate transformation:

$$\lambda_2 \mathbf{x}_2 = \lambda_1 R \mathbf{x}_1 + p.$$

If there exists $Y = A^{-1}A^{-T}$ such that $E^T Y E = \lambda^2 \widehat{p}^T Y \widehat{p}$ for some $\lambda \in \mathbb{R}$, then the matrix $F = A^{-T} E A^{-1} = A^{-T} R^T A^T \widehat{p'}$ is also an essential matrix with $p' = Ap$, that is, there exists $\tilde{R} \in SO(3)$ such that $F = \tilde{R}^T \widehat{p'}$ (see [10] for an account of properties of essential matrices). Under the new calibration A, the coordinate transformation is in fact:

$$\lambda_2 A \mathbf{x}_2 = \lambda_1 ARA^{-1}(A\mathbf{x}_1) + p'.$$

Since $F = \tilde{R}^T \widehat{p'} = A^{-T} R^T A^T \widehat{p'}$, we have $ARA^{-1} = \tilde{R} + p'v^T$ for some $v \in \mathbb{R}^3$. Then the above equation becomes: $\lambda_2 A \mathbf{x}_2 = \lambda_1 \tilde{R}(A\mathbf{x}_1) + \lambda_1 p'v^T(A\mathbf{x}_1) + p'$. Let $\beta = \lambda_1 v^T(A\mathbf{x}_1) \in \mathbb{R}$, we can further rewrite the equation as:

$$\lambda_2 A \mathbf{x}_2 = \lambda_1 \tilde{R} A \mathbf{x}_1 + (\beta + 1)p'. \tag{15}$$

Nevertheless, with respect to the solution A, the reconstructed images $A\mathbf{x}_1, A\mathbf{x}_2$ and $(\tilde{R}, p')$ must also satisfy:

$$\gamma_2 A \mathbf{x}_2 = \gamma_1 \tilde{R} A \mathbf{x}_1 + p' \tag{16}$$

---

[5] Nevertheless, extra *implicit* constraints on A may still be obtained from other algebraic facts. For example, the so called **modulus constraints** give three implicit constraints on A by introducing three extra unknowns, for more details see [13].

for some scale factors $\gamma_1, \gamma_2 \in \mathbb{R}$. Now we prove by contradiction that $v \neq 0$ is impossible for a valid Euclidean reconstruction. Suppose that $v \neq 0$ and we define the plane $N = \{q \in \mathbb{R}^3 | v^T q = -1\}$. Then for any $q = \lambda_1 A x_1 \in N$, we have $\beta = -1$. Hence, from (15), $A x_1, A x_2$ satisfy $\lambda_2 A x_2 = \lambda_1 \tilde{R} A x_1$. Since $A x_1, A x_2$ also satisfy (16) and $p' \neq 0$, both γ_1 and γ_2 in (16) must be ∞. That is, the plane N is "pushed" to the plane at infinity by the solution A. For points not on the plane N, we have $\beta + 1 \neq 0$. Comparing the two equations (15) and (16), we get $\gamma_i = \lambda_i / (\beta + 1), i = 1, 2$. Then for a point in the far side of the plane N, i.e., $\beta + 1 < 0$, the recovered depth scale γ is negative; for a point in the near side of N, i.e., $\beta + 1 > 0$, the recovered depth scale γ is positive. Thus, we must have that $v = 0$. ∎

Comment 4 (Quasi-affine Reconstruction) *Theorem 4 essentially implies the chirality constraints studied in [5]. According to the above theorem, if only finitely many feature points are measured, a solution of the calibration matrix A which may allow a valid Euclidean reconstruction should induce a plane N not cutting through the convex hull spanned by all the feature points and camera centers. Such a reconstruction is referred as quasi-affine in [5].*

It is known that, in general, all A's which make $A R A^{-1}$ a rotation matrix form a one parameter family [9]. Thus, following Theorem 4, a camera calibration can be *uniquely* determined by two independent rotations regardless of translation if enough feature points are available. An intuitive example is provided in Figure 2.

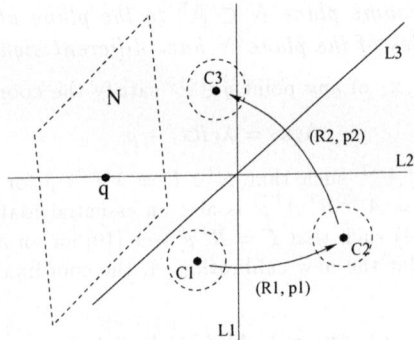

Fig. 2. A camera undergoes two motions (R_1, p_1) and (R_2, p_2) observing a rig consisting of three straight lines L_1, L_2, L_3. Then the camera calibration is uniquely determined as long as R_1 and R_2 have independent rotation axes and rotation angles in $(0, \pi)$, regardless of p_1, p_2. This is because, for any invalid solution A, the associated plane N (see the proof of Theorem 4) must intersect the three lines at some point, say q. Then the reconstructed depth of point q with respect to the solution A would be infinite (points beyond the plane N would have negative recovered depth). This gives us a criteria to exclude all such invalid solutions.

The significance of Theorem 4 is that it explains why we get only two constraints from one fundamental matrix even in the two special cases when the

Kruppa equations can be renormalized – extra ones are imposed by the structure, not the motion. The theorem also resolves the discrepancy between the Kruppa equations and the necessary and sufficient condition for a unique calibration: the Kruppa equations, although convenient to use, do not provide sufficient conditions for a valid calibration which allows a valid Euclidean reconstruction of both the camera motion and scene structure. However, the fact given in Theorem 4 is somewhat difficult to harness in algorithms. For example, in order to exclude invalid solutions, one needs feature points on or beyond the plane N.[6] Alternatively, if such feature points are not available, one may first obtain a **projective reconstruction** and then use the so called **absolute quadric constraints** to calibrate the camera [16]. However, in such a method, the camera motion needs to satisfy a stronger condition than requiring only two independent rotations, *i.e.*, it cannot be *critical* in the sense specified in [15].

4 Simulation Results

In this section, we test the performance of the proposed algorithms through different experiments. The error measure between the actual calibration matrix A and the estimated calibration matrix $\tilde{A}$ was chosen to be $error = \frac{\|A-\tilde{A}\|}{\|A\|} \times 100$. For all the simulations, field of view is chosen to be 90 degrees for a 500×500 pixel image size; a cloud of 20 points are randomly chosen with depths vary from 100 to 400 units of focal length; the number of trials is always 100 and the number of image frames is 3 to 4 (depending on the minimum number of frames needed by each algorithm). The calibration matrix A is simply the transformation from the original 2×2 (in unit of focal length) image to the 500×500 pixel image. For these parameters, the true A should be $A = \begin{pmatrix} 250 & 0 & 250 \\ 0 & 250 & 250 \\ 0 & 0 & 1 \end{pmatrix}$. The ratio of the magnitude of translation and rotation, or simply the T/R ratio, is compared at the center of the random cloud (scattered in the truncated pyramid specified by the given field of view and depth variation). For all simulations, the number of trials is 100.

Pure rotation case: For comparison, we here also implement the linear algorithm proposed by Hartley [4] for calibrating a pure rotating camera. Figures 3 and 4 show the experiments performed in the pure rotation case. The axes of rotation are X and Y for Figures 3 and 4. The amount of rotation is $20°$. The perfect data was corrupted with zero-mean Gaussian noise with standard deviation σ varying from 0 to 5 pixels. In Figures 3, it can be observed that the algorithm performs very well in the presence of noise, reaching errors of less than 6% for a noise level of 5 pixels. Figure 4 shows the effect of the amount of translation. This experiment is aimed to test the robustness of the pure rotation algorithm with respect to translation. The T/R ratio was varied from 0 to 0.5

---

[6] Some possible ways of harnessing the constraints provided by chirality have been discussed in [5]. Basically they give *inequality* constraints on the possible solutions of the calibration.

574

and the noise level was set to 2 pixels. It can be observed that the algorithm is not robust with respect to the amount of translation.

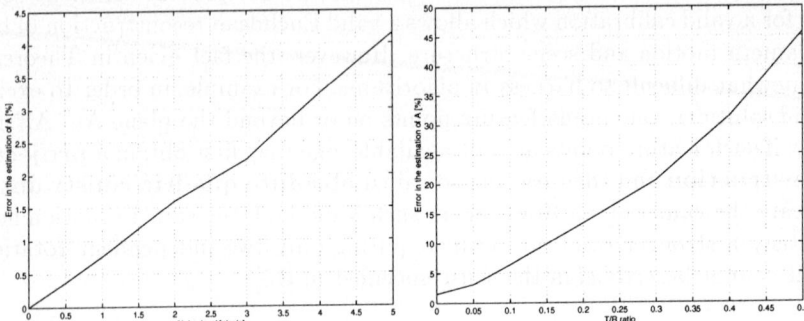

Fig. 3. Pure rotation algorithm. Rotation axes X-Y.

Fig. 4. Pure rotation algorithm in presence of translation. Rotation axes X-Y, $\sigma = 2$.

Translation parallel to rotation axis: Figures 5 and 6 show the experiments performed for our algorithm[7] when translation is parallel to the axis of rotation.[8] The non-isotropic normalization procedure proposed by Hartley [2] and statistically justified by Mühlich and Mester [12] was used to estimate the fundamental matrix. Figure 5 shows the effect of noise in the estimation of the calibration matrix for $T/R = 1$ and a rotation of $\theta = 20^o$ between consecutive frames. It can be seen that the normalization procedure improves the estimation of the calibration matrix, but the improvement is not significant. This result is consistent with that of [12], since the effect of normalization is more important for large noise levels. On the other hand, the performance of the algorithm is not as good as that of the pure rotation case, but still an error of 5% is reached for a noise level of 2 pixels. Figure 6 shows the effect of the angle of rotation in the estimation of the calibration matrix for a noise level of 2 pixels. It can be concluded that a minimum angle of rotation between consecutive frames is required for the algorithm to succeed.

Translation perpendicular to rotation axis: Figures 7 and 8 show the experiments performed for our algorithm when translation is perpendicular to the axis of rotation. It can be observed that this algorithm is much more sensitive to noise. The noise has to be less than 0.5 pixels in order to get an error of 5%. Experimentally it was found that Kruppa equations are very sensitive to the

---

[7] Although in this paper we do not outline the algorithm, it should be clear from Section 3.2.

[8] For specifying the Rotation/Translation axes, we simply use symbols such as "XY-YY-ZZ" which means: for the first pair of images the relative motion is rotation along X and translation along Y; for the second pair both rotation and translation are along Y; and for the third pair both rotation and translation are along Z.

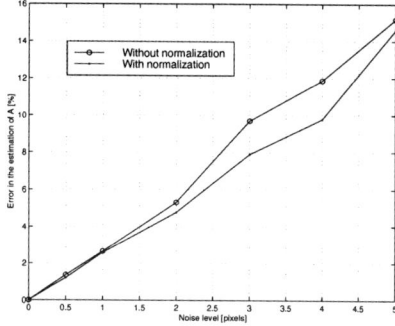

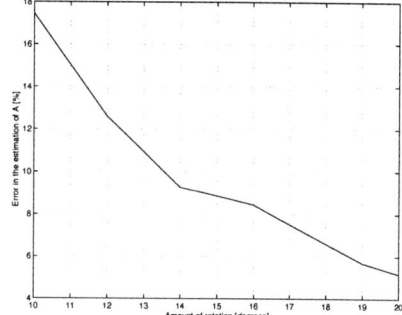

Fig. 5. Rotation parallel to translation case. $\theta = 20°$. Rotation/Translation axes: XX-YY-ZZ, T/R ratio $= 1$.

Fig. 6. Rotation parallel to translation case. $\sigma = 2$. Rotation/Translation axes: XX-YY-ZZ, T/R ratio $= 1$.

normalization of the fundamental matrix F and that the eigenvalues λ_1 and λ_2 of $F\widehat{p'}^T$ are close to each other. Therefore in the presence of noise, the estimation of those eigenvalues might be ill conditioned (even complex eigenvalues are obtained) and so might the solution of Kruppa equations. Another experimental problem is that more than one non-degenerate solution to Kruppa equations can be found. This is because, when taking all possible combinations of eigenvalues of $F\widehat{p'}^T$ in order to normalize F, the smallest eigenvalue of the linear map associated to "incorrect" Kruppa equations can be very small. Besides, the eigenvector associated to this eigenvalue can eventually give a non-degenerate matrix. Thus in the presence of noise, you can not distinguish between the correct and one of these incorrect solutions. The results presented here correspond to the best match to the ground truth when more than one solution is found. Finally it is important to note that large motions can significantly improve the performance of the algorithm. Figure 8 shows the error in the estimation of the calibration matrix for a rotation of $30°$. It can be observed that the results are comparable to that of the parallel case with a rotation of $20°$.

Robustness: We denote the angle between the rotation axis and translation by ψ. The two linear algorithms we have studied in the above are only supposed to work for the cases $\phi = 0°$ and $\phi = 90°$. In order to check how robust these algorithms are, we run them anyway for cases when ϕ varies from $0°$ to $90°$. The noise level is 2 pixels, amount of rotation is always $20°$ and the T/R ratio is 1. Translation and rotation axes are given by Figure 9. Surprisingly, as we can see from the results given in Figure 10, for the range $0° \leq \phi \leq 50°$, both algorithms give pretty close estimates. Heuristically, this is because, for this range of angle, the eigenvalues of the matrix $F\widehat{p'}^T$ are complex and numerically their norm is very close to the norm of the matrix $F\widehat{p'}F^T$. Therefore, the computed renormalization scale λ from both algorithms is very close, as is the calibration estimate. For $\phi > 50°$, the eigenvalues of $F\widehat{p'}^T$ become real and the performance of the two algorithms is no longer the same. Near the conditions under which

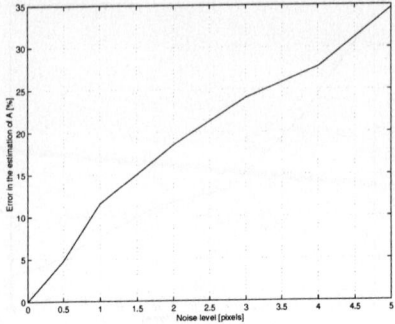

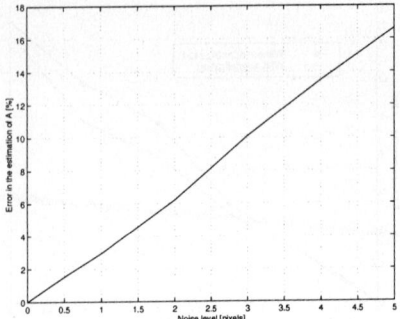

Fig. 7. Rotation orthogonal to translation case. $\theta = 20°$. Rotation/Translation axes: XY-YZ-ZX, T/R ratio $= 1$.

Fig. 8. Rotation orthogonal to translation case. $\theta = 30°$. Rotation/Translation axes: XY-YZ-ZX, T/R ratio $= 1$.

these algorithms are designed to work, the algorithm for the perpendicular case is apparently more sensitive to the perturbation in the angle ϕ than the one for the parallel case: As clear from the figure, a variation of $10°$ degree of ϕ results an increase of error almost 50%. We are currently conducting experiments on real images and trying to find ways to overcome this difficulty.

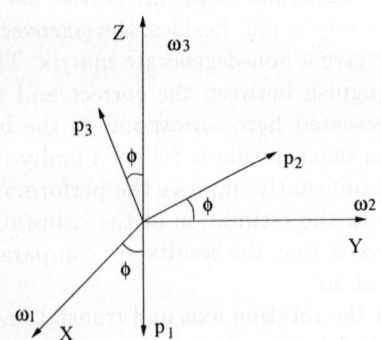

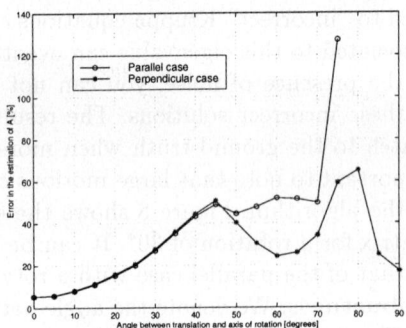

Fig. 9. The relation of the three rotation axes $\omega_1, \omega_2, \omega_3$ and three translations p_1, p_2, p_3.

Fig. 10. Estimation error in calibration w.r.t. different angle ϕ.

5   Conclusions

In this paper, we have revisited the Kruppa equations based approach for camera self-calibration. Through a detailed study of the cases when the camera rotation axis is parallel or perpendicular to the translation, we have discovered generic difficulties in the conventional self-calibration schemes based on directly solving the nonlinear Kruppa equations. Our results not only complete existing results in the literature regarding the solutions of Kruppa equations but also provide brand new linear algorithms for self-calibration other than the well-known one for a pure rotating camera. Simulation results show that, under the given conditions, these linear algorithms provide good estimates of the camera calibration despite the degeneracy of the Kruppa equations. The performance is close to that of the pure rotation case.

References

1. S. Bougnoux. From projective to Euclidean space under any practical situation, a criticism of self-calibration. In *Proceedings of IEEE conference on Computer Vision and Pattern Recognition*, pages 790–796, 1998.
2. R. I. Hartley. In defense of the 8-point algorithm. *IEEE Transactions on Pattern Analysis and Machine Intelligence*, 19(6), 1997.
3. R. I. Hartley. Kruppa's equations derived from the fundamental matrix. *IEEE Transactions on Pattern Analysis and Machine Intelligence*, 19(2):133–135, February 1997.
4. R. I. Hartley. Self-calibration of stationary cameras. *International Journal of Computer Vision*, 22(1):5–23, 1997.
5. R. I. Hartley. Chirality. *International Journal of Computer Vision*, 26(1):41–61, 1998.
6. A. Heyden and K. Astrom. Euclidean reconstruction from image sequences with varying and unknown focal length and principal point. In *Proceedings of IEEE Conference on Computer Vision and Pattern Recognition*, 1997.
7. Q.-T. Luong and O. Faugeras. Self-calibration of a moving camera from point correspondences and fundamental matrices. *IJCV*, 22(3):261–89, 1997.
8. Y. Ma, J. Košecká, and S. Sastry. Linear differential algorithm for motion recovery: A geometric approach. *International Journal of Computer Vision*, 36(1):71-89, 1998.
9. Y. Ma, René Vidal, J. Košecká, and S. Sastry. Camera self-calibration: geometry and algorithms. *UC Berkeley Memorandum No. UCB/ERL M99/32*, 1999.
10. S. J. Maybank. *Theory of Reconstruction from Image Motion*. Springer Series in Information Sciences. Springer-Verlag, 1993.
11. S. J. Maybank and O. D. Faugeras. A theory of self-calibration of a moving camera. *International Journal of Computer Vision*, 8(2):123–151, 1992.
12. M. Mühlich and R. Mester. The role of total least squares in motion analysis. In *Proceedings of European Conference on Computer Vision*, pages 305–321, 1998.
13. M. Pollefeys and L. Van Gool. Stratified self-calibration with the modulus constraint. *IEEE Transactions on Pattern Analysis and Machine Intelligence*, 21(8):707–24, 1999.
14. M. Pollefeys, R. Koch, and L. Van Gool. Self-calibration and metric reconstruction in spite of varying and unknown internal camera parameters. In *Proceedings of 6th International Conference on Computer Vision*, pages 90–95, 1998.
15. P. Sturm. Critical motion sequences for monocular self-calibration and uncalibrated Euclidean reconstruction. In *Proceedings of IEEE conference on Computer Vision and Pattern Recognition*, pages 1100–1105, 1997.
16. B. Triggs. Autocalibration and the absolute quadric. In *Proceedings of IEEE conference on Computer Vision and Pattern Recognition*, 1997.
17. C. Zeller and O. Faugeras. Camera self-calibration from video sequences: the Kruppa equations revisited. *Research Report 2793, INRIA, France*, 1996.

Registration with a Moving Zoom Lens Camera for Augmented Reality Applications

Gilles Simon and Marie-Odile Berger

LORIA- INRIA Lorraine
BP 101
54602 Villers les Nancy, France
email:{gsimon@loria.fr,berger@loria.fr}

Abstract. We focus in this paper on the problem of adding computer-generated objects in video sequences that have been shot with a zoom lens camera. While numerous papers have been devoted to registration with fixed focal length, little attention has been brought to zoom lens cameras. In this paper, we propose an efficient two-stage algorithm for handling zoom changing which are are likely to happen in a video sequence. We first attempt to partition the video into camera motions and zoom variations. Then, classical registration methods are used on the image frames labeled *camera motion* while keeping the internal parameters constant, whereas the zoom parameters are only updated for the frames labeled *zoom variations*. Results are presented demonstrating registration on various sequences. Augmented video sequences are also shown.

1   Introduction

Augmented Reality (AR) is a technique in which the user's view is enhanced or augmented with additional information generated from a computer model. In contrast to virtual reality, where the user is immersed in a completely computer-generated world, AR allows the user to interact with the real world in a natural way. This explains why interest in AR has substantially increased in the past few years and medical, manufacturing or urban planning applications have been developed [2, 5, 15, 18].

In order to make AR systems effective, the computer generated objects and the real scene must be combined seamlessly so that the virtual objects align well with the real ones. It is therefore essential to determine accurately the location and the optical properties of the cameras. The registration task must be achieved with special care because the human visual system is very good at detecting even small mis-registrations.

There has been much research in the field of vision-based registration for augmented reality [1, 12, 14, 18]. However these works assume that the internal parameters of the camera are known (focal length, aspect ratio, principal point) and they only address the problem of computing the pose of the camera. This is a strong limitation of these methods because zoom changing is likely to happen in a video sequence. A method is proposed in [11], which can retrieve metric reconstruction from image sequences obtained with uncalibrated zooming cameras. However, considering unknown principal point leads to unstable results if the projective calibration is not accurate enough, the sequence not long enough, or the motion sequence critical towards the set of constraints. More stable results are obtained when the principal point is considered as fixed in the centre of the image, but this assumption is not always fulfilled (see [19]) and is not accurate enough for image composition. Other attempts have been made to cope with varying internal parameters for AR applications [10]. However this approach uses targets arbitrarily positioned in the environment. It is therefore of limited use if outdoor scenes are considered.

In this paper we extend our previous works on vision based registration methods [12, 13] to the case of zoom-lens cameras. Zoom-lens camera calibration is still found to be very difficult for several reasons [16, 3]: modeling a zoom-lens camera is difficult due to optical and mechanical misalignments in the lens system of a camera. Moreover, zoom-lens variations can be confused with camera motions: for instance, it is difficult to discriminate a translation along the optical axis from a zoom.

In this paper, we take advantage of our application field to reduce the problem complexity. Indeed, we assume that the viewpoint and the focal length do not change at the same time. This assumption is compatible with the techniques used by professional movie-makers. We develop in this paper an original statistical approach: for each frame of the sequence, we test the hypothesis of a zoom against the hypothesis of a camera motion. If the motion hypothesis is retained, we still have to compute the camera pose with the old internal parameters. Otherwise, the internal parameters are computed assuming that the camera pose does not change. Camera parameters are supposed to be known in the first image of the sequence (they can be obtained easily from a set of at least 6 2D/3D point correspondences pointed out by the user).

This paper is organized as follows: first, we discuss in section 2 the pinhole camera model and we show the difficulties to recover both the camera pose and the internal parameters with varying focal lengths. Section 3 then describes our original method for zoom/motion partitioning of the sequence. Section 4 describes how registration is performed from this segmentation. Examples which demonstrate the effectiveness of our method are shown in section 5.

2 Registration difficulties with a zoom-lens camera

In this section, we first describe the pinhole model which is widely used for camera modeling. Then we describe our attempts to compute both the zoom and the motion parameters in a single stage. This task is called full calibration in the following. We show that classical registration methods fail to recover both the internal and the external parameters, even though some of the intrinsic parameters are fixed.

2.1 The pinhole camera model

Let (X, Y, Z) represent the coordinates of any visible point M in a fixed reference system (world coordinate system) and let (X_c, Y_c, Z_c) represent the coordinates of the same point in the camera centered coordinate system. The relationship between the two coordinate systems is given by

$$\begin{pmatrix} X_c \\ Y_c \\ Z_c \end{pmatrix} = R \begin{pmatrix} X \\ Y \\ Z \end{pmatrix} + T = [R\ T] \begin{pmatrix} X \\ Y \\ Z \\ 1 \end{pmatrix}$$

where $[R, T]$ is the 3D displacement (rotation and translation) from the world coordinate system to the camera coordinate system.

We assume that the camera performs a perfect perspective transform with center O at a distance f of the image plane. The projection of M on the image plane is $(x = f\frac{X_c}{Z_c}, y = f\frac{Y_c}{Z_c})$. If $1/k_u$ (resp $1/k_v$) is the size of the pixel along the x axes (resp. y axes), its pixel coordinates are:

$$m = (k_u f \frac{X_c}{Z_c} + u_0, k_v f \frac{Y_c}{Z_c} + v_0) \qquad (1)$$

where u_0, v_0 are the coordinates of the principal point of the camera (i.e. the intersection of the optical axis and the image plane).

The coordinates of a 3D point M in a world coordinate system and its pixel coordinates $m = \begin{pmatrix} u \\ v \end{pmatrix}$ are therefore related by $s \begin{bmatrix} u \\ v \\ 1 \end{bmatrix} = \underbrace{\begin{bmatrix} k_u f & 0 & u_0 \\ 0 & k_v f & v_0 \\ 0 & 0 & 1 \end{bmatrix}}_{A} [R\ T] \begin{pmatrix} X \\ Y \\ Z \\ 1 \end{pmatrix}$

Full camera calibration amounts to compute 10 parameters: 6 external parameters (3 for the rotation and 3 for the translation) and 4 internal parameters ($\alpha_u = k_u f$, $\alpha_v = k_v f$, u_0 and v_0). Internal and external parameters are collectively referred to as camera parameters in the following.

2.2 Direct full calibration

When the internal parameters are computed off-line, the registration process amounts to compute the displacement $[R, T]$ which minimizes the re-projection error, that is the error between the projection of known 3D features in the scene and their corresponding 2D features detected in the image. For sake of clarity, we only suppose that the 3D features are points but we can also consider free form curves [12]. Moreover, we show in section 4 that 2D/2D correspondences can be added to improve the viewpoint computation.

The camera pose is therefore the displacement $[R, T]$ which minimizes the reprojection error

$$\min_{R,T} \sum dist(proj(M_i), m_i)^2$$

where minimization is performed only on the 6 external parameters (Euler angles and translation).

Theoretically, zoom-lens variations during shooting can be recovered in the same way. We have therefore to compute not only the camera viewpoint but also the internal camera parameters (focal length, pixel size, optical center) which minimize the reprojection error.

$$\min_{R,T,\alpha_u,\alpha_v,u_0,v_0} \sum dist(proj(M_i), m_i)^2$$

As mentioned by several authors [3], this approach is unable to recover both the internal and external parameters. To overcome this problem, some authors have proposed to reduce the number of unknowns by fixing some of the internal parameters to predefined values. As several experimental studies proved that the ratio $\frac{\alpha_u}{\alpha_v}$ remains almost constant during zoom variations [4], the set of the internal parameters to be estimated is then reduced to α_u, u_0, v_0. Unfortunately this approach fails to recover the right camera parameters. Consider for instance Fig. 1 which exhibits the results when registration is achieved on the 6 external parameters and the 3 internal parameters. As the house stands on a calibration target, the internal and external parameters can be computed for each frame using classical calibration techniques [6]. They can therefore be compared to those computed with the registration method. The camera motions with respect to the turntable and zoom variations during the *cottage sequence* are shown in Table 3.a. The camera trajectory along with the focal length computed for each frame of the sequence are shown in Fig. 1 in dashed lines. They have to be compared to the actual parameters which are shown in solid lines on the same figure. Note that the trajectory is the position of the camera in the horizontal plane and the arrows indicates the optical axis. These results prove that some camera motions are confused with zoom variations: besides the common confusion between zoom and translation along the optical axis, other motions do not correspond to the actual one: between the frames 13 and 14, an unexpected translation is detected and is compensated by a camera zoom out.

Such confusions are also observed in [3], but Bougnoux considers that they do not really affect the quality of the reconstruction of the scene. Unfortunately, the conclusion is not the same for the quality of a composition: an augmented sequence of the cottage using the computed viewpoints and focal length is shown on our web site. Small errors on the camera parameters do not really affect the reprojection of the scene but they induce jittering effects which affect the realism of the composition.

To take into account the interdependance of the internal parameters, Sturm expresses u_0 and v_0 as polynomial functions of α_u [16]. As the aspect ratio α_u/α_v remains constant over the sequence, only one internal parameter α_u has to be determined. However, to determine the degrees and the coefficients of the polynomial models, the camera has to be pre-calibrated for several zoom positions.

Hence, resolving the general full calibration problem is difficult. In this paper, we propose a robust solution to the particular case of sequences where camera

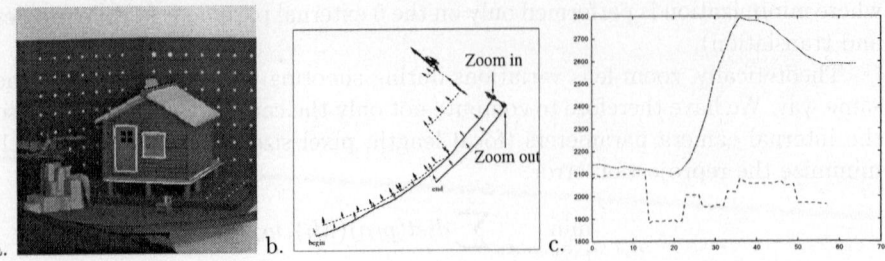

Fig. 1. (a) A snapshot of the cottage sequence and the reprojection of the 3D features. (b) The actual camera trajectory (solid line) and the computed one (dashed line). (c) The actual (solid line) and the estimated (dashed line) focal length during the sequence.

pose and zoom do not change at the same time. This particular case is very interesting for practical applications: indeed, when professional movie-makers make shootings, they generally avoid to mix camera motions and zoom variations. To take advantage of the structure of these sequences, we compute the reprojection error for each frame of the sequence in the two possible cases *zoom alone* and *camera motion alone*: (i) we consider that the internal parameters do not change and we search for the camera pose $[R, T]$ that minimizes the reprojection error (ii) we consider that the camera is fixed and we search for the internal parameters. Surprisingly, experiments we conducted show that the smallest of these two residuals does not always match the right camera parameters: Fig. 2 plots the reprojection error between frames 22 to 35 on a camera zoom sequence. For each frame i, the reprojection error between frame 20 and frame i is computed for the zoom and the motion hypothesis. This allows us to see the influence of the zoom magnitude on the criterion. The results prove that this method fails to recover the right camera parameters unless the magnitude of the zoom variation is high.

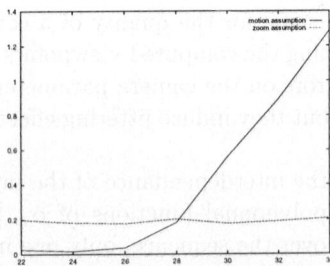

Fig. 2. Reprojection error with the zoom and the motion assumption for a camera zoom motion.

3 Discriminating between zoom variation and camera motion

The above results show that the classical registration methods cannot be used to cope with zoom-lens cameras. We therefore resort to a two-stage method: we first attempt to partition the video into camera motions and zoom variations. Then, our registration method is used on the image frames labeled *camera motion* while keeping the internal parameters constant, whereas the internal parameters are only computed for the frames labeled *zoom variations*. Unlike other methods for video partitioning which are based on the analysis of the optic flow [20], our method is only based on the analysis of a set of 2D corresponding points which are automatically extracted and matched between two consecutive images. The motion information brought by the key-point is very reliable and allows us to discriminate easily between zoom variation and translation along the optical axis. Our approach stands out from [20] in several points : in [20], the mean and the standard deviation of the optical flow are computed in seven non-overlapping sub-regions of the image. These values are compared with thresholds to discriminate between zoom, tilt, pan, Z-rotation, horizontal translation, vertical translation and Z-translation. However, it is not explained how the thresholds are computed, whereas it is the main point of the algorithm (furthermore, many confusions are observed in the final results). Moreover, to discriminate between a zoom and a Z-translation, the authors suppose that the center of the zoom is the center of the image, which is not true in practical situations [19].

Section 3.1 describes the way to extract key-points. Then we present the affine model of a zoom introduced in [4]. Finally we give our algorithm for zoom/motion automatic segmentation of the sequence (3.3).

3.1 Extracting and matching key-points

Key-points (or interest points) are locations in the image where the signal changes two dimensionally: corners, T-junctions or locations where the texture varies significantly. We use the approach developed by Harris and Stephens [7]: they exploit the autocorrelation function of the image to compute a measure which indicates the presence of an interest point. More precisely, the eigenvalues of the matrix

$$\begin{bmatrix} I_x^2 & I_x I_y \\ I_x I_y & I_y^2 \end{bmatrix} \quad (I_x = \frac{\partial I}{\partial x} \dots)$$

are the principal curvatures of the auto-correlation function. If these values are high, a key-point is declared.

We still have to match these key-points between two consecutive images. To do this, we use correlation techniques as described in [21].

Fig 3.a and 3.b exhibit the key-points which have been automatically extracted in two successive images in the *loria scene* and Fig. 3.c shows the matched key-points.

Fig. 3. (a,b) Key-points extracted in two consecutive frames. (c) The matched key-points.

3.2 Modeling zoom-lens cameras

Previous studies on zoom-lens modeling proved that the ratio $\frac{\alpha_u}{\alpha_v}$ is very stable over long time periods. On the contrary, the position of the principal point (u_0, v_0) depends on the zooming position of the camera. This point can vary up to 100 pixels while zooming! However, for most camera lens, it can be shown that the principal point varies on a line while zooming [4]. That is the reason why an affine model with 3 parameters C_0, a_0, b_0 can be used to describe zoom variations. Enciso and Vieville [4] show that if (u', v') and (u, v) are corresponding points after zooming, we have

$$\begin{cases} u' = C_0 u + a_0, \\ v' = C_0 v + b_0. \end{cases} \tag{2}$$

The current matrix of the internal parameters A' is therefore deduced from the previous one A by:

$$A' = \begin{pmatrix} C_0 & 0 & a_0 \\ 0 & C_0 & b_0 \\ 0 & 0 & 1 \end{pmatrix} A. \tag{3}$$

If we want to use this property to discriminate between a zoom and a camera motion, we must prove that a camera motion can not be approximated by the same model. This can be shown from the equations of the optical flow : the optical flow (or instantaneous velocity) of an image point $(x = f\frac{X_c}{Z_c}, y = f\frac{Y_c}{Z_c})$, is

$$\begin{cases} \dot{x} = -\frac{U}{Z_c} + x\frac{W}{Z_c} + Axy - B(x^2 + 1) + Cy, \\ \dot{y} = -\frac{V}{Z_c} + y\frac{W}{Z_c} + A(y^2 + 1) - Bxy - Cx, \end{cases}$$

where $(U, V, W)^T$ is the translational component of the motion of the camera, $(A, B, C)^T$ is its angular velocity and f is set to 1 [8]. The optical flow obtained for the basic motions T_x (horizontal translation), T_y (vertical translation), T_z (Z-translation), R_x (tilt), R_y (pan) and R_z (Z-rotation) are given in table 1.a. Theoretically, none of these motions can be described by an affine transformation with three parameters. However, if $Z_c = Z_0 + \Delta Z$ where $\Delta Z \ll Z_0$ for each model point, that is the depth of the object is small with regard to the distance from the object to the camera (case 1), then T_x, T_y and T_z can be approximated by a zoom model whose parameters C_0, a_0 and b_0 are given in table 1.b (we use the approximation $\dot{x} = \frac{\dot{u}}{k_u} = \frac{u'-u}{k_u \Delta t}$ and $\dot{y} = \frac{v'-v}{k_v \Delta t}$). Moreover, if $x \ll 1$ and $y \ll 1$, that is the focal length is large (case 2), then R_x and R_y can also be approximated by a zoom model (see table 1.b).

Hence, some camera motions can induce an image motion close to the model of the zoom. Fortunately, most of them can easily be identified as camera motions. Indeed, for a zoom motion, the invariant point of the affine model $(\frac{a}{1-C_0}, \frac{b}{1-C_0})$ is the principal point of the camera and lies approximately in the middle of the image. On the contrary, for T_x, T_y, R_x and R_y, this point is outside the image and goes to infinity because C_0 is close to 1. Finally, only the translation along the optical axis T_z is really difficult to discriminate from a zoom.

a.

Motion	$\dot{x}$	$\dot{y}$
T_x	$-\frac{U}{Z_c}$	0
T_y	0	$-\frac{V}{Z_c}$
T_z	$x\frac{W}{Z_c}$	$y\frac{W}{Z_c}$
R_x	Axy	$A(y^2+1)$
R_y	$-B(x^2+1)$	$-Bxy$
R_z	Cy	$-Cx$

b.

Case	(C_0, a_0, b_0)
$T_x + $ case1	$(1, -k_u \frac{U \Delta t}{Z_0}, 0)$
$T_y + $ case1	$(1, 0, -k_v \frac{V \Delta t}{Z_0})$
$T_z + $ case1	$(1 + \frac{W \Delta t}{Z_0}, -u_0 \frac{W \Delta t}{Z_0}, -v_0 \frac{W \Delta t}{Z_0})$
$R_x + $ case2	$(1, 0, A)$
$R_y + $ case2	$(1, -B, 0)$
-	-

Table 1. (a) Optical flow obtained for the basic motions. (b) Parameters of the approximating affine model for ambiguous cases.

3.3 Zoom/motion partioning

In this section, we present our approach for zoom/motion partioning. For each frame of the sequence, we test the hypothesis of a zoom against the hypothesis of a camera motion. We proceed as follows: key-points $(u_i, v_i)_{\{1 \leq i \leq N\}}$ and $(u'_i, v'_i)_{\{1 \leq i \leq N\}}$ are extracted and matched in two consecutive frames I_k and I_{k+1}. If we suppose that a zoom occurs, the model parameters C_0, a_0, b_0 which best fit the set of corresponding key-points are computed by minimizing the residual

$$r = \frac{1}{N} \sum_{i=1}^{N} (u'_i - C_0 u_i - a_0)^2 + (v'_i - C_0 v_i - b_0)^2. \qquad (4)$$

We must now estimate the goodness of fit of the data to the affine model of the zoom. We have to test if the discrepancy r is compatible with the noise magnitude on the extracted key-points. Otherwise the zoom hypothesis should be questioned.

Statistical tests, such as χ^2 tests, are often used to estimate the compatibility of the data with the model with a given significance level a (90% for instance).

However, the standard deviation is needed for each datum. In our case, it is very difficult to calculate an error on the location of the key points. The χ^2 test has also a serious drawback: how can we set the significance level a? For a very large value of a, the hypothesis is always admitted, while for a very small value of a the hypothesis is always rejected.

That is the reason why we resort to another criterion to assess the zoom hypothesis. An important thing to note is that a zoom variation does not introduce new features in the images whereas translation motion does: some features which are visible for a camera viewpoint are no longer visible for a neighboring camera position. In Fig. 4.a, point A is not visible from C_k because it is occluded by the object O_1. But point A becomes visible when the camera moves from C_k to C_{k+1}. Note that such a phenomenon also arises for translation along the optical axis (Fig. 4.b). These features which become visible due to the camera motion are very important for assessing the zoom hypothesis. As key-points are not necessarily detected in the areas which become visible or which disappear, the key-points are not well suited for zoom assessment. We therefore use the set of all the contours detected in image I_k to assess the parameters (if $C_0 < 1$ we use image I_{k+1}). We first compute a correlation score for each contour. This score belongs to $[-1, 1]$ and is all the better that the zoom hypothesis is fulfilled. If the zoom hypothesis is satisfied, the gray levels $I_k(u, v)$ and $I_{k+1}(C_0 u + a_0, C_0 v + b_0)$ must be nearly the same. Moreover the neighborhood of these two corresponding points must be similar. We therefore use the correlation score to evaluate the zoom hypothesis. First, we define the correlation for a given point $m = (u, v)$ in I_k:

$$score(m) = \frac{\sum_{i,j=-n}^{i,j=n} I_k(u + i, v + j) \times I_{k+1}(C_0(u + i) + a_0, C_0(v + j) + b_0)}{(2n + 1)^2 \sigma(I_k) \sigma(I_{k+1})},$$

where $\sigma(I_k)$ (resp. $\sigma(I_{k+1})$) is the standard deviation of I_k (resp. I_{k+1}) at point (u, v) in the neighborhood $(2n+1) \times (2n+1)$ of (u, v) (resp. $(C_0 u + a_0, C_0 v + b_0)$). The score ranges from -1 for two correlation windows which are not similar at all, to 1 for two correlation windows which are identical.

If a contour is given by the points $m_1, ..., m_p$, the score of a contour $\mathcal{C}$ is defined as the average of the scores of all points:

$$score(\mathcal{C}) = 1/p \sum_{i=1}^{i=p} score(m_i).$$

Finally the score of the *zoom hypothesis* is computed as the minimum of the score of each contour (note that only the strong contours are kept). This is a robust way to assess the zoom hypothesis. Indeed, if a zoom variation really happens, the score is high for each contour, and the global score is high too. On the contrary, if a camera motion happens, the score is generally low for nearly all the contours when the camera moves because the affine zoom model does not match the image transformation. Moreover, in case of a translating motion, the score is low for the contours of I_k which are occluded in I_{k+1}. Hence the global score is low too.

We still have to choose a threshold Th_{score} which allows us to distinguish between zoom variation and camera motion according to the global score. This

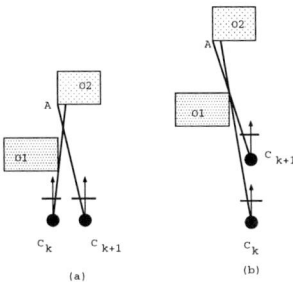

Fig. 4. New features appear under translating motion: point A is not visible from C_k but becomes visible from C_{k+1}.

value has been determined experimentally on various sequences. Experiments we have conducted (see section 5.2) prove that the value $Th_{score} = .5$ can be used for all the considered sequences to discriminate between zoom variation and camera motion even for the difficult case of a translation along the optical axis. Hence, if $global\_score > .5$ and if the invariant point of the affine model lies inside the image, then the zoom hypothesis is accepted, otherwise the camera motion hypothesis is retained.

4 Registration with a zoom lens camera

Once the zoom/motion partitioning has been achieved, registration can be performed. If the frame belongs to a camera zoom sequence, then registration is performed only on the set of the internal parameters. Otherwise, registration is performed only on the set of the external parameters. As described in [12], we use n 2D/3D curve correspondences. Once the curves corresponding to the 3D features have been detected in the first frame of the sequence, they are tracked from frame to frame.

4.1 Registration for a camera motion

If the frame belongs to a camera motion sequence, we perform a six-parameters optimization from the curve correspondences:

$$\alpha_u^{k+1} = \alpha_u^k, \alpha_v^{k+1} = \alpha_v^k,$$
$$u_0^{k+1} = u_0^k, v_0^{k+1} = v_0^k,$$
$$R^{k+1}, T^{k+1} = \underset{R,T}{argmin} \sum_i r_i^2,$$

where r_i is a robust distance between 2D curve i and the projection of its 3-D counterpart. The computation of the residual r_i is detailed in [12]. However, one of the limitations of using 2D/3D correspondences originates in the spatial distribution of the model features: the reprojection error is likely to be large far from the 3D features used for the viewpoint computation. An example is shown in Fig 5.a: the viewpoint has been computed using the buiding in the background of the scene (the Opera). If we add a computer generated car on the foreground of the the scene, this car seems to hover.

a.   b.

Fig. 5. (a) Registration using only 2D/3D correspondences. (b) Registration with the mixing method.

In order to improve viewpoint computation, we propose to use the key-points that have being matched for the partitionning stage. Previous approaches attempted to recover the viewpoint from 2D/2D correspondences alone [17]; unfortunately, this approach turns out to be very sensitive to noise in image measurements. For this reason, points correspondences between frames are here used to provide additional constraints on the viewpoint computation.

Our approach encompasses the strength of these two methods: the viewpoint is defined as the minimum of a cost function which incorporates 2D/3D correspondences between the image and the model as well as 2D/2D correspondences of key-points. Note that the extracted key-points bring information in areas where the 3D knowledge available on the scene are missing (fig. 5.b).

Given the viewpoint $[R_k, T_k]$ computed for a given frame k, we now explain how we compute the viewpoint in the next frame $k + 1$ using the 3D model as well as the matched key-points $(q_k^i, q_{k+1}^i)_{1 \leq i \leq N}$. Let q_k^i be a point in frame k. Its corresponding point in frame $k + 1$ belongs to the intersection of the image plane with the plane (C_k, C_{k+1}, q_k^i). This line is called the epipolar line. For two matched points (q_k^i, q_{k+1}^i), the quality of the viewpoint computed can be assessed by measuring the distance v_i between q_{k+1}^i and the epipolar line of q_k in frame k+1 [9]. Then, a simple way to improve the viewpoint computation using the interest points is to minimize

$$min_{R_{k+1}, T_{k+1}} \left(\frac{1}{n} \sum_{i=1}^{n} r_i^2 + \frac{\lambda}{N} \sum_{i=1}^{N} v_i^2 \right). \tag{5}$$

This way, any a priori information about the scene where the virtual object is going to sit on can be included in this model. The λ parameter controls the compromise between the closeness to the available 3D data and the quality of the 2D correspondences between the key-points. We use $\lambda = 1$ in our practical experiments. The minimum of equation 5 is computed by using an iterative algorithm for minimization such as Powell's algorithm, initialization being obtained from the parameters computed in the previous image of the sequence. More details about this method can be found in [13].

4.2 Registration for a zoom

If the frame belongs to a camera zoom sequence, we get the new intrinsic parameters of the camera from equation 3. However, as approximation errors can propagate from frame to frame, we prefer to perform a three-parameters optimization from the 2D/3D correspondences. Hence, the camera parameters in frame $k+1$ are deduced from the camera parameters in frame k by the relation:

$$R^{k+1} = R^k, T^{k+1} = T^k,$$
$$C_0^{k+1}, u_0^{k+1}, v_0^{k+1} = \underset{C_0, u_0, v_0}{arg min} \sum_i r_i^2,$$
$$\alpha_u^{k+1} = C_0^{k+1} \alpha_u^k,$$
$$\alpha_v^{k+1} = C_0^{k+1} \alpha_v^k.$$

5 Experimental results

In this section, we first justify experimentally the use of the threshold $Th_{score} = 0.5$ to discriminate between zoom variations and camera motions. Then, section 5.2 present results of the partitioning process. Finally, registration results are given and augmented scenes are shown.

5.1 Choosing Th_{score}

To prove that $Th_{score} = 0.5$ is well suited to discriminate between camera motion and zoom variation, we considered a variety of video sequences (see Fig. 6). Each sequence alternates zoom variations with camera motions, including translations along the optical axis T_Z. For each frame of the sequence, the labeling in terms of *zoom variation, rotation motion, translation motion* is known. This allows us to compare the results of our algorithm with the actual ones.

1:The cottage sequence 2:The cup sequence 3:The office sequence 4:The Loria sequence

Fig. 6. Snapshots of the scenes used for testing the zoom/motion partitioning algorithm.

We first compute the score of the zoom hypothesis for each frame of the four sequences. Then we compute the mean along with the standard deviation of the score for the frames of the sequence corresponding to *zoom variation, rotation and translation* and (more difficult cases) *Z-translation* and *panoramic motion*. These results are shown in table 2: the first column shows the kind of variation undergone by the camera. The second and third columns give the scene under consideration and the number of frames in the sequence corresponding to the camera variation. Columns 4 and 5 show the mean and the standard deviation of the residual computed from the corresponding key-points (see equation 4). Finally, columns 6 and 7 shows the mean and the standard deviation of the score of the *zoom hypothesis*. These results clearly show that the use of the residual defined in equation (4) does not permit to discriminate between zoom variations and translation along the optical axis. On the contrary, the score we have defined gives high values when zoom happens and much smaller results when camera motion happens, even in case of T_Z translation. Finally, these experiments prove that the value $Th_{score} = .5$ is appropriate to distinguish zoom variations from camera motions.

variation in the camera parameters	scene	nb frames	r	σ_r	mean score	σ_{score}
Zoom	1	6	0.617	0.030	0.747	0.055
	2	4	0.460	0.266	0.860	0.055
	3	32	0.860	0.057	0.677	0.133
	4	29	0.515	0.014	0.561	0.064
Rotation + translation	1	10	3.593	1.439	-0.591	0.171
Translation along the optical axis	1	2	0.651	0.020	0.393	0.066
	2	4	0.841	0.018	0.274	0.035
	3	16	1.380	0.190	0.047	0.277
Panoramic motion	4	15	0.630	0.066	-0.209	0.315

Table 2. Score of the zoom hypothesis for various camera parameters.

5.2 Results in zoom/motion partitioning

We now give detailed results of our algorithm on the *cottage sequence* and the *Loria sequence*. Note that the camera parameters are known for the *cottage sequence* because the house stands on a calibration target. The *Loria sequence* is a 700-frames sequence which has been shot outside our laboratory. The actual camera parameters are not available for this sequence, but we have manually partitioned the sequence (see table 3.b) to enable comparison with the algorithm.

For each of the two sequences (Fig. 7), we show the scores computed along the sequence, the results of our partitioning algorithm, and the computed zoom factor C_0. Also shown in the Fig. 7.b and 7.e is the actual partition of the sequence for comparison. For the *cottage sequence*, the algorithm performance is quite good and the computed parameters are very close to the actual parameters.

	image	motion/zoom
	0 → 20	rotation 40°
a.	20 → 35	zoom in
	35 → 40	translation 10cm
	40 → 55	zoom out
	55 → 65	rotation −20°

	Image frames	camera parameters
	0 → 120	panoramic motion
b.	121 → 344	Zoom in
	345 → 408	no motion, nor zoom
	409 → 600	Zoom out
	601 → end	panoramic motion

Table 3. Camera parameters during (a) the cottage sequence and (b) the Loria sequence.

For the *Loria sequence*, the reader can notice that some scores are higher than the threshold during the panoramic motion between frames 0 and 100 (Fig. 7.d). However, in Fig. 7.a and 7.d, the test on the invariant point is shown with the dash-dot lines: the value 1 indicates that the invariant point is inside the image, while the value 0 indicates that the invariant point is outside the image. Using this constraint, the results of the partition process is very good (Fig. 7.b and 7.e).

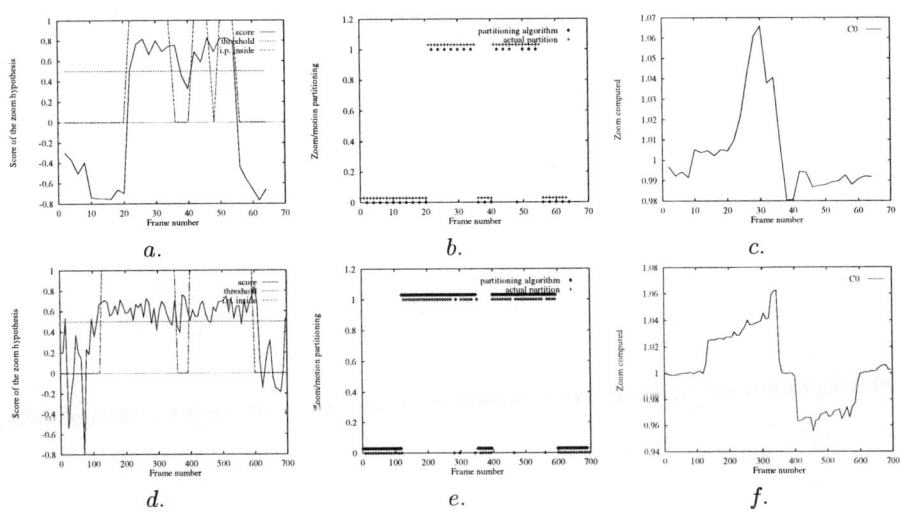

Fig. 7. Results for the cottage sequence (first row) and the Loria sequence (second row).

5.3 Registration results

In this section, registration results are shown for the *cottage sequence* and the *Loria sequence*. As the actual parameters are known for the *cottage sequence*, Fig.

8 shows the trajectory and the focal length computed with our algorithm (dashed lines) along with the actual parameters (solid lines). The reader can notice that the parameters obtained are in close agreement with the actual values. To prove the accuracy of the camera parameters, we have augmented the scene with a palm tree and a beach umbrella (Fig. 9). Note that the shadows between the scene and the computer generated objects greatly improve the realism of the composite images. They have been computed from a rough 3D reconstruction of the scene given by the corresponding key-points. The reprojection of the 3D model features with the computed camera parameters is also shown. The overall impression is very good.

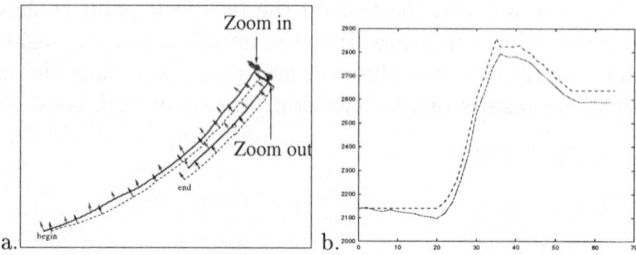

Fig. 8. Comparison of the actual trajectory (a) and focal length α_u (b) (solid lines) with the computed ones (dashed lines).

Fig. 9. Registration results on the cottage sequence: reprojection of the model (first row) and snapshots of the augmented scene (second row).

We do not have the actual camera parameters for the *Loria sequence*. Hence looking at the reprojection of the model features is a good way to assess the registration accuracy. Fig. 10 exhibits the reprojection of the model every hundred frames. The reader can notice that the reprojection error is small even at the end of the sequence, which proves the efficiency of our algorithm. Finally, we augment the sequence with the well known sculpture *La femme à la chevelure défaite* realized by *Miró*. The interested reader can look at the video sequences of our results at URL http://www.loria.fr/~gsimon/eccv2000.html.

Fig. 10. Registration results on the Loria sequence: the reprojection of the model every hundred frames (first row) and snapshots of the augmented scene (second row).

6   Conclusion

In this paper we have presented an efficient registration algorithm for a zoom lens camera. We restricted our study to the case of image sequences which alternate zoom variation alone and camera motion alone. This is a quite reasonable assumption which is always fulfilled by professional movie-makers. The performance of our algorithm is quite good and our algorithm is capable of discriminating between zoom variations and T_Z translations. However, our experiments show that some improvements and extensions can be made to our approach.

First, experiments on the *Loria sequence* show that the camera trajectory is somewhat jagged. Smoothing the trajectory afterwards is not appropriate because the correspondences between the image and the 3D model are not maintained. We currently investigate methods to incorporate regularity constraints on the trajectory inside the registration process.

Second, as was observed in our experiments, moving objects in the scene may perturb the partitioning process. Indeed, the correlation score is always low for moving objects and this may lead to false rejection of the zoom hypothesis. Detecting moving objects in the scene prior to the registration process could help to solve this problem.

References

1. R. T. Azuma and G. Bishop. Improving static and dynamic registration in an optical see through display. In *Proc. SIGGRAPH'94*, pages 194–204.
2. M.-O. Berger, C. Chevrier, and G. Simon. Compositing Computer and Video Image Sequences: Robust Algorithms for the Reconstruction of the Camera Parameters. In *Proc. Eurographics'96*, volume 15, pages 23–32.
3. S. Bougnoux. From Projective to Euclidiean Space under any Practical Situation, a Criticism of Self-calibration. In *Proc. ICCV'98*, pages 790–796.
4. R. Enciso and T. Vieville. Self-calibration from four views with possibly varying intrinsic parameters. *Image and Vision Computing*, 15(4):293–305, 1997.
5. G. Ertl, H. Müller-Seelich, and B. Tabatabai. MOVE-X: A System for Combining Video Films and Computer Animation. In *Proc. Eurographics'91*, pages 305–313.
6. O. D. Faugeras and G. Toscani. The Calibration Problem for Stereo. In *Proc. CVPR'86*, pages 15–20.
7. C. Harris and M. Stephens. A Combined Corner and Edge Detector. In *Proc. Alvey Conference*, 1988.
8. B. Horn and B. Schunck. Determining Optical Flow. *Artificial Intelligence*, 17:185–203, 1981.
9. Q. T. Luong. *Matrice fondamentale et calibration visuelle sur l'environnement, vers une plus grande autonomie des systèmes robotiques*. Thèse de doctorat, Université de Paris Sud, centre d'Orsay, December 1992.
10. J. Mendelsohn, K. Daniilidis, and R. Bajcsy. Constrained Self-Calibration for Augmented Reality Registration. In *Proc. IWAR'98*.
11. M. Pollefeys, R. Koch, and L. Van Gool. Self calibration and metric reconstruction in spite of varying and unknown camera parameters. In *Proc. ICCV'98*.
12. G. Simon and M.-O. Berger. A Two-stage Robust Statistical Method for Temporal Registration from Features of Various Type. In *Proc. ICCV'98*, pages 261–266.
13. G. Simon, V. Lepetit, and M.-O. Berger. Computer Vision Methods for Registration: Mixing 3D Knowledge and 2D Correspondences for Accurate Image Composition. In *Proc. IWAR'98*.
14. A. State, G. Hirota, D. Chen, W. garett, and M. Livingston. Superior Augmented Reality Registration by Integrating Landmark Tracking and Magnetic Tracking. In *Proc. SIGGRAPH'96*, pages 429–438.
15. A. State, M. Livingstone, W. Garett, G. Hirota, M. Whitton, and E. Pisan. Technologies for Augmented Reality Systems: Realizing Ultrasound Guided Needle Biopsies. In *Proc. SIGGRAPH'96*, pages 439–446.
16. Peter Sturm. Self Calibration of a moving Zoom Lens Camera by Pre-Calibration. In *Proc. BMVC'96*, pages 675–684.
17. C. Tomasi and T. Kanade. Shape and Motion from Image Streams under Orthography: A Factorization Method. *IJCV*, 9(2):137–154, 1992.
18. M. Uenohara and T. Kanade. Vision based object registration for real time image overlay. *Journal of Computers in Biology and Medecine*, 1996.
19. R. G. Willson and S. A. Shafer. What is the Center of the Image? In *Proc. CVPR'93*, pages 670–671.
20. W. Xiong and J.C.M. Lee. Efficient scene change detection and camera motion annotation for video classification. *Computer Vision and Image Understanding*, 71(2):166–181, 1998.
21. Z. Zhang, R. Deriche, O. Faugeras, and Q. Luong. A Robust Technique for Matching Two Uncalibrated Images Through the Recovery of the Unknown Epipolar Geometry. *Artificial Intelligence*, 78:87–119, 1995.

Calibration of a Moving Camera Using a Planar Pattern: Optimal Computation, Reliability Evaluation and Stabilization by Model Selection

Chikara Matsunaga[1] and Kenichi Kanatani[2]

[1] Broadcast Division, FOR-A Co. Ltd.,
2-3-3 Ohsaku, Sakura, Chiba 285-0802 Japan
matsunaga@for-a.co.jp
[2] Department of Computer Science, Gunma University,
Kiryu, Gunma 376-8515 Japan
kanatani@cs.gunma-u.ac.jp

Abstract. We present a scheme for *simultaneous calibration* of a continuously moving and continuously zooming camera: placing an easily distinguishable pattern in the scene, we calibrate the camera from an unoccluded portion of the pattern image in each frame. We describe an optimal method which provides an evaluation of the reliability of the solution. We then propose a technique for avoiding the inherent degeneracy and statistical fluctuations by *model selection* using the *geometric AIC* and the *geometric MDL*.

1   Introduction

Visually presenting 3-D shapes of real objects is one of the main goals of many Internet applications such as network cataloging and virtual museums. Today, generating virtual images by embedding graphics objects in real scenes or real objects in graphics scenes, known as *mixed reality*, is one of the central themes of image and media applications. In order to reconstruct the 3-D shapes of real objects or scenes for such applications, we need to know the 3-D position of the camera that we use and its internal parameters. Thus, camera calibration is a first step in all vision and media applications.

The standard method for it is *pre-calibration*: the camera internal parameters are determined from images of objects or patterns of known 3-D geometry in a controlled environment [1, 18, 29, 34, 36, 37]. Recently, techniques for computing both the camera parameters and the 3-D positions of the camera from an image sequence of the scene about which we have no prior knowledge have intensively been studied [3, 24]. Such a technique, known as *self-calibration*, may be useful in unknown environments such as outdoors. For stable reconstruction, however, it requires a long sequence of images taken from unconstrained camera positions and feature matching among frames. As a result, the amount of computation is too large for real-time applications, and it cannot be applied if the camera motion is constrained or the scene changes as the camera moves unless we are

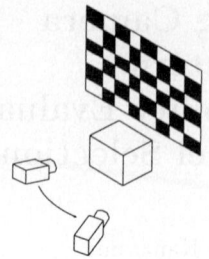 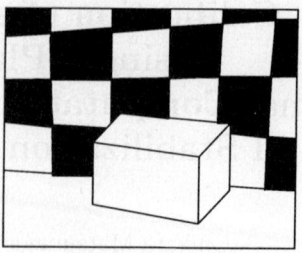

Fig. 1. Simultaneous calibration of a moving camera: we observe an unoccluded part of the image of a planar pattern placed in the scene.

given a priori information about the constraint or the scene change (see, e.g., [6, 9, 28] for self-calibration based on a priori information about the camera motion).

In this paper, we focus on *virtual studio* applications [7, 30]: we take images of moving objects such as persons and superimpose them in a graphics-generated background in real time by computing the 3-D positions and zooming of a moving camera. Since the scene as well as the position and zooming of the camera changes from frame to frame, we cannot pre-calibrate or self-calibrate the camera.

This difficulty can be overcome by placing an easily distinguishable planar pattern with a known geometry in the scene (Fig. 1): we detect an unoccluded portion of the pattern image in each frame, compute the 3-D position and zooming of the camera from it, and remove the pattern image by segmentation. We call this strategy *simultaneous calibration*. It has many elements that do not appear in pre-calibration:

1. While manual interventions can be employed in pre-calibration, simultaneous calibration must be completely automated. In particular, we must automatically identify the 3-D positions of the marker points that are unoccluded in each frame.
2. Since the number of unoccluded marker points is different in each frame, the accuracy of calibration is different from frame to frame. Hence, not only do we need an accurate computational procedure but also a scheme for evaluating the reliability of the computed solution.
3. Since we have no control over the camera position relative to the pattern, degenerate configurations can occur: when the camera optical axis is perpendicular to the pattern, the 3-D position and focal length of the camera are indeterminate because zooming out and moving the camera forward cause the same visual effect.
4. As the object moves in the scene, some unoccluded marker points become occluded while others become occluded. As a result, the computed camera position may not be the same even if the camera is stationary in the scene. This type of statistical fluctuations becomes conspicuous when the camera motion is small.

In this paper, we introduce a statistical model of image noise and describe a procedure for computing an optimal solution that attains the *Cramer-Rao lower bound* (*CRLB*) in the presence of noise. As a result, we can evaluate the reliability of the solution by computing an estimate of the CRLB.

We then show that degeneracy and statistical fluctuations can be avoided by *model selection*. At each frame, we predict the 3-D position and zooming of the camera in multiple ways from the past history. We then evaluate the goodness of each prediction, or *model*, and adopt the best one. In this paper, we use the *geometric AIC* introduced by Kanatani [12, 14] and the *geometric MDL* to be defined shortly as the model selection criterion.

The geometric MDL we use is different from the traditional MDL used in statistics and some vision applications [8, 11, 21, 22, 31]. We compare the performances of the geometric AIC and the geometric MDL by doing numerical simulations and real image experiments.

2 Basic Principle

We fix an XYZ world coordinate system in the scene and place a planar pattern in parallel to the XY plane at a known distance d. We imagine a hypothetical camera with a known focal length f_0 placed at the world origin O in such a way that the optical axis coincides with the Z-axis and the image x- and y-axes are parallel to the X- and Y-axes. The 3-D position of the actual camera is regarded as obtained by rotating the hypothetical camera by R (rotation matrix), translating it by t, and changing the focal length into f; we call $\{t, R\}$ the *motion parameters*. We regard the focal length f as a single unknown internal parameter, assuming that other parameters, such as the image skew and the aspect ratio, have already been pre-calibrated so that the imaging geometry can be modeled as a perspective projection.

Suppose N points on the planar pattern with known coordinates (X_α, Y_α, d) are observed at (x_α, y_α) in the image. If we define the 3-D vectors

$$\bar{x}_\alpha = \begin{pmatrix} X_\alpha/d \\ Y_\alpha/d \\ 1 \end{pmatrix}, \qquad x_\alpha = \begin{pmatrix} x_\alpha/f_0 \\ y_\alpha/f_0 \\ 1 \end{pmatrix}, \tag{1}$$

we have the following relationship:

$$x_\alpha = Z[H\bar{x}_\alpha]. \tag{2}$$

Here, $Z[\cdot]$ denotes normalization to make the third component 1, and H is the matrix in the following form [12]:

$$H = \text{diag}(1, 1, \frac{f_0}{f})R^\top \left(I - \frac{tk^\top}{d} \right). \tag{3}$$

Throughout this paper, i, j and k denote $(1,0,0)^\top$, $(0,1,0)^\top$, and $(0,0,1)^\top$, respectively, and $\text{diag}(\cdots)$ denotes the diagonal matrix with diagonal elements $\cdots$.

3   Optimal Computation

Eq. (2) defines an image transformation called *homography*. Since the unknown parameters are $\{t, R\}$ and f, the homography has seven degrees of freedom. If the homography is unconstrained with eight degrees of freedom, we can apply our statistically optimal renormalization-based algorithm [15]; its C++ code is available via the Web[3]. Here, however, the homography is constrained. So, we take the bundle-adjustment approach based on Newton iterations.

Let $V[x_\alpha]$ be the covariance matrix of the data vector x_α. We assume that it is known only up to scale and write

$$V[x_\alpha] = \epsilon^2 V_0[x_\alpha]. \tag{4}$$

We call the unknown magnitude ϵ the *noise level* and the matrix $V_0[x_\alpha]$ the *normalized covariance matrix*. Since the third component of x is 1, $V_0[x_\alpha]$ is a singular matrix of rank 2 with zeros in the third row and the third column. If the noise has no particular dependence on position and orientation, it has the form $\mathrm{diag}(1, 1, 0)$, which we use as the default value.

If the noise is Gaussian, an optimal estimate of H is obtained by *maximum likelihood estimation* [12]: we minimize the average squared *Mahalanobis distance*

$$J = \frac{1}{N} \sum_{\alpha=1}^{N} (x_\alpha - Z[H\bar{x}_\alpha], V_0[x_\alpha]^-(x_\alpha - Z[H\bar{x}_\alpha])), \tag{5}$$

where and throughout this paper the operation $(\cdot)^-$ denotes the (Moore-Penrose) generalized inverse and (a, b) denotes the inner product of vectors a and b. We define the following non-dimensional variables:

$$\phi = \frac{f}{f_0}, \quad \tau = \frac{t}{d}. \tag{6}$$

The first order perturbation of R is written as $R \to R + \Delta\Omega \times R$, where $\Delta\Omega$ is a 3-D vector and $\Delta\Omega \times R$ is a matrix whose columns are the vector products of $\Delta\Omega$ and each columns of R [12]. We define the gradient ∇J and the Hessian $\nabla^2 J$ with respect to $\{\phi, \tau, R\}$ in such a way that the Taylor expansion of J has the form

$$J(\phi + \Delta\phi, \tau + \Delta\tau, R + \Delta\Omega \times R)$$
$$= J(\phi, \tau, R) + (\nabla J, \begin{pmatrix} \Delta\phi \\ \Delta\tau \\ \Delta\Omega \end{pmatrix}) + \frac{1}{2}(\begin{pmatrix} \Delta\phi \\ \Delta\tau \\ \Delta\Omega \end{pmatrix}, \nabla^2 J \begin{pmatrix} \Delta\phi \\ \Delta\tau \\ \Delta\Omega \end{pmatrix}) + \cdots. \tag{7}$$

The solution that minimizes J is obtained by the following Newton iterations:
1. Give an initial guess of ϕ, τ, and R.
2. Compute the gradient ∇J and the Hessian $\nabla^2 J$ (their actual expressions are omitted).

---

[3] http://www.ail.cs.gunma-u.ac.jp/ kanatani/e

3. Compute $\Delta\phi$, $\Delta\tau$, and $\Delta\Omega$ by solving the linear equation

$$\left(\nabla^2 J\right)\begin{pmatrix} \Delta\phi \\ \Delta\tau \\ \Delta\Omega \end{pmatrix} = -\nabla J. \tag{8}$$

4. If $|\Delta\phi| < \epsilon_\phi$, $\|\Delta\tau\| < \epsilon_\tau$, and $\|\Delta\Omega\| < \epsilon_{\mathbf{R}}$, return ϕ, τ, and $\mathbf{R}$ and stop. Otherwise, update ϕ, τ, and $\mathbf{R}$ in the form

$$\phi \leftarrow \phi + \Delta\phi, \quad \tau \leftarrow \tau + \Delta\tau, \quad \mathbf{R} \leftarrow \mathcal{R}(\Delta\Omega)\mathbf{R}, \tag{9}$$

and go back to Step 2.

The symbol $\mathcal{R}(\Delta\Omega)$ denotes the rotation of angle $\|\Delta\Omega\|$ around $\Delta\Omega$; ϵ_ϕ, ϵ_τ, and $\epsilon_{\mathbf{R}}$ are thresholds for convergence.

The initial guess of ϕ, τ, and $\mathbf{R}$ can be obtained by computing the homography $\mathbf{H}$ between $\{\bar{\boldsymbol{x}}_\alpha\}$ and $\{\boldsymbol{x}_\alpha\}$, say, by least squares or by the renormalization-based method [15] without considering the constraint and approximately decomposing it into ϕ, τ, and $\mathbf{R}$ in the form of eq. (3) (an analytical procedure for this is given in [20]). However, this procedure is necessary only for the initial frame. For the subsequent frames, we can start from the solution in the preceding frame or an appropriate prediction from it, as we will describe shortly.

4 Reliability Evaluation

The squared noise level ϵ^2 can be estimated from the residual $\hat{J}$ (the minimum value of J) in the following form [12]:

$$\hat{\epsilon}^2 = \frac{\hat{J}}{2 - 7/N}. \tag{10}$$

Let $\nabla^2 \hat{J}$ be the resulting Hessian. The covariance matrix of $\{\hat{\phi}, \hat{\tau}, \hat{\mathbf{R}}\}$ is estimated in the following form:

$$V[\hat{\phi}, \hat{\tau}, \hat{\mathbf{R}}] = \frac{2\hat{\epsilon}^2}{N}\left(\nabla^2 \hat{J}\right)^{-1}. \tag{11}$$

This gives an estimate of the *Cramer-Rao lower bound (CRLB)* on $V[\hat{\phi}, \hat{\tau}, \hat{\mathbf{R}}]$ [12].

The (1,1) element of $V[\hat{\phi}, \hat{\tau}, \hat{\mathbf{R}}]$ gives the variance $V[\hat{\phi}]$ of ϕ. It follows that if the error distribution is approximated to be Gaussian, the 99.7% confidence interval of f has the form

$$\hat{\phi} - 3\sqrt{V[\hat{\phi}]} < \frac{f}{f_0} < \hat{\phi} + 3\sqrt{V[\hat{\phi}]}. \tag{12}$$

The submatrix of $V[\hat{\phi}, \hat{\tau}, \hat{\mathbf{R}}]$ defined by its second to fourth rows and columns gives the covariance matrix $V[\hat{\tau}]$ of τ. Let $\Delta\Omega$ and l be, respectively, the angle and axis of the rotation $\hat{\mathbf{R}}\bar{\mathbf{R}}^\top$ relative to the true rotation $\bar{\mathbf{R}}$. Let $\Delta\Omega = \Delta\Omega l$. The submatrix of $V[\hat{\phi}, \hat{\tau}, \hat{\mathbf{R}}]$ defined by its fifth to seventh rows and columns gives the covariance matrix $V[\hat{\mathbf{R}}]$ of $\Delta\Omega$.

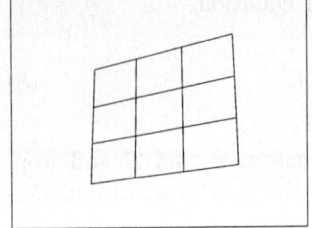

	empirical	CRLB
focal length (pixles)	33.4	34.0
translation (cm)	32.9	32.6
rotation (deg)	0.413	0.414

Fig. 2. Simulated image of a grid pattern (left); the standard deviations of the optimally computed solutions and estimates of their Cramer-Rao lower bounds (right).

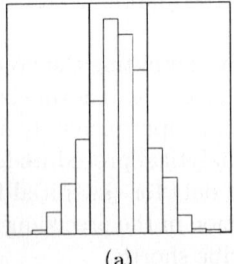　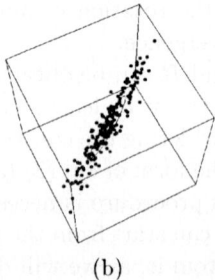　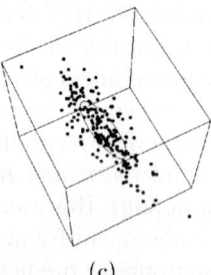

(a)　　　　　　　　　　(b)　　　　　　　　　　(c)

Fig. 3. (a) Histogram of the computed focal length. (b) Error distribution of the computed translation. (c) Error distribution of the computed rotation.

5　Examples of Reliability Evaluation

5.1　Numerical simulation

Fig. 2 shows a simulated image of a grid pattern viewed from an angle. We added Gaussian random noise of mean 0 and standard deviation 1 (pixel) to the x and y coordinates of the vertices independently and computed the focal length and the motion parameters 1,000 times, using different noise each time. The standard deviations of the computed solutions and estimates of their CRLBs are listed in Fig. 2.

Fig. 3(a) is the histogram of the computed focal length $\hat{f}$. The vertical lines indicate the estimated CRLB. Fig. 3(b) is a 3-D plot of the distribution of the error vector $\Delta t = \hat{t} - \bar{t}$ of translation. The ellipse indicates the estimated CRLB in each orientation. Fig. 3(c) is a 3-D plot of the error vector $\Delta\Omega$ of rotation depicted similarly.

From these results, we can confirm that the estimated CRLB can be used as a reliability measure of the solution.

5.2　Tennis court scene

Fig. 4(a) is a real image of a tennis court. Since the size of the court is stipulated by an international rule, we can compute the 3-D camera position and the focal length by using this knowledge. The focal length is estimated to be 955 pixels.

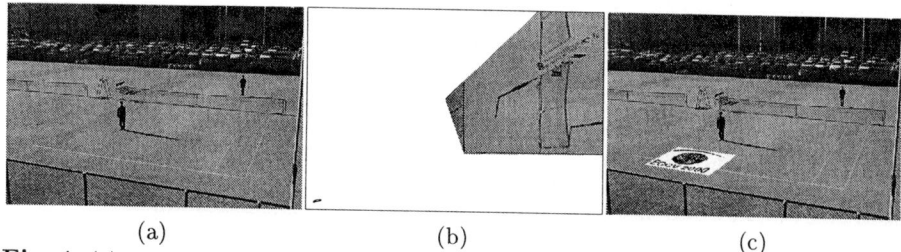

(a)   (b)   (c)

Fig. 4. (a) A real image of a tennis court. (b) The computed camera position viewed from above. (c) A virtual scene generated from (a).

The camera is estimated to be at 627cm above the ground. The standard deviations of the focal length, the translation, and the rotation are evaluated to be 6.99 pixels, 16.14cm, and 0.151 deg, respectively.

Fig. 4(b) shows the top view of the tennis court generated from Fig. 4(a). The estimated camera position is plotted there and encircled by an ellipse, which indicates three times the standard deviation of the estimated position in each orientation (actually it is an ellipsoid viewed from above).

The images of the poles and the persons in Fig. 4(b) can be regarded as their "shadows" on the ground cast by hypothetical light emitted from the camera, so we can compute their heights [5, 10]. The right pole is estimated to be 113cm in height. The person near the camera is estimated to be 171cm tall. This technique can be applied to 3-D analysis of sports broadcasting [25, 28]. Since we know the 3-D structure of the scene, we can generate a virtual view of a new object placed in the scene. Fig. 4(c) is a virtual view of a logo placed on the tennis court.

5.3 Virtual studio

Fig. 5(a) is a real image of a toy, behind which is placed a grid pattern colored light and dark blue. The grid pattern is placed on the floor perpendicularly. The camera optical axis is almost parallel to the floor. Unoccluded grid points in the image were matched to their true positions in the pattern by observing the cross ratio of adjacent points. This pattern is so designed that the cross ratio is different everywhere in such a way that matching can be done in a statistically optimal way in the presence of image noise [17, 19].

After separating the toy image from the background by using a chromakey technique, we computed the 3-D position and focal length of the camera by observing an unoccluded portion of the grid pattern (see [19] for the image processing details). The focal length is estimated to be 576 pixels. The standard deviations of the focal length, the translation, and the rotation are evaluated to be 38.3 pixels, 5.73cm, and 0.812 deg, respectively.

Fig. 5(b) is the top view of the estimated camera position and its uncertainty ellipsoid (three times the standard deviation in each orientation). Fig. 5(c) is a composition of the toy image and a graphics scene generated by VRML.

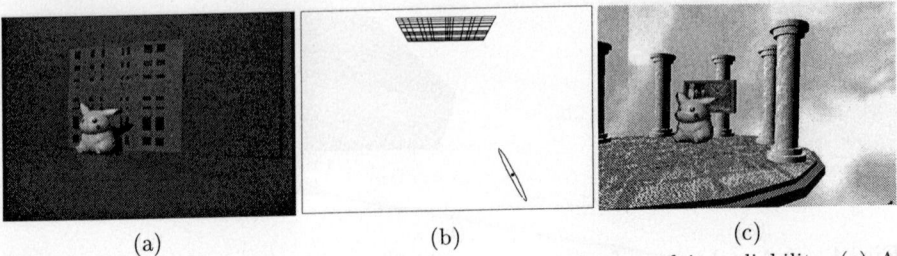

| (a) | (b) | (c) |

Fig. 5. (a) Original image. (b) Estimated camera position and its reliability. (c) A virtual scene generated from (a).

6 Trajectory Stabilization

If the camera optical axis is perpendicular to the planar pattern, the Hessian $\nabla^2 J$ in eq. (8) is a singular matrix, so the solution is indeterminate. This does not occur in practice due to image noise, but the resulting solution is numerically unstable. Also, as pointed out in Introduction, the computed camera position fluctuates when the camera motion is small. We now present a technique for avoiding degeneracy and statistical fluctuations by *model selection*.

6.1 Model selection criteria

The homography H given by eq. (3) is parameterized by $\{t, R\}$ and f, having seven degrees of freedom. If the motion and zooming of the camera are constrained in some way (e.g., the camera is translated without rotation or zooming), the homography H has a smaller degree of freedom, and a smaller number of parameters need to be estimated. In general, parameter estimation becomes stabler as the number of parameters decreases.

It follows that we can stably estimate the parameters or avoid degeneracy if we know the constraint on the camera motion or zooming [6, 9, 28]. In practice, however, we do not know how the camera is moving or zooming. Our strategy here is to assume probable constraints (translation only, etc.), which we call *models*, compare each other, and adopt the best one. A naive idea for this is to compute the residual $\hat{J}$ for each model and choose the one for which it is minimum. However, this does not work: the general model always has the smallest residual, since the residual decreases as the degree of freedom increases.

The best known criterion for balancing the residual and the degree of the freedom of the model is Akaike's *AIC* [2] designed for statistical estimation and used in some vision applications [4]. Kanatani's *geometric AIC* [12, 14] is a variant of Akaike's AIC specifically designed for geometric estimation and has been applied to a variety of vision applications [13, 16, 23, 31, 32, 33, 35]. In the present case, the geometric AIC for minimizing eq. (5) is written as

$$\text{G-AIC} = \hat{J} + 2k\epsilon^2, \tag{13}$$

where k is the degree of freedom of the homography $\boldsymbol{H}$. The square noise level ϵ^2 is estimated from the general model in the form of eq. (10).

Another well known criterion is Rissanen's *MDL* (*minimum description length*) based on the information theoretic code length of the model [26, 27]. It is derived by analyzing the function space of "stochastic models" identified with parameterized probability densities in the asymptotic limit of a large number of observations. Here, the models we want to compare are *geometric constraints*, not parameterized probability densities. Also, we are given only *one* set of data (i.e., one observation) for each frame. Hence, Rissanen's MDL cannot be used in its original form.

The starting point of Rissanen's MDL is the observation that encoding a real number requires an infinite code length. Rissanen's idea is to quantize the parameters to obtain a finite code length, taking into account the fact that real numbers cannot be estimated completely [27]. The quantization width is determined by attainable estimation accuracy, which in turn is determined by the data length n. Since the code length diverges as $n \to \infty$, asymptotic approximation comes into play. In this sense, the "minimum description length" actually means the "minimum growth rate" of the description length.

Suppose we hypothetically repeat independent observations, although the actual observation is done only once. The accuracy of estimation increases as the number of hypothetical observations, so we can define the MDL by asymptotic analysis. But increasing the number n of observations effectively reduces the noise level ϵ to $O(1/\sqrt{n})$. It follows that we can define the MDL as the "growth rate" of the description length as $\epsilon \to 0$. The final form is as follows (we omit the details of the code length analysis):

$$\text{G-MDL} = \hat{J} - k\epsilon^2 \log \epsilon^2. \tag{14}$$

We call this criterion the *geometric MDL*[4]. This form can also be obtained from Rissanen's MDL by replacing n by $1/\epsilon^2$ and is different from any MDLs used in statistics and vision applications [8, 11, 21, 22, 31] in that ours does *not* contain the logarithm of the number of the data.

6.2 Degeneracy detection

If degeneracy occurs, the confidence interval (12) expands infinitely wide if no noise exist. In the presence of noise, it has a finite width. We decide that degeneracy has occurred if the confidence interval (12) contains negative values of f. This means that we adopt the following criterion:

$$V[\hat{\phi}] > \frac{\hat{\phi}^2}{9}. \tag{15}$$

The variance $V[\hat{\phi}]$ equals the $(1,1)$ element of the covariance matrix $V[\hat{\phi}, \hat{\tau}, \hat{\boldsymbol{R}}]$ given by eq. (11), so it is equal to $2\hat{\epsilon}^2(\nabla^2 \hat{J})_{11}^\dagger / N \det(\nabla^2 \hat{J})$, where $(\nabla^2 \hat{J})_{11}^\dagger$ is the

---

[4] Since the additive terms can be ignored when $\epsilon \ll 1$, changing the unit of length does not affect the relative comparison of models asympotitically.

(1,1)-cofactor of the Hessian $\nabla^2 \hat{J}$ (the determinant of the submatrix obtained by removing the first row and the first column of $\nabla^2 \hat{J}$). Hence, eq. (15) can be rewritten in the form

$$\frac{18\hat{\epsilon}^2}{N} \left(\nabla^2 \hat{J}\right)_{11}^\dagger - \hat{\phi}^2 \det\left(\nabla^2 \hat{J}\right) > 0. \tag{16}$$

Since matrix inversion is no longer involved, this expression can always be stably evaluated.

6.3   Models of zooming and motion of the camera

We predict the focal length f and the motion parameters $\{t, R\}$ in the next frame from the values f_i and $\{t_i, R_i\}$ of the current frame and the values f_{i-1} and $\{t_{i-1}, R_{i-1}\}$ of the preceding frame. Here, we consider the following six models:

Stationary model: We assume that the camera is stationary: $f = f_i$, $t = t_i$, and $R = R_i$. Let $\hat{J}_*$ be the corresponding residual. This model has zero degrees of freedom.

t-fixed model: We assume that the camera only rotates. We let $f = f_i$ and $t = t_i$ and optimally compute the rotation R by Newton iterations starting from R_i. Let $\hat{J}_{s'}$ be the corresponding residual. This model has three degrees of freedom.

t-predicted model: Assuming that the zooming does not change, we linearly extrapolate the camera position and let $t = 2t_i - t_{i-1}$. Then, we optimally compute the rotation R by Newton iterations starting from $R_i R_{i-1}^\top R_i$. Let $\hat{J}_{p'}$ be the corresponding residual. This model has three degrees of freedom.

f-fixed model: Assuming that the zooming does not change, we optimally compute the motion parameters $\{t, R\}$ by Newton iterations starting from $\{t_i, R_i\}$. Let $\hat{J}_s$ be the corresponding residual. This model has six degrees of freedom. The square noise level ϵ^2 is estimated by

$$\hat{\epsilon}_s^2 = \frac{\hat{J}_s}{2 - 6/N}. \tag{17}$$

f-predicted model: We linearly extrapolate the focal length and let $f = 2f_i - f_{i-1}$. Then, we optimally compute the motion parameters $\{t, R\}$ by Newton iterations starting from $\{2t_i - t_{i-1}, R_i R_{i-1}^\top R_i\}$. Let $\hat{J}_p$ be the corresponding residual. This model has six degrees of freedom. The square noise level ϵ^2 is estimated by

$$\hat{\epsilon}_p^2 = \frac{\hat{J}_p}{2 - 6/N}. \tag{18}$$

General model: We optimally compute the focal length f and the motion parameters $\{t, R\}$ by Newton iterations starting from the solution obtained from the f-predicted model. Let $\hat{J}_g$ be the corresponding residual. This model has seven degrees of freedom.

Degeneracy is detected from the f-predicted model. Namely, we estimate the square noise level ϵ^2 by eq. (18) and evaluate the criterion (16). If degeneracy is not detected, we compare the stationary model, the f-fixed model, the f-predicted model, and the general model. Estimating the square noise level ϵ^2 by eq. (10), we evaluate the geometric AICs and the geometric MDLs of these models in the following form:

$$\text{G-AIC}_* = \hat{J}_*, \quad \text{G-AIC}_s = \hat{J}_s + \frac{12}{N}\hat{\epsilon}^2, \quad \text{G-AIC}_p = \hat{J}_p + \frac{12}{N}\hat{\epsilon}^2,$$

$$\text{G-AIC}_g = \hat{J}_g + \frac{14}{N}\hat{\epsilon}^2, \quad \text{G-MDL}_* = \hat{J}_*, \quad \text{G-MDL}_s = \hat{J}_s - \frac{6}{N}\hat{\epsilon}^2 \log \hat{\epsilon}^2,$$

$$\text{G-MDL}_p = \hat{J}_p - \frac{6}{N}\hat{\epsilon}^2 \log \hat{\epsilon}^2, \quad \text{G-MDL}_g = \hat{J}_g - \frac{7}{N}\hat{\epsilon}^2 \log \hat{\epsilon}^2. \tag{19}$$

The model that gives the smallest AIC or the smallest MDL is chosen.

If degeneracy is detected, we compare the stationary model, the t-fixed model, the t-predicted model, and the f-fixed model. Estimating the square noise level ϵ^2 by eq. (17), we evaluate the geometric AICs and the geometric MDLs of these models in the following form:

$$\text{G-AIC}_* = \hat{J}_*, \quad \text{G-AIC}_{s'} = \hat{J}_{s'} + \frac{6}{N}\hat{\epsilon}_s^2, \quad \text{G-AIC}_{p'} = \hat{J}_{p'} + \frac{6}{N}\hat{\epsilon}_s^2,$$

$$\text{G-AIC}_s = \hat{J}_s + \frac{12}{N}\hat{\epsilon}_s^2, \quad \text{G-MDL}_* = \hat{J}_*, \quad \text{G-MDL}_{s'} = \hat{J}_{s'} - \frac{3}{N}\hat{\epsilon}_s^2 \log \hat{\epsilon}_s^2,$$

$$\text{G-MDL}_{p'} = \hat{J}_{p'} - \frac{3}{N}\hat{\epsilon}_s^2 \log \hat{\epsilon}_s^2, \quad \text{G-MDL}_s = \hat{J}_s - \frac{6}{N}\hat{\epsilon}_s^2 \log \hat{\epsilon}_s^2. \tag{20}$$

The model that gives the smallest AIC or the smallest MDL is chosen.

7 Model Selection Examples

7.1 Numerical simulation

We simulate a camera motion in a plane perpendicular to a 3×3 grid pattern. In the course of its motion, the camera is rotated so that the center of the pattern is always fixed at the center of the image frame. First, the camera moves along a circular trajectory as shown in Fig. 8(a). It perpendicularly faces the pattern at frame 13 and stops at frame 20. The camera stays there for five frames (frames $20 \sim 24$) and then recedes backward for another five frames (frames $25 \sim 30$).

Adding random Gaussian noise of mean 0 and standard deviation 1 (pixel) to each coordinate of the grid points independently at each frame, we compute the focal length and the trajectory of the camera (Figs. 6(b) and 6(c)). Degeneracy is detected at frames 12 and 13. In order to emphasize the fact that the frame-wise estimation fails, we let f be ∞ and the camera position be at the center of the grid pattern in Figs. 6(b) and 6(c) when degeneracy is detected.

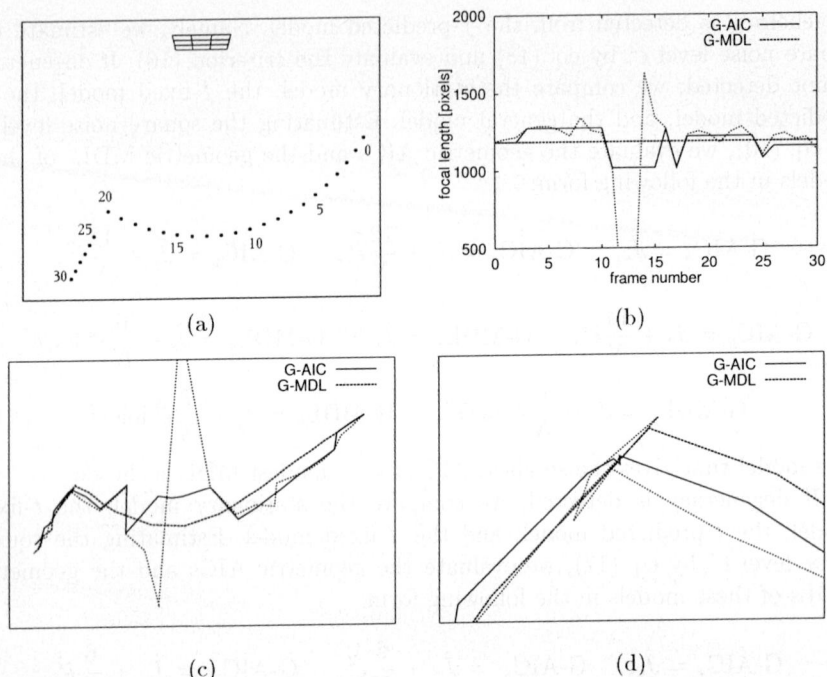

Fig. 6. (a) Simulated camera motion. (b) Estimated focal lengths. (c) Estimated camera trajectory. (d) Magnification of the portion of (c) for frames $20 \sim 24$. In (b)~(d), the solid lines indicate model selection by the geometric AIC; the thick dashed lines indicate model selection by the geometric MDL; the thin dotted lines indicate frame-wise estimation.

As we can see, both the geometric AIC and the geometric MDL produce a smoother trajectory than frame-wise estimation and that the computed trajectory smoothly passes through the degenerate configuration. Fig. 6(d) is a magnification of the portion for frames $20 \sim 24$ in Fig. 6(c). We can observe that statistical fluctuations exist if the camera position is estimated at each frame independently and that the fluctuations are removed by model selection.

From these results, it is clearly seen that the geometric MDL has a stronger smoothing effect than the geometric AIC. This is because the penalty $-\epsilon^2 \log \epsilon^2$ for each degree of freedom in the geometric MDL is generally larger than the penalty $2\epsilon^2$ in the geometric AIC (see eq. (13) and eq. (14)) so the geometric MDL tends to select a simpler model than the geometric AIC.

7.2 Virtual studio

Fig. 7 shows five sampled frames from a real image sequence obtained in the setting described in Section 5.3. The camera moves from right to left with a fixed focal length. The camera optical axis becomes almost perpendicular to the

Fig. 7. Sampled frames from a real image sequence.

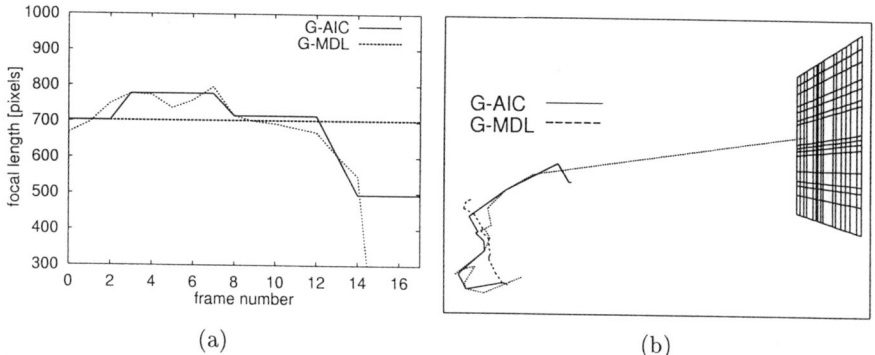

(a)   (b)

Fig. 8. (a) Estimated focal lengths. (b) Estimated camera trajectory. In (a) and (b), the solid lines indicate model selection by the geometric AIC; the thick dashed lines indicate model selection by the geometric MDL; the thin dotted lines indicate frame-wise estimation.

grid pattern in the 15th frame. Degeneracy is detected there and thereafter.

Fig. 8(a) shows the estimated focal lengths; Fig. 8(b) shows the estimated camera trajectory viewed from above. The frame-wise estimation fails when degeneracy occurs. In this case, the estimation by the geometric MDL is more consistent with the actual camera motion than the geometric AIC. But this is because we fixed the zooming and moved the camera smoothly. If we added variations to the zooming and the camera motion, the geometric MDL would still prefer a smooth motion. So, we cannot say which solution should be closer to the true solution; it depends on what kind of solution *we expect* is desirable for the application in question.

8   Concluding Remarks

Motivated by virtual studio applications, we have studied the technique for "simultaneous calibration" for computing the 3-D position and focal length of a continuously moving and continuously zooming camera from an image of a planar pattern placed behind the object. We have described a procedure for computing an optimal solution that provides an evaluation of the reliability of the solution.

Then, we showed that degeneracy of the solution and statistical fluctuations of computation can be avoided by model selection: we predict the 3-D position and focal length of the camera in multiple ways and select the best model using the geometric AIC and the geometric MDL. Doing numerical and real-image experiments, we have observed that the geometric MDL tends to select a simpler model than the geometric AIC, thereby producing a smoother and more cohesive estimation.

References

1. J. Batista, H. Araújo and A. T. de Almeida, Iterative multistep explicit camera calibration, *IEEE Trans. Robotics Automation*, **15**-5 (1999), 897–917.
2. H. Akaike, A new look at the statistical model identification, *IEEE Trans. Automation Control*, **19**-6 (1974), 716–723.
3. S. Bougnoux, From projective to Euclidean space under any practical situation, a criticism of self calibration, *Proc. 6th Int. Conf. Comput. Vision.*, January 1998, Bombay, India, pp. 790–796.
4. K. L. Boyer, M. J. Mirza and G. Ganguly, The robust sequential estimator: A general approach and its application to surface organization in range data, *IEEE Trans. Patt. Anal. Mach. Intell.*, **16**-10 (1994), 987–1001.
5. A. Criminisi, I. Reid and A. Zisserman, Duality, rigidity and planar parallax, *Proc. 5th Euro. Conf. Comput. Vision.*, June 1998, Freiburg, Germany, pp. 846–861.
6. L. de Agapito, R. I. Hartley and E. Hayman, Linear self-calibration of a rotating and zooming camera, *Proc. IEEE Conf. Comput. Vision Patt. Recog.*, June 1999, Fort Collins, CO, U.S.A., pp. 15–21.
7. S. Gibbs, C. Arapis, C. Breiteneder, V. Lalioti, S. Mostafawy and J. Speier, Virtual studios: An overview. *IEEE Multimedia*, **5**-1 (1998), 24–35.
8. H. Gu, Y. Shirai and M. Asada, MDL-based segmentation and motion modeling in a long image sequence of scene with multiple independently moving objects, *IEEE Trans. Patt. Anal. Mach. Intell.*, **18**-1 (1996), 58–64.
9. R. I. Hartley, Self-calibration of stationary cameras, *Int. J. Comput. Vision*, **22**-1 (1997), 5–23.
10. M. Irani, P. Anandan and D. Weinshall, From reference frames to reference planes: Multi-view parallax geometry and applications, *Proc. 5th Euro. Conf. Comput. Vision.*, June 1998, Freiburg, Germany, pp. 829–845.
11. Y. G. Leclerc, Constructing simple stable descriptions for image partitioning, *Int. J. Comput. Vision*, **3**-1 (1989), 73–102.
12. K. Kanatani, *Statistical Optimization for Geometric Computation: Theory and Practice*, Elsevier Science, Amsterdam, The Netherlands, 1996.
13. K. Kanatani, Self-evaluation for active vision by the geometric information criterion, *Proc. 7th Int. Conf. Computer Analysis of Images and Patterns (CAIP'97)*, September 1997, Kiel, Germany, pp. 247–254.
14. K. Kanatani, Geometric information criterion for model selection, *Int. J. Comput. Vision*, **26**-3 (1998), 171–189.
15. K. Kanatani and N. Ohta, Accuracy bounds and optimal computation of homography for image mosaicing applications, *Proc. 7th Int. Conf. Comput. Vision*, September, 1999, Kerkya, Greece, pp. 73–78.
16. Y. Kanazawa and K. Kanatani, Infinity and planarity test for stereo vision, *IEICE Trans. Inf. & Syst.* **E80-D**-8 (1997), 774–779.
17. Y. Kanazawa, C. Matsunaga and K. Kanatani, Best marker pattern design for recognition by cross ratio (in Japanese), *IPSJ SIG Notes*, 99-CVIM-115-13, March 1999, pp. 97–104.
18. D. Liebowitz and A. Zisserman, Metric rectification for perspective images of planes, *Proc. IEEE Conf. Comput. Vision Patt. Recog.*, June 1998, Santa Barbara, CA, U.S.A., pp. 482–488.

19. C. Matsunaga, K. Niijima and K. Kanatani, Best marker pattern design for recognition by cross ratio: Experimental investigation (in Japanese), *IPSJ SIG Notes*, 99-CVIM-115-14, March 1999, pp. 105–110.

20. C. Matsunaga and K. Kanatani, Stabilizing moving camera calibration from images by the geometric AIC, *Proc. 4th Asian Conf. Comput. Vision*, January 2000, Taipei, Taiwan, pp. 1168–1173.

21. B. A. Maxwell, Segmentation and interpretation of multicolored objects with highlights, *Comput. Vision Image Understand.*, 77-1 (2000), 1–24.

22. S. J. Maybank and P. F. Sturm, MDL, collineations and the fundamental matrix, *Proc. 10th British Machine Vision Conference*, September 1999, Nottingham, U.K., pp. 53–62.

23. N. Ohta and K. Kanatani, Moving object detection from optical flow without empirical thresholds, *IEICE Trans. Inf. & Syst.*, **E81-D**-2 (1998), 243–245.

24. M. Pollefeys, R. Koch and L. Van Gool, Self-calibration and metric reconstruction in spite of varying and unknown internal camera parameters, *Int. J. Comput. Vision*, **32**-1 (1999), 7–26.

25. I. Reid and A. Zisserman, Goal-directed video metrology, *Proc. 4th Euro. Conf. Comput. Vision*, April 1996, Cambridge, U.K., Vol. II, pp. 647–658.

26. J. Rissanen, Modeling by shortest data description, *Automatica*, **14** (1978), 465–471.

27. J. Rissanen, *Stochastic Complexity in Statistical Inquiry*, World Scientific, Singapore, 1989.

28. Y. Seo and K. S. Hong, About the self-calibration of a rotating and zooming camera: Theory and practice, *Proc. 7th Int. Conf. Comput. Vision*, September 1999, Kerkyra, Greece, pp. 183–189.

29. P. Sturm and S. Maybank, On plane-based camera calibration: A general algorithm, singularities, applications, *Proc. IEEE Conf. Comput. Vision Patt. Recog.*, June 1999, Fort Collins, CO, U.S.A., pp. 432–437.

30. M. Tamir, The Orad virtual set, *Int. Broadcast Eng.*, March (1996), 16–18.

31. P. H. S. Torr, An assessment for information criteria for motion model selection, *Proc. IEEE Conf. Comput. Vision Patt. Recog.*, June 1997, Puerto Ricco, pp. 47–52.

32. P. H. S. Torr, A. W. Fitzgibbon and A. Zisserman, Maintaining multiple motion model hypotheses over many views to recover matching and structure, *Proc. 6th Int. Conf. Comput. Vision*, January 1998, Bombay, India, pp. 485–491.

33. P. H. S. Torr, Geometric motion segmentation and model selection, *Phil. Trans. Roy. Soc.*, A-**356**-1740 (1998), 1321–1340.

34. B. Triggs, Autocalibration from planar scenes, *Proc. 5th Euro. Conf. Comput. Vision*, June 1998, Freiburg, Germany, pp. 89–105.

35. Iman Triono, N. Ohta and K. Kanatani, Automatic recognition of regular figures by geometric AIC, *IEICE Trans. Inf. & Syst.*, **E81-D**-2 (1998), 246–248.

36. R. Y. Tsai, A versatile camera calibration technique for high-accuracy 3D machine vision methodology using off-the-shelf TV cameras and lenses, *IEEE J. Robotics Automation*, **3**-4 (1987), 323–344.

37. Z. Zhang, Flexible camera calibration by viewing a plane from unknown orientations, *Proc. 7th Int. Conf. Comput. Vision*, September, 1999, Kerkya, Greece, pp. 666–673.

Multi-view constraints between collineations: application to self-calibration from unknown planar structures

Ezio Malis and Roberto Cipolla

Engineering Department, Cambridge University
Trumpington Street, CB2 1PZ Cambridge
{em240,cipolla}@eng.cam.ac.uk
http://www-svr.eng.cam.ac.uk

Abstract. In this paper we describe an efficient method to impose the constraints existing between the collineations which can be computed from a sequence of views of a planar structure. These constraints are usually not taken into account by multi-view techniques in order not to increase the computational complexity of the algorithms. However, imposing the constraints is very useful since it allows a reduction in the geometric errors in the reprojected features and provides a consistent set of collineations which can be used for several applications such as mosaicing, reconstruction and self-calibration. In order to show the validity of our approach, this paper focus on self-calibration from unknown planar structures proposing a new method exploiting the consistent set of collineations. Our method can deal with an arbitrary number of views and an arbitrary number of planes and varying camera internal parameters. However, for simplicity this paper will only discuss the case with constant camera internal parameters. The results obtained with synthetic and real data are very accurate and stable even when using only a few images.

Keywords: Self-calibration, Homography.

1 Introduction

The particular geometry of features lying on planes is often the reason for the inaccuracy of many computer vision applications (structure from motion, self-calibration) if it is not taken explicitly into account in the algorithms. Introducing some knowledge about the coplanarity of the features and about their structure (metric or topological) can improve the quality of the estimates [12]. However, the only prior geometric knowledge on the features that will be used here is their coplanarity. Two views of a plane are related by a collineation. Using multiple views of a plane we obtain a set of collineations which are not independent. If there are multiple planes in the scene there will be a set of collineations for each plane and again some constraints between the different sets. In order to avoid solving non-linear optimisation problems, the constraints existing within a set of collineation and between sets have often been neglected. However, these multi-view constraints can be used to improve the estimation of the collineations matrices as in [15], where multiple planes (≥ 2) are supposed to be viewed in the images. In this paper we analyse the constraints existing between a set of collineations induced by a simple plane in the image but it is very easy to extend our analysis to the case of multiple planes. Imposing the constraint is useful since it allows the reduction of the geometric error in the reprojected features and provides a consistent set of collineations which can be used for several applications as mosaicing, reconstruction and self-calibration.

In this paper we will focus on camera self-calibration. Camera self-calibration from views of a generic scene has been widely investigated and the two main approaches are based on the properties absolute conics [13] [10] or on some algebraic error [7] [4]. Depending on the a priori information provided the self-calibration algorithms can be classified as follows. Algorithms that use some knowledge of the observed scene: identifiable targets of known shape [8], metric structure of planes [11]. Algorithms that exploit particular camera motions: translating camera or rotating camera [5]. Algorithms that suppose known some of the camera parameters: some fixed camera parameters (i.e. skew zero, unit ratio ...), varying camera parameters [10] [9]. Camera self-calibration from planar scenes with known metric structure has been investigated in several papers. However, it is interesting to develop flexible techniques which do not need any a priori knowledge about the camera motion as in [5] or metric knowledge of the planar scene. A method for self-calibrating a camera from views of planar scenes without knowing their metric structure was proposed in [14]. Triggs developed a self-calibration technique based on some constraints involving the absolute quadric and the scene-plane to image-plane collineations. However, in practice it is not possible to estimate these collineations without knowing the metric structure of the plane. Only the collineations with respect to a reference view (a key image) can be used to self-calibrate a camera with constant internal parameters. As noticed by Triggs, inaccurate measurements or poor conditioning in the key image contribute to all the collineations reducing the numerical accuracy or the stability of the method. The aim of this paper is to investigate how to improve the self-calibration from planar scenes with unknown metric structure. We will not use any key image but all the images of the sequence are treated equally averaging the uncertainty over all of them.

This paper is organised as follows. In Section 2 we review the relationship existing between two views of coplanar features and some properties of the collineation matrices. In Section 3 we generalise the two-view geometry to multiple views introducing the super-collineation matrix to describe a set of collineations. Then, we describe a simple algorithm to impose the constraints existing between the collineation of the set. Finally, we describe some constraints on the camera internal parameters which can be used for self-calibration. In Section 4 we give the results obtained with both synthetic and real data.

2 Two-view geometry of a plane

In this section we describe the relationship between two views of a planar structure. Each camera performs a perspective projection of a point $\mathbf{x} \in \mathbb{P}^3$ (with homogeneous coordinates $\mathbf{x} = \begin{bmatrix} X \ Y \ Z \ 1 \end{bmatrix}^T$) to an image point $\mathbf{p} \in \mathbb{P}^2$ (with homogeneous coordinates $\mathbf{p} = \begin{bmatrix} u \ v \ 1 \end{bmatrix}^T$) measured in pixels: $\mathbf{p} \propto \mathbf{K} \begin{bmatrix} \mathbf{R} \ \mathbf{t} \end{bmatrix} \mathbf{x}$, where $\mathbf{R}$ and $\mathbf{t}$ represent the displacement between the frame $\mathcal{F}$ attached to the camera and an absolute coordinate frame $\mathcal{F}_0$, and $\mathbf{K}$ is a non-singular (3×3) matrix containing the intrinsic parameters of the camera:

$$\mathbf{K} = \begin{bmatrix} fk_u & -fk_u \cot(\theta) & u_0 \\ 0 & fk_v/\sin(\theta) & v_0 \\ 0 & 0 & 1 \end{bmatrix} \tag{1}$$

where u_0 and v_0 are the coordinates of principal point (in pixels), f is the focal length (in metres), k_u and k_v are the magnifications respectively in the $\vec{u}$ and $\vec{v}$ direction (in pixels/metres) and θ is the angle between these axes.

2.1 The collineation matrix in projective space

Let $\mathcal{F}_i$ and $\mathcal{F}_j$ be two frames attached respectively to the image $\mathcal{I}_i$ and $\mathcal{I}_j$. The two views of a planar object are related by a collineation matrix in projective space. Indeed, the image coordinates $\mathbf{p}_{ik}$ of the point $\mathcal{P}_k$ in the image $\mathcal{I}_i$ can be obtained from the image coordinates $\mathbf{p}_{jk}$ of the point $\mathcal{P}_k$ in the image $\mathcal{I}_j$:

$$\mathbf{p}_{ik} \propto \mathbf{G}_{ij}\mathbf{p}_{jk} \tag{2}$$

where the collineation matrix $\mathbf{G}_{ij}$ is a (3×3) matrix defined up to scalar factor which can be written as:

$$\mathbf{G}_{ij} \propto \mathbf{K}_i \mathbf{H}_{ij} \mathbf{K}_j^{-1} \tag{3}$$

where $\mathbf{H}_{ij}$ is the corresponding homography matrix in the Euclidean space. Homography and collineation are generally used to indicate the same projective transformation from $\mathbb{P}^n$ to $\mathbb{P}^n$ (in our case $n = 2$). In this paper we will use the term "homography" to indicate a collineation expressed in Euclidean space.

A relationship similar to equation (2) exists between the projections $\mathbf{l}_{ik}$ and $\mathbf{l}_{jk}$ in the two images $\mathcal{I}_i$ and $\mathcal{I}_j$ of a 3D line $\mathcal{L}_k$:

$$\mathbf{l}_{ik} \propto \mathbf{G}_{ij}^{-\top}\mathbf{l}_{jk} \tag{4}$$

The estimation of the collineation matrix is possible both from equation (2) and/or equation (4). However, for simplicity we will analyse only the case of points since the same results can be applied for lines.

2.2   The homography matrix in Euclidean space

The homography matrix can be written as a function of the camera displacement and the normal to the plane [2]:

$$\mathbf{H}_{ij} = \mathbf{R}_{ij} + \frac{\mathbf{t}_{ij}\,\mathbf{n}_j^\top}{d_j} \tag{5}$$

where $\mathbf{R}_{ij}$ and $\mathbf{t}_{ij}$ are respectively the rotation and the translation between the frames $\mathcal{F}_i$ and $\mathcal{F}_j$, $\mathbf{n}_j$ is the normal to the plane π expressed in the frame $\mathcal{F}_j$ and d_j is the distance of the plane π from the origin of the frame $\mathcal{F}_j$. From (3), $\mathbf{H}_{ij}$ can be estimated from $\mathbf{G}_{ij}$ if we know the camera internal parameters of the two cameras:

$$\mathbf{H}_{ij} \propto \mathbf{K}_i^{-1}\mathbf{G}_{ij}\mathbf{K}_j \tag{6}$$

Three important properties of the homography matrix will be extended to the multi-view geometry in the next section:

1. the Euclidean homography matrix is *not* defined up to a scale factor. If the homography is multiplied by a scalar γ ($\mathbf{H}' = \gamma\mathbf{H}$), this scalar can be easily recovered. If $\mathrm{svd}(\mathbf{H}') = \begin{bmatrix}\sigma_1 & \sigma_2 & \sigma_3\end{bmatrix}$ are the singular values of $\mathbf{H}'$ in decreasing order, $\sigma_1 \geq \sigma_2 \geq \sigma_3 > 0$, then γ is the median singular value of $\mathbf{H}'$: $\gamma = \mathrm{median}(\mathrm{svd}(\mathbf{H}')) = \sigma_2$. Indeed, the matrix $\mathbf{H}$ has a unit singular value [16] and this property can be used to normalise the homography matrix.

2. from equation (5) it is easy to show that the homography matrix satisfies the following equation $\forall k > 0$ (where $[\mathbf{n}_i]_\times$ and $[\mathbf{n}_j]_\times$ are the skew symmetric matrices associated with vectors $\mathbf{n}_i$ and $\mathbf{n}_j$ which represent the normal to the plane expressed respectively in the image frame $\mathcal{F}_i$ and $\mathcal{F}_j$):

$$[\mathbf{n}_i]_\times^k\,\mathbf{H}_{ji}^T = \mathbf{H}_{ij}\,[\mathbf{n}_j]_\times^k \tag{7}$$

This equation provides useful constraints. If $k = 1$, the matrix $[\mathbf{n}_i]_\times\,\mathbf{H}_{ji}^T = [\mathbf{n}_i]_\times\,\mathbf{R}_{ij}$ has similar properties to the essential matrix (i.e. $\mathbf{E} = [\mathbf{t}]_\times\,\mathbf{R}$). Indeed, this matrix has two equal singular values and one equal to zero. This means two constraints each homography on the camera internal parameters [6] which can be used for the self-calibration as in [9]. If $k = 2$, knowing that $[\mathbf{n}]_\times^2 = \mathbf{n}\mathbf{n}^\top - \mathbf{I}$, equation (7) can be written:

$$\mathbf{n}_i\mathbf{n}_i^T\mathbf{H}_{ji}^T - \mathbf{H}_{ij}\mathbf{n}_j\mathbf{n}_j^T = \mathbf{H}_{ji}^T - \mathbf{H}_{ij} \tag{8}$$

and provides equations that will be used to compute $\mathbf{n}_i$ and $\mathbf{n}_j$.

3. a very important relation can be obtained from equation (7) (with $k = 1$) and will be used to compute $\mathbf{n}_i$ and $\mathbf{n}_j$:

$$[\mathbf{n}_i]_\times = \mathbf{H}_{ij}\,[\mathbf{n}_j]_\times\,\mathbf{H}_{ij}^T \tag{9}$$

Indeed, since $\det(\mathbf{M})\mathbf{M}\,[\mathbf{v}]_\times\,\mathbf{M}^T = [\mathbf{M}^{-\top}\mathbf{v}]_\times$ then:

$$\mathbf{n}_i = \mathbf{Q}_{ij}\mathbf{n}_j \tag{10}$$

where:

$$\mathbf{Q}_{ij} = \det(\mathbf{H}_{ij})\,\mathbf{H}_{ij}^{-\top} \tag{11}$$

3 Multi-view geometry of a plane

In this section we describe the relationships between several views of a planar structure. We will point out that a super matrix of 2D collineations among m views has rank 3 and we will show how to enforce the rank property in an iterative procedure. The properties of the corresponding super matrix of 2D homographies provide the necessary constraint for the self-calibration of the camera internal parameters. In what follows we will describe the case when only one planar structure is used but the extension to more than one plane is straightforward.

3.1 The super-collineation matrix

If m images of an unknown planar structure are available, it is possible to compute $m(m-1)$ collineations (m collineations are always equal to the identity matrix). Let us define the super-collineation matrix as follows:

$$\mathbf{G} = \begin{bmatrix} \mathbf{G}_{11} & \cdots & \mathbf{G}_{1m} \\ \vdots & \ddots & \vdots \\ \mathbf{G}_{m1} & \cdots & \mathbf{G}_{mm} \end{bmatrix} \tag{12}$$

with $\dim(\mathbf{G}) = (3m, 3m)$ and $\text{rank}(\mathbf{G}) = 3$. The rank of $\mathbf{G}$ can not be less than three since $\mathbf{G}_{ii} = \mathbf{I}_3$ $i \in \{1, 2, 3, ..., m\}$, and cannot be more than three since each row of the matrix can be obtained from a linear combination of three others rows:

$$\mathbf{G}_{ij} = \mathbf{G}_{ik}\mathbf{G}_{kj} \qquad \forall i, j, k \in \{1, 2, 3, ..., m\} \tag{13}$$

This is a very strong constraint which is generally never imposed. Indeed, it would require a complex nonlinear minimisation algorithm over all the images. The constraints (13) can be summarised by the following equation:

$$\mathbf{G}^2 = m\,\mathbf{G} \tag{14}$$

Then, matrix $\mathbf{G}$ has 3 nonzero equal eigenvalues $\lambda_1 = \lambda_2 = \lambda_3 = m$ and $3(m-1)$ null eigenvalues $\lambda_4 = \lambda_5 = ... = \lambda_{3m} = 0$. If we can impose the constraint $\mathbf{G}^2 = m\,\mathbf{G}$ (with $\mathbf{G}_{ii} = \mathbf{I}_3$ $i = 1, 2, 3, ..., m$) then this is in fact equivalent to imposing the constraints $\mathbf{G}_{ij} = \mathbf{G}_{ik}\mathbf{G}_{kj}$.

Imposing the constraints In order to impose the constraint, we exploit the properties of the super-collineation matrix. Let $\mathbf{p}_{ij}$ be the j-th point ($j = \{1, 2, 3, ..., n\}$) of the i-th image ($i = \{1, 2, 3, ..., m\}$). The j-th point in all the images can be represented by the vector of dimension $(3m, 1)$ (which we will call a super-point): $\mathbf{p}_j^T = \begin{bmatrix} \mathbf{p}_{1j}^T & \mathbf{p}_{2j}^T & \cdots & \mathbf{p}_{mj}^T \end{bmatrix}$. Generalising equation (2) we obtain:

$$\boldsymbol{\Gamma}_j\mathbf{p}_j = \mathbf{G}\mathbf{p}_j \tag{15}$$

where $\boldsymbol{\Gamma}_j = \text{diag}(\gamma_{1j}\mathbf{I}_3, \gamma_{2j}\mathbf{I}_3, ..., \gamma_{mj}\mathbf{I}_3)$ is a diagonal matrix relative to the set of points j. Then, multiplying both sides of equation (15) by $\mathbf{G}$ we have:

$$\mathbf{G}\boldsymbol{\Gamma}_j\mathbf{p}_j = \mathbf{G}^2\mathbf{p}_j = m\mathbf{G}\mathbf{p}_j = m\boldsymbol{\Gamma}_j\mathbf{p}_j \tag{16}$$

The vector $\tilde{\mathbf{p}}_j = \boldsymbol{\Gamma}_j \mathbf{p}_j$ (representing the homogeneous coordinates of the point j in all the images) is an eigenvector of $\mathbf{G}$ corresponding to the eigenvalue m:

$$\mathbf{G}\tilde{\mathbf{p}}_j = m\tilde{\mathbf{p}}_j \tag{17}$$

As a consequence any super-point can be obtained as a linear combination of the eigenvectors of $\mathbf{G}$ corresponding to the eigenvalue $\lambda = m$:

$$\tilde{\mathbf{p}}_j = \alpha_1 \mathbf{x}_1 + \alpha_2 \mathbf{x}_2 + \alpha_3 \mathbf{x}_3 \tag{18}$$

The matrix $\mathbf{G}$ can always be diagonalised and thus three linearly independent eigenvectors always exist, i.e., $\exists \mathbf{X} : \mathbf{X}^{-1}\mathbf{G}\mathbf{X} = diag(\lambda_1, \lambda_2, ..., \lambda_{3m})$. The columns of the matrix $\mathbf{X}$ are in fact eigenvectors of $\mathbf{G}$. Since $\mathbf{X}$ is nonsingular, the eigenvectors of $\mathbf{G}$ are linearly independent and span the space $\mathbb{R}^{3m}$. That means that an initial estimation $\hat{\mathbf{p}} \in \mathbb{R}^{3m}$ of the super-point $\tilde{\mathbf{p}}$ can be written as $\hat{\mathbf{p}} = \alpha_1 \mathbf{x}_1 + \alpha_2 \mathbf{x}_2 + \alpha_3 \mathbf{x}_3 + ... + \alpha_{3m}\mathbf{x}_{3m}$. The real super-point $\tilde{\mathbf{p}}$ is an eigenvector of $\mathbf{G}$ corresponding to the largest eigenvalue $\lambda = m$. We can thus use a well-known algorithm to find an eigenvector of $\mathbf{G}$ starting from $\hat{\mathbf{p}}$. Lets multiply our vector by $\frac{1}{m}\mathbf{G}$:

$$\hat{\mathbf{p}}^1 = \frac{1}{m}\mathbf{G}\hat{\mathbf{p}} = \frac{1}{m}(\alpha_1 \mathbf{G}\mathbf{x}_1 + \alpha_2 \mathbf{G}\mathbf{x}_2 + \alpha_3 \mathbf{G}\mathbf{x}_3 + ... + \alpha_{3m}\mathbf{G}\mathbf{x}_{3m}) \tag{19}$$

and then replace each $\mathbf{G}\mathbf{x}_k$ with its corresponding $\lambda_k \mathbf{x}_k$. Factoring out λ_1 we have:

$$\hat{\mathbf{p}}^1 = \frac{\lambda_1}{m}\left(\alpha_1 \mathbf{x}_1 + \frac{\lambda_2}{\lambda_1}\alpha_2 \mathbf{x}_2 + \frac{\lambda_3}{\lambda_1}\alpha_3 \mathbf{x}_3 + ... + \frac{\lambda_{3m}}{\lambda_1}\alpha_{3m}\mathbf{x}_{3m}\right) \tag{20}$$

In a similar way, iterating the procedure k times we obtain:

$$\hat{\mathbf{p}}^k = \frac{\lambda_1^k}{m^k}\left(\alpha_1 \mathbf{x}_1 + \left(\frac{\lambda_2}{\lambda_1}\right)^k \alpha_2 \mathbf{x}_2 + \left(\frac{\lambda_3}{\lambda_1}\right)^k \alpha_3 \mathbf{x}_3 + ... + \left(\frac{\lambda_{3m}}{\lambda_1}\right)^k \alpha_{3m}\mathbf{x}_{3m}\right)$$
$$\tag{21}$$

This algorithm will converge to the eigenvector of $\mathbf{G}$ corresponding to the highest eigenvalue since all the fractions λ_k/λ_1 that are less than unit in magnitude become smaller as we raise to higher powers. In our case, if we knew exactly the super-collineation matrix, the algorithm would converge after only one iteration since we have $\lambda_1 = \lambda_2 = \lambda_3 = m$ and $\lambda_k = 0 \ \forall \ 3 < k \leq 3m$ and the new estimated super-point will satisfy the constraint of being an eigenvector of $\mathbf{G}$ which means that the noise has been reduced.

In practice, the real super-collineation matrix $\mathbf{G}$ is unknown and we must use an approximation $\hat{\mathbf{G}}$ estimated from the noisy points in the images. The algorithm used is the following. We start with a set of n points $\hat{\mathbf{p}}_j$ ($j = 1, 2, 3, ..., n$) and compute the super-collineation matrix $\hat{\mathbf{G}}$ solving independently the linear problem of estimating each block $\hat{\mathbf{G}}_{ij}$ from equation (2). It is not necessary that all the points are visible in all the images. Then, we compute a new set of super-points trying to impose the constraint. The better the estimate of $\mathbf{G}$ we obtain the faster the algorithm will converge and the more accurate will be the results. At iteration k the algorithm is:

(i) estimate the super-collineation matrix

$$\widehat{\mathbf{p}}_j(k) \ \Rightarrow \ \widehat{\mathbf{G}}(k) \qquad (22)$$

(ii) compute the new super-point

$$\widehat{\mathbf{p}}_j(k+1) = \frac{1}{m}\widehat{\mathbf{G}}(k)\widehat{\mathbf{p}}_j(k) \qquad (23)$$

This algorithm treats all the images with the same priority without using any key image and forces the rank 3 constraint on $\mathbf{G}$. We now show some simulation results which demonstrate the validity of our approach (we will describe in the next section 3.2 how to use the consistent set of collineation matrix in order to perform the self-calibration of the camera).

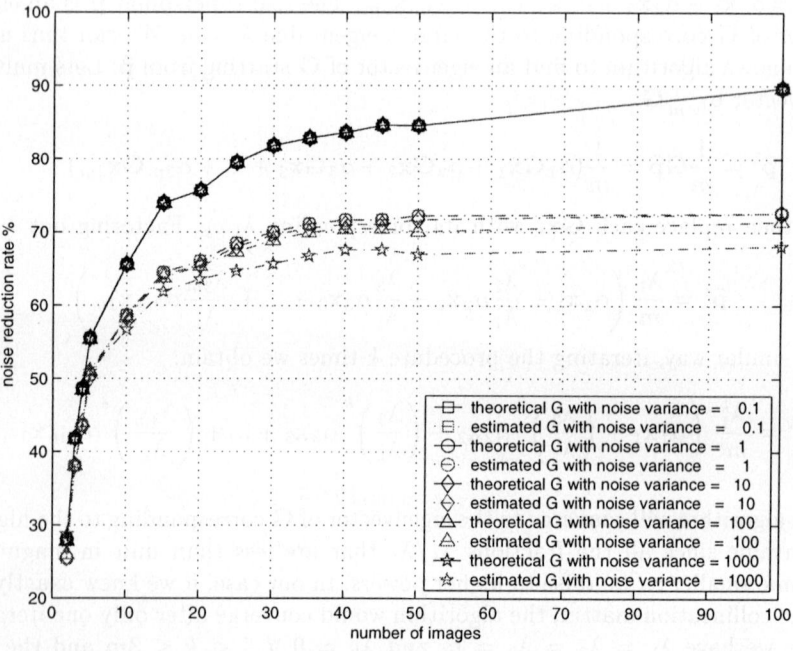

Fig. 1. Geometric noise reduction obtained imposing the rank 3 constraint on the super-collineation matrix.

Simulation results The algorithm was tested on a simulated planar grid of 64 points. It converges after 1 or 2 iterations imposing the constraint on the rank of the matrix $\mathbf{G}$. The error between the theoretical position of the points (which is never used in the algorithm but only for its evaluation) and the transformed coordinates is greatly reduced. Figure 1 shows the results obtained from random views with a random axis of rotation and a 30 degrees angle of rotation with respect to a fixed position. On the horizontal axis are given the number of images used and on the vertical axis the corresponding rate of noise reduction. The continuous line gives us an upper bound of the reduction rate that could be possible if the super-collineation was known exactly. This reduction is practically independent of the level of noise and all continuous lines are superposed in Figure 1. The dashed dotted lines represent the results obtained estimating the super-collineation matrix with differents level of noise ($0.1 \leq \sigma^2 \leq 1000$). The rate of noise reduction does not vary significantly with the amplitude of the noise. However, when the level of noise increases the reduction rate decreases since the estimation of the super-collineation matrix becomes less accurate. Finally, we obtain only a small improvement when increasing the number of the images from 50 to 100. In the simulation results described in section 4.1 we obtain very similar results varying the camera internal parameters and the angle of rotation between the images.

3.2 The super-homography matrix

Let us define the super-homography matrix in the Euclidean space as:

$$\mathbf{H} = \begin{bmatrix} \mathbf{H}_{11} & \cdots & \mathbf{H}_{1m} \\ \vdots & \ddots & \vdots \\ \mathbf{H}_{m1} & \cdots & \mathbf{H}_{mm} \end{bmatrix} \tag{24}$$

with $\dim(\mathbf{H}) = (3m, 3m)$ and $\mathrm{rank}(\mathbf{H}) = 3$. The super-homography matrix can be obtained from the super-collineation matrix and the camera parameters:

$$\mathbf{H} = \mathbf{K}^{-1}\mathbf{G}\mathbf{K} \tag{25}$$

where $(\dim(\mathbf{K}) = (3m, 3m)$ and $\mathrm{rank}(\mathbf{K}) = 3m)$:

$$\mathbf{K} = \begin{bmatrix} \mathbf{K}_1 & \cdots & 0 \\ \vdots & \ddots & \vdots \\ 0 & \cdots & \mathbf{K}_n \end{bmatrix} \tag{26}$$

is the matrix containing the internal parameters of all the cameras. It should be noticed that if the constraint $\mathbf{G}^2 = m\mathbf{G}$ was imposed, then the constraint $\mathbf{H}^2 = m\mathbf{H}$ is automatically imposed which means that the following constraints are satisfied:

$$\mathbf{H}_{ij} = \mathbf{H}_{ik}\mathbf{H}_{kj} \tag{27}$$

Unlike the super-collineation matrix, the super-homography matrix is *not* defined up to a diagonal similarity. Indeed, if σ_{ij} denotes the median singular value of the matrix $\mathbf{H}_{ij}$ we can build the following matrix which contain all the coefficients of normalisation: $\mathbf{D} = \mathrm{diag}(\sigma_{11}\mathbf{I}_3, \sigma_{12}\mathbf{I}_3, ..., \sigma_{1m}\mathbf{I}_3)$. The super homography matrix is thus normalised as follows:

$$\mathbf{H} = \mathbf{D}\tilde{\mathbf{H}}\mathbf{D}^{-1} \tag{28}$$

From this equation we can easily see that the constraint $\mathbf{H}^2 = m\mathbf{H}$ holds. In the presence of noise, normalising $\mathbf{H}$ with equation (28) will conserve the rank constraint of the matrix since it is a similarity transformation.

3.3 Super-homography decomposition

After normalisation, the homography matrix can be decomposed as:

$$\mathbf{H} = \mathbf{R} + \mathbf{T}\mathbf{N}^T \tag{29}$$

where:

$$\mathbf{R} = \begin{bmatrix} \mathbf{R}_{11} & \cdots & \mathbf{R}_{1m} \\ \vdots & \ddots & \vdots \\ \mathbf{R}_{m1} & \cdots & \mathbf{R}_{mm} \end{bmatrix}, \mathbf{T} = \begin{bmatrix} \dfrac{\mathbf{t}_{11}}{d_1} & \cdots & \dfrac{\mathbf{t}_{1m}}{d_m} \\ \vdots & \ddots & \vdots \\ \dfrac{\mathbf{t}_{m1}}{d_1} & \cdots & \dfrac{\mathbf{t}_{mm}}{d_m} \end{bmatrix}, \mathbf{N} = \begin{bmatrix} \mathbf{n}_1 & 0 & \cdots & 0 \\ 0 & \mathbf{n}_2 & \cdots & 0 \\ \vdots & \vdots & \ddots & \vdots \\ 0 & 0 & \cdots & \mathbf{n}_m \end{bmatrix} \tag{30}$$

with $\dim(\mathbf{R}) = (3m, 3m)$, $\text{rank}(\mathbf{R}) = 3$, $\dim(\mathbf{T}) = (3m, m)$ and $\dim(\mathbf{N}) = (3m, m)$. Matrix $\mathbf{R}$ is a symmetric matrix, $\mathbf{R} = \mathbf{R}^T$ and $\mathbf{R}^2 = m\mathbf{R}$. As a consequence not only are the three largest eigenvalues $\lambda_1 = \lambda_2 = \lambda_3 = m$ but also the three largest singular values are $\sigma_1 = \sigma_2 = \sigma_3 = m$. In [2] and [16] are presented two different methods for decomposing the homography matrix, computed from two views of a planar structure, following equation (5). In general, there are two possible solutions but the ambiguity can be resolved by adding more images. Here we present a method to decompose any set of homography matrices. Equation (10) can be generalised as follow:

$$\mathbf{Q} = \begin{bmatrix} \mathbf{Q}_{11} & \cdots & \mathbf{Q}_{1m} \\ \vdots & \ddots & \vdots \\ \mathbf{Q}_{m1} & \cdots & \mathbf{Q}_{mm} \end{bmatrix} = \mathbf{W}\mathbf{H}^T\mathbf{W}^{-1} \tag{31}$$

where $\mathbf{W} = \text{diag}(1, \det(\mathbf{H}_{21}), ..., \det(\mathbf{H}_{m1}))$ and $\dim(\mathbf{Q}) = (3m, 3m)$ and $\text{rank}(\mathbf{Q}) = 3$. Matrix $\mathbf{Q}$ has similar properties to the matrix $\mathbf{H}$, for example, it has an eigenvalue $\lambda = m$ of multiplicity three. The vector $\mathbf{n}$ is an eigenvector of $\mathbf{Q}$ corresponding to the eigenvalue $\lambda = m$:

$$\mathbf{Q}\mathbf{n} = m\mathbf{n} \tag{32}$$

where $\mathbf{n} = [\mathbf{n}_1^T \mathbf{n}_2^T ... \mathbf{n}_m^T]^T$. The vector can be written as a linear combination of the eigenvectors $\mathbf{n} = x\,\mathbf{v}_1 + y\,\mathbf{v}_2 + z\,\mathbf{v}_3 = \mathbf{V}\mathbf{x}$, where $\mathbf{x} = \begin{bmatrix} x & y & z \end{bmatrix}^T$ is a vector containing three unknowns and $\mathbf{V} = \begin{bmatrix} \mathbf{v}_1 & \mathbf{v}_2 & \mathbf{v}_3 \end{bmatrix}$ is a known matrix. Imposing the constraint $\|\mathbf{n}_k\| = 1$ and the constraints given by equation (8) we obtain:

$$\mathbf{V}_i\mathbf{x}\mathbf{x}^T\mathbf{V}_i^T\mathbf{H}_{ji}^T - \mathbf{H}_{ij}\mathbf{V}_j\mathbf{x}\mathbf{x}^T\mathbf{V}_j^T = \mathbf{H}_{ji}^T - \mathbf{H}_{ij} \tag{33}$$

from which is possible to compute the unknown matrix $\mathbf{x}\mathbf{x}^T$ and then, by singular values decomposition, the original unknown which is $\mathbf{x}$. Once find $\mathbf{x}$, the normals to the plane are extracted from $\mathbf{H}$ and knowing that $\mathbf{R}\mathbf{N} = \mathbf{N}\mathbf{O}_m$ we find:

$$\mathbf{T} = \mathbf{H}\mathbf{N} - \mathbf{0}_{3m}\mathbf{N} \tag{34}$$

$$\mathbf{R} = \mathbf{H}(\mathbf{N}\mathbf{N}^T - \mathbf{I}_{3m}) + \mathbf{N}^T\mathbf{0}_{3m}\mathbf{N} \tag{35}$$

3.4 Camera self-calibration

The super-homography can of course be used in many applications. In this section we use the properties of the set of homography matrices to self-calibrate the cameras. It should be noticed that we avoid the use of a bundle adjustment technique to impose the rank 3 constraint on the super-homography (as explained in section 3) and thus we considerably simplify the algorithm. In this case, the only unknowns are the camera internal parameters. Each independent homography will provide us two constraints on the parameters according to equation (7). Indeed, if σ_{ij}^I and σ_{ij}^{II} are the two non-zero singular values of $[\mathbf{n}_i]_\times \mathbf{H}_{ji}^T$ our self-calibration method is based on the minimisation of the following cost function [4][9]:

$$C = \sum_{i=1}^{m} \sum_{j=1}^{m} \frac{\sigma_{ij}^I - \sigma_{ij}^{II}}{\sigma_{ij}^I} \tag{36}$$

A minimum of 3 independent homography matrices (4 images) is sufficient to recover the focal length and the principal point supposing $r = 1$ and $\theta = \pi/2$ and a minimum of 4 independent homography matrices (5 images) is sufficient to recover all the parameters.

4 Experiments

The self-calibration algorithm has been tested on synthetic and real images. The results obtained with a calibration grid were compared with the standard Faugeras-Toscani method [3]. Our self-calibration algorithm is the following:

1. Match corresponding points in m images of a planar structure;
2. Compute the super-collineation imposing the rank 3 constraint using the algorithm described in Section 3.1;
3. Using an initial guess of the camera parameters compute the normalised super-homography matrix as described in Section 3.2;
4. Decompose the super-homography matrix and find the normal to the plane as described in Section 3.3;
5. Compute a new set of camera parameters which minimise the cost function given in Section 3.4 and go to step 3.

4.1 Simulations of a planar grid

The planar grid used for the simulations in section 3 was used to test the self-calibration algorithm. The experimental setup is as close as possible to the one proposed by Triggs [14]. The cameras roughly fixate a point on the plane from randomly generated orientations varying $\pm 30°$ in each of the three axes. The nominal camera calibration is $f = 1000$, $r = 1$, $\theta = 90°$, $u = 250$ and $v = 250$. The plane contains 64 points projected into a 500×500 image. The camera calibration varies randomly about the nominal values of $\sigma_f = \pm 30\%$, $\sigma_r = \pm 10\%$, $\sigma_\theta = 0.5°$ and $\sigma_u = \sigma_v = \pm 75$ pixels (σ_f and σ_r are standard deviations of log-normal distributions while σ_θ, σ_u and σ_v of normal ones).

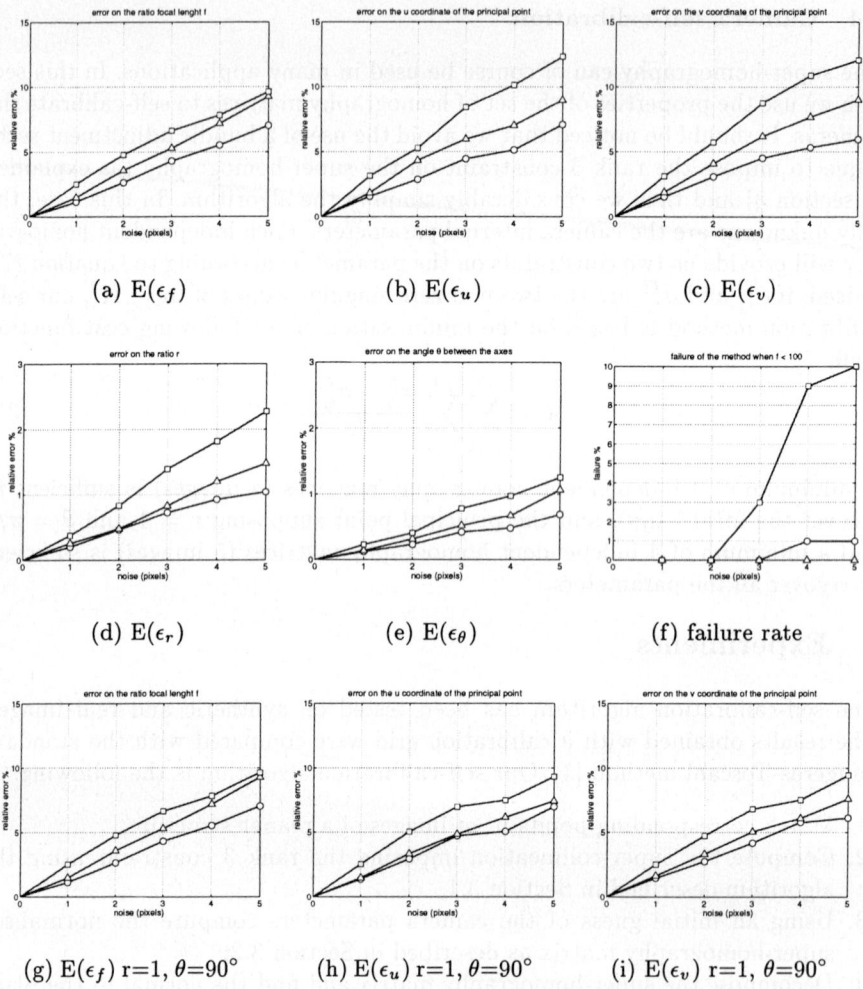

Fig. 2. Simulations results of camera self-calibration using a planar grid. The graphs (a), (b), (c), (d) and (e) show the mean of the errors on the camera internal parameters (respectively f, θ, r, u, v) obtained with the self-calibration algorithm. Graph (f) shows the failure rate of the algorithm. Finally, the graphs (g), (h) and (i) show the mean of the errors on the camera internal parameters (respectively f, u, v) obtained supposing $\theta = 90°$ and $r = 1$.

In Figure 2 we give the results obtained using 6 (lines marked with a square), 8 (lines marked with a triangle) and 10 (lines marked with a circle) images and supposing all the camera parameters unknowns. The figure represents the mean error computed on 100 trials with different parameters and different camera positions for each level of noise (the standard deviation of the Gaussian noise added to the coordinates of the points is increased from 0 to 5). The error on the principal point is given as a percentage of the focal length. The errors on the camera parameters increase with the noise and decrease with the number of images used for self calibration. Using six images the results are still satisfactory even if the failure rate of the method increases rapidly (a failure of the method occurs when the obtained focal length is less than 100 pixels). This can be explained since it is known that with few images there is the risk of degenerate configurations [11]. The results obtained compare very favourably to the results obtained by Triggs in [14], especially considering the failure rate of the method. For example, using 10 images we obtain a mean error more than 50 % smaller than the error obtained by Triggs. Finally, in Figure 2(g), (h) and (i) we give the results of our method when r and θ are fixed to their nominal values. The error on the focal length is practically the same. On the other hand, the error on the location of the principal point is reduced since the non-linear search is now done in a three-dimensional space reducing the risk of local minima.

4.2 Self-calibration from images of a grid and comparison with the standard Faugeras-Toscani calibration method

A sequence (26 images of dimension (640×480)) of a calibration grid was taken using a Fuji MX700 camera with a 7mm lens. Figure 3 shows three images of the sequence. The corners of the black squares are used to compute the super-collineation matrix in order to self-calibrate the camera with our method.

Fig. 3. Three images of the sequence taken with a digital camera. The calibration grid allows the "ground truth" to compare our method with the standard Faugeras-Toscani method. The main advantage of using our method is that we don't need any knowledge of the 3D structure of the grid to calibrate the camera. On the other hand, at least five images are needed.

Table 1 gives the results for the following experiment:

- non-planar calibration: the mean and the standard deviation on 26 images of the grid calibrated with the standard Faugeras-Toscani method initialised with the DLT linear method [1]. In this case we use both planes to calibrate the camera;

- planar self-calibration: the mean and the standard deviation on 50 tests using m images (m = 6,8,10) randomly chosen between the 26 images of the grid. The same tests are repeated using the right plane alone, the left plane alone and then again with r and θ fixed to nominal values.

The results are very good and agree with the simulations. They are more accurate than the results obtained by Triggs with a sequence of images of a calibration grid. In our case, the angle of rotation between the images of the sequence can be greater than 60° which has in general the effect to improve the results. However, this is not always true since the planes can be very close to the optical center of the camera (see in Figure 3) and in this case the estimation of the collineations is not accurate. The calibration obtained using the right plane is again very similar to the calibration obtained using the left plane. As we expected the accuracy decreases as we decrease the number of images but the worst result (obtained using only 6 images of the grid) is only an error of 2% on the focal length.

calibration method	f	r	θ	u	v
DLT linear	685 ± 3	1.0005 ± 0.0033	90.00 ± 0.14	322 ± 5	229 ± 4
Faugeras-Toscani	685 ± 3	1.0003 ± 0.0022	90.00 ± 0.16	322 ± 5	229 ± 4
right plane (10 im)	680 ± 8	0.9976 ± 0.0088	89.23 ± 0.59	318 ± 8	230 ± 8
left plane (10 im)	680 ± 6	0.9943 ± 0.0058	89.89 ± 0.30	320 ± 7	232 ± 4
right plane (8 im)	681 ± 12	0.9950 ± 0.0105	89.21 ± 0.80	315 ± 11	232 ± 9
left plane (8 im)	678 ± 12	0.9969 ± 0.0075	90.06 ± 0.24	327 ± 14	233 ± 3
right plane (6 im)	686 ± 13	0.9891 ± 0.0126	89.63 ± 0.69	312 ± 18	231 ± 11
left plane (6 im)	685 ± 10	0.9886 ± 0.0147	89.80 ± 0.59	339 ± 18	232 ± 7
Faugeras-Toscani	685 ± 3	1 ± 0	90 ± 0	322 ± 6	229 ± 4
right plane (10 im)	679 ± 6	1 ± 0	90 ± 0	318 ± 5	224 ± 8
left plane (10 im)	675 ± 6	1 ± 0	90 ± 0	325 ± 4	232 ± 4
right plane (8 im)	687 ± 6	1 ± 0	90 ± 0	323 ± 3	231 ± 6
left plane (8 im)	676 ± 4	1 ± 0	90 ± 0	343 ± 27	231 ± 12
right plane (6 im)	676 ± 8	1 ± 0	90 ± 0	314 ± 9	227 ± 5
left plane (6 im)	677 ± 18	1 ± 0	90 ± 0	327 ± 34	230 ± 31

Table 1. Results using digital images of the grid (statistics on 50 tests)

After the camera has been calibrated, the 3D reconstruction of the planes was realized. If $\mathbf{n}_{rj}$ and $\mathbf{n}_{lj}$ are respectively the normal to the right and left plane in the frame attached to the image $\mathcal{I}_j$, the angle between them is:

$$\phi_j = \cos^{-1}(\mathbf{n}_{rj}^T \mathbf{n}_{lj})$$

This angle should be the same for all the images $j = 1, 2, 3, ..., m$. In order to verify the quality of the reconstruction results we can compute the mean and the standard deviation σ over all the images. For example, the results obtained with a sequence of $m = 10$ images were:

$$\nu = \frac{1}{m} \sum_{j=1}^{m} \phi_j = 89.84, \qquad \sigma = \frac{1}{m} \sqrt{\sum_{j=1}^{m} (\phi_j - \nu)^2} = 0.21$$

4.3 Self-calibration from images of a facade

In this experiment, in order to test our algorithm in very extreme conditions, only four images of a facade (see Figure 4) were taken with the same digital camera. With such images the localisation of the corners was not accurate and with only four images we can only calibrate the focal length and the principal point (thus we fixed $r = 1$ and $\theta = 90°$). The results obtained using our self-calibration with 56 points (the corners of the windows on the facade) are $f = 678$ (1 % of the mean focal length obtained with the Faugeras-Toscani method and the calibration grid), $u = 355$ and $v = 216$. The results are very good even using images of a roughly planar structure.

Fig. 4. Four images of a facade. The corners of the windows (marked with a white cross) belong roughly to a plane. They are used to compute the super-collineation matrix from which it is possible to self-calibrate the camera.

5 Conclusion

In this paper we presented an efficient technique to impose the constraints existing within a set of collineation matrices computed from multiple views of a planar structure. The obtained set of collineations can be used for several applications such mosaicing, reconstruction and self-calibration from planes. In this paper we focused on self-calibration proposing a new method which does not need any a priori knowledge of the metric structure of the plane. The method was tested both with synthetic and real images and the obtained results are very good. However, the method could be improved by imposing further constraints in order to obtain not only a consistent set of collineations matrices but also a consistent set homography matrices. The method could also be improved using a probabilistic model for the noise.

Acknowledgements

This work was supported by an EC (ESPRIT) grant no. LTR26247 (VIGOR). We would like to thank Paulo Mendonca and Kenneth Wong for their kind help.

References

1. Y. I. Abdel-Aziz and H. M. Karara. Direct linear transformation into object space coordinates in close-range photogrametry. In *Proc. Symp. Close-Range Photogrametry*, pages 1–18, University of Illinois, Urbana, 1971.
2. O. Faugeras and F. Lustman. Motion and structure from motion in a piecewise planar environment. *International Journal of Pattern Recognition and Artificial Intelligence*, 2(3):485–508, 1988.
3. O.D. Faugeras and G. Toscani. The calibration problem for stereo. In *Proc. IEEE Int. Conf. on Computer Vision and Pattern Recognition*, pages 15–20, June 1986.
4. R. Hartley. Estimation of relative camera positions for uncalibrated cameras. In G. Sandini, editor, *Proc. European Conf. on Computer Vision*, volume 588 of *Lecture Notes in Computer Science*, pages 579–587. Springer-Verlag, May 1992.
5. R. Hartley. Self-calibration from multiple views with a rotating camera. In *Proc. European Conf. on Computer Vision*, pages 471–478, May 1994.
6. R. Hartley. Minimising algebraic error in geometric estimation problem. In *Proc. IEEE Int. Conf. on Computer Vision*, pages 469–476, 1998.
7. S. Maybank and O. Faugeras. A theory of self-calibration of a moving camera. *International Journal of Computer Vision*, 8(2):123–151, 1992.
8. J. Mendelsohn and K. Daniilidis. Constrained self-calibration. In *Proc. IEEE Int. Conf. on Computer Vision and Pattern Recognition*, pages 581–587, 1999.
9. P.R.S. Mendonca and R. Cipolla. A simple techinique for self-calibration. In *Proc. IEEE Int. Conf. on Computer Vision and Pattern Recognition*, pp. 500–505, 1999.
10. M. Pollefeys, R. Koch, and L. VanGool. Self-calibration and metric reconstruction inspite of varying and unknown intrinsic camera parameters. *International Journal of Computer Vision*, 32(1):7–25, August 1999.
11. P.F. Sturm and S.J. Maybank. On plane-based camera calibration: A general algorithm, singularities, applications. In *Proc. IEEE Int. Conf. on Computer Vision and Pattern Recognition*, pages 432–437, 1999.
12. R. Szeliski and P. Torr. Geometrically constrained structure from motion: Points on planes. In *European Workshop on 3D Structure from Multiple Images of Large-Scale Environments (SMILE)*, pages 171–186, Freiburg, Germany, June 1998.
13. B. Triggs. Autocalibration and the absolute quadric. In *Proc. IEEE Int. Conf. on Computer Vision and Pattern Recognition*, pages 609–614, 1997.
14. B. Triggs. Autocalibration from planar scenes. In *Proc. European Conf. on Computer Vision*, pages 89–105, 1998.
15. L. Zelnik-Manor and M. Irani. Multi-view subspace constraints on homographies. In *Proc. IEEE Int. Conf. on Computer Vision*, volume 1, pp. 710–715, Sept. 1999.
16. Z. Zhang and A. R. Hanson. Scaled euclidean 3D reconstruction based on externally uncalibrated cameras. In *IEEE Symposium on Computer Vision*, pp 37–42, 1995.

Stereo Autocalibration from One Plane

David Demirdjian[1], Andrew Zisserman[2], and Radu Horaud[1]

[1] INRIA Rhône-Alpes, 655 av. de l'Europe, 38330 Montbonnot, France
david.demirdjian@inrialpes.fr,radu.horaud@inrialpes.fr
[2] Dept. of Engineering Science, University of Oxford, Oxford OX13PJ, England
az@robots.ox.ac.uk

Abstract. *This paper describes a method for autocalibrating a stereo rig. A planar object performing general and unknown motions is observed by the stereo rig and, based on point correspondences only, the autocalibration of the stereo rig is computed. A stratified approach is used and the autocalibration is computed by estimating first the epipolar geometry of the rig, then the plane at infinity Π_∞ (affine calibration) and finally the absolute conic Ω_∞ (Euclidean calibration). We show that the affine and Euclidean calibrations involve quadratic constraints and we describe an algorithm to solve them based on a conic intersection technique. Experiments with both synthetic and real data are used to evaluate the performance of the method.*

1   Introduction

Autocalibration consists of retrieving the metric information of the cameras – their internal parameters and relative position and orientation – from images, without using special calibration objects. Additional constraints can also be introduced such as knowledge of some of the internal parameters of the two cameras (aspect ratio, image skew, ...).

Planar autocalibration has several advantages. Planar scenes are very easy to process, enable very reliable point matching by fitting inter-image homographies, and very accurate estimation of the homographies. It will be seen that only the homographies are required for the autocalibration.

Many approaches for autocalibration have been developed for monocular and binocular sensors in recent years. Faugeras, Luong and Maybank [5] proposed solving the Kruppa equations from point correspondences in 3 images. However, this requires non-linear solution methods. An alternative is to first recover affine structure and then solve for the camera calibration from this. Such a "stratified" approach [4] can be applied to a single camera motion [1, 7, 9, 12, 14] or to a stereo rig in motion [2, 10, 20] and requires no knowledge of the observed scene. The stratified approach applied to the autocalibration of a stereo rig involves the computation of projective transformations of 3-D space, that is the projective transformation that maps two different projective reconstructions of the same 3-D rigid scene. Unfortunately, these projective motions cannot be estimated when the 3-D scene is planar so those autocalibration approaches cannot be used.

Some approaches for calibration [11, 16, 18] and autocalibration [17] from planar scenes have also been developed. In [17], the author uses the constraint that the projections of the circular points of a 3-D plane must lie on the image of the absolute conic. The proposed criteria is non-linear and the associated optimization process must be bootstrapped. Unfortunately no general method is given to obtain this bootstrapping.

We show here that, using a stereo rig, the stratified paradigm is very well adapted for autocalibration from planar scenes and extend the idea developed in [17]. We prove the following results:

(1) *Affine calibration can be uniquely estimated from 3 views of a plane.*
(2) *Euclidean calibration can be uniquely estimated from 3 views of a plane if at least one of the cameras of the rig has zero image skew and known aspect ratio. Otherwise 4 views are required.*

2 Preliminaries

2.1 Camera model

A pinhole camera projects a point M from the 3-D projective space onto a point m of the 2-D projective plane. This projection can be written as a 3×4 homogeneous matrix $\mathbf{P}$ of rank equal to 3 :

$$m \simeq \mathbf{P}M$$

where $\simeq$ is the equality up to a scale factor. If we restrict the 3-D projective space to the Euclidean space, then it is well known that $\mathbf{P}$ can be written as :

$$\mathbf{P} = (\mathbf{KR} \ \mathbf{K}t)$$

$\mathbf{R}$ and t are the rotation and translation that link the camera frame to the 3-D Euclidean one. The most general form for the matrix of internal parameters $\mathbf{K}$ is :

$$\mathbf{K} = \begin{pmatrix} \alpha & r\alpha & u_0 \\ 0 & a\alpha & v_0 \\ 0 & 0 & 1 \end{pmatrix}$$

where α is the horizontal scale factor, a is the ratio between the vertical and horizontal scale factors, r is the image skew and u_0 and v_0 are the image coordinates of the principal point.

When the aspect ratio a is known and the image skew r is zero (*i.e.* the image axes are orthogonal), the matrix of internal parameters depends only on 3 parameters and becomes:

$$\mathbf{K} = \begin{pmatrix} \alpha & 0 & u_0 \\ 0 & a\alpha & v_0 \\ 0 & 0 & 1 \end{pmatrix} \qquad (1)$$

2.2 Stratified calibration

Autocalibration consists of recovering the metric information of the stereo rig. This information can be obtained through the recovery of the internal parameters and relative orientation and position of both cameras.

However, once the epipolar geometry of the stereo rig has been estimated and a projective basis has been defined, the metric information of the rig is fully encapsulated by the equation of the plane at infinity Π_∞ and the equation of absolute conic Ω_∞ [10, 20].

2.3 Notation

In this paper we assume that the cameras of the stereo rig have constant parameters under the motion, and that the rig acquired a sequence of n image pairs of a moving planar object.

We denote by $\Pi_1, ..., \Pi_k, ..., \Pi_n$ the geometric planes associated with the different positions of the planar object.

$\mathbf{H}_{ij}$ (resp. $\mathbf{H}'_{ij}$) denote the homographies between the left (resp. right) image of the stereo rig in position i and the left (resp. right) image of the stereo rig in position j. These 3×3 inter-image homographies can be computed from point correspondences.

We also denote by Γ_{ij} the geometric Euclidean transformation that maps the points of Π_i onto the points of Π_j. That is, if M_i is a 3-D point of the object at position i and M_j the same point at position j, then these two points are related by $M_j = \Gamma_{ij}(M_i)$.

$\mathbf{A}^\top$ denotes the transpose of the matrix $\mathbf{A}$. $[.]_\times$ denotes the matrix generating the cross product: $[\boldsymbol{x}]_\times \boldsymbol{y} = \boldsymbol{x} \wedge \boldsymbol{y}$.

2.4 Organization of the paper

The remainder of the paper is organized as follow. In Section 3, we explain how the epipolar geometry can easily be estimated from a sequence of image pairs of a planar object. In Section 4, the affine autocalibration is described and we show how the equation of the plane at infinity Π_∞ can be estimated. The Euclidean autocalibration (estimation of the absolute conic Ω_∞) is performed in Section 5. Section 6 shows some experiments with synthetic and real data in order to demonstrate the stability of the approach. Finally a brief discussion is given in Section 7.

3   Projective calibration

The projective calibration consists of estimating the epipolar geometry of the stereo rig. The epipolar geometry is assumed to be constant and can therefore be computed from many image pairs.

It is well known that the epipolar geometry cannot be estimated from a *single* image pair of a 3-D planar scene. However when the planar scene performs motions, all the image pairs (each corresponding to a different position of the planar scene) gathered by the stereo rig can be used and this makes the computation of the epipolar geometry possible.

The motions of the plane must be chosen so that they do not correspond to critical motions [13]. These are motions which are not sufficient to enable the epipolar geometry to be computed uniquely. In this case they are translations parallel to the plane of the scene, rotations orthogonal to the plane of the scene and combinations of the two. The plane is effectively fixed (as a set, not pointwise) relative to the rig under these motions.

The fundamental matrix $\mathbf{F}$ associated with the stereo rig is computed from all the left-to-right point correspondences from all the image pairs using a standard technique [19]. The projection matrices $\mathbf{P}$ and $\mathbf{P}'$ associated with the left and right cameras respectively can then be derived [8]. Without loss of generality these two 3×4 matrices can be written as:

$$\mathbf{P} \simeq (\mathbf{I}\ 0) \qquad \mathbf{P}' \simeq (\bar{\mathbf{P}}'\ \boldsymbol{p}') \tag{2}$$

where $\mathbf{I}$ is the 3×3 identity matrix, $\bar{\mathbf{P}}'$ is a 3×3 matrix and $\boldsymbol{p}'$ a 3-vector.

Using point correspondences it is therefore possible to obtain a projective reconstruction of the points of the planes. It is also possible to estimate the projective coordinates $\boldsymbol{\pi}_1,...,\boldsymbol{\pi}_k,...,\boldsymbol{\pi}_n$ of the planes $\Pi_1,...,\Pi_k,...,\Pi_n$ associated with the different positions of the planar object. In the following, $\boldsymbol{\pi}_k$ is the 4-vector:

$$\boldsymbol{\pi}_k = \begin{pmatrix} \bar{\boldsymbol{\pi}}_k \\ \alpha_k \end{pmatrix} \tag{3}$$

where $\bar{\boldsymbol{\pi}}_k$ is a 3-vector and α_k a real number.

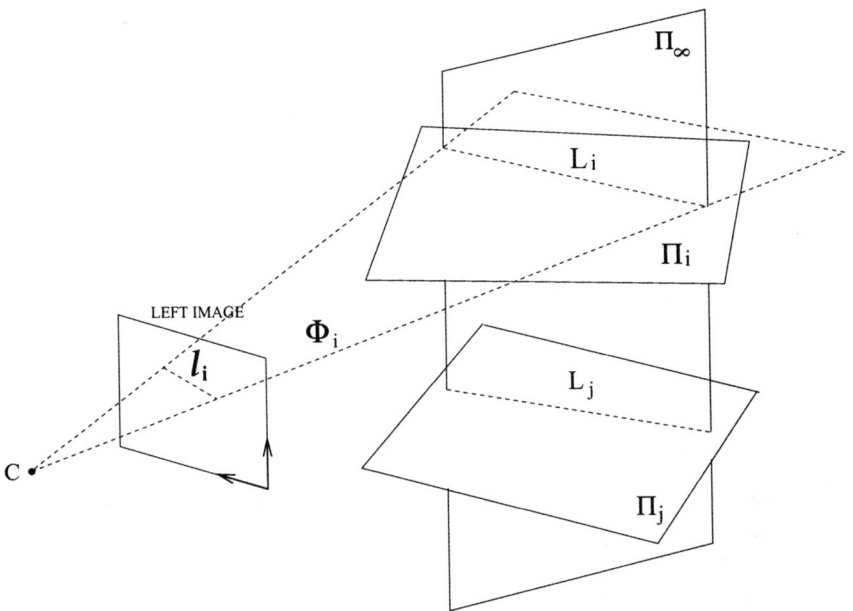

Fig. 1. The geometry of lines and planes involved in the affine autocalibration. The image line l_i is the vanishing line of the plane Π_i, which is the image of L_i.

4 Affine calibration

This section describes the affine autocalibration, which consists of estimating, in the projective basis determined previously (2), the coordinates π_∞ of the plane at infinity Π_∞. For this purpose we use here the vanishing line of the observed plane in each left view, and show how quadratic constraints on the coordinates of this vanishing line can be derived.

We will use the fact that Π_∞ is a particular plane: it is the only plane of projective space that remains globally invariant under *any* affine transformation, *i.e.* under the action of any affine transformation, any point lying on Π_∞ has its image lying on Π_∞ as well.

Let $L_1,...,L_k,...,L_n$ be the 3-D lines corresponding to the intersections of Π_∞ with $\Pi_1,...,\Pi_k,...,\Pi_n$ respectively, (see Figure 1). We use the following result:

Proposition 1. *Consider any two lines L_i and L_j among $L_1,...,L_n$. Γ_{ij} being the Euclidean transformation that maps Π_i onto Π_j as defined in Section 2.3, we have:*

$$L_j = \Gamma_{ij}(L_i).$$

Proof: The intersection of two planes is preserved by a Euclidean transformation (or indeed a projective transformation). However, a Euclidean transformation has the additional property that Π_∞ is fixed (as a set, not pointwise). Therefore, L_i (on Π_∞) is mapped to L_j (on Π_∞). In our notation this is written:

$$
\begin{aligned}
\Gamma_{ij}(L_i) &= \Gamma_{ij}(\Pi_\infty \cap \Pi_i) \\
&= \Gamma_{ij}(\Pi_\infty) \cap \Gamma_{ij}(\Pi_i) \\
&= \Pi_\infty \cap \Pi_j \\
&= L_j
\end{aligned}
$$

$\square$

This proves that, for all k, $1 \le k \le n$, L_k is the same line of the planar object in the different positions of the object, namely the line at infinity on the scene plane. An important feature of the lines $L_1,...,L_k,...,L_n$ is that they are all contained in the plane Π_∞ and therefore are coplanar. This provides a constraint that will be used to solve for π_∞. In fact we actually solve for the vanishing line l_k of each plane Π_k and parameterize the solution by l_1.

Let l_k be the vanishing line of Π_k which is the image of L_k in the left camera (see Figure 1). Let Φ_k be the 3-D plane going through L_k and the optical centre C of the left camera. The plane Φ_k also intersects the left image plane at l_k and it can easily be shown that, in the projective basis defined in Section 3, the equation of Φ_k is $\phi_k = \mathbf{P}^\top l_k$. With $\mathbf{P} = (\mathbf{I}\ 0)$ we have $\phi_k = (l_k^\top\ 0)^\top$.

L_k can be regarded as the intersection of Π_k and Φ_k. Π_k and Φ_k define a pencil of planes that contains L_k, and Π_∞ is in this pencil. Π_∞ is therefore common to all pencils (Π_k, Φ_k). In other words, there exist some reals $\lambda_1, \lambda_2,...,\lambda_n$ and $\mu_1, \mu_2,...,\mu_n$ such that for all k:

$$
\pi_\infty = \lambda_k \pi_k + \mu_k \phi_k \tag{4}
$$

Combining equation (4) for two pencils of planes (Π_i, Φ_i) and (Π_j, Φ_j) we obtain the constraint corresponding to the coplanarity on Π_∞ of two lines L_i and L_j:

$$
\lambda_i \pi_i + \mu_i \phi_i = \lambda_j \pi_j + \mu_j \phi_j \tag{5}
$$

Equation (5) means that π_i, ϕ_i, π_j and ϕ_j are linearly dependent and therefore is equivalent to $\det(\pi_i, \pi_j, \phi_i, \phi_j) = 0$. Using (3) for π_k, the condition for two lines L_i and L_j being coplanar becomes:

$$
\begin{vmatrix} \pi_i\ \pi_j\ l_i\ l_j \\ \alpha_i\ \alpha_j\ 0\ 0 \end{vmatrix} = 0 \tag{6}
$$

The lines $l_1,...,l_k,...,l_n$ represent the corresponding vanishing lines of the plane in the different images. Since all l_k are images of L_1 on Π_1, we have:

$$
l_k = \mathbf{H}_{1k}^{-\top} l_1 \tag{7}
$$

We can therefore express all the lines $l_2,...,l_n$ with respect to l_1. Expanding the determinant (6), we obtain the following quadratic equation:

$$l_1^\top \mathbf{C}_{ij}^\star l_1 = 0 \qquad (8)$$

where $\mathbf{C}_{ij}^\star$ is a 3×3 symmetric matrix such that $\mathbf{C}_{ij}^\star = \dfrac{\mathbf{A}_{ij} + \mathbf{A}_{ij}^\top}{2}$ and $\mathbf{A}_{ij}$ is a 3×3 matrix defined by $\mathbf{A}_{ij} = \mathbf{H}_{1j}^{-1}[\alpha_j \bar{\pi}_i - \alpha_i \bar{\pi}_j]_\times \mathbf{H}_{1i}^{-\top}$.

The coplanarity of L_i and L_j therefore defines a quadratic constraint on l_1. Once l_1 is estimated, the lines $l_2,...,l_n$ are estimated from (7), and the equations of the planes $\phi_1,...,\phi_n$ as well.

We will see that only the lines $l_1,...,l_n$ are required for Euclidean autocalibration. However π_∞ can also be estimated. π_∞ is computed as the common plane to all pencils of planes (Π_k, Φ_k). In practice, π_∞ is computed by solving the linear system defined by equations (4) where the unknowns are π_∞ and the reals $\lambda_1,...,\lambda_n$ and $\mu_1,...,\mu_n$. For n positions, this linear system has $2n + 4$ unknowns (n λ's, n μ's and 4 for π_∞) and $4n$ equations, and these can be solved using an SVD approach. To conclude:

- with 2 views of the planar object, we obtain a single constraint $\mathbf{C}_{12}^\star$ and there is a one-parameter family of solutions for l_1 (all the lines of the conic $\mathbf{C}_{12}^\star$). Therefore there is a one-parameter family of solutions for π_∞;
- with 3 views of the planar object, we obtain 3 independent constraints $\mathbf{C}_{12}^\star$, $\mathbf{C}_{13}^\star$ and $\mathbf{C}_{23}^\star$, and l_1 corresponds to the common intersection of these conics. The solution of the equations (8) can be found in Annex A. π_∞ is thus determined uniquely.

5 Euclidean calibration

Let Ω_∞ be the absolute conic and ω_∞ and ω_∞' its projection onto the left and right camera respectively. A fundamental property of Ω_∞, ω_∞ and ω_∞' is that they are all invariant to Euclidean transformations (provided that the internal parameters of the cameras are constant). Euclidean autocalibration consists of estimating the coordinates of Ω_∞. It is also equivalent, given Π_∞, to estimating the equation of one of the projections of Ω_∞. We can choose, for instance, to estimate its left projection ω_∞ whose expression is $\omega_\infty = (\mathbf{KK}^\top)^{-1}$ where $\mathbf{K}$ is the matrix of internal parameters of the left camera.

Consider the (complex) circular points $\mathcal{I}_k$ and $\bar{\mathcal{I}}_k$ of the plane Π_k. By definition $\mathcal{I}_k$ and $\bar{\mathcal{I}}_k$ are the intersections of Π_k with Ω_∞ and therefore are also the intersections of L_k with Ω_∞. Let $\boldsymbol{I}_k$ and $\bar{\boldsymbol{I}}_k$ be the projections of $\mathcal{I}_k$ and $\bar{\mathcal{I}}_k$ onto the left camera. As a consequence, $\boldsymbol{I}_k$ and $\bar{\boldsymbol{I}}_k$ are the intersections of l_k and ω_∞. Solving for ω_∞ then consists of the following steps:

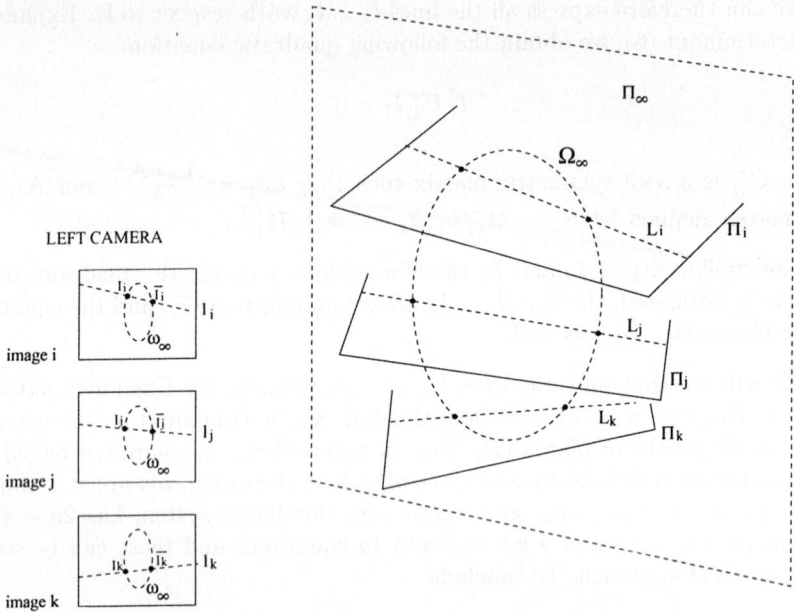

Fig. 2. The circular points lie on the absolute conic Ω_∞

1. Use the constraint that the points I_k and $\bar{I}_k$ lie on the lines l_k estimated by the affine autocalibration;
2. Express the constraint that all I_k and $\bar{I}_k$ lie on the same conic ω_∞;
3. Estimate ω_∞ from all I_k and $\bar{I}_k$;
4. Compute $\mathbf{K}$ from ω_∞.

Let p_1 and q_1 be two real points lying on l_1. I_1 can be parameterized by a complex λ such that $I_1 = q_1 + \lambda p_1$. As all I_k and $\bar{I}_k$ belong to the planar object, they are related by the inter-image homographies $\mathbf{H}_{ij}$ and therefore we have for all k:

$$I_k = \mathbf{H}_{1k}I_1 = \mathbf{H}_{1k}q_1 + \lambda\mathbf{H}_{1k}p_1$$
$$\bar{I}_k = \mathbf{H}_{1k}\bar{I}_1 = \mathbf{H}_{1k}q_1 + \bar{\lambda}\mathbf{H}_{1k}p_1 \tag{9}$$

A constraint can be expressed on λ that all points I_k and $\bar{I}_k$ lie on the same conic ω_∞. We will consider first the case of unrestricted $\mathbf{K}$.

5.1 General calibration K

Consider any 3 positions of the planar object associated with the planes Π_i, Π_j and Π_k and the projections I_i, $\bar{I}_i$, I_j, $\bar{I}_j$, I_k and $\bar{I}_k$ of their circular points onto the left camera.

Let $\boldsymbol{Y}_{ij}$, $\boldsymbol{Y}_{ik}$ and $\boldsymbol{Y}_{jk}$ be the respective intersections of the lines $(\boldsymbol{I}_i \bar{\boldsymbol{I}}_j)$ and $(\bar{\boldsymbol{I}}_i \boldsymbol{I}_j)$, $(\boldsymbol{I}_i \bar{\boldsymbol{I}}_k)$ and $(\bar{\boldsymbol{I}}_i \boldsymbol{I}_k)$, $(\boldsymbol{I}_j \bar{\boldsymbol{I}}_k)$ and $(\bar{\boldsymbol{I}}_j \boldsymbol{I}_k)$. One can show that the expression of $\boldsymbol{Y}_{ij}$ is:

$$
\begin{aligned}
\boldsymbol{Y}_{ij} &\simeq (\boldsymbol{I}_i \wedge \bar{\boldsymbol{I}}_j) \wedge (\boldsymbol{I}_j \wedge \bar{\boldsymbol{I}}_i) \\
&\simeq A_{ij} u + B_{ij} v + C_{ij}
\end{aligned}
\tag{10}
$$

where A_{ij}, B_{ij} and C_{ij} are three reals depending only on the entries of $\boldsymbol{p}_1$, $\boldsymbol{q}_1$, $\boldsymbol{H}_{1i}$ and $\boldsymbol{H}_{1j}$, and u and v are two real numbers such that $u = \lambda \bar{\lambda}$ and $v = \lambda + \bar{\lambda}$.

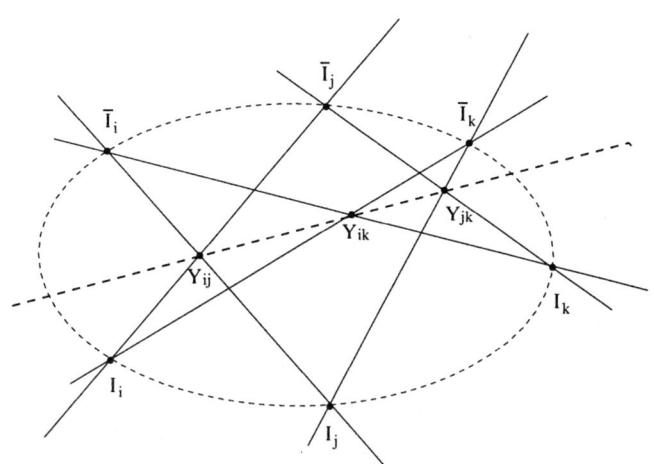

Fig. 3. Pascal's theorem : condition for 6 points to lie on a conic.

From Pascal's theorem, the six points $\boldsymbol{I}_i$, $\bar{\boldsymbol{I}}_i$, $\boldsymbol{I}_j$, $\bar{\boldsymbol{I}}_j$, $\boldsymbol{I}_k$ and $\bar{\boldsymbol{I}}_k$ lie on the same conic if and only if $\boldsymbol{Y}_{ik}$, $\boldsymbol{Y}_{jk}$ and $\boldsymbol{Y}_{ij}$ lie on a line (see Figure 3). This can be expressed as:

$$
\det(\boldsymbol{Y}_{ik}, \boldsymbol{Y}_{jk}, \boldsymbol{Y}_{ij}) = 0
\tag{11}
$$

Using the expression obtained in (10) for $\boldsymbol{Y}_{ij}$ it is clear that (11) – and therefore the constraint that the points $\boldsymbol{I}_i$, $\bar{\boldsymbol{I}}_i$, $\boldsymbol{I}_j$, $\bar{\boldsymbol{I}}_j$, $\boldsymbol{I}_k$ and $\bar{\boldsymbol{I}}_k$ are on a conic – is a cubic equation in u and v:

$$
\Gamma_{ijk}(u, v) = \sum_{N=0}^{N \leq 3} \sum_{m=0}^{m \leq N} \gamma_{m, N-m} u^m v^{N-m}
\tag{12}
$$

where $\gamma_{m, N-m}$ are some real numbers depending only on the entries of $\boldsymbol{p}_1$, $\boldsymbol{q}_1$, $\boldsymbol{H}_{1i}$, $\boldsymbol{H}_{1j}$ and $\boldsymbol{H}_{1k}$.

From 4 views, it is therefore possible to obtain 4 cubic constraints $\Gamma_{ijk}(u, v)$ such as (12). Solving simultaneously these cubic constraints [15] gives a solution for (u, v) from which λ and hence $\boldsymbol{\omega}_\infty$ may be computed.

5.2 Zero skew, known aspect ratio

In the case of a 3-parameter projective camera as described by the model (1), skew is zero and the aspect ratio a is known. These constraints can be imposed by introducing two complex points J and $\bar{J}$ such that $J = (1\ ai\ 0)^\top$ and $\bar{J} = (1\ -ai\ 0)^\top$. Then if skew is zero and the aspect ratio a is known J and $\bar{J}$ lie on ω_∞ (the intersection of ω_∞ with the line at infinity in the image).

The same approach as in the general case described above can be used. Using any two positions i and j of the planar object, a constraint derived from Pascal's theorem can be expressed that the 6 points I_i, $\bar{I}_i$, I_j, $\bar{I}_j$, J and $\bar{J}$ lie on the same conic ω_∞. Including J and $\bar{J}$ reduces the number of views required to solve for ω_∞. In this case the constraint (11) has the form:

$$(\lambda - \bar{\lambda})^2 x^\top \mathbf{Q}_{ij} x = 0$$

where x is a real 3-vector such that $x = (\lambda\bar{\lambda}, \lambda+\bar{\lambda}, 1)$ and $\mathbf{Q}_{ij}$ is a 3×3 symmetric matrix that depends only on the entries of p_1, q_1, $\mathbf{H}_{1i}$, $\mathbf{H}_{1j}$ and the aspect ratio a. As λ is a non-real complex number, then $\lambda \neq \bar{\lambda}$ and the constraint reduces to:

$$x^\top \mathbf{Q}_{ij} x = 0 \tag{13}$$

Then from two views we obtain a quadratic constraint on x. From 3 views or more, we obtain therefore at least 3 independent conics $\mathbf{Q}_{ij}$ corresponding to the quadratic constraints (13). The intersection of these conics gives, when the motions of the planar object are general, a unique solution for x.

Once x is computed (see details in Annex A), λ is known and then all the points I_k, $\bar{I}_k$ can be estimated as well. ω_∞ can then be computed as the conic going through all the points I_k, $\bar{I}_k$ and J and $\bar{J}$.

Finally $\mathbf{K}$ is estimated by the Cholesky decomposition of $\omega_\infty = (\mathbf{KK}^\top)^{-1}$.

5.3 Summary of the autocalibration algorithm

The complete algorithm can be summarized as follow:

1. Compute the fundamental matrix $\mathbf{F}$ and the projective coordinates $\pi_1,...,\pi_n$ of the planes $\Pi_1,...,\Pi_n$;
2. Estimate the inter-image homographies $\mathbf{H}_{ij}$;
3. *Affine autocalibration:* solve the quadratic constraints (8) for l_1;
4. *Euclidean autocalibration:* solve the quadratic constraints (13). Compute λ, I_k and $\bar{I}_k$ with (9). Then compute ω_∞ as the conic going through all I_k and $\bar{I}_k$ and finally compute $\mathbf{K}$ by Cholesky decomposition;
5. *Bundle adjustment (optional):* minimization of point backprojection errors onto the left and right cameras of the 3-D planar scene at its different locations.

6 Experiments

The stereo autocalibration algorithm has been implemented in matlab and applied to both synthetic and real data.

6.1 Synthetic data

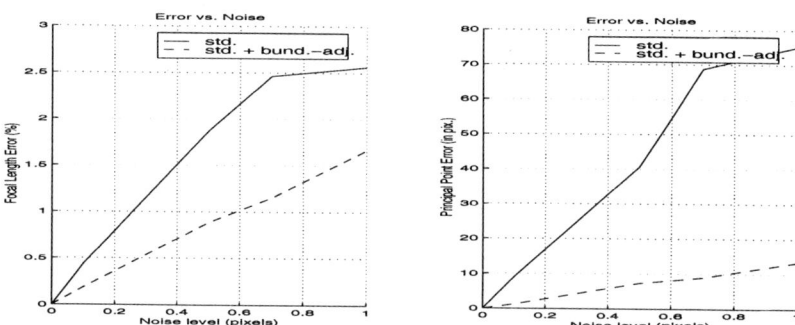

Fig. 4. Errors in the estimation of focal length (in %) and of principal point (in *pix.*) *vs.* level of noise.

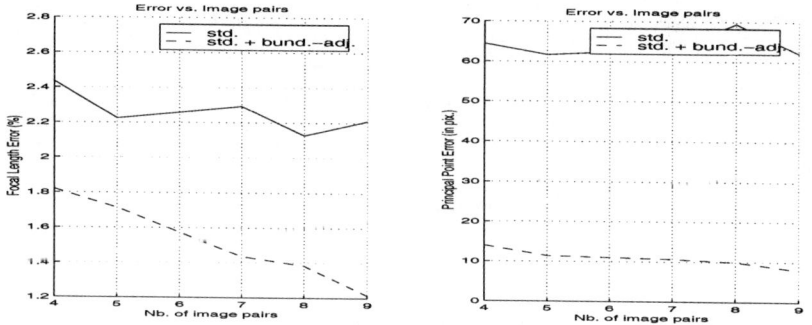

Fig. 5. Errors in the estimation of focal length (in %) and of principal point (in *pix.*) *vs.* number of image pairs.

Experiments with simulated data are carried out in order to assess the stability of the method against measurement noise.

A synthetic 3-D planar scene consisting of 100 points is generated and placed at different locations in 3-D space. The 3-D points of each position are projected onto the cameras of a stereo rig and Gaussian noise with varying standard deviation σ (from 0.0 to 1.0 pixel) is added to the image point locations. The cameras have a nominal focal length f of 1200 *pixels*, unit aspect ratio and zero image skew and the image size is 512 × 512. Image point locations are normalized as described in [6] and inter-image homographies $\mathbf{H}_{ij}$ are estimated. The autocalibration is then computed 100 times for each σ.

Figure 4 shows the resulting accuracy with varying noise and 7 image pairs. Figure 5 shows the resulting accuracy with a fixed noise level of 0.7 *pix.* and a varying number of image pairs.

The experiments show that the estimation provided by the method is quite accurate. Even for a level of noise of 1.0 *pix.*, the error in the estimation of the focal length is less than 2.5%. Moreover the approach gives sufficiently stable and accurate results to initialize a bundle adjustment procedure. With such a procedure, the accuracy of the estimation of both the focal length and the location of the principal point is increased as shown in Figures 4 and 5.

6.2 Real data

Fig. 6. One of the seven pairs gathered by the stereo rig

We gathered 7 image pairs of a planar scene (see Figure 6) with a stereo rig. Thirty points are matched between all images and the autocalibration algorithm applied using 4 to 7 image pairs from the whole sequence. In order to show the efficiency of the method, we show results before and after applying the bundle-adjustment procedure. The results are shown in Figure 7 where they are compared with the results of an off-line calibration [3].

As the number of views increases the estimated values approach ground truth. Although we used few points and all matches were made by hand, the method gives acceptable results. The bundle-adjustment procedure, initialized with these results, provides accurate enough calibration for metric reconstruction purposes.

637

| Autocalibration | | left camera | | | right camera | | |
nb. of image pairs	method	f	u_0	v_0	f	u_0	v_0
4 image pairs	std.	1008	420	275	1076	298	313
	w/ bund.-adj.	1058	373	304	1065	264	276
5 image pairs	std.	1088	503	286	1060	399	290
	w/ bund.-adj.	1060	421	221	1025	306	254
6 image pairs	std.	1008	320	300	1090	278	343
	w/ bund.-adj.	1020	399	274	1036	291	294
7 image pairs	std.	1048	345	247	1116	212	254
	w/ bund.-adj.	1022	400	279	1041	301	290
Off-line calibration		1030	399	269	1045	305	283

Fig. 7. Results of autocalibration algorithm for the real data of Figure 6 using different numbers of image pairs and off-line calibration.

7 Conclusion

We describe in this paper a new method for autocalibrating a stereo rig from several views of a plane.

We show that the epipolar geometry of the rig can easily be estimated with a planar scene in motion. We use the constraint that the projections of the circular points of a 3-D plane must lie on the image of the absolute conic. Then the autocalibration is performed by applying a stratified approach. Both autocalibration steps –affine and Euclidean– involve a set of quadratic constraints and we therefore designed a conic intersection method to solve for them.

Futhermore, our approach provides an algebraic solution (*i.e.* non-iterative) to Trigg's planar method [17] when vanishing lines are known, and this could be used for autocalibrating a camera from a monocular sequence of planes.

A Intersection of conics

Let $\mathbf{C}_1,...,\mathbf{C}_k,...,\mathbf{C}_n$ be n conics ($n \geq 3$) represented as 3×3 matrices. Let us suppose that these conics have a common intersection $\boldsymbol{x}$. For each k we have:

$$\boldsymbol{x}^\top \mathbf{C}_k \boldsymbol{x} = 0$$

Consider any two conics $\mathbf{C}_i$ and $\mathbf{C}_j$. Let ν_0 be a real number such that $\det(\mathbf{C}_i + \nu_0\mathbf{C}_j) = 0$ (ν_0 always exists because $\nu \mapsto \det(\mathbf{C}_i + \nu\mathbf{C}_j)$ is a degree-three polynomial with real factors). Let $\mathbf{D}_{ij}$ be such that $\mathbf{D}_{ij} = \mathbf{C}_i + \nu_0\mathbf{C}_j$. Then $\mathbf{D}_{ij}$ belongs to the pencil of conics generated by $\mathbf{C}_i$ and $\mathbf{C}_j$ and is degenerate ($\det(\mathbf{D}_{ij}) = 0$). Moreover $\boldsymbol{x}$ belongs to $\mathbf{D}_{ij}$ because:

$$\boldsymbol{x}^\top \mathbf{D}_{ij}\boldsymbol{x} = \boldsymbol{x}^\top(\mathbf{C}_i + \nu_0\mathbf{C}_j)\boldsymbol{x}$$
$$= \boldsymbol{x}^\top \mathbf{C}_i\boldsymbol{x} + \nu_0\boldsymbol{x}^\top\mathbf{C}_j\boldsymbol{x} = 0$$

638

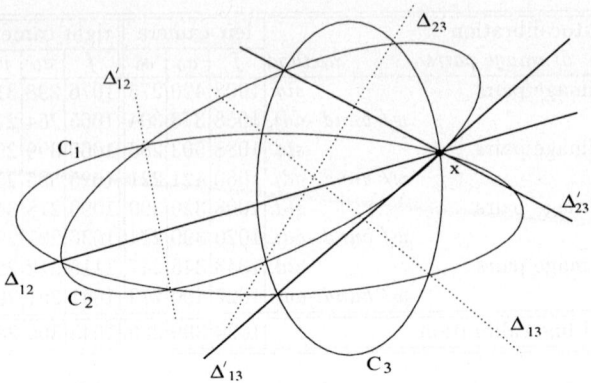

Fig. 8. Intersection of conics

As a degenerate conic, $\mathbf{D}_{ij}$ is the union of two lines Δ_{ij} and Δ'_{ij} and therefore x lies on one (at least) of these two lines. As a consequence, x can be estimated as the common intersection of all the pairs of lines Δ_{ij} and Δ'_{ij}.

Therefore the method we propose for solving simultaneously the quadratic constraints defined by the matrices $\mathbf{C}_k$ consists of the following steps:

- compute the degenerate conics $\mathbf{D}_{ij}$ and their associated pairs of lines Δ_{ij} and Δ'_{ij}. In practice, it is not necessary to compute all the possible $\mathbf{D}_{ij}$, we can choose to compute only n of them;
- intersect the pairs of lines Δ_{ij} and Δ'_{ij}, that is, find a point x such that it belongs to one line at least of each pair of lines Δ_{ij} and Δ'_{ij}. It is worth noticing that when data are noisy, the lines do not exactly intersect at the same point and an approach similar to linear least squares can be used to find the closest point x to all pairs of lines.

Acknowledgements

We are grateful for discussions with Frederik Schaffalitzky.

References

1. M. Armstrong, A. Zisserman, and R. Hartley. Self-calibration from image triplets. In B. Buxton and R. Cipolla, editors, *Proceedings of the 4th European Conference on Computer Vision, Cambridge, England*, volume 1064 of *Lecture Notes in Computer Science*, pages 3–16. Springer-Verlag, April 1996.

2. F. Devernay and O. Faugeras. From projective to euclidean reconstruction. In *Proceedings of the Conference on Computer Vision and Pattern Recognition, San Francisco, California, USA*, pages 264–269, June 1996.

3. O. Faugeras. *Three-Dimensional Computer Vision - A Geometric Viewpoint.* Artificial intelligence. The MIT Press, Cambridge, MA, USA, Cambridge, MA, 1993.

4. O. Faugeras. Stratification of three-dimensional vision: Projective, affine and metric representations. *Journal of the Optical Society of America*, 12:465–484, 1995.

5. O.D. Faugeras, Q.T. Luong, and S.J. Maybank. Camera self-calibration: Theory and experiments. In G. Sandini, editor, *Proceedings of the 2nd European Conference on Computer Vision, Santa Margherita Ligure, Italy*, pages 321–334. Springer-Verlag, May 1992.

6. R. Hartley. In defence of the 8-point algorithm. In *Proceedings of the 5th International Conference on Computer Vision, Cambridge, Massachusetts, USA*, pages 1064–1070, June 1995.

7. R.I. Hartley. Euclidean reconstruction from uncalibrated views. In *Proceeding of the* DARPA–ESPRIT *workshop on Applications of Invariants in Computer Vision, Azores, Portugal*, pages 187–202, October 1993.

8. R.I. Hartley. Projective reconstruction and invariants from multiple images. IEEE *Transactions on Pattern Analysis and Machine Intelligence*, 16(10):1036–1041, October 1994.

9. A. Heyden and K. Åström. Euclidean reconstruction from constant intrinsic parameters. In *Proceedings of the 13th International Conference on Pattern Recognition, Vienna, Austria*, volume I, pages 339–343, August 1996.

10. R. Horaud and G. Csurka. Self-calibration and euclidean reconstruction using motions of a stereo rig. In *Proceedings of the 6th International Conference on Computer Vision, Bombay, India*, pages 96–103, January 1998.

11. D. Liebowitz, A. Criminisi, and A. Zisserman. Creating architectural models from images. In *Proc. EuroGraphics*, volume 18, pages 39–50, September 1999.

12. Q.T. Luong and T. Vieville. Canonic representations for the geometries of multiple projective views. Technical report, University of California, Berkeley, EECS, Cory Hall 211-215, University of California, Berkeley, CA 94720, October 1993.

13. S. Maybank. *Theory of Reconstruction from Image Motion.* Springer-Verlag, 1993.

14. M. Pollefeys and L. Van Gool. A stratified approach to metric self-calibration. In *Proceedings of the Conference on Computer Vision and Pattern Recognition, Puerto Rico, USA*, pages 407–412. IEEE Computer Society Press, June 1997

15. J.G. Semple and G.T. Kneebone. *Algebraic Projective Geometry.* Oxford Science Publication, 1952.

16. P. Sturm and S. Maybank. On plane-based camera calibration: A general algorithm, singularities, applications. *Proceedings of the Conference on Computer Vision and Pattern Recognition, Fort Collins, Colorado, USA*, 1999.

17. B. Triggs. Autocalibration from planar scenes. In *Proceedings of the 5th European Conference on Computer Vision, Freiburg, Germany*, 1998.

18. Z. Zhang. A flexible new technique for camera calibration. In *Proceedings of the 7th International Conference on Computer Vision, Kerkyra, Greece*, September 1999.

19. Z. Zhang, R. Deriche, O. D. Faugeras, and Q-T. Luong. A robust technique for matching two uncalibrated images through the recovery of the unknown epipolar geometry. *Artificial Intelligence*, 78(1–2):87–119, October 1995.

20. A. Zisserman, P.A. Beardsley, and I.D. Reid. Metric calibration of a stereo rig. In *Workshop on Representation of Visual Scenes, Cambridge, Massachusetts, USA*, pages 93–100, June 1995.

Can We Calibrate a Camera Using an Image of a Flat, Textureless Lambertian Surface?

Sing Bing Kang[1] and Richard Weiss[2]

[1] Cambridge Research Laboratory, Compaq Computer Corporation,
One Kendall Sqr., Bldg. 700, Cambridge, MA 02139, USA
(currently with Microsoft Research, Redmond, WA 98052, USA)
[2] Alpha Development Group, Compaq Computer Corporation,
334 South St. SHR3-2/R28, Shrewsbury, MA 01545, USA

Abstract. In this paper, we show that it is possible to calibrate a camera using just a flat, textureless Lambertian surface and constant illumination. This is done using the effects of off-axis illumination and vignetting, which result in reduction of light into the camera at off-axis angles. We use these imperfections to our advantage. The intrinsic parameters that we consider are the focal length, principal point, aspect ratio, and skew. We also consider the effect of the tilt of the camera. Preliminary results from simulated and real experiments show that the focal length can be recovered relatively robustly under certain conditions.

1 Introduction

One of the most common activities prior to using the camera for computer vision analysis is camera calibration. Many applications require reasonable estimates of camera parameters, especially those that involve structure and motion recovery. However, there are applications that may not need accurate parameters, such as those that only require relative depths, or for certain kinds of image-based rendering (e.g., [1]). Having ballpark figures on camera parameters would be useful but not critical.

We present a camera calibration technique that requires only a flat, textureless surface (a blank piece of paper, for example) and uniform illumination. The interesting fact is that we use the camera optical and physical shortcomings to extract camera parameters, at least in theory.

1.1 Previous work

There is a plethora of prior work on camera calibration, and they can be roughly classified as *weak*, *semi-strong* and *strong* calibration techniques. This section is not intended to present a comprehensive survey of calibration work, but to provide some background in the area as a means for comparison with our work.

Strong calibration techniques recover all the camera parameters necessary for correct Euclidean (or scaled Euclidean) structure recovery from images. Many of such techniques require a specific calibration pattern with known exact dimensions. Photogrammetry methods usually rely on using known calibration points or structures [2, 15]. Brown [2], for example, uses plumb lines to recover distortion parameters. Tsai [15] uses corners of regularly spaced boxes of known dimensions for full camera calibration. Stein [13] uses point correspondences between multiple views of a camera that is rotated a full circle to extract intrinsic camera parameters very accurately. There are also proposed self-calibration techniques such as [6, 11, 16].

Weak calibration techniques recover a subset of camera parameters that will enable only projective structure recovery through the fundamental matrix. Faugeras' work [3] opened the door to this category of techniques. There are numerous other players in this field, such as [4, 12].

Semi-strong calibration falls between strong and weak calibration; it allows structures that are close to Euclidean under certain conditions to be recovered. Affine (e.g., [8]) calibration falls into this category. In addition, techniques that assume some subset of camera parameters to be known also fall into this category. By this definition, Longuet-Higgins' pioneering work [9] falls into this category. This category also includes Hartley's work [5] on recovering camera focal lengths corresponding to two views with the assumption that all other camera intrinsics are known.

The common thread of all these calibration methods is that they require some form of image feature, or registration between multiple images, in order to extract camera parameters. There are none that we are aware of that attempts to recover camera parameters from a single image of a flat, *textureless* surface. In theory, our method falls into the strong calibration category.

1.2 Outline of paper

We first present our derivation to account for off-axis camera effects that include off-axis illumination, vignetting, and camera tilt. We then present the results of our simulation tests as well as experiments with real images. Subsequently, we discuss the characteristics of our proposed method and opportunities for improvement before presenting concluding remarks.

2 Off-axis camera effects

The main simplifying assumptions made are the following: (1) entrance and exit pupils are circular, (2) vignetting effect is small compared to off-axis illumination effect, (3) surface properties of paper are constant throughout and can be approximated as a Lambertian source, (4) illumination is constant throughout (absolutely no shadows), and (5) a linear relation between grey level response of the CCD pixels and incident power is assumed. We are also ignoring the camera radial and tangential distortions. In this section, we describe three factors that result in change of pixel intensity distribution: off-axis illumination, vignetting, and camera tilt.

2.1 Off-axis illumination

If the object were a plane of uniform brightness exactly perpendicular to the optical axis, the illuminance of its image can be observed to fall off with distance away from the image center (to more precise, the principal point). It can be shown that the image illumination varies across the field of view in proportion with the fourth power of the cosine of the field angle (see, for example, [7, 10, 14]). We can make use of this fact to derive the variation of intensity as a function of distance from the on-axis projection. For completeness, we derive the relationship from first principles.

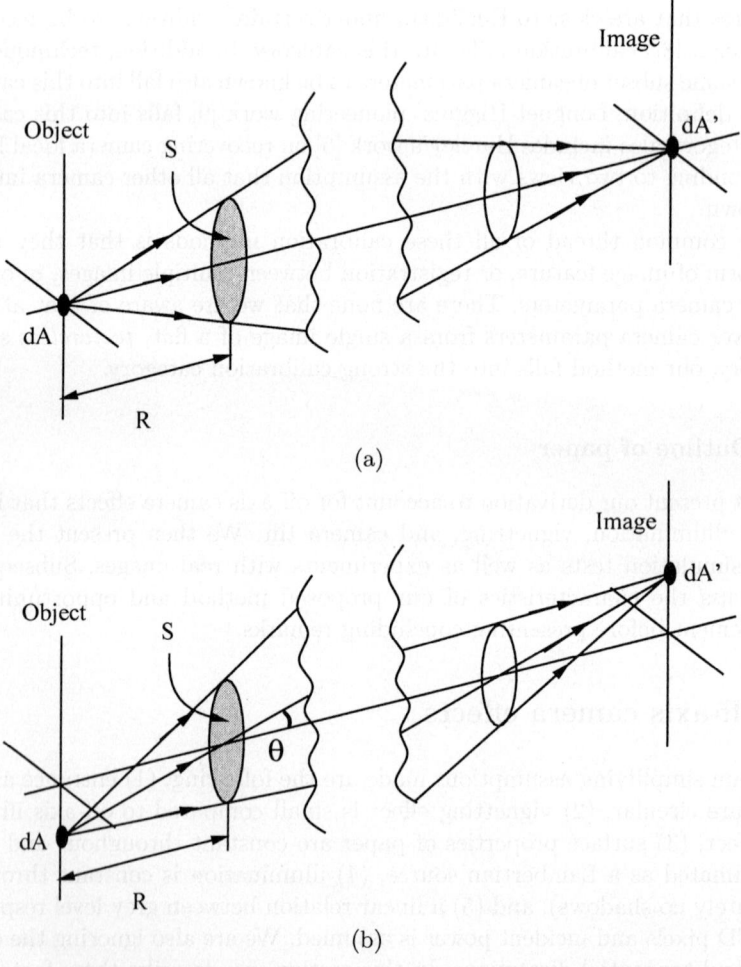

Fig. 1. Projection of areas: (a) On-axis, (b) Off-axis at entrance angle θ. Note that the unshaded ellipses on the right sides represent the lens for the imaging plane.

The illuminance on-axis (for the case shown in Figure 1(a)) at the image point indicated by dA' is

$$I_0' = \frac{LS}{(MR)^2} \tag{1}$$

L is the radiance of the source at dA, i.e., the emitted flux per unit solid angle, per unit projected area of the source. S is the area of the pupil normal to the optical axis, M is the magnification, and R is the distance of dA to the entrance lens. The flux Φ is related to the illuminance by the equation

$$I' = \frac{d\Phi}{dA'} \tag{2}$$

Now, the flux for the on-axis case (Figure 1(a)) is

$$d\Phi_0 = \frac{LdAS}{R^2} \tag{3}$$

However, the flux for the off-axis case (Figure 1(a)) is

$$d\Phi = \frac{L(dA\cos\theta)(S\cos\theta)}{(R/\cos\theta)^2} \tag{4}$$

$$= dA\frac{LS}{R^2}\cos^4\theta = dA'\frac{LS}{(MR)^2}\cos^4\theta$$

since $dA' = M^2 dA$.

As a result, the illuminance at the off-axis image point will be

$$I'(\theta) = I_0' \cos^4\theta \tag{5}$$

If f is the effective focal length and the area dA' is at image position (u, v) relative to the principal point, then

$$I'(\theta) = I_0'\left(\frac{f}{\sqrt{f^2 + u^2 + v^2}}\right)^4 \tag{6}$$

$$= I_0'\frac{1}{(1 + (r/f)^2)^2} = \beta I_0'$$

where $r^2 = u^2 + v^2$.

2.2 Vignetting effect

The off-axis behaviour of attenuation is optical in nature, and is the result of the intrinsic optical construction and design. In contrast, vignetting is caused by partial obstruction of light from the object space to image space. The obstruction occurs because the cone of light rays from an off-axis source to the entrance pupil may be partially cut off by the field stop or by other stops or lens rim in the system.

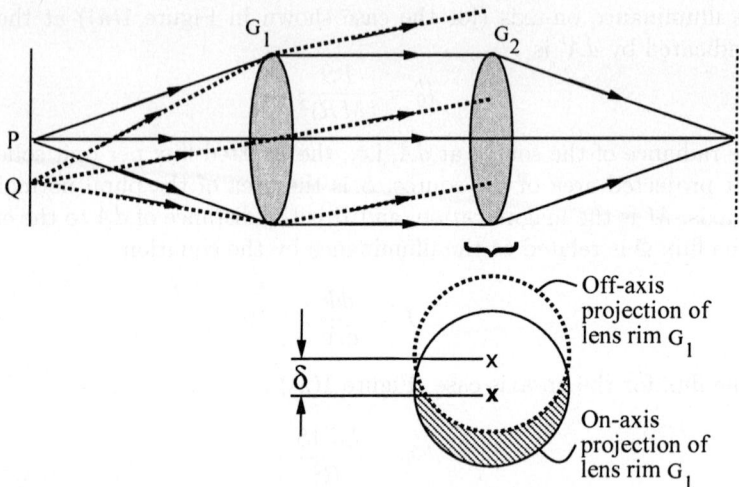

Fig. 2. Geometry involved in vignetting. Note that here there exists a physical stop. Contrast this with Figure 1, where only the effect of off-axis illumination is considered.

The geometry of vignetting can be seen in Figure 2. Here, the object space is to the left while the image space is to the right. The loss of light due to vignetting can be expressed as the approximation (see [14], pg. 346)

$$I'_{vig}(\theta) \approx (1 - \alpha r)I'(\theta) \tag{7}$$

This is a reasonable assumption if the off-axis angle is small. In reality, the expression is significantly more complicated in that it involves several other unknowns. This is especially so if we take into account the fact that the off-axis projection of the lens rim is elliptical and the original radius on-axis projection has a radius different from that of G_2 in Figure 2.

2.3 Tilting the camera

Since the center of rotation can be chosen arbitrarily, we use a tilt axis in a plane parallel to the image plane at an angle χ with respect to the x-axis (Figure 3). The tilt angle is denoted by τ. The normal to the tilted object sheet can be easily shown to be

$$\hat{\mathbf{n}}_\tau = (\sin\chi\sin\tau, \ -\cos\chi\sin\tau, \ \cos\tau)^{\mathrm{T}}. \tag{8}$$

The ray that pass through (u, v) has a unit vector

$$\hat{\mathbf{n}}_\theta = \frac{(\frac{u}{f}, \frac{v}{f}, 1)^{\mathrm{T}}}{\sqrt{1 + (\frac{r}{f})^2}} = \cos\theta(\frac{u}{f}, \frac{v}{f}, 1)^{\mathrm{T}}. \tag{9}$$

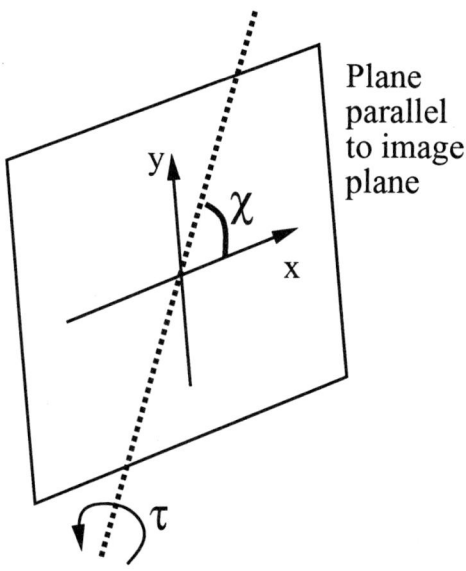

Fig. 3. Tilt parameters χ and τ. The rotation axis lies on a plane parallel to the image plane.

The foreshortening effect is thus

$$\hat{\mathbf{n}}_\theta \cdot \hat{\mathbf{n}}_\tau = \cos\theta \cos\tau \left(1 + \frac{\tan\tau}{f}(u\sin\chi - v\cos\chi)\right) \tag{10}$$

There are two changes to (4), and hence (5), as a result of the tilt:

- Foreshortening effect on local object area dA, where $dA\cos\theta$ is replaced by $dA(\hat{\mathbf{n}}_\theta \cdot \hat{\mathbf{n}}_\tau)$
- Distance to lens, where $(R/\cos\theta)^2$ is replaced by $(R/(\hat{\mathbf{n}}_\theta \cdot \hat{\mathbf{n}}_\tau/\cos\tau))^2$
  This is computed based on the following reasoning: The equation of the tilted object plane, originally R distance away from the center of projection, is

$$\mathbf{p} \cdot \hat{\mathbf{n}}_\tau = (0,0,R)^{\mathrm{T}} \cdot \hat{\mathbf{n}}_\tau = R\cos\tau \tag{11}$$

The image point (u, v), whose unit vector in space is $\mathbf{n}_\theta$, is the projection of the point $R_\tau \mathbf{n}_\theta$, where R_τ is the distance of the 3-D point to the point of projection. Substituting into the plane equation, we get

$$R_\tau = \frac{R\cos\tau}{\hat{\mathbf{n}}_\theta \cdot \hat{\mathbf{n}}_\tau} \tag{12}$$

Incorporating these changes to (5), we get

$$I'(\theta) = I_0'(\hat{\mathbf{n}}_\theta \cdot \hat{\mathbf{n}}_\tau)\left(\frac{\hat{\mathbf{n}}_\theta \cdot \hat{\mathbf{n}}_\tau}{\cos\tau}\right)^2 \cos\theta \tag{13}$$

$$= I'_0 \cos\tau \left(1 + \frac{\tan\tau}{f}(u\sin\chi - v\cos\chi)\right)^3 \cos^4\theta$$

$$= I'_0 \gamma \cos^4\theta = I'_0 \gamma\beta$$

from (6).

2.4 Putting it all together

Combining (13) and (7), we have

$$I'_{\mathrm{all}}(\theta) = I'_0(1 - \alpha r)\gamma\beta \qquad (14)$$

We also have to take into consideration the other camera intrinsic parameters, namely the principal point (p_x, p_y), the aspect ratio a, and the skew s. (p_x, p_y) is specified relative to the center of the image. If $(u_{\mathrm{orig}}, v_{\mathrm{orig}})$ is the original image location relative to the camera image center, then we have

$$\begin{pmatrix} u \\ v \end{pmatrix} = \begin{pmatrix} 1 & s \\ 0 & a \end{pmatrix}\begin{pmatrix} u_{\mathrm{orig}} \\ v_{\mathrm{orig}} \end{pmatrix} - \begin{pmatrix} p_x \\ p_y \end{pmatrix} \qquad (15)$$

The objective function that we would like to minimize is thus

$$\mathcal{E} = \sum_{ij} \left(I'_{\mathrm{all},ij}(\theta) - I'_0(1 - \alpha r)\gamma\beta\right)^2 \qquad (16)$$

Another variant of this objective function we could have used is the least median squared metric.

3 Experimental results

The algorithm implemented to recover both the camera parameters and the off-axis attenuation effects is based on the downhill Nelder-Mead simplex method. While it may not be efficient computationally, it is compact and very simple to implement.

3.1 Simulations

The effects of off-axis illumination and vignetting are shown in Figure 4 and 5. As can be seen, the drop-off in pixel intensity can be dramatic for short focal lengths (or wide fields of view) and significant vignetting effect. Our algorithm depends on the dynamic range of pixel variation for calibration, which means that it will not work with cameras with a very small field of view.

There is no easy way of displaying the sensitivity of all the camera parameters to intensity noise σ_n and the original maximum intensity level I'_0 (as in (14)). In our simulation experiments, we ran 50 runs for each value of σ_n and I'_0. In each run we randomize the values of the camera parameters, synthetically

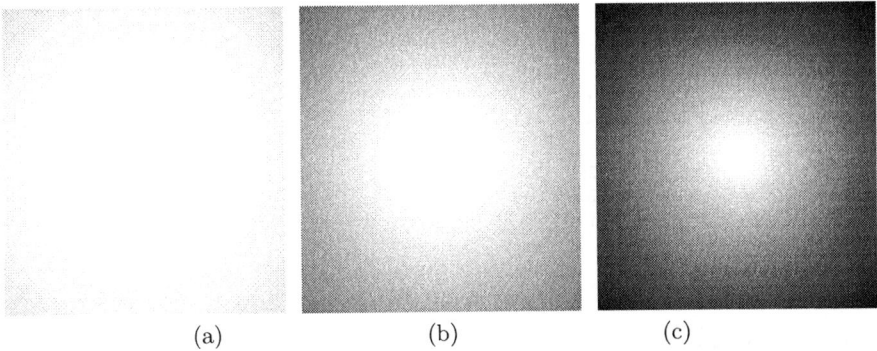

(a)   (b)   (c)

Fig. 4. Effects of small focal lengths (large off-axis illumination effects) and vignetting: (a) image with $f = 500$, (b) image with $f = 250$, and (c) image with $f = 500$ and $\alpha = 1.0^{-3}$. The size of each image is 240×256.

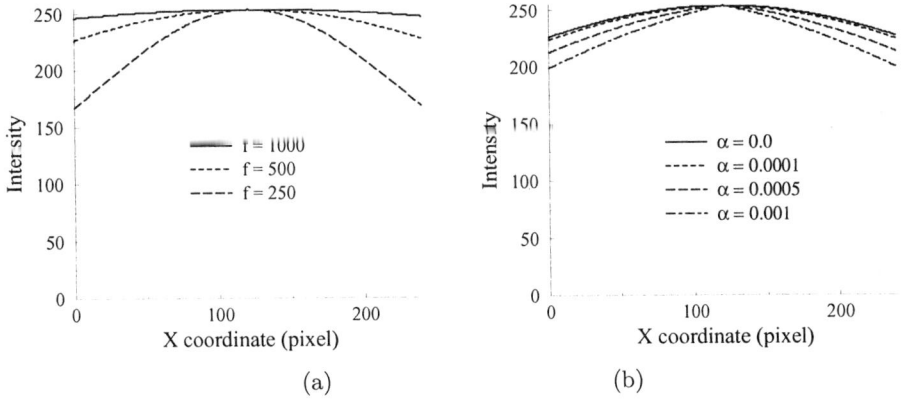

(a)   (b)

Fig. 5. Profiles of images (horizontally across the image center) with various focal lengths and vignetting effects: (a) varying f, (b) varying α (at $f=500$).

generate the appearance of the image, and use our algorithm to recover the camera parameters. Figure 6 shows the graphs of errors in the focal length f, location of the principal point $\mathbf{p}$, and the aspect ratio a. As can be seen, f and a are stable under varying σ_n and I'_0, while the error in $\mathbf{p}$ generally increases with increasing intensity noise. The error in $\mathbf{p}$ is computed relative to the image size.

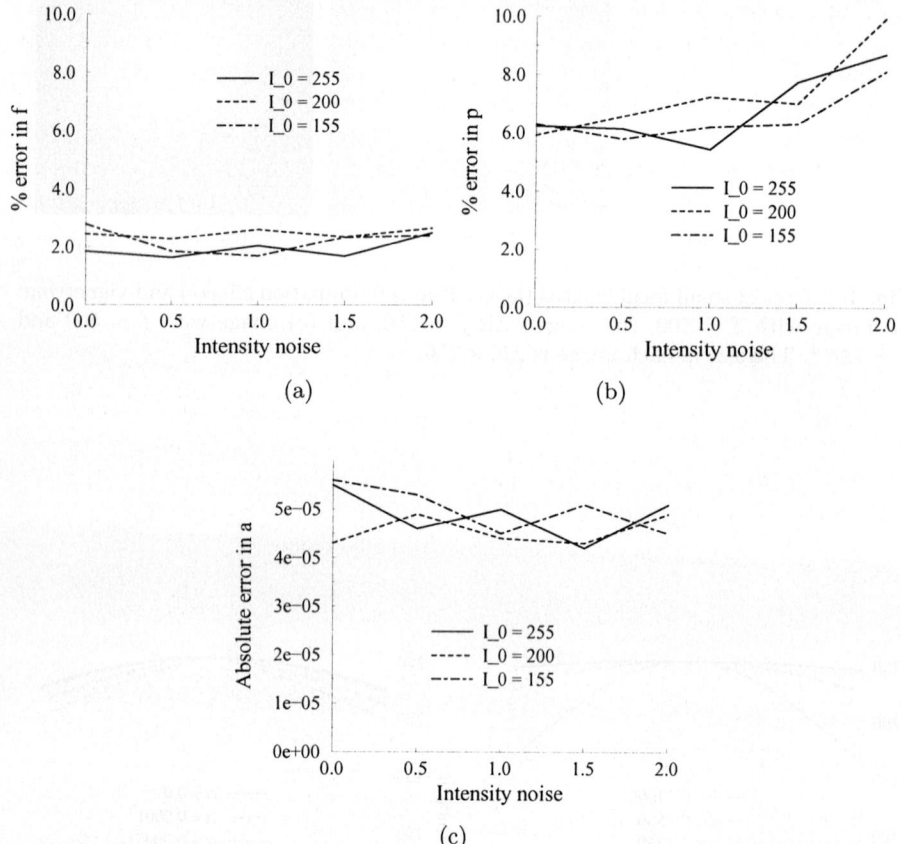

Fig. 6. Graphs of errors in selected camera parameters across different maximum intensity I_0 and intensity errors: (a) focal length f, (b) principal point location, (c) absolute error in aspect ratio.

3.2 Experiments with real images

We also used our algorithm on real images taken using two cameras, namely the Sony Mavica FD-91 and the Sharp Viewcam VL-E47. We conducted our experiments by first taking a picture of a known calibration pattern and then taking another picture of a blank paper in place of the pattern at the same camera pose. The calibration pattern is used to extract camera parameters as a means of "ground truth." Here, calibration is done using Tsai's algorithm [15]. Note that the experiments were conducted under normal conditions that are not highly controlled.

The results are mixed: The focal length estimated using our proposed technique range from 6% to 50% of the value recovered using Tsai's calibration technique. The results tend to be better for images taken at wider angles (and hence more pronounced off-axis illumination dropoff effects). It is also interesting to find that the focal length estimated using our method is consistently underestimated compared to that estimated using Tsai's algorithm. What is almost universal, however, is that the estimation of the principal point and camera tilt using our method is unpredictable and quite often far from the recovered "ground truth." *However, we should note that Tsai's calibration method for a single plane does not produce a stable value for the principal point when the calibration plane is close to being fronto-parallel with respect to the camera.*

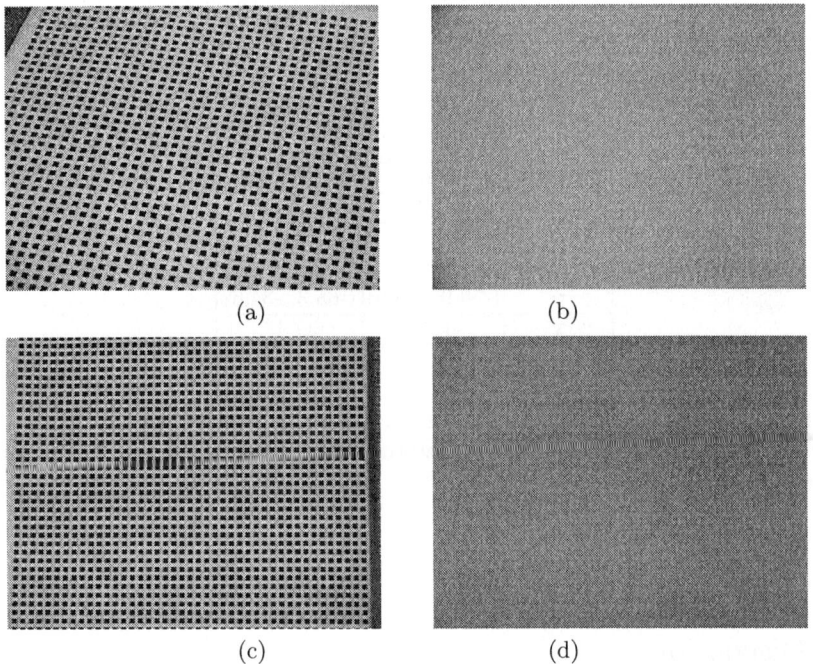

(a)   (b)

(c)   (d)

Fig. 7. Two real examples: images of calibration pattern (a,c) and their respective "blank" images (b,d). The image size for (a,b) is 512 × 384 while that for (c,d) is 640 × 486.

In this paper, we describe two of the experiments with real images. In experiment 1, the images in Figure 7(a,b) were taken with the Sony Mavica camera. In experiment 2, the images in Figure 7(c,d) were taken with the Sharp Viewcam camera. Notice that the intensity variation in (d) is much less than that of (b). Tables 1 and 2 summarize the results for these experiments. Note that we have converted Tsai's Euler representation to ours for comparison. Our values are quite different from those of Tsai's. There seems to be some confusion between the location of the principal point and the tilt parameters.

	Ours	Tsai's
f (pixels)	1389.0	1488.9
κ	—	3.56×10^{-8}
a	0.951	1.0
$\mathbf{p}$	(-4.5, 18.8)	(37.8, 14.7)
χ	1.8°	2.1°
τ	-0.3°	-40.0°

Table 1. Comparison between results from our method and Tsai's calibration for Experiment 1. κ is the radial distortion factor, $\mathbf{p}$ is the principal point, a is the aspect ratio, and χ and τ are the two angle associated with the camera tilt.

	Ours	Tsai's
f (pixels)	2702.9	3393.0
κ	—	-4.51×10^{-8}
a	1.061	1.0
$\mathbf{p}$	(-79.9, -56.9)	(-68.3, -34.6)
χ	1.6°	17.1°
τ	-0.2°	-9.1°

Table 2. Comparison between results from our method and Tsai's calibration for Experiment 2. κ is the radial distortion factor. Note that in this instance, the calibration plane is almost parallel to the imaging plane.

4   Discussion

In our work, we ignored the effect of radial distortion. This is for the obvious reason that its radial behaviour can misguide the recovery of off-axis drop-off parameters, which have radial behaviour as well. In addition, shadows, and possibly interreflection, will have a deleterious result on our algorithm. As a result, it is easy to introduce unwanted and unmodeled effects in the image acquisition process.

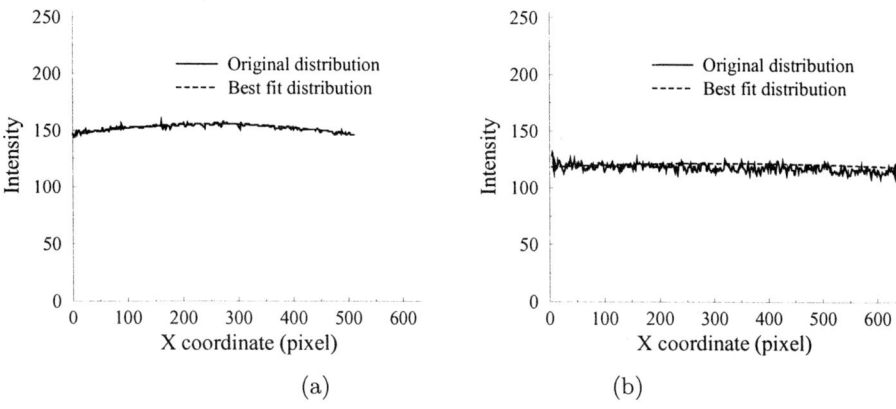

Fig. 8. Actual and fit profiles for the examples shown in Figure 7. (a) corresponds to Figure 7(a,b) while (b) corresponds to Figure 7(c,d).

The dynamic range of intensities is also important in our algorithm; this is basically a signal-to-noise issue. It is important because of the intrinsic errors of pixel intensity due to the digitization process. In a related issue, our algorithm works more reliably for wide-angled cameras, where the off-axis illumination and vignetting effects are more pronounced. This results in a wider dynamic range of intensities. One problem that we have faced in our experiments with real images is that one of our cameras used (specifically the Sony Viewcam) has the auto-iris feature, which has the unfortunate effect of globally dimming the image intensities.

Another unanticipated issue is that if paper is used and the camera is zoomed in too significantly, the fiber of the paper becomes visible, which adds to the texture in the resulting image. It is also difficult to have uniform illumination under normal, non-laboratory conditions.

On the algorithmic side, it appears that it is relatively easy to converge on a local minimum. However, if the data fit is good, the results are usually close to the values from Tsai's calibration method, which validates our model. We should also add that the value of the principal point cannot be stably recovered using Tsai's single-plane calibration method when the calibration plane is close to being fronto-parallel with respect to the camera. Our use of a simplified vignetting term may have contributed significantly to the error in camera parameter recovery.

We do admit that our calibration technique, in its current form, may not be practical. However, the picture may be radically different if images were taken under much stricter controls. This is one possible future direction that we can undertake, in addition to reformulating the vignetting term.

5 Conclusions

We have described a calibration technique that uses only the image of a flat textureless surface under uniform illumination. This technique takes advantage of the off-axis illumination drop-off behaviour of the camera. Simulations have shown that both the focal length and aspect ratio are robust to intensity noise and original maximum intensity. Unfortunately, in practice, under normal conditions, it is not easy to extract highly accurate camera parameters from real images. Under our current implementation, it merely provides a ballpark figure of the focal length. We do not expect our technique to be a standard technique to recover camera parameters accurately; there are many other techniques for that. What we have shown is that in theory, camera calibration using flat textureless surface under uniform illumination is possible, and that in practice, a reasonable value of focal length can be extracted. It would be interesting to see if significantly better results can be extracted under strictly controlled conditions.

References

1. S. Avidan and A. Shashua. Novel view synthesis in tensor space. In *Conference on Computer Vision and Pattern Recognition*, pages 1034–1040, San Juan, Puerto Rico, June 1997.
2. D. C. Brown. Close-range camera calibration. *Photogrammetric Engineering*, 37(8):855–866, August 1971.
3. O. D. Faugeras. What can be seen in three dimensions with an uncalibrated stereo rig? In *Second European Conference on Computer Vision (ECCV'92)*, pages 563–578, Santa Margherita Liguere, Italy, May 1992. Springer-Verlag.
4. R. Hartley. In defence of the 8-point algorithm. In *Fifth International Conference on Computer Vision (ICCV'95)*, pages 1064–1070, Cambridge, Massachusetts, June 1995. IEEE Computer Society Press.
5. R. Hartley, R. Gupta, and T. Chang. Estimation of relative camera positions for uncalibrated cameras. In *Second European Conference on Computer Vision (ECCV'92)*, pages 579–587, Santa Margherita Liguere, Italy, May 1992. Springer-Verlag.
6. R. I. Hartley. An algorithm for self calibration from several views. In *IEEE Computer Society Conference on Computer Vision and Pattern Recognition (CVPR'94)*, pages 908–912, Seattle, Washington, June 1994. IEEE Computer Society.
7. M. V. Klein and T. E. Furtak. *Optics*. John Wiley and Sons, 1986.
8. J. J. Koenderink and A. J. van Doorn. Affine structure from motion. *Journal of the Optical Society of America A*, 8:377–385538, 1991.
9. H. C. Longuet-Higgins. A computer algorithm for reconstructing a scene from two projections. *Nature*, 293:133–135, 1981.
10. P. Mouroulis and J. Macdonald. *Geometrical optics and optical design*. Oxford University Press, 1997.
11. M Pollefeys, R. Koch, and Van Gool L. Self-calibration and metric reconstruction in spite of varying and unknown internal camera parameters. In *International Conference on Computer Vision (ICCV'98)*, pages 90–95, Bombay, India, January 1998. IEEE Computer Society Press.

12. A. Shashua. Projective structure from uncalibrated images: Structure from motion and recognition. *IEEE Transactions on Pattern Analysis and Machine Intelligence*, 16(8):778–790, August 1994.
13. G. Stein. Accurate internal camera calibration using rotation, with analysis of sources of error. In *Fifth International Conference on Computer Vision (ICCV'95)*, pages 230–236, Cambridge, Massachusetts, June 1995.
14. J. Strong. *Concepts of Classical Optics*. W.H. Freeman and Co., San Francisco, CA, 1958.
15. R. Y. Tsai. A versatile camera calibration technique for high-accuracy 3D machine vision metrology using off-the-shelf TV cameras and lenses. *IEEE Journal of Robotics and Automation*, RA-3(4):323–344, August 1987.
16. A. Zisserman, P. Beardsley, and I. Reid. Metric calibration of a stereo rig. In *IEEE Workshop on Representations of Visual Scenes*, pages 93–100, Cambridge, Massachusetts, June 1995.

Underwater Camera Calibration

J.M.Lavest, G.Rives, J.T. Laprest

LASMEA, UMR 6602 du CNRS, Blaise-Pascal University of Clermont-Ferrand,
F.63177 Aubière cedex. France
lavest@lasmea.univ-bpclermont.fr

Abstract. This article deals with optical laws that must be considered when using underwater cameras. Both theoretical and experimental point of views are described, and it is shown that relationships between air and water calibration can be found.

1 Introduction

Use of vision systems in media in which the wave speed propagation is not that one of air is a subject seldom treated in the Vision community. However, any trial to localize or reconstruct an object observed by an underwater camera (for instance) has to go through a calibration phase.

This article presents some optical considerations relating to underwater cameras.

We show the relationship between the current pin-hole model of the camera and the general optical model of the lens combination for the same camera in air and under water.

The relations found are verified in simulation and by experiments. We prove that the calibration of a camera working under water does not have to be carried out under water.

The intrinsic parameters of a camera immersed in any fluid can be computed from an air-calibration as soon as the optical surface between the two fluids presents some simple geometrical properties.

2 Optics

The classical model used in artificial vision for description of image formation is the perspective projection and thus the pine-hole (or *sténopé*) model of projection.

Some links between this model and classical optical laws were established in [5], but the object and its image were both in the same homogeneous medium, namely the air.

Underwater camera calibration must involve a slightly more general optical model, taking account of the different fluids in which the object and the image are situated .

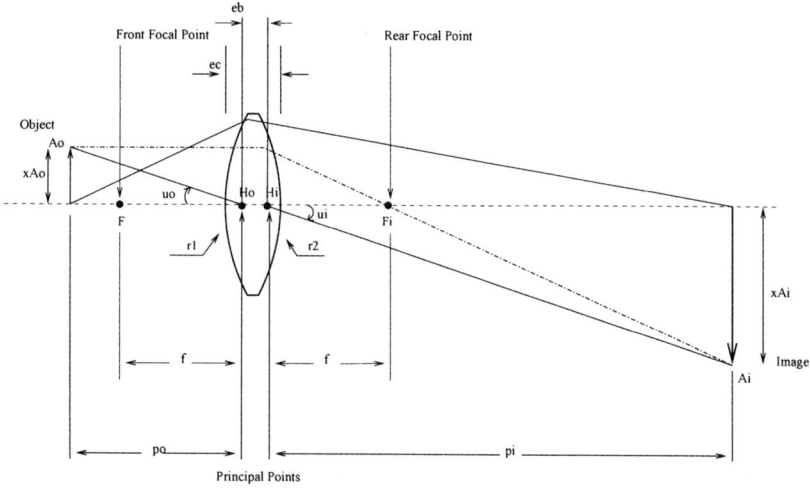

Fig. 1. Classical thick model, in an homogeneous fluid

2.1 Prerequisites

- **Conjugate planes:** if an optical system makes the rays from an object point A_o converge to a point A_i, then A_i is said to be the image or equivalently the conjugate of A_o.
- **Transversal magnification:** (Gt). If x_{Ao} and x_{Ai} are the respective distances of points A_o and A_i to the optical axis, the transversal magnification Gt is equal to the ratio of these distances:

$$Gt = \frac{x_{Ai}}{x_{Ao}}$$

- **Angular magnification:** (Ga). Angular magnification denotes the ratio of the incident and emergent angles (u_o, u_i) of an optical ray going through two conjugate points of the optical axis.

$$Ga = \left(\frac{u_i}{u_o}\right)_{x=0,y=0}$$

- **Principal planes and points:** object and image principal planes are conjugate planes orthogonal to the optical axis such that the transversal magnification is **one**. This definition implies that the rays between these two planes are parallel to the optical axis.
  Principal points are the intersection of the principal planes with the optical axis.
- **Focal length:** fi. This is the distance $(H_i F_i)$ where F_i is the image focal point. We recall that the image of an object located at infinity undergoes no blurring at the focal point.
- **Nodal points:** These are the pair of conjugate points on the optical axis N_o et N_i such that every ray through N_o emerges at N_i without change of direction (i.e. the angular magnification is **one**).

2.2 Thick model, for two different homogeneous fluids

Most vision applications deal with a camera immersed in an homogeneous fluid, namely *air*. Under such an hypothesis some simplifications arise and it can be shown [5] that nodal points and principal points coincide. The use of a pin-hole model consists in merging the two principal planes in order to only retain rays through the equivalent optical center.

Paraxial formulas for a lens located between two distinct homogeneous fluids are found in most handbooks of geometrical optics [7]. We recall the expressions that will be used hereafter.

These formulas extend the properties of the lenses to the arbitrary refractive index of the object (n_1) and of the image (n_2) media, also involving mechanical specification of the lenses in which glass has an index equals to n:

For opticians, refractive index is the ratio of the speed of light in air and the speed of light in the considered medium. When the situation involves two different extremal indices, the focal length f has two distinct values f_o for the object medium and f_i for the image medium. Moreover nodal and principal points are now distinct.

The following relations hold between the different optical variables (C.f. Figure 2.2).

1. Lens constant

$$k = \frac{n - n_1}{r_1} + \frac{n_2 - n}{r_2} - \frac{tc(n - n_1)(n_2 - n)}{n.r_1.r_2} \tag{1}$$

2. Focal lengths:

$$f_o = \frac{n_1}{k}, f_i = \frac{n_2}{k} \tag{2}$$

3. Gauss relation

$$\frac{n_1}{p_1} + \frac{n_2}{p_2} = k \tag{3}$$

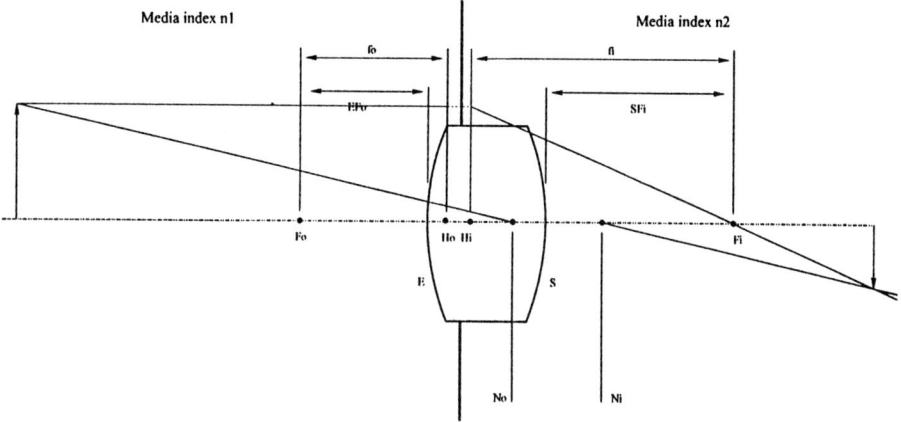

Fig. 2. Optical ways in fluids of different indices

4. Principal points locations

$$EH_o = \frac{n_1.tc}{k}\frac{(n_2 - n)}{n.r_2} \tag{4}$$

$$SH_i = \frac{-n_2.tc}{k}\frac{(n - n_1)}{n.r_1} \tag{5}$$

5. Nodal points locations

$$EN_o = EH_o + H_oN_o \tag{6}$$

$$SN_i = SH_i + H_iN_i \tag{7}$$

with

$$H_oN_o = H_iN_i = \frac{(n2 - n1)}{k} \tag{8}$$

2.3 Entry surface properties

For most applications involving an underwater camera, the lens system is set to be focused at infinity. This allows a focused image to be obtained from an infinite distance, up to a few centimeters of the entry surface (the minimum focused distance decreases with short focal lengths).The above consideration implies that the photosensitive matrix is almost always located at the image focal point.

Underwater cameras often possess an entry surface where the external surface is a plane. This property can be explained by the necessity of obtaining focused images in water as well as in air conditions.

In fact, an image will remain focused independently of the object medium index if and only if its image focal point remains unchanged through index variation. The image focal point is determined by the distance SF_i (where S denotes the exit surface of the last lens of the optical system).

$$SF_i = SH_i + H_iF_i = SH_i + f_i = \frac{-n_2.tc}{k}\frac{(n - n_1)}{n.r_1} + \frac{n_2}{k} \tag{9}$$

When r_1 grows to infinity (which is equivalent to obtaining a plane surface at the air/water interface), the expression becomes independent of n_1:

$$k = \frac{(n_2 - n)}{r_2}$$

and SF_i can be written:

$$SF_i = \frac{n_2}{k} = \frac{n_2.r_2}{(n_2 - n)} \tag{10}$$

This location of the image focal point related to the out surface (the one nearest to the CCD matrix) is also independent of n_1: the image is focused in air as well as in water.

2.4 From thick model to pin-hole model : the nodal points influence

The *pin-hole* model merely consists of using only one optical ray through an equivalent point called the optical center. The extension of the optical model to different media indices, shows that the role of the optical center will be played by the fusion of the two nodal points that conserve the angular magnification.

In the vision community the focal length is defined by the distance between the CCD sensor and the optical center. It can be seen in figure (2.2) that this distance is equivalent to N_iF_i if the object is at infinity.

$$N_iF_i = N_iH_i + HiF_i = \frac{(n_1 - n_2)}{k} + \frac{n_2}{k} = \frac{n_1}{k} = f_o$$

$$f_o = N_iF_i = n_1\frac{r_2}{(n_2 - n)} = n_1 * Ct \tag{11}$$

This last relation is a major one for our purpose. It can be noticed that the (vision community) 'focal length' is directly proportional to the object medium index n_1, because n (glass index), n_2 (CCD medium index $n_2 = 1$) and r_2 are constant.

When the camera is underwater, the focal length is equivalent to the value measured in air multiplied by a factor 1.333.

2.5 Distortions and changes of the view cone

It is obvious that the variation of the focal length implies a decrease of the solid angle of view, when the canera is immersed. This variation is directly proportional to the index because the image size (and hence the CCD size) is constant. (C.f. Figure 3)

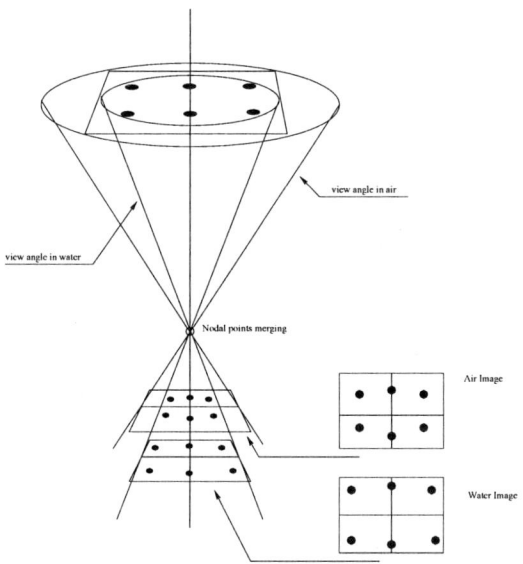

Fig. 3. *variation of the field of view, between air and water.*

What can be said about distortion ? How are air and water distortions related ?

Up to now we have not been able to determine in a theoretical way the mathematical relation between the two distortions, moreover it is doubtful if such a relation exists which does not involve the complete description of the lens systems. Even without any distortion, the image must be magnified with a factor 1.333.

Let u be the distorted image of a point in the air medium and du the distortion correction to obtain the perfect perspective projection. If now, in the same way u' is the distorted image of a point in the water medium and du' the new distortion correction, we must have:

$$1.333(u + du) = u' + du' \tag{12}$$

3 Camera Calibration

3.1 Protocol

This section briefly describes the camera calibration protocol we use in the experimental set-up in air as well as in water. The approach is mainly the photogrametric one [2] (i;e; *Bumble Adjustement*), and allows by the observation of a small number of views (approximately 10) the sensor calibration and the **calibration target reconstruction**. By this method, it is not necessary to take care in the calibration target measurement because, but the calibration sucess greatly depends on the accuracy of pattern detection in the calibration images set.The interested reader could refer to [6] for detailed issues.

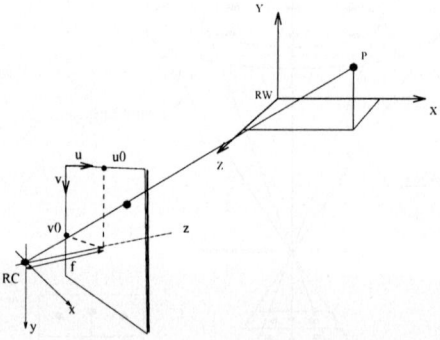

Fig. 4. *Coordinate systems.*

Under the perspective projection (pin-hole model), the relation between a point of an object and its image is given by the following expression:

$$\begin{pmatrix} x_i \\ y_i \\ z_i \end{pmatrix} = \lambda_i \left[\boldsymbol{R} \begin{pmatrix} X_i \\ Y_i \\ Z_i \end{pmatrix} + \boldsymbol{T} \right] \tag{13}$$

Where:

- (x_i, y_i, z_i) is a point defined in the camera frame (C.f. Figure 4 with $z(i) \equiv f$, i.e. the focal length of the camera,
- λ_i is a scale factor introduced when going from R^3 to R^2
- (X_i, Y_i, Z_i) are the coordinates of the target point in the world frame $W-XYZ$,

   – (T_x, T_y, T_z) are the coordinates of the translation vector $\boldsymbol{T}$,
   – $\boldsymbol{R}$ is the rotation matrix

Eliminating λ_i in (13) (and suppressing the i index for simplicity), we obtain the following expressions known as *colinearity equations* in photogrammetry:

$$\left.\begin{array}{l} x = f\frac{r_{11}X+r_{12}Y+r_{13}Z+T_x}{r_{31}X+r_{32}Y+r_{33}Z+T_z} \\[2mm] y = f\frac{r_{21}X+r_{22}Y+r_{23}Z+T_y}{r_{31}X+r_{32}Y+r_{33}Z+T_z} \end{array}\right\}$$

If we express (x, y) in the image frame, we get:

$$\left.\begin{array}{l} x = (u + e_x - u_0)dx - do_x \\ y = (v + e_y - v_0)dy - do_y \end{array}\right\} \tag{14}$$

In this expression e_x, e_y are the measure errors along coordinates x and y, (i.e., corrections to add to the measurements to fulfill the projection equations). do_x, do_y are the distortion components that can be split in two parts: *radial* and *tangential*, (i.e., $do_x = do_{xr} + do_{xt}$ and $do_y = do_{yr} + do_{yt}$).

   The two following expressions are commonly used in photogrammetry [1], [3] and we will be adopt them:

$$\left.\begin{array}{l} do_{xr} = (u - u_0)dx(a_1 r^2 + a_2 r^4 + a_3 r^6) \\ do_{yr} = (v - v_0)dy(a_1 r^2 + a_2 r^4 + a_3 r^6) \end{array}\right\} \tag{15}$$

$$\left.\begin{array}{l} do_{xt} = p_1[r^2 + 2(u - u_0)^2 dx^2] \\ \qquad + 2p_2(u - u_0)dx(v - v_0)dy \\[3mm] do_{yt} = p_2[r^2 + 2(v - v_0)^2 dy^2] \\ \qquad + 2p_1(u - u_0)dx(v - v_0)dy \end{array}\right\} \tag{16}$$

In these expressions (14), (15), et (16),

   – u, v are the image coordinates in the image frame,
   – u_0, v_0 are the coordinates of the principal point in the image frame,
   – u_1, a_2, a_3 are the radial distortion parameters,
   – p_1, p_2 are the tangential distortion parameters,
   – dx, dy are the sizes of the elementary pixel,
   – $r = \sqrt{(u - u_0)^2 dx^2 + (v - v_0)^2 dy^2}$ is the distance of the image from the principal point.

   Substituing (14), (15) and (16) in (3.1), we get the following system:

$$\left.\begin{array}{l} u + e_x = u_0 + (do_{xr} + do_{xt})/dx \\ \qquad + \left(\frac{f}{dx}\right)\frac{r_{11}X+r_{12}Y+r_{13}Z+T_x}{r_{31}X+r_{32}Y+r_{33}Z+T_z} = P(\boldsymbol{\Phi}) \\[4mm] v + e_y = v_0 + (do_{yr} + do_{yt})/dy \\ \qquad + \left(\frac{f}{dy}\right)\frac{r_{21}X+r_{22}Y+r_{23}Z+T_y}{r_{31}X+r_{32}Y+r_{33}Z+T_z} = Q(\boldsymbol{\Phi}) \end{array}\right\}$$

so we have:

$$\left.\begin{array}{l} e_x = P(\boldsymbol{\Phi}) - u \\ e_y = Q(\boldsymbol{\Phi}) - v \end{array}\right\} \boldsymbol{E}(\boldsymbol{\Phi}) \qquad (17)$$

Perspective projection is always defined up to a scale factor. Conventionally, we put $(dx = 1)$, then with $f_x = \frac{f}{d_x}$ and $f_y = \frac{f}{d_y}$, the parameter vector $\boldsymbol{\Phi}$ to estimate in the sensor/target joint calibration is:

$$\boldsymbol{\Phi}_{9+6m+3*n} = \left[u_0, v_0, a_1, a_2, a_3, p_1, p_2, f_x, f_y, \right.$$
$$X^1, Y^1, Z^1, \cdots, X^n, Y^n, Z^n,$$
$$\left. T_x^1, T_y^1, T_z^1, \alpha^1, \beta^1, \gamma^1, \cdots, T_y^m, T_z^m, \alpha^m, \beta^m, \gamma^m \right]^T$$

Where n is the target number of points and m the number of images.

3.2 Initial conditions

Optimisation of the non-linear system obtained is sensitive to the quality of the initial conditions. Generally the distortions coefficient are set to zero. The target is measured roughly (few millimeters); its planar structure eases the operation.

Initial locations of the camera in front of the target are estimated using Dementhon's algorithm [4] for planar objects. The principal point position is set at the image center, the focal length is set to the manufacturer estimate. Finally, the pixel size is set around 9 to 15 μm according to the camera manufacturer.

4 Experimentation

The experimental part consists of the self-calibration of an underwater camera in the two fluids air and water. We analyze results and try to express relations in regard with the previous theoretical developments.

4.1 Hardware

Two distinct cameras have been used for experiments. For the first one, the hardware system was an underwater camera made of a Sony CCD chip, a short focal length system and a special interface lens ensuring dry liaison between air and water. This lens allows an angular field of amplitude greater than 90 degrees. The whole video system is coupled with an automatic luminosity control device using two regulation loops, one for the mechanical regulation of the iris, the other being a gain controler for the video input signal.

The second one is also baseded on a sony CCD chip. However, all the optical system in this case, has been designed for experiments and the physical properties of each lens (index, size, position ...) is known. This permits a full optical simulation.

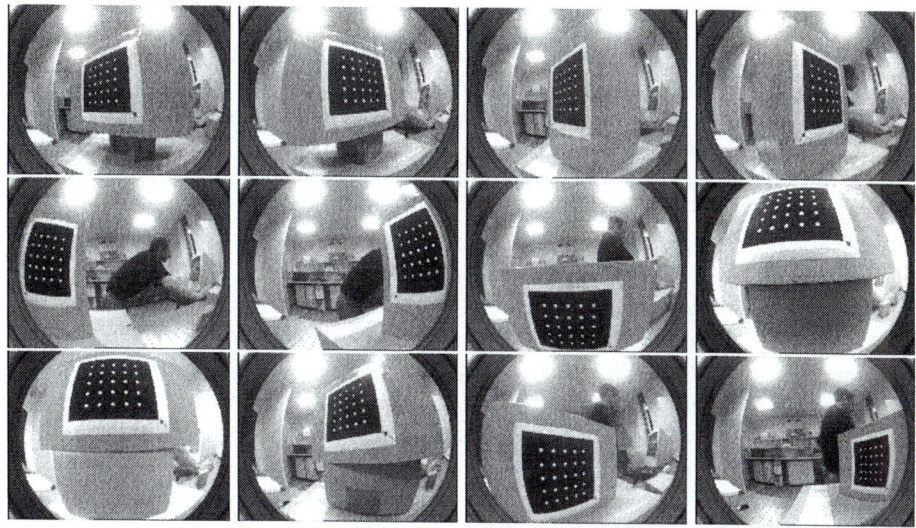

Fig. 5. Example of views for air calibration (768*576 pixels)

4.2 Air calibration

For this first experiment we calibrate the system out of the water medium from twelve images of a plane target. Figure (5) shows some of the shots. The important radial distortion is to be noted. The dark circle around the image is due to the air medium and disappears when the camera is immersed in water.

Results : air calibration (media index = 1) Under water camera 2	
camera2 : Sony + full optical system	
lens : 4mm	
digitizing card : Silicon Graphics	
algorithm : Self-calibration	
Number of images : 12	
Number of measures : 283	
Residuals mean e_x and σ (pixel)	2.69e-05 / 4.15e-02
Residuals mean e_y and σ (pixel)	1.49e-04 / 4.45e-02

		σ
fx(pix)	375.65	3.39e-01
fy(pix)	375.81	3.06e-01
u0(pix)	390.87	5.59e-02
v0(pix)	291.75	7.31e-02
a1	6.63e-01	7.52e-03
a2	-1.15e-00	5.02e-02
a3	6.83e+00	1.73e-01
a4	-1.20e+01	2.65e-01
a5	8.95e+00	1.56e-01
p1	-1.02e-03	1.98e-04
p2	1.22e-04	1.91e-04

Table 1. Self-Calibration in Air. Camera number 2

Notes:

– *The degree of the distortion polynomial has been increased in order to obtain a satisfactory fit with the image, due to this very distorted situation.*
– *The table (1) presents the computed values of the intrinsic parameters. It is to be noted that the residual at convergence is about 0.04 pixel along each*

coordinate: this is more than the usual results obtained with our method, which are turning at around 0.015 pixels. They denote the difficulty of a very accurate detection of the target point in the image corner, and also the difficulty for the polynomial to fit such a large distortion.
Nevertheless, the algorithm converges to a stable solution $f_x = 376$ pixels and $f_y = 376$ pixels, corresponding to an observed angular field of 110 degrees when the distortion is compensated.
- *The distortion polynomial can be seen in Figure 6. As we get further from the image center correction values become really high. As the target points measurements have been taken on a disk of radius of no more 320 pixels centered on the image (C.f. Figure 5), values of the distortion polynomial are mere extrapolation after this limit (Figure 6) and have no physical significance. The un-distorted view where the size has been increased by 400 pixels (line and columns) shows that inside the measurements field the distortion is properly corrected.*

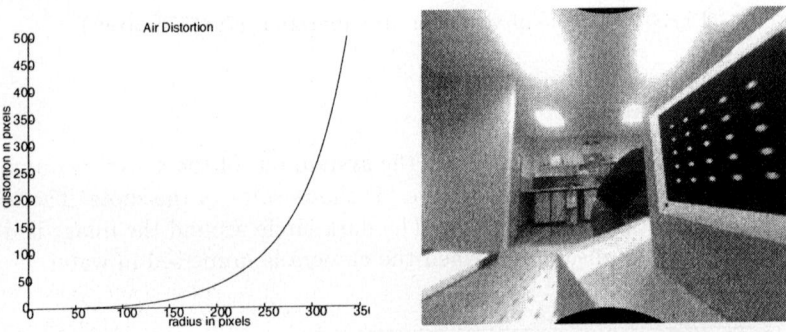

Fig. 6. radial distorsion and corrected image (1168*976 pixels)

4.3   Water calibration

In a similar way we have calibrated the system underwater from 10 images of the target. Each point has been detected and matched along the sequence. As previously emphasised, the dark circle also desappears in images. It shows that the intrinsic parameters have been modified. We can also notice that the angular field has shrunk under water as the distortion.

Notes:
For this second experiment, the focal length has increased to 500 pixels and leads to an expected field of view in water close to 90 degrees.
We have also drawn the distortion curve. Also as expected, the point displacement is less than in air. Figure (7) presents views obtained with the underwater camera. In order to constrain triangulation angles involved in the self calibration algorithm, it can be noticed that the calibration target is observed from quite different points of view.

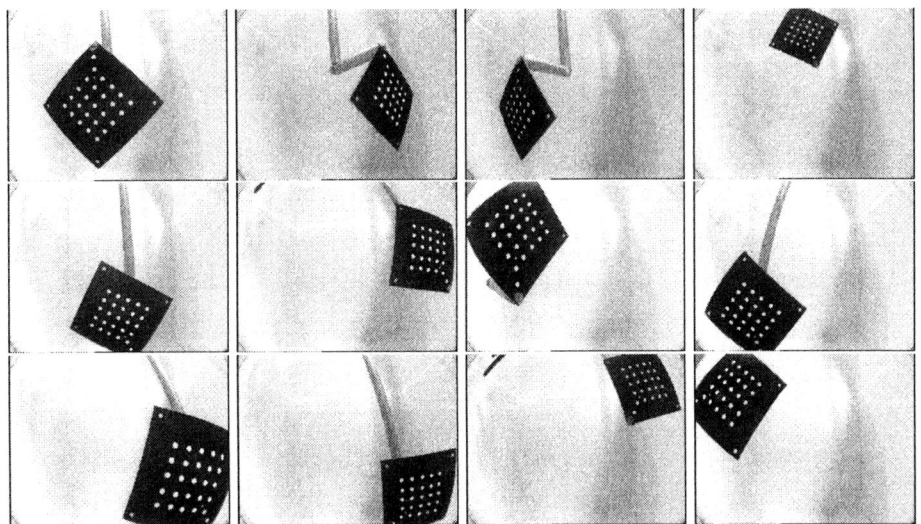

Fig. 7. Example of shots for underwater calibration, (768*576) pixels

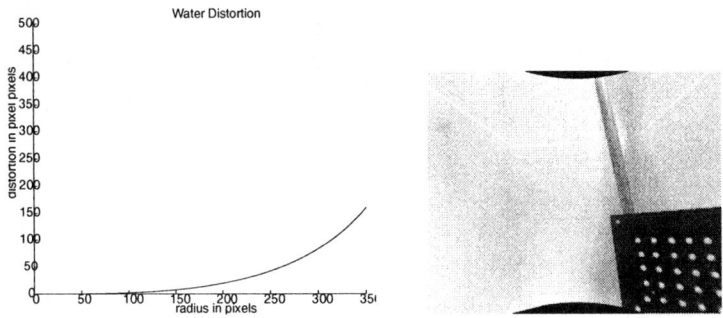

Fig. 8. radial distortion and corrected image in water, (968*776) pixels

Figure (8) shows one of the images after correction. The residuals remain at the same order of magnitude as in air. The black areas at the top and bottom correspond to image part that is not visible in the original view. (figure 7 number 10)

4.4 Relations between water and air calibrations

Focal length: It appears that the theoretical relation is almost completely fulfilled:

The distance between the image nodal point and the CCD matrix is multiplied by the water index.

Results of water calibration (media index = 1.333) underwater camera 2		
camera 2 : Sony + full optical system		
lens : 4mm		
digitizing card : Silicon Graphics		
algorithm : Self-calibration		
Number of images : 13		
Number of measures : 325		
Residuals mean e_x and σ (pixel)	1.36e-05	4.641e-02
Residuals mean e_y and σ (pixel)	-3.17e-05	5.164e-02

		σ
fx(pix)	499.12	5.51e-01
fy(pix)	501.97	5.22e-01
u0(pix)	391.81	9.27e-02
v0(pix)	292.30	1.25e-01
a1	7.52e-01	1.06e-02
a2	-1.84e-00	7.22e-02
a3	9.88e-00	2.54e-01
a4	-1.73e+01	4.11e-01
a5	1.30e+01	2.57e-01
p1	-1.66e-03	2.32e-04
p2	1.62e-03	1.76e-04

Table 2. Self-Calibration in Water. Camera number 2

	f-air	f-water	ratio (f-water/f-air)
fx(pix)	375.65	499.12	1.329
fy(pix)	375.81	501.97	1.336

Table 3. comparison of focal length in air and water media

Table (3) shows the ratio between the focal-length in water and air. If focal length uncertainties given by the calibration setup are taken into acccount, this ratio is almost $1,333$.

Self-calibration experiments have been carried out on many image sequences. The reproducibility of the results is ensured, but residuals at convergence are an order of magnitude larger than for calibration of a classical camera system.

(u_0, v_0) **location :**

	Air	Water
u0(pixels)	390.87	391.81
v0(pixels)	291.76	292.30

Table 4. comparison of principal point location in air and water media

The position of the image principal point (intersection of the optical axis and the CCD matrix) seems to remain unchanged between air and water calibrations (Table (4)).

However, it is well known that u_0 et v_0 are two parameters which are quite sensitive because they can (at a first order approximation) be compensated by object translation. The poor quality of the images delivered by the first underwater camera system has led to principal variation of up to 5 pixels.

Distortion:

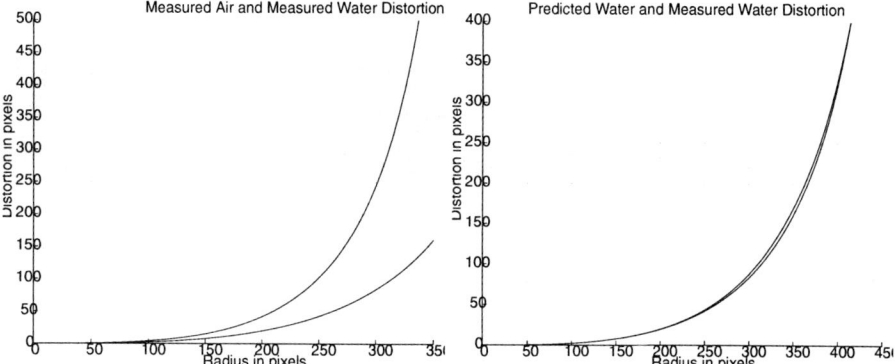

Fig. 9. Distortions: air and water curves (a), prediction of water distortion (b) from air data

Figure 9(a) shows a joint representation of the two distortion curves. As expected we can observe the large distortion in air medium compared with water measurements.

As seen in section 2.5, if we assume that the distortion is purely radial, the formula

$$1.333(u + d_a(u)) = u' + d_w(u')$$

would seem logical in order to give the natural relation between air and water distortion.

The right-hand part of Figure (10) shows the predicted water distortion compared to the measured one, according to the above expression. We can observe that the fit is quite good. Nevertheless, differences still remain if we try to overlap the two figures.

As the field of view in air is larger than in water, the predicted water distortion in the image border will correspond to very accurate data measured in the air sequence. This is not the case for the water sequence due to the difficulty in obtaining a full image in the image border.

5 Conclusion and Perspectives

This articles gives the basis of multi fluid sensor calibration and particularly air and water media. Different relations are shown between the index variation, the focal length, the field of view and the distortion function.

The fit between theoritical laws and measured data is almost completely fulfilled. For most applications that require an underwater camera, it is possible to carry out the sensor calibration in air and predict the intrinsic sensor parameters when the camera is immersed.

668

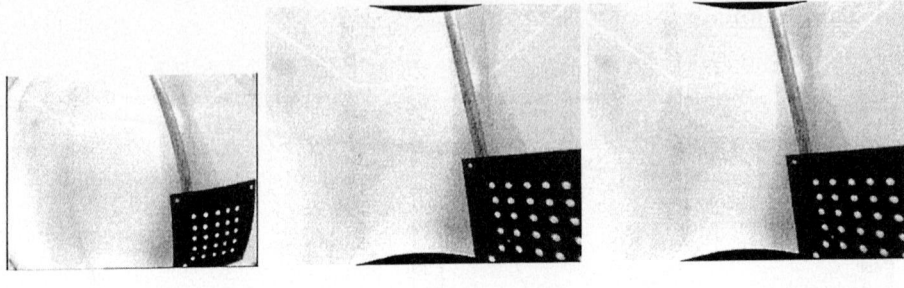

Fig. 10. Distortion: (a) Original view (768x576 pix), (b) Undistorted (968x776pix) from water data, (c) Undistorted from air data

To complete this study, we are working on a full optical simulation of the camera from the optical properties of each lens that compose the optical system. It will be possible to realize a more accurate comparison between simulated and real images.

Acknowledgements

This work has been done in collaboration with the french company POSEI-DON [8]. The authors gratefully acknowledge all the staff for lending the underwater cameras.

References

1. American Society for Photogrammetry. *Manual of Photogrammetry*, 4th edition, 1984.
2. H.A. Beyer. *Geometric and Radiometric Analysis of a CCD-Camera Based Photogrammetric Close-Range System*. PhD thesis, Institut fur Geodasie und Photogrammetrie, Nr 51, ETH, Zurich., May 1992.
3. D.C. Brown. Close-range camera calibration. *Photogrammetric Engineering*, 8(37):855–866, 1971.
4. L.S.Davis D.F.Dementhon. Model-based object pose in 25 lines of code. *International Journal of Computer Vison*, 15(2):123–141, 1995.
5. JM. Lavest, G. Rives, and M. Dhome. 3D Reconstruction by Zooming. *IEEE Trans. on Robotics and Automation*, Vol. 9(Nr 2):pp 196–207, April 1993.
6. JM. Lavest, M. Viala, and M. Dhome. Do we really need an accurate calibration pattern to achieve a reliable camera calibration. In *Proc. of ECCV98*, pages 158–174, Freiburg, Germany, 1998.
7. J.Ph. Perez. *Optique gomtrique et ondulatoire*. Masson,Paris, 1988.
8. Poseidon. *http://www.poseidon.fr*.

On Weighting and Choosing Constraints for Optimally Reconstructing the Geometry of Image Triplets

Wolfgang Förstner

Institut für Photogrammetrie, Universität Bonn
Nussallee 15, D-53115 Bonn, e-mail: wf@ipb.uni-bonn.de

Abstract. Optimally reconstructing the geometry of image triplets from point correspondences requires a proper weighting or selection of the used constraints between observed coordinates and unknown parameters. By analysing the ML-estimation process the paper solves a set of yet unsolved problems: (1) The minimal set of four linearly independent trilinearities (Shashua 1995, Hartley 1995) actually imposes only three constraints onto the geometry of the image triplet. The seeming contradiction between the number of used constraints, three vs. four, can be explained naturally using the normal equations. (2) Direct application of such an estimation suggests a pseudoinverse of a 4 × 4-matix having rank 3 which contains the covariance matrix of the homologeous image points to be the optimal weight matrix. (3) Instead of using this singluar weight matrix one could select three linearly dependent constraints. This is discussed for the two classical cases of forward and lateral motion, and clarifies the algebraic analyis of dependencies between trilinear constraints by Faugeras 1995.
Results of an image sequence with 800 images and an Euclidean parametrization of the trifocal tensor demonstrate the feasibility of the approach.

1 Motivation and Problem

Image triplets reveal quite some advantage over image pairs for geometric image analysis. Though the geometry of the image triplet is studied quite well, implementing an *optimal* estimation procedure for recovering the orientation and calibration of the three images from point, and possibly line, correspondencies still has to cope with a number of problems.

1.1 The Task

This paper discusses the role of the trilinear constraints between observed coordinates and unknown parameters [12, 13, 2, 8, 16] within an optimal estimation process for the orientation of the image triplet and shows an application within image sequence analysis.

The task formally can be described as following. We assume to have observed J sets $(P'(x',y'), P''(x'',y''), P'''(x''',y'''))_j, j = 1, ..., J$ of corresponding points in an image triplet. For each set of six coordinates $y_j = (x',y',x'',y'',x''',y''')_j^\mathsf{T}$ of three corresponding points we have a set of G_j generally nonlinear constraints, here the trilinear constraints $g_j(y_j,\beta) = 0$, which link the observed coordinates with the U parameters β of the orientation of the image triplet, specifically the $U = 27$ elements [16] of a $3 \times 3 \times 3$ tensor, termed trifocal tensor by [8]. There may be additional H constraints $h(\beta) = 0$ on the parameters alone, which in our case reduce the number of degrees of freedom of the trifocal tensor to 18 [8, 21, 3]. The task is to find optimal estimates for the parameters taking the uncertainty of the observed coordinates, e. g. captured in a covariance matrix Σ_{yy}, into account.

In this work, we are primarily interested in the optimal determination of the orientation and calibration of the three cameras, not in the elements of the trifocal tensor per se. We also assume some approximate values for the parameters to be known either by the camera setup, as e. g. in motion analysis or by some direct solutions. This is no severe restriction, as such techniques are available for a large class of setups. However, the optimal estimation of the orientation and calibration parameters, though used in [21], has not been treated in depth up to now.

1.2 Problems

There is a set of yet unsolved problems which are sketched here but worked out later:

P1: The number G_j of constraints: Shashua [16] showed that there exists a set of $G_j = 9$ constraints g_j with unique properties: They are linear in the coordinates of the three homologeous points and in the elements of the trifocal tensor. Up to four of them are linearly independent. However, as six coordiates are used to determine the three coordinates of the 3D-point only three of them actually constrain the orientation of the image triplet. Therefore the number of constraints to be used should be $G_j = 3$. Thus there seems to be a *contradiction* in counting independent constraints.

P2: Choosing G_j constraints: As the choice of these, three or four constraints depends on the numbering of the images we alltogether have 12 constraints. In addition we also could use the 3 epipolar constraints, being bilinear in the coordinates, for constraining the orientation. Though the algebraic relations between these constraints are analysed in [2], no generally valid rule is known how to select constraints. Therefore we have the problem to *choose* a small subset of $G_j = 3$ constraints from a total of 15, for determination of the orientation, thus, presuming problem P1 has been clarified. The problem is non trivial because a subset, which is well suited in one geometric situation may be unfavorable in another, leading to *singularities*.

P3: Weighting the constraints: Another way to look at the problem is to ask for the optimal weighting of the constraints, being more general than choosing [15]. Then the question arizes where to obtain the weights from, how to take the geometry into account, how to deal with singular cases and how to integrate the uncertainty of the matching procedure.

P4: Modelling and optimally estimating the geometry: There are several possibilities to *model* the geometry of the image triplet: (a) using the unconstrained $U = 27$ elements of the trifocal tensor as unknown parameters, (b) using the $U = 27$ elements of the trilinear tensor as parameters with $H = 9$ constraints on the parameters, (c) using a minimal parametrization with $H = 18$ parameters or (d) even restricting the geomtry to that of calibrated cameras, leading to an *Euclidean version* [13, 17] of the trifocal tensor involving $U = 11$ parameters for the relative orientation of the first two images and the 6 parameters of the orientation of the third image. The question then arises how an *optimal estimation* could be performed in each case, and how and under which conditions the estimates differ. Moreover, how are the above mentioned problems effected by the choice of the model?

We want to discuss these problems in detail.

1.3 Outline of the Paper

We first (section 2.1) present a generic model for representing parameter estimation problems. The resulting normal equation matrix, which represents the weights of the resulting parameters, can be used to analyse the quality of the result. The trilinear constraints on the observed coordinates can be interpreted geometrically (sect. 2.2) and allow a transparent visualization of the constriants within an image triplet (sect. 2.3). Based on different models for the image triplet (sect. 3.1) we discuss the number and the weighting of the contraints (sect. 3.2) and the optimal choice of the constraints for the classical cases of lateral and forward motion, leading to general selection rules (sect. 3.3). Sect. 4 presents an example on real data to prove the concept using a metric version of the trifocal tensor.

Notation: Normal vectors x and X and matrices R are given in italics, homogeneous vectors $\mathbf{x}$ and $\mathbf{X}$ and matrices P in upright letters. If necessary for clarity, stochastical variables are underscored, e. g. $\underline{x}$ being the model variable for the observed value x. True values are indicated with a tilde, e. g. $\tilde{x}$.

2 Basics

2.1 Modelling and Estimation

In this section we describe a broad class of estimation problems (cf. [20]) whose solution is obtained by solving an optimization problem of the same general form. In all cases the task is to infer the values of U non observable quantities $\tilde{\beta}_u$ from N given observations y_n fulfilling the constraints given by the geometrical, physical or other known relations. We treat these quantities as stochastic variables in order to be able to describe their uncertainty. As this takes place in our model of the actual setup, we distinguish stochastic variables $\underline{x}$ and their realizations (observed instances) x.

Modeling the Observation Process We assume that there are two vectors of unknown quantities, the N vector $\tilde{y} = (\tilde{y}_1, ..., \tilde{y}_n, ..., \tilde{y}_N)^\mathsf{T}$, and the U vector $\tilde{\beta} = (\tilde{\beta}_1, ..., \tilde{\beta}_u, ..., \tilde{\beta}_U)^\mathsf{T}$ participating in the G relations

$$g(\tilde{y}, \tilde{\beta}) = 0 \tag{1}$$

whose structural form is known. The values $\tilde{y}_n$ represent the true values for the observations, which according to the model are *intended* to be made. The parameters $\tilde{\beta}_u$ are assumed not to be directly observable. In our application these constraints are the trilinearities between observed image coordiantes and parameters of the geometry of the image triplet, worked out later.

In addition, it may be that the unknown parameters β have to fulfill certain constraints, e. g. $\beta^\mathsf{T}\beta = 1$. We represent these H constraints by

$$h(\tilde{\beta}) = 0 \tag{2}$$

In our application these may be 9 constraints on the 27 elements of the trifocal tensor (cf. [8]), to completely model the image geometry.

We now observe randomly perturbed values $\underline{y}$ of the unknown vector $\tilde{y}$. We model the random perturbation as an additive random perturbation assuming the random noise vector $\underline{e}$ is assumed to be normally distributed with mean $\mathbf{0}$ and covariance matrix $\Sigma_{ee} = \sigma^2 Q_{ee}$

$$\underline{y} = \tilde{y} + \underline{e} \qquad \underline{e} \sim N(\mathbf{0}, \Sigma_{ee}) = N(\mathbf{0}, \sigma^2 Q_{ee}) \tag{3}$$

The covariance matrix Σ_{ee} is separated in two factors: a positive definite symmetric matrix Q_{ee}, also called the cofactor matrix (cf. Mikhail & Ackermann 1976) being an *initial covariance matrix*, giving the structure of Σ_{ee}, and the multiplicative *variance factor* σ^2 to be estimated.

This separations has two reasons: One often only knows the ratios between the variances of the different observations and under certain conditions the estimation process is independent on the variance factor. The initial covariance matrix Q_{ee} is fixed and assumed to be known. It may result from previous experiments involving the same kinds of observations involved in the current observation. The initial covariance matrix Q_{ee} contains within it the scaling of the variables, their units, and the correlation structure of the observed variables. The *variance factor* σ^2 is an unknown variable for the multiplier on the known initial covariance matrix. It will be estimated using current data.

The complete model, represented by (1), (2) and (3), is called the GAUSS-HELMERT-*model* (cf. [9])

There are various special cases of this model. The most important one is the socalled GAUSS-MARKOFF-*model*, $\tilde{y} = \overline{g}(\tilde{\beta})$ (cf. [6], p. 213, [11], p. 218) where the observation process is made explicit, like in classical regression problems.

We will apply the complete model here for using the trilinear constraints on the coefficients of the trifocal tensor for estimating the relative orientation of the image triplet and especially for *analysing the ranks of the matrices involved for discussing the number of necessary constraints*.

Estimating Parameters The estimation problem we wish to solve now is: Given $\underline{y}$, estimate $\widehat{y}, \widehat{\beta}$, and $\widehat{\sigma}^2$ the most probable values for $\tilde{y}$, $\tilde{\beta}$ and $\tilde{\sigma}^2$.

We solve this problem by finding the value $(\widehat{y}, \widehat{\beta})$ for $(\tilde{y}, \tilde{\beta})$ that minimizes the weighted sum of squares of residuals, the weight matrix being the inverse covariance matrix $\phi(y, \tilde{y}) = 1/2\,(y - \tilde{y})^{\mathsf{T}} Q_{yy}^{-1}(y - \tilde{y})$ subject to the constraints $g(\tilde{y}, \tilde{\beta}) = 0$ and $h(\tilde{\beta}) = 0$. This is equivalent to finding the minimum of

$$\Phi(\tilde{y}, \beta, \lambda, \mu) = \frac{1}{2}(y - \tilde{y})^{\mathsf{T}} Q_{yy}^{-1}(y - \tilde{y}) + \lambda^{\mathsf{T}} g(\tilde{y}, \tilde{\beta}) + \mu^{\mathsf{T}} h(\tilde{\beta}) \qquad (4)$$

where λ and μ are G and H-vectors of Lagrangian multipliers. The solution is the ML-estimate, in case observations actually follow a normal distribution. Otherwise they are (locally) best linear unbiased estimates, i. e. estimates with smallest variance. The general solution of this optimization problem is given in the appendix.

We only need the normal equation matrix N here, which contains the *covarinace matrix $\Sigma_{\widehat{\beta\beta}}$ of the estimated unknown parameters $\widehat{\beta}$* in its inverse. With the Jacobians A and B of g with respect to the unknowns and the observations, and the Jacobian H of h with respect to the unknown parameters and the assumptions that these matrices have full rank we obtain the normal equation matrix

$$N = \begin{pmatrix} A^{\mathsf{T}}(B Q_{yy} B^{\mathsf{T}})^{-1} A & H^{\mathsf{T}} \\ H & 0 \end{pmatrix} = \begin{pmatrix} \overline{N} & H^{\mathsf{T}} \\ H & 0 \end{pmatrix} = \sigma^{-2} \begin{pmatrix} \Sigma_{\widehat{\beta\beta}} & S^{\mathsf{T}} \\ S & T \end{pmatrix}^{-1} \qquad (5)$$

with some matrices S and T, cf. (28) appendix.

We will be able to identify the rows of the matrix A with the Jacobian of the trilinear constraints w. r. t. the elements of the trifocal tensor, the matrix $(B Q_{yy} B^{\mathsf{T}})^{-1}$ with the sought weight matrix for the trilinearities containing the (initial) covariance matrix Q_{yy} of the observed coordintes and analyse the rank of these matrices.

2.2 Projection Matrices and their Interpretation

The geometric setup of three images is given by

$$x_i = P_i X \quad i = 1, 2, 3 \qquad (6)$$

which relate the coordinates $X^{\mathsf{T}} = (X, Y, Z, 1)$ of the object point to the three sets of coordiantes $x_i^{\mathsf{T}} = (u_i, v_i, w_i)$ with the (Euclidean) image coordinates $x' = u_1/w_1$, $y' = v_1/w_1$, $x'' = u_2/w_2$, etc. The three projection matrices are

$$P_1 = \begin{pmatrix} \mathbf{1}^{\mathsf{T}} \\ \mathbf{2}^{\mathsf{T}} \\ \mathbf{3}^{\mathsf{T}} \end{pmatrix}, \quad P_2 = \begin{pmatrix} \mathbf{4}^{\mathsf{T}} \\ \mathbf{5}^{\mathsf{T}} \\ \mathbf{6}^{\mathsf{T}} \end{pmatrix}, \quad P_3 = \begin{pmatrix} \mathbf{7}^{\mathsf{T}} \\ \mathbf{8}^{\mathsf{T}} \\ \mathbf{9}^{\mathsf{T}} \end{pmatrix} \qquad (7)$$

where the rows are indicated with bold face numbers. With the standard parametrization of the projection matrices

$$P_i = K_i R_i (I| - X_{oi}) \qquad (8)$$

Eq. (6) relates Euclidean object-space to Euclidean image space, capturing the (Euclidean) object coordiantes $\mathbf{X}_o$ of the projection centre, the rotation R and the calibration K, being an upper triangular matrix with 5 free parameters.

We now describe the geometry of the image triplet using the vectors $\mathbf{1}$, $\mathbf{2}$ etc. in detail. We use the following interpretation of the rows $\mathbf{1}$, $\mathbf{2}$ etc. of the projection matrices (cf. [2]): In case $u_1 = 0$ and (v_1, w_1) arbitrary, we have $\mathbf{1} \cdot \mathbf{X} = 0$, thus the vector $\mathbf{1}$ represents the homogeneous coordinates of the plane passing through the y'- and the z'-axis in the first camera; in the special case of K $= Diag(c_1, c_2, 1)$, i. e. reduced image coordinates but arbitrary focal lengths c_i, they are perpendicular to the x'-axis. By analogy, $\mathbf{4}$ and $\mathbf{7}$ are planes containing the $y^{(i)}$- and the $z^{(i)}$-axes in the second and the third camera, $\mathbf{2}$, $\mathbf{5}$ and $\mathbf{8}$ are planes containing the $x^{(i)}$- and the $z^{(i)}$-axes, and $\mathbf{3}$, $\mathbf{6}$ and $\mathbf{9}$ are planes containing the $x^{(i)}$- and the $y^{(i)}$-axes in the three cameras. Observe, all these planes pass through the corresponding projection centre.

As $u_1 : v_1 : w_1 = (\mathbf{1} \cdot \mathbf{X}) : (\mathbf{2} \cdot \mathbf{X}) : (\mathbf{3} \cdot \mathbf{X})$ and correspondingly for the other cameras, we have the following equivalent homogeneous constraints for the image coordinates:

$$
\begin{pmatrix}
\mathbf{A}_1^\mathsf{T} \\
\mathbf{B}_1^\mathsf{T} \\
\mathbf{D}_1^\mathsf{T} \\
\mathbf{A}_2^\mathsf{T} \\
\mathbf{B}_2^\mathsf{T} \\
\mathbf{D}_2^\mathsf{T} \\
\mathbf{A}_3^\mathsf{T} \\
\mathbf{B}_3^\mathsf{T} \\
\mathbf{D}_3^\mathsf{T}
\end{pmatrix}
\mathbf{X} \doteq
\begin{pmatrix}
u_1 \mathbf{3}^\mathsf{T} - w_1 \mathbf{1}^\mathsf{T} \\
v_1 \mathbf{3}^\mathsf{T} - w_1 \mathbf{2}^\mathsf{T} \\
u_1 \mathbf{2}^\mathsf{T} - v_1 \mathbf{1}^\mathsf{T} \\
u_2 \mathbf{6}^\mathsf{T} - w_2 \mathbf{4}^\mathsf{T} \\
v_2 \mathbf{6}^\mathsf{T} - w_2 \mathbf{5}^\mathsf{T} \\
u_2 \mathbf{5}^\mathsf{T} - v_2 \mathbf{4}^\mathsf{T} \\
u_3 \mathbf{9}^\mathsf{T} - w_3 \mathbf{7}^\mathsf{T} \\
v_3 \mathbf{9}^\mathsf{T} - w_3 \mathbf{8}^\mathsf{T} \\
u_3 \mathbf{8}^\mathsf{T} - v_3 \mathbf{7}^\mathsf{T}
\end{pmatrix}
\mathbf{X} \cong
\begin{pmatrix}
x' \mathbf{3}^\mathsf{T} - \mathbf{1}^\mathsf{T} \\
y' \mathbf{3}^\mathsf{T} - \mathbf{2}^\mathsf{T} \\
x' \mathbf{2}^\mathsf{T} - y' \mathbf{1}^\mathsf{T} \\
x'' \mathbf{6}^\mathsf{T} - \mathbf{4}^\mathsf{T} \\
y'' \mathbf{6}^\mathsf{T} - \mathbf{5}^\mathsf{T} \\
x'' \mathbf{5}^\mathsf{T} - y'' \mathbf{4}^\mathsf{T} \\
x''' \mathbf{9}^\mathsf{T} - \mathbf{7}^\mathsf{T} \\
y''' \mathbf{9}^\mathsf{T} - \mathbf{8}^\mathsf{T} \\
x''' \mathbf{8}^\mathsf{T} - y''' \mathbf{7}^\mathsf{T}
\end{pmatrix}
\mathbf{X} = 0 \qquad (9)
$$

The vectors $\mathbf{A}_i$, $\mathbf{B}_i$, $\mathbf{D}_i$ have a specific geometric meaning [18]:

The vectors $\mathbf{A}_i$ represent planes through the origin of the i-th camera, as they are linear combinations of the plane vectors; they pass through the v_i-axis of the i-th camera, as it is contained in both planes $\mathbf{1}$ and $\mathbf{3}$; they pass through the image point P_i, due to eq. (9); therefore they intersect the image plane in the line $u_i = const$. The vectors $\mathbf{B}_i$ represent planes through the origin of the i-th camera, pass through the $x^{(i)}$-axis of the i-th camera, pass through the image point P_i and thus intersect the image plane in the line $v_i = const$. Now, the vectors $\mathbf{D}_i$ represent planes through the origin of the i-th camera, pass through the $z^{(i)}$-axis of the i-th camera, pass through the image point P_i and thus intersect the image plane radially, fixing the *direction*, motivating the notation.

Observe, the planes $\mathbf{D}_i$ are not defined or are instable for points identical or close to the origin $(0, 0)$. Thus, planes $\mathbf{A}_i$, $\mathbf{B}_i$ and $\mathbf{D}_i$ fix the $x^{(i)}$-, the $y^{(i)}$- and the 'directional' coordinate. Only two of the three constraints for each camera are independent.

2.3 Constraints between Points of an Image Triplet

SHASHUA's **Four Constraints on the Trifocal Tensor Elements** We now easily can write down SHASHUA's constraints [16]. They can be formulated using the above mentioned planes, by establishing quadrupels of planes which should intersect in a 3D point, which is equivalent to requiring the 4×4 matrix of the 4 plane coordinate vectors to be singular or its determinant to vanish:

$$D_1^S \doteq |\mathbf{A}_1\,\mathbf{B}_1\,\mathbf{A}_2\,\mathbf{A}_3| = 0, \quad D_2^S \doteq |\mathbf{A}_1\,\mathbf{B}_1\,\mathbf{A}_2\,\mathbf{B}_3| = 0 \tag{10}$$
$$D_3^S \doteq |\mathbf{A}_1\,\mathbf{B}_1\,\mathbf{B}_2\,\mathbf{A}_3| = 0 \quad D_4^S \doteq |\mathbf{A}_1\,\mathbf{B}_1\,\mathbf{B}_2\,\mathbf{B}_3| = 0 \tag{11}$$

where $|\cdots|$ denotes the determinant of the vectors. The point-line-line constraint results from the fact that the first two vectors $\mathbf{A}_1$ and $\mathbf{B}_1$ fix the ray through the point in the first image and the two other vectors represent lines through the points in the second and the third image each (cf. the geometric interpretation above)[1].

Observe that these constraints are linear in all image coordinates, as each of these coordinates appears only once in the determinants and the w_i-coordinate can be set to 1 for all image image points, cf. (9c).

SHASHUA moreover showed that the constraints (10), (11) can be written as linear functions of the 27 entries of a $3 \times 3 \times 3$ tensor with elements $\mathbf{t}$, thus each is of the form

$$D_{lj}^S = \boldsymbol{\alpha}_{lj}^{S\,\mathsf{T}}\,\mathbf{t} = 0 \qquad l = 1, 2, 3, 4 \tag{12}$$

where the 27-vector $\boldsymbol{\alpha}_{lj}^S \doteq \boldsymbol{\alpha}_l^S(\mathbf{y}_j)$ only depends on the six coordinates of the point triple collected in the 6-vector $\mathbf{y}_j$ (here indexed with j to indicate the used point triple), and the 27-vector $\mathbf{t}$ contains the tensor coefficients. SHASHUA showed the 27×4 matrix

$$A_j^S = (\boldsymbol{\alpha}_{1j}^S, \boldsymbol{\alpha}_{2j}^S, \boldsymbol{\alpha}_{3j}^S, \boldsymbol{\alpha}_{4j}^S) = \left(\frac{\partial D_{lj}^S}{\partial t_k}\right)^{\mathsf{T}} \quad \begin{array}{l} k = 1, ..., 27; \ j = 1, ..., J \\ l = 1, ...4 \end{array} \tag{13}$$

to have rank four. Observe that A_j^S is the transposed Jacobian of the constraints (10 ff.) with respect to the parameters $\mathbf{t}$.

This suggests 4 constraints are necessary if one wants to exploit the full information of the image points for recovering the geometry of the image triplet.

Three Constraints between the Observations and the Triplet's Geometry However, we could argue only to need three constraints:

If one solves the basic projection equations (6) for the 6 observed coordinates one obtains 6 inhomogeneous equations. One now can take three of them and solve for the 3 coordinates of the object point. Substituting these object coordinates into the other three inhomogeneous equations yields *three* constraints between the six imge coordinates and the parameters of the geometry of the

---

[1] The four constraints correspond to those given in [8]: $\sum_k u_k'(u_i'' u_j''' T_{k33} - u_j''' T_{ki3} - u_i'' T_{k3j} + T_{kij}) = 0$ with the combinations $(1,1), (1,2), (2,1), (2,2)$, for the indices i and j and homogeneous coordinates (u_1', u_2', u_3') and $u_3' = 1$ etc.

image triplet, *independent* on the parametrization. Thus there can only be 3 independent constraints between the observed image coordiantes and the parameters of the geometry of the image triplet.

In a general setup one could argue that 1.) between the first two points P_1 and P_2 the epipolar constraints should be valid and that 2.) the 3D point, determined from the first two images, should map into the third image. This prediction was the basis for the derivation of the trifocal tensor in [8].

The epipolar constraint then reads as[2]

$$D_1^I \doteq |\mathbf{A}_1\,\mathbf{B}_1\,\mathbf{A}_2\,\mathbf{B}_2| = 0 \tag{14}$$

The first two vectors $\mathbf{A}_1$ and $\mathbf{B}_1$ span the ray in the first image, whereas the last two vectors span the the ray in the second image, which should intersect. The 3D point from the first two images could be determined as the intersection of the planes $\mathbf{A}_1$, $\mathbf{B}_1$ and $\mathbf{A}_2$ which should ly in the two planes $\mathbf{A}_3$ and $\mathbf{B}_3$, which gives rise to two further constraints, namely:

$$D_2^I \doteq |\mathbf{A}_1\,\mathbf{B}_1\,\mathbf{A}_2\,\mathbf{A}_3| = 0, \quad D_3^I \doteq |\mathbf{A}_1\,\mathbf{B}_1\,\mathbf{A}_2\,\mathbf{B}_3| = 0 \tag{15}$$

which are identical to the first two D_1^S and D_2^S of SHASHUA's constraints[3].

Singular Cases Unfortunately this set of constraints does not work in general.

First, assume the three images have collinear projection centres, establishing the X-axis in 3D and the rotation matrices are $R_i = I$. Then the two planes $\mathbf{A}_1$ and $\mathbf{A}_2$ intersect in a line parallel to the Y-axis, which, when intersected with $\mathbf{B}_1$ yields a well defined 3D point.

Now, if the three projection centres establish the Y-axis the two planes $\mathbf{A}_1$ and $\mathbf{A}_2$ are identical, as they are epipolar planes. Thus the 3D point *cannot* be determined using these two planes. In case the constraints D_2^I and D_3^I would be replaced by the last two constraints (11) of SHASHUA, we would be able to determine and predict the 3D-point in this case, but not in the previous one.

We therefore need to clarify the number of necessary constraints and discuss the selection or, more general, the weighing of the constraints.

3 Constraints within the Estimation Process

We now want to establish a statistical interpretation of such dependencies. Therefore we follow sect. (2.1), and model the reconstruction of the geometry of the image triplet.

3.1 Models

We distinguish three parametrizations:

M1: Tensor coefficients: We use the 27 elements $\mathbf{t}$ of the trifocal tensor as parameters to desrcibe the geometry. We therefore use (12) as constraints for each point triplet. We have to distinguish this model from the following:

---

[2] The superscript I indicates case I in the analysis later.
[3] and to Hartley's constraints with indices $(1,1)$ and $(1,2)$ cf. previous footnote .

M2: Projective parametrization: We use a minimal parametrization of the trifocal tensor with 18 parameters (cf. e. g. [21]). This leads to a projective reconstruction. We need not specify the parametrization for our analysis. Instead, we also could use the $U=27$ tensor coefficients and $H=9$ appropriate constraints between these parameters (cf. [3]).

M3: metric parametrization: We use a metric parametrization of the trifocal tensor with only 11 parameters in order to achieve an Euclidean reconstruction. The reason is: in our special application of image sequence analysis, we are able to calibrate the cameras in beforehand. Therefore we only have 11 parameters to specify the geometry of the image triplet, namely the 5 parameters of the relative orientation of the first two cameras as above and the 6 parameters of the exterior orientation of the third camera (cf. [12, 13, 17]). In our implementation we actually parametrize the orientation by the two translation vectors $\boldsymbol{X}_{o2}$ and $\boldsymbol{X}_{o3}$, and the two quaterions q_2 and q_3 for the rotations, fixing $\boldsymbol{X}_{o1} = \boldsymbol{0}$, and yielding $U = 14$ parameters with the $H = 3$ constraints $\tilde{\boldsymbol{X}}_{o2}^{\mathsf{T}}\tilde{\boldsymbol{X}}_{o2} = 1$, $\tilde{\mathsf{q}}_2^{\mathsf{T}}\tilde{\mathsf{q}}_2 = 1$ and $\tilde{\mathsf{q}}_3^{\mathsf{T}}\tilde{\mathsf{q}}_3 = 1$. This model will be used in the example.

In the last two cases M2 and M3 we may use the same constraints as above, by just replacing the 27 elements t_k of the trifocal tensor by 27 functions $t_k(\boldsymbol{\beta})$ of the 18 and 14 unknown parameters, thus the constraints (12) now read as

$$g_{lj}^S(\tilde{\boldsymbol{y}}_j, \tilde{\boldsymbol{\beta}}) = D_l^S(\tilde{\boldsymbol{y}}_j, \tilde{\boldsymbol{\beta}}) = \boldsymbol{\alpha}_l^S(\tilde{\boldsymbol{y}}_j)^{\mathsf{T}}\, \mathsf{t}(\tilde{\boldsymbol{\beta}}) = 0 \qquad l = 1, 2, 3, 4 \qquad (16)$$

The corresponding contraints of set A (14), (15) read as:

$$g_{lj}^A(\tilde{\boldsymbol{y}}_j, \tilde{\boldsymbol{\beta}}) = D_l^A(\tilde{\boldsymbol{y}}_j, \tilde{\boldsymbol{\beta}}) = \boldsymbol{\alpha}_l^A(\tilde{\boldsymbol{y}}_j)^{\mathsf{T}}\, \mathsf{t}(\tilde{\boldsymbol{\beta}}) = 0 \qquad l = 1, 2, 3 \qquad (17)$$

In case of model 3 we in addition have the $H = 3$ constraints between the parameters only:

$$\boldsymbol{h}^{\mathsf{T}}(\tilde{\boldsymbol{\beta}}) = (\tilde{\boldsymbol{X}}_{o2}^{\mathsf{T}}\tilde{\boldsymbol{X}}_{o2} - 1 \quad \tilde{\mathsf{q}}_2^{\mathsf{T}}\tilde{\mathsf{q}}_2 - 1 \quad \tilde{\mathsf{q}}_3^{\mathsf{T}}\tilde{\mathsf{q}}_3 - 1) = \boldsymbol{0} \qquad (18)$$

3.2 Number and Weighting of Constraints

We now discuss the left upper submatrix $\overline{N}$ from (5) in our context. In case of $j = 1, ..., J$ statistically independent triplets of points, thus $Q_{yy} = Diag(Q_{y_j y_j})$, which is no restriction in practical cases, it can be written as

$$\overline{N} = \sum_{j=1}^{J} \overline{N}_j = \sum_{j=1}^{J} A_j W_j A_j^{\mathsf{T}} = \sum_{j=1}^{J} A_j (B_j^{\mathsf{T}} Q_{y_j y_j} B_j)^{-1} A_j^{\mathsf{T}} \qquad (19)$$

using $A = (A_j^{\mathsf{T}})$ and $B = (B_j^{\mathsf{T}})$.

Each part $\overline{N}_j$ depends on three matrices, A_j, B_j and $Q_{y_j y_j}$. They have a very specific semantics. They give the key to the solution of the stated problems: **Coefficient matrix A_j:** The matrix A_j is the Jacobian of the constraints $g_j(y_j, \beta)$ with repect to the unknown parameters evaluated at the fitted values $\hat{\beta}$ and $\hat{y}_j$ of the parameters and the observations resp. (cf. App.).

In case the constraints are linear in the unknown parameters the matrix A_j only depends on the fitted coordinates $\widehat{y}_j$. Moreover, then one may use them for a direct solution of the unknowns β being the eigenvector corresponding to the smallest eigenvalue of $\dot{N} = A^\mathsf{T} A = \sum_j A_j A_j^\mathsf{T}$ minimizing the algebraic distance. This shows the close relation between the optimal nonlinear estimation and the direct solution: The constraints are not weighted; the direct solution obviously is an approximation. The weights W_j depend on B_j, which itself depends on the unknown parameters, thus are not available in a one-step solution. Due to the linear independency of the 4 constraints per point triplet, at least 7 points are necessary (cf. [16]) for the determination of the 27 tensor elements.

In case of 18 parameters the Jacobian A_j turns out have rank 3 in general, as can be shown using MAPLE. This is due to the projection of the 27 dimensional space of tensor parameters t to the 18 dimensional space of parameters β.

This can be geometrically visualized as follws: Without posing restrictions, assume the translation vector $X_{o2} = (X_{o2}, 0, 0)^\mathsf{T}$, and calibrated cameras with $K_i = I$, $R_i = I$. Then the two last constraints D_3^S and D_4^S *both* constrain the two first rays to follow the *epipolar geometry*, if the object point is in general position: this is because, $\mathbf{A}_1$ and $\mathbf{B}_1$ and the last plane $\mathbf{A}_3$ or $\mathbf{B}_3$ in (10) fix the object point. The plane $\mathbf{B}_2$ determined by the y_2-coordinate then has to pass through that point, in all three cases yielding the same constraint $y'' - y' = 0$.

Analytically, the two constraints in general are polynomials, which factor into, say, $u_3 v_3$ and $u_4 v_4$, where *in general position of the point* the first factors u_3 and u_4 are non zero and the second factors are identical, $v_3 \equiv v_4$, thus *both constraints, though algebraically different, impose the same restrictions onto the image geometry.*

This shows the two geometric setups, with 27 and 18 parameters resp., to differ in essence, solving problem P1, and explains why there is no real contradiction between the number of necessary constraints: SHASHUA's set of 4 constraints is necessary for estimating the geometry coded in the elements of the trifocal tensor, whereas only 3 constraints are necessary in case one wants to determine the projective geometry of the image triplet with 18 parameters. Observe, in this case one also could take the 27 elements of the trifocal tensor as unknowns β and introduce 9 constraints h on these parameters alone, this would not change the reasoning.

Coefficient matrix B_j: The matrix B_j is the Jacobian of the constraints with repect to the observations evaluated at the fitted values $\widehat{\beta}$ and $\widehat{y}_j$ of the parameters and the observations resp. (cf. App.).

It is implicitly used in the solution to determine the (preliminary) *covariance matrix* $Q_{g_j g_j} = B_j^\mathsf{T} Q_{y_j y_j} B_j$ of the contadictions $c = g_j(\underline{y}_j, \beta^{(0)}) \neq 0$, i. e. the deviation of the constraint evaluated at the observations $\underline{y}_j$ and the approximate values $\beta^{(0)}$ of the parameters by error propagation. The weightmatrix $W_j = Q_{g_j g_j}^{-1}$, being the inverse of this covariance matrix, therefore is the optimal choice. This solves problem P2, namely the choice of the weight matrix.

If model M1 with the 27 tensor coefficients as unknowns is chosen, the rank of this weight matrix in general is four, indicating that all 4 constraints actually are relevant and can be adequately weighted. However, for models M2 and M3 with 18 or less parameters describing the projective or Euklidean geometry the weightmatrix in general has rank 3. This confirms the fact that only three independent constraints are available. The Jacobians A_j and B_j have the same null space. Taking some generalized inverse

$$W_j = Q_{g_j g_j}^- = (B_j^{\mathsf{T}} Q_{y_j y_j} B_j)^- \tag{20}$$

when using more than 3 constraints does not lead to a different solution of the estimation problem.

This type of weighting with W_j has been used by [21]. The Jacobian B corresponds to Jacobian J in their eq. (20), which they state to have rank 3. They use the pseudo inverse $(J \Sigma_x^{1,2,3} J^{\mathsf{T}})^+$ (24) (via a SVD) instead of the normal inverse $(B_j \Sigma_{yy} B^{\mathsf{T}})^{-1}$ of a minimal set. This is more time consuming, compared to inverting a regular 3×3-matrix, especially if the number of used constraints is much larger than 3, as this computation has to be performed for every point triple in every iteration, which may be essential in real time applications.

However, the analysis confirms the direct 6-point solution of [21]to be a solution for the minimal number of points, as the number of free parameters of the trifocal tensor is 18 [16].

The weighing proposed in [15] is only an approximation as the rank of the weight matrix there is 4 instead of 3.

Covariance matrix $Q_{y_j y_j}$: As to expected, the weighting of the constraints depends on the uncertainty of the feature points or generally of the matching procedure. This uncertainty can be captured in the covariance matrix $Q_{y_j y_j}$ of the 6 coordiantes. Usually a diagonal matrix I will be sufficient. If the matching technique provides a realistic internal estimate of the variances this could be used to improve the result.

Observe, if $Q_{y_j y_j} = I$ then the direct solution would use the smallest eigenvector of $A^{\mathsf{T}}(B B^{\mathsf{T}})^{-1} A$. This *least squares solution* is identical to that given by [19], as $(B B^{\mathsf{T}})^{-1} = Diag(1/|\nabla g_j|^2)$ with the gradient magnitude of the constraints w. r. t. the observations. However, it here naturally follows from the general solution in a statistical estimation framework as a special case, and shows how to handle observed quantities which are *correlated*.

3.3 Choosing Independent Constraints

Instead of using a pseudo inverse for automatically getting the correct weight we also could choose a set of three independent constraints. The chosen set obviously will depend on the position of the object point with respect to the trifocal plane: If it is off the trifocal plane, three pairs of epipolar constraints would work. Thus we only analyse the important case where the projections centres are collinear. Then *all* object points lie on *a* trifocal plane, requiring at least one trilinear constraints on the tensor coefficients. We summarize the analysis from [5] here.

We assume image sequences with $R_i^{(0)} = I$, $K_i^{(0)} = Diag(c, c, 1)$, thus principal distance $c \doteq c^{(0)}$ and distinguish *forward motion* in Z-direction with $X_{o2}^{(0)} = (0, 0, B)^{\mathsf{T}}$, $X_{o3}^{(0)} = (0, 0, 2B)^{\mathsf{T}}$ and *lateral motion* in X-direction with

$X_{o2}^{(0)} = (B, 0, 0)^\mathsf{T}$, $X_{o3}^{(0)} = (2B, 0, 0)^\mathsf{T}$, thus base length $B = B^{(0)}$. We apply two different sets of constraints. The first is set A as in eq. (14) and (15). Trying to obtain full symmetry by using every coordinate twice and fixing each image ray in one of the three constraints [2, 18]) we obtain constraint set II:

$$D_1^{II} = |\mathbf{A}_1 \, \mathbf{B}_1 \, \mathbf{A}_2 \, \mathbf{B}_3| = 0, \; D_2^{II} = |\mathbf{B}_1 \, \mathbf{A}_2 \, \mathbf{B}_2 \, \mathbf{A}_3| = 0, \; D_3^{II} = |\mathbf{A}_1 \, \mathbf{B}_2 \, \mathbf{A}_3 \, \mathbf{B}_3| = 0$$

We give the determinants of the matrices $Q_{g_j g_j} = (B^\mathsf{T} Q_{y_j y_j} B)$, being proportional to the corresponding covariance matrices, in dependency of the object coordiantes (X, Y, Z) for lateral (l) and forward (f) motion and for set I and II, $d(Z)$ being a function of Z only:

$$|Q_{g_j g_j}^{(l,I)}| = 18B^2 c^6 \qquad |Q_{g_j g_j}^{(f,I)}| = X^4 (X^2 + Y^2) \cdot d(Z) \qquad (21)$$

$$|Q_{g_j g_j}^{(l,II)}| = 0 \qquad |Q_{g_j g_j}^{(f,II)}| = X^2 Y^2 (X^2 + Y^2) \cdot d(Z) \qquad (22)$$

Only if the determinat is not 0 the weightmatrix W_j has the proper rank. Therefore, the set I obviously is useful for all points in lateral motion, as the covariance matrix is regular, with a determinant *independent on the position*. The symmetric set II, however, is not useful at all in lateral motion. This is plausible, as only the y-coordinates are taken into account, i. e. this set then is a variation of the trifold use of the epipolar constraint. Both sets do quite a good job in forward motion, however lead to singularities if the points lie on the axes, on the x-axis for set I, on one of both for set II. Observe, that the origin $(0, 0)$ is the focus of expansion (FOE): points in the direction of the motion cannot be used at all, which is counter intuitive. They actually only constrain the rotation, not the translation, thus lead to only two constraints, causing the rank deficiency.

General rules for *choosing three constraints* are the following, solving problem P2 while distinuishing between 1, 2 and 3 trilinear constraints within the set:

1. One trilinear constraint and two epipolar constraints: The trilinear constraint in lateral motion needs to be one of $|\mathbf{A}_1, \mathbf{A}_2, \mathbf{A}_3, \mathbf{B}_i|$ $i = 1, 2, 3$. In forward motion we distinguish between points right or left of the FOE, for which the previous constraints works, and points above or below the FOE, for which one chooses one of $|\mathbf{B}_1, \mathbf{B}_2, \mathbf{B}_3, \mathbf{A}_i|, i = 1, 2, 3$[4].

2. Two trilinear constraints and one epipolar constraint: For lateral motion (X-direction) choose set I. For forward motion we again choose the sets according to position relative to the FOE, namely the determinants

$$D_1^{l,r} = |\mathbf{A}_1 \, \mathbf{B}_1 \, \mathbf{A}_2 \, \mathbf{B}_2|, \; D_2^{l,r} = |\mathbf{A}_1 \, \mathbf{B}_1 \, \mathbf{A}_2 \, \mathbf{A}_3|, \; D_3^{l,r} = |\mathbf{A}_1 \, \mathbf{B}_1 \, \mathbf{A}_2 \, \mathbf{B}_3|$$
$$D_1^{a,b} = |\mathbf{A}_1 \, \mathbf{B}_1 \, \mathbf{A}_2 \, \mathbf{B}_2|, \; D_2^{a,b} = |\mathbf{A}_1 \, \mathbf{B}_1 \, \mathbf{B}_2 \, \mathbf{A}_3|, \; D_3^{a,b} = |\mathbf{A}_1 \, \mathbf{B}_1 \, \mathbf{B}_2 \, \mathbf{B}_3|$$

   to be zero (l, r = left/right, a, b = above/below the FOE).

3. Three trilinear constraints *with the same ray fixed* in all constraints are generally independent *if* no constraint contains 3 planes parallel to a/the trifocal plane[5]. E. g. the set $D_1 = |\mathbf{A}_1, \mathbf{B}_1, \mathbf{A}_2, \mathbf{A}_3| = 0$, $D_2 = |\mathbf{A}_1, \mathbf{B}_1, \mathbf{A}_2, \mathbf{B}_3| = 0$, $D_3 = |\mathbf{A}_1, \mathbf{B}_1, \mathbf{B}_2, \mathbf{A}_3| = 0$ is independent in general; in lateral motion for all points, in forward motion at all points except with $X = 0$ or $Y = 0$.

---

[4] [13] proposes $|\mathbf{3}, \mathbf{D}_1, \mathbf{D}_2, \mathbf{D}_3| = 0$ in lateral motion only useful for points with $X \neq 0$.

[5] The set of constraints discussed in [2], p. 16 $T_{1,2,3,5} = |\mathbf{D}_1, \mathbf{B}_1, \mathbf{D}_2, \mathbf{D}_3|$, $T_{1,3,4,5} = |\mathbf{D}_1, \mathbf{D}_2, \mathbf{B}_2, \mathbf{D}_3|$, $T_{1,3,5,6} = |\mathbf{D}_1, \mathbf{D}_2, \mathbf{D}_3, \mathbf{B}_3|$ has rank 1 in lateral motion in x- or

4   Example

The usefulness of the estimation procedure for the metric version of the trifocal tensor is investigated [1]. An image sequence with 5300 images is taken from a car. The measured speed is shown in figure 1 top. The camera is looking ahead, establishing the case *forward motion*. A subsecquence of 800 images has been evaluated w. r. t. the geometric analysis of image pairs and image triplets. A subsection of 100 images was finally used for a bundle triangulation.

The Procedure: After initializing the procedure, interest points are selected in image i which promise good correspondence [4]. Using the correspondencies from the two previous frames we predict points in the current image using two trilinear constraints suited for that point. Thereby we assume *constant motion*, thus constant X_o and R. All interest points within an adaptive search area are checked for consistency using normalized crosscorrelation. Possibly their position is corrected based on the point in image $i - 1$ using a least squares matching procedure [7], chap. 16, at the same time yielding internal estimates for the uncertainty $\Sigma_{y_j y_j}$.

These point triplets are used for estimation. We applied the set of constraints I (14, 15) here and used a pseudo inverse to cope with singularities, which are possible (cf. (21b)). The 14 parameters with the 3 constraints of the third model are estimated using the GAUSS-HELMERT-model, however in a robustified version, by a reweighting scheme following [10]. Figure 1 bottom shows the number of used points per successfully determined image triplet, which excludes the images with velocity 0.

Finally, new points are detected and possibly linked to the previous image. The next image $i + 1$ is taken as third in the next image triplet, which uses the *metric parametrization* of the two previous images as approximate values. This chaining is not meant to be optimal not even consistent, as it only is used to yield approximate values for the image sequence, which then were to be optimally reconstructed in one process using a bundle adjustment.

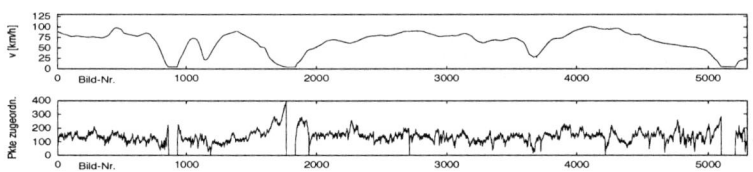

Fig. 1. *shows speed (top) and number of matched points over 5300 images (bottom)*

Results: Some results of the extensive experiments, documented in [1] can be summarized as follows:

---

y-direction, as the three planes $\mathbf{D}_i$ are parallel to the z-axis and should intersect in one ray, which is expressed equivalently by all three constraints; the set has rank 0 in forward motion in z-direction as they all contain three planes passing through the motion axis.

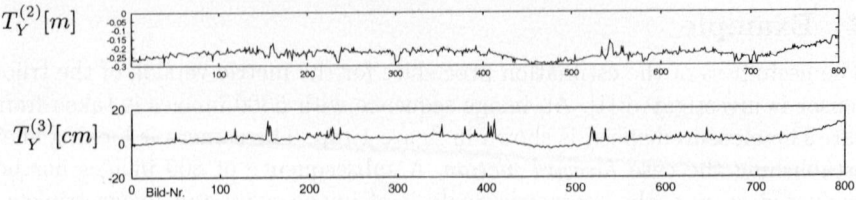

Fig. 2. *shows above the Y-coordinate of the translation vector $\boldsymbol{T}_2$ determined from the first 800 image pairs, revealing quite a number of erroneous values cause by mismatches. The lower row shows the Y-coordinate determined from image triplets, clearly demonstrating the effect of higher reliability from ([17])*

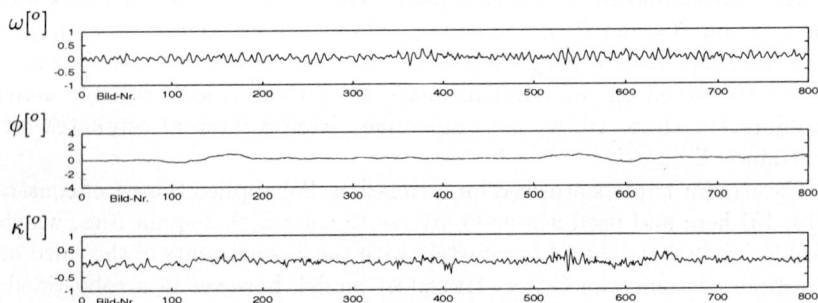

Fig. 3. *Estimated rotation angles of the second image w. r. t the first. Observe the typical vibration in the ω.*

Fig. 4. *Backprojection of trajectory of image sequence with 100 images and 3D point cloud together with trajectory*

- The quality of the motion parameters are much higher when using the image triplet than when only using image pairs (cf. fig. 2).
- The estimation of the rotation angles (cf. fig. 3) reflects the expected behaviour, especially vibrations in nick-angle, i. e. the oscillations of ω around the horizontal x-axis orthogonal to the speed vector.
- The approximate values obtained from the image triplets were sufficiently accurate to guarantee convergence of a global ML-estimation with a bundle adjustment (cf. fig. 4).

Appendix

We give the solution for the optimization problem (4) derived from the Gauss-Helmert-model. For solving this nonlinear problem in an iterative manner we need approximate values $\widehat{\beta}^{(0)}$ and $\widehat{y}^{(0)}$ for the unknowns $\widehat{\beta} = \widehat{\beta}^{(0)} + \widehat{\Delta\beta}$ and $\widehat{y} = \widehat{y}^{(0)} + \widehat{\Delta y}$ which obtain corrections $\widehat{\Delta\beta}$ and $\widehat{\Delta y}$ in an iterative manner. With the Jacobians

$$A = \left(\frac{\partial g(\beta, y)}{\partial \beta}\right)\Bigg|_{\substack{\beta=\widehat{\beta}^{(0)}\\y=\widehat{y}^{(0)}}}, B = \left(\frac{\partial g(\beta, y)}{\partial y}\right)\Bigg|_{\substack{\beta=\widehat{\beta}^{(0)}\\y=\widehat{y}^{(0)}}}, H = \left(\frac{\partial h(\beta)}{\partial \beta}\right)\Bigg|_{\beta=\widehat{\beta}^{(0)}} \quad (23)$$

and the relation $\widehat{\Delta y} = (y - \widehat{y}^{(0)}) - \widehat{e}$ we obtain the linear constraints $g(\widehat{\beta}, \widehat{y}) = g(\widehat{\beta}^{(0)}, \widehat{y}^{(0)}) + A\,\widehat{\Delta\beta} + B\,\widehat{\Delta y}$ or $g(\widehat{\beta}, \widehat{y}) = c_g + A\,\widehat{\Delta\beta} - B\widehat{e}$ and $h(\widehat{\beta}) = c_h + H\,\widehat{\Delta\beta}$ with $c_g = g(\widehat{\beta}^{(0)}, \widehat{y}^{(0)}) + B(y - \widehat{y}^{(0)})$ and $c_h = h(\widehat{\beta}^{(0)})$ are the contradictions between the approximate values for the unknown parameters and the given observations and among the approximate values for the unknowns.

Setting the partials of Φ (4) zero yields

$$\frac{\partial \Phi}{\partial \widehat{y}^{\mathsf{T}}} = -Q_{yy}^{-1}\widehat{e} + B^{\mathsf{T}}\lambda = 0 \qquad \frac{\partial \Phi}{\partial \widehat{\beta}^{\mathsf{T}}} = A^{\mathsf{T}}\lambda + H^{\mathsf{T}}\mu = 0 \qquad (24)$$

$$\frac{\partial \Phi}{\partial \lambda^{\mathsf{T}}} = c_g + A\,\widehat{\Delta\beta} - B\widehat{e} = 0 \qquad \frac{\partial \Phi}{\partial \mu^{\mathsf{T}}} = c_h + H\,\widehat{\Delta\beta} = 0 \qquad (25)$$

From (24a) follows the relation

$$\widehat{e} = Q_{yy}B^{\mathsf{T}}\lambda \qquad (26)$$

When substituting (26) into (25a), solving for λ yields

$$\lambda = (B\,Q_{yy}B^{\mathsf{T}})^{-1}(c_g + A\,\widehat{\Delta\beta}) \qquad (27)$$

Substitution in (24b) yields the symmetric normal equation system

$$\begin{pmatrix} A^{\mathsf{T}}(B\,Q_{yy}B^{\mathsf{T}})^{-1}A & H^{\mathsf{T}} \\ H & 0 \end{pmatrix} \begin{pmatrix} \widehat{\Delta\beta} \\ \mu \end{pmatrix} = \begin{pmatrix} -A^{\mathsf{T}}(B\,Q_{yy}B^{\mathsf{T}})^{-1}c_g \\ -c_h \end{pmatrix} \qquad (28)$$

The Lagrangian multipliers can be obtained from (27) which then yields the estimated residuals in (26). The estimated variance factor is given by

$$\widehat{\sigma}^2 = \frac{\widehat{e}^{\mathsf{T}}Q_{yy}^{-1}\widehat{e}}{G + H - U} \qquad (29)$$

The number R of contraints above the number $U - H$, which is nessessary for determinimg the unknown parameters, the *redundancy* is the denominator $R = G - (U - H)$. We finally obtain the *estimated* covariance matrix

$$\widehat{\Sigma}_{\widehat{\beta}\widehat{\beta}} = \widehat{\sigma}^2 Q_{\widehat{\beta}\widehat{\beta}} \qquad (30)$$

of the estimated parameters, where $Q_{\widehat{\beta}\widehat{\beta}}$ results from the inverted reduced normal equation matrix using $\overline{N} = A^{\mathsf{T}}(BQ_{yy}B^{\mathsf{T}})^{-1}A$

$$\begin{pmatrix} Q_{\widetilde{\beta\beta}} & S^{\mathsf{T}} \\ S & T \end{pmatrix} = \begin{pmatrix} \overline{N} & H^{\mathsf{T}} \\ H & 0 \end{pmatrix}^{-1} \tag{31}$$

This expression can be used even if $\overline{N}$ is singular.

References

[1] ABRAHAM, S. (2000): *Kamera-Kalibrierung und Metrische Auswertung von Bildfolgen.* Shaker Verlag, Aachen, 2000.

[2] FAUGERAS, O.; MOURRAIN, B. (1995): On the Geometry and Algebra of the Point and Line Correspondencies between N Images. Technical Report 2665, INRIA, 1995.

[3] FAUGERAS, O.; PAPADOPOULO, T. (1998): Grassmann-Cayley Algebra for Modeling Systems of Cameras and the Algebraic Equations of the Manifold of Trifocal Tensors. *Trans. of the ROYAL SOCIETY A*, 356:1123–1152, 1998.

[4] FÖRSTNER, W.; GÜLCH, E. (1987): A Fast Operator for Detection and Precise Location of Distinct Points, Corners and Circular Features. In: *Proc. of the Intercomm. Conf. on Fast Processing of Photogr. Data, Interlaken*, pages 281–305, 1987.

[5] FÖRSTNER, W. (1999): Choosing Constraints in Image Triplets. Technical report, Institut für Photogrammetrie, Universität Bonn, 1999.

[6] GAUSS, C. F. (1809): *Theoria Motus Corpum Coelestium.* Perthes und Besser, Hamburg, 1809.

[7] HARALICK, R. M.; SHAPIRO, L. G. (1993): *Computer and Robot Vision, Vol. II.* Addison-Wesley Publishing Company, 1993.

[8] HARTLEY, R. (1995): A Linear Method for Reconstruction from Lines and Points. In: *Proc. ICCV*, pages 882–887, 1995.

[9] HELMERT, F. R. (1872): *Die Ausgleichungsrechnung nach der Methode der Kleinsten Quadrate.* Teubner, Leipzig, 1872.

[10] HUBER, P. J. (1981): *Robust Statistics.* Wiley NY, 1981.

[11] MARKOFF, A. A. (1912): *Wahrscheinlichkeitsrechnung.* Teubner, Leipzig, 1912.

[12] MIKHAIL, E. M. (1962): Use of Triplets in Analytical Aerotriangulation. *Photogr. Eng*, 28:625–632, 1962.

[13] MIKHAIL, E. M. (1963): Use of Two-Directional Triplets in a Sub-Block Approach for Analytical Aerotriangulation. *Photogr. Eng*, 29:1014–1024, 1963.

[14] MIKHAIL, E. M.; ACKERMANN, F. (1976): *Observations and Least Squares.* University Press of America, 1976.

[15] SHASHUA, A.; ANANDAN, P. (1996): Trilinear Constraints Revisited: Generalized Trilinear Constraints and the Tensor Brightness Constraint. In: *Proc. Image Understanding Workshop*, 1996.

[16] SHASHUA, A. (1995): Algebraic Functions for Recognition. *IEEE T-PAMI*, 17(8):779–789, 1995.

[17] STEINES, B.; ABRAHAM, S. (1999): Metrischer Trifokaltensor für die Auswertung von Bildfolgen. In: FÖRSTNER/BUHMANN (Eds.), *Mustererkennung '99*, LNCS, 1999.

[18] STEINES, B. (1998): Bewegungsschätzung aus Bildfolgen. Diplomarbeit, Institut für Photogrammetrie, Universität Bonn, 1998.

[19] TAUBIN, G. (1993): An Improved Algorithm for Algebraic Curve and Surface Fitting. In: *Fourth ICCV, Berlin*, pages 658–665, 1993.

[20] TRIGGS, B. (1998): Optimal Estimation of Matching Constraints. In: *SMILE'98: European Workshop on 3D Structure from Multiple Images of Large-Scale Environments*, Springer, LNCS, pages 658–665, 1998.

[21] TORR, P. H. S.; ZISSERMAN, A. (1997): Robust Parametrization and Computation of the Trifocal Tensor. *Image Vision and Computing*, 15:591–605, 1997.

Computation of the Mid-Sagittal Plane in 3D Images of the Brain

Sylvain Prima, Sébastien Ourselin, and Nicholas Ayache

INRIA Sophia Antipolis, EPIDAURE Project,
2004, route des Lucioles, BP 93,
06902, Sophia Antipolis Cedex, France
{sprima,sourseli,na}@sophia.inria.fr

Abstract. We present a new symmetry-based method allowing to automatically compute, reorient and recenter the mid-sagittal plane in anatomical and functional 3D images of the brain. Our approach is composed of two steps. At first, the computation of local similarity measures between the two hemispheres of the brain allows to match homologous anatomical structures or functional areas, by way of a block matching procedure. The output is a set of point-to-point correspondences: the centers of homologous blocks. Subsequently, we define the mid-sagittal plane as the one best superposing the points in one side of the brain and their counterparts in the other side by reflective symmetry. The estimation of the parameters characterizing the plane is performed by a least trimmed squares optimization scheme. This robust technique allows normal or abnormal asymmetrical areas to be treated as outliers, and the plane to be mainly computed from the underlying gross symmetry of the brain. We show on a large database of synthetic images that we can obtain a subvoxel accuracy in a CPU time of about 3 minutes, for strongly tilted heads, noisy and biased images. We present results on anatomical (MR, CT), and functional (SPECT and PET) images.

1 Introduction

1.1 Presentation of the problem

A normal human head exhibits a rough bilateral symmetry. What is easily observable for external structures (ears, eyes, nose...) remains valuable for the brain and its components. It is split into two hemispheres, in which each substructure has a counterpart of approximately the same shape and location in the opposite side (frontal, occipital lobes, ventricles...). They are connected to each other by the corpus callosum, and separated by a grossly planar, mid-sagittal, fissure.

However, it has been reported since the late 19th century that conspicuous morphological differences between the hemispheres make the brain systematically asymmetrical. For example, the wider right frontal and left occipital lobes give rise to a torque effect of the overall brain shape (see Fig. 1). More subtly, the natural variability of the cortex translates into slight differences between hemispheres. In the same way, cerebral dominance has been demonstrated since the work of Paul Broca on the language lateralization (1861), and many brain functions are now thought or known to be located in mainly one of the hemispheres (handedness, visual abilities, *etc.*). The question of whether the anatomical and the functional brain asymmetries relate to each other remains debatable to the point, even if evidences of close connections have been demonstrated quite lately [5]. These studies suggest that symmetry considerations are key to the understanding of cerebral functioning.

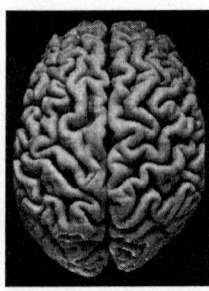 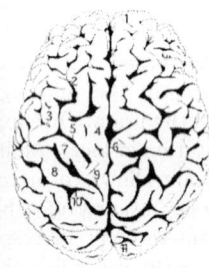

Fig. 1. Torque effect of the brain. The right frontal lobe (1) is larger than the left one, and this is the opposite for the occipital lobe (11). Description of the hemispheres: 1. Frontal pole 2. Superior frontal sulcus 3. Middle frontal gyrus 4. Superior frontal gyrus 5. Precentral sulcus 6. Longitudinal cerebral fissure 7. Precentral gyrus 8. Postcentral gyrus 9. Central sulcus 10. Postcentral sulcus 11. Occipital pole. This illustration comes from the Virtual Hospital [22].

Volumetric medical images convey information about anatomical (MR, CT) or functional (PET, SPECT) symmetries and asymmetries, but they are hidden by the usual tilt of the patient's head in the device during the scanning process. More precisely, the "ideal" coordinate system attached to the head, in which the inter-hemispheric fissure is conveniently displayed, differs from the coordinate system of the image by three angles around the bottom-top (yaw angle, axial rotation), the back-front (roll angle, coronal rotation) and the left-right (pitch angle, sagittal rotation) axes, and three translations along these directions (see Fig. 2). It means that the fissure is generally not displayed in the center of the image lattice. This prevents from further visual inspection or analysis, because the homologous anatomical structures or functional areas in both hemispheres are not displayed in the same axial or coronal slice in the 3D image.

It is of great interest to correctly reorient and recenter brain images, because normal (torque effect, intrinsic variability) and abnormal (unilateral pathologies) departures from symmetry appear more clearly and make the diagnosis easier in many cases: fractures of the skull in CT images, lesions, or bleed in MR images, asymmetries of perfusion in SPECT images, *etc.* Some diseases are assumed to be strongly linked with abnormalities of brain asymmetry, like schizophrenia: in this case, the brain is suspected to be more symmetrical than normal [4]. After the initial tilt has been corrected, it is easier to perform further manual or automatic measurements to compare the two sides of the brain, because relative locations of homologous structures become immediate to assess [6, 12, 19].

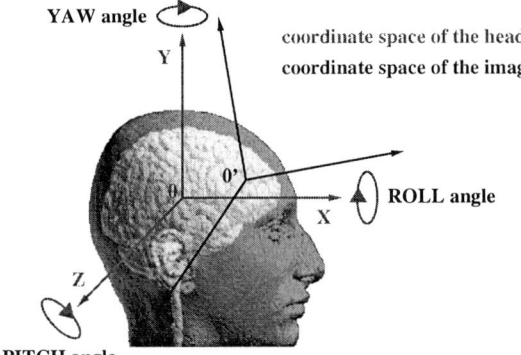

YAW angle

coordinate space of the head
coordinate space of the image

Y

0'

ROLL angle

X

Z

PITCH angle

Fig. 2. The "ideal" coordinate system attached to the head (in which the fissure is close to the plane $Z = 0$) and the coordinate system of the image are deduced to each other by way of three angles (yaw, roll and pitch) and a 3D translation ($\overrightarrow{OO'}$).

Several papers have previously considered the problem of correcting the axial and coronal rotations, and the translation along the left-right axis; we give a brief overview of the state-of-the-art in the next section. We do not tackle the problem of correcting the sagittal rotation (e.g., alignment along the AC-PC line) and the translations along the bottom-top and the back-front axes.

1.2 Existing methods

Most of the existing algorithms share a common methodology. First, a suitable mid-sagittal plane is defined in the brain. Then, this latter is rotated and centered, so that the estimated plane matches the center of the image lattice. There are mainly two classes of methods, differing in their definition of the searched plane. We briefly describe their advantages and drawbacks in the following.

Methods based on the inter-hemispheric fissure The basic hypotheses underlying these methods are that the inter-hemispheric fissure is roughly planar, and that it provides a good landmark for further volumetric symmetry analysis. Generally, the fissure is segmented in MR images, using snakes [6], or a Hough transform [3], and the plane best fitting the segmentation is estimated. As this approach focuses on the inter-hemispheric fissure, the resulting reorientation and recentering of the brain is insensitive to strong asymmetries. Conversely, as the global symmetry of the whole brain is not considered, the resulting algorithms are very sensitive to the often observed curvature of the fissure, which can lead to a meaningless plane (see Fig. 1). At last, these methods are not adaptable to other modalities, where the fissure is not clearly visible.

Methods based on a symmetry criterion There are relatively simple methods of finding a plane of reflective symmetry in case of perfectly symmetrical geometrical objects, in 2D or 3D. In this case, it can be demonstrated that any symmetry plane of a body is perpendicular to a principal axis. In case of medical images, the problem is different, because normal and abnormal asymmetries deviate the underlying symmetry of the brain: a perfect symmetry plane does not exist. To tackle this problem, an intuitive idea is to define the mid-sagittal plane as the one that maximizes the similarity between the image and its symmetric, i.e., the plane with respect to which the brain exhibits maximum symmetry. Practically, this approximate symmetry plane is to be close to the fissure, but is computed using the whole 3D image and no anatomical landmarks.

Most often, the chosen similarity criterion is the cross correlation, computed between either the intensities [1, 7, 8] or other features of the two symmetrical images with respect to a plane with given parameters. For example, the criterion can be computed between the derived Extended Gaussian Image (EGI) and its flipped version [17]: theoretically, if the brain is symmetrical, so is its EGI. Contrary to the first class of methods, the whole 3D volume is taken into account, which means that the overall gross symmetry of the brain is used. Consequently, these methods are less sensitive to the variability of the inter-hemispheric fissure and its curved shape. The trade-off is the need for the criterion to be robust with respect to departures from the gross underlying cerebral symmetry, i.e., the normal and pathological asymmetries of the brain. This robustness is difficult to achieve with global criteria such as the cross correlation, that is affected in the same way by areas in strong (i.e., symmetrical) and weak (i.e., asymmetrical) correlation. These latter can severely bias the estimation of the plane [1]. To overcome this issue, another similarity criterion is proposed in [10]: the stochastic sign change, previously shown to be efficient in case of rigid registration, even for quite dissimilar images [20]. In the same way, a specific symmetry measure introduced in [16] considers mainly strongly symmetrical parts of the brain.

One common drawback of these methods is the computational cost of the algorithms, due to the optimization scheme within the set of possible planes. However, this cost can be often reduced: the discretization of the parameters space (that limits the accuracy of the results) or a prior knowledge about the position of the optimal plane allow to investigate only a limited number of planes. Thus, the reorientation of the principal axes of the brain and the centering of its center of mass is often a useful preprocessing step. A multi-resolution scheme can also accelerate the process [1]. One important feature of these approaches is their ability to tackle other modalities than MR, in particular functional images.

1.3 Overview of the paper

In this article, we present a new symmetry-based method allowing to compute, reorient and recenter the mid-sagittal plane in anatomical and functional images of the brain. This method, generalizing an approach we previously described in [12, 19], is composed of two steps. At first, the computation of local rather than global similarity measures between the two sides of the brain allows to match homologous anatomical structures or functional areas, by way of a block matching procedure. The output is a set of point-to-point correspondences: the centers of homologous blocks. Subsequently, we define the mid-sagittal plane as the one best superposing the points in one hemisphere and their counterparts in the other hemisphere by reflective symmetry. The estimation of the parameters characterizing the plane is performed by a least trimmed squares optimization scheme. Then, the estimated plane is aligned with the center of the image lattice. This method is fully automated, objective and reproducible.

This approach deals with two severe drawbacks of classical symmetry-based methods. First, the computation of local measures of symmetry and the use of a robust estimation technique [15] allow to discriminate between symmetrical and asymmetrical parts of the brain, these latter being naturally treated as outliers. Consequently, the computation of the mid-sagittal plane mainly relies on the underlying gross symmetry of the brain. Second, the regression step yields an analytical solution, computationally less expensive than the maximization of the global similarity measures described in Section 1.2.

We describe this approach in Section 2. In Section 3, we show that we can cope with strongly asymmetrical and tilted brains, even in presence of noise and bias, with very good accuracy and low computation time. In Section 4, we present results on anatomical (MR, CT) and functional (PET, SPECT) images.

2 Description of the method

2.1 Presentation of the main principles

We recall the principles of the method presented in [12, 19]. Given I, an MR image of the head, the mid-sagittal plane P is defined as the one best superposing the pairs $\{a_i, S_P(b_i)\}$, where a_i is a brain voxel, b_i its anatomical counterpart in the other hemisphere, and S_P the symmetry with respect to P. Practically, P is obtained by minimization of the least squares (LS) criterion $\sum_i \|a_i - S_P(b_i)\|^2$; $\|.\|$ is the Euclidian norm. An analytical solution of this problem is described in the appendix. The pairs $\{a_i, b_i\}$ are obtained as follows (see also Fig. 3):

- The mid-sagittal plane K of the image grid (K is fixed to the grid) differs from the searched mid-sagittal plane P of the brain in the tilt of the head during the scanning process, but is usually a good first estimate. The original image I is flipped with respect to K, yielding $S_K(I)$.
- The "demons" algorithm [18] finds the anatomical counterpart b_i' in $S_K(I)$ of each point a_i in I, by way of non-rigid registration between the 2 images.
- $b_i = S_K(b_i')$ is the anatomical counterpart of a_i in the other hemisphere. For example, in I, the point a_i, located at the top of the right ventricle is matched with the point b_i, located at the top of the left ventricle.

Once P is computed, the transformation $R = S_K \circ S_P$ is a rotation if P and K are not parallel and a translation if P and K are parallel. The transformation $R^{1/2}$, when applied to the image I, automatically aligns the plane P with K [19]. Several difficulties and limitations arise when using this method:

- As many of the classical symmetry-based methods, normal and pathological asymmetries can severely disrupt the computation of the plane. Even

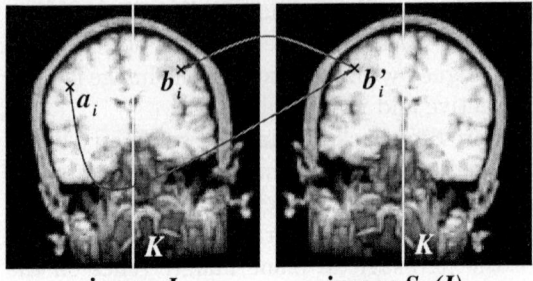

image *I*   **image $S_K(I)$**

Fig. 3. The non-rigid registration strategy. The point b_i' in $S_K(I)$ is matched with the point a_i in I; $b_i = S_K(b_i')$ is the counterpart of a_i in the other hemisphere.

though it is based on local instead of global measures of symmetry, the LS minimization is not robust with respect to outliers [15], and will be strongly affected by the departures from the underlying symmetry.

- The non-rigid registration algorithm will provide aberrant matchings when a structure is absent in one hemisphere (a lesion, one track of white matter, *etc.*), or when two structures are present but too different from each other; these failures are difficult if not impossible to detect. These meaningless correspondences can significantly affect the LS criterion and its minimization.
- At last, the "demons" algorithm mainly relies on the gradient of the image, and proved to be efficient for low-textured images like MR or CT. Consequently, this approach is not applicable to SPECT or PET images.

2.2 Modification based on a block matching strategy and a robust estimation technique

We propose a modification of this approach, allowing to compute the mid-sagittal plane mainly from correspondences between very symmetrical areas, and to tackle both functional and anatomical images. The methodology is twofold: we still find point-to-point correspondences between the two sides of the brain, and then derive the plane best superposing the pairs of matched points, but the matching and the optimization procedures significantly differ from Section 2.1.

Computation of inter-hemispheric correspondences by a block matching strategy. The pairs of correspondences $\{a_i, b_i'\}$ are obtained by way of a block matching strategy between the image I and its symmetric $S_K(I)$. This procedure is extensively described in [11], in case of rigid registration of anatomical sections. The common lattice of the 2 images (of size $X \times Y \times Z$) defines a set of rectangular parallelepipedic blocks of voxels $\{\mathcal{B}\}$ in I and $\{\mathcal{B}'\}$ in $S_K(I)$, given their size $N_x \times N_y \times N_z$: both images contain $(X - N_x + 1) \times (Y - N_y + 1) \times (Z - N_z + 1)$ such blocks. We aim at matching each block in $\{\mathcal{B}\}$ with the block in $\{\mathcal{B}'\}$ maximizing a given similarity measure, which yields a "displacement field" between I and $S_K(I)$. Practically, it is not computationally feasible to make an exhaustive search of matchings within $\{\mathcal{B}'\}$ for each block of $\{\mathcal{B}\}$. In addition, we have an *a priori* knowledge about the position of the correspondent $\mathcal{B}'$ of $\mathcal{B}$:

if the head is not too tilted, $\mathcal{B}'$ is to be located in a neighborhood of $\mathcal{B}$. Thus we constrain the search procedure to subsets defined as follows:

- We limit the search for correspondences to one block $\mathcal{B}$ every Δ_x (resp. Δ_y, Δ_z) voxels in the x (resp. y, z) direction, defining a subset of $\{\mathcal{B}\}$; $\Delta = (\Delta_x, \Delta_y, \Delta_z)$ determines the density of the computed "displacement field" between I and $S_K(I)$.
- For each block $\mathcal{B}$ in this subset, we define a sub-image in $S_K(I)$, centered on $\mathcal{B}$, which delimits a neighborhood of research. This sub-image is composed of the voxels in $S_K(I)$ located within a distance of Ω_x (resp. Ω_y, Ω_z) voxels in the x (resp. y, z) direction from $\mathcal{B}$. This yields a rectangular parallelepipedic sub-image of size $(N_x + 2\Omega_x) \times (N_y + 2\Omega_y) \times (N_z + 2\Omega_z)$ in $S_K(I)$, which contains $(2\Omega_x + 1) \times (2\Omega_y + 1) \times (2\Omega_z + 1)$ blocks $\mathcal{B}'$ (provided this sub-image is entirely located in $S_K(I)$).
- In this sub-image, we examine one block $\mathcal{B}'$ every Σ_x (resp. Σ_y, Σ_z) voxels in the x (resp. y, z) direction; $\Sigma = (\Sigma_x, \Sigma_y, \Sigma_z)$ determines the resolution of the displacement field.

Note that the subset of $\{\mathcal{B}\}$ in I and the subset of $\{\mathcal{B}'\}$ in the sub-image of $S_K(I)$ contain the following number of blocks, respectively:

$$\max\{n_x | (n_x - 1)\Delta_x + N_x \le X\}$$
$$\times \max\{n_y | (n_y - 1)\Delta_y + N_y \le Y\} \quad \text{and}$$
$$\times \max\{n_z | (n_z - 1)\Delta_z + N_z \le Z\}$$

$$\max\{n_x | (n_x - 1)\Sigma_x \le 2\Omega_x\}$$
$$\times \max\{n_y | (n_y - 1)\Sigma_y \le 2\Omega_y\}$$
$$\times \max\{n_z | (n_z - 1)\Sigma_z \le 2\Omega_z\}$$

We note $\mathcal{B}_{ijk}$ (resp. $\mathcal{B}'_{lnm}$) the block in I (resp. $S_K(I)$) containing the voxel (i, j, k) (resp. (l, n, m)) at its top left back corner. We summarize the features of the algorithm as follows:

- For $(i = 0; i \le X - N_x; i = i + \Delta_x)$
- For $(j = 0; j \le Y - N_y; j = j + \Delta_y)$
- For $(k = 0; k \le Z - N_z; k = k + \Delta_z)$
- We consider the block $\mathcal{B}_{ijk}$ in I
    - For $(l = i - \Omega_x; l \le i + \Omega_x; l = l + \Sigma_x)$
    - For $(m = j - \Omega_y; m \le j + \Omega_y; m = m + \Sigma_y)$
    - For $(n = k - \Omega_z; n \le k + \Omega_z; n = n + \Sigma_z)$
    - If the block $\mathcal{B}'_{lnm}$ in $S_K(I)$ is entirely located in the image lattice, we compute a similarity measure with $\mathcal{B}_{ijk}$
- We retain the block $\mathcal{B}'_{lnm}$ with maximal similarity measure, which defines the displacement vector between the center $(i + N_x/2, j + N_y/2, k + N_z/2)$ of $\mathcal{B}_{ijk}$ and the center $(l + N_x/2, n + N_y/2, m + N_z/2)$ of $\mathcal{B}'_{lnm}$.

A given choice of parameters $N = (N_x, N_y, N_z)$, $\Omega = (\Omega_x, \Omega_y, \Omega_z)$, $\Delta = (\Delta_x, \Delta_y, \Delta_z)$, $\Sigma = (\Sigma_x, \Sigma_y, \Sigma_z)$, whose interpretation will be given later, yields pairs of correspondences (a_i, b'_i) between I and $S_K(I)$, a_i and b'_i being the centers of matched blocks. The output of this scheme is a displacement field, which conveys local information about brain symmetry or asymmetry. The points $\{b'_i\}$

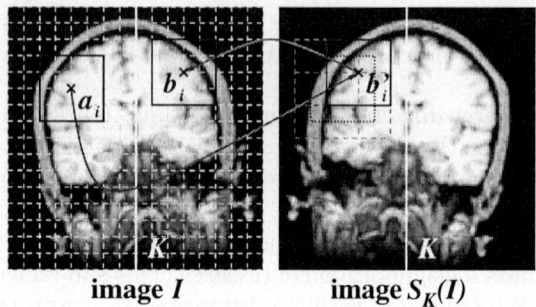

image *I*   **image $S_K(I)$**

Fig. 4. The block matching. The point b_i' in $S_K(I)$ is homologous to the point a_i in I; $b_i = S_K(b_i')$ is the counterpart of a_i in the other hemisphere. I contains 128^3 voxels. The chosen parameters are: $N = (32, 32, 32)$, $\Delta = (8, 8, 8)$, $\Omega = (8, 8, 8)$, $\Sigma = (16, 16, 16)$. In I, the subset of $\{\mathcal{B}\}$ is defined by the dashed grid (parameters Δ). Around the block of center a_i, superposed on $S_K(I)$ with dotted lines, a neighborhood of research is delimited (parameters Ω). In this sub-image of $S_K(I)$, the search is completed on the subset of $\{\mathcal{B}'\}$ defined by the small dashed grid (parameters Σ). For each of the $13^3 = 2197$ such defined blocks in I, the search is done on $2^3 = 8$ blocks in $S_K(I)$.

are then flipped back with respect to K, giving the points $\{b_i = S_K(b_i')\}$; b_i is the counterpart of a_i in the opposite side of the brain (see Fig. 4).

Different intensity-based criteria can be chosen as a similarity measure, such as the Correlation Coefficient (CC) [2], the Correlation Ratio (CR) [14] or the Mutual Information (MI) [21, 9]. Each of these measures assumes an underlying relationship between the voxel intensities of the 2 images, respectively affine (CC), functional (CR), or statistical (MI) [13]. Practically, the CR and the MI are well suited to multimodal registration, whereas the CC is suited to monomodal registration. In our case, I and $S_K(I)$ have the same "modality": an affine, or locally affine relationship can be assumed, and we use the CC.

This block matching approach, based on local similarity measures, allows to exclude very asymmetrical and meaningless areas from the computation of the plane. First, if no block $\mathcal{B}'$ in the subset defined in $S_K(I)$ exhibits a high |CC| with a given block $\mathcal{B}$ in the subset defined in I, its center is eliminated straightforwardly, by setting a convenient threshold. In practice, this happens when the structures existing in one given block in I are absent from any block in $S_K(I)$, which is the case for strongly asymmetrical areas. This elimination is not easily feasible in [12, 19], where it is difficult to detect where the non-rigid algorithm fails. Thus, the estimation step, performed with these preselected interhemispheric correspondences, is mainly based on symmetrical areas. The robust estimation technique we use (a least trimmed squares minimization) allows to exclude the remaining asymmetrical areas from the computation of the plane.

Robust estimation of the mid-sagittal plane. A least trimmed squares (LTS) strategy is used to find the plane P best superposing the points $\{a_i\}$ and their counterparts $\{b_i\}$. This minimization scheme has been proven to be far more robust to outliers than the classical LS method [15]. In our problem, we have to deal with two kinds of outlying measures. First, aberrant matchings can be obtained if the head is strongly tilted. Second, even after the initial short-listing that eliminates blocks with low |CC|, blocks conveying strong asymmetries can remain. This happens when a structure is present in both hemispheres, but in different locations: the two matched blocks containing this structure are likely to exhibit a high |CC|. The use of a robust estimation technique enables the computed plane to be only based on the underlying gross symmetry of the brain, the asymmetries being treated as outliers. The LTS scheme we use is:

- The plane P minimizing $\sum_i ||a_i - S_P(b_i)||^2$ is computed (see Appendix).
- The residuals $r_i = ||a_i - S_P(b_i)||$ are trimmed, and P is recomputed as previously, using only the voxels i with the 50% smaller residuals.
- After several iterations, the scheme stops when the angle between the normal vectors of two successively estimated planes is lower than a fixed threshold; we consider that they are "sufficiently close" to each other.

This strategy is able to cope with up to 50% of outliers [15]. To improve the accuracy of the estimation, we iterate the process (Fig. 5). As previously noted, after a first estimation P_1 of the mid-sagittal plane, the transformation $R_1 = (S_K \circ S_{P_1})^{1/2}$ is such that $P_1 = K$ in $R(I)$ (we recall that K is fixed to the image grid). We make a new block matching between $R_1(I)$ and $S_K(R_1(I))$, K being the firstly estimated plane P_1, and a new estimation P_2 by the LTS procedure. The transformation $R_2 = (S_K \circ S_{P_2})^{1/2}$ is such that $P_2 = K$ in $R_2 \circ R_1(I)$. After several iterations, the mid-sagittal plane P_n is computed from the image $(R_{n-1} \circ ... \circ R_1)(I)$. The final estimate is the plane K in $(R_n \circ ... \circ R_1)(I)$. The composition of the successively estimated rigid transformations R_i avoids multiple resampling. Usually, we choose a fixed number of iterations.

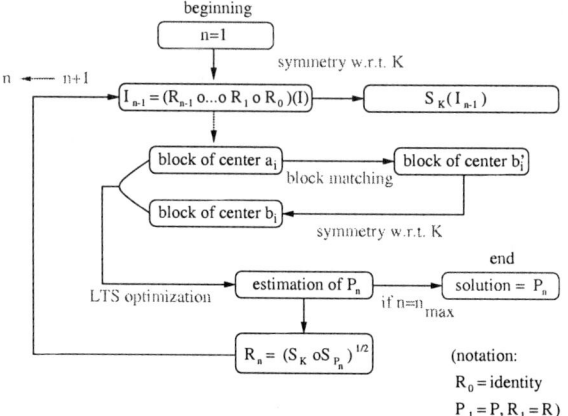

Fig. 5. General scheme. We describe the iterative process for one given choice of parameters (i.e., at one given scale). Usually, we fix the number of iterations: typically, $n_{max} = 5$ yields good results (see Section 3).

Multiscale scheme. Given a set of parameters N, Ω, Δ, Σ, the complexity of the block matching process is proportional to $\frac{(N_x N_y N_z)(\Omega_x \Omega_y \Omega_z)}{(\Delta_x \Delta_y \Delta_z)(\Sigma_x \Sigma_y \Sigma_z)}$ [11]. Intuitively, when I is strongly tilted, I and $S_K(I)$ are far from each other, and the neighborhood of research must be large (parameters Σ), to deal with strong differences in translation and rotation. We also expect large blocks (parameters N) to give more sensible CC than small ones. On the contrary, when I is already well aligned, we can restrict the neighborhood of research, and have more confidence in the CC computed on small blocks.

We implemented a multiscale scheme to achieve a good trade-off between accuracy and complexity. Initially, when the head is suspected to be strongly tilted, we make a first estimation of the mid-sagittal plane with large values of N, Ω, Δ, Σ. This raw estimate P_n^1, based on a displacement field with low density and low resolution, is the center of $(R_n^1 \circ ... \circ R^1)(I)$ (n is the number of iterations at a given scale). Then, we decrease the parameters so that the complexity remains constant: the new estimate P_n^2 is the center of $(R_n^2 \circ ... \circ R^2 \circ R_n^1 \circ ... \circ R^1)(I)$, and so on. At the last scale, the estimation is based on a displacement field of high density and high resolution, and is likely to be accurate. Usually, we make the following choices, for isotropic as well as anisotropic images:

- The initial values of the parameters are:
  - $N = ([X/4], [Y/4], [Z/4])$ or $N = ([X/8], [Y/8], [Z/8])$ (see Section 3)
  - $\Omega = N$, $\Delta = \Sigma = N/4$
- At each iteration, they are automatically updated as follows:
  $N \leftarrow N/2$, $\Omega \leftarrow \Omega/2$, $\Delta \leftarrow \Delta/2$, $\Sigma \leftarrow \Sigma/2$.
- The updating in the direction x (resp. y, z) stops when N_x (resp. N_y, N_z) is smaller than 4 at the next scale. At this level, the small block size makes the computed CC become meaningless. The whole process stops when there is no updating in any direction. For an image of size 128^3 and for each of the 2 choices we usually make for initial parameters, we get 4 and 3 scales respectively, and $\Delta = \Sigma = (1,1,1)$ at the last scale: this means that we obtain a displacement field of very high density and resolution.

3   Validation: robustness and accuracy analysis

3.1   Materials

In this section, we present a series of experiments on simulated data, to show the robustness and the accuracy of the algorithm. Moreover, we aim at finding a set of optimal parameters for the computation of the plane and showing that the algorithm is robust with respect to a relatively high level of noise and bias. This simulated dataset contains 1152 synthetic MR images, generated as follows.

First, a perfectly symmetrical image I_1 is created. We consider an original MR image I of size 256^3, with voxel size 0.78mm^3, provided by Dr. Neil Roberts, Magnetic Resonance and Image Analysis Research Centre (University of Liverpool, UK). Running our algorithm on very high resolution images implies a prohibitive computation time; we resample I to get a new image of size 128^3. In this latter, a mid-sagittal plane is determined by visual inspection, and matched with the center of the image grid. One half of the brain is removed; the other one is flipped with respect to the center, perfect symmetry plane of this new image I_1, which constitutes the ground truth for our validation experiments.

Second, artificial lesions with different grey levels and local expansions and shrinkings are added inside the brain to create strong focal asymmetries. Third, an additive, stationary, Gaussian white noise ($\sigma = 3$) is added, on top of the intrinsic noise in I_1. Fourth, a roll, a yaw angle and a translation along the left-right axis are applied. We choose the angles in the set $\{0, 3, 6,..., 21\}$ (in degrees), and the translations in the set $\{0, 4, 8,..., 20\}$ (in voxels): the 384 possible combinations constitute the dataset $\mathbf{A}$; the applied noise is different for each image. Resampling I_1 to the size 64^3 gives the image I_2. Adding the same lesions and deformations, random noise with the same characteristics, and applying the same rotations, and translations of 0, 2,..., 10 voxels, we get a second dataset ($\mathbf{B}$) of 384 images (the transformation with parameters (yaw,roll,translation)=$(\alpha, \beta, 2t)$ applied to I_1 and (α, β, t) applied to I_2 are the same). At last, a strong multiplicative bias field (linear in x, y and z) is added to I_2 before applying the transformation, which creates a third dataset ($\mathbf{C}$) of 384 images. In brief:

- dataset A: I_1 + lesions + deformations + noise + 2 rotations + 1 translation
- dataset B: I_2 + lesions + deformations + noise + 2 rotations + 1 translation
- dataset C: I_2 + lesions + deformations + noise + bias + 2 rotations + 1 translation

3.2 Methods

The following experiments are devised (with $n_{max} = 5$ iterations at each scale):

- Experiment 1: dataset A with $(N, \Omega, \Delta, \Sigma) = (32, 32, 8, 8)$
- Experiment 2: dataset A with $(N, \Omega, \Delta, \Sigma) = (16, 16, 4, 4)$
- Experiment 3: dataset B with $(N, \Omega, \Delta, \Sigma) = (16, 16, 4, 4)$
- Experiment 4: dataset C with $(N, \Omega, \Delta, \Sigma) = (16, 16, 4, 4)$

For each experiment, the computed roll, yaw angles and translation along the left-right axis aligning the estimated mid-sagittal plane are compared with the applied ones, giving a measure of **accuracy** of the algorithm. For this purpose, the computed rigid transformation is composed with the applied one. The norm of the yaw and roll angles of the rotation component of this composition and the norm of its translation component along the left-right axis are computed; the closer to zero these 3 parameters are, the more accurate the result is. Another measure of accuracy ϵ is described in Fig. 7. We consider that an experiment is successful when ϵ is lower than a given threshold, typically, 1 voxel. The maximal value δ_{max} of δ (which measures the initial tilt of the head) for which the algorithm succeeds gives an idea of the **robustness** of the algorithm.

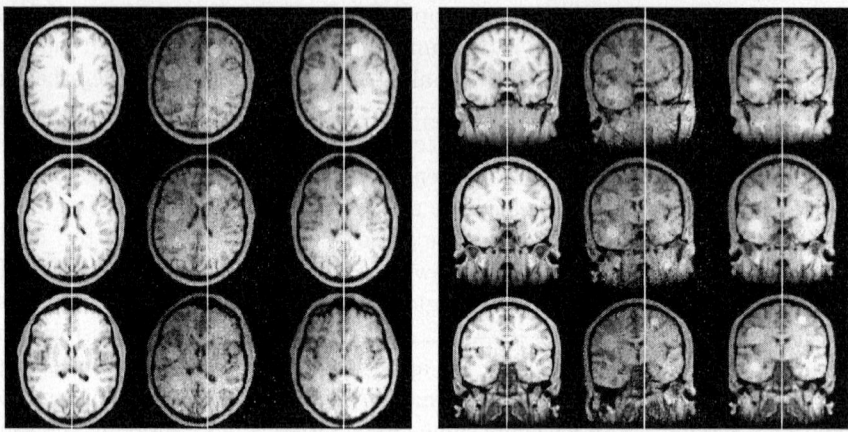

Fig. 6. Realignment of a synthetic MR image. Artificial lesions, local deformations, noise and bias are added to a perfectly symmetrical MR image of size 128^3. Roll and yaw angles of 6 degrees, and translation along the left-right axis of 6 voxels are applied to this image. The initial parameters of the block matching algorithm are $(N, \Omega, \Delta, \Sigma) = (16, 16, 4, 4)$. The errors of the computed transform, compared to the applied one are: 4.10^{-2} degrees (roll angle), 3.10^{-2} degrees (yaw angle), 10^{-1} voxels (translation), and 2.10^{-1} voxels (error ϵ, see Fig. 7). We display 2 panels with axial (left) and coronal (right) views. In each panel, from left to right, we have the original image with added lesions and deformations, the tilted image with added noise and bias, and the realigned and recentered image.

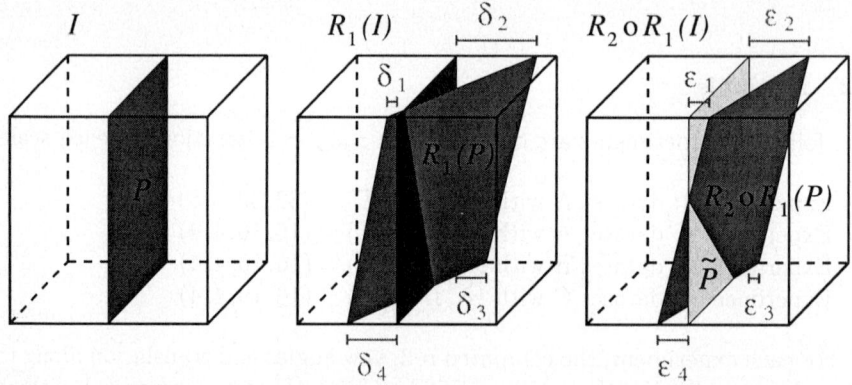

Fig. 7. A measure of accuracy. A synthetic image I is generated, in which the central plane P is the sought symmetry plane of the brain, as described in the text (left sketch). We apply yaw, roll angles, and a translation along the left-right axis, which yields a rigid transformation R_1. In $R_1(I)$, the real symmetry plane $R_1(P)$ is no longer aligned with the center of the image grid (central sketch). The maximum δ of the four distances $\delta_1, \delta_2, \delta_3, \delta_4$ measures the tilt of the head in $R_1(I)$ before we run the algorithm. We estimate a symmetry plane $\tilde{P}$ and a rigid transformation R_2 so that $\tilde{P}$ is displayed in the center of $R_2 \circ R_1(I)$ (right sketch). The estimated plane $\tilde{P}$ is generally different from the real one $R_2 \circ R_1(P)$. The maximum ϵ of the four distances $\epsilon_1, \epsilon_2, \epsilon_3, \epsilon_4$ gives a good idea of the maximal error in the whole volume of the image.

Comparing the experiments 1 and 2 (resp. 1 and 3) shows the influence of the initial size of the blocks (resp. subsampling) on the accuracy, the robustness and the computation time of the algorithm. This aims at indicating which set of parameters is best adapted to real medical images. Comparing the experiments 3 and 4 shows the sensitivity of the algorithm to bias effects. The experiments were led on a standard PC (OS Linux), 450 MHz, 256 MBytes of RAM.

3.3 Results and interpretation

Experiment 1 *vs* 2. The algorithm proved to be highly robust for the experiment 1. It never failed when δ was lower than 51 voxels, which corresponds (for example) to parameters (yaw,roll,translation)$=(15, 15, 16), (18, 18, 8)$ or $(21, 21, 0)$. In real images, the tilt of the head is usually smaller. We noticed that the convergence of the algorithm is the same for parameters (α, β, t) and (β, α, t): the yaw and roll angles play symmetric roles. Note that this convergence is not deterministic in our experiments, because the random noise is added separately on each image of the datasets. Thus, the algorithm did not fail systematically for more extreme parameters; for example, it succeeded for the parameters $(21, 21, 20)$. For the experiment 2, the rate of success is significantly reduced: it systematically succeeded when δ was lower than 42, which approximately corresponds to parameters $(12, 12, 16), (15, 15, 18)$ or $(18, 18, 0)$. The small initial block size and the restricted neighborhood of research explain that the algorithm is unable to deal with too tilted heads. Compared to experiment 1, there is one less scale to explore, and the average computation time is reduced, but still prohibitive (about 34 min). The obtained accuracy is about the same compared to experiment 1. Thus, the set of initial parameters $N = ([X/4], [Y/4], [Z/4])$ seems to be best adapted at a given resolution of the image.

Experiment 1 *vs* 3. For these two datasets, studied with optimal initial block size, the robustness is about the same, surprisingly. The subsampling does not reduce significantly the efficiency of the algorithm, which can fail when δ is superior to 25 voxels, which corresponds to parameters $(15, 15, 8), (18, 18, 4)$ or $(21, 21, 0)$, comparable with the parameters of experiment 1. The accuracy is divided by two in experiment 3 compared to experiments 1 and 2, but remains very high (see Table 1). At last, the computation time is strongly reduced (by a factor of 10). This suggests that highly subsampled images (from 256^3 to 64^3) are enough for a satisfying reorientation and recentering.

Experiment 3 *vs* 4. The algorithm is very robust with respect to a relatively high bias. This is an important feature of this local approach. Locally, the intensity variations are smaller than on the whole image, and the CC is still a sensible measure. The accuracy and the computation time are similar.

Conclusion. We draw several conclusions from these experiments: the accuracy is always very high when the algorithm succeeds. For a usual MR image of size

256^3, with voxel size 0.78mm^3 and with an initial tilt of δ lower than about 100 voxels, which corresponds to realistic conditions of $\delta = 50$ (resp. 25) voxels in the subsampled image of size 128^3 (resp. 64^3), our algorithm is likely to succeed. Using the subsampled image of size 64^3, with $(16, 16, 4, 4)$ as initial parameters and 5 iterations at each scale, we reach a precision of about $\epsilon = 10.10^{-2} \times 4 \times 0.78 \simeq 0.3$ mm (see Table 1 and Fig. 7) for successful experiments, within a CPU time of about 3 minutes. For strongly tilted images, an initial alignment along the principal axes of the brain can be a useful preprocessing.

Exp.	Robustness (δ_{max})	Accuracy (RMS errors)				CPU Time
		Roll Angle	Yaw Angle	Translation	ϵ	
1	51 voxels	4.10^{-2}	4.10^{-2}	5.10^{-2}	11.10^{-2}	45'
2	42 voxels	3.10^{-2}	4.10^{-2}	5.10^{-2}	10.10^{-2}	34'
3	25 voxels	11.10^{-2}	9.10^{-2}	6.10^{-2}	13.10^{-2}	3'
4	25 voxels	11.10^{-2}	8.10^{-2}	7.10^{-2}	11.10^{-2}	3'

Table 1. Validation on simulated data. The RMS errors (indicated for successful experiments only) are measured in degrees for the angles and voxels for the left-right translation and the value ϵ (see Fig. 7). The errors are doubled between experiments on 128^3 and 64^3 images, including for the translation and ϵ (the errors in voxels are about the same, and the errors in mm are doubled for half resolution images).

4 Results and acknowledgements

In this section, we present results for real anatomical (MR, CT) and functional (SPECT, PET) images. For each illustration, we present axial (top) and coronal (bottom) views, for the initial 3D image (left) and the reoriented and recentered version (right) (see Fig. 8). The MR image has been provided by Dr. Neil Roberts, Magnetic Resonance and Image Analysis Research Centre (University of Liverpool, UK), and is of size 256^3, with voxel size 0.78mm^3. The CT image comes from the Radiology Research Imaging Lab (Mallinckrodt Institute of Radiology, Saint Louis, Missouri, USA), and is of size $256 \times 256 \times 203$, with voxel size $0,6\text{mm}^3$. The SPECT image has been provided by Pr. Michael L. Goris, Department of Nuclear Medicine (Stanford University Hospital, USA), and is of size 64^3. At last, the PET image has been provided by the Hammersmith Hospital in London, UK, and the Unité 230 of INSERM, Toulouse, France. It is of size $128 \times 128 \times 15$, with voxel size $2.05\text{mm} \times 2.05\text{mm} \times 6.75\text{mm}$.

5 Conclusion

We have presented a new symmetry-based method allowing to compute, reorient and recenter the mid-sagittal plane in volumetric anatomical and functional images of the brain. Our approach relies on the matching of homologous anatomical structures or functional areas in both sides of the brain (or the skull), and a

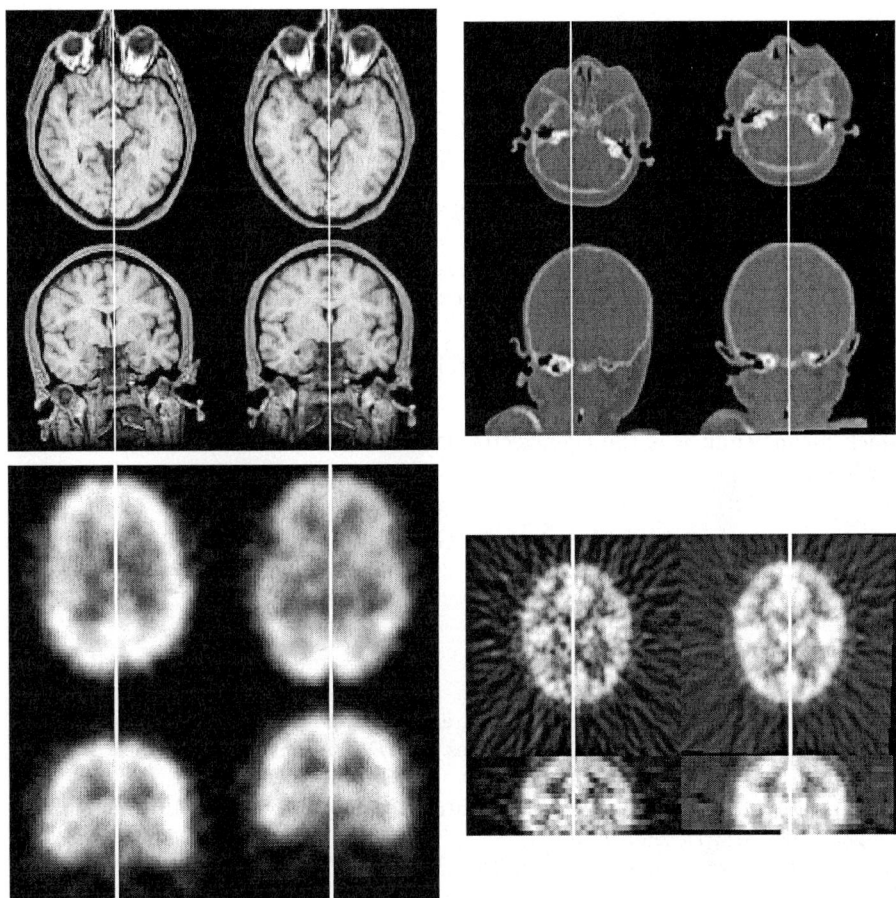

Fig. 8. Results on real images. From left to right, top to bottom: isotropic MR, CT, SPECT images, and anisotropic PET image. See Section 4 for details.

robust estimation of the plane best superposing these pairs of counterparts. The algorithm is iterative, multiscale, fully automated, and provides a useful tool for further symmetry-based analysis of the brain. We showed on a large database of synthetic images that we could obtain a subvoxel accuracy in a CPU time of about 3 minutes for strongly tilted heads, noisy and biased images. We have presented results on isotropic or anisotropic MR, CT, SPECT and PET images; the method will be tested on functional MR and ultrasound images in the future.

Appendix: LS estimation of the mid-sagittal plane

We want to minimize $C = \sum_i (S(b_i) - a_i)^2$, with $S(b_i) = b_i - 2((b_i - p)^\top n)n$ and where p is a point in the plane and n the unit normal vector to the plane. By differentiating C with respect to p, we get:

$$\frac{dC}{dp} = 4\sum_i (2p - b_i - a_i)^\top nn^\top$$

which demonstrates that the barycenter $G = \frac{1}{n}\sum_i \frac{(b_i+a_i)}{2}$ belongs to the plane. Substituting G in the first equation, we get:

$$C = \sum_i (b_i - a_i)^2 + 4[(b_i - G)^\top n][(a_i - G)^\top n]$$

which is minimized when the following expression is minimized:

$$\sum_i n^\top[(a_i - G)(b_i - G)^\top]n$$

which means than n is the eigenvector associated to the smallest eigenvalue of I, where:

$$I = \sum_i (a_i - G)(b_i - G)^\top$$

References

1. B.A. Ardenaki, J. Kershaw, M. Braun, and I. Kanno. Automatic Detection of the Mid-Sagittal Plane in 3-D Brain Images. *IEEE Transactions on Medical Imaging*, 16(6):947–952, December 1997.
2. L.G. Brown. A survey of image registration techniques. *ACM Computing Surveys*, 24(4):325–375, December 1992.
3. M.E. Brummer. Hough Transform Detection of the Longitudinal Fissure in Tomographic Head Images. *IEEE Transactions on Medical Imaging*, 10(1):74–81, March 1991.
4. T.J. Crow. Schizophrenia as an anomaly of cerebral asymmetry. In K. Maurer, editor, *Imaging of the Brain in Psychiatry and Related Fields*, pages 1–17. Springer-Verlag, Berlin Heidelberg, 1993.
5. N. Geschwind and W. Levitsky. Left-right asymmetry in temporal speech region. *Science*, 161:186–187, 1968.
6. R. Guillemaud, A. Marais, P. amd Zisserman, B. McDonald, and T.J. Crow. A 3-Dimensional Midsagittal Plane For Brain Asymmetry Measurement. *Schizophrenia Research*, 18(2-3):183–184, 1995.
7. L. Junck, J.G. Moen, G.D. Hutchins, M.B. Brown, and D.E. Kuhl. Correlation Methods for the Centering, Rotation, and Alignment of Functional Brain Images. *Journal of Nuclear Medicine*, 31:1220–1226, July 1990.
8. Y. Liu, R.T. Collins, and W.E. Rothfus. Automatic Bilateral Symmetry (Midsagittal) Plane Extraction from Pathological 3D Neuroradiological Images. In *SPIE, International Symposium on Medical Imaging*, San-Diego, CA, February 1998.
9. F. Maes, A. Collignon, Vandermeulen. D., G. Marchal, and P. Suetens. Multimodality Image Registration by Maximization of Mutual Information. *IEEE Transactions on Medical Imaging*, 16(2):187–198, April 1997.

10. S. Minoshima, K.L. Berger, K.S. Lee, and M.A. Mintun. An Automated Method for Rotational Correction and Centering of Three-Dimensional Functional Brain Images. *Journal of Nuclear Medicine*, 33:1579–1585, August 1992.

11. S. Ourselin, A. Roche, G. Subsol, and X. Pennec. Automatic Alignment of Histological Sections. In F. Pernuš, S. Kovačič, H.S. Stiehl, and M.A. Viergever, editors, *International Workshop on Biomedical Image Registration, WBIR'99*, pages 1–13, Bled, Slovenia, August 1999. Electronic version: http://www.inria.fr/RRRT/RR-3595.html.

12. S. Prima, J.-P. Thirion, G. Subsol, and N. Roberts. Automatic Analysis of Normal Brain Dissymmetry of Males and Females in MR Images. In W.M. Wells, A. Colchester, and S. Delp, editors, *First International Conference on Medical Image Computing and Computer-Assisted Intervention, MICCAI'98*, volume 1496 of *Lecture Notes in Computer Science*, pages 770–779, Boston, USA, October 1998. Springer.

13. A. Roche, G. Malandain, N. Ayache, and S. Prima. Towards a Better Comprehension of Similarity Measures Used in Medical Image Registration. In C. Taylor and A. Colchester, editors, *Second International Conference on Medical Image Computing and Computer-Assisted Intervention, MICCAI'99*, volume 1679 of *Lecture Notes in Computer Science*, pages 555–566, Cambridge, UK, September 1999. Springer. Electronic version: http://www.inria.fr/RRRT/RR-3741.html.

14. A. Roche, G. Malandain, X. Pennec, and N. Ayache. The Correlation Ratio as a New Similarity Measure for Multimodal Image Registration. In W.M. Wells, A. Colchester, and S. Delp, editors, *First International Conference on Medical Image Computing and Computer-Assisted Intervention, MICCAI'98*, volume 1496 of *Lecture Notes in Computer Science*, pages 1115–1124, Boston, USA, October 1998. Springer. Electronic version: http://www.inria.fr/RRRT/RR-3378.html.

15. P.J. Rousseeuw and A.M. Leroy. *Robust Regression and Outlier Detection*. Wiley Series In Probability And Mathematical Statistics, 1987.

16. S. Smith and M. Jenkinson. Accurate Robust Symmetry Estimation. In C. Taylor and A. Colchester, editors, *Second International Conference on Medical Image Computing and Computer-Assisted Intervention, MICCAI'99*, volume 1679 of *Lecture Notes in Computer Science*, pages 308–317, Cambridge, UK, September 1999. Springer.

17. C. Sun and J. Sherrah. 3D Symmetry Detection Using The Extended Gaussian Image. *IEEE Transactions on Pattern Analysis and Machine Intelligence*, 19(2):164–168, 1997.

18. J.-P. Thirion. Image matching as a diffusion process: an analogy with Maxwell's demons. *Medical Image Analysis (MedIA)*, 2(3):243–260, September 1998.

19. J.-P. Thirion, S. Prima, G. Subsol, and N. Roberts. Statistical Analysis of Normal and Abnormal Dissymmetry in Volumetric Medical Images. *Medical Image Analysis (MedIA)*, 4(2), 2000. Electronic version: http://www.inria.fr/RRRT/RR-3178.html.

20. A. Venot, J.F. Lebruchec, and J.C. Roucayrol. A New Class of Similarity Measures for Robust Image Registration. *Computer Vision, Graphics, and Image Processing*, 28(2):176–184, 1984.

21. W.M. Wells III, P. Viola, H. Atsumi, S. Nakajima, and R. Kikinis. Multi-modal volume registration by maximization of mutual information. In *Medical Image Analysis*, volume 1, pages 35–51. Oxford University Press, March 1996.

22. T.H. Williams, N. Gluhbegovic, and J.Y. Jew. Virtual Hospital. 1997. University of Iowa. WEB access: http://www.vh.org/Providers/Textbooks/BrainAnatomy/-BrainAnatomy.html.

Stochastic Tracking of 3D Human Figures Using 2D Image Motion

Hedvig Sidenbladh[1]   Michael J. Black[2]   David J. Fleet[2]

[1] Royal Institute of Technology (KTH), CVAP/NADA, S–100 44 Stockholm, Sweden
hedvig@nada.kth.se
[2] Xerox Palo Alto Research Center, 3333 Coyote Hill Rd., Palo Alto, CA 94304 USA
{black,fleet}@parc.xerox.com

Abstract. A probabilistic method for tracking 3D articulated human figures in monocular image sequences is presented. Within a Bayesian framework, we define a generative model of image appearance, a robust likelihood function based on image graylevel differences, and a prior probability distribution over pose and joint angles that models how humans move. The posterior probability distribution over model parameters is represented using a discrete set of samples and is propagated over time using particle filtering. The approach extends previous work on parameterized optical flow estimation to exploit a complex 3D articulated motion model. It also extends previous work on human motion tracking by including a perspective camera model, by modeling limb self occlusion, and by recovering 3D motion from a monocular sequence. The explicit posterior probability distribution represents ambiguities due to image matching, model singularities, and perspective projection. The method relies only on a frame-to-frame assumption of brightness constancy and hence is able to track people under changing viewpoints, in grayscale image sequences, and with complex unknown backgrounds.

1   Introduction

We present a Bayesian approach to tracking 3D articulated human figures in monocular video sequences. The human body is represented by articulated cylinders viewed under perspective projection. A *generative model* is defined in terms of the shape, appearance, and motion of the body, and a model of noise in the pixel intensities. This leads to a likelihood function that specifies the probability of observing an image given the model parameters. A prior probability distribution over model parameters depends on the temporal dynamics of the body and the history of body shapes and motions. With this likelihood function and temporal prior, we formulate the posterior distribution over model parameters at each time instant, given the observation history.

The estimation of 3D human motion from a monocular sequence of 2D images is challenging for a variety of reasons. These include the non-linear dynamics of the limbs, ambiguities in the mapping from the 2D image to the 3D model, the similarity of the appearance of different limbs, self occlusions, kinematic singularities, and image noise. One consequence of these difficulties is that, in general, we expect the posterior probability distribution over model parameters to be multi-modal. Also, we cannot expect to find an analytic, closed-form, expression for the likelihood function over model parameters. For these two reasons, we represent the posterior distribution non-parametrically using a discrete set of samples (i.e., states), where each sample corresponds to some hypothesized set of model parameters. Figure 1(a) illustrates this by showing a few samples from such a distribution over 3D model parameters projected into an image. This distribution is propagated in time using a particle filter [11, 13].

The detection and tracking of human motion in video has wide potential for application in domains as diverse as animation and human-computer interaction. For this reason there has been a remarkable growth in research on this problem. The majority of proposed methods rely on sources of information such as skin color or known backgrounds which may not always be available. Such cues, while useful, are not intrinsic to 3D human motion. We focus, instead, on the 3D motion of the figure and its projection into the image plane of the camera. This formulation, in terms of image motion, gives the tracker some measure of independence with respect to clothing, background clutter, and ambient lighting. Additionally, the approach does not require color images, nor does it require multiple cameras with different viewpoints. As a consequence, it may be used with archival movie footage and inexpensive video surveillance equipment. The use of perspective projection allows the model to handle significant changes in depth. Finally, unlike template tracking methods [6], the use of image motion allows tracking under changing viewpoint. These properties are illustrated with examples that include tracking people walking in cluttered images while their depth and orientation with respect to the camera changes significantly.

2 Related Work

Estimation of human motion is an active and growing research area [8]. We briefly review previous work on image cues, body representations, temporal models, and estimation techniques.

Image Cues. Methods for full body tracking typically use simple cues such as background difference images [4], color [22] or edges [7, 9, 10, 15]. However robust, these cues provide sparse information about the features in the image. Image motion (optical flow) [5, 14, 24] provides a dense cue but, since it only exploits relative motion between frames, it is sensitive to the accumulation of errors over multiple frames. The result is that these techniques are prone to "drift" from the correct solution over time. The use of image templates [6] can avoid this problem, but such approaches are sensitive to changes in view and illumination. Some of the most interesting work to date has combined multiple cues such as edges and optical flow [21]. The Bayesian approach we describe may provide a framework for the principled combination of such cues.

The approach here focuses on the estimation of 3D articulated motion from 2D image changes. In so doing we exploit recent work on the probabilistic estimation of optical flow using particle filtering [1, 2]. The method has been applied to non-linear spatial and temporal models of optical flow, and is extended here to model the motion of articulated 3D objects.

Body and Camera Models. Models of the human body vary widely in their level of detail. At one extreme are methods that crudely model the body as a collection of articulated planar patches [14, 24]. At the other extreme are 3D models in which the limb shapes are deformable [9, 15]. Additionally, assumptions about the viewing conditions vary from scaled orthographic projection [5] to full perspective [21, 25]. To account for large variations in depth, we model the body in terms of articulated 3D cylinders [12] viewed under perspective projection.

Temporal Models. Temporal models of body limb or joint motion also vary in complexity; they include smooth motion [7], linear dynamical models [18], non-linear models learned from training data using dimensionality reduction [3, 16, 23], and probabilistic Hidden Markov Models (HMM's) (e.g., [4]). In many of these methods, image measurements are first computed and then the temporal models are applied to either smooth or interpret the results. For example, Leventon and Freeman [16] proposed a Bayesian framework for recovering 3D human motion from the motion of a 2D stick figure. They learned a prior distribution over human motions using vector quantization. Given the 2D motion of a set of joints, the most plausible 3D motion could be found. They required a pre-processing step to determine the 2D stick figure motion and did not tie the 3D motion directly to the image. Their Bayesian framework did not represent multi-modal distributions and therefore did not maintain multiple interpretations.

Brand [4] learned a more sophisticated HMM from the same 3D training data used in [16]. Brand's method used binary silhouette images to compute a feature vector of image moments. The hidden states of the HMM represented 3D body configurations and the method could recover 3D models from a sequence of feature vectors. These weak image cues meant that the tracking results were heavily dependent on the prior temporal model.

Unlike the above methods, we explore the use of complex non-linear temporal models early in the process to constrain the estimation of low-level image measurements. In related work Yacoob and Davis [24] used a learned "eigencurve" model of image motion [23] to constrain estimation of a 2D articulated model. Black [1] used similar non-linear temporal models within a probabilistic framework to constrain the estimation of optical flow.

Estimation. Problems with articulated 3D tracking arise due to kinematic singularities [17], depth ambiguities, and occlusion. Multiple camera views, special clothing, and simplified backgrounds have been used to ameliorate some of these problems [5, 9, 15]. In the case of monocular tracking, body parts with low visibility (e.g. one arm and one leg) are often excluded from the tracking to avoid occlusion effects and also to lower the dimensionality of the model [5]. Cham and Rehg [6] avoid kinematic singularities and depth ambiguities by using a 2D model with limb foreshortening [17]. They also employ a multi-modal tracking approach related to particle filtering.

Bregler and Malik [5] assumed scaled orthographic projection and posed the articulated motion problem as a linear estimation problem. Yamamoto *et al.* [25] also formulated a linear estimation problem and relied on multiple camera views. These approaches elegantly modeled the image motion but did not account for imaging ambiguities and multiple matches.

Recently, Deutscher *et al.* [7] showed promising results in 3D tracking of body parts using a particle filtering method (the Condensation [13] algorithm). They successfully tracked an arm through kinematic singularities. We address the singularity problems in the same way but focus on image motion rather than edge tracking. We also employ learned temporal models to compensate for depth ambiguities and occlusion effects, and we show tracking results with more complex full-body motions.

3 Generative Model

A Bayesian approach to human motion estimation requires that we formulate a generative model of image appearance and motion. This model defines the state space representation for humans and their motion and specifies the probabilistic relationship between these states and observations. The generative model of human appearance described below has three main components, namely, shape, appearance, and motion. The human body is modeled as an articulated object, parameterized by a set of joint angles and an appearance function for each of the rigid parts. Given the camera parameters and the position and orientation of the body in the scene, we can render images of how the body is likely to appear. The probabilistic formulation of the generative model provides the basis for evaluating the likelihood of observing image measurements, $\mathbf{I}_t$ at time t, given the model parameters.

3.1 Shape: Human Body Model

As shown in Figure 1, the body is modeled as a configuration of 9 cylinders and 3 spheres, numbered for ease of identification. All cylinders are right-circular, except for the torso which has an elliptical cross-section. More sophisticated tapered cylinders [7, 21] or superquadrics [8] could be employed. Each part is defined in a part-centric coordinate frame with the origin at the base of the cylinder (or sphere). Each part is connected to others at joints, the angles of which are represented as Euler angles. The origin in each part's coordinate frame corresponds to the center of rotation (the joint position).

Rigid transformations, $\mathbf{T}$, are used to specify relative positions and orientations of parts and to change coordinate frames. We express them as a homogeneous transformation matrices:

$$\mathbf{T} = \begin{bmatrix} \mathbf{R}_z \mathbf{R}_y \mathbf{R}_x & \mathbf{t} \\ 0 & 1 \end{bmatrix} \tag{1}$$

where $\mathbf{R}_x$, $\mathbf{R}_y$ and $\mathbf{R}_z$ denote 3×3 rotation matrices about the coordinate axes, with angles θ_x, θ_y and θ_z, and $\mathbf{t} = [\tau_x, \tau_y, \tau_z]^T$ denotes the translation.

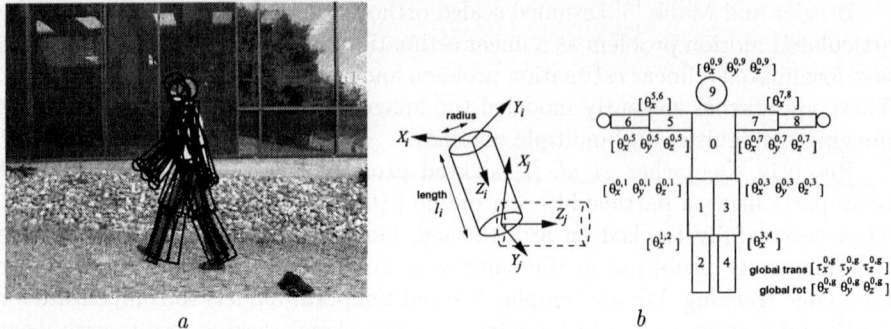

Fig. 1. *(a)* A few samples from a probability distribution over 3D model parameters projected into the image coordinate system. *(b)* Human body model. Each limb, i, has a local coordinate system with the Z_i axis directed along the limb. Joints have up to 3 angular DOF, expressed as rotations $(\theta_x, \theta_y, \theta_z)$.

A kinematic tree, with the torso at its root, is used to order the transformations between the coordinate frames of different limbs. For example, in Figure 1b, the point $\mathbf{P}_1$ in the local coordinate system of limb 1 (the right thigh) can be transformed to the corresponding point $\mathbf{P}_g$ in the global coordinate system as $\mathbf{P}_g = \mathbf{T}_{0,g}\mathbf{T}_{1,0}\mathbf{P}_1$. The global translation and rotation of the torso are represented by $\mathbf{T}_{0,g}$, while the translation and rotation of the right thigh with respect to the torso are represented by $\mathbf{T}_{1,0}$.

With these definitions, as shown in Figure 1b, the entire pose and shape of the body is given by 25 parameters, that is, angles at the shoulders, elbows, hips and knees, and the position and orientation of the torso in the scene. Let ϕ be the vector containing these 25 parameters.

Camera Model. The geometrical optics are modeled as a pinhole camera, with a transformation matrix $\mathbf{T}_c$ defining the 3D orientation and position of a 3D camera-centered coordinate system with a focal length f and an image center $\mathbf{c} = [x_{\mathbf{c}}, y_{\mathbf{c}}]^T$. The matrix maps points in scene coordinates to points in camera coordinates. Finally, points in 3D camera coordinates are projected onto the image at locations, $\mathbf{x} = [x, y]^T$, given by $\mathbf{x} = \mathbf{c} - f[\frac{Z_c}{X_c}, \frac{Y_c}{X_c}]^T$.

3.2 Appearance Model

For generality, we assume that each limb is textured mapped with an appearance model, $\mathbf{R}$. There are many ways in which one might specify such a model, including the use of low-dimensional linear subspaces [20]. Moreover, it is desirable, in general, to estimate the appearance parameters through time to reflect the changing appearance of the object in the image. Here we use a particularly simple approach in which the appearance function at time t is taken to be the mapping, $M(\cdot)$, of the image at time $t-1$ onto the 3D shape given by the shape parameters at time $t-1$:

$$\mathbf{R}_t = M(\mathbf{I}_{t-1}, \phi_{t-1}) \ .$$

In probabilistic terms, this means that the probability distribution over appearance functions at time t, conditioned on past shapes $\bar{\phi}_{t-1} = [\phi_{t-1}, \ldots, \phi_0]$, past image observations, $\bar{\mathbf{I}}_{t-1} = [\mathbf{I}_{t-1}, \ldots, \mathbf{I}_0]$, and past appearance functions $\bar{\mathbf{R}}_{t-1} = [\mathbf{R}_{t-1}, \ldots, \mathbf{R}_0]$, is given by

$$p(\mathbf{R}_t \mid \bar{\mathbf{I}}_{t-1}, \bar{\phi}_{t-1}, \bar{\mathbf{R}}_{t-1}) = p(\mathbf{R}_t \mid \mathbf{I}_{t-1}, \phi_{t-1}) = \delta(\mathbf{R}_t - M(\mathbf{I}_{t-1}, \phi_{t-1})) , \quad (2)$$

where $\delta(\cdot)$ is a Dirac delta function.

Our generative model of the image, $\mathbf{I}_t$, at time t is then the projection of the human model (shape and appearance) corrupted by noise:

$$\mathbf{I}_t(\mathbf{x}_j) = M^{-1}(\mathbf{R}_t, \phi_t, \mathbf{x}_j) + \eta \quad (3)$$

where $M^{-1}(\mathbf{R}_t, \phi_t, \mathbf{x}_j)$ maps the 3D model of limb j to image location $\mathbf{x}_j$ and $\mathbf{I}_t(\mathbf{x}_j)$ is the image brightness at pixel location $\mathbf{x}_j$. To account for "outliers", the noise, η, is taken to be a mixture of a Gaussian and a uniform distribution

$$p_\eta(\eta; \mathbf{x}_j, \phi_t) = (1 - \epsilon)\, G(\sigma(\alpha(\mathbf{x}_j, \phi_t))) + \epsilon\, c,$$

where $0 \leq \epsilon \leq 1$ and $c = 1/256$. The uniform noise is bounded over a finite interval of intensity values while $G(\cdot)$ is zero-mean normal distribution the variance of which may change with spatial position. In general, the variance is sufficiently small that the area of the Gaussian outside the bounded interval may be ignored.

The prediction of image structure, $\mathbf{I}_t$, given an appearance model, $\mathbf{R}_t$, estimated from the image at time $t - 1$ will be less reliable in limbs, or regions of limbs, that are viewed obliquely compared with those that are nearly fronto-parallel. In these regions, the image structure can change greatly from one frame to the next due to perspective distortions and self occlusion. This is captured by allowing the variance to depend on the orientation of the model surface.

Let $\alpha(\mathbf{x}_j, \phi_t)$ be a function that takes an image location, $\mathbf{x}_j$, and projects it onto a 3D limb position $\mathbf{P}$ and returns the angle between the surface normal at the point $\mathbf{P}$ and the vector from $\mathbf{P}$ to the focal point of the camera. The variance of the Gaussian component of the noise is then defined with respect to the expected image noise, σ_I, which is assumed constant, and $\alpha(\mathbf{x}_j, \phi_t)$:

$$\sigma^2(\alpha(\mathbf{x}_j, \phi_t)) = (\sigma_I / \cos(\alpha(\mathbf{x}_j, \phi_t)))^2 . \quad (4)$$

3.3 Temporal Dynamics

Finally we must specify the temporal dynamics as part the generative model. Towards this end we parameterize the motion of the shape in terms of a vector of velocities, $\mathbf{V}_t$, whose elements correspond to temporal derivatives of the shape and pose parameters in ϕ. Furthermore, we assume a first-order Markov model on shape and velocity. Let the entire history of the shape and motion parameters up to time t be denoted by $\bar{\phi}_t = [\phi_t, \ldots, \phi_0]$ and $\bar{\mathbf{V}}_t = [\mathbf{V}_t, \ldots, \mathbf{V}_0]$. Then, the temporal dynamics of the model are given by

$$p(\phi_t \mid \bar{\phi}_{t-1}, \bar{\mathbf{V}}_{t-1}) = p(\phi_t \mid \phi_{t-1}, \mathbf{V}_{t-1}) , \quad (5)$$

$$p(\mathbf{V}_t \,|\, \bar{\boldsymbol{\phi}}_{t-1}, \bar{\mathbf{V}}_{t-1}) = p(\mathbf{V}_t \,|\, \mathbf{V}_{t-1}) \;. \tag{6}$$

Humans move is a variety of complex ways, depending on the activity or gestures being made. Despite this complexity, the movements are often predictable. In Section 6, we explore two specific models of human motion. The first is a simple, general model of constant angular velocity. The second is an activity-specific model of walking.

4 Bayesian Formulation

The goal of tracking a human figure can now be formulated as the computation of the posterior probability distribution over the parameters of the generative model at time t, given a sequence of images, $\bar{\mathbf{I}}_t$; i.e., $p(\boldsymbol{\phi}_t, \mathbf{V}_t, \mathbf{R}_t \,|\, \bar{\mathbf{I}}_t)$. This can be expressed as a marginalization of the joint posterior over all states up to time t given all images up to time t:

$$p(\boldsymbol{\phi}_t, \mathbf{V}_t, \mathbf{R}_t \,|\, \bar{\mathbf{I}}_t) = \int p(\bar{\boldsymbol{\phi}}_t, \bar{\mathbf{V}}_t, \bar{\mathbf{R}}_t \,|\, \bar{\mathbf{I}}_t) d\bar{\boldsymbol{\phi}}_{t-1} d\bar{\mathbf{V}}_{t-1} d\bar{\mathbf{R}}_{t-1} \;. \tag{7}$$

Using Bayes' rule and the Markov assumptions above, it can be shown that the dependence on states at times before time $t-1$ can be removed, to give

$$p(\boldsymbol{\phi}_t, \mathbf{V}_t, \mathbf{R}_t \,|\, \bar{\mathbf{I}}_t) =$$
$$\kappa \, p(\mathbf{I}_t \,|\, \boldsymbol{\phi}_t, \mathbf{V}_t, \mathbf{R}_t) \int \big[p(\boldsymbol{\phi}_t, \mathbf{V}_t, \mathbf{R}_t \,|\, \boldsymbol{\phi}_{t-1}, \mathbf{V}_{t-1}, \mathbf{R}_{t-1}, \mathbf{I}_{t-1})$$
$$p(\boldsymbol{\phi}_{t-1}, \mathbf{V}_{t-1}, \mathbf{R}_{t-1} \,|\, \bar{\mathbf{I}}_{t-1}) \big] \, d\boldsymbol{\phi}_{t-1} d\mathbf{V}_{t-1} d\mathbf{R}_{t-1} \tag{8}$$

where κ is a normalizing constant that does not depend on the state variables. Here, $p(\mathbf{I}_t \,|\, \boldsymbol{\phi}_t, \mathbf{V}_t, \mathbf{R}_t)$, which we refer to as the "likelihood," is the probability of observing the image at time t, given the shape, motion and appearance states at time t. The integral in (8) is referred to as a temporal prior, or a prediction, as it is equivalent to the probability over states at time t given the image measurement history; i.e., $p(\boldsymbol{\phi}_t, \mathbf{V}_t, \mathbf{R}_t \,|\, \bar{\mathbf{I}}_{t-1})$. It is useful to understand the integrand as the product of two terms; these are the posterior probability distribution over states at the previous time, $p(\boldsymbol{\phi}_{t-1}, \mathbf{V}_{t-1}, \mathbf{R}_{t-1} \,|\, \bar{\mathbf{I}}_{t-1})$, and the dynamical process that propagates this distribution over states from time $t-1$ to time t.

Before turning to the computation of the posterior in (8), it is useful to simplify it using the generative model described above. For example, the likelihood of observing the image at time t does not depend on the velocity $\mathbf{V}_t$, and therefore $p(\mathbf{I}_t \,|\, \boldsymbol{\phi}_t, \mathbf{V}_t, \mathbf{R}_t) = p(\mathbf{I}_t \,|\, \boldsymbol{\phi}_t, \mathbf{R}_t)$. Also, the probability distribution over the state variables at time t, conditioned on those at time $t-1$, can be factored further. This is based on the generative model, and the assumption that the evolution of velocity and shape from time $t-1$ to t is independent of the evolution of appearance. This produces the following factorization

$$p(\boldsymbol{\phi}_t, \mathbf{V}_t, \mathbf{R}_t \,|\, \boldsymbol{\phi}_{t-1}, \mathbf{V}_{t-1}, \mathbf{R}_{t-1}, \mathbf{I}_{t-1}) =$$
$$p(\boldsymbol{\phi}_t \,|\, \boldsymbol{\phi}_{t-1}, \mathbf{V}_{t-1}) p(\mathbf{V}_t \,|\, \mathbf{V}_{t-1}) p(\mathbf{R}_t \,|\, \mathbf{I}_{t-1}, \boldsymbol{\phi}_{t-1}) \;.$$

Finally, these simplifications, taken together, produce the posterior distribution

$$p(\phi_t, \mathbf{V}_t, \mathbf{R}_t \,|\, \bar{\mathbf{I}}_t) =$$

$$\kappa\, p(\mathbf{I}_t \,|\, \phi_t, \mathbf{R}_t) \int \big[p(\phi_t \,|\, \phi_{t-1}, \mathbf{V}_{t-1}) p(\mathbf{V}_t \,|\, \mathbf{V}_{t-1}) p(\mathbf{R}_t \,|\, \mathbf{I}_{t-1}, \phi_{t-1})$$

$$p(\phi_{t-1}, \mathbf{V}_{t-1}, \mathbf{R}_{t-1} \,|\, \bar{\mathbf{I}}_{t-1}) \big]\, d\phi_{t-1} d\mathbf{V}_{t-1} d\mathbf{R}_{t-1}\,. \qquad (9)$$

4.1 Stochastic Optimization

Computation of the posterior distribution is difficult due to the nonlinearity of the likelihood function over model parameters. This is a consequence of self-occlusions, viewpoint singularities, and matching ambiguities. While we cannot derive an analytic expression for the likelihood function over the parameters of the entire state space, we can evaluate the likelihood of observing the image given a particular state $(\phi_t^s, \mathbf{V}_t^s, \mathbf{R}_t^s)$; the computation of this likelihood is described in Section 5.

Representation of the posterior is further complicated by the use of a non-linear dynamical model of the state evolution as embodied by the temporal prior. While we cannot assume that the posterior distribution will be Gaussian, or even unimodal, robust tracking requires that we maintain a representation of the entire distribution and propagate it through time. For these reasons we represent the posterior as a weighted set of state samples, which are propagated using a particle filter with sequential importance sampling. Here we briefly describe the method (for foundations see [11, 13], and for applications to 2D image tracking with non-linear temporal models see [1, 2]).

Each state, $\mathbf{s}_t$, is represented by a vector of parameter assignments, $\mathbf{s}_t = [\phi_t^s, \mathbf{V}_t^s]$. Note that in the current formulation we can drop the appearance model $\mathbf{R}_t^s$ from the state as it is completely determined by the shape parameters and the images. The posterior at time $t-1$ is represented by N state samples ($N \approx 10^4$ in our experiments). To compute the posterior (9) at time t we first draw N samples according to the posterior probability distribution at time $t-1$. For each state sample from time $t-1$, we compute $\mathbf{R}_t$ given the generative model. We propagate the angular velocities forward in time by sampling from the prior $p(\mathbf{V}_t \,|\, \mathbf{V}_{t-1})$. Similarly, the shape parameters are propagated by sampling from $p(\phi_t \,|\, \phi_{t-1}, \mathbf{V}_{t-1})$. At this point we have new values of ϕ_t and $\mathbf{R}_t$ which can be used to compute the likelihood $p(\mathbf{I}_t \,|\, \phi_t, \mathbf{R}_t)$. The N likelihoods are normalized to sum to one and the resulting set of samples approximates the posterior distribution $p(\phi_t, \mathbf{V}_t, \mathbf{R}_t \,|\, \bar{\mathbf{I}}_t)$ at time t.

5 Likelihood Computation

The likelihood $p(\mathbf{I}_t \,|\, \phi_t, \mathbf{R}_t)$ is the probability of observing image $\mathbf{I}_t$ given that the human model has configuration ϕ_t and appearance $\mathbf{R}_t$ at time t. To compare the image, $\mathbf{I}_t$, with the generative model, the model must be projected into the

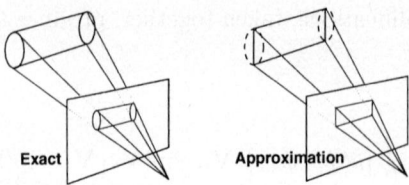

Fig. 2. Planar approximation of limbs improves efficiency.

image plane of the camera as described in Section 3. To reduce the influence of camera noise on the matching, the images, $\mathbf{I}_t$, are smoothed by a Gaussian filter with a standard deviation of $\sqrt{2}$. This has the effect of smoothing the likelihood function over model parameters and hence the posterior distribution.

Projection. The projection of limb surface points into the image plane and vice versa is computationally expensive. Given the stochastic sampling framework, this operation is performed many times and hence we seek a efficient approximation. To simplify the projection onto the image, we first project the the visible portion of the cylindrical surface onto a planar patch that bisects the cylinder, as shown in Figure 2. The projection of the appearance of a planar patch into the image can be performed by first projecting the corners of the patch via perspective projection. The projection of other limb points is given by interpolation. This approximation speeds up the likelihood computation significantly.

Recall that the variance in the generative model (3) depends on the angle, $\alpha(\mathbf{x}_j, \phi_t)$, between of the surface normal and the optical axis of the camera. With the planar approximation, α_j becomes the angle between the image plane and the Z axis of limb j.

Likelihood Model. Given the generative model we define the likelihood of each limb j independently. We sample, with replacement, $i = 1 \ldots n$ pixel locations, $\mathbf{x}_{j,i}$, uniformly from the projected region of limb j. According to (3), the grayvalue differences between points on the appearance model and the corresponding image values are independent and are modeled as a mixture of a zero-mean normal distribution and a uniform outlier distribution. We expect outliers, or unmatched pixels, to result from occlusion, shadowing, and wrinkled clothing.

The image likelihood of limb j is then expressed as:

$$p_{image} = \frac{\epsilon}{256} + \frac{1 - \epsilon}{\sqrt{2\pi}\sigma(\alpha_j)} \exp(-\sum_{i=1}^{n} \frac{(\mathbf{I}_t(\mathbf{x}_{j,i}) - \hat{\mathbf{I}}_t(\mathbf{x}_{j,i}))^2}{2\sigma^2(\alpha_j)}) \qquad (10)$$

where $\hat{\mathbf{I}}_t(\mathbf{x}_{j,i}) = M^{-1}(M(\mathbf{I}_{t-1}, \phi_{t-1}), \phi_t, \mathbf{x}_{j,i})$.

The likelihood must also account for occlusion which results from the depth ordering of the limbs or from the surface orientation. To model occluded regions we introduce the constant probability, $p_{occluded}$, that a limb is occluded. $p_{occluded}$ is currently determined empirically.

To determine self occlusion in the model configuration ϕ_t, the limbs are ordered according to the shortest distance from the limb surface to the image plane, using the camera parameters and ϕ_t. Limbs that are totally or partly covered by other limbs with lower depth are defined as occluded. This occlusion detection is sub-optimal and could be refined so that portions of limbs can be defined as occluded (cf. [21]).

Similarly as the limb is viewed at narrow angles (all visible surface normals are roughly perpendicular to the viewing direction) the linearized limb shape formulation makes the appearance pattern highly distorted. In this case, the limb can be thought of as occluding itself.

We then express the likelihood as a mixture between p_{image} and the constant probability of occlusion, $p_{occluded}$. The visibility q, (i.e. the influence of the actual image measurement), decreases with the increase of the angle α_j between the limb j principal axis and the image plane. When the limb is exactly perpendicular to the image plane, it is by this definition considered occluded. The expression for the image likelihood of limb j is defined as:

$$p_j = q(\alpha_j)p_{image} + (1 - q(\alpha_j))p_{occluded} \tag{11}$$

where $q(\alpha_j) = cos(\alpha_j)$ if limb j is non-occluded, or 0 if limb j is occluded.

According to the generative model, the appearance of the limbs are independent and the likelihood of observing the image given a particular body pose is given by the product of the limb likelihoods:

$$p(\mathbf{I}_t \mid \phi_t, \mathbf{R}_t) = \prod_j p_j . \tag{12}$$

6 Temporal Model

The temporal model encodes information about the dynamics of the human body. Here it is formulated as a prior probability distribution and is used to constrain the sampling to portions of the parameter space that are likely to correspond to human motions. General models such as constant acceleration can account for arbitrary motions but do not constrain the parameter space greatly. For a constrained activity such as walking or running we can construct a temporal model with many fewer degrees of freedom which makes the computational problem more tractable. Both types of models are explored below.

6.1 Generic Model: Smooth Motion

The smooth motion model assumes that the angular velocity of the joints and the velocity of the body are constant over time. Recall that the shape parameters are given by $\phi_t = [\tau_t^g, \theta_t^g, \theta_t^l]$ where τ_t^g and θ_t^g represent the translation and rotation that map the body into the world coordinate system and θ_t^l represents the relative angles between all pairs of connected limbs. Let $\mathbf{V}_t = [\dot{\tau}_t^g, \dot{\theta}_t^g, \dot{\theta}_t^l]$ represent the corresponding velocities. The physical limits of human movement are modeled as hard constraints on the individual quantities such that $\phi_t \in [\phi_{min}, \phi_{max}]$.

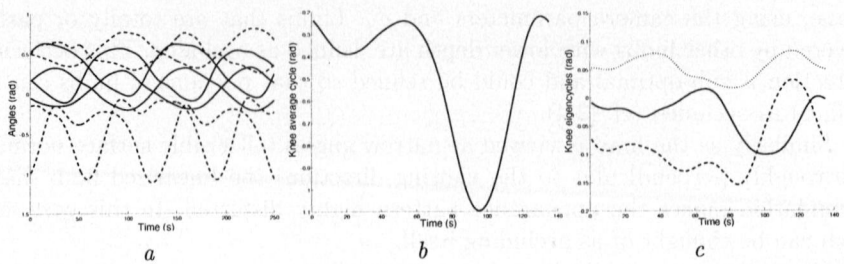

a b c

Fig. 3. Learning a walking model. *(a)* Joint angles of different people walking were acquired with a motion capture system. Curves are segmented into walking cycles manually and an eigenmodel of the cycle is constructed. *(b)* Mean angle of left knee as a function of time. *(c)* First three eigenmodes of the left knee $\mathbf{B}_j$, $j \in [1, 3]$, scaled by their respective variance λ_j. ($1 = solid, 2 = --, 3 = \cdots.$)

Our smooth motion model assumes that all elements $\phi_{k,t} \in \phi_t$ and $V_{q,t} \in \mathbf{V}_t$ are independent. The dynamics are represented by

$$p(\phi_{i,t} \mid \phi_{i,t-1}, V_{i,t-1}) = \begin{cases} G(\phi_{i,t} - (\phi_{i,t-1} + V_{i,t-1}), \sigma_i^\phi) & \text{if } \phi_{i,t} \in [\phi_{i,\min}, \phi_{i,\max}] \\ 0 & \text{otherwise} \end{cases}$$

$$p(V_{i,t} \mid V_{i,t-1}) = G(V_{i,t} - V_{i,t-1}, \sigma_i^V),$$

where $G(x, \sigma)$ denotes a Gaussian distribution with zero mean and standard deviation σ, evaluated at x. The standard deviations σ_i^ϕ and σ_i^V are empirically determined. The joint angles of heavy limbs typically have lower standard deviations than those in lighter limbs.

This model works well for tracking individual body parts that are relatively low dimensional. This is demonstrated in Section 7 for tracking arm motion (cf. [7]). This is a relatively weak model for constraining the motion of the entire body given the current sampling framework and limited computational resources. In general, one needs a variety of models of human motion and a principled mechanism for choosing among them.

6.2 Action Specific Model: Walking

In order to build stronger models, we can take advantage of the fact that many human activities are highly constrained and the body is often moved in symmetric and repetitive patterns. In what follows we consider the example of walking motion.

Training data corresponding to the 3D model parameters was acquired with a commercial motion capture system. Some of the data are illustrated in Figure 3. From the data, $m = 13$ example walking cycles from 4 different subjects (professional dancers) were segmented manually and scaled to the same length. These cycles are then used to train a walking model using Multivariate Principal Component Analysis (MPCA) [3, 19, 23]. In addition to the joint angles, we model the speed, $\mathbf{v}_i$ of the torso in the direction of the walking motion i. This speed, $v_{i,\mu}$, at time step μ in the cycle is $v_{i,\mu} = \|\tau^g_{i,\mu+1} - \tau^g_{i,\mu}\|$. The curves corresponding to the speed of the torso and the relative angles of the limbs, ϕ^l_i, are concatenated forming column vectors $\mathbf{A}_i$ for each training example $i = 1 \ldots m$. The mean vector $\hat{\mathbf{A}}$ is subtracted from all examples: $\mathcal{A}_i = \mathbf{A}_i - \hat{\mathbf{A}}$. Since the walking speed [m/frame] and the joint angles [radians] have approximately the same scales they need not be rescaled before applying MPCA.

The eigenvalues λ_j and eigenvectors $\mathbf{B}_j$, $j \in [1, m]$ of the matrix $\mathcal{A} = [\mathcal{A}_1, \cdots, \mathcal{A}_m]$ are now computed from $\mathcal{A} = \mathbf{B}\mathbf{\Sigma}\mathbf{D}^T$ using Singular Value Decomposition (SVD) where $\mathbf{B} = [\mathbf{B}_1, \cdots, \mathbf{B}_m]$ and $\mathbf{\Sigma}$ is a diagonal matrix with λ_j along the diagonal. The eigenvectors represent the principal modes of variation in the training set, while the eigenvalues reflect the variance of the training set in the direction of the corresponding eigenvector. The eigenvectors $\mathbf{B}_j$ can be viewed as a number of eigencurves, one for each joint, stacked together. Figure 3c shows three eigencurves corresponding to the left knee walking cycle.

The smallest number d of eigenvectors $\mathbf{B}_j$ such that $\sum_{j=1}^{d} \lambda_j^2 > 0.95$ is selected; in our case $d = 5$. With $\tilde{\mathbf{B}} = [\mathbf{B}_1, \cdots, \mathbf{B}_d]$ we can, with d parameters $\mathbf{c} = [c_1, \cdots, c_d]^T$, approximate a synthetic walking cycle $\mathbf{A}^*$ as:

$$\mathbf{A}^* = \hat{\mathbf{A}} + \tilde{\mathbf{B}}\mathbf{c}. \tag{13}$$

The set of independent parameters is now $\{\mathbf{c}_t, \mu_t, \tau^g_t, \theta^g_t\}$ where μ_t denotes the current position (or phase) in the walking cycle. Thus, this model reduces the original 25-dimensional parameter space, ϕ, to a 12-dimensional space.

Recall that the global translation and rotation, τ^g_t, θ^g_t, can be expressed as a homogeneous transformation matrix $\mathbf{T}$. We also define v_{t-1} to be the learned walking speed at time $t - 1$. The parameters are propagated in time as:

$$p(\mathbf{c}_t \mid \mathbf{c}_{t-1}) = G(\mathbf{c}_t - \mathbf{c}_{t-1}, \sigma^c I_d) \tag{14}$$

$$p(\mu_t \mid \mu_{t-1}) = G(\mu_t - \mu_{t-1}, \sigma^\mu) \tag{15}$$

$$p(\tau^g_t \mid \mathbf{T}_{t-1}, \mathbf{c}_{t-1}) = G([\tau^g_t, 1]^T - \mathbf{T}^{-1}_{t-1}[v_{t-1}\ 0\ 0\ 1]^T, \sigma^\tau I_3) \tag{16}$$

$$p(\theta^g_t \mid \theta_{t-1}) = G(\theta_t - \theta_{t-1}, \sigma^\theta I_3) \tag{17}$$

where σ^μ, σ^τ and σ^θ represent the empirically determined standard deviations, I_n is an $n \times n$ identity matrix, and $\sigma^c = \varepsilon\lambda$ where ε is a small scalar with $\lambda = [\lambda_1, \cdots, \lambda_d]^T$. ε is expected to be small since we expect the $\mathbf{c}$ parameters to vary little throughout the walking cycle for each individual

From a particular choice of $\{\mu_t, \mathbf{c}_t\}$, the relative joint angles are $\theta^l_t = \mathbf{A}^*(\mu_t) = \hat{\mathbf{A}}(\mu_t) + (\tilde{\mathbf{B}}\mathbf{c})(\mu_t)$, where $\mathbf{A}^*(\mu_t)$ indicates the interpolated value of each joint cycle, $\mathbf{A}^*_i$, at phase μ. The angular velocities, $\dot{\theta}^l_t = \mathbf{A}^*(\mu_t+1) - \mathbf{A}^*(\mu_t)$, are not estimated independently and the velocities $\dot{\tau}^g_t, \dot{\theta}^g_t$ are propagated as in the smooth motion case above. The Gaussian distribution over μ_t and $\mathbf{c}_t$ implies a Gaussian distribution over joint angles which defines the distribution $p(\phi_t \mid \phi_{t-1}, \mathbf{V}_{t-1})$ used in the Bayesian model.

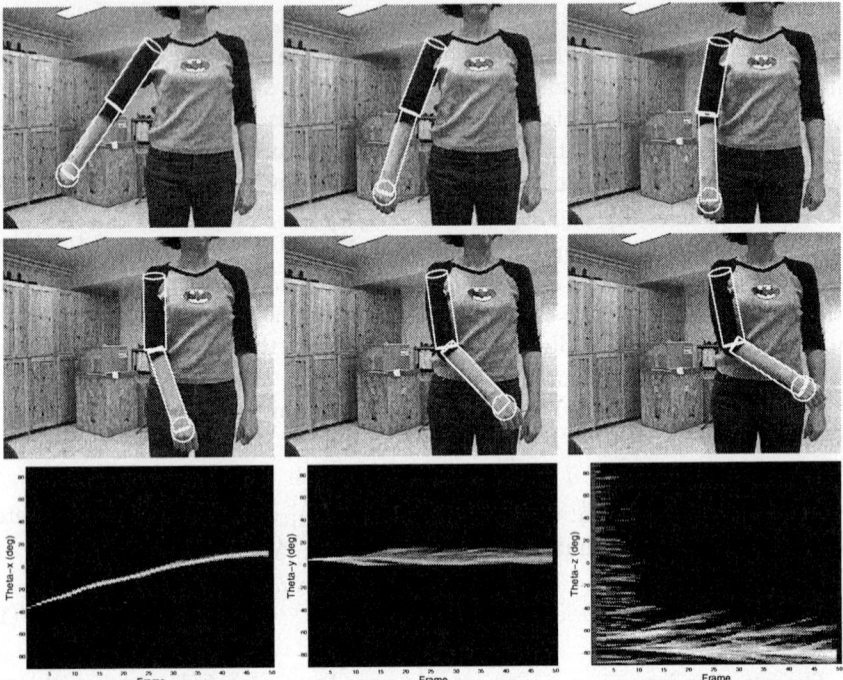

Fig. 4. Tracking of one arm (2000 samples). Upper rows: frames 0, 10, 20, 30, 40 and 50 with the projection of the expected value of model the model parameters overlaid. Frame 0 corresponds to the manual initialization. Lower row: distributions of the shoulder angles θ_x, θ_y and θ_z as function of frame number. Brightness values denote the log posterior distribution in each frame.

7 Experiments

We present examples of tracking people or their limbs in cluttered images. On an Ultra 1 Sparcstation the C++ implementation takes approximately 5 minutes/frame for experiments with 10,000 state samples. At frame 0, the posterior distribution is derived from a hand-initialized 3D model. To visualize the posterior distribution we display the projection of the 3D model corresponding to the expected value of the model parameters: $\frac{1}{N} \sum_{i=1}^{N} p_i \phi_i$ where p_i is the normalized likelihood of state sample ϕ_i.

Arm Tracking. The smooth motion prior is used for tracking relatively low dimensional models such as a single arm as illustrated in Figure 4. The model has 8 parameters corresponding to the orientation and velocity of the 3 shoulder angles and the elbow angle.

The twist of the upper arm θ_z is ambiguous when the arm is straight since the only information about the change in θ_z in that situation is the rotation of the texture pattern on the upper arm. If the upper arm texture is of low

Fig. 5. Tracking a human walking in a straight line (5000 samples, no rotation). Upper rows: projection of the expected model configuration at frames 0, 10, 20, 30, 40 and 50. Lower row: 3D configuration for the expected model parameters in the same frames.

contrast (as in Figure 4) this will provide a very weak cue. This ambiguity is easily represented in a particle filtering framework. In our case, θ_z is assigned a uniform starting distribution. Some frames later (around frame 20), the arm bends slightly, and the distribution over θ_z concentrates near the true value. The rotation of a straight arm is an example of a kinematic singularity [7, 17].

Tracking Walking People. The walking model described in Section 6.2 is used to track a person walking on a straight path parallel to the camera plane over 50 frames (Figure 5). The global rotation of the torso was held constant, lowering the number of parameters to 9: the 5 eigencoefficients, $\mathbf{c}$, phase, μ, and global 3D position, τ^g. All parameters were initialized manually with a Gaussian prior at time $t = 0$ (Figure 5, frame 0). As shown in Figure 5 the model successfully tracks the person although some parts of the body (often the arms) are poorly estimated. This in part reflects the limited variation present in the training set.

The next experiment involves tracking a person walking in a circular path and thus changing both depth and orientation with respect to the camera. Figure 6 shows the tracking results for frames from 0 to 50. In frame 50 notice that the model starts to drift off the person since the rotation is poorly estimated. Such drift is common with optical flow-based tracking methods that rely solely on the the relative motion between frames. This argues for a more persistent model of object appearance. Note that, while a constant appearance model (i.e. a template) would not suffer the same sort of drift it would be unable to cope with changes in view, illumination, and depth. Note also that the training data

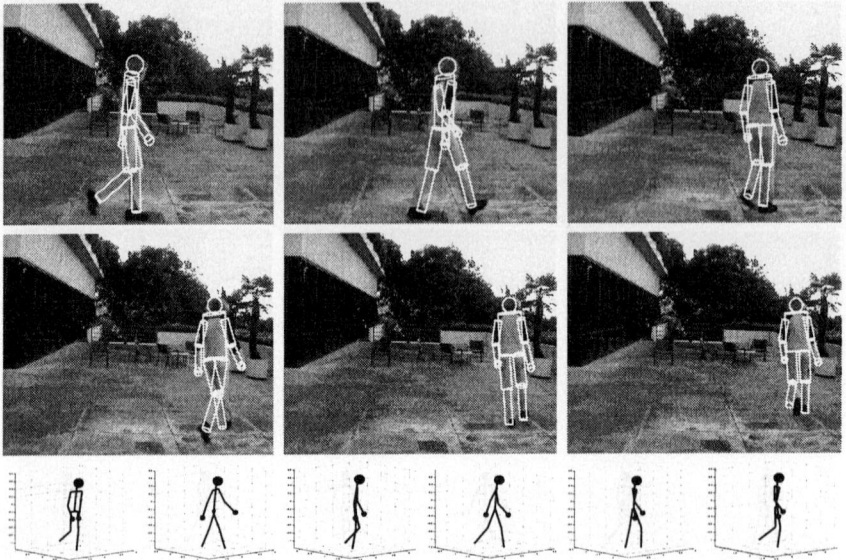

Fig. 6. Person walking in a circle (15000 samples). Upper rows: frames 0, 10, 20, 30, 40, 50 with the projection of the expected model configuration overlaid. Lower row: expected 3D configuration in the same frames.

only contained examples of people walking in a straight line. While the circular walking motion here differs significantly, the temporal model is sufficiently general that it can approximate this new motion.

How significant is the temporal walking prior model? Figure 7 illustrates the effect of repeating the above experiment with a uniform likelihood function, so that the evolution of the parameters is determined entirely by the temporal model. While the prior is useful for constraining the model parameters to valid walking motions, it does not unduly affect the tracking.

8 Conclusion

This paper has presented a Bayesian formulation for tracking of articulated human figures in 3D using monocular image motion information. The approach employs a generative model of image appearance that extends the idea of parameterized optical flow estimation to 3D articulated figures. Kinematic singularities, depth ambiguities, occlusion, and ambiguous image information result in a multi-modal posterior probability distribution over model parameters. A particle filtering approach is used to represent and propagate the posterior distribution over time, thus tracking multiple hypotheses in parallel. To constrain the distribution to valid 3D human motions we define prior probability distributions over the dynamics of the human body. Such priors help compensate for missing or noisy visual information and enable stable tracking of occluded

Fig. 7. How strong is the walking prior? Tracking results for frames 0, 10, 20, 30, 40 and 50, when no image information is taken into account.

limbs. Results were shown for a general smooth motion model as well as for an action-specific walking model.

A number of outstanding issues remain and are the focus of our research. The current model is initialized by hand and will eventually lose track of the object. Within a Bayesian framework we are developing a fully automatic system that samples from a mixture of initialization and temporal priors. We are also developing new temporal models of human motion that allow more variation than the eigencurve model yet are more constrained than the smooth motion prior. We are extending the likelihood model to better use information at multiple scales and to incorporate additional generative models for image features such as edges. Additionally, the likelihood computation is being extended to model the partial occlusion of limbs as in [21]. Beyond this, one might replace the cylindrical limbs with tapered superquadrics [9, 15] and model the prior distribution over these additional shape parameters. Finally, we are exploring the representation of the posterior as a mixture of Gaussians [6]. This provides a more compact representation of the distribution and interpolates between samples to provide a measure of the posterior in areas not covered by discrete samples.

Acknowledgments. This work was partially sponsored by the Foundation for Strategic Research under the "Center for Autonomous Systems" contract. This support is gratefully acknowledged. We would also like to thank Jan-Olof Eklundh, Dirk Ormoneit and Fernando De la Torre for helpful discussions and Michael Gleicher for providing the 3D motion capture data.

References

1. M. J. Black. Explaining optical flow events with parameterized spatio-temporal models. *CVPR*, pp. 326–332, 1999.

2. M. J. Black and D. J. Fleet. Probabilistic detection and tracking of motion discontinuities. *ICCV*, pp. 551–558, 1999.
3. A. Bobick and J. Davis. An appearance-based representation of action. *ICPR*, 1996.
4. M. Brand. Shadow puppetry. *ICCV*, pp. 1237–1244, 1999.
5. C. Bregler and J. Malik. Tracking people with twists and exponential maps. *CVPR*, 1998.
6. T-J. Cham and J. M. Rehg. A multiple hypothesis approach to figure tracking. *CVPR*, pp. 239–245, 1999.
7. J. Deutscher, B. North, B. Bascle, and A. Blake. Tracking through singularities and discontinuities by random sampling. *ICCV*, pp. 1144–1149, 1999.
8. D. M. Gavrila. The visual analysis of human movement: a survey. *CVIU*, 73(1):82–98, 1999.
9. D. M. Gavrila and L. S. Davis. 3-D model-based tracking of humans in action: A multi-view approach. *CVPR*, pp. 73–80, 1996.
10. L. Goncalves, E. Di Bernardi, E. Ursella, and P. Perona. Monocular tracking of the human arm in 3D. *ICCV*, 1995.
11. N. Gordon, D. J. Salmond, and A. F. M. Smith. A novel approach to nonlinear/non-Gaussian Bayesian state estimation. *IEE Proc. Radar, Sonar and Navigation*, 140(2):107–113, 1996.
12. D. Hogg. Model-based vision: A program to see a walking person. *Image and Vision Computing*, 1(1):5–20, 1983.
13. M. Isard and A. Blake. Contour tracking by stochastic propagation of conditional density. *ECCV*, pp. 343–356, 1996.
14. S. X. Ju, M. J. Black, and Y. Yacoob. Cardboard people: A parameterized model of articulated motion. *Int. Conf. on Automatic Face and Gesture Recognition*, pp. 38–44, 1996.
15. I. Kakadiaris and D. Metaxas. Model-based estimation of 3D human motion with occlusion based on active multi-viewpoint selection. *CVPR*, pp. 81–87, 1996.
16. M. E. Leventon and W. T. Freeman. Bayesian estimation of 3-d human motion from an image sequence. TR–98–06, Mitsubishi Electric Research Lab, 1998.
17. D. Morris and J. M. Rehg. Singularity analysis for articulated object tracking. *CVPR*, pp. 289–296, 1998.
18. V. Pavolvić, J. Rehg, T-J. Cham, and K. Murphy. A dynamic Bayesian network approach to figure tracking using learned dynamic models. *ICCV*, pp. 94–101, 1999.
19. J. O. Ramsay and B. W. Silverman. *Functional data analysis*. New York: Springer Verlag, 1997.
20. H. Sidenbladh, F. de la Torre, and M. J. Black. A framework for modeling the appearance of 3D articulated figures. *Int. Conf. on Automatic Face and Gesture Recognition*, 2000.
21. S. Wachter and H. H. Nagel. Tracking persons in monocular image sequences. *CVIU*, 74(3):174–192, 1999.
22. C. Wren, A. Azarbayejani, T. Darrell, and A. Pentland. Pfinder: Real-time tracking of the human body. *PAMI*, 19(7):780–785, 1997.
23. Y. Yacoob and M. J. Black. Parameterized modeling and recognition of activities in temporal surfaces. *CVIU*, 73(2):232–247, 1999.
24. Y. Yacoob and L. Davis. Learned temporal models of image motion. *ICCV*, pp. 446–453, 1998.
25. M. Yamamoto, A. Sato, S. Kawada, T. Kondo, and Y. Osaki. Incremental tracking of human actions from multiple views. *CVPR*, pp. 2–7, 1998.

Monocular Perception of Biological Motion – Clutter and Partial Occlusion

Yang Song[1], Luis Goncalves[1], and Pietro Perona[1,2]

[1] California Institute of Technology, 136-93,
Pasadena, CA 91125, USA
[2] Università di Padova, Italy
{yangs, luis, perona}@vision.caltech.edu

Abstract. The problem of detecting and labeling a moving human body viewed monocularly in a cluttered scene is considered. The task is to decide whether or not one or more people are in the scene (detection), to count them, and to label their visible body parts (labeling).

It is assumed that a motion-tracking front end is supplied: a number of moving features, some belonging to the body and some to the background are tracked for two frames and their position and velocity is supplied (Johansson display). It is not guaranteed that all the body parts are visible, nor that the only motion present is the one of the body.

The algorithm is based on our previous work [12]; we learn a probabilistic model of the position and motion of body features, and calculate maximum-likelihood labels efficiently using dynamic programming on a triangulated approximation of the probabilistic model. We extend those results by allowing an arbitrary number of body parts to be undetected (e.g. because of occlusion) and by allowing an arbitrary number of noise features to be present. We train and test on walking and dancing sequences for a total of approximately 10^4 frames. The algorithm is demonstrated to be accurate and efficient.

1 Introduction

Humans have developed a remarkable ability in perceiving the posture and motion of the human body ('biological motion' in the human vision literature). Johansson [7] filmed people acting in total darkness with small light bulbs fixed to the main joints of their body. A single frame of a Johansson movie is nothing but a cloud of bright dots on a dark field; however, as soon as the movie is animated one can readily detect, count, segment a number of people in a scene, and even assess their activity, age and sex. Although such perception is completely effortless, our visual system is ostensibly solving a hard combinatorial problem (which dot should be assigned to which body part of which person?).

Perceiving the motion of the human body is difficult. First of all, the human body is richly articulated – even a simple stick model describing the pose of arms, legs, torso and head requires more than 20 degrees of freedom. The body moves in 3D which makes the estimation of these degrees of freedom a challenge in a monocular setting [4, 6]. Image processing is also a challenge: humans typically wear clothing which may be loose and textured. This makes it difficult to identify limb boundaries, and even more so to segment the main parts of the body. In a general setting all that can be extracted reliably from the images is patches of texture in motion. It is not so surprising after all that the human visual system has evolved to be so good at perceiving Johansson's stimuli.

Perception of biological motion may be divided into two phases: first detection and, possibly, segmentation; then tracking. Of the two, tracking has recently been object of much attention and considerable progress has been made [10, 9, 4, 5, 2, 14, 3]. Detection (given two frames: is there a human, where?), on the contrary, remains an open problem. In [12], we have focused on the Johannson problem proposing a method based on probabilistic modeling of human motion and on modeling the dependency of the motion of body parts with a triangulated graph, which makes it possible to solve the combinatorial problem of labeling in polynomial time. Excellent and efficient performance of the method has been demonstrated on a number of motion sequences. However, that work is limited to the case where there is no clutter (the only moving parts belong to the body, as in Johansson's displays). This is not a realistic situation: in typical scenes one would expect the environment to be rich of motion patterns (cars driving by, trees swinging in the wind, water rippling... as in Figure 1). Another limitation is that only limited amounts of occlusion is allowed. This is again not realistic: in the typical situations little more than half of the body is visible, the other half being self-occluded.

Fig. 1. Perception of biological motion in real scenes: one has to contend with a large amount of clutter (more than one person in the scene, other objects in the scene are also moving), and a large amount of self-occlusion (typically only half of the body is seen). Observe that segmentation (arm vs. body, left and right leg) is at best problematic.

We propose here a modification of our previous scheme [12] which addresses both the problem of clutter and of large occlusion. We conduct experiments to explore its performance vis a vis different types and levels of noise, variable amounts of occlusion, and variable numbers of human bodies in the scene. Both the detection performance and the labeling performance are assessed, as well as the performance in counting the number of people in the scene.

In section 2 we first introduce the problem and some notation, then propose our approach. In section 3 we explain how to perform detection. In section 4 a simple method for aggregating information over a number of frames is discussed. In section 5 we explain how to count how many people there may be in the picture. Section 6 contains the experiments.

2 Labeling

In the Johansson scenario, each body part appears as a single dot in the image plane. Our problem can then be formulated as follows: given the positions and velocities of a number of point-features in the image plane (Figure 2(a)), we want to find the configuration that is most likely to correspond to a human body. Detection is done based on how human-like the best configuration is.

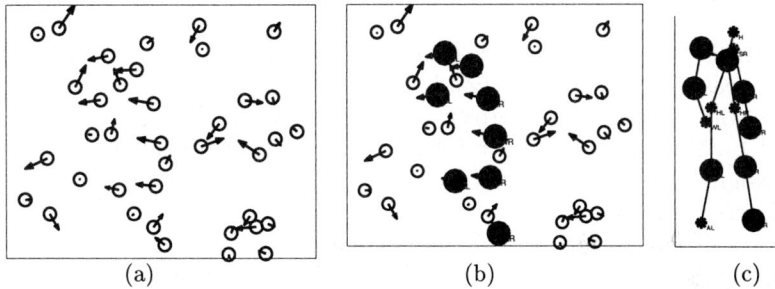

(a)   (b)   (c)

Fig. 2. Illustration of the problem. Given the position and velocity of point-features in the image plane (a), we want to find the best possible human configuration: filled dots in (b) are body parts and circles are background points. Arrows in (a) and (b) show the velocities. (c) is the full configuration of the body. Filled (blackened) dots represent the 'observed' points which appear in (b), and the '*'s are unobserved body parts. 'L' and 'R' in label names indicate left and right. H:head, N:neck, S:shoulder, E:elbow, W:wrist, H:hip, K:knee and A:ankle.

2.1 Notation

Suppose that we observe N points (as in Figure 2(a), where $N = 38$). We assign an arbitrary index to each point. Let $\mathcal{S}_{body} = \{LW, LE, LS, H \ldots RA\}$ be the set of M body parts, for example, LW is the left wrist, RA is the right ankle, etc. Then:

$$i \in 1, \ldots, N \qquad \text{Point index} \tag{1}$$

$$\overline{X} = [X_1, \ldots, X_N] \qquad \text{Vector of measurements (position and velocity)} \tag{2}$$

$$\overline{L} = [L_1, \ldots, L_N] \qquad \text{Vector of labels} \tag{3}$$

$$L_i \in \mathcal{S}_{body} \cup \{BG\} \qquad \text{Set of possible values for each label} \tag{4}$$

Notice that since there exist clutter points that do not belong to the body, the background label BG is added to the label set. Due to clutter and occlusion N is not necessarily equal to M (which is the size of S_{body}). We want to find $\overline{L}^*$, over all possible label vectors $\overline{L}$, such that the posterior probability of the labeling given the observed data is maximized, that is,

$$\overline{L}^* = \arg\max_{\overline{L} \in \mathcal{L}} P(\overline{L}|\overline{X}) \qquad (5)$$

where $P(\overline{L}|\overline{X})$ is the conditional probability of a labeling $\overline{L}$ given the data $\overline{X}$. Using Bayes' law:

$$P(\overline{L}|\overline{X}) = P(\overline{X}|\overline{L})\frac{P(\overline{L})}{P(\overline{X})} \qquad (6)$$

If we assume that the priors $P(\overline{L})$ are equal for different labelings, then,

$$\overline{L}^* = \arg\max_{\overline{L} \in \mathcal{L}} P(\overline{X}|\overline{L}) \qquad (7)$$

Given a labeling $\overline{L}$, each point feature i has a corresponding label L_i. Therefore each measurement X_i corresponding to body labels may also be written as X_{L_i}, i.e. the measurements corresponding to a specific body part associated with label L_i. For example if $L_i = LW$, i.e. the label corresponding to the left wrist is assigned to the ith point, then $X_i = X_{LW}$ is the position and velocity of the left wrist.

Let $\overline{\mathcal{L}}_{body}$ denote the set of body parts appearing in $\overline{L}$, $\overline{X}_{body}$ be the vector of measurements labeled as body parts, and $\overline{X}_{bg}$ be the vector of measurements labeled as background (BG). More formally,

$$\begin{aligned}
\overline{\mathcal{L}}_{body} &= \{L_i; i = 1, \ldots, N\} \cap S_{body} \\
\overline{X}_{body} &= [X_{i_1}, \ldots, X_{i_K}] & \text{such that } \{L_{i_1}, \ldots, L_{i_K}\} = \overline{\mathcal{L}}_{body} \\
\overline{X}_{bg} &= [X_{j_1}, \ldots, X_{j_{N-K}}] & \text{such that } L_{j_1} = \cdots = L_{j_{N-K}} = BG \quad (8)
\end{aligned}$$

where K is the number of body parts present in $\overline{L}$.

If we assume that the position and velocity of the visible body parts is independent of the position and velocity of the clutter points, then,

$$P(\overline{X}|\overline{L}) = P_{\overline{\mathcal{L}}_{body}}(\overline{X}_{body}) \cdot P_{bg}(\overline{X}_{bg}) \qquad (9)$$

where $P_{\overline{\mathcal{L}}_{body}}(\overline{X}_{body})$ is the marginalized probability density function of $P_{S_{body}}$ according to $\overline{\mathcal{L}}_{body}$. If independent uniform background noise is assumed, then $P_{bg}(\overline{X}_{bg}) = (1/S)^{N-K}$, where $N - K$ is the number of background points, and S is the volume of the space X_i lies in, which can be obtained from the training set. In the following sections, we will address the issues of estimating $P_{\overline{\mathcal{L}}_{body}}(\overline{X}_{body})$ and finding the $\overline{L}^*$ with the highest likelihood.

2.2 Approximation of the foreground probability density function

If no body part is missing, we can use the method proposed in [12] to get the approximation of the foreground probability density $P_{\overline{\mathcal{L}}_{body}}(\overline{X}_{body})$. By using the kinematic chain structure of human body, the whole body can be decomposed as in Figure 3(a). If the appropriate conditional independence (Markov property) is valid, then

$$
\begin{aligned}
& P_{\overline{\mathcal{L}}_{body}}(\overline{X}_{body}) \\
& = P_{S_{body}}(X_{LW}, X_{LE}, X_{LS}, X_H \dots X_{RA}) \\
& = P_{LW|LE,LS}(X_{LW}|X_{LE}, X_{LS}) \cdot P_{LE|LS,LH}(X_{LE}|\dots) \cdot \dots \\
& \quad \cdot P_{RK,LA,RA}(X_{RK}, X_{LA}, X_{RA}) \\
& = \prod_{t=1}^{T-1} P_t(X_{A_t}|X_{B_t}, X_{C_t}) \cdot P_T(X_{A_T}, X_{B_T}, X_{C_T})
\end{aligned}
\tag{10}
$$

Where T is the number of triangles in the decomposed graph in Figure 3(a), t is the triangle index, and A_t is the first label associated to triangle t, etc.

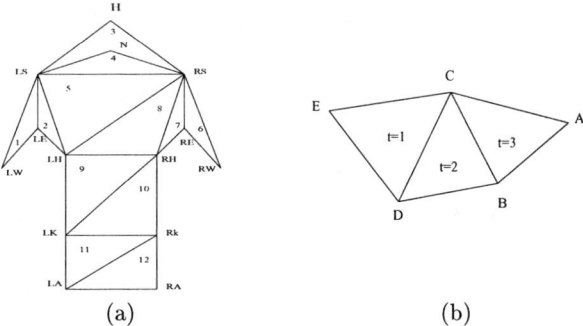

(a)   (b)

Fig. 3. (a) One decomposition of the human body into triangles [12]. The label names are the same as in Figure 2. The numbers inside triangles give the order in which dynamic programming proceeds. (b) An illustrative example used in section 2.2.

If some body parts are missing, then the foreground probability density function is the marginalized version of the above equation – marginalization over the missing body parts. Marginalization should be performed so that it is a good approximation of the true marginal probability density function and allows efficient computation such as dynamic programming. We propose that doing the marginalization term by term (triangle by triangle) of equation (10) and then multiplying them together is a reasonable way to get such an approximation. The idea can be illustrated by a simple example as in Figure 3(b). Considering the joint probability density function of 5 random variables $P(A, B, C, D, E)$, if these random variables are conditionally independent as described in the graph of Figure 3 (b), then

$$
P(A, B, C, D, E) = P(A, B, C)P(D|B, C)P(E|C, D)
\tag{11}
$$

If A is missing, then the marginalized PDF is $P(B, C, D, E)$. If the conditional independence as in equation (11) can hold, then,

$$P(B, C, D, E) = P(B, C) \cdot P(D|B, C) \cdot P(E|C, D) \tag{12}$$

In the case of D missing, the marginalized PDF is $P(A, B, C, E)$. If we assume that E is conditionally independent of A and B given C, which is a more demanding conditional independence requirement with the absence of D compared to that of equation (11), then,

$$P(A, B, C, E) = P(A, B, C) \cdot 1 \cdot P(E|C) \tag{13}$$

Each term on the right hand sides of equations (12) and (13) is the marginalized version of its corresponding term in equation (11). Similarly, if some stronger conditional independence can hold, we can obtain an approximation of $P_{\overline{\mathcal{L}}_{body}}(\overline{X}_{body})$ by performing the marginalization term by term of equation (10). For example, considering triangle (A_t, B_t, C_t), $1 \le t \le T - 1$, if all of A_t, B_t and C_t are present, then the tth term of equation (10) is $P_{A_t|B_t, C_t}(X_{A_t}|X_{B_t}, X_{C_t})$; if A_t is missing, the marginalized version of it is 1; if A_t and C_t are observed, but B_t is missing, it becomes $P_{A_t|C_t}(X_{A_t}|X_{C_t})$; if A_t exists but both B_t and C_t missing, it is $P_{A_t}(X_{A_t})$. For the Tth triangle, if some body part(s) are missing, then the corresponding marginalized version of P_T is used. The foreground probability $P_{\overline{\mathcal{L}}_{body}}(\overline{X}_{body})$ can be approximated by the product of the above (conditional) probability densities. Note that if too many body parts are missing, the conditional independence assumptions of the graphical model will no longer hold; it is reasonable to assume that the wrist is conditionally independent of the rest of the body given the shoulder and elbow, but if both shoulder and elbow are missing, this is no longer true. Nevertheless, we will use independence as an approximation. All the above (conditional) probability densities (e.g. $P_{LW|LE, LS}(X_{LW}|X_{LE}, X_{LS})$) can be estimated from the training data.

2.3   Cost functions and comparison of two labelings

The best labeling $(\overline{L}^*)$ can be found by comparing the likelihood of all the possible labelings. To compare two labelings $\overline{L}^1$ and $\overline{L}^2$, if we can assume that the priors $P(\overline{L}^1)$ and $P(\overline{L}^2)$ are equal, then by equation (9),

$$\frac{P(\overline{L}^1|\overline{X})}{P(\overline{L}^2|\overline{X})} = \frac{P(\overline{X}|\overline{L}^1)}{P(\overline{X}|\overline{L}^2)} = \frac{P_{\overline{\mathcal{L}}_{body}^1}(\overline{X}_{body}^1) \cdot P_{bg}(\overline{X}_{bg}^1)}{P_{\overline{\mathcal{L}}_{body}^2}(\overline{X}_{body}^2) \cdot P_{bg}(\overline{X}_{bg}^2)}$$

$$= \frac{P_{\overline{\mathcal{L}}_{body}^1}(\overline{X}_{body}^1) \cdot (1/S)^{N-K_1}}{P_{\overline{\mathcal{L}}_{body}^2}(\overline{X}_{body}^2) \cdot (1/S)^{N-K_2}}$$

$$= \frac{P_{\overline{\mathcal{L}}_{body}^1}(\overline{X}_{body}^1) \cdot (1/S)^{M-K_1}}{P_{\overline{\mathcal{L}}_{body}^2}(\overline{X}_{body}^2) \cdot (1/S)^{M-K_2}} \tag{14}$$

where $\overline{\mathcal{L}}_{body}^1$ and $\overline{\mathcal{L}}_{body}^2$ are the sets of observed body parts for $\overline{L}^1$ and $\overline{L}^2$ respectively, K_1 and K_2 are the sizes of $\overline{\mathcal{L}}_{body}^1$ and $\overline{\mathcal{L}}_{body}^2$, and M is the total number of body parts ($M = 14$ here). $P_{\overline{\mathcal{L}}_{body}^i}(\overline{X}_{body}^i)$, $i = 1, 2$, can be approximated as in section 2.2. From equation (14), the best labeling $\overline{L}^*$ is the $\overline{L}$ which can maximize $P_{\overline{\mathcal{L}}_{body}}(\overline{X}_{body}) \cdot (1/S)^{M-K}$. This formulation makes both search by dynamic programming and detection in different frames (possibly with different numbers of candidate features N) easy, as will be explained below.

The dynamic programming algorithm [1, 12] requires that the local cost function associated with each triangle (as in Figure 3(a)) should be comparable for different labelings: whether there are missing part(s) or not. Therefore we cannot only use the terms of $P_{\overline{\mathcal{L}}_{body}}(\overline{X}_{body})$, because, for example, as we discussed in the previous subsection, the tth term of $P_{\overline{\mathcal{L}}_{body}}(\overline{X}_{body})$ is $P_{A_t|B_tC_t}(X_{A_t}|X_{B_t}, X_{C_t})$ when all the three parts are present and it is 1 when A_t is missing. It is unfair to compare $P_{A_t|B_tC_t}(X_{A_t}|X_{B_t}, X_{C_t})$ with 1 directly. At this point, it is useful to notice that in $P_{\overline{\mathcal{L}}_{body}}(\overline{X}_{body}) \cdot (1/S)^{M-K}$, for each unobserved (missing) body part ($M - K$ in total), there is a $1/S$ term. $1/S$ (S is the volume of the space X_{A_t} lies in) can be a reasonable local cost for the triangle with vertex A_t (the vertex to be deleted) missing because then for the same stage, the dimension of the domain of the local cost function is the same. Also, $1/S$ can be thought of as a threshold of $P_{A_t|B_tC_t}(X_{A_t}|X_{B_t}, X_{C_t})$, namely, if $P_{A_t|B_tC_t}(X_{A_t}|X_{B_t}, X_{C_t})$ is smaller than $1/S$, then the hypothesis that A_t is missing will win. Therefore, the local cost function for the tth ($1 \le t \le T - 1$) triangle can be approximated as follows:
- if all the three body parts are observed, it is $P_{A_t|B_tC_t}(X_{A_t}|X_{B_t}, X_{C_t})$;
- if A_t is missing or two or three of A_t, B_t, C_t are missing, it is $1/S$;
- if either B_t or C_t is missing and the other two body parts are observed, then it is $P_{A_t|C_t}(X_{A_t}|X_{C_t})$ or $P_{A_t|B_t}(X_{A_t}|X_{B_t})$.
The same idea can be applied to the last triangle T. These approximations are to be validated in experiments. Notice that when two body parts in a triangle are missing, only velocity information for the third body part is available since we use relative positions. The velocity of a point alone doesn't have much information, so for two parts missing, we use the same cost function as the case of three body parts missing.

With the local cost functions defined above, dynamic programming can be used to find the labeling with the highest $P_{\overline{\mathcal{L}}_{body}}(\overline{X}_{body}) \cdot (1/S)^{M-K}$. The computational complexity is on the order of $M * N^3$.

3 Detection

Given a hypothetical labeling $\overline{L}$, the higher $P(\overline{X}|\overline{L})$ is, the more likely it is that the associated configuration of features represents a person. The labeling $\overline{L}^*$ with the highest $P_{\overline{\mathcal{L}}_{body}}(\overline{X}_{body}) \cdot (1/S)^{M-K}$ provides us with the most human-like configuration out of all the candidate labelings. Note that since the dimension of the domain of $P_{\overline{\mathcal{L}_{body}}}(\overline{X}_{body}) \cdot (1/S)^{M-K}$ is fixed regardless of the number of candidate features and the number of missing body parts in the labeling $\overline{L}$, we can directly compare the likelihoods of different hypotheses, even hypotheses from different images.

In order to perform detection we first get the most likely labeling, then compare the likelihood of this labeling to a threshold. If the likelihood is higher than the threshold, then we will declare that a person is present. This threshold needs to be set based on experiments, to ensure the best trade-off between false acceptance and false rejection errors.

4 Integrating temporal information [11]

So far, we have only assumed that we may use information from two consecutive frames, from which we obtain position and velocity of a number of features. In this section we would like to extend our previous results to the case where multiple frames are available. However, in order to maintain generality we will assume that tracking across more than 2 frames is impossible. This is a simplified model of the situation where, due to extreme body motion or to loose and textured clothing, tracking is extremely unreliable and each individual feature's lifetime is short.

Let $P(O|\overline{X})$ denote the probability of the existence of a person given $\overline{X}$. From equation (14) and the previous section, we use the approximation: $P(O|\overline{X})$ is proportional to $\Gamma(\overline{X}|\overline{L}^*)$ defined as $\Gamma(\overline{X}|\overline{L}^*) \overset{\text{def}}{=} \max_{\overline{L} \in \mathcal{L}} P_{\overline{\mathcal{L}_{body}}}(\overline{X}_{body}) \cdot (1/S)^{M-K}$, where $\overline{L}^*$ is the best labeling found from $\overline{X}$. Now if we have n observations $\overline{X}_1, \overline{X}_2, \ldots, \overline{X}_n$, then the decision depends on:

$$
\begin{aligned}
& P(O|\overline{X}_1, \overline{X}_2, \ldots, \overline{X}_n) \\
= \; & P(\overline{X}_1, \overline{X}_2, \ldots, \overline{X}_n|O) \cdot P(O)/P(\overline{X}_1, \overline{X}_2, \ldots, \overline{X}_n) \\
= \; & P(\overline{X}_1|O)P(\overline{X}_2|O) \ldots P(\overline{X}_n|O) \cdot P(O)/P(\overline{X}_1, \overline{X}_2, \ldots, \overline{X}_n) \quad (15)
\end{aligned}
$$

The last line of equation (15) holds if we assume that $\overline{X}_1, \overline{X}_2, \ldots, \overline{X}_n$ are independent. Assuming that the priors are equal, $P(O|\overline{X}_1, \overline{X}_2, \ldots, \overline{X}_n)$ can be represented by $P(\overline{X}_1|O) \ldots P(\overline{X}_n|O)$, which is proportional to $\prod_{i=1}^{n} \Gamma(\overline{X}_i|\overline{L}_i^*)$. If we set up a threshold for $\prod_{i=1}^{n} \Gamma(\overline{X}_i|\overline{L}_i^*)$, then we can do detection given $\overline{X}_1, \overline{X}_2, \ldots, \overline{X}_n$.

5 Counting

Counting how many people are in the scene is also an important task since images often have multiple people in them. By the method described above, we can first get the best configuration to see if it could be a person. If so, all the points belonging to the person are removed and the next best labeling can then be found from the rest of points. We repeat until the likelihood of the best configuration is smaller than a threshold. Then the number of configurations with likelihood greater than the threshold is the number of people in the scene.

6 Experiments

In this section we explore experimentally the performance of our system. The data were obtained from a 60 Hz motion capture system. The motion capture system can provide us with labeling for each frame which can be used as ground truth. In our experiments, we assumed that both position and velocity were available for each candidate point. The velocity was obtained by subtracting the positions in two consecutive frames.

Two different types of motions were used in our experiments, walking and dancing. Figure 4 shows sample frames of these two motions.

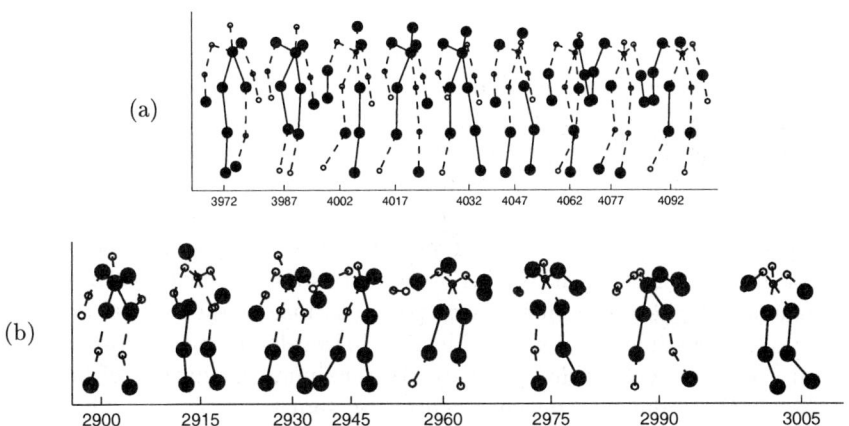

Fig. 4. Sample frames. (a) a walking sequence; (b) a dancing sequence. Eight Filled dots denote the eight observed body parts; the open circles mark points that are actually missing (not available to the program). The numbers along the horizontal axes indicate the frame numbers.

6.1 Training of the probabilistic models

The probabilistic models were trained separately for walking and dancing, and in each experiment the appropriate model was used. For the walking action, two sequences of 7000 frames were available. The first sequence was used for training, and the second sequence for testing. For the dancing action, one sequence of 5000 frames was available; the first half was used for training, and the second half for testing.

The training was done by estimating the joint (or conditional) probabilistic density functions (pdf) for all the triplets as described in section 2. For each triplet, position information was expressed within a local coordinate frame, i.e. relative positions, and velocities were absolute ones. As in [12], we assumed that all the pdfs were Gaussian, and the parameters for the Gaussian distribution were estimated from the training set.

6.2 Detection

In this experiment, we test how well our method can distinguish whether or not a person is present in the scene (Figure 2). We present the algorithm with two types of inputs (presented randomly in equal proportions); in one case only clutter (background) points are present, in the other body parts from the walking sequence are superimposed on the clutter points. We call 'detection rate' the fraction of frames containing a body that is recognized correctly. We call 'false alarm rate' the fraction of frames containing only clutter where our system detects a body.

We want to test the detection performance when only part of the whole body (with 14 body parts in total) can be seen. We generated the signal points (body parts) in the following way: for a fixed number of signal points, we randomly selected which body parts would be used in each frame (actually pair of frames, since consecutive frames were used to estimate the velocity of each body part). So in principle, each body part has an equal chance to be represented, and as far as the decomposed body graph is concerned, all kinds of graph structures (with different body parts missing) can be tested.

The positions and velocities of clutter (background) points were independently generated from uniform probability densities. For positions, we used the leftmost and rightmost positions of the whole training sequence as the horizontal range, and highest and lowest body part positions as the vertical range. For velocities, the possible range was inside a circle in velocity space (horizontal and vertical velocities) with radius equal to the maximum magnitude of body part velocities in the training sequences. Figure 2 (a) shows a frame with 8 body parts and 30 added background points with arrows representing velocities.

The six solid curves of Figure 5 (a) are the receiver operating characteristics (ROCs) obtained from our algorithm when the 'positive' test images contained 3 to 8 signal points with 30 added background points and the 'negative' test images contained 30 background points. The more signal points, the better the ROC. With 30 background points, when the number of signal points is more than 8, the ROCs are almost perfect.

When using the detector in a practical situation, some detection threshold needs to be set; if the likelihood of the best labeling exceeds the threshold, a person is deemed to be present. Since the number of body parts is unknown beforehand, we need to fix a threshold that is independent of (and robust with respect to) the number of body parts present in the scene. The dashed line in Figure 5 (a) shows the overall ROC of all the frames used for the six ROC curves in solid lines. We took the threshold when $P_{detect} = 1 - P_{false-alarm}$ on it as our threshold. The star ('*') point on each solid curve shows the point corresponding to that threshold. Figure 5 (b) shows the relation between detection rate and number of body parts displayed with regard to the fixed threshold. The false alarm rate is 12.97%.

When the algorithm can correctly detect whether there is a person, it doesn't necessarily mean that all the body parts are correctly labeled. Therefore we also studied the correct label rate when a person is correctly detected. Figure 5 (c) shows the result. While the detection rate is constant (with no errors) with 8 or more body parts visible, the correct label rate increases with the number of body parts. The correct label rates here are smaller than in [12] since we have less signal points but many more background points.

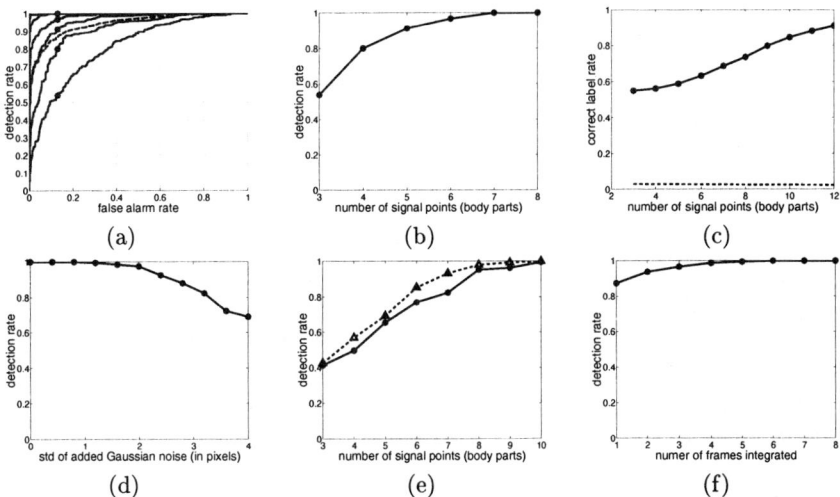

Fig. 5. (a) to (e) are detection results on 2 frames only, and (f) shows the result of using multiple frames. (a) ROC curves. Solid lines: 3 to 8 out of 14 body parts with 30 background points vs. 30 background points only. The more signal points, the better the ROC. Dashed line: overall ROC considering all the frames. The threshold corresponding to $P_D = 1 - P_{FA}$ on it was used for later experiments. The stars ('*') on the solid curves are the points corresponding to that threshold. (b) detection rate vs. number of body parts displayed with regard to the fixed threshold as in (a). The false alarm rate is 12.97%. (c) The solid line is correct label rate vs. number of body parts when a person is correctly detected. The chance level is shown in dashed line. (d) the detection rate vs. standard deviation (in pixels) when Gaussian noise was added to positions, using displays composed of 8 signal points and 30 background points in each frame. The standard deviation of the velocity error was one tenth of that of the position error. The detection threshold is the same as (b) and (c), with the false alarm rate 12.97%. (e) results for biological clutter (background points were obtained from the walking sequences): detection rate vs. number of signal points. Solid line (with stars): with 30 added background points, false alarm rate is 24.19%; Dashed line (with triangles): with 20 added background points, false alarm rate is 19.45%. (f) detection rate (when $P_{detect} = 1 - P_{false-alarm}$) vs. number of frames used with only 5 body parts present.

The data used above were acquired by an accurate motion capture system where markers were used to identify important features. In image sequences where people do not wear markers, candidate features can be obtained from a motion detector/feature tracker ([11, 13]), where extra measurement noise may be introduced. To test the performance of our method under that situation, independent Gaussian noise was added to the position and velocity of the signal points (body parts). We experimented with displays composed of 8 signal points and 30 background points in each frame. Figure 5 (d) shows the detection rate (with regard to the same threshold as Figure 5(b) and (c)) vs. standard deviation (in pixels) of added Gaussian noise to positions. The standard deviation of noise added to velocities is one tenth of that of positions, which reflects the fact that the position error, due to the inaccurate localization of a feature by a tracking algorithm ([11, 13]), is usually much larger than the velocity error which is due to the tracking error from one frame to the next.

We also tested our method by using biological clutter, that is, the background points were generated by independently drawing points (with position and velocity) of randomly chosen frames and body parts from the walking sequence. Figure 5(e) shows the results.

6.3 Using temporal information

The detection rate improves by integrating information over time as discussed in section 4. We tested this using displays composed of 5 signal points and 30 background points (the 5 body parts present in each frame were chosen randomly and independently). The results are shown in Figure 5(f).

6.4 Counting

We call 'counting' the task of finding how many people are present in a scene. Our stimuli with multiple persons were obtained in the following way. A person was generated by randomly choosing a frame from the sequence, and several frames (persons) can be superimposed together in one image with the position of each person selected randomly but not overlapped with each other. The statistics of background features was similar to that in section 6.2 (Figure 5(a)), but with the positions distributed on a window three times as wide as that in Figure 2 (a). Figure 6(a) gives an example of images used in this experiment, with three persons (six body parts each) and sixty background points.

Our stimuli contained from zero to three persons. The threshold from Figure 5(a) was used for detection. If the probability of the configuration found was above the threshold, then it was counted as a person. The curves in Figure 6(b) show the correct count rate vs. the number of signal points. To compare the results conveniently, we used the same number of body parts for different persons in one image (but the body parts present were randomly chosen). The solid line represents counting performance when one person was present in each image, the dashed line with circles is for stimuli containing two persons, and the dash-dot line with triangles is for three persons. If there was no person in the image, the correct rate was 95%. From Figure 6(b), we see that the result for displays containing fewer people is better than that with more people, especially when the number of observed body parts is small. We can explain it as follows. If the probability of counting one person correctly is P, then the probability of counting n people correctly is P^n if the detection of different people is independent. For

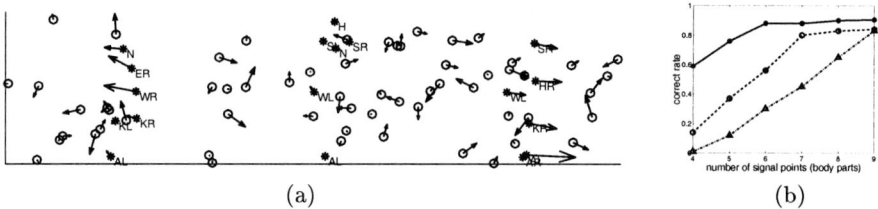

(a)   (b)

Fig. 6. (a) One sample image of counting experiments. '*'s denote body parts and 'o's are background points. There are three persons (six body parts for each person) with sixty superimposed background points. Arrows are the velocities. (b) Results of counting experiments: correct rate vs. number of body parts. Solid line (with solid dots): one person; dashed line (with open circles): two persons; dash-dot line (with triangles): three persons. Detection of a person is with regard to the threshold chosen from Figure 5(a). For that threshold the correct rate for recognizing that there is no person in the scene is 95%.

example, in the case of four body parts, for one person the correct rate is 0.6, then the correct rate for counting three person is $0.6^3 = 0.216$. This is just an approximation since body parts from different persons may be very close and the body part of one person may be perceived as belonging to another. Furthermore, the assumption of independence is also violated since once a person is detected the corresponding body parts are removed from the scene in order to detect subsequent people.

6.5 Experiments on dancing sequence

In the previous experiments, walking sequences were used as our data. In this section, we tested our model on a dancing sequence. Results are shown in Figure 7. The signal points (body parts) were from the dancing sequence and the clutter points were generated the same way as in section 6.2 (Figure 5(a)).

7 Conclusions

We have presented a method for detecting, labeling and counting biological motion in a Johansson-like sequence. We generalize our previous work [12] by extending the technique to work on arbitrary amounts of clutter and occlusion.

We have tested our implementation on two kinds of moving sequences (walking and dancing) and demonstrated that it performs well under conditions of clutter and occlusion that are possibly more challenging than one would expect in a typical real-life scenario. The motion clutter we injected in our displays was designed to resemble the motion of individual body parts, the number of noise points in our experiments far exceeded the number of signal points, the number of undetected/occluded signal features in some experiments exceeded the number of detected features. Just to quote one significant performance figure: 2-frame detection rate is better than 90% when 6 out of 14 body parts are seen

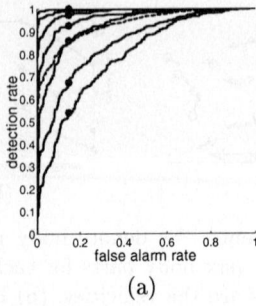 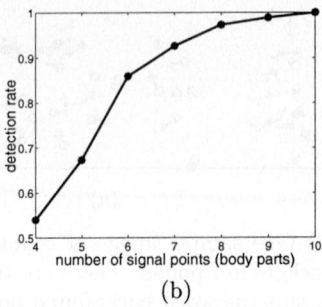

(a)   (b)

Fig. 7. Results of dancing sequences. (a) Solid lines: ROC curves for 4 to 10 body parts with 30 background points vs. 30 background points only. The more signal points, the better the ROC. Dashed line: overall ROC considering all the frames used in seven solid ROCs. The threshold corresponding to $P_D = 1 - P_{FA}$ on this curve was used for (b). The stars ('*') on the solid curves are the points corresponding to that threshold. (b) detection rate vs. the number of body parts displayed with regard to the fixed threshold. The false alarm rate is 14.67%. Comparing with the results in Figure 5 (a, b), we can see that more body parts must be observed during the dancing sequence to achieve the same detection rate as with the walking sequences, which is expected since the motion of dancing sequences is more active and harder to model. Nevertheless, the ROC curve with 10 out of 14 body parts present is nearly perfect.

within 30 clutter points (see Figure 5(b)). When the number of frames considered exceeds 5 then performance quickly reaches 100% correct (see Figure 5(f)). This means that even in high-noise conditions detection is flawless in 100ms or so (considering a 60 Hz imaging system), a figure comparable to the alleged performance of the human visual system [8]. Moreover, our algorithm is computationally efficient, taking order of 1 second in our Matlab implementation on a regular Pentium computer, which gives significant hope for a real-time C implementation on the same computer.

The next step in our work is clearly the application of our system to real image sequences, rather than Johansson displays. We anticipate using a simple feature/patch detector and tracker in order to provide the position-velocity measurements that are input in our system. Since our system can work with features that have a short life-span (in the limit 2-frame) this should be feasible without modifying the overall approach. A first set of experiments is described in [11]. Comparing in detail the performance of our algorithm with the human visual system is another avenue that we intend to pursue.

Acknowledgments

Funded by the NSF Engineering Research Center for Neuromorphic Systems Engineering (CNSE) at Caltech (NSF9402726), and by an NSF National Young Investigator Award to PP (NSF9457618).

References

1. Y. Amit and A. Kong, "Graphical templates for model registration", *IEEE Transactions on Pattern Analysis and Machine Intelligence*, 18:225–236, 1996.
2. C. Bregler and J. Malik, "Tracking people with twists and exponential maps", In *Proc. IEEE CVPR*, pages 8–15, 1998.
3. D. Gavrila, "The visual analysis of human movement: A survey", *Computer Vision and Image Understanding*, 73:82–98, 1999.
4. L. Goncalves, E. Di Bernardo, E. Ursella, and P. Perona, "Monocular tracking of the human arm in 3d", In *Proc. 5th Int. Conf. Computer Vision*, pages 764–770, Cambridge, Mass, June 1995.
5. I. Haritaoglu, D.Harwood, and L.Davis, "Who, when, where, what: A real time system for detecting and tracking people", In *Proceedings of the Third Face and Gesture Recognition Conference*, pages 222–227, 1998.
6. N. Howe, M. Leventon, and W. Freeman, "Bayesian reconstruction of 3d human motion from single-camera video", *Tech. Rep. TR-99-37, a Mitsubishi Electric Research Lab*, 1999.
7. G. Johansson, "Visual perception of biological motion and a model for its analysis", *Perception and Psychophysics*, 14:201–211, 1973.
8. P. Neri, M.C.Morrone, and D.C.Burr, "Seeing biological motion", *Nature*, 395:894–896, 1998.
9. J.M. Rehg and T. Kanade, "Digiteyes: Vision-based hand tracking for human-computer interaction", In *Proceedings of the workshop on Motion of Non-Rigid and Articulated Bodies*, pages 16–24, November 1994.
10. K. Rohr, "Incremental recognition of pedestrians from image sequences", In *Proc. IEEE Conf. Computer Vision and Pattern Recognition*, pages 8–13, New York City, June, 1993.
11. Y. Song, X. Feng, and P. Perona, "Towards detection of human motion", *To appear in IEEE Conference on Computer Vision and Pattern Recognition*, 2000.
12. Y. Song, L. Goncalves, E. Di Bernardo, and P. Perona, "Monocular perception of biological motion - detection and labeling", In *Proceedings of International Conference on Computer Vision*, pages 805–812, Sept 1999.
13. C. Tomasi and T. Kanade, "Detection and tracking of point features", *Tech. Rep. CMU-CS-91-132,Carnegie Mellon University*, 1991.
14. S. Wachter and H.-H. Nagel, "Tracking persons in monocular image sequences", *Computer Vision and Image Understanding*, 74:174–192, 1999.

3-D Motion and Structure from 2-D Motion Causally Integrated over Time: Implementation[*]

Alessandro Chiuso[†‡], Paolo Favaro[†], Hailin Jin[†], and Stefano Soatto[†]

† Washington University, One Brookings Dr. 1127, Saint Louis – MO 63130
‡ Università di Padova, Via Gradenigo 6/a 35131 Padova – Italy
email {chiuso,fava,hljin,soatto}@essrl.wustl.edu

Abstract. The causal estimation of three-dimensional motion from a sequence of two-dimensional images can be posed as a nonlinear filtering problem. We describe the implementation of an algorithm whose uniform observability, minimal realization and stability have been proven analytically in [5]. We discuss a scheme for handling occlusions, drift in the scale factor and tuning of the filter. We also present an extension to partially calibrated camera models and prove its observability. We report the performance of our implementation on a few long sequences of real images. More importantly, however, we have made our real-time implementation – which runs on a personal computer – available to the public for first-hand testing.

1 Introduction

Inferring the three-dimensional (3-D) shape of a moving scene from its two-dimensional images is one of the classical problems of computer vision, known by the name of "shape from motion" (SFM). Among all possible ways in which this can be done, we distinguish between *causal schemes* and *non-causal ones*. More than the fact that causal schemes use – at any given point in time – only information from the past, the main difference between these two approaches lies in their goals and in the way in which data are collected. When the estimates of motion are to be used in real time, for instance to accomplish a control task, a causal scheme must be employed since "future" data are not available for processing and the control action must be taken "now". In that case, the sequence of images is often collected sequentially in time, while motion changes smoothly under the auspices of inertia, gravity and other physical constraints. When, on the other hand, we collect a number of "snapshots" of a scene from disparate viewpoints and we are interested in reconstructing it, there is no natural ordering or smoothness involved; using a causal scheme in this case would be, in the end, highly unwise.

No matter how the data are collected, however, SFM is subject to fundamental tradeoffs, which we articulate in section 1.2. This paper aims at addressing

---

[*] Supported by NSF IIS-9876145 and ARO DAAD19-99-1-0139. We wish to thank Xiaolin Feng, Carlo Tomasi, Pietro Perona, Ruggero Frezza, John Oliensis and Philip McLauchlan for discussions.

such tradeoffs: it is possible to integrate visual information over time, hence achieving a global estimate of 3-D motion, while maintaining the correspondence problem local. Among the obstacles we encounter is the fact that individual points tend to become occluded during motion, while novel points become visible. In [5] we have introduced a wide-sense approximation to the optimal filter and proved that it is observable, minimal and stable. In this paper we describe a complete, real-time *implementation* of the algorithm, which includes an approach to handle *occlusions* causally.

1.1 A first formalization of the problem

Consider an N-tuple of points in the three-dimensional Euclidean space, represented as a matrix

$$\mathbf{X} \doteq \left[\mathbf{X}^1\ \mathbf{X}^2\ ...\ \mathbf{X}^N\right] \in \mathbb{R}^{3\times N} \tag{1}$$

and let them move under the action of a rigid motion represented by a translation vector T and a rotation matrix R. Rotation matrices are orthogonal with unit determinant $\{R \mid R^T R = RR^T = I\}$. Rigid motions transform the coordinates of each point via $R(t)\mathbf{X}^i + T(t)$. Associated to each motion $\{T, R\}$ there is a velocity, represented by a vector of linear velocity V and a skew-symmetric matrix $\widehat{\omega}$ of rotational velocity. Skew-symmetric 3×3 matrices are represented using the "hat" notation

$$\widehat{\mathbf{a}} = \begin{bmatrix} 0 & -a_3 & a_2 \\ a_3 & 0 & -a_1 \\ -a_2 & a_1 & 0 \end{bmatrix}. \tag{2}$$

Under such velocity, motion evolves according to

$$\begin{cases} T(t+1) = e^{\widehat{\omega}(t)}T(t) + V(t) \\ R(t+1) = e^{\widehat{\omega}(t)}R(t). \end{cases} \tag{3}$$

The exponential of a skew-symmetric matrix can be computed conveniently using Rodrigues' formula:

$$e^{\widehat{\omega}} = I + \frac{\widehat{\omega}}{\|\omega\|}\sin\left(\|\omega\|\right) + \frac{\widehat{\omega}^2}{\|\omega\|^2}\left(1 - \cos\left(\|\omega\|\right)\right). \tag{4}$$

We assume that - to an extent discussed in later sections - the *correspondence problem* is solved, that is we know which point corresponds to which in different projections (views). Equivalently, we assume that we can measure the (noisy) projection

$$\mathbf{y}^i(t) = \pi\left(R(t)\mathbf{X}^i + T(t)\right) + \mathbf{n}^i(t) \in \mathbb{R}^2 \quad \forall\, i = 1...N \tag{5}$$

where we know the correspondence $\mathbf{y}^i \leftrightarrow \mathbf{X}^i$. We take as projection model an ideal pinhole, so that $\mathbf{y} = \pi(\mathbf{X}) = \left[\frac{X_1}{X_3}\ \frac{X_2}{X_3}\right]^T$. This choice is not crucial and the discussion can be easily extended to other projection models (e.g. spherical, orthographic, para-perspective, etc.). We do not distinguish between $\mathbf{y}$ and its projective coordinate (with a 1 appended), so that we can write $\mathbf{X} = \mathbf{y}X_3$.

Finally, by organizing the time-evolution of the configuration of points and their motion, we end up with a discrete-time, non-linear dynamical system:

$$
\begin{cases}
\mathbf{X}(t+1) = \mathbf{X}(t) & \mathbf{X}(0) = \mathbf{X}_0 \\
T(t+1) = e^{\widehat{\omega}(t)}T(t) + V(t) & T(0) = T_0 \\
R(t+1) = e^{\widehat{\omega}(t)}R(t) & R(0) = R_0 \\
V(t+1) = V(t) + \alpha_V(t) & V(0) = V_0 \\
\omega(t+1) = \omega(t) + \alpha_\omega(t) & \omega(0) = \omega_0 \\
\mathbf{y}^i(t) = \pi\big(R(t)\mathbf{X}^i(t) + T(t)\big) + \mathbf{n}^i(t) & \mathbf{n}^i(t) \sim \mathcal{N}(0, \Sigma_n)
\end{cases}
\tag{6}
$$

where $\mathbf{v} \sim \mathcal{N}(M, S)$ indicates that a vector $\mathbf{v}$ is distributed normally with mean M and covariance S. In the above system, α is the relative acceleration between the viewer and the scene. If some prior modeling information is available (for instance when the camera is mounted on a vehicle or on a robot arm), this is the place to use it. Otherwise a statistical model can be employed. In particular, we can formalize our ignorance on acceleration by modeling α as a Brownian motion process[1]. In principle one would like - at least for this simplified formalization of SFM - to find the optimal solution. Unfortunately, as we explain in [5], there exists no finite-dimensional optimal filter for this model. Therefore, at least for this elementary instantiation of SFM, we would like to derive approximations that are provably stable and efficient.

1.2 Tradeoffs in structure from motion

The first tradeoff involves the magnitude of the baseline and the correspondence problem, and has been discussed extensively in [5]. When images are taken from disparate viewpoints, estimating relative orientation is simple, given the correspondence. However, solving the correspondence problem is difficult, for it amounts to a global matching problem – all too often solved by hand – which spoils the possibility of use in real-time control systems. When images are collected closely in time, on the other hand, correspondence becomes an easy-to-solve local variational problem. However, estimating 3-D motion becomes rather difficult since – on small motions – the noise in the image overwhelms the feeble information contained in the 2-D motion of the features.

No matter how one chooses to increase the baseline in order to bypass the tradeoff with correspondence, one inevitably runs into deeper problems, namely the fact that individual feature points can *appear and disappear due to occlusions*, or to changes in their appearance due to specularities, light distribution etc. To increase the baseline, it is necessary to associate the scale factor to an invariant of the scene. Therefore, in order to process that information, the scale factor must be included in the model. This tradeoff is fundamental and there is no easy way around it: information on shape can only be integrated as long as the shape is visible.

---

[1] We wish to emphasize that this choice is not crucial towards the conclusions reached in this paper. Any other model would do, as long as the overall system is observable.

1.3 Relation to previous work and organization of the paper

We are interested in estimating motion so that we can use the estimates to accomplish spatial control tasks such as moving, tracking, manipulation etc. In order to do so, the estimates must be provided *in real time and causally*, while we can rely on the fact that images are taken at adjacent instants in time and the relative motion between the scene and the viewer is somewhat smooth (rather than having isolated "snapshots"). Therefore, we do not compare our algorithms with batch multi-frame approaches to SFM. This includes iterative minimization techniques such as "bundle adjustment". If one can afford the time for processing sequences of images off-line, of course a batch approach that optimizes simultaneously on all frames will perform better![2]

Our work falls within the category of causal motion and structure estimation that has a long and rich history [10, 7, 18, 4, 23, 19, 32, 9, 30, 24, 8, 12, 26, 11, 31, 34, 33, 13, 25, 16, 1, 2, 22, 35, 15]. The first attempts to prove stability of the schemes proposed are recent [21]. The first attempts to handle occlusions in a causal scheme[3] came only a few years ago [19, 29]. Our approach is similar in spirit to the work of Azarbayejani and Pentland [2], extended to handle occlusions and to give correct weighting to the measurements.

The first part of this study [5] contains a proof of uniform observability and stability of the algorithm that we describe here. In passing, we show how the conditions we impose on our models are tight: imposing either more or less results in either a biased or an unstable filter. The second part, reported in this paper, is concerned with the *implementation* of a system working in real time on real scenes, which we have made available to the public [14].

2 Realization

In order to design a finite-dimensional approximation to the optimal filter, we need an observable realization of the original model[4]. In [5] we have proven the following claim.

Corollary 1 *The model*

$$
\begin{cases}
y_0^i(t+1) = y_0^i(t) & i = 4 \ldots N & y_0^i(0) = y_0^i \\
\rho^i(t+1) = \rho^i(t) & i = 2 \ldots N & \rho^i(0) = \rho_0^i \\
T(t+1) = \exp(\widehat{\omega}(t))T(t) + V(t) & & T(0) = T_0 \\
\Omega(t+1) = Log_{SO(3)}(\exp(\widehat{\omega}(t))\exp(\widehat{\Omega}(t))) & & \Omega(0) = \Omega_0 \\
V(t+1) = V(t) + \alpha_V(t) & V(0) = V_0 \\
\omega(t+1) = \omega(t) + \alpha_\omega(t) & \omega(0) = \omega_0 \\
y^i(t) = \pi\left(\exp(\widehat{\Omega}(t))y_0^i(t)\rho^i(t) + T(t)\right) + n^i(t) & i = 1 \ldots N.
\end{cases}
\tag{7}
$$

[2] One may argue that batch approaches are now fast enough that they can be used for real-time processing. Our take on this issue is exposed in [5], where we argue that speed is not the problem; robustness and delays are.

[3] There are several ways of handling missing data in a batch approach: since they do not extend to causal processing, we do not review them here.

[4] Observability in SFM has been addressed first in 1994 [6, 27] (see also [28] for a more complete account of these results). Observability is closely related to "gauge invariance" [20].

is a minimal realization of (6). The notation $Log_{SO(3)}(R)$ stands for Ω such that $R = e^{\widehat{\Omega}}$ and is computed by inverting Rodrigues' formula[5]. Ω is called the "canonical representation" of R.

Remark 1 *Notice that in the above claim the index for $\mathbf{y}_0^i$ starts at 4, while the index for ρ^i starts at 2. This corresponds to choosing the first three points as reference for the similarity group and is necessary (and sufficient) for guaranteeing that the representation is minimal. As explained in [5] this can be done without loss of generality, i.e. modulo a reordering of the states.*

2.1 Partial autocalibration

As we have anticipated, the models proposed can be extended to account for changes in calibration. For instance, if we consider an imaging model with focal length f[6]

$$\pi_f(\mathbf{X}) = \frac{f \begin{bmatrix} X_1 \\ X_2 \end{bmatrix}}{X_3} \tag{8}$$

where the focal length can change in time, but no prior knowledge on how it does so is available, one can model its evolution as a random walk

$$f(t+1) = f(t) + \alpha_f(t) \qquad \alpha_f(t) \sim \mathcal{N}(0, \sigma_f^2) \tag{9}$$

and insert it into the state of the model (6). As long as the overall system is observable, the conclusions reached in [5] will hold. The following claim shows that this is the case for the model (9) above. Another imaging model proposed in the literature is [2]: $\pi_\beta(\mathbf{X}) = \frac{[X_1 \ X_2]^T}{1+\beta X_3}$ for which similar conclusions can be drawn. The reader can refer to [5] for details on definitions and characterizations of observability.

Proposition 1 *Let $g = \{T, R\}$ and $v = \{V, \omega\}$. The model*

$$\begin{cases} \mathbf{X}(t+1) = \mathbf{X}(t) & \mathbf{X}(0) = \mathbf{X}_0 \\ g(t+1) = e^{\widehat{v}}g(t) & g(0) = g_0 \\ v(t+1) = v(t) & v(0) = v_0 \\ f(t+1) = f(t) & f(0) = f_0 \\ \mathbf{y}(t) = \pi_f(g(t)\mathbf{X}(t)) \end{cases} \tag{10}$$

is observable up to the action of the group represented by $\tilde{T}, \tilde{R}, \alpha$ acting on the initial conditions.

Proof: *Consider the diagonal matrix $F(t) = \text{diag}\{f(t), \ f(t), \ 1\}$ and the matrix of scalings $A(t)$ as in the proof of proposition 1 in [5]. Consider then two initial conditions*

---

[5] A Matlab implementation of $Log_{SO(3)}$ is included in the software distribution.

[6] This f is not to be confused with the generic state equation of the filter in section 3.3.

$\{\mathbf{X}_1, g_1, v_1, f_1\}$ and $\{\mathbf{X}_2, g_2, v_2, f_2\}$. For them to be indistinguishable there must exist matrices of scalings $A(k)$ and of focus $F(k)$ such that

$$\begin{cases} g_1 \mathbf{X}_1 = F(1)(g_2 \mathbf{X}_2) \cdot A(1) \\ e^{\widehat{v_1}} e^{(k-1)\widehat{v_1}} g_1 \mathbf{X}_1 = F(k+1) \left(e^{\widehat{v_2}} e^{(k-1)\widehat{v_2}} g_2 \mathbf{X}_2 \right) \cdot A(k+1) \quad k \geq 1. \end{cases} \quad (11)$$

Making the representation explicit we obtain

$$\begin{cases} R_1 \mathbf{X}_1 + \bar{T}_1 = F(1)(R_2 \mathbf{X}_2 + \bar{T}_2)A(1) \\ U_1 F(k)\tilde{\mathbf{X}}_k A(k) + \bar{V}_1 = F(k+1)(U_2 \tilde{\mathbf{X}}_k + \bar{V}_2)A(k+1) \end{cases} \quad (12)$$

which can be re-written as

$$\tilde{\mathbf{X}}_k A(k)A^{-1}(k+1) - F^{-1}(k)U_1^T F(k+1)U_2 \tilde{\mathbf{X}}_k = F(k)^{-1}U_1^T(F(k+1)\bar{V}_2 A(k+1) - \bar{V}_1)A^{-1}(k+1). \quad (13)$$

The two sides of the equation have equal rank only if it is equal to zero, which draws us to conclude that $A(k)A^{-1}(k+1) = I$, and hence A is constant. From $F^{-1}(k)U_1^T F(k+1)U_2 = I$ we get that $F(k+1)U_2 = U_1 F(k)$ and, since $U_1, U_2 \in SO(3)$, we have that taking the norm of both sides $2f^2(k+1) + 1 = 2f^2(k) + 1$, where f must be positive, and therefore constant: $FU_2 = U_1 F$. From the right hand side we have that $F\bar{V}_2 A = \bar{V}_1$, from which we conclude that $A = \alpha I$, so that in vector form we have $V_1 = \alpha F V_2$. Therefore, from the second equation we have that, for any f and any α, we can have $V_1 = \alpha F V_2$, $U_1 = F U_2 F^{-1}$ However, from the first equation we have that $R_1 \mathbf{X}_1 + T_1 = \alpha F R_2 \mathbf{X}_2 + \alpha F T_2$, whence - from the general position conditions - we conclude that $R_1 = \alpha F R_2$ and therefore $F = I$. From that we have that $T_1 = \alpha F T_2 = \alpha T_2$ which concludes the proof.

Remark 2 *The previous claim essentially implies that the realization remains minimal if we add into the model the focal parameter. Note that observability depends upon the structural properties of the model, not on the noise, which is therefore assumed to be zero for the purpose of the proof.*

2.2 Saturation

Instead of eliminating states to render the model observable, it is possible to design a nonlinear filter directly on the (unobservable) model (6) by *saturating* the filter along the unobservable component of the state space as we show in this section. In other words, it is possible to design the initial variance of the state of the estimator as well as its model error in such a way that it will never move along the unobservable component of the state space.

As proposition 2 in [5] suggests, one can saturate the states corresponding to $\mathbf{y}_0^1, \mathbf{y}_0^2, \mathbf{y}_0^3$ and ρ^1. We have to guarantee that the filter initialized at $\widehat{\mathbf{y}}_0, \widehat{\rho}_0, \widehat{g}_0, \widehat{v}_0$ evolves in such a way that $\widehat{\mathbf{y}}_0^1(t) = \widehat{\mathbf{y}}_0^1, \widehat{\mathbf{y}}_0^2(t) = \widehat{\mathbf{y}}_0^2, \widehat{\mathbf{y}}_0^3(t) = \widehat{\mathbf{y}}_0^3, \widehat{\rho}^1(t) = \widehat{\rho}_0^1$. It is simple, albeit tedious, to prove the following proposition.

Proposition 2 *Let $P_{\mathbf{y}^i}(0), P_{\rho^i}(0)$ denote the variance of the initial condition corresponding to the state $\mathbf{y}_0^i$ and ρ^i respectively, and $\Sigma_{\mathbf{y}^i}, \Sigma_{\rho^i}$ the variance of the model error corresponding to the same state, then $P_{\mathbf{y}^i}(0) = 0$, $\Sigma_{\mathbf{y}^i} = 0$ $i = 1 \ldots 3$ $\Sigma_{\rho^1} = 0$ implies that $\widehat{\mathbf{y}}_0^i(t|t) = \widehat{\mathbf{y}}_0^i(0)$, $i = 1 \ldots 3$, and $\widehat{\rho}^1(t|t) = \widehat{\rho}^1(0)$.*

2.3 Pseudo-measurements

Yet another alternative to render the model observable is to add pseudo-measurement equations with zero error variance.

Proposition 3 *The model*

$$
\begin{cases}
\mathbf{y}_0^i(t+1) = \mathbf{y}_0^i(t) & i = 1 \dots N & \mathbf{y}_0^i(0) = \mathbf{y}_0^i \\
\rho^i(t+1) = \rho^i(t) & i = 1 \dots N & \rho^i(0) = \rho_0^i \\
T(t+1) = \exp(\widehat{\omega}(t))T(t) + V(t) & & T(0) = 0 \\
\Omega(t+1) = Log_{SO(3)}(\exp(\widehat{\omega}(t))\exp(\widehat{\Omega}(t))) & & \Omega(0) = 0 \\
V(t+1) = V(t) + \alpha_V(t) & V(0) = V_0 \\
\omega(t+1) = \omega(t) + \alpha_\omega(t) & \omega(0) = \omega_0 \\
\mathbf{y}^i(t) = \pi\left(\exp(\widehat{\Omega}(t))\mathbf{y}_0^i(t)\rho^i(t) + T(t)\right) + n^i(t) & i = 1 \dots N \\
\rho^1 = \psi_1 \\
\mathbf{y}_0^i(t) = \phi^i & i = 1 \dots 3,
\end{cases}
\tag{14}
$$

where ψ_1 is an arbitrary (positive) constant and ϕ^i are three non-collinear points on the plane, is observable.

3 Implementation: occlusions and drift in SFM

The implementation of an extended Kalman filter based upon the model (7) is straightforward. However, for the sake of completeness we report it in section 3.3. The only issue that needs to be dealt with is the disappearing and appearing of feature points, a common trait of sequences of images of natural scenes. Visible feature-points may become occluded (and therefore their measurements become unavailable), or occluded points may become visible (and therefore provide further measurements). New states must be properly initialized. One way of doing so is described in the next section 3.1. Occlusion of point features do not cause major problems, unless the feature that disappears happens to be associated with the scale factor. This is unavoidable and results in a drift whose nature is explained in section 3.2.

3.1 Occlusions

When a feature point, say $\mathbf{X}^i$, becomes occluded, the corresponding measurement $\mathbf{y}^i(t)$ becomes unavailable. It is possible to model this phenomenon by setting the corresponding variance to infinity or, in practice $\Sigma_{n^i} = M I_2$ for a suitably large scalar $M > 0$. By doing so, we guarantee that the corresponding states $\hat{\mathbf{y}}_0^i(t)$ and $\hat{\rho}^i(t)$ are not updated:

Proposition 4 *If $\Sigma_{n^i} = \infty$, then $\hat{\mathbf{y}}_0^i(t+1) = \hat{\mathbf{y}}_0^i(t)$ and $\hat{\rho}^i(t+1) = \hat{\rho}^i(t)$.*

An alternative, which is actually preferable in order to avoid useless computation and ill-conditioned inverses, is to eliminate the states $\hat{\mathbf{y}}_0^i$ and $\hat{\rho}^i$ altogether, thereby reducing the dimension of the state-space. This is simple due to the diagonal structure of the model (7): the states ρ^i, $\mathbf{y}_0^i$ are decoupled, and therefore it is sufficient to remove them, and delete the corresponding rows from the gain matrix $K(t)$ and the variance $\Sigma_w(t)$ for all t past the disappearance of the feature (see section 3.3).

When a new feature-point appears, on the other hand, it is not possible to simply insert it into the state of the model, since the initial condition is unknown. Any initialization error will disturb the current estimate of the remaining states, since it is fed back into the update equation for the filter, and generates a spurious transient. We address this problem by running a separate filter in parallel for each point using the current estimates of motion from the main filter in order to reconstruct the initial condition. Such a "subfilter" is based upon the following model, where we assume that N_τ features appear at time τ:

$$
\begin{cases}
\mathbf{y}_\tau^i(t+1) = \mathbf{y}_\tau^i(t) + \eta_{y^i(t)} & i = 1\ldots N_\tau & \mathbf{y}_\tau^i(0) \sim \mathcal{N}(\mathbf{y}^i(\tau), \Sigma_{n^i}) & t > \tau \\
\rho_\tau^i(t+1) = \rho_\tau^i(t) + \eta_{\rho^i(t)} & i = 1\ldots N_\tau & \rho^i(0) \sim \mathcal{N}(1, P_\rho(0)) \\
\mathbf{y}^i(t) = \pi\left(\exp(\widehat{\Omega}(t|t)) \left[\exp(\widehat{\Omega}(\tau|\tau))\right]^{-1} \left[\mathbf{y}_\tau^i(t)\rho_\tau^i(t) - T\left(\tau|\tau\right)\right] + T(t|t) \right) + n^i(t)
\end{cases}
$$

$$(15)$$

where $\Omega(t|t)$ and $T(t|t)$ are the current best estimates of Ω and T, $\Omega(\tau|\tau)$ and $T(\tau|\tau)$ are the best estimates of Ω and T at $t = \tau$. In pracice, rather than initializing ρ to 1, one can compute a first approximation by triangulating on two adjacent views, and compute covariance of the initialization error from the covariance of the current estimates of motion. Several heuristics can be employed in order to decide when the estimate of the initial condition is good enough for it to be inserted into the main filter. The most natural criterion is when the variance of the estimation error of ρ_τ^i in the subfilter is comparable with the variance of ρ_0^j for $j \neq i$ in the main filter. The last step in order to insert the feature i into the main filter consists in bringing the coordinates of the new points back to the initial frame. This is done by

$$
\mathbf{X}^i = \left[\exp(\widehat{\Omega}(\tau|\tau))\right]^{-1} \left[\mathbf{y}_\tau^i\rho_\tau^i - T(\tau|\tau)\right]. \tag{16}
$$

3.2 Drift

The only case when losing a feature constitutes a problem is when it is used to fix the observable component of the state-space (in our notation, $i = 1, 2, 3$) as explained in [5] [7]. The most obvious choice consists in associating the reference to any other visible point. This can be done by saturating the corresponding state and assigning as reference value the current best estimate. In particular, if feature i is lost at time τ, and we want to switch the reference index to feature

---

[7] When the scale factor is not directly associated to one feature, but is associated to a function of a number of features (for instance the depth of the centroid, or the average inverse depth), then losing any of these features causes a drift. See [5] for more details.

j, we eliminate $\mathbf{y}_0^i$, ρ^i from the state, and set the diagonal block of Σ_w and $P(\tau)$ with indices $3j - 3$ to $3j$ to zero. Therefore, by proposition 2, we have that

$$\hat{\mathbf{y}}_0^j(\tau + t) = \hat{\mathbf{y}}_0^j(\tau) \quad \forall\, t > 0. \tag{17}$$

If $\hat{\mathbf{y}}_0^j(\tau)$ was equal to $\mathbf{y}_0^j$, switching the reference feature would have no effect on the other states, and the filter would evolve on the same observable component of the state-space defined by the reference feature i.

However, in general the difference $\tilde{\mathbf{y}}_0^j(\tau) \doteq \mathbf{y}_0^j(\tau) - \hat{\mathbf{y}}_0^j$ is a random variable with variance $\Sigma_\tau = P_{3j-3:3j-1,3j-3:3j-1}$. Therefore, switching the reference to feature j causes the observable component of the state-space to move by an amount proportional to $\tilde{\mathbf{y}}_0^j(\tau)$. When a number of switches have occurred, we can expect - on average - the state-space to move by an amount proportional to $\|\Sigma_\tau\|\#$switches. As we discussed in section 1.2, this is unavoidable. What we can do is at most try to keep the bias to a minimum by switching the reference to the state that has the lowest variance[8].

Of course, should the original reference feature i become available, one can immediately switch the reference to it, and therefore recover the original base and annihilate the bias.

3.3 Complete algorithm

The implementation of an approximate wide-sense nonlinear filter for the model (7) proceeds as follows:

Initialization Choose the initial conditions $\mathbf{y}_0^i = \mathbf{y}^i(0)$, $\rho_0^i = 1$, $rT_0 = 0$, $\Omega_0 = 0$, $V_0 = 0$, $\omega_0 = 0$, $\forall\, i = 1 \ldots N$. For the initial variance P_0, choose it to be block diagonal with blocks $\Sigma_{n^i}(0)$ corresponding to $\mathbf{y}_0^i$, a large positive number M (typically 100-1000 units of focal length) corresponding to ρ^i, zeros corresponding to T_0 and Ω_0 (fixing the inertial frame to coincide with the initial reference frame). We also choose a large positive number W for the blocks corresponding to V_0 and ω_0.

The variance $\Sigma_n(t)$ is usually available from the analysis of the feature tracking algorithm. We assume that the tracking error is independent in each point, and therefore Σ_n is block diagonal. We choose each block to be the covariance of the measurement $\mathbf{y}^i(t)$ (in the current implementation they are diagonal and equal to 1 pixel std.). The variance $\Sigma_w(t)$ is a design parameter that is available for tuning. We describe the procedure in section 3.4. Finally, set

$$\begin{cases} \hat{\xi}(0|0) \doteq [\mathbf{y}^{4^T}_{0}, \ldots \mathbf{y}^{N^T}_{0}, \rho_0^2, \ldots, \rho_0^N, T_0^T, \Omega_0^T, V_0^T, \omega_0^T]^T \\ P(0|0) \doteq P_0. \end{cases} \tag{18}$$

---

[8] Just to give the reader an intuitive feeling of the numbers involved, we find that in practice the average lifetime of a feature is around 10-30 frames depending on illumination and reflectance properties of the scene and motion of the camera. The variance of the estimation error for $\mathbf{y}_0^i$ is in the order of 10^{-6} units of focal length, while the variance of ρ^i is in the order of 10^{-4} units for noise levels commonly encountered with commercial cameras.

Transient During the first transient of the filter, we do not allow for new features to be acquired. Whenever a feature is lost, its state is removed from the model and its best current estimate is placed in a storage vector. If the feature was associated with the scale factor, we proceed as in section 3.2. The transient can be tested as either a threshold on the innovation, a threshold on the variance of the estimates, or a fixed time interval. We choose a combination with the time set to 30 frames, corresponding to one second of video.

The recursion to update the state ξ and the variance P proceed as follows: Let f and h denote the state and measurement model, so that equation (7) can be written in concise form as

$$\begin{cases} \xi(t+1) = f(\xi(t)) + w(t) & w(t) \sim \mathcal{N}(0, \Sigma_w) \\ y(t) = h(\xi(t)) + n(t) & n(t) \sim \mathcal{N}(0, \Sigma_n) \end{cases} \tag{19}$$

We then have

Prediction:

$$\begin{cases} \hat{\xi}(t+1|t) = f(\hat{\xi}(t|t)) \\ P(t+1|t) = F(t)P(t|t)F^T(t) + \Sigma_w \end{cases} \tag{20}$$

Update:

$$\begin{cases} \hat{\xi}(t+1|t+1) = \hat{\xi}(t+1|t) + L(t+1)\left(y(t+1) - h(\hat{\xi}(t+1|t))\right) \\ P(t+1|t+1) = \Gamma(t+1)P(t+1|t)\Gamma^T(t+1) + L(t+1)\Sigma_n(t+1)L^T(t+1). \end{cases} \tag{21}$$

Gain:

$$\begin{cases} \Gamma(t+1) \doteq I - L(t+1)H(t+1) \\ L(t+1) \doteq P(t+1|t)H^T(t+1)\Lambda^{-1}(t+1) \\ \Lambda(t+1) \doteq H(t+1)P(t+1|t)H^T(t+1) + \Sigma_n(t+1) \end{cases} \tag{22}$$

Linearization:

$$\begin{cases} F(t) \doteq \frac{\partial f}{\partial \xi}(\hat{\xi}(t|t)) \\ H(t+1) \doteq \frac{\partial h}{\partial \xi}(\hat{\xi}(t+1|t)) \end{cases} \tag{23}$$

Let $\mathbf{e}_i$ be the i-th canonical vector in $\mathbb{R}^3$ and define $Y^i(t) \doteq e^{\hat{\Omega}(t)} \mathbf{y}_0^i(t) \rho^i(t) + T(t)$, $Z^i(t) \doteq \mathbf{e}_3^T Y^i(t)$. The i-th block-row $(i = 1, \ldots, N)$ $H_i(t)$ of the matrix $H(t)$ can be written as $H_i = \frac{\partial y^i}{\partial Y^i}\frac{\partial Y^i}{\partial \xi} \doteq \Pi_i \frac{\partial Y^i}{\partial \xi}$ where the time argument t has been omitted for simplicity of notation. It is easy to check that $\Pi_i = \frac{1}{Z^i}\begin{bmatrix} I_2 & -\pi(Y^i) \end{bmatrix}$ and

$$\frac{\partial Y^i}{\partial \xi} = \begin{bmatrix} 0 & \cdots & \frac{\partial Y^i}{\partial y_0^i} & \cdots & 0 & 0 & \cdots & \frac{\partial Y^i}{\partial \rho^i} & \cdots & 0 & \frac{\partial Y^i}{\partial T} & \frac{\partial Y^i}{\partial \Omega} & \underbrace{0}_{3} & \underbrace{0}_{3} \\ & & \underbrace{\qquad\qquad}_{2N-6} & & & & & \underbrace{\qquad}_{N-1} & & & \underbrace{\ }_{3} & \underbrace{\ }_{3} & & \end{bmatrix}.$$

The partial derivatives in the previous expression are given by

$$\begin{cases} \frac{\partial Y^i}{\partial \mathbf{y}_0^i} = e^{\hat{\Omega}} \begin{bmatrix} I_2 \\ 0 \end{bmatrix} \rho^i \\ \frac{\partial Y^i}{\partial \rho^i} = e^{\hat{\Omega}} j\, \mathbf{y}_0^i \\ \frac{\partial Y^i}{\partial T} = I \\ \frac{\partial Y^i}{\partial \Omega} = \begin{bmatrix} \frac{\partial e^{\hat{\Omega}}}{\partial \Omega_1} \mathbf{y}_0^i \rho^i & \frac{\partial e^{\hat{\Omega}}}{\partial \Omega_2} \mathbf{y}_0^i \rho^i & \frac{\partial e^{\hat{\Omega}}}{\partial \Omega_3} \mathbf{y}_0^i \rho^i \end{bmatrix} \end{cases}$$

The linearization of the state equation involves derivatives of the logarithm function in SO(3) which is available as a Matlab function in the software distribution [14] and will not be reported here. We shall use the following notation:

$$\frac{\partial Log_{SO(3)}(R)}{\partial R} \doteq \left[\begin{array}{cccc} \frac{\partial Log_{SO(3)}(R)}{\partial r_{11}} & \frac{\partial Log_{SO(3)}(R)}{\partial r_{21}} & \cdots & \frac{\partial Log_{SO(3)}(R)}{\partial r_{33}} \end{array} \right]$$

where r_{ij} is the element in position (i,j) of R. Let us denote $R \doteq e^{\hat{\omega}} e^{\hat{\Omega}}$; the linearization of the state equation can be written in the following form:

$$F \doteq \left[\begin{array}{cccccc} I_{2N-6} & 0 & 0 & 0 & 0 & 0 \\ 0 & I_{N-1} & 0 & 0 & 0 & 0 \\ 0 & 0 & e^{\hat{\omega}} & 0 & I & \left[\frac{\partial e^{\hat{\omega}}}{\partial \omega_1} T \; \frac{\partial e^{\hat{\omega}}}{\partial \omega_2} T \; \frac{\partial e^{\hat{\omega}}}{\partial \omega_3} T \right] \\ 0 & 0 & 0 & \frac{\partial Log_{SO(3)}(R)}{\partial R} \frac{\partial R}{\partial \Omega} & 0 & \frac{\partial Log_{SO(3)}(R)}{\partial R} \frac{\partial R}{\partial \omega} \\ 0 & 0 & 0 & 0 & I & 0 \\ 0 & 0 & 0 & 0 & 0 & I \end{array} \right]$$

where

$$\frac{\partial R}{\partial \Omega} \doteq \left[\left(e^{\hat{\omega}} \frac{\partial e^{\hat{\Omega}}}{\partial \Omega_1} \right)^{\vee} \; \left(e^{\hat{\omega}} \frac{\partial e^{\hat{\Omega}}}{\partial \Omega_2} \right)^{\vee} \; \left(e^{\hat{\omega}} \frac{\partial e^{\hat{\Omega}}}{\partial \Omega_3} \right)^{\vee} \right]$$

and

$$\frac{\partial R}{\partial \omega} \doteq \left[\left(\frac{\partial e^{\hat{\omega}}}{\partial \omega_1} e^{\hat{\Omega}} \right)^{\vee} \; \left(\frac{\partial e^{\hat{\omega}}}{\partial \omega_2} e^{\hat{\Omega}} \right)^{\vee} \; \left(\frac{\partial e^{\hat{\omega}}}{\partial \omega_3} e^{\hat{\Omega}} \right)^{\vee} \right]$$

and the bracket $(\cdot)^{\vee}$ indicates that the content has been organized into a column vector.

Regime Whenever a feature disappears, we simply remove it from the state as during the transient. However, after the transient a feature selection module works in parallel with the filter to select new features so as to maintain roughly a constant number (equal to the maximum that the hardware can handle in real time), and to maintain a distribution as uniform as possible across the image plane. We implement this by randomly sampling points on the plane, searching then around that point for a feature with enough brightness gradient (we use an SSD-type test [17]).

Once a new point-feature is found (one with enough contrast along two independent directions), a new filter (which we call a "subfilter") is initialized based on the model (15). Its evolution is given by

Initialization:

$$\begin{cases} \hat{\mathbf{y}}_{\tau}^i(\tau|\tau) = \mathbf{y}_{\tau}^i(\tau) \\ \hat{\rho}_{\tau}^i(\tau|\tau) = 1 \\ \\ P_{\tau}(\tau|\tau) = \left[\begin{array}{ccc} \ddots & & \\ & \Sigma_{n^i}(\tau) & \\ & & \ddots \\ & & \qquad M \end{array} \right] \end{cases} \tag{24}$$

Prediction:

$$\begin{cases} \hat{\mathbf{y}}_\tau^i(t+1|t) = \hat{\mathbf{y}}_\tau^i(t|t) \\ \hat{\rho}_\tau^i(t+1|t) = \hat{\rho}_\tau^i(t|t) \\ P_\tau(t+1|t) = P_\tau(t+1|t) + \Sigma_w(t) \end{cases} \qquad t > \tau \qquad (25)$$

Update:

$$\begin{bmatrix} \hat{y}_\tau^i(t+1|t+1) \\ \hat{\rho}_\tau(t+1|t+1) \end{bmatrix} = \begin{bmatrix} \hat{y}_\tau^i(t+1|t) \\ \hat{\rho}_\tau(t+1|t) \end{bmatrix} + L_\tau(t+1) \left(y^i(t) - \pi(\exp(\widehat{\Omega}(t)) \left[\exp(\widehat{\Omega}(\tau))\right]^{-1} \left[y^i(t)\rho^i(t) - T(\tau)\right] + T(t)) \right)$$

$$(26)$$

and P_τ is updated according to a Riccati equation in all similar to (21).

After a probation period, whose length is chosen according to the same criterion adopted for the main filter, the feature is inserted into the state using the transformation (16). The initial variance is chosen to be the variance of the estimation error of the subfilter.

3.4 Tuning

The variance $\Sigma_w(t)$ is a design parameter. We choose it to be block diagonal, with the blocks corresponding to $T(t)$ and $\Omega(t)$ equal to zero (a deterministic integrator). We choose the remaining parameters using standard statistical tests, such as the Cumulative Periodogram of Bartlett [3]. The idea is that the parameters in Σ_w are changed until the innovation process $\epsilon(t) \doteq y(t) - h(\hat{\xi}(t))$ is as close as possible to being white. The periodogram is one of many ways to test the "whiteness" of a stochastic process. In practice, we choose the blocks corresponding to $\mathbf{y}_0^i$ equal to the variance of the measurements, and the elements corresponding to ρ^i all equal to σ_ρ. We then choose the blocks corresponding to V and ω to be diagonal with element σ_v, and then we change σ_v relative to σ_ρ depending on whether we want to allow for more or less regular motions. We then change both, relative to the variance of the measurement noise, depending on the level of desired smoothness in the estimates.

Tuning nonlinear filters is an art, and this is not the proper venue to discuss this issue. Suffices to say that we have only performed the procedure once and for all. We then keep the same tuning parameters no matter what the motion, structure and noise in the measurements.

4 Experiments

The complexity of SFM makes it difficult to demonstrate the performance of an algorithm by means of a few plots. This is what motivated us to (a) obtain analytical results, which are presented in [5], and (b) make our real-time implementation available to the public, so that the performance of the filter can be tested first-hand [14].

In this section, for the sake of exemplification, we present a small sample of the performance of the filter as characterized with a few experiments on our real-time platform.

4.1 Structure error

One of the byproducts of our algorithms is an estimate of the position of a number of point-features in the camera reference frame at the initial time. We use such estimates for a known object in order to characterize the performance of the filter. In particular, the distance between adjacent point on a checkerboard patter (see figure 1) is known to be 2cm. We have run the filter on a sequence of 200 frames and identified adjacent features, and plotted their distance (minus 2cm) in figure 1. It can be seen that the distance, despite an arbitrary initialization, remains well below 1mm.

 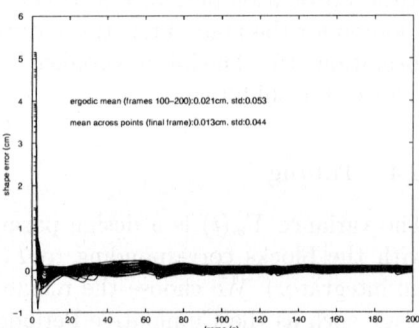

Fig. 1. *(Left)* **A display of the real-time system.** *Selected features are highlighted by asterisks, and a virtual object (a reference frame) is placed in the scene. As the camera moves, the image of the virtual object is modified in real time, according to the estimated motion and structure of the scene, so as to make it appear stationary within the scene. Other displays visualize the motion of the camera relative to an inertial reference frame, and a bird's eye view of the reconstructed position of the points tracked. (Right)* **Structure error:** *the error in mutual distance between a set of 20 points for which the relative position is known (the squares in the checkerboard box on the left) are plotted for a sequence of 200 frames. Mean and standard deviation, both computed across the set of points at the last frame and across the last 100 frames, are below one millimeter. The experiment is performed off-line, and only unoccluded features are considered.*

4.2 Motion error

Errors in motion are difficult to characterize on real sequences of images, for external means of estimating motion (e.g. inertial, magnetic sensors, encoders) are likely to be less accurate than vision. We have therefore placed a checkerboard box on a turntable and moved it for a few seconds, going back to its original position, marked with a accuracy greater than 0.5mm. In figure 2 we show the distance between the estimated position of the camera and the initial position. Again, the error is below 1mm.

Notice that in these experiments we have fixed the scale factor using the fact that the side of a square in the checkerboard is 2cm and we have processed the data off-line, so that only the unoccluded points are used.

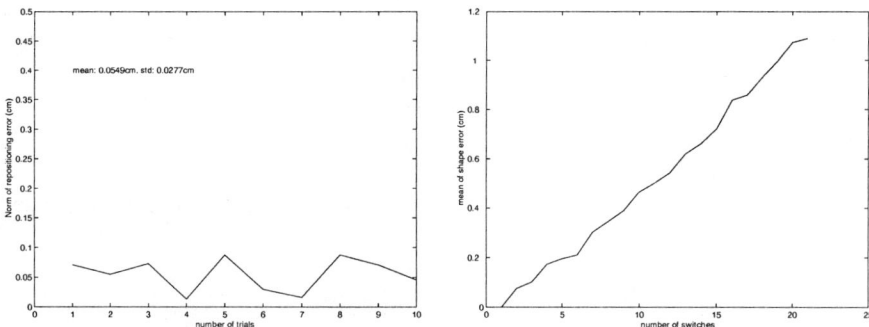

Fig. 2. *(Left)* **Motion error:** *a checkerboard box is rotated on a turntable and then brought back to the initial position 10 times. We plot the distance of the estimated position from the initial time for the 10 trials. The ergodic mean and std are below one millimeter. (Right)* **Scale drift:** *during a sequence of 200 frames, the reference feature was switched 20 times. The mean of the shape error increases drifts away, but at a slow pace, reaching about one centimeter by the end of the sequence*

4.3 Scale drift

In order to quantify the drift that occurs when the reference feature becomes occluded, we have generated a sequence of 200 frames and artificially switched the reference feature every 10 frames. The mean of the structure error is shown in figure 2. Despite being unavoidable, the drift is quite modest, around 1cm after 20 switches.

4.4 Use of the motion estimates for rendering

The estimates of motion obtained using the algorithm we have described can be used in order to obtain estimates of shape. As a simple example, we have taken an uncalibrated sequence of images, shown in figure 3, and estimated its motion and focal length with the model described in section 2.1, while fixing the optical center at the center of the image. We have then used the estimates of motion to perform a dense correlation-based triangulation. The position of some 120,000 points, rendered with shading, is shown in figure 3, along with two views obtained from novel viewpoints.

Although there is no ground truth available, the qualitative shape of the scene seems to have been captured. Sure there are several artifacts. However, we would like to stress that these results have been obtained entirely automatically.

Fig. 3. The "temple sequence" (courtesy of AIACE): one image out of a sequence of 46 views of an Etruscan temple (top-left): no calibration data is available. The motion estimated using the algorithm presented in this paper can be used to triangulate each pixel, thus obtaining a "dense" representation of the scene. This can be rendered with shading (top-right) or texture-mapped and rendered from an arbitrary viewpoint (bottom left and right). Although no ground truth is available and there are significant artifacts, the qualitative shape can be appreciated from the rendered views.

5 Conclusions

The causal estimation of three-dimensional structure and motion can be posed as a nonlinear filtering problem. In this paper we have described the implementation of an algorithm whose global observability, uniform observability, minimal realization and stability have been proven in [5].

The filter has been implemented on a personal computer, and the implementation has been made available to the public. The filter exhibits honest performance when the scene contains at least 20-40 points with high contrast, when the relative motion is "slow" (compared to the sampling frequency of the frame grabber), when the scene occupies a significant portion of the image and the lens aperture is "large enough" (typically more than $30°$ of visual field).

While it is relatively simple to design an experiment where the implementation fails to provide reliable estimates (changing illumination, specularities etc.), we believe that the algorithm we propose is close to the performance limits for causal, real-time algorithms to recover point-wise structure and motion[9]. In order to improve the performance of motion estimates, we believe that a more "global" representation of the environment is needed. Using feature-points alone, we think this is as good as it gets.

The next logical steps are in two directions. On one hand to explore more meaningful representations of the environment as a collection of surfaces with certain shape emitting a certain energy distribution. On the other hand, a theoretically sound treatment of nonlinear filtering for these problem involves estimation on Riemannian manifolds and homogeneous spaces. Both are open and challenging problems in need of meaningful solutions.

References

1. G. Adiv. Determining three-dimensional motion and structure from optical flow generated by several moving objects. *IEEE Trans. Pattern Anal. Mach. Intell.*, 7(4):348–401, 1985.
2. A. Azarbayejani and A. Pentland. Recursive estimation of motion, structure and focal length. *IEEE Trans. Pattern Anal. Mach. Intell.*, 17(6):562–575, 1995.
3. M.S. Bartlett. *An Introduction to Stochastic Processes.* Cambridge University Press, 1956.
4. T. Broida and R. Chellappa. Estimation of object motion parameters from noisy images. *IEEE Trans. Pattern Anal. Mach. Intell.*, Jan. 1986.
5. A. Chiuso and S. Soatto. 3-d motion and structure causally integrated over time: Theory. In *Tutorial lecture notes of IEEE Intl. Conf. on Robotics and Automation*, April 2000.
6. W. Dayawansa, B. Ghosh, C. Martin, and X. Wang. A necessary and sufficient condition for the perspective observability problem. *Systems and Control Letters*, 25(3):159–166, 1994.
7. E. D. Dickmanns and V. Graefe. Applications of dynamic monocular machine vision. *Machine Vision and Applications*, 1:241–261, 1988.
8. O. Faugeras. *Three dimensional vision, a geometric viewpoint.* MIT Press, 1993.
9. C. Fermüller and Y. Aloimonos. Tracking facilitates 3-d motion estimation. *Biological Cybernetics (67), 259-268*, 1992.
10. D.B. Gennery. Tracking known 3-dimensional object. In *Proc. AAAI 2nd Natl. Conf. Artif. Intell.*, pages 13–17, Pittsburg, PA, 1982.
11. J. Heel. Dynamic motion vision. *Robotics and Autonomous Systems*, 6(1), 1990.
12. X. Hu and N. Ahuja. Motion and structure estimation using long sequence motion models. *Image and Vision Computing*, 11(9):549–569, 1993.
13. A. Jepson and D. Heeger. Subspace methods for recovering rigid motion ii: theory. RBCV TR-90-35, University of Toronto – CS dept., November 1990. Revised July 1991.
14. H. Jin, P. Favaro, and S. Soatto. Real-time 3-d motion and structure from point features: a front-end system for vision-based control and interaction. In *Computer Vision and Pattern Recognition; code available from* http://ee.wustl.edu/~soatto/research/, June 2000.

---

[9] Of course we have no proof of this claim, and even comparisons with theoretical lower bounds are meaningless in this context, since the conditional density of the state is unknown and cannot be computed with a finite-dimensional algorithm, as explained in [5].

15. J. J. Koenderink and A. J. Van Doorn. Affine structure from motion. *J. Optic. Soc. Am.*, 8(2):377–385, 1991.
16. R. Kumar, P. Anandan, and K. Hanna. Shape recovery from multiple views: a parallax based approach. *Proc. of the Image Understanding Workshop*, 1994.
17. B.D. Lucas and T. Kanade. An iterative image registration technique with an application to stereo vision. *Proc. 7th Int. Joinnt Conf. on Art. Intell.*, 1981.
18. L. Matthies, R. Szelisky, and T. Kanade. Kalman filter-based algorithms for estimating depth from image sequences. *Int. J. of computer vision*, pages 2989–2994, 1989.
19. P. McLauchlan, I. Reid, and D. Murray. Recursive affine structure and motion from image sequences. *Proc. of the 3rd Eur. Conf. Comp. Vision*, Stockholm, May 1994.
20. P. F. McLauchlan. Gauge invariance in projective 3d reconstruction. In *IEEE Workshop on Multi-View Modeling and Analysis of Visual Scenes, Fort Collins, CO, June 1999*, 1999.
21. J. Oliensis. Provably correct algorithms for multi-frame structure from motion. In *Proceedings of the IEEE Conference on Computer Vision and Pattern Recognition (CVPR)*, 1996.
22. J. Oliensis and J. Inigo-Thomas. Recursive multi-frame structure from motion incorporating motion error. *Proc. DARPA Image Understanding Workshop*, 1992.
23. J. Philip. Estimation of three dimensional motion of rigid objects from noisy observations. *IEEE Trans. Pattern Anal. Mach. Intell.*, 13(1):61–66, 1991.
24. C. Poelman and T. Kanade. A paraperspective factorization method for shape and motion recovery. *Proc. of the 3 ECCV, LNCS Vol 810, Springer Verlag*, 1994.
25. H. S. Sawhney. Simplifying motion and structure analysis using planar parallax and image warping. *Proc. of the Int. Conf. on Pattern Recognition*, Seattle, June 1994.
26. L. Shapiro, A. Zisserman, and M. Brady. Motion from point matches using affine epipolar geometry. *Proc. of the ECCV94, Vol. 800 of LNCS, Springer Verlag*, 1994.
27. S. Soatto. Observability/identifiability of rigid motion under perspective projection. In *Proc. of the 33rd IEEE Conf. on Decision and Control*, pages 3235–3240, Dec. 1994.
28. S. Soatto. 3-d structure from visual motion: modeling, representation and observability. *Automatica*, 33:1287–1312, 1997.
29. S. Soatto and P. Perona. Reducing "structure from motion": a general framework for dynamic vision. part 1: modeling. *IEEE Trans. Pattern Anal. Mach. Intell.*, 20(9):993–942, September 1998.
30. M. Spetsakis and J. Aloimonos. A multi-frame approach to visual motion perception. *Int. J. Computer Vision 6 (3)*, 1991.
31. R. Szeliski. Recovering 3d shape and motion from image streams using nonlinear least squares. *J. visual communication and image representation*, 1994.
32. M. A. Taalebinezhaad. Direct recovery of motion and shape in the general case by fixation. *IEEE Trans. Pattern Anal. Mach. Intell.*, 14(8):847–853, 1992.
33. C. Tomasi and T. Kanade. Shape and motion from image streams under orthography: a factorization method. *Int. J. of Computer Vision*, 9(2):137–154, 1992.
34. J. Weng, N. Ahuja, and T. Huang. Optimal motion and structure estimation. *IEEE Trans. Pattern Anal. Mach. Intell.*, 15:864–884, 1993.
35. Z. Zhang and O. D. Faugeras. Three dimensional motion computation and object segmentation in a long sequence of stereo frames. *Int. J. of Computer Vision*, 7(3):211–241, 1992.

Non-parametric Model for Background Subtraction

Ahmed Elgammal, David Harwood, Larry Davis

Computer Vision Laboratory
University of Maryland, College Park, MD 20742, USA
{elgammal,harwood,lsd}@umiacs.umd.edu

Abstract. Background subtraction is a method typically used to segment moving regions in image sequences taken from a static camera by comparing each new frame to a model of the scene background. We present a novel non-parametric background model and a background subtraction approach. The model can handle situations where the background of the scene is cluttered and not completely static but contains small motions such as tree branches and bushes. The model estimates the probability of observing pixel intensity values based on a sample of intensity values for each pixel. The model adapts quickly to changes in the scene which enables very sensitive detection of moving targets. We also show how the model can use color information to suppress detection of shadows. The implementation of the model runs in real-time for both gray level and color imagery. Evaluation shows that this approach achieves very sensitive detection with very low false alarm rates.

Key words: visual motion, active and real time vision, motion detection, non-parametric estimation, visual surveillance, shadow detection

1   Introduction

The detection of unusual motion is the first stage in many automated visual surveillance applications. It is always desirable to achieve very high sensitivity in the detection of moving objects with the lowest possible false alarm rates. Background subtraction is a method typically used to detect unusual motion in the scene by comparing each new frame to a model of the scene background.

If we monitor the intensity value of a pixel over time in a completely static scene (i.e., with no background motion) , then the pixel intensity can be reasonably modeled with a Normal distribution $N(\mu, \sigma^2)$, given the image noise over time can be modeled by a zero mean Normal distribution $N(0, \sigma^2)$. This Normal distribution model for the intensity value of a pixel is the underlying model for many background subtraction techniques. For example, one of the simplest background subtraction techniques is to calculate an average image of the scene with no moving objects, subtract each new frame from this image, and threshold the result.

This basic Normal model can adapt to slow changes in the scene (for example, illumination changes) by recursively updating the model using a simple adaptive filter. This basic adaptive model is used in [1], also Kalman filtering for adaptation is used in [2–4].

In many visual surveillance applications that work with outdoor scenes, the background of the scene contains many non-static objects such as tree branches and bushes whose movement depends on the wind in the scene. This kind of background motion causes the pixel intensity values to vary significantly with time. For example, one pixel can be image of the sky at one frame, tree leaf at another frame, tree branch on a third frame and some mixture subsequently; in each situation the pixel will have a different color.

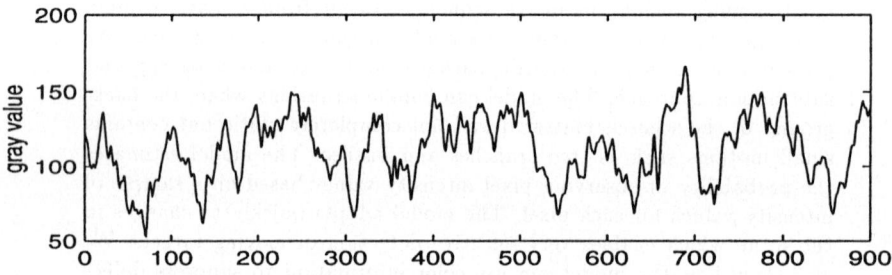

Fig. 1. Intensity value overtime

Fig. 2. Outdoor scene with a circle at the top left corner showing the location of the sample pixel in figure 1

Figure 1 shows how the gray level of a vegetation pixel from an outdoor scene changes over a short period of time (900 frames-30 seconds). The scene is shown at figure 2. Figure 3-a shows the intensity histogram for this pixel. It is clear that intensity distribution is multi-modal so that the Normal distribution model for the pixel intensity/color would not hold.

In [5] a mixture of three Normal distributions was used to model the pixel value for traffic surveillance applications. The pixel intensity was modeled as a weighted mixture of three Normal distributions: road, shadow and vehicle distribution. An incremental EM algorithm was used to learn and update the parameters of the model. Although, in this case, the pixel intensity is modeled with three distributions, still the uni-modal distribution assumption is used for the scene background, i.e. the road distribution.

In [6, 7] a generalization to the previous approach was presented. The pixel intensity is modeled by a mixture of K Gaussian distributions (K is a small number from 3 to 5) to model variations in the background like tree branch motion and similar small motion in outdoor scenes. The probability that a certain pixel has intensity x_t at time t is estimated as:

$$Pr(x_t) = \sum_{j=1}^{K} \frac{w_j}{(2\pi)^{\frac{d}{2}} \mid \Sigma_j \mid^{\frac{1}{2}}} e^{-\frac{1}{2}(x_t - \mu_j)^T \Sigma_j^{-1}(x_t - \mu_j)} \tag{1}$$

where w_j is the weight, μ_j is the mean and $\Sigma_j = \sigma_j^2 I$ is the covariance for the jth distribution. The K distributions are ordered based on w_j/σ_j^2 and the first B distributions are used as a model of the background of the scene where B is estimated as

$$B = \arg\min_{b} \left(\frac{\sum_{j=1}^{b} w_j}{\sum_{j=1}^{K} w_j} > T \right) \tag{2}$$

The threshold T is the fraction of the total weight given to the background model. Background subtraction is performed by marking any pixel that is more that 2.5 standard deviations away from any of the B distributions as a foreground pixel. The parameters of the distributions are updated recursively using a learning rate α, where $1/\alpha$ controls the speed at which the model adapts to change.

In the case where the background has very high frequency variations, this model fails to achieve sensitive detection. For example, the 30 second intensity histogram, shown in figure 3-a, shows that the intensity distribution covers a very wide range of gray levels (this would be true for color also.) All these variations occur in a very short period of time (30 seconds.) Modeling the background variations with a small number of Gaussian distribution will not be accurate. Furthermore, the very wide background distribution will result in poor detection because most of the gray level spectrum would be covered by the background model.

Another important factor is how fast the background model adapts to change. Figure 3-b shows 9 histograms of the same pixel obtained by dividing the original time interval into nine equal length subintervals, each contains 100 frames ($3\frac{1}{3}$ seconds.) From these partial histogram we notice that the intensity distribution is changing dramatically over very short periods of time. Using more "short-term" distributions will allow us to obtain better detection sensitivity.

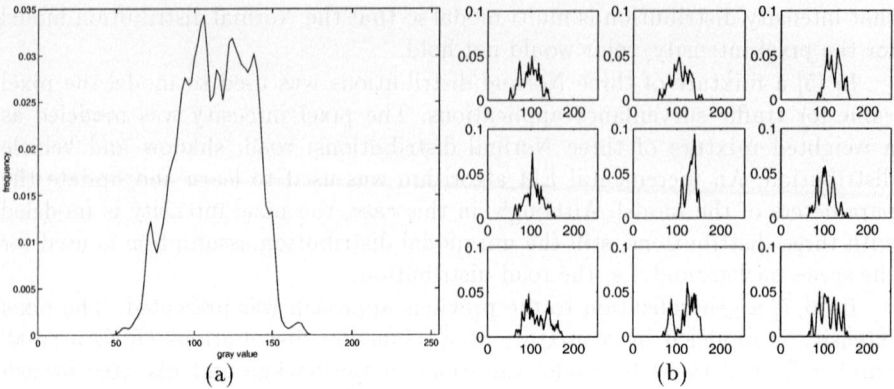

Fig. 3. (a) Histogram of intensity values, (b) Partial histograms

We are faced with the following trade off: if the background model adapts too slowly to changes in the scene, then we will construct a very wide and inaccurate model that will have low detection sensitivity. On the other hand, if the model adapts too quickly, this will lead to two problems: the model may adapt to the targets themselves, as their speed cannot be neglected with respect to the background variations, and it leads to inaccurate estimation of the model parameters.

Our objective is to be able to accurately model the background process non-parametrically. The model should adapt very quickly to changes in the background process, and detect targets with high sensitivity. In the following sections we describe a background model that achieves these objectives. The model keeps a sample for each pixel of the scene and estimates the probability that a newly observed pixel value is from the background. The model estimates these probabilities independently for each new frame. In section 2 we describe the suggested background model and background subtraction process. A second stage of background subtraction is discussed in section 3 that aims to suppress false detections that are due to small motions in the background not captured by the model. Adapting to long-term changes is discussed in section 4. In section 5 we explain how to use color to suppress shadows from being detected.

2 Basic Background Model

2.1 Density Estimation

In this section, we describe the basic background model and the background subtraction process. The objective of the model is to capture very recent information about the image sequence, continuously updating this information to capture fast changes in the scene background. As shown in figure 3-b, the intensity distribution of a pixel can change quickly. So we must estimate the density function of this distribution at any moment of time given only very recent history information if we hope to obtain sensitive detection.

Let $x_1, x_2, ..., x_N$ be a recent sample of intensity values for a pixel. Using this sample, the probability density function that this pixel will have intensity value x_t at time t can be non-parametrically estimated [8] using the kernel estimator K as

$$Pr(x_t) = \frac{1}{n} \sum_{i=1}^{N} K(x_t - x_i) \tag{3}$$

If we choose our kernel estimator function, K, to be a Normal function $N(0, \Sigma)$, where Σ represents the kernel function bandwidth, then the density can be estimated as

$$Pr(x_t) = \frac{1}{N} \sum_{i=1}^{N} \frac{1}{(2\pi)^{\frac{d}{2}} |\Sigma|^{\frac{1}{2}}} e^{-\frac{1}{2}(x_t - x_i)^T \Sigma^{-1} (x_t - x_i)} \tag{4}$$

If we assume independence between the different color channels with a different kernel bandwidths σ_j^2 for the jth color channel, then

$$\Sigma = \begin{pmatrix} \sigma_1^2 & 0 & 0 \\ 0 & \sigma_2^2 & 0 \\ 0 & 0 & \sigma_3^2 \end{pmatrix}$$

and the density estimation is reduced to

$$Pr(x_t) = \frac{1}{N} \sum_{i=1}^{N} \prod_{j=1}^{d} \frac{1}{\sqrt{2\pi\sigma_j^2}} e^{-\frac{1}{2} \frac{(x_{t_j} - x_{i_j})^2}{\sigma_j^2}} \tag{5}$$

Using this probability estimate the, pixel is considered a foreground pixel if $Pr(x_t) < th$ where the threshold th is a global threshold over all the image that can be adjusted to achieve a desired percentage of false positives. Practically, the probability estimation of equation 5 can be calculated in a very fast way using precalculated lookup tables for the kernel function values given the intensity value difference, $(x_t - x_i)$, and the kernel function bandwidth. Moreover, a partial evaluation of the sum in equation 5 is usually sufficient to surpass the threshold at most image pixels, since most of the image is typically sampled from the background. This allows us to construct a very fast implementation of the probability estimation.

Density estimation using a Normal kernel function is a generalization of the Gaussian mixture model, where each single sample of the N samples is considered to be a Gaussian distribution $N(0, \Sigma)$ by itself. This allows us to estimate the density function more accurately and depending only on recent information from the sequence. This also enables the model to quickly "forget" about the past and concentrate more on recent observation. At the same time, we avoid the inevitable errors in parameter estimation, which typically require large amounts of data to be both accurate and unbiased. In section 6.1, we present a comparison

(a)   (b)

Fig. 4. Background Subtraction. (a) original image. (b) Estimated probability image.

between the two models. We will show that if both models are given the same amount of memory, and the parameters of the two models are adjusted to achieve the same false positive rates, then the non-parametric model has much higher sensitivity in detection than the mixture of K Gaussians.

Figure 4-b shows the estimated background probability where brighter pixels represent lower background probability pixels.

2.2 Kernel Width Estimation

There are at least two sources of variations in a pixel's intensity value. First, there are large jumps between different intensity values because different objects (sky, branch, leaf and mixtures when an edge passes through the pixel) are projected to the same pixel at different times. Second, for those very short periods of time when the pixel is a projection of the same object, there are local intensity variations due to blurring in the image. The kernel bandwidth, Σ, should reflect the local variance in the pixel intensity due to the local variation from image blur and not the intensity jumps. This local variance will vary over the image and change over time. The local variance is also different among the color channels, requiring different bandwidths for each color channel in the kernel calculation.

To estimate the kernel band width σ_j^2 for the jth color channel for a given pixel we compute the median absolute deviation over the sample for consecutive intensity values of the pixel. That is, the median, m, of $\mid x_i - x_{i+1} \mid$ for each consecutive pair (x_i, x_{i+1}) in the sample, is calculated independently for each color channel. Since we are measuring deviations between two consecutive intensity values, the pair (x_i, x_{i+1}) usually comes from the same local-in-time distribution and only few pairs are expected to come from cross distributions. If we assume that this local-in-time distribution is Normal $N(\mu, \sigma^2)$, then the deviation $(x_i - x_{i+1})$ is Normal $N(0, 2\sigma^2)$. So the standard deviation of the first distribution can be estimated as

$$\sigma = \frac{m}{0.68\sqrt{2}}$$

Since the deviations are integer values, linear interpolation is used to obtain more accurate median values.

3 Suppression of False Detection

In outdoor environments with fluctuating backgrounds, there are two sources of false detections. First, there are false detections due to random noise which should be homogeneous over the entire image. Second, there are false detection due to small movements in the scene background that are not represented in the background model. This can occur, for example, if a tree branch moves further than it did during model generation. Also small camera displacements due to wind load are common in outdoor surveillance and cause many false detections. This kind of false detection is usually spatially clustered in the image and it is not easy to eliminate using morphology or noise filtering because these operations might also affect small and/or occluded targets.

The second stage of detection aim to suppress the false detections due to small and unmodelled movements in the scene background. If some part of the background (a tree branch for example) moves to occupy a new pixel, but it was not part of the model for that pixel, then it will be detected as a foreground object. However, this object will have a high probability to be a part of the background distribution at its original pixel. Assuming that only a small displacement can occur between consecutive frames, we decide if a detected pixel is caused by a background object that has moved by considering the background distributions in a small neighborhood of the detection.

Let x_t be the observed value of a pixel, x, detected as a foreground pixel by the first stage of the background subtraction at time t. We define the pixel displacement probability, $P_{\mathcal{N}}(x_t)$, to be the maximum probability that the observed value, x_t, belongs to the background distribution of some point in the neighborhood $\mathcal{N}(x)$ of x

$$P_{\mathcal{N}}(x_t) = \max_{y \in \mathcal{N}(x)} Pr(x_t \mid B_y)$$

where B_y is the background sample for pixel y and the probability estimation, $Pr(x_t \mid B_y)$, is calculated using the kernel function estimation as in equation 5. By thresholding $P_{\mathcal{N}}$ for detected pixels we can eliminate many false detections due to small motions in the background. Unfortunately, we can also eliminate some true detections by this process, since some true detected pixels might be accidentally similar to the background of some nearby pixel. This happens more often on gray level images. To avoid losing such true detections we add the constraint that the whole detected foreground object must have moved from a nearby location, and not only some of its pixels. We define the component displacement probability, $P_{\mathcal{C}}$, to be the probability that a detected connected component $\mathcal{C}$ has been displaced from a nearby location. This probability is estimated by

$$P_{\mathcal{C}} = \prod_{x \in \mathcal{C}} P_{\mathcal{N}(x)}$$

758

For a connected component corresponding to a real target, the probability that this component has displaced from the background will be very small. So, a detected pixel x will be considered to be a part of the background only if $(P_{\mathcal{N}}(x) > th_1) \wedge (P_{\mathcal{C}}(x) > th_2)$.

In our implementation, a diameter 5 circular neighborhood is used to determine pixel displacement probabilities for pixels detected from stage one. The threshold th_1 was set to be the same threshold used during the first background subtraction stage which was adjusted to produce a fixed false detection rate. The threshold, th_2, can powerfully discriminate between real moving components and displaced ones since the former have much lower component displacement probabilities.

Fig. 5. Effect of the second stage of detection on suppressing false detections

Figure 5 illustrates the effect of the second stage of detection. The result after the first stage is shown in figure 5-b. In this example, the background has not been updated for several seconds and the camera has been slightly displaced during this time interval, so we see many false detection along high contrast edges. Figure 5-c shows the result after suppressing detected pixels with high displacement probability. We eliminates most of the false detections due to displacement, and only random noise that is not correlated with the scene remains as false detections; but some true detected pixel were also lost. The final result of the second stage of the detection is shown in figure 5-d where the component displacement probability constraint was added. Figure 6-b shows another results where as a result of the wind load the camera is shaking slightly which results in a lot of clustered false detections especially on the edges. After the second stage of detection, figure 6-c, most of these clustered false detection are suppressed while the small target at the left side of the image remains.

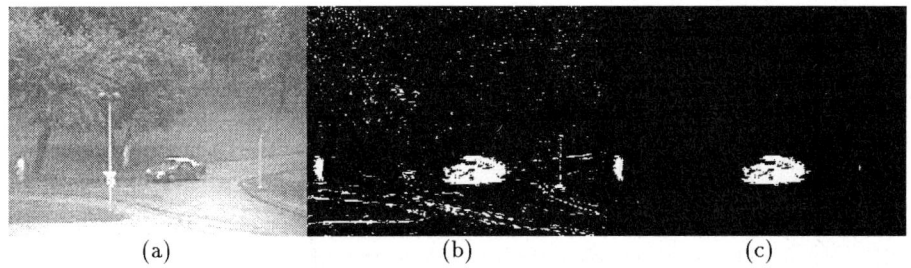

(a)   (b)   (c)

Fig. 6. b) Result after first stage of detection. (c) Result after second stage

4   Updating The Background

In the previous sections it was shown how to detect foreground regions given a recent history sample as a model of the background. This sample contains N intensity values taken over a window in time of size W. The kernel bandwidth estimation requires all the sample to be consecutive in time, i.e., $N = W$ or sample $\frac{N}{2}$ pairs of consecutive intensity values over time W.

This sample needs to be updated continuously to adapt to changes in the scene. The update is performed in a first-in first-out manner. That is, the oldest sample/pair is discarded and a new sample/pair is added to the model. The new sample is chosen randomly from each interval of length $\frac{W}{N}$ frames.

Given a new pixel sample, there are two alternative mechanisms to update the background:

1. Selective Update: add the new sample to the model only if it is classified as a background sample.
2. Blind Update: just add the new sample to the model.

There are tradeoffs to these two approaches. The first enhance detection of the targets, since target pixels are not added to the model. This involves an update decision: we have to decide if each pixel value belongs to the background or not. The simplest way to do this is to use the detection result as an update decision. The problem with this approach is that any incorrect detection decision will result in persistent incorrect detection later, which is a deadlock situations [2]. So for example, if a tree branch might be displaced and stayed fixed in the new location for a long time, it would be continually detected.

The second approach does not suffer from this deadlock situation since it does not involve any update decisions; it allows intensity values that do not belong to the background to be added to the model. This leads to bad detection of the targets (more false negatives) as they erroneously become part of the model. This effect is reduced as we increase the time window over which the sample are taken, as a smaller proportion of target pixels will be included in the sample. But as we increase the time window more false positives will occur because the adaptation to changes is slower and rare events are not as well represented in the sample.

Our objective is to build a background model that adapts quickly to changes in the scene to support sensitive detection and low false positive rates. To achieve this goal we present a way to combine the results of two background models (a long term and a short term) in such a way to achieve better update decisions and avoid the tradeoffs discussed above. The two models are designed to achieve different objectives. First we describe the features of each model.

Short-term model: This is a very recent model of the scene. It adapts to changes quickly to allow very sensitive detection. This model consists of the most recent N background sample values. The sample is updated using a selective-update mechanism, where the update decision is based on a mask $M(p,t)$ where $M(p,t) = 1$ if the pixel p should be updated at time t and 0 otherwise. This mask is driven from the final result of combining the two models.

This model is expected to have two kinds of false positives: false positives due to rare events that are not represented in the model, and persistent false positives that might result from incorrect detection/update decisions due to changes in the scene background.

Long-term model: This model captures a more stable representation of the scene background and adapts to changes slowly. This model consists of N sample points taken from a much larger window in time. The sample is updated using a blind-update mechanism, so that every new sample is added to the model regardless of classification decisions. This model is expected to have more false positives because it is not the most recent model of the background, and more false negatives because target pixels might be included in the sample. This model adapts to changes in the scene at a slow rate based on the ratio W/N

Computing the intersection of the two detection results will eliminate the persistence false positives from the short term model and will eliminate as well extra false positives that occur in the long term model results. The only false positives that will remain will be rare events not represented in either model. If this rare event persists over time in the scene then the long term model will adapt to it, and it will be suppressed from the result later.

Taking the intersection will, unfortunately, suppress true positives in the first model result that are false negatives in the second, because the long term model adapts to targets as well if they are stationary or moving slowly. To address this problem, all pixels detected by the short term model that are adjacent to pixels detected by the combination are included in the final result.

5 Shadow detection

The detection of shadows as foreground regions is a source of confusion for subsequent phases of analysis. It is desirable to discriminate between targets and their detected shadows. Color information is useful for suppressing shadows from detection by separating color information from lightness information. Given three color variables, R, G and B, the chromaticity coordinates r, g and b are $r = \frac{R}{R+G+B}, g = \frac{G}{R+G+B}, b = \frac{B}{R+G+B}$ where $r + g + b = 1$ [9]. Using the chromaticity coordinates in detection has the advantage of being more insensitive to small changes in illumination that are due to shadows. Figure 7 shows the results of detection using both (R, G, B) space and (r, g) space; the figure shows that using the chromaticity coordinates allow detection of the target without detecting their shadows. Notice that the background subtraction technique as described in section 2 can be used with any color space.

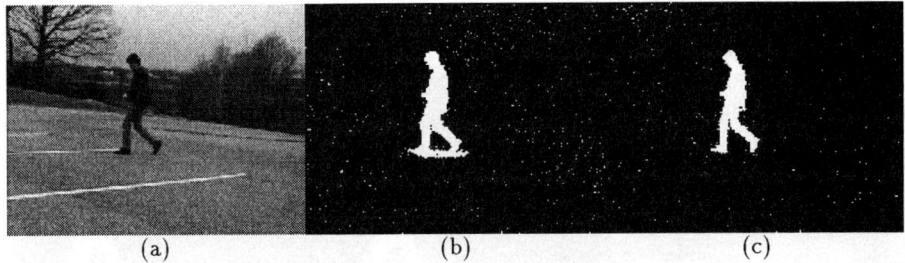

(a)   (b)   (c)

Fig. 7. b) Detection using (R,G,B) color space c) detection using chromaticity coordinates (r,g)

Although using chromaticity coordinates helps suppressing shadows, they have the disadvantage of losing lightness information. Lightness is related to the difference in whiteness, blackness and grayness between different objects [10]. For example, consider the case where the target wears a white shirt and walks against a gray background. In this case there is no color information. Since both white and gray have the same chromaticity coordinates, the target will not be detected.

To address this problem we also need to use a measure of lightness at each pixel. We use $s = R + G + B$ as a lightness measure. Consider the case where the background is completely static, and let the expected value for a pixel be $< r, g, s >$. Assume that this pixel is covered by shadow in frame t and let $< r_t, g_t, s_t >$ be the observed value for this pixel at this frame. Then, it is expected that $\alpha \leq \frac{s_t}{s} \leq 1$. That is, it is expected that the observed value, s_t, will be darker than the normal value s up to a certain limit, $\alpha s \leq s_t$, which corresponds to the intuition that at most $(1-\alpha)\%$ of the light coming to this pixel can be reduced by a target shadow. A similar effect is expected for highlighted background, where the observed value is brighter than the expected value up to a certain limit.

In the our case, where the background is not static, there is no single expected value for each pixel. Let A be the sample values representing the background for a certain pixel, each represented as $x_i = < r_i, g_i, s_i >$ and, let $x_t = < r_t, g_t, s_t >$ be the observed value at frame t. Then, we can select a subset $B \subseteq A$ of sample values that are relevant to the observed lightness, s_t. By relevant we mean those values from the sample which if affected by shadows can produce the observed lightness of the pixel. That is, $B = \{x_i \mid x_i \in A \wedge \alpha \leq \frac{s_t}{s_i} \leq \beta\}$. Using this relevant sample subset we carry out our kernel calculation, as described in section 2, based on the 2-dimensional (r, g) color space. The parameters α and β are fixed over all the image. Figure 8 shows the detection results for an indoor scene using both the (R, G, B) color space and the (r, g) color space after using the lightness variable, s, to restrict the sample to relevant values only. We illustrate the algorithm on indoor sequence because the effect of shadows are more severe than in outdoor environments. The target in the figure wears black pants and the background is gray, so there is no color information. However we still detect the target very well and suppress the shadows.

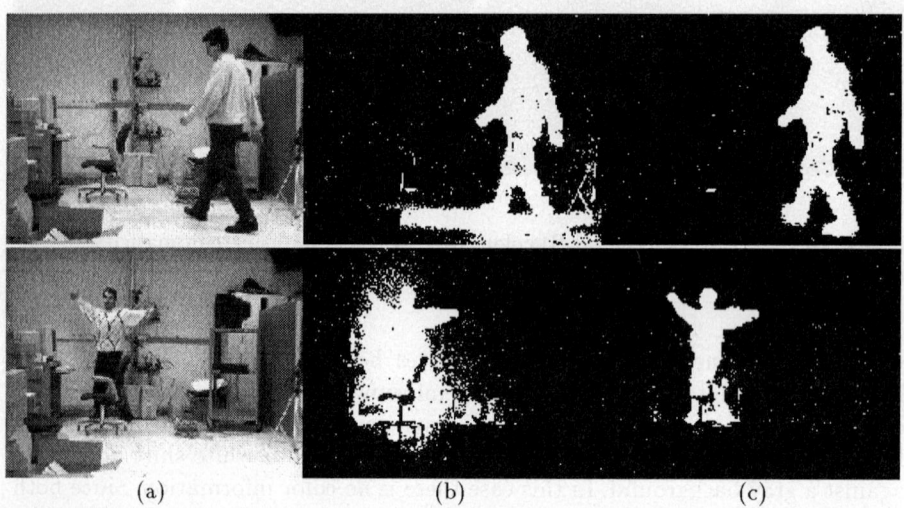

      (a)   (b)   (c)

Fig. 8. (b) Detection using (R,G,B) color space (c) detection using chromaticity coordinates (r, g) and the lightness variable s

6 Comparisons and Experimental Results

6.1 Comparison

In this section we describe a set of experiments performed to compare the detection performance of the proposed background model as described in section 2 and a mixture of Gaussian model as described in [6, 7]. We compare the ability of the two models to detect with high sensitivity under the same false positive rates and also how detection rates are affected by the presence of a target in the scene.

For the non-parametric model, a sample of size 100 was used to represent the background; the update is performed using the detection results directly as the update decision, as described in section 2. For the Gaussian mixture model, the maximum number of distributions allowed at each pixel was 10^1. Very few pixels reached that maximum at any point of time during the experiments. We used a sequence contains 1500 frames taken at a rate of 30 frame/second for evaluation. The sequence contains no moving targets. Figure 9 shows the first frame of the sequence.

Fig. 9. Outdoor scene used in evaluation experiments

The objective of the first experiment is to measure the sensitivity of the model to detect moving targets with low contrast against the background and how this sensitivity is affected by the target presence in the scene. To achieve this goal, a synthetic disk target of radius 10 pixels was moved against the background of the scene shown in figure 9. The intensity of the target is a contrast added to the background. That is, for each scene pixel with intensity x_t at time t that the target should occlude, the intensity of that pixel was changed to $x_t + \delta$. The experiment was repeated for different values of δ in the range from 0 to 40. The target was moved with a speed of 1 pixel/frame.

To set the parameters of the two models, we ran both models on the whole sequence with no target added and set the parameters of the two models to achieve an average of 2% false positive rate. To accomplish this for the non-parametric model, we adjust the threshold th; for the Gaussian mixture model we adjust two parameters T and α. This was done by fixing α to some value and finding the corresponding value of T that gives the desired false positive rates.

---

[1] this way the two models use almost the same amount of memory: for each distribution we need 3 floating point numbers a mean, a variance and a weight; for each sample in our method we need 1 byte

This resulted in several pairs of parameters (α, T) that give the the desired 2% rate. The best parameters were $\alpha = 10^{-6}, T = 98.9\%$. If α is set to be greater that 10^{-6}, then the model adapts faster and the false negative rate is increased, while if the α is less than this value, then the model adapts too slowly, resulting in more false positives and an inability to reach the desired 2% rate.

Using the adjusted parameters, both the models were used to detect the synthetic moving disk superimposed on the original sequence. Figure 10-a show the false negative rates obtained by the two models for various contrasts. It can be noticed that both models have similar false negative rates for very small contrast values; but the non-parametric model has a much smaller false negative rates as the contrast increases.

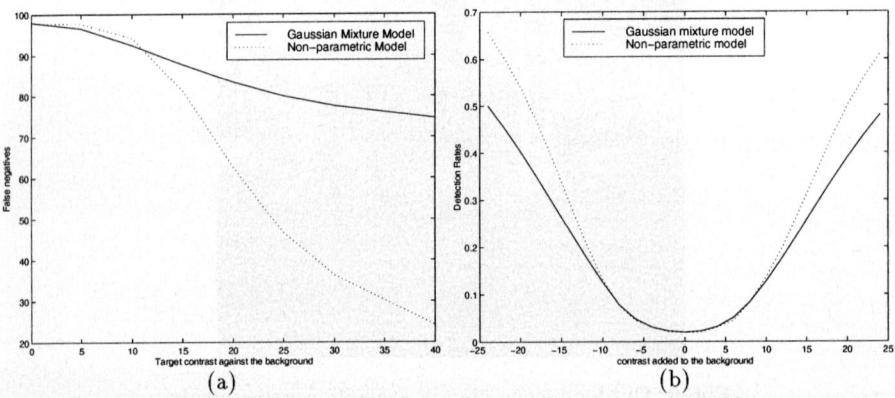

Fig. 10. (a) False Negatives with moving contrast target (b) Detection rates with global contrast added.

The objective of the second experiment is to measure the sensitivity of the detection without any effect of the target on the model. To achieve this a contrast value δ in the range -24 to +24 is added to every pixel in the image and the detection rates were calculated for each δ while the models were updated using the original sequence (without the added contrast.) The parameters of both the models were set as in the first experiment. For each δ value, we ran both the models on the whole sequence and the average detection rates were calculated, where the detection rate is defined as the percentage of the image pixels (after adding δ) that are detected as foreground. Notice that with $\delta = 0$ the detection rate corresponds to the adjusted 2% false positive rate. The detection rates are shown in figure 10-b where we notice better detection rates for the non-parametric model.

From these two experiments we notice that the non-parametric model is more sensitive in detecting targets with low contrast against the background; moreover the detection using the non-parametric model is less affected by the presence of targets in the scene.

6.2 Results

Video clips showing the detection results can be downloaded in either MPEG or
AVI formats from ftp://www.umiacs.umd.edu/pub/elgammal/video/index.htm.
Video clip 1 shows the detection results using 100 background samples. The video
shows the pure detection result without any morphological operations or noise
filtering. The video clip 2 shows the detection results for a color image sequence.
Figure 11-top shows a frame from this sequence. Video clip 3 shows the detection
results using both a short-term and a long-term model. The short-term model
contains the most recent 50 background samples while the long-term contains 50
samples taken over a 1000 frame time window. Figure 11-bottom shows a frame
from this sequence where the target is walking behind trees and is occluded by
tree branches that are moving.

Fig. 11. Example of detection results

Video clip 4 shows the detection result for a sequence taken using an omnidirectional camera[2]. A 100 sample short-term model is used to obtain these
results on images of size 320x240. One pass of morphological closing was performed on the results. All the results shows the detection result without any use

---

[2] We would like to thank T.E. Boult, EECS Department, Lehigh University, for providing us with this video

of tracking information of the targets. Figure 12-top shows a frame from this sequence with multiple targets in the scene. Video clip 5 shows detection result for outdoor scene on a rainy day. The video shows three different clips for different rain conditions where the system adapted to each situation and could detect targets with the high sensitivity even under heavy rain. Figure 12-bottom shows a frame from this sequence with a car moving under heavy rain.

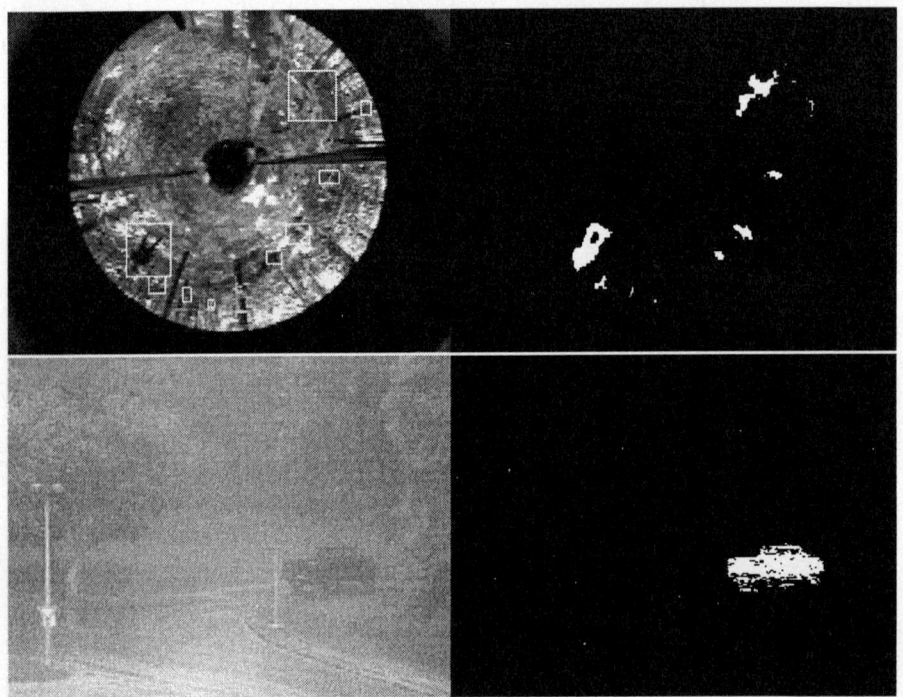

Fig. 12. Top:Detection result for an omni-directional camera. Bottom:Detection result for a rainy day.

7   Conclusion and Future Extensions

A robust, non-parametric background model and background subtraction mechanism that works with color imagery was introduced. The model can handle situations where the background of the scene is not completely static but contains small motions such as tree branch motion. The model is based on estimating the intensity density directly from sample history values. The main feature of the model is that it represents a very recent model of the scene and adapts to charges quickly. A second stage of the background subtraction was presented to suppress false detection that are due to small motions in the scene background based on spatial properties. We also showed how the model can use color information to suppress shadows of the targets from being detected. A framework was presented to combine a short-term and a long-term model to achieve more robust detection results. A comparison between the proposed model and a Gaussian mixture model [6, 7] was also presented.

The implementation of the approach runs at 15-20 frame per second on a 400 MHz pentium processor for 320x240 gray scale images depending on the size of the background sample and the complexity of the detected foreground. Precalculated lookup tables for kernel function values are used to calculate the probability estimation of equation 5 in an efficient way. For most image pixels the evaluation of the summation in equation 5 stops after very few terms once the sum surpasses the threshold, which allows very fast probability estimation.

As for future extensions, we are trying to build more concise representation for the long term model of the scene by estimating the required sample size for each pixel in the scene depending on the variations at this pixel. So, using the same total amount of memory, we can achieve better results by assigning more memory to unstable points and less memory to stable points. Preliminary experiments shows that we can reach a compression of 80-90% and still achieve the same sensitivity in detection.

References

1. C. R. Wern, A. Azarbayejani, T. Darrell, and A. P. Pentland, "Pfinder: Real-time tracking of human body," *IEEE Transaction on Pattern Analysis and Machine Intelligence*, 1997.
2. K.-P. Karmann and A. von Brandt, "Moving object recognition using and adaptive background memory," in *Time-Varying Image Processing and Moving Object Recognition*, Elsevier Science Publishers B.V., 1990.
3. K.-P. Karmann, A. V. Brandt, and R. Gerl, "Moving object segmentation based on adabtive reference images," in *Signal Processing V: Theories and Application*, Elsevier Science Publishers B.V., 1990.
4. D. Koller, J. Weber, T.Huang, J.Malik, G. Ogasawara, B.Rao, and S.Russell, "Towards robust automatic traffic scene analyis in real-time," in *ICPR*, 1994.
5. N. Friedman and S. Russell, "Image segmentation in video sequences: A probabilistic approach," in *Uncertainty in Artificial Intelligence*, 1997.
6. W.E.L.Grimson, C.Stauffer, and R.Romano, "Using adaptive tracking to classify and monitor activities in a site," in *CVPR*, 1998.
7. W.E.L.Grimson and C.Stauffer, "Adaptive background mixture models for real-time tracking," in *CVPR*, 1999.
8. D. W. Scott, *Mulivariate Density Estimation*. Wiley-Interscience, 1992.
9. M. D. Levine, *Vision in Man and Machine*. McGraw-Hill Book Company, 1985.
10. E. L. Hall, *Computer Image Processing and Recognition*. Academic Press, 1979.

Qualitative Spatiotemporal Analysis Using an Oriented Energy Representation

Richard P. Wildes and James R. Bergen

Sarnoff Corporation
Princeton, NJ 08543
USA

Abstract. This paper presents an approach to representing and analyzing spatiotemporal information in support of making qualitative, yet semantically meaningful distinctions at the earliest stages of processing. A small set of primitive classes of spatiotemporal structure are proposed that correspond to categories of stationary, coherently moving, incoherently moving, flickering, scintillating and "too unstructured to support further inference". It is shown how these classes can be represented and distinguished in a uniform fashion in terms of oriented energy signatures. Further, empirical results are presented that illustrate the use of the approach in application to natural imagery. The importance of the described work is twofold: (i) From a theoretical point of view a semantically meaningful decomposition of spatiotemporal information is developed. (ii) From a practical point of view, the developed approach has the potential to impact real world image understanding and analysis applications. As examples: The approach could be used to support early focus of attention and cueing mechanisms that guide subsequent activities by an intelligent agent; the approach could provide the representational substrate for indexing video and other spatiotemporal data.

1   Introduction

1.1   Motivation

When confronted with spatiotemporal data, an intelligent system that must make sense of the ensuing stream can be overwhelmed by its sheer quantity. Video and other temporal sequences of images are notorious for the vast amount of raw data that they comprise. An initial organization which affords distinctions that can guide subsequent processing would be a key enabler for dealing efficiently with data of this nature.

The current paper explores the possibility of performing qualitative analyses of spatiotemporal patterns that capture salient and meaningful categories of structure and which are easily recovered from raw data. These categories capture distinctions along the following lines: What is moving and what is stationary? Are the moving objects moving in a coherent fashion? Which portions of the data are best described as scintillating and which portions are simply too unstructured to support subsequent analysis? More generally, given a spatiotemporal region of interest, one may seek to decompose it into a combination of such components. Significantly, it is shown that all of these distinctions can be based on a unified representation of spatiotemporal information in terms of local (spatiotemporal) correlation structure.

The ability to parse a stream of spatiotemporal data into primitive, yet semantically meaningful, categories at an early stage of analysis can benefit subsequent processing in a number of ways. A parsing of this type could support cueing and focus of attention for subsequent analysis. Limited computational resources could thereby be focused on portions of the input data that will support the desired analysis. For example, areas that are too unstructured to support detailed analysis could be quickly discarded. Similarly, appropriate models to impose during subsequent analysis (such as for model-based motion estimation) could be selected and initialized. Further, the underlying representation could provide the basis of descriptors to support the indexing of video or other spatiotemporal data. The relative distribution of a spatiotemporal region's total energy across the defined primitives might serve as a characteristic signature for initial database construction as well as subsequent look-up. Also, in certain circumstances the proposed analysis could serve directly to guide intelligent action relative to the impinging environment. Certain primitive reactive behaviors (say, pursuit or flight) might be triggered by the presence of certain patterns of spatiotemporal structure (say, patterns indicative of large moving regions). As a step toward such applications, this paper presents an approach to qualitative spatiotemporal analysis and illustrates its representational power relative to a variety of natural image sequences.

1.2 Related research

Previous efforts that have attempted to abstract qualitative descriptors of motion information are of relevance to the research described in the current paper. Much of this work is motivated by observations suggesting the inherent difficulty of dealing with the visual motion field in a quantitative fashion [27] as well as the general efficacy of using motion in a qualitative fashion to solve useful tasks (e.g., boundary and collision detection) [26]. It should be noted, however, that the focus of most of this work is the qualitative interpretation of *visual motion* or *optical flow* while the current paper is about the analysis of *spatiotemporal structure*. The level of processing discussed here precedes that at which actual motion computation is likely to occur. Indeed, one possible use of low-level spatiotemporal structure information might be to determine where optical flow computation makes sense to perform.

Recent advances in the use of parameterized models characterizing motion information in terms of its projection onto a set of basis flows are also of interest. Some of this work makes use of principle components analysis to build the basis flows from training data with estimation for new data based on searching the space of admissable parameters [5]. Other work has defined steerable basis flows for simple events (e.g., motion of occluding edge or bar) with subsequent ability to both detect and estimate weights for a novel data set [9]. As a whole, this body of research is similar to the previously reviewed qualitative motion analysis literature in being aimed at higher-level interpretation.

Most closely related to the current work is prior research that has approached motion information as a matter for temporal texture analysis [17]. This research is similar in its attempt to map spatiotemporal data to primitive, yet meaningful patterns. However, it differs in significant ways: Its analysis is based on statistics (e.g., means and variances) defined over normal flow recovered from image sequence intensity data; whereas, the current work operates directly on the intensity data. Further, the patterns that it abstracts to (e.g., flowing water, fluttering leaves) are more specific and narrowly defined than those of the current work.

A large body of research has been concerned with effecting the recovery of image motion (e.g., optical flow) on the basis of filters that are tuned for local spatiotemporal orientation [1, 8, 11–13, 28]. Filter implementations that have been employed to recover estimates of spatiotemporal orientation include angularly tuned Gabor, lognormal and derivative of Gaussian filters. Also of relevance is the notion of opponency between filters that are tuned for different directions of motion [1, 21, 23]. An essential motivation for taking such an operation into account is the close correspondence between the difference in the response of filters tuned to opposite directions of motion (e.g., leftward vs. rightward) and optical flow along the same dimension (e.g., horizontal). While the current work builds directly on methods for recovering local estimates of spatiotemporal orientation, it then takes a different direction in moving directly to qualitative characterization of structure rather than the computation of optical flow.

Previous work also has been concerned with various ways of characterizing local estimates of spatiotemporal orientation. One prominent set of results along these lines has to do with an eigenvalue analysis of the local orientation tensor [11, 14]. Here the essential point is to characterize the dimensionality of the local orientation as being isotropic, line- or plane-like in order to characterize the local spatial structure with respect to motion analysis (e.g., distributed vs. oriented spatial structure with uniform motion). Other work of interest along these lines includes interpretation of opponent motion operators as indicative of motion salience [30] and the exploitation of multiscale analysis of temporal change information for detection and tracking purposes [2]. Overall, while these lines of investigation are similar to the subject of the current paper, none of this work has proposed and demonstrated the particular and complete set of spatiotemporal abstractions that are the main subject of the current paper.

In the light of previous research, the main contribution of the current paper is that it shows how to abstract from spatiotemporal data a number of qualitative structural descriptions corresponding to semantically meaningful distinctions (e.g., what is stationary, what is moving, is the exhibited motion coherent or not, etc.). Further, a formulation is set forth that captures all of the distinguished properties of spatiotemporal structure in a unified fashion.

2   Technical approach

In this section, the proposed approach to spatiotemporal analysis is presented, accompanied by natural image examples. For the purposes of exposition, the presentation begins by restricting consideration to one spatial dimension plus time. Subsequently, the analysis is generalized to encompass an additional spatial dimension and issues involving spatiotemporal boundaries.

2.1   Analysis in one spatial dimension plus time

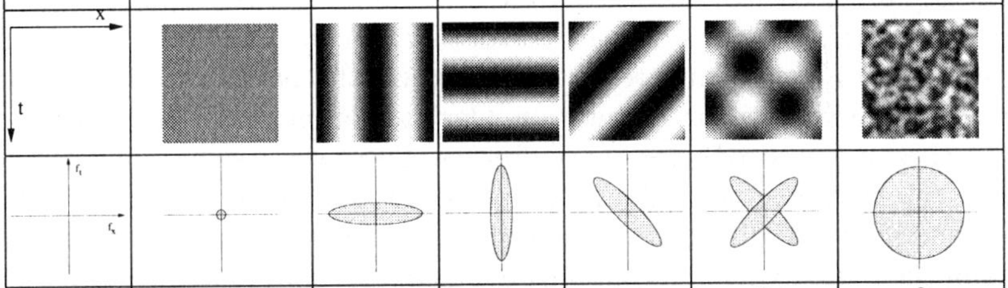

	Unstructured	Static	Flicker	Coherent Motion	Incoherent Motion	Scintillation
$|R - L|$	0	0	0	++	0	0
$R + L$	0	++	++	++	++++	++
S_x	0	++	0	+	+	+
F_x	0	0	++	+	+	+

Fig. 1. Primitive Spatiotemporal Patterns. The top row of images depict prototypical patterns that comprise the proposed qualitative categorization of spatiotemporal structure. For display purposes the images are shown for a single spatial dimension, x, plus time, t. The second row of plots shows the corresponding frequency domain structure, with axes f_x and f_t. As suggested by their individual titles, the categories have semantically meaningful interpretations. The lower part of the figure shows the predicted distribution of energy for each pattern as it is brought under the proposed oriented energy representation. The representation consists of four energy images components, $|R - L|$, $|R + L|$, S_x and F_x that are derived from an input image via application of a bank of oriented filters. For the purpose of qualitative analysis the amount of energy that is contributed by the underlying filter responses, R, L, S_x and F_x, is taken as having one of three values: (approximately) zero, moderate and large, symbolized as 0, + and ++, respectively.

Primitive spatiotemporal patterns   The local orientation (or lack thereof) of a pattern is one of its most salient characteristics. From a purely geometric point of view, orientation captures the local first-order correlation structure of a pattern. In the realm of image analysis, local spatiotemporal orientation often can be interpreted in a fashion that has additional ramifications. For example, image velocity is manifest as orientation in space-time [14]. We now explore the significance of this structure in one spatial dimension, the horizontal image axis,

x, and time, t. Fig. 1 shows x-t-slices of several prototypical spatiotemporal patterns that are of particular interest.

Perhaps the simplest situation that might hold is that a region is essentially devoid of structure, i.e., image intensity is approximately constant or slowly varying in both the spatial and temporal directions. In the spatiotemporal frequency domain, such a pattern would have the majority of its energy concentrated at the origin. When such regions occur where local contrast is small they can indicate an underlying smoothness in the material that is being imaged. For subsequent processing operations it is important to flag such areas as lacking enough information to support stable estimates of certain image properties. For example, image registration can be led astray by blindly attempting to align structureless regions. This category will be referred to as "unstructured".

Locally oriented structures are quite common in spatiotemporal data. Here, there are several situations that are useful to distinguish. From a semantic point of view, it is of particular interest to categorize the patterns according to the direction of their dominant orientation. One case of interest is that which arises for the case of (textured) stationary objects. These cases show elongated structure in the spatiotemporal domain that is parallel to the temporal axis, i.e., features exhibit no shift in position with the passage of time. In the frequency domain, their energy will be concentrated along the spatial frequency axis. This case will be referred to as "static". A second case of interest is that of homogeneous spatial structure, but with change in intensity over time (for example, overall change in brightness due to temporal variation in illumination). Here, the spatiotemporal pattern will be oriented parallel to the spatial axis. Correspondingly, in the frequency domain the energy will be concentrated along the temporal frequency axis. This case will be referred to as "flicker". A third case of interest is that of objects that are in motion. As noted above, such objects trace a trajectory that is slanted in the spatiotemporal domain in proportion to their velocity. Their energy in the frequency domain also exhibits a slant corresponding to their having both spatial and temporal variation. Such simple motion that is (at least locally) manifest by a single dominant orientation will be referred to as "coherent motion". Finally, it is useful to distinguish a special case of oriented structure, that of multiple local orientations intermixed or superimposed within a spatial region. In this regard, there is motivation to concentrate on the case of two structures both indicative of motion. Such a configuration has perceptual significance corresponding to oscillatory motion, shear and occlusion boundaries, and other complex motion phenomena that might be generally thought of as dynamic local contrast variation with motion. Interestingly, it appears that human vision represents this category as a special case as suggested by the perception of counterphase flicker [6]. In the frequency domain the energy distribution will be the sum of the distributions that are implied by the component motions. This case will be referred to as "incoherent motion". In comparison, there does not seem to be anything significant about something that is both static and flickering, beyond its decomposition into those primitives.

The final broad class of spatiotemporal pattern to be considered is that of isotropic structure. In this case, no discernable orientations dominate the local region; nevertheless, there is significant spatiotemporal contrast. The frequency domain manifestation of the pattern also lacks a characteristic orientation, and is likewise isotropic. Situations that can give rise to this type of structure are characteristically stochastic or chaotic in nature. Natural examples include turbulence and the glint of specularities on water. Owing to the perceptual manifestation of these phenomena, this case will be referred to as "scintillation".

The essence of the proposed approach is to analyze any given sample of spatiotemporal data as being decomposed along the dimensions of the adduced categories: unstructured, static, flicker, coherent motion, incoherent motion and scintillation. While it is possible to make finer distinctions (e.g., exactly what the numerical value of the space-time orientation is), at the level of qualitative semantics these are fundamental distinctions to be made: Is something structured or not? If it is structured, does it exhibit a characteristic orientation or is it more isotropic and thereby scintillating in nature? Are oriented patterns indicative of something that is stationary, flickering or moving? Is the motion coherent or incoherent? It should be noted that each of the descriptions identified above is attached to the visual signal within a specified spatiotemporal region. The choice of this region generally affects the description assigned. For example, the motion of leaves in the wind may be coherent if analyzed over a very small area and time but incoherent over a larger area or time. An alternative way to think about the proposed decomposition is to consider it from the point of view of signal processing: In particular, what sort of decomposition (e.g., in the frequency domain) does it imply. This topic is dealt with in the next section in terms of a representation that captures the proposed distinctions.

Oriented energy representation Given that the concern is to analyze spatiotemporal data according to its local orientation structure, a representation that is based on oriented energy is appropriate. Such a representation entails a filter set that divides the spatiotemporal signal into a set of oriented energy bands. In general, the size and shape of the filter spectra will determine the way that the spatiotemporal frequency domain is covered. In the present case, a family of relatively broadly tuned filters is appropriate due the interest in qualitative analysis. The idea is to choose a spatial frequency band of interest with attendant low pass filtering in the temporal domain. This captures orientation orthogonal to the spatial axis. On the basis of this choice, a temporal frequency band can be specified based on the range of dynamic phenomena that are of interest for the given spatial band. This captures structure that is oriented in directions indicative of motion, e.g., a spatiotemporal diagonal. Finally, these characteristics can be complemented by considering just the temporal frequency band while spatial frequency is covered with a low-pass response. This captures structure that is oriented orthogonal to the temporal axis. Thus, it is possible to represent several principle directions in the spatiotemporal domain while systematically covering the frequency domain. The simplification realized by analyzing

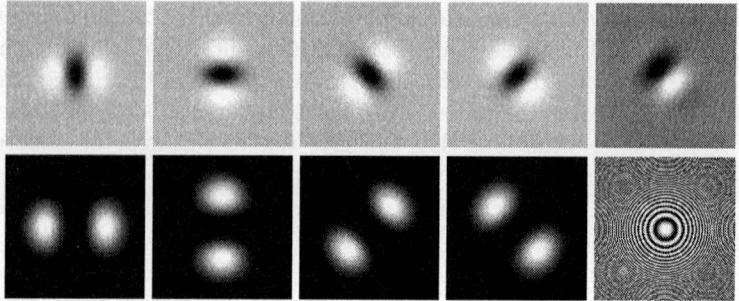

Fig. 2. Oriented Energy Filters for Spatiotemporal Analysis. The top row shows synthesized profiles for second derivative of Gaussian filters oriented to capture static, flicker, rightward and leftward motion structure (left to right). The last plot is the Hilbert transform of the leftward motion filter. (These plots are shown greatly enlarged for clarity). The bottom row indicates the frequency response of the corresponding quadrature pair filters via application of an energy calculation to the zone plate at the far right. The proposed approach to representing spatiotemporal structure builds on such filtering operations.

spatiotemporal structure in a two dimensional representation (i.e. one spatial and one temporal dimension) requires somehow addressing the remaining spatial dimension since the input data consists of a three dimensional volume. This is done by lowpass filtering the data in the orthogonal spatial direction using the 5-tap binomial filter $[1\ 4\ 6\ 4\ 1]/16$. This filtering allows for analysis of the other spatiotemporal plane (i.e. that containing the orthogonal spatial dimension) in an exactly analogous manner.

In the remainder of this section a choice of filters is presented for a given frequency response, i.e., scale of spatial structure.

The desired filtering can be implemented in terms of second derivative of Gaussian filters, G_{2_θ} at orientation θ (and their Hilbert transforms, H_{2_θ}) [14]. The motivation for this choice is twofold. First, while selective for orientation, the tuning of these filters is moderately broad and therefore well suited to the sort of qualitative analysis that is the focus of the current research. Second, they admit a steerable and separable implementation that leads to compact and efficient computation. The filters are taken in quadrature (i.e., for any given θ, G_{2_θ} and H_{2_θ} in tandem) to eliminate phase variation by producing a measure of local energy, $E_\theta(x,t)$ within a frequency band, according to

$$E_\theta(x,t) = (G_{2_\theta}(x,t) * I(x,t))^2 + (H_{2_\theta}(x,t) * I(x,t))^2. \qquad (1)$$

In particular, to capture the principle orientations that were suggested above, filtering is applied (i) oriented orthogonally to the spatial axis, (ii) orthogonally to the temporal axis and (iii, iv) along the two spatiotemporal diagonals, see Fig. 2. Notice that the frequency response plots show how the filters sweep out an annulus in that domain; this observation can provide the basis for allowing a multiscale extension to systematically alter the inner and outer rings of the annulus to effectively cover the frequency domain. Finally, note that at a given frequency the value of any one oriented energy measure is a function of both orientation and contrast and therefore rather ambiguous. To avoid this confound and get a purer measure of orientation the response of each filter should be normalized by the sum of the consort, i.e.,

$$\hat{E}_{\theta_i}(x,t) = \frac{E_{\theta_i}}{\Sigma_i E_{\theta_i(x,t)} + \epsilon} \tag{2}$$

where ϵ is a small bias to prevent instabilities when overall energy is small. (Empirically we set this bias to about 1 % of the maximum (expected) energy.)

The necessary operations have been implemented in terms of a steerable filter architecture [10, 15]. The essential idea here is to convolve an image of interest with a set of n basis filters, with $n = 3$ for the second derivative of Gaussians of concern. Subsequently the basis filtered images are combined according to interpolation formulas to yield images filtered at any desired orientation, θ. Processing with the corresponding Hilbert transforms is accomplished in an analgous fashion, with $n = 4$. To remove high frequency components that are introduced by the squaring operation in forming the energy measurement (1), the previously introduced 5-tap binomial low-pass filter is applied to the result, E_θ. Details of the filter implementation (e.g., specification of the basis filters and the interpolation formulas) are provided in [10, 15].

The final oriented energy representation that is proposed is based directly on the basic filtering operations that have been described. Indeed, given the class of primitive spatiotemporal patterns that are to be distinguished, one might imagine simply making use of the relative distribution of (normalized) energies across the four proposed orientation tuned bands as the desired representation. In this regard, it is proposed to make use of two of these bands directly. In particular, the result of filtering an input image with the filter oriented orthogonally to the spatial axis will be one component of the representation, let it be called the "S_x-image" (for static). Second, let the result of filtering an input image with the filter oriented orthogonally to the temporal axis be the second component of the representation and call it the "F_x-image" (for flicker). Due to their characteristic highlighting of particular orientations, these (filtered) images are well suited to capturing the essential nature of the patterns for which they are named.

The information provided individually by the remaining two bands is ambiguous with respect to the desired distinctions between, e.g., coherent and incoherent motion. This state of affairs can be remedied by representing these bands as summed and differenced (i.e., opponent) combinations. Thus, let $R - L$ and $R + L$ stand for opponent and summed images (resp.) formed by taking the pointwise arithmetic difference and sum of the images that result from filtering an input image with the energy filters oriented along the two diagonals. It can be shown that the opponent image (when appropriately weighted for contrast) is proportional to image velocity [1] and has a strong signal in areas of coherent motion. It is for this reason that the notation R and L is chosen to underline the relationship to rightward and leftward motion. For present purposes the absolute value of the opponent signal, $|R - L|$, will be taken as the third component of the proposed representation since this allows for coherency always to be positive. Finally, the fourth component of the representation is the summed (motion) energy $R + L$. This image is of importance as it captures energy distributions that contain multiple orientations that are individually indicative of motion and is therefore of importance in dealing with incoherent motion phenomena.

At this point it is interesting to revisit the primitive spatiotemporal patterns of interest and see how they project onto the four component oriented energy representation comprised of S_x, F_x, $|R - L|$ and $R + L$, see Fig. 1. In the unstructured case, it is expected that all of the derived images will contain vanishingly small amounts of energy. Notice that for this to be true and stable, the presence of the bias factor, ϵ, in the normalization process is important in avoiding division by a very small factor. For the static case, not surprisingly the S_x-image contains the greatest amount of energy. Although, there also is a moderate energy from the $R + L$-image as the underlying R and L responses will be present due to the operative orientation tuning. In contrast, these responses will very nearly cancel to leave the $|R - L|$-image essentially zero. Similarly, the orthogonal F_x-image should have essentially no intensity. The flicker case is similar to the static case, with the S_x and F_x-images changing roles. For the case of coherent motion, it is expected that the $|R - L|$-image will have a large amount of energy present. Indeed, this is the only pattern where the image is expected to contain any significant energy. The $R + L$-image also should show an appreciable response, with the other images showing more moderate responses. For the case of incoherent motion, the $R + L$- image should dominate as both the underlying R and L responses should be appreciable. Again, due to finite bandwidth tuning the S and F images also should show moderate responses. Once again the $|R - L|$-image should be very nearly zero. Finally, for the case of scintillation the S and F images should show modest, yet still appreciable responses. The $R + L$-image response should be somewhat larger, perhaps by a factor of two as each of the modest R and L responses sum together. Essentially no response is expected from the $|R - L|$-image. Significantly, when one compares all of the signatures, each is expected to be distinct from the others, at least for the idealized prototypical patterns. The question now becomes how well the representation captures the phenomena of interest in the face of natural imagery.

Natural image examples A set of natural image sequences have been gathered that provide one real world example of each of the proposed classes of spatiotemporal structure, see Fig. 3. For the unstructured case the image sequence shows a featureless sky. For the static case the image sequence shows a motionless tree. (Note that for each of these first two cases, a single image was not simply duplicated multiple times to make the sequence, an actual video sequence of images was captured.) The third case, flicker, is given as a smooth surface of human skin as lightning flashes over time. Coherent motion is captured by a field of flowers that appear to move diagonally upward and to the right due to camera motion. Incoherent motion is captured by a sequence of images of overlapping legs in very complex motion (predominantly, but not entirely, horizontal motion). The last case, scintillation, is shown via a sequence of rain striking a puddle. All of the image sequences had horizontal, x, and vertical, y, length both equal to 64 while the temporal length (i.e., number of frames) was 40. All of the spatiotemporal image volumes were processed in an identical fashion by bringing them under the proposed oriented energy representation, as described in the previous section. This resulted in each original image begin decomposed along the four dimensions, $|R - L|$, $R + L$, S_x and F_x.

The results of the analysis are shown in Fig. 3. For each of the natural image examples a representative spatial slice shows the recovered energy along each of the dimensions, $|R - L|$, $R + L$, S_x and F_x. In each cell, the average (normalized) energy is shown for the entire spatiotemporal volume. (Note that due to the presence of the bias, ϵ, the sum of $R + L$, S_x and F_x does not necessarily sum exactly to unity.) In reviewing the results it is useful to compare the recovered distribution of energies with the predictions that are shown in Fig. 1. Beginning with the unstructured case, it is seen that all of the recovered energies are vanishingly small, exactly as predicted. The static case also follows the pattern predicted in Fig. 1. For this case it is interesting to note that the deviation from zero in the F_x component is due to some fluttering (i.e., scintillation) in the leaves of the tree. The flicker case also performs much as expected, with a bit more energy in the F_x component relative to the $R + L$ component than anticipated. For the case of coherent motion the pattern of energy once again follows the prediction closely. Here it is important to note that the depicted motion is not strictly along the horizontal axis, rather it is diagonal. This accounts for the value of $R + L$ being somewhat larger than $|R - L|$ as the underlying L channel has a nonzero response. For the incoherent case, it is seen that while the general trend in the distribution of energies is consistent with predictions, the magnitude of $R + L$ is not as large as expected. Examination of the data suggests that this is due to the F_x component taking on a larger relative value than expected due to the imposition of some flicker in the data as some bright objects come into and go out of view (e.g., bright props and boots that the people wear). Finally, the case of scintillation follows the predictions shown in Fig. 1 quite well. Taken on the whole, these initial empirical results support the ability of the proposed approach to make the kinds of distinctions that have been put forth. Clearly the utility of the representation depends on its ability to distinguish and identify populations of samples corresponding to the various semantic categories described. Demonstration of this ability will require a quantitative analysis of energy signatures across an appropriate collection of samples and is beyond the scope of this paper.

2.2 Adding an additional spatial dimension

The approach that has been developed so far can be extended to include the vertical dimension, y, by augmenting the representation with a set of components that capture oriented structure in y-t image planes. The same set of oriented filters that were used previously are now applied to y-t planes, as before with the addition of a low-pass characteristic in the orthogonal spatial dimension, now x. This will allow for (normalized) oriented energy to be computed in the four directions: (i) oriented orthogonally to the spatial axis, y, (ii) oriented orthogonally to the temporal axis, t and (iii,iv) along the two y-t diagonals. These energy computations are performed for an input image using the y-t counterparts of formulas (1) and (2). The resulting filtered images are then used to complete the representation in a way entirely analogous to that used for the horizontal case except with U and D (for up and down) replacing R and L.

To illustrate these extensions, Fig. 4 shows the results of bringing the same set of natural image examples that were used with the x-t analysis under the $|U-D|$, $U+D$, S_y, F_y extensions to the representation. Here it is useful to refer to both the a priori predictions of Fig. 1 as well as the previously presented x-t empirical results. By and large the results once again support the ability of the approach to distinguish the six qualitative classes that have been put forth. Note, however, that for the incoherent motion case the depicted movement is predominant in the x direction and the value of $U + D$ is correspondingly relatively low.

2.3   Boundary analysis

As an example of how the proposed representation can be used for early segmentation of the input stream, we consider the detection of spatiotemporal boundaries. Differential operators matched to the juxtaposition of different kinds of spatiotemporal structure can be assembled from the primitive filter responses, $R - L$, $R + L$, S_x, F_x and their vertical (i.e., y-t) counterparts. To illustrate this concept, consider the detection of (coherent) motion boundaries. Here, the intent is not to present a detailed discussion of motion boundary detection, which has been extensively treated elsewhere (see, for example [3, 7, 9, 19]), but to use it as an example of the analysis of spatiotemporal differential structure in general.

Coherent motion is most directly related to the opponent filtered images $R - L$ and $U - D$. Correspondingly, the detection of coherent motion boundaries is based on the information in these images. As shown in Fig. 5, combining a difference of Gaussians

$$G(x, y, \sigma_1) - G(x, y, \sigma_2) \qquad (3)$$

operator (where $G(x, y, \sigma)$ is a Gaussian distribution with standard deviation σ) with motion opponent signals yields a double opponency: The pointwise opponency $R - L$ is combined with a spatial opponency provided by the difference of Gaussians and similarly for $U - D$. As in difference of Gaussian based edge-detection [14], the zero-crossings in the convolution of (3) with $R - L$ and $U - D$ are indicative of boundaries in these inputs. Final boundary detection is based on the presence of a zero-crossing in either of the individual results $(G(x, y, \sigma_1) - G(x, y, \sigma_2)) * (R - L)$ or $(G(x, y, \sigma_1) - G(x, y, \sigma_2)) * (U - D)$.

An example is shown in Fig. 5. Here, the difference of Gaussians (3) was realized in terms of binomial approximations to low-pass filters with cut-off frequencies at $\pi/8$ and $\pi/16$. A sequence of aerial imagery showing a tree canopy with movement relative to undergrowth due to camera motion serves as input.

Due to the homogeneous texture of the vegetation, the boundary of the tree is not visible in any one image from the sequence. Opponent motion images $R - L$ and $U - D$ were derived from this input and difference of Gaussian processing was applied to each of the motion opponent images. Finally, the zero-crossings in the results are marked. For purposes of display, the slope magnitude is calculated for the zero-crossings and summed between the two (double opponent) images to given an indication of the strength of the boundary signal. The result accurately captures one's visual impression upon viewing the corresponding image sequence where the apparent boundary can be traced along the left side as an irregular contour, then along a diagonal and finally across the top where it has a pronounced divot.

3 Discussion

3.1 Implications

The work that has been described in this paper builds on a considerable body of literature on spatiotemporal filtering. The main implication of the current effort is that the output of such filtering can be interpreted directly in terms of rather abstract information, i.e., the 6 proposed categories of spatiotemporal structure: structureless, static, flicker, coherent motion, incoherent motion and scintillation. Based on the analysis presented, not all of these classes are equally discriminable under the proposed representation. The signatures for the classes structureless, static, flicker and coherent motion are quite distinct, but those for incoherent motion and scintillation (while distinct from the other four) differ from each other only in the amount of energy expected in the summed energies $R + L$ and $U + D$. This state of affairs suggests that these last two categories might be best distinguished from each other in relative comparisons, while all other distinctions might be accomplished in a more independent and absolute fashion. This difference has implications for how the signatures can be used: The stronger form of distinctness supports categorical decisions about signal content across imaging situations; because it depends on a metric comparison, the weaker form probably does not.

Operations have been described at a single spatiotemporal scale; however, the proposed representation is a natural candidate for multiscale extensions [16, 31]. Indeed, such extensions might support finer distinctions between categories of spatiotemporal structure as characteristic signatures could be manifest across scale. Two kinds of extension can be distinguished. The first is concerned with varying the region of (spatiotemporal) integration that is applied to the oriented energy measures. The second type of multiscale extension concerns the frequency tuning of the underlying oriented filters. A systematic extension in this regard would operate at a number of spatial frequency bands and, for each of these bands, perform the analysis for a number of temporal frequency bands. It would thereby be possible to tile the frequency domain and correspondingly characterize the local orientation structure of an input spatiotemporal volume. These two extensions serve distinct purposes that are perhaps best understood with respect to a simple example. Consider a typically complex outdoor scene containing a tree blowing in a gusty wind and illuminated by a sunny sky with a few drifting clouds in it. As the tree branches sway back and forth, the corresponding image motion will be locally and temporarily coherent. However, over longer periods of time or over larger areas it will be incoherent or oscillatory. Thus, the characterization of the spatiotemporal structure will shift from one category to the other as the region of analysis is extended. Now consider the effect of a cloud shadow passing across the tree. At a fine spatial scale (i.e. for a high spatial frequency underlying filter) it will look like an illumination variation thus having a component in the "flicker" category. At the scale of the shadow itself (i.e. at low spatial frequency) it will look like coherent motion as the cloud passes over. The pattern of spatiotemporal signatures taken as a function of scale thus captures both the structural complexities of the dynamic scene and the quasitransparency of complex illumination. These two types of scaling behavior are complimentary and taken in tandem serve to enrich the descriptive vocabulary of the approach.

In contrast to the main message of this paper regarding the abstraction of spatiotemporal information to the level of qualitative descriptors, the details of the particular filtering architecture that have been employed are less important. A variety of alternatives could be employed, including oriented Gabor (e.g., [13]) and lognormal (e.g., [11]) filters. Similarly, one might be concerned with issues of causality and use oriented spatiotemporal filters that respect time's arrow [1, 8, 28]. Also, one might consider a more uniform sampling of orientation in x-y-t-space, rather than relying on x-t and y-t planes. Nevertheless, it is interesting that the fairly simple filters that were employed in the current effort have worked reasonably well for a variety of natural image examples.

The type of qualitative analysis described here seems particularly suited to processing in biological vision systems because of the apparently hierarchical nature of biological computation and the importance of such factors as attention. It is interesting therefore to note aspects of biological processing that relate to the current approach. With respect to fineness of sampling in the spatiotemporal domain, it appears that humans employ only about 2 to 3 temporal bands, while making use of 6 or more spatial bands [4, 25, 29]. Also, there is evidence that biological systems combine motion tuned channels in an opponent fashion [24], as is done in the current work. Regarding the degree to which filter responses are spatially integrated (i.e., as part of computing aggregate properties of a region) biological systems seem to be rather conservative: Physiological recordings of visual cortex complex cells indicate integration regions on the order of 2 to 5 cycles of the peak frequency [20], suggesting a preference for preservation of spatial detail over large area summation. It also is interesting to note that human contrast sensitivity is on the order of 1 % [18], an amount that has proven useful analogously in the current work as a choice for the bias in the process of energy normalization (2). With regard to border analysis, part of a purported mechanism for the detection of relative movement in the fly makes use of spatially antagonistic motion comparisons [22], in a fashion suggestive of the approach taken in the current paper.

Based on the ideas of this paper, a number of applications can be envisioned falling into two broad areas of potential impact. The first type of application concerns front end processing for real-time vision tasks. In this capacity, it could provide an initial organization, thereby focusing subsequent processing on portions of the data most relevant to critical concerns (e.g., distinguishing static, dynamic and low information regions of the scene). The second type of application concerns issues in the organization and access of video sequences. Here, the proposed representation could be used to define feature vectors that capture volumetric properties of spatiotemporal information (e.g., space-time texture) as an aid to the design and indexing of video databases. More generally, the proposed approach would be appropriate to a variety of tasks that could benefit from the early organization of spatiotemporal image data.

3.2 Summary

This paper has presented an approach to representing and analyzing spatiotemporal data in support of making qualitative yet semantically meaningful distinctions. In this regard, it has been suggested how to ask and answer a number in simple, yet significant questions, such as: Which spatiotemporal regions are stationary? Which regions are moving in a coherent (or incoherent) fashion? How much of the variance in the spatiotemporal data is due to overall changes in intensity. Where is the spatiotemporal structure isotropic and indicative of scintillation? Where is the data stream simply lacking in sufficient structure to support further inference? Also indicated has been an approach to issues regarding the analysis of spatiotemporal boundaries. Further, all of these matters have been embodied in a unified oriented energy representation. A variety of empirical results using natural image data suggest that the approach may have the representational power to support the desired distinctions. On the basis of these results, it is conjectured that the developed representation and analysis can subserve a variety of vision-based tasks and applications. More generally, the approach provides an integrated framework for dealing with spatiotemporal data in terms of its abstract information content at the earliest stages of processing.

References

1. Adelson, E., Bergen, J.: Spatiotemporal energy models for the perception of motion. JOSA A **2** (1985) 284–299
2. Anderson, C., Burt, P., van der Wal, G.: Change detection and tracking using pyramid transform techniques. Proc. SPIE Conf. on Intell. Rob. and Comp. Vis. (1985) 300–305
3. Beauchemin, S., Barron, J.: The computation of optical flow. ACM Comp. Surv. **27** (1995) 433–467
4. Bergen, J., Wilson, H.: Prediction of flicker sensitivities from temporal three pulse data. Vis. Res. (1985) 284–299

5. Black, M., Yacoob, Y., Jepson, A., Fleet, D.: Learning parameterized models of image motion. Proc. IEEE CVPR (1997) 561–567
6. Bruce, V., Green, B., Georgeson, M.: Visual Perception. East Sussex: Earlbaum (1996)
7. Chou, G.: A model of figure-ground segregation from kinetic occlusion. Proc. ICCV (1995) 1050–1057
8. Fleet, D., Jepson, A.: A Cascaded Approach to the Construction of Velocity Selective Mechanisms. RBCV Tech. Rep., TR-85-6, Dept. of Comp. Sci., University of Toronto (1985)
9. Fleet, D., Black, M., Jepson, A.: Motion feature extraction using steerable flow fields. Proc. IEEE CVPR (1998) 274–281
10. Freeman, A., Adelson, E.: The design and use of steerable filters. IEEE PAMI **13** (1991) 891–906
11. Granlund, G., Knutsson, H.: Signal Processing for Computer Vision. Boston: Kluwer (1995)
12. Grzywacz, N., Yuille, A.: A model for the estimation of local velocity by cells in the visual cortex. Proc. Roy. Soc. Lond. B **239** (1990) 129–161
13. Heeger, D.: A model for the extraction of image flow. JOSA A **4**, (1997) 1455–1471
14. Jähne, B.: Digital Image Processing. Berlin: Springer-Verlag (1993)
15. Knutsson, H., Wilson, R., Granlund, G.: Anisotropic non-stationary image estimation and its applications – part I: Restoration of noisy images. IEEE TC **31** (1983) 388–397
16. Koenderink, J.: Scale-time. Bio. Cyb. **58** (1988) 159–162
17. Nelson, R., Polana, R.: Qualitative recognition of motion using temporal texture. CVGIP-IU **56** (1992) 78–89
18. van Ness, R., Bouman, M.: Spatial modulation transfer in the human eye. JOSA **57** (1967) 401–406
19. Niyogi, S.: Detecting kinetic occlusion. Proc. ICCV (1995) 1044–1049
20. Movshon, J., Thompson, I., Tolhurst, D.: Receptive field organization of complex cells in the cat's striate cortex. J. Physiol. Lond. **283** (1978) 79–99
21. Reichardt, W.: Autocorrelation, a principle for the evaluation of sensory information by the central nervous system. In W. Rosenblith (Ed.) Sensory Communication, NY: Wiley (1961)
22. Reichardt, W., Poggio, T.: Figure-ground discrimination by relative movement in the visual system of the fly. Bio. Cyb. **35** (1979) 81-100
23. van Santen, J., Sperling, G.: Temporal covariance model of human motion perception. JOSA A **1** (1984) 451–473
24. Stromeyer, C., Kronauer, R., Madsen, J., Klein, S.: Opponent mechanisms in human vision. JOSA A **1** (1984) 876–884
25. Thompson, P.: The coding of the velocity of movement in the human visual system. Vis. Res. **24** (1984) 41–45
26. Thompson, W., Kearney, J.: Inexact vision. Proc. Workshop on Motion Rep. and Anal. (1986) 15–22
27. Verri, A., Poggio, T.: Against quantitative optical flow. IEEE PAMI **9** (1987) 171–180
28. Watson, A., Ahumada, A.: Model of human motion sensing. JOSA A **2** (1985) 322–341
29. Watson, A., Robson, J.: Discrimination at threshold: Labelled detectors in human vision. Vis. Res. **21** (1981) 1115–1122
30. Wildes, R.: A measure of motion salience. Proc. IEEE ICIP (1988) 183–187
31. Witkin, A.: Scale-space filtering. Proc. IJCAI (1983) 1019–1021

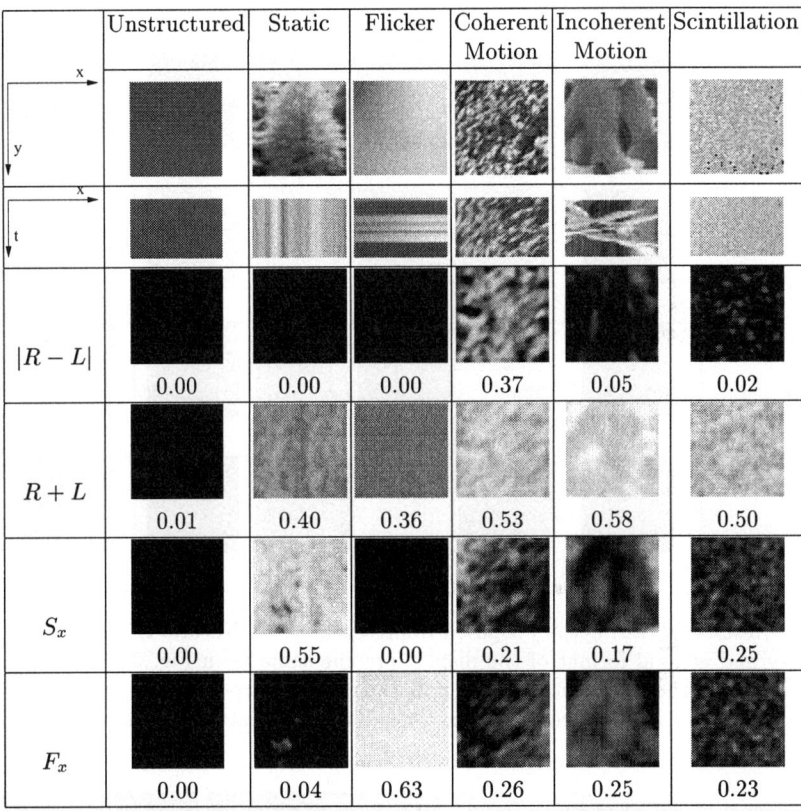

	Unstructured	Static	Flicker	Coherent Motion	Incoherent Motion	Scintillation
$\|R-L\|$	0.00	0.00	0.00	0.37	0.05	0.02
$R+L$	0.01	0.40	0.36	0.53	0.58	0.50
S_x	0.00	0.55	0.00	0.21	0.17	0.25
F_x	0.00	0.04	0.63	0.26	0.25	0.23

Fig. 3. Results of Testing the Proposed Representation on Natural Imagery. For each of the proposed primitive classes, a sequence of images that displays the associated phenomena was selected. Top row, left to right: featureless sky, a motionless tree, lightning flashing on (motionless) skin, a field of flowers in diagonal motion due to camera movement, legs of multiple cheerleaders in overlapping motion and rain striking a puddle. Each sequence has x, y, t dimensions of 64, 64, 40, respectively. The second row shows corresponding x-t-slices. The next four rows show the recovered energies in each of four components of the representation. Each cell shows a representative spatial, i.e., x, y, slice of the processed data as well as the average value for the energy across the entire spatiotemporal volume. Overall, the results are in accord with the predictions of Fig. 1.

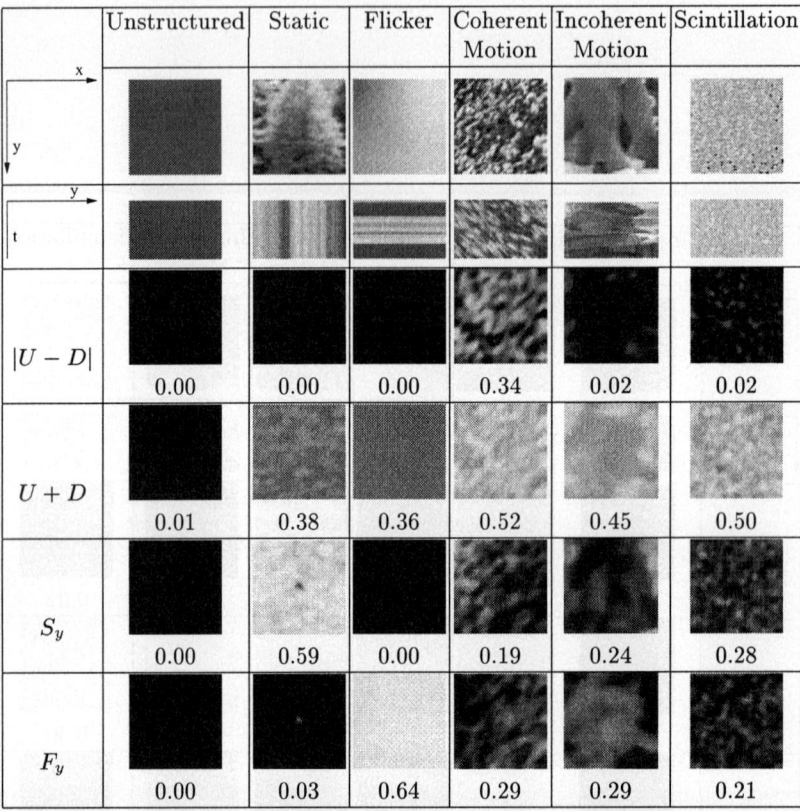

	Unstructured	Static	Flicker	Coherent Motion	Incoherent Motion	Scintillation
$|U - D|$	0.00	0.00	0.00	0.34	0.02	0.02
$U + D$	0.01	0.38	0.36	0.52	0.45	0.50
S_y	0.00	0.59	0.00	0.19	0.24	0.28
F_y	0.00	0.03	0.64	0.29	0.29	0.21

Fig. 4. Results of Testing the Proposed Representation on Natural Imagery. The input imagery and general format of the display are the same as in Fig. 3. Four additional components of the representation are now shown to incorporate information in the y spatial dimension. The overall pattern of results are consistent with predictions.

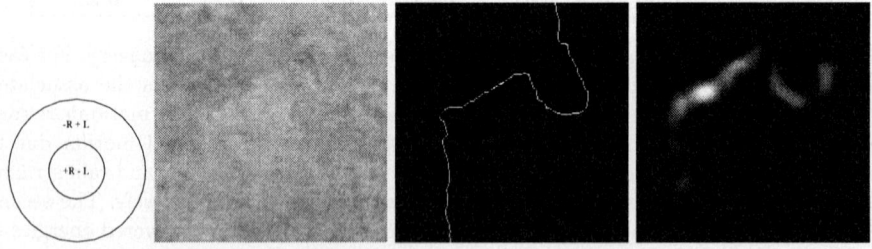

Fig. 5. Motion Boundary Detection. Left to right: A schematic of a double opponent motion operator for motion boundary detection. An aerial image of a tree canopy moving against undergrowth with relative motion due to camera movement. The hand marked outline of the motion boundary. The magnitude of the boundary signal. The result accurately localizes the edge of the tree against the background.

Regularised Range Flow

Hagen Spies[1,2], Bernd Jähne[1], and John L. Barron[2]

[1] Interdisciplinary Center for Scientific Computing,
University of Heidelberg, INF 368, 69120 Heidelberg, Germany,
{Hagen.Spies,Bernd.Jaehne}@iwr.uni-heidelberg.de
[2] Dept. of Comp. Science, University of Western Ontario,
London, Ontario, N6G 5B7 Canada,
barron@csd.uwo.ca

Abstract. Extending a differential total least squares method for range flow estimation we present an iterative regularisation approach to compute dense range flow fields. We demonstrate how this algorithm can be used to detect motion discontinuities. This can can be used to segment the data into independently moving regions. The different types of aperture problem encountered are discussed. Our regularisation scheme then takes the various types of flow vectors and combines them into a smooth flow field within the previously segmented regions. A quantitative performance analysis is presented on both synthetic and real data. The proposed algorithm is also applied to range data from castor oil plants obtained with the Biris laser range sensor to study the 3-D motion of plant leaves.

Keywords. *range flow, range image sequences, regularisation, shape, visual motion.*

1 Introduction

We are concerned with the estimation of local three-dimensional velocity from a sequence of depth maps. Previously we introduced a total least squares (TLS) algorithm for the estimation of this so called *range flow* [1]. It is shown that the result of this TLS algorithm can be used to detect boundaries between independently moving regions, which enables a segmentation. However, within these regions the computed flow fields are not generally dense. To amend this we present an iterative regularisation method to compute dense full flow fields using the information available from the TLS estimation.

Most previous work on range sequence analysis focuses on the estimation of the 3D motion parameters of either a moving sensor or an object [2–6]. Such approaches implicitly assume global rigidity. In contrast we are dealing with only locally rigid objects moving in an environment observed by a stationary sensor. As with optical flow calculation we initially assume that the flow field can be approximated as being constant within a small local aperture [7, 8]. In a second processing step this is replaced by requiring the flow field to be smooth. The work presented here is related to previously reported model based range flow estimation on non-rigid surfaces [9, 10]. The 3D range flow can also be recovered from optical flow if other surface properties such as depth or correspondences are available [11]. Some other work includes 2D range flow obtainable from a radial range sensor [12] and car tracking in range image sequences [13].

The underlying constraint equation is introduced in Sect. 2. Then Sect. 3 recapitulates the TLS estimation technique, in particular it is described how sensible parameters can be estimated even if not enough constraints are available, see Sect. 3.2. This is a generalisation of the known normal flow estimation in optical flow algorithms. It is also demonstrated how boundaries in the motion field between differently moving regions can be detected. Section 4 then shows how a dense parameter field can be obtained exploiting the previously calculated information. In Sect. 5 we proceed towards a quantitative performance analysis, where we introduce appropriate error measures for range flow. The methods potential is exploited on both synthetic (Sect. 5.2) and real data (Sect. 5.3). Results of applying our algorithm to sequences of range scans of plant leaves are given in Sect. 6.

The work reported here was performed with data gathered by a *Biris* laser range sensor [14]. The algorithm introduced could, however, be equally well used on dense depth maps obtained from structured lighting, stereo or motion and structure techniques.

2   Constraint Equation

Depth is taken as a function of space and time $Z = Z(X, Y, T)$. From the total derivative with respect to time we derive the *range flow motion constraint equation* [3, 9]

$$Z_X \dot{X} + Z_Y \dot{Y} - \dot{Z} + Z_T = 0 \ . \tag{1}$$

Here partial derivatives are denoted by subscripts and time derivatives by using a dot. We call the 3D motion vector *range flow* f and introduce the following abbreviation $f = [U \ V \ W]^T = [\dot{X} \ \dot{Y} \ - \dot{Z}]^T$. The range flow motion constraint (1) then becomes

$$Z_X U + Z_Y V + W + Z_T = [Z_X \ Z_Y \ 1 \ Z_T]^T \begin{bmatrix} U \\ V \\ W \\ 1 \end{bmatrix} = 0 \ . \tag{2}$$

As this gives only one constraint equation in three unknowns we need to make further assumptions, this is the aperture problem revisited.

Equation (2) describes a plane in velocity space. If there are three mutually independent planes in a local neighbourhood we can compute *full flow* under the assumption of locally constant flow fields. Obviously this could easily be extended to incorporate linear flow variations. If there is only one repeated constraint in the entire considered neighbourhood only the normal flow can be recovered. As this occurs on planar surfaces we call this *plane flow*. When two planes meet in the aperture we get two constraint classes, in this case it is possible to determine all but the part of the flow in the direction of the intersection. The flow with minimal norm perpendicular to the intersecting line will be called *line flow* [1]. The following section describes how we can compute the described flow types using a total least squares (TLS) estimator.

3 Total Least Squares Estimation

The TLS solution presented here is an extension of the *structure tensor* algorithm for optical flow estimation [15, 8]. The method may also be viewed as a special case of a more general technique for parameter estimation in image sequences [16].

Assuming constant flow in a region containing n pixel we have n equations (2). With $d = [Z_X \; Z_Y \; 1 \; Z_T]^T$, $u = [U \; V \; W \; 1]^T$ and the data matrix $D = [d_1 \ldots d_n]^T$, the flow estimation in a total least squares sense can be formulated as

$$\|Du\|_2 \to \min \quad \text{subject to} \quad u^T u = 1 \;. \tag{3}$$

The solution is given by the eigenvector $\hat{e}_4$, corresponding to the smallest eigenvalue λ_4 of the generalised structure tensor

$$F = D^T D = \begin{bmatrix} <Z_X Z_X> & <Z_X Z_Y> & <Z_X> & <Z_X Z_T> \\ <Z_Y Z_X> & <Z_Y Z_Y> & <Z_Y> & <Z_Y Z_T> \\ <Z_X> & <Z_Y> & <1> & <Z_T> \\ <Z_T Z_X> & <Z_T Z_Y> & <Z_T> & <Z_T Z_T> \end{bmatrix} \;. \tag{4}$$

Here $< \cdot >$ denotes local averaging using a Box or Binomial filter. The desired range flow is then given by

$$f_f = \frac{1}{e_{44}} \begin{bmatrix} e_{14} \\ e_{24} \\ e_{34} \end{bmatrix} \;. \tag{5}$$

As F is real and symmetric the eigenvalues and eigenvectors can easily be computed using Jacobi-Rotations [17]. In order to save execution time we only compute range flow where the trace of the tensor exceeds a threshold τ_1. This eliminates regions with insufficient magnitude of the gradient. The regularisation step described in Sect. 4 subsequently closes these holes.

3.1 Detecting Motion Discontinuities

In the above we are really fitting a local constant flow model to the data. The smallest eigenvalue λ_4 directly measures the quality of this fit. In particular at motion discontinuities the data can not be described by a single flow and the

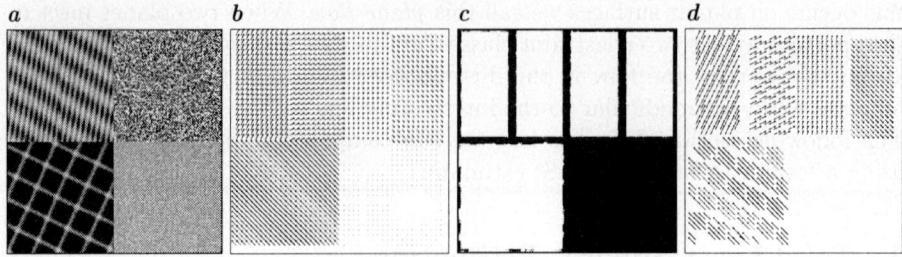

Fig. 1. Using the confidence measure to detect motion discontinuities: **a** synthetic depth map, the lower right quarter contains random noise without coherent motion. **b** X, Y–component of the correct flow field, **c** confidence measure ($\tau_2 = 0.1$) and **d** TLS full flow.

fit fails. This is also the case for pure noise without any coherent motion. To quantify this we introduce a confidence measure

$$
\omega = \begin{cases} 0 & \text{if } \lambda_4 > \tau_2 \text{ or } tr(\boldsymbol{D}) < \tau_1 \\ \left(\frac{\tau_2 - \lambda_4}{\tau_2 + \lambda_4}\right)^2 & \text{else} \end{cases} . \tag{6}
$$

Figure 1 shows the obtained confidence measure for a synthetic sequence of depth maps. Clearly motion discontinuities and pure noise can be identified. Also the estimated full flow is very close to the correct flow, however this full flow can not be computed everywhere regardless of ω. The next section explains why and how to deal with such situations.

3.2 Normal Flows

Let the eigenvalues of $\boldsymbol{F}$ be sorted: $\lambda_1 \geq \lambda_2 \geq \lambda_3 \geq \lambda_4$. Thus if $\lambda_3 \approx \lambda_4$ no unique solution can be found [18]. More general any vector in the nullspace of $\boldsymbol{F}$ is a possible solution. In this case it is desirable to use the solution with minimal norm. Towards this end the possible solutions are expressed as linear combinations of the relevant eigenvectors and that with minimal Euclidean norm is chosen, see App. A for details.

On planar structures all equations (2) are essentially the same. Only the largest eigenvalue is significantly different ($> \tau_2$) from zero. The so called plane flow can then be found from the corresponding eigenvector $\hat{e}_1 = [e_{11}\ e_{21}\ e_{31}\ e_{41}]^T$ as follows

$$
\boldsymbol{f}_p = \frac{e_{41}}{e_{11}^2 + e_{21}^2 + e_{31}^2} \begin{bmatrix} e_{11} \\ e_{21} \\ e_{31} \end{bmatrix} . \tag{7}
$$

Linear structures exhibit two types of constraints within the considered aperture, the minimum norm solution (line flow) is found from the eigenvectors $\hat{e}_1$, $\hat{e}_2$

$$
\boldsymbol{f}_l = \frac{1}{1 - e_{41}^2 - e_{42}^2} \left[e_{41} \begin{bmatrix} e_{11} \\ e_{21} \\ e_{31} \end{bmatrix} + e_{42} \begin{bmatrix} e_{12} \\ e_{22} \\ e_{32} \end{bmatrix} \right] . \tag{8}
$$

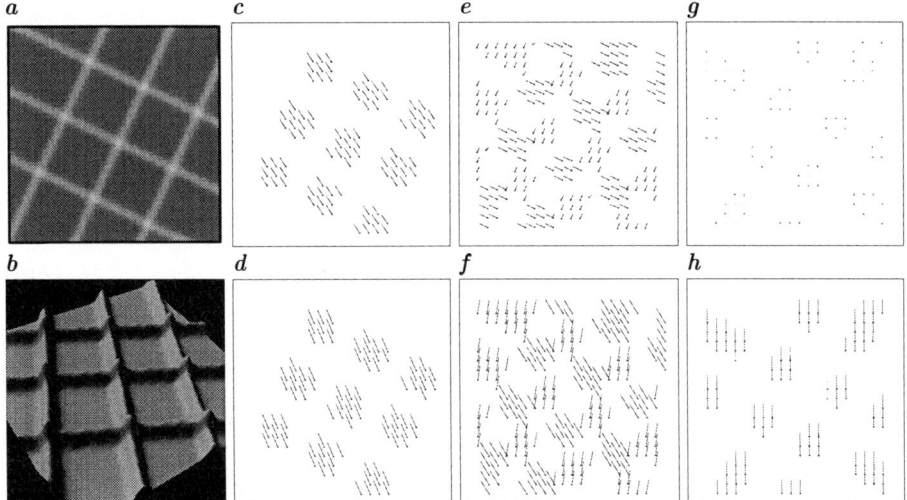

Fig. 2. Example flow types: **a** synthetic depth map, **b** rendered. $X - Y$ components of the estimated flow fields: **c** full flow, **e** line flow and **g** plane flow and $X - Z$ components of the estimated flow fields: **d** full flow, **f** line flow and **h** plane flow.

Figure 2 shows an example of the various flow types.

4 Flow Regularisation

We now introduce a simple iterative regularisation algorithm that computes smoothly varying flow fields in some previously segmented area A. Segmentation of the data into regions of different motions is best accomplished by means of the previously described threshold on the lowest eigenvalue of $\boldsymbol{F}$, see Sect. 3.1. However, if additional knowledge about the scene is available other segmentation schemes may be employed. As we are given depth data such a segmentation is often feasible.

We seek to estimate a dense and smooth flow field $\boldsymbol{v} = [U \ V \ W]^T$. In places where flow estimations from the above TLS algorithm exist we denote them $\boldsymbol{f}$, computed from (5,7,8) as appropriate. As we are now working in 3 dimensions and from the structure of the TLS solution given by (38) we can use the reduced eigenvectors as, not necessarily orthogonal, basis for the desired solution

$$\boldsymbol{b}_i = \frac{1}{\sum_{k=1}^{3} e_{ki}^2} \begin{bmatrix} e_{1i} \\ e_{2i} \\ e_{3i} \end{bmatrix} \quad i = 1, 2, 3 . \tag{9}$$

Using this notation we define a projection matrix which projects onto the subspace that was determined by our TLS algorithm

$$\boldsymbol{P} = \bar{\boldsymbol{B}}_p \bar{\boldsymbol{B}}_p^T \quad \text{where} \quad \lambda_p > \lambda_{p+1} \approx \ldots \approx \lambda_4 \approx 0 , \tag{10}$$

$$\bar{\boldsymbol{B}}_p = [\hat{b}_1 \ \ldots \ \hat{b}_p] . \tag{11}$$

Each estimated flow vector $\boldsymbol{f}_{f,p,l}$ constrains the solution within this subspace. We therefore require the regularised solution to be close in a least squares sense

$$(\boldsymbol{Pv} - \boldsymbol{f})^2 \to \min . \tag{12}$$

At locations where no solution has been computed obviously no such data term exists. To ensure smoothly varying parameters we use a smoothness term

$$\sum_{i=1}^{3} (\nabla v_i)^2 \to \min . \tag{13}$$

Obviously the use of this simple membrane model is only justified because we have already segmented the data into differently moving objects. If no such segmentation were available more elaborate schemes would have to be considered [19, 20]. The above smoothness term usually considers only spatial neighbourhoods ($\nabla = [\partial x, \partial y]^T$), however this is easily extended to enforce temporal smoothness as well ($\nabla = [\partial x, \partial y, \partial t]^T$).

Combining the data (12) and smoothness (13) terms in the considered area A yields the following minimisation problem

$$\int_A \underbrace{\left\{ \omega \, (\boldsymbol{Pv} - \boldsymbol{f})^2 + \alpha \sum_{i=1}^{3} (\nabla v_i)^2 \right\}}_{h(\boldsymbol{v})} \mathrm{d}\boldsymbol{r} \to \min . \tag{14}$$

Where ω, given by equation (6), captures the confidence of the TLS solution. The overall smoothness can be regulated by the constant α. The minimum of (14) is reached when the Euler-Lagrange equations are satisfied

$$\frac{\partial h}{\partial v_i} - \frac{\mathrm{d}}{\mathrm{d}x} \frac{\partial h}{\partial (v_i)_x} - \frac{\mathrm{d}}{\mathrm{d}y} \frac{\partial h}{\partial (v_i)_y} = 0 \quad ; \; i = 1, \ldots, m . \tag{15}$$

If an extension in the temporal domain is anticipated another term $-\dfrac{\mathrm{d}}{\mathrm{d}t} \dfrac{\partial h}{\partial (v_i)_t}$ has to be added. Subscripts x, y, t denote partial differentiation. Using vector notation we write the Euler-Lagrange equations as follows:

$$\frac{\partial h}{\partial \boldsymbol{v}} - \frac{\mathrm{d}}{\mathrm{d}x} \frac{\partial h}{\partial (\boldsymbol{v}_x)} - \frac{\mathrm{d}}{\mathrm{d}y} \frac{\partial h}{\partial (\boldsymbol{v}_y)} = 0 . \tag{16}$$

Computing the derivatives yields

$$2\omega \boldsymbol{P}(\boldsymbol{Pv} - \boldsymbol{f}) - 2\alpha \left[\frac{\mathrm{d}}{\mathrm{d}x}(\boldsymbol{v}_x) + \frac{\mathrm{d}}{\mathrm{d}y}(\boldsymbol{v}_y) \right] = 0 . \tag{17}$$

Introducing the Laplacian $\Delta \boldsymbol{v} = \boldsymbol{v}_{xx} + \boldsymbol{v}_{yy}$ we get

$$\omega \boldsymbol{Pv} - \omega \boldsymbol{Pf} - \alpha \Delta \boldsymbol{v} = 0 , \tag{18}$$

where the idempotence of the projection matrix $\boldsymbol{PP} = \boldsymbol{P}$ is used. The Laplacian can be approximated as $\Delta \boldsymbol{v} = \bar{\boldsymbol{v}} - \boldsymbol{v}$, where $\bar{\boldsymbol{v}}$ denotes a local average. In principle this average has to be calculated without taking the central pixel into consideration. Using this approximation we arrive at

$$(\omega \boldsymbol{P} + \alpha \mathbb{1})\, \boldsymbol{v} = \alpha \bar{\boldsymbol{v}} + \omega \boldsymbol{P} \boldsymbol{f} \; . \tag{19}$$

This enables an iterative solution to the minimisation problem. We introduce $\boldsymbol{A} = \omega \boldsymbol{P} + \alpha \mathbb{1}$ and get an update $\boldsymbol{v}^{k+1}$ from the solution at step k

$$\boldsymbol{v}^{k+1} = \alpha \boldsymbol{A}^{-1} \bar{\boldsymbol{v}}^{k} + \omega \boldsymbol{A}^{-1} \boldsymbol{P} \boldsymbol{f} \; . \tag{20}$$

Initialisation is done as $\boldsymbol{v}^0 = \boldsymbol{0}$. The matrix $\boldsymbol{A}^{-1}$ only has to be computed once, existence of the inverse is guaranteed by the Sherman-Morrison-Woodbury formula [21], see Appendix B.

4.1 Direct Regularisation

Instead of performing a TLS analysis first one might want to directly try to find the flow field by imposing the smoothness constraint, in analogy to the well known optical flow algorithm by Horn and Schunk [22]. As mentioned before this simple smoothness term is not generally advisable, mainly because problematic locations ($\lambda_4 > 0$) are equally taken into account. In particular it smoothes across motion discontinuities. On the other hand this regularisation works very well when a segmentation, if at all necessary, can be achieved otherwise.

However, if the TLS algorithm is used for segmenting the data, it makes sense to use the thus available information. The scheme described in Sect. 4 does usually converge much faster than direct regularisation. Yet, it is sometimes advisable to use the direct regularisation as a final processing step. The already dense and smooth flow field is used to initialise this step. Especially on real data, where the TLS estimate occasionally produces outliers, this post-processing improves the result, see Sect. 5.3.

Therefore we briefly discuss how such a direct regularisation can be applied to sequences of depth maps. The minimisation in this case reads

$$\int_A \underbrace{\left\{ (\boldsymbol{d}^T \boldsymbol{u})^2 + \alpha \sum_{i=1}^{3} (\nabla v_i)^2 \right\}}_{h(\boldsymbol{v})} \mathrm{d}r \to \min \; . \tag{21}$$

Here we only work on the first n-1 components of $\boldsymbol{u} = [\boldsymbol{v}^T, 1]^T$. Looking at the Euler-Lagrange equations (15) we get

$$2\boldsymbol{d}'(\boldsymbol{d}'^T \boldsymbol{v} - d_4) - 2\alpha \Delta \boldsymbol{v} = 0 \quad \text{where} \quad \boldsymbol{d} = [\boldsymbol{d}'^T, d_4]^T \; . \tag{22}$$

Again approximating the Laplacian as difference $\Delta \boldsymbol{v} = \bar{\boldsymbol{v}} - \boldsymbol{v}$ this can be rewritten as

$$(\boldsymbol{d}'\boldsymbol{d}'^T)\boldsymbol{v} - \alpha \bar{\boldsymbol{v}} + \alpha \boldsymbol{v} = \boldsymbol{d}' d_4 \tag{23}$$

$$\underbrace{\alpha \mathbb{1} + \boldsymbol{d}'\boldsymbol{d}'^T}_{\boldsymbol{A}_1} \boldsymbol{v} = \alpha \bar{\boldsymbol{v}} + \boldsymbol{d}' d_4 \; . \tag{24}$$

Table 1. Results on synthetic data using $\alpha = 10$, $\tau_1 = 15$ and $\tau_2 = 0.1$.

sequence	iterations	E_r [%]	E_d [°]	E_b [%]
Fig. 1	100	0.6 ± 2.6	0.4 ± 1.6	-0.4
Fig. 1	500	0.5 ± 2.6	0.4 ± 1.6	-0.3
Fig. 1	1000	0.5 ± 2.6	0.4 ± 1.6	-0.3
Fig. 2	100	5.3 ± 4.3	6.4 ± 5.5	-5.3
Fig. 2	500	0.7 ± 0.8	0.6 ± 0.8	-0.5
Fig. 2	1000	0.4 ± 0.3	0.2 ± 0.2	-0.2

An iterative solution is found using the following update

$$v^{k+1} = \alpha A_1^{-1} \bar{p}^k + d_4 A_1^{-1} d' \ . \tag{25}$$

Initialisation can be done by the direct minimum norm solution n to $d^T p = 0$ given by:

$$n = \frac{-d_4}{\sum_{i=1}^{3} d_i^2} \begin{bmatrix} d_1 \\ d_2 \\ d_3 \end{bmatrix} = \frac{-Z_T}{Z_X^2 + Z_Y^2 + 1} \begin{bmatrix} Z_X \\ Z_Y \\ 1 \end{bmatrix} \ . \tag{26}$$

The existence of the inverse of A_1 is guaranteed, see Appendix B.

5   Quantitative Performance Analysis

We now give a quantitative analysis of the proposed algorithm. Even though our algorithm can be used with any kind of differential depth maps we focus on depth maps taken with a laser range finder. In particular we are concerned with a *Biris* sensor [14]. First we introduce the error measures used. Due to experimental limitations the available real data with known ground truth only contains pure translational movements. Thus we also look at one synthetic sequence with a motion field that exhibits some divergence and rotation.

5.1   Error Measures

In order to quantify the obtained results three error measures are used. Let the correct range flow be called f_c and the estimated flow f_e. The first error measure describes the relative error in magnitude

$$E_r = \frac{|(\|f_c\| - \|f_e\|)|}{\|f_c\|} \cdot 100 \ [\%] \ . \tag{27}$$

The deviation in the direction of the flow is captured by the directional error

$$E_d = \arccos\left(\frac{f_c \cdot f_e}{\|f_c\| \ \|f_e\|}\right) \ [°] \ . \tag{28}$$

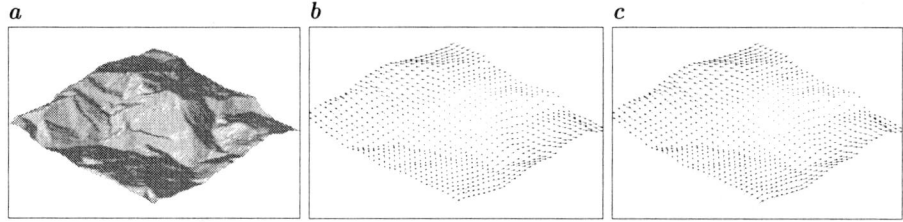

Fig. 3. Synthetic sequence generated from a real depth map. **a** rendered depth map, **b** correct flow and **c** estimated flow field ($\alpha = 10$, $\tau_1 = 25$ and $\tau_2 = 0.01$).

Even though both E_r and E_d are available at each location we only report their average values in the following. It is also interesting to see if the flow is consistently over- or underestimated. This is measured by a bias error measure

$$E_b = \frac{1}{N} \sum_{}^{N} \left(\frac{\|\mathbf{f}_e\| - \|\mathbf{f}_c\|}{\|\mathbf{f}_c\|} \cdot 100 \right) \ [\%] \ , \tag{29}$$

where the summation is caried out over the entire considered region. This measure will be negative if the estimated flow magnitude is systematically smaller than the correct magnitude.

5.2 Synthetic Test Data

The performance of the TLS algorithm, described in Sect. 3, has previously been analysed on synthetic data [1]. Here we simply repeat the results that for low noise levels of less than 2%, laser range data is typically a factor 10 less noisy, all flow types (full, line, plane) can be estimated with less than 5% relative error E_r and less than 5° error E_d in the velocity range of 0.5 to 3 units per frame. Here unit stands for the mean distance between adjacent data points, typically ≈ 0.3mm.

The regularisation algorithm produces excellent results on pure synthetic data. Instead of giving numerous such results we simply state that for the sequences shown in figures 1 and 2 we achieve the results given in table 1. It can be seen that when starting with a relatively dense flow field as in Fig. 1 the use of 100 iterations provides good results. The remaining error here is mainly due to small mistakes in the segmentation into different regions. On data like that of Fig. 2, where we have large areas to be filled in, far more iterations are necessary. Convergence can be accelerated by starting with an interpolated full flow field instead of a zero flow field or by employing a hierarchical method [23].

As we are unable to make real test data with other than translational motion, we took the depth map from one scan and warped the data[1] with a known flow field. Figure 3a shows the depth map taken from a crumpled sheet of paper. It can be seen that the estimated flow is very close to the correct flow. In numbers

---
[1] Using bicubic interpolation.

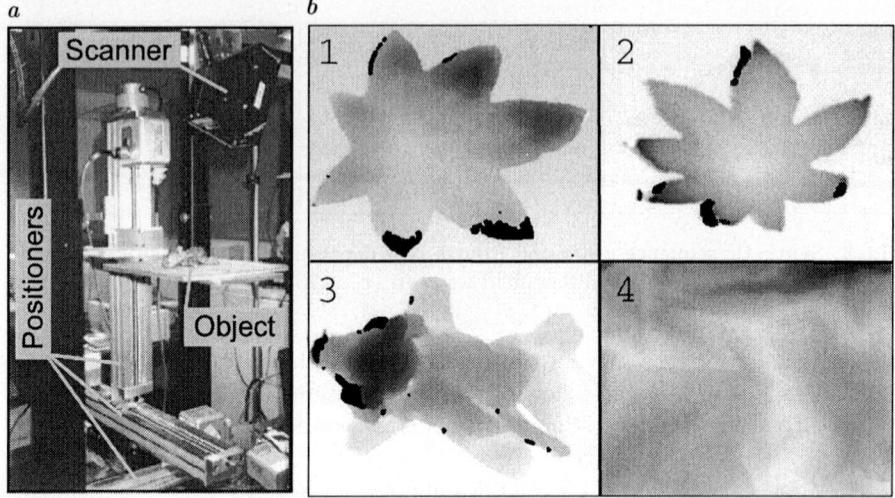

Fig. 4. Real test data: **a** laser scanner and positioners and **b** depth maps of the used test objects. Object 1 and 2 are freshly cut castor bean leaves, object 3 a toy tiger and object 4 a sheet of crumpled newspaper.

we get $E_r = 2.1 \pm 1.6\%$, $E_d = 2.3 \pm 0.8°$ and $E_b = 1.9\%$ after 100 iterations. From the last number we see that in this particular example the estimated flow is systematically larger than the correct flow, this can be attributed to the very small velocities present in this case.

5.3 Real Test Data

In order to get real test data we placed some test objects on a set of linear positioners, see Fig. 4. The positioners allow for translations along all three axes. As the objects are placed on a flat surface we segmented them prior to any computation. There is no motion discontinuity in this case and without segmenting we would have to use the background as well. Due to the lack of structure there this would make convergence extremely slow. Table 2 gives some results, here first the indirect regularisation (Sect. 4) is employed for 300 iterations with $\alpha = 10$, $\tau_1 = 15$ and $\tau_2 = 0.01$. Then the direct regularisation (Sect. 4.1) is used for another 200 iterations with $\alpha = 5$.This post-processing typically improves the result (E_r) by about 1-2%.

Given the fact that we are dealing with real data these results are quite encouraging. The average distance between two data points is 0.46mm in X-direction and 0.35mm in Y-direction, which shows that we are able to estimate sub-pixel displacements. One has to keep in mind that even slight misalignments of the positioner and the laser scanner introduce systematic errors.

Table 2. Results on real data.

object	correct flow [mm]	E_r [%]	E_d [°]	E_b [%]
1	$[0.0\ 0.0\ 0.48]^T$	3.0 ± 3.2	4.5 ± 3.0	1.5
1	$[0.32\ -0.38\ 0.32]^T$	9.2 ± 5.9	11.2 ± 6.0	1.3
2	$[-0.32\ 0.0\ 0.0]^T$	8.0 ± 11.6	7.5 ± 4.6	2.2
2	$[-0.64\ 0.0\ 0.0]^T$	6.1 ± 8.5	6.0 ± 3.8	-0.3
3	$[-0.16\ -0.19\ -0.32]^T$	3.5 ± 2.5	3.2 ± 2.4	-2.7
4	$[0.25\ 0.31\ 0.0]^T$	8.8 ± 5.4	4.3 ± 3.3	5.1

6 Plant Leaf Motion

This section finally presents some flow fields found by observing living castor oil leaves. Figure 5 shows four examples of the type of data and flow fields encountered in this application. The folding of the outer lobes is clearly visible, also a fair bit of lateral motion of the leaf. The data sets considered here are taken at night with a sampling rate of 5 minutes. Analysis is done using the same parameters as in the previous section. In Fig. 5a two overlapping leaves are observed, it is such cases that makes a segmentation based on the TLS algorithm very useful. If the leaves are actually touching each other it is quite involved to separate them otherwise.

In collaboration with the botanical institute at the University of Heidelberg and the Agriculture and Agri-Food Canada research station in Harrow, Ontario we seek to establish the leafs diurnal motion patterns. We also hope to examine the growth rate of an undisturbed leaf with a previously impossible spatial and temporal resolution. Up to now related experiments required the leaf to be fixed in a plane [15].

7 Conclusions

An algorithm to compute dense 3D range flow fields from a sequence of depth maps has been presented. It is shown how the sparse information from a TLS based technique can be combined to yield dense full flow fields everywhere within a selected area. The segmentation into regions corresponding to different motions can easily be done based on the quality of the initial TLS estimation. The performance is quantitatively assessed on synthetic and real data and the algorithm is found to give excellent results. Finally it could be shown that the motion of a living castor oil leaf can be nicely captured.

Future work includes the interpretation of the obtained flow fields from a botanical point of view. We also plan to test the method on depth data from structured lighting and stereo.

Acknowledgements. Part of this work has been funded under the DFG research unit "Image Sequence Analysis to Investigate Dynamic Processes" (Ja395/6) and by the federal government of Canada via two NSERC grants.

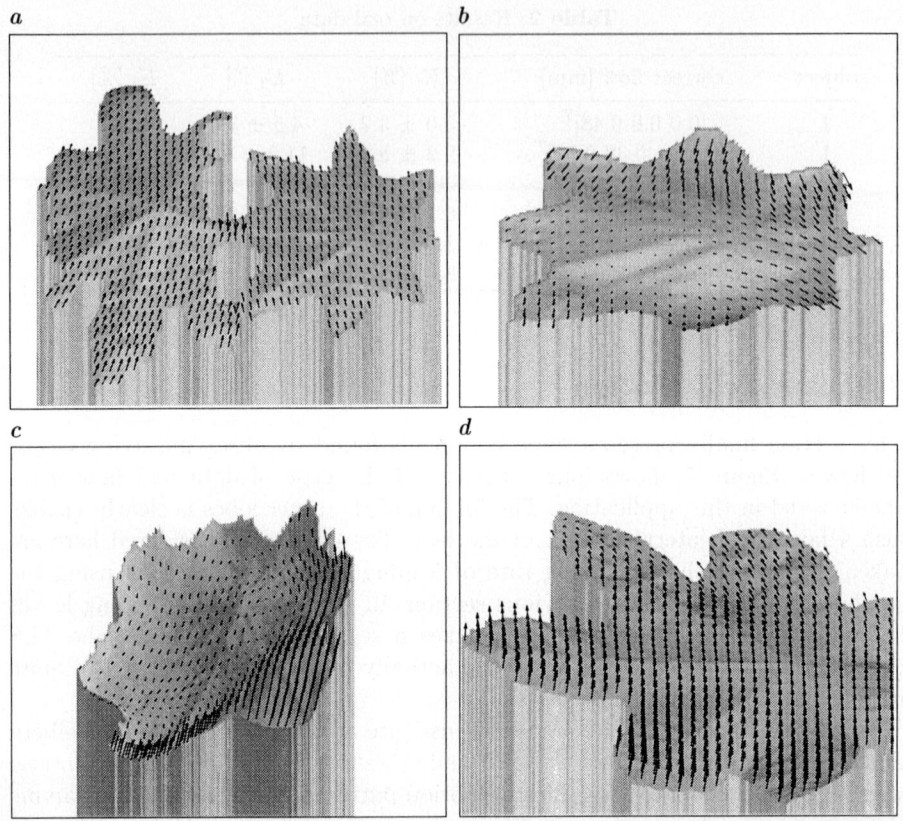

Fig. 5. Example movements of castor oil plant leaves.

A Minimum Norm Solution

Let's assume we have $\lambda_1 > \ldots > \lambda_p > \lambda_{p+1} \approx \ldots \approx \lambda_n \approx 0$ then any linear combination of the eigenvectors $\hat{e}_i$; $i > p$ is a solution to (3). Following [18] (Theorem 3.8) we now describe a way to find the minimum norm solution.

First the possible solutions are expressed as linear combinations of the relevant eigenvectors

$$ \boldsymbol{p} = \sum_{i=p+1}^{n} g_i \hat{e}_i = \boldsymbol{E}_p \boldsymbol{g} \quad \text{where} \quad \boldsymbol{E}_p = [\hat{e}_{p+1}, \ldots, \hat{e}_n] = \begin{bmatrix} e_{1(p+1)} & \cdots & e_{1n} \\ \vdots & \ddots & \vdots \\ e_{n(p+1)} & \cdots & e_{nn} \end{bmatrix}. $$
(30)

The norm of $\boldsymbol{p}$ is then given by

$$ \|\boldsymbol{p}\| = \boldsymbol{g}^T \boldsymbol{E}_p^T \boldsymbol{E}_p \boldsymbol{g} = \boldsymbol{g}^T \boldsymbol{g} = \sum_i g_i^2 . $$
(31)

The additional constraint $p_n = 1$ can be expressed as

$$p_n = \left(\sum_{i=p+1}^{n} g_i \hat{e}_i \right)_n = \sum_{i=p+1}^{n} g_i e_{ni} = \boldsymbol{v}_n^T \boldsymbol{E}_p \boldsymbol{g} = 1 \ , \tag{32}$$

where $\boldsymbol{v}_n = [0, \ldots, 0, 1]^T$. Equations (31) and (32) can be combined using a Lagrange multiplier

$$F(\boldsymbol{g}) = \boldsymbol{g}^T \boldsymbol{g} + \lambda(\boldsymbol{v}_n^T \boldsymbol{E}_p \boldsymbol{g}) \ . \tag{33}$$

The minimum is found by setting the partial derivatives of F with respect to the g_i to zero. Doing so yields

$$2g_i + \lambda e_{ni} = 0 \quad \rightarrow \quad g_i = -\frac{\lambda}{2} e_{ni} \quad \rightarrow \quad \boldsymbol{g} = -\frac{\lambda}{2} \boldsymbol{E}_p^T \boldsymbol{v}_n \ . \tag{34}$$

Substitution into (32) gives

$$-\frac{\lambda}{2} \sum_{i=p+1}^{n} e_{ni} e_{ni} = 1 \quad \rightarrow \quad \lambda = \frac{-2}{\sum_i e_{ni} e_{ni}} = \frac{-2}{\boldsymbol{v}_n^T \boldsymbol{E}_p \boldsymbol{E}_p^T \boldsymbol{v}_n} \ . \tag{35}$$

The minimum norm solution then equates to

$$\boldsymbol{p} = \begin{bmatrix} \boldsymbol{p}' \\ 1 \end{bmatrix} = \frac{\boldsymbol{E}_p \boldsymbol{E}_p^T \boldsymbol{v}_n}{\boldsymbol{v}_n^T \boldsymbol{E}_p \boldsymbol{E}_p^T \boldsymbol{v}_n} \ . \tag{36}$$

In components this equals

$$p_k = \frac{\sum_{i=p+1}^{n} e_{ki} e_{ni}}{\sum_{i=p+1}^{n} e_{ni}^2} , \tag{37}$$

or as vector equation

$$\boldsymbol{p}' = \frac{\sum_{i=p+1}^{n} e_{ni} [e_{1i}, \ldots, e_{(n-1)i}]^T}{\sum_{i=p+1}^{n} e_{ni}^2} = \frac{\sum_{i=1}^{p} e_{ni} [e_{1i}, \ldots, e_{(n-1)i}]^T}{1 - \sum_{i=1}^{p} e_{ni}^2} \ . \tag{38}$$

Where we used $\boldsymbol{E}_p \boldsymbol{E}_p^T = \mathbb{1} - \bar{\boldsymbol{E}}_p \bar{\boldsymbol{E}}_p^T$, with $\bar{\boldsymbol{E}}_p = [\boldsymbol{e}_1, \ldots, \boldsymbol{e}_p]$, in the last equality.

B   Inversion of $\boldsymbol{A}$

To show that $\boldsymbol{A}$ is always regular we use the Sherman-Morrison-Woodbury Lemma [21]. It states that for a regular (n,n) matrix $\boldsymbol{Q}$, two (n,m) matrices $\boldsymbol{R}, \boldsymbol{T}$ and a regular (m,m) matrix $\boldsymbol{S}$ the combination

$$\bar{\boldsymbol{Q}} = \boldsymbol{Q} + \boldsymbol{R} \boldsymbol{S} \boldsymbol{T}^T \tag{39}$$

is regular if it can be shown that $U := S^{-1} + T^T Q^{-1} R$ is regular. To apply this to $\bar{Q} = A = \alpha \mathbb{1} + \omega P$ we rewrite A as

$$A = \mathbb{1}_n + \bar{B}_p \mathbb{1}_m \bar{B}_p^T . \tag{40}$$

Here we dropped the constants α and ω without loss of generality. Thus we have to examine

$$U = \mathbb{1}_m + \bar{B}_p^T \mathbb{1}_n \bar{B}_p . \tag{41}$$

The off-diagonal elements of U are given by $b_i^T b_j = \cos(\beta_{ij}) \leq 1$, where β_{ij} is the angle between b_i and b_j. Thus U is diagonal dominant with all diagonal elements stricly positive and hence a symmetric positive definite matrix [21]. This implies U is regular. Thus we conclude that for $\alpha > 0$ the matrix A can always be inverted.

In the direct regularisation case described in Sect. 4.1 we encounter $A_1 = \mathbb{1}_3 + d' \mathbb{1}_1 d'^T$. Thus we have to look at $U = \mathbb{1}_1 + d'^T \mathbb{1}_3 d'$ which is simply a scalar. Hence A_1 can always be inverted provided $\alpha > 0$.

References

1. H. Spies, H. Haußecker, B. Jähne and J. L. Barron: Differential Range Flow Estimation. 21.Symposium für Mustererkennung DAGM'1999. Bonn (1999) 309–316
2. R. Szeliski: Estimating Motion from Sparse Range Data without Correspondence. ICCV'88. (1988) 207–216
3. B.K.P. Horn and J.G. Harris: Rigid Body Motion from Range Image Sequences. CVGIP: Image Understanding. **53**(1) (1991) 1–13
4. B. Sabata and J.K. Aggarwal: Estimation of Motion from a Pair of Range Images: A Review. CVGIP: Image Understanding. **54**(3) (1991) 309–324
5. L. Lucchese, G.M. Cortelazzo and A. Vettore: Estimating 3-D Roto-translations from Range Data by a Frequency Domain Technique. Conf. on Optical 3-D Measurement Techniques IV. Zürich (1997) 444–453
6. M. Harville, A. Rahimi, T. Darrell, G. Gordon and J. Woodfill: 3D Pose Tracking with Linear Depth and Brightness Constraints. ICCV'99, (1999) 206–213
7. B. Lucas and T. Kanade: An Iterative Image Registration Technique with an Application to Stereo Vision. Int. Joint Conf. on Artificial Intelligence. (1981) 674–679
8. H. Haußecker and H. Spies: Motion. In Handbook on Computer Vision and Applications, Eds.: B, Jähne, H. Haußecker and P. Geißler. Academic Press. (1999)
9. M. Yamamoto, P. Boulanger, J. Beraldin and M. Rioux: Direct Estimation of Range Flow on Deformable Shape from a Video Rate Range Camera. PAMI. **15**(1) (1993) 82–89
10. L.V Tsap, D.B. Goldgof and S. Sarkar: Model-Based Force-Driven Nonrigid Motion Recovery from Sequences of Range Images without Point Correspondences. Image and Vision Computing, **17**(14) (1999) 997–1007
11. S. Vedula, S. Baker, P. Rander, R. Collins and T. Kanade: Three-Dimensional Scene Flow. ICCV'99, (1999) 722–729
12. J. Gonzalez: Recovering Motion Parameters from a 2D Range Image Sequence. ICPR'96. (1996) 82–89

13. L. Zhao and C. Thorpe: Qualitative and Quantitative Car Tracking from a Range Image Sequence. CVPR'98, (1998) 496–501
14. J.-A. Beraldin, S.F. El-Hakim and F. Blais: Performance Evaluation of three Active Vision Systems Built at the National Research Council of Canada. Conf. on Optical 3-D Measurement Techniques III. Vienna (1995) 352–361
15. B. Jähne, H. Haußecker, H. Scharr, H. Spies, D. Schmundt and U. Schurr: Study of Dynamical Processes with Tensor-Based Spatiotemporal Image Processing Techniques. ECCV '98. (1998) 322–336
16. H. Haußecker, C. Garbe, H. Spies and B. Jähne: A Total Least Squares Framework for Low-Level Analysis of Dynamic Scenes and Processes. 21.Symposium für Mustererkennung DAGM'1999. (1999) 240–249
17. W. H. Press, S. A. Teukolsky, W.T. Vetterling and B.P. Flannery: Numerical Recipes in C: The Art of Scientific Computing. Cambridge University Press. (1992)
18. S. Van Huffel and J. Vandewalle: The Total Least Squares Problem: Computational Aspects and Analysis. Society for Industrial and Applied Mathematics. (1991)
19. Ch. Schnörr: Variational Methods for Adaptive Image Smoothing and Segmentation. In Handbook on Computer Vision and Applications, Eds.: B, Jähne, H. Haußecker and P. Geißler. Academic Press. (1999)
20. J. Weickert: On Discontinuity-Preserving Optic Flow. Proc. CVMR '98. (1998) 115–122
21. G. H. Golub and C. F. van Loan: Matrix Computations (3rd edition). The Johns Hopkins University Press. (1996)
22. B.K.P. Horn and B.G. Schunk: Determining Optical Flow. Artificial Intelligence 17 (1981) 185–204
23. J.R. Bergen, p. Anandan, K.J. Hanna and R. Hingorani: Hierarchical Model-Based Motion Estimation. ECCV'92. (1992) 237–252

Visual Encoding of Tilt from Optic Flow: Psychophysics and Computational Modelling

Huiying Zhong[1], Valérie Cornilleau-Pérès[2, 3, 4], Loong-Fah Cheong[1],
Jacques Droulez[3]

[1] Department of Electrical Engineering, The National University of Singapore, 10 Kent
Ridge Crescent, Singapore 119260
{engp8927, eleclf}@nus.edu.sg
[2] Singapore Eye Research Institute, W212, 500 Dover Road, Singapore 139651
[3] Laboratoire de Physiologie de la Perception et de l'Action, CNRS-Collège de France, 11 pl
Marcelin Berthelot, 75005 Paris, France
{vcp, jdr}@moka.ccr.jussieu.fr
[4] Optometry Center, Singapore Polytechnic, 500 Dover Road, Singapore 139651

Abstract. Many computational models indicate ambiguities in the recovery of
plane orientation from optic flow. Here we questioned whether psychophysical
responses agree with these models. We measured the perceived tilt of a plane
rotating in depth with two-view stimuli for 9 human observers. Response
accuracy was higher under wide-field perspective projection (60°) than in small
field (8°). Also, it decreased when the tilt and frontal translation were
orthogonal rather than parallel. This effect was stronger in small field than in
large field. Different computational models focusing on the recovery of plane
orientation from optic flow can account for our results when associated with a
hypothesis of minimal translation in depth. However, the twofold ambiguity
predicted by these models is usually not found. Rather, most responses show a
shift of the reported tilts toward the spurious solution with concomitant
increase in response variability. Such findings point to the need for further
simulations of the computational models.

1   Introduction

Plane orientation can be defined by the tilt (τ) and slant (σ). We call **N** the vector
normal to a plane. Slant is the angle between **N** and the frontoparallel plane, while tilt
is the orientation of **N** as projected in this plane (Fig.1). Determining the tilt of a
planar surface is required for navigation, when climbing a slope for instance, or for
actions like grasping flat objects. In these situations, motion parallax is a depth cue
that reveals the 3D structure of the visual scene to biological or machine vision
systems [19], [15].

The perception of tilt from optic flow has been addressed by few psychophysical
studies. Domini and Caudek [6] found that observers estimate tilt more accurately
than slant in multiple-view stimuli. Cornilleau-Pérès et al [4] defined the winding
angle W as the angle between the tilt and the component of the frontal translation

They found that the accuracy in tilt reports decreases as W increases, this effect being particularly strong in small-field (8° visual angle).

A more systematic exploration of this question is found in the theoretical domain, where several models of tilt computation have been proposed [10], [13], [16] and give a thorough account for the existence of multiple solutions in the problem of tilt computation from optic flow. However, these studies give little information on the performance of the corresponding algorithms in terms of accuracy and robustness to noise. While many have developed error analyses of the structure from motion problem [1], [18],[5], [3], little is known on the accuracy of orientation estimates for a planar scene. In general, the recovery of the motion and structure parameters seems to have a maximal sensitivity to image noise when the 3D translation is parallel to **N** [18], [5]. Baratoff [2] is the only author addressing the sensitivity of tilt and slant estimates from binocular parallax. He finds that tilt is less sensitive than slant to variations of the viewing geometry, and that both variables are seriously affected by image noise. Contrary to slant estimates, tilt computation does not require a metric of the visual space, and the recent interest for an ordinal, rather than metrical, representation of depth [12], [8] warrants a deeper understanding of the properties of tilt perception.

In this respect, the human performance may help at designing simulation tests, since it points to two critical variables in tilt perception, namely the size of the field of view (FOV) and the orientation of the plane relative to its 3D motion [4]. Because the previous results were obtained with multiple-frame stimuli, which provides complementary acceleration information [9], our first goal was to develop a systematic exploration of human tilt perception with two-view stimuli. We evaluated the errors in tilt estimation, and also the position of the perceived tilt with respect to the stimulus tilt and the direction of frontal translation (as is well-known and shown in the appendix, these are the two possible solutions for tilt). Our second objective was to test the predictions of different computational models so as to propose new directions of research on tilt perception in both biological and machine vision.

2 Preliminaries

If the position of the eye is the origin of a XYZ coordinate system, and the Z axis lies along the line of sight (Fig. 1), a plane is given by the equation:

$$Z = Z_X X + Z_Y Y + Z_0 \tag{1}$$

In what follows, we suppose that the plane moves with a rotation $\Omega = (\Omega_X, \Omega_Y, \Omega_Z)$ around the eye, and a translation $\mathbf{T} = (T_X, T_Y, T_Z)$. Thus, $\mathbf{T'} = (T_X, T_Y)$ is the frontal translation and $\mathbf{T'} = \tan^{-1} \dfrac{T_Y}{T_X}$ is the angle between $\mathbf{T'}$ and the X axis in the frontoparallel plane. The normalized **N** and **T** are $\bar{n}$ and $\bar{t}$, respectively.

Under perspective projection, $p = \dfrac{1}{Z}$ can be written as

$$p = p_x x + p_y y + p_0 \qquad (2)$$

where

$$x = \frac{X}{Z}, \; y = \frac{Y}{Z}, \; p_x = -Z_X p_0, \; p_y = -Z_Y p_0, \text{ and } p_0 = \frac{1}{Z_0}.$$

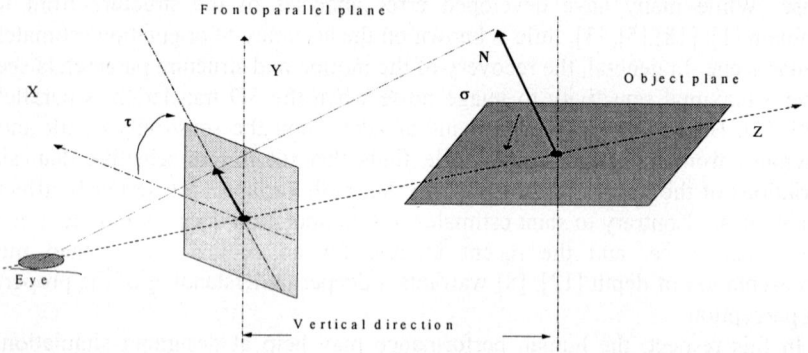

Fig. 1. The tilt and slant of an object plane. N is the normal to the plane. τ is tilt. σ is slant.

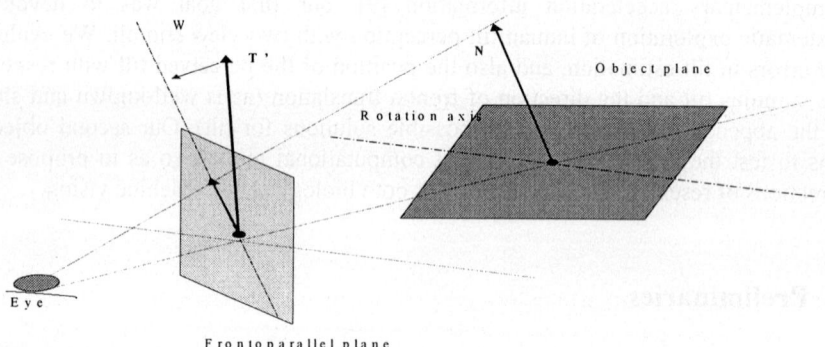

Fig. 2. The winding angle of a moving plane. **T'** is the frontal translation, orthogonal to the optical axis. N is the normal to the plane. The winding angle (W) is the unsigned angle between the tilt (τ) direction and **T'**.

The tilt τ and the slant σ can be expressed as:

$$\tau = \tan^{-1} \frac{p_y}{p_x} \qquad (3)$$

$$\sigma = \tan^{-1} \frac{\sqrt{p_x^2 + p_y^2}}{p_0} \tag{4}$$

Under orthographic projection,

$$\tau = \tan^{-1} \frac{Z_Y}{Z_X} \tag{5}$$

$$\sigma = \tan^{-1} \sqrt{Z_X^2 + Z_Y^2} \tag{6}$$

3 Experiment and Results

3.1 Method

- *Participants*

Nine observers aged between 21 and 28 served as naïve subjects for this experiment. All of them had normal or corrected-to-normal vision.

- *Design*

We examined the effects of two variables on the judgments of plane orientation in terms of tilt and slant: (1) the size of the visual stimulus (diameters 8° or 60° visual angle) and (2) the winding angle (W) randomized between 0° and 90° (here W is unsigned). The tilt τ was randomly chosen between 0° and 360°. The angle of the rotation axis was such that the angle between the tilt and the frontal translation was +W or −W, and thus ranged randomly between 0° and 360°. The slant of the plane was 35° and the rotation amplitude between the two views was 3°. There were 8 sessions of 108 trials for each field size. The sessions in small field and large field were performed alternately in random order.

- *Apparatus*

The stimulus patterns were generated on a PC, and displayed either on the 19-in. monitor for small visual field or on a glass-fabric screen using the Marquee Ultra 8500 projector for large visual field. The diameter of the small stimuli was 27.5 cm (8° visual angle) or 2 m (60° visual angle). Both large-field and small-field displays had a spatial resolution of 768 pixels for the stimulus diameter, and we used an anti-aliasing software to achieve subpixel accuracy, each dot covering a 3×3 pixels area. The refresh rate was 85 Hz.

- *Stimuli*

The viewing distance was 1.96 m in small field, and 1.73 m in large field. The stimuli in the experiment were perspective projections of dotted planes, with dots spread uniformly within a circular area of the display window (Fig. 3). Each plane rotated about a frontoparallel axis. In this case the component of frontal translation **T'** is orthogonal to the rotation axis. A probe was presented in the center of the screen and could be adjusted by the subjects to indicate the perceived plane orientation, using the computer mouse. A uniform dot density was achieved in the position of the surface corresponding to the intermediate position between the 2 views. The stimuli were generated with the appropriate perspective for visual angles of 8°and 60°. The motion sequence was composed of two views corresponding to rotational angles of − 1.5° and 1.5°. The duration of the two views was 0.38 ± 0.015 s. The dot number for each stimulus was 572 ± 17. Trial duration was determined by the subject and usually ranged around 8 s. The luminance was adjusted to 0.23 cd/m^2.

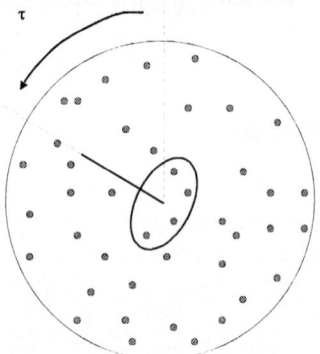

Fig. 3. Reporting tilt and slant through probe adjustment. The probe is made of a needle and an ellipse. Subjects adjust the orientation of the needle and the small-width of the ellipse with the computer mouse to indicate the perceived tilt (direction of the needle) and slant (width of the ellipse).

- *Procedure*

The subjects were seated with head maintained in a chinrest, and the experimental room was dark. With an eye patch to cover the non-dominant eye, he/she was asked to fixate the center of the stimulus. Each stimulus was displayed in a continuous way, and after 3 seconds of presentation, the subjects could adjust the XY position of the mouse to modify the orientation of the probe superimposed on the stimulus. Upon completion of the adjustment, they clicked on the mouse, and proceeded to the next trial.

- *Data Analysis*

We partitioned the winding angles in nine intervals: 0°-10°, 10°-20°, ... 80°-90°. The average number of trials for each subject in each W interval was 96 (standard deviation 7).

We measured the ambiguity on the tilt sign (tilt reversal) by calculating the percentage of trials where the unsigned tilt error ranged between 90° and 180°. Having corrected the responses for this ambiguity, we then used the corrected absolute tilt error as a measure of the performance, ranging between 0° and 90°.

In order to assess the influence of T' (the direction of frontal translation) on the reported tilt, we imposed a polarity on our data and calculated a 'asymmeterized' distribution of the responses, where the angle between the tilt and T' is always positive. Initially, the frontal translation is at angle +W or −W from the tilt. In the second case, we replace T' and the reported tilt by their symmetrical values relative to τ. Hence we obtain a new distribution, where the angle between τ and T' is always +W. As the distribution is not Gaussian, we did the non parametric tests using a software of Statistica.

We used circular statistics to find the mean of the distributions of the reported tilt.[1]

3.2 Results

- *Effect of the field of view (FOV) on the reported tilt sign*

We find 41% of tilt reversals in small field and only 2.4% in large field. This confirms previous results showing that large-field perspective projection disambiguates the sign of the perceived tilt [4]. All subsequent results are corrected with respect to the sign of the tilt.

- *Effect of the FOV on the absolute tilt error*

The average absolute tilt error, as presented in Fig. 4, is always lower in large field than in small field, especially for large values of W. This effect (median test, $\chi^2 = 52$ to 297, p<0.001) of the FOV is significant for every subject

- *Effect of the winding angle on the absolute tilt error and variability in reported tilt*

Fig. 4 shows the average absolute tilt error with respect to W in each of the W intervals. In small field, the average absolute tilt error increases dramatically as W increases. This effect is smaller in large field. The Spearman correlation of the absolute tilt error with W is significant for each subject in small field (overall value: 0.572) and for 8 of the 9 subjects in large field (overall value: 0.115).

Fig. 5 indicates that the variability in reported tilt (width of the distribution) increases rapidly with W in small field but less in large field. In small field, the order of magnitude of the variability in the tilt report corresponds roughly to W/2 (from 50% to 72% of W for $10° < W < 80°$).

- *Effect of the FOV on the asymmeterized tilt distributions*

Fig. 5 and 6 shows that the trend of the reported tilt toward T' is stronger in small field than in large field. The FOV has a significant effect (median test with $\chi^2 = 77$ to 344, p<0.001) on the asymmeterized distributions for 8 of the 9 subjects.

- *Effect of the winding angle on the asymmeterized tilt distributions*

W has a significant effect on the asymmeterized distributions of the reported tilt (median test $\chi^2 = 821.5$, p<0.001, in small field, and $\chi^2 = 179.2$, p<0.001, in large field). The factor 'subject' has also a significant, although less prominent, effect ($\chi^2 = 138.1$, p<0.001, in small field, and $\chi^2 = 129.4$, p<0.001, in large field).

The effect of W could be due to the fact that, during an oscillation, the tilt is constant in time if W=0, but varies more as W increases with a span reaching $3°$ when W=90°. This effect is small, however, and cannot account for the large standard deviations observed when W increases (typically above $16°$).

Fig. 5 shows the histograms of the asymmeterized tilt reports for each W interval. Here, the origin of the abscissae is the bisector between the tilt and the frontal

---

[1] Due to the periodicity of tilt, we iteratively flipped the reported tilt into a single period and calculated the mean until we achieved the minimum variance.

translation. Hence, the angle –W/2 corresponds to the stimulus tilt, and W/2 to the direction of frontal translation T'.

In small field, we usually observe a one-peak distribution in Fig. 5A except for W=80°-90°, where the distribution is flattened and tends to present two peaks at –W/2 and +W/2. For other W ranges, the decline in the peak height and the shift of the peak toward W/2 increase with W (Fig. 5A). The means of the distribution are plotted in Fig. 6 for all subjects. In small-field (Fig. 6A), the means of tilt responses are significantly shifted towards the frontal translation direction (Wilcoxon Matched Pair Test, z=17.02, n=7776, p<0.001). Hence the perceived tilt lies between the stimulus tilt and the translation direction T'. Overall, the distributions of the reported tilt are centered near the bisector of the stimulus tilt and T'.

In large field, the distribution of reported tilts presents one peak (Fig. 5B), which is significantly shifted toward T' (z=55.167, n=7776, p<0.001). This shift is, in average, equal to only a fraction of W (5% to 33% when W<50°), hence the dominant direction is the stimulus tilt, rather than the frontal translation direction. Also, this effect is weaker than in small-field, and significant for each category of W range only when W ≤ 50°. When W is higher than 50°, the shift toward T' is not significant and it can even be reversed for some subjects. Thus, the dominant reported tilt is the stimulus tilt, although it is shifted slightly but significantly toward T' for W ≤ 50°.

- *Shape of the response distributions*

We found a considerable positive skewness for all the distributions except for W in the range 80-90° in small-field. Therefore, subjects' responses cannot be considered as being spread symmetrically about an average direction. Rather, we find that the presence of the translation direction tends to distort the shape of the distribution.

For W<60° in small-field and all W ranges in large-field, the shape of the distributions in Fig.5 was found to be significantly sharper than the normal distribution, and well fitted by Laplace distributions. We did the Laplace fittings on

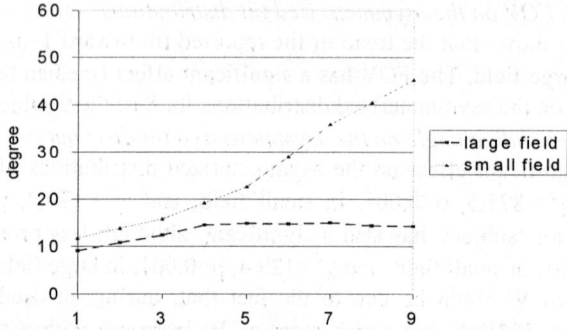

Fig. 4. Average absolute tilt error in each W category (2 views) 1:W=0°-10°, 2:W=10°-20°, 3:W=20°-30°, 4:W=30°-40°, 5:W=40°-50°, 6:W=50°-60°, 7:W=60°-70°, 8:W=70°-80°, 9: W=80°-90°.

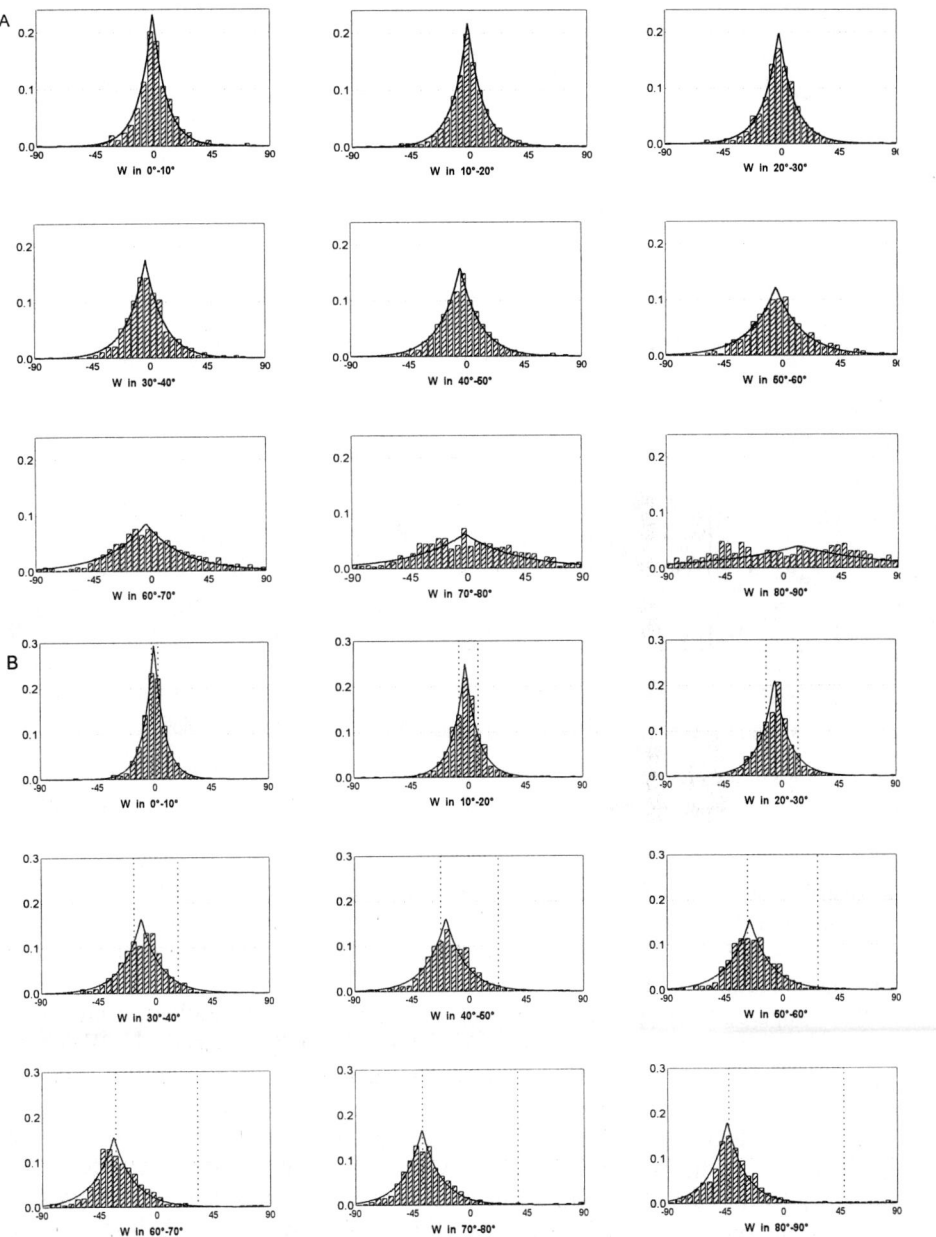

Fig. 5. Histograms of the reported tilt. The left dashed line is the position of the stimulus tilt, and the right one is position of the frontal translation The continuous line is the fitted Laplace Distribution. Abscissae: reported tilts in degrees. Ordinates: the fraction of the number of trials. A and B: results in small and large field respectively. Each box corresponds to a 10°-wide W interval.

808

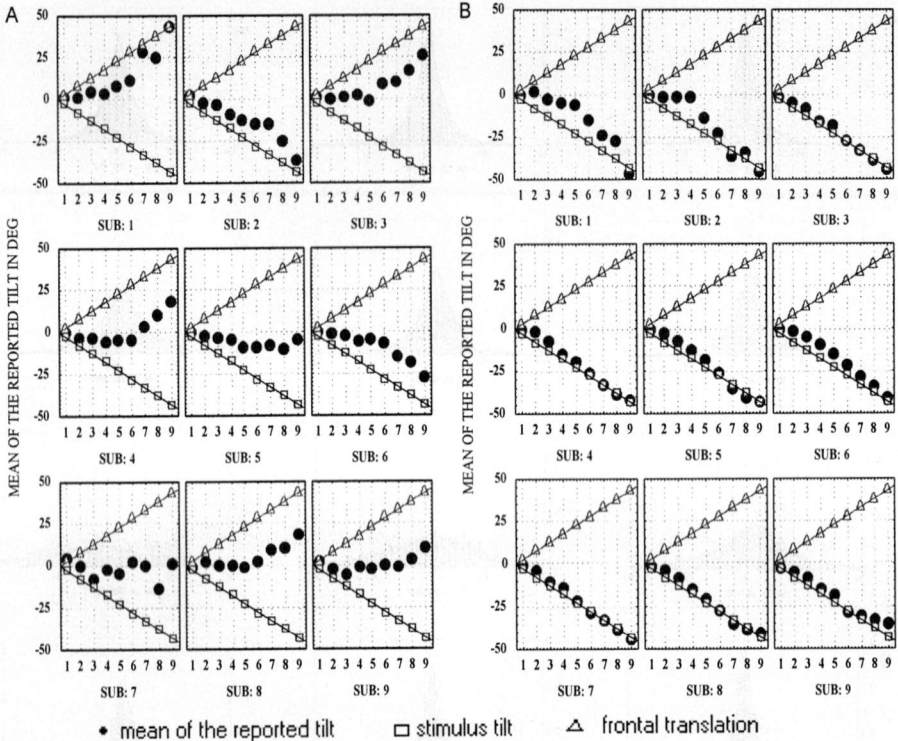

Fig. 6. Means of the reported tilt in each W interval for each subject in small field (A) and large field (B). Abscissae: the W categories, 1: W=0°-10°, ... 9: W=80°-90°. Ordinates: reported tilts in degrees

the distributions in a new coordinate system with the mean as the origin.

Hence the Laplace distributions give a first approximation of the response distributions, but the observed skewness that we observe in general precludes its use for a full modelling of the data.

We compared the responses to the sum of two Laplace distributions, centered on the stimulus tilt, and on the direction of frontal translation **T'**, respectively. We chose the width as equal to the width found for the range 0-10° of W, which yields the smallest dispersion of the responses.

In small-field this modelling predicts a distinct peak in the direction of **T'** (at abscissa +W/2 on fig.5), which is not observed in our results when W<80°. Hence the modelling by the sum of 2 distributions would require parameterizing the variance of each distribution. For W ranging between 80° and 90°, however, the tilt distribution in Fig. 5 presents two peaks in the direction of the stimulus tilt and of T'.

These peaks are shallower than Laplace-type peaks, but present a good symmetry about the bisector of the stimulus tilt and T'.

In large-field, for W>50°, the values of the distribution for +W/2 (the direction of **T'**) are close to zero, which means that the 2-peak distribution model does not hold in this case.

In conclusion, in all cases except in small-field for the W range 80-90°, the positive skewness of the distributions indicates a role of the translation direction, and precludes the modelling of the responses by a unique symmetric distribution. However, within these cases, our large-field data does not support the existence of a 2-peak underlying distribution, with peaks centered on the stimulus tilt and the direction of the frontal translation. As for the small-field, other variables such as the increase of the variance for each of the separate distribution would have to be modelled to account for our results.

- *Verbal Reports*

All nine subjects found the task more difficult in small field than in large field. Eight of them reported a perception of curved surfaces, rather than planes, for large values of W, particularly in large field.

4 Computational Interpretation

This section gives a computational interpretation of the preceding results. We examine the optic flow equations for a plane moving in the 3D space, with application to the particular case of rotation in depth, which is the motion used in our experiments.

4.1 Choice of Projection Model and Assumptions

For a plane rotating in depth, the second-order optic flow is small, as compared to the first-order optic flow. The ratio of the magnitude of second-order flow, divided by the magnitude of the first-order flow is equal to $x/\tan(\sigma)$, where x is the angular eccentricity. This ratio is 0.1 and 0.82 for our small field and large field stimuli respectively. Therefore, the second-order flow is likely to play little role in small field. Hence we distinguish here the affine and full-flow processing for perspective projection.

Many authors have used the orthographic projection as an approximation to small-field perspective projection [11]. However, this approximation does not hold for translations in depth, which create no optic flow in orthographic projection, but do yield an image expansion or contraction in perspective projection, even in small-field.

Therefore the advantage of the perspective affine scheme is that it is quantitatively valid in small field for our stimuli, yet makes no a priori hypothesis on the 3D movement used. Note that, the perspective affine approximation would not hold for a curved surface, which can induce large second-order flows even in small field [7].

- *Perspective projection and full flow*

The optic flow field is [13],[16]

$$u = a_1 + a_2 x + a_3 y + a_7 x^2 + a_8 xy$$

$$v = a_4 + a_5 x + a_6 y + a_7 x\, y + a_8 y^2$$

where

$$a_1 = T_X p_0 + \Omega_Y$$

(7)

$$a_2 = T_X p_x - T_Z p_0$$

$$a_3 = T_X p_y - \Omega_Z ,$$

$$a_4 = T_y p_0 - \Omega_X ,$$

$$a_5 = T_Y p_x + \Omega_Z ,$$

$$a_6 = T_Y p_y - T_Z p_0 ,$$

$$a_7 = \Omega_Y - T_Z p_x ,$$

$$a_8 = -\Omega_X - p_y T_z .$$

Solving these nonlinear equations leads to a twofold ambiguity, with an interchangeable role of vectors $\vec{n}$ and $\vec{t}$ [14]. Since the Z components of these vectors are the cosinus of the slant (for $\vec{n}$) and the translation in depth (for $\vec{t}$), respectively, it follows that

(1) because our stimuli have no translation in depth, the wrongly perceived orientation should correspond to a slant of 90°, i.e. a surface normal to the frontoparallel plane, which normally yields no optic flow ;

(2) if the subject assumes that $T_Z = 0$, he should perceive the correct tilt (the same conclusion is reached for the hypothesis $\Omega_Z = 0$).

Therefore the theoretical analysis of the full second order flow indicates that under large field, the perceived tilt should always be unambiguous if the subject uses one of the above hypotheses, or if he rules out the case of the spurious orientation.

• *Perspective projection and affine flow*

Using the affine flow alone will yield an infinite number of solutions. The affine flow is characterized by the six coefficients of the optic flow equations: $a_1, a_2, a_3, a_4, a_5, a_6$. Denoting $T_z = T_Z p_0$, and from a_2, a_3, a_5, a_6, we obtain

$$\frac{a_2 + a_6}{2} + T_z = \frac{T_X p_x + T_Y p_y}{2}$$

$$\frac{a_5 - a_3}{2} - \Omega_Z = \frac{T_Y p_x - T_X p_y}{2}$$

which can be simplified to

$$(T_z - C_T)^2 + (\Omega_Z - C_\Omega)^2 = R^2$$

(8)

where

$$C_T = -\frac{a_2 + a_6}{2}, \ C_\Omega = \frac{a_5 - a_3}{2} \ \text{and} \ R^2 = \frac{(a_2 - a_6)^2 + (a_5 + a_3)^2}{4}$$

Thus, the infinite number of solutions to the 3D problem is parameterized by the position of the point (T_z, Ω_Z) on the circle C given by equation (8).

In our experiment, we have $T_Z = \Omega_Z = 0$, which means that the circle C of equation (8) passes through the origin.

As demonstrated in the Appendices (I and II), under the a priori assumption $T_Z = 0$, we obtain two solutions for the tilt if $W \neq 0$ and one solution only if $W=0$. Alternatively, if the hypothesis is that $\Omega_Z = 0$, we find two solutions for $W \neq 90$ and only one for $W=90$. Hence, the tendency of observers to report an erroneous tilt direction might have an interpretation in terms of the a priori position of the couple (Ω_Z, T_z) on this circle C.

- *Orthographic Projection*

Under orthographic projection, the optic flow is equal to the frontal translation of the 3D point:

$$U = T_X + \Omega_Y Z_0 + \Omega_Y Z_X X + (\Omega_Y Z_Y - \Omega_Z)Y \qquad (9)$$

$$V = T_Y - \Omega_X Z_0 + (\Omega_Z - \Omega_X Z_X)X - \Omega_X Z_Y Y$$

We can subtract from the optic flow the velocity vector in the center of the image (at X=Y=0). The resulting flow is as if

$$\Omega_X = \frac{T_Y}{Z_0}$$

$$\Omega_Y = -\frac{T_X}{Z_0}$$

Substituting these values of Ω_X and Ω_Y into (9) leads to a system equivalent to

Table 1. Number of solutions for the computation of tilt from optic flow. The numbers in each triplet indicate the numbers of solution for τ when W=0°, 0°<W<90°, and W=90°, respectively.

	No Assumption	Hypothesis: $T_Z = 0$	Hypothesis: $\Omega_Z = 0$
projection Type	Number of solutions for τ		
Perspective Full Flow	(1, 2, 2)	(1, 1, 1)	(1, 1, 1)
Perspective Affine Flow	(∞, ∞, ∞)	(1, 2, 2)	(2, 2, 1)
Orthographic	(1, 2, 2)	(1, 2, 2)	(1, 1, 1)

the perspective affine scheme associated with the hypothesis $T_Z = 0$. Hence, there are generally two solutions for the tilt direction if $W \neq 0$. These two merge in one if $W=0$. If we make the hypothesis that $\Omega_Z = 0$, the alternative 'spurious' solution is eliminated.

• *Summary*

A summary of the number of solutions with respect to the projection type and a priori conditions is listed in Table 1.

4.2 Comparison with our results

In our results, we distinguish three possible directions for the reported tilt, namely the stimulus tilt, the direction of frontal translation T', and their bisector. The distributions of reported tilt tend to be centered
- on the stimulus tilt in large-field,
- on the stimulus tilt for W ranging between 0 and 10° in small-field,
- on the bisector for W>10° in small-field.

We can interpret our results as the consequence of a twofold ambiguity when the stimulus tilt and frontal translation are not colinear in small-field, and of a single tilt percept in all other cases. In this sense, our results support the validity of the hypothesis $T_Z=0$, because it yields a unique solution in the perspective full flow model, and an ambiguity on the computed tilt for W>0° in the perspective affine scheme (Table 1).

However this modelling is too simple to explain our results in more details. First, even when the presence of the frontal translation has a strong effect (small-field, W>10°), we usually do not observe a clear 2-peak distribution of the reported tilt, except for the W range 80-90°. Rather, the variability of the responses increases strongly with W, and a general flattening of the distributions is observed. Also, if there exists a twofold ambiguity, the influence of the stimulus tilt solution is stronger than that of the T' solution. Indeed, for 10°<W<80°, the distribution is asymmetric and shifted slightly from the bisector toward the stimulus tilt. Second, for intermediate values of W (lower than 50°) in large-field, the distribution center is close to the stimulus tilt, with a significant shift toward the frontal translation direction.

5 Discussion

In summary, we find that

(1) The FOV has a critical influence on the tilt reports. The accuracy of tilt reports increases in large-field, and tilt report distributions differ strongly in small and large field.

(2) Tilt reversals are observed in small field but not in large field. When corrected with respect to tilt reversals, the average absolute tilt errors are smaller in large field than in small field.

(3) The winding angle W significantly affects the performance on tilt perception in small field, and to a lesser extent, in large field. The absolute tilt error increases rapidly in small field when W increases.

(4) W has a significant effect on the asymmeterized distributions of the perceived tilt. The reported tilt is generally shifted toward the direction of frontal translation. In

small field, when W ranges between 80° and 90° the distribution of tilts presents one peak at the stimulus tilt and one peak at the frontal translation direction. Such two-peak shape is not found for other W ranges, or in large-field.

(5) The results in large-field are well predicted by the second-order full flow modelling with additional constraints. However, the increase of the variability of the responses, and their shift toward the direction of frontal translation direction for W<50°, still remain to be explained theoretically.

(6) In small-field, the perspective affine approach with the hypothesis $|T_Z|$ minimum, and the orthographic modelling account for the two-peak distribution observed for when W is higher than 80°. For lower values of W, an explicit two-peak distribution is not found. Rather, the responses are centered at the bisector of the stimulus tilt and direction of the frontal translation, and their variability increases. However, the absence of a hidden twofold ambiguity for 10°<W<80° in small field still remains to be demonstrated.

Our results fully confirm those obtained by Cornilleau-Pérès et al. [4], despite the difference in number of views displayed (72 in their studies, 2 in ours). There is a similar dependence of the accuracy in the tilt report on W. The agreement is also quantitative, as the average absolute tilt errors are similar (Table 2). Our results are also in good agreement with those obtained by Domini, et al.'s [6] in spite of the difference in number of views (1-83 in their studies). The tilt reports found by these authors show standard deviations that can be estimated at around 20° from their figure. Our standard deviations are slightly worse (31.5°) in similar conditions (small-field, all W confounded). This could be due to the choice of the direction of the rotation, which is random in our experiment, and fixed in theirs. In the latter case the subjects may have been helped by predetermining this direction, thereby improving their tilt perception across trials.

Table 2. Average absolute tilt error in our and Cornilleau-Pérès, et al's results. W1: W=0°-30°, W2: W=30°-60°, W3: W=60°-90°.

		Average Absolute Tilt Error (deg)					
		Small Field			Large Field		
		W1	W2	W3	W1	W2	W3
Our results σ=35°		13.8	23.7	40.41	10.7	14.7	14.53
CP, et al' results	σ=30°	11	19.5	45	12	17	23
	σ=45°	13	19	34	9	12.5	16

The results of this paper have consequences for the experimental evaluation of plane recovery algorithms. To have an appropriately stringent test of an algorithm, one should assess it against known hard situations. Our results provide psychophysical hints of such problem conditions. Therefore, while it has been claimed that under small field of view, weak perspective algorithms should be used because of their robustness, *a more complete comparison should also test against the algorithm's behavior under different winding angles.* Only by carrying out such motivated and controlled experiments, one will understand an algorithm's limits of applicability.

In conclusion, our results demonstrate a strong effect of the stimulus size, and a clear anisotropy of tilt perception related to the orientation of the plane with respect to its movement. There is a general tendency for the perceived tilt to shift toward T'. Our results point to the crucial need for extensive sensitivity analysis of the computation of orientation from motion. The models proposed so far express the computation in terms of the presence or absence of a twofold ambiguity, whereas the distributions of reported tilt usually present a shift toward the spurious solution, rather than an explicit split into the two ambiguous solutions.

Reference

1. Adiv, G.: Inherent ambiguities in recovering 3-D motion and structure from a noisy flow field. IEEE Trans. Pattern Analysis and Machine Intelligence, Vol. 11. (1989) 477-489.
2. Baratoff, G.: Ordinal and metric structure of smooth surfaces form parallax. Proceedings of the 13th International Conference on Pattern Recognition (1996) 275-279, Vienna, Austria.
3. Cheong, L.F., Fermüller, C., & Aloimonos, Y.: Effects of errors in the viewing geometry on shape estimation. Computer Vision and Image Understanding, Vol. 71 (1998). 5, 356-372
4. Cornilleau-Pérès, V., Wexler, M., Marin, E, Droulez, J.: The perception of surface orientation from motion in small and wide-field. Invest Ophthalmol Vis Sci, 40(4): B781. Abstract 3923. (1999)
5. Daniilidis, K. & Nagel, H.-H.: The coupling of rotation and translation in motion estimation of planar surfaces. IEEE Conf. On Computer Vision and Pattern Recoginition (1993) 188-193, New York, NY.
6. Domini, F & Caudek,C.: Perceiving surface slant from deformation of Optic flow. Journal of Experimental Psychology, Vol. 25, (1999) 426-444.
7. Droulez, J. & Cornilleau-Pérès, V.: Visual perception of surface curvature. The Spin variation and its physiological implications. Biological Cybernetics, Vol. 62. (1990) 211-224.
8. Garding, J., Porrill, J., Mayhew, J.E.W. & Frisby, J.P.: Stereopsis, vertical disparity and relief transformations. Vision Research, Vol. 5. (1995) 703-722
9. Hoffman, D. D.: Inferring local surface orientation from motion fields. Journal of the Optical Society of America, Vol. A72, (1982) 888-892.
10. Koenderink, J.J. & Doorn, A.J.: Local structure of movement parallax of the plane. Journal of the Optical Society of America, Vol. 66. (1976) 717-723
11. Koenderink, J.J. & Doorn, A.J.: Affine structure from motion. J. Opt. Soc. Am. A., 8, No.2. (1991)
12. Koenderink, J.J. & Doorn, A.J.: Relief: Pictorial and otherwise. Image and Vision Computing, Vol. 5. (1995) 321-334.
13. Longuet-Higgins, H.C. & Prazdny, K.: The interpretation of a moving retinal image. Proceedings of the Royal Society of London, B 208, (1980) 385-397.
14. Longuet-Higgins, H.C.: The visual ambiguity of a moving plane. Proceedings of the Royal Society of London, B 223, (1984) 165-175.
15. Rogers,B., &Graham,M.: Motion parallax as an independent cue for depth perception. Perception, Vol. 8. (1979) 125-134.
16. Subbarao, M.: Interpretation of Visual Motion: A computational Study. Morgan Kaufmann Publishers (1988)

17. Todd,T. & Bressan, P.: The perception of 3-dimensional affine structures from minimal motion sequences. Perception & Psychophysics, Vol. 48. (1991) 419-430.
18. Tsai, R.Y. & Huang, T.S.: Uniqueness and estimation of three-dimensional motion parameters of rigid objects with curved surfaces. IEEE Trans. Pattern Analysis and Machine Intelligence, Vol. 6. (1984) 13-27.
19. Wallach, H., & O'Connell, D.N.: The kinetic depth effect. Journal of Experimental Psychology, Vol. 45, (1953) 205-217

Appendix

I. Solutions under the perspective affine scheme with $T_Z=0$

We only have the first order terms. Using a_2, a_3, a_5, a_6, we have

$$a_2 = T_X p_x,$$
$$a_3 + a_5 = p_y T_X + p_x T_Y,$$
$$a_6 = T_Y p_y$$

When $a_2 \neq 0$, we get two equations with two unknowns $\dfrac{p_y}{p_x}$ and $\dfrac{T_Y}{T_X}$

$$\frac{a_6}{a_2} = \frac{p_y}{p_x} \frac{T_Y}{T_X},$$
$$\frac{a_3 + a_5}{a_2} = \frac{p_y}{p_x} + \frac{T_Y}{T_X}.$$

Due to the quadratic nature of the equations, we usually get two solutions for the tilt. They can be shown to be the true tilt and an alternative solution corresponding to T', up to 180°. If the tilt is parallel to the frontal translation, i.e., the winding angle is zero, the two tilt solutions merge as one.

As we can express T' in terms of τ and W as $\tau + W$, the alternative solution for the tilt can be written as $\tau + W$.

If $a_2 = T_X p_x = 0$, it is still the same case:

(1). If $a_3 + a_5 \neq 0$, which indicates that **T'** is not parallel to the tilt direction, as $(T_X, T_Y) \bullet (p_y, p_x) \neq 0$, we still have two solutions:

$$\begin{cases} \theta_{T'} = 90° \\ \dfrac{p_y}{p_x} = \dfrac{a_6}{a_3 + a_5} \end{cases} \quad \text{or} \quad \begin{cases} \tau = 90° \\ \dfrac{T_Y}{T_X} = \dfrac{a_6}{a_3 + a_5} \end{cases}$$

(2). If $a_3 + a_5 = 0$, which indicates **T'** is parallel to τ direction, thus winding angle is zero, there is a unique solution: $\tau = $ T' $=90°$.

In summary, when $T_Z = 0$, we usually have two solutions for tilt direction, unless when W=0°.

II. Solutions under perspective affine scheme with $\Omega_z = 0$

Using a_2, a_3, a_5, a_6, we have

$$a_3 = T_X p_y,$$

$$a_2 - a_6 = T_X p_x - T_Y p_y,$$

$$a_5 = T_Y p_x$$

Following the same method as in Appendix I, we will have one solution when W=90° and two when W≠90°.

III. Solutions under orthographic scheme

We denote the coefficients of the optic flow under orthographic projection as:

$$a'_1 = T_X + \Omega_Y Z_0$$

$$a'_2 = \Omega_Y Z_X$$

$$a'_3 = \Omega_Y Z_Y - \Omega_Z$$

$$a'_4 = T_Y - \Omega_X Z_0$$

$$a'_5 = \Omega_Z - \Omega_X Z_X$$

$$a'_6 = -\Omega_X Z_Y$$

We can subtract from the optic flow the velocity vector in the center of the image (X=Y=0). The resulting flow is such that

$$\Omega_X = \frac{T_Y}{Z_0}$$

$$\Omega_Y = -\frac{T_X}{Z_0}$$

Substituting these values of Ω_X and Ω_Y into a'_2, a'_3, a'_5, a'_6 and following the same method as in Appendix I, we usually have two solutions except at W=0°, when they merge as one.

Visual Motion

IMPSAC: Synthesis of Importance Sampling and Random Sample Consensus

P. H. S. Torr and C. Davidson

Microsoft Research Ltd, 1 Guildhall St, Cambridge CB2 3NH, UK
philtorr@microsoft.com

Abstract. This paper proposes a new method for effecting feature correspondence between images. The method operates from coarse to fine and is superior to previous methods in that it can solve the wide baseline stereo problem, even when the image has been deformed or rotated. At the coarsest level a RANSAC-style estimator is used to estimate the two view image constraint $\mathcal{R}$ which is then used to guide matching. The two view relation is an augmented fundamental matrix, being a fundamental matrix plus a homography consistent with that fundamental matrix. This is akin to the plane plus parallax representation with the homography being used to help guide matching and to mitigate the effects of image deformation.

In order to propagate the information from coarse to fine images, the distribution of the parameters θ of $\mathcal{R}$ is encoded using a set of particles and an importance sampling function. It is not known in general how to choose the importance sampling function, but a new method "IMPSAC" is presented that automatically generates such a function. It is shown that the method is superior to previous single resolution RANSAC-style feature matchers.

Keywords: Structure from motion, Stereoscopic vision.

1   Introduction

The goal of this work is to obtain accurate matches and image relations between consecutive images, with the ultimate aim of recovering 3D structure and camera projection matrices from an uncalibrated image sequence (such as might be obtained from a hand-held camcorder) where the motion is unlikely to be smooth or known *a priori*. Once the matches and two view image relation have been recovered, they can be used for image compression, or as a basis for building 3D graphical models from an image sequence [2, 22, 28]. These are underpinned by the need to match tokens/features (usually interest points) successfully through image sequences with a large number of frames. It transpires that the correspondence problem is one of the most difficult parts of structure recovery, especially when these images are far apart (the *wide baseline* problem) or when they undergo large rotations (the *image deformation* problem). Small baseline image matching technology has made large advances over the past decade [1–3, 11, 17, 22, 26, 30], but there has been comparatively little progress in wide baseline matching technology. Furthermore, the small baseline methods do not work on every image pair. For example, feature based cross correlation methods may fail if (1) there are insufficient features in the image pair, (2) there is too much repeated structure for features to get a good match, or (3) there is an image deformation that causes the cross correlation to fail.

There has been some work on rectifying these problems. Pritchett and Zisserman [19] present a set of recipes for special cases, but no unified theory of how to solve the problem in general. Cham and Cipolla [5] present a multi scale method for feature matching when making mosaics. The work is valid only if there is no parallax, i.e. if the image motion is governed by a homography. Furthermore the formulation is flawed as it propagates parameters using the estimate at the coarser level as a prior for the estimate at the finer, but since the images at fine and coarse resolution are not independent, the prior and likelihood are not independent. This leads to an erroneous posterior, which is then used (in their method) as a prior for the next level, compounding the error.

The method presented here solves the image deformation and wide baseline matching problems. It also requires no camera calibration. A coarse to fine approach is adopted in which information about the epipolar geometry is passed from the coarser levels to the finer. Ideally, the information to be transmitted would be the posterior distribution of the parameters at the coarser level. Encoding this posterior distribution and its relation to the finer level is an intricate task, not least because the normalization constant of the distribution is unknown. Three powerful statistical methods are enlisted to create a solution: (1) to represent the distributions as a set of particles, (2) the use of importance sampling to generate unbiased draws from the posterior distribution, (3) RANSAC to generate the importance sampling function. In this way the posterior distribution at the coarse level is used as an importance sampling function to draw samples from the posterior distribution at the finer level. As a result, the epipolar geometry is estimated by using features at many different scales, solving the problem of having to select this scale manually.

A fundamental component of several existing algorithms is the use of epipolar geometry to simplify the search for correspondences between view pairs, particularly because epipolar geometry and matches consistent with this geometry may be computed simultaneously, using only features in each view. Two images of a rigid object are related by a fundamental matrix, or in special cases just by a homography. The types of two view relations that might arise are described in Section 2, and the likelihood of the matches given these relations in Section 2.1. Existing geometry based matching methods are reviewed in Section 3, they comprise two stages: (a) estimate best cross correlation matches, (b) estimate epipolar geometry using a robust estimator. However this approach breaks down for the image deformation and wide base line cases. In Section 4 the coarse to fine algorithm is outlined, and the wide base line problem overcome, but cross correlation still fails if there is image deformation. This is because matches are initially scored by a combination of their cross correlation score and their agreement with epipolar geometry. However in order to calculate the cross correlation the deformation of each image patch must be known. Thus an image deformation homography is estimated in addition to the epipolar geometry, leading to a plane plus parallax representation. Local patches may be warped by the image deformation homography to establish cross correlation scores. This combined set of parameters is referred to as the augmented fundamental matrix and is described in Section 5. The results are given in Section 7, where the algorithm is demonstrated on the wide baseline and the image deformation problems.

Notation The image of a 3D scene point $\mathbf{X}$ is $\mathbf{x}^1$ in the first view and $\mathbf{x}^2$ in the second, where $\mathbf{x}^1$ and $\mathbf{x}^2$ are homogeneous three vectors, $\mathbf{x} = (x, y, 1)^\top$. The correspondence $\mathbf{x}^1 \leftrightarrow \mathbf{x}^2$ will also be denoted as $\mathbf{x}^{1,2}$. Throughout, underlining a symbol $\underline{x}$ indicates the perfect or noise-free quantity, distinguishing it from $x = \underline{x} + \Delta x$, which is the measured value corrupted by noise.

2 The Two View Relations

Within this section the possible relations $\mathcal{R}$ on the motion of points between two views are summarized. Four examples of $\mathcal{R}$ are considered: (a) the Fundamental matrix [7, 12], (b) the affine fundamental matrix [18] (c) the planar projective transformation (a homography), and (d) the affinity. All these two view relations are estimable from image correspondences alone.

The epipolar constraint is represented by the Fundamental matrix [7, 12]. This relation applies for general motion and structure with uncalibrated cameras; consider the movement of a set of point image projections from an object which undergoes a rotation and non-zero translation between views. After the motion, the set of homogeneous image points $\{\underline{\mathbf{x}}_i\}, i = 1, \ldots n$, as viewed in the first image is transformed to the set $\{\mathbf{x}_i'\}$ in the second image, with the positions related by

$$\underline{\mathbf{x}}_i'^\top \mathbf{F} \underline{\mathbf{x}}_i = 0 \tag{1}$$

where $\underline{\mathbf{x}} = (\underline{x}, y, 1)^\top$ is a homogeneous image coordinate and $\mathbf{F}$ is the Fundamental Matrix. The affine fundamental matrix $\mathbf{F}_A$ is the linear version of $\mathbf{F}$. The affine camera is applicable when the data is viewed under orthographic conditions and gives rise to a fundamental matrix with zeroes in the upper 2 by 2 submatrix[1], and it is studied in detail by Shapiro [20].

In the case where all the observed points lie on a plane, or the camera rotates about its optic axis and does not translate, then all the correspondences lie on a homography:

$$\underline{\mathbf{x}}' = \mathbf{H}\underline{\mathbf{x}} \ . \tag{2}$$

The affinity $\mathbf{H}_A$ is a special case of the homography with zeros for the first two elements of the bottom row. Again it is valid under uncalibrated orthographic conditions.

2.1 Likelihood of a Match Given a Relation

In this section, the maximum likelihood formulation is given for computing any of the multiple view relations, given a set of matches. Later this formalism will be extended to include the case when the matches themselves are unknown and must be estimated. In the following we make the assumption that the noise in the two images is Gaussian on

---

[1] Actually $\mathbf{F}_A$ occurs in the non-orthographic case when the optical planes of the two cameras coincide [23]. Affine reconstruction in this case gives projectively correct results.

each image coordinate with zero mean and uniform standard deviation σ. Thus, given a true correspondence, the probability density function of the noise perturbed data is

$$p(\mathbf{x}^{1,2}|\mathcal{R}) = \prod_{i=1\ldots n} \left(\frac{1}{\sqrt{2\pi}\underline{\sigma}}\right)^n e^{-\left(\sum_{j=1,2}(\underline{x}_i^j - x_i^j)^2 + (\underline{y}_i^j - y_i^j)^2\right)/(2\underline{\sigma}^2)} , \qquad (3)$$

where n is the number of correspondences and $\mathcal{R}$ is the appropriate 2 view relation, e.g. the fundamental matrix or projectivity.

The above derivation assumes that the errors are Gaussian. Often, however, features are mismatched and the error on the match is not Gaussian. Thus the error can be modelled as a mixture model of Gaussian and uniform distribution:-

$$p(e) = \left(\gamma \frac{1}{\sqrt{2\pi\sigma^2}} \exp(-\frac{e^2}{2\sigma^2}) + (1-\gamma)\frac{1}{v}\right) \qquad (4)$$

where γ is the mixing parameter and v is just a constant, σ is the standard deviation of the error on each coordinate. To correctly determine γ and v entails some knowledge of the outlier distribution; here it is assumed that the outlier distribution is uniform, with $-\frac{v}{2}..+\frac{v}{2}$ being the pixel range within which outliers are expected to fall (for feature matching this is dictated by the size of the search window for matches). Therefore the error minimized is the negative log likelihood:

$$-L = -\sum_i \log\left(\gamma\left(\frac{1}{\sqrt{2\pi}\sigma}\right)^n \exp\left(-\sum_{j=1,2}\frac{((x_i^j - x_i^j)^2 + (y_i^j - y_i^j)^2)}{2\sigma^2} + (1-\gamma)\frac{1}{v}\right)\right) .$$
$$(5)$$

Given a suitable initial estimate there are several ways to estimate the parameters of the mixture model, most prominent being the EM algorithm [6, 16], but gradient descent methods could also be used. Because of the presence of outliers in the data the standard method of least squares estimation is often not suitable as an initial estimate, and it is better to use a robust estimate such as RANSAC which is described in the next section.

3 Random Sampling Guided Matching

Within this section the state of the art in feature matching is described. This computation requires initial matching of points (e.g. corners detected to sub-pixel accuracy by the Harris corner detector [10]) between two images; the aim is then to compute the relation from these image correspondences. Given a corner at position (x, y) in the first image, the search for a match considers all corners within a region centred on (x, y) in the second image with a threshold on maximum disparity. The strength of candidate matches is measured by sum of squared differences in intensity. At this stage, the threshold for match acceptance is deliberately conservative in order to minimise incorrect matches. Nevertheless, many mismatches will occur because the matching process is based only on proximity and similarity. These mismatches (called outliers) are sufficient to render standard least squares estimators useless. Consequently robust methods must be adopted, which can provide a good estimate of the solution even if some of the data are outliers.

There are potentially a significant number of mismatches amongst the initial matches. Since correct matches will obey the epipolar geometry, the aim is to obtain a set of "inliers" consistent with the epipolar geometry using a robust technique. In this case "outliers" are putative matches which are inconsistent with the epipolar geometry. Robust estimation by random sampling (such as MLESAC, LMS or RANSAC) have proven the most successful [8, 24, 29, 26]. These algorithms are well known and briefly summarized in Fig. 1.

---

1. Detect corner features using the Harris corner detector [10].
2. Putative matching of corners over the two images using proximity and cross correlation to get best set of matches.
3. Repeat for a fixed number of samples or until "jump out" [25] occurs
   (a) Select a random sample without replacement of the minimum number of correspondences $\{x_i^{1,2}\}$ required to estimate the relation $\mathcal{R}$
   (b) Estimate the unique image relation $\mathcal{R}$ consistent with this minimal set.
   (c) Calculate the error $-L$ for all matches (MLESAC), or the median of residuals (LMS), or the number of inliers (RANSAC).
4. Select the best solution over all the samples i.e. that which minimizes $-L$ (MLESAC), or that which minimized the median error (LMS), or that which maximized the number of inliers (RANSAC).
5. Minimize robust cost function over all correspondences using gradient descent.

Table 1. *A brief summary of all the stages of random sampling guided matching*

3.1 Problems with Conventional Matching

There are two types of failure mode for the class of matching algorithms in Table 1. The first is the wide baseline case, see Figure 1, which shows two images taken at the same time instant [2] where the disparity is 160 pixels. In the conventional algorithm, described above, a search window must be set for putative matches. If this search window is too large (which it must be in this case to guarantee that the correct match lies within it), then there is a combinatorial explosion of putative matches. This leads to a catastrophic failure of correlation matching as there are too many potential false matches for each corner. The second failure mode is caused when the image is rotated (see Figure 2). In this case, standard correlation matching cannot be expected to succeed, because the correlation score is not rotationally invariant. Using a rotationally invariant correlation score does not correct this problem; instead it reduces the discriminating power of the score, increasing the number of mismatches even when the second image is not rotated. The answer to both these problems, presented here, is to adopt a coarse to fine strategy. The coarse to fine strategy has been used successfully for small baseline homography matching [4], but neglected for feature matching.

---

[2] Kindly provided by Dayton Taylor

824

Fig. 1. Wide Baseline Failure of MLESAC/LMS/RANSAC: *50 matches from the first and last images of the Samsung sequence. The images are were imaged at the same time instance and are two of 50 taken from a 50 camera stereo rig. The features are shown in each image (circles) together with the line joining them to their correspondence in the other image, and are matched with an affine fundamental matrix. Although several of the features with small disparities have been correctly matched, features with large disparities are incorrectly matched. This is because, as the disparity increases, so does the number of potential mismatches.*

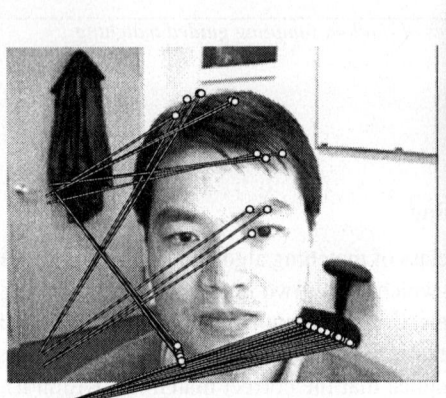

Fig. 2. Catastrophic Failure of MLESAC/LMS/RANSAC **Due To Rotation:** *the second image in the Zhang sequence has been rotated by 90 degrees, in addition there is a slight change of pose of the head. The image correlation used is not invariant to rotation, so there are too many mismatches for* MLESAC *to converge. Rotation-invariant correlation is not a solution to this problem, because it is less discriminating and thus results in too many mismatches even when the second image is not rotated.*

4 Coarse to Fine

In the coarse to fine strategy, an image pyramid is formed by subsampling the image repeatedly by a factor of 2. At the coarsest level of this pyramid (level $l = 0$), the distribution of the parameters $\boldsymbol{\theta}$ of the relation $\mathcal{R}$ given the data $\mathbf{D}_l$ is $p(\boldsymbol{\theta} | \mathbf{D}_l)$. The information contained in this posterior distribution should be propagated down to the finer levels. One way to propagate information from one level to the next is to simply propagate down the mode of this distribution. However, at the coarsest levels this distribution is not expected to have a strong peak and often propagation of the mode does not convey sufficient information. Too soon a commitment to a single hypothesis may cause the algorithm to converge to the wrong solution. Rather, it is desirable to pass as much of the distribution as possible from one level to the next.

The coarse to fine strategy is beneficial for a number of reasons. It furnishes a solution to the wide baseline problem because the search window, and thus the number of potential false matches per corner, is reduced at the coarser levels. Furthermore, at the coarser level, it is less computationally intensive to estimate the global image deformation (e.g. cyclorotation), by testing different hypotheses for the deformation of the cross correlation between image patches.

Two problems arise with this. First, the parametric form of the distribution is not known. Second, the normalizing factor of the distribution is not known. The first problem is overcome by representing the distribution by a set of particles $\{\boldsymbol{\theta}_1 \ldots \boldsymbol{\theta}_m\}$ with weights $\{w_1 \ldots w_m\}$. This sort of representation has been used with a good deal of success in the tracking literature [14]. Ideally the set of particles would be drawn from the posterior distribution. One way to achieve this is via importance sampling, which is defined next.

4.1 Importance Sampling

Importance sampling [9] is a key step in drawing approximate samples from complicated high dimensional posterior distributions for which the normalization factor is unknown. Suppose it is of interest to draw samples from such a distribution $q(\boldsymbol{\theta})$, and there exists a normalized positive density function (the importance sampling function) $g(\boldsymbol{\theta})$ from which it is possible to draw samples. The algorithm proceeds as follows:

1. Generate a set of M draws $S^t = \{\boldsymbol{\theta}_1, \ldots \boldsymbol{\theta}_M\}$ from $g(\boldsymbol{\theta})$.
2. Evaluate $q(\boldsymbol{\theta})$ for each element of S^t.
3. Calculate importance weights $w_i = \dfrac{q(\boldsymbol{\theta}_i)}{g(\boldsymbol{\theta}_i)}$ for each element of S^t.
4. Sample a new draw from S^{t+1} from S^t where the probability of taking a new $\boldsymbol{\theta}_i$ is proportional to its weight w_i.

Iterating this procedure from step 2 is called *sampling importance resampling* (SIR). This process, in the limit, produces a fair sample from the distribution $q(\boldsymbol{\theta})$ [9]. The rate of convergence is determined by the suitability of the importance function $g(\boldsymbol{\theta})$. The worst possible scenario occurs when the importance ratios are small with high probability and large with low probability. There is no general purpose method for choosing a good importance sampling function, but in the next section it will be explained how RANSAC can be used to construct one.

4.2 Using RANSAC to Generate the Importance Sampling Function: IMPSAC

The success of RANSAC-style methods proves that at least some of the generated samples lie in areas of high posterior probability. It would be nice to be able to harness the RANSAC mechanism in order to generate a good importance sampling function with which to propagate information from coarse to fine levels. There are several ways in which this can be done. The method we favour is to model the importance function $g(\theta)$ as a mixture of Gaussians, each centred at a RANSAC sample, with the mixing parameters being in proportion to the posterior likelihood of each sample: $p(\theta \,|\mathbf{D})$. This presents a new method for propagating probabilities: generate a density function $g(\theta)$ via RANSAC and use this as an importance sampling function to draw samples from the posterior. This method is dubbed "IMPSAC".

Speed Up 1. Using all the particles to generate the mixture of Gaussians can be slow. Generally if the distribution is to be represented by L particles then a particle can be excluded from the computation if it contains less than $1/L$ of the mass of the density function.

Speed Up 2. Often the artifice of constructing the mixture of Gaussians can be computationally onerous. A simpler device can be obtained under the assumption that the initial set of particles generated by the random sampling of minimal match sets is uniform. Although this assumption is not realistic in theory, unless we are interested in calculating integrals or exact expectations under the distribution, it is safe to make in practise (when all we are interested in is finding the mode of the distribution). One case when the exact posterior would be of interest would be if one was evaluating the evidence to effect model selection (e.g. choosing whether $\mathbf{F}$ or $\mathbf{H}$ best modelled the data. This is the subject of a forthcoming paper).

5 The Augmented Fundamental Matrix

In [27] it was shown that using $\mathbf{H}$ to guide matches throughout the sequence leads to fewer matches being extracted in the part of the sequence undergoing a general motion, as might be expected since the model underfits this part. However, when a loose threshold of 3 pixels was used (as opposed to a threshold of 1.25 pixels which is the two sigma window arising from interest point measurement noise) the homography is able to carry correct matches even when the planar assumption is broken. The explanation lies in the "plane plus parallax" model of image motion [13]: the estimated homography often behaves as if induced by a 'scene average' plane, or indeed is induced by a dominant scene plane; the homography map removes the effects of camera rotation and change in internal parameters, and is an exact map for points on the plane. The only residual image motion (which is *parallax* relative to this homography) arises from the scene relief relative to the plane. Often this parallax is less than the loose displacement threshold, so that all correspondences may still be obtained. Thus the homography provides strong disambiguation for matching and the parallax effects do not exceed the loose threshold.

This suggests a new method for matching, in which one (or more) homographies *and* a fundamental matrix are estimated for the data. The homographies estimated at the coarser level are used to guide the search windows in order to detect matches for the features at the finer level. They can also be used to guide the cross correlation matching at the finer level in that the patches that are correlated can be corrected by transformation under the homography. This representation is referred to as the *augmented* fundamental $\mathbf{F}^+$ or affine fundamental matrix $\mathbf{F}_A^+$. For the examples presented in this paper, one homography is sufficient to guide matching. This leads to a 10 parameter estimation problem for $\mathbf{F}^+$ (8 for the homography and 2 for the epipole, alternatively: 7 for the fundamental matrix and 3 for the plane of the homography), and 7 for $\mathbf{F}_A^+$ (6 for the affinity and 1 for the epipole, alternatively 4 for the affine fundamental matrix and 3 for the plane). Future work will consider the use of several planes to augment the fundamental matrix, but for many image sequences one seems to be sufficient to get good matches.

In order to estimate the augmented relation, the likelihood for a match given this relation (Section 2.1) is decomposed into two parts: the first is the usual likelihood of the fundamental matrix (4), the second is the likelihood of the parallax in the image given the homography. This is assumed to be Gaussian with large variance. This has the effect in general that if two equally good matches happen to lie along an epipolar line the one closer to the base plane represented by the homography is favoured.

5.1 Augmented Likelihood Formulation

Previously the optimisation was done on only the "best" set of matches found under cross correlation. If the image deformation is unknown, this is no longer acceptable and the likelihoods must be extended to incorporate a term for the probability of the correlation conditioned on a given match and a given homography. Given the set of images (the data) $\mathbf{D}_l$ at level l of the image pyramid, both the parameters of the relation θ and the set of matches δ_i, $i = 1 \ldots n$ need to be estimated. Here the ith match is encoded by δ_i, which is the disparity of the ith feature of the first image. The set of disparities of all the features is Δ. The laws of probability give:

$$p(\theta, \Delta|\mathbf{D}_l) \propto p(\mathbf{D}_l|\theta, \Delta)p(\theta, \Delta) = p(\mathbf{D}_l|\theta, \Delta)p(\Delta|\theta)p(\theta) . \tag{6}$$

Under the assumption that the errors in each match are independent, and that the the distribution of matches are independent:

$$p(\theta, \Delta|\mathbf{D}_l) = \prod_i p(\theta, \delta_i|\mathbf{D}_l) \propto \prod_i p(\mathbf{D}_l|\theta, \delta_i)p(\delta_i|\theta)p(\theta) . \tag{7}$$

This is the criterion to be optimised. However, only the augmented relation θ is propagated from the coarser level, and the matches are encoded by the homography part of θ and the disparity assigned to the parallax.

The probability of θ can be calculated by integrating out the disparity parameters. Note the following identity: $\int_{-\infty}^{\infty} p(\mathbf{X}, \mathbf{Y}|\mathbf{I})d\mathbf{Y} = p(\mathbf{X}|\mathbf{I})$. Then

$$p(\theta|\mathbf{D}_l) \propto \int p(\mathbf{D}_l|\theta, \delta_1)p(\delta_1|\theta)p(\theta)d\delta_1 \times \ldots \times \int p(\mathbf{D}_l|\theta, \delta_n)p(\delta_n|\theta)p(\theta)d\delta_n. \tag{8}$$

Since δ_i may take only a finite number of values, corresponding to the features $j = 1 \ldots m$ of the second image (see below for the case of occlusion),

$$p(\theta|\mathbf{D}_l) \propto \prod_i \sum_j p(\mathbf{D}_l|\theta, \delta_i = j)p(\delta_i = j|\theta)p(\theta) \tag{9}$$

Each term in this expression is the product of three elements. First, $p(\mathbf{D}_l|\boldsymbol{\theta}, \delta_i = j)$ is the likelihood of the image (patches) given the augmented fundamental matrix $\mathbf{F}^+$ and the match $\delta_i = j$. This is evaluated from the cross correlation score after warp under the homography part of $\mathbf{F}^+$ under the assumption that the image intensities have Gaussian error mean zero and standard deviation σ_D. The second term $p(\delta_i = j|\boldsymbol{\theta})$ is the likelihood of the match given the relation, given by equation (3) (account for occlusion is made below). The third term $p(\boldsymbol{\theta})$ is the prior on the relation, assumed uniform here, but this can be altered to include any appropriate prior knowledge.

Thus the decomposition above is useful in two ways: (1) it yields $p(\boldsymbol{\theta}|\mathbf{D}_l)$ without having to commit to a set of matches and (2) the likelihood $p(\mathbf{D}_l|\boldsymbol{\theta}, \delta_i)$ takes account of the different hypothesised image deformations.

Occlusion To take account of occlusion, the disparity δ_i for a given match can take a null value, representing the fact no match can be found with a finite probability, that is $p(\delta_i = \emptyset) = \rho_1$. For this value of δ_i, the conditional probability of the image patch correlation $p(\mathbf{D}_l|\boldsymbol{\theta}, \delta_i)$ is also set to a constant value ρ_2. The resulting estimate of $\boldsymbol{\theta}$ remains constant over a large range of $\rho_{1,2}$. Smaller values of these constants tend to peak the distribution, while larger values flatten it.

6 Feature Matching Algorithm Using IMPSAC

The algorithm is summarized in Fig. 2. The first stage is to generate the features at all levels. Then, at the coarsest scale, cross correlation scores are generated between all features, with each patch undergoing 16 evenly space rotations (this is only necessary if image deformation is expected). Random sampling of minimal match sets is used to generate an initial set of putative solutions, each match being picked in proportion to its correlation likelihood.

After the coarsest level $l = 0$, two options are considered for generation of the subsequent importance sampling functions, both valid. The first method (importance sampling) is to use the mixture of Gaussian methods described above. This has the advantage that new particles are generated across the whole parameter space, the disadvantage that it is slow to compute. The second method (importance resampling) represents $g_l(\boldsymbol{\theta})$, $l > 0$ using the set of particles S^l each assigned probability $p(\boldsymbol{\theta}_i) = \pi_i$ where $\pi_i = \frac{w(\boldsymbol{\theta}_i)}{\sum_j w(\boldsymbol{\theta}_j)}$ and $w(\boldsymbol{\theta}_i) = \frac{p(\boldsymbol{\theta}_i|\mathbf{D}_l)}{g_{l-1}(\boldsymbol{\theta}_i)}$. A problem with the resampling approach is that one particle $\boldsymbol{\theta}_{max}$ may come to represent all the probability mass at a given level and hence all the particles at the finer level will be replicas of it. One solution to this problem in a different setting is justified by Sullivan and Blake [21] in which a small amount of noise (compensated for by subtracting it from the prior $p(\boldsymbol{\theta})$) is added to each particle as it is transmitted to the next level. This can be intuitively explained in this case by the fact that the resolution of the match-coordinates changes as the image is subsampled (here by a factor of 2). For instance, if the features are not represented to sub-pixel accuracy, then change of scale introduces some uncertainty into where the features should lie at the next scale of the order 0-1 pixel. Each particle was estimated from a minimal set of feature matches. Thus, to add uncertainty to $\boldsymbol{\theta}$, noise from 0-1 pixel is added to the minimal set used to estimate it. In this case, each particle represents a distribution over $\boldsymbol{\theta}$-space, determined by the level of uncertainty in the coordinates.

1. At each scale: Detect features.
2. Putative matching of corners over the coarsest two images using proximity and cross correlation under a variety of rotations.
3. At the **coarsest level**. Generate a set of particles $S^0 = \{\theta^0_m\}$ and weights $\{w^0_m\}$, $m = 1 \ldots M$ as follows:
   (a) Select a random sample without replacement of the minimum number of correspondences required to estimate the relation $\mathcal{R}$
   (b) Calculate θ^0_i from this minimal set.
   (c) Calculate $w^0_i = p(\theta | \mathbf{D}_0)$ for each sample.
4. For $l = 1$ to l = finest level
   (a) Generate an importance sampling function $g_l(\theta)$ from S^{l-1}.
   (b) Generate M draws from g_l, to generate S^l.
   (c) For each θ^l_i, calculate $w^l_i = p(\theta^l_i | \mathbf{D}_l)/g_l(\theta^l_i)$.
5. The particle with the maximum posterior probability is taken as the MAP estimate. This can then be used as a starting point for a gradient descent algorithm.

Table 2. *Feature Matching Algorithm using* IMPSAC.

7 Results

The final stage of the algorithm in Table 2 is to select the most likely particle at the finest level as the most likely hypothesis. This is the particle θ_{imax} which maximises $p(\theta_i | \mathbf{D})$. The ith feature in the first image is matched to the feature j in the second image which maximises $p(\delta_i = j | \theta_{imax})$. Figure 3 shows the successful matching of two images with up to 160 pixels disparity, demonstrating the capacity of IMPSAC for wide baseline matching. Figure 4 shows how IMPSAC is robust to large rotations of the image. In figure 5, mismatches of MLESAC are corrected by rematching with the augmented likelihood, doubling the number of matched features.

8 Future Work

Due to space constraints, model selection is not the topic of this paper. However it will be briefly illustrated how importance sampling can be used to evaluate the marginal likelihoods required for model comparison. Given a set of k models $\mathbf{M}_1 \ldots \mathbf{M}_k$ that can explain the data $\mathbf{D}$ (here the models are fundamental matrix, homography, augmented fundamental matrix etc.) then Bayes rule leads us to

$$p(\mathbf{M}_i | \mathbf{DI}) = \frac{p(\mathbf{D} | \mathbf{M}_i \mathbf{I}) p(\mathbf{M}_i | \mathbf{I})}{p(\mathbf{D} | \mathbf{I})}, \tag{10}$$

where $\mathbf{I}$ is the prior information assumed about the world. Note $p(\mathbf{D} | \mathbf{I})$ is the same for all models. Assuming that all the models are equally likely *a priori* i.e. $\mathbf{M}_i = \frac{1}{k}$, the key posterior likelihood of each model is the evaluation of $p(\mathbf{D} | \mathbf{M}_j \mathbf{I})$, which is called

Fig. 3. Wide Baseline Success of IMPSAC: *the first and last images from the Samsung sequence, captured at the same time but from different positions. The disparity between the images is up to 160 pixels, yet only 3 or 4 of the 50 example matches shown are mismatched.*

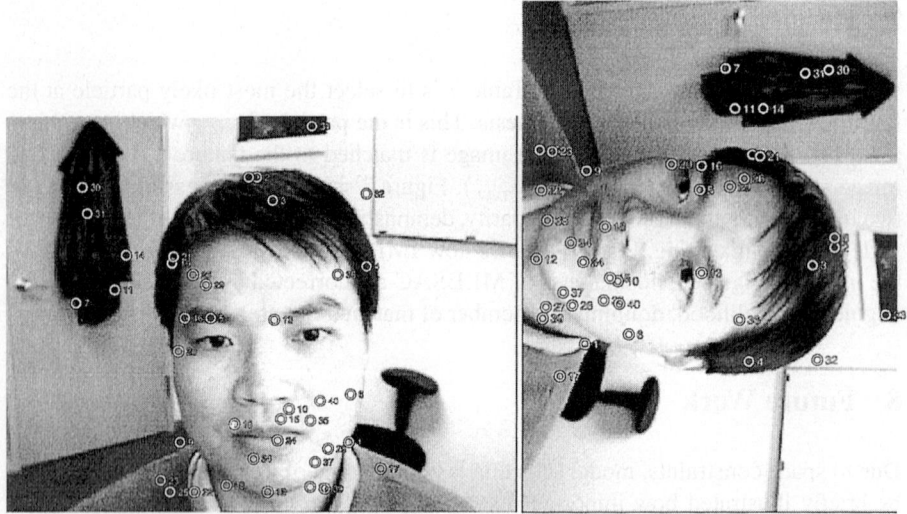

Fig. 4. Rotation Success of IMPSAC: *Despite the combination of a rotation of 90 degrees and the change in pose of the face, the features are correctly matched. Although just 40 features are shown for clarity, over 1000 were matched.*

Fig. 5. MLESAC **Mismatches Corrected by Augmented Likelihood:** *(Above)* MLESAC *matches with affine fundamental matrix include numerous mismatches. (Below) From the same* MLESAC *hypothesis, rematching with augmented likelihood increases number of matches from 509 to 1274, also reducing mismatches.*

the evidence. This is the integral of the likelihood over all possible values of the model's parameters:

$$p(\mathbf{D}|\mathbf{M}_j\mathbf{I}) = \int p(\mathbf{D}|\mathbf{M}_j\boldsymbol{\theta}\,\mathbf{I})p(\boldsymbol{\theta}\,|\mathbf{M}_j\mathbf{I})\partial\boldsymbol{\theta} \qquad (11)$$

where $\boldsymbol{\theta}$ are the jth model's parameters, and $p(\boldsymbol{\theta}\,|\mathbf{M}_j\mathbf{I})$ is the prior distribution of parameters of the model. One method for numerically evaluating this integral would be to uniformly sample the parameter space and sum the posteriors of the samples. Unfortunately the high dimensionality of the parameter space precludes this. One could draw samples from the prior and sum the posterior of these samples, but typically the prior is too diffuse to yield samples around the peak of the distribution. Importance sampling furnishes a Monte Carlo method for performing this integration [9], the advantage of which is that samples can be taken more densely around the expected peak of the posterior and less densely in areas of little interest. If the importance sampling function is

$g(\boldsymbol{\theta})$ ($g(\boldsymbol{\theta})$ is a normalized density), then given a set of M particles drawn from $g(\boldsymbol{\theta})$

$$p(\mathbf{D}|\mathbf{M}_j\mathbf{I}) \rightarrow \sum_{i=1}^{i=M} \frac{p(\mathbf{D}|\mathbf{M}_j\boldsymbol{\theta}\,\mathbf{I})p(\boldsymbol{\theta}\,|\mathbf{M}_j\mathbf{I})}{g(\boldsymbol{\theta})} \text{ as } M \rightarrow \infty \qquad (12)$$

Evaluation of this leads to the selection of an augmented fundamental matrix model for the Samsung sequence shown in Figure 3, a homography model for the Zhang sequence shown in Figure 4, and an augmented affine fundamental matrix for Figure 5.

9 Conclusion

Within this paper coarse to fine estimation of structure and motion has been demonstrated. This has been achieved through the synthesis of powerful statistical techniques. The concept of using a random sampling estimator to generate the importance sampling function, IMPSAC, is a general mechanism that can be used in a wide variety of statistical problems beyond this. It provides a solution to the general problem of how to create importance sampling functions for outlier corrupted data. The coarse to fine strategy helps overcome the wide baseline problem, and this combined with the plane plus parallax representation (the augmented fundamental matrix) overcomes the image deformation problem. The resultant is a general purpose and powerful image matching algorithm that can be used for 3D reconstruction or compression. Finally how the importance sampling can also be used for automatic model selection is explained.

References

1. Ayache N. *Artificial vision for mobile robots*. MIT Press, Cambridge, 1991.
2. Beardsley P., Torr P., and Zisserman A. 3D model acquisition from extended image sequences. In *Proc. European Conference on Computer Vision*, LNCS 1064/1065, pages 683–695. Springer-Verlag, 1996.
3. Beardsley P., Zisserman A., and Murray D. Navigation using affine structure and motion. In *Proc. European Conference on Computer Vision*, LNCS 800/801, pages 85–96. Springer-Verlag, 1994.
4. J. R. Bergen, P. Anandan, K. Hanna, and R. Hingorani. Hierarchical model-based motion estimation. In *Proc. 2nd European Conference on Computer Vision, LNCS 588, Santa Margherita Ligure*, pages 237–252, 1992.
5. T. Cham and R. Cipolla. A statistical framework for long range matching in uncalibrated image mosaicing. In *Conference on Computer Vision and Pattern Recognition*, pages 442–447, 1998.
6. A. P. Dempster, N. M. Laird, and D. B. Rubin. Maximum likelihood from incomplete data via the em algorithm. *J. R. Statist. Soc.*, 39 B:1–38, 1977.
7. O.D. Faugeras. What can be seen in three dimensions with an uncalibrated stereo rig? In G. Sandini, editor, *Proc. 2nd European Conference on Computer Vision, LNCS 588, Santa Margherita Ligure*, pages 563–578. Springer–Verlag, 1992.
8. M. Fischler and R. Bolles. Random sample consensus: a paradigm for model fitting with application to image analysis and automated cartography. *Commun. Assoc. Comp. Mach.*, vol. 24:381–95, 1981.

9. A. Gelman, J. Carlin, H. Stern, and D. Rubin. *Bayesian Data Analysis*. Chapman and Hall, 1995.

10. C. Harris and M. Stephens. A combined corner and edge detector. In *Proc. Alvey Conf.*, pages 189–192, 1987.

11. Harris C. Determination of ego-motion from matched points. In *Third Alvey Vision Conference*, pages 189–192, 1987.

12. R. I. Hartley. Estimation of relative camera positions for uncalibrated cameras. In *Proc. 2nd European Conference on Computer Vision, LNCS 588, Santa Margherita Ligure*, pages 579–587. Springer-Verlag, 1992.

13. Irani M. and Anandan P. Parallax geometry of pairs of points for 3d scene analysis. In Buxton B. and Cipolla R., editors, *Proc. 4th European Conference on Computer Vision, LNCS 1064, Cambridge*, pages 17–30. Springer, 1996.

14. M. Isard and A. Blake. Condensation — conditional density propagation for visual tracking. *International Journal of Computer Vision*, 28(1):5–28, 1998.

15. E. T. Jaynes. Probability theory as extended logic. Not yet published a postscript version of this excellent book is available at ftp://bayes.wustl.edu/pub/Jaynes/, 1999.

16. G.I. McLachlan and K. Basford. *Mixture models: inference and applications to clustering.* Marcel Dekker. New York, 1988.

17. McLauchlan P. and Murray D. A unifying framework for structure from motion recovery from image sequences. In *Proc. International Conference on Computer Vision*, pages 314–320, 1995.

18. J. Mundy and A. Zisserman. *Geometric Invariance in Computer Vision*. MIT press, 1992.

19. P. Pritchett and A. Zisserman. Wide baseline stereo matching. In *Proc. 6th International Conference on Computer Vision, Bombay*, pages 754–760, January 1998.

20. L. S. Shapiro. *Affine Analysis of Image Sequences*. PhD thesis, Oxford University, 1993.

21. J. Sullivan, A. Blake, M. Isard, and J. MacCormick. Bayesian correlation. In *Seventh International Conference on Computer Vision*, volume 2, pages 1068–1075, 1999.

22. C. Tomasi and T. Kanade. Shape and motion from image streams under orthography: A factorisation approach. *International Journal of Computer Vision*, 9(2):137–154, 1992.

23. P. H. S. Torr. *Outlier Detection and Motion Segmentation*. PhD thesis, Dept. of Engineering Science, University of Oxford, 1995.

24. P. H. S. Torr and D. W. Murray. Outlier detection and motion segmentation. In P. S. Schenker, editor, *Sensor Fusion VI*, pages 432–443. SPIE volume 2059, 1993. Boston.

25. P. H. S. Torr and D. W. Murray. The development and comparison of robust methods for estimating the fundamental matrix. *Int Journal of Computer Vision*, 24(3):271–300, 1997.

26. P. H. S. Torr and A. Zisserman. Robust computation and parametrization of multiple view relations. In U Desai, editor, *ICCV6*, pages 727–732. Narosa Publishing House, 1998.

27. P.H.S. Torr, A. Fitzgibbon, and A. Zisserman. The problem of degeneracy in structure and motion recovery from uncalibrated image sequences. *IJCV*, 32(1):27–45, 1999. Marr Prize Paper ICCV 1999.

28. Zeller, C. *Projective, Affine and Euclidean Calibration in Compute Vision and the Application of Three Dimensional Perception*. PhD thesis, RobotVis Group, INRIA Sophia-Antipolis, 1996.

29. Z. Zhang, R. Deriche, O. Faugeras, and Q. T. Luong. A robust technique for matching two uncalibrated images through the recovery of the unknown epipolar geometry. *AI Journal*, vol.78:87–119, 1994.

30. Z. Zhang and O. Faugeras. *3D Dynamic Scene Analysis*. Springer-Verlag, 1992.

Egomotion Estimation Using Quadruples of Collinear Image Points*

Manolis I.A. Lourakis

INRIA Sophia-Antipolis, 2004 route des Lucioles
BP 93 06902 Sophia-Antipolis Cedex, FRANCE
mlouraki@sophia.inria.fr
http://www-sop.inria.fr/robotvis/personnel/Manolis.Lourakis/

Abstract. This paper considers a fundamental problem in visual motion perception, namely the problem of egomotion estimation based on visual input. Many of the existing techniques for solving this problem rely on restrictive assumptions regarding the observer's motion or even the scene structure. Moreover, they often resort to searching the high dimensional space of possible solutions, a strategy which might be inefficient in terms of computational complexity and exhibit convergence problems if the search is initiated far away from the correct solution. In this work, a novel linear constraint that involves quantities that depend on the egomotion parameters is developed. The constraint is defined in terms of the optical flow vectors pertaining to four collinear image points and is applicable regardless of the egomotion or the scene structure. In addition, it is exact in the sense that no approximations are made for deriving it. Combined with robust linear regression techniques, the constraint enables the recovery of the FOE, thereby decoupling the 3D motion parameters. Extensive simulations as well as experiments with real optical flow fields provide evidence regarding the performance of the proposed method under varying noise levels and camera motions.

1 Introduction

Knowledge of the velocity of a mobile system with respect to its environment is essential for various servoing tasks that are based on visual feedback, e.g. collision avoidance, docking, image stabilization, etc. Given a sequence of images acquired by a monocular observer pursuing unrestricted rigid motion, the problem of egomotion estimation can be defined as the problem of recovering the linear and angular velocities comprising the motion of the observer. Although simply stated, the problem of estimating egomotion using visual input is particularly difficult. This difficulty primarily stems from the fact that the only information available from images is related to the observed 2D motion of image points, which depends both on the sought egomotion and the unknown 3D structure of

* This work has been carried out while the author was with the Computer Science Dept, Univ. of Crete and the Inst. of Computer Science, FORTH, Heraklion, Crete, Greece. Funding was partially supplied by the VIRGO research network of the TMR Programme (EC Contract No ERBFMRX-CT96-0049).

the viewed scene. Since the dependence of the 2D image motion on the scene structure is nonlinear, small errors in the estimates of 2D motion can have a significant impact on the accuracy of the recovered 3D motion [4]. In addition, the confounding of translation and rotation makes the problem of estimating unrestricted egomotion much harder compared to the problem of estimating pure translation or rotation [4].

Due to its importance, many algorithms dealing with the problem of estimating egomotion have appeared in the literature. The following paragraphs provide a short review of a few representative methods; more detailed discussions can be found in [7, 8, 10]. Most of the methods reviewed here rely on the availability of a dense optical flow field to describe 2D motion. Prazdny [19], for example, assumes that surfaces in the viewed scene are smooth and recovers rotation through numerical optimization techniques using a set of nonlinear equations that are independent of translation. Prazdny [20] and later Burger and Bhanu [2] also suggested solving for rotation first and employed a search in the space of rotational parameters. For each hypothesized rotation, the corresponding rotational field was subtracted from the optical flow and the remaining field was tested for conformance to a purely translational flow field. Bruss and Horn [1] combine information from the whole visual field to determine the 3D motion that is the best least squares fit to the observed velocity field. They developed three different algorithms, the first two of which give closed form solutions for translation and rotation when the motion is purely translational or rotational respectively. The third algorithm applies to the case of general motion and estimates translation by minimizing an appropriate residual function using iterative numerical procedures. Reiger and Lawton [21] solve for translation by exploiting the phenomenon of *motion parallax*. By subtracting the optical flow vectors at two image locations whose corresponding 3D points have sufficiently different depths, a flow vector that is approximately pointing towards the FOE[1] is obtained. The main drawback of this approach stems from the fact that most optical flow algorithms cannot give accurate estimates of optical flow in areas with large depth variations. Recently, Irani et al [9] alleviated some of the difficulties related to the estimation of motion parallax by decomposing image motion into the sum of the motion of a planar surface and a residual planar parallax field that is purely translational.

Heeger and Jepson [7] also make use of the residual function introduced in [1] and propose an efficient search technique for locating its minimum. Hummel and Sundareswaran [8] present an algorithm for finding the rotational motion and one for locating the FOE. The first algorithm is based on the observation that the curl of the optical flow field is approximately a linear function whose coefficients are proportional to the desired rotational parameters of motion. The algorithm for locating the FOE extends the work of Heeger and Jepson [7] by considering for each candidate FOE the projection of the optical flow along vectors emanating from the former. Da Vitoria Lobo and Tsotsos [10] develop a constraint (the *Collinear Point Constraint - CPC*) involving flow projections at three collinear

---

[1] The FOE gives the direction of translation and is defined more rigorously in the following.

image points, which provides a means for canceling rotation and at the same time constraining the FOE to lie on the line defined by the collinear points. The CPC is discussed in more detail in Section 3. Optical flow projections are also used in [13] and the FOE is recovered through their pairwise differences. Daniilidis [3] employs fixation on a scene point to reduce the number of motion parameters to be estimated from five to four. The associated spherical motion field is projected on two latitudinal directions and the motion parameters are then found by two one-dimensional searches along meridians of the image sphere.

In this paper, it is assumed that either the viewed scene is static or the independently moving objects have been identified and masked out [14]. The motivation behind our egomotion estimation method is twofold. First, we are interested in estimating egomotion by means of linear constraints. Second, we want to avoid making any restrictive assumptions regarding the egomotion or the scene structure. Hence, we have developed a novel linear constraint regarding the motion parameters, defined in terms of four collinear image points. The constraint is applicable regardless of the egomotion or the scene structure and combined with robust linear regression techniques, permits the recovery of the direction of translation, thereby decoupling the 3D motion parameters. The rest of this paper is organized as follows. Section 2 presents an overview of some preliminary results that are essential for the development of the proposed method. Section 3 develops the proposed constraint and shows how it can be employed to recover egomotion. Experimental results from an implementation of the method are presented in Section 4. The paper is concluded with a brief discussion in Section 5. A more detailed version can be found in [12].

2 Visual Motion Representation

Before proceeding with the description of the proposed method, issues related to motion representation are discussed. Consider a coordinate system $OXYZ$ positioned at the optical center (nodal point) of a pinhole camera, such that the OZ axis coincides with the optical axis. Suppose that the camera is moving rigidly with respect to its 3D static environment with translational motion (U, V, W) and rotational motion (α, β, γ). Under perspective projection, the 3D point $P(X, Y, Z)$ projects to image point $p(x, y)$ which moves on the image plane with velocity (u, v), given by [11]:

$$u = \frac{(-Uf + xW)}{Z} + \alpha \frac{xy}{f} - \beta \left(\frac{x^2}{f} + f \right) + \gamma y$$

$$v = \frac{(-Vf + yW)}{Z} + \alpha \left(\frac{y^2}{f} + f \right) - \beta \frac{xy}{f} - \gamma x \qquad (1)$$

Equations (1) describe the optical flow field, which relates the 3D motion of points to their projected 2D motion on the image plane. The problem of estimating the optical flow from an image sequence is fundamental to motion analysis. However, due to space limitations, it will not be discussed further here. An excellent introduction to the problem as well as a review of the state of the art can be found in [18]. Several observations regarding Eqs. (1) can be made. First, the effect of translation on the observed 2D motion is independent from that of rotation, i.e. the translational and rotational components of motion are separable. Second, the rotational component of motion is independent of scene structure, since the depth Z influences the translational component only. Third, the vectors defined by the translational components of the motion field, lie on lines going through the point $(x_0, y_0) \equiv (Uf/W, Vf/W)$, which is known as the *Focus Of Expansion* (FOE). The FOE defines the direction of the translational motion, and is of central importance for several motion analysis problems. Finally, if the quantities W and Z are multiplied by the same scale factor, the flow defined by Eqs. (1) remains the same. In other words, there exists a scale ambiguity that prevents us from differentiating between a close object moving slowly and a distant one that is moving fast. Thus, the information related to the translational component of egomotion that can be recovered from Eqs. (1) is at most its direction, i.e. the FOE. The ratio $\frac{Z}{W}$ is often referred to as the *time-to-contact* [16].

3 Using Quadruples of Collinear Points to Constrain the FOE

In the following, it is assumed that the camera has been intrinsically calibrated, so that the retinal transformations among pixel and image coordinate systems are known [15]. Before proceeding to the description of the proposed method, we state two theorems which are essential for its derivation. The proofs, which are omitted due to space limitations, can be found in [12].

3.1 Two precursory theorems

Theorem 1 *Suppose that two image points* $\mathbf{p_1} = (x_1, y_1)$ *and* $\mathbf{p_2} = (x_2, y_2)$ *lie on a line that goes through the origin of the image coordinate system (i.e. the principal point). The difference of the projections of their corresponding optical flow vectors along the direction* $\mathbf{n} = (n_x, n_y)$ *that is normal to the line is equal to*

$$un_1 - un_2 = DW\left(\frac{1}{Z_1} - \frac{1}{Z_2}\right) + \frac{\gamma}{n_y}(x_2 - x_1), \tag{2}$$

where $un_i = u_i n_x + v_i n_y$, $i = 1, 2$ *and* $D = (x_1 - x_0)n_x + (y_1 - y_0)n_y$.

Theorem 2 *Let* $\mathbf{p_1} = (x_1, y_1)$, $\mathbf{p_2} = (x_2, y_2)$ *and* $\mathbf{p_3} = (x_3, y_3)$ *be three collinear image points lying on a line whose equation is* $y = \kappa x + \nu$. *Let also* (x_0, y_0) *be the FOE and assume that* $\mathbf{p_2}$ *divides the line segment* $\overrightarrow{\mathbf{p_1}\,\mathbf{p_3}}$ *in ratio* λ. *For the projections* $un_i, i = 1 \ldots 3$ *of the optical flow vectors at points* $\mathbf{p_1}, \mathbf{p_2}$ *and* $\mathbf{p_3}$ *along an arbitrary direction* (n_x, n_y), *the following holds*

$$un_2 - \frac{1}{1+\lambda}un_1 - \frac{\lambda}{1+\lambda}un_3 = D_2W\left(\frac{1}{Z_2} - \frac{1}{1+\lambda}\frac{1}{Z_1} - \frac{\lambda}{1+\lambda}\frac{1}{Z_3}\right) +$$
$$\frac{d_{21}}{1+\lambda}W\left(\frac{1}{Z_1} - \frac{1}{Z_3}\right) + \frac{\kappa d_{21}(x_2 - x_3)}{f}\alpha - \frac{d_{21}(x_2 - x_3)}{f}\beta \tag{3}$$

In the above equation, $D_2 = (x_2 - x_0)n_x + (y_2 - y_0)n_y$ and $d_{21} = (x_2 - x_1)n_x + (y_2 - y_1)n_y$.

By inspecting Eq. (3), it can easily be seen that in the case that the direction of projection (n_x, n_y) is perpendicular to the line defined by the points $\mathbf{p_i}$, the term d_{21} is zero, thus the sum of the rotational components vanishes. The remaining terms are identical to the expression for the Collinear Point Constraint (CPC) that was derived by Da Vitoria Lobo and Tsotsos in [10]. The CPC states that when an appropriate linear combination of the projections of optical flow vectors in the direction perpendicular to the line joining them is zero, there exist two possible situations. Either the three 3D points whose projections form the collinear triplet are also collinear in the scene (i.e. $\frac{1}{Z_2} - \frac{1}{1+\lambda}\frac{1}{Z_1} - \frac{\lambda}{1+\lambda}\frac{1}{Z_3} = 0$), or the line defined by the collinear triplet passes through the FOE (i.e. $D_2 = 0$). By employing a voting scheme to differentiate between these two cases, the CPC has been combined in [10] with exhaustive image based search for locating the FOE.

3.2 The proposed constraint on egomotion

Assume now a mobile observer undergoing rigid motion in a static environment. Let $\mathbf{p_1} = (x_1, y_1)$, $\mathbf{p_2} = (x_2, y_2)$ and $\mathbf{p_3} = (x_3, y_3)$ be three collinear image points lying on a line $\mathcal{L}$ through the image principal point. Let also (n_x, n_y) be the direction normal to $\mathcal{L}$ and (n'_x, n'_y) and (n''_x, n''_y) two other directions that are not perpendicular to $\mathcal{L}$. According to Theorem 2, for the projections of the optical flow vectors along the direction (n'_x, n'_y) the following holds

$$un'_2 - \frac{1}{1+\lambda}un'_1 - \frac{\lambda}{1+\lambda}un'_3 = D'_2 W(\frac{1}{Z_2} - \frac{1}{1+\lambda}\frac{1}{Z_1} - \frac{\lambda}{1+\lambda}\frac{1}{Z_3}) + \tag{4}$$

$$\frac{d'_{21}}{1+\lambda}W(\frac{1}{Z_1} - \frac{1}{Z_3}) + (\kappa\alpha - \beta)\frac{d'_{21}(x_2 - x_3)}{f},$$

where the primed terms are defined analogously to the unprimed ones in Eq. (3). Similarly, for the projections along the normal direction (n_x, n_y), Eq. (3) gives

$$un_2 - \frac{1}{1+\lambda}un_1 - \frac{\lambda}{1+\lambda}un_3 = D_2 W(\frac{1}{Z_2} - \frac{1}{1+\lambda}\frac{1}{Z_1} - \frac{\lambda}{1+\lambda}\frac{1}{Z_3}) \tag{5}$$

Dividing Eq. (4) with Eq. (5) yields

$$\frac{un'_2 - \frac{1}{1+\lambda}un'_1 - \frac{\lambda}{1+\lambda}un'_3}{un_2 - \frac{1}{1+\lambda}un_1 - \frac{\lambda}{1+\lambda}un_3} = \frac{D'_2}{D_2} + \frac{d'_{21}}{1+\lambda}\frac{\frac{1}{Z_1} - \frac{1}{Z_3}}{D_2(\frac{1}{Z_2} - \frac{1}{1+\lambda}\frac{1}{Z_1} - \frac{\lambda}{1+\lambda}\frac{1}{Z_3})} + \tag{6}$$

$$(\kappa\alpha - \beta)\frac{d'_{21}(x_2 - x_3)}{f}\frac{1}{un_2 - \frac{1}{1+\lambda}un_1 - \frac{\lambda}{1+\lambda}un_3}$$

Applying Eq. (2) for points $\mathbf{p_1}$ and $\mathbf{p_3}$ results in $un_1 - un_3 = D_2 W(\frac{1}{Z_1} - \frac{1}{Z_3}) + \frac{\gamma}{n_y}(x_3 - x_1)$. Solving this equation for $\frac{1}{Z_1} - \frac{1}{Z_3}$, dividing in terms by Eq. (5) and substituting the result into Eq. (6) yields

$$\frac{un_2' - \frac{1}{1+\lambda}un_1' - \frac{\lambda}{1+\lambda}un_3'}{un_2 - \frac{1}{1+\lambda}un_1 - \frac{\lambda}{1+\lambda}un_3}\frac{1}{d_{21}'} = \frac{D_2'/d_{21}'}{D_2} + \frac{1}{1+\lambda}\frac{un_1 - un_3 - \frac{x_3-x_1}{n_y}\gamma}{D_2(un_2 - \frac{1}{1+\lambda}un_1 - \frac{\lambda}{1+\lambda}un_3)} +$$

$$(\kappa\alpha - \beta)\frac{(x_2 - x_3)}{f}\frac{1}{un_2 - \frac{1}{1+\lambda}un_1 - \frac{\lambda}{1+\lambda}un_3} \qquad (7)$$

Let now $\mathbf{p_4} = (x_4, y_4)$ be a fourth point collinear with the triplet $\mathbf{p_1}, \mathbf{p_2}$ and $\mathbf{p_3}$ and such that point $\mathbf{p_2}$ divides the segment $\overrightarrow{\mathbf{p_1}\,\mathbf{p_4}}$ in ratio μ. Eq. (7) gives for the projections along the direction (n_x'', n_y'')

$$\frac{un_2'' - \frac{1}{1+\mu}un_1'' - \frac{\mu}{1+\mu}un_4''}{un_2 - \frac{1}{1+\mu}un_1 - \frac{\mu}{1+\mu}un_4}\frac{1}{d_{21}''} = \frac{D_2''/d_{21}''}{D_2} + \frac{1}{1+\mu}\frac{un_1 - un_4 - \frac{x_4-x_1}{n_y}\gamma}{D_2(un_2 - \frac{1}{1+\mu}un_1 - \frac{\mu}{1+\mu}un_4)} +$$

$$(\kappa\alpha - \beta)\frac{(x_2 - x_4)}{f}\frac{1}{un_2 - \frac{1}{1+\mu}un_1 - \frac{\mu}{1+\mu}un_4} \qquad (8)$$

Subtracting Eq. (8) from Eq. (7) and noting that $\frac{x_1-x_3}{1+\lambda} = x_2 - x_3$ and $\frac{x_1-x_4}{1+\mu} = x_2 - x_4$, results in

$$\frac{un_2' - \frac{1}{1+\lambda}un_1' - \frac{\lambda}{1+\lambda}un_3'}{un_2 - \frac{1}{1+\lambda}un_1 - \frac{\lambda}{1+\lambda}un_3}\frac{1}{d_{21}'} - \frac{un_2'' - \frac{1}{1+\mu}un_1'' - \frac{\mu}{1+\mu}un_4''}{un_2 - \frac{1}{1+\mu}un_1 - \frac{\mu}{1+\mu}un_4}\frac{1}{d_{21}''} = \frac{D_2'/d_{21}' - D_2''/d_{21}''}{D_2} +$$

$$\frac{1}{D_2}(\frac{1}{1+\lambda}\frac{un_1 - un_3}{un_2 - \frac{1}{1+\lambda}un_1 - \frac{\lambda}{1+\lambda}un_3} - \frac{1}{1+\mu}\frac{un_1 - un_4}{un_2 - \frac{1}{1+\mu}un_1 - \frac{\mu}{1+\mu}un_4}) + \qquad (9)$$

$$(\frac{\gamma f}{D_2 n_y} + \kappa\alpha - \beta)(\frac{x_2 - x_3}{f(un_2 - \frac{1}{1+\lambda}un_1 - \frac{\lambda}{1+\lambda}un_3)} - \frac{x_2 - x_4}{f(un_2 - \frac{1}{1+\mu}un_1 - \frac{\mu}{1+\mu}un_4)})$$

The term $\frac{D_2'/d_{21}' - D_2''/d_{21}''}{D_2}$ in Eq. (9) is independent of the FOE and can be computed using the point retinal coordinates only. Indeed, it can be shown that

$$\frac{D_2'/d_{21}' - D_2''/d_{21}''}{D_2} = \frac{(n_x''n_y' - n_x'n_y'')n_y}{(n_x n_y' - n_x'n_y)(n_x n_y'' - n_x''n_y)(x_2 - x_1)} \qquad (10)$$

Equation (9) is independent of the scene depths and linear in the two unknowns $\frac{1}{D_2}$ and $\frac{\gamma f}{D_2 n_y} + \kappa\alpha - \beta$, therefore forms the basis for the development of the proposed egomotion estimation method: Given a line $\mathcal{L}$ through the image principal point, Eq. (9) is employed for estimating the term $\frac{1}{D_2^{\mathcal{L}}}$ corresponding to $\mathcal{L}$. In theory, two quadruples of image points lying on $\mathcal{L}$ suffice to provide estimates of the unknown parameters $\frac{1}{D_2}$ and $\frac{\gamma f}{D_2 n_y} + \kappa\alpha - \beta$. However, to enhance noise immunity, multiple quadruples of points on $\mathcal{L}$ are selected at random and robust estimates of the two unknowns are computed using the LMedS robust estimator [22]. Knowledge of the term $D_2^{\mathcal{L}}$ for a line $\mathcal{L}$ provides one constraint on the location of the FOE, namely

$$x_0 n_x^{\mathcal{L}} + y_0 n_y^{\mathcal{L}} = x^{\mathcal{L}} n_x^{\mathcal{L}} + y^{\mathcal{L}} n_y^{\mathcal{L}} - D_2^{\mathcal{L}}, \qquad (11)$$

where (x_0, y_0) is the sought FOE, $(n_x^{\mathcal{L}}, n_y^{\mathcal{L}})$ is the unit normal for line $\mathcal{L}$ and $(x^{\mathcal{L}}, y^{\mathcal{L}})$ is a point on $\mathcal{L}$. Noting that each line $\mathcal{L}$ through the image principal point supplies one constraint of the form of Eq. (11) regarding the FOE, the constraints arising from multiple such lines can be combined to yield the FOE. More specifically, using many lines through the image principal point, robust estimates of the corresponding distances $\frac{1}{D_2^{\mathcal{L}}}$ are obtained as previously outlined. For each of the obtained distance estimates, Eq. (11) gives rise to a linear constraint regarding the FOE. The LMedS estimator is then applied once again on these constraints to give a robust estimate of the FOE. If required, estimates of the rotational velocity can be obtained in a similar manner by employing robust regression for (α, β, γ) on the constraints derived from the terms $\frac{\gamma f}{D_2^{\mathcal{L}} n_y} + \kappa\alpha - \beta$ computed for each line through the image principal point. Alternatively, rotation can be estimated using optical flow projections along directions that are normal to lines through the estimated FOE and therefore are independent of translation.

4 Experimental Results

The proposed method has been extensively tested with the aid of simulated and real flow fields. Representative results from these experiments are given in this section. In all the experiments reported here, at most 180 lines through the image principal point and 400 quadruples of points along each line have been employed.

4.1 Synthetic flow fields

The use of simulated data is justified by the fact that knowledge of the ground truth facilitates a quantitative assessment of the accuracy of the results. Besides, simulation enables us to vary in a controlled manner subsets of the parameters involved in the problem of egomotion estimation and then study their effect on the recovered motion. Therefore, a simulator has been constructed, which given appropriate values for the intrinsic parameters of the simulated camera (focal length and principal point), the translational and rotational motion parameters, the dimensions of the retina and the depth corresponding to each image point, employs Eqs. (1) to synthesize an optical flow field. The depths of image points are generated by random variables following various distributions. For the experiments reported here, a uniform distribution in the range $[Z_{min}, Z_{max}]$ and a Gaussian distribution with nonzero mean have been employed. All distances and sizes used by the simulator are specified in units of pixels. To account for the fact that optical flow fields might be sparse, their *density*, i.e. a percentage specifying the fraction of image points for which optical flow vectors have been computed, can be supplied. To make the simulated optical flow fields more realistic, noise is added to the synthetic optical flows. The noise we employ is generated according to the model suggested in [10]:

$$u_{noisy} = u + sign_1 * N(a, b) * 0.01 * u \ , \quad v_{noisy} = v + sign_2 * N(a, b) * 0.01 * v$$

where $sign_1$ and $sign_2$ are binary values (i.e. 1 or -1) that are randomly chosen with equal probability and $N(a, b)$ is a Gaussian random variable with mean a and standard deviation b. This noise model is referred to as "Gaussian noise with mean $a\%$ and $\sigma = b\%$". As noted in [10], 8% and 2% are realistic values for the noise mean and the standard deviation respectively, accounting for most of the errors observed in actual flow fields.

Throughout all experiments, image size was 512×512 pixels and the principal point was assumed to be in the center of the image. Also, in all but the third set of experiments, the focal length was 256 pixels, amounting to a field of view of 90 degrees. The density of the optical flow fields was 70%. Two different scenarios for the scene depth were simulated. The first uses a random variable that is uniformly distributed in the range $[10000, 50000]$ pixels to model the depth of a scene with large depth variations. The second scenario employs a Gaussian distribution with mean 15000 pixels and standard deviation 3000, to emulate a scene with less depth variation, in which the majority of the points lie at a dominant depth rather close to the camera. To ensure that the results are independent of the exact depth values used to synthesize the optical flow field, each experiment was run 100 times, each time using a different depth population drawn from the distributions described above.

In the first set of experiments, the effect of noise on the accuracy of the estimated FOE is examined. Employing increasing noise levels, Figures 1 (a) and (b) illustrate the mean and the standard deviation respectively of the FOE error for both depth distributions. Each point in the plots summarizes error statistics computed from 100 runs. If f is the focal length and the true FOE is at (x_0, y_0) while the estimated is at $(\hat{x_0}, \hat{y_0})$, the error in the FOE estimate is defined as the angle between the vectors (x_0, y_0, f) and $(\hat{x_0}, \hat{y_0}, f)$, given by $cos^{-1}(\frac{(x_0,y_0,f)\cdot(\hat{x_0},\hat{y_0},f)}{||(x_0,y_0,f)||\ ||(\hat{x_0},\hat{y_0},f)||})$. The 3D motion parameters used to synthesize flow were $(U, V, W) = (-120, 100, 150)$ (measured in pixels per frame) and $(\alpha, \beta, \gamma) = (0.005, 0.004, 0.002)$ (measured in radians per frame). The egomotion parameters and the depth values are such that the magnitude of the average translational component of the flow fields is comparable to that of the average rotational component. The angle between the direction of translation and the optical axis is about 46 degrees. The noise mean was increased to 12% in steps of 1% and the standard deviation was kept equal to 2%. As expected, the error increases with noise but remains acceptable even with very large amounts of noise. The error in the case of Gaussian depths is smaller since in this case the translational component of motion is larger than that in the case of uniformly distributed depths; this is further explained in the discussion of the experiments related to the magnitude of translation below.

It has been observed in previous work on egomotion estimation that the error of the estimated FOE increases with the angle between the direction of translation and the direction of gaze (i.e. the direction defined by the optical axis) [4]. The second set of experiments studies the dependence of the FOE error on this angle for the proposed method. Figures 2 (a) and (b) show the mean and standard deviation of the FOE error with respect to the angle between the direction of

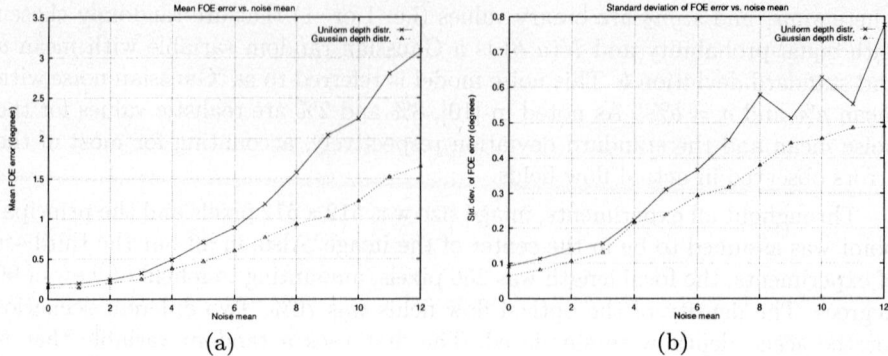

Fig. 1. (a) Mean FOE error versus noise and (b) Standard deviation of FOE error versus noise.

translation and the direction of gaze. The direction of translation was varied from $(0, 0, f)$ to $(f, 0, f)$, where f is the focal length. In other words, the translations considered range from a straight ahead motion to a sideways motion forming an angle of 45 degrees with the direction of gaze. The rotation parameters were again equal to $(\alpha, \beta, \gamma) = (0.005, 0.004, 0.002)$ and the magnitude of translation has been kept constant, equal to 216.565 pixels per frame, which is the magnitude of translation used in the first set of experiments. Each point in the graphs has been computed from 100 trials, performed with Gaussian noise of mean 8% and standard deviation of 2%. As can be seen from Fig. 2 (a), the FOE error does not vary considerably when the angle between the direction of translation and the direction of gaze is increased. This is a desirable characteristic of the proposed method, since it implies that the observer does not need to fixate on the estimated FOE to ensure small errors in the FOE estimates.

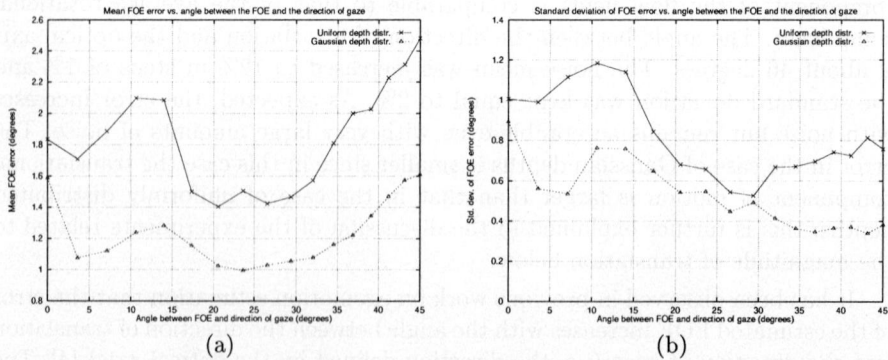

Fig. 2. (a) Mean FOE error versus the angle between the direction of translation and the direction of gaze and (b) Standard deviation of FOE error versus the angle between the direction of translation and the direction of gaze.

The third set of experiments investigates the dependence of the FOE error on the field of view size. Figures 3 (a) and (b) show the mean and standard deviation of the FOE error with respect to the size of the field of view. The field of view size was varied by adjusting the focal length while keeping the image size constant. More specifically, the former was decreased by a multiplicative factor of 0.5 from 2048 to 64 pixels while the image size remained equal to 512×512 pixels. This change of the focal length amounts to the field of view being increased from 14.250 to 151.927 degrees. Recall that a focal length of 256 pixels used in the previous experiments corresponds to a field of view equal to 90 degrees. The simulated 3D velocity was identical to that of the first set of experiments, i.e. translation was equal to $(-120, 100, 150)$ and rotation to $(0.005, 0.004, 0.002)$. Gaussian noise of mean 8% and standard deviation of 2% was added to the simulated flows and each point in the graphs was again computed from 100 trials. As can be seen from Figs. 3, the error in the recovered FOE is almost identical for both depth distributions. More specifically, the FOE error is very large for small fields of view but becomes acceptable when the latter are larger than 25 degrees. This observation agrees with the theoretical findings of [6, 5], which conclude that the inhomogeneous flow characteristics of a large field of view make it more helpful for determining the singularities of the flow field (i.e. the FOE and axis of rotation) compared to a narrow field of view. This conclusion holds independently of the particular algorithm that is employed to recover 3D motion.

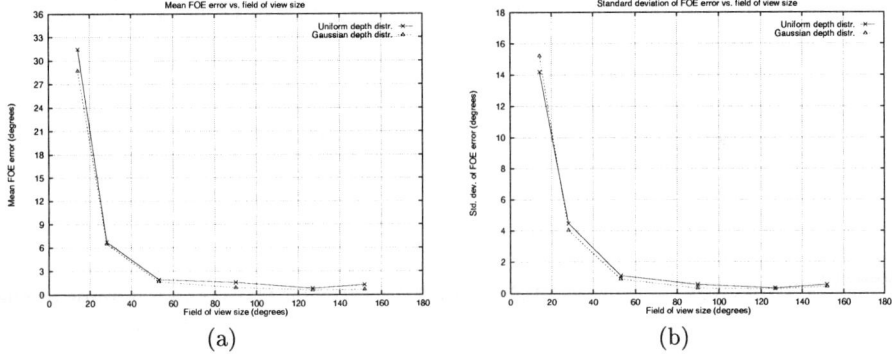

Fig. 3. (a) Mean FOE error versus the size of the field of view and (b) Standard deviation of FOE error versus the size of the field of view.

The last set of experiments evaluates the performance of the method when the ratio between the magnitude of translation and that of rotation is varied. More specifically, assuming that the rotation is constant, Figures 4 (a) and (b) depict the effect of variable translation magnitude on the mean and the standard deviation of the FOE error. In this series of experiments, the direction of translation is identical to that defined by $(U, V, W) = (-120, 100, 150)$, but its magnitude is increased by a multiplicative factor of 1.5 between successive experiments. The

844

rotation has been kept constant at $(\alpha, \beta, \gamma) = (0.005, 0.004, 0.002)$ and 100 runs were made for each set of motion parameters. The noise was Gaussian with mean 8% and standard deviation 2%. As can be clearly seen from the plots, the FOE error is significant when the translation magnitude is small (less than 130 pixels per frame in Fig. 4 (a)). This is due to the fact that in this case, the translational components of the optical flow vectors are negligible compared to the rotational ones. Therefore, noise has a more pronounced effect on the translational components from which the FOE is recovered. However, as the magnitude of translation increases beyond 130 pixels per frame, the translational parts become comparable or even larger than the rotational ones. Thus, the translational parts are more immune to noise, giving rise to small FOE errors which are almost constant with respect to the magnitude of translation. Assuming constant translation, Fig-

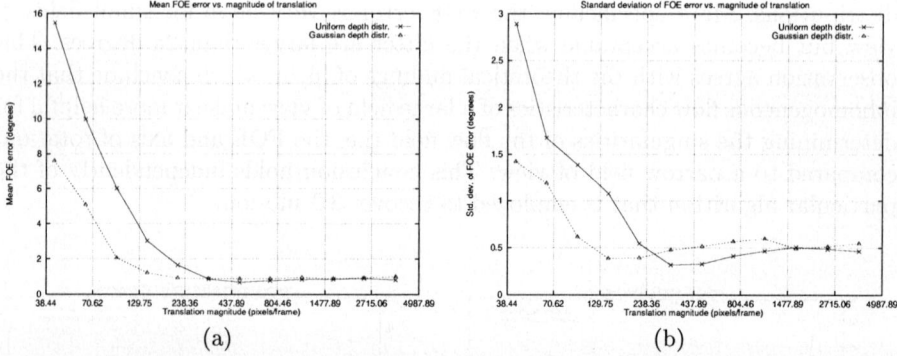

Fig. 4. (a) Mean FOE error versus magnitude of translation (b) Standard deviation of FOE error versus magnitude of translation. Note that the scale on the horizontal axes is logarithmic with base 1.5.

ures 5 (a) and (b) show the effects on the mean and the standard deviation of the FOE error induced by altering the rotation magnitude. Here, the behavior of the method is the converse of that observed in the case of constant rotation investigated in the previous paragraph. As can be seen from Fig. 5 (a), the error in the FOE estimates is almost constant for realistic amounts of rotation (less than 0.5 degrees per frame). When the rotation increases too much, the flow field becomes mainly rotational, with the rotational components accounting for a large fraction of the full flow field. Thus, noise has an increased impact on the translational parts, resulting in large errors for the FOE estimates. During the experiments outlined in Fig. 5, translation was kept fixed at $(U, V, W) = (-120, 100, 150)$, the rotation magnitude was increased by a multiplicative factor of 2.0 between successive experiments and 100 runs were made for each experiment. As before, the noise was Gaussian with mean 8% and standard deviation 2%. Note that a rotation of $(\alpha, \beta, \gamma) = (0.005, 0.004, 0.002)$ has a magnitude of 0.3845 degrees. When assuming continuous image motion (i.e. fine time sampling), rotations having

845

magnitudes larger than one degree per frame are very large and thus unrealistic.

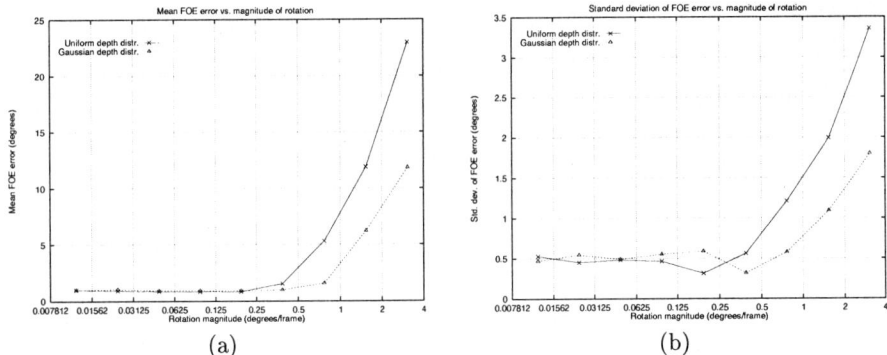

Fig. 5. (a) Mean FOE error versus magnitude of rotation and (b) Standard deviation of FOE error versus magnitude of rotation. Note that the scale on the horizontal axes is logarithmic with base 2.0.

4.2 Real Image Sequences

The method has also been tested using flow fields computed from real imagery for which the ground truth was known a priori. Throughout all experiments, optical flow was computed using an implementation of the Lucas & Kanade algorithm [17]. The first experiment employed the "yosemite" image sequence, one frame of which is shown in Fig. 6 (a). This sequence contains both translation and rotation and depicts a flight through Yosemite valley. Since the clouds are moving independently, only the optical flow vectors computed at the lower portion of the images have been employed. This portion of the original images corresponds to a field of view equal to 49.6 degrees horizontally and 29 degrees vertically. The true FOE is rather close to the center of the field of view, namely at $(0, 58)^2$ while the estimate computed by the proposed method was (-17.3, 72.3), a value that corresponds to an error of 22.4 pixels or 3.7 degrees. This amount of error compares favorably to errors in the "yosemite" FOE estimates appearing in the literature. More specifically, Heeger and Jepson [7] report an error of 3.5 degrees for the "yosemite" sequence and Daniilidis [3] reports an error of 4.0 degrees. The rotation recovered by the proposed method using robust regression on projections of flow vectors that are perpendicular to lines through the recovered FOE, was equal to $(0.000906, 0.002116, 0.000481)$ (in radians/frame). As mentioned in [7], the actual rotational velocity for the "yosemite" sequence is $(0.00023, 0.00162, 0.00028)$.

---

[2] These are "calibrated" image coordinates, defined with respect to the image principal point.

Fig. 6. (a)-(d) the "yosemite" image sequence, (b)-(e) the "marbled block" image sequence and (c)-(f) the "nasa" image sequence. One frame from each sequence is shown in the top row, while the optical flow fields used for egomotion estimation are shown in the bottom row.

The second experiment refers to the "marbled block" sequence, one frame of which is shown in Fig. 6 (b). The sequence was captured by a translating camera mounted on a robot arm that was moving above a textured floor in a right to left direction and contains many sharp discontinuities in depth and motion. The four dark blocks that lie on the floor are stationary, while the white block in the middle of the scene is moving independently with a right to left direction. The images of the "marbled block" sequence subtend 25.6 degrees of visual angle. The primary difficulty when estimating the egomotion for this sequence stems from the fact that the true FOE is outside the field of view, specifically at (777, 95.6). Thus, the angle between the direction of translation and the optical axis is about 35 degrees. The proposed method estimated the FOE at (625.0, 111.4), in error by 152.7 pixels or 5.65 degrees. For comparison, the FOE estimate reported by Daniilidis in [3] amounts to an error of 7.17 degrees. The rotation estimated by the proposed method was equal to $(-0.000748, 0.000291, 0.000031)$, close to being zero as expected.

The last experiment is based on the "nasa" image sequence, shown in Fig. 6 (c). Since the camera undergoes a purely translational motion, a rotation of $(\alpha, \beta, \gamma) = (-0.00025, -0.0018, 0.00030)$ was added synthetically in order to make the experiment more challenging[3]. The ground truth for the FOE is (-5, -8) while the recovered FOE was (2.21, 49.29), in error by 57.74 pixels or 5.5 degrees. For reference, the images of the "nasa" sequence subtend 24 degrees of visual angle. The rotation estimated by the proposed method was equal to $(-0.000176, -0.001918, 0.000138)$. The rather large error in the recovered FOE for the "nasa" sequence is due to the proximity between the true FOE and the image principal point. Therefore, in this case, the distance D_2 (see Eq. (9)) of the FOE from every line through the principal point is very small and thus difficult to estimate accurately.

5 Conclusions

Accurate estimation of camera motion is important for many vision based tasks. In this paper, a novel constraint regarding the parameters of 3D motion has been presented. This constraint was used to develop a method for egomotion estimation that has several advantages. First, the method does not impose any constraints on the egomotion that can be recovered or on the structure of the viewed scene. Second, egomotion is computed through closed form solutions of linear equations, avoiding searching the space of possible solutions. The use of such linear constraints permits the exploitation of overdetermined linear systems through the application of robust linear regression techniques. The egomotion estimate computed by the proposed method can either be used as is, or, optionally, for bootstrapping more elaborate, iterative nonlinear egomotion estimation methods for refining it. Third, instead of employing local information derived from small image regions, redundancy is exploited by combining information across the whole visual field. Fourth, the method does not assume the availability of a dense optical flow field. This is very important for practical applications, since image sequences often have uniform, textureless areas that give rise to sparse optical flow fields. Finally, the use of a robust estimator such as LMedS safeguards against errors in the input, which could otherwise have a significant effect on the accuracy of the computations. Experimental results collected from extensive simulations as well as real image sequences indicate the effectiveness and robustness of the proposed method.

References

1. A. R. Bruss and B.K.P. Horn. Passive Navigation. *CVGIP*, 21:3–20, 1983.
2. W. Burger and B. Bhanu. Estimating 3D Egomotion from Perspective Image Sequences. *IEEE Trans. on PAMI*, 12(11):1040–1058, Nov. 1990.

---

[3] This is possible since the rotational component of motion is independent of the (unknown) scene structure; see Eqs. (1).

3. K. Daniilidis. Fixation Simplifies 3D Motion Estimation. *CVIU*, 68(2):158–169, Nov. 1997.

4. K. Daniilidis and M.E. Spetsakis. Understanding Noise Sensitivity in Structure From Motion. In Y. Aloimonos, editor, *Visual Navigation: From Biological Systems to Unmanned Ground Vehicles*, chapter 4. Lawrence Erlbaum Associates, Hillsdale, NJ, 1997.

5. S. Fejes and L.S. Davis. Direction-Selective Filters for Egomotion Estimation. Technical Report CS-TR-3814, University of Maryland, Jul. 1997.

6. C. Fermüller and Y. Aloimonos. The Confounding of Translation and Rotation in Reconstruction from Multiple Views. In *Proceedings of CVPR'97*, pages 250–256, 1997.

7. D.J. Heeger and A.D. Jepson. Subspace Methods for Recovering Rigid Motion I: Algorithm and Implementation. *IJCV*, 7(2):95–117, 1992.

8. R. Hummel and V. Sundareswaran. Motion Parameter Estimation from Global Flow Field Data. *IEEE Trans. on PAMI*, 15(5):459–476, May 1993.

9. M. Irani, B. Rousso, and S. Peleg. Recovery of Ego-Motion Using Region Alignment. *IEEE Trans. on PAMI*, 19(3):268–272, Mar. 1997.

10. N. V. Lobo and J. K. Tsotsos. Computing Egomotion and Detecting Independent Motion from Image Motion Using Collinear Points. *CVIU*, 64(1):21–52, July 1996.

11. H.C. Longuet-Higgins and K. Prazdny. The Interpretation of a Moving Retinal Image. In *Proceedings of the Royal Society*, pages 385–397. London B, 1980.

12. M.I.A. Lourakis. Egomotion Estimation Using Quadruples of Collinear Image Points. Technical Report 240, ICS/FORTH, Greece, Dec. 1998. Available at ftp://ftp.ics.forth.gr/tech-reports/1998.

13. M.I.A. Lourakis. Using Constraint Lines for Estimating Egomotion. In *Proc. of ACCV'2000*, volume 2, pages 971–976, Taipei, Taiwan, Jan 2000.

14. M.I.A. Lourakis, A.A. Argyros, and S.C. Orphanoudakis. Independent 3D Motion Detection Using Residual Parallax Normal Flow Fields. In *Proceeedings of ICCV'98*, pages 1012–1017, Bombay, India, Jan. 1998.

15. M.I.A. Lourakis and R. Deriche. Camera Self-Calibration Using the Singular Value Decomposition of the Fundamental Matrix: From Point Correspondences to 3D Measurements. Research Report 3748, INRIA Sophia-Antipolis, Aug. 1999.

16. M.I.A. Lourakis and S.C. Orphanoudakis. Using Planar Parallax to Estimate the Time-to-Contact. In *Proc. of CVPR'99*, volume 2, pages 640–645, Fort Collins, CO, June 1999.

17. B.D. Lucas and T. Kanade. An Iterative Image Registration Technique with an Application to Stereo Vision. In *Proceedings DARPA IU Workshop*, pages 121–130, 1981.

18. A. Mitiche and P. Bouthemy. Computation and Analysis of Image Motion: A Synopsis of Current Problems and Methods. *IJCV*, 19(1):29–55, Jul. 1996.

19. K. Prazdny. Egomotion and Relative Depth from Optical Flow. *Biological Cybernetics*, 36:87–102, 1980.

20. K. Prazdny. Determining the Instantaneous Direction of Motion From Optical Flow Generated by a Curvilinearly Moving Observer. *CVGIP*, 17:238–248, 1981.

21. J.H. Reiger and D.T. Lawton. Processing Differential Image Motion. *Journal of the Optical Society of America A*, 2:354–359, 1985.

22. P.J. Rousseeuw. Least Median of Squares Regression. *Journal of American Statistics Association*, 79:871–880, 1984.

Geometric Driven Optical Flow Estimation and Segmentation for 3D Reconstruction

Lionel Oisel, Étienne Mémin, and Luce Morin

IRISA, Campus de Beaulieu, Rennes, France

Abstract. We present a method for fully automatic 3D reconstruction from a pair of uncalibrated images in order to deal with the modeling of complex rigid scenes. A 2D triangular mesh model of the scene is calculated using a two-step algorithm mixing sparse matching and dense motion estimation approaches. The 2D mesh is iteratively refined to fit any arbitrary 3D surface. At convergence, each triangular patch corresponds to the projection of a 3D plane. The algorithm proposed here relies first on a dense disparity field. The dense field estimation modelized within a robust framework is constrained by the epipolar geometry. The resulting field is then segmented according to homographic models using iterative Delaunay triangulation. In association with a simplified self-calibration algorithm, this 2D planar model is used to obtain a VRML-compatible 3D model of the scene.

Many recent works attempt to deal with 3D reconstruction from set of images. Two different classes of approaches are generally proposed using different types of information: the first one includes model-based methods and the second one deals with model-free methods.

In model-based approaches, the scene information is assumed to be composed of large polygonal objects described by a limited set of 3D points characterizing the vertices of each 3D plane. This model can be computed in the 2D space without 3D information. This can be done by extracting, matching and 3D reconstructing points of interest[6] or edges [7]. One of the main limitations of these methods is that effective planarity of generated facets is assumed but not always satisfied. To enforce a global planarity, a manual intervention is even usually necessary to indicate reliable coplanar points. Another way of estimating the model is to use disparity maps (or alternatively depth maps). In [9], Koch *et al.* suggest computing differential properties from a dense disparity map. Images are then segmented according to similar surface orientation at each point of a region. The underlying strongly polyhedral assumption is indeed the major limitation of model-based techniques.

To enlarge the variety of treated scenes, model-free representations (second class of approaches) have been proposed. Such methods generally rely on a dense disparity map. This map can be combined with weak or strong calibration information to provide a depth map that can be manipulated for view synthesis [6, 8]. The major limitation consists here in the estimation of reliable dense disparity information allowing occlusion areas and spatial discontinuities to be coped with efficiently.

The main objective of our study is to propose an entirely automatic approach for the reconstruction of not necessarily polyhedral textured scenes. In addition to this non-specialized goal, we impose to have the ability of an easy and real time visualization. This latter requirement dismisses practically the use of methods based entirely on a dense depth map. On the other hand, the removal of the polyhedral scenes assumption favors such approaches. Following these two remarks and in order to comply with the previously described goals, our aim is to suggest a compromise between model-free and model-based methods. We first propose to describe the 3D scene by a triangular mesh which can be displayed by most visualization dedicated systems. Our method therefore belongs to the first class (model-based approaches) but as this triangular mesh is automatically computed from a dense disparity field, it is also related to the second class.

The key point of our method is to segment the images into regions which are actually planar in the 3D scene and to extract the planarity propriety from the image data (and not from a user intervention). This is indeed equivalent to realizing motion segmentation according to an homographic model. As the homographic model describing the set of admissible transformations of planar patches is non-linear, a direct region-based segmentation method is hardly feasible. We have therefore designed a two-step method. The first step provides a geometrically constrained dense depth map and an associated discontinuity map. This dense information is then used to initialize the second step: homographic model estimation and segmentation.

The outline of the paper is the following. The first section briefly describes geometric definitions associated with perspective projection of two images. In this context, epipolar geometry is presented. This important geometric constraint is used in all the following steps of our method and has to be previously estimated.

In the second section, in order to facilitate a subsequent planar facet segmentation step, we present a geometrically constrained disparity field estimation. This technique is derived from a robust optical flow estimation approach. Unlike classical correlation methods, it provides a reliable piecewise smooth motion field [2, 12]. Moreover the disparity estimation is constrained by the associated epipolar geometry so that the estimated field is explicitly forced to be geometrically consistent with a perspective projection model and with the fixed scene assumption. This constraint also yields a substantial computational cost decrease (the 2D disparity estimation problem is reduced to a 1D problem).

The third section presents the planar facet segmentation step of our method. To ensure the effective planarity of each reconstructed triangle, an adaptive iterative triangulation based on homographic models estimation is computed from the disparity field.

By arbitrarily fixing intrinsic parameters, 3D rotation and translation parameters can be extracted from the epipolar geometry. Using this 3D information, the resulting 2D model is then re-projected in the 3D space to be visualized as a VRML representation.

This method has been validated on synthetic and real world images. Comparison with existing classical techniques are presented in the last section of the paper.

Remark: in the following, vectors will be represented by bold letters.

1 Epipolar geometry

1.1 Definition

The characterization of the geometry associated with the two cameras is of key importance in order to build a 3D model of the scene. In our case, we deal with two uncalibrated cameras (or alternatively one moving camera shooting a rigid scene) assuming a pinhole camera model. This model characterizes the projection of a 3D point $\mathbf{P}(X, Y, Z)$ on a point $\mathbf{p}(x, y)$ of the image plane. In the case of two images, the projection model is defined by a system of two equations linking a 3D point $\mathbf{P}(X, Y, Z)$ to its projections $\mathbf{p_1}(x, y)$ in the first image and $\mathbf{p_2}(x', y')$ in the second one. Without lost of generality, we assume that the world coordinate system coincides with the first camera coordinate system. The resulting system can be written using homogeneous coordinates as follows (where $\tilde{\ }$ denotes homogeneous coordinates):

$$
\begin{aligned}
\tilde{\mathbf{p}}_1 &= A_1 [I\ 0] \tilde{\mathbf{P}} \\
\tilde{\mathbf{p}}_2 &= A_2 [R\ \mathbf{t}] \tilde{\mathbf{P}}
\end{aligned}
\tag{1}
$$

R is the rotation matrix and $\mathbf{t}$ the translation vector between the first and the second camera location (extrinsic parameters). Matrix A contains internal camera parameters (intrinsic parameters).

Eliminating $\tilde{\mathbf{P}}$ in equations (1) leads to a relation linking the projections of a 3D point in both images:

$$
\tilde{\mathbf{p}}_2^T A_2^{-T} [\mathbf{t}]_\times R A_1^{-1} \tilde{\mathbf{p}}_1 = 0,
\tag{2}
$$

where $[\mathbf{t}]_\times$ denotes the cross product matrix associated with the translation vector.

This constraint called epipolar geometry has been first introduced by Longuet-Higgins [11]. It is entirely defined by a 3×3 homogeneous matrix called the *fundamental matrix* formulated as $F_{12} = A_2^{-T} [\mathbf{t}]_\times R A_1^{-1}$. By construction, this matrix is of rank 2 and is defined up to a non-zero scalar factor. A fundamental matrix has therefore only seven degrees of freedom.

The epipolar constraint can be used to determine the epipolar line $\mathbf{l_2}$ in the second image associated to the point $\mathbf{p_1}$. It represents the line of $\mathbf{p_1}$ potential correspondences in the second image. Line $\mathbf{l_2}$ is given by:

$$
\tilde{\mathbf{l}}_2 = \mathbf{F}_{12} \tilde{\mathbf{p}}_1
\tag{3}
$$

where $\tilde{\mathbf{l}}_2$ denotes homogeneous coordinates of $\mathbf{l_2}$, i.e. all points in $\mathbf{l_2}$ satisfy $\tilde{\mathbf{l}}_2 \tilde{\mathbf{p}}_2 = 0$.

1.2 Case specific application

The issue we are concerned is the recovery of 3D information from sets of 2D images. It consists in solving system (1) to obtain the 3D point $\mathbf{P}$. To that end, corresponding points $\mathbf{p_1}$ and $\mathbf{p_2}$ and calibration parameters (extrinsic and intrinsic parameters) giving A_1, A_2, R, $\mathbf{t}$ have to be recovered. The first issue can be greatly simplified by constraining the matching process with the epipolar geometry while the second one can be achieved using a decomposition of the fundamental matrix (see section 4). The epipolar geometry estimation is indeed a crucial key point of our method. The next paragraph will present the method we use to recover the fundamental matrix from two uncalibrated images.

1.3 Fundamental matrix estimation

We assumed here that corresponding points have been extracted and matched using an Harris and Stephens detector associated with a cross correlation process. This first step is equivalent to the one developed by Zhang [17].

To take into account the nullity of the fundamental matrix determinant, we followed a method proposed by Boufama *et al.* based on the virtual parallax [4]. This method may be briefly described as follow. The fundamental matrix is first estimated from 8 matches: three of them are selected to perform a projective change of basis to constraint the matrix to be of rank 2. A fourth arbitrary pair is also added to complete the projective change of basis [4]. The four last pairs are then used to provide a unique fundamental matrix solution which respects the rank 2 constraints (determinant of null value).

In association with the determinant nullity constraint, the change of basis provides a normalization effect on points coordinates: the coordinates of the three points selected to characterize the new basis are assigned to values between 0 and 1. This involves that coordinates of points belonging to the triangle defined by these points, also belong to the range of 0 to 1. In order to perform an optimal normalization, the pairs of points are chosen as near as possible to image corners.

Besides, to cope with erroneous matches, a robust estimation based on least median squares estimation is incorporated [14].

2 Dense disparity field estimation

2.1 Constrained optical flow expression

Let $I_i(s)$ be the intensity in the ith image, where $s(x, y) \in S$ denotes the spatial position on grid S. Assuming a constant intensity along motion trajectories, the brightness constancy assumption is expressed as:

$$DFD(\mathbf{s}, \mathbf{d}_s) = I_1(\mathbf{s}) - I_2(\mathbf{s} + \mathbf{d}_s) = 0 \, , \tag{4}$$

where DFD stands for the Displaced Frame Difference function and $\{\mathbf{d}_s = (d_x, d_y), \mathbf{s} \in S\}$ for the image displacements from position 1 to position 2. In the general case, this is a 2D problem: for each pixel, d_x and d_y have to be recovered.

Using the epipolar constraint, it is possible to decompose the displacement vector $\mathbf{d}_s$ into normal and tangential components with respect to the epipolar line (see Figure 1). The brightness constancy assumption is therefore rewritten as: $DFD(\mathbf{s}, \mathbf{d}_s) = I_1(\mathbf{s}) - I_2(\mathbf{s} + \mathbf{n}_s + \lambda_s \mathbf{v}_s) = 0$. The normal component $\mathbf{n}_s$ and the unit vector on the epipolar line $\mathbf{v}_s$ can be computed from the fundamental matrix for any position $\mathbf{s}$ (see eq. 3). The enforcement of the epipolar constraint at every point reduces the original 2D estimation problem to a 1D problem: the estimation of $\lambda = \{\lambda_s, \ s \in S\}$ along epipolar lines.

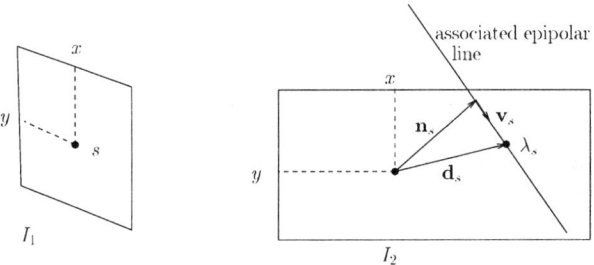

Fig. 1. *Displacement vector decomposition.*

The DFD expression is highly non linear with respect to the displacements. To avoid a tough non linear estimation, a Taylor expansion of this equation is considered around point $\mathbf{s} + \mathbf{n_s}$. This linearization leads to a constrained optical flow equation:

$$I_1(\mathbf{s}) - I_2(\mathbf{s} + \mathbf{n}_s) - \lambda_s \mathbf{v}_s \nabla I_2(\mathbf{s} + \mathbf{n}_s) = 0$$

where ∇ is the spatial gradient.

This equation relies nevertheless on an inherent ambiguity. The fundamental matrix defining epipolar lines is well known to be far more reliably estimated for large displacement between two camera view points. This large displacement assumption somewhat contradicts the infinitesimal disparity hypothesis. To overcome this incompatibility, the estimation is embedded in a coarse-to-fine multiresolution scheme.

2.2 Multiresolution scheme

At a given level k, the disparity $\lambda_s = \{\lambda_s^k, \ \mathbf{s} \in S\}$ is decomposed into a previously estimated disparity λ_s^{k-1} (coming from a coarser level $k-1$ or a previous iteration) and a refinement $d\lambda_s = \{d\lambda_s^k, \ \mathbf{s} \in S\}$ to be estimated. Considering the brightness constancy assumption for the total displacement yields the following equation:

$$I_1^k(\mathbf{s}) - I_2^k(\mathbf{s} + \mathbf{n}_s^k + [\lambda_s^{k-1} + d\lambda_s^k]\mathbf{v}_s^k) = 0, \tag{5}$$

to be solved with respect to $d\lambda_s^k$.

This equation involves pyramids of images $I_i^k = \{I_i^k(s), \ \mathbf{s} \in S\}$, $k = 0, ..., K$, $i = 1, 2$, and pyramids of tangent and normal vectors $\mathbf{n}^k = \{\mathbf{n}_s^k, \ \mathbf{s} \in S\}$, $\mathbf{v}^k = \{\mathbf{v}_s^k, \ \mathbf{s} \in S\}$ with k spanning from K (the coarsest resolution) to 0 (the finest resolution). The image pyramids I_i^k are derived from the original images I_i^0 by successive Gaussian smoothing and regular subsampling by a factor of two in each direction.

As for pyramid $\mathbf{n}^k$ and $\mathbf{v}^k$, we consider fundamental matrices $\{F^k\}$, $k = 0, ..., K$ deduced for each level from the initial matrix F and a change of coordinates. More precisely, we have:

$$F^k = M^{kT} F M^k,$$

where $M^k = \text{diag}(2^k, 2^k, 1)$ is the matrix associated with the considered change of basis involved in the pyramidal representation. The matrix F^k allows to compute $\mathbf{n}_s^k$ and $\mathbf{v}_s^k$ at resolution k for each position s.

To insure that the previously estimated disparity at level $k - 1$ follows the current epipolar geometry at a given level k, λ^k is deduced by projecting disparity $d\lambda^{k-1}$ (with a multiplying factor of 2) onto the epipolar lines at level k (see Fig. 2).

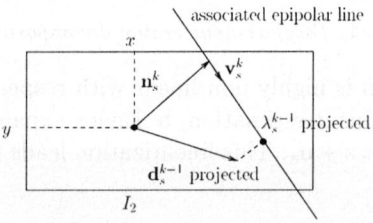

Fig. 2. *Projection of the disparity vector $d\lambda^{k-1}$ according to epipolar geometry at level k.*

2.3 Global estimation method

For sake of clarity, we will omit the resolution upper-script k in all expressions throughout the reminder of this paper. All the expressions will be meant to concern level k. Following the same principle as previously, the DFD expression (5) is linearized around point $\mathbf{s} + \mathbf{n}_s + \lambda_s \mathbf{v}_s$. This leads to a displaced version of the constrained optical flow equation:

$$d\lambda_s \mathbf{v}_s \nabla \tilde{I}_2(\mathbf{s}) + \tilde{I}_2(\mathbf{s}) - I_1(\mathbf{s}) = 0.$$

Assuming this equation is almost satisfied everywhere and that the disparity field is piecewise smooth, the disparity estimation problem may be addressed by the following minimization problem:

$$\widehat{d\lambda} = \arg\min_{d\lambda \in \mathbb{R}^{|s|}} H(d\lambda) = \arg\min_{d\lambda \in \mathbb{R}^{|s|}} (H_1(d\lambda, I_s) + \alpha[H_2(d\lambda)]), \qquad (6)$$

where α is an arbitrary fixed constant. The first term H_1 of the objective function H represents the data model:

$$H_1(d\lambda, I_s) = \sum_{s \in S} \rho \left[d\lambda_s \mathbf{v}_s \nabla \tilde{I}_2(\mathbf{s}) + \tilde{I}_2(\mathbf{s}) - I_1(\mathbf{s}) \right], \tag{7}$$

where $\tilde{I}_2 \triangleq \{I_2(\mathbf{s} + \mathbf{n}_s + \lambda_s \mathbf{v}_s), \ \mathbf{s} \in S\}$ is the backward registered version of the second image. The second prior H_2 is the smoothness term which favors piecewise smooth disparity solutions. This term is expressed over all pairs $<s, r> \in \mathcal{C}$ of mutual neighbors (according to a 4-neighborhood system in our implementation):

$$H_2(d\lambda) = \sum_{<s,r> \in \mathcal{C}} \rho(\|\mathbf{d}_s - \mathbf{d}_r\|).$$

To cope with large deviations from the data model (resp. to allow disparity depth discontinuities), H_1 (resp. H_2) includes a M–estimator, ρ. Under some simple conditions [3, 5], (mainly the concavity of $\phi(v) \triangleq \rho(\sqrt{u})$), any multidimensional minimization of the form "find $\arg\min_{x_i} \sum_i \rho(g_i(x))$" is equivalent to an optimization problem of the form "find $\arg\min_{x,z_i} \sum_i \tau z_i g_i(x)^2 + \psi(z_i)$" involving auxiliary variables (or weights) z_i's continuously lying in $(0, 1]$. The function ψ (which is never used in practice) is a decreasing function depending on ρ. In our case, the weights are of two natures: (a) the data outliers weights, $\delta = \{\delta_s, \ \mathbf{s} \in S\}$ (provided by the semi-quadratic formulation of H_1, and (b) the discontinuity weights $\beta = \{\beta_{sr}, \ < s, r > \in \mathcal{C}\}$ related to the semi-quadratic formulation of H_2 and lying on the dual edge grid. The estimation problem is now expressed as a global minimization in $(d\lambda, \beta, \delta)$ of $\mathcal{H} = \mathcal{H}_1 + \alpha \mathcal{H}_2$ where:

$$\begin{cases} \mathcal{H}_1 = \sum_{s \in S} \tau_1 \delta_s [d\lambda_s \mathbf{v}_s . \nabla \tilde{I}_2(\mathbf{s}) + \tilde{I}_2(\mathbf{s}) - I_1(\mathbf{s})]^2 + \psi(\delta_s) \\ \mathcal{H}_2 = \sum_{<s,r> \in \mathcal{C}} \tau_2 \beta_{sr} \| d\lambda_s \mathbf{v}_s + \lambda_s \mathbf{v}_s + \mathbf{n}_s - \mathbf{d}_r \|^2 + \psi(\beta_{sr}) \end{cases},$$

where $\mathbf{d}_r = (\lambda_r + d\lambda_r)\mathbf{v}_r + \mathbf{n}_r$. The scalar τ_i a parameter depending on the M–estimator chosen.

The energy contribution of a point $\mathbf{s}$ to $\mathcal{H}_1$ is thus weighted by a factor $\delta_s \in (0, 1]$: the larger the contribution, the smaller the weight. Similarly, each pair of neighbors $< s, r > \in \mathcal{C}$ contributes to $\mathcal{H}_2$ with a weight $\beta_{sr} \in (0, 1]$ depending on their displacement vector difference $\|\mathbf{d}_s - \mathbf{d}_r\|$. The larger the difference, the smaller the weight.

The resulting semi-quadratic minimization problem is conducted alternatively with respect to the different variables (here the scalar field $d\lambda$ and the two weight fields δ and β). The minimization with respect to weights are given in the following closed from [3, 5]:

$$\arg\min_{z_i} \sum_i z_i g_i(x)^2 + \psi(z_i) = \frac{\rho'(g_i(x))}{2g_i(x)}.$$

Now considering weights as being frozen, the minimization with respect to $d\lambda_s$ is a classical weighted quadratic problem solved using an iterative method. Using a Gauss-Seidel scheme, the local update $d\lambda_s^{(n)}$ at iteration n of the iterative solver is given by:

$$d\lambda_s^{(n)} = \frac{\alpha(-\lambda_s\bar{\beta}_s + \mathbf{v}_s.\boldsymbol{\omega}_s^{n-1}) - \delta_s\mathbf{v}_s.\nabla\tilde{I}_2(\mathbf{s}).I_t(\mathbf{s})}{\delta_s(\mathbf{v}_s.\nabla\tilde{I}_2(\mathbf{s})^2 + \alpha\bar{\beta}_s}, \tag{8}$$

where $\boldsymbol{\omega}_s^{n-1}$ is the weighted average of neighboring disparity vectors at iteration $n-1$ and $\bar{\beta}_s$ is the sum the spatial discontinuity variables between s and its neighbors.

Let us note that in case of long range disparity, an initial disparity field is necessary to avoid solutions corresponding to undesirable local minima. In our case, we consider an initialization derived from the interpolation of the initial matched points of interest used for the computation of the fundamental matrix. We have used here a bilinear interpolation based on a Delaunay triangulation. The resulting field is projected on the top level of the pyramid to provide an initial disparity field for the coarsest resolution level with respect to the associated epipolar geometry (projection on the associated epipolar lines (see fig. 2)).

3 Segmentation

As our final goal is to provide a 3D reconstruction of the scene easy to handle, we now introduce a segmentation method of the dense disparity field obtained at the previous step. The method we propose is based on a adaptive triangular mesh structure. The idea of our technique consists in recursively splitting an initial mesh until each triangular element corresponds to a 3D planar element. The associated splitting criterion is based on the homographic parametric model-description of the disparity field. It can be easily shown that, according to a pinhole camera model, the disparity associated with a planar surface projected respectively as Π_1 in the first image and Π_2 in the second image satisfies an homographic model. This model is linear using homogeneous coordinates. For sake of clarity, all the following expressions are meant to be expressed in homogeneous coordinates. The homographic model links two corresponding points $\mathbf{s}$ and $\mathbf{s} + \mathbf{d}_s$ of Π_1 and Π_2 with a 3×3 homogeneous homography matrix named H up to a scalar factor μ:

$$\forall \mathbf{s} \in \Pi_1, H\mathbf{s} = \mu(\mathbf{s} + \mathbf{d}_s).$$

The segmentation step we propose consists thus in triangulating the disparity map until the disparity vectors associated with each patch correspond to a single representative homographic model. An initial Delaunay triangulation is first performed by taking four arbitrary points near to the corner of the image. This triangulation is then refined until each triangle verifies a distance criterion between the dense estimation disparity and an homographic model estimated within the considered triangle.

3.1 Homography estimation

The homography estimation is performed using a method proposed by Robert and Faugeras [13]. The method relies on the epipolar geometry to efficiently estimate the homography matrix from three or more corresponding pairs of points.

For H to be consistent with epipolar geometry, the homogeneous symmetric matrix $F^T H + H^T F$ must be null. This leads to 6 homogeneous equations with unknowns h_{ij} (the coefficient of H). In our case, each point of a considered triangle T accounts for one scalar equation. we have therefore the following system of equation:

$$\forall \mathbf{s} \in T, \ [\mathbf{s} + \mathbf{d}_s, F\mathbf{s}, H\mathbf{s}] = 0,$$

where $[a, b, c]$ denotes the triple product.

This over-constrained system can be rewritten in matrix notation as $A\mathbf{h} = 0$, where $\mathbf{h}$ is a 8 components vector gathering the unknown coefficients of H and A is a $(|\{\mathbf{s} \in T\}| + 6) \times 8$ matrix. An estimate of $\mathbf{h}$ is computed using a SVD (singular value decomposition) of the matrix $A^t A$.

To be robust to problematic situations where the estimated disparities are likely to be biased or erroneous (such as occlusion areas or range discontinuities), we exclude from this system points which are not simultaneously in accordance with the data model and the smoothing model (points for which the data outliers and the discontinuity weights approach zero).

3.2 Splitting criterion

The distance criterion we chose to handle the splitting of the triangular mesh is decomposed in two terms:

- The first one measures the adequacy of H to the disparity field. The influence of each point $\mathbf{s}$ of the triangle is weighted by the data model weight $\delta_\mathbf{s}$ coming from the robust estimator associated with the data model of the dense disparity estimator (occlusion areas do not influence the distance measurement). The resulting adequacy term is given by:

$$C_1(T, H, \mathbf{d}) = \frac{1}{\sum_{\mathbf{s} \in T} \delta_\mathbf{s}} \sum_{\mathbf{s} \in T} \delta_\mathbf{s}[\|H\mathbf{s} - (\mathbf{s} + \mathbf{d}_s)\|^2 + \|H^{-1}(\mathbf{s} + \mathbf{d}_s) - \mathbf{s}\|^2],$$

$$(9)$$

where $\| \ \|$ denotes the Euclidean distance.
- The second term is related to the presence of disparity discontinuities within the considered triangle. This term is defined as the mean of discontinuity weights included in the considered triangle. It is expressed as follows:

$$\begin{cases} C_2(T, \beta) = \frac{\sum_{<\mathbf{s}, \mathbf{r}> \in \mathcal{C}_T} \beta_{\mathbf{s}, \mathbf{r}}}{|\mathcal{C}_T|} \\ \mathcal{C}_T \overset{\triangle}{=} \{< \mathbf{s}, \mathbf{r} >, \mathbf{s} \in T, \mathbf{r} \in T\}, \mathcal{C}_T \subset \mathcal{C} \end{cases} \qquad (10)$$

where $< \mathbf{s}, \mathbf{r} >$ denotes neighboring pixel of image 1.

More precisely, a given triangle T is split if the global criterion $C_1(T, H, \mathbf{d}) + \gamma C_2(T, \beta)$ exceeds a given threshold ϵ. The parameter γ is an arbitrary fixed positive constant.

3.3 Triangulation refinement

A given triangle is refined by adding a point located at its "center of mass"; the mass of each point being given by the value of their associated data outliers weights. The iterative triangulation refinement is performed until the distance measure $C(T)$ computed for each triangle decreases below ϵ.

4 3D reconstruction

So far we have obtained a 2D triangulation of the first image and an associated disparity information. The last step of our method consists in recovering 3D information in order to build the final 3D model. To that end, the calibration parameters of the cameras have to be estimated. As the aim is not an accurate reconstruction but a visually satisfactory 3D representation we have used a simplified self-calibration technique. This approach consists to fix to some arbitrary values the intrinsic parameters (represented by the A matrix) and then to estimate the extrinsic parameters. The intrinsic parameters are chosen in order to respect the following assumptions: the projection of the optical center is supposed to be at the center of the image, coordinate image axes are perpendicular, horizontal and vertical pixel sizes are fixed and equal to one and the focal length is assigned to a realistic value. The fundamental matrix F allows to access to the essential matrix E. This matrix only depends on the extrinsic parameters composed of the rotation matrix R and the translation vector between the first and the second camera location:

$$E = A^T F A = [\mathbf{t}]_\times R, \tag{11}$$

where $[\mathbf{t}]_\times$ is an antisymmetric cross product matrix associated to the translation vector $\mathbf{t}$. As shown by Tsai and Huang in [16], the essential matrix can be decomposed in order to recover rotation and translation parameters. Using a singular value decomposition, E can be written as follows:

$$E = \Delta E' \Theta^t, \tag{12}$$

where Δ and Θ are two orthogonal matrices and E' is a diagonal matrix. It can be shown that an essential matrix has one null singular value, while the two others have the same value (they can be assigned to 1 because of the homogeneous property) [16]. Matrix E' can thus be rewritten as follows:

$$
\begin{aligned}
E' &= T_1 R_1 \\
&= \begin{pmatrix} 0 & 0 & 0 \\ 0 & 0 & 1 \\ 0 & -1 & 0 \end{pmatrix} \begin{pmatrix} 1 & 0 & 0 \\ 0 & 0 & -1 \\ 0 & 1 & 0 \end{pmatrix}.
\end{aligned} \tag{13}
$$

Injecting this decomposition in equation (12) leads to write the matrix E as a product of an antisymmetric matrix by an orthogonal one. By identification with equation (11), we can extract rotation and translation matrices:

$$E = \underbrace{\Delta T_1 \Delta}_{[\mathbf{t}]_\times} \underbrace{\Delta^t R_1 \Theta^t}_{R}$$

We must notice that this decomposition is not unique. The rotation is only defined up to π while the translation is defined up to a scalar factor. The adequate pair of matrices is obtained by ensuring a 3D reconstructed point to be in view of the camera.

The resulting intrinsic and extrinsic parameters lead to two projection matrices. The nodes of the triangulation are then re-projected into the 3D space by solving the system (1) according to the dense disparity field. The 3D mesh is coded in the VRML language to allow real time interactivity. To avoid texture projection artifacts due to affine mapping, a preliminary simple correction is processed (an homographic transformation is performed to set the texture collinear to the image plane).

5   Results

The proposed method has been applied on different kinds of image sequences. It has been run both on real world sequences and synthetic sequences for which a ground truth exits.

The first sequence we are considering here is the well known synthetic "Yosemite sequence" (fig. 3). In order to satisfy the rigidity assumption, a major part of the sky containing moving clouds has been removed. Two different image pairs of this sequence have been considered. In the first one, which is composed of two consecutive images (images 9 and 10) the small range of the displacements (not more than 4 pixels) makes critical the estimation of the epipolar geometry. The second image pair, composed of far apart images in the sequence, constitutes a difficult benchmark towards the differential aspect of our method (up to 30 pixels of displacement).

As expected and shown on the recovered disparity map (fig. 3d), the disparities are larger in the mountain area in the foreground and continuously decreases while we move towards the valley. The global aspect of this map is in accordance with what could be expected from visual inspection.

Following [1], we provide quantitative comparative results on this pair of images. Angular deviations with respect to the actual flow field have been computed. Table 5 lists the mean angular value error and associated the standard deviation. It gathers some results presented in [1], and by other authors (only the higher and the lower mean square error obtained by state of the art methods are presented in comparison with the classical Horn and Schunck algorithm). Let us note, we report here only performances of similar algorithms (energy based dense estimators). Other results of more complex method combining motion estimation with a joint segmentation may be found in the literature. As may be

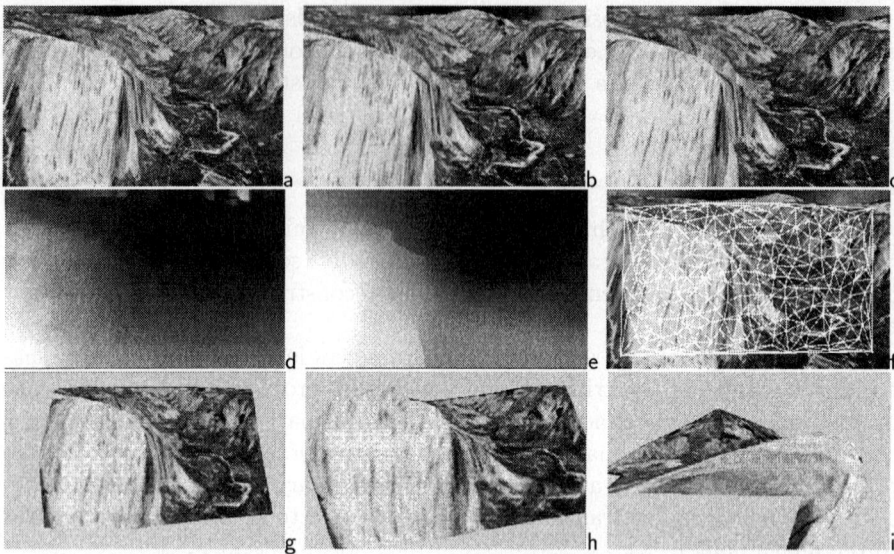

Fig. 3. Original images 3 (a), 11 (b) and 12 (c) of the "Yosemite" sequence; disparity map for images 11 and 12 (d) and 3 and 12 (e) (the darker the smaller the disparity value) and final triangulation (f); reconstructed images for translation along Z axis (small (g), important (h)) and for a complex motion (viewpoint on the left of the foreground mountain (i)

Technique	Mean error	Standard deviation
Horn and Schunck [1]	9.78^o	16.19^o
Black [2]	3.52^o	3.25^o
Lai and Vemuri[10]	1.99^o	1.45^o
Our method	4.82^o	3.27^o

Table 1. Comparative results on Yosemite

observed, compared to others our method yields to a higher angular discrepancy. Let us note meanwhile, it stays satisfactory. A few remarks must be done at this point. First at the opposite of the best methods mentioned in the table, our method uses a simple iterative solver (Gauss-Seidel). It could be therefore improved by using more efficient solvers. Second, it must be pointed out, that our method is a *one-dimensional method*. It is therefore far more faster than the others. Besides, due to small motion the epipolar geometry is quite difficult to estimate accurately.

Let us now consider the second sequence, composed of far apart images (images 3 and 12) of the "Yosemite" sequence. Experiments on this sequence have shown that, due to the presence of very large displacements (up to 30 pixels of displacement), non constrained optical flow estimators (even embedded in a multiresolution framework) do not converge towards acceptable solutions. As shown in the disparity map presented figure 3e our method provides consistent results. The foreground mountain is characterized by important disparity values whereas in the background, disparities decrease smoothly. The dense disparity field estimation performs well for an image presenting both small and large displacements. The resulting field is globally smooth but presents discontinuities on important depth changes.

The disparity field computed from images 3 and 12 has been then iteratively triangulated to obtain a 2D model of the valley. The associated VRML model has been computed by arbitrarily fixing the focal length to 1000. Figure 3 presents some interpolated and extrapolated images. The camera displacement along the z-axis is not far away from the real 3D motion in images 3g and 3h. The resulting images are visually satisfactory. Image 3i exemplifies more complex displacements illustrating occlusion problems.

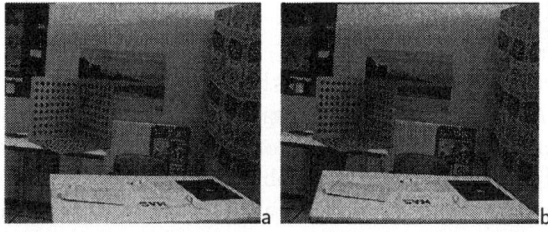

Fig. 4. Two original images of an indoor sequence (a) and (b)

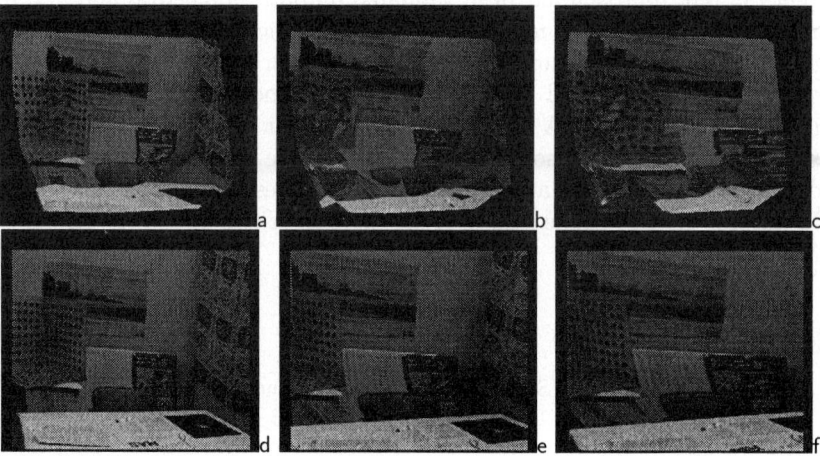

Fig. 5. Three synthesized views from the same view point: model computed directly from automatically extracted and matched points (a, (b and (c; same 3D motion simulation as previously with the model obtained by our method ((d corresponds to (a, (e to (b and (f to (c)

Some reconstruction results obtained for a static scene shot by a moving commercial camera (fig. 4) are shown in figure 5. Two kind of reconstruction are presented here. The first one comes from the "image-matching" software, developed by Zhang [17], which gives a list of matching points of interest that respect the epipolar geometry. These points are triangulated and re-projected to obtain a 3D model. The examples presented in figure 5a 5b and 5c are constructed from 89 automatically extracted matching points. The synthesized views outline the presence of outliers points that make the model visually uncomfortable. This effect can mostly be explained by the presence of spurious matches that respect both the epipolar geometry and the luminance consistency. The second 3D model results from our algorithm (fig. 5d, 5e and 5f). A visual inspection of the reconstructed images shows far less artifacts for the same 3D displacements of the virtual camera. Such results could now be used in the context of video manipulation applications.

6 Conclusion

In this paper we have presented a method for the reconstruction of complex scene from a pair of uncalibrated images. This method relies on the estimation of a dense disparity field. The estimator proposed here is constrained by the epipolar geometry and incorporates robust function. We have experimentally demonstrated that the recovered fields are of good quality even in unfavorable case (very close views). The final 3D reconstruction is obtained through a segmentation process handled as a recursive adaptation of a triangular mesh. The outliers informations provided by the dense robust estimation are also used in the segmentation step to improve the quality of the final reconstruction. The efficiency of our approach has been validated on both polyhedral and non polyhedral complex scenes. The models obtained are sufficiently good to be used in a comfortable way in the context of video manipulation applications. Nevertheless, more accurate results could be expected using the best self-calibration method available in the literature. A natural extension of our algorithm would consist in considering the trifocal tensor (associated with three images [15]) instead of the fundamental matrix F, to avoid many degenerate estimation cases of F. This could naturally lead to take into account more than two images to improve the VRML model quality.

References

1. J. Barron, D. Fleet, and S. Beauchemin. Performance of optical flow techniques. *International Journal on Computer Vision*, 12(1):43–77, 1994.
2. M. Black. Recursive non-linear estimation of discontinuous flow fields. In *Proceedings of the European Conf. on Computer Vision*, pages 138–145, Stockholm, Sweden, 1994.
3. M.J. Black and A. Rangarajan. On the unification of line processes, outlier rejection, and robust statistics with applications in early vision. *International Journal on Computer Vision*, 19(1):57–91, July 1996.

4. B. Boufama and R. Mohr. Epipole and fundamental matrix estimation using the virtual parallax property. In *Proc. Int. Conf. Computer Vision*, pages 1030–1036, Cambridge, Massachusetts, 1995.

5. P. Charbonnier, L. Blanc-Féraud, G. Aubert, and M. Barlaud. Deterministic edge-preserving regularization in computed imaging. *IEEE Trans. on Image Processing*, 6(2):298–311, 1997.

6. O. Faugeras and S. Laveau. Representing three-dimensional data as a collection of images and fundamental matrices for image synthesis. In *Proceedings of International Conf. on Pattern Recognition*, pages 689–691, Jerusalem, Israel, 1994.

7. P. Havaldar, M-S. Lee, and G. Medioni. View synthesis from unregistered 2-d images. In *Graphics Interface*, pages 61–69, Toronto, Canada, May 1996.

8. T. Kanade, P.J. Narayanan, and P.W. Rander. Virtualized reality: Concept and early results. In *Workshop on Representation of Visual Scenes*, Cambridge, USA, 1995.

9. R. Koch, M. Pollefeys, and L. Van Gool. Automatic 3d model acquisition from uncalibrated image sequences. In *Computer Graphics International*, pages 597–604, Hannover, 1998.

10. S. Lai and B. Vemuri. Reliable and efficient computation of optical flow. *IJCV*, 29(2):87–105, 1998.

11. H.C. Longuet-Higgins. The reconstruction of a scene from two projections: configurations that defeat the 8-point algorithm. In *Proceedings of the 1st Conference on Artificial intelligence applications*, pages 395–397, Denver, 1984.

12. L. Robert and R. Deriche. Dense depth map reconstruction: A minimization and regularization approach which preserves discontinuities. In *Proceedings of the 4th European Conf. on Computer Vision*, volume 1, pages 439–451, 1996.

13. L. Robert and O. Faugeras. Relative 3-D positioning and 3-D convex hull computation from a weakly calibrated stereo pair. *Image and Vision Computing*, 13(3):189–197, 1995.

14. P.J. Rousseeuw and A.M. Leroy. *Robust Regression and Outlier Detection*. John Wiley & Sons, New York, 1987.

15. P.H.S. Torr and A. Zisserman. Robust parameterization and computation of the trifocal tensor. *Image and Vision Computing*, 15:591–605, 1997.

16. R. Tsai and T. Huang. Uniqueness and estimation of three dimensional motion parameters of rigid objects with curved surface. *Transaction on Pattern Analysis ans Machine intelligence*, 6:13–26, 1984.

17. Z. Zhang. Estimating motion and structure from correspondences of line segments between two perspective images. *IEEE Transactions on Pattern Analysis and Machine Intelligence*, 17(12):1129–1139, 1995.

Camera Pose Estimation and Reconstruction from Image Profiles under Circular Motion

Paulo R. S. Mendonça, Kwan-Yee K. Wong, and Roberto Cipolla

Department of Engineering, University of Cambridge
Trumpington Street, Cambridge, UK, CB2 1PZ
{prdsm2, kykw2, cipolla}@eng.cam.ac.uk

Abstract. This paper addresses the problem of motion estimation and reconstruction of 3D models from profiles of an object rotating on a turntable, obtained from a single camera. Its main contribution is the development of a practical and accurate technique for solving this problem from profiles alone, which is, for the first time, precise enough to allow the reconstruction of the object. No correspondence between points or lines are necessary, although the method proposed can be equally used when these features are available, without any further adaptation. Symmetry properties of the surface of revolution swept out by the rotating object are exploited to obtain the image of the rotation axis and the homography relating epipolar lines, in a robust and elegant way. These, together with geometric constraints for images of rotating objects, are then used to obtain first the image of the horizon, which is the projection of the plane that contains the camera centres, and then the epipoles, thus fully determining the epipolar geometry of the sequence of images. The estimation of the epipolar geometry by this sequential approach (image of rotation axis — homography — image of the horizon — epipoles) avoids many of the problems usually found in other algorithms for motion recovery from profiles. In particular, the search for the epipoles, by far the most critical step, is carried out as a simple one-dimensional optimisation problem. The initialisation of the parameters is trivial and completely automatic for all stages of the algorithm. After the estimation of the epipolar geometry, the Euclidean motion is recovered using the fixed intrinsic parameters of the camera, obtained either from a calibration grid or from self-calibration techniques. Finally, the spinning object is reconstructed from its profiles, using the motion estimated in the previous stage. Results from real data are presented, demonstrating the efficiency and usefulness of the proposed methods.

1 Introduction

Methods for motion estimation and 3D reconstruction from point or line correspondences in a sequence of images have achieved a high level of sophistication, with impressive results [12, 8]. Nevertheless, if corresponding points are not available the current techniques cannot be applied. That is exactly the case when the scene being viewed is composed by non-textured smooth surfaces, and in this situation the predominant feature in the image is the *profile* or *apparent contour* of the surface [13]. Besides, even when point correspondences can be established, the profile still offers important clues for determining both motion and shape, and therefore should be used whenever available.

This work presents a method for motion estimation and reconstruction of an object rotating around a fixed axis from information provided by its profiles. It makes use of symmetry properties of the surface of revolution swept out by the rotating object to overcome the main difficulties and drawbacks present in other methods which have attempted to estimate motion from apparent contours, namely: the need for a very good initialisation for the epipolar geometry and an unrealistic demand of a large number of *epipolar tangencies* [5, 1, 2] (here as few as two epipolar tangencies are needed), restriction to linear motion [18] (whereas circular motion is a more practical situation), or the use of an affine approximation [14, 22] (which may be used only for shallow scenes). After obtaining the motion, the reconstruction can be achieved by a simple technique, based on the epipolar parameterisation [6], which extends the common triangulation methods from points to profiles.

The first attempts to approach the problem of motion estimation from apparent contours date back to Rieger, in 1986 [17], who introduced the concept of *frontier point*, interpreted as "centres of spin" [*sic*] of the image motion. The paper dealt with the case of fronto-parallel orthographic projection, which is a rather restrictive situation. This idea was further developed by Porrill [16], who recognised the frontier point as a fixed point on the surface, corresponding to the intersection of two consecutive *contour generators* [6]. The connection between the epipolar geometry and the frontier points was established in [10], and an algorithm for motion estimation from profiles was introduced in [5].

Related works also include [1], where a technique based on registering the images using a planar curve was first developed. This method was implemented in [7], which also showed results of reconstruction from the estimated motion. In [14] the algorithm presented in [5] is specialised to the affine case.

The first steps towards a solution for the problem of reconstruction from apparent contours with known camera motion were given by Barrow and Tenenbaum, in 1981 [3], where a technique to compute surface normals was introduced. Koenderink [13] established relations between the differential geometry of a surface and the differential geometry of its profiles. This work was extended in [9], where algorithms for computing the curvature of a surface from its profiles were developed and implemented for orthographic projection.

In [20] a reconstruction method based on parameterising the surface by *radial curves* was developed. Better results can be achieved by using an *epipolar parameterisation*, together with an interpolation using the *osculating circle*, as introduced in [6]. Further refinements were obtained in [4], and a simple technique was developed in [22], based on a finite-difference implementation of [6]. Despite its simplicity, the method developed in [22] renders results comparable to those in [4] and [6], and was thus the technique chosen to be used here.

An interesting comparison can be made between the work presented here and [8]. Both papers tackle the same problem, but while in [8] hundreds of points are tracked and matched for each pair of adjacent images, it is shown here that a solution can be obtained even when only two epipolar tangencies are available, with at least comparable results.

Section 2 presents a summary of the theoretical background and notation used in the remaining of the paper. It reviews the symmetry properties of images of surfaces of revolution related to the *harmonic homology*, and presents two useful parameterisations of the fundamental matrix. These parameterisations allow the estimation of the epipoles to be carried out as independent one-dimensional searches, avoiding points of local minima. This greatly reduces the computational complexity of the estimation. Section 3 presents the algorithm for motion recovery, and the implementation of the algorithm for real data is shown in Section 4, which also makes comparisons with previous works. The reconstruction technique is described in Section 5, together with experimental results for reconstruction.

2 Theoretical Background

This section is a concise review of the mathematical background necessary for the rest of the paper, and only the main results will be presented. Details of the derivations can be found in [15].

2.1 Symmetry Properties of Images of Surfaces of Revolution

A 2D homography that keeps the pencil of lines through a point $\mathbf{u}$ and the set of points on a line $\mathbf{l}$ fixed is called a *perspective collineation* with centre $\mathbf{u}$ and axis $\mathbf{l}$. A *homology* is a perspective collineation whose centre and axis are not incident (otherwise the perspective homology is called *elation*). Let $\mathbf{x}$ be a point mapped by an homology onto a point $\mathbf{x}'$ and let $\mathbf{q}$ be the line passing through these points. The point of intersection of $\mathbf{q}$ and $\mathbf{l}$ is denoted by $\mathbf{v}$. If $\mathbf{x}$ and $\mathbf{x}'$ are harmonic conjugates with respect to $\mathbf{u}$ and $\mathbf{v}$, i.e., their cross-ratio is one, the homology is said to be a *harmonic homology* (see details in [19, Chapter IX]). A curve or set of points invariant to a harmonic homology will be henceforth called *harmonically symmetric*.

Consider an object rotating about a fixed axis. The surface of the object sweeps out a surface of revolution S. The image of S taken by a pinhole camera $\mathbf{P}$ is a curve s. Let $\mathbf{l_s}$ be the image of the axis of rotation of the surface S in the camera $\mathbf{P}$. The optical centre of $\mathbf{P}$ and the axis of rotation define a plane $\varPsi$, whose normal direction is $\mathbf{n}_\varPsi$. The image of the point at infinity in the direction $\mathbf{n}_\varPsi$ is the vanishing point $\mathbf{v}_x$.

If $\mathbf{v}_x$ and $\mathbf{l_s}$ are represented in homogeneous coordinates, the 2D collineation $\mathbf{W}$ given by

$$\mathbf{W} = \mathbb{I} - 2\frac{\mathbf{v}_x \mathbf{l}_s^{\mathrm{T}}}{\mathbf{v}_x^{\mathrm{T}} \mathbf{l}_s} \tag{1}$$

is a harmonic homology, and s is harmonically symmetric with respect to $\mathbf{W}$. It is worth remembering that $\mathbf{W}$ is an involutary matrix, i.e., $\mathbf{W}^2 = \mathbb{I}$. It can be shown that if the camera $\mathbf{P}$ points towards the axis of rotation, the harmonic homology $\mathbf{W}$ reduces to a skew symmetry transformation, and the curve s will simply be skew symmetric about $\mathbf{l_s}$. Furthermore, if the camera aspect ratio is one and the skew is zero, the skew symmetry transformation becomes a mirroring, and the curve s will be bilaterally symmetrical about $\mathbf{l_s}$, as shown in Figure 1.

2.2 Parameterisations of the Fundamental Matrix

Consider a pair of camera matrices $\mathbf{P}_1$ and $\mathbf{P}_2$ related by a rotation with an angle $\theta \neq 0$ about an axis $\mathbf{a}$ not passing through their optical centres, represented as the matrix $\mathbf{R}_\mathbf{a}^\theta$. The image of the plane containing the optical centres of the cameras and orthogonal to the axis a is the *horizon*, and it is represented as the line $\mathbf{l}_\mathrm{h}$ in homogeneous coordinates. The fundamental matrix $\mathbf{F}$ relating $\mathbf{P}_1$ and $\mathbf{P}_2$ is given by (see [21, 8])

$$\mathbf{F} = [\mathbf{v}_x]_\times + k \tan\frac{\theta}{2}(\mathbf{l_s}\mathbf{l}_\mathrm{h}^{\mathrm{T}} + \mathbf{l}_\mathrm{h}\mathbf{l}_s^{\mathrm{T}}), \tag{2}$$

with $\mathbf{l}_\mathrm{h}^{\mathrm{T}}\mathbf{v}_x = 0$, using the notation of Section 2.1. The parameter k is unknown but fixed for any angle θ, and cannot be obtained from two images alone. This should be expected, since the terms in (2) are in homogeneous coordinates, and thus defined only up to arbitrary scale factors.

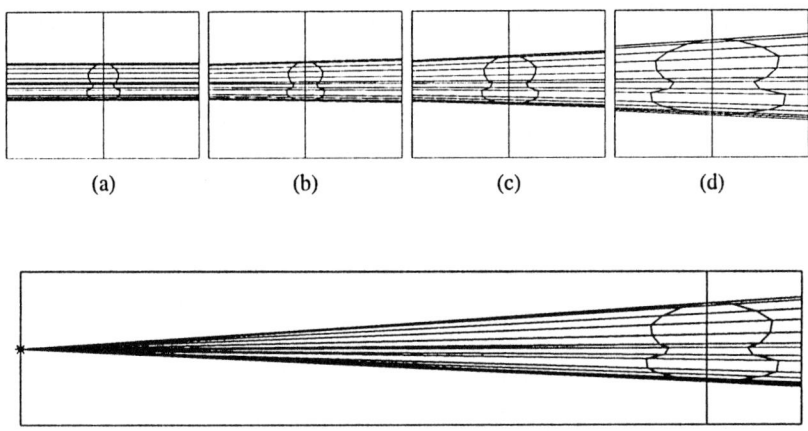

(a)　　　　　(b)　　　　　(c)　　　　　(d)

(e)

Fig. 1. Lines joining points which are symmetric about the image of rotation axis l_s (images are scaled and translated independently for better observation). (a) The optical axis points directly towards the rotation axis. (b) The camera is rotated about its optical centre by an angle ρ of $20°$ in a plane orthogonal to the rotation axis. (c) $\rho = 40°$. (d) $\rho = 60°$. (e) Same as (d), but the vanishing point $\mathbf{v}_x$ is also shown.

From (2) it is easy to prove that the epipole $\mathbf{e}_i$, formed in the image of camera $\mathbf{P}_i$, is given by

$$\mathbf{e}_i = \mathbf{v}_x - (-1)^i k \tan \frac{\theta}{2} [l_s]_\times l_h. \tag{3}$$

From (3) it can be seen that all the epipoles lie on the horizon l_h, independently of the value of θ. It can also be shown that the parameterisation given by (2) is equivalent to

$$\mathbf{F} = [\mathbf{e}_2]_\times \mathbf{W}, \tag{4}$$

where $\mathbf{W}$ is given by (1), and, moreover, $\mathbf{e}_1 = \mathbf{W}\mathbf{e}_2$. The result in (4) shows that there is a plane in space that induces the homology $\mathbf{W}$. The proof of the following theorem does not appear anywhere else, and it will be shown here in more detail.

Theorem 1. *The planar homology $\mathbf{W}$ relating the cameras $\mathbf{P}_1$ and $\mathbf{P}_2$ with $\theta \neq n\pi$, $n \in \mathbb{Z}$, is induced by the plane Ξ that contains the axis of rotation $\mathbf{a}$ and bisects the segment joining the optical centres of the cameras.*

Proof. The existence and uniqueness of Ξ satisfying the hypothesis of the Theorem are trivial. Let $\mathbf{x}_1 = [1\ 0\ 0]^T$, $\mathbf{x}_2 = [0\ 1\ 0]^T$, and $\mathbf{x}_3 = [0\ 0\ 1]^T$. Without loss of generality, let

$$\mathbf{P}_1 = \mathbf{K}\mathbf{R}[\mathbb{I}\,|\,\mathbf{x}_3] \quad \text{and}$$
$$\mathbf{P}_2 = \mathbf{K}\mathbf{R}[\mathbf{R}_y^\theta\,|\,\mathbf{x}_3], \tag{5}$$

where $\mathbf{K}$ is the intrinsic parameters matrix of $\mathbf{P}_1$ and $\mathbf{P}_2$, $\mathbf{R}$ is the rotation matrix relating the orientation of the coordinate system of $\mathbf{P}_1$ to the world coordinate system, and $\mathbf{R}_y^\theta$ is a rotation by θ about the y-axis of the world coordinate system, i.e.,

$$\mathbf{R}_y^\theta = \begin{bmatrix} \cos\theta & 0 & \sin\theta \\ 0 & 1 & 0 \\ -\sin\theta & 0 & \cos\theta \end{bmatrix}. \tag{6}$$

Therefore, $\forall \alpha, \beta \in \mathbb{R}$, the point $\mathbf{X} = [-\alpha\sin(\theta/2) \; \beta \; \alpha\cos(\theta/2)]^T$ lies on Ξ. Projecting $\mathbf{X}$ using $\mathbf{P}_1$ and $\mathbf{P}_2$, one obtains $\mathbf{u}_1 = \mathbf{KR}(\mathbf{X} + \mathbf{x}_3)$ and $\mathbf{u}_2 = \mathbf{KR}(\mathbf{R}_y^\theta \mathbf{X} + \mathbf{x}_3)$. Since

$$\mathbf{R}_y^\theta \mathbf{X} = \begin{bmatrix} \alpha\sin\theta\cos(\theta/2) - \alpha\cos\theta\sin(\theta/2) \\ \beta \\ \alpha\sin\theta\sin(\theta/2) + \alpha\cos\theta\cos(\theta/2) \end{bmatrix}$$

$$= \begin{bmatrix} \alpha\sin(\theta/2) \\ \beta \\ \alpha\cos(\theta/2) \end{bmatrix} = \begin{bmatrix} -1 & 0 & 0 \\ 0 & 1 & 0 \\ 0 & 0 & 1 \end{bmatrix} \mathbf{X}, \tag{7}$$

or $\mathbf{R}_y^\theta \mathbf{X} = (\mathbb{I} - 2\mathbf{x}_1\mathbf{x}_1^T)\mathbf{X}$, we have $\mathbf{u}_2 = \mathbf{KR}[(\mathbb{I} - 2\mathbf{x}_1\mathbf{x}_1^T)\mathbf{X} + \mathbf{x}_3]$, or $\mathbf{u}_2 = (\mathbb{I} - 2\mathbf{KR}\mathbf{x}_1\mathbf{x}_1^T\mathbf{R}^{-1}\mathbf{K}^{-1})\mathbf{u}_1$. It can be shown [15] that $\mathbf{KR}\mathbf{x}_1 = \mathbf{v}_x$ and $\mathbf{x}_1^T\mathbf{R}^{-1}\mathbf{K}^{-1} = \mathbf{l}_8^T$, and thus the result follows. $\qquad\square$

2.3 Epipolar Geometry and Apparent Contours

Consider a surface S of type C^1 viewed by two pinhole cameras $\mathbf{P}_1$ and $\mathbf{P}_2$. The following definitions are presented as a quick review:

- a *contour generator* associated with the surface S and the camera $\mathbf{P}_1$ corresponds to the space curve $\mathcal{C} \subset S$ such that for all points $c \in \mathcal{C}$ the line passing through the optical centre of $\mathbf{P}_1$ and c is tangent to S at c;
- the image of the contour generator associated with a camera $\mathbf{P}_1$ on this same camera is a *profile* or *apparent contour*;
- if two contour generators associated with the surface S and the cameras $\mathbf{P}_1$ and $\mathbf{P}_2$ intersect, the points of intersection are denoted *frontier points*;
- the epipolar plane Π defined by the optical centres of the two cameras $\mathbf{P}_1$ and $\mathbf{P}_2$ and the frontier point is tangent to the associated surface S;
- the epipolar lines corresponding to the epipolar plane Π are tangent to their associated apparent contours and are called *epipolar tangents*;

The tangent point of associated epipolar tangencies corresponds to the image of the same point on the surface S, namely the frontier point. All the above definitions can be better understood by looking at Figure 2.

3 Motion Estimation

Consider an object that undergoes a full rotation around a fixed axis. The envelope ϵ of its profiles is found by overlapping the images of the sequence and applying a Canny edge detector to the resultant image (Figure 3(b)). This envelope corresponds to the image of a surface of revolution, and thus it is harmonically symmetric. The homography $\mathbf{W}$ related to ϵ is then found by sampling N points $\mathbf{x}_i$ along ϵ and optimising the cost function

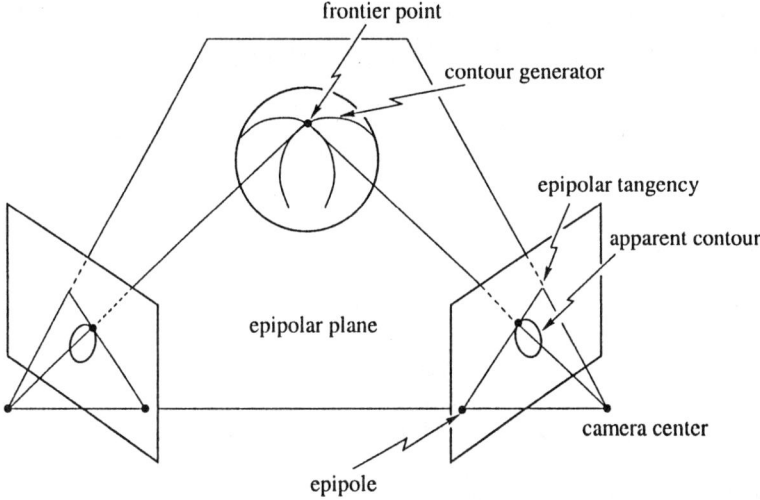

Fig. 2. The frontier point is a fixed point on the surface, corresponding to the intersection of two contour generators. The epipolar lines corresponding to the frontier point are tangent to the profile.

$$f_{\mathbf{W}}(\mathbf{v}_x, \mathbf{l}_s) = \sum_{i=1}^{N} \operatorname{dist}(\epsilon, \mathbf{W}(\mathbf{v}_x, \mathbf{l}_s)\mathbf{x}_i)^2, \tag{8}$$

where $\operatorname{dist}(\epsilon, \mathbf{W}(\mathbf{v}_x, \mathbf{l}_s)\mathbf{x}_i)$ is the distance between the curve ϵ and the transformed sample point $\mathbf{W}(\mathbf{v}_x, \mathbf{l}_s)\mathbf{x}_i$.

The initialisation of the line $\mathbf{l}_s$ and the point $\mathbf{v}_x$ can be made very close to the global minimum by automatically locating one or more pairs of corresponding bitangents on the envelope. The estimation of $\mathbf{W}$ is summarised in Algorithm 1.

Algorithm 1 Estimation of the harmonic homology $\mathbf{W}$.

---

overlap the images in sequence;
extract the envelope ϵ of the profiles using a Canny edge detector;
sample N points $\mathbf{x}_i$ along ϵ;
initialise the axis of symmetry $\mathbf{l}_s$ and the vanishing point $\mathbf{v}_x$ using bitangents
while not converged **do**
    transform the points $\mathbf{x}_i$ using $\mathbf{W}$;
    compute the distances between ϵ and the transformed points;
    update $\mathbf{l}_s$ and $\mathbf{v}_x$ to minimise the function in (8);
end while

After obtaining a good estimation of $\mathbf{W}$, one can then search for *epipolar tangencies* between pairs of images in the sequence using the parameterisation given by (4). To obtain a pair of corresponding epipolar tangents in two images, it is necessary to find a line tangent

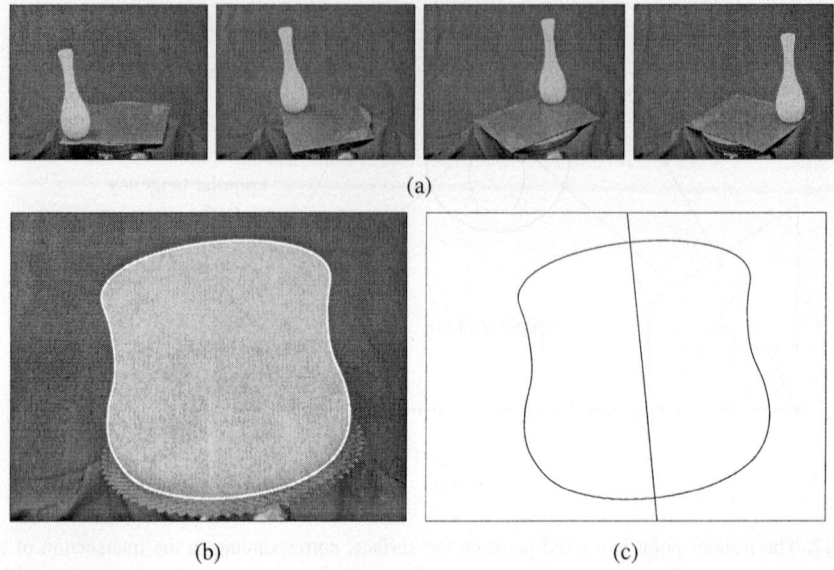

(a)

(b)   (c)

Fig. 3. (a) Image 1, 8, 15 and 22 in the sequence of 36 images of a rotating vase. (b) Envelope of apparent contours produced by overlapping all images in the sequence. (c) Estimation of the image of the rotation axis.

to one profile which is transformed by $\mathbf{W}^{-T}$ onto a line tangent to the profile in the other image (see Figure 4). The search for corresponding tangents may be carried out as a one-dimensional optimisation problem. The single parameter is the angle α that defines the orientation of the epipolar line $\mathbf{l}$ in the first image, and the cost function is given by

$$f_\alpha = \text{dist}(\mathbf{W}^{-T}\mathbf{l}(\alpha), \mathbf{l}'_{\parallel}(\alpha)), \tag{9}$$

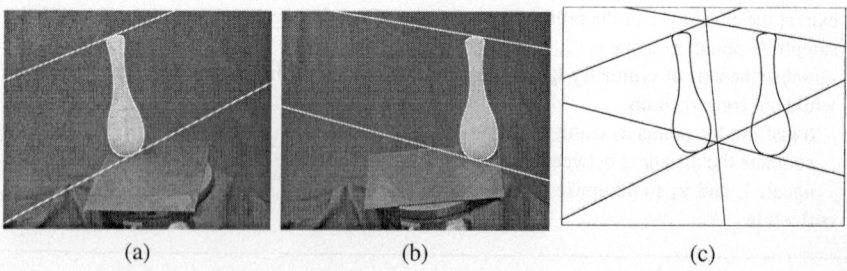

(a)   (b)   (c)

Fig. 4. A pair of images of an object undergoing circular motion with a rotation of $80°$ is shown in (a) and (b). The overlapping of the two images can be seen in (c). Corresponding epipolar lines intersect at the image of the rotation axis, and all epipoles lie on a common horizon.

where $\mathrm{dist}(\mathbf{W}^{-T}\mathbf{l}(\alpha), \mathbf{l}'_{\|}(\alpha))$ is the distance between the transformed line $\mathbf{l}' = \mathbf{W}^{-T}\mathbf{l}$ and a parallel line $\mathbf{l}'_{\|}$ tangent to the profile in the second image. Typical values of α lie between -0.5 rad and 0.5 rad, or $-30°$ and $30°$. The shape of the cost function (9) for the profiles in Figure 4 can be seen in Figure 5.

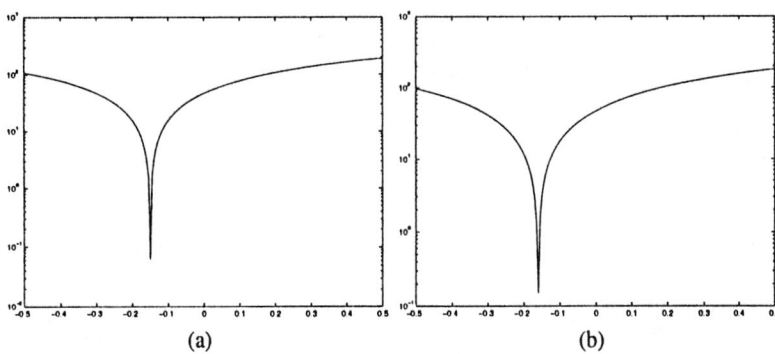

(a)   (b)

Fig. 5. Plot of the cost function (9) for a pair of images in the sequence. (a)/(b) Cost function for a pair of corresponding epipolar tangents near the top/bottom of the profile in Figure 4.

Algorithm 2 Estimation of the orientation of the epipolar lines.

extract the profiles of two adjacent images using a Canny edge detector;
fit b-splines to the top and the bottom of the profiles;
initialise α;
while not converged **do**
    find $\mathbf{l}$, $\mathbf{l}'$ and $\mathbf{l}'_{\|}$;
    compute the distance between $\mathbf{l}'$ and $\mathbf{l}'_{\|}$;
    update α to minimise the function in (9);
end while

The epipoles can then be computed as the intersection of epipolar lines at the same image. After obtaining this first estimate for the epipoles, the image of the horizon can then be found by robustly fitting a line $\mathbf{l}_h$ to the initial set of epipoles, such that $\mathbf{l}_h^T \mathbf{v}_x$.

An alternative method to compute the epipoles is to register the profiles using the homology $\mathbf{W}$, eliminating the effects of rotation on the images, and then apply any of the methods in [1, 18, 7], in a *plane + parallax* approach. However, no advantage has been obtained by doing so, since to use this method it is necessary to search for a common tangent between two profiles, which involves a search at least as complex as the one in Algorithm 2.

Figure 7 shows a typical output of Algorithm 2, together with the horizon $\mathbf{l}_h$ fitted to the epipoles. After estimating the horizon, the only missing term in the parameterisation of the fundamental matrix shown in (2) is the scale factor $k\tan\theta/2$. This parameter can be found by, again, a one-dimensional search that minimises the geometric error of transformed epipolar lines as shown in Fig 6.

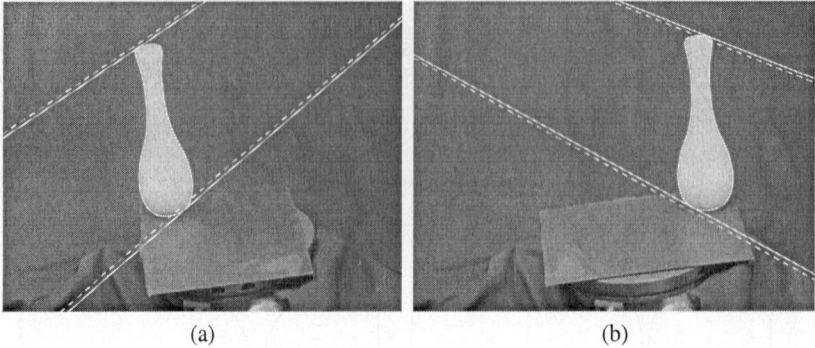

(a)   (b)

Fig. 6. Geometric error for transformed epipolar lines, with the scale factor $k \tan \theta/2$ in (3) set to 100, for better visualisation. The terms $\mathbf{v}_x$, $\mathbf{l}_s$ and $\mathbf{l}_h$ were obtained from Algorithm 1 and Algorithm 2. The solid lines in each correspond to tangents to the profile passing through the epipoles, and the dashed lines correspond to lines transferred from the one image to the other by applying the harmonic homology $\mathbf{W}$. The distance between transformed lines and the corresponding tangent points is the cost function that drives the search for the scale factor $k \tan \theta/2$ in (3).

4 Implementation and Experimental Results

The algorithms described in the previous session were tested using a set of 36 images of a vase placed on a turntable (see Figure 3(a)) rotated by an angle of $10°$ between successive snapshots. To obtain $\mathbf{W}$, Algorithm 1 was implemented with 100 evenly spaced sample points along the envelope ($N = 100$). Bitangents were used to find an initial guess for homology $\mathbf{W}$. Less then 10 iterations of the Levenberg-Marquadt algorithm are necessary, with derivatives computed by finite differences. The final configuration of the rotation axis can be seen in Figure 3(c).

In the implementation of Algorithm 2, 70 pairs of images were selected by uniformly sampling the indexes of the images, and the resultant estimate for the epipoles is shown in Figure 7, which also shows the horizon $\mathbf{l}_h$ found by a robust fit. To get $\mathbf{l}_h$ a minimisation of the median of the squares of the residuals was used, followed by removal of outliers and orthogonal least-squares regression using the remaining points (inliers). The epipolar geometry was then re-estimated with the epipoles constrained to lie on $\mathbf{l}_h$. The resulting camera configurations are presented in Figure 8.

The object was rotated on a manual turntable with resolution of $0.01°$, but the real precision achieved is highly dependent on the skills of the operator. The RMS error in the estimated angles is less than $0.2°$, as can be seen from Figure 9, demonstrating the accuracy of the estimation.

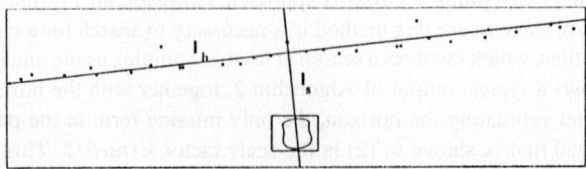

Fig. 7. Epipoles estimated by Algorithm 2. The horizon is found by doing a robust fit to the cloud of epipoles.

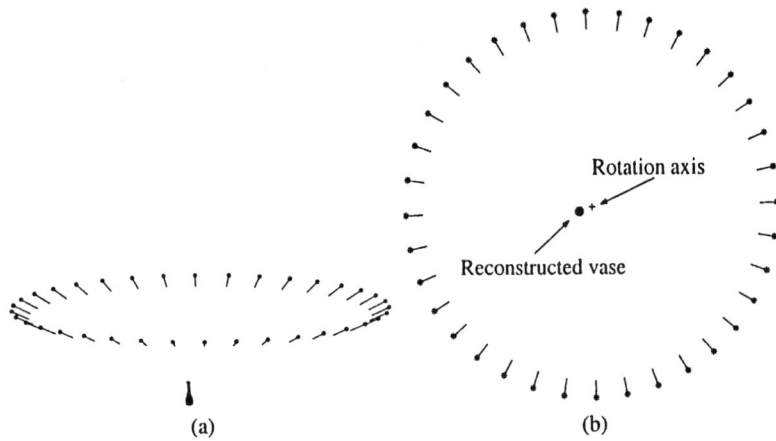

Fig. 8. Lateral and top view of the estimated configuration of the cameras. The technique to reconstruct the object shown at the bottom in (a) and in the centre in (b) is described in Section 5.

It is interesting to compare this result with the ones shown in [8, pg. 166] for the "Head", "Freiburg" and "Dinosaur" sequences, where the average number of point matches per image pair varies from 137 to 399, depending on the sequence. It should be stressed that only two epipolar tangents were used for each pair of images in the experiments presented in this paper, with comparable results.

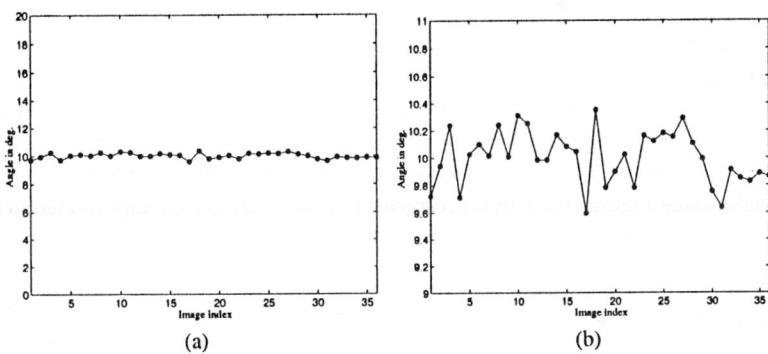

Fig. 9. Estimated angle of rotation between successive views. The RMS error is $0.2°$, for a maximum resolution of $0.01°$ for the manual turntable.

5 Reconstruction from Image Profiles

The algorithm for motion estimation introduced here can perfectly be used even when point correspondences can be established. On the other hand, methods as the ones in [8] and [12] cannot deal with situations where profiles are the only available features in the scene, and it is therefore natural to use the motion recovered by the technique shown in this paper to the problem of reconstruction from apparent contours. To solve this problem under known motion, the main algorithms can be found in [20, 6, 4, 22]. Results reported in [22] compare the last three, and although it slightly favours the one in [4], the simplicity of the method proposed in [22] justifies its choice for evaluating the accuracy of the motion estimated here.

5.1 Description of the Method

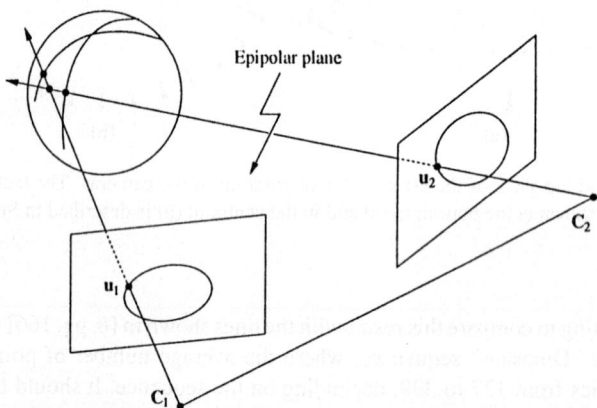

Fig. 10. The correspondence between the points u_1 and u_2 is established via the epipolar parameterisation. The result of the triangulation of u_1 and u_2 is *not* a point on the surface, but if the motion is small, the error will be negligible.

The algorithm for reconstruction from apparent contours introduced in [22] is based on the assumption that, if the motion is small, the error in triangulating correspondences on images of successive contour generators, established via the epipolar parameterisation, will be negligible (see Figure 10). This corresponds to a finite-difference approximation of the technique shown in [6]. A summary of the procedure is shown in Algorithm 3.

Algorithm 3 Reconstruction from image profiles.

---
  for $i = 1$ to $N - 1$ do
    sample M points u_j along the profile if image i;
    for $j = 1$ to M do
      compute the epipolar line l at image $i + 1$ corresponding to the point u_j;
      find the intersection u_j' of the line l with the profile in image $i + 1$;
      triangulate the points u_j and u_j';
    end for
  end for

5.2 Implementation and Experimental Results

A B-spline was fitted to the left side of the profile in the sequence of images shown in Figure 3(a). From the top to the bottom, 18 points were sampled on the spline in the first image (see Figure 11(a)), from which the corresponding epipolar lines in the second image were computed, and associated points where then triangulated. The intersection of the epipolar lines with the profile at the second image is shown in Figure 11(b). Since the points satisfy the epipolar constraint by construction, the triangulation will be exact, i.e., the rays associated with the points at the first image will exactly intersect the corresponding rays at the second image. As pointed in [11], in this case the choice of triangulation method becomes irrelevant, and a simple least-squares solution was adopted.

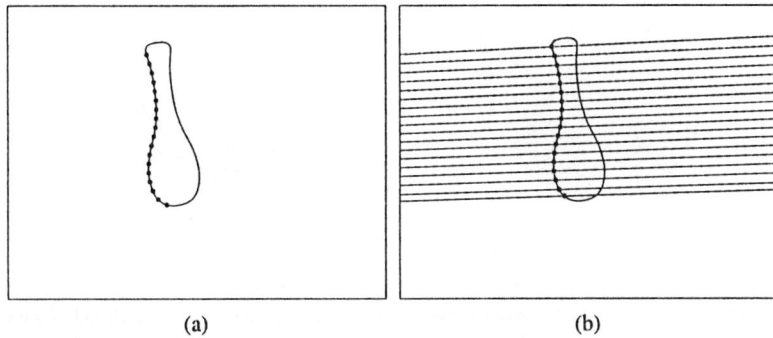

(a)   (b)

Fig. 11. (a) Points sampled at the first image. (b) Corresponding epipolar lines at the second image. The triangulation is carried out between a point in the first image and the intersection of its correspondent epipolar line and the profile in the second image.

Figure 8 shows the relative position of the reconstructed object. Incidentally, the camera is far away, making both the motion estimation and the reconstruction an even more challenging problem, since the most appropriate model to deal with such situations is the affine model, instead of the projective model used throughout this paper. Details of the 3D reconstruction of the object are shown in Figure 12 and Figure 13.

6   Summary and Conclusions

This paper introduces a novel technique for motion estimation from image profiles. It does not make use of expensive search procedures, such as bundle adjustment, although it naturally integrates data from multiple images. The method is mathematically sound, practical and highly accurate. From the motion estimation to the model reconstruction, no point tracking is required and it does not depend on having point correspondences beforehand.

The convergence to local minima, a critical issue in most non-linear optimisation problems, is avoided by a divide-and-conquer approach which keeps the size of the problem manageable. Moreover, a search space with lower dimension results in fewer iterations before convergence. The quality of model reconstructed is remarkable, in particular if one considers that only the least possible amount of information has been used.

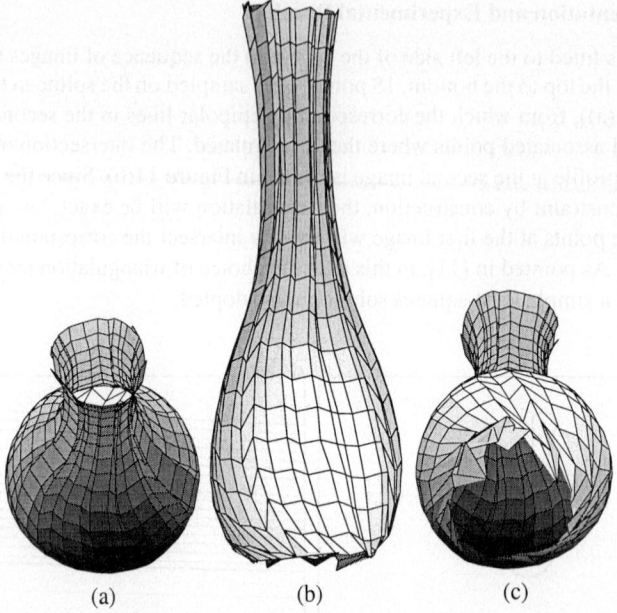

(a)   (b)   (c)

Fig. 12. Details of the reconstruction of the object in Figure 3(a). The reconstructed model is smooth, even considering that the epipolar parameterisation is degenerate in the neighbourhood of the frontier points. The views in (a) correspond to an angle ψ of $10°$ with respect to the y-axis. (b) $\psi = 0°$. (c) $\psi = 170°$. The original viewing direction, computed from the estimated motion, is $\psi = 24.35°$.

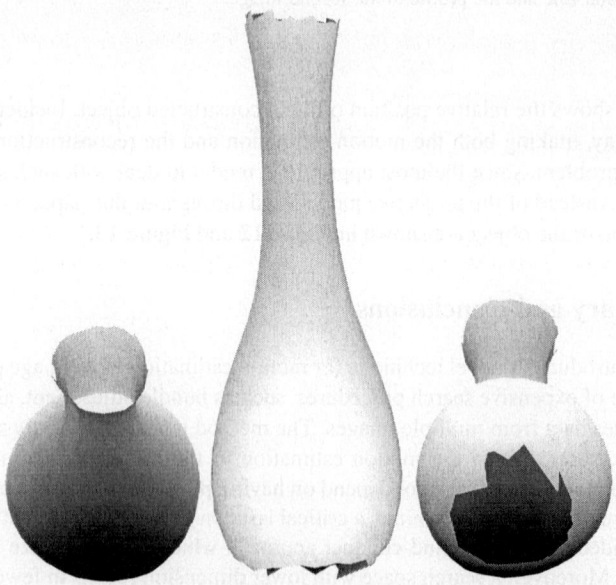

Fig. 13. Reconstruction of the object in Figure 3(a), showing the shaded surface. The view points are the same as in Figure 12.

References

1. K. Åström, R. Cipolla, and P. J. Giblin. Generalised epipolar constraints. In B. F. Buxton and R. Cipolla, editors, *Proc. 4th European Conf. on Computer Vision*, volume II, pages 97–108. Springer–Verlag, 1996.

2. K. Åström and F. Kahl. Motion estimation in image sequences using the deformation of apparent contours. *IEEE Trans. Pattern Analysis and Machine Intell.*, 21(2):114–127, February 1999.

3. H. G. Barrow and J. M. Tenenbaum. Interpreting line drawings as three-dimensional surfaces. *Artificial Intelligence*, 17:75–116, 1981.

4. E. Boyer and M. O. Berger. 3D surface reconstruction using occluding contours. *Int. Journal of Computer Vision*, 22(3):219–233, 1997.

5. R. Cipolla, K. Åström, and P. J. Giblin. Motion from the frontier of curved surfaces. In *Proc. 5th Int. Conf. on Computer Vision*, pages 269–275, 1995.

6. R. Cipolla and A. Blake. Surface shape from the deformation of apparent contours. *Int. Journal of Computer Vision*, 9(2):83–112, 1992.

7. G. Cross, A. Fitzgibbon, and A. Zisserman. Parallax geometry of smooth surfaces in multiple views. In *Proc. 7th Int. Conf. on Computer Vision*, volume I, pages 323–329, 1999.

8. A. W. Fitzgibbon, G. Cross, and A. Zisserman. Automatic 3D model construction for turntable sequences. In *3D Structure from Multiple Images of Large-Scale Environments, European Workshop SMILE'98*, Lecture Notes in Computer Science 1506, pages 155–170, 1998.

9. P. J. Giblin and R. Weiss. Reconstruction of surfaces from profiles. In *Proc. 1st Int. Conf. on Computer Vision*, pages 136–144, London, 1987.

10. P. J. Giblin and R. S. Weiss. Epipolar fields on surfaces. In J-O. Eklundh, editor, *Proc. 3rd European Conf. on Computer Vision*, volume I, pages 14–23. Springer–Verlag, 1994.

11. R. I. Hartley and P. Sturm. Triangulation. *Computer Vision and Image Understanding*, 68(2):146–157, November 1997.

12. R. Koch, M. Pollefeys, and L. Van Gool. Multi viewpoint stereo from uncalibrated video sequences. In *Proc. 5th European Conf. on Computer Vision*, volume I, pages 55–71, 1998.

13. J. J. Koenderink. What does the occluding contour tell us about solid shape? *Perception*, 13:321–330, 1984.

14. P. R. S. Mendonça and R. Cipolla. Estimation of epipolar geometry from apparent contours: Affine and circular motion cases. In *Proc. Conf. Computer Vision and Pattern Recognition*, volume I, pages 9–14, 1999.

15. P. R. S. Mendonça, K-Y. K. Wong, and R. Cipolla. Circular motion recovery from image profiles. In B. Triggs, R. Szeliski, and A. Zisserman, editors, *ICCV Vision and Algorithms Workshop: Theory and Practice*, Corfu, Greece, 21–22 September 1999. Springer–Verlag.

16. J. Porrill and S. B. Pollard. Curve matching and stereo calibration. *Image and Vision Computing*, 9(1):45–50, 1991.

17. J. H. Rieger. Three dimensional motion from fixed points of a deforming profile curve. *Optics Letters*, 11:123–125, 1986.

18. J. Sato and R. Cipolla. Affine reconstruction of curved surfaces from uncalibrated views of apparent contours. In *Proc. 6th Int. Conf. oon Computer Vision*, pages 715–720, 1998.

19. J. G. Semple and G. T. Kneebone. *Algebraic Projective Geometry*. Oxford University Press, 1952.

20. R. Vaillant and O. D. Faugeras. Using extremal boundaries for 3D object modelling. *IEEE Trans. Pattern Analysis and Machine Intell.*, 14(2):157–173, 1992.

21. T. Vieville and D. Lingrand. Using specific displacements to analyze motion without calibration. *Int. Journal of Computer Vision*, 31(1):5–29, February 1999.

22. K-Y. K. Wong, P. R. S. Mendonça, and R. Cipolla. Reconstruction and motion estimation from apparent contours under circular motion. In *Proc. British Machine Vision Conference*, pages 83–92, Nottingham, UK, 1999.

Author Index

Lecture Notes in Computer Science

For information about Vols. 1–1744
please contact your bookseller or Springer-Verlag

Vol. 1785: S. Graf, M. Schwartzbach (Eds.), Tools and Algorithms for the Construction and Analysis of Systems. Proceedings, 2000. XIV, 552 pages. 2000.

Vol. 1786: B.H. Haverkort, H.C. Bohnenkamp, C.U. Smith (Eds.), Computer Performance Evaluation. Proceedings, 2000. XIV, 383 pages. 2000.

Vol. 1787: J. Song (Ed.), Information Security and Cryptology – ICISC'99. Proceedings, 1999. XI, 279 pages. 2000.

Vol. 1789: B. Wangler. L. Bergman (Eds.), Advanced Information Systems Engineering. Proceedings, 2000. XII, 524 pages. 2000.

Vol. 1790: N. Lynch, B.H. Krogh (Eds.), Hybrid Systems: Computation and Control. Proceedings, 2000. XII, 465 pages. 2000.

Vol. 1792: E. Lamma, P. Mello (Eds.), AI*IA 99: Advances in Artificial Intelligence. Proceedings, 1999. XI, 392 pages. 2000. (Subseries LNAI).

Vol. 1793: O. Cairo, L.E. Sucar, F.J. Cantu (Eds.), MICAI 2000: Advances in Artificial Intelligence. Proceedings, 2000. XIV, 750 pages. 2000. (Subseries LNAI).

Vol. 1795: J. Sventek, G. Coulson (Eds.), Middleware 2000. Proceedings, 2000. XI, 436 pages. 2000.

Vol. 1794: H. Kirchner, C. Ringeissen (Eds.), Frontiers of Combining Systems. Proceedings, 2000. X, 291 pages. 2000. (Subseries LNAI).

Vol. 1796: B. Christianson, B. Crispo, J.A. Malcolm, M. Roe (Eds.), Security Protocols. Proceedings, 1999. XII, 229 pages. 2000.

Vol. 1800: J. Rolim et al. (Eds.), Parallel and Distributed Processing. Proceedings, 2000. XXIII, 1311 pages. 2000.

Vol. 1801: J. Miller, A. Thompson, P. Thomson, T.C. Fogarty (Eds.), Evolvable Systems: From Biology to Hardware. Proceedings, 2000. X, 286 pages. 2000.

Vol. 1802: R. Poli, W. Banzhaf, W.B. Langdon, J. Miller, P. Nordin, T.C. Fogarty (Eds.), Genetic Programming. Proceedings, 2000. X, 361 pages. 2000.

Vol. 1803: S. Cagnoni et al. (Eds.), Real-World Applications and Evolutionary Computing. Proceedings, 2000. XII, 396 pages. 2000.

Vol. 1805: T. Terano, H. Liu, A.L.P. Chen (Eds.), Knowledge Discovery and Data Mining. Proceedings, 2000. XIV, 460 pages. 2000. (Subseries LNAI).

Vol. 1806: W. van der Aalst, J. Desel, A. Oberweis (Eds.), Business Process Management. VIII, 391 pages. 2000.

Vol. 1807: B. Preneel (Ed.), Advances in Cryptology – EUROCRYPT 2000. Proceedings, 2000. XVIII, 608 pages. 2000.

Vol. 1810: R.López de Mántaras, E. Plaza (Eds.), Machine Learning: ECML 2000. Proceedings, 2000. XII, 460 pages. 2000. (Subseries LNAI).

Vol. 1811: S.W. Lee, H.. Bülthoff, T. Poggio (Eds.), Biologically Motivated Computer Vision. Proceedings, 2000. XIV, 656 pages. 2000.

Vol. 1815: G. Pujolle, H. Perros, S. Fdida, U. Körner, I. Stavrakakis (Eds.), Networking 2000 – Broadband Communications, High Performance Networking, and Performance of Communication Networks. Proceedings, 2000. XX, 981 pages. 2000.

Vol. 1816: T. Rus (Ed.), Algebraic Methodology and Software Technology. Proceedings, 2000. XI, 545 pages. 2000.

Vol. 1817: A. Bossi (Ed.), Logic-Based Program Synthesis and Transformation. Proceedings, 1999. VIII, 313 pages. 2000.

Vol. 1818: C.G. Omidyar (Ed.), Mobile and Wireless Communications Networks. Proceedings, 2000. VIII, 187 pages. 2000.

Vol. 1819: W. Jonker (Ed.), Databases in Telecommunications. Proceedings, 1999. X, 208 pages. 2000.

Vol. 1821: R. Loganantharaj, G. Palm, M. Ali (Eds.), Intelligent Problem Solving. Proceedings, 2000. XVII, 751 pages. 2000. (Subseries LNAI).

Vol. 1822: H.H. Hamilton, Advances in Artificial Intelligence. Proceedings, 2000. XII, 450 pages. 2000. (Subseries LNAI).

Vol. 1823: M. Bubak, H. Afsarmanesh, R. Williams, B. Hertzberger (Eds.), High Performance Computing and Networking. Proceedings, 2000. XVIII, 719 pages. 2000.

Vol. 1824: J. Palsberg (Ed.), Static Analysis. Proceedings, 2000. VIII, 433 pages. 2000.

Vol. 1825: M. Nielsen, D. Simpson (Eds.), Application and Theory of Petri Nets 2000. Proceedings, 2000. XI, 485 pages. 2000.

Vol. 1830: P. Kropf, G. Babin, J. Plaice, H. Unger (Eds.), Distributed Communities on the Web. Proceedings, 2000. X, 203 pages. 2000.

Vol. 1831: D. McAllester (Ed.), Automated Deduction – CADE-17. Proceedings, 2000. XIII, 519 pages. 2000. (Subseries LNAI).

Vol. 1835: D. N. Christodoulakis (Ed.), Natural Language Processing – NLP 2000. Proceedings, 2000. XII, 438 pages. 2000. (Subseries LNAI).

Vol. 1839: G. Gauthier, C. Frasson, K. VanLehn (Eds.), Intelligent Tutoring Systems. Proceedings, 2000. XIX, 675 pages. 2000.

Vol. 1840: F. Bomarius, M. Oivo (Eds.), Product Focused Software Process Improvement. Proceedings, 2000. XI, 426 pages. 2000.

Vol. 1842: D. Vernon (Ed.), Computer Vision – ECCV 2000. Part I. Proceedings, 2000. XVIII, 953 pages. 2000.

Vol. 1843: D. Vernon (Ed.), Computer Vision – ECCV 2000. Part II. Proceedings, 2000. XVIII, 881 pages. 2000.

Vol. 1845: H.B. Keller, E. Plöderer (Eds.), Reliable Software Technologies Ada-Europe 2000. Proceedings, 2000. XIII, 304 pages. 2000.

Vol. 1846: H. Lu, A. Zhou (Eds.), Web-Age Information Management. Proceedings, 2000. XIII, 462 pages. 2000.

Vol. 1848: R. Giancarlo, D. Sankoff (Eds.), Combinatorial Pattern Matching. Proceedings, 2000. XI, 423 pages. 2000.

Vol. 1849: C. Freksa, W. Brauer, C. Habel, K.F. Wender (Eds.), Spatial Cognition II. XI, 420 pages. 2000. (Subseries LNAI).

Vol. 1850: E. Bertino (Ed.), ECOOP 2000 – Object-Oriented Programming. Proceedings, 2000. XIII, 493 pages. 2000.

Vol. 1857: J. Kittler, F. Roli (Eds.), Multiple Classifier Systems. Proceedings, 2000. XII, 404 pages. 2000.